Dreaming
of
Florence

Dreaming of Florence

⚜ *Where to Find the Best There Is* ⚜

Renaissance Treasures • Rooms with a View
Exquisite Shops • Secret Gardens • Stylish Restaurants
Artisanal Crafts • Delightful Day Trips

Barbara Milo Ohrbach

PHOTOGRAPHS BY OVIDIO GUAITA

RIZZOLI
NEW YORK

First Published in the United States of America in 2009 by
Rizzoli International Publications, Inc.
300 Park Avenue South, New York, NY 10010
www.rizzoliusa.com

2009 2010 2011 2012 / 10 9 8 7 6 5 4 3 2 1

Distributed in the U.S. trade by Random House, New York

Designed by Jan Derevjanik
Map of Florence © 2008 Melanie Marder Parks

Printed in China
ISBN-13: 978-0-8478-3331-3
Library of Congress Control Number: 2009924940

The photograph on the cover is a view of Florence from Torre di Bellosguardo.
The endpapers are engravings of Florence by G.B.Probst, printed in Augsburg, Germany
in the late eighteenth century. Courtesy of Libreria Gozzini, Florence.

—————————— Also by Barbara Milo Ohrbach ——————————

The Scented Room

*The Scented Room
Gardening Notebook*

Antiques at Home

Simply Flowers

A Token of Friendship

Memories of Childhood

A Bouquet of Flowers

A Cheerful Heart

The Spirit of America

Merry Christmas

Happy Birthday

*All Things Are Possible . . .
Pass the Word*

Food for the Soul

Tabletops

*If You Think You Can . . .
You Can*

Roses for the Scented Room

A Token of Love

Love Your Life

You're the Best

A Passion for Antiques

Dreaming of Tuscany

Grazie Mille

St. Augustine once wrote, "The world is a book, and those who do not travel read only a page." The making of a book is always an adventure, especially making a book in a foreign place. Florence is a city that I have visited many times but living and working there on this project was a revelation and a joy. I'm indebted to everyone who participated and helped make *Dreaming of Florence* a reality.

I have to thank my husband Mel who, because he speaks Italian like an Italian, happily charmed everyone he met in the city of Florence opening many doors and without whom this book would not have been possible; Ovidio Guaita, who followed me into every nook and cranny of the city photographing with avid curiosity and unflappable professionalism; Jan Derevjanik who approached the design of this project with her usual calm and special talent and Deborah Geltman and Gayle Benderoff who have seen me through twenty-two books with unstinting support and advice. Thank you to Rita Singer who helped through a week of jet lag and rain, always with a smile, and Beth Allen, who diligently guided me through the mysteries of Italian food measurements. Everyone at Rizzoli always does such a remarkable job bringing these books to reality, I'm grateful to my editor Kathleen Jayes and Charles Miers, Ellen Nidy, Jennifer Pierson, Pam Sommers, and Kaija Markoe.

I'd like to take a page out of Mary McCarthy's book *The Stones of Florence* by thanking the city of Florence and all the Florentines past and present. The genius and creativity that flowered here over the centuries is unique in the world and the warmth and generosity of its inhabitants today continue to make it a glorious place indeed. My appreciation to everyone on the following list. Grazie alla vostra gentilezza: Chiara Adami, Albiera Antinori, Allegra Antinori, Allesia Antinori, Piero and Francesca Antinori, Duccio Banchi, Lamberto Banchi, Paolo Basagni, Pietro Bazzanti, Daniele Benci, Elena Branchini, Ginevra Brandolini d'Adda, Simonetta Brandolini d'Adda, Claudia Buccellati, Lorenzo Buccellati, Luca Buccellati, The Budini Gattai Family, Eleonora Burci, Jane Camilloni, Letezia Campana, Loretta Caponi, Lucia Caponi, Angela Caputi, Elena Carradori, Marilena Carradori, Christina N. Caughlan, Marcella Cagnoli, Marco Castorina, Maria di Caterina, Francesco Chellini, Pietro Chellini, Dedy Ferrari Clerici, Danytza Contreras, Prince and Princess Corsini, Sabina Corsini, Elisabetta di Costanzo, Claudio Delli, Attilio di Fabrizio, Wanny di Filippo, the Ferragamo family, especially, Ferruccio, Giovanna Gentile, Leonardo, Massimo, Salvatore, and Wanda, Sally Fischer, Amerigo Franchetti, Elisa Francini, the Frescobaldi family, especially, Bona, Cristiana, Diana, Diletta, Dino, Eleonora, Ferdinando, Lamberto, Leonardo, Livia, Maria Benini, Rosaria, Tiziana, and Vittorio, Francesa Gavoni, Giulio Gentile, Sibilla della Gherardesca, Ugo Gherardi, Caia Gibson, Luca Giovanelli, Vittoria Gondi, Simone Guaita, Dominique Guihenneuc, Ori Kafri, Atsuko Kato, Barrie Kerper, Francesca and Walter Lotti, Laura Lorimer, Livia and Lorenzo Magnelli, Duccio Magni, Carlo and Stefania Martelli, Davide Monni, Giordano Monni, Dario Nardella, Filippo and Ginevra Niccolini di Camugliano, Maria Anna Paoletti, Barbara Pardini, Annalisa Passigli, Michela Passigli, Cristina Petrelli, Angela Pescarolo, Sabrina Pestelli, Fabio Picchi, Giulio Picchi, Sabine Pretsch, Cristina Pucci, Franco Rovigli, Lastrucci Saverio, Alina Scarcelli, Cristiana Segato, Staci Smith, Diana Stefani, Adele Tognaccia, Neri Torrigiani, Angelica Visconti, Sabrina Zadro, Miriam Zamparella, Marilena Zinatti.

1

2

Table of Contents

5

6

3

4

7

8

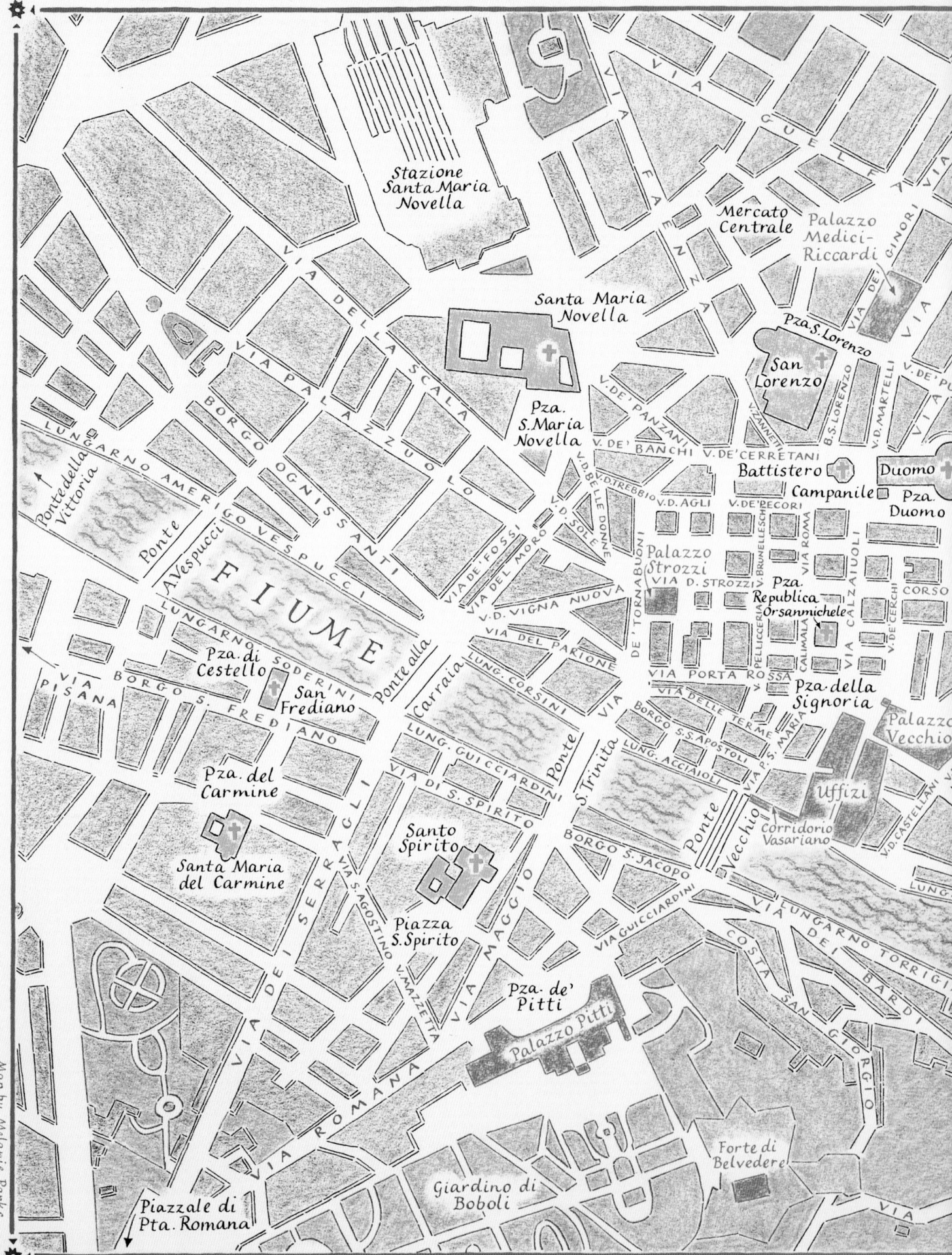

Map by Melanie Parks

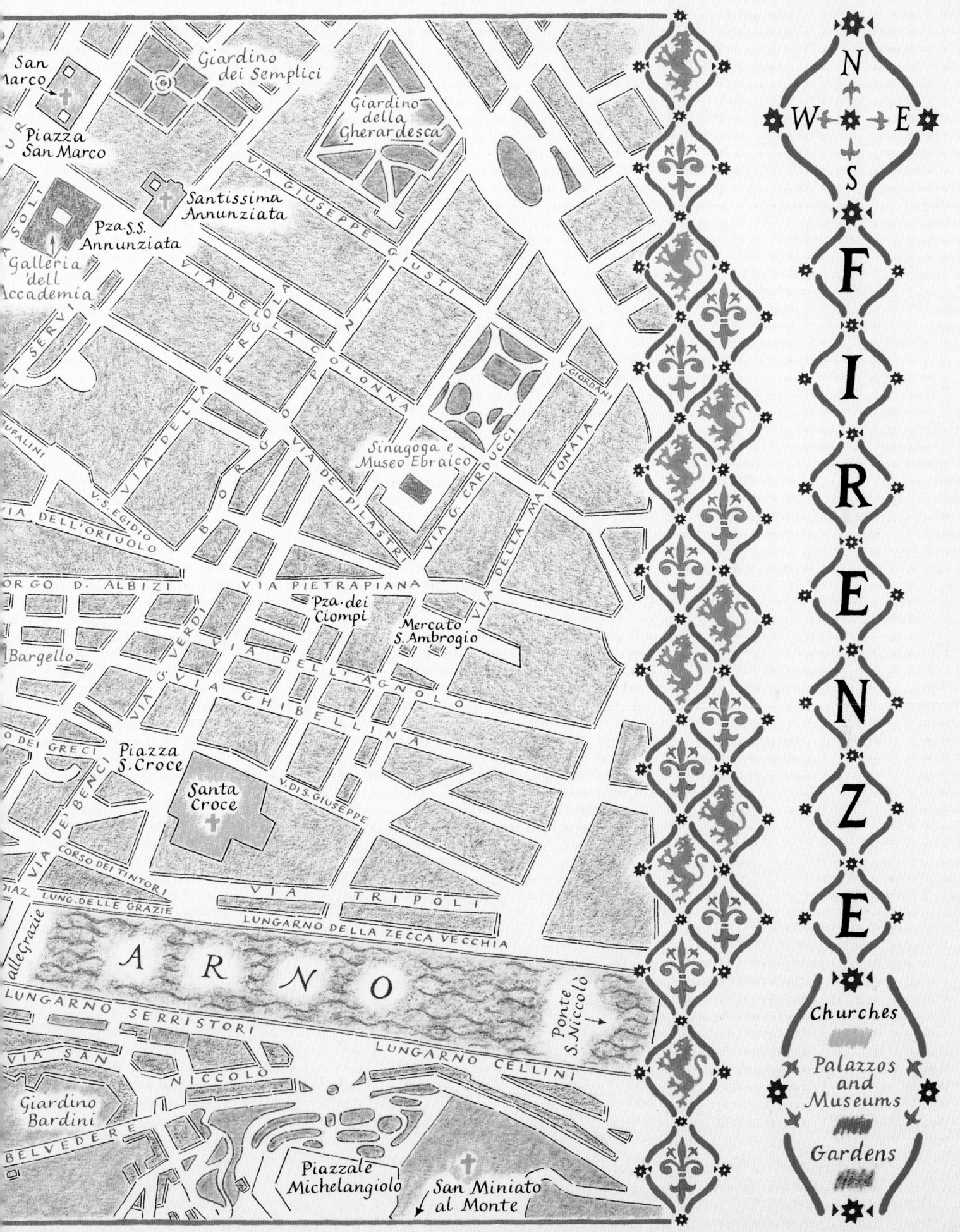

Introduction

"Everything about Florence pleases me, its name, its sky, its river,
its setting and surroundings—I love it all."

—Hector Berlioz

There was only enough room for a single chapter on Florence in my last book, *Dreaming of Tuscany*. So, for the many readers who enjoyed it and in order to try and correct the injustice to this special city, I'm now happy to be writing the introduction to *Dreaming of Florence*. When I started working on this book, I decided that, to get in the mood, I would reread all the superb Florentine mysteries by Magdalen Nabb—a real treat. That was when I came across this tribute in *Death in Springtime* written by the respected novelist and fellow mystery writer Georges Simenon: "What a pleasure it is to wander with you through the streets of Florence, with their carabinieri, working people, trattoria, even their noisy tourists. It is all so alive: its sounds audible, its smells as perceptible as the light morning mist above the Arno's swift current…there is never a false note. You even capture that shimmer in the air which is so peculiar to this city and to the still untamed countryside close at hand."

Nabb's novels were remarkable in that they impeccably captured the essence of the city and the spirit of its inhabitants. Reading her books, I could almost smell the aroma of early-morning espresso wafting out the doorways of its *caffès*. She recently died, and we will miss her salt-of-the-earth police hero, Marshal Guarnaccia and, even more, her talent for being able to connect us, magically, to one of the most exceptional cities in the world.

For decades I have loved Florence and its many guises. I first visited, like many, during college, focusing as an art history major on its abundant cultural treasures. Then I returned and worked there in the early days of my fashion career. The first fashion shows in the Pitti Palace's elegant Sala Bianca (White Room) featuring Emilio Pucci's colorful, happy creations opened the window to a fresh and exciting fashion direction for Italian design in the 1960s. Gucci began and had one of its first boutiques here, and you could (and still can) buy gorgeous shoes in Ferragamo's Palazzo Spini Feroni on the Arno. There were two CIGA hotels owned by the dashing Aga Khan that luxuriously accommodated all the sophisticated travelers whose globe-trotting always included a stop in Florence to enjoy its culture and shopping.

Some things have changed and some things haven't. The art is still there in all its glory, looking better than it has in years. Funds from international organizations like Friends of Florence have augmented government budgets and revitalized the city's museums, monuments, and buildings. And you can still shop until you drop in more beautiful stores than ever.

But today, everyday life can sometimes be frustrating. The city is noisy. For every 1,000 residents there are 1,200 motor vehicles. Even though a street is one-way or for pedestrians only, you have to look both ways before crossing because there is usually a Vespa or a bicycle heading straight for you. During high season, there are tour groups and people blocking pavements really only wide enough for one person.

That said, there are so many treasures that, even if the city is packed and there seems to be someone in every nook and cranny, you can always find a quiet refuge. If you walk off the beaten path, you'll often find a street or little square that is charming, like the Piazza del Limbo, with its precious Romanesque church.

There are many extraordinary museums—the Museo dell'Opera del Duomo, the Bargello, or the

RIGHT, CLOCKWISE: Flea market souvenirs—good luck horseshoes for five Euros; this sign says, "It is prohibited to park a bicycle in the courtyard"; a scene on Via dei Servi that hasn't changed in hundreds of years; the ultimate Italian delicacy, a hand-crafted silver fig; my husband, Mel, and I taking a break between photos.

ABOVE: Sabina Corsini and I take a walk from the magnificent Palazzo Corsini al Prato to the two grand ancient *limonai* at the end of the garden, and right, an elegant doorway on the portico at Villa San Michele in Fiesole.

Opificio delle Pietre Dure, for example—that are so sparsely visited that you may find yourself alone in one of these gems. A giddy feeling!

Amazingly, Florence has half the artistic treasures of Italy. Everywhere you look—up, down, and around a corner—is something notable and usually beautiful. After all, this was the center of the Renaissance in Europe. Just imagine what these somber buildings and cobbled squares have seen over the years.

Although the architecture of the city may be stolid, the people are the opposite. They say that in the Middle Ages travelers deliberately took a route through Florence because of the hospitality they knew they would receive there. The tradition survives. There wasn't a stop we made where someone didn't make a gracious offer of a drink or something to eat, or offer us a place to sit comfortably.

The Florentines are generous and rarely forget their manners. The day starts with *buon giorno* and a smile, and ends with *buona notte*, punctuated by *grazie*, *prego*, and *per favore* in between. These niceties are delivered

sometimes in the Florentine dialect, in which the "c" is often pronounced as an "h," for example, "Hoca-Hola" instead of "Coca-Cola." And when we asked directions to little-known places, many locals simply walked us there, and I am indebted to all the delightful people we met in the city who made such good suggestions and helped us ferret out so many of the great discoveries that are on the pages of this book.

I spent a misty morning in the Corsini Gardens, with Sabina Corsini describing all the nuances of this spectacular green place in the very heart of the city (see chapter 3). Albiera Antinori took us to her family's new vineyard, in Monteloro, in the hills just above the city. We walked along ancient stone terraces planted with grapes and with lunch sampled several bottles of the their first vintage of Mezzo Braccio, a lovely white wine (see chapter 6). We visited the other major Florentine winemaking family, the Frescobaldis, who graciously put together a traditional alfresco party in their spectacular garden in Santo Spirito.

The artisans I encountered demonstrated with

pride and infinite patience their expertise in etching a piece of glass, restoring a three-hundred-year-old painting, or even hand-crafting a ripe solid-silver fig. The same perfection affects almost everything done in a city known for its artisan traditions. Loretta Caponi, whose shop has been offering the most desirable handmade bed and table linens, baby clothes, and lingerie for years, spent a morning sharing with me her precious collection of sixteenth- to twentieth-century lace, including Alençon, Bruges, and Point Venise —the examples were breathtaking.

The Florentines are not only generous, they are also perfectionists. When we were working on this book, we took an apartment in Florence. It was lovely to be able to have breakfast at home every morning. Then we would hit the streets and stop at our favorite *caffè* to share a *bombolino* (cream donut) with our coffee. It was always presented precisely cut in half, with each half wrapped in its own crisp paper napkin—a telling example of the Florentine attention to detail. A gilt frame is packed neatly into kraft paper folded like a piece of origami so that the package stays tightly closed without any Scotch tape. Shop windows are cleaned until they gleam, doorways are swept clean—all done with pride every morning. There's always a way to do things properly.

I know Florence well, have great affection for it, and have tried to create a book that is a how-to of navigating this cornucopia of a city, filled to the brim with endless beauty and pleasures, so you can get the most out of it. *Dreaming of Florence* is not meant to be all-inclusive. Instead, it is a carefully edited collection of recommendations, with an emphasis on quality, not necessarily price. I've included "the best of the best," whether simple or grand, including insider information. Out-of-the-way places that you might not easily discover are included, too.

I have tried to answer the eternal question of "too much art, too little time" by editing a list of museums which should not be missed (it's still too many to see on one trip!). I have stayed in irresistible hotels, tracked down fun and glamorous shops, discovered delicious new restaurants, big and small, found talented artisans, and put together a list of my favorite gardens and places to visit outside the city center if you have the time. And you will learn to dine like a Florentine in a chapter devoted to food and wine that includes traditional Tuscan recipes re-interpreted by Florence's most famous chefs.

In each chapter there is a special section called "Florentine Notes" that highlights important practical information, including places to go with children and restaurants open on Sundays.

I hope you find this book helps you to plan your trip so that you can savor every amazing moment that you spend in this city. Indulge yourself in the luxury of going slowly. Return to Florence, as I have, again and again to walk its empty streets in the early morning accompanied by church bells chiming, and perhaps feel the magic that journalist Oriana Fallaci always felt for her city when she wrote, "The first music I heard when I came into this world was the music of the bells. In that music, that landscape, that church to which even great minds like Dante Alighieri and Leonardo da Vinci and Michelangelo and Galileo Galilei bent, I have grown up. Through it I have learnt what sculpture and architecture and painting and poetry and literature are, what beauty combined with knowledge is."

Barbara Milo Ohrbach
Florence, Italy 2009

ONE

Renaissance Jewel

"The Florentines, in fact, invented the Renaissance, which is the same as saying that they invented the modern world . . . ."
—Mary McCarthy, *The Stones of Florence*

QUESTA EFFIGIE DEL DIVINO GALILE
FECE PORRE NEL MDCCCXLIII
ANTONFILIPPO MARCHIONNI

A DANTE ALIGHIERI
L'ITALIA
M·DCCC·LXV

In most people's minds the Renaissance equals Florence. "The Athens of Italy," "Cradle of the Renaissance," and "Mother of Tuscany" trip off the tongue. Historians are still disputing and wondering how, after the Dark and the Medieval Ages, such an outpouring of brilliant thought and so many profound achievements could have occurred in one exuberant era. The reawakening of humanistic ideals, the one fundamental idea of civilization, and the optimism of man's unlimited possibilities made the small town of Florence the center of creativity for sculpture, painting, architecture, astronomy, science, exploration, banking, trade, poetry, music, law, philosophy, and political idealism. A rediscovery of the classics of ancient Rome and Greece created a "rebirth" of the human spirit.

The fourteenth, fifteenth, and part of the sixteenth centuries in this capital of the Italian Renaissance saw vigorous achievements in every phase of human activity taking place: the writing of the *Divine Comedy* by Dante Alighieri (1302), *The Decameron* by Giovanni Boccaccio (1349), *The Prince* by Niccolo Machiavelli (1532), and the works of "the father of the Renaissance," Petrarch; the minting, in 1252, of the first gold coin, the *fiorino d'oro* (the gold florin), which was to become the stablest currency in Europe; the creation of the census and the first bank in the world, in 1492; the establishing of basic financial systems still in use today, including checks, life insurance, and double-entry bookkeeping!

In 1434, Filippo Brunelleschi built and completed the first dome in the world, at the cathedral of Santa Maria del Fiore (from then on, known as the Duomo); Lorenzo Ghiberti completed the Baptistery doors in-corporating the art of foreshortening and perspective; Leonardo da Vinci (1452) and Michelangelo Buonarroti (1455) were born; Sandro Botticelli painted *Primavera* and the *Birth of Venus* (1480-1485); Galileo Galilei refuted Aristotelian physics, invented the telescope, and discovered that the sun is the center of the solar system. A dictionary, the first of any modern language, was written, in Italian, in 1612; the first opera, *Euridice* by Jacopo Peri, was performed in the Pitti Palace, in 1598; the first piano was invented by Bartolomeo Cristofori, in 1709; and the first museum in the world, the Galleria degli Uffizi, was assembled in the late sixteenth century by Francesco I de' Medici with precious family works of art.

This is not to mention the masterpieces of painters like Raffaello, Fra Angelico, Giotto, Andrea del Sarto, Masaccio, Masolino da Panicale, Piero della Francesca, Domenico Ghirlandaio, Filippo Lippi, Cimabue; sculptors like Donatello, Benvenuto Cellini, the Della Robbia family, Giambologna, Andrea del Verrocchio; and architects such as Giorgio Vasari, Arnolfo di Cambio, Leon Battista Alberti, Bernardo Buontalenti, and Bartolomeo Ammannati.

To try to describe, or even mention, everything is just not possible here. See chapter 2 for a look at the city's treasures. And if you are inclined to do a little reading, start with Mary McCarthy's *The Stones of Florence*. It will inspire you to know more and go further to some of the other many books written on this subject (see "Suggested Reading").

This golden age was made possible by the leadership of the Medici, the powerful banking family. They were the world's first true art patrons, who, fueled by their wealth, supported all aspects of the

OPENING PICTURE: Marble horses in the Fountain of Neptune by Bartolomeo Ammannati in the Piazza della Signoria.
OVERLEAF, LEFT: A fresco-decorated salon at Palazzo Niccolini overlooks the Duomo, and right, an antique doorbell.
LEFT, CLOCKWISE: Three famous Florentine statues: *Primavera* (Spring), Galileo Galilei, and Dante Alighieri.

fine and decorative arts, pushing and expanding the sciences, encouraging Platonic ideals and scholarly thought. All the while, they were commissioning some of the greatest works of art ever created—many of which we see in Florence still today.

We should not forget, however, that the sophisticated Etruscans, who ruled Tuscany for one thousand years, were the first with the foresight to settle in the cool, verdant Fiesole hills overlooking the city. For this reason, Fiesole was called the "Mother City of Florence." The Etruscans predated the Romans, who created *Florentia* in 59 B.C. as a military camp on the banks of the Arno River.

Charlemagne traveled to Florence in 781 A.D. and ruled the city for a time. Violent power struggles and ruinous wars between the Florentines and their neighboring city-states, including Pistoia, Fiesole, Siena, and Arezzo, followed. The conflicts between the most powerful Florentine families—the Guelphs, supporters of the Pope and the House of Anjou, and the Ghibellines, who supported the Suevians and the Holy Roman Empire—went on for hundreds of years, occasionally interrupted by floods, famines, and fires, not to mention the Black Death, a plague that ravaged half the city's population from 1348 to 1393.

Papal bankers, the Medici family came to power under Cosimo de' Medici (1389-1464) and continued to rule Florence for the next three centuries. Cosimo the Elder was called "the father of his city," and he was an intellectual who enriched Florence and its citizenry by expanding the philosophy of humanism, patronizing the finest artists and sculptors, commissioning elegant architects to design and adorn buildings, creating an academy of learning, and, generally, planting the seeds for the flowering of the

RIGHT: The sculptures in the niches of the Piazzale degli Uffizi include the two most remarkable Medici men.

COSIMO PATER PATRIAE

LORENZO IL MAGNIFICO

Renaissance, an example for all of Europe. He gave generously to charities, introduced the income-tax system, and built the first public library in Europe.

His grandson, the legendary statesman Lorenzo de' Medici (1449-1492), known as Lorenzo the Magnificent, followed, and made Florence the first city of the world. As an accomplished poet himself, he saw to it that scholars and intellects flourished. As a result, he ruled Florence at the pinnacle of its greatness.

After Lorenzo's death, Florence entered an unstable era. Charles VIII of France invaded Florence in 1494 and Savonarola seized power, burning paintings and books—the famous "Bonfire of the Vanities"—in the Piazza della Signoria. He was burned at the stake four years later on the same spot.

Calm returned with Cosimo I (1519-1574). He restored stability to Florence becoming the Grand Duke of Tuscany in 1570 and ruling over all the city-states, continuing to expand the sciences, and creating two of the first botanical gardens in Pisa (1543) and Florence (1545), still there today (see page 86). He was a long time defender of Galileo Galilei, who was accused of heresy and excommunicated from the church for what it considered his controversial discoveries.

The Medici ruled for another one hundred fifty years, until the line became extinct in 1737, and Anna Maria Luisa Ludovica, the last member of the Medici family, signed a treaty giving Florence to Duke Francis of Lorraine. He later became the Emperor of Austria and united Florence with that country. At her death, Anna Maria Luisa generously transferred all of the immense Medici collections of art and treasures to the city of Florence in perpetuity, on the condition that they never leave the city. Thus the Pitti Palace, Boboli Gardens, and the Uffizi Gallery are still there today to be an inspiration to all of us.

Napoleon appears briefly and is then driven out of Florence. In 1860, Florence becomes part of the newly united Italy and in 1865 is named its capital until being replaced by Rome five years later. During this time, there were major changes in the city's architecture—unfortunately not for the better. The ancient walls were torn down leaving only the isolated gates that stand today. The Piazza Beccaria and Piazza della Libertà were created as green spaces that have now become traffic islands. And even more devastating, the Roman and medieval center of Florence was razed to make room for the innocuous Piazza della Repubblica.

In the late eighteenth and nineteenth centuries, Florence was described by the Goncourt brothers as the *"ville toute anglaise,"* because it was invaded by British and American visitors and other Europeans who came under its spell. Many moved into grand palazzi, restored villas and gardens in the surrounding hills, and generally made the city their home and again a center of the arts in the nineteenth and twentieth centuries. The names are legend: artists such as John Singer Sargent, Benjamin West, and Thomas Cole; writers and poets such as Robert and Elizabeth Barrett Browning, Mark Twain, Wolfgang von Goethe, Henri-Marie Beyle Stendhal, George Sand, Feodor Dostoevsky, Walt Whitman, Henry James, George Eliot, Sinclair Lewis, Edith Wharton, Henry Wadsworth Longfellow, Ralph Waldo Emerson, Nathaniel Hawthorne, and Charles Dickens; composers such as Franz Liszt, Giuseppe Verdi, George Frideric Handel, Felix Mendelssohn, Hector Berlioz, Richard Wagner, and Tchaikovsky; and collectors such as J.P.

PREVIOUS PAGE: Reminders of the flood at Antico Setificio Fiorentina. Left, there is a mark where water rose over the door, and right, a sculpture by Guy Sanders.

Morgan, Bernard Berenson, Isabella Stewart Gardner, Charles Augustus Strong, James Jackson Jarves, the Goncourt brothers, and Mable Dodge Luhan.

In June 1940, Italy entered World War II on the side of Germany. The Florentines felt secure in their belief that the city would never be attacked because of all its artistic treasures, and, for a time, this was the case. But, just to be sure, many people took their own measures. Some of the most valuable paintings from the city's museums, especially the Uffizi, were stored in the Castello di Montegufoni. It was chosen because the windows and doors were large enough to allow the largest pictures to be carried in without being damaged. At the same time hundreds of people from the surrounding Tuscan countryside had taken refuge in the fortified castle's cellars.

There is a wonderful description of the arrival of journalists just after the Germans had fled in 1944. The refugees ran out of their hiding places shouting the names of the Renaissance painters whose treasures lay within. When the journalists entered the castle, they stopped short in surprise, for in front of them was Botticelli's *Primavera*, casually propped up against a wall in all its glory—ready to go home along with the hundreds of paintings stored for safekeeping in the rooms beyond.

The only bridge over the Arno not destroyed by the retreating Germans in August 1944 was the oldest, the Ponte Vecchio. Especially distressing to the Florentines was the bombing of the Ponte Santa Trinità. The "Four Seasons" statues that defined each corner of the bridge were thought to be totally lost, but eventually all were found by divers scouring the bottom of the Arno. Sadly, the beautiful head of *Spring* was missing. Posters reading "Have you seen this woman?" and offering a reward went up all over

the city (a photo of the poster is pictured in the first edition of Mary McCarthy's book). The bridge was rebuilt exactly as it had been, and the missing head was found twenty years later (see page 20).

In November 1966, the Florentines pulled together again, this time because the Arno River burst its banks. It had done so in 1296, 1333, 1466, 1557, and 1844, but never with this violent intensity. At dawn, after many days of torrential rain and the opening of the sluice gates above the city to prevent collapse of a dam, the river swelled, engulfing the streets and piazzas all the way to the city center. Houses, businesses and even more devastating, museums, churches, and libraries were inundated with tons of mud and water mixed with heating oil. Cars floated in the streets. The river's force was so turbulent that the five bronze panels dislodged from the Baptistery doors were later found over a mile away. The tragic result was the death of many and the destruction of priceless artworks, ancient books, and buildings.

If you look up as you walk through the city, you will see small plaques, some with wavy lines on them, marking the height, sometimes over 20 feet, to which the Arno rose. At the corner of Via San Remigio and Via de' Neri are two plaques, one commemorating the flood of 1333, the other the flood of 1966, both of

ABOVE: There are many plaques in the city marking the height of water level of the periodic flooding of the Arno River. This one in marble is dated the year 1844.

which took place on the same day, November 4!

People from across Italy and around the world came to Florence to rescue her Renaissance masterpieces. Hundreds of paintings and sculptures and over 700,000 rare books and manuscripts in the Biblioteca Nazionale were submerged. The thousands of students and young people who arrived to help were called "mud angels," and many stayed on.

One of the good things to come out of this tragedy was the importance taken on by the Opificio delle Pietre Dure e Laboratori di Restauro, the conservation center of Florence. It was established in 1588 by Ferdinando I de' Medici as the Galleria dei Lavori to create luxurious *pietre dure* and other semiprecious hard stone objects that reflected the extraordinary workmanship of the time. In the nineteenth century, it began to specialize in conservation and restoration work. As a result of the flood, in 1975 all of Florence's state restoration laboratories were merged together into the historic Opificio, making it into one of the most distinguished and cutting edge conservation centers in the world. It contains scientific research laboratories, a library and archives, and a museum which is open to the public (see page 55).

The Opificio recently completed a twenty-five-year restoration of the gilded panels of the Baptistery doors, returning them to their original glory after five hundred years of exposure to the elements. They are now in the Museo dell'Opera del Duomo, after traveling to the United States—the only time they have been outside of Florence since Ghiberti created them. Be sure to visit this extraordinary museum, never crowded, to enjoy all the glorious treasures within.

In the 1890s, when Queen Victoria visited Florence, she stood in front of the Duomo and held up an open locket containing a miniature of Prince Albert

because she thought he would enjoy seeing how it had been restored! Remarkably, Florence looks pretty much the same today. After all, this is a city where the past lives on in the present: an open-air museum with public buildings, noble palaces, churches, and medieval alleyways that are all masterpieces you can wander through and touch, enabling you to travel back in time in a blink.

Mary McCarthy wrote that, in this city, the past is "near and indifferently real." It is a contrast of old and new, whose 360,000 residents go about their daily lives in the midst of a heritage of beauty and the millions of tourists that visit each year. They are sophisticated, some with deep roots that go back many hundreds of years, not intimidated by their past but living with it as custodians, calling upon their Florentine characteristics of hard work and pride to ensure that the city retains its individuality. This independent Florentine spirit was noted by Pope Alexander VI in the fifteenth century, when he said, "The world is made up of five elements: earth, air, fire, water and the Florentines."

Several summers ago, I was lucky enough to see Roberto Benigni give a spectacular performance in Piazza Santa Croce. Over a period of two weeks, he read the entire *Divine Comedy* by Dante. It was over 100 degrees, even at 9:00 P.M. on the night I went. But, despite this, more than five thousand people, mostly Florentines beautifully dressed in crisp cottons and linens, sat for hours with their well-worn leather copies of the book, enjoying his wonderful interpretation of this astonishing fourteenth-century poem. The large, devoted audience prompted the city's mayor to say that the event would inspire its citizens to "rediscover the soul of Florence—Universal City that springs from Dante, our Universal Poet."

Even the feisty journalist and writer Oriana Fallaci, who was born and died here, had a soft spot for the genius Dante in her angry book, *The Rage and the Pride*, published before she died several years ago. She said about her critics, "I always follow the advice of an illustrious compatriot of mine, the overly exiled Dante Alighieri, who said, *"Non ti curar di lor, ma guarda e passa."* Don't care about them just look and walk on.

Florence today is a study in contrasts, and you have to learn to work around its vexing problems of too many tourists and too much noise and almost too much art. Bypass the well-worn paths: nothing is farther then a twenty-minute walk away, so explore to your heart's content the ancient streets and alleyways in parts of the city not frequented by tourists.

Florence has entered the twenty-first century. In 1988, cars were banned from the city center. It is putting in a new public-transport system, called the Tramvia, to further reduce traffic. A new opera house is in the works for the Maggio Musicale Fiorentino, whose conductor-for-life is Zuben Mehta. At the same time, the artisan tradition continues, and you can get your watchband fixed while you wait or a zipper replaced in a favorite old handbag, without anyone acting as if you asked for the moon. Sheets and pillowcases are starched to buttery perfection. Ham or salami is shaved so thin that you can almost see through it; melon is served so sweet that you can't stop eating it. Over a hundred years ago, Henry James said about Florence, "The past seems to have left a sensible deposit, an aroma, an atmosphere." It's still true today. You just have to look a little harder.

PREVIOUS PAGE, CLOCKWISE: Some street scenes: Saying "cheese," on the Ponte Santa Trinità; two local shoppers in Piazza Santo Spirito; a narrow medieval street; police on the Ponte Vecchio; wrapping the first tulips of spring.

It is said that half of Italy's art treasures are in one city—Florence! So you can imagine the enormous amounts of money and expertise needed to ensure that all these treasures are safeguarded and maintained. Recognizing this enormous responsibility, Friends of Florence was formed in 1998 to help protect the city's cultural legacy. Founder Contessa Simonetta Brandolini d'Adda started this international non profit foundation to bring together both Americans who love Florence and prominent Florentines who care about their city. Their mission says it all: "As we enter the third millennium, it is ever more important that the legacy of Florence and the Tuscany Region be preserved, enhanced where possible, and protected. Many of the unique treasures found in and around Florence are in danger of being ruined from neglect or sporadic preservation. The city itself is a work of art, rich and beautiful palaces, churches, museums, secret corners, and splendid gardens. All must be carefully protected so that Florence and Tuscany will remain a symbol of humanism and man's creativity and genius for centuries to come."

The organization's first project was the cleaning and restoring of all the marble statues in the Loggia della Signoria on the main square of Florence, including important extraordinary works by Giambologna and Cellini. Today, it's amazing to sit in the Piazza della Signoria and enjoy these gleaming sculptures which must look as they did when they were created. The second project, in the Galleria dell'Accademia, was completed in 2003 and included restoring all of the painting which surround Michelangelo's David. The very next year, the organization took part in the actual restoration of this famous sculpture and also created a website which covers all phases of the cleaning, analysis and research regarding the masterpiece.

Work continued with the Sala della Niobe in the Uffizi Gallery entirely restored in 2006, including seventeen statues and an extraordinary Roman sarcophagus from the Medici collections as well as a large, long lost painting by Grissoni. Current projects include the restoration of Ghiberti's Gates of Paradise on the Baptistery, work in the cloister in San Marco which contains Fra Angelico's frescoes, and projects in the Pitti Palace.

As if this weren't enough, the organization has put together wonderful educational programs. They arrange visits to private collections not usually open to the public and current restoration projects that are underway so you can actually see the experts at work.

If you love the city and would like to become a true citizen of Florence, why not join Friends of Florence? A gift of any amount will put you on its mailing list. You can also become a Patron or Founding Patron, which allows you to participate in many unique programs. Then, the next time you visit this wonderful city, you'll know you've helped in preserving its magnificent treasures.

ABOVE: The world famous sculpture, *David* by Michelangelo, on display in the Galleria dell'Accademia.

Friends of Florence
4545 W Street, NW
Washington, DC 20007
202-333-3705

Friends of Florence
Via Ugo Foscolo, 72
50124 Florence, Italy
011-39-055-223-064
www.friendsofflorence.org

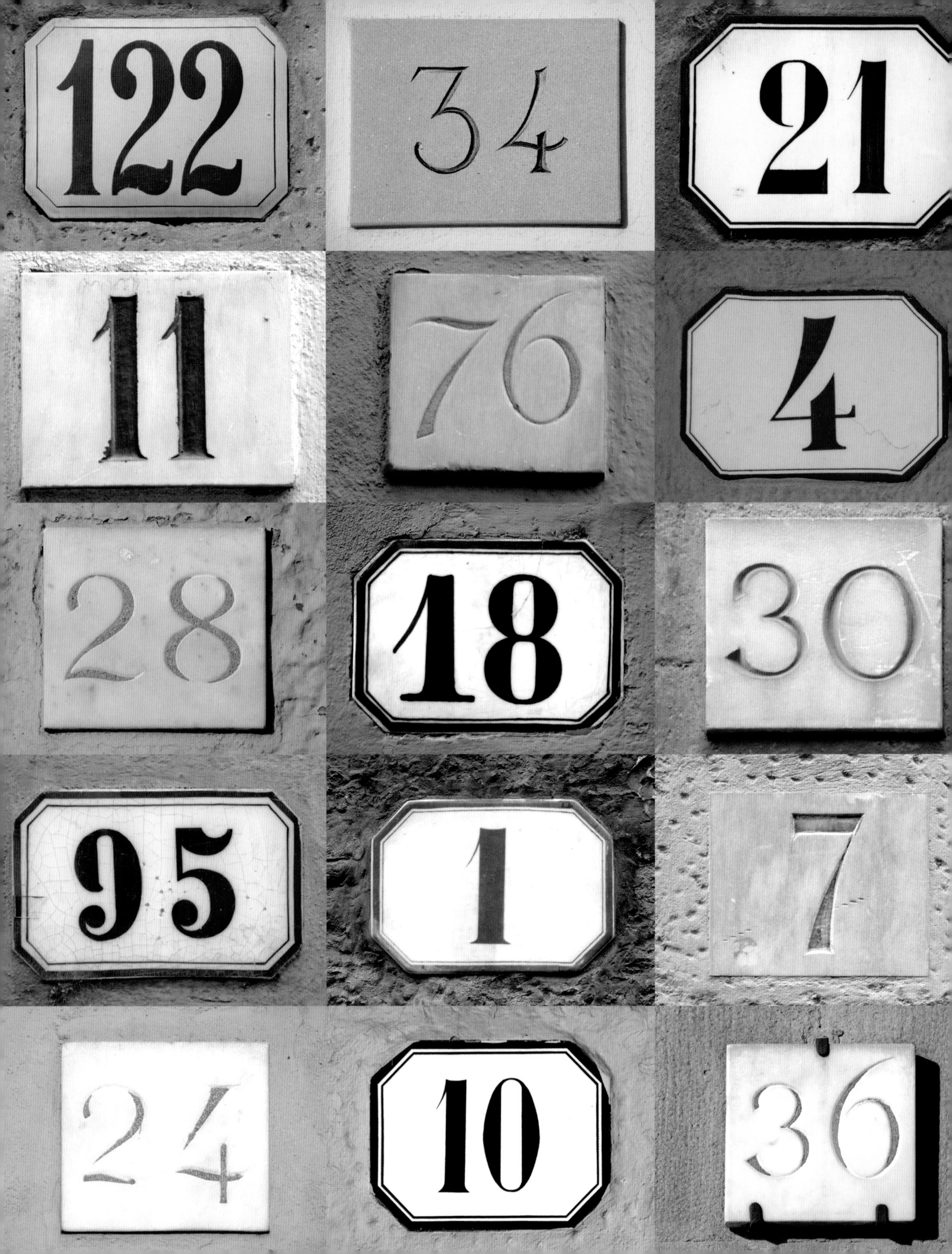
122
34
21
11
76
4
28
18
30
95
1
7
24
10
36

Finding Your Way

In *Dreaming of Tuscany* I wrote that "Florence is a wonderful walking city with surprises at every turn." However there can be more surprises than anticipated because of the confusing, idiosyncratic numbering system of its street addresses. This first started when the city experienced tremendous growth in the nineteenth century when many new numbers were added. This creates much confusion for the visitor.

Firstly, there are two independent sets of numbers on plaques on the building façades: black (*nero*) or blue numbers for residences and red (*rosso*) numbers for businesses or commercial properties. The red sometimes fades to pink and the black to pale grey, further confusing the issue.

Secondly, the numbers on the street do not run in consecutive order. For example a red number 88, which you would expect to be next to or near 87, could instead be next door to 25! This means that the same number can appear twice on the same street—one black and the other red, so you must know whether you are looking for a residence or a business before you set out.

To save time and reduce stress and taxi fares always try to call ahead and ask what is next door or across the street so that you have a landmark to look for. An "r", sometimes printed on the address plaque, is usually printed after the street number on business cards and stationery.

Obtaining a Good Street Map

Be aware that to further complicate this, the same street as it wends its way through the city, can change its name several times. For example, the street directly leading from the Ponte Vecchio is called the Via Por Santa Maria. As it passes the Straw Market, the name changes to Via Calimala then the Via Roma. As it passes the Duomo, it

LEFT: The variety of street numbers in marble, ceramic, and enamel, can sometimes be bewildering—black or blue are reserved for residences and red for businesses.
RIGHT: Vespas, vespas everywhere—the ultimate transportation choice for many Florentines on the go.

becomes the Borgo San Lorenzo, then the Via de'Ginori and then Via San Gallo. The same goes for the street names (*lungarnos*) along the Arno River, which change with every bridge.

This is a good reason to buy a proper map of the city either before or as soon as you arrive. Be sure to get one with a separate listings on the back with all the streets in alphabetical order. The maps that you can get from your hotel are usually fine for general orientation (as is ours on pages 8-9), but if you really want to know where you are going, you will need something more detailed.

Taxis

Florence is easy to negotiate but it's simple to get a taxi for those few times when you might need one. There are basically three numbers you can call from anywhere in the city. They are: 055-4242, 055-4798 and 055-4390. You can always walk to the nearest taxi rank where the white Florentine taxis with ID numbers painted on the door are lined up. Or you can go to the nearest hotel and ask the concierge to call you one.

TWO

The City of Art

*"Every wall tells a story, every house is a palace,
every palace a masterpiece and a legend."*
—Théophile Gautier

I mentioned in my book *Dreaming of Tuscany* that upon arriving in Florence, the French novelist Stendhal found himself overwhelmed when thinking about all the art and beauty he was about to see in this museum city. The stricken Stendhal said, "My soul, affected by the very notion of being in Florence…was already in a state of trance. I had palpitations of the heart…I walked with the fear of falling…." In fact, sitting down to write this chapter, I felt as though I, too, had Stendhal's syndrome. Even though I have been in Florence many, many times, it is still somewhat difficult to come to terms with this city, which has more artistic treasures per square foot than any other in the world, most of which have been here since the Renaissance. It is often very hard for visitors to focus—to know how to organize their day and not be overcome by the art and architecture. After all, you are on vacation—shouldn't you be enjoying yourself, instead of dealing with cultural overload? So how do you navigate what Henry James called "the richest little city in the world"?

Everyone who loves Florence has a list of the things that he or she meant to visit but was unable to get to. You will never be able to see everything you want to see in one trip (unless you stay a year or two!). So, my first suggestion is to make a list of those things that you absolutely do not want to miss. Try to plan your day with variety in mind—a combination of culture and fun.

The good news is that Florence is a walking city, and everything is close by. Even so, it makes sense to coordinate your daily plans by neighborhood. There is no sense exhausting yourself by running from one side of the city to the other, retracing your steps.

There is something else to be considered: Florence is reaching its saturation point as a tourist destination. At certain times of the year, it becomes thronged with crowds. In fact, just recently there were several newspaper articles about a new idea of moving Michelangelo's *David* and some of the more popular of the Uffizi's masterpieces to a location out of town, to cut down on the traffic and crowds in the city center! Really! It sounds like a crazy idea, but that's how bad things have gotten.

There are still many, many lesser-known museums and churches for the motivated visitor to focus on—places where you will be either alone or with just several other people gazing at important art.

My husband and I usually prefer sightseeing in the mornings, when we've got lots of energy and most churches and museums are open. Then we stop for a delicious lunch. You should always spend time choosing a place to have an enjoyable—and delectable—meal in this food lover's Mecca. Then we take a short siesta like the locals. After everything reopens around 4:00 P.M., we're content to wander the city's squares and narrow streets, people-watching, window-shopping, and popping in and out of some of the most wonderful little stores in the world.

When you arrive at your hotel, immediately ask for a complimentary copy of *Florence Concierge Information*. This monthly booklet lists everything happening in the city and is available from your concierge. I also find it invaluable because it more importantly has up-to-date opening and closing times of galleries, historic sites, museums, churches, and gardens. Pick one up on your arrival, and you will get

OPENING PICTURE: An opulent fresco angel by Benozzo Gozzoli at the altar in the Chapel of the Magi.
OVERLEAF, LEFT: Thousands of mosaics by Jacopo da Torrita glitter in the cupola of the Baptistery, and right, ornate armillary from the comprehensive collection in the Museo di Storia della Scienza.

the most out of each day. (Most hotels will give you a copy if you ask—even if you are not staying there.) You can also get one at the Florence Tourist Office, Via Cavour, 1r, 50129 Florence, telephone 011-39-055-290-832, www.firenzeturismo.it.

There is also a recent development, a terrific little newspaper published in English, called *The Florentine*. It's available free throughout the city, including at most bookstores, tourist offices, the airport and train station, and other locations. It contains current information and interesting editorial features and also lists what's happening around the city, including special events, markets, festivals, concerts, lectures, and sports. I usually find some wonderful things in it.

If you want to avoid the hordes of tourists and absorb the essence of the city, explore beyond the popular Duomo, Santa Croce, and Piazza Signoria areas. Wander in the charming neighborhoods of the Oltrarno—Via San Niccolò and Santo Spirito—for example. Take a walk on the winding back streets around Sant' Ambrogio (the organic food market) where Florentines actually live. I guarantee you will experience something unexpected—an artisan carving a delicate gilded frame in an ancient workroom or a tiny corner bakery just putting out fragrant treats.

I've tried to organize this chapter in a way that will help you get the most enjoyment out of the city. Let's start with the piazzas that interrupt the grid of streets in the center of the city that the Romans laid out many years ago. Each anchors a neighborhood, so I've listed them first and have suggested things nearby in order to orient you. Florence's bridges are important not only because they connect one side of the city to the other over the Arno River, which divides the city, but also because they are, in themselves, notable architectural sites. As I've said, the list

ABOVE: You can pick up a guide to the city of Florence, in almost language, on almost any street corner.

of art is inexhaustible, so I've put together an edited selection of the important museums and churches.

One caveat: Each year the museums of Florence are visited by six million people! Certain ones get very crowded and the ticket lines can be extremely long. This can be frustrating, not to mention time-consuming, shortening the valuable time you have available. So if you want to visit the Uffizi or Accademia Gallery, for example, it makes good sense to buy your tickets before your trip, even though it will cost a little extra. It's easy to do on the Internet, and this information is provided on page 48. By doing so, you will go directly to the ticket holders' line, which is usually much shorter and moves faster. Keep in mind, too, that most museums empty out in the late afternoon, when the tour buses leave. A growing number of museums are also open late one night a week and on Mondays (see www.polomuseale.firenze.it/english/musei/musei.asp or www.florence.tickets.com).

The reason I'm giving you websites, instead of listing museum hours, is because Italian museums are famous for their undependable hours. For example, this is what is printed in the tourist information for the Museum of San Marco: "Hours: Monday–Friday, 8:15 A.M.–1:50 P.M., Saturdays, 8:30 A.M.–6:50 P.M., Sundays and holidays, 8:15 A.M.–7:00 P.M. Closed first, third, and fifth Sundays, second and fourth Mondays of month." This is why I'm suggesting you check the museums' websites first, as you certainly wouldn't want to miss the breathtaking works of Fra Angelico housed in this museum, or the opportunity to walk across the square to Pugi for a piece of the best pizza in town.

The Piazza

In Italy, the piazzas are the heart of the country. In Florence, which highly prizes community values, they are the center of city life. A piazza is the same thing as a public square or green, except in Italy it is not necessarily square and, unlike those in England or the United States, does not have much vegetation. In most cases, major buildings and churches anchor these piazzas. They're places where neighbors have been congregating for centuries and weekly open-air markets are held. The active Piazza Santo Spirito is a perfect example, with its daily fresh-food stalls and monthly organic country market.

One of the joys of being in Florence is sitting at a *caffè* table in one of these piazzas. It's the perfect spot to people-watch and enjoy the after-dinner *passeggiata* of Italians, arm in arm and going nowhere in particular—just greeting old friends, window-shopping and walking off a wonderful dinner.

Like all Italian cities, Florence has numerous piazzas, each part of a small neighborhood, so keep your eyes open as you wander. Listed here are some larger ones you will inevitably encounter as you explore the city, but all are worth visiting, if you have the time. Each has its share of prominent buildings and churches, which I have tried to mention.

Piazza della Signoria

D.H. Lawrence once said that when he was in Piazza della Signoria he felt as if he were in one of the living centers of the world, and, in fact, since the fourteenth century, this square has been at the center of Florentine political life. It's one of my favorites, because most of the time, its unusual, large shape absorbs the horde of tourists that occupy it, so it never seems overcrowded. It's nice to arrive in this sunny oasis after wandering Florence's narrow, dim streets.

During the Middle Ages, it was tiny, and has expanded over the years to include the *piazzale* in front of the Uffizi Gallery, all the way to the Arno River. The piazza has been at the center of the many ups and downs of Florence's history, from Roman times to the Medici—Savonarola was burned at a stake in the center during the Inquisition, on May 3, 1498.

The square is dominated by the majestic Palazzo Vecchio and its Gothic bell tower. The statues in front are well known, and include an equestrian bronze statue of Grand Duke Cosimo de' Medici; the Neptune Fountain; and a copy of Michelangelo's *David* that replaced the original, which stood in the piazza for 350 years and, in 1873, was moved to the Galleria dell'Accademia where it still is.

To its east side is the Gothic arched Loggia dei Lanzi, or Loggia della Signoria, a gem of an outdoor

ABOVE: This early morning picture of the Duomo is unique because no one is waiting on line yet!

Piazza del Duomo

From Piazza della Signoria, you can walk directly down Via dei Calzaiuoli to the most famous cathedral in Florence, the Duomo of Santa Maria del Fiore, in Piazza del Duomo. This busy street lined with shops and gelato stands will prepare you for the crowds that you will see in front of the huge Duomo, which anchors this piazza. The street scene in this square is sometimes overwhelming, with schoolchildren and tourists led by umbrella-waving guides. It reminds me of St. Mark's Square in Venice, in that it contains an immense concentration of beauty that is sometimes diluted by the ever-present noise and crowds.

My suggestion is to visit the magnificent Duomo, the Campanile, and the oldest building in the city, the Baptistery, in early morning or late afternoon, when you can actually see and savor the lavish beauty of these distinctive landmarks. Michelangelo is said to have described the Baptistery doors as the "Gates of Paradise" because they were so magnificent. After you have explored these three buildings (see pages 62-3), be sure to walk around the back of the Duomo and visit one of the most wonderful museums in Florence, the Museo dell'Opera del Duomo (see page 59), which contains many significant masterpieces, including works by Michelangelo and Donatello. Most people don't get this far, so the museum is usually empty and a heavenly place to reflect on all the beauty that surrounds you.

DON'T MISS: While you are here, don't miss Nante, at 52r, a dusty shop where you can buy old-fashioned enamel numbers for your house, and Pegna, a gourmet food store extraordinaire masquerading as a supermarket behind the Baptistery (see page 200).

sculpture gallery that is often overlooked. It features several notable works, including Benvenuto Cellini's bronze masterpiece, Perseus, and Giambologna's Rape of the Sabine Women. It was recently restored, with help from Friends of Florence (see page 31).

DON'T MISS: This is the first place you should go to get the true heartbeat of the city and orient yourself. In late afternoon, there are fewer people, and things are quieter. Have a leisurely cup of rich hot chocolate at the famous Caffè Rivoire, stop in next door at Pneider to admire the heavy embossed stationery, and, if you are in the mood for nostalgia, take a horse-carriage ride into the surrounding narrow streets.

ABOVE: A bird's-eye view of the Piazza della Signoria includes the Loggia dei Lanzi and outdoor *caffès*.

Piazza della Repubblica

Despite it never being a favorite with the locals, you will often find yourself walking through this large, nondescript square with its overwhelming arch, which replaced the old market in the late nineteenth century, when Florence became the capital of Italy.

DON'T MISS: The main post office and the large Edison bookstore are on one side, Rocco Forte's trendy Hotel Savoy on the opposite, a perfect place to meet someone for a drink in the early evening. Gilli, the belle époque *caffè* and tea room is here, at 39r, where we like to stop for a morning cappuccino and delicious pastry.

Piazza Santa Croce

This large piazza has been home to many public events since the Middle Ages. Today, ceremonies and festivities, even the annual games of *calcio fiorentino* (a form of sixteenth-century soccer), still take place here. The star of this square is the Church of Santa Croce, a very special place indeed. The city's most eminent residents are buried here, in addition to luminaries such as Michelangelo, Machiavelli, and Galileo, and though Dante's sarcophagus is inside, it is empty, because he died a political exile in Ravenna, and that is where he was buried. Undaunted, the citizens of Florence erected a huge marble statue of him in front of the church (see page 63 for more about this interesting church).

DON'T MISS: Though Piazza Santa Croce has touristy shops facing both sides, walk to the rear on the left side of the church and visit the Scuola del Cuoio (Leather School— see page 193). It was founded after World War II by the Franciscan friars of

ABOVE: The famous church of Santa Croce dominates the piazza with its statue, left, of Dante Alighieri.

the Monastery of Santa Croce and several Florentine families who were master craftsmen in leather. This is a terrific spot to buy good-quality, handcrafted leather gifts to bring home. Florentines love the many flavors of gelato at nearby Vivoli, on Via delle Stinche, 7r. You'll easily find it because there is always a line of people all the way out the front door.

Piazza della Santissima Annunziata

This piazza is off the beaten path but worth going out of your way for. It was planned by Brunelleschi, who then went on to design the adjacent Ospedale degli Innocenti (orphanage) which gives this square a certain grace. You will recognize the building by the loggia, which is decorated with glazed pottery medallions of babies by Andrea della Robbia. The Church of Santissima Annunziata was founded in the thirteenth century and contains an important group of frescoes by notable artists of the sixteenth century, including Jacopo Pontormo. The tabernacle was commissioned by the Medici and designed by Michelozzo. In the center of the square is Giambologna's equestrian statue of Grand Duke Ferdinando I.

DON'T MISS: Look up, and you will see the vast side of the Duomo at the end of the Via dei Servi. Stop at Robiglio, 112r, a *pasticceria* with some of the most delicious sandwiches and cakes in town. They also have a restaurant where you can have lunch.

Piazza San Lorenzo

Also called Piazza del Mercato Centrale, this piazza is lined with open-air stalls and always thronged with people. Vendors are hawking everything from inexpensive T-shirts and souvenirs to colorful silk

scarves and leather coats. It's the location of the active Mercato Centrale, or central market, which is the food basket of Florence, selling everything from fruit to vegetables, meat, fish, pastas, cheeses, and everything in between (see page 167).

It's also the home of the parish church of the Medici, the Church of San Lorenzo, designed by Brunelleschi and said to be the oldest in Florence. Located here are the Medici Chapels and the Laurentian Library—two of the most amazing treasures in this city. You can easily spend an entire day here being inspired by the church, wandering the outdoor and indoor markets, and stopping for lunch at one of several, good family-run trattorias.

DON'T MISS: All the little outdoor stalls where you can get good hot snacks as you wander—from tripe sandwiches, a Florentine specialty, to the *friggitore* at Via di Sant'Antonio, 50r, who offers hot donuts. Try Mario, Via Rosina, 2, open only for lunch serving reasonably priced Tuscan specialties.

Piazza Santa Maria Novella

This piazza is near the railroad station and is not terribly attractive. Ironically, it is one of the few squares in Florence with some greenery, but it's a place that is rather unappealing, usually being occupied by transients and tourists taking one last break before dragging their suitcases across the wide street to the station. However, after such bad press, the square is now being totally renovated and, hopefully, by the time you read this, will be finished. One very good reason to come to this piazza, however, is to visit the exceptional Church of Santa Maria Novella. Note its magnificent marble façade, and plan to spend some time viewing its Renaissance treasures, including the museum and cloisters (see page 68).

DON'T MISS: After visiting the church, walk around the corner to Via della Scala, 16, for the olfactory experience of a lifetime. This is where you'll find the Farmaceutica di Santa Maria Novella, located in a gorgeous fourteenth-century, fresco-decorated chapel displaying ancient vases, perfume bottles, and mortars, and selling the most divinely fragrant perfumes, soaps, and creams (see pages 185-7).

Piazza de' Pitti

This immense cobblestone piazza is the starting place for tourists entering one of the most fabulous museums in the world—the Pitti Palace, designed by Brunelleschi (see page 48). Mystery buffs who read Magdalen Nabb's books will know that the Police Department is also located here.

DON'T MISS: It looks touristy, but in front of the piazza are some artists who routinely show their work, some of which is quite good. My favorites are Adelina Quadri, from whom you can buy beautiful watercolors of the surrounding Tuscan countryside, and Joseph Moussa, an artist who does architectural interpretations of the landmarks in Florence by using pen and ink and watercolors. The shops across from the Pitti are some of the oldest in town. You'll find nicely crafted leather goods, pottery, and my favorite tiny postcard shop, at 39r. If you are lucky, Casa Guidi at Piazza San Felice, 8, home to poets Robert and Elizabeth Browning, will be open (see page 54).

Piazza Santo Spirito

This is my favorite piazza in all of Florence, situated in my favorite area, the Oltrarno. It is planted with shade trees and always filled with children riding bikes, neighbors chatting, and other daily activity in this congenial neighborhood. In the morning, there is

an outdoor market selling fresh fruit and vegetables, clothing and household goods. You have left most tourists behind and can sit gazing up at the simple but elegant façade of the Church of Santo Spirito.

DON'T MISS: Stop in at Caffè Ricchi for espresso and wonderful pastry—be sure to go into the side room to see all the artists' framed renditions of the church's façade. I always buy packets of arugula, and other Italian seeds, next door at Morganti. At night, all the restaurants and bars are open, making it a lively place for people to congregate.

The Bridges

The bridges of Florence are one of its most distinctive and graceful architectural elements. They all cross the brown, swirling Arno River, which has been alternately criticized (Mark Twain) and appreciated (André Gide) by visitors throughout the years. For centuries, the river has been the city's life blood, providing water from the surrounding mountains for the leather and textile trades, which were responsible for its prosperity. There are seven bridges, some of which you will encounter as you wander the winding streets of Florence. Starting in the west with the Ponte della Vittoria to the Ponte Vespucci, the Ponte alla Carraia, the Ponte Santa Trinità, the Ponte Vecchio, the Ponte alle Grazie, and the Ponte San Niccolò, in that order. These bridges have been the victim of floods and wars but they have always been rebuilt.

Ponte Vecchio

What John Ruskin described as the "Old Treasure Bridge" is probably one of the best-known landmarks in the world, and synonymous with Florence.

So ancient that it was known even in the tenth century as the "old bridge," it was for years the only way Florentines could get from one side of the city to the other. Neri di Fioravante designed the bridge you see today after the 1345 flood swept away the previous one. It inspired Longfellow to write a poem, it was spared when the Nazis destroyed every other bridge in the city to thwart the advancing Allies, and it even survived the disastrous floods of 1966—so it really should be considered a little Florentine miracle!

During the day, this pedestrian bridge is overflowing with activity with browsing tourists, residents and noisy street vendors. But if you wander over in the early morning or early evening, the view is transformed because the closed jewelry shops still have their old-fashioned awnings and evocative wood shutters harking back to medieval times.

Originally, the bridge was home to butchers and fish sellers, who conveniently dumped their waste through the arches into the river, then to the tanners, who soaked their hides in the water. In the mid-sixteenth century, Grand Duke Cosimo I decided to avoid the smell and the crowds by commissioning Giorgio Vasari to build a second story above the shops on the east side of the bridge called the Corridoio Vasariano, so he could leave his home in the Pitti Palace and walk to work at the Uffizi and Palazzo Vecchio, avoiding the hoi polloi. It is now an art gallery (see page 50).

In the sixteenth century, the tanners were replaced by goldsmiths, who are there to this day, a must-stop for those of us who love baubles. In honor of the jewelers on the bridge, there is a statue of Benvenuto Cellini, craftsman extraordinaire, which has become an informal meeting place for the many college students from abroad who study in Florence.

Ponte della Vittoria

I've never walked over this bridge, but I have driven over it when I picked up a rental car and wanted to get out of town fast. It takes you over the Arno on the outskirts of the city, enabling you to avoid one-way streets. In no time, you are through the Porta Romana and on your way to southern Tuscany.

Ponte A. Vespucci

If you are at the Grand Hotel, the Hotel Excelsior, or the American Consulate and want to go to the Oltrarno, this is the bridge to use. On the other side, you will find yourself in the midst of restoration workshops—craftsmen carving, sanding, and hammering. Many of the small, family-run restaurants we like are in this area (see chapter 6).

Ponte alla Carraia

This is the second-oldest bridge in Florence and was sometimes called the "new bridge" to differentiate it from the Ponte Vecchio. Originally made of wood, it was rebuilt many times, notably in 1304, when it collapsed beneath the weight of dense crowds assembled to watch a play taking place on boats in the river below it. It was destroyed during World War II. Its name derives from the carts that were used, when it was first built, to transport silk and woolen textiles from the Borgo Ognissanti to the Oltrarno.

Ponte Santa Trinità

You may often find yourself on this graceful bridge because it traverses the Arno from Piazza dei Frescobaldi on the Oltrarno to Via de' Tornabuoni, the chic

LEFT, ABOVE: A rooftop view, facing west, of the Ponte Santa Trinità and the Ponte alla Carraia, and below, boaters row on the Arno River under the Ponte Vecchio.

shopping street in Florence. Like the Ponte Vecchio, it has a long story to tell. Originally built in the sixteenth century by Bartolomeo Ammannati, it is said to be based on a design by Michelangelo. Its total destruction in 1944 by the retreating Germans was one of the greatest of the many losses suffered by the Florentines during the war. In *The Stones of Florence*, Mary McCarthy called the bridge "the most beautiful in Florence, the most beautiful perhaps in the world...." Concerned Americans and organizations, including Bernard Berenson and the Samuel Kress Foundation, joined with the city and vowed to reconstruct the much-loved bridge exactly as it had been before. It was.

Ponte alle Grazie

Named after the Church of Santa Maria delle Grazie, which once stood nearby, this thirteenth-century bridge was rebuilt in the modern style after World War II. If you take it from Piazza Santa Croce over the Arno to the Oltrarno, you avoid the city center. From the middle, you have a lovely view of the Ponte Vecchio. The other side feels like another city—the countrified neighborhood of San Niccolò. Nearby is Piazza Demidoff, a charming little square with two gazebos and trees where you can sit and enjoy a view of the river. Piazzale Michelangelo is not too far away, and it's a lovely walk, albeit uphill.

Ponte San Niccolò

This is another bridge I've driven over many times in an effort to avoid the maze of one-way streets of Florence. If you are heading south, it will take you to Piazzale Michelangelo and the Church of San Miniato al Monte (see page 69). If you are heading northeast, it will take you to Fiesole (see page 128).

The Museums

Already by 1804, when Madame de Staël visited the Uffizi, the museums in the city were open to the public. In her book *Corrine*, she writes, "The fine arts are very republican in Florence. The statues and pictures are on show at all hours, with the utmost ease of entry. Attendants, trained and paid by the government, are on hand to explain the masterpieces." Although today there is staff, their role has changed, and in most cases, if you are interested in the masterpieces, you will have to buy a guidebook or rent a headset.

The guidebook that the Tourist Board issues says that "opening times of museums are not indicated due to the fact that they change rather frequently." An understatement, which is why I've listed the following websites. Though recently some hours have been standardized, the important thing is that there are so many wonderful museums that you can never see everything in them, no matter how many times you come to Florence. Unlike many other European cities, Florence does not have a museum-card system. So since Tuscany is said to have the highest density of museums in the world and Florence has at least sixty-five, this further complicates things.

The best way to approach this "feast of art" is to be selective initially. I've listed my favorites here, and you will have your own, as well. An asterisk next to the museum name means it should be on your "do-not-miss list," especially if you are in the city for a limited time. The following websites could help your decision-making:

- www.museumsinflorence.com Go to this website to get the most up-to-date hours of museums, as well as other important details, including telephone numbers and admission fees.

- www.polomuseale.firenze.it/english/musei/musei.asp Use this for accessing all details of the state museums, many of which have special seniors and children's admission prices.

- www.weekendafirenze.com If you are going to visit popular museums such as the Uffizi, you can save yourself valuable time by preordering your tickets on this website.

Palazzo Pitti*
Pitti Palace
Piazza de' Pitta
Via Romana
011-39-055-238-8611
www.polomuseale.firenze.it/english/musei/musei.asp

In a city of fabulous museums, this is the grandest of all. It was built for the Pitti family in 1457 based on designs by Brunelleschi. The Pittis sold it to the Medici in the mid-sixteenth century, and they engaged Bartolomeo Ammannati to remodel the façade and create the courtyard that we see today.

For three centuries, this was the seat of the Lorraine Dynasty, and after the unification of Italy, it was the headquarters of the Savoy kings. Florence was the capital of Italy for the five years from 1865 to 1870. Standing in the piazza and looking at this immense building can give one an overwhelming feeling: all that art, so little time.

But in fact the Pitti Palace houses four smaller museums within its walls and two just outside that contain some of the most outstanding treasures of the Medici. In the nineteenth century, Henry James said that the masterpieces "jostle each other in their splendor." You enter the museum through a huge archway into a large courtyard. If this is your first visit, my suggestion is to go directly into the corner

bookshop and pick up a catalog, which is available for each collection, to act as your guide. Here's a short rundown on each of the museums:

Galleria Palatina and Appartamenti Reali

Palatine Gallery and Royal Apartments

011-39-055-238-8614

On the left as you enter, this collection of artworks ranges from the sixteenth to the eighteenth century. Floor-to-ceiling paintings cover the walls, gallery-style, in the sumptuous rooms including the Royal Apartments. Make sure you look for masterpieces by

Titian, Caravaggio, Rubens, Veronese, and Raphael scattered throughout. Miniatures of sixteenth-century fruits and flowers by my favorite watercolorist, Giovanna Garzoni, are in good company!

Museo degli Argenti

Silver Museum

011-39-055-238-8709

As a longtime antiques collector, I never tire of visiting this museum. It is the Medici "Cabinet of Curios," containing not only an astounding group of rare, ornate Renaissance silver but amazing objets d'art: ewers, vases, and serving pieces, all made from rock crystal, shells, semiprecious stones, and mother-of-pearl; cameos and intaglios; tortoiseshell and ivory boxes; luminous jewels highlighting those of Anna Maria Luisa, the last Medici; and tapestries that will leave any collector breathless. New additions include an important collection of contemporary jewelry and Japanese and Chinese porcelain.

Galleria d'Arte Moderna

Modern Art Museum

011-39-055-238-8601

If you are a fan of art that is a bit more contemporary, visit these galleries, featuring Tuscan paintings and sculptures of the eighteenth century to World War I.

Museo del Costume

Costume Museum

011-39-055-238-8763

This gallery, located in a wing that overlooks the Boboli Gardens, features fashion accessories and textiles from the sixteenth through the early twentieth century. They often have specific exhibitions, like the one on Roman fashion designer Simonetta.

Museo della Porcellana

Porcelain Museum

011-39-055-238-8709

On display in this pink villa, used by scholars during the Renaissance, is a small collection of porcelain—Meissen, Sevres, Doccia—made for the Medicis and the House of Lorraine. Located in the Garden of the Cavaliere at the top of the Boboli Gardens, it has a heart-stopping view of the hills surrounding Florence. Stroll in the little garden, whose parterres are filled with roses and peonies in the spring.

Galleria degli Uffizi*

Uffizi Gallery

Piazzale degli Uffizi, 6

011-39-055-238-8651

www.polomuseale.firenze.it/english/musei/musei.asp

The Tuscan state government was finally located in one central place in 1560, when Cosimo I de' Medici commissioned Giorgio Vasari to build these offices (Uffizi). Shortly after, Francesco I de' Medici created what would be the first art museum in the world, on the top floor. Now the Uffizi contains more than forty-five glorious rooms exhibiting approximately 2,000 works of art at any one time, the greatest collection of Renaissance art in the world, including *Primavera* by Sandro Botticelli and Duccio's *Madonna Enthroned*, for a start.

Though the art is hung in chronological order, starting with the Renaissance, you will definitely need a guide book, comfortable shoes, and several days to see it all. Present is art from every major Italian master from the thirteenth to the eighteenth century, including Cimabue, Duccio, Giotto, Masaccio, Filippo Lippi, Botticelli, Caravaggio, Canaletto, Uccello, Tiepolo, Titian, Leonardo da Vinci, and Michelangelo, not to mention the Mannerist, Flemish, Spanish, French, and German schools. And let's not forget the furniture, tapestry, and objects that complement it all.

In *Italian Hours*, Henry James wrote that "the long outer galleries of the Uffizi had never beguiled me more; sometimes there were not more than two or three figures standing there, Baedeker in hand." Unfortunately, today over 1.5 million visit the museum every year. Even on my first visit, one could just walk in and savor. But ever since the terrible bombing in 1993 and all the attendant publicity, the Uffizi has been mobbed with visitors. To avoid wasting valuable time in the never-ending line waiting to enter, you can reserve tickets in advance. Pick them up the day of your visit and enter the Uffizi—stress free (almost)! There are several websites available, but we used the following one last year and it worked just fine: www.weekendafirenze.com or call Firenze Musei at 011-39-055-294-883.

Corridoio Vasariano

Vasari Corridor

This overhead passageway on the east side of the Ponte Vecchio, connecting the Palazzo Vecchio to the Pitti Palace, was built in 1565 by Vasari. It enabled the Medici rulers to walk from the Pitti Palace through the Uffizi to the Palazzo Vecchio. Several years ago, limited guided tours of the *corridoio* were started. Lately, they have been changing the rules so it's always best to check in advance. One caveat: you may get more of a thrill from the views of the Arno River and the surrounding hills from this unique vantage point than from the paintings and the tour is about a half mile through unheated hallways with no place to stop off in between, so freshen up and have an espresso or a cup of tea before you start.

Museo della Fondazione H. P. Horne*

Horne Foundation Museum
Via de' Benci, 6
011-39-055-244-661

You can almost feel what it would be like to live in the Renaissance as you wander from room to room in this small fifteenth-century palazzo. It was left to the state in 1917 by English collector Herbert Percy Horne and is decorated with furnishings with an emphasis on domestic use, even to the antique cooking utensils in the kitchen. There are masterpieces, too, by Giotto, Masaccio, and Lippi.

Museo Stibbert

Stibbert Museum
Via Federico Stibbert, 26
011-39-055-475-520

This museum is a little bit out of town, so you will need to take a bus or taxi. It's home to the collection of Frederick Stibbert, a Scotsman who, in the nineteenth century, put together a personal, some say eccentric, collection of approximately 50,000 items. Notable is the collection of arms and armor from Europe, Asia, Africa, and India, said to be unique.

Museo Nazionale Alinari della Fotografia*

Alinari Museum of Photography
Piazza Santa Maria Novella, 14a
011-39-055-216-310
www.alinarifondazione.it

This museum is part of the world's oldest photographic company, founded in 1852 by the Alinari brothers. It is easy to believe, as, over the years, many of their images have become icons. The museum's exhibits are created from the photographs in its archives, copies of which you can purchase (see page 199).

Museo Salvatore Ferragamo*

Ferragamo Shoe Museum
Via dei Tornabuoni, 2
011-39-055-336-0456
www.salvatoreferragamo.it

Anyone who loves shoes (don't we all?) will enjoy this gem of a museum, which is around the corner from the shop at the Palazzo Spini Feroni and documents the work of master designer Salvatore Ferragamo. The collection of over 10,000 pairs of shoes dates from Ferragamo's 1927 return from Hollywood. See handcrafted fashion statements made for the likes of Audrey Hepburn, Sophia Loren, and Ingrid Bergman to name just a few. Admission is free. After the museum, visit the shop and indulge.

Villa Bardini

Costa San Giorgio, 2
011-39-055-265-4321

The Bardini Museum, housing Stefano Bardini's collection, is still not open to the public, but the Villa Bardini, above, has been beautifully restored and now features changing exhibits, the first being dedicated to design maestro Roberto Capucci's sculptural clothing and archives.

Casa Buonarroti

Buonarroti House
Via Ghibellina, 70
011-39-055-241-752

Michelangelo bought this house in 1508, but he never actually lived here, although his descendants lived in it until the mid-nineteenth century. On display are the memorabilia of his life, including a model of the *Madonna della Scala*, his earliest known work, and an important collection of his drawings.

PREVIOUS PAGE: The glorious *The Birth of Venus*, painted by Sandro Botticelli, is in the Uffizi Gallery.
ABOVE: The powerful statue of Hercules by Bacio Bandinelli, is in front of the Palazzo Vecchio nearby.

Museo Marino Marini

Marino Marini Museum
Piazza San Pancrazio
011-39-055-219-432

Works by this vigorous twentieth-century sculptor and painter are displayed in the sleekly renovated Church of San Pancrazio, behind Via dei Tornabuoni.

Casa di Dante

Dante's House
Via Santa Margherita, 1
011-39-055-219-416

Though not the original house of Dante, this reconstruction was built in the early twentieth century on what was thought to be the site of the Alighieri family home. Skip the ground floor, and go up to the top of this modest museum, where you'll find memorabilia from Dante's life, including rare antique editions of his masterpiece, *The Divine Comedy*.

Casa Guidi*

Piazza San Felice, 8
011-39-055-354-457

A visit to this charming suite of rooms, once occupied by the poets Robert and Elizabeth Barrett Browning, is well worth it, despite its short opening hours and the fact that it is usually closed for the winter. When we were last there, it was open Mondays, Wednesdays, and Fridays, 3:00 P.M. to 6:00 P.M., April through November. If you are a romantic, take a short walk past the Pitti Palace, turn right at Piazza San Felice where it meets Via Maggio,

and you are gazing at the place where the Brownings worked and lived happily for fourteen years, part of a thriving English colony in Florence. It is now owned by Eton College, which engaged the Landmark Trust of England to help with the renovations. It's a lovely way to spend the afternoon on the Oltrarno, and if you have a mind to stay longer, ask to see the next-door apartment, which can be rented through the Holiday Division of the Landmark Trust; www.landmarktrust.co.uk.

Museo dell Opificio delle Pietre Dure*

Museum of the Semiprecious-Stone Works
Via degli Alfani, 78
011-39-055-265-1357
www.opificio.arte.beniculturali.it

This museum is unique, as it showcases the carving of semiprecious hard stones used in the magnificently ornate inlaid mosaics for which Florence is famous. Established in 1558 by the Medici, this workshop moved to its present location in 1796 and was renovated in 1995 into this glittering gem, containing rare, colorful, and precious objects. It also houses the Opificio delle Pietre Dure, one of the leading and most prestigious laboratories in the world, restoring everything from tapestries to paintings to sculpture.

Museo Zoologico della Specola

Zoological Museum
Via Romana, 17
011-39-055-228-8251
www.specola.unifi.it

Opened in 1775, this is one of the oldest science museums in Europe—and one of the most bizarre! Named for the observatory on its roof, this is really a zoology museum, filled with exhibits that range

ABOVE: You can walk from the Arno to the Palazzo Vecchio through the classical Piazzale degli Uffizi.

from stuffed and pickled animals to an anatomically realistic wax collection made in the eighteenth century and including gory depictions of the plague. It is definitely not for the squeamish or very young.

Museo di Storia della Scienza

History of Science Museum
Piazza dei Giudici, 1
011-39-055-293-493/ 055-265-311
www.imss.fi.it

If you have a passion for science, this is the place for you. Its impressive collections make us realize that Tuscany was the center of a scientific Renaissance, as well as an artistic one. Galileo lived and worked in Florence, and the museum pays homage to his discoveries by featuring the telescopes he used in many

of his noteworthy experiments. Even one of his fingers is preserved! Antiques lovers will be inspired by the dazzling, beautifully crafted objects on display: scientific instruments, exquisite maps, delicate glass thermometers, intricate clocks, etched astrolabes, and even a medieval pharmacy. It is currently closed for renovations, so check before heading over.

Sinagoga e Museo di Arte e Storia Ebraica
Synagogue and Museum of Jewish Art and History
Via Farini, 4
011-39-055-234-6654
The original Jewish ghetto in Florence was demolished in the 1860s, and this ornate Spanish-Moorish building, constructed in the 1870s, is easily recognized by its tall copper domes. The museum contains memorabilia, objects, furniture, and photographs that document the history of Florence's Jewish population, which dates back to Roman times.

Museo della Casa Fiorentina Antica*
The Ancient Florentine House Museum
or Palazzo Davanzati
Via Porta Rossa, 13
011-39-055-238-8610
www.polomuseale.firenze.it/musei/davanzati/
Restored by Elia Volpi at the turn of the twentieth century, this eccentric, little house museum is furnished with objects from the Middle Ages, Renaissance, and Baroque periods. Sometimes called the Palazzo Davanzati Museum, it was originally built in the

fourteenth century and is one of the most important medieval palazzi in the city. It has just been restored. The main rooms feature amazing trompe-l'oeil frescoed walls imitating rich Renaissance fabrics, a small collection of rare Montelupo ceramics, circa 1620, and a *cassaforte* (strong box) with twenty-four locks!

Museo di Firenze com'era
Museum of Florence as It Was
Via dell' Oriuolo, 24
011-39-055-239-8483
Flemish artist Justus Utens painted the twelve lunettes (half-moon-shaped aerial views) of the Medici family's estates and gardens in 1599, and they are on display here in this small museum behind the Duomo which charts the everyday life of fifteenth-century Florence through engravings and paintings.

Museo Archeologico
Archeological Museum
Via della Colonna, 36/38
011-39-055-235-75
www.comune.firenze.it
Located off Piazza S.S. Annunziata, this museum houses some of the most important collections of Etruscan art and artifacts in Italy, including the masterpiece the *Chimera*, a bronze Etruscan sculpture restored by Benvenuto Cellini. Roman and Greek antiquities are on display here, along with Egyptian treasures that rank second in all of Italy.

RIGHT ABOVE: As you are walking on the Via dello Studio near the Duomo, take a peek into the workshop of the Museo dell'Opera del Duomo, where artisan stone masons are constantly busy.
BELOW RIGHT: The inner courtyard colonnade of the Museo Nazionale del Bargello, one of the most notable museums in Florence with its extraordinary architecture and memorable masterpieces.
BELOW LEFT: The Capella dei Pazzi in the Church of Santa Croce designed by Brunelleschi is considered a classic.

Palazzo Medici-Riccardi*

Medici-Riccardi Palace

Via Cavour, 1

011-39-055-276-0340

www.palazzo-medici-it

The heavily rusticated architecture of this palace, commonly known as the first Renaissance building in Florence, was designed in 1444 by Michelozzo, Cosimo Medici's favorite architect. It set the trend for buildings made of huge, roughly hewn stones. (The Palazzo Pitti and Palazzo Strozzi are just two somber examples.) As you enter, take the steps that lead up to the small chapel, the Capella dei Magi. You'll discover the masterpiece *The Journey of the Magi*, a fresco by Benozzo Gozzoli, a student of Fra Angelico. It depicts opulently dressed nobles (members of the Medici family, including Lorenzo the Magnificent) riding through a lush Renaissance landscape filled with charming animals. Be sure not to miss the inner courtyard, decorated with medallions, carved in Donatello's workshop, of the Medici coats of arms.

Palazzo Strozzi

Strozzi Palace

Piazza degli Strozzi, 1

011-39-055-285-395

This immense palace was commissioned by the wealthy Strozzi family, who had to clear a substantial amount of central Florence in order to have enough space to erect it. It sits as a somber reminder of the Palazzo Medici-Riccardi across town. It has been recently revitalized, housing noteworthy museum shows, and is used for special exhibitions, lectures, and programs. Be sure to stop by to check out what is currently happening and to look at the graceful loggia by Cronaca.

The two most well-known Davids in the world are in Florence. **ABOVE**: the marble giant by Michelangelo, and below, the graceful bronze beauty by Donatello.

Museo Nazionale del Bargello*

Bargello Museum
Via del Proconsolo, 4
011-39-055-238-8606
www.sbas.firenze.it/bargello

This museum has been my refuge in Florence, despite its most eccentric daily schedule, open only in the morning and closed on various days of the week. Originally built as the Palace of the Podestà, seat of the chief magistrate and law courts, before being turned over to the Chief of Police, or Bargello, in the sixteenth century, it officially opened as a museum in 1865 and now features Italy's most impressive collection of important Renaissance sculpture and ceramics. Its depressing history belies its entrance into an elegant courtyard and the fact that it is usually, inexplicably, not too crowded. Buying the guide book as you first walk in, is a good idea.

The museum is on three floors, just one masterpiece after another. The crème de la crème includes four works by Michelangelo, featuring his *Bacchus,* carved when he was just twenty-two; Donatello's significant bronze *David*—a must-see—and fierce *Saint George,* originally in the Orsanmichele; Giambologna's iconic bronze *Mercury*; and works by Cellini—just the tip of the iceberg. So you will understand why it's easy to overlook two amazing pieces, the bronze panels sculpted by Filippo Brunelleschi and Lorenzo Ghiberti for their entries in the design competition for the Baptistery doors, on display here. And don't miss the glittering glazed terracotta masterpieces by the Della Robbia brothers on the third floor. Oh, and be sure not to skip the fabulous ancient textiles, rare ceramics, arms and armor, ivories, and miniature bronzes—you get the picture.

Galleria dell'Accademia*

Accademia Gallery
Via Ricasoli, 60
011-39-055-238-8609
www.sbas.firenze.it/accademia

Of course, you have to visit the Accademia to see again what a genius Michelangelo really was. Expect to stand in line, because every other tourist has the same idea. You will not be disappointed. The statue of *David* has not a flaw—it is majestic and overwhelming because of its sheer size. Originally in Piazza della Signoria, it was moved here in 1873 to protect it from the environment (a copy was substituted). On either side of *David* are a group of Michelangelo's powerful unfinished works, struggling for five hundred years to free themselves from the raw marble.

Museo dell'Opera del Duomo*

Museum of the Cathedral Works
Piazza del Duomo, 9
011-39-055-230-2885
www.operaduomo.firenze.it

Many people think this museum, known officially as the Museum dell'Opera di Santa Maria del Fiore, has to do with singing, but it is really something very different, because the word *opera* in Italian means "works." This workshop opened in this ancient palazzo when construction on the Duomo was started. Its mission was to care for and maintain all the artwork and sculpture of both the Duomo and the Baptistery. In fact, Michelangelo carved his famous *David* in what was the original courtyard here! In 1891, it was converted into a formal museum in order to more properly display its treasures.

Though I have been here many times, there are never more than several people wandering around

under the elegant glass roof of the courtyard—a pleasure, especially during the crowded, hot summer months, and an opportunity to see masterpieces up close. The star attraction is one of Michelangelo's last sculptures, *The Bandini Pietà*, which, though intended for his tombstone, was unfinished when he died. Many say the face of Nicodemus on the piece is that of Michelangelo.

Be amazed by the original "Gates of Paradise" Baptistery bronze door panels by Ghiberti. Fifteenth-century choir stalls by Donatello and Luca della Robbia sit side by side with the tools and machinery actually used by Brunelleschi and his artisans to build the dome, including architectural models of it in various stages of development.

Palazzo Vecchio
Old Palace Town Hall
Piazza della Signoria
011-39-055-276-8465
www.comune.firenze.it

The Palazzo Vecchio, created by Arnolfo di Cambio in the thirteenth century, is probably the most recognizable building in Florence because of its ancient Gothic bell tower (the highest in the city). It serves as Piazza Signoria's landmark, a fortress that signaled Florence's emergence into the Renaissance. For seven centuries, it was the seat of the city's political power. The Town Council still meets here today in rooms that are closed to the public. Most people stop in front to view the sculptures (see pages 40-1 and 54) but, in their rush to get to the Uffizi, don't go inside.

LEFT: A tin-glazed earthenware plaque of the Madonna and Child, hallmark of the Florentine workshops of the della Robbia family, in San Giovannino del Cavalieri.

Admire the sculptures on the first floor, and visit the Salone del Cinquecento, the Studiolo of Francesco I, and the Quartiere degli Elementi, all by Vasari. If you have children, stop in at the Museo dei Ragazzi (see "Traveling with Children," page 72).

Churches

Throughout history, Florence's churches have been the focus of city life and, as a result, are filled with many important artworks and precious objects. I've always thought of them as "church-museums." Their architecture ranges from the Romanesque to the contemporary. Many were commissioned by the Medici and designed by major Florentine masters. A visit to one of the following can be a wonderful refuge, because not only will you be seeing some of the most distinguished art in the city but in many cases you will be seeing it in solitude and have time to really savor the experience. Remember that most of these churches still function as such, and masses are held not only on Sundays but throughout the week. Be a respectful visitor, and heed the signs on church doors asking people to dress properly and enter quietly.

Orsanmichele
Church and Museum of Orsanmichele
Via dell'Arte della Lana
011-39-055-284-944

This unique name stems from the fact that the church—the original home of Florence's grain market—was constructed on the site of the vegetable garden, or *orto*, of the Monastery of San Michele, hence Orsanmichele. In 1339 each of the leading guilds in the city was asked to commission a statue of

its patron saint reflecting stature and wealth, to decorate the external niches of the building's walls. They took their time, completing the project almost a hundred years later. A fortuitous delay, as some of the statues were created by the most prestigious early-Renaissance sculptors of the day—Della Robbia, Ghiberti, and Donatello. Today, the statues are all copies, the originals in the museum that occupies the top two stories of the building. (*St. George*, by Donatello, is in the Bargello.) To get relief from the shoppers outside on Via dei Calzaiuoli, stop into the dark church to view Andrea Orcagna's *Tabernacle*.

Duomo*

Duomo, or Cathedral, of Santa Maria del Fiore
Piazza del Duomo
011-39-055-230-2885
www.duomo.firenze.it

It is said that when Michelangelo was working on the cupola of St. Peter's in Rome, he would visit Florence and, gazing up at Brunelleschi's soaring Duomo, say "*Come te non voglio, meglio di te non posso*" (Similar to thee I will not, better than thee I cannot). From the moment it was conceived as a project, the Duomo was considered something of great importance.

This green-and-pink marble masterpiece, with its stupendous dome, the first in Europe, has become an icon of cathedrals because of the miraculous way in which Brunelleschi designed and engineered it. It is so huge that Henry James said that approaching it from one of the narrow city streets was like greeting "the side of a mountain when you move in the gorge."

In the thirteenth century, Florence's power was growing, both on the mercantile and the political levels, and the city's church, Santa Reparata, was no longer considered impressive enough. The Florentines leveled over three hundred buildings to create a site where the esteemed Tuscan architect Arnolfo di Cambio could design a new cathedral. He based it on the cloverleaf model of the famous cathedrals in France but died just as the foundation was being laid. In 1418, Filippo Brunelleschi won the competition to design the dome, and the rest is history.

On the other hand, the interior of the Duomo is relatively simple. While you are inside, visit Brunelleschi's tomb, which was discovered in the crypt of Santa Reparata in 1972. It is where you can also see the ruins of the original church. The world's largest fresco, the Last Judgment, by Giorgio Vasari, decorates the vast interior of the dome. There have been thousands of books written about this church and its dome—one of the most intriguing and miraculous feats in the history of architecture—so you can do more research on your own. Visit the Museo dell'Opera del Duomo (which I've written about on page 59) behind the Duomo to see wood models of the cupola, and the some of the actual tools and original machinery used to build it.

Campanile di Giotto*

Giotto's Bell Tower
Piazza del Duomo
011-39-055-230-2885

The slender, graceful bell tower of the Duomo is commonly called the "Campanile." "The model and mirror of perfect architecture," said John Ruskin of it. It was designed and begun in 1334 by the painter Giotto and finished by Francesco Talenti in 1359. There are 414 steep steps to the top, but definitely worth the climb because of the remarkable 360 degree views of Florence. You are really on top of the world here!

Battistero di San Giovanni*

Baptistery

Piazza del Duomo

011-39-055-230-2885

This renowned building, with its splendid interior, probably the most revered in Florence, is one of its oldest—its foundation dates from the sixth or seventh century. Many Florentines, including Dante, were baptized here. They say his spirit pervades the building, because he called it *"il mio bel San Giovanni"* in his masterpiece, *The Divine Comedy*. The green-and-white marble exterior is punctuated with three important sets of gilded-bronze doors.

Andrea Pisano designed the first set of doors on the south side in 1336. In 1424 Lorenzo Ghiberti won the competition to design those on the north side. (His winning panel and the masterpiece runner-up by Filippo Brunelleschi are now in the Bargello Museum.) They were so successfully received that he was then engaged to design the east doors about which Ghiberti humbly wrote, "I executed that work with the greatest diligence and the greatest love!"

These ten monumental, glittering bas-relief panels are so remarkable and called the "Gates of Paradise," a phrase attributed to Michelangelo, who said they inspired his work on the Sistine Chapel in Rome. The originals are now in the Museo dell'Opera del Duomo, just around the corner. Be sure to set time aside to explore the splendid interior, with its amazing mosaic ceiling.

Santa Croce*

Church of the Holy Cross

Piazza Santa Croce

011-39-055-244-619

Sometimes called the "pantheon of Florence," this vast Gothic church is well known because it is the resting place of so many of the city's illustrious citizens, with grandiose tombs of luminaries ranging from Michelangelo and Machievelli to Galileo and Ghiberti—even Marconi, who invented the radio. Madame de Staël wrote that the church "contains the most brilliant assembly of corpses in perhaps the whole of Italy."

There is also an elaborate cenotaph to Dante Alighieri, who, though born in Florence, is buried in Ravenna to the chagrin of the Florentines who tried unsuccessfully to have him moved back. The airy interior is simply magnificent, with its soaring pillars and monumental sculptures by Rossellino, Canova, Donatello, and da Maiano. Don't miss the tomb of the poet Alfieri, which is thought to be one of Canova's best works. Some of Giotto's most exquisite frescoes are in the Bardi and Peruzzi chapels adjacent to the altar. They depict the lives of St. John the Baptist, St. John the Evangelist, and St. Francis of Assisi, who preached here.

Chiostri di Santa Croce*

Cloisters of the Holy Cross and Pazzi Chapel

Piazza Santa Croce

011-39-055-244-619

Facing the church on the right is the gem, the Cappella dei Pazzi, which you reach by walking though Santa Croce. This Renaissance masterpiece is quintessential Brunelleschi, and it is decorated with terra-cotta *tondi* reliefs of the twelve apostles by Luca della Robbia. Stop in at the adjacent museum to admire Cimabue's crucifix, severely damaged in the flood of 1966, and enjoy the quiet in the tranquil green cloister garden outside, which features a sculpture by Henry Moore.

San Lorenzo*

Church of San Lorenzo
Piazza San Lorenzo
011-39-055-216-634

This is the Medici family's church, which was built by Brunelleschi in 1419. Its façade has a very austere look because of the rough exterior, which was to have been covered by a design by Michelangelo. Unfortunately, it never happened, but you can view his original wood model in Casa Buonarroti (see page 51). The interior of the church, however, is polished, and finished down to the last detail. Filippo Lippi's vividly painted *Annunciation* is here, as is Brunelleschi's Old Sacristy. There are two dramatic bronze pulpits with intricate bas-reliefs which are famous because Savonarola preached his sermons from one of them. They were designed by Donatello, who also created the eight circular reliefs and the doors for the Old Sacristy. Located in Piazza San Lorenzo, this church complex contains two extraordinary gems: the Laurentian Library and, behind, the Medici Chapels.

Biblioteca Laurenziana*

Laurentian Library
011-39-055-210-760

On the way out of the church, take a right through the cloisters and you are met by the stately masterpiece, the Laurentian Library, designed by Michelangelo. It is an amazing space, renowned the world over. First you enter the vestibule, designed as an elegant courtyard in white plaster and gray-green *pietra serena* stone. Then ascend the most graceful staircase imaginable (designed by Michelangelo and completed by Ammaneti in 1559, when the former was called to Rome to work on the Sistine Chapel). It leads to the library, with its red-and-yellow floor designed by

Michelangelo's pupil, Niccolò Tribolo. Monumental wood benches, desks, and original glass cases with their Medici crests host priceless Medici treasures: manuscripts, books, and archives. Horace's Odes annotated by Petrarch, Aristotle's Logica, and a copy of *The Divine Comedy* are just several examples of what is in this astounding collection.

Cappelle Medicee*

Medici Chapels
Piazza Madonna degli Aldobrandini
011-39-055-238-8602

After you have savored the beauties of Michelangelo's library, walk around to the back of the church to enter the Medici Chapels, a dazzling space that is deemed one of Michelangelo's most famous masterpieces—a mausoleum honoring one of Italy's most aristocratic and powerful Florentine families, the Medici.

It is made up of two parts, the Chapel of the Princes and the New Sacristy. The chapel is an octagonal building topped by a lofty dome. It is obvious at first glance that no expense was spared in decorating this resting place of six Medici grand dukes. The inlaid *pietra dura* floor, Medici crest and decorations, marbles and semiprecious stones of every color and texture from all over Europe—lapis lazuli, agate, red coral, alabaster, chalcedony all meticulously carved—create an atmosphere of unbelievable opulence.

Michelangelo's mausoleum for the Medici family, the New Sacristy, is voluptuous in a very different way. Michelangelo was entrusted with designing the total picture—the architecture, sculpture, and painting. He didn't finish it, but every detail bears his mark

RIGHT: A view of the gable atop the Church of Santa Maria Novella contains a marble inscription dedicated to the Rucellai family's generous contribution.

of genius. The remains of Lorenzo the Magnificent and his brother Giuliano are marked here by the sculpture *Virgin and Child*, made by Michelangelo in 1521. Later, Lorenzo, the Duke of Urbino, and another Giuliano, the Duke of Nemours—two Medici to die in the flower of youth—were movingly commemorated by sculptures, probably among the most recognizable allegorical figures in art: the reclining *Day and Night* and *Dawn and Dusk*. "It is a miracle," said the novelist Nathaniel Hawthorne when he saw them for the first time.

Santa Maria del Carmine*
Church of Santa Maria del Carmine
Piazza del Carmine
011-39-055-212-331

This simple Baroque church of rough stone, in a piazza in the Oltrarno, owes its fame to the Cappella Brancacci (Brancacci Chapel) within. In 1425, Felice Brancacci, the Florentine ambassador to Egypt, commissioned the artist Masolino to paint a series of frescoes to illustrate the life of St. Peter. He collaborated with Masaccio, who took over when he died. These frescoes chart the movement of art from the traditional, late-Gothic style of Masolino to the powerful innovation of Masaccio, who used the new science of perspective and realism. *The Expulsion of Adam and Eve*—a statement about the eternal agony of man that transcends time—is said by art historians to document the beginning of Renaissance painting. In the 1980s, the frescoes were restored, and there is a time limit for viewing this masterpiece. It is always best to make a reservation.

LEFT: The Frescobaldi family's palazzo has this original window overlooking the altar of the Church of Santo Spirito which allows them to see mass from above.

Santa Maria Novella*
Church of Santa Maria Novella
Piazza di Santa Maria Novella
011-39-055-210-113

The immense fresco-decorated interior of this magnificent church, designed by Leon Battista Alberti, is said to be the most important Gothic church in Tuscany. It was from this pulpit that Galileo was first denounced for saying that the earth circled the sun, not the opposite. It is also the setting for the opening pages of the *Decameron*, by Giovanni Bocaccio.

These days, however, it is appreciated for its impressive masterpieces, including the groundbreaking *Holy Trinity* by Masaccio and Domenico Ghirlandaiao's fresco cycle of St. John the Baptist. The Cappella di Filippo Strozzi, by Lippi was sponsored by the fifteenth-century banker of the same name.

There are several famous crucifixes here. The one in the Gondi Chapel is by Filippo Brunelleschi. The other is by Giotto and is considered a seminal work in Western art, opening the door for realism. It was recently restored and is back on display in the church. Before you leave the site, go outside the church—more frescoes! Back in the green cloister (Chiostro Verde) is a series of pale, exquisite frescoes by Paolo Uccello.

San Frediano in Cestello
Church of San Frediano
Piazza di Cestello, 4
011-39-055-215-816

This Baroque church, with its unfinished façade by Cerutti, has a small dome by Antonio Maria Ferri visible atop the roofs of Florence. There are several frescoes by Gabbiani and Gherardini within.

Santo Stefano al Ponte
Church of St. Stephen
Piazzetta Santo Stefano
011-39-055-290-832

This Romanesque church, dating from 969, is on the way to the Ponte Vecchio—hence its name. Concerts and other musical events are often held here.

Santo Spirito*
Church of the Holy Spirit
Piazza Santo Spirito
011-39-055-210-030

When I take an unplanned walk in Florence, I usually end up here. I love this early-Renaissance church by Brunelleschi, with its simple, creamy façade, which exudes a sense of peace and gracefulness. It faces the active piazza, with its morning market, *caffès*, and easygoing neighborhood feeling. The façade was never finished after Brunelleschi's death, which is why it's so plain, but inside he designed a colonnade of continuous arches which elegantly highlights altar pieces by Sansovino and Lippi. The coffered ceiling is by Cronaca. The *Cenacolo di Santo Spirito* (Last Supper of the Holy Spirit) by Andrea Orcagna, is a much-visited masterpiece in the refectory to the left.

Santissima Annunziata
Church of the Holy Annunciation
Piazza della Santissima Annunziata
011-39-055-239-8034

First founded in 1250, this church was redesigned by Michelozzo in 1444. It was known as the "Church of the Miracles." Today, the interior is mostly Baroque with Andrea del Sarto's frescoes in the atrium and the cloister. (You may need to ask to see them.) Andrea del Castagno's frescoes should also not be missed.

Ospedale degli Innocenti

Foundling Hospital and Museum

011-39-055-203-7308

www.istitutodeglinnocenti.it

Just steps from this church is Europe's first foundling hospital, started as a charity by the Silk Weavers' Guild of Florence. You will recognize it by its beautifully proportioned, graceful loggia topped with ten glazed terra-cotta medallions of wrapped infants by Andrea della Robbia. Though the building still operates as an orphanage, you can enter it to see a worthwhile collection of paintings in the upper Galleria del Ospedale, including Ghirlandaio's *Adoration of the Magi,* which was commissioned for the hospital's church.

San Miniato al Monte*

Viale Galileo, near Piazzale Michelangelo

011-39-055-234-2733

This elegant Romanesque church sits atop Piazzale Michelangelo, its front faced with white Carrera and green Prato marble. As you walk up the steps, leaving the hurly-burly below, stop and look back at the magnificent view of Florence, especially at the end of the day. The tranquil interior of the church is quite impressive—starting with the floor, which is inlaid with geometric motifs intended to replicate oriental carpets and on up to the ornate roof, with its Gothic trusses and flying buttresses. The oldest part is the crypt housing the tomb of San Miniato, who became Florence's first martyr, after being beheaded and walking all the way up to this site. (It's the least they could have done!) The mosaic in the apse dates from 1297, and the crucifix above the altar is attributed to Luca della Robbia. Gregorian chants accompany the afternoon service of Vespers.

Badia Fiorentina

Abbey of Florence

Via del Proconsolo (across from the Bargello)

011-39-055-287-386

www.badiafiorentina.it

The hexagonal campanile of this church is as recognizable as its pealing bell, which rings with regularity throughout the day. This is the oldest monastery in the city, and Mino da Fiesole sculpted the elaborate marble tomb inside for the Marquis Ugo of Tuscany, whose mother founded the abbey. Dante is said to have fallen in love with Beatrice Portinari here.

Santa Felicita

Church of St. Felicity

Piazza Santa Felicità

011-39-055-213-018

This church is located in a little square at the beginning of the Ponte Vecchio, on the site of one of the oldest established churches in the city. Its façade was added by Vasari in the sixteenth century to support his Vasari Corridor, which runs above the portico. Turn right as you enter, to see the large, unexpectedly colorful *Deposition,* by Mannerist painter Pontormo.

Santa Trinità

Church of the Holy Trinità

Piazza Santa Trinità, Via de' Tornabuoni

011-39-055-216-912

Within this church is the Cappella Sassetti decorated with frescoes by Domenico Ghirlandaio that illustrate the life of St. Francis. Many of the background locations are set in fifteenth-century Florence and recognizable even today, including Piazza della Signoria. Don't miss Luca della Robbia's glazed terracotta monument, the Tomb of Benozzo Federighi.

Santissimi Apostoli*

Church of the Holy Apostles
Piazza del Limbo
011-39-055-290-642

A favorite of Florentine residents, this ancient church is in a charming medieval square next to the Arno River and still has its eleventh-century Romanesque façade. It features a terra-cotta tabernacle by Andrea della Robbia and a painting of the Immaculate Conception by Giorgio Vasari. A serene and very special spot attributed to Charlemagne.

Museo di San Marco*

Church and Monastery of St. Mark
Piazza San Marco
011-39-055-238-8608
www.sbas.firenze.it/sanmarco

A visit here is a must. This church and monastery was rebuilt in the fifteenth century by Michelozzo, and it's the monastery museum, dedicated to Fra Angelico, that you will want to head for. "Beato Angelico" (Blessed Angel), as the Florentines call him, lived here as a monk and produced some magical masterpieces, including the familiar golden *Annunciation*. Then there are the *Tabernacle of the Madonna dei Linaiuoli* and the *Last Judgment*. Be sure to look in the monks' cells to see the gorgeous frescoes in each one. There is a plaque to mark where Girolamo Savonarola, who was a monk here, was detained and arrested in 1498.

Before you leave the monastery, visit the library (considered one of the finest Renaissance interiors in Florence), whose shelves contain books of exquisite illuminations painted by the monks. The small refectory contains the *Last Supper* by Ghirlandaio in, inexplicably, the gift shop. On the way out, take a peek at the ornate marble friezes and architectural fragments on the walls of the Museo di Firenze Antica (Museum of Ancient Florence), in the back.

Though Leonardo da Vinci's is the most famous, Florence is the place where the tradition of Last-Supper paintings (*Cenacoli*) started. Most are in churches so if you want to spend a lovely afternoon in solitude, this is the way to go. My favorites are:

Cenacolo di Sant'Apollonia

Via XXVII Aprile,1
011-39-055-238-85

Located in a former Benedictine monastery, this great fresco by Andrea del Castagno, which covers a wall, is said to rival Leonardo da Vinci's version in Milan.

Cenacolo di Santo Spirito

Piazza di Santo Spirito, 29
011-39-055-287-043

I enjoy visiting this Cenacolo, by Andrea Orcagna, because, though in a fragmentary state, it is in the monastery of Santo Spirito, on the Oltrarno.

Cenacolo di Ognissanti

Borgo Ognissanti, 42
011-39-055-239-8700

On the square facing the Grand Hotel and the Excelsior is the Church of the Ognissanti, founded in the mid-thirteenth century by the monks who established the wool industry in Florence. Ghirlandaio painted his fresco here of the *Last Supper* in 1480.

After reading these pages, many of you will be heading out the door in comfortable shoes, guidebooks in hand, but there are those of us who might like

an alternative, a little help to sort it all out—perhaps someone to smooth our path and plan our itinerary for us. Well, in Florence you are in luck. It is easy to engage the services of people or companies that will happily help you. They will meet with you (or you can do it online) to find out where your interest lies. They will then customize a program for you that can last several hours, an entire day, or longer. They can book a car, if necessary, and supply guides who speak English (or any other language), if desired. Here are three that come highly recommended:

Città Nascosta means "hidden city," and this cultural group was created in 1994 in order to highlight the secret treasures of Florence and Tuscany. It organizes the famous "Toscana Esclusiva," a day in May in which Florence opens to the public its private palazzi, courtyards, and gardens. It is an opportunity to see private properties and the event is free. The Associazione Dimore Storiche Italiane (www.adsito-scana.it) promotes the event, which also includes concerts and activities in the area surrounding Florence. Check its website for next year's dates.

In addition, the delightful founders of Citta Nascosta, Marcella Cangioli, Tiziana Frescobaldi, and Maria de Pepperelli, specialize in guided tours and personalized itineraries to exclusive venues—aristocratic palazzi, gardens, and events, many of which are in private hands. They will take you anywhere you want to go in Florence and beyond.

Florentines Sabina Corsini and Jane Camilloni will take you "where we tell our best friends to go," and in style. Since 2000, their company, Inventing Itineraries, has been known for custom-designing trips. They say, "So often, one returns from a trip having seen all the monuments and having understood so little about a place, its people, its customs."

They aim to make sure that you will see Florence from a different viewpoint than the average traveler, and they can call upon all their wonderful contacts in the city to make sure that you don't miss a thing.

Eleonora Burci is the Managing Director of Viandando, a company she created that is dedicated to a philosophy of unique travel. She has a wonderful list of adventures in Tuscany, from truffle hunting and the "Terracotta Trail" in Impruneta to a private viewing of see Siena's famous Palio from an elegant palazzo. She gets especially creative in Florence, with adventures that include "The Artisans of Florence" (see chapter 8) and even "Drifting on the Waters of the River Arno," and will set up wine tastings, cooking lessons, and children's activities.

If you would like a lovely and informative way to become acquainted with Florence for the first time, do call Alessandra Marchetti. She has her masters in art history, has been a guide for fourteen years after living in the U.S., and is now doing research in the Michelangelo family archives. She also offers special visits to places like the Uffizi Galleries on Mondays when it is closed.

Città Nascosta
Lungarno Benvenuto
Cellini, 25
50125 Florence
011-39-055-680-2590
www.cittanascosta.com

Viandando
Via dell'Eremo, 3
50013 Bagno a Ripoli
011-39-055-698-337
www.viandando.it

Inventing Itineraries
Piazzale di Porta al Prato, 37
50123 Florence
011-39-338-619-3763
www.inventingitineraries.
com

Alessandra Marchetti
Via Della Capponcina, 83
011-39-37-386-9837
www.tuscanvillasandcastles.
com

Visiting Florence with children can be great fun. The Italians love children and can be very patient and tolerant. We experienced this when we decided on Easter years back to go with four nieces and nephews in order to visit the fifth, who was spending her junior year abroad. We had a great time, despite the fact that it was the busiest week of the year and Easter vacation for schoolchildren from everywhere. The Duomo was a sea of denim and we were glued to little hands as we traversed the narrow sidewalks in rhythm—up down, up down. Everywhere we went, locals leaned over to pinch cheeks and admire the *tesori* (treasures), just another name for children in this lovely country.

Following are some tips that may come in handy. Remember to ask for a children's discount (*sconto bambino*) in museums, as most state (and some private) museums allow children under eighteen to be admitted free. In most cases, restaurants do not have children's menus, but no one will mind if you order a half-portion of pasta or a main course. There are also many events during the year, and especially in summer, just made for kids. Check out the Florence Tourist Office, or get a free copy of *Florence Concierge* from the front desk in your hotel or pensione.

Another good idea is to contact Eleonora Burci (see page 71) to set up unique activities for you and your children. For example, how about a picnic in the garden of a Renaissance villa? Or a "Pinocchio" party? Or pizza or chocolate classes, where your children can learn to make some of their favorite treats while you take a wine-and-cheese tasting course at the same time?

David

The story of young David defying the giant Goliath has lasting value, especially for children. They will be awed by this huge heroic figure in the Galleria dell'Accademia. Then you can take them to see the other copies in the Piazza della Signoria and up on Piazzale Michelangelo (see pages 40 and 59).

Stibbert Museum

Medieval knights on armored horses—the G.I. Joes of their day—are the centerpiece of this museum and will intrigue all the little and big boys in your group. They'll love the fascinating collection of ancient weapons, swords, and armor, too. Afterwards, everyone can let off steam in the nice garden (see page 51).

Museo Zoologico della Specola

Florence's Zoological Museum, one of the most ancient in Europe, offers over 5,000 specimens of birds, mammals, fish, and reptiles that children will enjoy seeing. One note of caution: only older children should be allowed to see the realistic anatomical wax models of human bodies and vignettes of the plague in Florence, which are gruesome (see page 55).

Museo di Storia della Scienza

Any family with a budding scientist should visit the History of Science Museum. A large section is dedicated to the genius Galileo. On display is his personal telescope, and—something that will delight children—his preserved finger! There is also a dazzling display of scientific instruments, collected by the Medici, that will appeal to adults, too (see page 55).

Musei dei Ragazzi

This museum for children of all ages is located in the Palazzo Vecchio. There's a puppet theater, plus arts-and-crafts workshops, games, and all kinds of multimedia activities based on Renaissance themes (see page 61).

Mercato Nuovo

You may not want to hassle with the crowds in the Straw Market, but your children will definitely enjoy seeing *Il Porcellino*, a bigger-than-life-size bronze boar for which this market is famous. A pat on his well-worn snout ensures that they will return to Florence someday (see page 180).

Giardino di Boboli

Florence is known for not having many open green spaces, so if you want to spend a morning or afternoon in the fresh air, you should visit the Boboli Gardens, behind the Pitti Palace. Enter through the door at the end of the palace courtyard, and you are in another world, where children can run and play to their hearts' content in a park-like setting while you give your feet a rest (see page 83).

Top of the World

Kids love to climb steps, which is easy to do in Florence. Here are three sets you should try: the top of Giotto's Bell Tower—414 steps—to Florence's most famous landmark, the Duomo (you can also climb to the top of the dome of the Duomo, through the separate side entrance); the Terazza di Saturno, an open terrace at the top of the Palazzo Vecchio; and Piazzale Michelangelo, with its classic views of Florence. And you can climb even higher by taking the steps up to the nearby Church of San Miniato.

Gelato

And what do kids like more than anything? Ice cream, of course! And Florence has some of the creamiest gelato in Italy. There are four famous places, with so many flavors (pear with caramel, tiramisù) that your head will spin. They also offer *granite*, drinks with fruit syrups drizzled atop shaved ice. All you need to know is how to say cone (*cono*) and cup (*coppa*). You'll easily recognize these spots, because there is usually a line out the front door.

Vivoli
Via Isola della Stinche, 7r
(Near Santa Croce)
011-39-055-292-334

Gelateria Carabè
Via Ricasoli, 60r
(Near the Accademia)
011-39-055-289-476

Perchè No!
Via dei Tavolini, 19r
(Near the Uffizi)
011-39-055-239-8969

Vestri Cioccolato
Borgo Deglialbizi, 11r
(Near Sant'Ambrogio)
011-39-055-234-0374

BELOW: Florentines call children *tesori*. Here are two adorable local treasures enjoying the sunny afternoon.

I thought it would be fun (and informative) to ask some longtime residents and native Florentines to share with me their favorite spots in the city. Here's what they said:

"It goes without saying that the entire city of Florence is a treasure. I always advise visitors to look up, look into every doorway, into every alley. If I'm not in a hurry when I'm walking and the sun is shining, I invariably see something I've never seen before, even after all these many decades of living here."
—Harold Gibson, co-founder of the International (American) School of Florence.

"I love La Specola (the Zoology Museum) because it has not been changed much since it was founded in the 18th century. My children, 4 and 9 years old, love it too. Each weekend they want to visit the stuffed animals."
—Marcella Cagnoli, co-founder of Città Nascosta

"I actually rediscovered the Bargello Museum recently. It was always special, and now it has a new director, and it is as if the place has been revived. It is a gem and is, inexplicably, never crowded."
—Albiera Antinori, Director of Sales, Marketing, and Communication, Marchesi Antinori

"I'm afraid I'm being very grand to say I love Forte Belvedere and would like to live in it! I treasure my friends, I love meeting people, and I like to entertain. It's an ideal home; to have the best view of the city I love from the front windows and yet be in the country would be so rare—just too perfect."
—Bona Frescobaldi, president of the Consortium of Laudemio and president of Friends of FAI

"Although I get inspiration from flowers and gardens, I'm really interested in the streets of Florence—the big, majestic doors of the palaces and the small terraces jutting out from the buildings. All the little streets have the story of Florence in their pavements. I especially like those near Via dei Serragli—I constantly see surprises there."
—Angela Caputi, jewelry designer

"It's hard to narrow down. I think I'd have to say it would be when we arrange a private tour of the Uffizi on Mondays, when it is closed. You are alone with the masterpieces while those around you are dusting light bulbs, rehanging paintings, and generally straightening the galleries for the crowds that will arrive the next day."
—Simonetta Brandolini, founder of The Best in Italy, and Friends of Florence

"The eleventh-century Castello di Vincigliata, just outside of Florence, is a very special place. It was in ruins when Sir John Temple Leader had it rebuilt in the nineteenth century in the spirit of the Renaissance, employing a team of fine artisans of every type—painters, carvers, sculptors, glass blowers. It is an inspiration."
—Adele Tognaccini, interior designer

"My favorite walk starts just above Florence on one of its most charming streets, Via San Leonardo, which begins in the country hills planted with olive trees. You pass beautiful old villas, a tiny church called San Leonardo, and Forte Belvedere. Then you continue through Costa San Giorgio, past the Bardini Museum, with its stunning gardens, and Gaileo's house. At the bottom is the Church of Santa Felicità, in a little square, which features the Deposition from the Cross, by Pontormo, painted with the most incredible colors we can imagine."
—Sibilla della Gherardesca, public relations director of Pitti Immagine and author of *La Mia Toscana*

"The Museum of San Marco, with its Fra Angelico masterpieces. It has a silent, contemplative atmosphere—the Renaissance in a nutshell."
—Jane Camilloni, co-founder of Inventing Itineraries

"Masaccio's frescoes in the Church of the Carmine—they symbolize the beginning of the revolution of the Renaissance."
—Paolo Parisi, abstract painter

Because Florence is surrounded by hills there are several places to experience breathtaking views of the city.

- *Campanile al Duomo—Walk all the way up to the top of this bell tower just next to the main cathedral, Santa Maria del Fiore.*

- *Loggia di Lanzi Caffè—Have an espresso in this Uffizi caffè, whose terrace overlooks Piazza della Signoria.*

- *Forte di Belvedere—This sixteenth century Medici fortress built by Buontalenti is on the Via San Leonardo behind the Pitti Palace and the Boboli Gardens.*

- *Garden of the Cavaliere—Enjoy unchanged Renaissance views from the top of the Boboli Gardens, where the Porcelain Museum is situated within a rose garden.*

- *The Bardini Garden—These beautiful gardens and a terrific new restaurant have reopened at the top of Costa San Giorgio and afford a stunning view of the city.*

- *Piazzale Michelangelo and San Miniato al Monte—You can take the bus or hike up to this piazza, dedicated to Michelangelo, for the classic view of Florence. Walk up to the Church of San Miniato for an even better view and fewer tourists.*

- *There are several hotels in the surrounding hills that have memorable views of the city. Ensconce yourself in Villa San Michele, La Vedetta, or Torre di Bellosguardo and enjoy a beautiful eyeful of Florence with your morning caffè. You can also visit the first two for a drink or an elegant meal even if you are not a hotel guest (see chapter 4 for more).*

RIGHT, TOP: As you leave the Boboli gardens, take a peek over the balustrade for a striking view.
BOTTOM: Wide vistas from the Bardini Garden include the Arno River and the Church of Santa Croce.

THREE

The City of Flowers

*"The roses are quiet for the moment, after their summer bloom…
but oleanders make a rosy tracery against the blue sky."*

—Charles Latham, *The Gardens of Italy*

Florence has often been called the "City of Flowers" and its name is said to come from the Italian word for flower, *fiore*. Its symbol, the fleur-de-lis, is the Florentine iris. The original standard of Florence had a white iris on a red field, but in 1266 the colors were reversed, and to this day the standard insignia reflects this ancient image. You see it everywhere—etched in brass on manhole covers, painted bright red on "do not litter" signs and carved into old stone buildings. Each spring the city fills with flowers. Dramatic sculptures in front of the Palazzo Vecchio are surrounded almost up to their knees in colorful blooms. Tubs of bright pink azaleas march across the Ponte Vecchio. Camellias are in bloom everywhere and on display in special shows around the city. And in May, the beloved iris is celebrated with a unique show and competition held by the Italian Iris Society in the Iris Garden at the Piazzale Michelangelo, open only one month a year. The Maggio Musicale welcomes the season, too, with special concerts celebrating spring. Botticelli painted *Primavera* here for a very good reason.

Florence has been often criticized for not having much green space. This may be true, when compared to the parks of London or Paris, but, in fact, it does have some of world's most outstanding Renaissance gardens. Some are still in private hands, but one of Italy's most important public parks, the Boboli Gardens of the Pitti Palace, is located here. Created in the sixteenth century, it typifies the Roman ideal that a country home should be a retreat for its sophisticated owners.

In 1450, Florentine scholar Leon Battista Alberti wrote in his *De Re Aedificatoria* that *villegiatura* glori-fied the rural lifestyle. This popular book encouraged many Tuscans to build large estates in the country, surrounded by magnificent gardens. (At the time the Pitti Palace was built, it was in the country.)

The powerful Medici family followed this advice by renovating the Pitti and the Boboli Gardens behind it. They also built some of the grandest country estates around Florence, engaging some of the most outstanding architects of the time and commissioning sophisticated gardens to be planted around them—gardens which were then copied throughout Italy, Europe, and Great Britain. They also created the first botanical gardens in Florence and Pisa, and collected rare plants with the same passion and intellect as they did art. (See the Giardino dei Semplici and Giardino dell'Orticoltura, listed below.)

The Boboli Gardens are woven into the fabric of Florentines' life. In *The Innocent*, Magdalen Nabb's last mystery, the author gives her usual deft description of a local's view of this well-loved garden: "A stroll around Boboli was usually an extra, somewhere for tourists to relax after an exhausting visit to the big galleries in the Pitti Palace. Somewhere, too, for students from the language schools to eat a slice of pizza…the mothers of Florence had their own well-worn routes. They showed their children Poseidon stirring the waters, threatening the orderly lines of potted lemons with his trident, or the ferocious marble Oceano, ruling his island, and bright goldfish, bigger than the pointing toddlers, who appeared out of the green gloom, hoping for a crust of bread."

Florence is also privileged to be the site of the handsome Giardino Bardini, on a hill overlooking the Piazza dei Mozzi. Created by antiquarian Stefano

OPENING PICTURE: Bordering the main axis of the Corsini al Prato's garden are statues of the Roman gods.
OVERLEAF, LEFT: The Garden Club of Florence's Camellia Festival in March, and right, a perfect camellia, and right, the Boboli Gardens is cherished by everyone who enjoys winding pathways and statuary-filled avenues.

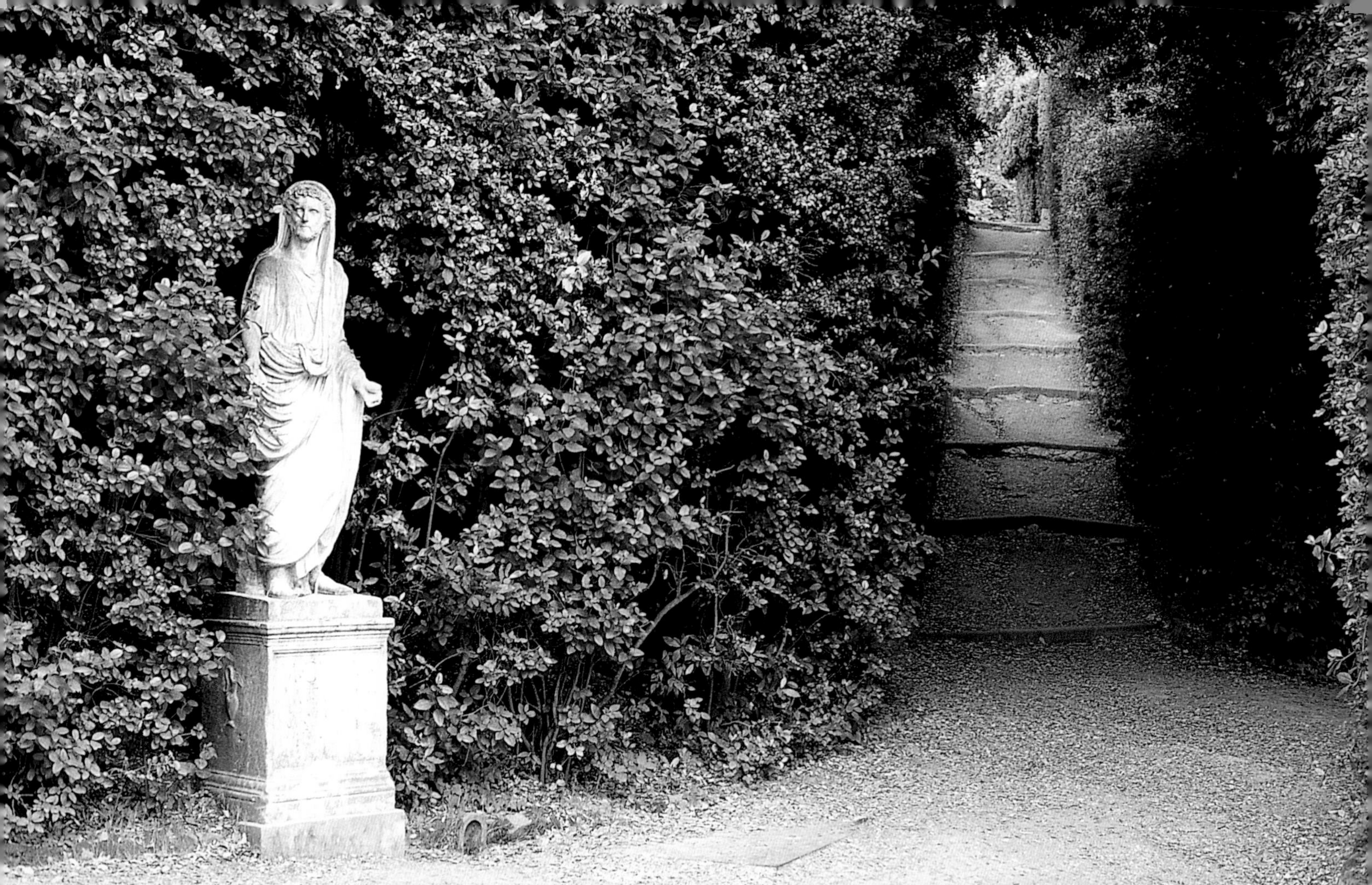

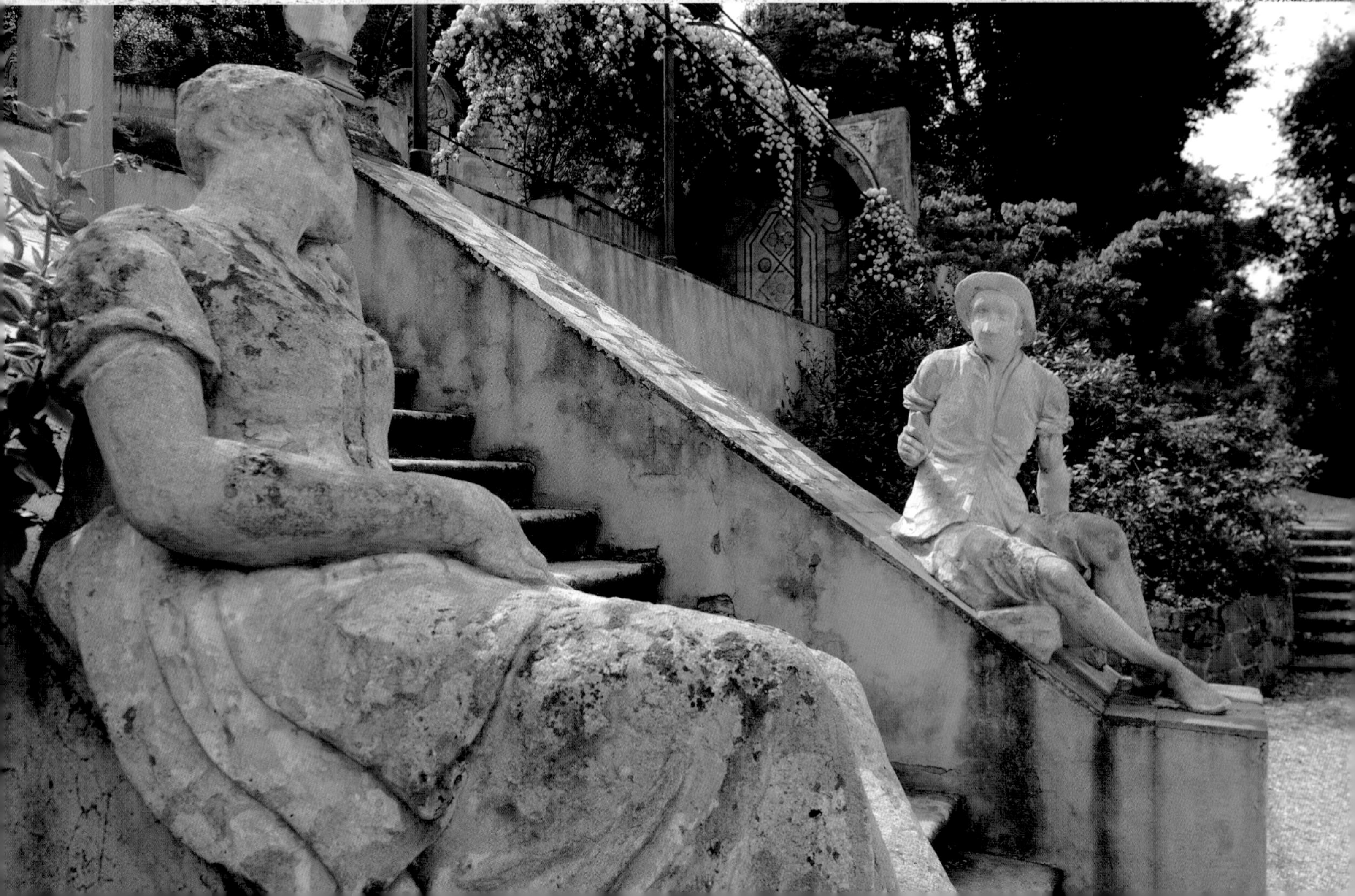

Bardini almost a hundred years ago, it has just re-opened, after being closed for three decades. It is beautifully laid out on terraces lushly planted with rare botanicals and architectural treasures, affording some of the most breathtaking views of the city as a surprising dividend.

Both the Boboli and Bardini illustrate the classic design ideals of the Italian Renaissance garden. The focus was always on harmony and order. A main axis generally extends from the villa outward, to create vast vistas that intersect. Garden rooms are created, linked together by terraces, stone paths, and steps joined by allées of dignified trees or laurel hedges. Water is a highlight, featured in cascading fountains, grottoes and pools creating cool corners in which to escape Italy's summer heat.

There is an emphasis on architectural elements—stone urns, carved statues, obelisks, balustrades, and garden furniture—rather than flowers. In *Italian Hours*, Henry James wrote of the Boboli, "The garden is in the Italian manner, with flowers rather remarkably omitted, as too flimsy and easy and cheap, and without lawns that are too smart, paths that are too often swept and shrubs that are too closely trimmed."

Other green Florentine escapes are the cool cloisters adjacent to some of the city's churches, many of which date from the Renaissance. They are quiet, tranquil spots with small verdant gardens: perfect places to take a moment to relax and savor the beauty around you, especially in the hot summertime. Some of my favorites are the cloister of Brunelleschi's Pazzi Chapel at the Church of Santa Croce; the cloister of the Church of Ognissanti, or

LEFT ABOVE: A hidden corner in the Boboli Gardens.
BELOW AND NEXT PAGE: Three views of the Bardini Garden as you climb up the enchanted green hills.

All Saints, on the Borgo Ognissanti; the little cloister of San Lorenzo, the Chiostro dei Canonici, designed by Antonio Manetti; and the cloisters at Santa Maria Novella, especially the Chiostro Verde. (See churches listed in chapter 2.)

The gardens located in the countryside near Florence are almost as famous as the ones in it. The mild weather and lovely surroundings were magnets for the American and British expatriates who invaded Italy in the mid-nineteenth century. They bought villas, which they restored, and created unique and personal gardens, many surviving to this day. Enjoy visiting some of the gardens listed below and then turn to chapter 5 to read about more of them, none more than a half hour outside of Florence.

Giardino di Boboli

Boboli Gardens
Piazza de' Pitti
011-39-055-218-741
www.polomuseale.firenze.it/english/musei/boboli
Grand Duke Cosimo de' Medici and his wife, Eleonora di Toledo, started this garden in 1549, after they had decided to make the Pitti Palace their royal residence. It was designed by the important architect Niccolò Pericoli, also known as Tribolo, and later refined by Vasari, Ammannati, and Buontalenti, and continued to be enlarged in the seventeenth, eighteenth, and nineteenth centuries.

In 1766, it was opened to the public and is today one of the few spots that Florentines can go to enjoy a park-like setting, with its lovely, uneven meadows and tree-lined avenues. For the visitor, it's the perfect spot to take a break, being just behind the Pitti Palace (the entrance is at the very end of the museum's large courtyard).

ABOVE: Florence's top nursery makes a plant delivery.
RIGHT CLOCKWISE: The canine population ranges from statuary in the Villa Gamberaia to trompe l'oeil painted by Nencia and Fiona Corsini in the Corsini al Prato.

As you enter the garden, the first thing you see is the large amphitheater, designed by Giulio Parigi around 1630. It was created by the removal of sandstone for the building of the Pitti Palace. Its scale sets the tone for the Boboli, which is really rather formal but retains most of its Renaissance and Baroque design, and features a plethora of Roman and sixteenth- and seventeenth-century garden statuary, plus a second-century Egyptian obelisk, fountains, small lakes, and ornate grottoes that can be visited on your climb up to the top for one of the most spectacular panoramic views of Florence and the surrounding hills.

If you have taken your vitamins that day, you should walk up to Michelangelo's ramparts, built in 1529—one of my favorite spots in the city. It's called the Garden of the Cavaliere, and the pink building is now home to the Porcelain Museum. The surrounding view is breathtaking and looks like it must have done in Renaissance times.

Giardino Bardini
Bardini Garden
Via dei Bardi, 1r
Piazza dei Mozzi
011-39-055-294-883
www.bardinipeyron.it

If you love gardens, a visit here is a must because it has just reopened after being closed for decades. It is adjacent to the Boboli Gardens, but it is comparatively small, a ten-acre site planted with imaginative things including rare roses, hydrangeas, peonies, and camellias. It features fountains, grottoes, dramatic garden statuary, and architectural fragments collected by antiquarian Stefano Bardini, who bought the property in 1913. There are two ways of entering this garden, the first by Via dei Bardi, 1r, off the Piazza dei Mozzi. Take your time, because you will be walking up steep stone steps most of the time—your reward is one of the most spectacular views of Florence. The other entrance is on top, at Costa San Giorgio, 4. It's the way to go for those who would like a less strenuous climb, because you can take a taxi there and walk down. The Roberto Capucci Museum, with the designer's clothes, is also here at the top.

Giardino dei Semplici
Botanical Garden
Via Micheli, 3
011-39-055-275-7402

The Giardino dei Semplici at the botanical gardens of the University of Florence, was created in 1545, when Grand Duke Cosimo I de' Medici purchased the land from the Dominican Sisters. It was so called because medicinal plants with therapeutic properties were cultivated here. Niccolò Tribolo, who designed many gardens for the Medici, designed the original

layout for this small garden located just near the Church of San Marco, dividing it into parterre beds containing flowers and special plants. Most notable are the very old trees, some with thick, impressive trunks and dating from the early eighteenth century. Orchids, ferns, and a large collection of azaleas and citrus trees are just some of the gems that draw gardeners to its large greenhouses.

Palazzo Budini Gattai

Piazza S.S. Annunziata, 1

011-39-055-210-832

www.budinigattai.it

Part of a unique palazzo designed by Bartolomeo Ammannati in 1563, this small courtyard garden features a stone seventeenth-century wall fountain with a statue of Venus surrounded by old camellias and majestic banana trees. The palazzo has been owned by the Budini Gattai family since 1890. Call for an appointment to visit the garden, which is especially beautiful in March, when the lush varieties of camellias are blooming in profusion and the Garden Club of Florence Camellia Show takes place here.

Palazzo Corsini al Prato

Via del Prato, 58

011-39-055-218-994

This is one of the most charming gardens I've visited anywhere, made more so by the fact that it is in the center of a city. Set behind the Palazzo Corsini, between Via del Prato and Via della Scala, sits this extraordinary rarity, a late-Renaissance garden that

PREVIOUS PAGE: A classic boxwood parterre planted with various herbs and flowers is flanked by lemon trees. LEFT: Blooms photographed in the Iris Garden, Piazzale Michelangelo, and center, a Florentine *giglio* in marble.

when designed, was in the countryside. The bisecting pathways are lined with giant terra-cotta lemon pots and graceful garden statuary. Within the clipped parterres are fragrant herbs, including thyme, catmint, lavender, and rosemary. Shade trees and laurel hedges create an island of calm and tranquility in this magical space. This garden is owned and beautifully maintained by the Corsini family, and you can call for an appointment.

Giardino dell'Orticoltura

Horticultural Garden

Via Bolognese, 17

011-39-055-483-698

This horticultural garden was started in the late nineteenth century and is known for its grand steel-and-glass *tepidarium*, or pavilion, designed by Giacomo Roster for the Tuscan Horticultural Society. A tradition every spring is a flower festival held here that is open to the public.

Il Giardino del Museo Archeologico Nazionale di Firenze

Via della Colonna, 36-38

011-39-055-235-75

www.comune.firenze.it

This lovely little garden sits behind the archeological museum, in the far corner of Piazza S.S. Annunziata. It features statuary and archeological remnants and is lushly planted with verdant shrubs and flowers. You can look through the iron railings on Via della Collona to glimpse the garden, or arrive Saturday between 9:30 P.M. and 12:30 A.M. (the only time the garden is open to the public) and take a guided tour, if the tours are on schedule that morning—not a given.

Spring, when the whole town seems to burst out into flowers everywhere you look, is a lovely time to be in Florence. The Flower Market, located under the loggia along the side of Piazza della Repubblica, is at its peak at this time of year. The popular and precious camellias are in bloom in gardens throughout the city, and a visit to Piazzale Michelangelo yields more varieties of irises and roses than tourists. So, if you are a flower lover look in a copy of *Florence Concierge Information* for scheduled flower events in March, April, and May.

Flower Markets

Mercato delle Piante
Flower Market
Loggiati di Via Pellicceria
Thursdays from 8 A.M. to 5 P.M. there is a little market selling cut flowers and plants in the Piazza della Repubblica.

Flower Festivals

Giardino dell'Orticultura
Horticultural Garden Show
Via Bolognese, 17
011-39-055-483-698
A popular flower show is held here the last week of April, highlighting plants, garden tools and accessories.

Il Giardino dell'Iris
Iris Garden
Piazzale Michelangelo (West side)
011-39-055-483-112
www.irisfirenze.it
The iris has been the symbol of Florence since the thirteenth century. The Iris Garden is on terraces on the side of Piazzale Michelangelo and is planted with 2,500 special varieties of irises from every part of the world. Since the 1950s, an international competition, "Il Premio Firenze," has been held here one month each year—usually May. It is open to the public and there is no admission charge.

LEFT: Colorful azalea bushes line a pathway in the Giardino dei Semplice of the University of Florence.
RIGHT: A yellow sign points the way in the Italian style.

Giardini delle Rose
Rose Gardens
Viale Giuseppe Poggi, 2 (Piazzale Michelangelo)
011-39-055-262.5305
This garden was designed in the late nineteenth century and features beautiful varieties of roses planted on the terraced hillside. Call ahead to find when the roses will be at their peak, usually during the months of May and June.

Mostra della Camelia in Giardino di Boboli
Camellias in Flower at the Boboli
Boboli Gardens
Piazza Pitti
011-39-055-294-883
www.polomuseale.firenze.it/english/musei
This March event featuring hundred-year-old camellias takes place in the Boboli Gardens. Inquire there about tours in English and Italian.

Mostra della Camelia
Camellia Festival of The Garden Club of Florence
Palazzo Budini Gattai
Piazza S.S. Annuziata, 1
Contact The Garden Club: 011-39-055-282-245
This annual event, in March, has taken place for decades in the loggia of one of the oldest palazzi in Florence. It features magnificent camellias grown by horticulturalists and enthusiasts from all over Tuscany. Prizes are awarded for some of the most interesting and beautiful examples.

FOUR

Rooms with a View

"The Signoria had no business to do it," said Miss Bartlett.
"No business at all. She promised us south rooms with a view close
together, instead of which here are north rooms, looking into
a courtyard, and a long way apart. Oh, Lucy!"

—E.M. Forster, *A Room with a View*

I know exactly how Miss Bartlett felt. I don't understand those who say that where they stay doesn't matter—"We leave early in the morning, so we are never in the room, all we do is sleep there, etc." For those of us who still have a romantic view of travel, a wonderful room in a hotel is one of the most important parts of a trip. In a strange place, it's where we call home—a place to relax and recharge. A hotel doesn't have to be grand or pretentious. It can be simple and charming. It should have a friendly, caring staff. The linens should be fresh and crispy, the towels fluffy. There are also other advantages: though I always go through my files and make long lists before I leave, if the hotel concierge is good, it means I'll find out about "insider places" that I might have missed. In some hotels, the food alone is worth the stay (the Hotel Cipriani in Asolo in years gone by comes to mind), although in Florence this is not a consideration, because there are so many outstanding places to dine. In any case, you should choose a place you will absolutely love coming home to.

A visit to Florence is a hotel maven's dream. The city has always had its traditional grand hostelries: the Grand, the Excelsior and the Helvetia and Bristol. In the hills, the legendary Villa Corer is now undergoing a much-needed restoration, and the Villa San Michele is looking as chic as ever. Then there are the classic *pensioni* celebrated in novels, like the Pensione Bertolini in E.M. Forster's book on the previous page. They offer the traveler an Italian experience— charming (or not so charming) rooms, one or two meals a day, and usually affordable rates. I stayed

OPENING PICTURE: I love the sumptuous rose salon in Palazzo Niccolini where I feel I'm in a Florentine home. OVERLEAF, LEFT: The library at JK Place and right, keys, and right, the view from a terrace at the Lungarno Suites.

ABOVE: A Renaissance bedroom overlooking Florence and the Tuscan hills in the evocative Torre di Bellosquardo.
RIGHT: JK Place, known for its sophisticated décor, includes distinctively designed rooms like this one in neutrals.

at the Pensione Hermitage decades ago at $8.25 a night—breakfast and dinner included! It's still there, renovated, and "Hotel" now replaces "Pensione" in the name. Though it's, sadly, no longer the same price, it is still reasonable, and in the same terrific location.

Happily, there are lots of new hotels that have recently opened. Several years ago, Rocco Forte bought and totally updated the Savoy Hotel, and the Ferragamo family, the Hotel Lungarno. They started a trend, and now there are many new boutique hotels with their own contemporary point of view. Then there are B & B's (in Italy this is a room in a private home that is usually not lived in by the owners) and *residenze d'epoca* (restored historical palaces with twelve or fewer rooms), like my very favorite, the Palazzo Niccolini al Duomo, which is beautifully

situated and decorated, friendly and oh-so-comfortable. In a city that hadn't seen a new hotel in years, Florence's hotel scene continues to grow—the newest addition is the Four Seasons just recently opened. One caveat: even with the new choices, advance reservations are always a must, especially from Easter through June and during the month of September.

The specific hotels I have recommended in this chapter have passed my *very* fussy standards. For me, décor is important—chic, elegant—or it must be charming and have a personality. It can also be absolutely simple but fresh. It must be spotlessly clean, and the bath and bed linens pristine. The staff should be friendly and, if possible—especially those in Reception and at the Concierge Desk—knowledgeable about their city. It doesn't have to be perfect, and I truly dis-

like pretentiousness, but there has to be something special about a hotel for me to return.

Italian hotels are officially graded from one to five stars, based on a rigid rating system of their facilities. This is only half the story, you should consider much more. Take noise, for example. The Florentines' love of the Vespa and the narrow medieval streets that amplify sound make Florence a noisy city. A room with a beautiful view may turn out to be unbearable at three in the morning because of loud street noise. If this is an issue, consider booking a quieter room overlooking an inner courtyard.

The city can be very hot in the summer, so you must be sure, when you are making your reservation, to ask if there is air-conditioning. Location is important. Florence is a walking city and taxi cabs are expensive, so a bargain hotel on the outskirts may not be a wise choice if you have a tendency to carry heavy cameras or totes, or dislike walking for hours on uneven cobblestones. Today, many Italian hotels serve a substantial complimentary breakfast which is included in your room rate. Be sure to ask about this when making your reservation. Since most Italians grab just a pastry and a quick *caffè* for breakfast, this is a welcome perk for most Americans.

It is impractical and unnecessary to have a car in this congested city. Most hotels do not have parking, but many have an arrangement with a nearby garage. If you are renting a car in Florence to drive to your next destination or explore the countryside, plan to pick it up and leave the city directly. You will then avoid the maze of inexplicable and ever-changing one-way streets and unexpected "pedestrian only" closures—GPS or not!

Returning from Siena on a recent trip, we needed to drop off our luggage. We were almost within

LEFT: Top right, a bathroom with a view at the Continentale; top left, towels at Villa San Michele; below, Acqua di Parma at the Grand Hotel.
ABOVE: Ginevra Niccolini at Palazzo Niccolini al Duomo.

sight of our apartment when two workmen walked in front of our car, put up blockades and started fixing the street! Because of the one-way-street system, we spent another twenty minutes driving round trying to find our way home. After our mission was accomplished, we decided to short-circuit the navigation nightmare, and hired a taxi to follow back to the rental office to return the car. When we told our Florentine friends the story, they just laughed and said it happens all the time.

As I've mentioned, Florence has long, humid summers, so if you can, avoid the months of July and August. But, for many of us it's the only time we can get away. Those "in the know" head for the cool,

breezy hills and a collection of gorgeous hotels with swimming pools, beautiful gardens, and magnificent views. All are less than thirty minutes from the city center. Most have frequent shuttle service to the center of Florence so that you can easily go back and forth and enjoy the best of both worlds.

And hotels are not the only option. Starting with the Grand Tour in the early nineteenth century, visitors have come to Florence and fallen in love with it, returning again and again for longer periods of time. As a result, there is a thriving network of rental apartments available for as little as several days, or a week or longer. It's a great opportunity to live like the locals—going to the open air markets, buying crisp produce and fresh bread, and trying out some of the wonderful Tuscan recipes you've picked up along the way. If you can share with friends, it becomes a reasonable way to extend your trip.

Hotels

LUXURY

Casa Howard Florence
Via della Scala, 18
011-39-06-924-555
www.casahoward.com
This twelve-room hotel, sister to the Casa Howard Rome, always gets a lot of press because of its décor—rather dramatic and just a little bit quirky. Vivid colors and decorator fabrics cover antique and custom-designed pieces, creating a pleasing effect in the high-ceilinged rooms of this palazzo. It's located almost next door to the fragrant Farmaceutica di

Santa Maria Novella (which is where the amenities in the bathrooms come from). Both are located on the noisy Via della Scala.

Continentale
Vicolo dell'Oro, 6r
011-39-055-272-62
www.lungarnohotels.com
Part of the Ferragamo family hotel group, located on the corner of the Ponte Vecchio and the Arno River. Architect Michele Bönan put an emphasis on detail, balancing high tech and soft design in designing the forty-three rooms, which are light and airy because of the blonde wood and pale pastel colors used. There is a "relaxing room" with large windows, where you can sit and read overlooking the river (the front rooms with terraces all have the same view); a roof garden, the perfect place to have a drink at sunset; and even a small spa downstairs. Stop here if you want to be in the thick of things.

Four Seasons Hotel Florence
Borgo Pinti, 99
011-39-055-262-61
www.fourseasons.com/florence
The second Four Seasons in Italy opened here in the spring of 2008 and occupies two very special buildings, the fifteenth-century Palazzo della Gheradesca and the sixteenth-century convent next door, set in a lush, eleven-acre botanical garden, the Giardino della Gheradesca. One of the most breathtaking hidden treasures in the city, it features rare species, including a giant evergreen sequoia and a century-old thuja tree, also known as the "tree of life." The hotel has been sumptuously restored—five-hundred-year-old

LEFT: The majestic sixteenth century *piano nobile* at Residenza del Moro features a suite with a sumptuous bath.

frescoes, carvings, bas-reliefs, and architectural details—have been returned to their original glistening state. The 117 bedrooms and suites are luxuriously appointed, including lotions and potions by the Farmaceutica di Santa Maria Novella and the Coty Perfume Prize-winner Lorenzo Villoresi. All the Four Seasons trademarks are in place—beautiful extra-large bathrooms; knowledgeable, friendly service; a chic spa; a terrific-looking bar and restaurant; and something found only in a few places in Florence—quiet, quiet, quiet.

Gallery Hotel Art

Vicolo dell'Oro, 5

011-39-055-272-63

www.lungarnohotels.com

The sister hotel of the Continentale, just across a tiny courtyard, was conceived with a cutting-edge, contemporary-Asian influence in mind. The hotel's sleek lobby is furnished with deep orange ottomans and dark Wengé-wood walls hung with giant, abstract insect watercolors by Alberto Reggianini. The space is often a venue for periodic art and photographic exhibitions. A large, comfortable library is filled with coffee-table books and cashmere throws. The rooms have clean lines, neutral colors, and beautiful bathrooms. Reserve the penthouse or a junior suite facing the river for views of Bellosguardo and the surrounding hills. The "Fusion Bar" off the lobby, with its outdoor café, is a favorite late-night spot.

Grand Hotel

Piazza Ognissanti, 1

011-39-055-288-781

www.grandhotel.hotelinfirenze.com

The Grand Hotel was the first hotel I stayed in when

I graduated from my little *pensione*. In those days, it was part of the chic CIGA group. Now the Grand is part of the Starwood chain, as is the Westin Excelsior across Piazza Ognissanti. The Westin is the prime destination for large tour groups, so try the Grand if you prefer to stay in a large hotel. The 107 Florentine-style bedrooms and suites are decorated with frescoes and coffered-wood ceilings. Book a room on a high floor overlooking the Arno—breathtaking and quiet. The large marble Art Deco–style bathrooms have amenities from scrumptious Acqua di Parma. Concierge Paolo Basagni, who has been there for many years, knows where everything is in Florence.

Hotel Helvetia & Bristol

Via de' Pescione, 2

011-39-055-266-51

www.hotelhelvetiabristolfirenze.it

This hotel has been a fixture in Florence since the late nineteenth century. Its old-world feeling meets you in the lobby, with its cozy fireplace, leaded-glass windows, and antique furnishings, and continues in the charming, belle-époque Winter Garden and the forty-nine luxurious bedrooms. The staff has always been helpful, so, if you like tradition, you'll enjoy this peaceful oasis in the center of bustling Florence.

Hotel Lungarno

Borgo San Jacopo, 14

011-39-055-272-61

www.lungarnohotels.com

We stayed at the old Lungarno Hotel when it was on its last legs—a bit tatty but, oh that view! At that

PREVIOUS PAGE: The Penthouse at Gallery Hotel Art.
RIGHT CLOCKWISE: The Four Seasons lobby; the reading rooms at Residenza del Moro and Four Seasons.

ABOVE: The tranquil, monochromatic Spa in the Four Seasons Hotel is situated in its own building in their famous gardens.

time, it was one of the few accommodations on the Oltrarno. In 1997, the Ferragamo family bought it and gave it a much-needed face-lift. The decorating scheme of the lobby and sixty-nine bedrooms—crisp, cream linen trimmed in navy blue—always reminds me of Ralph Lauren. In fact, you can buy almost everything in your room at their shop, Lungarno Details, across the river (see chapter 7). The rooms are on the small side but comfortable, and the bathrooms are nicely appointed. The lobby, filled with fresh flowers, serves breakfast in the morning and drinks all day long—a great place to meet business associates and friends. Reserve a room with a terrace overlooking the river, and dine upstairs on the balcony in the Borgo San Jacopo Restaurant.

Hotel Santa Maria Novella

Piazza di Santa Maria Novella, 1
011-39-055-271-840
www.hotelsantamarianovella.it
This new, thirty-eight-room addition to the hotel scene was opened several years ago, just down the block from JK Place. It's decorated in the Empire style, with marble floors and two cozy teal green rooms in the lobby, both with fireplaces and one filled with Napoleonic furniture and mementos. The bedrooms are a nice size, brightly decorated, and the marble bathrooms feature Farmaceutica di Santa Maria Novella amenities. Piazza di Santa Maria Novella, just in front, is undergoing a very timely face-lift and should be completed soon.

ABOVE: A very luxurious Renaissance bedroom at the Grand Hotel overlooks the historic Church of San Frediano.

Hotel Savoy

Piazza della Repubblica, 7

011-39-055-273-51

www.roccofortehotels.com

Sir Rocco Forte bought this hotel in the 1990s, and his sister Olga Polizzi, the interior designer, has recreated this sleek neoclassic landmark in the heart of Florence. It's very popular with business people and celebrities who enjoy L'Incontro, the outdoor terrace on the lively Piazza della Repubblica, the perfect place to have their signature martini or a Florentine specialty, the Negroni (see page 172). The 102 bedrooms and suites are extremely stylishly decorated—a neutral palette accented with colors like purple or chartreuse, but some are on the small side.

The most desirable rooms overlooking the piazza have two sets of shutters and thick glazed windows, but the din of the square still seeps through sometimes until the early morning hours. The back rooms are much quieter. This hotel is beautifully run, with excellent service and attention to detail.

JK Place

Piazza di Santa Maria Novella, 7

011-39-055-264-5181

www.jkplace.com

The first time I entered this sophisticated lobby, I thought I had stumbled into a chic Parisian hotel. The common rooms, library, lounge, and dining room are smartly decorated in neoclassic style, with

antique prints, marble busts, and elegant fireplaces. The twenty bedrooms and suites, each different, are comfortable and luxuriously furnished in muted tones. The hotel expanded its popular restaurant, "The Lounge," which is the place to go for a delicious light lunch (Chianti beef supplied by famed Tuscan butcher Dario Cecchini and creamy gelato from Vivoli). The downstairs bar is on the hip-nightlife list. The hotel's location, is in front of Piazza di Santa Maria Novella, which is being renovated, so it will be more attractive than ever.

Palazzo Niccolini al Duomo

Via dei Servi, 2

011-39-055-282-412

www.niccolinidomepalace.com

I wish I could live full-time at the Palazzo Niccolini al Duomo. This jewel of a hotel has been carved out of the grand Palazzo Niccolini, which sits directly across from the Duomo. In fact, Donatello had his workshop here in the beginning of the fifteenth century. Filippo and Ginevra Niccolini di Camugliano have renovated these twelve rooms with taste and sensitivity. They have high ceilings, painted frescoes, and large bathrooms. The staff is cordial, friendly, and helpful. And the Grand Salon, which is decorated with family heirlooms, coffee-table books, and big bouquets of flowers, is a lovely place to have breakfast or afternoon tea. Overall, a very comfortable and elegant home away from home.

Residenza del Moro

Via del Moro, 15

011-39-055-290-884

www.residenzadelmoro.com

This hotel, a one of a kind, is situated in the Palazzo

LEFT ABOVE: The lobby at Hotel Lungarno next to the Arno River, and below, a green salon in the Hotel Santa Maria Novella adorned with Napoleonic memorabilia. **ABOVE:** The Grand Hotel's longtime concierge Paolo Basagni.

Niccolini-Bourbon, a sixteenth-century building, almost directly across from the famous restaurant Garga. As you walk in off the quiet street, you enter a courtyard and an arched loggia. There are eleven huge, high-ceilinged suites, each decorated differently with ancient frescoes, antique pieces, and a spectacular collection of contemporary art—an interesting juxtaposition. The rooms open off large common areas where contemporary-art installations and sculpture are showcased. There is a third-floor garden, featuring an ancient tree, where you can have breakfast or something prepared by their in-house chef. It's so quiet that you could spend an entire afternoon there just reading.

MODERATE

Albergotto

Via de' Tornabuoni, 13

011-39-055-239-6464

www.albergotto.com

Friends seem to enjoy staying in this hotel, located right on the main shopping street of Florence. The décor is traditional, and there's a cozy feeling about the place. If you reserve the suite at the top of the hotel, the views are wonderful.

Antica Dimora Firenze

Via San Gallo, 72

011-39-055-462-7296

www.anticadimorafirenze.it

Antica Dimora Johlea

Via San Gallo, 80

011-39-055-463-3292

www.johanna.it

Residenza Johlea

Via San Gallo, 76

011-39-055-462-7296

www.johanna.it

These three hotels are owned by the same group and are located next to each other on Via San Gallo, a peaceful street near the Church of San Marco. I have friends who frequently visit Florence who wouldn't stay anywhere else. They like it because it's like staying in your own suite and prices are reasonable. The décor is traditional and unpretentious, with predominantly pastel colors. Everything is comfortable, and some rooms even have balconies. The bathrooms are new.

Hotel Beacci Tornabuoni

Via dei Tornabuoni, 3

011-39-055-212-645

www.tornabuonihotels.com

This small pensione has been here forever, and we have friends who have stayed here for years. It's decorated with large Italian antiques and comfortable furniture. The location is great. It occupies the top floors of a fifteenth-century palazzo, so the views from its lovely roof garden are a real treat—a delightful place to sip your cappuccino in the morning.

Hotel Hermitage

Vicolo Marzio, 1

011-39-055-287-216

www.hermitagehotel.com

This was the first place I stayed in Florence as a student and when I returned to work in fashion. I loved it because it was owned by two nice old ladies, was just steps away from the Ponte Vecchio, and had the best roof garden in Florence, where continental breakfast was served under the verdant pergola and the railings were hung with coral-geranium-filled window boxes. It had a view of the Duomo and the Palazzo Vecchio from one side and the Arno River and the Vasari Corridoio from the other. Though the hotel has new owners and updated interiors, those things have not changed. The staff is lovely, and every time I visit to say hello, it still feels a little like home.

In Piazza della Signoria

Via dei Magazzini, 2

011-39-055-239-9546

www.inpiazzadellasignoria.com

This *residenza d'epoca* is owned by friendly young couple Alessandro and Sonia Pini. They bought this

fourteenth-century palazzo in 2000 and have restored the eleven rooms and three apartments with sensitivity, even finding a six-hundred-year-old woman's shoe in one of the walls during the renovation. The décor is very Italian, with simple, elegant pieces, terra-cotta floors and beautiful frescoes on the walls and ceilings. There is a nice feeling throughout, because everyone is so friendly and helpful.

J & J Hotel

Via di Mezzo, 20
011-39-055-263-121
www.jandjhotel.com

If you want to stay somewhere that is just off the beaten path and yet close to everything, the J & J fits the bill. It's situated on a quiet street in a Florentine neighborhood near the Sant' Ambrogio organic market and the delicious Cibrèo group of restaurants. It was transformed from a sixteenth-century convent into a twenty-room hotel decorated with period Italian antiques and comfortable furniture crisply covered in pretty fabrics. Settle in the courtyard, a great place to relax and have tea or a drink, and you will feel that you really are living in the past.

Residence Hilda

Via dei Servi, 40
011-39-055-288-021
www.residencehilda.com

Midway between the Duomo and Piazza S.S. Annunziata, the location of this hotel is ideal for those who want to explore the San Marco part of the city, where locals live. There are twelve sleek designer apartment suites, brand new and nicely done with living and dining areas. Maid service and a concierge staff are also available.

ABOVE: Stay in the gentle countryside just above Florence at the Villa Poggio San Felice and enjoy its verdant gardens.

Residenza Santo Spirito

Piazza Santo Spirito, 9
011-39-055-265-8376
www.residenzasspirito.com

This is the perfect place for anyone who loves the Oltrarno and Piazza Santo Spirito, as it sits just at the corner. It has just three rooms, but they are grand— big and beautifully restored, with antiques and original floors and ceilings. The bathrooms are spacious and modern. It is owned by Ferdinando and Laura Budini Gattai, who will be enlarging it shortly by renovating the top floor. The loggia at the top offers a wonderful view of the city and the very lively piazza below.

HOTELS IN THE HILLS

Grand Hotel Villa Cora

Viale Machiavelli, 18

011-39-055-229-8451

www.villacora.it

No more than ten minutes outside of Florence, this extravagant neoclassic hotel has been popular since the turn of the century. Built in 1865, it was originally called the Villa Oppenheim, after the baron who built it when Florence was the capital of Italy. At one time, Napoleon III's widow, Eugenia, was a resident. It has recently been closed for renovation and updating.

Relais Marignolle

Via di San Quirichino a Marignolle, 16

011-39-055-228-6910

www.marignolle.com

Though situated very close to the city, when you are here you feel as if you were in the deep Tuscan countryside. Seven bedrooms are decorated in fresh, colorful country fabrics and pristinely maintained. Breakfast is served every morning in the garden's large gazebo, and the pretty grounds and swimming pool are other good reasons to just relax in this family-run inn.

Torre di Bellosguardo

Via Roti Michelozzi, 2

011-39-055-229-8145

www.torrebellosguardo.com

The setting of this hotel above Florence is simply spectacular. Originally the home of Guido Caval-

RIGHT: The view from the garden planted with wisteria and colorful flower beds at Villa San Michelle.

canti, a friend of Dante, who built it in the twelfth century, it has expanded and changed over the years. It was a private school during and after the war and was finally turned into a hotel by the owner Amerigo Franchetti, who inherited it from his grandmother many years ago. The surrounding gardens and the views are breathtakingly beautiful. There is a *limonaia*, a swimming pool, and sixteen guest rooms simply decorated in the Florentine Renaissance style. Breakfast is the only meal served, so you are on your own for meals, either walking down to Florence on the secret path (about thirty minutes) or taking a taxi into the city since the hotel does not supply transportation.

Villa La Vedetta

Viale Michelangelo, 78

011-39-055-681-631

www.villalavedettahotel.com

This handsome eighteen-room hotel is set in a patrician villa built in the late 1800s. Its creamy exterior is surrounded by balustrades, impeccably groomed Italian-style gardens, and a gorgeous swimming pool. Its best asset, a large terrace, overlooks one of the most magnificent panoramas of Florence. The hotel's décor is stunning—gray and white with accents of bright red in a contemporary blending of modern furniture and antiques. The staff is helpful, and there is a car service down into Florence whenever you wish to go. Even if you are not staying at the hotel, it's the perfect spot to visit for lunch, dinner, or a drink on a beautiful day.

LEFT: The lofty *limonaia* at Torre di Bellosguardo, originally used in winter for storing lemon trees, is now the perfect place to have a drink or read a good book.

Villa La Massa

Via della Massa, 24

Candeli

011-39-055-626-11

www.villadeste.it

If you have ever stayed on Lake Como at the Villa d'Este then you can imagine how blissful it is to stop here, as it is owned by the same hotel group. Purchased in 1999, this stunning sixteenth-century villa and its thirty-eight rooms have been tastefully restored. It is in the midst of a large private park with manicured grounds and a tranquil terrace sitting right at the edge of the Arno. There is a swimming pool set gracefully under the trees. You may feel that you are miles from civilization, but you're really only about twenty minutes from Florence, and the hotel has a shuttle to take you there.

Villa Poggio San Felice

Via San Mattteo in Arcetri, 24

011-39-055-220-016

www.villapoggiosanfelice.com

This gracious two-story Tuscan villa is in the tiny town of Arcetri, just above Florence. It was inherited by the owner Livia Puccinelli from her great-great-grandfather, Gerardo Kraft, who once owned the Grand and Excelsior hotels in town. The cool, simple-but-charming interiors include five bedrooms—most with balconies—lovely flower-filled gardens, and a small swimming pool. You can walk into Arcetri to see Galileo's house and have lunch at Omero. The last lines in the hotel's brochure are the clincher: "Free accommodation is offered to children under the age of three. So as to make you feel at home, we also speak English and French. Small and well-behaved dogs are welcome."

LEFT: Villa La Vedetta's swimming pool and formal terrace overlooking an unforgettable view of the Duomo.
ABOVE: Taking a swim in the stylish pool at Villa San Michele under sun-dappled olive trees is a bit of heaven.

Villa San Michele

Via Doccia, 4

Fiesole

011-39-055-567-8200

www.villasanmichele.orient-express.com

I've been in love with this romantic hotel for a very long time, ever since we had a memorable lunch on the loggia one spring afternoon when we were just married. It is nestled into the hills of Fiesole, just fifteen minutes from Florence. The magic starts as you approach, up a narrow, winding road. The fragrance of lemon trees and flowers comes to meet you as you enter the hotel, a fifteenth-century Franciscan monastery, whose façade is said to have been designed by Michelangelo. Stroll through the elegant ancient cloister and restaurant to the terraced garden, with its beige umbrellas, comfortable chaise lounges, roses, wisteria, and fragrant herbs. The pool is at the top, above two rows of junior suites, which are roomy and comfortable and have terraces overlooking the spectacular panorama of Florence. The bathrooms and dressing rooms are large and beautifully appointed with Bulgari and Penhaligon amenities tucked into baskets filled with fluffy towels. The staff couldn't be nicer. Do try to stay here, but if you can't, put lunch, dinner, or a drink on the loggia on your to-do list.

APARTMENT AND HOUSE RENTALS

Family Estates in Tuscany

Piazzale di Porta al Prato, 37

011-39-055-268-123

www.familyestatesintuscany.com

The Corsini family has some beautiful, very special rental properties in the city of Florence. We looked at everything from a well-designed cottage in their magnificent city garden to an apartment overlooking the river that was quiet and private.

Gidec

Piazza Antinori, 2

011-39-055-213-138

www.gidec.it

Many of the apartments managed by Gidec that we looked at were in the elegant Palazzo Antinori or next door. This means you step out of your flat and you are on the Via Tornabuoni. The apartments are nicely decorated, and some have terraces with views.

Lungarno Suites

Lungarno Acciaiuoli, 4

011-39-055-2726-8000

www.lungarnohotels.com

Part of the Ferragamo Group, these apartments are handsomely decorated in neutral tones and contain kitchens with everything you need, including an espresso machine. All the hotel services are available to you, including housekeeping, reception, and a concierge to guide your way.

LEFT: The huge painting in the reception area of Lungarno Suites gives new meaning to the words "big bird."
ABOVE: A dream come true. You can rent this splendid Corsini apartment from Family Estates in Tuscany.

Owners Direct

www.ownersdirect.co.uk/city-of-florence.htm
This website has some adorable apartments. Most have character and are in interesting neighborhoods. One had a terrace overlooking the river and the Uffizi Galleries and was steps from the Ponte Vecchio.

St. James Guest House

Via Bernardo Rucellai, 9
011-39-055-294-417
www.stjames.it
St. James, the Episcopal church in Florence, was founded by J.P. Morgan and has some wonderful programs for visitors, including a library and terrific thrift shop. They also have a guest house with a spacious three-bedroom, threebath apartment overlooking the church garden. Minimum booking is one week.

Windows on Italy

Via dei Serragli, 6r
011-39-055-268-510
www.windowsonitaly.com
This company has a vast selection of interesting apartments. We prefer the ones on the Oltrarno and, in fact, rented one for a month when we were working on *Dreaming of Tuscany*. It was a nice change from staying in a hotel.

A Day in the Country

"I should like you to see Florence itself and the surrounding country and the situation of the town, for you would say that one should live and die here."

—Leopold Mozart, writing to his wife in Salzburg

Whether you are sitting in an outdoor *caffè* in the quiet San Niccolò neighborhood or having lunch at a trattoria on Via Bartolini, all you have to do is look around—you are almost in the country. The city of Florence lies in a hollow which is surrounded by countryside—some of it breathtakingly beautiful. In some sections of the city, it bumps up against the stone buildings and busy streets without warning. In *The Merchant of Prado*, Iris Origo wrote, "Always the Tuscan cities have held their arms wide open to the country, and….it was often difficult to tell where one ended and the other one began."

In Florence, it's still that way today. Just shortly out of town on your way to Fiesole, you can feel this happening. This is one of its biggest advantages. A thirty-minute drive in any direction from the center will put you in almost another world. So if you want a break from the hustle and bustle of the city, take Mr. Beebe's advice to Lucy in *A Room with a View* and "don't neglect the country round." You can take a drive, a tour, or a public bus from the Santa Maria Novella train station to one of these spots where history and culture reside.

Fiesole and Settignano

North and east of Florence are several charming hill towns. Old narrow roads, verdant vegetation, and superb views await you in Fiesole and Settignano. All this beauty, the mild weather, and the culture were magnets for the Americans and British who flocked to Italy in the mid-nineteenth century. Many

OPENING PICTURE: Charming statuary at Villa Peyron.
OVERLEAF, LEFT: A gardener tidies up the parterres at Villa Peyron, and right, a Tuscan scene from Certosa.

were artists, like Benjamin West and Thomas Cole. Others were authors, like Mark Twain, Nathaniel Hawthorne, and Henry James. Then there were the educated and wealthy people, like Hortense Acton, Sybil Cutting, James Jackson Jarves, Bernard Berenson, Charles Augustus Strong, and Charles Loeser, who restored crumbling villas and created personal and unique gardens.

Many of these villas survive to this day, including three with lovely gardens, bequeathed to American universities by their owners—Villa I Tatti (Harvard), Villa le Balze (Georgetown), and Villa la Pietra (New York University). You can make an appointment to tour their gardens. Others, like the magnificent Villa Gamberaia, are open to the public.

Be sure to leave some time to visit the little village of Fiesole. Aside from the spectacular views, the fact that Fiesole was an Etruscan colony and was important in Roman times gives it another dimension. There's a little square in the town center called Piazza Mino da Fiesole. The Duomo of San Romolo, begun in 1028, is here, and just behind is the Museo Bandini, with its ceramics, ivory, and painting collections. Just beyond is the archeological park, with a civic museum highlighting the excavated Etruscan and Roman treasures found in the area and the Constantini Collection of Greek vases. The 3,000-seat Roman amphitheater, built in the first century B.C., is still used during the town's summer music festival, Estate Fiesolana.

When you are in Fiesole, don't forget to visit the tiny hamlet of San Domenico, just a five-minute walk away. The fifteenth-century church houses several beautiful paintings by Fra Angelico, who was a monk here until 1437. A short walk away down the Via della Badia is the Badia Fiesolana—originally the

ABOVE: The sunny town square in the center of Fiesole surrounded by historic buildings and casual restaurants.

town's cathedral—with its Romanesque façade. If you walk a little way out of town, there is a marble memorial that marks the place where Leonardo da Vinci made his flying experiments in 1488.

Indulge yourself and make reservations to have lunch at the romantic Villa San Michele, set in the nearby hills (see page 121). It's a delightful spot to dine alfresco on the elegant loggia while enjoying the stunning view of Florence. Or you can have a simpler meal at either of two other spots: Tullio a Montebene, a country trattoria near Fiesole; or La Sosta del Rossellino, a rustic *enoteca* in Settignano.

Villa I Tatti

Via di Vincigliata, 26
Fiesole
011-39-055-603-251
www.itatti.it

Set near Settingnano, a short, twenty-minute drive from Florence, Villa I Tatti was the longtime home of art historian Bernard Berenson, who purchased it in 1900. The villa, a former farmhouse, was decorated by Berenson, who carefully arranged his collections there—furniture, oriental rugs, and, of course, important Italian paintings. A photography archive and fine library of 100,000 volumes constitute what Berenson felt was "my most important legacy to the future." The garden was designed by English architect and landscape designer Cecil Pinsent in the Italian Renaissance–revival style with Baroque details—terraces, fountains, flower beds, box hedges, stone paths, and a limonaia. Berenson bequeathed the handsome villa and its gardens to Harvard when he died. It is currently closed for renovations, but you can call or go online to learn more.

Villa Le Balze

Via Vecchia Fiesolana, 26
Fiesole
011-39-055-592-08
www.villalebalze.org
By appointment only
Located on the southern slope of Fiesole, Le Balze
is the property of Georgetown University, and you
must make an appointment to visit. Le Balze was
designed by Cecil Pinsent, who was famous for so
many Tuscan gardens created between 1910 and
the Second World War, including my favorite, La
Foce. This particular garden was commissioned by
Charles Augustus Strong, the American philosopher,
and consists of a succession of stanze di verdure, or
garden rooms—one leading into the other, and each
more beautiful than the last.

Villa Peyron al Bosco di Fontelucente

Via di Vincigliata, 2
Fiesole
011-39-055-264-321
www.bardinipeyron.it
The garden, not the villa, is open to the public, and
it's well worth a visit. The Peyron family bought
the property in 1914, and Paolo Peyron is credited
with creating a distinctive garden that has evolved
over the years. Water is an important feature, with
twenty-nine fountains on the property and a lovely
lake devoted to music and dedicated to conductor
Riccardo Muti. Beautiful antique statuary from the
Veneto is everywhere, including in the surrounding
woods. Try to view the garden in the spring, when
the graceful wisteria is in bloom everywhere.

Villa Gamberaia

Via del Rossellino, 72
Settingnano
011-39-055-697-205
www.villagamberaia.com
I have been coming to visit this garden for many
years, and each time, I enjoy it more because of its
intimacy and being small enough—three acres—to
be explored easily. There are beautiful pathways
through parterres of boxwood, a rippling pond, a
charming grotto, a huge *limonaia*, and the best views
of Florence and the Arno valley. It has been for many
years a favorite of garden-lovers, including enthusiasts like Edith Wharton and Bernard Berenson, who
both wrote glowingly about it. This is the reason
why so many people were deeply affected when it
was destroyed during the Second World War. The
Zalum family restored the garden and impeccably
maintains it today.

Also north of Florence, if you have time, are two
beautiful spots:

Villa Stibbert

Via Stibbert, 26
011-39-055-475-520
www.museostibbert.it/visita.htm
Villa Stibbert was owned by Frederick Stibbert, who
inherited the house from his parents. He then bought
the neighboring mansion, turned it into a museum,
and left it all to the city of Florence in 1906. Just ten
minutes from the city center, the Stibbert Museum
houses one of the biggest collections of ancient
weapons in all of Europe. Early antique furniture,
rare costumes and textiles, and some notable paint-

RIGHT: Spectacular views of three special gardens, clockwise from left: the pool at Villa Gamberaia; the entrance of
cypresses at Villa la Pietra; and formal stone steps into the garden around a graceful fountain at Villa Peyron.

ABOVE: The dramatic, larger-than-life statue of Appennino done in 1580 by Giamblogna at Parco di Villa Demidoff.

ings by Botticelli and Bronzino, to name a few, are just some of the treasures. Stibbert was a collector extraordinaire who not only amassed but made sure these objects were properly displayed in the villa's sixty rooms.

The vast park surrounding the museum features a garden designed by Girolamo Passeri and Giuseppe Poggi in 1859 and includes a limonaia, an Egyptian temple, and a man-made lake. It's a perfect place to get some air after you have spent several hours viewing some of the 50,000 objects within the museum.

Villa La Pietra

Via Bolognese, 120
011-39-055-500-7210
www.nyu.edu/lapietra
By appointment only
Sir Harold Acton left Villa La Pietra to New York University, and it is now their center for Italian studies, so you must call or go online to make an appointment. The garden was originally designed

in 1908 for Harold Acton's father, Arthur, by French landscaper Henri Duchene, then updated by Diego Suarez about five years later. It is a magical place, defined by majestic bay hedges, tall cypresses, stately umbrella pines, and ancient garden statuary.

Parco di Villa Demidoff

Via Fiorentina, 282
Pratolino
011-39-055-409-427
www.cultura.toscana.it/architetture/giardini/firenze/parco_villa_demidoff.shtml
Located near Pratolino, seven miles from Florence, and created by Buontalenti in 1569 for Francesco de' Medici, the original villa was demolished in the nineteenth century, and the large servants' quarters renovated. The garden, too, has undergone many changes and in the late nineteenth century was redesigned in the English-garden style. The statue called Appennino, by Giambologna, of a giant sadly gazing at his image in the water below, was created in 1580. The sculpture is a fountain in this garden, famous for its *giochi d'acqua*, or water features.

Restaurants

La Sosta del Rossellino
Via del Rossellino, 2r
Settignano
011-39-055-697-245

Tullio a Montebene
Ontignano, 48
Fiesole
011-39-055-597-354

Villa San Michele
Via Doccia, 4
Fiesole
011-39-055-567-8200
www.villasanmichele.com

Museum

Museo Bandini
Via Depre, 1
Fiesole
011-39-055-594-77

Medici Villas

Florence is known for the beautiful villas and gardens in the countryside that surrounds it. In the sixteenth century, the powerful ruling Medici family embarked on a program of renovating ancient castles and building extravagant villas as country escapes from political strife and the city's summer heat. It was called *villeggiatura*. These refuges were also another place where the family's accumulated collections could be shown and enjoyed.

These villas evolved into cultural centers where the humanistic ideas of the Renaissance could be celebrated. Learned thinkers, scientists, astronomers and writers rubbed shoulders with the most dynamic artists and sculptors of the age. They became centerpieces, surrounded by their gardens, farmlands, vineyards, and olive groves. Leon Battista Alberti said of them: "How blessed it will be staying in a country villa: an unknown happiness!"

A bird's-eye view of these villas, including Castello Careggi, Il Trebbio, Petraia, Artimino and their gardens, can be seen in paintings on display in Florence's Museo di Firenze com'era (see page 56), where a series of lunettes painted for the Medici by Flemish artist Justus Utens are displayed. You can visit some of these Medici villas, just a car ride from Florence. The ones I've listed are managed by the Italian government and open to the public.

Villa Medicea di Castello

Via di Castello

011-39-055-454-791

www.polomuseale.firenze.it/english/musei/villacastello

This is the oldest of the Medici villas, built in 1477 by Lorenzo de' Medici's cousin, who was Botticelli's

patron. It is said that the paintings *Primavera* and the *Birth of Venus* were hanging here before being moved to the Uffizi, in 1815. Unfortunately, only the garden is open to the public, but it is considered one of the most beautiful gardens in Tuscany.

Cosimo de' Medici engaged Tribolo in 1537 to design the garden as an allegory, and it contains many statues by prominent Renaissance artists like Giambologna, Ammannati, and Tribolo. It is divided into compartments featuring parterres, which include displays of heirloom flowers and old roses. The Lemon Garden features two limonaie, where over five hundred citrus trees—some of the oldest in Italy—spend the winter in enormous terra cotta pots.

The extraordinary grotto, the "Grotto degli Animali," by Tribolo and Vasari, is famous for its ornate decorations of animals, fish, shells, and unicorns cavorting around stone-and-seashell-encrusted walls, all bathed in water that cascades everywhere. Be sure to visit the *ortaccio*, a Renaissance herb garden planted with aromatic specimens. Then take the short walk to La Petraia next door.

The Accademia della Crusca, started in 1582 to standardize the purity of the Italian language, is located in this Medici villa. In 1612, the members produced the Vocabolario, a dictionary of pure Italian—the first of its kind in Europe. This year, the Academy reprinted the dictionary, and you can read about it on its website, www.accademiadellacrusca.it.

Villa Medicea della Petraia

Via della Petraia, 40

011-39-055-452-691

www.polomuseale.firenze.it/english/musei/petraia

This Renaissance villa was transformed from an ancient castle in the sixteenth century by Buontalenti

LA PRETAIA

for Grand Duke Ferdinando I de' Medici. It was re-modeled again by the House of Savoy, in 1861, when Florence became the capital of Italy. La Petraia was the royal palace at this time, and the notable interior features extraordinary frescoes, ornate furniture, paintings, and sculpture, including the king's former apartments, which are open to the public.

The garden is on three terraces that were laid out with a focus on parterres that feature flowers, dwarf fruit trees, and a large collection of roses—even Renaissance wild flowers. The original 1590 fish pond is still the source of water for irrigating the garden. A fountain by Tribolo with a bronze statue by Giambologna dating from the Renaissance was restored and is on display inside the studiolo.

Villa Corsi Salviati

Via Gramsci, 462
Sesto Fiorentino
011-39-055-443-805
www.gicas.net/villa.html
By appointment only

Near the Medici villas in the center of the industrial town of Sesto Fiorentino, is this beautiful old garden privately owned by the Guicciardini Corsi Salviati family. It is now also the Florence headquarters of the University of Michigan. Surrounded by trees that screen out the city, you can quietly enjoy this formal garden and its special details, like stone statues, reflecting pools and walls decorated with marble pietra spugna, and a small boxwood maze modeled after the one at Hampton Court in England.

LEFT: Three Medici villas: above, a lunette of the exterior and gardens of Villa La Petraia painted by Justus Utens in 1599; below, at Villa Medicea di Castello, left, an ornate interior view and right, the unusual grotto.

The Monastery of Certosa

Certosa del Galluzzo
Via della Buca di Certosa, 2
Galluzzo
011-39-055-204-9226, 204-8167

This Chartreuse or Carthusian monastery, once the most powerful in all Europe, sits high on a hill overlooking Florence. It was commissioned in 1841 by Niccolò Acciaioli, a prominent Florentine banker, and once had over five hundred works of art and a lavish library within its walls. It's visible to all who leave the city by car heading to southern Tuscany through the Porta Romana. It is now run by a small group of Cistercian monks. When you arrive, leave your car in the parking lot at the bottom of the battlements, and follow the vintage 1950s tin signs with arrows pointing up the hill.

The first little piazza you encounter is home to the *farmacia* (pharmacy), stocked with liquors, teas, elixirs, essential oils, and many other magical potions and lotions—all distilled by the monks from fragrant botanicals. Don't forget to stop here on your way down to pick up a bottle of the Gran Liquore della Certosa—aged liquor made with fragrant herbs that comes in several flavors. I always buy the classic, which tastes a little like Grand Marnier. If it's not too busy, ask if you can sample some of them. I became a devotee a long time ago, when my husband and I walked there from Florence (five kilometers—a trek), passing meadows and farms. Now the road is lined with ugly gas stations, but the magic starts working once you arrive.

One of the main reasons to visit Certosa is the group of five splendid lunette frescoes representing Christ's passion, painted by Mannerist artist Jacopo

ABOVE: 1950s vintage directions to the treasures in the Monastery of Certosa and their monks' famous liquors.

Pontormo. Pontormo came to the monastery to escape the plague, and it took him three years, from 1522 to 1525, to paint these masterpieces. Also in the Picture Gallery, or Pinacoteca, on the top floor is a collection of paintings from the fourteenth to the seventeenth century, many donated by prominent Florentines of the time.

Then there is the important Church of San Lorenzo with its rich frescoes, ornate marble altar, and large Renaissance cloister decorated with sixty-six maiolica tondi depicting portraits of the saints, by Andrea and Giovanni della Robbia. There are daily tours of the monastery and one of the monk's cells overlooking the cloister. Sunday morning is a quiet time to visit, as Certosa opens at 9:00 A.M. and there is a lovely mass at 10:00 A.M.

Montelupo Fiorentino

If you are crazy about Tuscan ceramics and want to see some beautiful examples, this is the place. The entire town of Montelupo Fiorentino is dedicated to the art of pottery. The streets are lined on both sides with ceramics stores and galleries featuring examples painted and glazed with skill. Workshops and kilns have been producing high-quality, sophisticated ceramics here for years. The companies of Dolfi and Flavia, with fine worldwide reputations, are just two examples of the best of Montelupo pottery. Every June, there is a ceramics festival in the town center, with exhibits, demonstrations, and outdoor workshops.

The Pottery and Archeological Museum of Montelupo houses an impressive collection of ceramics, with artifacts from prehistoric times through the twentieth century. The centerpiece of the museum is a stunning collection of maiolica. The museum's restoration laboratory is well known and open by appointment.

Nearby is the town of Artimino, the location of Villa di Artimino Trevilla. It can be recognized by its extraordinary rooftop, which is crowned by many chimneys, all different. It is often called the "house

ABOVE: After strolling down the main street in Montelupo Fiorentino, be sure to visit the comprehensive museum.

of a thousand chimneys," or "La Ferdinanda," as it was built for Ferdinando I by Bernardo Buontalenti in his old age. This is where the seventeen lunettes in the series painted by Justus Utens between 1599 and 1602—"The Medici Villas"—were originally hung (the lunettes are now in Florence). You can make an appointment to visit the villa and take a guided tour.

When it's time for lunch, you have a treat in store. One of the best restaurants in Tuscany, Da Delfina, is in the hamlet of Artimino. You will have an unforgettable meal in this cozy farmhouse, which features traditional Tuscan dishes like *ribollita* and *fritto misto*. Even though it is well known, it's not the least bit touristy, and you'll usually find locals with discerning palates enjoying the fare.

If you feel like having a picnic instead, you have another treat. Stop in at Peruzzi Alimentari and choose from a gourmet selection of local crostini, artisanal cheeses and *salumi*, vegetable confits, and good local wines. The heavenly aromas are so appetizing that we usually eat our picnic lunch right there, at one of the small tables in this friendly place.

Restaurants

Peruzzi Alimentari
Via 5 Martiri, 21
Artimino
011-39-055-871-8124

Ristorante da Delfina
Via della Chiesa, 1
Artimino, Carmignano
011-39-055-871-8119
www.dadelfina.it

Museums

Museum of Montelupo
Via Bartolomeo
Sinibaldi, 45
Montelupo
011-39-0571-513-352

Villa di Artimino
Viale Papa Giovanni
XXIII, 1
Artimino, Carmignano
011-39-055-875-1427

Festival

International Ceramics Festival
Ufficio Turistico
Via Baccio da Montelupo, 43
Montelupo
011-39-0571-518-993

SIX

The Food of Florence

"Does a well-fed race produce more geniuses than others?"
—Anonymous, Fifteenth Century

In his definitive book, *The Food of Italy*, Waverley Root introduces the intriguing thought on the previous page when discussing the Renaissance in Tuscany. The region, and specifically Florence, nurtured so many outstanding scientists, painters, sculptors, poets, musicians, artisans, astronomers, engineers, and architects, that even today their achievements seem extraordinary. The question is definitely food for thought.

But the city's Renaissance splendors, a stunning feast for the eye, have always had competition from its splendid food. Fruit markets, food stores, pastry shops, and *enoteche* line the streets of the city, their windows overflowing with mouthwatering offerings. The outdoor markets and fruit stalls always reflect abundance and are crowded with people talking about food—pointedly sharing their expertise and favorite recipes.

"I don't think you need to have been born with a casserole for a hat . . . always select the finest ingredients to start with, and you're sure to make a good impression." This advice was taken to heart by middle-class cooks who made Pelligrino Artusi's *La Scienza in Cucina e l'Arte di Mangiar Bene* (The Science of Cookery and the Art of Eating Well) a bestseller. The book, published in 1891, featured easily understood recipes that were practical, encouraging the reader to make nourishing, delicious dishes. Written in the Florentine dialect, to this day it reflects the cuisine of the region—robust food prepared without fussiness, unadorned, and with an emphasis on freshness, quality, and, above all, simplicity.

All you have to do is visit a tiny trattoria down the steps in the shadow of the Ponte Vecchio to sample some of this philosophy. We've been enjoying delicious meals at Buca dell'Orafo for over thirty years

now. Giordano Monni is the fourth generation of his family to run the restaurant, now with his brother-in-law Mirko in the kitchen and his nephew Davide in the dining room. They specialize in the flavorful food you would expect on a Tuscan kitchen table (many of the recipes come from Giordano's grandmother). Even the accessories for your *bistecca alla fiorentina* are local—handcrafted knives with buffalo-horn handles by Colteria Saladini in Scarperia, a town near Florence, famous since the fifteenth century for its cutlers.

Ask to see a copy of *A Typical Tuscan Food Affair,* their book published in 2007 with Apicius, one of the top cooking schools in Florence. The photos were taken by the students and accompany this landmark restaurant's delicious recipes.

Judith Jones, the esteemed cookbook editor, noted in her lovely book, *The Tenth Muse: My Life in Food,* "How little Americans understand of Italian ingenuity when it comes to food." Traditionally, cooks in Italy don't waste anything, and in Florence most restaurant menus still reflect "*la cucina povera,*" frugal home cooking—an economical cuisine that utilizes seasonal local produce, rather than expensive imports, to create simple, tasty dishes based on recipes passed down from generation to generation. Fusion cuisine and globalization have recently opened the door to new food trends, but even so, in this city tradition prevails, with most menus reflecting hearty Tuscan home cooking using the best ingredients.

OPENING PICTURE: A mouth-watering selection of tasty pecorino cheeses, honey, and wine from the Antinori farms and vineyards are served at Cantinetta Antinori. OVERLEAF, LEFT: Fabio Picchi in front of his newest restaurant, and right, a glass of crisp Mezzo Braccio. RIGHT, ABOVE: Giordano Monni and his staff eating before Buca dell'Orafo opens for lunch, and below, their famous Tuscan *bistecca alla fiorentina*.

One of those ingredients is extra-virgin olive oil, and the finest is produced in Tuscany. Extra virgin comes from the first pressing and is tested (and tasted) to assure the very best. Some oils are sharp and peppery, others sweet and fruity. All are flavorful and distinctive. The fresher the oil, the more intense is its taste. There are millions of silvery olive trees in Tuscany, but, because of local demand, a comparatively small percentage of olive oil from them is exported. So take the opportunity when you are in Florence to sample some of the many delicious local selections available.

Bread has always been a staple of the local diet. Tuscan bread, *pane toscano*, is made without salt (*sciocco*) because of the salt taxes originally levied on Florentine bakers in the twelfth century. This is one of the reasons that the bread lasts so long. Even when it starts to become hard, it is used as the basis for many favorite dishes—the perfect complement to the region's salty, savory food. *Schiacciata*, a flat loaf with olive oil liberally drizzled on top, is a local mouthwatering specialty.

There is more organic farming in Italy than any other European country, with over two million acres in production. In order to protect local farmers and encourage a natural-food philosophy, many worthwhile changes have taken place. In the 1980s, Carlo Petrini, an Italian, started Slow Food to counteract globalization and the spread of fast food. Its goal is to preserve the art of enjoying the good, healthy food of the past. Petrini says, "Make more time. Not just for food, but for family, friends, and poetry." The organization is now international, with a member-

LEFT: The organic Sant'Ambrogio market offers Florentines the freshest of everything from cheeses to new greens to prosciutto sold by the friendliest vendors in town.

ship approaching 80,000, and you will see its logo, a small snail, on the doors of many restaurants and food stores in Florence.

Working on this book was an opportunity to revisit many restaurants, big and small, pricey and inexpensive, trendy and traditional. Though we hadn't been in some for many years, we are happy to say that Florence has remained true to herself and that the Tuscan-based cuisine served in most is very much alive and well.

In a conversation I had recently with Emily Wise Miller, the author of *The Food Lover's Guide to Florence*, she explained why there are so many regional cuisines in this country, saying, "In Italy there's a word *campanilismo*, meaning that a person's loyalty doesn't extend beyond the parish *campanile* (bell tower). The same idea applies to Tuscan cooking. Every town has its own signature foods: In Siena you eat *pici* pasta; go north to Lucca, and it's *tortelli con ragù;* head to the coastal town of Livorno, and you will enjoy the seafood stew known as *cacciucco*. As the regional capital, Florence absorbs a little of all these foods but also has its own specialties."

The restaurant Cantinetta Antinori is a good example. Attractive, comfortable, and located in the Antinori family's palazzo on Via Tornabuoni, it's a perfect place to drop after you've shopped! The food is distinctive, in the best Tuscan way. Flavorful *crostini*, rich *ribollita* (see recipe, page 171), and satisfying pastas are preludes to fortifying chicken and beef dishes. Even more special are the outstanding wines you can enjoy from all the Antinori vineyards. Their new one, Tenuta Monteloro, is just to the north, in the hills overlooking Florence. One spring morning, we visited the vineyard with Albiera Antinori and brought back several bottles of the first vintage to

ABOVE: Tripe and *lampredotto* carts everywhere are a Florentine institution, and right, Cibreo's gourmet specialties.

enjoy with lunch at Cantinetta Antinori. It's called Mezzo Braccio and was light and delicious.

Cibrèo also carries on the Tuscan tradition. It's named after the old Florentine recipe of a chicken neck stuffed with giblets, coxcombs, and other chicken parts. Catherine de' Medici is said to have indulged—and over indulged—in this, her favorite dish. Ristorante Cibrèo is a Florentine treasure. It was started thirty years ago by Fabio Picchi and Benedetta Vitale, who set out to revitalize rustic, traditional Tuscan cooking, but with a refreshing twist—and they did!

When it opened, the restaurant was an immediate success, and I remember how hard it was to get a reservation. It was in an area of Florence that then seemed like the end of the world. Now, all these years later, it's the center of the universe. The little Piazza

Ghiberti is now home to the original restaurant, in addition to the smaller Trattoria Cibrèo (called Cibrèino) next door. Across are Cibrèo Caffè and Teatro del Sale. There's even a small shop selling Picchi's delicious gourmet specialties, many made in the restaurant. The Sant'Ambrogio market (see page 167) and my favorite shop, Lisa Corti (see pages 188-9), are around the corner.

The food at Ristorante Cibrèo is as legendary as the chef. Your meal will start with a selection of "surprise" antipasti, perhaps including spring fava beans with diced pecorino cheese in olive oil; fresh tomatoes and basil in a savory aspic (see recipe page 170); a delicate tripe salad with baby carrots, celery, and onions; and a flan of frothy ricotta cheese blended with herbs—a symphony of freshness and intense flavor reflecting Fabio Picchi's now-well-known food

ABOVE: Mouth-watering *prosciutto crudo* is freshly carved at the abundant breakfast buffet at Villa San Michele.

serving; and *zuppa di fagioli*, the ever-present beans simmered with vegetables and bread.

Though soup reigns, pastas still make an important appearance. *Pappardelle* and *tagliatelle*, ribbon-shaped strips, and *maltagliati*, irregularly cut pasta, are served with meat ragùs made from hare, wild boar, duck, and veal, or fresh-vegetable toppings like pumpkins, tomatoes, artichokes, and mushrooms. *Ravioli* and *tortellini,* typically filled with ricotta cheese, are usually served with creamy sauces like butter and sage or sweet baby peas and cream.

The main course, or second course, in any meal is called the **SECONDO PIATTO** and includes meat, fish, or fowl, usually roasted or grilled but sometimes fried. The best-loved main course will always be *bistecca alla fiorentina*, the legendary grilled Chianina beef. This specially thick, cut steak is seasoned with salt, pepper, and olive oil and served rare, rendering it tender and juicy. On most menus, you will see this dish priced by weight, so you can specify how large a portion you want and will be charged accordingly. While we are on beef, I should mention **stracotto**, slowly cooked pot roast with tomatoes and red wine that should be mouthwateringly tender when served and is fortifying on a winter's day. My favorite is served at Buca dell'Orafo, mentioned above.

The Florentines are avid hunters and also enjoy eating the fruits of their labor, so you will often see wild boar (*cinghiale*), hare (*lepre*), and venison (*cervo*) on the menu. *Fritto misto* often includes the expected

zucchini, cauliflower, mushrooms, and artichokes, with the addition of various other meats like rabbit or chicken, battered and fried.

Another Florentine favorite is *trippe alla fiorentina*, small pieces of tripe stewed with tomatoes and vegetables and covered with parmesan cheese. Tripe is such a Florentine favorite that it is sold in sandwiches at outdoor stands, like hot dogs in New York City. Another important meat is pork. *Arista di maiale*, moist pork roasted with garlic and rosemary, is a dish that should not be missed.

Pollo alla diavola, or *pollo al mattone*, is a classic chicken dish. The chicken is split, pressed flat—traditionally with a brick—then grilled over a hot fire and usually served with rosemary-scented potatoes, as is simple roast chicken, another favorite.

Even though Florence is landlocked, Tuscany is not, so there are some delicious fish dishes to consider, especially *cacciucco alla livornese*, a classic fish stew from Livorno, and tender, small shrimp (*gamberetti*) are often served.

The word *CONTORNI* literally means "contours," a side dish, giving the meal shape and interesting flavors. Beans, asparagus, squash, eggplant, and mushrooms are just a few of the many local and seasonal vegetables on the Florentine menu. Tuscans, including Florentines, are often laughingly called *mangiafagioli*, or bean eaters, harking back to their humble roots and affinity for all types of pulses. Cannellini and toscanelli are the most-often-used *fagioli*. The two most popular recipes are *fagioli all'olio*—white beans, olive oil, and rosemary, and *fagioli all'uccelletto*—white beans cooked in olive oil with sage, garlic, and tomatoes. There is also the recipe that Elizabeth David, the English food writer, repopularized in the 1960s, called *fagioli al fiasco*—beans cooked slowly over a low fire in a straw-covered Chianti bottle. Seasonal vegetables deep fried in batter are a Florentine favorite and include artichokes, sliced squash, cardoons, cauliflower, black kale, and, especially, *fiori di zucchini fritti*, zucchini flowers in season.

After the *secondi piatti*, a small green or mixed salad (*insalata verde*) is sometimes eaten in order to cleanse the palate. *Panzanella*, another local favorite, is a cold salad of chopped tomatoes, basil, and pieces of softened stale bread mixed with olive oil and vinegar. *Pinzimonio* is the name for a platter of fresh raw vegetables to be dipped in olive oil seasoned with salt and pepper.

Now we come to *DOLCE* or dessert. Florentines, like most Italians, do not generally eat many sweets. In many cases, they prefer to end the meal with a ripe piece of fruit, a *macedonia* (fresh-fruit cup), *frutti di bosco* (tiny sweet berries of the season), or sweet pears cooked in red wine. Or, they may choose cheese—a treat in this fertile region, where sheep dot almost every verdant hillside not covered with grapevines.

The word *cacio*, the ancient name for cheese, has been used since Etruscan times interchangeably with *pecorino*, the sheep's milk cheese of Tuscany. There are many different types of *pecorino*, including the mild, soft, very flavorful *pecorino marzolino*, made in early spring from pure ewes' milk, and *pecorino stagionato*, which is aged for six months, hard and tangy, and often served with sweet pears. In between is the exceptional *pecorino delle crete senese* (from the chalky terrain of southern Tuscany near Pienza), *pecorino nero* (coated with ash), *pecorino rosso* (coated with tomato paste), and even *pecorino tartufato* (with truffles), and *pecorino di grotta* (aged in a cave), just to name a few. The taste of each reflects the grazing areas of the sheep from which this distinctive cheese is made.

PREVIOUS PAGE: An appetizing platter of delicious maltagliati and tortelloni pastas at Cantinetta Antinori.
ABOVE: Chef Attilio di Fabrizio, in the sunny glass-enclosed kitchen of Villa San Michele in Fiesole, preparing to teach one of their popular cooking classes. Their famous herb garden, featuring Italian varieties, is just outside.

If a Florentine is in the mood for something sweeter, there are always *cantucci* (hard biscotti) to be dipped in a small glass of **Vin Santo**; *ricciarelli*, almond-flavored cookies, and various other assortments on a theme. Cakes take the form of the *zuccotto*, a dome-shaped, liquor-soaked sponge cake inspired by the Duomo. The light Florentine cheese tart, **torta della nonna**, made with cheese custard and almonds or pine nuts, and *castagnaccio*, a flat cake made with chestnut flower, raisins, and nuts, are also features on the dessert cart, next to *panna cotta*, *tiramisù*, and *gelato,* even though they are not Florentine in origin.

Every meal in Italy ends with a tiny, strong cup of coffee and is always served after the dessert. Italians order *espresso*—called simply *un caffè*—which is never served with a lemon peel—an American affectation. Italians consider *cappuccino* a breakfast drink, a sub-stantial way to start the day. It is never, ever ordered after a meal, as the milk does not aid in digestion.

And we can't possibly end a Florentine meal without talking about one of the most important components, the wine. An old adage says that Tuscany was baptized with wine. In fact, the Greeks called this region "Enotria," the land of wine. For the visitor to Florence, this is an opportunity to sample the selection of great wines, since some of them are not exported.

The famous enologist Giacomo Tachis, who created Sassicaia—often called the "perfect wine"—said this about the region: "Here there is light, the sun. Radiant sunlight and the right soil are the soul of wine. But the tradition of the countryside and the memory of men are the solid basis of the extraordinary Tuscan wine culture."

ABOVE: Albiera Antinori and her estate director in the new vineyard Tenuta Monteloro, in the ancient hills above Fiesole.

Although many of the best wines in the world come from Tuscany, it wasn't always the case. In the early to middle part of the twentieth century, through about the 1950s, Tuscan wines were produced in small vineyards, generally with little concern for real quality, and large quantities of mediocre wine were often produced.

During the early 1960s, the Italian government decided to improve the situation and developed a system to standardize the country's wines. Two major classifications were created: DOC and DOCG. DOC (*Denominazione di Origine Controllata*) established minimum requirements a wine had to meet to earn this rating. For DOCG (*Denominazione di Origine Controllata e Garantita*), the requirements were even more rigorous.

Super-Tuscan was the name given in the 1970s to the early wines that did not fit to the specific requirements of DOC and DOCG. The name Super-Tuscan was created as a category by winemakers who wanted to experiment with nontraditional blends like one of the first, the wine Solaia, that did not fit into an existing category. Super-Tuscan has now been replaced in most cases by the designation IGT (*Indicazione Geografica Tipica*), and the category includes some of the very best wines in Italy.

These categories are very much in use today, and they do ensure quality and consistency. In addition

Nipozzano, a red Frescobaldi wine, and served with sweet heavy cream. If you would like to try it, see the recipe on page 173.

Italian wines are typically known by the region in Italy they come from, instead of the grape used in their production. The wines of Tuscany fall into several major categories:

Chianti is probably the most instantly recognizable name in Italian wine. Chianti, the place, whose boundaries were established in the 1930s is the largest wine-making area in Italy. Chianti, the wine, is today produced by more than a thousand winemakers. For years, it was thought of as the straw-covered wine bottle with a candle in it, on the table of your local Italian-American restaurant. All this has changed.

The **Chianti Classico** area lies in the fertile countryside between Florence and Siena. A wine labeled Chianti Classico must meet more rigid requirements than Chianti and is usually better and more costly. The *Gallo Nero* (Black Rooster) label on the neck of its bottle means it has met the established standards of the regulating committee, the *Gallo Nero Consortium*. The term *riserva* is applied to a Chianti Classico that has been aged longer, either in French-oak barrels or in the bottle, and is released only after three years of aging. Riservas are not produced every year, only from the best harvests of an especially good season.

Many people call ***Brunello di Montalcino,*** made from the Sangiovese Grosso grape, the superior wine of Tuscany. As it needs ten to fifteen years of aging, it has somewhat limited production. Introduced by the Biondi-Santi family in 1970, it is made by more than a hundred vineyards around Montalcino today.

LEFT: The Frescobaldi women meet for an elegant alfresco luncheon in Bona Frescobaldi's verdant flower-filled garden in the heart of Florence's Oltrarno.

A delicious, dry, elegant red wine, ***Carmignano***, with up to 10% Cabernet Sauvignon, must be aged up to two years. Coming from the smallest DOCG in Tuscany, just west of Florence, it was, along with Chianti, the first wine to be protected by stringent rules.

Vino Nobile di Montepulciano, the king of wines, rivals the best of the Chianti Classicos, and is made from the Prugnolo Gentile grape, a clone of the Sangiovese grape. It has often been compared to Brunello di Montalcino but is just a bit lighter.

Tuscany has never been known for its white wines. A notable exception is ***Vernaccia di San Gimignano***, named for the walled city of the same name. It has a DOCG rating and has been the dominant white wine of the area. It is made from ancient vinestock and was mentioned in Michelangelo's writings. As I mentioned before, Antinori has just come out with a new white wine called Mezzo Braccio.

Said to have gotten its name from Cardinal Bessarione—who, in 1440, exclaimed, when served ***Vin Santo***, "Now this is a holy wine"—this sweet dessert wine is usually served with simple cakes and the Florentine favorite *cantucci*, hard cookies which are dipped in it. It's produced from pressed semi-dried Malvasia and Trebbiano grapes that have been laid on straw mats or hung up to dry for several months to concentrate the sugars.

The joy and mystery of wine comes down to us through the ages. Even Galileo Galilei, who lived in Florence and was, among his many other accomplishments, court mathematician to the Medici, pondered the question, saying, "The sun with all those planets revolving around it and dependent on it, can still ripen a bunch of grapes as if it had nothing else in the universe to do."

Dining

Whether it's at a five-star restaurant or a humble trattoria, you can always count on dining well in Florence. Italians are very serious about what they eat—and Florentines even more so—and the choice of restaurants reflects this.

One thing to be wary of is that tourists are sometimes taken advantage of with mediocre food, bad service, and high prices. Do your homework before you leave on your trip. Network with fellow Italophiles to get their suggestions. Read guidebooks written by travel writers whose taste you respect (see "Suggested Reading," page 219). You should also look for a decal on the restaurant's door from "Slow Food," "Gambero Rosso," or "Veronelli," which means it comes highly recommended. Avoid places with tourist menus, written in English and several other languages, displayed in their window. But remember to leave yourself open to the unexpected. When you are in Florence, if you walk by a place that looks good and is filled with the locals, it probably is good!

The lines have blurred, and there are many different types of eating establishments that you can choose from—everything from restaurants and trattorie to small *caffès,* wine bars and even pastry shops. We have edited the following list to what we consider the "best of the best"—places that we have enjoyed eating in for years.

RESTAURANTS

This list ranges from formal restaurants, and all that implies, to trattorias, usually simple, family-run establishments with robust home-style cooking. I've not included restaurants serving international cuisine—only those that serve Italian/Tuscan food with an emphasis on local ingredients from the region surrounding Florence. I've tried to incorporate more trattorie that are good—and reasonably priced—especially considering the dollar-versus-Euro ratio.

Another thing to remember is to make reservations, as many popular spots get especially crowded at dinnertime and on weekends. Most restaurants open for lunch between 12:30 and 1:00 and for dinner between 7:00 and 7:30 (although the locals tend to eat later). Buon appetito!

All'Antico Ristoro di Cambi
Via Sant'Onofrio, 1r
011-39-055-217-134
www.anticoristorodicambi.it
Everyone orders the meat, especially the *bistecca alla fiorentina.*

Alle Murate
Via del Proconsolo, 6
011-39-055-240-618
The place to go for an elegant, candlelit dinner.

Al Tranvai
Piazza Tasso, 14r
011-39-055-225-197
Always crowded with locals because it's reasonable.

Antico Fattore
Via Lambertesca, 1/3r
011-39-055-288-975
Nicely old-fashioned and near the Uffizi Gallery.

Belle Donne Osteria
Via Belle Donne, 16r
011-39-055-238-2609
www.belledonneosteria.com

Borgo San Jacopo
Hotel Lungarno
Borgo San Jacopo, 14
011-39-055-272-61
Reserve a table on the balcony at the top of the hotel.

Buca dell'Orafo

Volta dei Girolami, 28r
011-39-055-213-619
My favorite—try any delicious
Tuscan specialty, especially
the *bistecca alla fiorentina*.

Buca Lapi

Via del Trebbio, 1r
011-39-055-213-768
www.bucalapi.com
Another place to order the
Chianina *bistecca alla fiorentina*.

Cammillo Trattoria

Borgo San Jacopo, 57r
011-39-055-212-427
Old standby—have the tagliolini
with fresh garden peas.

Cantinetta Antinori

Piazza Antinori, 3r
011-39-055-292-234
www.antinori.it
Order the humble *ribollita* in
this chic wine-making family's
restaurant.

Cavalo Nero

Via Ardiglione, 22
011-39-055-294-744
Everybody loves this tiny
place—eat in the garden
in the summer.

Cibrèo

Via A. del Verrocchio, 8r
011-39-055-234-1100
www.fabiopicchi.it
Do not miss this legendary
restaurant and its creative
legendary chef.

Cibrèo Trattoria

Via de' Macci, 122r
011-39-055-234-1100
www.fabiopicchi.it
Cibrèo fare in a less formal
atmosphere—no reservations.

Coco Lezzone

Via del Parioncino, 6r
011-39-055-287-178
Ribollita and *papa al pomadoro*
served in one bowl.

Da Burde

Via Pistoiese, 6r
011-39-055-317-206
Family-run trattoria several miles
out of town; locals like it.

Da Mario

Via Rosina, 2r
011-39-055-218-550
Trattoria open only for lunch at
the Mercato Centrale.

Da Sergio

Piazza San Lorenzo, 8r
011-39-055-281-941
Traditional dishes, including tripe.

Enoteca Pinchiorri

Via Ghibellina, 87
011-39-055-242-777
www.enotecapinchiorri.com
Elegant ambiance and service,
and three Michelin stars.

Frescobaldi Ristorante

Via dei Magazzini, 2
011-39-055-284-724
The wine family's smart addition
to the restaurant scene.

Fuor d'Acqua

Via Pisana, 37r
011-39-055-222-999
Top quality seafood, especially
fresh on Friday night.

Garga Trattoria

Via del Moro, 48r
011-39-055-239-8898
www.garga.it
Contemporary art and creative
dishes by Giuliano Gargani.

Gilda Bistro

Piazza Lorenzo Ghiberti, 40r
011-39-055-234-3885
A local favorite for lunch at
the Sant'Ambrogio market.

Il Guscio

Via dell'Orto, 49
011-39-055-224-421
Lively trattoria in San Frediano.

Il Latini

Via dei Palchetti, 6r
011-39-055-210-916
www.illatini.com
Share a table and dine in a
boisterous atmosphere.

Il Profeta

Via Borgo Ognissanti, 93r
011-39-055-212-265
www.ristoranteilprofeta.com
Old-fashioned and cozy; near
the Grand Hotel.

La Baraonda

Via Ghibellina, 67r
011-39-055-234-1171
Authentic, traditional classics.

La Giostra
Borgo Pinti, 12r
011-39-055-241-341
www.ristorantelagiostra.com
Traditional menu.

La Loggia
Via delle Oche, 12r
Piazzale Michelangelo
011-39-055-218-747
www.ristorantelaloggia.com
Enjoy the most sensational
view of Florence.

Nanamuta
Corso Italia, 35
011-39-055-265-7881
www.nanamuta.it
Reserve a table for an
after-theater treat.

Nella
Via delle Terme, 19r
011-39-055-218-925
Simple dishes, reasonable prices.

BELOW: The splendid soft peach dining
room at the Frescobaldi Restaurant.

Oliviero
Via delle Terme, 51r
011-39-055-287-643
Sophisticated ambiance.

Omero
Via Pian de' Giullari, 11r
Arcetri
011-39-055-220-053
www.ristoranteomero.it
Perfect for Sunday lunch in the
hills above Florence.

Ora d'Aria Ristorante
Via Ghibellina, 3r
011-39-055-200-169
www.oradariaristorante.com
Sleek, sophisticated setting—
worth the price.

Osteria delle Belle Donne
Via delle Belle Donne, 16r
011-39-055-238-2609
Simple Tuscan fare, good value.

Osteria del Cinghiale Bianco
Borgo San Jacopo, 43r
011-39-055-215-706
www.cinghialebianco.it
Always crowded, friendly service,
and good food.

Pandemonio
Via del Leone
011-39-055-224-002
Don't miss mamma's sauce in
this family trattoria.

Pennello
Via Dante Alighieri, 4r
011-39-055-294-848
A little touristy, but good and
affordable dining.

4 Leoni
Via dei Vellutini, 1r
011-39-055-218-562
www.4leoni.com
Convenient and comfortable,
though touristy.

Sabatini Ristorante
Via Panzani, 9a
011-39-055-282-802
Since the 1930s, formal,
dignified, and expensive.

Sostanza Trattoria
Via della Porcellana, 25r
011-39-055-212-691
Order the chicken *al burro* in
this Florentine landmark.

Taverna del Bronzino
Via delle Ruote, 25r
011-39-055-495-220
Treat yourself to some of the
best Tuscan cooking.

Teatro del Sale
Via dei Macci, 111r
011-39-055-200-1492
www.teatrodelsale.com
Become a member and enjoy food
and theater performances.

13 Gobbi
Via della Porcellana, 9r
011-39-055-284-015
Simple, good Tuscan food.

Zibibbo
Via di Terzollina, 3r
011-39-055-433-383
www.zibibbonline.com
Delicious food in a country setting,
worth the short taxi ride.

WINE BARS

When you're in the mood for something light, try an alternative to a restaurant or trattoria, an *enoteca*. It's anything from a wine store to a hole-in-the-wall bar serving little snacks and regional wines by the glass to a chic, casual eatery where you can enjoy light fare and vast wine selections. The Frescobaldi Wine Bar is a good example. Here you can order the family's wines from their vineyards around the world, accompanied by *stuzzichini*, little, appetizing Florentine snacks, including mixed *salume*, cheeses, a tasty selection of *mostarde di frutta* (fruit mustards), and *crostini* with various toppings. Or stop at the counter at I Fratellini and enjoy your lunch standing outside.

Cantinetta dei Verrazzano
Via dei Tavolini, 18r
011-39-055-268-590
Order the focaccia sandwich board.

Enoteca Fuori Porta
Via Monte alle Croci, 10r
011-39-055-234-2483
www.fuoriporta.it
In charming San Niccolò, nice wines and delicious snacks.

Frescobaldi Wine Bar
Via de' Magazzini, 2r
011-39-055-284-724
www.frescobaldiwinebar.it
Sophisticated antipasti and excellent Frescobaldi wines.

Golden View Open Bar
Via de' Bardi, 58r
011-39-055-272-9343
www.goldenviewopenbar.com
Overlook the Arno in this sunny, attractive space.

I Fratellini
Via dei Cimatori, 38r
011-39-055-239-6096
Tasty panini with wine at this tiny place since 1875.

'Ino
Via dei Georgofili, 38r
011-39-055-219-208
www.ino-firenze.com
The best panini sandwiches, behind the Uffizi.

Le Volpi e L'Uva
Piazza dei Rossi, 1r
011-39-055-239-8132
www.levolpieluva.com
Sit at a table in the piazza, and sample good wines.

Osteria de L'Ortolano
Via degli Alfani, 91r
011-39-055-239-6466
www.osteriafirenze.com
Friendly couple, freshest antipasti.

ABOVE: At the Frescobaldi Wine Bar you can order wines by the glass.

Procacci
Via dei Tornabuoni, 64r
011-39-055-211-656
www.antinori.it
A Florentine landmark—sip Antinori wines with your delicate truffle sandwich.

Rifrullo
Via San Niccolò, 55r
011-39-055-234-2621
Wonderful place for light fare or a drink in San Niccolò.

Santo Bevitore
Via di Santo Spirito, 64r
011-39-055-211-264
Order the interesting antipasti, and enjoy the young crowd.

CAFFÈS

In *Italy for the Gourmet Traveler*, Fred Plotkin gives this good definition of an Italian *caffè*: "A bar with table and waiter service for which you will pay a higher price." It's the place where most Italians stop to grab a quick cappuccino and *cornetto* first thing in the morning, then return to again during the day for that quick shot of espresso—always standing at the bar.

On the other hand, many *caffès*, especially those built at the turn of the century, are beautiful spots for tourists to sit and relax, preferably outside. For the price of a hot chocolate, a glass of prosecco, or a dessert—all of which can be pricey—you can sit for as long as you like, just watching the world go by.

If you crave something light for lunch—a salad or sandwich—a *caffè* is the perfect place. Two things to remember: it's more expensive (sometimes double) to sit at a table rather than stand at the bar. Second, the bar ritual: one checks out the selection and pays the cashier first for what you want to eat, then take your receipt back to the bar and place your order.

Caffè Giacosa
Via della Spada, 10r
011-39-055-277-6328
Roberto Cavalli updates Giacosa, still delicious for light lunches.

Caffè Ricchi
Piazza di Santo Spirito, 8r
011-39-055-215-864
Have coffee in shady
Piazza di Santo Spirito.

Cibrèo Caffè
Via A. del Verrocchio, 5r
011-39-055-234-5853
www.fabiopicchi.it
Delicious cappuccino, pastries, and tiny sandwiches.

Da Scudieri al Battistero
Piazza San Giovanni, 19r
011-39-055-210-733
Just in front of the Duomo.

Gilli
Piazza della Repubblica, 39r
011-39-055-213-896
www.gilli.it
Have an espresso in a beautiful belle-époque setting.

LEFT: Fresh truffle sandwiches piled high at charming landmark Proccaci.

Hemingway
Piazza Piattelline, 9r
011-39-055-284-781
Coffee, tea, and desserts on the Oltrarno.

Paskowski
Piazza della Repubblica, 6
011-39-055-210-236
www.paskowski.it
A literary *caffè* since 1846.

Rivoire
Piazza della Signoria
011-39-055-214-412
www.rivoire.it
Splurge and watch the world go by with a hot chocolate or peach iced tea, since 1872.

Robiglio
Via dei Servi, 122r
011-39-055-214-501
The best, and prettiest, cappuccino and the creamiest pastries.

ICE CREAM

What would Italy be without gelato? Florence has some of the richest offerings—an endless selection of flavors ranging from triple-dark chocolate to rice! A delicious way to cool off during the hot summer months is to sample the icy coffee *granite* at Carabè or the fresh-fruit gelati at Vivoli.

Gelateria Carabé

Via Ricasoli, 60r
011-39-055-289-476
www.gelatocarabe.com
Try the Sicilian specialty, pistachio.

Gelateria Grom

Via delle Oche, 24r
011-39-055-216-158
www.grom.it
Gelato from Torino; try hometown favorite, *gianduja* (chocolate and hazelnut).

Gelateria Neri

Via dei Neri, 20r
011-39-055-210-034
Around the corner from Vivoli—
almost as good and less expensive.

Perchè No!

Via dei Tavolini, 19r
011-39-055-239-8969
A favorite with the locals—tourists, too!

Vestri Cioccolato

Borgo degli Albizi, 11r
011-39-055-234-0374
www.vestri.it
The creamiest gelato and most divine chocolate shop, too.

ABOVE: We often stop at Vivoli when we take an evening stroll. There is usually a line, but it moves quickly.

Vivoli

Via Isola delle Stinche, 7
011-39-055-292-334
www.vivoli.it
A nonstop line outside; in summer try their chilled-fruit gelati in mouthwatering flavors.

PASTRY SHOPS

You're in luck if you are celebrating your birthday in Florence, because the cakes and sweets in these places can be divine. Here's my list of favorite pastry shops (*pasticcerie*)—tiny places with mouthwatering selections of pretty, festive confections. Most have one or two tables for those of us who can't wait to get home to bite into something sweet!

Dolceforte

Via della Scala, 21r
011-39-055-219-116
Delightful sweets featuring
rich Tuscan chocolates
and many other candies.

Dolci & Dolcezze

Piazza C. Beccaria, 8r
011-39-055-234-5458
Enchanting colorful candy-box
interior—tempting cakes,
fruit tarts, and chocolates.

Dolcissimo

Via Maggio, 61r
011-39-055-239-6268
www.caffeitaliano.it
Fluffy cakes and tarts, plus tiny
pastries and sweets.

Panificio Palatresi

Borgo Ognissanti, 102r
011-39-055-294-969
Beautiful biscotti, pastries, and bread.

Pasticceria Ballerini

Borgo Ognissanti, 132r
011-39-055-215-094
Wonderful selection of cakes
and biscotti.

Robiglio

Via dei Servi, 112r
011-39-055-214-501
Near S.S. Annunziata, enjoy the
creamiest pastries anywhere.

Robiglio

Via dei Tosinghi, 11r
011-39-055-215-013
Another Robiglio, near the
Hotel Savoy, very good.

PIZZERIAS

If you get the urge, you can stop for a delicious piece of thin-crust pizza in these two favorites. Just for good measure, I've also included a casual sit-down restaurant that has the Neapolitan version, too.

Caffè Italiano

Via Isola delle Stinche, 11r
011-39-055-289-368
Have delicious Neapolitan-style pizza
next door to the restaurant.

Focacceria Pugi

Piazza San Marco, 10
011-39-055-280-981
www.focacceria-pugi.it
Pizza and *schiacciata* every way imaginable
to take out or eat at a tiny table in the back.

Il Gatto e La Volpe

Via Ghibellina, 151r
011-39-055-289-264
Dependable pizza and a variety of pastas.

COCKTAIL BARS

Florence nightlife is lively. There are new bars opening all the time, and some open as early as 7:00 in the evening. Have an *aperitivo* (how about a classic Negroni?—recipe on page 172), and enjoy buffets featuring snacks of delicious canapés, crostini, tapas, or sushi. A nice prelude to an evening on the town, especially if you are sitting outside watching the sunset.

Dolce Vita

Piazza del Carmine, 6r
www.dolcevitaflorence.com
Still hip, have an *apertivo* in the piazza.

Fusion Bar

Gallery Hotel Art
Vicolo dell'Oro, 2
011-39-055-272-63
Fashionista headquarters—
good sushi, too.

L'Incontro

Savoy Hotel
Piazza della Repubblica, 7
011-39-055-283-313
www.hotelsavoy.com
Chic decor, celebrity crowd.

Negroni alla Martelli

Via Martelli, 22
011-39-055-200-1497
Named after the inventor of the
cocktail—try one here.

The Lounge

JK Place
Piazza di Santa Maria Novella, 9r
011-39-055-264-5282
www.lounge-bar.it
Head downstairs to the all-white
leather banquettes, which turn colors.

The Noir

Lungarno Corsini, 12r
011-39-055-210-751
www.noirfirenze.com
There's no sign, so be advised.

Roses

Via del Parione, 26r
011-39-055-287-090
Hottest sushi bar in the city.

Zoe

Via dei Renai, 13r
011-39-055-243-111
Try the cocktail hour with tasty snacks.

ABOVE: The menu is Asian-inspired at the Fusion Bar which is located in the Gallery Hotel Art.

The Markets

Mercato Centrale di San Lorenzo
Via dell'Ariento, 10
Open Monday to Saturday, 7:00 A.M. to 2:00 P.M.
The *Mercato Centrale* or Central Market is Florence's largest. It is around the corner from the Church of San Lorenzo, which includes the Medici Chapel and Laurentian Library and is surrounded by stalls selling T-shirts, leather jackets, handbags, and souvenirs. The market, built in 1874, was designed by Giuseppe Mengoni (who conceived the elegant Galleria in Milan) and occupies a two-story cast-iron, glass-enclosed space. It is home to food vendors selling meats, fish, fruit, vegetables, cheeses, olives, pasta and rice, dried fruit, and nuts—literally, a taste of Tuscany. You could easily spend the entire day in this quarter enjoying a little bit of everything.

Here you'll find Florentine favorites like *cinghiale* (wild boar), tripe, every type of pecorino cheese, *salumi*, plus the freshest seafood. Ripe seasonal fruits and vegetables taste as sweet as those you remember from your childhood. Make sure you get to Da Nerbone before the hordes arrive at noon, for a mouthwatering *bollito* (boiled beef) sandwich. Order the panino *bagnato*, which means the bread is soaked in the meat's cooking juices first. Top it off with a deep-fried donut from the *friggitore* on the Via di Sant'Antonio, 50. If you would rather sit down and have lunch, stop around the corner at Da Sergio, at Piazza San Lorenzo, 8. It's a family-run trattoria with good, simple food.

Mercato di Sant'Ambrogio
Piazza Sant'Ambrogio
Open Monday to Saturday, 7:00 A.M. to 2:00 P.M.
I enjoy this market for several reasons: firstly, it's organic with farmers displaying their fresh seasonal vegetables and fruits in rows of tables outside; secondly, it's smaller and more manageable than the *Mercato Centrale*. Inside there are excellent butchers and fish sellers and a tantalizing selection of pastas, cheeses, honey, dried beans, and rice.

On the side is a small market that offers inexpensive paper goods, household items, funny T-shirts, and anything you don't need but buy anyway because it's so reasonable. Have a yummy pastry and frothy cappuccino at Cibrèo Caffè on the way into the market in the morning and when you are done shopping, treat yourself to lunch at one of the three delicious Cibrèo restaurants just steps away.

Fierucoline di Santo Spirito
Piazza Santo Spirito
Open third Sunday each month, 8:00 A.M. to 6:00 P.M.
This interesting market is located under the shady trees in front of the Church of Santo Spirito. Market farmers come from the surrounding countryside to sell their organic offerings: fragrant cheeses, whole-grain bread, and *ciabatta*, spicy salamis, jams made of everything from figs to pumpkins, wine, and good things to eat. It's also a lovely place to pick up unique gifts like carved olive-wood soap dishes, fragrant soaps and potpourris, handmade toys, and hand-knitted sweaters to bring home.

LEFT: Stopping at the butcher in the organic Sant'Ambrogio market, and above, early morning marketing in shady Piazza Santo Spirito for the freshest produce possible.

Historically, dining out in Florence on Sunday has been a problem, as most of the restaurants were closed. Lately, some of the nicer places have been staying open. Here is my list of favorites. Be sure to book in advance, as most are usually packed.

Alle Murate
Via del Proconsolo, 6
011-39-055-240-618

Baldovino
Via San Giuseppe, 22r
011-39-055-241-773

Beccofino
Piazza degli Scarlatti, 1r
011-39-055-290-076

Borgo San Jacopo
Hotel Lungarno
Borgo San Jacopo, 14
011-39-055-272-61

Cammillo Trattoria
Borgo San Jacopo, 57r
011-39-055-212-427

Enoteca Boccadama
Piazza Santa Croce, 25r
011-39-055-243-640
www.boccadama.it

Fusion Bar
Gallery Hotel Art
Vicolo dell'Oro, 2
011-39-055-272-63

RIGHT: A floral welcome in front of Osteria del Cinghiale Bianco.

Il Cavaliere
Viale Lavagnini, 20
011-39-055-471-914

Il Latini
Via dei Palchetti, 6r
011-39-055-210-916
www.illatini.com

La Giostra
Borgo Pinti, 12r
011-39-055-241-341
www.ristorantelagiostra.com

La Loggia
Via delle Oche, 12r
011-39-055-218-747
www.ristorantelaloggia.com

L'Incontro
Savoy Hotel
Piazza della Repubblica, 7
011-39-055-283-313
www.hotelsavoy.com

Omero
Via Pian de' Giullari, 11r
011-39-055-220-053
www.ristoranteomero.it

Osteria del Cinghiale Bianco
Borgo San Jacopo, 43r
011-39-055-215-706
www.cinghialebianco.it

4 Leoni
Via dei Vellutini, 1r
011-39-055-218-562
www.4leoni.com

Santo Bevitore
Via di Santo Spirito, 64r
011-39-055-211-264

The Lounge
JK Place
Piazza di Santa Maria Novella, 9r
011-39-055-264-5282
www.lounge-bar.it

The first cooking academy was started in Florence during the Renaissance, and its members were all artists who had to create a new dish for every meeting, so it's natural that this fascination with food would have grown. Now, five hundred years later, there is a large choice of cooking schools available to anyone who wants to experience the how-to of Italian cooking. Listed below is my selection of some of the most professional cooking classes in Florence. They offer a variety of programs aimed at those interested in short- or long-term study. Check out their websites to see the myriad possibilities available. Buon appetito!

Villa San Michele, School of Cookery

Via Doccia, 4 (Fiesole)
011-39-055-567-8200, USA 1-800-237-1236
www.villasanmichele.com
What could be more enjoyable than staying at the luxurious Orient-Express hotel, the Villa San Michele, and taking cooking lessons? The program is extensive. You can work directly in hands-on sessions with their chef in morning and afternoon classes. There's also the opportunity to pick up pointers from internationally renowned gourmet cooks, including Raymond Blanc and Giuliano Hazan. Particular programs for children, wine lovers, and chocoholics, among others, are available. One of the nicest parts is choosing some of your ingredients from their beautiful herb and vegetable gardens and enjoying the fruits of your labor at lunch or dinner with the chef of twenty-two years, Attilio di Fabrizio.

La Cucina del Garga

Via delle Belle Donne, 3
011-39-055-211-396
www.garga.it
Sharon Oddson and Giuliano Gargani opened their trend-setting restaurant, Trattoria Garga, in 1979. If you like eating here, you'll be happy to know that you can learn how to duplicate some of their delicious signatures dishes. Sharon teaches small groups in intimate classes on weekday afternoons in the restaurant's kitchen. Afterwards,

you'll enjoy the meal you have cooked, accompanied by appropriate wines. If you have more time, she can also arrange excursions to southern Tuscany.

Apicius

Via Guelfa, 85
011-3-055-365-8135
USA 800-655-8965
www.tuscancooking.com
This school's extensive curriculum is mainly geared to those who are interested in careers in the food industry. However, in addition to the professional courses, there are hands-on lessons for vacationers and people who are only visiting the city for a short time. The school will also customize programs for small groups and will even set up private lessons.

Cordon Bleu

Via dei Mezzo, 55r
011-39-055-234-5468
www.cordonbleu.it
Not connected with the Cordon Bleu in Paris, Gabriella Mari and Cristina Blasi started this school in 1985. Both have a deep background in Italian cooking and wine. They offer an intensive, week-long course, taught in English, that will fill you in on all the basics, in addition to shorter courses and even lessons at night.

Zibibbo

Via di Terzollina, 3r (Careggi)
011-39-055-433-383
www.trattoriazibibbo.it
Have you ever wondered what it would be like to cook in a functioning restaurant kitchen next to one of the most respected Florentine chefs? Benedetta Vitale, co-founder of the famous Cibrèo and current owner of Zibibbo, is giving "Total Immersion" cooking courses in her restaurant. Her philosophy of sharing her passion for cooking starts with basics like *soffritto*, the classic vegetable base of many Italian dishes, and goes all the way to desserts.

Tomato Surprise

Fabio Picchi, the owner and chef of the Cibrèo restaurants, is known for taking traditional dishes and creating something connected but just a little bit different—and always delicious. Leave it to him to take the simple tomato, beloved by all Italians, especially Tuscans, and create a surprise—a cool, refreshing tomato aspic that reminds you of the happy days of summer with your first bite. Another surprise is how simple and easy it is to make.

10 ounces fine quality peeled Italian plum tomatoes
1 ounce of gelatin
1 clove garlic, chopped
4 sprigs fresh basil, chopped
1 sprig fresh Italian parsley, chopped
Salt and Pepper
⅛ teaspoon red pepper flakes
1 cup extra virgin olive oil

- Drain the canned tomatoes in a bowl, crushing them with your hands to release liquid inside.
- Pour off liquid into medium saucepan and place over low heat until warm, not hot.
- Add the gelatin to the warm tomato liquid and mix with wood spoon until dissolved.
- Stir in tomatoes, olive oil, garlic, basil, parsley, red-pepper flakes, and salt and pepper to taste.
- Process all ingredients in a blender until smooth.
- Pour mixture into small ramekins and chill in refrigerator for at least 4 hours, or until set.
- To remove from ramekin, dip the bottom of the ramekin into warm water and turn it over onto a dinner plate.
- Garnish with a sprig of basil.

Serves 4

Ribollita

Cantinetta Antinori opened on the ground floor of stately Palazzo Antinori in 1957, and the menu still offers some of the most classic dishes from Tuscany. One of the most popular is ribollita, *an entire meal in a bowl. This hearty, thick, vegetable and bean soup is made by Cantinetta's chef, Franco Rovigli, with the freshest ingredients, including olive oil from the Antinori estates. There are many variations, but this version is true to the original recipe, a densely textured, flavorful dish.*

10 tablespoons extra virgin olive oil

2 tablespoons chopped fresh rosemary, sage, thyme and basil

1 onion, coarsely chopped

2 tablespoons tomato paste

1 cup canned whole tomatoes

1 small bunch kale, shredded

2 small bunches chard, shredded

½ head of green cabbage, shredded

2 carrots, coarsely chopped

½ celery stalk, coarsely chopped

1 pound cannellini beans, soaked overnight and drained

4 cups vegetable broth

salt and pepper

½ loaf sliced day-old country bread (unsalted)

- Pour ½ of the oil into a large saucepan and sauté the herbs and chopped onion over medium heat.
- Add tomato paste, canned tomatoes, the vegetables, and the drained cannelli beans.
- Mix and cook five minutes, then add the vegetable broth.
- Bring to a boil, cover, and reduce heat. Simmer for 1½ hours. Add salt and pepper.
- When ready, layer the vegetable soup and bread slices in another saucepan. Add the remaining olive oil.
- Cook uncovered on a low flame for another 10 minutes.
- Remove from heat. Cover and allow to stand for 10 minutes.
- Serve in bowls, drizzling a last touch of olive oil on top.

Serves 6

The Negroni

This aperitivo *is the official Florentine drink, and every bartender in the city knows how to make one. They say that it was created around the turn of the century, when a debonair count wanted a bartender to add gin to his favorite drink, the* Americano. *His name was Count Camillo Negroni, and the rest is history. For some people, it's an acquired taste, but this red and refreshing cocktail can become a habit. Just witness the elegant locals sitting in the city's outdoor caffès, enjoying the sunset and a Negroni before dinner. This one is a specialty at L'Incontro at the Savoy Hotel.*

1 ounce London Dry Gin
1 ounce bitter Campari
1 ounce sweet red vermouth
1 orange slice

- Pour the first three ingredients in an old-fashioned glass and stir.
- Add ice cubes and garnish with a slice of orange.

Serves 1

Pears Cooked in Red Wine

Florentines love fruit (frutta). In fact, in Italy there is a tradition of making a wish the first time you eat a piece of sweet, ripe fruit that has just come into season. In 1699, Bartolomeo Bimbi painted a huge canvas for Cosimo de' Medici which illustrated every kind of pear produced in Tuscany at that time—115 of them! One of the nicest ways to cook pears is in a lovely red wine with some spices. Here, Bona Frescobaldi shares her recipe for this simple, but visually beautiful, way to end a meal, using the famous Frescobaldi Tuscan Chianti Rùfina wine, Nipozzano.

6 firm pears
1 bottle of full-bodied red wine
¾ cup sugar

1 tablespoon whole cloves
2 cinnamon sticks

- Carefully peel the pears, leaving stems on.
- Stand upright in a saucepan.
- Add red wine, sugar, cinnamon, and cloves.
- Cook uncovered for about 20 minutes.
- Leave the pears to rest in wine for 30 minutes.
- Carefully remove with slotted spoon and set on a serving platter.
- Serve with whipped cream or crème fraiche on the side.

Serves 6

SEVEN

Shopping Florentine Style

"You are aware of the joy of wealth, the feeling for everyday luxury, in Florence's clothes, its handbags and shoes and innumerable touches of vanity."

—Hugh Johnson, *Tuscany and its Wines*

Last Christmas, a dear friend gave me a copy of the book *Shopping in the Renaissance*, by Evelyn Welch. It was heavy reading but interestingly noted that even in the Renaissance women played a big role as consumers. Many were powerful purchasers who made a big impact on the Renaissance market. So, when you are in this happy hunting ground, you have another reason to shop—keeping up the centuries-old tradition. As a lifelong retailer I love when I'm in a city like Florence where I always feel "spoiled by choice," especially when it comes to beautiful clothing and accessories.

Some trace the birth of the Italian fashion industry to the early fifties, when Marchese Giovanni Battista Giorgini founded Moda Italiana, an organization to promote Italian fashion design. He held a fashion show introducing, for the first time, Italy's designers to the international press and store buyers. Held in his elegant palazzo in Florence, the show put a spotlight on designers like Gucci, Ferragamo, and Pucci, who have endured and become iconic symbols of not only Florentine but Italian style. The fashion shows then went on to be held in the exquisite Sala Bianca of the Pitti Palace, focusing the world's attention on the Renaissance code of *sprezzatura*—that above all attention should be paid to beauty. Mary McCarthy said that Florence was the only Italian town whose name naturally became a word, *fiorentinità*, meaning "taste" and "fine quality." The tradition continues with Pitti Immagine, which puts together all the fashion, textile, and fragrance fairs still held in the city.

The city has its fashionable designer boutiques on Via Tornabuoni, Via della Vigna Nuova, and Via Calzaiuoli—Versace, Valentino, Tod's, Dolce & Gabbana, and, of course, Pucci, Gucci, and Ferragamo, which have their roots here. But another reason to love—really love—shopping in Florence is all the smaller shops and boutiques everywhere. Some are barely able to hold more than three customers at a time but each is unique in its own way. Many are still run by the same family that started them generations ago—gems that you won't see anywhere else— shops carrying items that are stylish, finely crafted, absolutely luscious, and made with pride.

I just read in a newspaper about how terribly expensive fashion has become. It stated (wistfully) that in the sixties and seventies, "you didn't need to be rich to dress well—you just needed some money." Very true. We could always afford to buy good clothes then—it's much harder to do today. But even with

OPENING PICTURE: This mascot in Wanny Di Filippo's shop, Il Bisonte, is familiar to all his devoted fans.
OVERLEAF, LEFT: Art Noveau at Loretta Caponi, and right, gold chianti flasks and turquoise at Angela Caputi.
LEFT: A Ferragamo get together at Palazzo Spini Feroni: Giovanna, Leonardo, Salvatore and Ferruccio on either side of co-founder, Wanda Ferragamo and granddaughter Angelica Visconti.
RIGHT: The Shoe Museum, a tribute to the genius of patriarch Salvatore Ferragamo. To visit, see page 51.

the weakness of the dollar, in Florence it's still possible to find the affordable—shoes, handbags, belts, ties, gloves, and ready-to-wear (especially in January, which is traditionally dedicated to sales, or *saldi*, with very tempting prices). As if that's not enough, one must mention ceramics and all the other categories of glorious luxury goods—bed and table linens, sleek kitchen utensils, tabletop accessories, rich tassels, trims and tiebacks, delicate crystal, heavy silver. Add to that creamy soaps, fragrant perfumes, and food specialties that range from never-to-be-forgotten olive oils to unusual jams and chocolates.

The choice has never been more varied, and you can unearth these treasures everywhere from luxurious shops to open-air markets. Florence is truly a shopper's paradise, which it has been since the Middle Ages, when jewelers and shoemakers were regarded with the same level of respect as artists.

This is what I suggest you buy when you come to Florence: quality handbags and shoes; small leather goods; shawls, scarves, and ties; fine and costume jewelry; handmade paper; ceramics; food specialties; and soaps, elixirs, and perfumes. And don't forget exquisite lingerie, baby clothes, and bed and table linens—all made by hand.

I have to start with leather. In the fourteenth century, hundreds of tanneries crammed the tiny streets of the city. In fact, one of the city's streets, Via dei Calzaiuoli, is named after shoemakers. The pungent odor finally got them evicted from the Ponte Vecchio, which has since been populated by elegant goldsmiths. Today, there are still many leather workshops in Florence, from small ateliers on up to Il Bisonte, Gucci, and Ferragamo. You shouldn't leave the city without buying a handbag, belt, gloves, or especially shoes.

ABOVE: The Straw Market with its famous bronze boar. Rub its snout and you'll surely return to Florence

If you are looking for beautifully crafted small leather items, especially for gifts, do visit the leather school, Scuola del Cuoio, in the former monastery behind the Church of Santa Croce (you enter through the lovely garden cloisters on the left). Here you can watch the craftsmen make everything from handbags and totes to wallets and credit-card cases. They say the Queen of England buys her picture frames here. Afterwards, you can visit the Church of Santa Croce and see the tombs of Michelangelo and Galileo and special memorials to Dante and Machiavelli (see chapter 2).

ABOVE: Luxurious temptations for the shopper include colorful silk shawls, intricately designed gloves, and, next page, rare deep red Sardinian coral necklaces from U.Gherardi and glittering faux chokers by Angela Caputi.

Jewelry comes next. In 1252, Florence was one of the first cities to mint its own gold coin, the florin. (The jewelry store Torrini makes a beautiful gold copy which you can buy as a memento of your trip.) Brunelleschi and Cellini were initially trained as goldsmiths, setting the standard for innovative jewelry design hundreds of years ago. That's why it's so much fun to look in the luminous shop windows of jewelers such as Buccellati and U. Gherardi, to name just a few. And don't overlook the fabulous costume jewelry that the city has always been famous for. For years, I always had to stop at the end of the Ponte Vecchio to look in the windows of Bijoux Cascio, now, sadly, gone. But not to worry. Prolific designer Angela Caputi and all the others on my list have filled the gap nicely with their innovative and creative costume jewelry.

If you love paper, you had better bring an extra suitcase. The craft of printing and bookmaking began in Italy. Your head will spin when you walk through the doors of Antica Baccani, Giulio Giannini, or the sophisticated Pneider and see all the thick, creamy papers, hand-blocked blank books, wrapping papers, and cards.

Scarves have always been an Italian specialty (it's why the women always look so put-together), but I've always found the best in Florence. I still have an Hermès knockoff, bought years ago, that I would never part with. You'll find scarves, from heavy twill squares printed in gorgeous designs to colorful, textured raw silks, tussah oblongs, and buttery-soft cashmeres everywhere, from shops like the venerable Zuffanelli to the open-air stalls in the San Lorenzo and the Straw Markets. And don't overlook the sumptuous, heavy silk ties perfect for "hard-to-buy-for" male friends.

Catherine de' Medici took her master perfumer with her when she left Florence to marry Henry II of France—even then, Florence was already famous for its *farmacie*. Much more than just drugstores or pharmacies, many of these places today are filled with intoxicating scents and magical elixirs and housed in magnificent environments. Take, for example, the Officina Profumo Farmaceutica di Santa Maria Novella, which looks more like a museum than a shop. I don't know what I expected when I first walked in years ago but I was thunderstruck. The salesroom was in fact the chapel of the monastery once connected to the Church of Santa Maria Novella. The monks who arrived in the thirteenth century were famous for creating remedies from herbs and plants.

In the late nineteenth century, the Stefani family took over from a close relative who was the last Dominican monk left. And it continues today, enabling us to enjoy a shopping experience known nowhere else, and to take a little bit of it home. In fact, in the 1980s we were able to carry the products in our New York City shop, Cherchez. It was a real coup, as we were the only place you could purchase it

LEFT: Voluptuous fruits in hand-hammered silver include lemons, pomegranates and squash. They make perfect gifts, all from the elegant shop of jeweler Mario Buccellati. **ABOVE:** A rainbow of men's silk ties are displayed on an entire wall at the very chic Ferragamo Palazzo.

outside of Florence. I'm still hooked and you will be, too, when you try their intoxicating ancient aromas such as Acqua di Santa Maria Novella, pomegranate soap (one of many scents available), scented burning papers fragrant when lit, elixirs for the digestion or hysteria, and pungent potpourris that never seem to lose their scent. Be sure to check out every nook and cranny of this magnificent place.

Another not-to-be-missed visit is to the fifteenth-century palazzo and studio of Lorenzo Villoresi. I wrote about him in my book *Dreaming of Tuscany*.

If you still have any energy—or Euros—left, wonderful Tuscan ceramics and food specialties make great gifts. The newest peppery olive oils from the olive groves around Florence, unusual jams, honeys, and flaky cheeses like pecorino, redolent of the Tuscan countryside, are available. And you can buy a ceramic or terra cotta piece in traditional, as well as modern, designs to hold them.

And for the ultimate Florentine shopping experience, be sure to visit the magical shop Loretta Caponi. It has two entrances, one on Piazza Antinori and, the one I prefer, another on Via delle Belle Donne. To me, it is like entering a dream. It was started by Loretta Caponi and is now run with her daughter Lucia. The shop has for decades featured the most extraordinary, creamiest table and bed linens in the finest fabrics; lacy, delicate lingerie and nightgowns in elegant silks and satin charmeuse; and the most adorable children's clothes with special smocked details, tiny mother-of-pearl buttons, and embroidered motifs, all done in miniature and by hand. The last time I was there, Lucia took out a box of seventeenth-century Venetian lace to show me. It was the first time I'd seen such rare things outside of a museum. Her mother's collection of antique textiles and lace could fill a museum and is used for inspiration for all the precious things in their shop.

The last thing you need or want to do in this specialty-shopping city is to go browsing in a department store. However, there are times when you may need to replace a lost Chanel lipstick or a pair of laddered hose, so I should mention that there are

PREVIOUS PAGE: Views of the Farmaceutica di Santa Maria Novella: the entrance hall, antique decanters containing precious essential oils, and creamy soaps.
LEFT: One of my favorite shops, Lisa Corti, stocks bright, colorful Indian clothing and gifts for the home.

ABOVE: This luxurious banquet cloth, embroidered with Tuscan trees at Loretta Caponi, is so large that Lucia Caponi needs help showing it. The shop carries irresistible frocks like this delicate child's lacey batiste pinafore at right.

two department stores in Florence. La Rinascente is on Piazza della Repubblica, almost next door to the Hotel Savoy. It has an excellent cosmetics counter with almost every brand available, and nice hosiery and accessories. After the umpteenth time that Alitalia lost my husband's luggage, he was easily able to buy the basics, as well as some good-looking classic sportswear, there. La Rinascente is also open on Sundays, as is the other department store, Coin, on Via dei Calzaiuoli. It has a nice MAC cosmetics boutique and an endless assortment of reasonable costume jewelry.

At the other end of the spectrum are the open-air markets. They should be approached with a sharp eye, because there is now a disproportionate amount of tourist junk sold there. But nobody loves a bargain more than I do, so for me these markets are filled with potential finds. One of the unexpected pleasures of Florence is just wandering, stumbling upon these stalls, and finding something—a great shawl perhaps (Pashmina! Really?)—that perks up your day. I especially like the San Lorenzo Market, which features leather goods, paper and stationery, T-shirts, shawls and scarves. It's situated right next

to the famous Central Market (wonderful fresh food; see chapter 6) and the Church of San Lorenzo (home of the Laurentian Library and the Medici Chapel). So you can spend a lovely morning absorbing some culture, pick up a few gifts, and then relax over a good, simple lunch at any of the good trattorias in this busy neighborhood.

The Mercato Nuovo, also called the Straw Market, is on Via Por Santa Maria, on the main route to the Ponte Vecchio. Also called the Mercato del Porcellino because of its life-size bronze boar statue, which always has tourists rubbing its nose, ensuring their return to Florence. The prices are higher here, but I have been known to find some unexpected treasures. Besides, it doesn't close for lunch!

There are also the stalls in front of the Church of Santa Croce. Their specialty is leather jackets of dubious quality and cheap souvenirs. However, on the corner of the square when you are facing the church is one of my favorite shops for buying the typical Florentine hand-painted gold trays and boxes, Giorgi, at 32r. They're a wee bit old-fashioned, but still nice to bring home. The last outdoor market I'll mention is in the Parco delle Cascine. Held only on Tuesday mornings from 8 A.M. to 2 P.M., it's filled with mostly household items, inexpensive ready-to-wear, acces-

BELOW: Pietro Chellini and his son Francesco carry on a five-generation tradition of rare book collecting at Libreria Gozzini established in 1850 and located in the Palazzo Alfani across from the reknowned Galleria dell'Accademia.

sories, and Florentine housewives. I've never found anything there, and, as it's in a rather seedy area on the edge of the city which is under construction now, I'd pass for the time being.

The next stop would normally be the traditional artisans of Florence, known worldwide for their generational workshops, some hundreds of years old. The fact that these ateliers still exist and thrive is even more noteworthy today, in our increasingly mechanized world. These are the wood carvers, furniture makers, gilders, metalworkers, bronze specialists, framers, mosaic and *pietra dura* specialists, silversmiths, and ceramic, terra-cotta, and fine-crystal designers. There are so many handcraftsmen working in Florence today that, in order to properly cover the subject, I've decided it needs its own chapter, "Artisans and Antiques," which follows, starting on page 204.

So here's my list of what I think are some of the best Florentine shops. Each is special in its very own way. I've browsed and bought in some of these stores for decades, and it's always been fun. I've listed them in the "Insider's Address Book" by category and have highlighted some of my most favorites with an asterisk. There is never anything better than a word-of-mouth recommendation!

BELOW: I love to visit Nante for a peek into the past. Established in 1879, this filled-to-the-brim sign shop just behind the Duomo, sells address numbers, emblems, shields, and every manner of sign made in materials from enamel to brass.

Fashion

READY TO WEAR WOMENS

Armani
Via dei Tornabuoni, 48r
011-39-055-219-041
www.giorgioarmani.com
Sleek, contemporary clothes.

Aspesi
Via Porta Rossa, 83
011-39-055-287-987
Snappy r-t-w for men and women.

*Emilio Pucci
Via dei Tornabuoni, 20r
011-39-055-265-8082
www.pucci.com
Since 1950, brilliantly colored
R-T-W and accessories.

*Gucci
Via dei Tornabuoni, 73r
011-39-055-264-011
www.gucci.it
Where it all started, still
stylish leather and clothing.

Jain
Sdrucciolo de'Pitti, 25r
011-39-055-230-2985
Ethnic jewelry and beautiful
pashmina shawls.

*L'Elefante Verde
Borgo La Croce, 70r
011-39-055-234-882
Colorful ethnic clothes in
a teeny space.

Laura Nutini
Via Lambertesca, 8r
011-39-055-239-6563
Exquisite handmade trousseaus
and feminine lingerie.

*Loretta Caponi
Piazza Antinori, 4r
011-39-055-213-668
www.lorettacaponi.com
The ultimate art of hand
embroidery on baby clothes,
lingerie, bed and table linens.

Luisa Via Roma
Via Roma, 19r
011-39-055-217-826
www.luisaviaroma.com
Trendy, cutting edge fashion.

Max Mara
Via dei Pecori, 23r
011-39-055-239-6590
Classic, well-made, man-
tailored sportswear.

Michele Negri
Via Roma, 24r
011-39-055-216-524
www.michelenegri.com
Trendy, classic R-T-W.

*Old England Stores
Via Vecchietti, 28r
011-39-055-211-983
Everything from Marmite to
Harris Tweeds.

*Prada
Via dei Tornabuoni, 51r
011-39-055-283-439
www.prada.it
Still the most creative
clothing on the planet.

Raspini
Via Roma, 25r
011-39-055-213-077
www.raspini.com
Designer shopping in one
location.

Stile Biologico
Via dello Sprone, 25r
011-39-055-277-6275
www.stilebiologico.it
Everything designed in
organic fabrics

*White
Via de'Benci, 32r
011-39-055-247-8274
www.whiteshop.eu
Chic, contemporary R-T-W
and accessories

Zuffanelli
Via dei Lamberti, 1r
011-39-055-239-6174
www.zuffanelli.it
My scarf collection owes a lot
to this shop.

⚜

Vintage

Boutique Nadine
Lungarno Acciaiuoli, 22r
011-39-055-287-851
www.boutiquenadine.it
Near the Ponte Vecchio.

Ceri Vintage
Via de'Serragli, 26r
011-39-055-217-978
Terrific selection of designer
accessories.

Pitti Vintage
Sdrucciolo dei Pitti, 19r
011-39-055-230-2676
Fun and kitschy.

Mens

Alfreda e Manuela Evangelisti
Borgo dei Greci, 33r
011-39-055-292-772
Where to buy a tie for the
man in your life.

AteSeta
Via dei Calzaiuoli, 1r
011-39-055-214-959
www.ateseta.com
Handsome selection of shirts and ties.

*Bemporad
Via Calzaiuoli, 11r
011-39-055-216-833
You don't have to go to Vienna for
men's and women's loden coats.

Eredi Chiarini
Via Roma, 16r
011-39-055-284-478
www.eredichiarini.com
Where the Florentines buy
their classic menswear.

Liverano & Liverano
Via dei Fossi, 43
011-39-055-239-6436
Bespoke quality tailoring.

Matucci
Via del Corso, 71r
011-39-055-239-6420
Men's designer collections.

Simone Abbrachi
Borgo SS. Apostoli, 16
011-39-055-210-552
Order the suit of your dreams
to be shipped to you.

Shoes

*Ferragamo
Via dei Tornabuoni, 14r
011-39-055-292-123
www.salvatoreferragamo.com
Shop in the Palazzo Spini
Feroni, then visit the shoe
museum, downstairs.

*Guido Longinotti
Via Guicciardini, 9r
011-39-055-214-787
My current favorite, affordable
and very fashionable.

*JP Tod's
Via de' Tornabuoni, 103r
011-39-055-219-423
www.tods.com
Where I buy my
favorite classic loafers.

Mondo Albion
Via Nazionale, 121r
011-39-055-282-451
www.mondoalbion.it
Hand designs the most
eccentric, fun shoes.

Roberto Ugolini
Via Michelozzi, 17r
011-055-39-216-246
Elegant custom made men's shoes.

*Saskia
Via di Santa Lucia, 24r
011-39-055-293-291
Graceful handmade shoes.

*Stefano Bemer
Borgo San Frediano, 143r
011-39-055-222-558
www.stefanobemer.it
Extraordinary hand crafted shoes
for men and women of more than
180 kinds of leather.

Leather Accessories

Cellerini
Via del Sole, 37r
011-39-055-282-533
Custom made bags in rare
beautiful leathers.

*Giotti
Borgo Ognissanti, 3r
011-39-055-294-265
Terrific handbags and luggage next
door to the Grand Hotel.

*Il Bisonte
Via del Parione, 31r
011-39-055-215-722
www.ilbisonte.net
Soft unlined cowhide bags,
briefcases and accessories
in natural tones.

Infinity
Borgo SS. Apostoli, 18r
011-39-055-239-8405
www.infinityfirenze.com
Add your own details to a
vast selection of belts and bags.

Luciano
Via Por. S. Maria, 10r
011-39-055-210-635
Gloves in many styles and colors.

*Madova
Via de'Guicciardini, 1r
011-39-055-239-6526
www.madova.com
This tiny favorite overflows
with beautifully designed
affordable gloves.

*Scuola del Cuoio
Via San Giuseppe, 5r
011-39-055-244-533
www.leatherschool.com
A fascinating place to watch the
artisans at work.

Jewelry

COSTUME JEWELRY

*Angela Caputi
Borgo SS. Apostoli, 44
011-39-055-292-993
www.angelacaputi.com
Fabulous costume jewelry you'll
treasure forever.

*Aprosio e Co.
Via Santa Spirito, 11
011-39-055-265-4077
www.aprosio.it
Ephemeral jewelry made
from small glass beads.

Falsi Gioielli
Via de'Ginori, 34r
011-39-055-287-237
Color, color, and more color.

Oromatto
Via dei Servi, 49r
011-39-055-216-768
Chock full of fabulous fakes.

*Tharros
Borgo SS. Apostoli, 28r
011-39-055-289-388
www.tharros.com
Too, too tempting.

FINE JEWELRY

Alessandro Dari
Via San Niccolò, 115r
011-39-055-244-4747
www.alessandrodari.com
Exotic, extraordinary jewels.

Mario Buccellati
Via della Vigne Nuova, 71r
011-39-055-239-6579
Gold and silver jewelry made
in the delicate Renaissance style.

Bulgari
Via de'Tornabuoni, 61r
011-39-055-239-6786
www.bulgari.com
Status symbol pieces.

Parenti
Via de'Tornabuoni, 93r
011-39-055-214-438
www.parentifirenze.it
Always a brilliant collection
of desirable designs.

*Pomellato
Piazza Antinori, 8r
011-39-055-213-200
www.pomellato.it
Stunning designs, sublime stones.

Santini
Via Guicciardini, 62r
011-39-055-284-624
www.santinigioelli.it
Watches, jewelry and repairs—all
with a smile.

Torrini
Piazza Duomo, 10r
011-39-055-230-2401
www.torrinishop.it
Since 1369. Buy a florin for your
charm bracelet.

*U. Gherardi
Ponte Vecchio, 5r
011-39-055-211-809
A unique collection of pearls
and very rare coral.

Ugo Piccini
Via Por Santa Maria, 9r
011-39-055-214-511
Specializes in custom design.

Vincenti
Ponte Vecchio, 16r
011-39-055-291-065
Since 1887, regal handmade jewelry.

Home Style & Gifts

Al Portico
Piazza S. Firenze, 1
011-39-055-213-716
www.semialportico.it
In and out of the garden—
seeds, plants, pots, and baskets.

*Antico Setificio Fiorentino
Via L. Bartolini, 4
011-39-055-213-861
www.anticosetificiofiorentina.com
Step into the past for lustrous
silk fabrics and accessories.

Apostolato Liturgico
Piazza Duomo, 14r
011-39-055-214-592
Religious mementos and
the best non-drip candles.

*Arte Creta
Via del Proconsolo, 63r
011-39-055-284-341
Fresh, charming pottery designs.

Baroni
Via de'Tornabuoni, 9r
011-39-055-210-562
www.baroni-firenze.com
Precious baby clothes and
embroidered linens since 1912.

Bartolini
Via dei Servi, 30r
011-39-055-211-895
Every kitchen accessory imaginable
starting with Alessi.

Bartolucci
Via Condotta, 12r
011-39-055-239-8596
www.bartolucci.com
Enchanting toys handcrafted
in natural wood.

Brandimarte
Viale L. Ariosto, 11cr
011-39-055-230-41
www.brandimarte.com
Florentine brides register here
for their silver—great gifts.

*Castorina
Via Santa Spirito, 13r
011-39-055-212-885
www.castorina.net
If you like baroque you'll love
their carved gold and wooden
moldings and frames.

Ducci
Lugarno Corsini, 24r
011-39-055-214-550
www.duccishop.com
Choose some marble figs
to bring home as a souvenir.

*Duccio Banchi
Via dei Serragli, 10r
011-39-055-294-694
Intricate, beautifully made bronze
frames and lamps.

Elisabetta Manzani
Via delle Porte Nuove, 9
011-39-333-863-0699
The art of decoupage.

*Flair
Piazza Scarlatti, 2r
011-39-055-267-0154
Chic mixture of accessories and furniture for the contemporary lifestyle.

Galleria Romanelli
Borgo San Frediano, 70
011-39-055-239-6662
www.raffaelloromanelli.com
Since 1860, superb statuary.

Giorgi
Piazza Santa Croce, 32r
Old fashioned hand painted wood
Florentine trays, mirrors, etc.

Il Paralume
Borgo San Frediano, 47
011-39-055-239-6760
www.ilparalume.it
Lamps, chandeliers, and sconces.

Lastrucci
Borgo Ognissanti, 11r
011-39-055-238-1836
www.bottegalastrucci.it
The quintessential souvenir
shop, Florentine style and
so friendly.

*Lisa Corti
Via de' Bardi, 58
011-39-055-264-5600
And Piazza Ghiberti, 33r
011-39-055-200-1860
www.lisacorti.com
Cheerful Indian caftans,
quilted jackets, bedcovers and
pillows in colorful hand prints
Italian style.

*Lugarno Details
Lungarno Acciaiuoli, 4
011-39-055-2726-4095
www.lungarnodetails.com
If you liked it at the Lungarno
Hotel, you can buy it here.

Manetti e Masini
Via Bronzino, 125r
011-39-055-700-445
Terrific collection of crafted
Tuscan ceramics.

*Marco Fancelli
Via dello Sprone, 14r
011-39-055-215-150
Good selection of Shefield
silver, he restored Cellini statue
on the Ponte Vecchio.

Mazzoni
Via Orsanmichele, 14r
011-39-055-215-153
www.mazzonicasa.it
Fine bed and table linens since 1889.

Mesticheria Mazzanti
Borgo La Croce, 101r
011-39-055-248-0663
You'll never have so much fun
in a hardware store.

*Molarie Locchi
Via D. Burchiello, 10
011-39-055-229-8371
www.lochi.com
Still making exquisite glass
objects inspired by old designs.

Nante
Piazza del Duomo, 52r
011-39-055-239-6002
Making enamel address plaques
since the nineteenth century.

*Pampaloni
Borgo SS. Apostoli, 47r
011-39-055-289-094
The place to register for
magnificent wedding silver.

*Paolo Pagliai
Borgo San Jacopo, 41r
011-39-055-282-840
www.paolopagliai.com
Long time makers of elegant
silver and repairers for the Vatican.

Parenti
Via dei Tornabuoni. 93r
011-39-055-214-438
Chic Florentines shop here
for home accessories.

Passamaneria Valmar
Via Porta Rossa, 53r
011-39-055-284-493
www.valmar-florence.com
Tassels, tiebacks, and trimmings.

*Peter Bazzanti & Son
Via Parione, 37r
011-39-055-215-649
www.galleriabazzanti.it
Fabulous marble statues and
bronzes.

Pratesi
Lungarno Corsini, 32r
011-39-055-289-488
Luxurious bed linens.

Rampini Ceramics
Borgo Ognissanti, 32
011-39-055-219-720
www.rampiniceramics.com
Sophisticated versions of classic
Tuscan pottery.

Riccardo Barthel
Via dei Serragli, 234r
011-39-055-228-0721
www.riccardobarthel.it
An Italian version of a small
department store with everything
for the home.

Richard Ginori
Via Rondinelli, 17r
011-39-055-210-041
www.richardginori1735.com
Makers of the famous classic china.

*Sbigoli Terrecotte
Via San Egidio, 4r
011-39-055-247-9713
www.sbigoliterrecotte.it
Sophisticated pottery shapes and
designs made on the premises.

T & T
Via de'Ginori, 2r
011-39-055-280-123
A vast selection of Italian fabrics,
table and bed linens.

Artisans

All artisans shops are listed in
chapter 8.

Books

*Alinari
Largo Alinari, 15
011-39-055-239-5232
www.alinari.it
Prestigious photography books and
prints of its historic archives.

Assolibri
Via del Sole, 3r
011-39-055-284-533
A discriminating selection of
beautiful coffee table books.

*BM Book Shop
Borgo Ognissanti, 4r
011-39-055-294-575
email: bmbookshop@dada.it
Quality selection and extensive
choice of British authors.

Edison Bookstore
Piazza della Repubblica, 27r
011-39-055-213-110
www.libreriaedison.it
Four floors of books.

Fashion Room
Via dei Palchetti, 3
011-39-055-213-270
www.fashionroom.it
Fashionistas will never want to
leave—I didn't.

Feltrinelli International
Via Cavour, 12r
011-39-055-219-524
www.feltrinelli.it
A bookshop for everyone.

Libreria Babele
Via della Belle Donne, 41
011-39-055-283-312
Specializes in beautiful art books,
limited editions, and the luscious
FMR publications.

*Libreria Antiquaria Gozzini
Via Ricasoli, 49
011-39-055-212-433
www.gozzini.it
Italian books galore in the eighteenth century Palazzo Alfani.

Libreria Martelli
Via dei Martelli, 22r
011-39-055-265-7603
Books plus a wonderful rooftop
terrace.

*Paperback Exchange
Via delle Oche, 4r
011-39-055-293-460
www.papex.it
Swap your paperbacks here.

Florentine & Tuscan Food Specialties

*Cibreo Teatro del Sale
Via de'Macci, 11r
011-39-055-200-1492
www.teatrodelsale.com
Mouthwatering products by
restaurateur owner Fabbio Picchi.

Dolceforte
Via della Scala, 21r
011-39-055-219-116
Couture chocolate indulgences.

La Bottega dell'Olio
Piazza del Limbo, 2r
011-39-055-267-0468
Everything made from olives—oils
and soaps to kitchen accessories.

Olio & Convivium
Via Santo Spirito, 4
011-39-055-265-8198
www.conviviumfirenze.it
Shop for Tuscan prosciuttos and
cheeses—try the restaurant.

*Pegna
Via dello Studio, 8
011-39-055-282-701
www.pegna.it
The Florentine version of a gourmet
supermarket.

*Vestri
Borgo degli Albizi, 11r
011-39-055-234-0374
www.vestri.it
Sip a sublime hot chocolate and
buy a box of handmade chocolates.

Lotions and Potions

*Alessandro Bizzarri
Via Condotta, 32r
011-39-055-211-580
Old Florentine remedies in a
nineteenth century shop.

Antica Erboristeria San Simone
Via Ghibellina, 190r
011-39-055-215-980
Good varied selection.

*Farmacista Dr. Vranjes
Via San Gallo, 63r
011-39-055-494-537
www.drvanjes.it
Elegant luxurious fragrances
and aromatherapy.

Farmacia SS. Annunziata
Via dei Servi, 80r
011-39-055-210-738
Have fun trying all the original products in this sixteenth century shop.

*Lorenzo Villoresi
Via de'Bardi, 14
011-39-055-234-1187
Design your own fragrance in
a palazzo with a stunning view
of the city.

Monastica
Via Ghibellina, 127r
011-39-055-211-006
Email: monastica@email.it
Lotions potions and liquors made
in Italian monasteries.

*Officina di Santa Maria Novella
Via della Scala, 16
011-39-055-216-276
www.smnovella.com
Shop for soaps eau de colognes
and creams in a magical thirteenth
century chapel.

Stationery Paper Goods

*Antica Baccani
Via Porta Rossa, 99r
011-39-055-215-448
I favor their cards, papers and
little paper surprises.

*Giulio Giannini & Figlio
Piazza Pitti, 37r
011-39-055-212-621
email: giannini@giuliogiannini.it
Making beautiful paper and leather
books since 1856.

Johnsons & Relatives
Via Cavour, 49r
011-39-055-265-8103
Email: joandrefi@yahoo.it
Off the beaten track.

Landi di Giuliano Martini
Piazza Pitti, 39r
My favorite postcard shop with
a staggering selection.

*Pineider
Piazza della Signoria, 13r
011-39-055-284-655
www.pineider.it
Creamy engraved paper and
splendid leather accessories.

Scriptorium
Via dei Servi, 5r
011-39-055-211-804
www.scriptoriumfirenze.com
Beautiful accessories for
sophisticated desks including
leather bound books.

Department Stores

Coin
Via dei Calzaiuoli, 56r
011-39-055-280-531
www.coin.it

La Rinascente
Piazza della Repubblica, 1
011-39-055-219-113
www.rinascente.it

Store hours

The Florentines still respect the traditional Italian hours for business. Almost everything is open from 9:00 A.M. to 12:30 or 1:00 P.M., closes for lunch, reopens at 3:30 or 4:00 P.M., and closes at 7:30 P.M. More stores tend to be open through the lunch hour than ever before, but they are usually ones that cater to tourists.

- On Saturdays, most stores are open only in the morning and close at 1:00 P.M. Many still follow tradition and do not open on Monday until 3:30 P.M.
- Remember that in August, when all Italians head for the beach, almost everything shuts down for a month. As a result, most of your favorite restaurants and shops will probably be closed. Also check the calendar for religious holidays. In many cases, everyone takes the day off. This is part of the charm of *la dolce vita* in Italy.

Getting it all home

If you really plan to do a lot of shopping, then bring an extra suitcase. I always put an empty nylon suitcase flat in the bottom of mine before I start packing. If I have room, I add several lengths of bubble wrap, which saves me having to waste valuable shopping/museum time searching for packing supplies when I'm there.

Sometimes it's just easier to mail your purchases home. There are two Mail Boxes Etc. stores in Florence which will ship everything with no hassle. Just bring everything over in shopping bags, and they will take care of the rest! Oh, and bring money, too, as it can be pricey—but worth it in the end.

Mail Boxes Etc.
Corso Tintori, 39
011-39-055-246-6660

Mail Boxes Etc.
Via della Scala, 13r
011-39-055-268-173

Tax refunds

When you are purchasing an expensive item, always ask if you qualify for a tax refund. In Italy and the EU countries, foreigners who buy merchandise and take it out of the country qualify for this if they meet the minimum amount in a single purchase. The store personnel will show you how to fill out the form (you will need your passport) and tell you what to do when you get to the airport. I just received a 13% credit (the amount changes) to my charge card from my last trip's purchases—a nice surprise that can really add up. Pick up a copy of a brochure called *Global Refund*, which will tell you about this system, from the store or your hotel concierge.

Customs

The first day of my trip, I start putting in a separate envelope my receipts for purchases I intend to bring home. That way, they are handy when I'm filling out the customs form on the plane home.

Taxis

Of course you are going to need a taxi sometime, especially if you plan to "shop till you drop." Taxi service in Florence is mostly organized. You can call one from anywhere in the city, and they usually arrive within minutes (except during rush hour or when there are special events taking place). In a pinch, you can ask the shop to call one, which I have always found they will graciously do. Or walk to the nearest taxi rank. You can also go into a hotel and ask a kind concierge to call one for you. Licensed Florentine taxicabs are white, with the ID number painted on the door; be sure to use one of these. I have used several companies, and they have all been dependable. The numbers to use are 011-39-055-4242, 011-39-055-4798, and 011-39-055-4390.

✦

I've heard the story over and over again: "For years, I resisted going to the outlets. Miss a day in Florence or Tuscany—no way! Not with all the fabulous shopping in Florence." However, times change, and when I recently interviewed a cross section of my savvy fashionista friends, they all said, "Go." There are several reasons to go now— the biggest being the devaluation of the dollar, followed by the recently disappointing merchandise in the January and July sales that were fabulous in the past.

So if you have a free morning, you might find something wonderful. Those in the know hire a car with a driver for four or five hours to wait while you are shopping. Raugei, 011-39-055-411-363 or 011-39-339-147-4836, dimitriraugei@yahoo.it, is dependable and has everything from cars to minivans, or you can ask your hotel concierge. Most have a flat fee, which I've found runs between 200 and 300 Euros for five hours. That way, you can keep going back to the car with your bulging totes again and again. So gather all your friends together and split the cost. It's well worth it in terms of wear and tear. If you are there after Christmas, you are in luck. Merchandise will be marked down again, on top of the original markdown, and labeled with a sign that says, "occasionissima," which means "great bargain!"

The Mall

Via Europa, 8
Leccio Regello
011-39-055-865-7775
Hours: Monday-Sunday 10-8
Thirty minutes from Florence, The Mall features a cross section of the best designers: Gucci, Yves St. Laurent, Giorgio Armani, Stella McCartney, Loro Piana, Alexander McQueen, Balenciaga, Fendi, Tod's, Emilio Pucci, Ferragamo, Ungaro, Marni, Bottega Veneta, Valentino, Agnona, and more. If you only have time to go to one outlet, this is the place for you. One caveat: mixed in are some regular shops that are not outlets, so be aware of what you are willing to pay for something. Everyone who

has been here has a story of buying something special, so enjoy. The Dot.Com Cafè is a nice spot to periodically revive yourself. There is also a twice-daily shuttle bus from Florence, so check the above phone number for details.

I Pellettieri d'Italia

Localita Levanella-SS69
Montevarchi
011-39-055-919-01
Hours: Monday-Friday 10-7, Saturday 9:30-7, Sunday 2-7
This was the first designer outlet I ever heard about, and it's still very popular because it features the fabulous Prada, Miu Miu, Helmut Lang, and Jil Sander—all at a nice discount. So if you can, avoid going on the weekends, when you will have to pick up a ticket and probably stand in line for several hours before getting in. But if you must, you will often find a chic bargain.

Barberino McArthur Glen

Via Meucci
Mugello
011-39-055-842-161
www.mcarthurglen.it
Hours: Tuesday-Friday 10-8, Saturday and Sunday 10-9, open Mondays in January, June, July, August September and December from 2-8
This is the newest of the outlet groups, with ninety shops featuring designers like J.P. Gaultier, Malo, Missoni, Benetton, Bruno Magli, Frette, Furla, Guess, and more, just thirty minutes from Florence.

The Roberto Cavalli Outlet

Via Volturno,3/3
Osmannoro, Sesto Fiorentino
011-39-055-317-754
If you are a big Cavalli fan and so motivated, you can stop at his outlet, which is located in his offices on the way to the Florence Airport—how convenient!

RIGHT: The outlets near Florence are known for their chic fashions and accessories by designer names like these.

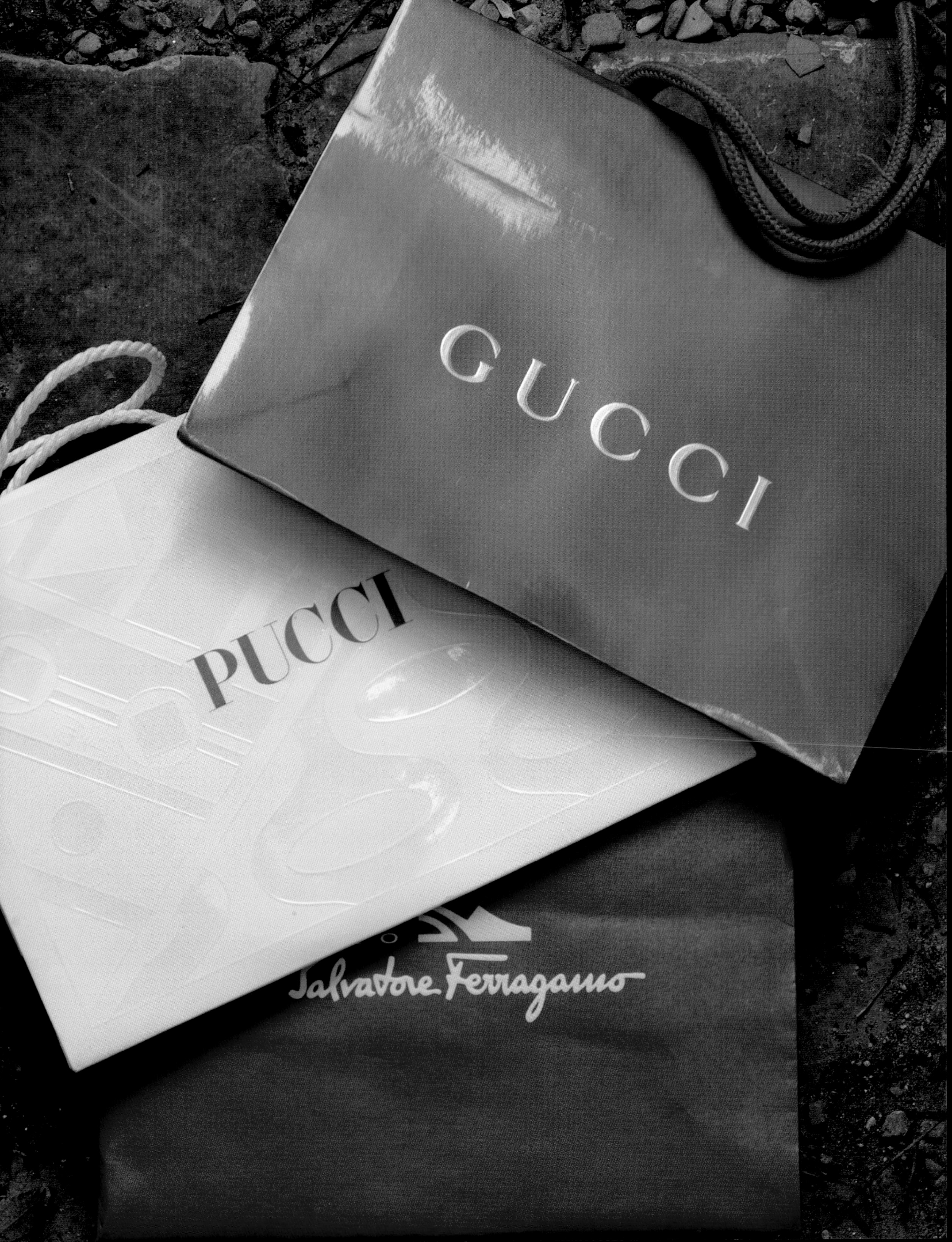
GUCCI
PUCCI
Salvatore Ferragamo

EIGHT

Artisans and Antiques

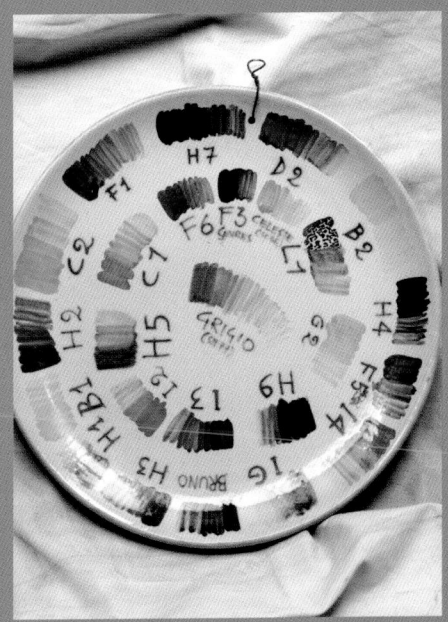

"Like the wise woman who lived in the portico of Santissima Annunziata and sewed pretty patches on her clothes, the modern Florentines are extremely gifted in repair work—mending and fixing old things to make them last."
—Mary McCarthy, *The Stones of Florence*

Working on this book has been a wonderful voyage of discovery, but it has had its ups and downs. On one trip, I actually fell off a curb into the street and fractured my foot. It wasn't only the narrow sidewalks but because I was distracted by the looks of an artisan's workshop and lost my balance trying to take a peek inside. It was worth it!

Italy is a country that excels in design and splendid workmanship, and Florence is the natural home to this cherished tradition—one that began in the twelfth century, when craft guilds were first established and creativity flowered. The "art of making"—crafts, antiques, and restoration—all are typical activities that keep the past connected to the present. The artisans and craftsmen who live and work in Florence today are using the same ancient methods, tools, and skills passed down from generation to generation—making things of high quality and irresistible beauty, by hand. For centuries, humble materials have been made into desirable objects because of the artisan tradition, which has a long history.

Ferdinando I de' Medici in 1593 moved all the jewelry makers and silversmiths over to the Ponte Vecchio. There are still streets in Florence named after the craftsmen, like Via dell'Ariento, the "street of silver." The arts and crafts were treated with the same degree of respect, and artists like Benvenuto Cellini created celebrated works of art at the same time that they were making objects for the Medici to use in their everyday lives. When you look around Florence, it is impossible to ignore the sconces, lamps, and other decorations—made with skill by the artisans of the city—that embellish the old palazzi.

OPENING PICTURE: A copy of Raphael's *Madonna della Seggiola* being restored by Carla Martelli.
OVERLEAF, LEFT: Lamberto and son Duccio Banchi at their shop, and right, color swatches at Sbiglio Terracotta.

Today, young people from all around the world come to this city to participate in the apprentice/mentoring system that has survived here since the Middle Ages and serves as a link between the past and the present. If you value the past and respect the effort that goes into crafting precious objects, then you will enjoy wandering the maze of old, winding streets in the Oltrarno and discovering the spirit of the past flourishing in artisans' ateliers and workshops, many that have been here for centuries.

Florentine Eleonora Burci creates interesting itineraries for people who visit Florence. A friend of mine loved her tour, "The Artisans of Florence" (see page 71), so I asked Eleonora if she would take me to some of the favorites on her list. On a rainy day last spring, we walked around the district where cabinetmakers, wood-carvers, gilders, silversmiths, bronzers, glassmakers, paint restorers, and artisans working in ceramics and *pietre dure* were busily working in every nook and cranny. The scent of wood, paint, and glue mingled with the humid air.

Our first stop was the tiny shop of Lamberto and Duccio Banchi, father and son working together in making beautiful bronze objects using traditional lost-wax-casting methods and cold-finishing each piece by hand. The workshop on Via dei Serragli still has its original furnishings. It was opened in 1925 by Vasco Cappuccini, one of the foremost bronze artisans, and passed on to his pupil Lamberto in 1946. Lamberto and Duccio were recently awarded the prestigious "Bottega Artigiana Fiorentina 2008" prize for their outstanding frames, table lamps, sconces, and boxes.

We then walked over to Via Maggio and stopped in to say hello at Bartolozzi and Maioli. I've been coming here for decades, and it's still an intriguing

ABOVE: A skilled artisan trained in gold leaf restoration works restoring an antique frame at C & S Martelli.
NEXT PAGE: Left, wood carving is a Florentine specialty at legendary Bartolozzi e Maioli on the Via Maggio.
Right, frames and more since 1895 at Castorina, and below, well-used tools lined up at Duccio Banchi.

place—almost a museum—filled with wood carvings, models, and prototypes, some dating from the seventeenth century. Maria di Caterina now runs the studio, laboratory, and store, located here since 1938, and the artisans here continue working on prestigious commissions from places like the Kremlin and the Palazzo del Quirinale in Rome.

Around the corner is the studio of Carla and Stefania Martelli. They specialize in painting and gold-leaf restoration, and they have done work for many museums, including the Pitti Palace, the Bargello, and the Uffizi. A good example of their restoration work is the *Carro del Fuoco,* an ornately decorated cart that is the focal point of a traditional fireworks display at the Duomo that has occurred

every Easter Sunday since about 1300. You can also attend their school, Oro e Colore, and take courses in various painting and gold leaf-techniques. They will even prepare you to take the admission test to attend the Opificio delle Pietre Dure, the prestigious, state-run Florentine school of restoration.

Many artisans offer courses and workshops, supporting the apprentice/mentoring tradition of this city. Sbigilio Terracotta, a shop on Via San Egidio, offers courses in pottery making and decoration. If you are interested, they will customize a schedule for you, even if you are visiting for only a short period of time. The pottery designs are sophisticated, and the artisans here do wonderful patterns of tableware inspired by the lovely Tuscan countryside.

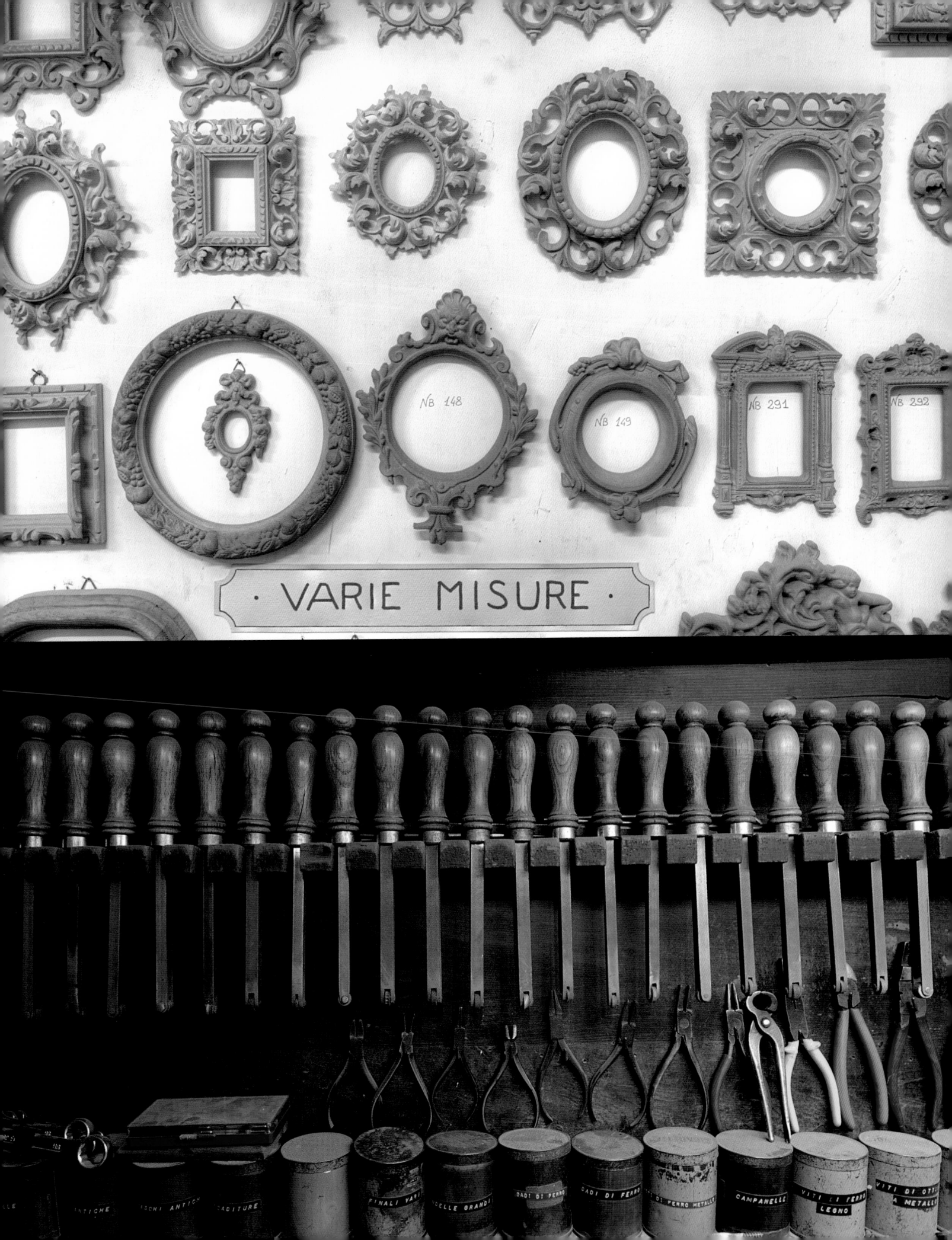

· VARIE MISURE ·

Another favorite of mine is Elizabetta di Constanzo, who sells her designs in a tiny shop called Arte Creta. Her ceramics are whimsical and charming, reflecting the sun and joy of Tuscany. I could buy everything in her shop, especially those pieces painted with brightly colored birds.

As I wrote in *Dreaming of Tuscany*, wandering the back streets between the Pitti Palace and the Arno River, you'll find someone who can craft, repair, or restore almost anything. For anyone who loves antiques, this is a wonderful opportunity. As we walked by the Studio Santo Spirito, we watched Francesca Lotti restoring a Chinese Tang-dynasty horse brought by a client all the way from London.

And, if you don't need anything fixed, you can just order irresistible fabrics, woven on looms designed five hundred years ago at the Antico Setificio Fiorentino; sample pungent perfumes and oils based on ancient formulas at the Farmaceutica di Santa Maria Novella; choose from Renaissance or modern designs at silversmiths Pampaloni, Pagliai, Parenti, Buccelati, or Brandimarte; watch soft leather handbags being made from scratch at the Leather School at Santa Croce; or buy a handblown-glass olive-oil pourer from Locchi that will be the envy of all your friends back home.

May is a wonderful month to be in Florence. The Maggio Musicale opens the concert season, the Iris Festival takes place in Piazzale Michelangelo (see chapter 3), and the Artigianato e Palazzo, a top-notch artisans' fair, takes place the third weekend in May. In 1994, Neri Torrigiani and Princess Giorgiana Corsini had the idea of creating an event featuring top-quality artisans. Today, over a hundred talented master craftsmen, chosen from hundreds of applicants from Florence, other parts of Italy, and abroad, get together in the exceptionally elegant Italian gardens of the Palazzo Corsini to show and share their talents with visitors from far and wide.

Sabina Corsini, Giorgiana's daughter, told me, "What makes this event unique is that the artisans move part of their workshops here, doing demonstrations so you can see their work in progress and appreciate the talent and effort it takes to make something by hand." A perfect example is Marco Viviani of Plissettatura Milady, who pleats fabrics using old, traditional techniques and creating complex designs. The results are amazing, and designers like Roberto Capucci, one of the first couturiers in Italy, has used these fabrics in his sculptural clothing. If you want more information and to find the details for next year, log on to www.artigianatoepalazzo.it.

There is a wonderful little market called *La Fierucola* that takes place the third Sunday of every month in Piazza Santo Spirito. The square is charming, and the market features artisans ranging from my favorite basket maker, Marianna Baldasseroni, to someone who carves olive wood into beautiful bowls and serving utensils. There is a weaver who uses thatchy wool from Tuscan sheep, a soap maker, not to mention all the artisanal food—tasty cheeses, condiments, local oils, and wines from the surrounding Tuscan countryside.

Florence is filled with too many wonderful artisans to list here but I'm giving you a start by including this list of people I've enjoyed visiting for many years—they put tradition and quality first.

RIGHT, CLOCKWISE: Florence is known for its artisans including pottery and ceramics at Sbiglio, printmaking at Il Bisonte, fine art restoration at Studio Santo Spirito, textile weaving at Antico Setificio Fiorentino, and fashion design at innovator Roberto Capucci.

Artisans

Bookbinding and Handmade Paper

Giulio Giannini & Figlio
Piazza dei Pitti, 37r
011-39-055-212-947

Bruscoli Pelletteria-Legatoria
Via Montebello, 58r
011-39-055-212-947
www.bruscoli.it

Bronze

Duccio Banchi
Via dei Serragli, 10r
011-39-055-294-694

F.lli Ugolini Bronzisti
Via del Drago D'Oro, 25r
011-39-055-215-343
www.flliugolinibronzistisrl.com

Ceramics

Art Creta
Via del Proconsolo, 6r
011-39-055-284-341

Marta Cangioli
Via della Scala, 42
011-39-328-695-5903

Sbiglio
Via Sant' Egidio, 4r
011-39-055-247-9713
www.sbiglioterracotta.it

Romano Pampaloni
Via di Montughi, 55
011-39-055-475-006

Ceramic Restoration

Studio Santo Spirito
Via dello Sprone, 19r
011-39-055-214-873

Clocks & Watches

Puliti
Piazza Sant'Elisabetta, 6
011-39-055-230-2528

Fabric

Antico Setificio Fiorentino
Via L. Bartolini, 4
011-39-055-213-861
www.anticosetificiofiorentino.com

Tessilarte
Via Toselli, 100
011-39-055-364-097

Fabric Pleating

Plissettatura Milady
Via Giuliani, 158B
011-39-055-415-493
www.plissettaturamilady.it

Fabric Restoration

Antica Tappezzeria Borsellini
Via Maggio, 54r
011-39-055-212-051

Furniture Restoring

Enrico Morandi
Via dello Sprone, 23r
011-39-055-287-207

Ponziani Lo Studiolo
Via di Santo Spirito, 27r
011-39-055-287-958
www.ponzianilostudiolo.com

Glass and Crystal

Moleria Locchi
Via D. Burchiello, 10
011-39-055-229-8371
www.locchi.com

Handbags and Small Leather Items

Scuola del Cuoio
Via San Giuseppe, 5r
011-39-055-244-533
www.leatherschool.com

Jewelry Making

Beaded Lily Glassworks
Via Toscanella, 33r
011-39-334-976-3949
www.beadedlilyglassworks.com

Marble Statues and Bronzes

Peter Bazzanti & Son
Via Parione, 37r
011-39-055-215-649
www.galleriabazzanti.it

Mosaics

Pitti Mosaici
Piazza de' Pitti, 23r
011-39-055-282-127
www.pittimosaici.it

Raffaello Romanelli
Lungarno Acciaioli, 72r
011-39-055-239-6662

Painting Restoration

C & S Martelli
Via Toscanella, 18r
011-39-055-28-415
www.oroecolore.com

ABOVE, LEFT: Neri Torrigiani and Princess Giorgiana Corsini at the Artigianato e Palazzo in the Corsini gardens.
RIGHT: There are many works in progress at the artisans' show including the making of beautiful Florentine shoes.

Painted Furniture

Autentiqua di Leonardo Cappellini
Via del Presto di San Martino, 20r
011-39-055-282-935
www.autentiqua.it

Perfume

Lorenzo Villoresi
Via de' Bardi, 14
011-39-055-234-5893
www.lorenzovilloresi.it

Officina Profumo Farmaceutica di Santa Maria Novella
Via della Scala, 16
011-39-055-216-276
www.smnovella.it

Printmaking

Il Bisonte
Via San Niccolo, 24r
011-39-055-234-2585
www.ilbisonte.it/scuola.htm

Scagliola

Pietra di Luna
Via Maggio, 4r
011-39-055-265-8257

Shoes

Stefano Bemer
Borgo San Frediano, 143r
011-39-055-222-558
www.stefanobemer.it

Saskia
Via di Santa Lucia, 24r
011-39-055-293-291

Silver

Brandimarte
Viale L. Ariosto, 11r
011-39-055-230-41
www.brandimarte.com

Marco Fancelli
Via dello Sprone, 14r
011-39-055-215-150

Mario Buccelati
Via della Vigna Nuova, 71r
011-39-055-239-6579

Pampaloni
Borgo S.S. Apostoli, 47r
011-39-055-289-094
www.pampaloni.com

Paolo Pagliai Argentiere
Borgo San Jacopo, 41r
011-39-055-282-840

Parenti
Via dei Tornabuoni, 93r
011-39-055-214-438

Penko
Via F. Zannetti, 14r
011-39-055-211-661
www.penkofirenze.it

Woodcarving and Frames

Bartolozzi e Maioli
Via Maggio, 13r
011-39-055-232-8633
www.bartolozzi.net

Castorina
Via di Santo Spirito, 13r
011-39-055-212-885
www.castorina.net

Sernissi Massimiliano "Leone"
Via Il Prato, 46r
011-39-055-282-090
www.leonecornici.com

"When I am alone with antiques I don't feel alone anymore," said industrialist, composer and collector Alberto Bruni Tedeschi. He was one of a group of prestigious Italian collectors who emerged during the late nineteenth and twentieth centuries to continue the antiquarian tradition many trace back to the city of Florence and Francesco I, who started the first museum here, the Uffizi.

If you are passionate about collecting antiques put Florence on your list because, in addition to the magnificent Renaissance architecture and treasure-filled museums displaying everything from antique musical instruments to the first telescopes, there are fine antiques shops located on several streets: the Via dei Fossi and Borgo Ognissanti near the Grand Hotel and the Via Maggio on the Oltrarno. The Associazione Antiquari Fiorentini lists the names and addresses of their members in Florence and you can log on to their website, www.antiquarifiorentini.com.

There are also several antiques markets and the prestigious Biennale Antiques Show held here every other year. Following is a list of some of the shops we enjoy:

Antichità Dei Bardi
Via dei Fossi, 8r
011-39-055-215-688

Bacarelli Antichità
Via dei Fossi, 33r
011-39-055-215-457
www.bacarelli.com

Botticelli Via Maggio
Via Maggio, 47r
011-39-055-230-2095

Casa d'Arte Bruschi di
Anita Almehagen
Via dei Fossi, 42r
011-39-055-280-970

Damiano Lapiccirella
Borgognissanti, 56r
011-39-055-284-902
www.lapiccirella.com

Di Clemente Antichità
Palazzo Cosimo Ridolfi
Via Maggio, 19r
011-39-055-239-6649

Enrico Frascione
Via dei Fossi, 61r
011-39-055-294-087

Enzo Marianelli e
FiglioAntiquari
Via dei Fossi, 11r
011-39-055-264-257

Galleria Pasti Bencini
Via Maggio, 26r
011-39-055-282-384
www.pastibencini.com

Gallori Turchi Antichità
Via Maggio, 14r
011-39-055-282-279

Giovanni Pratesi
Antiquario
Via Maggio 13r
011-39-055-239-6568

Il Cartiglio
Via Maggio, 78r
011-39-055-287-961

Massimo Vezzosi
Via Maggio, 60r
011-39-055-294-549

Moretti
Piazza Ottaviani, 17r
011-39-055-265-4277
www.morettigallery.com

Parronchi Dipinti '800-'900
Via dei Fossi, 18r
011-39-055-215-109

Piacenti Art Gallery
Via Maggio, 17r
011-39-055-285-232
www.piacentiart.com

Sandro Morelli
Via Maggio, 51r
011-39-055-282-789

Silvio Varando
Via Maggio, 45r
011-39-055-213-279

Tettamanti Antichità
Via Maggio, 22r
011-39-055-218-044

Velona Antichità & C.
Via dei Fossi, 31r
011-39-055-287-069

Zecchi Antichità di Mara
Masini
Via Maggio, 34r
011-39-055-293-368

CLOCKWISE FROM LEFT: Avid collectors entering the grand archway of the Palazzo Corsini. Flea market and antiques finds at the Mercato del Pulci in Piazza dei Ciompi include vintage engravings and magazines, late nineteenth century furniture, hand-tinted etchings, woodworking tools, Italian table silver and, center, an assortment of porcelain.

ABOVE: The Loggia del Pesce by Vasari, created in 1568, now occupies the Piazza dei Ciompi, where a flea and antiques market is held the first Sunday of each month.

Antiques Shows

Biennale in Florence
Mostra Mercato Internazionale del Antiquariato
Palazzo Corsini
Lungarno Corsini
011-39-055-282-283
www.mostraantiquariato.it

Every other year Florence and the elegant Palazzo Corsini host one of the most extraordinary antiques shows held in the world, the International Antiques Show or Biennale. The cream of international antiques dealers, displaying their sophisticated treasures and collectors from around the world, descend on Florence for this elegant event. It usually occurs the end of September.

Antiques Markets

Mercato delle Pulci
Piazza dei Ciompi
Last Sunday of each month.
This market is fun and you can find anything from heavy table silver and delicate porcelain to vintage table linens and kitsch costume jewelry.

Mercato di Santo Spirito
Piazza Santo Spirito
Second Sunday of each month.
This market abounds in flea market finds—vintage clothing and accessories, old postcards, boxes filled with ceramic odds and ends, and hand wrought hardware. You never know!

Suggested Reading

"Books are beautiful things."

— George Bernard Shaw

One of the additional pleasures of traveling is reading about it—either before or after your trip. If you love Florence and Tuscany, there are more books than one can possibly imagine on the subject. Here are some of my favorites, both old and new, starting with the Renaissance and up to present day Florence. Some are out of print but worth searching for on the Internet. Happy reading!

Acton, Harold. *The Last Medici*. London: MacMillan, 1980.

-----------------. *Florence: A Traveller's Companion*. London: Constable & Co., 1986.

Alighieri, Dante. *The Divine Comedy*. New York: Knopf, 1995.

Anderson, Burton. *Treasures of the Italian Table*. New York: William Morrow, 1994.

---------------------. *The Wines & Winemakers of Italy*. New York: Little Brown and Company, 1980.

Andres, Glenn, John Hunisak and A. Richard Turner. *The Art of Florence*. New York: Abbeville Press, 1988.

Artom Treves, Giuliana. *The Golden Ring: The Anglo-Florentines, 1847–1862*. London: Longmans, Green, 1956.

Barzini, Luigi. *The Italians*. New York: Atheneum, 1985.

Bell Italia. *Historic Houses & Gardens Open to the Public*. Milano: Giorgio Mondadori, 1996.

Berenson, Bernard. *The Italian Painters of the Renaissance*. New York: Phaidon Press, 1959.

Boccaccio, Giovanni. *The Decameron*. New York: Penguin, 2003.

Borsook, Eve. *The Companion Guide to Florence*. London: Collins, 1973.

Browning, Elizabeth Barrett. *Casa Guidi Window*. Cedar City: Classic Books, 2001.

Calvino, Italo. *Invisible Cities*. New York: Harcourt Brace Jovanovich, 1978.

Campanello, Thomas. *A Defense of Galileo, the Mathematician from Florence*. Notre Dame: Notre Dame Press, 1994.

Cardini, Franco. *Tuscany: Landscape, History, Art*. Florence: Scala, 2003.

Clarke, Ethne and Raffaello Bencini. *The Gardens of Tuscany*. London: Weidenfeld & Nicolson, 1990.

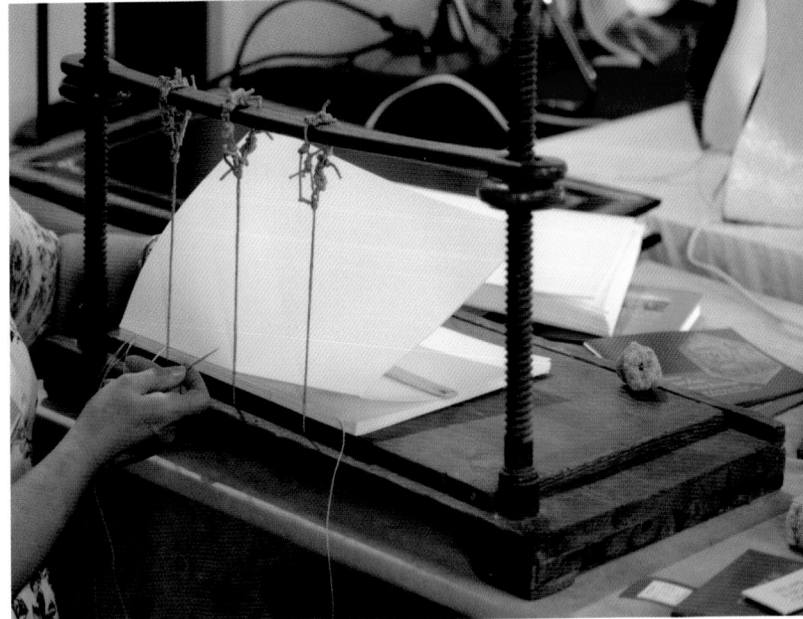

ABOVE: A how-to demonstration of the art of bookmaking at the Artigianato e Palazzo artisans' fair in May.

David, Elizabeth. *Italian Food*. New York: Harper & Row, 1987.

De' Medici, Lorenza. *Florentines, A Tuscan Feast*. New York: Random House, 1992.

Dentler, Clara Louise. *Famous Americans in Florence*. Florence: Giunti, 1976.

Dibdin, Michael. *A Rich Full Death*. New York: Vintage, 1999.

---------------------. *Rat King*. New York: Vintage, 1997.

Forster, E.M. *A Room with a View*. New York: Bantam, 1988.

Freson, Robert. *Savoring Italy*. New York: HarperCollins, 1992.

Goethe, Johann Wolfgang Von. *Italian Journey, 1786–1788*. London: Penguin Books, 1970.

Gombrich, E.H. *The Story of Art*. London: Phaidon Press Ltd., 1995.

Grant, George and Karen. *Just Visiting*. Nashville: Cumberland House, 1999.

Hartt, Frederick and David Wilkins. *The History of Italian Renaissance Art*. New York: Prentice Hall, 2006.

Hale, J.R. *A Concise Encylopaedia of Italian Renaissance*. London: Thames & Hudson, 1981.

Hawthorne, Nathaniel. *The Marble Faun*. Boston: Ticknor & Fields, 1860.

Hazan, Marcella. *The Classic Italian Cookbook*. New York: Alfred A. Knopf, 1983.

Suggested Reading

Hazan, Victor. *Italian Wine*. New York: Alfred A. Knopf, 1982.

Harrison, Barbara Grizzuti. *Italian Days*. New York: Grove Press, 1989.

Hibbert, Christopher. *The House of Medici: Its Rise and Fall*. New York: Perennial, 1999.

Highet, Gilbert. *Poets in a Landscape*. Pleasantville, New York: Akadine Press, 1996.

Hobhouse, Penelope. *The Gardens of Italy*. London: Mitchell Beazley, 1998.

James, Henry. *Italian Hours*. New York: Penguin Classics, 1995.

---------------. *Roderick Hudson*. New York: Penguin Classics, 1986.

Johnson, Hugh. *Tuscany and Its Wines*. San Francisco: Chronicle, 2000.

Jones, Irene Marchegiani & Haeussler, Thomas. *The Poetics of Place: Florence Imagined*. Florence: L.S. Olschki, 2001.

Kerper, Barrie. *The Collector Traveler, Central Italy*. New York: Three River Press, 2000.

Levey, Michael. *Florence, A Portrait*. Boston: Harvard University Press, 1998.

Lewis, Richard, W.B. *The City of Florence, Historical Vistas and Personal Sightings*. New York: Farrar Straus & Giroux, 1991.

King, Ross. *Brunelleschi's Dome: How Renaissance Genius Reinvented Architecture*. New York: Penguin, 2001.

Macadam, Alta. *American in Florence*. Florence: Giunti Editore, 2003.

Machiavelli, Niccolo. *The Prince*. New York: Penguin, 1999.

Mariano, Nicky. *Forty Years with Berenson*. New York: Knopf, 1966.

McCarthy, Mary. *The Stones of Florence*. New York: Harcourt Brace Jovanovich, 1963.

McAleer, Edward C. *Brownings of Casa Guidi*. London: Browning Institute, 1979.

Miller, Emily Wise. *The Food Lover's Guide to Florence*. Berkeley: Ten Speed Press, 2007.

Moorehead, Caroline. *Iris Origo: Marchesa of Val d'Orcia*. London: John Murray, 2000.

Murray, Peter. *The Architecture of the Italian Renaissance*. New York: Schocken Books, 1986.

---------------. *The Art of the Renaissance*. Oxford: Oxford University Press, 1963.

Nabb, Magdalen. *Death in Springtime*. New York: Penguin, 1983.

------------------- *Vita Nuova*. New York: Soho Press, 2008. (There are fourteen wonderful mysteries in this series. We have listed the first and the last.)

Olson, Roberta. *Italian Renaissance Sculpture*. London: Thames & Hudson, 1992.

Origo, Iris. *War in Val d'Orcia: An Italian War Diary, 1943-1944*. Boston: David R. Godine, 2002.

Pope-Hennessy, John. *Italian Gothic Sculpture, Italian Renaissance Sculpture, Italian High Renaissance and Baroque Sculpture*. London: Phaidon Press Ltd., 1955.

Powers, Alice. *Italy in Mind*. New York: Vintage, 1997.

Root, Waverley. *The Food of Italy*. New York: Vintage, 1971.

Russell, Vivian. *Edith Wharton's Italian Gardens*. New York: Bullfinch Press, 1997.

Satkowski, Leon. *Giorgio Vasari: Architect & Courtier*. Princeton: Princeton University Press, 1994.

Scott, Rupert. *Florence Explored*. New York: New Amsterdam Press, 1987.

Shepard, J.C. & G.A. Jellicoe. *Italian Gardens of the Renaissance*. Princeton: Princeton Architectural Press, 1993.

Simon, Kate. *Italy, The Places In Between*. New York: Harper & Row, 1970.

Sobel, Dava. *Galileo's Daughter*. New York: Penguin, 2000.

Stone, Irving. *The Agony and the Ecstasy*. New York: Penguin, 2004.

Toman, Rolf. *The Art of the Italian Renaissance*. New York: Konemann, 1995.

Turner, A. Richard. *Renaissance Florence, The Invention of a New Art*. New York: Prentice Hall, 2005.

Twain, Mark. *The Innocents Abroad*. Mineola, New York: Dover Press, 2003.

Welch, Evelyn. *Shopping in the Renaissance*. New Haven: Yale University Press, 2005.

Wells, Patricia. *Trattoria*. New York: William Morrow, 1993.

Wharton, Edith. *Italian Villas and Their Gardens*. New York: Rizzoli, 2008.

Willinger, Faith. *Red, White and Greens: The Italian Way with Vegetables*. New York: Harper Collins, 1996.

Wirtz, Rolf. *Art & Architecture Florence*. Cologne, Germany: Barnes & Noble, 2000.

Wright, Sarah Bird. *Edith Wharton Abroad, Selected Travel Writings, 1818-1920*. New York: St. Martin's Press, 1995.

Index

Page numbers in *italics* refer to illustrations.

*"The world is made up of five elements:
earth, air, fire, water and the Florentines."*
—Pope Alexander VI (1492-1503)

Volume 2 • 2005

WHAT DO I READ NEXT?

A Reader's Guide
to Current
Genre Fiction

- Fantasy
- Popular Fiction
- Romance
- Horror
- Mystery
- Science Fiction
- Historical
- Inspirational
- Western

ISSN 1052-2212

Volume 2 • 2005

WHAT DO I READ NEXT?

A Reader's Guide
to Current
Genre Fiction

- Fantasy
- Popular Fiction
- Romance
- Horror
- Mystery
- Science Fiction
- Historical
- Inspirational
- Western

NEIL BARRON
TOM BARTON
DANIEL S. BURT
MELISSA HUDAK
D.R. MEREDITH
KRISTIN RAMSDELL
TOM AND ENID SCHANTZ

THOMSON

GALE

Detroit • New York • San Francisco • San Diego • New Haven, Conn. • Waterville, Maine • London • Munich

THOMSON
GALE

What Do I Read Next? 2005. Volume 2

Project Editor
Beverly Baer

Editorial
Dana Ferguson
Kathy Meek

Editorial Support Services
Tom Potts

Data Capture
Katrina Coach
Beverly Jendrowski
Elizabeth Pilette
Beth Richardson

Manufacturing
Drew Kalasky

LIBRARY OF CONGRESS CATALOG CARD NUMBER 82-15700
ISBN 0-7876-9022-8
ISSN 1052-2212

Printed in the United States of America
10 9 8 7 6 5 4 3 2 1

Contents

Introduction

Thousands of books are published each year intended for devoted fans of genre fiction. Dragons, outlaws, lovers, murderers, monsters, and aliens abound on our own world or on other worlds, throughout time—all featured in the pages of fantasy, western, romance, mystery, horror, science fiction, historical, inspirational, and popular fiction. Given the huge variety of titles available each year, added to the numbers from previous years, readers can be forgiven if they're stumped by the question "What do I read next?" And that's where this book comes in.

Designed as a tool to assist in the exploration of genre fiction, *What Do I Read Next?* guides the reader to both current and classic recommendations in nine widely read genres: Mystery, Romance, Western, Fantasy, Horror, Science Fiction, Historical, Inspirational, and Popular Fiction. *What Do I Read Next?* allows readers quick and easy access to specific data on recent titles in these popular genres. Plus, each entry provides alternate reading selections, thus coming to the rescue of librarians and booksellers, who are often unfamiliar with a genre, yet must answer the question frequently posed by their patrons and customers "What do I read next?"

Details on 1,247 Titles

Volume 2 of this year's edition of *What Do I Read Next?* contains entries for titles published mostly in 2005. These entries are divided into sections for Mystery, Romance, Western, Fantasy, Horror, Science Fiction, Historical, Inspirational, and Popular Fiction. Experts in each field compile the entries for their respective genres. The experts also discuss topics relevant to their genres in essays that appear at the beginning of each section.

The criteria for inclusion of specific titles vary somewhat from genre to genre. In genres such as Romance and Mystery, where large numbers of titles are published each year, the inclusion criteria are more selective, and the experts attempted to select the recently published books they considered the best. In genres such as Horror and Western, where the amount of new material is relatively small, a broader range of titles is represented, including many titles published by small or independent houses and some young adult books.

The entries are listed alphabetically by main author in each genre section. Most provide the following information:

- **Author or editor's name** and real name if a pseudonym is used. Co-authors, co-editors, and illustrators are also listed where applicable.

- **Book title.**
- **Date and place of publication; name of publisher.**
- **Series name.**
- **Story type:** Specific categories within each genre, identified by the compiling expert. Definitions of these types are listed in the "Key to Genre Terms" section.
- **Subject(s):** Gives the subject matter covered by the title.
- **Major character(s):** Names and brief descriptions of up to three characters featured in the title.
- **Time period(s):** Tells when the story takes place.
- **Locale(s):** Tells where the story takes place.
- **What the book is about:** A brief plot summary.
- **Where it's reviewed:** Citations to reviews of the book, including the source of the review, date of the source, and the page on which the review appears. Reviews are included from genre-specific sources such as *Locus* and *Affaire de Coeur*, as well as more general reviewing sources such as *Booklist* and *Publishers Weekly*.
- **Other books by the author:** Titles and publication dates of other books the author has written, useful for those wanting to read more by a particular author.
- **Other books you might like:** Titles by other authors written on a similar theme or in a similar style. These titles further the reader's exploration of the genre.

Indexes Answer Readers' Questions

The nine indexes in *What Do I Read Next?* used separately or in conjunction with each other, create many pathways to the featured titles, answering general questions or locating specific titles. For example:

"Are there any new Eve Dallas books?"

The SERIES INDEX lists entries by the name of the series of which they are a part.

"I like Regency Romances. Can you recommend any new ones?"

The GENRE INDEX breaks each genre into story types or more specialized areas. In the Romance genre for example, there is a story type heading "Regency." For the definitions of story types, see the "Key to Genre Terms."

"I'm looking for a story set in Paris."

The GEOGRAPHIC INDEX lists titles by their locale. This can help readers pinpoint an area in which they may have a particular interest, such as their hometown, another country, or even Cyberspace.

"Do you know of any science fiction stories set during the 23rd century?"

The TIME PERIOD INDEX is a chronological listing of the time settings in which the main entry titles take place.

"What books are available that feature teachers?"

The CHARACTER DESCRIPTION INDEX identifies the major characters by occupation (e.g. Accountant, Editor, Librarian) or persona (e.g. Cyborg, Noblewoman, Stowaway).

"Has anyone written any new books with Sherlock Holmes in them?"

The CHARACTER NAME INDEX lists the major characters named in the entries. This can help readers who remember some information about a book, but not an author or title.

"What has Debra White Smith written recently?"

The AUTHOR INDEX contains the names of all authors featured in the entries and those listed under "Other books you might like."

"I want to read a book that's similar to Michael Chabon's The Amazing Adventures of Kavalier & Clay."

The TITLE INDEX includes all main entry titles and all titles recommended under "Other books by the author" and "Other books you might like" in one alphabetical listing. Thus a reader can find a specific title, new or old, then go to that entry to find out what new titles are similar.

"I'm interested in books that depict military life."

The SUBJECT INDEX is an alphabetical listing of all the subjects covered by the main entry titles.

The indexes can also be used together to narrow down or broaden choices. A reader interested in Mysteries set in New York during the 19th century would consult the TIME PERIOD INDEX and GEOGRAPHIC INDEX to see which titles appear in both. Time Travel is a common theme in Science Fiction but occasionally appears in other genres such as Fantasy and Romance. Searching for this theme in other genres would enable a reader to cross over into previously unknown realms of reading experiences. And with the AUTHOR and TITLE indexes, which include all books listed under "Other books by the author" and "Other books you might like," it is easy to compile an extensive list of recommended reading, beginning with a recently published title or a classic from the past.

Also Available Online

The entries in this book can also be found in the online version of *What Do I Read Next?* on GaleNet. This electronic product encompasses over 100,000 books, including genre fiction, mainstream fiction, and nonfiction. All the books included in the online version are recommended by librarians or other experts, award winners, or appear on bestseller lists. The user-friendly functionality allows users to refine their searching by using several criteria, while making it easy to identify similar titles for further research and reading. The online version is updated with new information two times a year. For more information about *What Do I Read Next?* Online or GaleNet, please contact Gale Group, Inc.

Suggestions Are Welcome

The editors welcome any comments and suggestions for enhancing and improving *What Do I Read Next?* Please address correspondence to the Editors, *What Do I Read Next?*, at the following address:

Gale Group
27500 Drake Rd.
Farmington Hills, MI 48331-3535
Phone: 248-699-GALE
Toll-free: 800-347-GALE
Fax: 248-699-8054

About the Genre Experts

Neil Barron Barron, the coordinator of the Science Fiction, Fantasy, and Horror Fiction sections, is the editor of the reader guides *Anatomy of Wonder: A Critical Guide to Science Fiction* (Libraries Unlimited, 5th ed., 2004) and *Fantasy and Horror: A Critical and Historical Guide to Literature, Illustration, Film, TV, Radio, and the Internet* (Scarecrow Press, 1999).

Tom Barton Barton (Popular Fiction) is a reference librarian at the Rebecca Crown Library, Dominican University in River Forest, Illinois. A former journalist and community organizer, Barton lives in the West Beverly neighborhood of Chicago.

Daniel S. Burt Burt (Historical Fiction) is a writer and college professor who teaches graduate literature courses at Wesleyan University in Middletown, Connecticut, where he was a dean for nine years. He is the author of *The Chronology of American Literature* (Houghton Mifflin, 2004), *What Historical Novel Do I Read Next?* Volumes 1-3 (Gale, 1997-2003), *The Novel 100* (Facts on File, 2003), *The Literary 100* (Facts on File, 2001), *The Biography Book* (Greenwood/Oryx, 2001), and the forthcoming *Drama 100* (Facts on File, 2006). He lives with his wife on Cape Cod, Massachusetts.

Melissa Hudak Hudak (Inspirational Fiction) is a medical librarian for Methodist Medical Center in Peoria, Illinois. She was previously employed in public libraries and wrote a column on inspirational literature for *Library Journal*.

D.R. Meredith Meredith (Western Fiction) is a full time writer of western historical novels and three mystery series. The award-winning Sheriff series are western mysteries set in rural Texas. *The Sheriff and the Panhandle Murders* and *The Sheriff and the Branding Iron Murders* were actually first published as Westerns (Walker, 1984 and 1985). *Murder by Impulse* (Ballantine, 1988) and *Murder by Deception* (Ballantine, 1989) were both nominated for the Anthony Award. Her latest title in the Megan Clark series is *By Hook or by Book* (Berkley, 2000). In addition to writing, she is book review editor for *Roundup Magazine*, reviews western literature for the *Amarillo Globe-News*, is a speaker at writers' conferences, colleges and universities, libraries, and civic clubs, and is Liaison Chairperson for the American Crime Writers League. She is a member of Western Writers of America, Mystery Writers of America, and Sisters in Crime.

Kristin Ramsdell Ramsdell (Romance Fiction) is a librarian at California State University, Hayward and is a nationally known speaker and consultant on the subject of romance fiction. Besides writing articles about the romance genre, she writes a romance review column for *Library Journal* and is the author of *Romance Fiction: A Guide to the Genre* (Libraries Unlimited, 1999) and its predecessor, *Happily Ever After: A Guide to Reading Interests in Romance Fiction* (Libraries Unlimited, 1987). She was named Librarian of the Year by Romance Writers of America in 1996.

Tom & Enid Schantz This couple (Mystery Fiction) has been in the mystery business for nearly 35 years. From 1970 to 1980 they ran a rare and out of print mail order business as The Aspen Bookhouse and later as The Rue Morgue Mystery Bookshop. Between 1980 and 2000, they operated a retail mystery bookstore, The Rue Morgue, in Boulder, Colorado. During that same period, they edited a monthly publication, *The Purloined Letter*, which reviews all new mystery titles. They have written a monthly crime fiction column for the *Denver Post* since 1982. In the 1970s, they operated The Aspen Press, which published books of detective stories and items of Sherlockiana. In 1997, they founded The Rue Morgue Press, which continues to publish reprints of classic mysteries from the turn of the century to the 1960s. They continue to operate a mail order book business as The Rue Morgue, which specializes in vintage mystery fiction, and are the recipients of the 2001 Raven from the Mystery Writers of America in honor of their distinguished contribution to mystery bookselling and publishing.

Contributors

John Charles Charles (Romance Fiction), a reference librarian and retrospective fiction selector for the Scottsdale Public Library, was named 2002 Librarian of the Year by the Romance Writers of America. Charles reviews books for *Library Journal*, *Booklist*, and *VOYA* (*Voice of Youth Advocates*) and co-authors *VOYA's* annual "Clueless: Adult Mysteries with Young Adult Appeal" column. John Charles is co-author of *The Mystery Readers' Advisory: The Librarian's Clues to Murder and Mayhem* (ALA, 2001). Along with co-author Shelley Mosley, Charles has twice been the recipient of the Romance Writers of America's Veritas Award.

Don D'Ammassa D'Ammassa (Science Fiction and Fantasy) has been reading SF and fantasy for almost 40 years and has been the book reviewer for the *Chronicle*, formerly the *Science Fiction Chronicle*, for many years. He has had fiction published in fantastic magazines and anthologies and has contributed essays to a variety of reference books dealing with fantastic literature. D'Ammassa is the author of the novels *Blood Beast* (Windsor, 1988), *Servants of Chaos* (Leisure, 2002), *Scarab* (Five Star, 2004), *Haven* (Five Star, 2004), and the nonfiction work *Encyclopedia of Science Fiction* (Facts on File, 2005).

Stefan Dziemianowicz Dziemianowicz (Horror Fiction) is a medical editor for a New York-based law book publisher. He authored the definitive study, *The Annotated Guide to Unknown and Unknown Worlds* (Starmont House, 1991) and is also the author of *Bloody Mary and Other Tales for a Dark Night* (Barnes and Noble, 2000). He has co-edited numerous horror and mystery anthologies—among them the Bram Stoker Award-winning *Horrors! 365 Scary Stories* (Barnes and Noble, 1998). Dziemianowicz also writes features on horror fiction for *Publishers Weekly*.

Shelley Mosley Mosley (Romance Fiction), a library manager and romance genre specialist for the Glendale (AZ) Library System, was named 2001 Librarian of the Year by the Romance Writers of America. She writes romantic comedies with Deborah Mazoyer under the pen name Deborah Shelley. Their book, *Talk about Love*, was a Holt Medallion finalist for Best First Book. With John Charles, also a *What Do I Read Next?* contributor, she has won two Romance Writers of America's Veritas Awards. In addition to two newspaper columns, she reviews romance for *Booklist*. Mosley has written articles for *Wilson Library Bulletin*, *Library Journal*, *Romance Writer's Report*, and *VOYA*.

Key to Genre Terms

The following is a list of terms used to classify the story type of each novel included in What Do I Read Next? along with brief definitions of the terms. To find books that fall under a particular story type heading, see the Genre Index.

Action/Adventure ▮ Minimal detection; not usually espionage, but can contain rogue police or out of control spies.

Adult ▮ Fiction dealing with adult characters and mature, developed ideas.

Adventure ▮ The character(s) must face a series of obstacles, which may include monsters, conflict with other travelers, war, interference by supernatural elements, interference by nature, and so on.

Alternate History ▮ A story dealing with how society might have evolved if a specific historical event had happened differently, e.g., if the South had won the American Civil War.

Alternate Intelligence ▮ Story featuring an entity with a sense of identity and able to self-determine goals and actions. The natural or manufactured entity results from a synergy, generally unpredictable, of individual elements. This subgenre frequently involves a computer-type intelligence.

Alternate Universe ▮ More accurately, in most cases, alternate history, in which the South won the Civil War, the Nazis triumphed, etc. The idea is a venerable one in SF.

Alternate World ▮ The story starts out in the everyday world, but the main character is transported to an alternate/parallel world by supernatural means.

Amateur Detective ▮ Detective work is performed by a non-professional rather than by police or a private detective.

Americana ▮ A romance set in the present that features themes that are particularly American; often focuses on small-town life.

Ancient Evil Unleashed ▮ The evils may take familiar forms, like vampires undead for centuries, or malevolent ancient gods released from bondage by careless humans, or ancient prophecies wreaking havoc on today's world. The so-called *Cthulhu Mythos* originated by H.P. Lovecraft, in which *Cthulhu* is prominent among a pantheon of ancient evil gods, is a specific variation of this.

Anthology ▮ A collection of short stories by different authors, usually sharing a common theme.

Apocalyptic Horror ▮ Traditionally, horrors that signal or presage the end of the world, or the world of the characters, and the establishment of a new, possibly very sinister order.

Arts ▮ Fiction that incorporates some aspect of the arts, whether it be music, painting, drama, etc.

Biblical Fiction ▮ Novels that take their plots or characters from the Bible.

Black Magic ▮ Magic directed toward malevolent ends, as distinct from white magic, which is directed toward benevolent ends. Witch-craft is commonly thought of as a black art. Voodoo consists of mysterious rites and practices, including sorcery, magic and conjuration, and often has evil goals.

Carnival-Circus Horror ▮ Derived from its setting, especially the freakish world of the sideshow, in which the distorted or horrific is the norm and is sometimes used as a distorting mirror to reveal hidden selves.

Chase ▮ A traditional Western in which the action of the plot is based on some form of pursuit.

Child-in-Peril ▮ The innocence of childhood is often used to heighten the intensity and unpredictability of evil.

Collection ▮ A book of short stories by a single author.

Coming-of-Age ▮ A story in which the primary character is a young person, usually a teenager. The growth of maturity is chronicled.

Contemporary ▮ A story set in the present.

Contemporary/Exotic ▮ Set in the present but with an especially unusual or exotic setting, e.g., the tent of a desert sheik or a boat on the Amazon.

Contemporary/Fantasy ▮ A contemporary story that makes use of fantasy or supernatural elements.

Contemporary/Innocent ▮ Story set in the present that contains little or no sex.

Contemporary/Mainstream ▮ A story set in the present that would be more properly categorized as general fiction rather than a work in a specific genre.

Contemporary Realism ▮ An accurate representation of characters, settings, ideas, themes in the present day. Not idealistic in nature.

Curse ▮ Words said when someone wishes evil or harm on someone or something, such as a witch's or prophet's curse.

Cyberpunk ▮ Usually applied to the stories by a group of writers who became prominent in the mid-1980s, such as William Gibson and his *Necromancer* (1984). The "cyber" is derived from cybernetics, nominally the study of control and communications in machines. These books also feature a downbeat, punk sensibility reminiscent of the hardboiled school of detective fiction writers.

Disaster ▮ A tale recounting some event or events seriously disruptive of the social fabric but not as serious as a holocaust.

Domestic ▮ Fiction relating to household and family matters. Concerned with psychological and emotional needs of family members.

Doppelganger ▮ A double or alter ego, popularized in the works of E.T.A. Hoffmann, Edgar Allan Poe, and Robert Louis Stevenson.

Dystopian ∎ The antonym of utopian, sometimes called anti-utopian, in which traditionally positive utopian themes are treated satirically or ironically and the mood is downbeat or satiric.

End of the World ∎ A story that concerns the last events following some sort of disaster.

Erotic Horror ∎ Sexuality and horror are often argued to be inextricably linked, as in Bram Stoker's *Dracula* and Sheridan Le Fanu's "Carmilla," although others have argued that they are antithetical. Sexuality became increasingly explicit in the 1980s, sometimes verging on the pornographic, as in Brett Easton Ellis' *American Psycho*.

Espionage ∎ Involving the CIA, KGB, or other organizations whose main focus is the collection of information from the other side. Can be either violent or quiet.

Espionage Thriller ∎ Plot contains a high level of action and suspense relating to espionage.

Ethnic ∎ A work in which the ethnic background of the characters is integral to the story. Usually the focus is on an American ethnic minority group (e.g., African American, Asian American, Native American, Latino) and the two main characters are members of this group.

Evil Children ∎ The presumed innocence of a child is replaced with adult-like malevolence and cunning, contradicting the reader's usual expectations.

Family Saga ∎ Stories focusing on the problems or concerns of a family; estrangement and reunion are common themes.

Fantasy ∎ A story that contains some fantasy or supernatural elements.

Femme Fatale ∎ A seductress for whom men abandon careers, families, and responsibilities and who feels no pity or compunction in return; a common figure in history and literature.

First Contact ∎ Any story about the initial meeting or communication of humans with extraterrestrials or aliens. The term may take its name from the eponymous 1945 story by Murray Leinster.

Future Shock ∎ A journalistic term derived from Alvin Toffler's 1970 book and which refers to the alleged disorientation resulting from rapid technological change.

Futuristic ∎ A story with a science fiction setting. Often these stories are set on other planets, aboard spaceships or space stations, or on Earth in an imaginary future or, in some cases, past.

Gay/Lesbian Fiction ∎ Stories portraying homosexual characters or themes.

Generation Starship ∎ If pseudoscientific explanations involving faster-than-light drives are rejected, then the time required for interstellar travel will encompass many human generations.

Genetic Manipulation ∎ Sometimes called genetic engineering, this assumes that the knowledge exists to shape creatures, human or otherwise, using genetic means, as in *Brave New World* (1932).

Ghost Story ∎ The spirits of the dead, who can be benevolent, as in Charles Dickens, or malevolent, as in the tales of M.R. James.

Gothic ∎ A story with a strong mystery suspense plot that emphasizes mood, atmosphere, and/or supernatural or paranormal elements. Unexplained events, ancient family secrets, and a general feeling of impending doom often characterize these tales. These stories are most often set in the past.

Gothic Family Chronicle ∎ A story often covering several generations of a family, many of whose members are typically evil, perverted, or loathsome, and in which family violence is common. The family may live in a decaying mansion suggestive of those in 18th-century Gothic novels.

Hard Science Fiction ∎ Stories in which the author adheres with varying degrees of rigor to scientific principles believed to be true at the time of writing, principles derived from hard (physical, biological) rather than soft (social) sciences.

Haunted House ∎ Literally, a house visited by ghosts, usually with evil intentions in horror fiction, but sometimes the subject of comedy.

Historical ∎ Set in an earlier time frame than the present.

Historical/American Civil War ∎ Set during the American Civil War, 1861-1865.

Historical/American Revolution ∎ Set during the American Revolutionary period.

Historical/American West ∎ Set in the Western portion of the United States, usually during the second half of the 19th century. Stories often involve the hardships of pioneer life (Indian raids, range wars, climatic disasters, etc.) and the main characters (most often the hero) can be of Native American extraction.

Historical/American West Coast ∎ Set in the American Far West (California, Oregon, Washington, or Alaska). Stories often focus on the Gold Rush and the tension between Spanish Land Grant families and immigrants from the Pacific Rim, usually China.

Historical/Americana ∎ A story dealing with themes unique to the American experience.

Historical/Ancient Egypt ∎ A novel set during the time of the pharaohs from the fourth century B.C. to the first century A.D. and the absorption of Egypt into the Roman Empire.

Historical/Ancient Greece ∎ Set during the flowering of the ancient Greek civilization, particularly during the age of Periculos in the 5th century B.C.

Historical/Ancient Rome ∎ Covering the history of Rome from its founding and the Roman Republic before Augustus through the decline and fall of the Roman Empire in the fifth century.

Historical/Antebellum American South ∎ Set in the American Old South (prior to the Civil War).

Historical/Canadian West ∎ Set in the western or frontier portions of Canada, usually during the 19th century. Stories most often revolve around the hardships of frontier life.

Historical/Colonial America ∎ Set in America before the American Revolution, 1620-1775. Stories featuring the Jamestown Colony, the Salem Witch Trials, and the French and Indian Wars are especially popular.

Historical/Depression Era ∎ Set mainly in America during the period of economic hardship brought on by the 1929 Stock Market Crash that continued throughout the 1930s.

Historical/Edwardian ∎ Set during the reign of Edward VII of England, 1901-1910.

Historical/Elizabethan ∎ A novel set during the reign of Elizabeth I of England (1558-1603). There is some overlap with the last part of the Historical Renaissance category but the emphasis is British.

Historical/Exotic ∎ Setting is an unusual or exotic place.

Historical/Fantasy ∎ A historical work that makes use of fantasy or supernatural elements.

Historical/French Revolution ∎ Set during the French Revolution, 1789-1795.

Historical/Georgian ∎ Set during the reigns of the first three "Georges" of England. Roughly corresponds to the 18th century. Stories often focus on the Jacobite Rebellions and the escapades of Bonnie Prince Charlie.

Historical/Mainstream ❚ Historical fiction that would be more properly categorized as fiction rather than a specific genre.

Historical/Medieval ❚ Set during the Middle Ages, approximately the fifth through the fifteenth centuries. Stories feature battles, raids, crusades, and court intrigues; plot-lines associated with the Battle of Hastings (1066) are especially popular.

Historical/Napoleonic Wars ❚ Set between 1803-1815 during the wars waged by and against France under Napoleon Bonaparte.

Historical/Post-American Civil War ❚ Set in the years following the Civil War/War Between the States, generally from 1865 into the 1870s.

Historical/Post-American Revolution ❚ Set in the years immediately following the Civil War, 1865-1870s.

Historical/Post-French Revolution ❚ Set during the years immediately following the French Revolution; stories usually take place in France or England.

Historical/Pre-History ❚ Set in the years before the Middle Ages.

Historical/Regency ❚ A novel that is set during the Regency period (1811-1820).

Historical/Renaissance ❚ Novel set in the years of the Renaissance in Europe, generally lasting from the 14th through the 17th centuries.

Historical/Roaring Twenties ❚ Usually has an American setting and takes place in the 1920s.

Historical/Russian Revolution ❚ These stories are set around and during the 1917 Russian Revolution.

Historical/Seventeenth Century ❚ A work of fiction set during the 17th century. Stories of this type often center around the clashes between the Royalists and the Cromwellians and the Restoration.

Historical/Victorian ❚ Set during the reign of Queen Victoria, 1837-1901. This designation does not include works with a predominately American setting.

Historical/Victorian America ❚ Set in America, usually the Eastern part, during the Victorian Period, 1837-1901.

Historical/War of 1812 ❚ Set during the British-U.S. conflict which lasted from 1812 to 1814.

Historical/World War I ❚ Set during the First World War, 1914-1918.

Historical/World War II ❚ Set in the years of the Second World War, 1939-1945.

Holiday Themes ❚ Fiction that focuses on or is set during a particular holiday or holiday season (e.g., Christmas, Valentine's Day, Mardi Gras).

Horror ❚ Refers to stories in which interest in the events, the intellectual puzzle characteristic of much of SF, is subordinated to a feeling of terror or horror by the reader, which could result from a variety of causes, including a disaster or an invasion of earth.

Humor ❚ Story with an amusing story line.

Immortality ❚ Usually includes extreme longevity, resulting from fountains of youth, elixirs, or something with a pseudoscientific basis.

Indian Culture ❚ These novels center on the lives, customs, and cultures of characters who are American Indians or who lived among the Indians.

Indian Wars ❚ Often traditional Westerns, these stories are set during the period of the Indian wars and rely on this warfare for plots, characters, and themes.

Inspirational ❚ A novel with an uplifting, often Christian theme, and usually considered "innocent."

Invasion of Earth ❚ An extremely common theme, often paralleling historical events and reflecting fears of the time. Most invasions are depicted as malign, only occasionally benign.

Legal ❚ Main focus is on a lawyer, though it does not always involve courtroom action.

Legend ❚ A story based on a legend, myth, or fairy tale that has been rewritten.

Lesbian/Contemporary ❚ A story with lesbian protagonists set in the present.

Lesbian/Historical ❚ Historical fiction with lesbian protagonists.

Light Fantasy ❚ There is a great deal of humor throughout the story and it is almost guaranteed to have a happy ending.

Literary ❚ Relates to the nature and knowledge of literature; can be applied to setting or characters.

Lost Colony ❚ Stories centering around a colony on another world that loses contact with or is abandoned by its parent civilization and the type of society that evolves under those conditions. Conflict usually arises when contact is re-established between the colony and its home world.

Magic Conflict ❚ The main conflict of the story stems from magical interference. Protagonists may be caught in the middle of a conflict between sorcerers or may themselves be engaged in conflict with other sorcerers.

Magic Realism ❚ A style of prose fiction writing in which the author blends the realism of describing ordinary places and incidents with fantastic, dreamlike, or mythical events and does not differentiate between the real and the magical.

Man Alone ❚ A lone man, alienated from the society that would normally support him, faces overwhelming dangers.

Medical ❚ Stories in which medical themes are dominant.

Military ❚ Stories have a military theme; may deal with life in the armed forces or military battles.

Modern ❚ Reflection of the present time period.

Mountain Man ❚ Any story in which the principal characters are mountain men and women, living in mountain areas remote from civilization and depending upon their own resourcefulness for survival.

Multicultural ❚ A romance in which the ethnic background of the characters is integral to the story.

Mystery ❚ Usually a story where a crime occurs or a puzzle must be solved.

Mystical ❚ Fiction dealing with spiritual elements. Miraculous or supernatural characteristics of events, characters, settings, and themes.

Nature in Revolt ❚ Tales in which normally docile plants or animals suddenly turn against humankind, sometimes transformed (giant crabs resulting from radioactivity, predatory rats, plagues, blobs that threaten London or Miami, etc.).

Occult ❚ An adjective suggesting fiction based on a mystical or secret doctrine, but sometimes referring to supernatural fiction generally. Implies that there is a reality beyond the perceived world that only adepts can penetrate.

Paranormal ❚ Novel contains supernatural elements. Story may include ghosts, UFOs, aliens, demons, and haunted houses among other unexplained phenomena.

Parody ❚ A narrative that follows the form of the original but usually changes its sense to nonsense, thus making fun of the original or its ideas.

Police Procedural ▮ A story in which the action is centered around a police officer.

Political ▮ The novel deals with political issues that are skewed by the use and presence of fantastic elements.

Possession ▮ Domination, usually of humans, by evil spirits, demons, aliens, or other agencies in which one's own volition is replaced by an outside force.

Post-Disaster ▮ Story set in a much degraded environment, frequently involving a reduction in population and the resulting loss of access to processes, resources, technology, etc.

Post-Holocaust ▮ The events following a world-wide disaster, often the result of human folly rather than natural events (collision with a meteor, etc.).

Post-Nuclear Holocaust ▮ The events following a world-wide nuclear disaster.

Private Detective ▮ Usually detection, involving a professional for hire.

Psychic Powers ▮ Parapsychological or paranormal powers.

Psychological ▮ Fiction dealing with mental or emotional responses.

Psychological Suspense ▮ Tales in which the psychological exploration and quirks of characters generate suspense and plot.

Quest ▮ The central characters are on a journey filled with dangers to reach some worthwhile goal.

Ranch Life ▮ The basic cowboy story, in which the plot and characters are inextricably bound up in the workings of a ranch.

Reanimated Dead ▮ These can take many forms, such as mummies and zombies (often the result of Voodoo).

Regency ▮ A light romance involving the British upper classes, set during the Regency Period, 1811-1820. During this time, the Prince of Wales acted as Prince Regent because of the incapacity of his father, George III. In 1820, "Prinny" became George IV. These stories, in the style of Jane Austen, are essentially comedies of manners and the emphasis is on language, wit, and style. Georgette Heyer set the standard for the modern version of this genre. This designation is also given to stories of similar type that may not fit precisely within the Regency time period.

Reincarnation ▮ A tale in which the horror arises in connection with the reincarnation of one of the characters.

Religious ▮ Religion of any sort plays a primary role in the plot.

Revenge ▮ A character who has suffered an unjust loss returns to take vengeance. This is one of the most common traditional themes.

Robot Fiction ▮ From the Jewish Golem to the traditional clanking bucket of bolts to the human-like android, robots in various guises have been among us for centuries. The term comes from Karl Capek's play, *R.U.R.*, which stands for Rossum's Universal Robots. Robots are often surrogates for humans and may be treated seriously or comically.

Romance ▮ Stories involving love affairs and love stories; deals with the emotional attachments of the characters.

Romantic Suspense ▮ Romance with a strong mystery suspense plot. This is a broad category including works in the tradition of Mary Stewart, as well as the newer women-in-jeopardy tales by writers such as Mary Higgins Clark. These stories usually have contemporary settings but some are also set in the past.

Saga ▮ A multi-generational story that usually centers around one particular family and its trials, tribulations, successes, and loves.

Satanism ▮ Suggests worship of evil rather than benevolent gods, the antithesis of conventional theism, whether Christianity or other religions. Evil demons are Satan writ small and usually lack the awful majesty of their parent.

Satire ▮ Fiction written in a sarcastic and ironic way to ridicule human vices or follies; usually using an exaggeration of characteristics to stress a point.

Science Fantasy ▮ A somewhat vague term in which there are "rational" elements from SF and "magical" or "fanciful" elements from fantasy, which hopefully cohere in a plausible story.

Science Fiction ▮ Although the story has been classified in another genre, there are strong elements of science fiction.

Serial Killer ▮ A multiple murderer, going back to Bluebeard and up to Ed Gein, who inspired Robert Bloch's *Psycho*.

Series ▮ A number of books united either by continuing characters and situations or by a common theme. Series books may appear under a single author's name or each book in the series may be by a different author.

Small Town Horror ▮ The coziness and intimacy of a small community is disrupted by some sort of horrific happening, suggesting an unjustified placidity and complacency on the part of the citizens.

Space Colony ▮ A permanent space station, usually orbiting Earth but in principal located in deep space or near other planets or stars.

Space Opera ▮ Intergalactic adventures; westerns in space; a specialized form of the genre type Adventure.

Supernatural Vengeance ▮ Punishment inflicted by God or a god-like creature, whether justly or capriciously.

Sword and Sorcery ▮ Often a muscle-bound swordsman, who is innocent of thought and common sense, up against evil sorcerers and sorceresses, who naturally lose in the end because they are evil.

Techo-Horror ▮ Suggests a catastrophe with horrific elements resulting from a scientific miscalculation or technological hubris; Victor Frankenstein's unnamed monster or a plague resulting from a laboratory mishap.

Techno-Thriller ▮ Stories in which a technological development, such as an invention, is linked to a series of suspenseful (thrilling) events.

Theological ▮ Stories in which religion or religious belief plays an important role.

Time Travel ▮ A story in which characters from one time are transported either literally or in spirit to another time period. The time shifts are usually between the present and another historical period.

Traditional ▮ Traditional stories may deal with virtually any time period or situation, but they are related by shared conventions of setting and characterization.

Trail Drive ▮ Any story in which a cattle drive (or, more rarely, a drive of sheep or horses) is a major plot component.

UFO ▮ Unidentified Flying Objects, literally, although sometimes used more generally to refer to any object of mysterious origin or intent.

Urban ▮ Stories set in large cities; usually the tone of the novel is gritty and realistic and may involve issues such as drugs and gangs.

Utopia ▮ A large, often influential, story type that takes its name from Thomas More's 1516 book. Usually refers to a society considered better by the author, even if not perfect. Aldous Huxley's *Island* (1962) is a utopia, whereas his more famous *Brave New World* (1932) is a dark twin, a dystopia.

Vampire Story ▮ Based on mythical bloodsucking creatures possessing supernatural powers and various forms, both animal and human. The concept can be traced far back in history, long before Bram Stoker's famous novel, *Dracula*.

Wagon Train ▮ A book that deals with wagon trains traveling across the American West.

Werewolf Story ▮ *Were* is Old English for man, suggesting the ancient lineage of a creature that once dominated a world in which witches and sorcerers were equally feared. Sometimes used to refer to any shape shifter, whether wolves or other animals.

Wild Talents ▮ The phrase comes from Charles Fort's writings and usually refers to parapsychological powers such a telepathy, psychokinesis, and precognition, collectively called psychic or psi phenomena.

Witchcraft ▮ Characters either profess to be or are stigmatized as witches or warlocks, and practitioners of magic associated with witchcraft. This can include black magic or white magic (e.g., Wicca).

Young Adult ▮ A marketing term for publishers; one or more of the central characters is a teenager often testing his or her skills against adversity to achieve a greater degree of maturity and self-awareness. A category used by librarians to shelve books of likely appeal to teenage readers.

Young Readers ▮ A novel with characters, plot, and vocabulary primarily aimed at juveniles.

Award Winners

Mystery Awards
by Tom and Enid Schantz

The Agatha Awarded on April 30, 2005 at Malice Domestic XVII for works published in 2004. Nominations and voting by the membership. Books must be traditional mysteries that do not rely on excessive violence. The award is a teapot and is named, of course, for Agatha Christie.

Best Novel: *Birds of a Feather* by Jacqueline Winspear

Best First Novel: *Dating Dead Men* by Harley Jane Kozak

The Edgar Nominations and final voting by five-person committees composed of active members of the Mystery Writers of America. The awards for books published in 2004 were announced at the MWA annual banquet in New York City on April 28, 2005. The award is a statue of Edgar Allan Poe.

Grand Master: Marcia Muller

Best Novel: *California Girl* by T. Jefferson Parker

Best First Novel by an American Author: *Country of Origin* by Don Lee

Best Paperback Original: *The Confession* by Domenic Stansberry

Best Critical/Biographical: *The New Annotated Sherlock Holmes* edited by Leslie S. Klinger

Mary Higgins Clark Award: *Grave Endings* by Rochelle Krich

Gumshoe Awards Nominations and voting by the staff of Mystery Ink, an Internet mystery web forum. Their fourth annual awards were announced in March 2005.

Best Mystery: *Hard, Hard City* by Jim Fusilli

Best Thriller: *Rain Storm* by Barry Eisler

Best European Crime Novel: *The Return of the Dancing Master* by Henning Mankell

Best First Novel: *Misdemeanor Man* by Dylan Schaffer

Left Coast Crime Awards Nominations and voting by the membership of Left Coast Crime, at an annual convention held in February or March in a city in either the Mountain or Pacific time zones.

Bruce Alexander Award for the Best Historical Mystery: *The Witch in the Well* by Sharon Newman

The Calavera (special award given for the best mystery in the region defined by Left Coast Crime): *Grave Endings* by Rochelle Krich

The Lefty (for the best humorous mystery by an American): Two books tied for the award: *We'll Always Have Parrots* by Donna Andrews and *Blue Blood* by Susan McBride

Ross Thomas Award Named for the late thriller writer, this award is presented by the Midwest Chapter of the Mystery Writers of America at its annual "Dark and Stormy Nights Conference" for the best first line in a mystery or thriller published in 2004.

The Winner: *Ninja Soccer Moms* by Jennifer Apodaca. The line: "The thing about revenge is that it takes a woman who is well and truly pissed to get it right."

Romance Awards
by Kristin Ramsdell

As romance fiction has attained increased recognition as a legitimate literary genre, various publications, organizations, and groups have developed to support the interests of its writers and readers. As part of this mission, a number of these offer awards to recognize the accomplishments of the practitioners. Some awards are juried and are presented for excellence in quality and style of writing; others are based on popularity and are selected by the readers. Usually awards are given for a particular work by a particular writer; however, some awards are presented for a body of work produced over a number of years (a type of career award) and others are given for various types of contributions to romance fiction in general. The Romance Writers of America, *Romantic Times*, and RRA-L listserv are the sponsors of most of the awards listed below.

Romance Writers of America Awards These awards for excellence in romance fiction writing are presented by the Romance Writers of America at the annual RWA conference in July. The following awards were presented at the 2005 conference in Reno, Nevada.

RITA Awards for Published Novels These awards are presented by the Romance Writers of America for the best ro-

What Do I Read Next? 2005 • Volume 2

mance novel published during 2004. Named for Rita Clay Estrada, RWA's first president, RITAs for published works are given in a number of categories, some of which have changed over the years. This year's winners are as follows:

First Book: *Time Off for Good Behavior* by Lani Diane Rich

Traditional: *Christmas Eve Marriage* by Jessica Hart

Short Contemporary: *Miss Pruitt's Private Life* by Barbara McCauley

Long Contemporary: *John Riley's Girl* by Inglath Cooper

Regency Romance: *A Passionate Endeavor* by Sophia Nash

Romantic Suspense: *I'm Watching You* by Karen Rose

Paranormal: *Blue Moon* by Lori Handeland

Short Historical: *A Wanted Man* by Susan Kay Law

Single Title Contemporary: *Bet Me* by Jennifer Crusie

Long Historical: *Shadowheart* by Laura Kinsale

Inspirational: *Grounds to Believe* by Shelley Bates

Novella: "Her Best Enemy" by Maggie Shayne (included in the anthology *Night's Edge*)

Novel with Strong Romantic Elements: *A.K.A. Goddess* by Evelyn Vaughn

Golden Heart Awards Presented by the Romance Writers of America for the best romance novel manuscript by an unpublished writer. Golden Hearts are given in a number of categories, some of which have changed over the years. The 2005 awards are as follows:

Traditional: "Snow-White Wedding" by Jenna Ness

Short Contemporary: "Venus Rising" by Karina A. Bliss

Long Contemporary: "Finding Hope" by Kimberly M. Fisk

Romantic Suspense: "Dancing in the Dark" by Holli S. Bertram

Paranormal: "Sapphire Dreams" by Pamela P. Poulson

Regency: "Lady Wicked" by Nadele Jacobs

Long Historical: "Ruined" by Victoria H. Grondahl

Single Title Contemporary: "Hard Lies" by S. Lorelle Marinello

Short Historical: "Secrets of All Hearts" by Christine R. Merrill

Inspirational: "Autumn Rains" by Myra Langley Johnson

Young Adult: "Almost Cool: Confessions of the Popular Girl's Best Friend" by Julie Ann Linker

Novel with Strong Romantic Elements: "Viva Las Vegas" by Robin Flury

ARTemis Awards Presented by RWA in previous years for the best published romance novel cover. As of 2005, these awards have been discontinued.

WaldenBook/Borders Awards Presented by Walden-Book and Borders (BGI) separately and combined for the best-selling romances of the previous year. The following awards were for 2004 and were presented at the 2005 RWA Annual conference.

WaldenBook/Borders Awards

Historical Romance: *Slightly Tempted* by Mary Balogh

Contemporary Romance: *Blue Skies* by Catherine Anderson

Series Romance: *Pretending with the Playboy* by Cathleen Galitz

Contemporary Hardcover: *White Hot* by Sandra Brown

Historical Hardcover: *The Paid Companion* by Amanda Quick

Multicultural Author: *Edge of Midnight* by Beverly Jenkins

Paranormal Romance: *Night Play* by Sherrilyn Kenyon

Romantic Suspense: *Morning After* by Lisa Jackson

Romantic Comedy: *Code Name: Princess* by Christina Skye

Hardcover Debut: *Immortal Highlander* by Karen Marie Moning

Continuing Series: *Vision in Death* (21st in series) by J.D. Robb

Anthology: *Hot Blooded* by Christine Feehan, Maggie Shayne, Emma Holly, and Angela Knight

Borders Awards

Contemporary Romance: *The Secret Life of Bryan* by Lori Foster

Contemporary Hardcover: *Ain't She Sweet* by Susan Elizabeth Phillips

Romantic Suspense: *Dead Wrong* by Mariah Stewart

Romantic Comedy: *Hot and Bothered* by Susan Andersen

Romantic Times Bookclub *Reviewer's Choice Awards* Presented by *Romantic Times Bookclub Magazine* for outstanding romances published in the previous year. Selection is done by the *RT* romance reviewers. Categories may vary from year to year. The awards for books published in 2004 and announced at the *Romantic Times* Booklovers Convention in St. Louis, Missouri, April 28-May 1, 2005, are listed below.

Best First Series Romance: *I Shocked the Sheriff* by Mara Fox

Best Harlequin American: *The Wedding Rescue* by Dianne Castell

Best Harlequin Blaze: *Hot Sheets* by Jeanie London

Best Harlequin Flipside: *Found and Lost* by Holly Jacobs

Best Harlequin Intrigue: *Situation: Out of Control* by Debra Webb

Best Harlequin Presents: *The Stephanides Pregnancy* by Lynne Graham

Best Harlequin Romance: *A Family of His Own* by Liz Fielding

Best Harlequin Superromance: *The Unknown Daughter* by Anna DeStefano

Best Harlequin Temptation: *How to Be the Perfect Girlfriend* by Heather MacAllister

Best Silhouette Bombshell: *A.K.A. Goddess* by Evelyn Vaughn

Best Silhouette Desire: *Fit for a Sheikh* by Kristi Gold

Best Silhouette Intimate Moments: *Ghost of a Chance* by Nina Bruhns

Best Silhouette Romance: *The Marine Meets His Match* by Cathie Linz

Best Silhouette Special Edition: *The Other Brother* by Janis Reams Hudson

Best Steeple Hill Love Inspired: *Hosea's Bride* by Dorothy Clark

Best Inspirational Romance: *King's Ransom* by Jan Beazely and Thom Lemmons

Historical Romance of the Year: *Obsession* by Katherine Sutcliffe

Best First Historical Romance: *Rules of Engagement* by Kathryn Caskie

Best Historical Love & Laughter: *Miss Wonderful* by Loretta Chase

Best American-Set Historical Romance: *Moon in the Water* by Elizabeth Grayson

Best British Isles-Set Historical Romance: *Guilty Pleasures* by Laura Lee Guhrke

Best Regency-Set Historical Romance: *A Visit from Sir Nicholas* by Victoria Alexander

Best Medieval-Set Historical Romance: *Under a Wild Sky* by Sasha Lord

Best Historical Paranormal Fantasy: *Kiss of Fate* by Mary Jo Putney

Best Historical Romantic Adventure: *Heart of the Hunter* by Tina St. John

Best Historical Anthology: *The One That Got Away* by Victoria Alexander, Liz Carlyle, Eloisa James, and Cathy Maxwell

Best Sensual Historical Romance: *The Bookseller's Daughter* by Pam Rosenthal

Best Historical Fiction: *The Lady and the Unicorn* by Tracy Chevalier

Best Historical Saga: *The Princes of Ireland* by Edward Rutherford

Best Historical K.I.S.S. Hero: Duncan MacRae from *The Sweetest Sin* by Mary Reed McCall

Best Historical Romantic Mystery: *A Deal with the Devil* by Liz Carlyle

Best Erotic Romance: *The Forever Kiss* by Angela Knight

Best Regency Romance: *A Passionate Endeavor* by Sophia Nash

Best Science Fiction Novel: *Angel-Seeker* by Sharon Shinn

Best Fantasy Novel: *Dead Witch Walking* by Kim Harrison

Best Epic Fantasy Novel: *Wellspring of Chaos* by L.E. Modesitt, Jr.

Best Contemporary Romance: *Ring around My Heart* by Pat White

Best Romantic Suspense: *Lady Justice* by Vicki Hinze

Best Romantic Intrigue: *Falling Awake* by Jayne Ann Krentz

Best Futuristic Romance: *The Scarlet Empress* by Susan Grant

Best Vampire Romance: *Undead and Unemployed* by MaryJanice Davidson

Best Contemporary Paranormal Romance: *Industrial Magic* by Kelley Armstrong

Best Contemporary Novel (with romantic elements): *Northern Lights* by Nora Roberts

Best Multicultural Romance: *Finding Love Again* by AlTonya Washington

Best First Multicultural Romance: *Sweet Desire* by Christine Townsend

Best Small Press Paranormal & Futuristic: *Kindred Spirits* by CB Scott

Best Small Press Romance: *Deadly Obsession* by Jaycee Clark

Best Women's Fiction Novel: *Dance with Me* by Luanne Rice

Best Chick Lit: *Can You Keep a Secret?* by Sophie Kinsella

Best Young Adult: *The Truth about Forever* by Sarah Dessen

Best Contemporary Mystery: *Body Double* by Tess Gerritsen

Best P.I. Novel: *By a Spider's Thread* by Laura Lippman

Best Historical Mystery: *The Shifting Tide* by Anne Perry

Best First Mystery: *Skinny-Dipping* by Claire Matturro

Best Suspense: *Head Games* by Eileen Dreyer

Best Amateur Sleuth Novel: *Double Shot* by Diane Mott Davidson

Romantic Times Bookclub *Career Achievement Awards* Presented by *Romantic Times Bookclub Magazine* for outstanding career achievement. Awards announced at the *Romantic Times* Booklovers Convention in St. Louis, Missouri, April 28-May 1, 2005, are listed below.

Historical Romance: Maggie Osborne

British Isle Historical: Amanda Scott

Historical Storyteller of the Year: Lois Greiman

Innovative Historical Romance: Laura Kinsale

Series Romance: Lindsay McKenna

Series Romantic Suspense: Susan Kearney

Series Romantic Adventure: Amy J. Fetzer

Series Romance Love & Laughter: Holly Jacobs

Series Storyteller of the Year: Jean Brashear

Contemporary Romance: Catherine Anderson

Contemporary Novel: Kristin Hannah

Contemporary Romantic Suspense: Christina Skye

Contemporary New Reality: Deb Stover

Historical Mystery: Barbara Hambly

Mystery Series: Jan Burke

Female Sleuth Series: Sue Grafton

Suspense: Beverly Connor

Inspirational Romance: Catherine Palmer

Regency Romance: Allison Lane

Multicultural Romance: Bette Ford

RRA-L Awards Selected by the members of the RRA-L (Romance Readers Anonymous) electronic mailing list, these awards are usually published on the list in midwinter. The awards for books published in 2004 were listed in Volume 1 of *What Do I Read Next? 2004* and will not be repeated here. The awards for 2005 have not yet been determined and are not available as of this writing.

Awards information courtesy of Romance Writers of America, *Romantic Times* Publishing Group, and the RRA-L listserv.

Western Awards
by D.R. Meredith

Western Heritage Awards The Western Heritage Awards, more commonly called the Wranglers because they are replicas of a Charles Russell bronze of that name, are given by the National Cowboy Hall of Fame to the entries in western literature, music, film, and television which best represent matters relating to the American West or the western experience.

2005 Outstanding Novel: *And Not to Yield* by Randy Lee Eickhoff

Spur Awards The most widely known and perhaps the most beneficial to both author and publisher for that reason are the Spur awards presented by the Western Writers of America. They are presented at the annual Spur banquet in June of each year for novels published the previous calendar year. To avoid confusion, the Spurs are designated by the year of presentation rather than the year of publication. Thus the Spurs for 2005 are actually awarded to books published in 2004.

The number of Spurs awarded has not always remained constant, as the organization debates whether fiction should be divided into numerous categories, or whether a single Best Western Novel be designated regardless of its length or binding. In other words, should the Best Western Novel stand alone whether it is 100,000 or 65,000 words, historical or traditional, hardbound or paperback original? Or should the novel be categorized by length and binding?

At present, the Western Writers of America recognize three categories of Western novels: Best Western Novel, Best Novel of the West, and Best Paperback Original. The first two categories are divided by length; the Western Novel is defined as a novel of less than 100,000 words, while longer works are considered to be Novels of the West. Best Paperback Original is any book of any length which first appeared in soft cover.

Western Writers of America also awards Spurs to western nonfiction, juvenile fiction, short stories, short nonfiction, cover art, movie and television scripts, and poetry. The organization also presents the Medicine Pipe Award to the Best First Western Novel, and the Owen Wister Award for Lifetime Achievement in the Western field. Below are the winners in fiction categories for 2005 awarded to books published in 2004.

Best Western Novel: *Buy the Chief a Cadillac* by Rick Steber

Finalists: *Whose Names Are Unknown* by Sanora Babb, *Useful Girl* by Marcus Stevens

Best Novel of the West: *People of the Raven* by Kathleen O'Neal Gear and W. Michael Gear

Finalists: *Blood Kin* by Henry Chappell, *The Indian Agent* by Dan O'Brien

Best Original Mass-Market Paperback Novel: *Vengeance Valley* by Richard S. Wheeler

Finalists: *Brotherhood of Blood* by J. Lee Butts, *Staring Down the Devil* by Peter Brandvold

Best First Novel: *Field of Honor* by D.L. Birchfield

Finalists: *Santa Fe Passage* by Jon R. Bauman, *The Ghost Ocean* by Richard Benke

Best Juvenile Fiction: *Fire in the Hole!* by Mary Cronk Farrell

Finalists: *Worth* by Alexandria LaFaye, *Nothing Here but Stones* by Nancy Oswald

Fantastic Fiction Awards
by Neil Barron

Locus provides full listings of dozens of awards given throughout the year and provides a comprehensive historical and current list on its Web site, www.locusmag.com/SFawards. This

volume lists the awards given in 2005, and most books listed here are discussed in earlier volumes of *What Do I Read Next?*

Nebula Awards Given by the Science Fiction and Fantasy Writers of America, an organization with about 1,500 members, 1,100 of whom are eligible to vote for the Nebulas, although only a small fraction vote. The awards, in four fiction categories of varying length, are announced several months before the Hugos and may influence voting for them. Because of the Nebula rules, some books listed here were published prior to 2004. Only novels are listed here.

Best Novel: *Paladin of Souls* by Lois McMaster Bujold

Runners-up: *Down and Out in the Magic Kingdom* by Cory Doctorow, *Omega* by Jack McDevitt, *Cloud Atlas* by David Mitchell, *Perfect Circle* by Sean Stewart, and *The Knight* by Gene Wolfe

Damon Knight Memorial Grand Master: Anne McCaffrey

Bram Stoker Awards Active members of the Horror Writers Association vote for this award in 12 categories "for superior achievement" at an annual summer conference. See also the World Fantasy awards in Volume 1 of *What Do I Read Next? 2005*, whose nominated books often overlap this award.

Best Novel: *In the Night Room* by Peter Straub

Runners-up: *The Wind Caller* by P.D. Cacek, *The Dark Tower VII: The Dark Tower* by Stephen King, *Deep in the Darkness* by Michael Laimo

Best First Novel: (tie) *Covenant* by John Everson and *Stained* by Lee Thomas

Runners-up: *Black Fire* by James Kidman and *Move under Ground* by Nick Mamatas

Best Collection: *Fearful Symmetries* by Thomas F. Monteleone

Runners-up: *100 Jolts: Shockingly Short Stories* by Michael Arnzen, *The Machinery of Night* by Douglas Clegg, *Demonized* by Christopher Fowler, *Fears Unnamed* by Tim Lebbon

Best Anthology: *The Year's Best Fantasy and Horror: 17th Annual Collection* edited by Ellen Datlow, Kelly Link, and Gavin J. Grant

Runners-up: *Quietly Now* edited by Kealan-Patrick Burke, *The Many Faces of Van Helsing* edited by Jeanne Cavelos, *Shivers III* edited by Richard Chizmar, *Acquainted with the Night* edited by Barbara and Christopher Roden

Works for Younger Readers: (tie) *The Year's Best Fantasy and Horror: 17th Annual Collection* edited by Ellen Datlow, Kelly Link, and Gavin J. Grant and *Oddest Yet* by Steve Burt

Runners-up: *Robot Santa: The Further Adventures of Santa's Twin* by Dean Koontz and *Witch Season: Fall* by Jeff Mariotte

Lifetime Achievement Award: Michael Moorcock

International Horror Guild Award Normally presented each spring, but in 2005 presented late in the fall, too late for this volume.

Inspirational Fiction Awards
by Melissa Hudak

Gold Medallion Awards The Evangelical Christian Publishers Association has been presenting Gold Medallion Awards for over twenty-five years. Given in twenty categories, including Bibles, biographies, and reference works, there is one category for fiction. Publishers submit entries for consideration, which judges then narrow to five finalists. A panel of editors, retailers, and ministry leaders then selects the winners.

2005 Fiction Winner: *Oceans Apart* by Karen Kingsbury

Finalists: *The Yada Yada Prayer Group Gets Down* by Neta Jackson, *Rejoice* by Karen Kingsbury with Gary Smalley, *Reunion* by Karen Kingsbury with Gary Smalley, *Second Touch* by Bodie & Brock Thoene

Christy Awards The Christy Awards were implemented in 2000 to both encourage writers of inspirational fiction and to bring awareness to an often overlooked genre. The awards, named after the novel *Christy* by Catherine Marshall, are presented annually at the CBA International Convention. Publishers submit titles for consideration. Those titles are then judged by an expert panel. This year, three finalists were chosen in six categories.

General Winner: *Bad Ground* by W. Dale Cramer

Finalists: *No Dark Valley* by Jamie Langston Turner, *Tiger Lillie* by Lisa Samson

Visionary Winner: *The Shadow Within* by Karen Hancock

Finalists: *Beyond the Summerland* by L.B. Graham, *Dragonspell* by Donita K. Paul

Historical Winner: *King's Ransom* by Jan Beazely and Thom Lemmons

Finalists: *Retribution* by Randall Ingermanson, *Third Watch* by Bodie & Brock Thoene

Romance Winner: *Secrets* by Kristen Heitzmann

Finalists: *Wild Heather* by Catherine Palmer, *Winter Winds* by Gayle Roper

Suspense Winner: *Tiger in the Shadows* by Debbie Wilson

Finalists: *The Assignment* by Mark Andrew Olsen, *River's Edge* by Terri Blackstock

First Novel Winner: *The Mending String* by Cliff Coon

Finalists: *The Dead Don't Dance* by Charles Martin, *There Is a Wideness* by Mark McAllister

Popular Fiction Awards
by Tom Barton

Book Sense of the Year Award The American Booksellers Association, a non-profit trade association, gives an annual award for the book their members most enjoyed selling.

2005 Adult Fiction Winner: *Jonathan Strange & Mr. Norrell* by Susanna Clarke

Finalists: *Eventide* by Kent Haruf, *The Birth of Venus* by Sarah Dunant, *The Plot Against America* by Philip Roth, *The Shadow of the Wind* by Carlos Ruiz Zafon

National Book Critics Circle Award The award is given annually by the National Book Critics Circle, an organization of approximately 700 book reviewers, at an award ceremony recognizing the best book of the previous year.

2004 Winner: *Gilead* by Marilynne Robinson

Finalists: *The Dew Breaker* by Edwidge Danticat, *The Line of Beauty* by Alan Hollinghurst, *Cloud Atlas* by David Mitchell, *The Plot Against America* by Philip Roth

Pen/Faulkner Award The award is given annually to a distinguished work of fiction by a contemporary American author.

2005 Winner: *War Trash* by Ha Jin

Finalists: *The Green Lantern* by Jerome Charyn, *The Dew Breaker* by Edwidge Danticat, *Gilead* by Marilynne Robinson, *Prisoners of War* by Steve Yarbrough

Pulitzer Prize for Fiction The Pulitzer Prize, established in 1917, is awarded annually to an American author for fiction, preferably about American life.

2005 Winner: *Gilead* by Marilynne Robinson

Finalists: *War Trash* by Ha Jin, *An Unfinished Season* by Ward Just

Mystery Fiction in Review
by
Tom and Enid Schantz

In 1941, upon the 100th anniversary of the publication of the first recognized detective story, "Murders in the Rue Morgue" by Edgar Allan Poe, Howard Haycraft's groundbreaking history of detective fiction, *Murder for Pleasure*, was released. Never revised or truly updated, this useful and entertaining reference book remained in print into the 1990s. Mystery fiction is as popular today as it was then, but if Haycraft were alive in 2005 to update his history, it's doubtful he'd keep the same title. What he called mystery fiction has turned into crime fiction with angst seemingly replacing the puzzle as the key weapon in the mystery writer's arsenal. Today's writer usually ignores fair play and replaces it with the gross-out, believing that an inflated body count is more important than a carefully planted clue. The modern detective, whether amateur or professional, does very little detecting and is often more flawed than the villain. Perhaps this is just a natural reflection of our times as fiction imitates life. Violence is all about us, from Oklahoma City to the Twin Towers. Amber alerts flash across our television screens and freeways. Sadly, after Columbine and Green River, it's hard to use "murder" and "pleasure" in the same sentence.

Hard, that is, until you remember that mysteries are supposed to be escape fiction, a way to push those bloody headlines out of your mind and bring a quiet end to the day. Today, reading Patricia Cornwell or Kathy Reichs might induce nightmares, but only the most fragile of constitutions could be frightened from sleep by the exploits of Nero Wolfe or Hercule Poirot, where the murders, more often than not, took place offstage, and blood and gore were merely hinted at by a neat little bullet hole or an empty vial of arsenic. These traditional mysteries were not supposed to be realistic. They were intended to be fun and to provide a little intellectual diversion for readers who liked to match their sleuthing skills with those of the fictional detective. Books like these dominated the mystery bookshelves well into the 1980s. And they still write 'em like that, in many cases much better than they did during the Golden Age (1913-1947).

The people who write and read them gather each year in late April or early May in the Washington D.C. area at the Malice Domestic convention to celebrate the traditional mystery.

A commonly held misconception is that Malice Domestic showcases only "cozies," mysteries in which little old ladies who run knitting shops solve bloodless crimes with the aid of their feisty Siamese cat. Nothing could be further from the truth. Some of the finest mysteries of the past fifteen years have been honored at the convention. Winners of the Agatha for the best novel or best first novel include *Track of the Cat* by Nevada Barr, *Bootlegger's Daughter* (also an Edgar-winner) by Margaret Maron, *A Great Deliverance* by Elizabeth George, *Butcher's Hill* by Laura Lippman, *The Devil in Music* by the late Kate Ross (acknowledged by her peers as one of the best historical mystery writers of all time), *The Salaryman's Wife* by Sujata Massey, *She Walks These Hills* by Sharyn McCrumb, and *In the Bleak Midwinter* by Julia Spencer- Fleming. Many of these books, as well as other Agatha-nominated titles, have received considerable critical acclaim and have also been honored with Edgars, Anthonys, Leftys, and various other awards. Carolyn Hart's 2004 winner, *Letter from Home*, was also nominated for a Pulitzer Prize. This year's winners, Jacqueline Winspear's *Birds of a Feather* and Harley Jane Kozak's *Dating Dead Men*, made our own list of the best mysteries of the year in a past edition of *What Do I Read Next?* Other distinguished writers who have earned lifetime achievement awards from Malice Domestic are Tony Hillerman, Dick Francis, Mary Stewart, and Emma Lathen. Robert Barnard, the Evelyn Waugh of mystery fiction and a frequent Edgar nominee, will join their ranks in 2006. Peter Lovesey, recipient of the British Crime Writers Association's Diamond Dagger and perhaps the most accomplished mystery writer of his generation, made a special trip to the U.S. to attend this year's Malice Domestic where the Lifetime Achievement Award was bestowed upon H.R.F. Keating.

Early in 2005, David Morrell and Gayle Lynds formed Thriller Writers Inc., an organization modeled somewhat after the Private Eye Writers of America. In England, ''thriller'' is a term used to describe most crime fiction, but in the U.S. it is more commonly used to describe books in which action drives the plot, as in a Robert Ludlum book. The organization intends to present its own, as yet unnamed, awards.

Thrillers and traditional mysteries were both pretty much ignored when the Mystery Writers of America handed out its Edgars in late April 2005. Top honor for the best book of the year went to the very talented T. Jefferson Parker for *California Girl*. It's an undeniably good book, one that made our own *What Do I Read Next?* list, but no match for his 2002 winner, *Silent Joe*, unquestionably the best book in its year. Nor was it markedly superior to this year's Agatha winner, Winspear's *Birds of a Feather*, or several others that also failed even to be nominated, including Lisa Scottoline's *Killer Smile*, John Shannon's *Terminal Island*, John Lawton's *Bluffing Mr. Churchill*, or Laurie R. King's *The Game*. Don Lee's *Country of Origin* won for Best First Novel. It's a book that we somehow missed and it may well deserve to have won. But we fail to understand how Jeff Lindsay's extraordinary debut, *Darkly Dreaming Dexter*, failed even to be nominated in this category, given it has that dark subtexture so dearly loved by the Edgar committees. The pick for best paperback original, Domenic Stansberry's *The Confession*, produced a bit of controversy as well, with one of the female judges on the panel openly breaking from protocol and condemning the choice.

Speaking of women, while three women—Rhys Bowen for *Evan's Gate*, Laura Lippman for *By a Spider's Thread*, and Julia Spencer-Fleming for *Out of the Deep I Cry*—received best-novel nominations, not a single woman writer received an Edgar nomination in the Best First Novel or Best Paperback Original category. Women writers did dominate—as you would expect—the short list for the Mary Higgins Clark Award for the best book of the year in that bestselling author's style, which was announced by sponsor Simon & Schuster as part of the MWA weekend.

But enough of last year's best books. The first half of 2005 produced a number of equally excellent mysteries, including a few that may still be popular when this century comes to a close. For the most part, we've tried to avoid listing some of the bigger names (Michael Connelly, Harlan Coben, Lee Child, Robert Crais, George P. Pelecanos, for example), figuring that these authors have already found their audience. The following list contains comic extravaganzas, tales of gripping suspense, clever puzzles, promising debuts, and books with strong literary aspirations. But some of them, we're not ashamed to admit, are just for fun.

Owl's Well That Ends Well by Donna Andrews. With a title like this, you know this is one that falls into our ''just for fun'' category. In just a few short years, Andrews has established herself as the reigning queen of the screwball comedy. Meg Langslow is a plucky, in-your-face heroine with a large, extended dysfunctional family, all of whom are deftly showcased.

The Poet's Funeral by John M. Daniel. If you thought the world of small press poetry publishing was a gentleman's game, Daniel, a small press publisher himself, will set you straight. Set in Las Vegas in 1990 at the American Booksellers Association Convention (now Book Expo USA), it involves the murder of a poet who is more—and less—that she appears to be. Briskly paced and filled with irreverent digs at the publishing industry, it's a treat for bibliophiles and lovers of the satirical mystery.

Dating Is Murder by Harley Jane Kozak. The former actress (*Parenthood, Arachnophobia*) shows no sign of a sophomore jinx in this screwball tale involving a reality dating television show. Marketed as chick lit, it's much more, and Wollie Shelley is one of the more endearing mystery heroines to come along in quite a while.

Cavalcade by Walter Satterthwait. You may not think that the rise of Adolph Hitler could be fodder for a comic mystery, but this latest in the author's well-researched series about two 1920s-era Pinkerton agents would prove you wrong. His eye for the absurd has never been sharper, but there is a darkly haunting undercurrent to the story that will stay with you a long while.

The Point in the Market by Michael Pearce. The Mamur Zapt is the title given to a ranking British civil servant in colonial Egypt. The Great War casts its shadow on this installment, which may be the last in the series. The humor here is as dry as the Sahara.

Ruddy Gore by Kerry Greenwood. This wonderful series featuring a 1920s amateur Australian sleuth bombed when it was first published in the United States, perhaps because the title of the first book in the series, *Cocaine Blues*, failed to capture the flavor of the books. But the amusing adventures of the outrageously appealing Phryne Fisher, a sort of cross between Harriet Vane and Auntie Mame, are finding a new audience here with a new publisher.

The Circle by Peter Lovesey. One of Lovesey's best books, *Bloodhounds*, involved a club composed of mystery fans. Much the same flavor can be found in this tale set among members of a writers' critique group. Further, the author—who has always excelled at writing women characters—has given Henrietta Mallon, a police detective who played a supporting part in an earlier Peter Diamond mystery, the lead role here.

No Corners for the Devil by Olive Etchells. The title refers to an isolated round-shaped house in Cornwall, where a newly arrived family realizes that one of the villagers who welcomed them into their community just might be a murderer. A compassionate police inspector sorts

things out, and we're hoping it's the first book in a long series.

The Water Room by Christopher Fowler. Filled with arcane information about the hidden rivers than flow beneath the streets of London, this thoroughly entertaining book features the detectives of the Peculiar Crimes Unit, including an elderly odd-couple pair whose crotchety exchanges often had us laughing out loud. This original and inventive series is one of our favorite new discoveries.

To Kingdom Come by Will Thomas. As with the Kozak, there's no sophomore jinx here. Thomas brings 19th-century London alive in this vastly entertaining tale of Irish dynamiters who are foiled by a pair of resourceful private enquiry agents. The author owes a debt to the Sherlock Holmes stories, but the books in this series are uniquely his own.

Blood from a Stone by Donna Leon. New York publishing houses gave up on Leon when she failed to sell her first time out. Her atmospheric, traditional mysteries set in Venice and featuring a sophisticated, caring police detective appear to be gaining an ever-widening audience.

Mr. Lucky by James Swain. This is a fast, very funny look at high stakes gambling—and cheating—in Las Vegas by an author who knows what he's talking about. In addition, there's a satisfying father-son subplot.

Suicide Squeeze by Victor Gischler. This entertaining comedy features an unlikely hero, Conner Samson, who specializes in repossessing boats from owners who have defaulted on their payments. This time, however, it's what is on the boat that is truly valuable—a 1954 baseball card signed by Joe DiMaggio, Marilyn Monroe, and Billy Wilder.

The Italian Secretary by Caleb Carr. It may be sacrilege to say so, but this book is an example of a Sherlock Holmes pastiche that comes close to improving on the original model.

By this point, you may have noticed that all of the books recommended so far are either traditional mysteries or mysteries laced with a good deal of humor. If grim, hard-edged crime fiction is more to your liking, the following books are sure to please.

The Devil of Nanking by Mo Hayder. This is a gripping, nightmarish novel dealing with the atrocities committed by the Japanese during World War II, made even more appalling by the fact that the Japanese government still refuses to apologize for—or acknowledge—what happened. The story is told through the eyes of a fragile young Englishwoman who is trying to trace a bit of film footage shot in Nanking in 1937, and through journal entries written by an elderly survivor of the carnage.

Alibi by Joseph Kanon. The Venice of 1946 seems strangely unaffected by World War II. The victorious Allies are treated as just another wave of tourists, which is much the way Venetians treated the occupying Germans. Once again, Kanon excels at capturing the atmosphere of the World War II era. As a bonus, there's his trademark—a passionate love affair, this time between a former war crimes investigator and a holocaust survivor.

Dangerous Games by John Shannon. For our money, Shannon writes the Southern California private eye novel better than anyone else, but his books have never gotten the exposure they deserve. Much of this one is set against the sordid background of the adult film industry in the San Fernando Valley, but the strengths of its various characters usually outweigh their flaws, and there are some genuinely moving moments.

Hard Truth by Nevada Barr. Set in Rocky Mountain National Park, this is the darkest entry to date in the Anna Pigeon park ranger series, dealing with serial killers and pedophilia. But those who read her books for the breathtaking portraits she paints of our most beautiful national parks won't be disappointed.

Savage Garden by Denise Hamilton. The multiethnic neighborhoods of modern day Los Angeles come alive as reporter Eve Diamond looks into the murder of a Latina actress. This isn't Raymond Chandler's Southern California; if anything, it's far more dangerous.

Dead Run by P.J. Tracy. The three female members of Monkeewrench—a quirky Minneapolis software firm that has designed a program t track down serial killers—find themselves trapped in a small Minnesota town w population has been wiped out by nerve gas. The resourceful women acquit themsel very nicely in this latest book from a mother-daughter writing team.

Nightcrawlers by Bill Pronzini. Pronzini once thought about bringing an end to his Nameless Detective series, fearing the series might grow stale with age. Instead, he introduced two new regular characters and experimented with multiple points of view, giving the series a fresh new life. Here his private detectives investigate incidents of gay-bashing in San Francisco's Castro district.

Before the Frost by Henning Mankell. New York editors insist that Americans will only read mysteries set in either the United States or England. This innovative Swedish series just might prove them wrong. Series character Kurt Wallander takes a back seat to his rookie cop daughter in this installment.

The Magdalen Martyrs by Ken Bruen. Jack Taylor is a former Irish cop who got kicked off the force for alcoholism. He's still drinking, but if he can stay sober long enough to find out who once helped a friend's mother escape from a home for unwed mothers, he might find some redemption.

Desert Blood by Alicia Gaspar de Alba. The well-known Chicana poet explores social injustice along the border in this story about the murders of several young Mexican women whose bodies have been dumped in the desert. The murders are investigated by a lesbian Chicana academic who has come to Mexico to adopt a child.

Trip Wire by Charlotte Carter. This murder mystery set in 1968 Chicago with a young African-American protagonist paints a vivid portrait of a society still reeling from the police riots at the Democratic National Convention, as well as the assassinations of Martin Luther King and Robert Kennedy.

As good as those books are, a quick look at the publishers' catalogs of forthcoming titles gives us hope of discovering even better books in the second half of 2005. Mystery fiction is a hugely inclusive genre, encompassing a wide variety of books. The key to finding good mysteries is to set aside preconceived prejudices and at least sample all the genre has to offer. You'll be glad you did.

Mystery Titles

1

MEGAN ABBOTT

Die a Little

(New York: Simon & Schuster, 2005)

Story type: Amateur Detective
Subject(s): Brothers and Sisters; Secrets
Major character(s): Lora King, Teacher, Detective—Amateur
Time period(s): 1950s (1954)
Locale(s): Pasadena, California; Hollywood, California

Summary: Orphaned when they were young, Lora and her brother Bill have lived together contentedly for years. Then Bill, an investigator for the D.A.'s office, falls for Alice Steele, a smoldering beauty who's a seamstress in a Hollywood studio. Lora wants to like the mysterious Alice but can't, even after Bill and Alice marry and she and Alice play at being sisters. There's just something about the woman that sets off warning bells for Lora. So she starts investigating Alice's dark past, taking enormous risks and becoming dangerously fascinated by the increasingly ugly secrets she turns up. *Noir* in tone and concept, it's the author's first novel.

Where it's reviewed:
Booklist, January 1, 2005, page 824
Entertainment Weekly, February 18, 2005, page 81
Publishers Weekly, January 10, 2005, page 39

Other books you might like:
Andrew Bergman, *Tender Is LeVine*, 2001
James Ellroy, *L.A. Confidential*, 1990
Terence Faherty, *Come Back Dead*, 1997
Joe Gores, *Cases*, 1998
Richard Rayner, *The Devil's Wind*, 2005

2

BORIS AKUNIN (Pseudonym of Grigory Chkhartishvili)

The Turkish Gambit

(New York: Random House, 2005)

Story type: Historical/Victorian
Series: Erast Fandorin
Subject(s): War; Russian Empire; Espionage
Major character(s): Erast Fandorin, Diplomat, Detective—Police; Varvara Andreevna ''Varya'' Suvorova, Worker (telegraphist)
Time period(s): 1870s (1877)
Locale(s): Bulgaria

Summary: The quiet, diffident Fandorin plays a secondary role in this novel of intrigue and espionage during the war between Russia and Turkey in 1877. He's on a mission to the Bulgarian front when he meets up with Varya, a liberated young woman who has traveled from Moscow to find her fiance, a cryptographer who's been court-martialed for treason. She and Fandorin must prove him innocent in order to save his life and discover who is really spying on the Russian encampment. The third Fandorin novel to be published in the U.S., it's really the second in the series, and there are a total of 11 in print in Akunin's native Russia, where he is a mega-bestselling author. Translated from the Russian by Andrew Broomfield.

Where it's reviewed:
Entertainment Weekly, March 1, 2005, page 109
Library Journal, March 1, 2005, page 74
Publishers Weekly, February 21, 2005, page 161

Other books by the same author:
Murder on the Leviathan, 2004
The Winter Queen, 2003

Other books you might like:
Tom Braby, *The Master of Rain*, 2002
Robert Goddard, *In Pale Battalions*, 1988
Laurie R. King, *O Jerusalem*, 1999
Michael Pearce, *Dmitri and the Milk-Drinkers*, 1997

Arturo Perez-Reverte, *The Fencing Master*, 1999

3

SUSAN WITTIG ALBERT

Dead Man's Bones

(New York: Berkley, 2005)

Story type: Amateur Detective; Domestic
Series: China Bayles. Book 14
Subject(s): Small Town Life; Marriage; Theater
Major character(s): China Bayles, Herbalist, Detective—Amateur
Time period(s): 2000s
Locale(s): Pecan Springs, Texas

Summary: When China's teenage stepson turns up some 30-year-old skeletal remains while on an archaeological dig at a nearby cave, China is only mildly interested in the discovery, being preoccupied with the effects of the declining tourist trade on her business, her best friend Ruby's budding romance with a professor at the local college, and the opening of a new community theater in Pecan Springs. When a local handyman is shot and killed by one of the theater's elderly benefactors, China wonders if it was really an act of self-defense, as Jane Obermann claims, and she eventually comes to suspect that the skeleton discovered in the cave may be the key to the present-day mystery. Much herbal lore is woven into the pleasant story, which continues the chronicles of this former fast-track lawyer from Austin who gave it all up to open a small-town herb shop and tea room and has never looked back. Recipes from China's kitchen are included. The author has also begun a historical series featuring Beatrix Potter as the detective and, under the pseudonym Robin Paige, writes, with her husband Bill, a series set in Victorian times featuring American writer Kathryn Ardleigh.

Where it's reviewed:
Mystery News, April/May 2005, page 26
Publishers Weekly, March 21, 2005, page 39

Other books by the same author:
A Dilly of a Death, 2004
An Unthymely Death and Other Gardening Mysteries, 2003 (short stories)
Indigo Dying, 2003
Bloodroot, 2001
Mistletoe Man, 2000

Other books you might like:
Laura Childs, *The Theodosia Browning Series*, 2001-
Monica Ferris, *The Betsy Devonshire Series*, 1999-
Earlene Fowler, *The Benni Harper Series*, 1994-
Sarah Graves, *The Jacobia Tiptree Series*, 1998-
Janis Harrison, *The Bretta Solomon Series*, 1999-

4

BRUCE ALEXANDER (Pseudonym of Bruce Cook)

Rules of Engagement

(New York: Putnam, 2005)

Story type: Historical/Georgian

Series: Sir John Fielding. Book 11
Subject(s): Social Classes; Suicide
Major character(s): Sir John Fielding, Historical Figure, Judge (magistrate); Jeremy Proctor, Assistant
Time period(s): 1770s (1775)
Locale(s): London, England

Summary: Jeremy Proctor is a former guttersnipe who was plucked from the streets and saved from a life of poverty and crime by the legendary blind magistrate Sir John Fielding, brother of novelist Henry Fielding and founder of the Bow Street Runners. Jeremy became his ward and assistant in crime-solving and gradually took over more of the sleuthing in this splendid historical series, which was cut short by the author's death in 2003. Here, the detecting duo investigate the strange death of Lord Francis Lammermoor, who was working on legislation to quell the rebellion fomenting in America. In full view of at least a dozen witnesses, Lammermoor plunged into the Thames from Westminster Bridge. Ruled a suicide, the bizarre act is eventually linked with the arrival in London of a doctor who is a student of Dr. Anton Mesmer and whose patron is Lammermoor's widow. Did some form of hypnotism play a part in the apparent suicide? This final posthumous installment was ably completed from the author's unfinished manuscript by his widow Judith Aller and crime novelist John Shannon.

Where it's reviewed:
Library Journal, February 1, 2005, page 56
Publishers Weekly, January 10, 2005, page 41

Other books by the same author:
The Price of Murder, 2003
An Experiment in Treason, 2002
Smuggler's Moon, 2001
The Color of Death, 2000
Death of a Colonial, 1999

Other books you might like:
Diana Gabaldon, *Lord John and the Private Matter*, 2003
Janet Gleeson, *The Grenadillo Box*, 2002
Robert Lee Hall, *The Benjamin Franklin Series*, 1988-
Deryn Lake, *The John Rawlings Series*, 1994-
Hannah March, *The Complaint of the Dove*, 2003

5

CONRAD ALLEN (Pseudonym of Keith Miles)

Murder on the Salsette

(New York: St. Martin's Minotaur, 2005)

Story type: Historical
Series: George Porter Dillman/Genevieve Masefield. Book 6
Subject(s): Ships; Voyages and Travels
Major character(s): George Porter Dillman, Detective—Private; Genevieve Masefield, Gentlewoman, Detective—Private
Time period(s): 1900s (1909)
Locale(s): *Salsette*, At Sea

Summary: George and Genevieve (now secretly married) are aboard the beautiful small luxury liner, the *Salsette*, as it sails from Bombay to Aden. Posing as passengers, they are really private detectives hired by the P & O line to keep an eye out

for smuggling, theft, and other crimes aboard the company's ships. Also on board are two Englishmen who obviously know and detest each other, an Indian mystic whom the detectives suspect of being a fraud, and a young woman traveling with her wheelchair-using mother. Before the ship reaches its destination, all these people are involved in some way in a murder, and it's up to George and Genevieve to find out who. As Edward Marston and Keith Miles, the author writes several other series set in a variety of time periods, mostly historical.

Where it's reviewed:
Booklist, January 1, 2005, page 824

Other books by the same author:
Murder on the Marmora, 2004
Murder on the Caronia, 2003
Murder on the Minnesota, 2002
Murder on the Mauretania, 2000
Murder on the Lusitania, 1999

Other books you might like:
Mary Kruger, *Honeymoon for Death*, 1995
Peter Lovesey, *The False Inspector Dew*, 1982
Sam McCarver, *The Case of Cabin 13*, 1999
Walter Satterthwait, *The Phil Beaumont/Jane Turner Series*, 1995-

---

6

RUDOLFO ANAYA

Jemez Spring

(Albuquerque: University of New Mexico Press, 2005)

Story type: Private Detective
Series: Sonny Baca. Book 4
Subject(s): Mexican Americans; Cultures and Customs; Supernatural
Major character(s): Sonny Baca, Detective—Private
Time period(s): 2000s
Locale(s): Albuquerque, New Mexico

Summary: From the dean of Chicano literature comes this long-awaited final installment in the Sonny Baca quartet, in which the Albuquerque private eye does battle again with his archenemy, the witch Raven. When the former governor of New Mexico is found dead at the Jemez Springs with four black feathers beside him, Sonny goes searching for Raven, after first communing with the spirit of his mentor Don Eliseo, who, along with the dreaming dog Chica, accompanies him on his quest. This time his enemy has set a nuclear device to go off in the Jemez Mountains, and Sonny must stop him before he succeeds.

Where it's reviewed:
Library Journal, December 2004, page 96

Other books by the same author:
Shaman Winter, 1999
Rio Grande Fall, 1996
Zia Summer, 1995

Other books you might like:
George Chesbro, *The Mongo Series*, 1977-
James D. Doss, *The Shaman Series*, 1994-

Tony Hillerman, *The Joe Leaphorn/Jim Chee Series*, 1970-
Jake Page, *The Stolen Gods*, 1993
Manuel Ramos, *The Luis Montez Series*, 1993-

7

DONNA ANDREWS

Owl's Well That Ends Well

(New York: St. Martin's Minotaur, 2005)

Story type: Humor; Amateur Detective
Series: Meg Langslow. Book 6
Subject(s): Collectors and Collecting; Family Life; Animals/Owls
Major character(s): Meg Langslow, Artisan (blacksmith), Detective—Amateur; Michael Waterston, Professor (drama), Actor (part-time)
Time period(s): 2000s
Locale(s): Caerphilly, Virginia

Summary: Whenever large numbers of Meg's eccentric extended family converge on one site, there's sure to be trouble, as well as plenty of laughs. Meg and Michael have just bought a large old Victorian house near Caerphilly, at a bargain price—not only because of its state of disrepair but because of the vast amount of junk that its previous owner accumulated in the house and its various outbuildings. So they are holding a gigantic, multi-family, two-acre yard sale, which is interrupted by the murder of a particularly greedy dealer in books and antiques, known to all as Gordon-you-thief. The presence of the police only increases attendance at the sale, which is temporarily shut down but is soon surrounded by secondary vendors along its perimeter. Meg's father is on hand, guarding the owls that are nesting in the barn, and so are her imperious mother and nerdy brother, the famously ill-tempered little dog Spike, and all the other familiar characters from this clever, award-winning series.

Other books by the same author:
We'll Always Have Parrots, 2004
Crouching Buzzard, Leaping Loon, 2003
Revenge of the Wrought Iron Flamingoes, 2001
Murder with Puffins, 2000
Murder with Peacocks, 1999

Other books you might like:
Joan Hess, *The Maggody Series*, 1987-
Toni L.P. Kelner, *Tight as a Tick*, 1998
Charlotte MacLeod, *The Sarah Kelling Series*, 1979-1998
Sharyn McCrumb, *The Elizabeth MacPherson Series*, 1984-
Gillian Roberts, *The Amanda Pepper Series*, 1987-

8

JENNIFER APODACA

Batteries Required

(New York: Kensington, 2005)

Story type: Amateur Detective; Humor
Series: Samantha Shaw. Book 4
Subject(s): Dating (Social Customs); Small Town Life; Romance

Major character(s): Samantha Shaw, Businesswoman, Detective—Amateur
Time period(s): 2000s
Locale(s): Lake Elsinore, California

Summary: Even though her own marriage went sour, Samantha has thrown herself into her dating-service business, Heart Mates, and into a new relationship with ex-cop Gabe Pulizzi. The business has as many downs as ups, things are a little rocky with Gabe, and her newly divorced friend Angel is starting her own lingerie business and has samples of some nifty sex toys she wants Sam to look at. Then Angel disappears and Sam looks to homicide detective Logan Vance (who moonlights as romance novelist R.V. Logan) to help find her. Sam doesn't think that Angel's ex-husband could have done it, but she's got her hands full keeping the naughty toys away from her two sons and dealing with the pressure to commit Gabe is putting on her.

Where it's reviewed:
Library Journal, April 1, 2005, page 74

Other books by the same author:
Ninja Soccer Moms, 2004
Dying to Meet You, 2003
Dating Can Be Murder, 2002

Other books you might like:
Nancy Bartholomew, *The Sierra Lavatoni Series*, 1998-
Nancy J. Cohen, *The Marla Shore Series*, 1999-
Selma Eichler, *The Desiree Shapiro Series*, 1994-
Judy Fitzwater, *The Jennifer March Series*, 1998-
Harley Jane Kozak, *The Wollie Shelley Series*, 2004-

9

NANCY ATHERTON

Aunt Dimity and the Next of Kin

(New York: Viking, 2005)

Story type: Amateur Detective
Series: Aunt Dimity. Book 10
Subject(s): Rural Life; Ghosts; Winter
Major character(s): Lori Shepherd, Volunteer, Detective—Amateur; Dimity Westwood, Spirit
Time period(s): 2000s
Locale(s): Finch, England (Cotswolds)

Summary: After a storybook marriage and a set of adorable twins (now five), Lori Shepherd still occasionally finds herself seeking guidance from Dimity Westwood, the benevolent spirit who brought Lori to her snug cottage in the Cotswolds and made possible her comfortable lifestyle. In need of a little break from her daily routine, kind-hearted Lori decides to volunteer at the local hospital, where she befriends patient Elizabeth Beacham, a retired secretary who appears to have no friends or family. When she dies, Miss Beacham leaves Lori the keys to her apartment and an invitation to take a keepsake from it. What Lori finds is a luxurious penthouse filled with valuable antiques—and a lot of questions about why a missing brother hasn't claimed his inheritance and who Miss Beacham really was. Turning to Aunt Dimity for help, Lori eventually manages to unravel the mystery. A recipe for Miss Beacham's raisin bread is included.

Where it's reviewed:
Booklist, January 1, 2005, page 825
Deadly Pleasures, Winter 2005, page 43
Publishers Weekly, January 17, 2005, page 38

Other books by the same author:
Aunt Dimity, Snowbound, 2004
Aunt Dimity Takes a Holiday, 2003
Aunt Dimity, Detective, 2001
Aunt Dimity Beats the Devil, 2000
Aunt Dimity's Christmas, 1999

Other books you might like:
Mignon F. Ballard, *The Augusta Goodnight Series*, 1999-
Simon Brett, *The Carol Seddon Series*, 2000-
Dorothy Cannell, *The Ellie Haskell Series*, 1984-
Charles Mathes, *The Girl at the End of the Line*, 1999
Mary Stewart, *Rose Cottage*, 1997

10

MIGNON F. BALLARD

Too Late for Angels

(New York: St. Martin's Minotaur, 2005)

Story type: Amateur Detective
Series: Augusta Goodnight. Book 5
Subject(s): Small Town Life; American South; Angels
Major character(s): Augusta Goodnight, Angel, Detective—Amateur; Lucy Nan Pilgrim, Widow(er)
Time period(s): 2000s
Locale(s): Stone's Throw, South Carolina

Summary: At loose ends since her husband died, Lucy Nan Pilgrim has just decided to rent out a room in her capacious old house when an elderly woman shows up at her door, insisting it's her house and that her mother lives there. The woman, who calls herself Shirley, may well be the long-lost cousin of Lucy's best friend Ellis, who vanished when she was a child over half a century ago. Before Lucy can get help for her strange visitor, the woman disappears, only to be found dead in the Methodist church parking lot. Then an even stranger visitor arrives at Lucy's house, wanting to rent her room: Augusta Goodnight, her substitute guardian angel, who brings strawberry muffins and an offer to help Lucy and Ellis solve the mystery. Recipes included.

Where it's reviewed:
Publishers Weekly, February 21, 2005, page 161
Romantic Times, April 2005, page 90

Other books by the same author:
The Angel Whispered Danger, 2003
Shadow of an Angel, 2002
An Angel to Die For, 2000
Angel at Troublesome Creek, 1999

Other books you might like:
Nancy Atherton, *The Aunt Dimity Series*, 1992-
Carolyn Haines, *The Sarah Booth Delaney Series*, 1999-
Charles Mathes, *The Girl at the End of the Line*, 1999
Sharyn McCrumb, *The Ballad Series*, 1990-
Susan Wade, *Walking Rain*, 1996

11

ROBERT BARNARD

The Graveyard Position

(New York: Scribner, 2005)

Story type: Traditional; Police Procedural
Series: Charlie Peace. Book 9
Subject(s): Family Relations; Inheritance
Major character(s): Merlyn Docherty, Lawyer; Charlie Peace, Police Officer
Time period(s): 2000s
Locale(s): London, England

Summary: After two decades abroad, his whereabouts unknown to all but his Aunt Clarissa, Merlyn Docherty returns to England for her funeral. He gets a chilly and skeptical reception from his assorted relatives, mostly because he has been named Clarissa's sole heir, and several members of this quarrelsome, highly dysfunctional clan even go so far as to challenge his identity. Merlyn left England and Clarissa, a self-styled clairvoyant, kept his whereabouts a secret because someone in the family wanted to see him dead. Merlyn, who's been living in Brussels and employed by the European Union, just wants to get his business over with and return to his sweetheart in Belgium, but an attempt on his life that destroys another complicates matters. To establish his identity and find out who's trying to kill him, he enlists the aid of Scotland Yarder Charlie Peace. There's the usual acerbic Barnard wit and enough good writing and characterization to make the story enjoyable despite the uncharacteristically static plot. The author has also written many stand-alones as well as a series about young Scotland Yard detective Perry Trethowan.

Where it's reviewed:
Mystery Scene, Spring 2005, page 74
Publishers Weekly, April 11, 2005, page 37

Other books by the same author:
The Mistress of Alderly, 2003
The Bones in the Attic, 2002
Unholy Dying, 2001
The Corpse in the Haworth Tandoori, 1999
The Bad Samaritan, 1995

Other books you might like:
Colin Dexter, *The Inspector Morse Series*, 1975-2000
Kate Ellis, *The Wesley Peterson Series*, 1999-
Reginald Hill, *The Dalziel/Pascoe Series*, 1970-
Peter Lovesey, *The Peter Diamond Series*, 1991-
Peter Robinson, *The Inspector Alan Banks Series*, 1987-

12

MICHAEL BARON (Pseudonym of Michael Kahn)

The Mourning Sexton

(New York: Doubleday, 2005)

Story type: Legal
Subject(s): Judaism; Law; Redemption
Major character(s): David Hirsch, Lawyer
Time period(s): 2000s
Locale(s): St. Louis, Missouri

Summary: The deeply flawed protagonist of this book (being misleadingly promoted as a first novel) is David Hirsch, once a powerful attorney with a top law firm who let his taste for risky pleasures destroy his career. After serving seven years in federal prison for embezzling over a million dollars from his firm, Hirsch is now working as a bankruptcy lawyer and rediscovering his Jewish faith. He's a *gabbai* at his local synagogue, where he rounds up the ten members needed to make up the *minyan* at the morning prayers. When an elderly member of the *minyan* asks for help in suing the corporation he thinks is responsible for his daughter's death in a car accident years earlier, Hirsch runs up against powerful adversaries involved in a deadly cover-up. With some help from an altruistic defense attorney the accident victim once worked for, he resolves to set things right, no matter what the cost to himself. Under his own name, the author has written a series of mysteries featuring St. Louis attorney Rachel Gold.

Where it's reviewed:
Booklist, February 1, 2005, page 944
Library Journal, February 15, 2005, page 113

Other books you might like:
John Grisham, *The Rainmaker*, 1995
John Lescroart, *The Dismas Hardy Series*, 1990-
Ronald Levitsky, *The Nate Rosen Series*, 1991-
Steve Martini, *The Paul Madriani Series*, 1992-
Scott Turow, *Reversible Errors*, 2002

13

NEVADA BARR

Hard Truth

(New York: Putnam, 2005)

Story type: Psychological Suspense; Action/Adventure
Series: Anna Pigeon. Book 13
Subject(s): Wilderness; Serial Killers; Abuse
Major character(s): Anna Pigeon, Ranger (National Park Service)
Time period(s): 2000s
Locale(s): Rocky Mountain National Park, Colorado

Summary: Ranger Anna Pigeon's latest assignment is beautiful Rocky Mountain National Park, and she's no sooner settled in than two teenage girls who have been missing for weeks appear at the campsite of Heath Jarrod, a woman climber who was paralyzed in a fall. A third girl who disappeared from the same religious retreat is still missing, and neither Heath nor Anna can find out what happened. Although they clash initially, Heath and Anna come to respect each other and team up to solve the mystery. It's a darker book than most in this outstanding series, dealing with such issues as pedophilia, religious cults, and serial murders, but the author still works in breathtaking descriptions of the mountain wilderness and creates believable and sympathetic characters as well.

Where it's reviewed:
Booklist, January 1, 2005, page 782
Library Journal, February 1, 2005, page 57
New York Times Book Review, March 27, 2005, page 21
Publishers Weekly, February 14, 2005, page 57

Other books by the same author:
High Country, 2004
Flashback, 2003
Hunting Season, 2002
Blood Lure, 2001
Deep South, 2000

Other books you might like:
C.J. Box, *The Joe Pickett Series*, 2001-
Steve Hamilton, *Winter of the Wolf Moon*, 2000
Clinton McKinzie, *Trial by Ice and Fire*, 2003
Jessica Speart, *The Rachel Porter Series*, 1997-
Dana Stabenow, *The Kate Shugak Series*, 1992-

14

STEPHANIE BARRON (Pseudonym of Francine Mathews)

Jane and His Lordship's Legacy

(New York: Bantam, 2005)

Story type: Historical/Regency
Series: Jane Austen. Book 8
Subject(s): Authors and Writers
Major character(s): Jane Austen, Historical Figure, Writer
    (novelist)
Time period(s): 1800s (1809)
Locale(s): Hampshire, England

Summary: Jane and her mother move into Chawton Cottage in
Hampshire, a converted alehouse owned by her brother. She's
then surprised to receive an unusual bequest from the late
Lord Harold Trowbridge: a large Bengal chest filled with his
personal papers, from which she is expected to write an
intimate biography of a man known as the Gentleman Rogue,
whom she once loved. The discovery of a body in the cottage
cellar quickly takes precedence over this bittersweet task.
Told in the form of a journal kept by Jane, the story incorporates historical events of the day and is always true to what is
known of Austen's whereabouts and personal life. As
Francine Mathews, the author also writes the Merry Folger
series about a young Nantucket police officer, as well as
stand-alone thrillers.

Where it's reviewed:
Library Journal, February 1, 2005, page 57
Publishers Weekly, February 14, 2005, page 57

Other books by the same author:
Jane and the Ghosts of Netley, 2003
Jane and the Prisoner of Wool House, 2001
Jane and the Stillroom Maid, 2000
Jane and the Genius of the Place, 1999
Jane and the Wandering Eye, 1998

Other books you might like:
T.F. Banks, *The Bow Street Runner Series*, 2001-
Carrie Bebris, *The Mr. & Mrs. Darcy Series*, 2004-
Wilder Perkins, *The Bartholomew Hoare Series*, 1998-2001
S.K. Rizzolo, *The Penelope Wolfe/John Chase Series*, 2002-
Kate Ross, *The Julian Kestrel Series*, 1993-1997

15

CYNTHIA BAXTER

Lead a Horse to Water

(New York: Bantam, 2005)

Story type: Amateur Detective
Series: Jessica Popper. Book 3
Subject(s): Animals/Dogs; Animals/Horses; Sports
Major character(s): Jessica Popper, Veterinarian, Detective—
    Amateur
Time period(s): 2000s
Locale(s): Long Island, New York

Summary: Jessica is called out to an elegant Long Island estate
owned by wealthy Andrew MacKinnon to check out the
sprained tendon of a prize horse and is distracted by the
handsome polo player who's taking his morning practice
nearby. The horse recovers, but the Argentine polo player is
poisoned to death, and Jessie can't get the incident out of her
mind. She manages to get herself invited to various events
hosted by the MacKinnons, where she does some discreet
snooping to find out who killed the handsome horseman. An
intricate plot and interesting animal lore keep this one going.

Where it's reviewed:
Publishers Weekly, April 18, 2005, page 49

Other books by the same author:
Dead Canaries Don't Sing, 2004
Putting on the Dog, 2004

Other books you might like:
Lydia Adamson, *The Dr. Deirdre Nightingale Series*, 1994-
Laura Crum, *The Gail McCarthy Series*, 1994-
Patricia Guiver, *The Delilah Doolittle Series*, 1997-
Lillian M. Roberts, *The Andi Pauling Series*, 1996-
Karen Ann Wilson, *The Samantha Holt Series*, 1994-

16

HOLLY BAXTER (Pseudonym of Paula Gosling)

Tears of the Dragon

(Scottsdale, Arizona: Poisoned Pen Press, 2005)

Story type: Historical/Depression Era; Amateur Detective
Series: Elodie Browne. Book 1
Subject(s): Radio; Chinese; Depression (Economic)
Major character(s): Elodie Browne, Writer (radio), Detec-
    tive—Amateur
Time period(s): 1930s
Locale(s): Chicago, Illinois

Summary: Elodie is one of four daughters living with their
widowed mother in 1930s Chicago. She's lucky to have a
good job, having been newly promoted from advertising
copywriter to working on a radio show she created with two
veteran radio writers. One night, to earn a little extra cash, she
helps a friend out by serving food at a party held by Lee
Chang, a wealthy importer of jade and other antiquities. A
murder that takes place on the premises is effectively hushed
up, and the ever-curious Ellie wonders why. There's a touch
of romance and plenty of background on Depression-era Chicago, riddled with crime and corruption, but the real charm of

this first in a new series is its pert, resilient young heroine. Under her real name, the author has written many mysteries, set in both her adopted England and her native Michigan.

Where it's reviewed:
Library Journal, May 1, 2005, page 65
Publishers Weekly, April 4, 2005, page 46

Other books you might like:
Jill Churchill, *The Grace & Favor Series*, 1999-
Max Allan Collins, *True Crime*, 1984
Sandra Dallas, *The Persian Pickle Club*, 1995
Hal Glatzer, *The Katy Green Series*, 2002-
Robert Goldsborough, *Three Strikes You're Dead*, 2005

17

M.C. BEATON (Pseudonym of Marion Chesney)

Death of a Bore
(New York: St. Martin's Minotaur, 2005)

Story type: Police Procedural; Traditional
Series: Hamish Macbeth. Book 21
Subject(s): Small Town Life; Authors and Writers; Romance
Major character(s): Hamish Macbeth, Police Officer (village constable)
Time period(s): 2000s
Locale(s): Lochdubh, Scotland

Summary: A serpent insinuates itself into the paradise of Lochdubh, a picture-perfect village in the Scottish Highlands, in the form of John Heppel, a visiting writer who invites the town's aspiring writers to join his writing circle. The villagers' initial enthusiasm turns to hatred when the dozen who join his group are humiliated by Heppel's arrogant criticism and bored to death with his egotistical ranting. It's no surprise when Heppel turns up dead, but village constable Hamish Macbeth is dismayed when the case brings his new boss, the fearsome Heather Meikle, to Lochdubh. As usual, Hamish keeps on dodging women and promotions, all the while refusing to play along with his superiors. The author also writes a series of English-village cozies featuring equally stubborn amateur sleuth Agatha Raisin.

Where it's reviewed:
Booklist, November 15, 2004, page 563
Library Journal, January 2005, page 38
Mystery News, February/March 2005, page 10
Publishers Weekly, January 1, 2005, page 84
Romantic Times, March 2005, page 86

Other books by the same author:
Death of a Poison Pen, 2004
Death of a Village, 2003
Death of a Celebrity, 2002
Death of a Dustman, 2001
A Highland Christmas, 2000

Other books you might like:
Rhys Bowen, *The Evan Evans Series*, 1997-
Gerald Hammond, *The Keith Calder Series*, 1979-
Jonathan Harrington, *The Danny O'Flaherty Series*, 1996-
Frank Parrish, *The Dan Mallett Series*, 1977-1993
Graham Thomas, *Malice in the Highlands*, 1998

18

CARRIE BEBRIS

Suspense and Sensibility
(New York: Forge, 2005)

Story type: Historical/Regency
Series: Mr. & Mrs. Darcy. Book 2
Subject(s): Literature; Country Life; Romance
Major character(s): Elizabeth Bennet Darcy, Gentlewoman, Spouse (of Fitzwilliam); Fitzwilliam Darcy, Gentleman, Spouse (of Elizabeth)
Time period(s): 1810s (1813)
Locale(s): Derbyshire, England; London, England

Summary: Although they long to enjoy the serenity of their country home, Pemberley, newlyweds Elizabeth and Fitzwilliam Darcy are obligated to return to London for the Season in order to introduce their younger sisters, Kitty Bennet and Georgina Darcy, to society—in other words, find suitable matches for them. Kitty is a particular problem as she has no money or social connections, so the Darcys are pleased when well-to-do Harry Dashwood shows an interest in her. However, the couple is no sooner engaged than Harry begins acting strangely and there are rumors of gambling and other imprudent behavior on his part.

Where it's reviewed:
Library Journal, February 1, 2005, page 57
Publishers Weekly, January 24, 2005, page 224

Other books by the same author:
Pride and Prescience, 2004

Other books you might like:
Stephanie Barron, *The Jane Austen Series*, 1996-
Wilder Perkins, *The Bartholomew Hoare Series*, 1998-2001
S.K. Rizzolo, *The Penelope Wolfe/John Chase Series*, 2002-
Rosemary Stevens, *The Beau Brummell Series*, 2000-
James Tully, *The Crimes of Charlotte Bronte*, 1999

19

STEVE BERRY

The Third Secret
(New York: Ballantine, 2005)

Story type: Action/Adventure
Subject(s): Catholicism; Papacy; Secrets
Major character(s): Colin Michener, Religious (priest), Secretary (to pope)
Time period(s): 2000s
Locale(s): Vatican City; Medjugorje, Bosnia-Hercegovina; Bamberg, Germany

Summary: In 1917, the Virgin Mary appeared to three children in Fatima, Portugal, and revealed to them three secrets, two of which were soon disclosed. The third remained hidden until the year 2000, but many still wonder if it was revealed in its entirety. In this novel set in the near future, a caretaker pope, Clement XV, installed upon the death of John Paul II, becomes obsessed with this third secret and finally sends his secretary, a conflicted young priest named Colin Michener, abroad to explore the matter. Meanwhile, a cardinal who

hopes to become the pope someday sees his chance to destroy Clement XV when a Romanian priest who has a connection to the secret is murdered. Michener eventually realizes that to reveal the third secret in its entirety will shake the foundations not only of the Roman Catholic Church but the world.

Where it's reviewed:
Booklist, March 15, 2005, page 45
Publishers Weekly, April 25, 2005, page 35

Other books by the same author:
The Romanov Prophecy, 2004
The Amber Room, 2003

Other books you might like:
Dan Brown, *The Da Vinci Code*, 2003
Daniel Easterman, *The Brotherhood of the Tomb*, 1990
Thomas Gifford, *The Assassini*, 1990
Katharine Neville, *The Eight*, 1989
Lewis Perdue, *Daughter of God*, 2000

20

SALLIE BISSELL

Legacy of Masks
(New York: Bantam, 2005)

Story type: Psychological Suspense
Series: Mary Crow. Book 4
Subject(s): Native Americans; Appalachia; Prejudice
Major character(s): Mary Crow, Lawyer, Indian (half-Cherokee)
Time period(s): 2000s (2004)
Locale(s): Pisgah County, North Carolina

Summary: Mary Crow, an assistant district attorney from Atlanta, returns to her native North Carolina mountains to be near the man she loves, Jonathan Walkingstick. She's been all but promised a job with the district attorney's office, but when she shows up for the interview, the position has been mysteriously filled, no doubt because of her Cherokee heritage and her history in the town. She has no choice but to enter into private practice, and her first client is Deke Keener, a pillar of the community who's a softball coach, church deacon, and successful businessman, and whom Mary thoroughly detests. When young Bethany Daws is found dead with a tomahawk buried in her head, everybody assumes her Cherokee boyfriend, Ridge Standingdeer, killed her. Mary wonders why Bethany seemed to be in fear of Keener and why so many young girls have gone missing in the region. It's evident early on that Keener is a vicious sexual predator who specializes in young girls, and the story hinges on how Mary goes after him and at the same time clears young Standingdeer of the murder.

Where it's reviewed:
Booklist, March 1, 2005, page 1144
Library Journal, December 2004, page 96
Mystery Scene, Spring 2005, page 72
Publishers Weekly, February 28, 2005, page 43
Romantic Times, April 2005, page 85

Other books by the same author:
Call the Devil by His Oldest Name, 2004
A Darker Justice, 2002
In the Forest of Harm, 2001

Other books you might like:
James W. Hall, *Forests of the Night*, 2005
Laurie R. King, *With Child*, 1996
Sharyn McCrumb, *The Ballad Series*, 1990-
Kathy Reichs, *Fatal Voyage*, 2001
Michael C. White, *A Dream of Wolves*, 2001

21

CARA BLACK

Murder in Clichy
(New York: Soho, 2005)

Story type: Private Detective
Series: Aimee Leduc. Book 5
Subject(s): Nuns; Vietnamese; Meditation
Major character(s): Aimee Leduc, Detective—Private; Rene Friant, Computer Expert
Time period(s): 2000s
Locale(s): Paris, France

Summary: Having recovered from the temporary blindness that struck her in her previous case, Aimee, at the urging of her partner Rene Friant, has taken up meditation under the tutelage of a Vietnamese nun, Linh. She's promised to avoid dangerous undertakings, but she unwittingly becomes involved in one when she agrees to do a favor for Linh and exchange an envelope for a package in Clichy, a Parisian neighborhood. The envelope's recipient, Thadee Baret, is shot before the exchange is made, and Aimee is left with a dead man in her arms, as well as a check for 50,000 francs and a bag full of precious jade. Next, Linh disappears, Aimee finds herself under surveillance, Rene is kidnapped, and if she's going to get out of this mess unharmed, she has to find out what's going on. As usual, the Parisian scene is vividly rendered.

Where it's reviewed:
Mystery News, February/March 2005, page 21
Publishers Weekly, December 20, 2004, page 39

Other books by the same author:
Murder in the Bastille, 2003
Murder in the Sentier, 2002
Murder in Belleville, 2000
Murder in the Marais, 1999

Other books you might like:
Norman Bogner, *To Die in Provence*, 1998
Dean Fuller, *A Death in Paris*, 1992
Jane Jakeman, *Death at Versailles*, 2003
Jake Lamar, *Rendezvous Eighteenth*, 2003
Peter Steiner, *A French Country Murder*, 2003

22

LAWRENCE BLOCK

All the Flowers Are Dying
(New York: William Morrow, 2005)

Story type: Private Detective
Series: Matt Scudder. Book 16
Subject(s): Serial Killers; Crime and Criminals; Violence

Major character(s): Matt Scudder, Detective—Private
Time period(s): 2000s
Locale(s): New York, New York (Manhattan)

Summary: Now in his sixties, semi-retired from his work as a private detective and long fully retired from drinking, Matt Scudder spends most of his time hanging out in AA meetings and coffee shops and relaxing with his wife Elaine, a former call girl. The good times come to a halt when a very nasty serial killer emerges to match wits with Scudder, one linked to the unresolved crimes in Scudder's last case, *Hope to Die.* This time it soon becomes obvious that Matt and Elaine will become his next targets if Matt doesn't find the psychopath first. All the old familiar characters from the series are present, and as is often the case, the violence is graphic and unsettling. The author, who has won numerous awards over the course of his long career, also writes several other series, including one featuring burglar/bookseller/detective Bernie Rhodenbarr, as well as numerous non-series crime novels.

Where it's reviewed:
Entertainment Weekly, February 25, 2005, page 106
Publishers Weekly, February 14, 2005, page 56
Romantic Times, April 2005, page 84

Other books by the same author:
Hope to Die, 2001
Everybody Dies, 1998
Even the Wicked, 1997
A Long Line of Dead Men, 1994
The Devil Knows You're Dead, 1993

Other books you might like:
Thomas Adcock, *The Neal Hockaday Series*, 1989-
James Lee Burke, *The Dave Robicheaux Series*, 1987-
Tucker Coe, *The Mitch Tobin Series*, 1966-1972
John Connolly, *The Charlie Parker Series*, 1999-
Stephen Greenleaf, *The John Marshall Tanner Series*, 1979-

23

ELIZABETH BLOOM (Pseudonym of Beth Saulnier)

See Isabelle Run

(New York: Mysterious, 2005)

Story type: Amateur Detective
Series: Isabelle Leonard. Book 1
Subject(s): Journalism; Business Enterprises
Major character(s): Isabelle Leonard, Journalist, Detective—Amateur
Time period(s): 2000s
Locale(s): New York, New York

Summary: Isabelle came to New York to be married, only to be left behind at the altar when her would-be groom ran off with another woman. Not one to stare a lemon in the face without whipping up some lemonade, Isabelle proceeded to dance on the table-tops at what was supposed to have been her reception. This got her noticed by the media (''Give 'Em Hell Isabelle!'') and landed her a job with the magazine arm of Becky Belden Enterprises, run by a sort of exuberant Martha Stewart type. It's a good thing, too, as Isabelle is broke and saddled with an expensive apartment she can't afford. The job is sweet, except that her supervisor and various co-workers

get themselves murdered, and then Isabelle finds herself in danger. Under her maiden name of Beth Saulnier, the author has published four novels featuring reporter Alex Bernier.

Where it's reviewed:
Booklist, January 1, 2005, page 825
Library Journal, January 2005, page 85
Publishers Weekly, February 7, 2005, page 46
Romantic Times, March 2005, page 87

Other books you might like:
Donna Andrews, *The Meg Langslow Series*, 1999-
Janet Evanovich, *The Stephanie Plum Series*, 1994-
Nancy Martin, *The Blackbird Sisters Series*, 2002-
Susan McBride, *Blue Blood*, 2004
Sarah Strohmeyer, *The Bubbles Yablonsky Series*, 2001-

24

GILES BLUNT

Black Fly Season

(New York: Putnam, 2005)

Story type: Police Procedural
Series: John Cardinal/Lise Delome. Book 3
Subject(s): Memory Loss; Cults; Gangs
Major character(s): John Cardinal, Detective—Homicide; Lise Delome, Detective—Homicide
Time period(s): 2000s
Locale(s): Algonquin Bay, Ontario, Canada

Summary: When a young woman stumbles into a tavern in the remote Ontario town of Algonquin Bay, covered with black flies and with a bullet hole in her skull, homicide detectives John Cardinal and Lise Delome are called in to find out what happened. Unfortunately, the woman is suffering from amnesia, with no recollection of what happened or who she is. As the homicide team investigates, they turn up links to a local motorcycle gang, drugs, and grisly ritual killings. Based on a true case on the U.S./Mexican border which involved a Cuban cult, but transposed to a rural Ontario setting, this haunting novel also features Red Bear, a man who proclaims himself to be an Ojibway shaman but is really the son of a Cuban prostitute and one of the more memorable sociopathic killers in the genre. His pursuers are not faceless cops, but very human characters with strengths, flaws, and problems of their own.

Where it's reviewed:
Maclean's, May 9, 2005, page 53
Publishers Weekly, May 9, 2005, page 44

Other books by the same author:
The Delicate Storm, 2003
Forty Words for Sorrow, 2001

Other books you might like:
Alex Abella, *Final Acts*, 2000
Arnaldo Correa, *Cold Havana Ground*, 2003
Donald Harstad, *The Carl Houseman Series*, 1998-
William Kent Krueger, *The Cork O'Connor Series*, 1998-
Ted Wood, *The Reed Bennett Series*, 1983-1995

25

PETER BOWEN

Stewball

(New York: St. Martin's Minotaur, 2005)

Story type: Amateur Detective
Series: Gabriel Du Pre. Book 12
Subject(s): American West; Small Town Life; Animals/ Horses
Major character(s): Gabriel Du Pre, Musician (roadhouse fiddler), Detective—Amateur
Time period(s): 2000s
Locale(s): Toussaint, Montana

Summary: Toussaint is one of those fictional small towns that's a microcosm of the larger world it occupies, and the part-Metis Indian fiddler and homespun philosopher Gabriel Du Pre is a sort of cockeyed Everyman. When his much-married Aunt Pauline shows up in town and tells her nephew that her current husband, Badger, has disappeared, Du Pre agrees to go looking for him. Badger turns up dead in the middle of the wilderness, and Du Pre's search for the killer leads him to the world of illegal brush racing, where huge bets are wagered by traveling horsemen on horse races held way out in the boondocks. The author's mannered but graceful prose is one of the hallmarks of this series, which is truly *sui generis* and definitely habit-forming.

Other books by the same author:
The Tumbler, 2004
Badlands, 2003
Ash Child, 2002
Cruzette and Maria, 2001
Stick Game, 2000

Other books you might like:
James Lee Burke, *Black Cherry Blues*, 1989
Margaret Coel, *Spirit Woman*, 2000
Hartley GoodWeather, *DreadfulWater Shows Up*, 2003
Jamie Harrison, *The Jules Clement Series*, 1995-
John Straley, *The Cecil Younger Series*, 1992-

26

RHYS BOWEN (Pseudonym of Janet Quin-Harkin)

In Like Flynn

(New York: St. Martin's Minotaur, 2005)

Story type: Historical/Edwardian; Private Detective
Series: Molly Murphy. Book 4
Subject(s): Irish Americans; Spiritualism; Kidnapping
Major character(s): Molly Murphy, Immigrant, Detective— Private
Time period(s): 1900s (1902)
Locale(s): New York, New York; Hudson Valley, New York

Summary: Recent immigrant Molly Murphy is now a full-fledged detective, having taken over the agency of her employer and mentor Paddy Riley following his death. Business has been slow, since few potential clients have any confidence in a woman investigator. So when her former boyfriend, NYPD Captain Daniel Sullivan, asks her to go undercover in the household of a wealthy Irish-American senator to expose a pair of spiritualist sisters whom the police suspect of being con artists, she agrees, especially with a typhoid epidemic raging in the city. When she arrives at the senator's Hudson Valley mansion, she discovers a kidnapping as well as fraud. The author also writes a charming contemporary series set in a Welsh village, featuring police constable Evan Evans.

Where it's reviewed:
Library Journal, February 1, 2005, page 57
Publishers Weekly, February 28, 2005, page 45

Other books by the same author:
For the Love of Mike, 2003
Death of Riley, 2002
Murphy's Law, 2001

Other books you might like:
Jeanne M. Dams, *The Hilda Johansson Series*, 1999-
Maan Meyers, *The House on Mulberry Street*, 1996
Cynthia Peale, *The White Crow*, 2002
Troy Soos, *Island of Tears*, 2001
Victoria Thompson, *The Sarah Brandt Series*, 1999-

27

DOROTHY BOWERS

Postscript to Poison

(Lyons, Colorado: Rue Morgue Press, 2005)

Story type: Traditional; Police Procedural
Series: Inspector Dan Pardoe. Book 1
Subject(s): Family Relations; Inheritance
Major character(s): Dan Pardoe, Police Officer (chief inspector); Tommy Salt, Police Officer (detective sergeant)
Time period(s): 1930s (ca. 1938)
Locale(s): Minsterbridge, England

Summary: Scotland Yarders Pardoe and Salt are called to the English cathedral town of Minsterbridge to work with the local constabulary when Cornelia Lackland, an old lady who ruled her household with an iron fist, is found dead from an apparent poisoner. Once a great beauty, she has used her late husband's fortune to control his granddaughters, and there is no shortage of suspects for Pardoe and Salt to investigate. Originally published in 1938, it marked the debut of a writer whom contemporaries hailed as the next Dorothy Sayers but whose career was cut short when she died of tuberculosis in 1948. This edition marks its first U.S. publication.

Where it's reviewed:
Library Journal, May 1, 2005, page 129

Other books by the same author:
The Bells of Old Bailey, 1947 (non-series)
Fear and Miss Betony, 1941
Deed Without a Name, 1940
Shadows Before, 1939 (reprinted in 2005)

Other books you might like:
Christianna Brand, *The Inspector Cockrill Series*, 1942-1955
Agatha Christie, *The Hercule Poirot Series*, 1920-1975
Ngaio Marsh, *The Roderick Alleyn Series*, 1934-1982
Dorothy L. Sayers, *The Lord Peter Wimsey Series*, 1923-1937
Josephine Tey, *The Inspector Alan Grant Series*, 1929-1952

28

DOROTHY BOWERS

Shadows Before

(Lyons, Colorado: Rue Morgue Press, 2005)

Story type: Traditional; Police Procedural
Series: Inspector Dan Pardoe. Book 2
Subject(s): Family Relations; Inheritance; Small Town Life
Major character(s): Dan Pardoe, Police Officer (chief inspector); Tommy Salt, Police Officer (detective sergeant)
Time period(s): 1930s (1939)
Locale(s): Cottlebury, England

Summary: Professor Matthew Weir was acquitted of poisoning his meddlesome sister-in-law in 1937 and moved his family to a Tudor manor house in the quiet village of Cottlebury, not far from Oxford. Then, in the spring of 1939, his own wife, an amateur herbalist, dies of poisoning, and the local police call for Inspector Pardoe and Sergeant Salt from Scotland Yard to make certain the case is thoroughly investigated. It's a case complicated by many suspects and a confusing will, and Pardoe and Salt are far from certain that the professor is the culprit in either case. Strong characterizations and a well-realized setting support the predictions of many contemporary critics that the author might have rivaled Dorothy Sayers or Agatha Christie had she lived longer. Originally published in 1939.

Other books by the same author:
The Bells of Old Bailey, 1947 (non-series)
Fear and Miss Betony, 1941
Deed Without a Name, 1940
Postscript to Poison, 1938 (reprinted in 2005)

Other books you might like:
Christianna Brand, *The Inspector Cockrill Series*, 1942-1955
Agatha Christie, *The Hercule Poirot Series*, 1920-1975
Ngaio Marsh, *The Roderick Alleyn Series*, 1934-1982
Dorothy L. Sayers, *The Lord Peter Wimsey Series*, 1923-1937
Josephine Tey, *The Inspector Alan Grant Series*, 1929-1952

29

C.J. BOX

Out of Range

(New York: Putnam, 2005)

Story type: Action/Adventure; Psychological Suspense
Series: Joe Pickett. Book 5
Subject(s): American West; Environment; Wildlife Conservation
Major character(s): Joe Pickett, Game Warden
Time period(s): 2000s
Locale(s): Jackson Hole, Wyoming

Summary: Joe Pickett is called away from his backwater post in a remote county of Wyoming when a fellow game warden and close friend commits suicide in trendy Jackson, in the heart of the spectacular Grand Tetons and a major draw for tourists and the rich and beautiful who yearn for the simple life. Unfortunately the new job means being separated from his wife Marybeth, who faces the pressures of keeping her family and business going in Joe's absence, as well as dealing with threatening phone calls that force her to turn to another man for support. Meanwhile, Joe has his own problems, with environmentalists and developers squaring off and hunters and animal rights activists clashing. Joe also disbelieves the official verdict that his friend's death was a suicide, and as he begins experiencing the same problems Jake did before he died—blackouts, amnesia, mood swings—he comes to believe that not only was Jake murdered but that he's the next likely target. Like the other books in this impressive series, it's strongly grounded in the natural landscape of the American West.

Where it's reviewed:
Library Journal, May 1, 2005, page 67
New York Times Book Review, May 8, 2005, page 23
Publishers Weekly, April 11, 2005, page 37

Other books by the same author:
Trophy Hunt, 2004
Winterkill, 2003
Savage Run, 2002
Open Season, 2001

Other books you might like:
Nevada Barr, *The Anna Pigeon Series*, 1993-
Gregory Bean, *The Harry Starbranch Series*, 1995-
Peter Bowen, *The Gabriel Du Pre Series*, 1994-
Michael McGarrity, *The Kevin Kerney Series*, 1996-
Clinton McKinzie, *The Edge of Justice*, 2002

30

LAURA BRADLEY (Pseudonym of Linda Zimmerhanzel)

Sprayed Stiff

(New York: Pocket, 2005)

Story type: Amateur Detective; Humor
Series: Reyn Marten Sawyer. Book 2
Subject(s): Beauty; Hair
Major character(s): Reyn Marten Sawyer, Hairdresser, Detective—Amateur; Jackson Scythe, Detective—Homicide
Time period(s): 2000s
Locale(s): San Antonio, Texas

Summary: Still mourning the loss of her mentor, Reyn has barely gotten back into the swim of things when she gets a late-night call from a wealthy client who can't get her hair to behave. Reluctantly she heads for Alexandra Barrister's palatial home, only to find Alexandra's mother with a hole in her chest and her hair arranged standing straight out from her head. Since she found the body, Reyn becomes a suspect in the murder, and as she snoops to solve it she keeps running into handsome homicide detective Jackson Scythe at every turn.

Other books by the same author:
The Brush-Off, 2004

Other books you might like:
Ellen Byerrum, *Killer Hair*, 2003
Nancy J. Cohen, *The Marla Shore Series*, 1999-
Sophie Dunbar, *The Claire Claiborne Series*, 1993-
Janet Evanovich, *The Stephanie Plum Series*, 1994-
Sarah Strohmeyer, *The Bubbles Yablonsky Series*, 2001-

31

LILIAN JACKSON BRAUN

The Cat Who Went Bananas

(New York: Putnam, 2005)

Story type: Amateur Detective
Series: Cat Who. Book 27
Subject(s): Animals/Cats; Small Town Life; Theater
Major character(s): James "Qwill" Qwilleran, Journalist, Detective—Amateur; Koko, Animal (Siamese cat), Detective—Amateur; Yum Yum, Animal (Siamese cat), Detective—Amateur
Time period(s): 2000s
Locale(s): Pickaxe, Michigan (Moose County)

Summary: Moose County is still 400 miles north of everywhere, Qwill is still rich and adorable, and the cats still have a keen nose for crime. Qwill is writing a history of the Hibbard House, whose heiress suddenly marries a newly arrived amateur actor, Alden Wade, the star of a local production of Oscar Wilde's *The Importance of Being Earnest*. The question is: who was the mysterious sniper who killed Wade's first wife, and should his much older and very wealthy new wife be worried?

Where it's reviewed:
Booklist, December 15, 2004, page 710
Publishers Weekly, November 22, 2004, page 41
Romantic Times, March 2005, page 88

Other books by the same author:
The Cat Who Talked Turkey, 2004
The Cat Who Brought Down the House, 2003
The Cat Who Went Up the Creek, 2002
The Cat Who Smelled a Rat, 2001
The Cat Who Robbed a Bank, 2000

Other books you might like:
Garrison Allen, *The Big Mike Series*, 1994-
Rita Mae Brown, *The Mrs. Murphy Series*, 1990-
Barbara Collins, *Too Many Tomcats and Other Feline Tales of Suspense*, 2000
   editor; short stories
Carole Nelson Douglas, *The Midnight Louie Series*, 1992-
Shirley Rousseau Murphy, *The Joe Grey Series*, 1996-

32

RITA MAE BROWN

Cat's Eyewitness

(New York: Bantam, 2005)

Story type: Amateur Detective
Series: Mrs. Murphy. Book 13
Subject(s): Animals/Cats; Small Town Life; American South
Major character(s): Mary Minor "Harry" Haristeen, Postal Worker (former postmistress), Detective—Amateur; Mrs. Murphy, Animal (cat), Detective—Amateur; Tee Tucker, Animal (dog), Detective—Amateur
Time period(s): 2000s
Locale(s): Crozet, Virginia; Blue Ridge Mountains, Virginia

Summary: At a crossroads in her life since quitting her job as postmistress of Crozet because she was no longer allowed to bring her animal companions to work with her, Harry is visiting a statue of the Virgin Mary high atop the Blue Ridge Mountains at Greyfriars monastery. With her are her best friend Susan Tucker; her beloved cats, Mrs. Murphy and Pewter; and her Welsh corgi, Tee Tucker. As she and Susan discuss the directions their lives might be taking, they see tears of blood falling from the statue's eyes. Then Susan's great-uncle, a Greyfriars monk, is found dead at the foot of the statue, and the reporter who filed the original story on the tears is murdered. As usual, the animals do most of the detecting, discuss the investigation with each other, make wry observations about their human friends, and generally steal the show.

Where it's reviewed:
Publishers Weekly, January 31, 2005, page 52

Other books by the same author:
Whisker of Evil, 2004
The Tail of the Tip-Off, 2003
Catch as Cat Can, 2002
Claws and Effect, 2001
Pawing through the Past, 2000

Other books you might like:
Garrison Allen, *The Big Mike Series*, 1994-
Lilian Jackson Braun, *The Cat Who Series*, 1966-
Barbara Collins, *Too Many Tomcats and Other Feline Tales of Suspense*, 2000
   editor
Carole Nelson Douglas, *The Midnight Louie Series*, 1992-
Shirley Rousseau Murphy, *The Joe Grey Series*, 1996-

33

MAGGIE BRUCE, Editor

Murder Most Crafty

(New York: Berkley, 2005)

Story type: Anthology
Subject(s): Short Stories; Crafts

Summary: Crafts ranging from needlework to paper-making to knitting to basketry to fly-tying to candle-making provide the subject matter for these 15 original stories, from authors who either already have series focusing on crafts of one sort or another (Susan Wittig Albert, Tim Myers, Monica Ferris, Victoria Houston) or who are showing this side of themselves for the first time (Sujata Massey, Sue Dunlap, Parnell Hall, Margaret Maron, Sharan Newman, Gillian Roberts, Dorothy Cannell). Instructions for a crafts project accompany each story. The editor, who under her own name, Marilyn Wallace, edited five Sisters in Crime anthologies and wrote a number of mystery novels, contributes a short story featuring gourd crafting with a character, Lili Marino (the Gourdmother), who is the heroine of a forthcoming new series.

Where it's reviewed:
Publishers Weekly, March 14, 2005, page 49

Other books you might like:
Susan Wittig Albert, *The China Bayles Series*, 1992-
Monica Ferris, *The Betsy Devonshire Series*, 1999-
Victoria Houston, *The Doc Osborne Series*, 2000-

Tim Myers, *The Harrison Black Series*, 2004-
Maggie Sefton, *Knit One, Kill Two*, 2005

34

KEN BRUEN

The Magdalen Martyrs

(New York: St. Martin's Minotaur, 2005)

Story type: Private Detective
Series: Jack Taylor. Book 3
Subject(s): Alcoholism; Drugs; Substance Abuse
Major character(s): Jack Taylor, Detective—Private, Alcoholic
Time period(s): 2000s
Locale(s): Galway, Ireland

Summary: Boozy, sardonic Jack Taylor, a sort of unofficial private detective who was kicked off the Garda Siochana for his hard drinking, is still battling his private demons of alcohol and drugs when he's yanked back into sobriety by a call from a thug to whom he owes a favor. Bill Cassell wants Jack to find the woman who long ago helped his mother escape from a notorious home for pregnant Catholic girls. However, Jack can only stay sober for so long, Cassell's motives for hiring him aren't what they seem to be, and before long Jack is in big trouble. The author's highly mannered style works well for his brand of anguished *noir* realism, and he also writes an equally mordant series about an ensemble of cynical London cops, three of which are collected in *The White Trilogy*.

Where it's reviewed:
Booklist, January 1, 2005, page 826
Library Journal, January 2005, page 85
Mystery News, February/March 2005, page 11
Mystery Scene, Winter 2005, page 70
Publishers Weekly, February 14, 2005, page 57

Other books by the same author:
The Killing of the Tinkers, 2004
The Guards, 2003
The White Trilogy, 2003 (collection)

Other books you might like:
John Brady, *The Matt Minogue Series*, 1988-
Bartholomew Gill, *The Peter McGarr Series*, 1977-
Bill James, *The Harpur and Iles Series*, 1985-
Eugene McEldowney, *The Cecil Megarry Series*, 1994-
Ian Rankin, *The Inspector John Rebus Series*, 1987-

35

EDNA BUCHANAN

Shadows

(New York: Simon & Schuster, 2005)

Story type: Police Procedural
Series: Cold Case Squad. Book 2
Subject(s): Law Enforcement; Adoption
Major character(s): Craig Burch, Detective—Homicide
Time period(s): 2000s
Locale(s): Miami, Florida

Summary: Homicide detective Craig Burch, head of the Miami police department's Cold Case Squad, who was introduced as a supporting character in *The Ice Maiden*, now has a series of his own. He works with various other squad members, all of whom have personal difficulties which furnish subplots to the principal story, which involves an effort to save a historic Miami beachfront mansion, Shadows. One of the preservationists convinces the Cold Case Squad that there's a key to the unsolved 1961 murder of a former Miami mayor inside the mansion, and when they search the house they indeed find a trunk full of mummified infants. The author, who began her writing career as a crime reporter in Miami, has also written various true-crime books and non-series thrillers in addition to a series featuring Miami crime reporter Britt Montero.

Where it's reviewed:
Publishers Weekly, May 23, 2005, page 60

Other books by the same author:
Cold Case Squad, 2004
The Ice Maiden, 2002

Other books you might like:
Carolina Garcia-Aguilera, *The Lupe Solano Series*, 1996-
Carl Hiaasen, *Sick Puppy*, 2000
Elmore Leonard, *Riding the Rap*, 1995
Les Standiford, *The John Deal Series*, 1993-
Charles Willeford, *The Hoke Moseley Series*, 1984-1988

36

JOHN BURDETT

Bangkok Tattoo

(New York: Knopf, 2005)

Story type: Police Procedural
Series: Sonchai Jitpleecheep. Book 2
Subject(s): Cultures and Customs; Crime and Criminals; Prostitution
Major character(s): Sonchai Jitpleecheep, Detective—Police
Time period(s): 2000s
Locale(s): Bangkok, Thailand

Summary: The son of a Thai prostitute and an unknown American G.I., Sonchai (a devout Buddhist) grew up in Bangkok speaking English and French as well as his native language, and put his street smarts to the good when he became one of the few honest cops in the city. This time he's called by his crusty supervisor to investigate the murder of a CIA agent whose mutilated, disemboweled corpse was discovered in his hotel room. A beautiful bar girl, Chanya, to whom Sonchai is attracted and who is the chief rainmaker at his mother's brothel, seems to be the chief suspect, and Sonchai and his boss try to steer the investigation elsewhere. The author spares no lurid details about the Thai sex trade, including the inroads AIDS has made among its workers, and throws in an assortment of Japanese gangsters, Asian drug lords, Muslim fundamentalists, corrupt government officials, and clueless American tourists. It's a brisk, cynical, darkly comic book, steeped in the culture and atmosphere of a complex and alien country.

Where it's reviewed:
Entertainment Weekly, May 20, 2005, page 78
New York Times Book Review, June 5, 2005, page 37
Publishers Weekly, April 25, 2005, page 40

Other books by the same author:
Bangkok 8, 2003

Other books you might like:
Gopal Baratham, *Moonrise, Sunset*, 1996
Martin Limon, *The Ernie Bascom/George Sueno Series*, 1992-
Francine Mathews, *The Secret Agent*, 2002
Eliot Pattison, *The Shan Tao Yun Series*, 1998-
David Rotenburg, *The Zhong Fong Series*, 1998-

37

JAN BURKE

Bloodlines
(New York: Simon & Schuster, 2005)

Story type: Psychological Suspense
Series: Irene Kelly. Book 9
Subject(s): Journalism; Missing Persons
Major character(s): Irene Kelly, Journalist (newspaper reporter); Jack Corrigan, Journalist (newspaper reporter); Conn O'Connor, Journalist (newspaper reporter)
Time period(s): 20th century (1958; 1978; 1998)
Locale(s): Las Piernas, California

Summary: A crime that baffles three generations of journalists in the Southern California town of Las Piernas is at the heart of this ambitious and complex novel. In 1958, hard-drinking veteran reporter Jack Corrigan is nearly killed after having witnessed the burial of a car on a farm, but his credibility is questioned by his colleagues. The same night a yacht disappears in a storm, there is a home invasion in which a servant is killed, and the young heir, Max Ducane, disappears. Corrigan becomes a mentor to greenhorn reporter Conn O'Connor, who 20 years later takes another rookie, Irene Kelly, under his wing. At a routine groundbreaking for a shopping mall, the missing car is unearthed, its trunk containing human remains. They could be those of Max Ducane or he could be very much alive, as a young man calling himself Max Ducane claims to be the kidnapped heir. Another 20 years pass, O'Connor is dead, and Irene herself is mentoring two young reporters and is married to homicide detective Frank Harriman, who picks up the case and brings it to its eventual resolution.

Where it's reviewed:
Library Journal, December 2004, page 94
Mystery News, February/March 2005, page 18
Publishers Weekly, December 20, 2004, page 40
Romantic Times, January 2005, page 81

Other books by the same author:
Flight, 2001
Bones, 1999
Liar, 1998
Hocus, 1997
Remember Me, Irene, 1996

Other books you might like:
Michael Connelly, *The Harry Bosch Series*, 1992-

Robert Crais, *L.A. Requiem*, 1999
T. Jefferson Parker, *California Girl*, 2004
John Shannon, *The Jack Liffey Series*, 1996-
Mary Willis Walker, *The Molly Cates Series*, 1994-

38

LESLIE CAINE (Pseudonym of Leslie O'Kane)

False Premises
(New York: Dell, 2005)

Story type: Amateur Detective; Humor
Series: Erin Gilbert. Book 2
Subject(s): Antiques; Friendship
Major character(s): Erin Gilbert, Interior Decorator, Detective—Amateur; Steve Sullivan, Interior Decorator
Time period(s): 2000s
Locale(s): Crestview, Colorado (thinly disguised Boulder)

Summary: When interior designer Erin Gilbert learns that her glamorous new best friend and client, Laura Smith, is really a well-known con artist, she turns to her friend and sometime rival Steve Sullivan for help. He's out for revenge, having been scammed himself by the beautiful Laura, and when bodies start piling up, it's Sullivan the police suspect, and it's up to Erin to clear his name. Decorating tips are sprinkled throughout. Under her own name, the author has written equally light-hearted series featuring Allie Babcock, a Boulder dog psychologist, and Mollie Masters, a greeting card designer living in an upstate New York suburb.

Other books by the same author:
Death by Inferior Design, 2004

Other books you might like:
Kate Collins, *Mum's the Word*, 2004
Jerrilyn Farmer, *The Madeline Bean Series*, 1998-
Sarah Graves, *The Jacobia Tiptree Series*, 1998-
Maddy Hunter, *The Emily Andrew Series*, 2003-
Dean James, *Decorated to Death*, 2004

39

DANA CAMERON

More Bitter than Death
(New York: Avon, 2005)

Story type: Amateur Detective
Series: Emma Fielding. Book 5
Subject(s): Archaeology; History; Winter
Major character(s): Emma Fielding, Archaeologist, Detective—Amateur
Time period(s): 2000s
Locale(s): Green Bank, New Hampshire; Penitence Point, Maine

Summary: Historical archaeologist Emma is one of the attendees at a small conference being held at a small, isolated historic inn to celebrate the life and works of the legendary Julius Garrison. She's no sooner arrived, in the midst of a relentless winter storm, than Garrison's corpse is discovered on the grounds. Emma herself, as well as other guests, becomes a suspect in the old man's death, and as they are cut off

from the outside world as the snow continues to fall, Emma must clear herself and find out who is the murderer in their midst.

Other books by the same author:
A Fugitive Truth, 2004
Past Malice, 2003
Grave Consequences, 2002
Site Unseen, 2002

Other books you might like:
Margot Arnold, *The Penny Spring/Toby Glendower Series*, 1979-
Beverly Connor, *The Lindsay Chamberlain Series*, 1996-
Aaron Elkins, *The Gideon Oliver Series*, 1982-
Mary Anna Evans, *Artifacts*, 2003
Malcolm Shuman, *The Alan Graham Series*, 1998-

40

ANDREA CAMILLERI

Excursion to Tindari

(New York: Viking, 2005)

Story type: Police Procedural
Series: Salvo Montalbano. Book 5
Subject(s): Humor; Law Enforcement; Crime and Criminals
Major character(s): Salvo Montalbano, Police Officer (inspector)
Time period(s): 2000s
Locale(s): Sicily, Italy

Summary: Inspector Montalbano has two seemingly unrelated cases on his hands when an old couple visiting the ancient site of Tindari go missing and a young man is found murdered in town. When it turns out that all lived in the same apartment building, and when an old Mafia warrior comes to Montalbano wanting to turn in both himself and his grandson, Montalbano realizes something out of the ordinary is going on. Although mysteries set in Italy are popular in the U.S., this is about the only such series published here which is by an Italian author, who is a best-seller in his native land. Nicely translated from the Italian by Stephen Sartarelli, who provides helpful notes for American readers.

Where it's reviewed:
Deadly Pleasures, Winter 2005, page 3

Other books by the same author:
The Snack Thief, 2003
The Voice of the Violin, 2003
The Shape of Water, 2002
The Terra-Cotta Dog, 2002

Other books you might like:
Marshall Browne, *The Wooden Leg of Inspector Anders*, 2001
Michael Dibdin, *The Aurelio Zen Series*, 1988-
John Spencer Hill, *The Carlo Arbati Series*, 1995-1997
Donna Leon, *The Guido Brunetti Series*, 1992-
Magdalen Nabb, *The Marshal Guarnaccia Series*, 1981-

41

CALEB CARR

The Italian Secretary

(New York: Carroll & Graf, 2005)

Story type: Historical/Victorian; Private Detective
Series: Sherlock Holmes
Subject(s): Castles; Nationalism; Ghosts
Major character(s): Sherlock Holmes, Detective—Private; John Watson, Doctor, Sidekick; Mycroft Holmes, Spy
Time period(s): 1890s (ca. 1890)
Locale(s): Edinburgh, Scotland

Summary: Mycroft Holmes calls for his younger brother Sherlock, along with his ubiquitous sidekick Dr. Watson, to board a royal train headed for Scotland in aid of their Queen. Two of her servants have just been killed while working on the renovation of Holyrood, Victoria's royal palace in Edinburgh, a stopover where she can be viewed by her loyal subjects en route to Balmoral. Mycroft believes the murders may be the work of Scottish nationalists, but Sherlock is reminded of the murder centuries earlier of David Rizzio, the Italian secretary of the title, at the same palace when it was occupied by a young Mary, Queen of Scots. An afterword by Sherlockian expert Jon Lellenberg points out the similarities between Holmes and the author's series character, the American psychologist (or alienist), Dr. Kreizler.

Where it's reviewed:
Entertainment Weekly, April 22, 2005, page 69
Library Journal, April 15, 2005, page 74
New York Times Book Review, May 22, 2005, page 15
Publishers Weekly, April 4, 2005, page 44

Other books by the same author:
Killing Time, 2000 (non-series)
The Angel of Darkness, 1997
The Alienist, 1994

Other books you might like:
Anita Janda, *The Secret Diary of Dr. Watson*, 2001
Larry Millett, *The Disappearance of Sherlock Holmes*, 2002
Barrie Roberts, *Sherlock Holmes and the Crosby Murder*, 2002
Donald Thomas, *Sherlock Holmes and the Voice from the Crypt*, 2002
Alan Vanneman, *Sherlock Holmes and the Hapsburg Tiara*, 2004

42

CHARLOTTE CARTER

Trip Wire

(New York: Ballantine, 2005)

Story type: Amateur Detective
Series: Cassandra Lisle. Book 2
Subject(s): African Americans; Race Relations; Family
Major character(s): Cassandra Lisle, Student—College, Detective—Amateur
Time period(s): 1960s (1968)
Locale(s): Chicago, Illinois (North Side)

Summary: Rebellious Cassandra, still a college student, has moved out of her great-uncle's Hyde Park home into a hippie commune in a ramshackle apartment on Chicago's North Side, blissed out on love, sharing, rock music, anti-war politics, and recreational drugs. Then two of her roommates are murdered and her Uncle Woody, who still loves her fiercely though alarmed by her lifestyle, calls in a favor from a cop he knows to oversee the investigation. The author also writes a contemporary mystery series about Nanette Hayes, a free-spirited young black musician.

Where it's reviewed:
Library Journal, February 1, 2005, page 56
Publishers Weekly, February 21, 2005, page 161

Other books by the same author:
Jackson Park, 2003

Other books you might like:
Thomas H. Cook, *Streets of Fire*, 1989
David Daniel, *White Rabbit*, 2003
Gary Hardwick, *Cold Medina*, 1996
Walter Mosley, *The Easy Rawlins Series*, 1990-
Kris Nelscott, *War at Home*, 2005

43

NORA CHARLES (Pseudonym of Noreen Wald)

Who Killed Swami Schwartz?

(New York: Berkley, 2005)

Story type: Amateur Detective; Humor
Series: Kate Kennedy. Book 2
Subject(s): Beaches; Small Town Life; Animals/Dogs
Major character(s): Kate Kennedy, Widow(er), Detective—Amateur
Time period(s): 2000s
Locale(s): Palmetto, Florida

Summary: It wasn't Kate's idea to retire from upstate New York to sunny Florida, but when her ex-cop husband Charlie dropped dead the very same day they signed on their beachfront condo, there was no going back. She's still mourning Charlie's death but is beginning to adjust to life on her own when her yogi, Swami Schwartz, dies suddenly after dining with his financial backers. Kate and her former sister-in-law, Marlene, do a little research, which leads them to a questionable cryogenics firm and a large number of suspects. A remarkable West Highland terrier named Ballou contributes to the fun. Under her own name, the author has written a series about ghostwriter Jake O'Hara.

Where it's reviewed:
Mystery Scene, Winter 2005, page 64

Other books by the same author:
Death with an Ocean View, 2004

Other books you might like:
Patricia Guiver, *The Delilah Doolittle Series*, 1997-
Carolyn Hart, *The Henrie O Series*, 1993-
Carl Hiaasen, *Tourist Season*, 1986
Corinne Holt Sawyer, *The Angela Benbow/Caledonia Wingate Series*, 1988-

Kathy Hogan Trocheck, *The Truman Kicklighter Series*, 1996-

44

MARION CHESNEY

Sick of Shadows

(New York: St. Martin's Minotaur, 2005)

Story type: Historical/Edwardian; Traditional
Series: Lady Rose Summer. Book 3
Subject(s): Social Classes; Women's Rights; Romance
Major character(s): Lady Rose Summer, Noblewoman, Detective—Amateur; Captain Harry Cathcart, Detective—Private
Time period(s): 1900s
Locale(s): London, England

Summary: Desperate to escape being shipped off to India by her parents, rebellious Lady Rose enters into a mock engagement with dashing Captain Harry Cathcart. Although disappointed that their daughter has become betrothed to a man in trade, her parents are forced to accept the arrangement, not knowing they are being deceived. However, Cathcart is so busy with his private enquiry work that he spends little or no time with his supposed fiancee, which causes much gossip in London society. Bored, Lady Rose makes friends with a young debutante, Dolly Tremaine, who is feeling uncomfortably pressured by her parents to marry well. Then Dolly turns up drowned, threats are made on Rose's life, and she and Cathcart must find the killer. The author, who also writes Regency romances under her real name, is better known to mystery readers as M.C. Beaton, author of the Hamish Macbeth and Agatha Raisin series.

Where it's reviewed:
Library Journal, April 1, 2005, page 73

Other books by the same author:
Hasty Death, 2004
Snobbery with Violence, 2003

Other books you might like:
Clare Curzon, *Guilty Knowledge*, 2000
David Dickinson, *The Lord Francis Powerscourt Series*, 2002-
Kate Kingsbury, *The Pennyfoot Hotel Series*, 1993-
Gillian Linscott, *Dead Man Rising*, 2002
Robin Paige, *The Kathryn Ardleigh Series*, 1994-

45

LEE CHILD

One Shot

(New York: Delacorte, 2005)

Story type: Action/Adventure; Psychological Suspense
Series: Jack Reacher. Book 10
Subject(s): Memory Loss; Crime and Criminals
Major character(s): Jack Reacher, Drifter, Military Personnel (former military police)
Time period(s): 2000s
Locale(s): Indiana (small unnamed town)

Summary: When army veteran James Barr goes on a killing spree in a small Indiana town, the only words he will utter to the cops are, ''Get Jack Reacher for me.'' Almost before the authorities can find out who Reacher is, he arrives on the scene after learning about the incident on the news. He's not there to help Barr, but to explain that he investigated a similar incident involving Barr 14 years earlier in Kuwait, when they were in the military together. Then Barr is attacked by a fellow inmate and falls into a coma followed by amnesia. Some very wicked villains and surprising plot twists, along with the usual downplayed heroics from Reacher, draw the suspense out until the very end.

Where it's reviewed:
Library Journal, March 15, 2005, page 68
Publishers Weekly, May 23, 2005, page 59

Other books by the same author:
The Enemy, 2004
Persuader, 2003
Without Fail, 2002
Echo Burning, 2001
Running Blind, 2000

Other books you might like:
Michael Connelly, *The Harry Bosch Series*, 1992-
Robert Crais, *The Elvis Cole Series*, 1987-
James W. Hall, *The Thorn Series*, 1987-
Stephen Hunter, *The Bob Swagger Series*, 1993-
Randy Wayne White, *The Doc Ford Series*, 1990-

46

LAURA CHILDS (Pseudonym of Gerry Schmitt)

Chamomile Mourning

(New York: Berkley, 2005)

Story type: Amateur Detective
Series: Theodosia Browning. Book 6
Subject(s): American South; Restaurants; Food
Major character(s): Theodosia Browning, Store Owner (tea shop), Detective—Amateur
Time period(s): 2000s
Locale(s): Charleston, South Carolina

Summary: Former advertising executive Theodosia Browning loves her life as owner of the Indigo Tea Shop in Charleston's picturesque historic district, and as hard as she works, she still likes to contribute some of her time to the city's worthy causes. This time she and her crew are serving up tea and treats at the first-ever Poet's Tea at the Heritage Society as part of Spoleto, the city's annual arts and music festival. Intended to be an outdoor event, the tea is forced indoors because of inclement weather, and then interrupted when an auction house owner falls from a balcony onto Theo's six-layer almond cake during an Edgar Allan Poe slide show. Lots of tea lore and tempting recipes are included. The author also writes a series of scrapbooking mysteries set in New Orleans.

Where it's reviewed:
Library Journal, May 1, 2005, page 66
Publishers Weekly, April 18, 2005, page 47

Other books by the same author:
The Jasmine Moon Murder, 2004

Shades of Earl Grey, 2003
The English Breakfast Murder, 2003
Gunpowder Green, 2002
Death by Darjeeling, 2001

Other books you might like:
Susan Wittig Albert, *The China Bayles Series*, 1992-
Sandra Balzo, *Uncommon Grounds*, 2004
Cleo Coyle, *The Clare Cosi Series*, 2003-
Yasmine Galenorn, *Ghost of a Chance*, 2003
Tamar Myers, *The Abigail Timberlake Series*, 1996-

47

CAROL HIGGINS CLARK

Burned

(New York: Scribner, 2005)

Story type: Private Detective; Humor
Series: Regan Reilly. Book 8
Subject(s): Vacations; Islands
Major character(s): Regan Reilly, Detective—Private
Time period(s): 2000s
Locale(s): Waikiki, Hawaii

Summary: With her recent engagement about to result in marriage, Regan decides she needs one last fling as a single person and heads to Hawaii with her best friend, Kit. It's lucky for Will Brown, manager of the resort hotel where they're staying, that she's on hand, for he definitely needs a resident private investigator when the body of Dorinda Dawes, a gossipy hotel employee, washes up on the beach. Around her neck is a rare and valuable seashell lei that was recently stolen from an island museum. Regan's investigation takes her from Oahu to the big island and provides a pleasant travelogue, as well as a light-hearted detective puzzle.

Where it's reviewed:
Booklist, March 15, 2005, page 1269

Other books by the same author:
Popped, 2003
Jinxed, 2002
Fleeced, 2001
Twanged, 1998
Iced, 1995

Other books you might like:
Jerrilyn Farmer, *The Madeline Bean Series*, 1998-
Jacquelyn Girdner, *The Kate Jasper Series*, 1991-2002
Laura Levine, *The Jaine Austen Series*, 2002-
Marlys Millhiser, *The Charlie Greene Series*, 1992-
Katy Munger, *The Casey Jones Series*, 1997-

48

HARLAN COBEN

The Innocent

(New York: Dutton, 2005)

Story type: Psychological Suspense
Subject(s): Secrets; Marriage
Major character(s): Matt Hunter, Paralegal, Spouse
Time period(s): 2000s

Locale(s): New Jersey

Summary: Matt Hunter, happily married to Olivia (who is expecting a baby), is an ordinary guy in every way except one: nine years earlier, in the process of breaking up a fight at a fraternity party, he accidentally killed a young man and served four years in prison for it. Now things are going just fine, until he gets a call on his camera phone showing Olivia in bed with another man. Next, an autopsy on a beloved nun reveals breast implants, implying a somewhat more adventuresome past than would be expected, and her murder and that of a man who's been tailing Matt lead the cops to suspect him of the crimes. In addition to his stand-alone thrillers, the author has written a series about New Jersey sports agent Myron Bolitar.

Where it's reviewed:
Entertainment Weekly, March 29, 2005, page 155
Library Journal, April 1, 2005, page 84
Publishers Weekly, March 7, 2005, page 50

Other books by the same author:
Just One Look, 2004
No Second Chance, 2003
Gone for Good, 2002
Tell No One, 2001

Other books you might like:
Lee Child, *The Jack Reacher Series*, 1997-
Michael Connelly, *The Harry Bosch Series*, 1992-
Dennis Lehane, *Mystic River*, 2001
T. Jefferson Parker, *Silent Joe*, 2001
Ridley Pearson, *The Body of David Hayes*, 2004

49

REED FARREL COLEMAN

The James Deans

(New York: Plume, 2005)

Story type: Private Detective
Series: Moe Prager. Book 3
Subject(s): Politics; Missing Persons; Grief
Major character(s): Moe Prager, Detective—Private (former cop), Businessman (wine merchant)
Time period(s): 1980s (1983)
Locale(s): New York, New York

Summary: After his wife Katy had a miscarriage, wine merchant and sometime private eye Moe Prager is relieved they're gradually putting their loss behind them and beginning to enjoy life again. At a party at a Long Island country club, Moe is approached by a spokesman for Steve Brightman, a rising state senator whose career crashed and burned when a pretty young intern he was associated with disappeared two years earlier. His backers want Moe to investigate, and sure enough he turns up a plausible suspect, but there's something about it that puts Moe off. A man of unassailable integrity blessed with a strong marriage and a beloved daughter, Moe is not your stereotypical angst-ridden loner, and all the more refreshing and believable for it. The author has also written a three-book series about a former insurance investigator turned *noir* novelist, Dylan Klein.

Where it's reviewed:
Mystery News, February/March 2005, page 9
Publishers Weekly, November 15, 2004, page 44

Other books by the same author:
Redemption Street, 2004
Walking the Perfect Square, 2001

Other books you might like:
David Daniel, *The Alex Rasmussen Series*, 1993-
Jim Fusilli, *The Terry Orr Series*, 2001-
Bill Pronzini, *The Nameless Detective Series*, 1971-
John Shannon, *The Jack Liffey Series*, 1996-
John Straley, *The Cecil Younger Series*, 1992-

50

BARBARA COLLEY

Wiped Out

(New York: Kensington, 2005)

Story type: Amateur Detective; Domestic
Series: Charlotte LaRue. Book 4
Subject(s): Sisters; American South; Gardens and Gardening
Major character(s): Charlotte LaRue, Businesswoman (owner, house cleaning service), Detective—Amateur
Time period(s): 2000s
Locale(s): New Orleans, Louisiana

Summary: Sixtyish Charlotte LaRue, owner of Maid for a Day, a busy house-cleaning agency in New Orleans, has just lost one of her biggest clients, so she's delighted when a new one comes along. Society figure Mimi Adams is scheduled to host an upcoming meeting of the prestigious Horticultural Heritage Society, and Charlotte is anticipating lots of gardening talk at the well-attended meeting, but instead there's mainly gossip, most of it about Mimi. So when Mimi turns up dead from poisoning, Charlotte has many suspects to sort through to find the killer. Cleaning tips included.

Where it's reviewed:
Library Journal, February 1, 2005, page 57
Mystery Scene, Winter 2005, page 77
Publishers Weekly, January 24, 2005, page 226

Other books by the same author:
Polished Off, 2004
Death Tidies Up, 2003
Maid for Murder, 2002

Other books you might like:
Nancy J. Cohen, *The Marla Shore Series*, 1999-
Sophie Dunbar, *The Claire Claiborne Series*, 1993-
Charlaine Harris, *The Lily Bard Series*, 1996-
Robert J. Randisi, *The Masks of Auntie Laveau*, 2001
    Christine Matthews, co-author
Kathy Hogan Trocheck, *The Callahan Garrity Series*, 1992-

51

KATE COLLINS (Pseudonym of Linda Tsoutsouris)

Slay It with Flowers

(New York: Signet, 2005)

Story type: Amateur Detective
Series: Abby Knight. Book 2
Subject(s): Small Town Life; Gardens and Gardening
Major character(s): Abby Knight, Store Owner (flower shop), Detective—Amateur
Time period(s): 2000s
Locale(s): New Chapel, Indiana

Summary: Life dealt Abby Knight a double whammy when she flunked out of law school and got jilted by her fiance, but she's pulled herself together, returned to her hometown in Indiana, and bought a small flower shop, Bloomers. She's thrilled when her cousin Jillian asks her not only to be a bridesmaid at her upcoming wedding but to design and furnish the floral arrangements. Jillian, the proverbial runaway bride who's broken any number of engagements, actually nearly makes it to the altar this time, but the ceremonies are stalled when one of the groomsmen disappears and another member of the wedding party is murdered. Family and friends, including a sexy bar owner, help Abby find the murderer.

Where it's reviewed:
Romantic Times, March 2005, page 88

Other books by the same author:
Mum's the Word, 2004

Other books you might like:
Susan Wittig Albert, *The China Bayles Series*, 1992-
Janis Harrison, *The Bretta Solomon Series*, 1999-
Denise Swanson, *The Scumble River Series*, 2000-
Leann Sweeney, *A Wedding to Die For*, 2005
Heather Webber, *A Hoe Lot of Trouble*, 2004

52

SUSAN CONANT

Scratch the Surface

(New York: Berkley, 2005)

Story type: Amateur Detective; Traditional
Series: Felicity Pride. Book 1
Subject(s): Animals/Cats; Authors and Writers; Humor
Major character(s): Felicity Pride, Writer, Detective—Amateur
Time period(s): 2000s
Locale(s): Brighton, Massachusetts (Boston suburb)

Summary: Returning to her Boston area home one night after a local book signing, mystery author Felicity Pride (who writes a series of cat lovers' mysteries) is surprised to find a dead body lying next to a large gray cat in her vestibule. She's never seen either of them before, and even as she's calling 911 the devious Felicity is plotting ways to use her discovery to her advantage, imagining the great publicity she'd get if she solved a real-life crime herself. It turns out to be a lot harder than it is for her popular series character, but she muddles

through. Along the way Conant provides some sly fun about the mystery publishing world and those who inhabit it. The author has also written a long-running series of dog lovers' mysteries featuring Holly Winter and her two malamutes.

Where it's reviewed:
Publishers Weekly, May 9, 2005, page 50

Other books by the same author:
Bride and Groom, 2004
The Dogfather, 2003
The Wicked Flea, 2002
Creature Discomfort, 2000
Evil Breeding, 1999

Other books you might like:
Garrison Allen, *The Big Mike Series*, 1994-
Lilian Jackson Braun, *The Cat Who Series*, 1966-
Rita Mae Brown, *The Mrs. Murphy Series*, 1990-
Carole Nelson Douglas, *The Midnight Louie Series*, 1992-
Shirley Rousseau Murphy, *The Joe Grey Series*, 1996-

53

MICHAEL CONNELLY

The Closers

(New York: Little, Brown, 2005)

Story type: Police Procedural; Psychological Suspense
Series: Harry Bosch. Book 11
Subject(s): Law Enforcement; Grief; Crime and Criminals
Major character(s): Hieronymus "Harry" Bosch, Detective—Homicide
Time period(s): 2000s
Locale(s): Los Angeles, California

Summary: Having realized that he needs the badge and the gun if he's going to fight crime, Harry Bosch has given up the idea of being a private detective and returned to the fold of the Los Angeles Police Department, where he's relegated to working on cold case files. One in particular turns out to be anything but cold, when a new DNA match reopens the case of a 16-year-old girl who went missing and then was found dead in 1988. A thorough investigation failed to turn up any leads. Bosch finds that the girl's death had repercussions still being felt today, and he also finds his own colleagues aren't as cooperative as they might be.

Where it's reviewed:
Booklist, March 15, 2005, page 1245
Entertainment Weekly, May 20, 2005, page 81
Library Journal, May 15, 2005, page 71
New York Times Book Review, May 8, 2005, page 23
Publishers Weekly, April 4, 2005, page 313

Other books by the same author:
The Narrows, 2004
Lost Light, 2003
City of Bones, 2002
A Darkness More than Night, 2001
Angels Flight, 1999

Other books you might like:
James Lee Burke, *The Dave Robicheaux Series*, 1987-
Robert Crais, *L.A. Requiem*, 1999

Jeffery Deaver, *The Lincoln Rhyme Series*, 1997-
Dennis Lehane, *The Patrick Kenzie/Angela Gennaro Series*, 1994-1999
George P. Pelecanos, *Right as Rain*, 2001

54

JOHN CONNOLLY

The Black Angel
(New York: Atria, 2005)

Story type: Private Detective
Series: Charlie Parker. Book 5
Subject(s): Missing Persons; World War II; Supernatural
Major character(s): Charlie Parker, Detective—Private
Time period(s): 2000s
Locale(s): Scarborough, Maine; New York, New York

Summary: Although he's now remarried with an infant daughter, Parker is still haunted by the memory of his first wife and daughter, whose murders he attributes in part to his heavy drinking at the time. Now sober and retired from the Brooklyn police force, Parker is asked to investigate the disappearance of a young prostitute from New York, and despite the risks inherent in the job, he feels compelled to take it. The girl's abduction is connected to events in the past, including a slaughter at a French monastery in 1944 and the existence of a mysterious object known as the Black Angel. Supernatural elements are woven into the dark story line, with the solution to the mystery leading Parker back to the secret of his own origins.

Where it's reviewed:
Publishers Weekly, May 30, 2005, page 38

Other books by the same author:
The White Road, 2002
The Killing Kind, 2001
Dark Hollow, 2000
Every Dead Thing, 1999

Other books you might like:
Lawrence Block, *The Matt Scudder Series*, 1976-
James Lee Burke, *The Dave Robicheaux Series*, 1987-
George Chesbro, *The Veil Kendry Series*, 1986-
Lee Child, *The Jack Reacher Series*, 1997-
William Hjortsberg, *Falling Angel*, 1978

55

PHILIP R. CRAIG
WILLIAM G. TAPPLY, Co-Author

Second Sight
(New York: Scribner, 2005)

Story type: Private Detective
Series: J.W. Jackson. Book 2
Subject(s): Islands; Concerts; Cults
Major character(s): J.W. Jackson, Beachcomber, Detective—Private; Brady Coyne, Lawyer, Detective—Private
Time period(s): 2000s
Locale(s): Martha's Vineyard, Massachusetts

Summary: The second felicitous collaboration between these two veteran private eye writers again has Tapply's long-running series character, Boston lawyer Brady Coyne, paying a visit to Nantucket Island, home of laid-back private eye J.W. Jackson, Craig's engaging series protagonist. Coyne is doing a favor for an old friend who is dying and wants to be reconciled with his runaway daughter Christa, who may be on the island. Meanwhile, Jackson is serving as driver to a visiting pop star, Evangeline, there for a much-hyped musical extravaganza. It turns out that Christa may have been abducted by the leader of a religious cult and is being held in his compound against her will, and Evangeline may be in danger from whoever has just murdered her show's director. The two friends find time to get in a little fishing despite the demands of their assignments, and there are even a few manly recipes thrown in.

Where it's reviewed:
Booklist, January 1, 2005, page 825
Deadly Pleasures, Winter 2005, page 32
Library Journal, December 2004, page 95
Mystery News, February/March 2005, page 27
Mystery Scene, Winter 2005, page 68

Other books by the same author:
First Light, 2002

Other books you might like:
Rick Boyer, *The Doc Adams Series*, 1982-
Sally Gunning, *The Peter Bartholomew Series*, 1990-
David Osborn, *Murder on Martha's Vineyard*, 1989
Cynthia Riggs, *Deadly Nightshade*, 2001
Kelley Roos, *Murder on Martha's Vineyard*, 1981

56

PHILIP R. CRAIG

Vineyard Prey
(New York: Scribner, 2005)

Story type: Private Detective
Series: J.W. Jackson. Book 16
Subject(s): Islands; Spies; Winter
Major character(s): J.W. Jackson, Beachcomber, Detective—Private; Zee Jackson, Nurse; Joe Begay, Veteran (Vietnam), Spy
Time period(s): 2000s
Locale(s): Martha's Vineyard, Massachusetts

Summary: Former cop J.W. Jackson and his family are just settling in for a long, quiet winter on the island when his old Vietnam buddy and fishing companion Joe Begay asks J.W. to meet him in Cape Cod and smuggle him onto the island. Begay was no ordinary soldier, and he's been doing top secret work for the government since the war. He and five other agents were on a failed mission several years ago, and since then all but Joe and one other have been killed by a terrorist known as the Easter Bunny. Then Kate MacLeod, the other surviving agent, arrives on Martha's Vineyard, suggesting that the Easter Bunny's not far behind. As much as J.W. wants to help them, he wants to keep his family safe, and the only way to do that may be to enter the fray himself. Set during

scallop season, the book also contains three recipes for scallop dishes from J.W.'s kitchen.

Where it's reviewed:

Publishers Weekly, May 2, 2005, page 179

Other books by the same author:

Murder at a Vineyard Mansion, 2004
A Vineyard Killing, 2003
Vineyard Enigma, 2002
Vineyard Shadows, 2001
Vineyard Blues, 2000

Other books you might like:

Francine Mathews, *The Merry Folger Series*, 1994-
David Osborn, *Murder on Martha's Vineyard*, 1989
Katherine Hall Page, *The Body in the Lighthouse*, 2003
Cynthia Riggs, *The Victoria Trumbull Series*, 2001-
Kelley Roos, *Murder on Martha's Vineyard*, 1981

57

ROBERT CRAIS

The Forgotten Man

(New York: Doubleday, 2005)

Story type: Private Detective
Series: Elvis Cole. Book 10
Subject(s): Identity; Fathers and Sons; Friendship
Major character(s): Elvis Cole, Detective—Private (ex-cop); Joe Pike, Detective—Private, Veteran (Vietnam); Carol Starkey, Police Officer (ex-bomb technician)
Time period(s): 2000s
Locale(s): Los Angeles, California; San Diego, California

Summary: The author's ground-breaking eighth novel, *L.A. Requiem*, disclosed a great deal about the troubled past of Elvis Cole's enigmatic and often lethal sidekick, Joe Pike. Now a few things about Elvis' history come to light. When a homeless man dies in a Los Angeles alley, his dying request is that the cops find his son, Elvis Cole. He just might be Elvis' father, whom Elvis never knew and whom his mentally unbalanced mother always refused to discuss. Not knowing who his father was has always haunted Elvis. With the help of Pike and Carol Starkey, the former bomb squad technician from *Demolition Angel*, he sets out to find the truth about this stranger. Unfortunately, their search brings Elvis closer and closer to a psychopath connected to his father's past who now believes that Elvis is after him and is prepared to kill him before he can be killed himself. The author has also written two non-series crime novels.

Where it's reviewed:

Booklist, January 1, 2005, page 782
Entertainment Weekly, February 18, 2005, page 80
Library Journal, February 15, 2005, page 114
Publishers Weekly, January 24, 2005, page 221

Other books by the same author:

The Last Detective, 2003
L.A. Requiem, 1999
Indigo Slam, 1997
Sunset Express, 1996
Voodoo River, 1995

Other books you might like:

Lee Child, *The Jack Reacher Series*, 1997-
Michael Connelly, *The Harry Bosch Series*, 1992-
James Ellroy, *The Lloyd Hopkins Series*, 1984-
Robert B. Parker, *The Spenser Series*, 1973-
John Shannon, *The Jack Liffey Series*, 1996-

58

FRANCES CRANE

The Golden Box

(Lyons, Colorado: Rue Morgue Press, 2005)

Story type: Private Detective
Series: Pat & Jean Abbott. Book 2
Subject(s): Small Town Life; World War II; Family
Major character(s): Jean Holly, Store Owner; Pat Abbott, Detective—Private
Time period(s): 1940s (1941)
Locale(s): Elm Hill, Illinois

Summary: Jean Holly leaves her new home in New Mexico to be with an ailing aunt in her childhood home in Illinois, arriving just in time to see the town tyrant, Claribel Lake, murdered. Many people in Elm Hill are glad to see the arrogant old lady dead, so there is no shortage of suspects. Luckily Jean's boyfriend, lanky San Francisco private detective Pat Abbott, shows up in time to help out in the investigation. When the dead woman's maid is found hanged in a room in the mansion, Pat renews his efforts to find the killer. Set shortly before the attack on Pearl Harbor, this 1942 mystery is a carefully realized portrait of small-town America on the eve of World War II. It's the second of 26 mysteries to feature the soon-to-be-wed detecting team of Pat and Jean Abbott.

Other books by the same author:

The Amethyst Spectacles, 1944
The Pink Umbrella, 1944
The Applegreen Cat, 1943
The Yellow Violet, 1942
The Turquoise Shop, 1941 (reprinted in 2004)

Other books you might like:

Carolyn Hart, *Letter from Home*, 2003
Frances Lockridge, *The Pam & Jerry North Series*, 1940-1963
   Richard Lockridge, co-author
Lenore Glen Offord, *The Todd McKinnon Series*, 1943-1959
Kelley Roos, *The Jeff & Haila Troy Series*, 1940-1966
Margaret Scherf, *The Henry & Emily Bryce Series*, 1949-1963

59

JAMES CRUMLEY

The Right Madness

(New York: Viking, 2005)

Story type: Private Detective
Series: C.W. Sughrue. Book 4
Subject(s): Alcoholism; Drugs; Friendship
Major character(s): C.W. Sughrue, Detective—Private

Time period(s): 2000s
Locale(s): Missoula, Montana; Seattle, Washington; El Paso, Texas

Summary: Montana private eye C.W. Sughrue, a grumpy Vietnam vet with a wildly checkered past, seems to finally have his life together, married to a lady lawyer and buddies with a shrink on his over-50 softball team. Then his friend, Dr. Will MacKinderick, hires C.W. to locate some missing office files with sensitive information about his clients, and everything goes to pieces. Mac's patients start dying horrible deaths, C.W.'s wife goes back to her temporary job in Minneapolis, and C.W. takes to the road after the files and the murderer, succumbing to one temptation after another in the way of booze, recreational drugs, women, and cigarettes (yes, he'd even given up smoking). One of the last of a vanishing breed of unreconstructed bad-boy private eyes, C.W. has miraculously survived the ruinous lifestyle he keeps inflicting upon himself, even as the gray overtakes the blond of his ponytail and his friends and wives betray or desert him. There is, of course, the author's lyrical writing to carry the reader effortlessly through the wild times, and the memory of the brilliance of C.W.'s first outing. The author also writes a similar series about another aging Missoula private eye, Milo Milodragovitch.

Where it's reviewed:
Booklist, March 1, 2005, page 1102
New York Times Book Review, May 8, 2005, page 13
Publishers Weekly, April 11, 2005, page 37

Other books by the same author:
Bordersnakes, 1996
The Mexican Tree Duck, 1993
The Last Good Kiss, 1978

Other books you might like:
Richard Barre, *The Wil Hardesty Series*, 1995-
James Lee Burke, *The Dave Robicheaux Series*, 1987-
Dennis Lehane, *The Patrick Kenzie/Angela Gennaro Series*, 1994-1999
George P. Pelecanos, *The Nick Stefanos Series*, 1992-
Walter Satterthwait, *The Joshua Croft Series*, 1989-

60

MARY DAHEIM

The Alpine Quilt

(New York: Ballantine, 2005)

Story type: Amateur Detective
Series: Emma Lord. Book 17
Subject(s): Small Town Life; Catholicism; Journalism
Major character(s): Emma Lord, Editor (newspaper), Detective—Amateur; Milo Dodge, Police Officer (sheriff)
Time period(s): 2000s
Locale(s): Alpine, Washington

Summary: Quilting plays a very small part in this case for newspaper editor/publisher Emma Lord. She teams up with Sheriff Milo Dodge to solve the murder by poisoned cheesecake of a former Alpine resident back in town for a visit and to attend a reunion of her quilting circle. The chief suspect is church organist Annie Jean Dupre, but since she was the

victim's best friend, it's hard to figure her motive. Emma's brother Ben, a Catholic priest, has agreed to substitute for old Father Kelly for six months, and he lends a helpful hand in the investigation. The author also writes a Seattle-based bed-and-breakfast series featuring innkeeper Mary McMonigle Flynn.

Where it's reviewed:
Booklist, March 15, 2005, page 1269
Library Journal, April 1, 2005, page 74
Publishers Weekly, March 28, 2005, page 60

Other books by the same author:
The Alpine Pursuit, 2004
The Alpine Obituary, 2002
The Alpine Nemesis, 2001
The Alpine Legacy, 2000
The Alpine Menace, 2000

Other books you might like:
Carol Cail, *The Maxey Burnell Series*, 1993-
Jo Dereske, *The Miss Zukas Series*, 1994-
Earlene Fowler, *The Benni Harper Series*, 1994-
Linda French, *The Teddy Morelli Series*, 1998-
Carolyn Hart, *The Henrie O Series*, 1993-

61

JOHN M. DANIEL

The Poet's Funeral

(Scottsdale, Arizona: Poisoned Pen Press, 2005)

Story type: Amateur Detective
Subject(s): Publishing; Authors and Writers; Books and Reading
Major character(s): Guy Mallon, Publisher, Detective—Amateur
Time period(s): 1990s (1990)
Locale(s): Santa Barbara, California; Las Vegas, Nevada

Summary: Set in 1990 in Las Vegas during the American Booksellers Association's annual convention, this is a deliciously wicked look at the book world by an industry insider. Like his hero, the five-foot-tall Guy Mallon, the author himself is a bookseller turned small press publisher. Mallon got his start in the book business when he stumbled across an extremely rare Jack Kerouac book of poetry at a Santa Barbara used bookstore's going-out-of-business sale. He bought the shop on the spot, and then sold the Kerouac for enough money to put the bookstore back on its feet. Guy's first employee (who became his lover), Heidi Yamada, talked him into publishing her first book of poetry, and his publishing firm grew into one of the most respected small presses in the country while Yamada became the most publicized poet of her generation. Years later their paths cross again at the Las Vegas ABA when Heidi is found dead of an apparent drug overdose. It's murder, of course, and Guy makes a great amateur sleuth, but the real fun of the book lies in the author's irreverent, wisecracking look at the world of books and, more importantly, the deeply flawed people who produce them.

Where it's reviewed:
Publishers Weekly, March 14, 2005, page 48

Other books by the same author:
Play Melancholy Baby, 1986

Other books you might like:
Isaac Asimov, *Murder at the ABA*, 1976
John Dunning, *The Bookman's Wake*, 1995
David Handler, *The Man Who Would Be F. Scott Fitzgerald*, 1990
Julie Kaewert, *The Alex Plumtree Series*, 1994-
Hubert Montheilet, *Murder at the Frankfurt Book Fair*, 1975

62

CLAIRE DANIELS (Pseudonym of Jacqueline Girdner)

Cruel and Unusual Intuition
(New York: Berkley, 2005)

Story type: Amateur Detective
Series: Cally Lazar. Book 3
Subject(s): Healing; Psychic Powers; Paranormal
Major character(s): Cally Lazar, Healer (intuitive), Detective—Amateur
Time period(s): 2000s
Locale(s): Fiebre, California

Summary: A self-styled ''recovering attorney,'' Cally Lazar has chucked life in the fast lane to follow her bliss, in this case her New Age calling: reading people's auras and staging karmic interventions. She and others of her ilk are taking an intensive workshop from energy healer Dr. Aurora Hart, who proceeds to dismay her students with her own negative vibes and all-around rudeness. When Dr. Hart dies mysteriously, the cops suspect the workshop members, so Cally and her friends and family turn sleuth to find the real killer. Under her own name the author wrote a 12-book series featuring Marin County gag gift entrepreneur Kate Jasper.

Other books by the same author:
Strangled Intuition, 2004
Body of Intuition, 2002

Other books you might like:
Catherine Dain, *The Mariana Morgan Series*, 1999-
Yasmine Galenorn, *The Emerald O'Brien Series*, 2003-
Kate Green, *The Theresa Fortunato Series*, 1986-
Christine T. Jorgensen, *The Stella the Stargazer Series*, 1994-
Victoria Laurie, *Abby Cooper, Psychic Eye*, 2005

63

KYRA DAVIS

Sex, Murder and a Double Latte
(Don Mills, Ontario: Red Dress Ink, 2005)

Story type: Amateur Detective; Humor
Series: Sophie Katz. Book 1
Subject(s): African Americans; Authors and Writers; Books and Reading
Major character(s): Sophie Katz, Writer (mystery novelist), Detective—Amateur
Time period(s): 2000s
Locale(s): San Francisco, California

Summary: Bestselling mystery writer Sophie Katz (who's half black and half Jewish) may be the target of a killer who has offed a famous rapper and a movie producer who were interested in optioning her latest novel. The San Francisco police think she's paranoid, so she turns to her wide circle of friends for help in finding the murderer, who just could be the sexy Russian-Israeli hunk who's been saving her life on a more or less regular basis and could easily become her next boyfriend. Chick lit through and through (the publisher is a new imprint of Harlequin), this debut novel is full of Sophie's sassy humor.

Where it's reviewed:
Library Journal, May 1, 2005, page 65
Publishers Weekly, April 11, 2005, page 34

Other books you might like:
Elizabeth Bloom, *See Isabelle Run*, 2005
Janet Evanovich, *The Stephanie Plum Series*, 1994-
Harley Jane Kozak, *The Wollie Shelley Series*, 2004-
Joanne Pence, *The Angelina Amalfi Series*, 1993-
Sarah Strohmeyer, *The Bubbles Yablonsky Series*, 2001-

64

JEFFERY DEAVER

The Twelfth Card
(New York: Simon & Schuster, 2005)

Story type: Psychological Suspense; Police Procedural
Series: Lincoln Rhyme. Book 8
Subject(s): History; Civil Rights; Stalking
Major character(s): Lincoln Rhyme, Criminologist, Handicapped (quadriplegic); Amelia Sachs, Detective—Homicide, Lover
Time period(s): 2000s
Locale(s): New York, New York

Summary: The author, who wrote a splendid historical thriller about prewar Germany in *Garden of Beasts* (2004), again turns to a historical background to give weight and substance to this contemporary police procedural. Series character Lincoln Rhyme and his assistant/lover Amelia Sachs try to trap the man who attacked a young Harlem schoolgirl, Geneva Settle. Geneva has been researching the history of an ancestor, Charles Singleton, a former slave and early civil rights advocate who was disgraced after being arrested for theft. Actually, two people are stalking Geneva, a white hit man and a black ex-con, and Lincoln (who's a quadriplegic) and Amelia do their best to protect Geneva, find her would-be assassins, and solve the mystery of what happened to Charles Singleton in 1868. The usual plot twists abound and Geneva is a wonderfully realized character.

Where it's reviewed:
Entertainment Weekly, June 10, 2005, page 115
Publishers Weekly, April 18, 2005, page 42

Other books by the same author:
The Vanished Man, 2003
The Stone Monkey, 2002
Speaking in Tongues, 2001
The Empty Chair, 2000
The Devil's Teardrop, 1999 (Rhyme makes a cameo appearance)

Other books you might like:
Ethan Black, *The Conrad Voort Series*, 1999-

Michael Connelly, *The Harry Bosch Series*, 1992-
William Heffernan, *Beulah Hill*, 2001
Ridley Pearson, *The Lou Boldt Series*, 1988-
John Sandford, *The Lucas Davenport Series*, 1989-

65

DAVID DICKINSON

Death of a Chancellor

(New York: Carroll & Graf, 2005)

Story type: Historical/Victorian
Series: Lord Francis Powerscourt. Book 4
Subject(s): Cathedrals; Victorian Period; Anglicans
Major character(s): Lord Francis Powerscourt, Detective—
Private, Nobleman; Lady Lucy Powerscourt, Spouse (of
Francis), Sidekick
Time period(s): 1900s (1901)
Locale(s): West Country, England

Summary: Upon his return to England after a delicate mission
to South Africa during the Boer War, Powerscourt is asked by
the haughty sister of the recently deceased chancellor of
Compton Cathedral to investigate her brother's death, which
occurred on the eve of the thousand-year anniversary of the
ancient building. She thinks his death was not from natural
causes, as ruled. Powerscourt begins to agree as he uncovers
links between the chancellor's death and the disappearances
of members of the choir and the murder of a parishioner. The
chancellor also turns out to be one of the richest men in
England, and the disposition of his fortune is complicated by
the presence of three separate wills. As usual, Powerscourt's
astute wife, Lucy, aids him in his investigations.

Where it's reviewed:
Library Journal, January 2005, page 84
Publishers Weekly, December 13, 2004, page 49

Other books by the same author:
Death of an Old Master, 2004
Death & the Jubilee, 2003
Goodnight, Sweet Prince, 2002

Other books you might like:
Ray Harrison, *The Sergeant Bragg/Constable Morton Series*,
1983-
Peter Lovesey, *The Bertie, Prince of Wales Series*, 1987-1993
Robin Paige, *The Kathryn Ardleigh Series*, 1994-
Anne Perry, *The Thomas and Charlotte Pitt Series*, 1979-
Gerald Williams, *The Dr. Mortimer Series*, 2000-

66

DEBORAH DONNELLY (Pseudonym of Deborah Wessell)

Death Takes a Honeymoon

(New York: Dell, 2005)

Story type: Amateur Detective; Humor
Series: Carnegie Kincaid. Book 4
Subject(s): Weddings; Romance; Fires
Major character(s): Carnegie Kincaid, Consultant (wedding
planner), Detective—Amateur
Time period(s): 2000s

Locale(s): Seattle, Washington; Sun Valley, Idaho

Summary: Seattle wedding planner Carnegie Kincaid is to be a
guest at the wedding of her old friend Tracy, now a movie
actress, who's marrying hotshot firefighter Jack Packard, a
man Carnegie has long lusted after. This means traveling back
to her childhood home of Sun Valley, Idaho, where she's
roped into helping with last-minute preparations for the celeb-
rity-studded ceremony. Then her cousin Brian, a smoke
jumper, dies in the line of duty, and Carnegie becomes
involved in investigating his death.

Where it's reviewed:
Publishers Weekly, March 21, 2005, page 40

Other books by the same author:
May the Best Man Die, 2003
Died to Match, 2002
Veiled Threats, 2002

Other books you might like:
Donna Andrews, *Murder with Peacocks*, 1999
Paula Carter, *The Hillary Scarborough Series*, 1999-
Laura Durham, *Better Off Wed*, 2005
Jerrilyn Farmer, *Killer Wedding*, 2000
Leslie Meier, *Wedding Day Murder*, 2001

67

TIM DORSEY

Torpedo Juice

(New York: William Morrow, 2005)

Story type: Humor; Psychological Suspense
Series: Serge A. Storms. Book 7
Subject(s): Crime and Criminals; Organized Crime
Major character(s): Serge A. Storms, Serial Killer
Time period(s): 2000s
Locale(s): Key West, Florida; Big Pine Key, Florida

Summary: Serge A. Storms, a genial serial killer who only offs
really bad guys, has decided it's time to get married, and he
heads to the Florida Keys to find himself a wife. He lands in
Big Pine Key, a less developed stop on the way to Key West,
and takes a job as social director of the No Name Pub, named
for an even more obscure Florida key. He also woos and wins
Molly, the mousy librarian of his dreams. The bartender at the
pub has hooked up with a woman on the run named Anna,
who is being pursued by some bad guys in a white Mercedes,
while someone driving a brown Plymouth Duster is trying to
kill Serge. There's the usual supporting cast of zany characters, including the improbably resurrected Coleman, perhaps
the most socially maladapted of Serge's misfit friends. Along
the way, the author manages to skewer the many factions
intent on destroying his beloved state of Florida, and if the
humor is a little more self-referential than in earlier books,
there are still a lot of laughs in the story.

Where it's reviewed:
Library Journal, January 2005, page 95
Publishers Weekly, January 17, 2005, page 36

Other books by the same author:
Cadillac Beach, 2004
The Stingray Shuffle, 2003

Orange Crush, 2002
Triggerfish Twist, 2002
Hammerhead Ranch Motel, 2000

Other books you might like:
Dave Barry, *Tricky Business*, 2002
Carl Hiaasen, *Tourist Season*, 1986
Jeff Lindsay, *Darkly Dreaming Dexter*, 2004
Laurence Shames, *The Key West Series*, 1992-
Randy Wayne White, *The Doc Ford Series*, 1990-

`68`

CAROLE NELSON DOUGLAS

Cat in a Hot Pink Pursuit

(New York: Forge, 2005)

Story type: Amateur Detective; Humor
Series: Midnight Louie. Book 17
Subject(s): Animals/Cats; Beauty; Television
Major character(s): Midnight Louie, Animal (cat), Detective—Amateur; Temple Barr, Public Relations, Detective—Amateur
Time period(s): 2000s
Locale(s): Las Vegas, Nevada

Summary: Petite PR consultant Temple Barr agrees to do a favor for her friend, homicide lieutenant Carmen Molina, and pose as a contestant on the TV reality show, "Teen Queen." Carmen is concerned for the safety of the contestants, including her own 13-year-old daughter Mariah, when mutilated Barbie dolls start appearing all over Vegas. Temple wonders how she's going to pull it off when her romance writer aunt is named one of the judges, so she dyes her hair black and punks out in order to fool her. With her boyfriend, ex-magician Max Kinsella, investigating a group of terrorist magicians, Temple is pretty much on her own here. Except, of course, for her dear companion, Midnight Louie, who does his best to protect both Temple and Mariah. The author also writes a historical series featuring Irene Adler, a contemporary of Sherlock Holmes.

Where it's reviewed:
Publishers Weekly, April 4, 2005, page 46

Other books by the same author:
Cat in an Orange Twist, 2004
Cat in a Neon Nightmare, 2003
Cat in a Midnight Choir, 2002
Cat in a Leopard Spot, 2001
Cat in a Kiwi Con, 2000

Other books you might like:
Garrison Allen, *The Big Mike Series*, 1994-
Lilian Jackson Braun, *The Cat Who Series*, 1966-
Rita Mae Brown, *The Mrs. Murphy Series*, 1990-
Harley Jane Kozak, *Dating Is Murder*, 2005
Shirley Rousseau Murphy, *The Joe Grey Series*, 1996-

`69`

JOHN DUNNING

The Sign of the Book

(New York: Scribner, 2005)

Story type: Private Detective
Series: Cliff Janeway. Book 4
Subject(s): Collectors and Collecting; Books and Reading; Small Town Life
Major character(s): Cliff Janeway, Store Owner (bookseller), Detective—Private (former cop); Erin D'Angelo, Lawyer
Time period(s): 1980s (ca. 1989)
Locale(s): Denver, Colorado; Paradise, Colorado

Summary: Ex-cop turned antiquarian bookseller Cliff Janeway is having a good day at his used bookstore on Denver's seedy East Colfax Avenue and reflecting happily on his relationship with lawyer Erin D'Angelo, now also his business partner. Everything is soon to change, however, after Erin asks him to look into a murder in the small western Colorado mountain town of Paradise—not just any murder, but the slaying of a book collector who was once Erin's lover, and whose accused murderer, Laura Marshall, was Erin's best friend. Once he gets there, Janeway isn't sure he wants any part of the case, but he's eventually drawn into it because of the books in Bobby Marshall's collection. The story is deliberately set in the past, before the face of antiquarian bookselling was changed forever by the Internet.

Where it's reviewed:
Booklist, January 1, 2005, page 825
Publishers Weekly, January 3, 2005, page 30

Other books by the same author:
The Bookman's Promise, 2004
Two O'Clock, Eastern Wartime, 2001 (non-series)
The Bookman's Wake, 1995
Booked to Die, 1992

Other books you might like:
Julie Kaewert, *The Alex Plumtree Series*, 1994-
Roy Lewis, *The Matthew Coll Series*, 1980-
Marianne Macdonald, *Death's Autograph*, 1997
Judith Van Gieson, *The Claire Reynier Series*, 2000-
Wayne Warga, *Hard Cover*, 1985

`70`

LAURA DURHAM (Pseudonym of Laura Weatherly)

Better Off Wed

(New York: Avon, 2005)

Story type: Amateur Detective
Series: Annabelle Archer. Book 1
Subject(s): Weddings; Social Classes
Major character(s): Annabelle Archer, Consultant (wedding planner), Detective—Amateur
Time period(s): 2000s
Locale(s): Washington, District of Columbia

Summary: This debut mystery introduces Annabelle Archer who, like the author, is a professional wedding planner in Washington, D.C. Her latest project is the most harrowing

she's ever undertaken, as the mother of the bride is poisoned at the crowded reception at a Georgetown museum. Since the victim, a well-known socialite, was despised by many of the wedding guests, there are plenty of suspects, and Annabelle's own business partner and friend Richard Gerard is one of them. They turn detective to find the killer, in order to save Richard from prison and salvage Annabelle's budding career as a society wedding planner.

Where it's reviewed:
Library Journal, October 1, 2004, page 64
Romantic Times, March 2005, page 85

Other books you might like:
Donna Andrews, *Murder with Peacocks*, 1999
Paula Carter, *The Hillary Scarborough Series*, 1999-
Deborah Donnelly, *The Carnegie Kincaid Series*, 2002-
Jerrilyn Farmer, *Killer Wedding*, 2000
Leann Sweeney, *A Wedding to Die For*, 2005

71

MARJORIE ECCLES

Killing a Unicorn
(New York: St. Martin's Minotaur, 2005)

Story type: Police Procedural; Traditional
Subject(s): Family Problems; Rural Life; Secrets
Major character(s): Dave Crouch, Detective—Homicide (inspector); Kate Colville, Detective—Homicide (sergeant)
Time period(s): 2000s
Locale(s): Felsborough, England (Chilterns)

Summary: The author introduces two new police detectives here, Inspector Dave Crouch and Sergeant Kate Colville. They investigate a complicated murder in the Calvert family, who have long lived at Membery Place, an imposing country home. One of the three Calvert sons, Chip, has brought the beautiful and enigmatic Bianca Morgan and her nine-year-old son to live with him at Membery, and another son, Mark, and his wife, Francesca, have built a modern house on the premises. When Bianca is found dead beneath a waterfall, it turns out that all three of the brothers, including Jonathan, a cellist, have ties to her, past and present. When Bianca's son Jasie goes missing, the investigation takes a new turn. The author of this cleverly plotted stately-home detective novel has also written a stand-alone mystery with police officer Tom Richmond, *Echoes of Silence* (2003), as well as a long-running series featuring Superintendent Gil Mayo and Inspector Abigail Moon.

Where it's reviewed:
Publishers Weekly, January 3, 2005, page 39
Romantic Times, April 2005, page 90

Other books by the same author:
Untimely Graves, 2004
A Sunset Touch, 2001
The Superintendent's Daughter, 1999
Killing Me Softly, 1998
A Species of Revenge, 1996

Other books you might like:
Jo Bannister, *The Castlemere Series*, 1993-
Clare Curzon, *The Mike Yeadings Series*, 1983-

Caroline Graham, *The Tom Barnaby Series*, 1987-
Christine Green, *The Connor O'Neill/Fran Wilson Series*, 1993-
Jill McGown, *The Inspector Lloyd/Judy Hill Series*, 1983-

72

SELMA EICHLER

Murder Can Mess Up Your Mascara
(New York: Signet, 2005)

Story type: Private Detective; Humor
Series: Desiree Shapiro. Book 12
Subject(s): Food; Adolescence
Major character(s): Desiree Shapiro, Detective—Private, Widow(er)
Time period(s): 2000s
Locale(s): New York, New York

Summary: Food-loving and unapologetically full-figured private eye Desiree Shapiro is asked by Gordon Curry to find the person who has twice tried to kill him. Before Dez can find the villain—her client has thoughtfully provided her with his name—a third attempt on Gordon's life is successful. However, the man whom Gordon thought was trying to kill him is dead, too, having committed suicide before the murder attempts began. It's almost enough to put a girl off her feed, but Dez manages to keep body and soul together while interviewing suspects and sifting through the evidence.

Where it's reviewed:
Publishers Weekly, January 10, 2005, page 44

Other books by the same author:
Murder Can Botch Up Your Birthday, 2004
Murder Can Rain on Your Show, 2003
Murder Can Cool Off Your Affair, 2002
Murder Can Upset Your Mother, 2001
Murder Can Spoil Your Appetite, 2000

Other books you might like:
Carole Lea Benjamin, *The Rachel Alexander and Dash Series*, 1996-
Ruth Birmingham, *The Sunny Childs Series*, 1998-
G.A. McKevett, *The Savannah Reid Series*, 1995-
Katy Munger, *The Casey Jones Series*, 1997-
Lynne Murray, *The Josephine Fuller Series*, 1997-

73

BARRY EISLER

Killing Rain
(New York: Putnam, 2005)

Story type: Action/Adventure; Espionage
Series: John Rain
Subject(s): Spies; Suspense; Japanese Americans
Major character(s): John Rain, Spy, Murderer
Time period(s): 2000s
Locale(s): Manila, Philippines

Summary: John Rain is a Japanese-American freelance assassin and martial arts expert who tries to justify his profession by pointing out (to himself) that he only kills bad people: no

women, no children, no innocents. He always makes it look accidental, and always gets away with it. Based in Asia, Rain has been hired by the Mossad, the Israeli intelligence agency, to take out Israeli arms dealer Manheim Levi. Distracted by the appearance of Levi's young son on the scene, Rain winds up shooting the man's bodyguards, who turn out to be ex-CIA agents. Rain is working with a new partner, Dox, a deadly sniper whose true nature is masked by his laid-back, good ole boy persona. Because he failed to carry out his assignment, the Mossad puts a contract out on Rain, and he must use all his secret skills and awareness to stay alive.

Where it's reviewed:
Publishers Weekly, May 16, 2005, page 40

Other books by the same author:
Rain Storm, 2004
Hard Rain, 2003
Rain Fall, 2002

Other books you might like:
Lawrence Block, *The John Keller Series*, 1998-
Lee Child, *The Jack Reacher Series*, 1997-
Loren D. Estleman, *The Peter Macklin Series*, 1984-
Robert Ludlum, *The Jason Bourne Series*, 1980-
Richard Stark, *The Parker Series*, 1962-

74

AARON ELKINS

Where There's a Will

(New York: Berkley, 2005)

Story type: Amateur Detective
Series: Gideon Oliver. Book 12
Subject(s): Islands; Ranch Life; Anthropology
Major character(s): Gideon Oliver, Anthropologist (forensic), Detective—Amateur
Time period(s): 2000s
Locale(s): Hawaii

Summary: While vacationing on the Big Island, Gideon Oliver is called upon by his friend, FBI agent John Lau, to help in a case involving the deaths of two elderly Swedish cattle ranchers ten years earlier. One of the Torkelsson brothers was clearly murdered, and the other disappeared along with his airplane and pilot on the same night. Now divers have found the wreckage of the aircraft in a remote lagoon, with some skeletal remains scattered nearby. This, of course, is where forensic anthropologist Oliver's expertise is required. As the puzzle unfolds, a long-standing feud between rival ranches, a mysterious will, and the identity of the skeletal remains are all revealed. The author has also written non-series mysteries as well as another series with Seattle art curator Chris Norgren and, with his wife Charlotte, a series featuring female golf pro Lee Ofsted.

Where it's reviewed:
New York Times Book Review, April 24, 2005, page 21
Publishers Weekly, February 21, 2005, page 160

Other books by the same author:
Good Blood, 2004
Skeleton Dance, 2000
Twenty Blue Devils, 1997

Dead Men's Hearts, 1994
Make No Bones, 1991

Other books you might like:
Margot Arnold, *The Menehune Murders*, 1989
Beverly Connor, *One Grave Too Many*, 2003
Jerrilyn Farmer, *The Flaming Luau of Death*, 2005
Juanita Sheridan, *The Mamo Murders*, 1952 reprinted in 2000
Deborah Turrell, *Primitive Secrets*, 2002

75

DAVID ELLIS

In the Company of Liars

(New York: Putnam, 2005)

Story type: Psychological Suspense
Subject(s): Terrorism; Law Enforcement; Trials
Major character(s): Allison Pagone, Writer (of mysteries); Jane McCoy, FBI Agent
Time period(s): 2000s
Locale(s): Midwest (large unnamed city)

Summary: The author has written an ingeniously constructed tour de force here, told in reverse chronological order, with the ending presented first and the narrative working backward to the beginning. Several plot threads intertwine: the trial of mystery writer Allison Pagone for murdering her lobbyist lover, Sam Dillon; the investigation into her ex-husband's role in expediting the release of a potentially dangerous new drug; and a scheme by Pakistani terrorists to kill millions of people. Much of the story is told from the viewpoint of dedicated FBI agent Jane McCoy, and although there is a trial, the book is less concerned with legal issues than its predecessors.

Where it's reviewed:
Library Journal, March 15, 2005, page 68
Mystery News, April/May 2005, page 17
Mystery Scene, Spring 2005, page 68
Publishers Weekly, February 28, 2005, page 41

Other books by the same author:
Jury of One, 2004
Line of Vision, 2004
Life Sentence, 2003

Other books you might like:
Donald Harstad, *A Long December*, 2003
Francine Mathews, *Blown*, 2005
James Patterson, *3rd Degree*, 2004
    Andrew Gross, co-author
Ridley Pearson, *Cut and Run*, 2005
Carsten Stroud, *Cobraville*, 2004

76

EARL EMERSON

The Smoke Room

(New York: Ballantine, 2005)

Story type: Psychological Suspense; Action/Adventure
Subject(s): Arson; Fires; Blackmail

Major character(s): Jason Gum, Fire Fighter
Time period(s): 2000s
Locale(s): Seattle, Washington

Summary: Jason Gum is a 24-year-old rookie firefighter whose ambition is eventually to become chief of the department, but events, and his own slacker tendencies, conspire against this ever happening. The tone of the book is set with the opening, in which a hog falls from 11,000 feet into a West Seattle home with unhappy consequences. Then Jason, who shows up late at a fire but is nonetheless given the hero treatment after making a daring rescue, is blackmailed by two of his fellow firefighters over this dereliction of duty and expected to cover up for them in turn when they steal $12 million worth of bearer bonds. Chicanery, deadpan humor, and exciting firefighting sequences are served up in equal measure in this offering from an author, a Seattle firefighter himself, who has also written a series about Seattle private eye Thomas Black and another about firefighter Mac Fontana.

Where it's reviewed:
Publishers Weekly, March 21, 2005, page 36

Other books by the same author:
Pyro, 2004
Into the Inferno, 2003
Vertical Burn, 2002

Other books you might like:
Suzanne Chazin, *The Fourth Angel*, 2001
Peter Lance, *First Degree Burn*, 1997
Ridley Pearson, *Beyond Recognition*, 1997
Shelley Reuben, *Spent Matches*, 1996
Don Winslow, *California Fire and Life*, 1999

KATHY LYNN EMERSON

Face Down Below the Banqueting House

(McKinleyville, California: Perseverance, 2005)

Story type: Historical/Elizabethan
Series: Susanna, Lady Appleton. Book 8
Subject(s): Kings, Queens, Rulers, etc.; Women; History
Major character(s): Lady Susanna Appleton, Herbalist, Detective—Amateur
Time period(s): 16th century (1573)
Locale(s): England

Summary: As honored as she is to learn that Queen Elizabeth I is planning a summer visit to her home, Leigh Abbey, Susanna is dismayed at the prospect, as it will necessitate rearranging not only the entire house for the queen's comfort but Susanna's own life as well. When a murder occurs, it's almost welcome, for at least it gives Susanna something else to think about in this lively and well-researched novel of daily life in bygone times. The chaos of a royal visit is described in fascinating detail, from the 500 horses required to be on hand for Her Majesty to the wealth of personal belongings that accompany the queen wherever she goes, including her own bed and bathtub. A glossary of Elizabethan terms is included. The author has also begun a new historical series set in turn-of-the-century New York featuring journalist Diana Spaulding.

Where it's reviewed:
Library Journal, March 1, 2005, page 71

Other books by the same author:
Murders and Other Confusions, 2004 (short stories featuring Susanna, Lady Appleton)
Face Down Across the Western Sea, 2002
Face Down Before the Rebel Hooves, 2001
Face Down Beneath the Eleanor Cross, 2000
Face Down under the Wych Elm, 2000

Other books you might like:
Fiona Buckley, *The Ursula Blanchard Series*, 1997-
Judith Cook, *The Simon Forman Series*, 1997-
P.C. Doherty, *The Soul Slayer*, 1997
Ann Dukthas, *Time for the Death of a King*, 1994
Karen Harper, *The Elizabeth I Series*, 1999-

LOREN D. ESTLEMAN

Little Black Dress

(New York: Forge, 2005)

Story type: Psychological Suspense
Series: Peter Macklin. Book 5
Subject(s): Crime and Criminals; Violence; Marriage
Major character(s): Peter Macklin, Criminal (former hit man for the mob)
Time period(s): 2000s
Locale(s): Hilliard, Ohio

Summary: The trouble with being a retired hit man is that your past keeps catching up with you. Tired of the life, Peter Macklin has quit killing people for a living, married a young, beautiful, and intelligent woman, and moved from Detroit to a small Ohio town, buying the farm that his wife, Laurie, had grown up on. He's also survived an ordeal more harrowing than any professional challenge he's ever faced: he's spent an evening with Laurie's eccentric mother. Unfortunately, his mother-in-law has a boyfriend, Benjamin Grinnell, who works as a spotter for a group of armed robbers, and he fell down on the job one day and failed to spot a shop owner with a shotgun. Now he's in danger from his disgruntled employers, and that means both Macklin's mother-in-law and his wife are in danger too, unless he can get to the robbers first. The author also writes a long-running series about Detroit private eye Amos Walker as well as a loosely connected group of mysteries chronicling the history of that city.

Where it's reviewed:
Mystery News, April/May 2005, page 22
Publishers Weekly, March 28, 2005, page 61

Other books by the same author:
Something Borrowed, Something Black, 2002
Any Man's Death, 1986
Roses Are Dead, 1985
Kill Zone, 1984

Other books you might like:
Lawrence Block, *The John Keller Series*, 1998-
Barry Eisler, *The John Rain Series*, 2002-
Patricia Highsmith, *The Tom Ripley Series*, 1954-1991
Thomas Perry, *The Butcher's Boy*, 1982

Richard Stark, *The Parker Series*, 1962-

79

OLIVE ETCHELLS

No Corners for the Devil

(New York: Carroll & Graf, 2005)

Story type: Traditional; Police Procedural
Subject(s): Rural Life; Farm Life; Family
Major character(s): Channon, Detective—Homicide (detective chief inspector); Bowles, Detective—Homicide (sergeant)
Time period(s): 2000s
Locale(s): Cornwall, England

Summary: Sally and Rob Baxter and their children have escaped Manchester for a quiet farming community on south Cornwall's beautiful Roseland Peninsula, where they live in a historical round house overlooking the sea (round so there will be no corners for the devil to hide in). The villagers have welcomed them and all is going well until their youngest child, Ben, discovers the body of a teenage girl on the beach below their house. The discovery sets off all kinds of turmoil in the quiet village. The Baxter's older son, Luke, is initially suspected of killing the victim, a young temptress who's one of his schoolmates. Like many of the other locals whose lives are disrupted by the event, he has secrets he wants to keep from the police, which makes it difficult for them to do their job. Kindly, compassionate Inspector Channon leads the investigation, assisted by the resentful Sergeant Bowles, who'd very much like to see Luke found guilty. There is another murder before matters are resolved, and more than one family is transformed by the killings. The author of this first mystery (she's written historical fiction previously) handles the interplay among the large cast of well-delineated characters with great skill and insight. She also encouragingly leaves the door open for a sequel.

Where it's reviewed:
New York Times Book Review, May 8, 2005, page 23
Publishers Weekly, May 9, 2005, page 49

Other books you might like:
Janie Bolitho, *The Rose Trevelyan Series*, 1997-
Stephen Booth, *The Ben Cooper/Diane Fry Series*, 2000-
Caroline Graham, *The Tom Barnaby Series*, 1987-
John Harvey, *Flesh and Blood*, 2004
Peter Robinson, *The Inspector Alan Banks Series*, 1987-

80

JANET EVANOVICH

Eleven on Top

(New York: St. Martin's Press, 2005)

Story type: Humor; Private Detective
Series: Stephanie Plum. Book 11
Subject(s): Crime and Criminals; Family; Stalking
Major character(s): Stephanie Plum, Bounty Hunter; Joe Morelli, Detective—Police; Carlos ''Ranger'' Manoso, Bounty Hunter

Time period(s): 2000s
Locale(s): Trenton, New Jersey

Summary: Tired of being shot at, attacked by dogs, fire-bombed, and otherwise assaulted in the line of duty, Stephanie decides to quit the bounty-hunting business for good and get a respectable job that won't upset her family. The problem is that she has no other job skills, and after a succession of low-paying dead-end jobs, Stephanie not only gets fed up with her new life but realizes that no matter what she does, trouble follows her. She's being stalked by a psycho murderer who's ready to kill her when he gets the chance, so Steph takes an office job with her long-time colleague Ranger, hoping to gain some new skills that will help her find her stalker before he does her in. This doesn't sit well with her boyfriend, Trenton cop Joe Morelli, who's always been jealous of Ranger—with reason. The author recycles many of the jokes, gags, and attitudes from previous books in the series, which should suit her fans just fine.

Other books by the same author:
Ten Big Ones, 2004
To the Nines, 2003
Visions of Sugarplums, 2003
Hard Eight, 2002
Seven Up, 2001

Other books you might like:
Nancy Bartholomew, *The Sierra Lavatoni Series*, 1998-
Sparkle Hayter, *The Robin Hudson Series*, 1994-
Harley Jane Kozak, *The Wollie Shelley Series*, 2004-
Sarah Strohmeyer, *The Bubbles Yablonsky Series*, 2001-
Elaine Viets, *The Helen Hawthorne Series*, 2003-

81

ROBERT EVERSZ

Digging James Dean

(New York: Simon & Schuster, 2005)

Story type: Psychological Suspense; Humor
Series: Nina Zero. Book 4
Subject(s): Animals/Dogs; Photography; Crime and Criminals
Major character(s): Nina Zero, Photographer (paparazza), Criminal (former)
Time period(s): 2000s
Locale(s): Los Angeles, California; Fairmount, Indiana

Summary: Once Nina was a cute blonde children's photographer named Mary Alice Baker. Then she accidentally sets off a bomb at the Los Angeles International Airport while doing a favor for the wrong guy. While in prison she reinvented herself as a punk, pierced brunette and, on parole, became a paparazza, sharing a funky apartment in Venice Beach with a toothless Rottweiler and selling most of her work to a third-rate tabloid. Here she and her employer get wind of some scandalous doings in James Dean's hometown of Fairmount, Indiana, where some of his bones have gone missing from his grave. From there she follows a convoluted trail to a weird Los Angeles cult known as the Church of Divine Thespians. She's also disastrously reunited with her long-lost older sister, who winds up stealing Nina's driver's license and checkbook.

Lots of action, some sharp satire, and an appealing anti-heroine make this an entertaining read.

Where it's reviewed:
Mystery Scene, Winter 2005, page 68
Publishers Weekly, November 22, 2004, page 41
Romantic Times, March 2005, page 86

Other books by the same author:
Burning Garbo, 2003
Killing Paparazzi, 2002
Shooting Elvis, 1996

Other books you might like:
Jen Banbury, *Like a Hole in the Head*, 1998
Elizabeth Cosin, *The Zen Moses Series*, 1998-
Alan Russell, *Exposure*, 2002
Barbara Seranella, *No Human Involved*, 1997
Jenny Siler, *Iced*, 2001

82

TERENCE FAHERTY

The Confessions of Owen Keane

(Norfolk, Virginia: Crippen & Landru, 2005)

Story type: Collection; Amateur Detective
Series: Owen Keane. Book 8
Subject(s): Short Stories
Major character(s): Owen Keane, Researcher (law firm), Detective—Amateur
Time period(s): 2000s
Locale(s): Boston, Massachusetts

Summary: Owen Keane is a moody ex-seminarian who feels an enormous sense of failure for not having become the priest he set out to be. He works at meaningless jobs, mostly as a researcher at a Boston law firm, and fills his life with solving mysteries. This volume brings together a novella and six short stories detailing his investigations, from solving a gang murder to dealing with a loss of faith. Two of the stories have never been published before, including "St. Jimmy," the first Owen Keane story, and "On Pilgrimage," written specifically for this collection. There is also an introduction by the author and a checklist of his works, which include a historical series set in postwar Hollywood featuring actor turned private eye Scott Elliott.

Other books by the same author:
Orion Rising, 1999
The Ordained, 1996
Die Dreaming, 1994
The Lost Keats, 1993
Live to Regret, 1992

Other books you might like:
Jon L. Breen, *Kill the Umpire*, 2004
    short stories
William L. DeAndrea, *Murder—All Kinds*, 2004
    short stories
Brendan DuBois, *Tales from the Dark Woods*, 2000
    short stories
Joe Gores, *Stakeout on Page Street*, 2000
    short stories

John Lutz, *The Nudger Dilemmas*, 2001
    short stories

83

LINDA FAIRSTEIN

Entombed

(New York: Scribner, 2005)

Story type: Police Procedural; Psychological Suspense
Series: Alexandra Cooper. Book 7
Subject(s): Rape; Literature; Crime and Criminals
Major character(s): Alexandra Cooper, Lawyer (assistant district attorney); Mercer Wallace, Detective—Homicide; Mike Chapman, Detective—Homicide
Time period(s): 2000s
Locale(s): New York, New York

Summary: Manhattan sex crimes prosecutor Alex Cooper searches for a serial killer and rapist with help from her usual sidekicks, NYPD homicide detectives Mercer Wallace and Mike Chapman. The skeleton of a young woman is found walled up in an East Village building once occupied by Edgar Allen Poe. The victim has been dead for over 20 years but was alive when she was sealed up within the building's walls in a manner eerily reminiscent of Poe's short story, "The Cask of the Amontillado." She appears to have been a victim of the Silk Stocking rapist, who seems to have disappeared from the city. Then a freelance writer who belonged to a secret society devoted to Poe turns up dead, apparently his latest victim. It quickly becomes obvious that her murder was the work of a copycat, and the search for answers takes Alex and her team to the Bronx Botanical Gardens, where they meet the head of the mysterious Raven Society. Details about Poe's life and work continually enrich the narrative, which is also enhanced by solid police work from Mercer and Mike and the unwavering determination of Alex to find the truth.

Where it's reviewed:
People Weekly, February 14, 2005, page 164
Publishers Weekly, November 22, 2004, page 36
Romantic Times, March 2005, page 81

Other books by the same author:
The Kills, 2004
The Bone Vault, 2003
The Deadhouse, 2001
Cold Hit, 1999
Likely to Die, 1997

Other books you might like:
Patricia Cornwell, *The Kay Scarpetta Series*, 1990-
Laura Lippman, *In a Strange City*, 2001
Carol O'Connell, *The Kathleen Mallory Series*, 1994-
Kathy Reichs, *The Tempe Brennan Series*, 1997-
Marianne Wesson, *The Cinda Hayes Series*, 1998-

84

JERRILYN FARMER

The Flaming Luau of Death

(New York: William Morrow, 2005)

Story type: Amateur Detective; Humor
Series: Madeleine Bean. Book 7
Subject(s): Weddings; Cooks and Cooking; Islands
Major character(s): Madeleine Bean, Caterer (event planner), Detective—Amateur
Time period(s): 2000s
Locale(s): Los Angeles, California; Hawaii

Summary: Madeleine Bean, party organizer extraordinaire, has decided to surprise one of her long-time employees (and close friend) Holly Nichols with a surprise bridal shower at an exclusive spa resort on Hawaii's Big Island. The only catch is that Holly might not actually be divorced from her high school prom date, whom she married during a high-spirited fling in Las Vegas shortly after the dance. Maddie, Holly, and various of their friends, family, and co-workers decide to go through with it anyway, despite the threatening e-mails Holly has begun to get. Once on the island, murder follows, and so do a lot of laughs, information on Hawaii's history, and many descriptions of drink and food, especially wasabi.

Where it's reviewed:
Booklist, February 1, 2005, page 945
Library Journal, March 1, 2005, page 70
Publishers Weekly, February 21, 2005, page 161
Romantic Times, March 2005, page 85

Other books by the same author:
Perfect Sax, 2004
Mumbo Gumbo, 2003
Dim Sum Dead, 2001
Killer Wedding, 2000
Immaculate Reception, 1999

Other books you might like:
Paula Carter, *The Hillary Scarborough Series*, 1999-
Isis Crawford, *A Catered Murder*, 2003
Diane Mott Davidson, *The Goldy Bear Schulz Series*, 1990-
Aaron Elkins, *Where There's a Will*, 2005
Lou Jane Temple, *The Heaven Lee Series*, 1996-

85

MONICA FERRIS (Pseudonym of Mary Monica Kuhlfeld)

Embroidered Truths

(New York: Berkley, 2005)

Story type: Amateur Detective
Series: Betsy Devonshire. Book 9
Subject(s): Crafts; Homosexuality/Lesbianism; Sewing
Major character(s): Betsy Devonshire, Store Owner (needlework shop), Detective—Amateur
Time period(s): 2000s
Locale(s): Excelsior, Minnesota

Summary: Since taking over her late sister's needlework shop, Crewel World, in the small Minnesota town of Excelsior, Betsy Devonshire has thrown herself into the business and has forged friendships with her employees and customers. When Godwin, her gay shop manager, has a falling out with his boyfriend John, Betsy is only too happy to let Godwin move in with her. Then, when John is found dead and Godwin arrested for his murder, Betsy is determined to help him prove his innocence. An embroidery pattern is included.

Where it's reviewed:
Publishers Weekly, May 9, 2005, page 50

Other books by the same author:
Crewel Yule, 2004
Cutwork, 2004
Hanging by a Thread, 2003
A Murderous Yarn, 2002
Unraveled Sleeve, 2001

Other books you might like:
Susan Wittig Albert, *The China Bayles Series*, 1992-
Laura Childs, *The Carmela Bertrand Series*, 2003-
Mary Kruger, *Died in the Wool*, 2005
Tamar Myers, *The Abigail Timberlake Series*, 1996-
Maggie Sefton, *Knit One, Kill Two*, 2005

86

BILL FITZHUGH

Highway 61 Resurfaced

(New York: William Morrow, 2005)

Story type: Humor; Private Detective
Series: Rick Shannon. Book 2
Subject(s): Radio Broadcasting; Music and Musicians; American South
Major character(s): Rick Shannon, Radio Personality (disc jockey), Detective—Private
Time period(s): 2000s
Locale(s): Vicksburg, Mississippi

Summary: Classic rock disc jockey Rick Shannon is moonlighting as a private eye, having opened his own agency, Rockin'Vestigations. He's hired by a young woman named Lollie Woolfolk to locate the grandfather she never knew, Tucker Woolfolk, who turns out to be a former blues producer, making this a case after Rick's own heart. They locate Woolfolk in his shack in the Mississippi Delta country, but someone's gotten to him first. Lollie, who keeps handing Rick envelopes full of cash to pursue the investigation, disappears shortly after, and then a different woman claiming to be Lollie Woolfolk turns up and joins him in a journey that takes them through the Delta and its rich history of blues. There is a tremendous amount of background on blues, rock, and soul, some extremely funny (and extremely raunchy) scenes, plenty of memorable villains, and a very needy little kitten named Crusty.

Where it's reviewed:
Library Journal, December 2004, page 96

Other books by the same author:
Radio Activity, 2004 (Rick Shannon. Book 1)
Heart Seizure, 2003
Fender Bender, 2001
Cross Dressing, 2000
The Organ Grinders, 1998

Other books you might like:
Ace Atkins, *Crossroad Blues*, 1998
Pete Hautman, *The Mortal Nuts*, 1996
Carl Hiaasen, *Basket Case*, 2002
Corson Hirschfeld, *Freeze Dry*, 2003
Elmore Leonard, *Mr. Paradise*, 2004

87

JOANNE FLUKE

Peach Cobbler Murder

(New York: Kensington, 2005)

Story type: Amateur Detective
Series: Hannah Swensen. Book 7
Subject(s): Weddings; Cooks and Cooking; Small Town Life
Major character(s): Hannah Swensen, Baker, Detective—Amateur
Time period(s): 2000s
Locale(s): Lake Eden, Minnesota

Summary: Hannah Swensen, owner of The Cookie Jar Bakery in the small Minnesota town of Lake Eden, has a formidable competitor in the new Magnolia Blossom Bakery which has opened just across the street from her, run by two Southern sisters. Although she has her hands full working on her business partner's wedding, Hannah is determined to do what she must to keep her business going. Then Shawna Lee, one of the sisters (who has also been making a play for Hannah's sometime boyfriend, police detective Miles Kingston), is found dead in the new bakery. Since she had a great deal to gain by Shawna's death, naturally Hannah is a prime suspect. In order to clear herself, she starts looking for the real killer. Recipes included.

Where it's reviewed:
Library Journal, March 1, 2005, page 71
Romantic Times, April 2005, page 143

Other books by the same author:
Fudge Cupcake Murder, 2004
Sugar Cookie Murder, 2004
Lemon Meringue Pie Murder, 2003
Blueberry Muffin Murder, 2002
Strawberry Shortcake Murder, 2001

Other books you might like:
JoAnna Carl, *The Chocolate Cat Caper*, 2002
Laura Childs, *The Theodosia Browning Series*, 2001-
Isis Crawford, *A Catered Murder*, 2003
Diane Mott Davidson, *The Goldy Bear Schulz Series*, 1990-
Nancy Fairbanks, *The Carolyn Blue Series*, 2001-

88

RICHARD FORREST

Death in the Secret Garden

(New York: Severn House, 2005)

Story type: Amateur Detective; Police Procedural
Series: Lyon Wentworth. Book 9
Subject(s): Small Town Life; Mental Illness

Major character(s): Lyon Wentworth, Writer (children's books), Detective—Amateur; Bea Wentworth, Political Figure (state senator), Detective—Amateur; Rocco Herbert, Police Officer (police chief)
Time period(s): 2000s
Locale(s): Connecticut (small town)

Summary: It's good to have this amiable crime-solving trio back. When the body of a young woman is found in the woods, all evidence points to Spook, a Vietnam veteran with a long history of alcoholism and mental illness. Rocco doesn't think Spook is guilty and turns to his old friends, Lyon and Bea Wentworth, to help him prove it. As more people are killed, the list of suspects grows, and the quiet little town is soon rocked to its foundations by the unhappy events. With a strong plot and even stronger characterizations, this is on par with earlier works in this pleasantly old-fashioned series.

Where it's reviewed:
Booklist, December 1, 2004, page 639

Other books by the same author:
The Pied Piper of Death, 1997
Death on the Mississippi, 1989
Death under the Lilacs, 1985
The Death at Yew Corner, 1980
The Death in the Willows, 1979

Other books you might like:
Philip R. Craig, *The J.W. Jackson Series*, 1989-
Aaron Elkins, *The Gideon Oliver Series*, 1982-
David Handler, *The Berger & Mitry Series*, 2001-
Jane Langton, *The Homer Kelly Series*, 1964-
Justin Scott, *The Ben Abbott Series*, 1994-

89

CHRISTOPHER FOWLER

The Water Room

(New York: Bantam, 2005)

Story type: Police Procedural; Traditional
Series: Peculiar Crimes. Book 2
Subject(s): Aging; Humor; Law Enforcement
Major character(s): Arthur Bryant, Detective—Police; John May, Detective—Police
Time period(s): 2000s
Locale(s): London, England

Summary: This old-fashioned, fair-play mystery offers up a classic impossible crime for the elderly detectives Arthur Bryant and John May of Scotland Yard's Peculiar Crimes Unit. The reclusive sister of a friend and former colleague of Bryant dies of drowning in the basement of her house, immaculately attired and dry as a bone. Bryant, an irascible, technologically challenged old coot who lives as much in the past as in the present, has no idea what to make of the case and turns to his slightly younger and far more personable partner, John May, for assistance. Always on hand to help them is the unflappable Sergeant Janice Longbright. Other strange deaths follow in an elaborate plot that offers as much fun as do the unusual personalities of the detectives and the improbable workings of their Peculiar Crimes Unit. The author is also noted for his tales of urban horror.

Where it's reviewed:
Publishers Weekly, May 23, 2005, page 62

Other books by the same author:
Full Dark House, 2004

Other books you might like:
Carter Dickson, *The Sir Henry Merrivale Series*, 1934-1953
Kenneth Hopkins, *The William Blow and Gideon Manciple Series*, 1957-1962
Peter Lovesey, *The Peter Diamond Series*, 1991-
John Mortimer, *The Horace Rumpole Series*, 1978-
John Sladek, *The Thackeray Phin Series*, 1977-1979

90

EARLENE FOWLER

Delectable Mountains
(New York: Berkley, 2005)

Story type: Amateur Detective
Series: Benni Harper. Book 12
Subject(s): Children; Quilts; Religion
Major character(s): Benni Harper, Museum Curator (folk art), Detective—Amateur
Time period(s): 1990s (1996)
Locale(s): San Celina County, California

Summary: When Benni's beloved Grandma Dove calls her to tell her that Lily Sanders, the music director at San Celina Baptist Church, has been called away, she knows it can mean only one thing. Grandma Dove wants Benni to help her take over directing the children's musical adaptation of John Bunyan's *Pilgrim's Progress* in Lily's absence. No sooner do they start rehearsing than the body of the church handyman is found, beaten to death, in front of the altar; a rare antique violin goes missing from the San Celina mission; and an unsavory cousin of her police chief husband Gabe makes an appearance in town.

Where it's reviewed:
Publishers Weekly, April 18, 2005, page 46

Other books by the same author:
Broken Dishes, 2004
Sunshine and Shadow, 2003
Steps to the Altar, 2002
Arkansas Traveler, 2001
Seven Sisters, 2000

Other books you might like:
Susan Wittig Albert, *The China Bayles Series*, 1992-
Laura Crum, *The Gail McCarthy Series*, 1994-
Diane Mott Davidson, *The Goldy Bear Schulz Series*, 1990-
Monica Ferris, *Unraveled Sleeve*, 2001
Janet LaPierre, *The Meg Halloran Series*, 1987-

91

MARGARET FRAZER (Pseudonym of Gail Frazer)

The Widow's Tale
(New York: Berkley, 2005)

Story type: Historical/Medieval

Series: Dame Frevisse. Book 14
Subject(s): Middle Ages; Nuns; Politics
Major character(s): Dame Frevisse, Religious (nun)
Time period(s): 15th century (1449)
Locale(s): Oxfordshire, England

Summary: After wealthy landowner Edward Helyngton dies, his treacherous cousin Laurence seizes his estate, kidnaps his children, and imprisons his widow Cristiana in St. Frideswide's, the convent that houses shrewd Dame Frevisse. The poor widow is made to do penance by lying face down on the cold floor of the chapel, subsisting on only bread and water, having been charged with unnamed sins by Laurence. Dame Frevisse hears Cristiana out and comes to believe her tragic story, which prompts the inquisitive nun to do some investigating into the matter. Eventually a secret Cristiana learned from her husband on his deathbed sets the wheels of justice in motion, even though it threatens to bring about a civil war.

Where it's reviewed:
Mystery News, February/March 2005, page 19
Publishers Weekly, December 20, 2004, page 40

Other books by the same author:
The Hunter's Tale, 2004
The Bastard's Tale, 2003
The Clerk's Tale, 2002
The Squire's Tale, 2000
The Reeve's Tale, 1999

Other books you might like:
Alys Clare, *The Abbess Helewise Series*, 1999-
C.L. Grace, *A Shrine of Murder*, 1993
Sheri Holman, *A Stolen Tongue*, 1997
Candace Robb, *The Nun's Tale*, 1995
Priscilla Royal, *The Eleanor of Wynethorpe Series*, 2003-

92

KINKY FRIEDMAN

Ten Little New Yorkers
(New York: Simon & Schuster, 2005)

Story type: Private Detective; Humor
Series: Kinky Friedman. Book 17
Subject(s): Serial Killers; Friendship; Animals/Cats
Major character(s): Kinky Friedman, Detective—Private, Singer (country singer)
Time period(s): 2000s
Locale(s): New York, New York; Medina, Texas

Summary: Still mourning the loss of his cat, the Kinkster decides to leave Greenwich Village for his other home in the Texas hill country, where he runs an animal shelter and likes to chill out. Little does he know that in the eyes of the police, particularly NYPD homicide detective Sgt. Mort Cooperman, he's the chief suspect in four murders in the Village. The wallet of one of the victims has been found in Kinky's loft, and when he returns to New York, four more killings occur. If the murderer isn't Kinky (and naturally it isn't), he's almost certainly one of his inner circle. It's giving nothing away to reveal that this somewhat melancholy adventure, a somewhat

twisted homage to Agatha Christie, is being billed as the Kinkster's final case.

Where it's reviewed:
Mystery News, February/March 2005, page 76
Publishers Weekly, January 17, 2005, page 37
Texas Monthly, March 2005, page 76

Other books by the same author:
The Prisoner of Vandam Street, 2004
Meanwhile Back at the Ranch, 2002
Steppin' on a Rainbow, 2001
The Mile High Club, 2000
Spanking Watson, 1999

Other books you might like:
Lawrence Block, *The Bernie Rhodenbarr Series*, 1977-
Stan Cutler, *The Rayford Goodman Series*, 1991-
Parnell Hall, *The Stanley Hastings Series*, 1987-
Ben Rehder, *The John Marlin Series*, 2002-
Roger L. Simon, *The Moses Wine Series*, 1973-

93

DAVID FULMER

Jass

(Orlando, Florida: Harcourt, 2005)

Story type: Historical; Private Detective
Series: Valentin St. Cyr. Book 2
Subject(s): Music and Musicians; Race Relations; Serial Killers
Major character(s): Valentin St. Cyr, Detective—Private; Jelly Roll Morton, Historical Figure, Musician; Tom Anderson, Historical Figure, Political Figure
Time period(s): 1900s (1909)
Locale(s): New Orleans, Louisiana (Storyville)

Summary: Creole detective Valentin St. Cyr, formerly a New Orleans cop, is now on the payroll of political boss Tom Anderson, the infamous ''King of Storyville'' (New Orleans' red-light district). When four jazz musicians who all once played for the same band are murdered, St. Cyr starts to investigate, at the behest of his friend, legendary jazz great Jelly Roll Morton. He's warned off the case not only by Anderson but by the police and city officials, including the mayor, who have their own reasons for not wanting to see it solved. The author expertly weaves historical details, including real-life characters and the development of the new music called ''jass,'' into his narrative without ever overwhelming the story.

Where it's reviewed:
Booklist, January 1, 2005, page 826
Library Journal, December 2004, page 94
Mystery News, February/March 2005, page 26
Mystery Scene, Winter 2005, page 70
Publishers Weekly, November 29, 2004, page 26

Other books by the same author:
Chasing the Devil's Tail, 2001 (Shamus Award winner for Best First P.I. Novel)

Other books you might like:
John Dickson Carr, *The Ghosts' High Noon*, 1970

Barbara Hambly, *The Benjamin January Series*, 1997-
Bill Moody, *The Evan Horne Series*, 1994-
James Sallis, *The Lew Griffin Series*, 1992-
Robert Skinner, *The Wesley Farrell Series*, 1997-

94

LUIZ ALFREDO GARCIA-ROZA

A Window in Copacabana

(New York: Henry Holt, 2005)

Story type: Police Procedural
Series: Inspector Espinosa. Book 4
Subject(s): Crime and Criminals; Morality
Major character(s): Espinosa, Police Officer (inspector)
Time period(s): 2000s
Locale(s): Rio de Janeiro, Brazil

Summary: Espinosa, who heads up the Copacabana precinct of Rio, is a police officer of a somewhat bookish, existentialist bent, with a weakness for beautiful women. When three cops are murdered on the mean streets of his precinct, and then their three mistresses are slain, Espinosa forms a confidential task force to investigate the crimes and the policemen's private lives. Evidence points to a killer within the police force, as well as corruption and a cover-up. Not exactly a conventional police procedural, it's rich in atmosphere and psychological detail, and is capably translated from the Portuguese by Benjamin Moser.

Where it's reviewed:
Booklist, November 1, 2004, page 95
Library Journal, December 2004, page 95
New York Times Book Review, January 9, 2005, page 17
Publishers Weekly, November 29, 2004, page 26

Other books by the same author:
Southwesterly Wind, 2004
December Heat, 2003
The Silence of the Rain, 2002

Other books you might like:
Jorge Luis Borges, *Six Problems for Don Isidro Parodi*, 1942
Ruben Fonseca, *High Art*, 1986
Gabriel Garcia Marquez, *Chronicle of a Death Foretold*, 1982
Marcio Souza, *Death Squeeze*, 1984
Mario Vargas Llosa, *Death in the Andes*, 1996

95

ASHLEY GARDNER (Pseudonym of Jennifer Ashley)

The Sudbury School Murders

(New York: Berkley, 2005)

Story type: Historical/Regency
Series: Captain Gabriel Lacey. Book 4
Subject(s): Social Classes; Gypsies; Schools/Boarding Schools
Major character(s): Captain Gabriel Lacey, Military Personnel (former), Veteran
Time period(s): 1810s (1816)
Locale(s): Sudbury, England

Summary: Captain Gabriel Lacey, a cashiered cavalry officer and veteran of the Peninsular War takes a position as secretary to the headmaster of the Sudbury School, where London's wealthy merchant class sends its sons to be trained as gentlemen. A series of vicious pranks are plaguing the school, culminating in the murder of a groom whose body is found in a canal. Another stable hand, a gypsy named Sebastian, of whom the headmaster's daughter is enamored, is the chief suspect, but Lacey believes him to be innocent and sets out to prove it.

Other books by the same author:
A Regimental Murder, 2004
The Hanover Square Affair, 2004
The Glass House, 2004

Other books you might like:
T.F. Banks, *The Thief-Taker,* 2001
S.K. Rizzolo, *The Penelope Wolfe/John Chase Series,* 2002-
Madeleine E. Robins, *Point of Honour,* 2003
Kate Ross, *The Julian Kestrel Series,* 1993-1997
Rosemary Stevens, *The Beau Brummell Series,* 2000-

96

ALICIA GASPAR DE ALBA

Desert Blood

(Houston: Arte Publico, 2005)

Story type: Psychological Suspense
Subject(s): Mexican Americans; Adoption; Serial Killers
Major character(s): Ivon Villa, Professor (women's studies), Lesbian
Time period(s): 1990s (1998)
Locale(s): El Paso, Texas; Juarez, Mexico

Summary: For several years somebody has been terrorizing and murdering young Mexican women and dumping their bodies in the Chihuahuan desert outside of Juarez. When Ivon Villa arrives in her native El Paso to adopt a baby for herself and her lover, she finds the pregnant young *maquiladora* worker she had made the arrangements with has been brutally murdered by the unknown killer. Then Ivon's younger sister is kidnapped in Juarez, and she vows to find her, no matter what the cost. It's a powerful indictment of social injustice along the border, and the first mystery by a well-regarded Chicana poet, essayist, and novelist.

Where it's reviewed:
Library Journal, March 1, 2005, page 70

Other books you might like:
Lucha Corpi, *The Gloria Damasco Series,* 1992-
Allana Martin, *The Texana Jones Series,* 1996-
James C. Mitchell, *Choke Point,* 2004
Janice Steinberg, *Death Crosses the Border,* 1995
Judith Van Gieson, *North of the Border,* 1988

97

BRAD GEAGLEY

Year of the Hyenas

(New York: Simon & Schuster, 2005)

Story type: Historical/Ancient Egypt; Private Detective
Subject(s): Kings, Queens, Rulers, etc.; Ancient History; Egyptian Religion
Major character(s): Semerket, Detective—Police
Time period(s): 12th century B.C. (1153 B.C.)
Locale(s): Egypt

Summary: The so-called Harem Conspiracy of Ramses III, a historical event well-known to Egyptologists, provides the backdrop to this detective novel set in ancient Egypt. The principal investigator is Semerket, a man no longer young, too fond of strong drink, down on his luck, and desperately trying to win back his ex-wife. Formerly the Clerk of Investigations and Secrets, he's hired by higher-ups to investigate the murder of an aging priestess; what they don't tell him is that they fully expect him to fail. Set in Thebes in the court of the great Pharaoh Ramses III, it's essentially a modern private eye novel transposed to ancient times, with Semerket working doggedly to solve a crime that nobody wants solved. First novel.

Where it's reviewed:
Booklist, January 1, 2005, page 826
Deadly Pleasures, Winter 2005, page 42
Library Journal, January 2005, page 83
Mystery News, Winter 2005, page 26

Other books you might like:
P.C. Doherty, *The Lord Amerotke Series,* 1998-
Lauren Haney, *The Lieutenant Bak Series,* 1997-
Lee Levin, *King Tut's Private Eye,* 1996
Lynda S. Robinson, *The Lord Meren Series,* 1994-
Carol Thurston, *The Eye of Horus,* 2000

98

CHRISTINE GENTRY

Carnosaur Crimes

(Scottsdale, Arizona: Poisoned Pen Press, 2005)

Story type: Amateur Detective
Series: Ansel Phoenix. Book 2
Subject(s): Paleontology; American West; Native Americans
Major character(s): Ansel Phoenix, Artist, Detective—Amateur
Time period(s): 2000s
Locale(s): Big Toe, Montana

Summary: Ansel Phoenix, a paleoartist who makes her living drawing dinosaurs, is called to the scene when a charred corpse is found hanging from the mouth of a life-sized Allosaurus replica she constructed outside the natural history museum in Big Toe. It turns out to be the remains of an Indian poacher who was cutting out fossilized dinosaur tracks along the Redwater River, and the feds are threatening to close the museum while the FBI have taken over for the local police. Ansel, who is half-Blackfoot with ties to both native and

Anglo communities, devises a sting operation to help the FBI nail the fossil poachers. There's plenty of action, as well as a vivid portrayal of the wild Montana landscape.

Where it's reviewed:
Booklist, March 1, 2005, page 1144
Mystery News, Spring 2005, page 77
Publishers Weekly, March 21, 2005, page 39

Other books by the same author:
Mesozoic Murder, 2003

Other books you might like:
Sarah Andrews, *Bone Hunter*, 1999
Nevada Barr, *The Anna Pigeon Series*, 1993-
Peter Bowen, *The Gabriel Du Pre Series*, 1994-
James D. Doss, *The Shaman's Bones*, 1997
Sandra West Prowell, *The Killing of Monday Brown*, 1994

99

ELIZABETH GEORGE

With No One as a Witness

(New York: HarperCollins, 2005)

Story type: Police Procedural; Psychological Suspense
Series: Inspector Thomas Lynley. Book 13
Subject(s): Serial Killers; Social Classes; Racism
Major character(s): Thomas Lynley, Police Officer (acting superintendent); Barbara Havers, Police Officer (constable)
Time period(s): 2000s
Locale(s): London, England

Summary: Thomas Lynley and his assistant, Barbara Havers (newly demoted from sergeant to constable) are being pressured to solve the serial killings of four teenage boys, three of them black or of mixed parentage. The newest victim is white, and there are murmurs of racism within the department because of its failure to solve the three earlier murders. Havers is smarting over her demotion, Lynley is having to deal with a reporter and a profiler his boss has unleashed upon his team, and red herrings and plot twists abound, with an ending that presages some major life changes for various of the series characters.

Where it's reviewed:
Entertainment Weekly, March 18, 2005, page 74
Publishers Weekly, February 21, 2005, page 161
Romantic Times, March 2005, page 82

Other books by the same author:
A Place of Hiding, 2003
A Traitor to Memory, 2001
In Pursuit of the Proper Sinner, 1999
Deception on His Mind, 1997
In the Presence of the Enemy, 1996

Other books you might like:
Stephen Booth, *The Ben Cooper/Diane Fry Series*, 2000-
Deborah Crombie, *The Duncan Kincaid/Gemma James Series*, 1993-
Martha Grimes, *The Inspector Jury Series*, 1981-
P.D. James, *The Adam Dalgliesh Series*, 1962-
Ruth Rendell, *The Inspector Wexford Series*, 1964-

100

VICTOR GISCHLER

Suicide Squeeze

(New York: Delacorte, 2005)

Story type: Private Detective; Humor
Subject(s): Boats and Boating; Crime and Criminals; Arson
Major character(s): Conner Samson, Detective—Private (repo man)
Time period(s): 2000s
Locale(s): Pensacola, Florida

Summary: Conner Samson is a not terribly successful repo man who specializes in reclaiming boats from defaulting owners. This time it's a sloop, the *Electric Jenny*, being leased by Teddy Folger, who plans to sail away in it and leave his ex-wife far behind. He's collected a fat insurance check after burning down his comic book/baseball card store, a good part of the money in compensation for a 1954 Joe DiMaggio card signed by Joe, Marilyn Monroe, and Billy Wilder. The only problem is that Folger still has the card, on the sloop, and not only would his insurance company and ex-wife like to have it, but so would a couple of competing Japanese collectors. Samson does succeed in repossessing the boat, so now he has all of the above people after him, as well as his bookie to whom he owes a great deal of money. Fast, funny, and filled with eccentric characters and improbable situations, it's another entertaining comedy of bad manners from this Edgar-nominated author.

Where it's reviewed:
Booklist, March 1, 2005, page 1144
Library Journal, December 2005, page 96
Publishers Weekly, March 14, 2005, page 481

Other books by the same author:
The Pistol Poets, 2002
Gun Monkeys, 2001

Other books you might like:
Lawrence Block, *The Burglar Who Traded Ted Williams*, 1994
Tim Dorsey, *The Serge O. Storms Series*, 1999-
Bill Eidson, *The Repo*, 2003
Kinky Friedman, *The Kinky Friedman Series*, 1986-
Joe Gores, *The DKA Series*, 1972-

101

JANET GLEESON

The Serpent in the Garden

(New York: Simon & Schuster, 2005)

Story type: Historical/Georgian
Subject(s): Gardens and Gardening; Social Classes; Art
Major character(s): Joshua Pope, Artist (portrait painter)
Time period(s): 1760s (1766)
Locale(s): London, England; Richmond, England

Summary: Still mourning the untimely death of his wife and young son, portrait painter Joshua Pope accepts a commission and leaves London for a lavish estate in Richmond. There he is to paint the wedding portrait of wealthy Herbert Bentnick's

betrothed, Sabine Mercer, an exotic beauty from the West Indies. Sabine's passion is horticulture, particularly the cultivation of pineapples (a fruit the English were obsessed with at the time), and Pope has no sooner arrived on the scene than Sabine finds a dead man in her beloved conservatory. Soon after, Sabine's prized emerald necklace disappears and Pope is suspected of stealing it. If he can't prove his innocence, Pope—at 33, already the equal of Reynolds and Gainsborough—stands to lose his reputation, and with it, his livelihood.

Where it's reviewed:
Booklist, January 1, 2005, page 827
Library Journal, January 2005, page 85
Publishers Weekly, January 24, 2005, page 225

Other books by the same author:
The Grenadillo Box, 2002

Other books you might like:
Bruce Alexander, *The Sir John Fielding Series*, 1994-2005
Diana Gabaldon, *Lord John and the Private Matter*, 2003
Robert Lee Hall, *The Benjamin Franklin Series*, 1988-
Deryn Lake, *The John Rawlings Series*, 1994-
Hannah March, *The Complaint of the Dove*, 2003

102

KAT GOLDRING

The Eye That Is Divine

(New York: Berkley, 2005)

Story type: Amateur Detective
Series: Willi Gallagher. Book 4
Subject(s): Buddhism; Religious Life; Small Town Life
Major character(s): Wilhelmina "Willi" Gallagher, Teacher (high school), Detective—Amateur; Quannah Lassiter, Police Officer (Texas Ranger), Indian (part Sioux)
Time period(s): 2000s
Locale(s): Nickleberry, Texas; Serenity Lake Island, Texas

Summary: Willi's best friend Kenzie Francis, fed up with being stalked by her interfering ex-husband, persuades Willi to accompany her to a Buddhist retreat led by Zen monks. Quannah, Willi's boyfriend, is conducting a sweat-lodge ceremony for some of the participants who want a multicultural spiritual experience. It's a good thing he's there, because the retreat turns out to be anything but peaceful, with some sinister Japanese businessmen in attendance, as well as a thief intent on liberating the monks' sacred gem, The Eye That Is Divine.

Other books by the same author:
Work of the Angels, 2003
Death Medicine, 2002
All Signs Point to Murder, 2001

Other books you might like:
Susan Wittig Albert, *Rueful Death*, 1996
Earlene Fowler, *The Benni Harper Series*, 1994-
Yasmine Galenorn, *The Emerald O'Brien Series*, 2003-
Nancy Herndon, *The Elena Jarvis Series*, 1995-
Denise Swanson, *The Scumble River Series*, 2000-

103

ROBERT GOLDSBOROUGH

Three Strikes You're Dead

(Memphis: Echelon, 2005)

Story type: Historical/Depression Era
Subject(s): Organized Crime; Politics; Journalism
Major character(s): Steve Malek, Journalist (police reporter)
Time period(s): 1930s (1938)
Locale(s): Chicago, Illinois

Summary: Steve Malek is a police reporter for the *Chicago Tribune*, the leader in the fiercely competitive newspaper wars raging in the Windy City. He sees his chance for journalistic glory when a reform candidate mayor is shot down by an unidentified gunman, and despite his editor's warning to stay away from the story, he starts an investigation in which he encounters many real-life figures of the day, including Helen Hayes, Richard Daley, Al Capone, and the legendary pitching phenomenon Dizzy Dean. The author has also written a series continuing the adventures of Rex Stout's great detective, Nero Wolfe.

Other books by the same author:
The Missing Chapter, 1994
Silver Spire, 1992
Fade to Black, 1990
The Last Coincidence, 1989
The Bloodied Ivy, 1988

Other books you might like:
Holly Baxter, *Tears of the Dragon*, 2005
Max Allan Collins, *The Nate Heller Series*, 1983-
Ron Goulart, *The Groucho Marx Series*, 1998-
Stuart M. Kaminsky, *The Toby Peters Series*, 1977-
Lise McClendon, *One O'Clock Jump*, 2001

104

PHILIP GOODEN

An Honorable Murder

(New York: Carroll & Graf, 2004)

Story type: Historical/Renaissance
Series: Nicholas Revill. Book 6
Subject(s): Theater; Actors and Actresses; Political Prisoners
Major character(s): Nicholas Revill, Actor, Detective—Amateur
Time period(s): 17th century (1604)
Locale(s): London, England

Summary: Like its predecessors, this latest case for actor/manager Nick Revill is closely tied to current events of the day. Following the defeat of the Armada, the Spanish have arrived in London intent on negotiating a peace treaty, while their archfoe, Sir Walter Raleigh, is being held prisoner in the Tower of London. Nick's theater company, renamed the King's Men now that James I has succeeded Elizabeth I to the throne, is invited by Ben Jonson to take part in a masque at Somerset House, where the Spaniards are staying. Allies of Sir Walter are actively working to stall the peace negotiations,

and Nick and his men soon find themselves in the midst of a conspiracy not of their making.

Other books by the same author:
Mask of Night, 2004
Alms for Oblivion, 2003
The Pale Companion, 2002
Death of Kings, 2001
Sleep of Death, 2000

Other books you might like:
Judith Cook, *The Slicing Edge of Death*, 1993
Simon Hawke, *The Smythe/Shakespeare Series*, 2000-
Tony Hays, *Murder on the Twelfth Night*, 1993
Faye Kellerman, *The Quality of Mercy*, 1989
Edward Marston, *The Nicholas Bracewell Series*, 1988-

105
ANN GRANGER
That Way Murder Lies
(New York: St. Martin's Minotaur, 2005)

Story type: Amateur Detective; Traditional
Series: Mitchell & Markby. Book 15
Subject(s): Small Town Life; Secrets; Weddings
Major character(s): Meredith Mitchell, Civil Servant, Detective—Amateur; Alan Markby, Police Officer (detective superintendent), Fiance(e) (of Meredith)
Time period(s): 2000s
Locale(s): Bamford, England (Cotswolds)

Summary: Although Meredith is delighted when Toby Smythe, an old friend from her consular days, turns up in her office between assignments, her fiance, Alan Markby, is less pleased. He likes Toby well enough, but knows that trouble follows him, and this time is no exception. Alison Jenner, Toby's cousin's wife, who was acquitted of the murder of her aunt, Frieda Kemp, 25 years ago, has been getting hate mail from an anonymous correspondent who insists that Allison is guilty and threatens to destroy her life. So at Toby's behest, Meredith and Alan take time out from their wedding preparations to look into the matter, and it will come as no surprise that this seemingly simple favor soon turns into a full-fledged murder investigation.

Where it's reviewed:
Booklist, January 1, 2005, page 826
Library Journal, February 1, 2005, page 57
Publishers Weekly, January 24, 2005, page 226

Other books by the same author:
A Restless Evil, 2002
Shades of Murder, 2001
Beneath These Stones, 2000
Call the Dead Again, 1998
A Touch of Mortality, 1996

Other books you might like:
Deborah Crombie, *The Duncan Kincaid/Gemma James Series*, 1993-
Caroline Graham, *The Inspector Barnaby Series*, 1987-
Christine Green, *The Connor O'Neill/Fran Wilson Series*, 1993-
Jill McGown, *The Inspector Lloyd/Judy Hill Series*, 1983-

Janet Neel, *The John McLeish/Francesca Wilson Series*, 1988-

106
PIP GRANGER
Trouble in Paradise
(Scottsdale, Arizona: Poisoned Pen Press, 2005)

Story type: Historical/World War II; Humor
Series: Rosa Featherby
Subject(s): Singing; Crime and Criminals; World War II
Major character(s): Zelda Fluck, Spouse; Zinnia Makepeace, Healer
Time period(s): 1940s (1945)
Locale(s): London, England (Soho)

Summary: In this heart-warming prequel to earlier books in the series, little Rosie, who narrated the previous stories, doesn't make her appearance until the very end, when she is born. The war has just ended, but shortages and social turmoil are making life almost as difficult as the Blitz did, especially for the working classes. Waitress Zelda Fluck (Madame Zelda in later books) is dreading the return of her abusive husband Charlie, whom she was well rid of during the war, and her new boss is giving her a hard time on the job. Her best friend, healer Zinnia Makepeace, is being threatened, her house broken into, and her beloved cats stolen. Zelda's nephew Tony has fallen in with a young thug and is on his way to joining the criminal class. However, he does have a gift for music: he can sing like an angel, and Zinnia finds him a voice coach in Soho, where kindly Bert and Maggie Featherby (who become little Rosie's guardians) take Zelda and Tony under their wing and in the process turn their lives around.

Where it's reviewed:
Booklist, December 15, 2004, page 711
Mystery News, February/March 2005, page 22
Publishers Weekly, December 20, 2004, page 40

Other books by the same author:
The Widow Ginger, 2003
Not All Tarts Are Apple, 2002

Other books you might like:
Meredith Blevins, *The Hummingbird Wizard*, 2003
Tony Broadbent, *The Smoke*, 2002
John Lawton, *Bluffing Mr. Churchill*, 2004
Peter Lovesey, *On the Edge*, 1989
Andrew Taylor, *The Lydmouth Series*, 1994-

107
SARAH GRAVES (Pseudonym of Mary Kittredge)
Tool & Die
(New York: Bantam, 2005)

Story type: Amateur Detective
Series: Jacobia Tiptree. Book 8
Subject(s): Small Town Life; Friendship; Holidays
Major character(s): Jacobia Tiptree, Housewife, Detective—Amateur
Time period(s): 2000s

Locale(s): Eastport, Maine

Summary: Still hard at work renovating her 1823 home in a tranquil Maine village, former fast-track stockbroker Jacobia ''Jake'' Tiptree tackles the front porch, which needs rebuilding, and the tool shed, which needs a new roof. To free up the time to do this, she hires a housekeeper, Bella Diamond, a neat freak who soon has the entire family on edge. Jake's home improvement projects get put on hold when Bella tells her she's been receiving death threats. Further, Jake's teenage son has dumped his nice girlfriend for one who's nothing but trouble, and a pack of relatives are about to descend on Jake for the Fourth of July holidays. Home repair hints are sprinkled throughout.

Where it's reviewed:
Library Journal, December 2004, page 95
Publishers Weekly, November 1, 2004, page 46
Romantic Times, January 2005, page 81

Other books by the same author:
Mallets Aforethought, 2004
Unhinged, 2002
Repair to Her Grave, 2001
Wreck the Halls, 2001
Wicked Fix, 2000

Other books you might like:
Susan Wittig Albert, *The China Bayles Series*, 1992-
Donna Andrews, *The Meg Langslow Series*, 1999-
Diane Mott Davidson, *The Goldy Bear Schulz Series*, 1990-
Leslie Meier, *The Lucy Stone Series*, 1993-
Katherine Hall Page, *The Body in the Lighthouse*, 2003

108

KERRY GREENWOOD

Away with the Fairies

(Scottsdale, Arizona: Poisoned Pen Press, 2005)

Story type: Historical/Roaring Twenties; Private Detective
Series: Phryne Fisher. Book 11
Subject(s): Publishing; Authors and Writers; Chinese
Major character(s): Phryne Fisher, Detective—Private; Lin Chung, Businessman
Time period(s): 1920s (1928)
Locale(s): Melbourne, Australia

Summary: Phryne Fisher is the free-spirited daughter of a baronet who early on fled her domineering father to strike out on her own, with a healthy trust fund to smooth over life's rough edges. Now she's settled in Melbourne with her two adopted daughters, loyal servants, assorted pets, and her lover Lin Chung, who is off to China on a silk buying trip. One morning her friend, Detective Inspector Jack Robinson, calls upon her with news of the murder of Miss Marcella Lavender, the beloved author and illustrator of scores of children's books about flower fairies. She also wrote an advice column for a women's magazine, and to help him solve Miss Lavender's murder, Jack asks Phryne to go undercover at *Women's Choice* as its fashion editor in order to observe the victim's co-workers. Meanwhile, Lin Chung is late returning from his mission, and Phryne is horrified to learn that he's been captured by pirates. The double plot resolves itself satisfactorily,

but it's the kindly, shrewd, flamboyant Phryne, a sort of cross between Harriet Vane and Auntie Mame, with a heart as big as her bank account, who really stands out. The book was originally published in Australia in 2001 and makes its first U.S. appearance here. (Note: the series is being published out of sequence in the U.S.)

Where it's reviewed:
Booklist, December 15, 2004, page 711
Mystery News, February/March 2005, page 17
Mystery Scene, Winter 2005, page 70

Other books by the same author:
Murder at Montparnasse, 2004
The Castlemaine Murders, 2002
Death Before Wicket, 1999
Raisins and Almonds, 1997
Urn Burial, 1996

Other books you might like:
K.K. Beck, *The Iris Cooper Series*, 1984-
Carola Dunn, *The Daisy Dalrymple Series*, 1994-
Laurie R. King, *The Mary Russell/Sherlock Holmes Series*, 1994-
Walter Satterthwait, *The Phil Beaumont/Jane Turner Series*, 1995-
Jacqueline Winspear, *The Maisie Dobbs Series*, 2003-

109

KERRY GREENWOOD

Ruddy Gore

(Scottsdale, Arizona: Poisoned Pen Press, 2005)

Story type: Historical/Roaring Twenties; Private Detective
Series: Phryne Fisher. Book 12
Subject(s): Theater; Prejudice; Chinese
Major character(s): Phryne Fisher, Detective—Private; Lin Chung, Businessman
Time period(s): 1920s (1928)
Locale(s): Melbourne, Australia

Summary: The Hon. Phryne Fisher is on the way to the theater one night, elegantly clad in silver brocade and prepared to enjoy a rousing performance of Gilbert and Sullivan's light opera, *Ruddygore*, when she and her companion interrupt an assault on two Chinese, an old woman and a handsome young man. She puts an effective stop to it without even soiling her dress, and proceeds to the opera, but not until she has invited the young man, Lin Chung, to her house for dinner later in the week. Readers of the series (which is being published out of sequence here) will know that Lin soon becomes Phryne's devoted lover. Besides the romance, which is frowned upon in 1928 Melbourne, there are multiple killings among the opera's cast which seem to be the work of a ghost, although Phryne suspects a more mundane explanation. Originally published in Australia in 1995, the book makes its first U.S. appearance here.

Where it's reviewed:
Publishers Weekly, May 9, 2005, page 50

Other books by the same author:
Away with the Fairies, 2005
The Castlemaine Murders, 2002

Death Before Wicket, 1999
Raisins and Almonds, 1997
Urn Burial, 1996

Other books you might like:
K.K. Beck, *The Iris Cooper Series*, 1984-
Carola Dunn, *The Daisy Dalrymple Series*, 1994-
Laurie R. King, *The Mary Russell/Sherlock Holmes Series*, 1994-
Walter Satterthwait, *The Phil Beaumont/Jane Turner Series*, 1995-
Jacqueline Winspear, *The Maisie Dobbs Series*, 2003-

110

MICHAEL GRUBER

Valley of Bones
(New York: William Morrow, 2005)

Story type: Psychological Suspense; Police Procedural
Series: Jimmy Paz. Book 2
Subject(s): Cuban Americans; Catholicism; Mental Illness
Major character(s): Jimmy Paz, Detective—Homicide; Lorna Wise, Doctor (psychiatrist)
Time period(s): 2000s
Locale(s): Miami, Florida

Summary: This is no ordinary Miami cop story. Jimmy Paz, a Cuban-American homicide detective, thinks he may have an open and shut case when Emmylou Dideroff, found kneeling in the room of an Nigerian oilman whose body is impaled on a gate ten stories below, produces a four-page confession acknowledging that she killed him. Her narrative, however, is so bizarre that Jimmy is forced to turn Emmylou over to his psychiatrist girlfriend, Dr. Lorna Wise, who diagnoses her as unfit to stand trial and places her under observation in a psychiatric hospital. For Emmylou has not only confessed to a murder but she's told a tale of a bleak, abusive childhood, a descent into prostitution and drug addiction, and a rebirth as a Nursing Sister of the Blood of Christ. Whether she's simply a religious fanatic gone wrong or something closer to a saint is left unanswered. The author for many years was the ghost writer for the Butch Karp/Marlene Ciampi series of legal thrillers credited to his cousin, Robert Tanenbaum.

Where it's reviewed:
Booklist, December 1, 2004, page 639
Entertainment Weekly, January 21, 2005, page 93
Library Journal, January 2005, page 85
Mystery News, February/March 2005, page 12
Publishers Weekly, November 8, 2004, page 33

Other books by the same author:
Tropic of Night, 2003

Other books you might like:
Daniel Easterman, *The Judas Testament*, 1994
Carolina Garcia-Aguilera, *A Miracle in Paradise*, 1999
Greg Iles, *The Footprints of God*, 2003
Arturo Perez-Reverte, *The Seville Communion*, 1998
Robert Wilson, *The Company of Strangers*, 2001

111

ELIZABETH GUNN

Crazy Eights
(New York: St. Martin's Minotaur, 2005)

Story type: Police Procedural
Series: Jake Hines. Book 6
Subject(s): Small Town Life; Crime and Criminals; Law Enforcement
Major character(s): Jake Hines, Detective—Homicide
Time period(s): 2000s
Locale(s): Rutherford, Minnesota

Summary: Chief of detectives Jake Hines is chagrined when the charges against a murderous thug, Benny Niemeyer, are dismissed, but when Benny's body is found in the local skateboard park, his murder has to be investigated just like anyone else's. The search for his killer takes Jake and his team all across the small city of Rutherford (based closely on Rochester), into some of the nicest and ugliest parts of town. Off-duty, he looks forward to relaxing with his girlfriend, forensics expert Trudy Hanson, in the farmhouse they've bought together halfway between Rutherford and St. Paul, where she works—that is, if you can call tending their huge vegetable garden, the produce from which they barter for help in renovating the rundown house, relaxing. It's a refreshingly low-key series, both believable and appealing, with the solid police work nicely offset by the engaging characters.

Where it's reviewed:
Booklist, February 15, 2005, page 1064
Library Journal, March 1, 2005, page 70
Publishers Weekly, February 28, 2005, page 46

Other books by the same author:
Seventh-Inning Stretch, 2002
Six-Pound Walleye, 2001
Five Card Stud, 2000
Par Four, 19998
Triple Play, 1997

Other books you might like:
Susan Rogers Cooper, *The Milton Kovak Series*, 1988-
Jamie Harrison, *The Jules Clement Series*, 1995-
Donald Harstad, *The Carl Houseman Series*, 1998-
Steven F. Havill, *The Posadas County Series*, 1991-
William Kent Krueger, *The Cork O'Connor Series*, 1998-

112

PETER GUTTRIDGE

A Ghost of a Chance
(Denver: Speck, 2005)

Story type: Amateur Detective; Humor
Series: Nick Madrid. Book 2
Subject(s): Haunted Houses; Journalism; Spiritualism
Major character(s): Nick Madrid, Journalist, Detective—Amateur; Bridget Frost, Editor
Time period(s): 2000s
Locale(s): Sussex, England

Summary: Freelance journalist and hapless amateur sleuth Nick Madrid has been commissioned by his friend and editor Bridget ''Bitch of the Broadsheets'' Frost to spend a night at supposedly haunted Ashcombe Manor, formerly the home of black magician Aleister Crowley, and write it up for her weekly magazine. The manor house itself has been turned into a New Age conference center, so Nick chooses to spend his night in the nearby graveyard, where he's being kept company by a dead man hanging upside down from a tree. When he calls the police, they fail to understand what is so unusual about finding a corpse in a graveyard. After he finally convinces them to take a look, they naturally see him as a suspect. Full of New Age devotees, including modern-day druids, satanists, spiritualists, priests and priestesses, the book is a delightful send-up of the classical English village mystery. Originally published in England in 1998, it's making its first U.S. appearance here.

Where it's reviewed:
Mystery Scene, Winter 2005, page 75

Other books by the same author:
No Laughing Matter, 2004

Other books you might like:
Colin Bateman, *The Dan Starkey Series*, 1995-
Rhys Bowen, *Evans to Betsy*, 2002
Ruth Dudley Edwards, *The Robert Amiss Series*, 1981-
Carl Hiaasen, *Basket Case*, 2002
Colin Watson, *Kissing Covens*, 1972

113

JANE HADDAM (Pseudonym of Orania Papazoglou)

The Headmaster's Wife

(New York: St. Martin's Press, 2005)

Story type: Psychological Suspense
Series: Gregor Demarkian. Book 20
Subject(s): Schools/Boarding Schools; Adolescence; Secrets
Major character(s): Gregor Demarkian, FBI Agent (former)
Time period(s): 2000s
Locale(s): Philadelphia, Pennsylvania; Windsor, Massachusetts

Summary: Gregor Demarkian, who used to be the head of the FBI's behavioral sciences unit, has been kept busy since his retirement exploring a variety of cases, but lately he's been feeling burned out. He has also been wondering if he and his partner, Bennis Hannaford, will ever get married. When he gets a call for help from Mark Deavecca, the brilliant but troubled son of well-known cable news commentator Liz Tolliver (from *Somebody Else's Music*), he puts personal concerns aside and travels to Windsor Academy, an elite prep school near Boston, to help out. Mark's drug-dealing roommate, Michael Feyre, has been found hanged in his room, and his apparent suicide may have been connected to the affair he was having with the promiscuous wife of the headmaster. Then Mark himself, who has lately been feeling that he's losing his grip on reality, is the victim of an attempted poisoning. While investigating the corruption and deceit at the school, Demarkian wins Mark's trust and helps steer him back on course. As usual, this underrated author gives full measure

with this complex story of adolescent angst and adult folly. Under her real name, the author wrote a more light-hearted series about true-crime and romance writer Patience McKenna.

Where it's reviewed:
Booklist, March 1, 2005, page 1147
Library Journal, March 1, 2005, page 71
Publishers Weekly, February 28, 2005, page 45

Other books by the same author:
Conspiracy Theory, 2003
Somebody Else's Music, 2002
True Believers, 2001
Skeleton Key, 2000
Deadly Beloved, 1997

Other books you might like:
Thomas H. Cook, *Breakheart Hill*, 1995
Thomas H. Cook, *The Chatham School Affair*, 1996
Carol Goodman, *The Lake of Dead Languages*, 2002
Elizabeth Hartman, *The Truth about Fire*, 2002
Laurie R. King, *A Darker Place*, 1999

114

JAMES W. HALL

Forests of the Night

(New York: St. Martin's Minotaur, 2005)

Story type: Psychological Suspense; Action/Adventure
Subject(s): Indians of North America; History; Identity
Major character(s): Charlotte Monroe, Detective—Homicide; Parker Monroe, Lawyer
Time period(s): 2000s
Locale(s): Great Smoky Mountains, North Carolina; Coral Gables, Florida

Summary: In most of Hall's books, an innocent is suddenly struck down by a cold-blooded killer who shows absolutely no human emotion, instilling in the reader a blood lust to see the murderer punished. If this one departs somewhat from that pattern, it is only in that the victims are Cherokees, the killers are U.S. troops and the initial killings take place a century and a half in the past. The fact that the incident is based on an actual historical event makes it all the more chilling. How— and more importantly why—that incident brings Charlotte Monroe, a Coral Gables cop with extrasensory abilities; her criminal defense attorney husband Parker; and their schizophrenic daughter to an isolated camp in the Great Smoky Mountains of North Carolina is deftly handled in clean, yet elegant prose. Hall used to be a poet; in all the important ways, he still is.

Where it's reviewed:
Booklist, November 15, 2004, page 531
Library Journal, November 1, 2004, page 63
Mystery News, February/March 2005, page 13
Publishers Weekly, October 25, 2004, page 25

Other books by the same author:
Rough Draft, 2000
Body Language, 1998
Hard Aground, 1994
Bones of Coral, 1993

Mystery

Other books you might like:
Sallie Bissell, *The Mary Crow Series*, 2001-
G.D. Gearino, *Blue Hole*, 1999
Sharyn McCrumb, *The Ballad Series*, 1990-
Kathy Reichs, *Fatal Voyage*, 2001
Michael C. White, *A Dream of Wolves*, 2001

115

OAKLEY HALL

Ambrose Bierce and the Ace of Shoots

(New York: Viking, 2005)

Story type: Historical/Victorian America
Series: Ambrose Bierce. Book 5
Subject(s): Authors and Writers; Entertainment; Literature
Major character(s): Ambrose Bierce, Historical Figure, Writer; Tom Redmond, Sidekick
Time period(s): 1890s (1892)
Locale(s): San Francisco, California

Summary: Cynical journalist Ambrose Bierce and his young sidekick, Tom Redmond, investigate the murder of Colonel Studely, shot to death in a parade down Market Street as he was introducing his Wild West show to San Francisco. Train robber Oswald ''Oz'' Bird is an immediate suspect, since his former wife, Dora, became Studely's lover while Oz was in prison. However, Dora herself is a sharpshooter, as are any number of the show's cast. Bierce makes a caustic, keenly intelligent detective, and the period details are convincingly handled.

Where it's reviewed:
Booklist, March 15, 2005, page 1269
Publishers Weekly, March 7, 2005, page 53

Other books by the same author:
Ambrose Bierce and the Trey of Pearls, 2004
Ambrose Bierce and the One-Eyed Jacks, 2003
Ambrose Bierce and the Death of Kings, 2001
Ambrose Bierce and the Queen of Spades, 1998

Other books you might like:
Peter J. Heck, *The Mark Twain Series*, 1995-
Peter King, *The Jack London Series*, 2001-
Walter Satterthwait, *Wilde West*, 1994
Steven Saylor, *A Twist at the End*, 2000
Harold Schechter, *The Edgar Allan Poe Series*, 1998-

116

PATRICIA HALL (Pseudonym of Maureen O'Connor)

Dead Reckoning

(New York: St. Martin's Minotaur, 2005)

Story type: Police Procedural; Traditional
Series: Michael Thackeray/Laura Ackroyd. Book 10
Subject(s): Muslims; Labor and Labor Classes; Racial Conflict
Major character(s): Michael Thackeray, Police Officer (detective chief inspector), Widow(er); Laura Ackroyd, Journalist (newspaper reporter)
Time period(s): 2000s
Locale(s): Bradfield, England (Yorkshire)

Summary: The romantic relationship between widowed police officer Michael Thackeray and investigative reporter Laura Ackroyd continues to grow in this installment, which focuses on a threatened strike at Earnshaw's Mill, a longtime institution in the town which faces an uncertain future. Many of Bradfield's large Muslim community are employed at the mill, and racial tensions are rising with the threat of massive layoffs. Meanwhile, Laura is researching a story on the subject and learns about a young Pakistani woman with a bright future who's gone missing.

Other books by the same author:
Death in Dark Waters, 2004
Deep Freeze, 2003
Skeleton at the Feast, 2002
Dead on Arrival, 2001
The Italian Girl, 2000

Other books you might like:
Deborah Crombie, *The Duncan Kincaid/Gemma James Series*, 1993-
Clare Curzon, *The Mike Yeadings Series*, 1983-
Ann Granger, *The Alan Markby/Meredith Mitchell Series*, 1991-
Reginald Hill, *The Dalziel/Pascoe Series*, 1970-
Peter Robinson, *The Inspector Alan Banks Series*, 1987-

117

DENISE HAMILTON

Savage Garden

(New York: Scribner, 2005)

Story type: Psychological Suspense
Series: Eve Diamond. Book 4
Subject(s): Journalism; Multicultural; Smuggling
Major character(s): Eve Diamond, Journalist (newspaper reporter), Detective—Amateur
Time period(s): 2000s
Locale(s): Los Angeles, California

Summary: Eve, a reporter for the *Los Angeles Times*, becomes embroiled in the murder of a Latina actress, Catarina Velosi, who is a friend of her new love, Silvio Aguilar. When Catarina first goes missing, Silvio is asked by his friend Alfonso, a former gang member turned playwright, to check things out, and Eve becomes aware that Silvio is no stranger to Catarina's home. Eve is determined to cover the story for her newspaper, despite her editor's misgivings because of her involvement with the principal players. At the same time she's asked to mentor a hotshot young African-American reporter, Felice Morgan, of whom she is both resentful and suspicious. Eve Diamond's 21st-century Los Angeles, as the author points out, is not Raymond Chandler's, but she paints it with the same loving care and is particularly strong at depicting the city's many ethnic neighborhoods and cultural diversity.

Where it's reviewed:
Booklist, February 15, 2005, page 1064
Library Journal, March 1, 2005, page 72
Publishers Weekly, February 28, 2005, page 39

Other books by the same author:
Last Lullaby, 2004

Sugar Skull, 2003
The Jasmine Trade, 2001

Other books you might like:
Jan Burke, *The Irene Kelly Series*, 1993-
Wendy Hornsby, *Midnight Baby*, 1993
Rochelle Krich, *The Molly Blume Series*, 2000-
Nina Revoyr, *Southland*, 2003
John Shannon, *The Jack Liffey Series*, 1996-

118

LYN HAMILTON

The Moai Murders
(New York: Berkley, 2005)

Story type: Amateur Detective
Series: Lara McClintoch. Book 9
Subject(s): Travel; Archaeology; Islands
Major character(s): Lara McClintoch, Antiques Dealer, Detective—Amateur
Time period(s): 2000s
Locale(s): Toronto, Ontario, Canada; Easter Island, Chile (Rapa Nui)

Summary: Toronto-based antiquities dealer Lara McClintoch is accustomed to traveling the world over in search of artifacts for her business, but here she does something unusual: she takes a vacation with her best friend Moira, to Easter Island (Rapa Nui), home of the mysterious stone carvings of gigantic heads that have long puzzled archaeologists. It's been a lifelong dream of Moira's to hug one of these statues, or Moai, and Lara gladly indulges her. They arrive on the tiny, remote island to find a quasi-academic congress going on which they are allowed to crash in order to learn more about the origins of the Moai. When one of the conference participants, a documentary filmmaker with his own theories about the Moai, is murdered, Lara turns sleuth to find out who did it. As usual with this engaging travelogue series, the author provides enough information on the locale to satisfy armchair travelers.

Where it's reviewed:
Booklist, March 1, 2005, page 1147
Publishers Weekly, March 14, 2005, page 48
Romantic Times, April 2005, page 1147

Other books by the same author:
The Magyar Venus, 2004
The Thai Amulet, 2003
The Etruscan Chimera, 2002
The African Quest, 2001
The Celtic Riddle, 2000

Other books you might like:
Margot Arnold, *The Penny Spring/Toby Glendower Series*, 1979-
Aaron Elkins, *The Gideon Oliver Series*, 1982-
Sharyn McCrumb, *Paying the Piper*, 1988
Barbara Michaels, *The Sea King's Daughter*, 1975
Aaron Marc Stein, *The Tim Mulligan/Elsie Mae Hunt Series*, 1940-1955

119

KAREN HARPER

The Fyre Mirror
(New York: St. Martin's Minotaur, 2005)

Story type: Historical/Elizabethan
Series: Elizabeth I. Book 7
Subject(s): Kings, Queens, Rulers, etc.; Phobias; Arson
Major character(s): Elizabeth I, Historical Figure, Ruler (Queen of England)
Time period(s): 16th century (1565)
Locale(s): Surrey, England

Summary: Young Elizabeth Tudor has fled hectic London for the tranquility of Nonsuch Palace in Surrey, where she plans to rest and sit for her official portrait, with the artist to be selected from those competing for the honor. One of them is Gil Sharpe, her young court artist, just back from Italy where he has been attending school, as well as spying for the crown. The queen's plan begins to go horribly wrong when a series of fires are set at the castle, taking the lives of two people and damaging the work of one of the artists. Could Gil be to blame for the arsons, which began shortly after his return from Italy? Or is Elizabeth's archrival for the throne, the Roman Catholic Mary, Queen of Scots, who well knows her fear of fire, to blame? Although she can't trust even her closest advisors, Elizabeth calls a meeting of her privy council to find the arsonist.

Where it's reviewed:
Library Journal, February 1, 2005, page 56
Publishers Weekly, January 31, 2005, page 52

Other books by the same author:
The Queene's Christmas, 2003
The Thorne Maze, 2003
The Queene's Cure, 2002
The Twylight Tower, 2001
The Tidal Poole, 2000

Other books you might like:
Fiona Buckley, *The Ursula Blanchard Series*, 1997-
P.C. Doherty, *The Soul Slayer*, 1997
Ann Dukthas, *Time for the Death of a King*, 1994
Kathy Lynn Emerson, *The Susanna, Lady Appleton Series*, 1997-
Edward Marston, *The Nicholas Bracewell Series*, 1988-

120

TOM HARPER

The Mosaic of Shadows
(New York: St. Martin's Minotaur, 2005)

Story type: Historical/Medieval
Subject(s): Crusades; Byzantine Empire; Cultures and Customs
Major character(s): Demetrios the Apokalyptor, Detective—Private
Time period(s): 11th century (1096)
Locale(s): Constantinople, Byzantine Empire

Summary: For centuries after Rome itself fell, the Holy Roman Empire continued to stand, based now in the city of Constantinople in Byzantium. Its borders are being threatened by enemies from all quarters: Normans, Venetians, Bulgarians, Germans, and especially Turks. The empire faces danger from within as well, and when the Emperor Alexios is nearly killed by an assassin's arrow, shot with tremendous force, Demetrios the Apokalyptor, the unveiler of mysteries, is called upon to find the assailant. In the meantime, the emperor has implored the pope to send mercenaries to protect his empire, and to his surprise a great force of tens of thousands of western knights show up at the city gates—the first crusaders. First novel.

Where it's reviewed:
Publishers Weekly, May 16, 2005, page 43

Other books you might like:
Simon Beaufort, *Death in the Holy City*, 1998
Alan Gordon, *A Death in the Venetian Quarter*, 2002
Bernard Knight, *The Sir John de Wolfe Series*, 1998-
Edward Marston, *The Domesday Book Series*, 1993-
Mary Reed, *The John the Eunuch Series*, 1999-

121

CHARLAINE HARRIS

Dead as a Doornail

(New York: Ace, 2005)

Story type: Amateur Detective; Humor
Series: Sookie Stackhouse. Book 5
Subject(s): Vampires; Mental Telepathy; Witches and Witchcraft
Major character(s): Sookie Stackhouse, Telepath, Detective—Amateur
Time period(s): 2000s
Locale(s): Bon Temps, Louisiana

Summary: Cocktail waitress and reluctant telepath Sookie Stackhouse has a soft spot in her heart for vampires. After all, they saved her life once, so they've become a part of her circle of friends and customers at Sam Merlotte's bar. When her own brother, who's recently discovered that he's a were-panther, is suspected of killing others in the shape-shifting community, Sookie puts her talents to use in searching for the real murderer. It's the usual inventive, funny, and charming blend of mystery, romance, and horror fiction by the author of the Lily Bard and Aurora Teagarden mystery series, also set in the American South.

Where it's reviewed:
Library Journal, April 1, 2005, page 74
Publishers Weekly, April 4, 2005, page 47

Other books by the same author:
Dead to the World, 2004
Club Dead, 2003
Living Dead in Dallas, 2002
Dead Until Dark, 2001

Other books you might like:
Rosemary Edghill, *The Karen Hightower Series*, 1994-
Barbara Hambly, *The James Asher Series*, 1988-
Laurell K. Hamilton, *The Anita Blake Series*, 1993-

Dean James, *The Simon Kirby-Jones Series*, 2002-
David Thurlo, *Second Sunrise*, 2002
   Aimee Thurlo, co-author

122

LEE HARRIS

Murder in Alphabet City

(New York: Fawcett, 2005)

Story type: Police Procedural
Series: Jane Bauer. Book 2
Subject(s): Brothers and Sisters; Mental Illness; Suicide
Major character(s): Jane Bauer, Detective—Homicide
Time period(s): 2000s
Locale(s): New York, New York

Summary: Jane Bauer, detective first-grade with the NYPD, is back at work after recovering from a near-death experience at the hands of a serial killer. She's assigned to a cold case going back eight years, when a mentally ill man, Anderson Stratton, apparently starved himself to death in his apartment. His sister, wealthy and socially prominent Flavia Constantine, wants the case reopened, as she doesn't accept the official verdict that Andy's death was a suicide. After conducting a series of interviews, Jane learns that Andy's social worker also died of an apparent suicide at roughly the same time, and that the she was also a friend of Andy's building super. When both cases are officially reopened as murder investigations, it soon becomes clear that somebody doesn't want the police to go any further and that Jane and her partners are in danger if they continue. The author also writes a somewhat lighter series about a former nun turned suburban housewife, Christine Bennett.

Other books by the same author:
Murder in Hell's Kitchen, 2003

Other books you might like:
Edna Buchanan, *Cold Case Squad*, 2004
Robin Burcell, *The Kate Gillespie Series*, 2001-
Laurie R. King, *The Kate Martinelli Series*, 1993-
Rochelle Krich, *The Jessie Drake Series*, 1993-
Margaret Maron, *The Sigrid Harald Series*, 1981-

123

CAROLYN HART

Murder Walks the Plank

(New York: William Morrow, 2004)

Story type: Amateur Detective
Series: Death on Demand. Book 16
Subject(s): Books and Reading; Islands
Major character(s): Annie Laurance Darling, Store Owner (mystery bookstore), Detective—Amateur; Max Darling, Detective—Private, Spouse (of Annie)
Time period(s): 2000s
Locale(s): Broward's Rock, South Carolina (island in the Low Country); Golden Silk, South Carolina (private island)

Summary: It's appropriate that Annie, proprietor of the Death on Demand mystery bookstore, should find herself in a situa-

tion right out of one of her favorite vintage mysteries. Her detective husband Max Darling has been hired by a wealthy woman to investigate the recent death of her late sister's husband, a major media tycoon. They're off to the family's private island along with a group of selected guests, one of whom is almost certainly the man's murderer. When the island is cut off from the outside world and the guests are marooned with a killer, what had seemed like a relaxing working vacation turns out to be anything but. The author also writes a series about senior sleuth Henrietta O'Dwyer (Henrie O), a retired journalist.

Where it's reviewed:
Library Journal, December 2004, page 96

Other books by the same author:
Engaged to Die, 2003
April Fool Dead, 2002
Sugar Plum Dead, 2000
White Elephant Dead, 1999

Other books you might like:
Donna Andrews, *The Meg Langslow Series*, 1999-
Laura Childs, *The Theodosia Browning Series*, 2001-
Joan Hess, *The Claire Malloy Series*, 1986-
Toni L.P. Kelner, *The Laura Fleming Series*, 1993-
Margaret Maron, *The Deborah Knott Series*, 1992-

124

ELLEN HART (Pseudonym of Patricia Boenhardt)

No Reservations Required
(New York: Fawcett, 2005)

Story type: Amateur Detective
Series: Sophie Greenway. Book 8
Subject(s): Food; Revenge
Major character(s): Sophie Greenway, Critic (restaurant reviewer), Detective—Amateur
Time period(s): 2000s
Locale(s): St. Paul, Minnesota; Minneapolis, Minnesota

Summary: When Twin Cities businessman Ken Loy is executed during one of his daily bike rides, his murder is followed almost immediately by the shooting death of newspaper owner Bob Fabian. Both murders follow a year after Fabian's wife was killed in an auto accident, after being hit by a car driven by none other than Ken Loy. Sophie Greenway, restaurant critic for the *Minneapolis Times Register*, doesn't think the connection between the two men is just a coincidence, and sifts through gossip and rumors to find the truth. The author also writes a series featuring lesbian restaurateur Jane Lawless.

Other books by the same author:
Death on a Silver Platter, 2003
Dial M for Meat Loaf, 2001
Slice and Dice, 2000
Murder in the Air, 1997
The Oldest Sin, 1996

Other books you might like:
Nancy Fairbanks, *The Carolyn Blue Series*, 2001-
Claire M. Johnson, *Beat Until Stiff*, 2002
Joanne Pence, *The Angelina Amalfi Series*, 1993-

Phyllis Richman, *The Chas Wheatley Series*, 1997-
Lou Jane Temple, *The Heaven Lee Series*, 1996-

125

PATRICIA HARWIN

Slaying Is Such Sweet Sorrow
(New York: Pocket, 2005)

Story type: Amateur Detective; Traditional
Series: Far Wychwood. Book 2
Subject(s): Small Town Life; Academia
Major character(s): Catherine Penny, Librarian, Detective—Amateur
Time period(s): 2000s
Locale(s): Far Wychwood, England (Gloucestershire)

Summary: Sixtyish American transplant Catherine Penny has started life anew, after her husband dumped her for a younger woman, in the quaint English village of Far Wychwood. Her daughter Emily, a psychotherapist with a practice in Oxford, and her son-in-law Peter Tyler, a lecturer at the university, live nearby with their young son Archie. Catherine's new-found serenity is shattered when her ex-husband arrives in the village with his new girlfriend to attend an awards ceremony honoring Peter, and then Peter is passed over for a promotion by an unpopular colleague, Edgar Stone. When Edgar is murdered, Peter is a logical suspect, and Catherine turns sleuth to help him clear his name.

Where it's reviewed:
Mystery Scene, Spring 2005, page 64
Romantic Times, March 2005, page 86

Other books by the same author:
Arson and Old Lace, 2004

Other books you might like:
M.C. Beaton, *The Agatha Raisin Series*, 1992-
Simon Brett, *The Carol Seddon Series*, 2000-
Kate Charles, *The Lucy Kingsley Series*, 1991-
Jeanne M. Dams, *The Dorothy Martin Series*, 1995-
Hazel Holt, *The Mrs. Malory Series*, 1989-

126

MO HAYDER

The Devil of Nanking
(New York: Grove, 2005)

Story type: Psychological Suspense
Subject(s): China; History; Crime and Criminals
Major character(s): Grey Hutchins, Young Woman
Time period(s): 1990s (1990); 1930s (1937)
Locale(s): Tokyo, Japan; Nanking, China

Summary: An emotionally vulnerable young Englishwoman, Grey Hutchins, comes to Tokyo in 1990 in search of a lost snippet of film supposedly shot during the infamous Rape of Nanking in 1937. The only person who can help her find it is elderly professor Shi Chongming, a survivor of the massacre in which 400,000 Chinese civilians were tortured and killed, but he refuses to do so unless she can help him in a terrible quest of his own. While waiting for his instructions, she

moves into a decaying house and takes a job as a hostess in a Tokyo nightclub, where she meets an aged Japanese gangster seeking desperately to prolong his life. The story is told partly in Grey's voice, in which she gradually reveals the harrowing chain of events that led to her obsession, and partly in Shi's, in the form of a journal which graphically recounts the atrocities committed by the conquering Japanese, deeds so horrible that they have been largely withheld from the Japanese people. There is a terrible beauty to both narratives as they unfold toward an agonizing but inevitable conclusion, with the two stories dovetailing exquisitely. It won't be to everyone's taste, but *The Devil of Nanking* (published in England as *Tokyo*) just may be one of the best books of the year. The author's two earlier books, noted for their relentlessly graphic forensic detail, feature the moody English police detective Jack Caffery.

Where it's reviewed:
Booklist, February 15, 2005, page 1064
Entertainment Weekly, April 15, 2005, page 86
Library Journal, April 1, 2005, page 86
Publishers Weekly, January 31, 2005, page 48

Other books by the same author:
The Treatment, 2001
Birdman, 1999

Other books you might like:
Tom Braby, *The Master of Rain*, 2002
Naomi Hirahara, *Gasa-Gasa Girl*, 2005
Susanna Jones, *The Earthquake Bird*, 2001
Natsuo Kirino, *Out*, 2005
Patricia McFall, *Night Butterfly*, 1992
Caroline Petit, *The Fat Man's Daughter*, 2005

SUE HENRY

Murder at Five Finger Light

(New York: New American Library, 2005)

Story type: Amateur Detective
Series: Jessie Arnold. Book 11
Subject(s): Animals/Dogs; Lighthouses; Islands
Major character(s): Jessie Arnold, Animal Trainer (musher), Detective—Amateur
Time period(s): 2000s
Locale(s): Five Finger Island, Alaska

Summary: Jessie is invited by her friends to be part of a work party helping them to restore their recently acquired historic lighthouse on Five Finger Island in Alaska's Inside Passage. On the way to the remote island, she meets a woman who's being stalked and invites her along. Once on the island, she stumbles across a dead body and one of the guests disappears. When both the radio and the phone lines go down, Jessie and the rest of the renovation crew realize there's a killer on the tiny island who means business. The author has recently begun a spinoff series featuring a nomadic sixty-something widow, Maxie McNabb, and her dachshund Stretch, who were introduced in earlier titles in the Jessie Arnold series.

Where it's reviewed:
Booklist, March 15, 2005, page 1270

Mystery Scene, Spring 2005, page 77
Publishers Weekly, March 14, 2005, page 49

Other books by the same author:
Death Trap, 2003
Cold Company, 2002
Beneath the Ashes, 2000
Murder on the Yukon Quest, 1999
Deadfall, 1998

Other books you might like:
Stan Jones, *The Nathan Active Series*, 1999-
Bill Pronzini, *The Lighthouse*, 1987
  Marcia Muller, co-author
Marcia Simpson, *The Liza Romero Series*, 2000-
Dana Stabenow, *The Kate Shugak Series*, 1992-
John Straley, *The Cecil Younger Series*, 1992-

JOAN HESS

The Goodbye Body

(New York: St. Martin's Minotaur, 2005)

Story type: Amateur Detective; Humor
Series: Claire Malloy. Book 15
Subject(s): Mothers and Daughters; Small Town Life
Major character(s): Claire Malloy, Store Owner (bookstore), Detective—Amateur
Time period(s): 2000s
Locale(s): Farberville, Arkansas

Summary: Life is never dull in Farberville, the small Arkansas university town where Claire is still eking out a living as a bookseller and enduring the withering sarcasm of her teenage daughter Caron. Their life is turned topsy-turvy when rats invade their apartment and they must seek other lodgings while the exterminator does his work. Luckily, one of Claire's wealthiest customers offers them a house-sitting gig at her palatial mansion while she's away on a trip. Of course there's a catch, in the form of suspicious characters who are looking for the house's owner, who is apparently not who she says she is, and finally a body that keeps appearing and disappearing on the spacious grounds. The story is fun, and so is Claire's wry and always engaging take on life. The author also writes another, more broadly comic series set in the tiny Arkansas hamlet of Maggody and featuring its long-suffering police chief, Arly Hanks.

Where it's reviewed:
Booklist, March 15, 2005, page 1270
Mystery News, April/May 2005, page 27
Publishers Weekly, March 7, 2005, page 53

Other books by the same author:
Out on a Limb, 2002
A Conventional Corpse, 2000
A Holly, Jolly Murder, 1997
Closely Akin to Murder, 1996
Busy Bodies, 1995

Other books you might like:
Donna Andrews, *The Meg Langslow Series*, 1999-
Toni L.P. Kelner, *The Laura Fleming Series*, 1993-
Harley Jane Kozak, *The Wollie Shelley Series*, 2004-

Margaret Maron, *The Deborah Knott Series*, 1992-
Gillian Roberts, *The Amanda Pepper Series*, 1987-

129

NAOMI HIRAHARA

Gasa-Gasa Girl

(New York: Delta, 2005)

Story type: Amateur Detective
Series: Mas Arai. Book 2
Subject(s): Japanese Americans; Revenge; Multicultural
Major character(s): Mas Arai, Gardener, Detective—Amateur
Time period(s): 2000s (2000)
Locale(s): Altadena, California; New York, New York

Summary: Mas Arai is a Hiroshima survivor, a *Kibei* who was born in the U.S. but raised in Japan only to return to his birthplace after World War II. He's long worked as a gardener in the Los Angeles suburb of Altadena, where he is just barely getting by, the heyday of the Japanese gardener being long over. Widowed and alone, with his only daughter, Mari, living in New York with her white husband and new baby, Mas welcomes the opportunity to go to visit them when she calls upon him for help. When he arrives in the strange city, he finds both Mari and his grandson Takei have disappeared and his son-in-law Lloyd frantic to find them. Mari, always a fretful, restless child—a *gasa-g asa* girl—turns up in time, but their baby is very ill, and Lloyd, a landscape designer, becomes a suspect in the murder of his boss at a garden they are designing for a half-Japanese millionaire. Mas is an unusual, endearing character, whose unique perspective on a culture he has always felt detached from is both entertaining and thought-provoking.

Where it's reviewed:
Booklist, March 1, 2005, page 1147
Mystery News, April/May 2005, page 15
Publishers Weekly, February 28, 2005, page 45
Romantic Times, April 2005, page 89

Other books by the same author:
The Summer of the Big Bachi, 2004

Other books you might like:
Leonard Chang, *The Allen Choice Series*, 2000-
E.V. Cunningham, *Masuto Investigates*, 2000
Dale Furutani, *The Ken Tanaka Series*, 1996-
Sujata Massey, *The Rei Shimura Series*, 1997-
Nina Revoyr, *Southland*, 2003

130

RUPERT HOLMES

Swing

(New York: Random House, 2005)

Story type: Historical
Subject(s): Fairs; Bands; Music and Musicians
Major character(s): Ray Sherwood, Musician (jazz saxophonist); Gail Prentice, Composer, Student—College
Time period(s): 1940s (1940)

Locale(s): San Francisco, California; Berkeley, California; Treasure Island, California

Summary: When music student and composer Gail Prentice turns to big band saxophonist Ray Sherwood for help in arranging her original composition, *Swing around the Sun*, commissioned for the Golden Gate Exposition on Treasure Island, he finds himself attracted to her. Shortly after they first meet, a young woman leaps to her death from the fair's landmark attraction, the Tower of the Sun. The incident draws the two musicians closer together, but as Ray finds out more about Gail and her family, he learns there is a connection between them and the dead woman. Set on the eve of World War II, the story brilliantly evokes the era of big bands, swing music, and the gala Exposition on the newly created Treasure Island, and is further enhanced by period photographs of places mentioned in the book as well as a CD of big band music, which contains further clues to the mystery. Among his many other accomplishments in the worlds of music and letters, the author wrote the book and music for the Tony-winning Broadway musical *The Mystery of Edwin Drood*, based on Charles Dickens' unfinished novel.

Where it's reviewed:
Publishers Weekly, January 31, 2005, page 49

Other books by the same author:
Where the Truth Lies, 2003

Other books you might like:
John Dunning, *Two O'Clock, Eastern Wartime*, 2001
Hal Glatzer, *Too Dead to Swing*, 2002
M.T. Jefferson, *In the Mood for Murder*, 2000
Lise McClendon, *One O'Clock Jump*, 2001
John Mersereau, *Murder Loves Company*, 1940
    reprinted in 2004

131

DAVID HOUSEWRIGHT

Tin City

(New York: St. Martin's Minotaur, 2005)

Story type: Private Detective
Series: Mac McKenzie. Book 2
Subject(s): Animals/Bees; Crime and Criminals; African Americans
Major character(s): Rushmore McKenzie, Detective—Private (former police officer)
Time period(s): 2000s
Locale(s): Minneapolis, Minnesota; St. Paul, Minnesota; Norwood Young America, Minnesota

Summary: Former cop Rushmore McKenzie, who prefers to be called Mac, quit the force in order to collect a huge cash reward for capturing a swindler. He would probably never have to work again, but he's a big-hearted guy who can't help doing favors for people in trouble. This time he goes to the aid of Mr. Mosley, an elderly black man and old family friend whose livelihood as a beekeeper is being threatened when large numbers of his bees start dying off. An unregulated pesticide seems to be behind it, and Mac traces it to a small-time hood, Frank Crosetti, who is Mosley's new neighbor. Murder, rape, a rogue FBI agent, and all kinds of trouble

follow, with Mac going underground in his attempt to solve the puzzle.

Where it's reviewed:
Publishers Weekly, April 18, 2005, page 47

Other books by the same author:
A Hard Ticket Home, 2004
Penance, 1995 (Edgar Award winner)

Other books you might like:
Robert Crais, *The Elvis Cole Series*, 1987-
Steve Hamilton, *The Alex McKnight Series*, 1998-
William Kent Krueger, *The Cork O'Connor Series*, 1998-
Walter Satterthwait, *The Joshua Croft Series*, 1989-
Steve Thayer, *The Weatherman*, 1995

132

VICTORIA HOUSTON

Dead Jitterbug

(New York: Berkley, 2005)

Story type: Amateur Detective
Series: Lew Ferris/Doc Osborne. Book 6
Subject(s): Small Town Life; Fishing; Campaigns, Political
Major character(s): Llewellyn ''Lew'' Ferris, Police Officer (police chief), Fisherman; Paul ''Doc'' Osborne, Dentist (retired), Fisherman
Time period(s): 2000s
Locale(s): Loon Lake, Wisconsin

Summary: Hope McDonald is a syndicated advice columnist read by millions of readers worldwide, as well as by her own friends and neighbors in the small Wisconsin town of Loon Lake. When she's found murdered in her home, police chief Lew Ferris can only suppose that somewhere along the way Hope angered some unhinged reader enough to kill her. As usual, Lew turns to her best fishing buddy, retired dentist Doc Osborne, for help. Between the murder investigation and Lew's campaign to be elected county sheriff, there's less fishing lore than usual, but still plenty of local atmosphere and a warm look at small-town life.

Other books by the same author:
Dead Hot Mama, 2004
Dead Frenzy, 2003
Dead Water, 2002
Dead Creek, 2001
Dead Angler, 2000

Other books you might like:
Rick Boyer, *The Doc Adams Series*, 1982-
Bartholomew Gill, *Death on a Cold, Wild River*, 1993
Macdonald Hastings, *Cork on the Water*, 1951 reprinted in 1999
David Leitz, *The Max Addams Series*, 1996-
Bill Stackhouse, *Stream of Death*, 2001

133

ROBERTA ISLEIB

Fairway to Heaven

(New York: Berkley, 2005)

Story type: Amateur Detective
Series: Cassie Burdette. Book 4
Subject(s): Sports/Golf; Weddings; Family Problems
Major character(s): Cassie Burdette, Sports Figure (golfer), Detective—Amateur
Time period(s): 2000s
Locale(s): Pinehurst, North Carolina

Summary: Cassie joins her estranged father, Chuck, and her moody boyfriend, Mike Callahan, for the Pine Straw Three Tour Challenge, possibly not the best move she could have made. Although her game is improving dramatically, this only emphasizes the weaknesses of her teammates, which leads to a lot of tension and ill feeling. Worse, she's agreed to be maid of honor at a friend's wedding shortly after the tournament. Before the ceremony takes place, the bride's father is kidnapped, and her friend asks Cassie to investigate. A useful glossary of golf terms is included.

Other books by the same author:
Putt to Death, 2004
Buried Lie, 2003
Six Strokes Under, 2002

Other books you might like:
James Y. Bartlett, *Death from the Ladies' Tee*, 1992-
Conor Daly, *Buried Lies*, 1996
Charlotte Elkins, *The Lee Ofsted Series*, 1981-
Aaron Elkins, co-author
John Logue, *The John Marris Series*, 1979-
Keith Miles, *The Alan Saxton Series*, 1986-

134

DEAN JAMES

Baked to Death

(New York: Kensington, 2005)

Story type: Amateur Detective; Humor
Series: Simon Kirby-Jones. Book 4
Subject(s): Vampires; Fairs; Homosexuality/Lesbianism
Major character(s): Simon Kirby-Jones, Vampire, Detective—Amateur
Time period(s): 2000s
Locale(s): Snupperton Mumsley, England (Bedfordshire)

Summary: Being a vampire and requiring little sleep gives Simon Kirby-Jones plenty of time to write, and he's been successful enough at it to live out his very American fantasy of settling into a quaint English village where nobody knows he's a vampire (thanks to some miracle pills he pops) or that he writes romance novels under a pseudonym. A medieval fair is coming to town, and with it Simon's former lover, Tristan Lovelace, the man who turned him into a vampire (and who bequeathed him the charming cottage where he now lives). Simon's life becomes even more complicated when the new ''king'' of the fair succumbs to a poisoned fig pastry. A

witty variation on the classic English-village mystery, this light-hearted effort also pokes gentle fun at historical reenactments. Recipes for medieval delicacies are included.

Where it's reviewed:
Library Journal, January 2005, page 83
Publishers Weekly, January 31, 2005, page 52

Other books by the same author:
Decorated to Death, 2004
Faked to Death, 2003
Posted to Death, 2002

Other books you might like:
Nancy Atherton, *The Aunt Dimity Series*, 1992-
Diane Mott Davidson, *Sticks and Scones*, 2001
Laurell K. Hamilton, *The Anita Blake Series*, 1993-
Charlaine Harris, *The Sookie Stackhouse Series*, 2001-
Mary Monica Pulver, *Murder at the War*, 1987

135

SUSAN S. JAMES

The Siren of Solace Glen

(New York: Berkley, 2005)

Story type: Amateur Detective
Series: Flip Paxton. Book 2
Subject(s): Stalking; Small Town Life
Major character(s): Flip Paxton, Businesswoman, Detective—Amateur
Time period(s): 2000s
Locale(s): Solace Glen, Maryland

Summary: Flip Paxton's housecleaning business has taken off to the point that she's looking to hire some help, and she and her lawyer boyfriend Tom plan to get married as soon as their busy schedules permit. They're building a new house together, Flip's house is on the market, and she even has a buyer—gorgeous Stewart Larkin, a client of Tom who's just arrived in Solace Glen with her millionaire father. Unfortunately Stewart is being pursued by a vicious stalker, whose identity Flip is determined to uncover after one of the townspeople turns up dead.

Other books by the same author:
The Belles of Solace Glen, 2004

Other books you might like:
Kate Borden, *The Peggy Turner Series*, 2004-
Barbara Colley, *The Charlotte LaRue Series*, 2002-
Earlene Fowler, *The Benni Harper Series*, 1994-
Rett MacPherson, *The Torie O'Shea Series*, 1997-
Kathy Hogan Trocheck, *The Callahan Garrity Series*, 1992-

136

EMYL JENKINS

Stealing with Style

(Chapel Hill, North Carolina: Algonquin, 2005)

Story type: Amateur Detective
Series: Sterling Glass. Book 1
Subject(s): Antiques; American South; Small Town Life

Major character(s): Sterling Glass, Appraiser (antiques), Detective—Amateur
Time period(s): 2000s
Locale(s): Leemont, Virginia; New York, New York

Summary: Sterling Glass makes a comfortable living as an antiques appraiser in her small Virginia town, for she not only knows antiques but she's able to keep people's secrets and has a well-deserved reputation for honesty. She's puzzled when some extremely valuable pieces start turning up where they're not expected—a rare silver tea urn in the otherwise unexceptional estate of an ordinary woman, an antique diamond brooch in the local Goodwill store—and eventually ends up working with the Leemont police in uncovering a group of scammers working to cheat families out of their cherished heirlooms. A side story involves an old man in New York trying to protect his family heritage of hand-carved antique dolls. A well-known antiques expert herself, the author weaves a great deal of information on the subject into her narrative in this debut novel.

Where it's reviewed:
Library Journal, April 1, 2005, page 73

Other books you might like:
Ann Campbell, *The Annie O'Hara Series*, 2000-
Sharon Fiffer, *The Jane Wheel Series*, 2001-
Elaine Flinn, *The Molly Doyle Series*, 2003-
Deborah Morgan, *The Jeff Talbot Series*, 2001-
Tamar Myers, *The Abigail Timberlake Series*, 1996-

137

LINDA O. JOHNSTON

Sit, Stay, Slay

(New York: Berkley, 2005)

Story type: Amateur Detective
Series: Kendra Ballentyne. Book 1
Subject(s): Animals/Dogs; Romance; Law
Major character(s): Kendra Ballentyne, Lawyer (disgraced), Detective—Amateur
Time period(s): 2000s
Locale(s): Los Angeles, California

Summary: When Kendra Ballentyne resigns from her law firm in disgrace, having been accused of malfeasance, she's forced to declare bankruptcy and rent out her luxurious home. Broke and at loose ends, she goes to work for her friend Darryl, owner of an upscale kennel, who hires her as a pet-sitter for his wealthy clients. She keeps walking into houses with dead bodies in them and the police start getting suspicious. Kendra forges an alliance with a private detective, who helps her clear herself of the current crimes and restore her good name in the legal profession. First mystery.

Where it's reviewed:
Romantic Times, January 2005, page 82

Other books you might like:
Laurien Berenson, *The Melanie Travis Series*, 1995-
Melissa Cleary, *The Jackie Walsh & Jake Series*, 1992-
Susan Conant, *The Holly Winter Series*, 1989-
Lee Charles Kelley, *The Jack Field Series*, 2003-
Leslie O'Kane, *The Allie Babcock Series*, 1998-

138

SUSAN KANDEL

Not a Girl Detective

(New York: William Morrow, 2005)

Story type: Amateur Detective; Humor
Series: Cece Caruso. Book 2
Subject(s): Books and Reading; Authors and Writers; Clothes
Major character(s): Cece Caruso, Writer (biographer), Detective—Amateur
Time period(s): 2000s
Locale(s): West Hollywood, California

Summary: A 39-year-old former beauty queen from New Jersey who has a passion for vintage clothing and dead mystery writers, Cece Caruso cut her teeth on the Nancy Drew mysteries and is now busy researching the girl detective's pseudonymous creator, Carolyn Keene (actually a literary syndicate). In the process she crosses paths with an avid collector of the original editions of the series, who lends her his vacation house in Palm Springs when she attends the annual Nancy Drew fan convention there with a couple of her girlfriends. There turns out to be a catch: the collector's body is found near the swimming pool, and his much younger boyfriend has disappeared. The obligatory Italian-American homicide cop boyfriend, a well worked-out plot, and lots of interesting information on the Nancy Drew phenomenon, make this a successful follow-up to 2004's series debut, *I Dreamed I Married Perry Mason*.

Where it's reviewed:
Entertainment Weekly, May 27, 2005, page 146
Publishers Weekly, April 25, 2005, page 42

Other books by the same author:
I Dreamed I Married Perry Mason, 2004

Other books you might like:
Donna Andrews, *The Meg Langslow Series*, 1999-
Sharon Fiffer, *The Jane Wheel Series*, 2001-
Joan Hess, *The Claire Malloy Series*, 1986-
Lindsay Maracotta, *The Lucy Freers Series*, 1996-
Ellen Pall, *The Juliet Bodine Series*, 2001-

139

JOSEPH KANON

Alibi

(New York: Henry Holt, 2005)

Story type: Historical/World War II
Subject(s): World War II; Jews; Lovers
Major character(s): Adam Miller, Military Personnel (World War II); Claudia Grassini, Survivor (Holocaust)
Time period(s): 1940s (1945)
Locale(s): Venice, Italy

Summary: In four novels Joseph Kanon has become a preeminent name among writers of World War II-era historical fiction. This time his setting is postwar Venice, a beautiful, mysterious, never-bombed city that seems eerily untouched by the war and to which indolent expatriates have returned in droves now that peace has been declared. Adam Miller's widowed mother is one of them, and she has become engaged to a powerful Italian with a shadowy past, Gianno Maglione, of whom she desperately wants Adam's approval. Adam, recently a war crimes investigator for the U.S. Army, wrongly suspects Gianno of being a fortune hunter, but when he meets Holocaust survivor Claudia Grassini, he finds that Gianno may be something much more evil. Adam and Claudia, an Italian Jew, fall passionately in love, but her past has doomed the affair, and soon the lovers are caught up in murder, treachery, and anguishing moral dilemmas. Meanwhile Venice goes on, accommodating the return of the international set as willingly as the city accommodated the German invaders during the war. It's a haunting book in which the author does for his characters much what Ernest Hemingway did for an earlier postwar generation in *The Sun Also Rises*.

Where it's reviewed:
Booklist, March 1, 2005, page 1102
Library Journal, March 15, 2005, page 72
New York Times Book Review, April 10, 2005, page 24
Publishers Weekly, March 14, 2005, page 46

Other books by the same author:
The Good German, 2001
The Prodigal Spy, 1998
Los Alamos, 1997

Other books you might like:
Jeffery Deaver, *Garden of Beasts*, 2004
Alan Furst, *Kingdom of Shadows*, 2001
Philip Kerr, *German Requiem*, 1991
John Lawton, *Bluffing Mr. Churchill*, 2004
Robert Wilson, *The Company of Strangers*, 2001

140

H.R.F. KEATING

A Detective at Death's Door

(New York: St. Martin's Minotaur, 2005)

Story type: Police Procedural
Series: Harriet Martens. Book 5
Subject(s): Law Enforcement; Women; Serial Killers
Major character(s): Harriet Martens Piddock, Police Officer (detective superintendent)
Time period(s): 2000s
Locale(s): Birchester, England

Summary: Harriet Martens has become a seasoned and successful police officer, nicknamed the "Hard Detective" because of her tough stance on crime. Now happily married to John Piddock and relaxing at poolside at their club, she nearly becomes the victim of a poisoner when somebody drops a lethal dose into her cold drink. Fortunately John is reading an Agatha Christie novel in which the same poison is used, and his quick action saves his wife's life. She's bedridden for a while before making a full recovery, and then her colleagues doubt her contention that her poisoner is a serial killer. They think his victims have too little in common, and it's up to Harriet to find a recognizable pattern to the murder. This veteran author has also written a long-running series about Bombay detective Ganesh Ghote as well as numerous standalone mysteries.

Where it's reviewed:
Publishers Weekly, April 18, 2005, page 47

Other books by the same author:
A Detective under Fire, 2004
A Dreaming Detective, 2004
A Detective in Love, 2002
The Hard Detective, 2000

Other books you might like:
Judith Cutler, *The Kate Power Series*, 2003-
Lucy Harkness, *The Happy Pigs*, 2002
Lynda La Plante, *Prime Suspect*, 1993
Gay Longworth, *The Jessie Driver Series*, 2003-
Peter Lovesey, *The Promise*, 2005

141

SIMON KERNICK

The Crime Trade

(New York: St. Martin's Minotaur, 2005)

Story type: Police Procedural; Psychological Suspense
Subject(s): Crime and Criminals; Drugs; Law Enforcement
Major character(s): Stegs Jenner, Police Officer; John Gallan, Police Officer (detective inspector); Tina Boyd, Police Officer (detective sergeant)
Time period(s): 2000s
Locale(s): London, England

Summary: When a police sting intended to catch Colombian drug dealers ends in disaster, maverick undercover cop Stegs Jenner is suspected of having sabotaged it. Suspended from duty, he determines to go after the man really responsible, even if he has to do it alone. After all, his best friend was killed in the shootout. Meanwhile, partners John Gallan (last seen in *The Murder Exchange*) and Tina Boyd of the Serious Crimes Squad are officially assigned the case, which turns out to be far more dangerous than they suspect. The author, a rising young star of the British noir school, writes loosely linked police procedures which are not actually a series, although some characters are carried over.

Other books by the same author:
The Murder Exchange, 2004
The Business of Dying, 2003

Other books you might like:
Ken Bruen, *The White Trilogy*, 2003
John Harvey, *The Charlie Resnick Series*, 1989-1998
Bill James, *The Colin Harpur Series*, 1985-
Quintin Jardine, *The Robert Skinner Series*, 1993-
Ian Rankin, *The John Rebus Series*, 1987-

142

PHILIP KERR

Hitler's Peace

(New York: Putnam, 2005)

Story type: Historical/World War II; Espionage
Subject(s): World War II; Nazis; Spies
Major character(s): Willard Mayer, Spy, Professor (philosophy)

Time period(s): 1940s (1943)
Locale(s): Washington, District of Columbia; Berlin, Germany; Teheran, Iran

Summary: Willard Mayer is a cynical, disaffected professor of philosophy at Princeton who's volunteered to serve in the OSS during World War II. The son of a German Jew and an American heiress, he was a member of the Communist Party in Vienna and Berlin before the war, and ended up spying on German intelligence for the Soviets. He's severed all his European ties and returned to the U.S., where he's managed to keep his youthful indiscretions a secret. Now he's been recruited by President Franklin Roosevelt to accompany him to the Big Three meeting in Teheran with Winston Churchill and Josef Stalin. At the same time, one faction of the German high command is planning to sabotage this meeting and another is escorting Adolf Hitler to Teheran for secret peace negotiations. There are plots, counterplots, double-crosses, triple-crosses, and intimate looks at most of the major players on both sides of the war, as well as a truly surprising ending, but the book takes its sweet time getting there. Besides his non-series books, the author is best known for his Berlin Noir trilogy, featuring a Nazi-hating private eye, Bernie Gunther, in 1936-1947 Berlin.

Where it's reviewed:
Library Journal, April 15, 2005, page 74
Publishers Weekly, April 18, 2005, page 44

Other books by the same author:
Dark Matter, 2002
The Second Angel, 1999
The Shot, 1999
A Five Year Plan, 1997
Esau, 1997

Other books you might like:
Len Deighton, *SS-GB*, 1979
Brian Garfield, *The Paladin*, 1979
Jack Higgins, *The Eagle Has Landed*, 1975
Joseph Kanon, *The Good German*, 2001
John Lawton, *Bluffing Mr. Churchill*, 2004
Robert Wilson, *The Company of Strangers*, 2001

143

JONATHON KING

A Killing Night

(New York: Dutton, 2005)

Story type: Private Detective
Series: Max Freeman. Book 4
Subject(s): Illegal Immigrants; Relationships
Major character(s): Max Freeman, Detective—Private (former police detective)
Time period(s): 2000s
Locale(s): Everglades, Florida; Fort Lauderdale, Florida; Philadelphia, Pennsylvania

Summary: Former Philadelphia cop turned private eye Max Freeman has left his shack at the edge of the Everglades for a beach cottage in Fort Lauderdale. He's helping out his old pal, attorney Billy Manchester, in a case involving a group of illegal immigrants working for a cruise ship, as well as

coming to the aid of Sherry Richards, a homicide detective and old flame who needs to find a Philadelphia ex-cop who may have killed several female bartenders.

Where it's reviewed:
Booklist, January 1, 2005, page 827
Library Journal, March 1, 2005, page 72
Mystery News, April/May 2005, page 12
Publishers Weekly, February 7, 2005, page 46

Other books by the same author:
Shadow Men, 2004 (Max Freeman. Book 3)
A Visible Darkness, 2003 (Max Freeman. Book 2)
Blue Edge of Midnight, 2002 (Max Freeman. Book 1; Edgar Award winner)

Other books you might like:
James Lee Burke, *The Dave Robicheaux Series*, 1987-
Lee Child, *The Jack Reacher Series*, 1997-
Michael Connelly, *The Harry Bosch Series*, 1992-
Randy Wayne White, *The Doc Ford Series*, 1990-
Daniel Woodrell, *The Rene Shade Series*, 1986-

144

LAURIE R. KING

Locked Rooms

(New York: Bantam, 2005)

Story type: Historical/Roaring Twenties
Series: Mary Russell/Sherlock Holmes. Book 8
Subject(s): Childhood; Memory Loss; Fires
Major character(s): Mary Russell, Detective—Private; Sherlock Holmes, Detective—Private
Time period(s): 1920s (1924)
Locale(s): San Francisco, California

Summary: Following their fling at espionage in colonial India, recounted in *The Game*, Sherlock Holmes and his much younger wife and soulmate Mary Russell are en route to San Francisco, where pressing family matters relating to her late parents' estate can wait no longer. Mary, who lost her family in an apparent car accident in 1915 when she was very young, is strangely reluctant to revisit her past, having been haunted by terrifying dreams of locked rooms that make no sense to her but which seem to reflect lost memories of her childhood. The family home has been closed all these years, waiting for her to come and reclaim it, and a visit to it begins to release painful buried memories, some of them relating to the earthquake and fire of 1906, which she had long believed she wasn't present in the city to witness. When she narrowly escapes an attempt on her life, Holmes engages Pinkerton agent Dashiell Hammett to help them unravel the mystery. More leisurely than many others in the series, it fills in important gaps in Mary's history and proves her to be an even more remarkable woman.

Where it's reviewed:
Library Journal, May 1, 2005, page 67
Publishers Weekly, April 25, 2005, page 42

Other books by the same author:
The Game, 2004
Justice Hall, 2002
O Jerusalem, 1999

The Moor, 1998
A Letter of Mary, 1996

Other books you might like:
K.K. Beck, *The Revenge of Kali-Ra*, 1999
Carole Nelson Douglas, *The Irene Adler Series*, 1990-
Elizabeth Peters, *The Amelia Peabody Series*, 1975-
Lora Roberts, *The Affair of the Incognito Tenant*, 2004
Walter Satterthwait, *The Phil Beaumont/Jane Turner Series*, 1995-

---

145

LAURENCE KLAVAN

The Shooting Script

(New York: Ballantine, 2005)

Story type: Psychological Suspense
Series: Roy Milano. Book 2
Subject(s): Movies; Romance; Humor
Major character(s): Roy Milano, Editor (film newsletter)
Time period(s): 2000s
Locale(s): New York, New York; Amsterdam, Netherlands; Los Angeles, California

Summary: Roy Milano likes to call himself a trivial man, or one who is obsessed with trivia, in this case movies. He edits a newsletter on the subject, and he's especially fascinated with films that were either unfinished or never released. Second to the original director's version of *The Magnificent Ambersons* (which figured in his first case), the holy grail of lost movies is Jerry Lewis' *The Day the Clown Cried*, shot in Sweden in 1972 but never completed. When Roy gets wind of the existence of a bootleg tape of the film, he naturally drops everything else to go looking for it—not a wise move as it very nearly gets him killed several times over. He goes to the Hamptons, Los Angeles, Maine, and Amsterdam (not always of his own volition) and meets a host of showbiz types, including a Seinfeld-type retired comic who prides himself on being a stay-at-home dad but can't last 20 minutes at the playground with his son. In 1984 the author, who is also a playwright, won an Edgar under the pseudonym Margaret Trace for best paperback original, *Mrs. White*.

Where it's reviewed:
Booklist, December 1, 2004, page 639
Library Journal, December 2004, page 182
Romantic Times, March 2005, page 87

Other books by the same author:
The Cutting Room, 2004

Other books you might like:
Charles Benoit, *Relative Danger*, 2004
Lee Goldberg, *My Gun Has Bullets*, 1995
Lev Grossman, *Codex*, 2004
David Handler, *The Berger & Mitry Series*, 2001-
William Jefferies, *The Location Scout Series*, 1992-

146

HARLEY JANE KOZAK

Dating Is Murder

(New York: Doubleday, 2005)

Story type: Humor; Amateur Detective
Subject(s): Television; Women; Dating (Social Customs)
Major character(s): Wollstonecraft ''Wollie'' Shelley, Store Owner (greeting card), Detective—Amateur
Time period(s): 2000s
Locale(s): Los Angeles, California

Summary: Actress-turned-writer Kozak delivers up an entertaining bit of murderous chick lit set against the background of a third-rate reality television series. Struggling greeting card artist Wollie Shelley is closing in on 40 faster than the altar when she's tricked into appearing on ''Biological Clock'', a low-budget show in which three couples date with an eye toward future procreation. Sure it's tacky and humiliating, but it's also an easy $500 for a few hours work two nights a week. Then the young German *au pair* who was tutoring her in math disappears and Wollie finds herself mixed up with drug dealers, as well as an LAPD detective with more than crime on his mind. It's pure screwball fun all the way as Wollie escapes at one point from a menacing goose, later encounters a cat with a very odd choice in a toy, and finally goes undercover to help nab the bad guys. With a little encouragement, she also just might nab a good guy.

Where it's reviewed:
Booklist, November 1, 2004, page 468
Library Journal, November 1, 2004, page 63
Mystery Scene, Winter 2005, page 77
Publishers Weekly, February 7, 2005, page 45
Romantic Times, March 2005, page 80

Other books by the same author:
Dating Dead Men, 2004

Other books you might like:
Janet Evanovich, *The Stephanie Plum Series*, 1994-
Sparkle Hayter, *The Robin Hudson Series*, 1994-
Lindsay Maracotta, *The Dead Hollywood Moms Society*, 1996
Sarah Strohmeyer, *The Bubbles Yablonsky Series*, 2001-
Elaine Viets, *The Helen Hawthorne Series*, 2003-

147

VICTORIA LAURIE

Better Read than Dead

(New York: Signet, 2005)

Story type: Amateur Detective
Series: Psychic Eye. Book 2
Subject(s): Psychic Powers; Weddings; Organized Crime
Major character(s): Abby Cooper, Psychic, Detective—Amateur; Dutch Rivers, FBI Agent
Time period(s): 2000s
Locale(s): Detroit, Michigan

Summary: Abby is settling into her nearly renovated new house when a client fails to heed a warning not to put off a shopping trip and becomes the latest victim of a serial rapist when she finally makes it to the grocery store. Then, when pressed by a friend to read tarot cards at a wedding, Abby senses the presence of a hit man among the family of the bride. Finally, she's asked by a mob boss who's related to the bride to help him in some business matters, and the police want her to help in tracking down the rapist. While working for both sides of the law, Abby is dismayed when her boyfriend, FBI agent Dutch Rivers, seems to be falling for his sexy new partner. The author is a professional psychic.

Other books by the same author:
Abby Cooper, Psychic Eye, 2005

Other books you might like:
Lucha Corpi, *The Gloria Damasco Series*, 1992-
Catherine Dain, *The Mariana Morgan Series*, 1999-
Claire Daniels, *The Cally Lazar Series*, 2002-
Yasmine Galenorn, *The Emerald O'Brien Series*, 2003-
Kate Green, *The Theresa Fortunato Series*, 1986-

148

JOYCE LAVENE
JIM LAVENE, Co-Author

Pretty Poison

(New York: Berkley, 2005)

Story type: Amateur Detective
Series: Peggy Lee. Book 1
Subject(s): Gardens and Gardening; Animals/Dogs
Major character(s): Peggy Lee, Store Owner (garden shop), Detective—Amateur
Time period(s): 2000s
Locale(s): Charlotte, North Carolina

Summary: Widowed in her fifties when her police detective husband was killed in the line of duty, Peggy Lee retired from her job as a botany professor and opened The Potting Shed, a garden shop for urban gardeners in the historic district of Charlotte. She's had to go back to part-time teaching to offset the store's expenses, both at the university and more informally, as with her morning cafe lectures on a variety of gardening topics. She's just wrapped one of these up and opened the shop when she finds the very dead body of one of the town's wealthiest and most socially prominent men, whose wife is one of her clients. The police suspect a local homeless man, but Peggy isn't so sure. She's also not sure about how she feels about an attractive man she ran into on her bike that same morning, or about the enormous Great Dane that has taken a fancy to her. Gardening tips are included in this first in a new series by two authors who have written ten books about small-town North Carolina sheriff Sharyn Howard.

Other books by the same author:
Last One Down, 2005
Last Fires Burning, 2003
Dreams Don't Last, 2002
For the Last Time, 2002
Until Our Last Embrace, 2001

Other books you might like:
Kate Collins, *The Abby Knight Series*, 2004-

Mary Freeman, *The Rachel O'Connor Series*, 1999-
Janis Harrison, *The Bretta Solomon Series*, 1999-
Ann Ripley, *The Louise Eldridge Series*, 1994-
Heather Webber, *The Nina Quinn Series*, 2004-

149

JOHN LAWTON

Flesh Wounds

(New York: Atlantic Monthly, 2005)

Story type: Historical/World War II; Police Procedural
Series: Frederick Troy. Book 4
Subject(s): World War II; Organized Crime; Friendship
Major character(s): Frederick Troy, Police Officer; Kitty Stilton, Police Officer (former), Lover (Freddie's former); Calvin McCormack, Political Figure (presidential hopeful), Spouse (of Kitty)
Time period(s): 1940s (1944); 1950s (1959)
Locale(s): London, England

Summary: Sergeant Frederick Troy of Scotland Yard, the scion of a family of Russian aristocrats, has moved up in the police ranks since his wartime years, and in 1959 he is chief superintendent. The past is brought back to him when his former lover, the sexually insatiable Kitty Stilton, arrives in England with her husband, U.S. presidential hopeful Calvin McCormack, also an old friend of Troy's from 1944. Since those days, London and its many nightclubs have become a favorite spot for jet-set gamblers and celebrities, and Kitty appears to have become involved not only with a Frank Sinatra-like crooner but a Meyer Lansky-type gangster. The action moves back and forth between 1944 and 1959, and the book's place in the chronology of the series is a bit confusing, although it definitely follows up on characters introduced in *Bluffing Mr. Churchill*. Published in 2004 in England as *Blue Rondo*, it's a memorable portrait of London at two different points in its history.

Where it's reviewed:
Publishers Weekly, January 24, 2005, page 219

Other books by the same author:
Bluffing Mr. Churchill, 2004
Old Flames, 2003
Black Out, 1995

Other books you might like:
Tony Broadbent, *The Smoke*, 2002
Frederick Forsyth, *The Day of the Jackal*, 1971
Brian Garfield, *The Paladin*, 1979
Pip Granger, *The Widow Ginger*, 2003
Robert Harris, *Enigma*, 1995

150

DONNA LEON

Blood from a Stone

(New York: Atlantic Monthly, 2005)

Story type: Police Procedural
Series: Guido Brunetti. Book 14
Subject(s): Law Enforcement; Illegal Immigrants; Christmas

Major character(s): Guido Brunetti, Police Officer
Time period(s): 2000s
Locale(s): Venice, Italy

Summary: Guido Brunetti, an honest cop in a system rife with corruption, is also a devoted husband and father and a man who appreciates beauty and culture. As frustrating as it is, he also enjoys the challenges of his job. Here, shortly before Christmas, he investigates the murder of a seemingly harmless Senegalese street vendor who eked out a living selling knockoff designer goods in Campo San Stefano. A search of the man's room turns up a cache of uncut diamonds, as well as evidence that somebody else had searched the room earlier. Before he can go further, Brunetti is warned off the case by his superior officer, which only makes him more eager to continue. Along the way he uncovers widespread prejudice against illegal immigrants, even within his own family. As usual, the author (an American expatriate living in Venice) has written a book that is uniquely Italian in flavor but still addresses social and political issues being debated in her native country. This outstanding series, hugely popular in Europe, has just recently resumed publication in the U.S.

Where it's reviewed:
Entertainment Weekly, May 13, 2005, page 92
Library Journal, April 1, 2005, page 76
Mystery News, April/May 2005, page 15
New York Times Book Review, May 22, 2005, page 21
Publishers Weekly, March 21, 2005, page 38

Other books by the same author:
Doctored Evidence, 2004
Uniform Justice, 2003
Wilful Behavior, 2002
A Sea of Trouble, 2001
Friends in High Places, 2000

Other books you might like:
Marshall Browne, *The Inspector Anders Series*, 2001-
Michael Dibdin, *The Aurelio Zen Series*, 1988-
Magdalen Nabb, *The Marshal Guarnaccia Series*, 1981-
Iain Pears, *The Titian Committee*, 1993
Edward Sklepowich, *The Urbino McIntyre Series*, 1990-

151

JOHN LESCROART

The Motive

(New York: Dutton, 2005)

Story type: Legal; Psychological Suspense
Series: Dismas Hardy/Abe Glitsky. Book 13
Subject(s): Law; Politics; Arson
Major character(s): Dismas Hardy, Lawyer; Abe Glitsky, Police Officer (deputy police chief); Dan Cuneo, Detective—Homicide (sergeant)
Time period(s): 2000s
Locale(s): San Francisco, California

Summary: What initially seems like a simple case of arson is soon determined to be a double homicide when the lead arson investigator discovers that both victims were shot to death before their bodies were burned beyond recognition. The victims turn out to be a wealthy, politically ambitious business-

man, Paul Hanover, and his fiancee, Missy D'Amiens. Homicide detective Dan Cuneo is handed the investigation, but the mayor herself, dissatisfied with his performance, takes him off the case and assigns it to Glitsky, a half-black, half-Jewish cop who is a longtime adversary of Cuneo. Attorney Dismas Hardy, Glitsky's old friend and former colleague, agrees to represent Hanover's widow Catherine, whom the resentful Cuneo regards as a prime suspect (and with whom Hardy was once romantically involved). Cuneo regards Hardy's decision to defend Catherine as further proof that he and Glitsky are attempting a cover-up.

Where it's reviewed:
Booklist, November 15, 2004, page 532
Entertainment Weekly, December 24, 2004, page 73
Mystery News, December 2004/January 2005, page 18
Publishers Weekly, November 29, 2004, page 22

Other books by the same author:
The Second Chair, 2004
The First Law, 2002
The Oath, 2002
The Hearing, 2001
Nothing but the Truth, 2000

Other books you might like:
William Bernhardt, *The Ben Kincaid Series*, 1991-
Robert Heilbrun, *Offer of Proof*, 2003
Philip Margolin, *Wild Justice*, 2002
Steve Martini, *The Paul Madriani Series*, 1992-
Richard North Patterson, *Conviction*, 2005

152

CLYDE LINSLEY

Die Like a Hero
(New York: Berkley, 2005)

Story type: Historical/Victorian America
Series: Josiah Beede. Book 3
Subject(s): Politics; Missing Persons; Slavery
Major character(s): Josiah Beede, Lawyer, Farmer
Time period(s): 1840s (1841)
Locale(s): Warrensboro, New Hampshire; Washington, District of Columbia

Summary: Josiah Beede, a former war hero who fought with Andrew Jackson in the War of 1812, is called by Secretary of State Daniel Webster to Washington, D.C., following the death of President William Henry Harrison. There is some speculation that Harrison, who expired after only 30 days in office, may have been poisoned, with Henry Clay pointing a finger at the vice president, John Tyler, but Beede's investigations turn up an unexpected suspect. However, he's forced to suspend his inquiries when he learns that the husband of a woman he once hoped to marry, Deborah Tompkins, has disappeared. The role of freed slaves in New England society also makes up one of the plot threads.

Other books by the same author:
Saving Louisa, 2003
Death of a Mill Girl, 2002

Other books you might like:
M.J. Adamson, *The Burning Tree*, 2000

Patricia Cohen, *The Murder of Helen Jewett*, 1990
Barbara Hambly, *The Benjamin January Series*, 1997-
Miriam Grace Monfredo, *North Star Conspiracy*, 1993
Harold Schechter, *Nevermore*, 1999

153

LAURA LIPPMAN

To the Power of Three
(New York: William Morrow, 2005)

Story type: Psychological Suspense; Police Procedural
Subject(s): Adolescence; Schools/High Schools; Friendship
Major character(s): Harold Lenhardt, Detective—Homicide; Kevin Infante, Detective—Homicide
Time period(s): 2000s
Locale(s): Glendale, Maryland (suburb of Baltimore)

Summary: Now high school seniors, Josie, Katarina, and Petrie have been inseparable since the third grade. However, their bond is beginning to weaken, until just days before graduation it disintegrates entirely in an inexplicable incident which leaves one of them dead and two wounded, including the girl who did the shooting. Only one of them can talk, and it's up to Harold Lenhardt and Kevin Infante of the Baltimore police to determine how much of what she's telling them is the truth. It's the second non-series novel by the prize-winning creator of Baltimore private eye Tess Monaghan.

Where it's reviewed:
Publishers Weekly, May 16, 2005, page 35

Other books by the same author:
Every Secret Thing, 2003

Other books you might like:
Thomas H. Cook, *Breakheart Hill*, 1995
Carol Goodman, *The Lake of Dead Languages*, 2002
Jane Haddam, *The Headmaster's Wife*, 2005
Dennis Lehane, *Mystic River*, 2001
T. Jefferson Parker, *California Girl*, 2004

154

CONSTANCE LITTLE
GWENYTH LITTLE, Co-Author

The Black Smith
(Lyons, Colorado: Rue Morgue Press, 2005)

Story type: Humor; Amateur Detective
Subject(s): Nursing; Hospitals; Doctors
Major character(s): Judith Onslow, Nurse, Detective—Amateur
Time period(s): 1950s (1950)
Locale(s): East Coast

Summary: Judith Onslow takes the job of head nurse at a small country hospital after being named corespondent in a nasty divorce, only to discover that the doctor in charge is her former lover's brother-in-law. She's determined to do her job as professionally as possible, but the staff and patients are a challenging lot. The trampy new switchboard operator seems to be undergoing a personality transplant, and one of the doctors wanders the corridors of the hospital with a lethally

sharp knife. First published in 1950,it's the usual merriment and mayhem from this Australian-born team of writing sisters.

Other books by the same author:
The Black House, 1950 (reprinted in 2004)
The Black Coat, 1948 (reprinted in 2001)
The Black Piano, 1948 (reprinted in 2004)
The Black Goatee, 1947 (reprinted in 2004)
The Black Stocking, 1946 (reprinted in 2000)

Other books you might like:
Donna Andrews, *The Meg Langslow Series*, 1999-
Elizabeth Dean, *The Emma Marsh Series*, 1939-1944
    reprinted 1998-2001
Joan Hess, *The Claire Malloy Series*, 1986-
Charlotte MacLeod, *The Sarah Kelling Series*, 1979-1998
Craig Rice, *Home Sweet Homicide*, 1944
    reprinted in 2002

155

RANDYE LORDON

Son of a Gun

(New York: St. Martin's Minotaur, 2005)

Story type: Private Detective
Series: Sydney Sloane. Book 7
Subject(s): Adoption; Homosexuality/Lesbianism; Family Problems
Major character(s): Sydney Sloane, Detective—Private, Lesbian
Time period(s): 2000s
Locale(s): New York, New York

Summary: After her old college friend Peggy confides that the son she had given up for adoption when she was a teenager has tried to contact her and that she's afraid not so much for her own life but for that of her young daughter Lucy, Sydney has no choice but to get involved. Then Peggy's husband, NYPD Captain John Cannady, is shot and critically wounded. There is a pattern of hereditary violence in Peggy's family, with the first-born child over several generations exhibiting psychopathic tendencies, and it looks as if it's continued with her own first-born. At the same time, Sydney's lover Leslie is concerned about her mother, who has married a man whose previous wives have all died shortly after marriage. Sydney's sexual orientation is not central to the story, just another characteristic of who she is.

Where it's reviewed:
Library Journal, January 2005, page 84
Publishers Weekly, January 17, 2005, page 38

Other books by the same author:
East of Niece, 2001
Mother May I, 1998
Say Uncle, 1998
Father Forgive Me, 1997
Sister's Keeper, 1994

Other books you might like:
Ellen Hart, *The Jane Lawless Series*, 1988-
Elizabeth Pincus, *The Nell Fury Series*, 1992-
J.M. Redmann, *The Mickey Knight Series*, 1990-

Sandra Scoppettone, *The Lauren Laurano Series*, 1991-
Mary Wings, *The Emma Victor Series*, 1986-

156

PETER LOVESEY

The Circle

(New York: Soho, 2005)

Story type: Police Procedural
Series: Hen Mallin. Book 1
Subject(s): Authors and Writers; Humor; Serial Killers
Major character(s): Henrietta Mallin, Police Officer (chief inspector)
Time period(s): 2000s
Locale(s): Chichester, England (Sussex)

Summary: The formidable Henrietta ''Hen'' Mallin, who had a memorable supporting role in *The House Sitter*, a Peter Diamond mystery, makes her first solo appearance here, investigating a serial killer who is preying on members of the quirky Chichester Writers' Circle. Hen is a small, resolute woman, given to smoking wicked little cigars, who learned years earlier how to succeed in a male-dominated profession without giving up her essential womanliness. Diamond, her opposite number on the Bath police force, makes a brief appearance, but much of this fair-play puzzle is worked out by competing members of the writing circle, although it's Hen who is clearly in charge of the investigation and who sorts all the material out. Lovesey has always written women well, and it's high time one of them became a leading character. The author has also written other series and stand-alone mysteries, most of them historicals.

Where it's reviewed:
Publishers Weekly, March 28, 2005, page 59

Other books by the same author:
The House Sitter, 2003
Diamond Dust, 2002
The Vault, 2000
Upon a Dark Night, 1997
Bloodhounds, 1996

Other books you might like:
Robert Barnard, *The Charlie Peace Series*, 1990-
Colin Dexter, *The Inspector Morse Series*, 1975-2000
Reginald Hill, *The Dalziel/Pascoe Series*, 1970-
H.R.F. Keating, *The Harriet Martens Series*, 2000-
Peter Robinson, *The Inspector Alan Banks Series*, 1987-

157

RETT MACPHERSON (Pseudonym of Lauretta Allen)

Thicker than Water

(New York: St. Martin's Minotaur, 2005)

Story type: Amateur Detective
Series: Torie O'Shea. Book 8
Subject(s): Genealogy; Small Town Life; Inheritance
Major character(s): Torie O'Shea, Genealogist, Detective—Amateur
Time period(s): 2000s

Locale(s): New Kassell, Missouri

Summary: When Torie returns to her hometown from a visit to Minnesota, she is grieved to learn that her beloved mentor and employer, Sylvia Pershing, has died at the age of 102. Much to her surprise, Torie finds that Sylvia has left her everything she owned, including the Gaheimer House, home of the local historical society. As Torie begins sorting through Sylvia's personal effects, she's intrigued by a postcard from the 1920s that bears a threatening message. The puzzle deepens when Torie also learns that Sylvia had hired a private detective and installed an elaborate security system before she died. Torie begins to wonder if the old lady's death was really from natural causes. While she investigates the mystery, she has to deal with issues at home, not the least of which is an unexpected visit from her mother-in-law.

Where it's reviewed:
Publishers Weekly, February 21, 2005, page 161
Romantic Times, March 2005, page 81

Other books by the same author:
In Sheep's Clothing, 2004
Blood Relations, 2003
Killing Cousins, 2002
A Misty Mourning, 2000
A Comedy of Heirs, 1999

Other books you might like:
Earlene Fowler, *The Benni Harper Series*, 1994-
Sara Hoskinson Frommer, *Witness in Bishop Hill*, 2002
Susan Holtzer, *Black Diamond*, 1997
Eugene Aubrey Stratton, *Killing Cousins*, 1989
Denise Swanson, *The Scumble River Series*, 2000-

`158`

HENNING MANKELL

Before the Frost

(New York: New Press, 2005)

Story type: Police Procedural
Series: Kurt Wallander. Book 10
Subject(s): Terrorism; Cults; Missing Persons
Major character(s): Linda Wallander, Police Officer; Kurt Wallander, Police Officer
Time period(s): 2000s (2001)
Locale(s): Ystad, Sweden

Summary: The internationally bestselling author has refreshed his Kurt Wallander series by giving center stage to a supporting character from earlier books, Kurt's daughter Linda, a rookie cop whose first case proves to have global implications. After her best friend goes missing and the mutilated body of another woman is discovered, Linda and her father uncover links to international terrorism, the mass suicides in Jonestown in 1978, and fundamentalist religious cults. The author has also written a non-series mystery, *The Return of the Dancing Master* (2004), featuring homicide detective Stefan Lindman, who plays a supporting role here.

Where it's reviewed:
Booklist, January 1, 2005, page 828
Library Journal, February 15, 2005, page 124
Mystery News, April/May 2005, page 11

New York Times Book Review, January 23, 2005, page 21
Publishers Weekly, January 31, 2005, page 52

Other books by the same author:
The Dogs of Riga, 2003
Firewall, 2002
One Step Behind, 2002
The Fifth Woman, 2000
Sidetracked, 1999

Other books you might like:
K. Arne Blom, *The Moment of Truth*, 1977
Kersten Ekman, *Blackwater*, 1996
Paul Orum, *Nothing but the Truth*, 1976
Maj Sjowall, *The Martin Beck Series*, 1968-1976
   Per Wahloo, co-author
Helen Tursten, *The Detective Inspector Huss Series*, 2003-

`159`

NANCY MARTIN

Cross Your Heart and Hope to Die

(New York: New American Library, 2005)

Story type: Amateur Detective; Humor
Series: Blackbird Sisters. Book 4
Subject(s): Fashion Design; Organized Crime; Romance
Major character(s): Nora Blackbird, Journalist (society page columnist), Detective—Amateur
Time period(s): 2000s
Locale(s): Philadelphia, Pennsylvania

Summary: Nora, the middle of the three widowed Blackbird sisters and arguably the most sensible, took a job as a journalist when their irresponsible parents fled the country, leaving the family estate and the two million dollar tax lien that went with it. Her latest assignment is to cover the introduction of a miraculous new bra, but when she attends the unveiling ceremonies she's shocked to see her half-naked sister Emma is one of its models. It's not that Nora is a prude, it's just that Emma is supposed to be in rehab. Next Nora's boss Kitty is found shot execution-style and Nora's boyfriend Michael Abruzzo, the white-sheep scion of a Mafia family, is a prime suspect. Nora, however, suspects Brinker Holt, the bra's designer, a psychopath she knew as a child and who has a vendetta against Kitty.

Where it's reviewed:
Mystery News, February/March 2005, page 14
Romantic Times, March 2005, page 82

Other books by the same author:
Some Like It Lethal, 2004
Dead Girls Don't Wear Diamonds, 2003
How to Murder a Millionaire, 2002

Other books you might like:
Donna Andrews, *The Meg Langslow Series*, 1999-
Janet Evanovich, *The Stephanie Plum Series*, 1994-
Susan McBride, *The Debutante Dropout Series*, 2004-
Gillian Roberts, *The Amanda Pepper Series*, 1987-
Sarah Strohmeyer, *The Bubbles Yablonsky Series*, 2001-

160

ROSEMARY MARTIN (Pseudonym of Rosemary Stevens)

It's a Mod, Mod, Mod, Mod Murder

(New York: Signet, 2005)

Story type: Amateur Detective
Series: Bebe Bennett. Book 1
Subject(s): Rock Music; Bands; City and Town Life
Major character(s): Bebe Bennett, Secretary, Detective—Amateur
Time period(s): 1960s (1964)
Locale(s): New York, New York

Summary: Thoroughly modern Bebe Bennett arrives in New York City fresh out of secretarial school and finds a dream job at Rip-City Records, as well as a fun-loving stewardess, Darlene, for a roommate. Bebe loves everything about the Big Apple, except the dead bodies, that is. Darlene's new boyfriend, Philip Royal (lead singer for the English group, the Beefeaters), is found electrocuted to death by his own guitar in his bathtub, and the police suspect free-spirited Darlene. To protect her friend and her boss, who was ready to sign the Beefeaters for his record label, Bebe turns detective. The author, who writes Regency detective novels under her own name, recreates the go-go world of the 1960s, with characters who are totally focused on their own lives and never seem to be concerned about civil rights or Vietnam. First in a series.

Where it's reviewed:
Publishers Weekly, March 7, 2005, page 55
Romantic Times, April 2005, page 85

Other books you might like:
Sheryl J. Anderson, *Killer Heels*, 2004
Cleo Coyle, *The Clare Cosi Series*, 2003-
Isis Crawford, *The Bernie Simmons Series*, 2004-
Robert Levinson, *The Elvis and Marilyn Affair*, 1999
Amanda Matetsky, *Murderers Prefer Blondes*, 2003

161

MICHELE MARTINEZ

Most Wanted

(New York: William Morrow, 2005)

Story type: Legal; Psychological Suspense
Series: Melanie Vargas. Book 1
Subject(s): Law Enforcement; Stalking
Major character(s): Melanie Vargas, Lawyer (federal prosecutor), Single Parent
Time period(s): 2000s
Locale(s): New York, New York

Summary: One summer night while trying to calm her restless baby, Melanie Vargas hears sirens and decides to take little Maya for an impromptu stroll. She walks right into a crime scene, the burning home of a high-profile former prosecutor who turns out to have been murdered before the fire was set. With her career at a standstill and her marriage in shambles (she can't even bring herself to tell her family that she's kicked her cheating husband out), Melanie fights hard to get the case, which she thinks will put her back on a fast track in the department. Intimidated by her strong-willed nanny, she can barely cobble together the hours she needs to crack the case, and she doesn't bargain on being stalked herself by the killer. The author, who was for years a Manhattan federal prosecutor and, like her protagonist, is half-Puerto Rican, brings authenticity and a fresh, often funny voice to her narrative. First novel.

Where it's reviewed:
Library Journal, February 15, 2005, page 119
Publishers Weekly, January 24, 2005, page 219
Romantic Times, March 2005, page 81

Other books you might like:
Edna Buchanan, *The Britt Montero Series*, 1992-
Linda Fairstein, *The Alexandra Cooper Series*, 1996-
Kathy Reichs, *The Tempe Brennan Series*, 1997-
Lisa Scottoline, *The Rosato & Associates Series*, 1993-
Marianne Wesson, *The Cinda Hayes Series*, 1998-

162

FRANCINE MATHEWS

Blown

(New York: Bantam, 2005)

Story type: Espionage
Series: Caroline Carmichael. Book 2
Subject(s): Terrorism; Identity, Concealed; Neo-Nazis
Major character(s): Caroline Carmichael, Spy (CIA analyst)
Time period(s): 2000s
Locale(s): Washington, District of Columbia; Berlin, Germany

Summary: After a breathless beginning in which a terrorist hands out ricin-laced water to runners in the Washington, D.C., marathon, resulting in hundreds of deaths, this sequel to *The Cutout* picks up where its predecessor left off. Caroline Carmichael, a CIA analyst whose husband Eric is presumed dead, becomes the terrorist's next target after he does away with her boss. It turns out that Eric is alive but that his cover has been blown and he's been accused by high-ranking CIA officials of belonging to a neo-Nazi terrorist cell called 30 April (after the date of Adolf Hitler's death). The only person who believes in Eric and could possibly save him is Caroline. While he searches for a safe haven in Europe she goes after terrorists in the U.S. and tries to find a way to get him home alive, both of them facing betrayal and treachery at every turn. The author has written a very different series featuring Nantucket police officer Merry Folger and, as Stephanie Barron, a historical series featuring Jane Austen as the detective.

Where it's reviewed:
Library Journal, May 1, 2005, page 75
Mystery News, April/May 2005, page 28
Publishers Weekly, April 11, 2005, page 33

Other books by the same author:
The Secret Agent, 2002 (non-series thriller)
The Cutout, 2001

Other books you might like:
Margaret Duffy, *The Ingrid Langley Series*, 1987-
John Le Carre, *The George Smiley Series*, 1961-
Gayle Lynds, *Masquerade*, 1996

Thomas Perry, *The Jane Whitefield Series*, 1995-
Maureen Tan, *The Jane Nichols Series*, 1997-

163

CLAIRE MATTURRO

Wildcat Wine

(New York: William Morrow, 2005)

Story type: Legal; Humor
Series: Lilly Cleary. Book 2
Subject(s): American South; Law; Trials
Major character(s): Lilly Bell Rose Cleary, Lawyer
Time period(s): 2000s
Locale(s): Sarasota, Florida

Summary: Lilly is the only female partner in a Sarasota law firm, specializing in medical malpractice suits. She's six feet tall, a devout vegetarian, and blessed with a wry outlook on life and an appreciation of the weirdness around her, as well as an appetite for romance. Her current case involves not only a pet psychic but an alien abductee, and she's also dealing with a cranky neighbor and the murder of one of the partners in her law firm, which the police think could be Lilly's work. Then her childhood sweetheart shows up and things really get complicated.

Other books by the same author:
Skinny-Dipping, 2004

Other books you might like:
Tim Dorsey, *The Serge O. Storms Series*, 1999-
Janet Evanovich, *Metro Girl*, 2004
Carl Hiaasen, *Skinny Dip*, 2004
Lisa Scottoline, *Killer Smile*, 2004
Randy Wayne White, *The Doc Ford Series*, 1990-

164

SUSAN MCBRIDE

The Good Girl's Guide to Murder

(New York: Avon, 2005)

Story type: Amateur Detective; Humor
Series: Debutante Dropout. Book 2
Subject(s): Crime and Criminals; Social Classes; Mothers and Daughters
Major character(s): Andrea ''Andy'' Kendricks, Consultant (web designer), Heiress
Time period(s): 2000s
Locale(s): Dallas, Texas

Summary: Independent Andy Kendricks disappointed her society mother Cissy by refusing to become the debutante she had been groomed to be. Instead she headed off to art school, became a web designer, and is quite happy with her modest lifestyle. Then her mother bribes her into managing a website for local domestic diva Marilee Mabry, whose reputation for being difficult to work with is well deserved. During a webcast of the first show, a fire breaks out in the studio and Andy finds Marilee's daughter Kendall unconscious in the bathroom. Then a body is found, Marilee's personal trainer becomes a suspect, and Andy turns sleuth to get to the bottom

of things. The author has also written two books about former Dallas police officer Maggie Ryan.

Where it's reviewed:
Mystery News, December 2004/January 2005, page 27
Publishers Weekly, January 24, 2005, page 227

Other books by the same author:
Blue Blood, 2004

Other books you might like:
Mary Kay Andrews, *Little Bitty Lies*, 2003
Nancy Bartholomew, *The Sierra Lavatoni Series*, 1998-
Nancy J. Cohen, *The Marla Shore Series*, 1999-
Janet Evanovich, *The Stephanie Plum Series*, 1994-
Sarah Strohmeyer, *The Bubbles Yablonsky Series*, 2001-

165

ALEXANDER MCCALL SMITH

In the Company of Cheerful Ladies

(New York: Pantheon, 2005)

Story type: Private Detective
Series: No. 1 Ladies' Detective Agency. Book 6
Subject(s): Africa; Women; Cultures and Customs
Major character(s): Precious Ramotswe, Detective—Private
Time period(s): 2000s
Locale(s): Botswana

Summary: Precious, who operates the No. 1 Ladies' Detective Agency, has married her long-time suitor, town mechanic J.L.B. Matekoni, who is distressed when one of his employees takes up with a rich older married woman. Precious surprises an intruder in their home, who flees without his trousers, and is visited by a man from her past with a strange request. These, and other everyday mysteries involving the No. 1 Lady Detective and her friends, family, and neighbors, are solved by common sense and an understanding of human nature, all against the sunny, exotic backdrop of her native Botswana. The author also writes the Sunday Philosophy Club series featuring Edinburgh ethics scholar Isabel Dalhousie.

Where it's reviewed:
Booklist, February 1, 2005, page 918
Entertainment Weekly, May 27, 2005, page 103
Mystery News, April/May 2005, page 27
Mystery Scene, Spring 2005, page 78
People, May 30, 2005, page 46

Other books by the same author:
The Full Cupboard of Life, 2003
The Kalahari Typing School for Men, 2002
Morality for Beautiful Girls, 2001
Tears of the Giraffe, 2000
The No. 1 Ladies' Detective Agency, 1998

Other books you might like:
Dennis Casley, *Death Underfoot*, 1994
Gaylord Dold, *The World Beat*, 1994
Karen McQuillan, *The Jazz Jasper Series*, 1990-
Donald E. Westlake, *Kahawa*, 1982
John Wyllie, *The Samuel Quarshie Series*, 1975-1981

166

VAL MCDERMID

The Torment of Others

(New York: St. Martin's Minotaur, 2005)

Story type: Psychological Suspense; Police Procedural
Series: Tony Hill and Carol Jordan. Book 4
Subject(s): Children; Serial Killers; Law Enforcement
Major character(s): Tony Hill, Police Officer, Psychologist (criminal profiler); Carol Jordan, Police Officer (detective chief inspector)
Time period(s): 2000s
Locale(s): Bradfield, England

Summary: Criminal profiler Tony Hill is just winding up a university teaching appointment and glad to be back on the job again. Inspector Carol Jordan and her team need his expertise in a particularly baffling case: a murder victim has just been discovered, killed in exactly the same fashion as the victims of a serial killer who is now locked up in a mental institution. It has to be the work of a copycat killer, but Hill's instincts tell him it isn't. Meanwhile, there are children being kidnapped and murdered. Carol, who is still traumatized by an attack in an earlier case, is edgy and apprehensive, and Hill remains desperately in love with her—just to further complicate matters. Shortlisted for the Crime Writers Association of England Silver Dagger award (for best crime novel of the year), it's an intelligent and suspenseful addition to this first-rate (if often creepy) series. In addition to stand-alone thrillers, the author also writes two other series, one featuring Manchester private eye Kate Brannigan and another with lesbian journalist Lindsey Gordon.

Where it's reviewed:
Entertainment Weekly, May 27, 2005, page 144
Publishers Weekly, May 2, 2005, page 179

Other books by the same author:
The Last Temptation, 2002
The Wire in the Blood, 1998
The Mermaids Singing, 1995

Other books you might like:
Mo Hayder, *The Jack Caffery Series*, 2002-
Denise Mina, *The Garnethill Trilogy*, 1999-2002
Ian Rankin, *The John Rebus Series*, 1987-
Manda Scott, *No Good Deed*, 2002
Minette Walters, *The Sculptress*, 1993

167

JILL MCGOWN

Unlucky for Some

(New York: Ballantine, 2005)

Story type: Police Procedural; Traditional
Series: Inspector Lloyd/Judy Hill. Book 13
Subject(s): Serial Killers; Marriage; Parenthood
Major character(s): Lloyd, Police Officer (detective chief inspector), Spouse (to Judy); Judy Hill, Police Officer (detective chief inspector), Spouse (to Lloyd)
Time period(s): 2000s

Locale(s): Stansfield, England; Malworth, England

Summary: For much of their long and intimate relationship, police detectives Lloyd and Judy lived apart, finally combining their households when they married and became parents of a daughter, now two years old. They are partners in their professional life as well. The unusual murder of a bingo player who was walking home with her winnings presents them with a perplexing problem, for the victim's money was not stolen but fanned out across her chest. A second and then a third murder that echo this first one follow, and Tony Baker, a celebrity journalist and expert on serial killers, becomes involved in the case as well. This excellent series focuses equally on the solid but sometimes challenging relationship between Lloyd and Judy and the intricacies of the puzzle they are trying to solve. The author, who also wrote one non-series mystery as Elizabeth Chapin, deserves to be more widely read.

Where it's reviewed:
Entertainment Weekly, January 29, 2005, page 89
Library Journal, January 2005, page 85
Mystery Scene, Winter 2005, page 67
Publishers Weekly, December 13, 2004, page 48

Other books by the same author:
Death in the Family, 2003
Scene of Crime, 2001
Plots and Errors, 1999
Picture of Innocence, 1998
Verdict Unsafe, 1996

Other books you might like:
Deborah Crombie, *The Duncan Kincaid/Gemma James Series*, 1993-
Caroline Graham, *The Inspector Barnaby Series*, 1987-
Patricia Hall, *The Laura Ackroyd/Michael Thackeray Series*, 1993-
Peter Lovesey, *The Peter Diamond Series*, 1991-
Janet Neel, *The John McLeish/Francesca Wilson Series*, 1988-

168

PAT MCINTOSH

The Nicholas Feast

(New York: Carroll & Graf, 2005)

Story type: Historical/Medieval
Series: Gil Cunningham. Book 2
Subject(s): Theater; Middle Ages; Universities and Colleges
Major character(s): Gil Cunningham, Lawyer; Maistre Pierre, Artisan (master mason)
Time period(s): 15th century (1492)
Locale(s): Glasgow, Scotland

Summary: The young lawyer Gil Cunningham returns to his alma mater, Glasgow University, for the annual Nicholas Feast, where he dons his full academic robes for the ceremony, much to the pleasure of his fiancée, Alys, and her father, the French stonemason Maistre Pierre. Gil and his colleagues are entertained by a play performed by some of the students, and when one of them, William Irvine, is later found murdered, Gil investigates. It soon becomes apparent that

someone is desperately searching for some missing papers, and a Dominican priest who is the university chaplain is a suspect. Alys and Pierre help Gil in his search for the truth, unexpectedly aided by his mother and the victim's wolfhound pup, Socrates, who becomes a vital player in the game.

Other books by the same author:
The Harper's Quine, 2004

Other books you might like:
C.L. Grace, *A Feast of Poisons*, 2004
Sheri Holman, *A Stolen Tongue*, 1997
Alanna Knight, *The Dagger in the Crown*, 2001
Candace Robb, *A Trust Betrayed*, 2001
Kate Sedley, *The Roger the Chapman Series*, 1991-

169

G.A. MCKEVETT (Pseudonym of Sonja Massie)

Murder a la Mode

(New York: Kensington, 2005)

Story type: Private Detective; Humor
Series: Savannah Reid. Book 10
Subject(s): Television; Romance; Contests
Major character(s): Savannah Reid, Detective—Private; Lance Roman, Model
Time period(s): 2000s
Locale(s): San Carmelita, California

Summary: Knowing that she has a crush on the handsome male model Lance Roman, several of Savannah Reid's friends have arranged for the amply proportioned private detective to compete for his affections in a TV reality show called ''Man of My Dreams.'' Savannah and four other contestants will live in a phony medieval castle with Lance, but things get off to a bad start when Tess Jarvis, the show's obnoxious producer, turns up dead in a walk-in freezer. Throughout the proceedings, Savannah remains both good-humored and good-natured and focused equally on her twin passions: food and Lance Roman.

Where it's reviewed:
Library Journal, January 2005, page 84
Mystery Scene, Winter 2005, page 69
Publishers Weekly, December 6, 2004, page 46
Romantic Times, January 2005, page 82

Other books by the same author:
Cereal Killer, 2004
Death by Chocolate, 2003
Peaches and Screams, 2002
Sour Grapes, 2001
Sugar and Spite, 2000

Other books you might like:
Dorothy Cannell, *The Thin Woman*, 1984
Carol Higgins Clark, *Popped*, 2003
Selma Eichler, *The Desiree Shapiro Series*, 1994-
Harley Jane Kozak, *Dating Is Murder*, 2005
Lynne Murray, *The Josephine Fuller Series*, 1997-

170

ADRIAN MCKINTY

Hidden River

(New York: Scribner, 2005)

Story type: Private Detective
Subject(s): Drugs; Redemption
Major character(s): Alex Lawson, Detective—Private, Addict (heroin)
Time period(s): 2000s
Locale(s): Belfast, Ireland, Northern; Colorado

Summary: Alex Lawson was once a young detective fast-tracked with the Royal Ulster Constabulary, Northern Ireland's police force. His career got derailed when he stepped on too many toes uncovering corruption within the force, his mother died, and he became addicted to heroin. Now on the dole and living in a small village, he learns that his childhood sweetheart was murdered in America, and the girl's Indian father sends him to Denver to investigate. Alex quickly becomes enamored of Colorado (and its superior dope), and just as quickly gets in trouble with the law. In denial about his addiction, caught up in a web of politics he doesn't understand, and on the run from the cops, he still persists in searching for a solution to the murder and in seeking a personal redemption that doesn't come easily. Despite a somewhat sketchy understanding of Colorado locales and politics, it's an absorbing study of a life gone wrong but still worth saving.

Where it's reviewed:
Booklist, November 1, 2004, page 468
Library Journal, October 15, 2004, page 54
Mystery News, December 2004/January 2005, page 13
New York Times Book Review, January 9, 2005, page 17
Publishers Weekly, December 6, 2004, page 44

Other books by the same author:
Dead I Well May Be, 2003

Other books you might like:
Ken Bruen, *The Jack Taylor Series*, 2003-
Lee Child, *The Jack Reacher Series*, 1997-
John Connolly, *The Charlie Parker Series*, 1999-
Bill James, *The Colin Harpur Series*, 1985-
Ian Rankin, *The Inspector John Rebus Series*, 1987-

171

CLINTON MCKINZIE

Badwater

(New York: Delacorte, 2005)

Story type: Action/Adventure
Series: Antonio Burns. Book 5
Subject(s): Sports/Rock Climbing; Brothers; American West
Major character(s): Antonio Burns, Police Officer (special agent); Roberto Burns, Addict
Time period(s): 2000s
Locale(s): Badwater, Wyoming

Summary: Two brothers couldn't be more different. Upright Antonio Burns is a special agent for the Wyoming Division of Criminal Investigation, and volatile Roberto is an addict and

sometime drug runner. Despite all their differences, they are extraordinarily close, and when Antonio gets into trouble, it's Roberto he turns to. Antonio is on loan to the police in the tiny town of Badwater, where a tourist is on trial for murdering a 10-year-old boy. He misses his infant daughter (who's with his estranged wife in Denver), his job is in jeopardy for the way he mishandled a prisoner, and he's at odds with the hotshot lawyer who's defending the accused killer. Once again he seeks out Roberto and ends up putting his own life in danger. The character's addiction to danger, especially in the form of rock climbing, enhances an already strong story.

Where it's reviewed:
Publishers Weekly, April 11, 2005, page 35

Other books by the same author:
Crossing the Line, 2004
Point of Law, 2003 (prequel to the series)
Trial by Ice and Fire, 2003
The Edge of Justice, 2002

Other books you might like:
Nevada Barr, *The Anna Pigeon Series*, 1993-
C.J. Box, *The Joe Pickett Series*, 2001-
Jeff Long, *Angels of Light*, 1987
Michael McGarrity, *The Kevin Kerney Series*, 1996-
Les Standiford, *Black Mountain*, 2000

172

ÇAMILLE MINICHINO

The Nitrogen Murder

(New York: St. Martin's Minotaur, 2005)

Story type: Amateur Detective
Series: Gloria Lamerino. Book 7
Subject(s): Weddings; Italian Americans; Physics
Major character(s): Gloria Lamerino, Scientist (retired physicist), Detective—Amateur; Matt Gennaro, Detective—Homicide
Time period(s): 2000s
Locale(s): Revere, Massachusetts; Berkeley, California

Summary: After a 30-year career as a physicist, Gloria returned to the Boston suburb where she was raised and acquired a new boyfriend (her second since the Kennedy administration), homicide detective Matt Gennaro, to whom she has recently become engaged. Now she is returning to Berkeley, where she used to work, to attend the wedding of her best friend, with Matt in tow. They've no sooner arrived than the groom disappears, along with some of the top-secret research he's doing on nitrogen, and a colleague of his daughter is killed. Gloria, who has been filling in her retirement by consulting with the police department back home, teams up with Matt to do their part in the investigation.

Where it's reviewed:
Booklist, January 1, 2005, page 833
Publishers Weekly, February 9, 2005, page 62

Other books by the same author:
The Carbon Murder, 2004
The Boric Acid Murder, 2002
The Beryllium Murder, 2000
The Lithium Murder, 1999

The Helium Murder, 1998

Other books you might like:
Monica Ferris, *The Betsy Devonshire Series*, 1999-
Sara Hoskinson Frommer, *The Joan Spencer Series*, 1986-
Carolyn Hart, *The Henrie O Series*, 1993-
Wendi Lee, *The Angela Matelli Series*, 1994-
Patricia T. Westfall, *The Molly West Series*, 1996-

173

GLADYS MITCHELL

Sleuth's Alchemy

(Norfolk, Virginia: Crippen & Landru, 2005)

Story type: Collection
Subject(s): Short Stories
Time period(s): 20th century
Locale(s): England

Summary: Of the 31 short detective stories collected here, only a handful feature the author's durable series character, Beatrice Bradley, an eccentric psychiatrist with an interest in English folklore, prehistory, and the supernatural who appeared in some 66 novels. Described as reptilian in appearance but with a honeyed voice, Mrs. Bradley (later Dame) was no sweet little old lady, but was impatient, demanding, and keenly intelligent. Her short cases (and all the other tales in this volume) were originally commissioned, with one exception, by the *Evening Standard* in the 1930s through the 1950s and for the most part make their first book appearance here, along with an introduction by Mitchell scholar Nicholas Fuller.

Other books by the same author:
No Winding-Sheet, 1984
The Crozier Pharaohs, 1984
Cold, Lone and Still, 1983
The Greenstone Griffins, 1983
Death of a Burrowing Mole, 1982

Other books you might like:
Anthony Berkeley, *The Avenging Chance and Other Mysteries from Roger Sheringham's Casebook*, 2004
Christianna Brand, *The Spotted Cat and Other Mysteries from the Casebook of Inspector Cockrill*, 2002
John Dickson Carr, *The Door to Doom and Other Detections*, 1980
Ngaio Marsh, *The Collected Short Fiction of Ngaio Marsh*, 1989
Dorothy L. Sayers, *Lord Peter*, 1972

174

GWEN MOFFAT

Dying for Love

(New York: Carroll & Graf, 2005)

Story type: Traditional; Police Procedural
Subject(s): Small Town Life; Kidnapping; Blackmail
Major character(s): Vince Bell, Police Officer (detective inspector); Helen Dodd, Police Officer (detective sergeant)
Time period(s): 2000s

Locale(s): Culchet, England (Lake District)

Summary: The premise here, as with many a traditional mystery, was first formulated by Sherlock Holmes: the smiling English countryside conceals viler crimes than the back alleys of London. Culchet is a postcard-perfect village in England's Lake District, but its tranquility is shattered when two suspicious deaths take place in a short period of time and are followed by the kidnapping of a small boy. Inspector Vince Bell, who is nearing retirement, and ambitious young Sergeant Helen Dodd take over the investigation. Despite their mistrust of each other's lifestyle—she thinks Vince is a slob, he thinks Helen is a workaholic—they function smoothly together and respect each other's ability. The author is best known for her long-running series about the resourceful mountain-climbing novelist, Melinda Pink.

Other books by the same author:
Running Dogs, 2000
A Wreath of Dead Moths, 1998
The Lost Girls, 1998 (Miss Pink series)
Veronica's Sisters, 1992 (Miss Pink series)
The Raptor Zone, 1990 (Miss Pink series)

Other books you might like:
Stephen Booth, *The Ben Cooper/Diane Fry Series*, 2000-
Olive Etchells, *No Corners for the Devil*, 2005
Caroline Graham, *The Inspector Barnaby Series*, 1987-
Christine Green, *The Connor O'Neill/Fran Wilson Series*, 1993-
Sheila Radley, *The Inspector Quantrill Series*, 1978-1994

175

SHIRLEY ROUSSEAU MURPHY

Cat Cross Their Graves

(New York: HarperCollins, 2005)

Story type: Amateur Detective
Series: Joe Grey. Book 10
Subject(s): Animals/Cats; Small Town Life; Children
Major character(s): Joe Grey, Animal (cat), Detective—Amateur; Dulcie, Animal (cat), Detective—Amateur
Time period(s): 2000s
Locale(s): Molena Point, California

Summary: When aging movie star Patty Rose decides to make peaceful Molena Point her permanent home and even buys the village inn, the town decides to honor her with a retrospective festival of her films. These plans are abruptly halted when Patty is savagely murdered. Patty's feline friends, Joe Grey and his companion Dulcie, immediately get to work on the case. Both are descendants of ancient intelligent Celtic cats who are blessed with the gift of speech (to certain humans) and other abilities (such as analytical thought), and they have the advantage of being able to snoop around without arousing suspicion where human investigators could never go. Their investigation is complicated by the kidnapping of a child and Dulcie's harboring of a runaway teenager in the local library. The underlying darkness of the crimes, in particular the presence of a child predator in Molena Point, is somewhat at odds with the book's fanciful premise.

Where it's reviewed:
Booklist, December 15, 2004, page 712
Library Journal, January 2005, page 84
Publishers Weekly, December 13, 2004, page 48

Other books by the same author:
Cat Fear No Evil, 2004
Cat Seeing Double, 2003
Cat Laughing Last, 2002
Cat Spitting Mad, 2001
Cat to the Dogs, 2000

Other books you might like:
Garrison Allen, *The Big Mike Series*, 1994-
Lilian Jackson Braun, *The Cat Who Series*, 1966-
Rita Mae Brown, *The Mrs. Murphy Series*, 1990-
Barbara Collins, *Too Many Tomcats and Other Feline Tales of Suspense*, 2000
  editor
Carole Nelson Douglas, *The Midnight Louie Series*, 1992-

176

BEVERLE GRAVES MYERS

Painted Veil

(Scottsdale, Arizona: Poisoned Pen Press, 2005)

Story type: Historical/Georgian
Series: Tito Amato. Book 2
Subject(s): Opera; Music and Musicians; Jews
Major character(s): Tito Amato, Singer (castrato)
Time period(s): 1730s (1734)
Locale(s): Venice, Italy

Summary: Tito Amato, who was castrated as a boy to preserve his soprano voice and taught to be an opera singer, has had to relinquish his position as lead singer with the Teatro San Marco after a period of debauchery and self-indulgence. In order to get back into the good graces of the opera company's director, he agrees to search for the person who strangled a gifted set designer and dumped his body in a canal. Everybody immediately suspects the man's lover, a Jewish woman named Liya Del'Vecchio, to whom Tito himself is attracted. With the help of his new friend August Rumbolt, a young English nobleman taking the Grand Tour, he explores the ancient Jewish ghetto, where he is appalled at the conditions and restrictions its inhabitants must endure. Having experienced no small degree of prejudice himself, he takes a most sympathetic view of this historically mistreated minority.

Where it's reviewed:
Booklist, February 15, 2005, page 1066
Mystery News, April/May 2005, page 25
Publishers Weekly, February 28, 2005, page 46

Other books by the same author:
Interrupted Aria, 2004

Other books you might like:
Thomas Godfrey, *Murder at the Opera*, 1989
  anthology
Deryn Lake, *Death at the Beggar's Opera*, 1995
Donna Leon, *Death at la Fenice*, 1992
David Liss, *The Coffee Trader*, 2003
Kate Ross, *The Devil in Music*, 1997

177

TAMAR MYERS

Assault and Pepper

(New York: New American Library, 2005)

Story type: Amateur Detective; Humor
Series: Magdalena Yoder. Book 13
Subject(s): Mennonites; Hotels and Motels; Cooks and Cooking
Major character(s): Magdalena Yoder, Innkeeper, Detective—Amateur
Time period(s): 2000s
Locale(s): Hernia, Pennsylvania

Summary: Magdalena Yoder, proprietor of the PennDutch Inn, is working along with other members of the Beechy Grove Mennonite Church preparing for its annual chili supper cook-off. Just as everyone is about to dig in, their popular pastor collapses after taking a bite of the chili. It turns out the dish has been laced with peanut butter, a substance everyone knew the Reverend Schrock was fatally allergic to, and his grieving widow asks Magdalena to investigate. Bossy and outspoken, Magdalena rides roughshod over anyone who gets in the way of her finding the murderer, and she discovers that Schrock was nowhere nearly as universally beloved as everyone thought. Recipes are included, mostly for chili and chili-related dishes. The author also writes a series about antiques store owner Abigail Timberlake.

Where it's reviewed:
Library Journal, January 2005, page 84
Mystery News, February/March 2005, page 28
Publishers Weekly, January 24, 2005, page 226

Other books by the same author:
Thou Shalt Not Grill, 2004
Custard's Last Stand, 2003
Gruel and Unusual Punishment, 2002
The Crepes of Wrath, 2001
The Hand That Rocks the Ladle, 2000

Other books you might like:
Susan Wittig Albert, *Chile Death*, 1998
Mary Daheim, *The Judith McMonigle Flynn Series*, 1991-
Valerie Malmont, *The Tori Miracle Series*, 1994-
Tim Myers, *The Alex Winston Series*, 2001-
Nancy Pickard, *The 27-Ingredient Chile Con Carne Murders*, 1983
    based on an uncompleted manuscript by Virginia Rich

178

TAMAR MYERS

Monet Talks

(New York: Avon, 2005)

Story type: Amateur Detective
Series: Abigail Timberlake. Book 12
Subject(s): Antiques; American South; Art
Major character(s): Abigail Timberlake Washburn, Antiques Dealer, Detective—Amateur
Time period(s): 2000s
Locale(s): Charleston, South Carolina

Summary: Abigail Timberlake Washburn, who owns the Den of Antiquities antique shop in historic Charleston, is pleased to have acquired a fabulous jeweled birdcage at an estate auction. A loquacious mynah bird named Monet comes with it, who Abby is not thrilled about but who quickly charms her customers, so she figures she might as well keep him. Then the bird is kidnapped and held for ransom. Its abductor is demanding a genuine Monet in exchange for the bird, so Abby decides to just ignore it all—until her own mother is kidnapped, too. The author writes another cozy series about Magdalena Yoder, proprietor of the PennDutch bed and breakfast.

Other books by the same author:
Statue of Limitations, 2004
Tiles and Tribulations, 2003
Splendor in the Glass, 2002
Nightmare in Shining Armor, 2001
A Penny Urned, 2000

Other books you might like:
Ann Campbell, *The Annie O'Hara Series*, 2000-
Sharon Fiffer, *The Jane Wheel Series*, 2001-
Elaine Flinn, *The Molly Doyle Series*, 2003-
Emyl Jenkins, *Stealing with Style*, 2005
Deborah Morgan, *The Jeff Talbot Series*, 2001-

179

BARBARA NADEL

The Ottoman Cage

(New York: St. Martin's Minotaur, 2005)

Story type: Police Procedural
Series: Inspector Ikmen. Book 2
Subject(s): Middle East; Cultures and Customs; Drugs
Major character(s): Cetin Ikmen, Detective—Homicide (inspector)
Time period(s): 1990s
Locale(s): Istanbul, Turkey

Summary: The murder of a young man in a wealthy neighborhood of Istanbul is the latest case for Turkish homicide inspector Cetin Ikmen, a man not noted for his patience and whose chief vices are cigarettes and brandy in plentiful quantities. Despite his education, Ikmen lives the life of a working-class Turk, struggling to make ends meet with a large family and an aging father to support, and his professional life is marked by an ongoing struggle with modern technology, in particular a temperamental cell phone. The victim was a drug addict who died of what might have been a medically administered overdose of a synthetic form of heroin. With his female boss and his Jewish and Armenian colleagues on the police force, the beleaguered Ikmen is a sort of everyman for modern Turkey and Istanbul in particular, a surprisingly cosmopolitan, diverse, and progressive city.

Where it's reviewed:
Mystery Scene, Winter 2005, page 69

Other books by the same author:
Belshazzar's Daughter, 2004

Other books you might like:
Charles B. Child, *The Sleuth of Baghdad*, 2002
    short stories
Joan Fleming, *The Nuri Iskirlak Series*, 1962-1965
Batya Gur, *The Michael Ohayon Series*, 1988-
Julian Rathbone, *The Nur Bey Series*, 1966-1972
Robert Rosenberg, *The Avram Cohen Series*, 1991-

180

KRIS NELSCOTT (Pseudonym of Kristine Kathryn Rusch)

War at Home
(New York: St. Martin's Minotaur, 2005)

Story type: Private Detective; Historical
Series: Smokey Dalton. Book 5
Subject(s): Vietnam War; African Americans; Race Relations
Major character(s): Smokey Dalton, Detective—Private; Jimmy, Ward (of Smokey)
Time period(s): 1960s (1969)
Locale(s): Chicago, Illinois; New Haven, Connecticut; New York, New York

Summary: Anyone who thinks the 1960s were all flower power and love-ins will be sobered to read this series, which recounts the flight of African-American private eye Smokey Dalton from Memphis with his young ward, Jimmy, who is hiding out from the FBI because he witnessed who really killed Martin Luther King. They've taken refuge in Chicago where they have put down roots, and in the summer of 1969 Smokey agrees to look for Daniel Kirkland, a young black militant who is the son of one of Jimmy's teachers and who failed to show up for his spring semester at Yale. His disappearance may be connected with his activities with the antiwar movement, and Smokey and Jimmy go to New Haven and New York to find out. Under her own name, the author is a noted science fiction and fantasy writer.

Where it's reviewed:
Entertainment Weekly, March 25, 2005, page 76
Publishers Weekly, February 28, 2005, page 46

Other books by the same author:
Stone Cribs, 2004
Thin Walls, 2002
Smoke-Filled Rooms, 2001
A Dangerous Road, 2000

Other books you might like:
Charlotte Carter, *Trip Wire*, 2005
Thomas H. Cook, *Streets of Fire*, 1989
Gary Hardwick, *Cold Medina*, 1996
Chester Himes, *Cotton Comes to Harlem*, 1965
Walter Mosley, *Bad Boy Brawly Brown*, 2002

181

ALBERT NOYER

The Cybelene Conspiracy
(New Milford, Connecticut: Toby, 2005)

Story type: Historical/Ancient Rome
Series: Getorius Asterius. Book 2

Subject(s): Roman Empire; Cultures and Customs; Cults
Major character(s): Getorius Asterius, Doctor; Arcadia Asterius, Spouse (of Getorius), Sidekick
Time period(s): 5th century (440)
Locale(s): Ravenna, Italy

Summary: Getorius and his wife Arcadia are drawn into an investigation of the pagan cult of Cybele, an order of self-mutilated eunuchs served by vestal virgins and led by the archpriest Diotar. Their inquiries into the death of a young castrated youth lead to Claudia, an epileptic, pregnant vestal virgin, and eventually to a counterfeiting and smuggling ring led by Senator Publius Maximin, who leases a galley from Claudia's father.

Other books by the same author:
The Secundus Papyrus, 2003
The Saint's Day Deaths, 2000

Other books you might like:
Ron Burns, *Roman Nights*, 1991
Anthony Clarke, *Ordeal at Lichfield*, 1998
Lindsey Davis, *The Marcus Didius Falco Series*, 1989-
Jane Finnis, *Get Out or Die*, 2004
Mary Reed, *The John the Eunuch Series*, 1999-

182

NEIL OLSON

The Icon
(New York: HarperCollins, 2005)

Story type: Action/Adventure
Subject(s): Art; Religion; Nazis
Major character(s): Matthew Spear, Museum Curator (assistant); Ana Kessler, Collector (art)
Time period(s): 2000s (2000); 1940s (1944)
Locale(s): New York, New York; Katarini, Greece

Summary: In 1944, during the German occupation of the tiny Greek village of Katarini, a German commander makes a deal which nets him possession of a mysterious Byzantine icon said to have supernatural powers. However, the deal goes wrong and the icon vanishes, only to resurface 56 years later in New York City as part of the inheritance Ana Kessler received from her grandfather, a recently deceased Swiss banker known for his illicit collection of stolen Nazi art. Matthew Spear, a curator of Greek descent employed at the Metropolitan Museum, is stunned by the icon when he arrives at her home to appraise it. When news gets out of the icon's existence, many are interested in acquiring it, from the Greek Orthodox Church to a very old Nazi war criminal. With both Matthew and Ana now in danger, they race against time to save themselves and find out what really happened 56 years ago in Greece. First novel.

Where it's reviewed:
Library Journal, April 1, 2005, page 87
Publishers Weekly, March 21, 2005, page 35

Other books you might like:
Steve Berry, *The Amber Room*, 2003
Dan Brown, *The Da Vinci Code*, 2003
Ian Caldwell, *The Rule of Four*, 2004
    Dustin Thomason, co-author

Katharine Neville, *The Eight*, 1989
Peter Watson, *Landscape of Lies*, 1989

183

DENISE OSBORNE

Evil Intentions

(McKinleyville, California: Perseverance, 2005)

Story type: Amateur Detective
Series: Salome Waterhouse. Book 4
Subject(s): Arson; Crime and Criminals
Major character(s): Salome Waterhouse, Consultant (feng shui), Detective—Amateur
Time period(s): 2000s
Locale(s): Washington, District of Columbia

Summary: *Feng shui* practitioner Salome Waterhouse uses the principles of this ancient Chinese art and science to help her solve a mystery involving members of a privileged Washington, D.C., family and a deadly underworld organization involved in white slavery and murder. She must track the villains down with no thought of revenge, only a wish to see justice done, for "evil intentions" would undermine the entire karma of the investigation. The author, a *feng shui* expert, has also written a mystery series involving screenwriter Queenie Davilov. Tips on *feng shui* (the art of harmonious placement of furniture and objects within the home) are included.

Where it's reviewed:
Mystery Scene, Spring 2005, page 67

Other books by the same author:
Designed to Kill, 2003
Positioned to Die, 2002
A Deadly Arrangement, 2001

Other books you might like:
Leslie Caine, *The Domestic Bliss Series*, 2004-
Paula Carter, *The Hillary Scarborough Series*, 1999-
Jerrilyn Farmer, *The Madeline Bean Series*, 1998-
Jacqueline Girdner, *The Kate Jasper Series*, 1991-2002
Dean James, *Decorated to Death*, 2004

184

LEONARDO PADURA (Pseudonym of Leonardo Padura Fuentes)

Havana Red

(London: Bitter Lemon, 2005)

Story type: Police Procedural
Series: Mario Conde. Book 1
Subject(s): Homosexuality/Lesbianism; Cultures and Customs; Social Conditions
Major character(s): Mario Conde, Detective—Homicide; Alberto Marques, Writer
Time period(s): 1980s (1989)
Locale(s): Havana, Cuba

Summary: When the body of a transvestite wearing a red evening gown and strangled with a matching ribbon is found in the Havana Woods, Lieutenant Mario Conde is put in charge of investigating the murder. He's dismayed to learn that the victim is the son of a prominent diplomat, making the case a politically sensitive one. The investigation takes him to the home of Alberto Marques, a disgraced playwright who was formerly a giant in Cuban letters and with whom the young man was living. Marques joins forces with Conde to solve the murder. The first in the author's prizewinning Havana quartet, the book offers a compelling portrait of his native country, the appalling shortages his people must live with, and the aftereffects of the Angolan war. Under his full name, Leonardo Padura Fuentes, the author has also written a fifth book in the series, available in English as *Adios Hemingway* (2005).

Other books you might like:
Daniel Chavarria, *Adios Muchachos*, 2001
Arnaldo Correa, *Cold Havana Ground*, 2003
Carolina Garcia-Aguilera, *Havana Heat*, 2000
Jose Latour, *Outcast*, 1999
Thomas Sanchez, *King Bongo*, 2003

185

KATHERINE HALL PAGE

The Body in the Snowdrift

(New York: William Morrow, 2005)

Story type: Amateur Detective
Series: Faith Fairchild. Book 15
Subject(s): Food; Sports/Skiing; Cooks and Cooking
Major character(s): Faith Sibley Fairchild, Caterer (part-time), Detective—Amateur
Time period(s): 2000s
Locale(s): Pine Slopes, Vermont

Summary: Faith Fairchild has mixed feelings about the family's upcoming reunion at the struggling Pine Slopes ski resort, where her husband Tom's family has been vacationing for years and where his father is treating the extended Fairchild family to a full week to celebrate his 70th birthday. They've become good friends of the owners, and when the resort's chef mysteriously disappeared, Faith is pressed into filling in for him. Other puzzling events occur: a family friend dies of an apparent heart attack on the cross-country trails, Faith's condo is broken into, and a chairlift is sabotaged. Worst of all, a body somehow finds its way into the water supply for the snow-making equipment, spraying the slopes red. Family secrets and feuds further complicate the story. Some recipes from Faith's kitchen are included.

Where it's reviewed:
Library Journal, May 1, 2005, page 66
New York Times Book Review, April 24, 2005, page 21
Publishers Weekly, April 18, 2005, page 46

Other books by the same author:
The Body in the Attic, 2004
The Body in the Lighthouse, 2003
The Body in the Bonfire, 2002
The Body in the Moonlight, 2001
The Body in the Big Apple, 1999

Other books you might like:
Susan Wittig Albert, *The China Bayles Series*, 1992-

Diane Mott Davidson, *The Goldy Bear Schulz Series*, 1990-
Earlene Fowler, *The Benni Harper Series*, 1994-
Sarah Graves, *The Jacobia Tiptree Series*, 1998-
Jane Langton, *The Homer Kelly Series*, 1964-

186

ROBIN PAIGE (Pseudonym of Susan Wittig Albert and Bill Albert)

Death at Blenheim Palace
(New York: Berkley, 2005)

Story type: Historical/Edwardian
Series: Kathryn Ardleigh. Book 11
Subject(s): Authors and Writers; Kings, Queens, Rulers, etc.; Burglary
Major character(s): Lady Kathryn Ardleigh Sheridan, Writer (novelist), Noblewoman; Lord Charles Sheridan, Scientist, Nobleman
Time period(s): 1900s (1903)
Locale(s): England

Summary: The Duke and Duchess of Marlborough have invited Lord Charles Sheridan and his wife Kate to be their guests at Blenheim Palace. Kate is working on a book about a long-ago scandal at the site (formerly Marlborough Hall) when a housemaid is kidnapped and their hosts disappear. In addition to the philandering duke and his unhappy American wife, Consuelo Vanderbilt, the book features historical figures T.E. Lawrence and Winston Churchill. Before the story is over, a burglary ring has been exposed, Lawrence has gone undercover as a household servant, and a royal visit from King Edward VII and Queen Alexandra has been announced. Under her own name, co-author Susan Wittig Albert writes a popular series about Texas hill country herbalist China Bayles and has begun another historical series featuring Beatrix Potter.

Where it's reviewed:
Publishers Weekly, January 17, 2005, page 38
Romantic Times, April 2005, page 90

Other books by the same author:
Death in Hyde Park, 2004
Death at Glamis Castle, 2003
Death at Dartmoor, 2002
Death at Epsom Downs, 2001
Death at Whitechapel, 2000

Other books you might like:
David Dickinson, *The Lord Francis Powerscourt Series*, 2002-
Peter Lovesey, *The Bertie, Prince of Wales Series*, 1987-1993
J.P. Morrissey, *A Weekend at Blenheim*, 2002
Anne Perry, *The Thomas and Charlotte Pitt Series*, 1979-
Elizabeth Peters, *The Amelia Peabody Series*, 1975-

187

LINDA PALMER

Love Her to Death
(New York: Berkley, 2005)

Story type: Amateur Detective; Humor
Series: Morgan Tyler. Book 2
Subject(s): Television; Television Programs; Actors and Actresses
Major character(s): Morgan Tyler, Producer, Detective—Amateur
Time period(s): 2000s
Locale(s): New York, New York

Summary: Former playwright and wildlife photographer Morgan Tyler turned to writing soap operas after her beloved husband of six years was killed in Kenya. Now she's just been promoted to co-executive producer of the wildly popular series "Love of My Life." This means, that in addition to her regular scriptwriting duties, Morgan is now expected to clean up the messes everybody else makes. She's approached by the show's leading lady, Cybelle Carter, who's certain her estranged husband is out to kill her. When another actress in the show is murdered, it looks as if the leading lady had been the intended target. To further complicate matters, when Cybelle's husband actually shows up, Morgan finds herself dangerously attracted to him.

Other books by the same author:
Love Is Murder, 2004

Other books you might like:
Sheryl J. Anderson, *Killer Heels*, 2004
Jerrilyn Farmer, *Mumbo Gumbo*, 2003
Eileen Fulton, *The Nina McFall Series*, 1988-
Sparkle Hayter, *The Robin Hudson Series*, 1994-
Lindsay Maracotta, *The Lucy Freers Series*, 1996-

188

SARA PARETSKY

Fire Sale
(New York: Putnam, 2005)

Story type: Private Detective
Series: V.I. Warshawski. Book 13
Subject(s): Sports/Basketball; Schools/High Schools; Social Conditions
Major character(s): V.I. Warshawski, Detective—Private
Time period(s): 2000s
Locale(s): Chicago, Illinois

Summary: The author's ground-breaking mysteries featuring tough Chicago private eye V.I. Warshawski have always been informed by a social conscience, and this is no exception. Here the author explores the contrast between the working-class poor, who can barely make ends meet, and the conscienceless corporate rich, whose primary concern is to get even richer. The framework of the story is V.I.'s decision to fill in temporarily as coach of the girls' basketball team at her old South Chicago high school, where she's put in charge of an assortment of gang members, Christian fundamentalists,

and dispirited teen moms. The mother of one of the players, Josie Dorrado, hires V.I. to investigate industrial sabotage in the flag factory where she works, fearing the loss of her job and her ability to eke out a living for herself and her four children if the plant is destroyed—which it is. V.I.'s search for a team sponsor leads her to the Bysen family, whose patriarch founded a mammoth discount department store chain and whose idealistic grandson has run off with Josie.

Where it's reviewed:
Publishers Weekly, May 16, 2005, page 36

Other books by the same author:
Blacklist, 2004
Total Recall, 2002
Hard Time, 1999
Windy City Blues, 1995 (short stories)
Tunnel Vision, 1994

Other books you might like:
Linda Barnes, *The Carlotta Carlyle Series*, 1987-
Barbara D'Amato, *The Cat Marsala Series*, 1990-
Sue Grafton, *The Kinsey Millhone Series*, 1982-
Laura Lippman, *The Tess Monaghan Series*, 1997-
Marcia Muller, *The Sharon McCone Series*, 1977-

189

BARBARA PARKER

Suspicion of Rage

(New York: Dutton, 2005)

Story type: Legal; Psychological Suspense
Series: Gail Connor. Book 8
Subject(s): Cuban Americans; Marriage; Politics
Major character(s): Gail Connor, Lawyer (corporate litigator); Anthony Quintana, Lawyer (criminal)
Time period(s): 2000s
Locale(s): Florida Keys, Florida; Cuba

Summary: There's little of the legal shenanigans usual to this series here, but plenty of suspense and atmosphere, including lots of information on Cuba, past and present. Gail and her lawyer lover, Anthony Quintana, have finally gotten married in the Florida Keys and are planning a Cuban honeymoon so she can meet his family. It doesn't prove to be as simple as they expected, however, for the CIA tries to recruit Anthony to get his brother-in-law to defect, and he's caught between his family, who supported the revolution, and his friends, passionate political dissidents.

Where it's reviewed:
Library Journal, February 15, 2005, page 120

Other books by the same author:
Suspicion of Madness, 2003
Suspicion of Vengeance, 2001
Suspicion of Malice, 2000
Suspicion of Betrayal, 1999
Suspicion of Deceit, 1998

Other books you might like:
Edna Buchanan, *The Britt Montero Series*, 1992-
Carolina Garcia-Aguilera, *Havana Heat*, 2000
Lia Matera, *Havana Twist*, 1998

Les Standiford, *Havana Run*, 2003
Randy Wayne White, *North of Havana*, 1997

190

ROBERT B. PARKER

Cold Service

(New York: Putnam, 2005)

Story type: Private Detective
Series: Spenser. Book 32
Subject(s): Revenge; Organized Crime; Friendship
Major character(s): Spenser, Detective—Private; Hawk, Detective—Private
Time period(s): 2000s
Locale(s): Boston, Massachusetts; Marshport, Massachusetts

Summary: Spenser's seemingly indestructible sidekick Hawk is gravely injured while protecting a bookie client in an incident that leaves the bookie, his wife, and two of his three children dead. Now the proud and independent Hawk has to depend on doctors and friends, notably Spenser, if he's to make a full recovery. While this happens, Spenser tries to find a way to penetrate the Ukrainian mob who made the hit, not an easy task given their insularity and power. They control the Boston suburb of Marshport, where much of the action takes place. Hawk is anxious for revenge, not only for himself, but for his client's surviving child. The author writes two other series, one with small-town police chief Jesse Stone and another with Spenser's female counterpart, Boston private eye Sunny Randall, as well as having written several stand-alones.

Where it's reviewed:
Booklist, January 1, 2005, page 783
New York Times Book Review, March 14, 2005, page 28
Publishers Weekly, February 7, 2005, page 45

Other books by the same author:
Bad Business, 2004
Back Story, 2003
Widow's Walk, 2002
Potshot, 2001
Hugger Mugger, 2000

Other books you might like:
Lee Child, *The Jack Reacher Series*, 1997-
Robert Crais, *The Elvis Cole Series*, 1987-
Dennis Lehane, *The Patrick Kenzie/Angela Gennaro Series*, 1994-1999
Rick Riordan, *The Tres Navarre Series*, 1997-
Walter Satterthwait, *The Joshua Croft Series*, 1989-

191

OWEN PARRY (Pseudonym of Ralph Peters)

Rebels of Babylon

(New York: William Morrow, 2005)

Story type: Historical/American Civil War
Series: Abel Jones. Book 6
Subject(s): Slavery; Civil War; Voodoo
Major character(s): Abel Jones, Military Personnel, Spy
Time period(s): 1860s (1863)

Locale(s): New Orleans, Louisiana

Summary: Abel Jones, a Union army major who also works as an agent for President Abraham Lincoln, is sent to New Orleans to investigate the murder of Susan Peabody, an heiress and ardent abolitionist. Although the diminutive and staunchly puritanical Welshman is dismayed by the exotic and sinful ambience of New Orleans, he gamely pursues his investigation, dealing with voodoo rituals, a kidnapping, poison charms, and the mysterious disappearance of blacks from their neighborhoods, as well as a burgeoning movement to send former slaves back to Africa. Throughout, Abel maintains his rigorous moral code and ardent nationalism, seeing everything not Methodist or Welsh as highly suspect, which makes for a number of entertaining and amusing situations.

Where it's reviewed:
Publishers Weekly, February 28, 2005, page 42

Other books by the same author:
The Bold Sons of Erin, 2003
Honor's Kingdom, 2002
Call Each River Jordan, 2001
Shadows of Glory, 2000
Faded Coat of Blue, 1999

Other books you might like:
Ava Dianne Day, *Cut to the Heart*, 2002
Michael Kilian, *The Harrison Raines Series*, 2000-
Ann McMillan, *The Narcissa Powers Series*, 1998-
Miriam Grace Monfredo, *The Cain Trilogy*, 2000-2002
Anne Perry, *Slaves of Obsession*, 2000

192

REBECCA PAWEL

The Watcher in the Pine

(New York: Soho, 2005)

Story type: Historical/World War II; Police Procedural
Series: Carlos Tejada. Book 3
Subject(s): Civil War/Spanish; Marriage; Political Movements
Major character(s): Carlos Tejada Alonso y Leon, Police Officer (lieutenant); Elena Fernandez, Spouse (Carlos' pregnant wife)
Time period(s): 1940s (1940)
Locale(s): Potes, Spain

Summary: At the end of the Spanish Civil War in 1940, Carlos Tejada of the Guardia Civil is transferred from Salamanca to the isolated mountain village of Potes, his first independent command. He takes with him his pregnant wife Elena, whose Republican sympathies had made her unpopular at his previous post. Their arrival is met with hostile indifference, and Tejada soon realizes that the villagers are still waging guerrilla warfare against the Fascist regime. Further, he finds that his predecessor was murdered by rebel forces and his killer has still not been found—perhaps because nobody has been looking for him. The Edgar-winning author tells her story in spare prose, befitting the bleakness of the political and physical landscape. The pace may be leisurely, but the richness of historical detail and the loving but uneasy relationship between Tejada and Elena offer their own rewards.

Where it's reviewed:
Booklist, December 15, 2004, page 712
Mystery News, February/March 2005, page 21
Mystery Scene, Winter 2005, page 73
Publishers Weekly, November 29, 2004, page 26

Other books by the same author:
Law of Return, 2004
Death of a Nationalist, 2003

Other books you might like:
Stephen Burger, *Walking the Lions*, 2003
J. Robert Janes, *The Jean-Louis St-Cyr/Hermann Kohler Series*, 1992-
Manuel Vazquez Montalban, *Murder in the Central Committee*, 1984
Robert Wilson, *The Blind Man of Seville*, 2003
James Garcia Woods, *The General's Dog*, 2000

193

MICHAEL PEARCE

The Point in the Market

(Scottsdale, Arizona: Poisoned Pen Press, 2005)

Story type: Historical/World War I
Series: Mamur Zapt. Book 15
Subject(s): Politics; Cultures and Customs; World War I
Major character(s): Gareth Owen, Government Official (head of secret police)
Time period(s): 1910s (1914)
Locale(s): Cairo, Egypt

Summary: Gareth Owen, the canny Welshman who holds the position of Mamur Zapt, or head of the Cairo secret police in colonial Egypt, has at last married his longtime sweetheart Zeinab, the pasha's daughter. The Great War has begun, casting its shadow over Egypt, which has been ruled by Britain since 1881, with its hereditary ruler, the khedive, in a largely ceremonial role. It's a social and political order whose days are numbered, but in the meantime life goes on for Owen and his bride, neither of whom is fully accepted by the other's culture. This may well be the last book in the series, although it's possible a further and final book will be published detailing the final days of the British protectorate. Like the best historical fiction, this admirable series illuminates the present by explaining the past, and entertains as well as educates.

Where it's reviewed:
Mystery News, April/May 2005, page 26

Other books by the same author:
A Cold Touch of Ice, 2004
Death of an Effendi, 2004
The Face in the Cemetery, 2004
The Last Cut, 2004
The Snake Catcher's Daughter, 2003

Other books you might like:
Conrad Allen, *Murder on the Marmora*, 2004
Barbara Cleverly, *The Last Kashmiri Rose*, 2001
Laurie R. King, *The Game*, 2004
Eric Lawlor, *Murder on the Verandah*, 1999
Elizabeth Peters, *Guardian of the Horizon*, 2004

194

RIDLEY PEARSON

Cut and Run

(New York: Hyperion, 2005)

Story type: Psychological Suspense
Subject(s): Federal Witness Security Program; Organized Crime; Law Enforcement
Major character(s): Roland Larson, Police Officer (U.S. marshal); Hope Stevens, Consultant (to the Justice Department), Single Parent
Time period(s): 2000s
Locale(s): St. Louis, Missouri; Seattle, Washington

Summary: When a mob family hijacks a computer disc with the names of thousands of participants in the witness protection program on it, and then kidnaps the person who encrypted it, U.S. Marshal Roland Larson once again gets a chance to work with Justice Department consultant Hope Stevens, whom he once loved and who was forced to go undercover in the program herself. One of the names on the list is that of her own daughter. It's a roller coaster ride of a book, with Hope—who has been in hiding for six years waiting to testify against the deadly Romero family—the chief target of one of their assassins, a very scary guy named Paolo, who is after Hope's daughter as well. The author also writes a Seattle-based series featuring homicide detective Lou Boldt and police psychologist Daphne Matthews, as well as another series written under the pseudonym Wendell McCall.

Where it's reviewed:
Booklist, February 15, 2005, page 1037
Mystery Scene, Spring 2005, page 79
New York Times Book Review, April 10, 2005, page 35
Publishers Weekly, March 14, 2005, page 46
Romantic Times, April 2005, page 85

Other books by the same author:
Parallel Lines, 2001
Chain of Evidence, 1995
Hard Fall, 1992
Probable Cause, 1990
Hidden Charges, 1987

Other books you might like:
Harlan Coben, *Tell No One*, 2001
Jeffery Deaver, *The Blue Nowhere*, 2001
Jon A. Jackson, *Badger Games*, 2002
Alan Russell, *Exposure*, 2002
Stephen White, *The Program*, 2001

195

GEORGE P. PELECANOS

Drama City

(New York: Little, Brown, 2005)

Story type: Psychological Suspense
Subject(s): City and Town Life; Crime and Criminals; Animals, Treatment of
Major character(s): Lorenzo Brown, Convict (former); Rachel Lopez, Parole Officer

Time period(s): 2000s
Locale(s): Washington, District of Columbia

Summary: Lorenzo Brown is one of the few of parole officer Rachel Lopez's clients to be making it in the outside world, and they're both happy with his progress. A former small-time drug dealer, Lorenzo has taken a job with the Washington, D.C., Humane Society, patrolling the streets for animal abuse cases. He likes his job, just as Rachel is satisfied with hers, but they both have their demons to fight. Lorenzo's is the constant pressure to go back to his old life, and Rachel's is her compulsion to drink herself into having dangerous sex with strange men. Although the odds are against it, both protagonists survive a local drug war and series of revenge killings to emerge with their integrity, at least, intact. It's an unusual plot twist for this author, whose characters usually are overcome by their own hard luck. Among his other works are several stand-alone mysteries, a series featuring D.C. private detectives Derek Strange and Terry Quinn, and another, set largely in the past, featuring bartender/private eye Nick Stefanos.

Where it's reviewed:
Booklist, February 15, 2005, page 1037
Entertainment Weekly, March 25, 2005, page 78
Library Journal, March 15, 2005, page 76
Mystery News, Spring 2005, page 68
Publishers Weekly, February 21, 2005, page 158

Other books by the same author:
Shame the Devil, 2000
The Sweet Forever, 1998
King Suckerman, 1997
The Big Blowdown, 1996

Other books you might like:
Lee Child, *The Jack Reacher Series*, 1997-
Michael Connelly, *The Harry Bosch Series*, 1992-
Dennis Lehane, *Mystic River*, 2001
T. Jefferson Parker, *Silent Joe*, 2001
John Shannon, *Dangerous Games*, 2005

196

SHARON KAY PENMAN

Prince of Darkness

(New York: Putnam, 2005)

Story type: Historical/Medieval
Series: Justin de Quincy. Book 4
Subject(s): Middle Ages; Kings, Queens, Rulers, etc.
Major character(s): Justin de Quincy, Agent, Bastard Son
Time period(s): 12th century (1193)
Locale(s): France

Summary: Justin de Quincy, Eleanor of Aquitaine's loyal servant, is summoned by his nemesis, Prince John (Eleanor's younger son), who has been falsely (but plausibly) accused of plotting to kill his brother, King Richard the Lionhearted. Plots and counterplots abound as Justin reluctantly agrees to help clear John of the charges, once he realizes that to do so will be helping Eleanor as well. The author also writes mainstream historical novels.

Where it's reviewed:
Library Journal, December 2004, page 96

Mystery News, April/May 2005, page 18
Publishers Weekly, March 7, 2005, page 54

Other books by the same author:
Dragon's Lair, 2003
Cruel as the Grave, 1998
The Queen's Man, 1996

Other books you might like:
Alys Clare, *The Helewise of Hawkenlye Series*, 1999-
Judith Koll Healey, *The Canterbury Papers*, 2003
Domini Highsmith, *Master of the Keys*, 1996
Bernard Knight, *The Sir John de Wolfe Series*, 1998-
Ellis Peters, *The Brother Cadfael Series*, 1977-1994

197

ANNE PERRY

Long Spoon Lane

(New York: Ballantine, 2005)

Story type: Historical/Victorian; Police Procedural
Series: Thomas and Charlotte Pitt. Book 24
Subject(s): Victorian Period; Terrorism; Politics
Major character(s): Thomas Pitt, Police Officer (superintendent); Charlotte Pitt, Socialite, Spouse
Time period(s): 1890s (1893)
Locale(s): London, England

Summary: In the summer of 1893, anarchists set off a bomb in a working-class neighborhood in protest of a police protection racket, destroying a number of homes. Thomas Pitt of Special Branch is summoned to the scene, and a long chase leads to the capture of the bombers in an abandoned warehouse in Long Spoon Lane. The body of a young aristocrat is found there, shot to death. Pitt's inquiries into the shooting lead him to a secret society known as the Inner Circle, led by a rogue police officer, Inspector Wetron of Bow Street. Wetron is using the press to strike fear of terrorism in the populace and to influence Parliament to suspend certain civil liberties in order to curtail terrorist activities, raising obvious parallels to post-9/11 America. The author also writes other historical series, one set in mid-Victorian times featuring private investigator William Monk and another set during the World War I era.

Where it's reviewed:
Booklist, December 15, 2004, page 691
Publishers Weekly, February 14, 2005, page 57

Other books by the same author:
Seven Dials, 2003
Southampton Row, 2002
The Whitechapel Conspiracy, 2001
Half Moon Street, 2000
Bedford Square, 1999

Other books you might like:
David Dickinson, *The Lord Francis Powerscourt Series*, 2002-
Ray Harrison, *The Sergeant Bragg/Constable Morton Series*, 1983-
Maureen Jennings, *The William Murdoch Series*, 1997-
Peter Lovesey, *The Sergeant Cribb/Constable Thackeray Series*, 1970-1978

Robin Paige, *The Kathryn Ardleigh Series*, 1994-

198

ELIZABETH PETERS (Pseudonym of Barbara Mertz)

The Serpent on the Crown

(New York: William Morrow, 2005)

Story type: Historical; Amateur Detective
Series: Amelia Peabody. Book 17
Subject(s): Archaeology; Family; Egyptian Antiquities
Major character(s): Amelia Peabody, Archaeologist, Detective—Amateur; Radcliffe Emerson, Archaeologist, Spouse (Amelia's husband)
Time period(s): 1920s (1922)
Locale(s): Luxor, Egypt

Summary: With the world at peace and the Valley of the Kings reopened to archaeologists, Amelia and Emerson, at home with their family, receive an unexpected visitor. It's Magda Petherick, a well-known novelist and the widow of a noted collector, who has an unusual request: she wants Emerson to dispose of the solid gold statuette she has brought, claiming it carries a curse and is responsible for her husband's death. If it's not returned to the tomb from whence it came, more lives could be endangered. Word of the statuette travels fast and soon journalists, collectors, dealers in antiquities, and museum curators descend upon the household. There may be some silver threads among Amelia's raven tresses these days, but she's as sharp—and stubborn—as ever, and as devoted to her irascible husband, known to the natives as the Father of Curses.

Where it's reviewed:
Booklist, March 1, 2005, page 1102
Library Journal, April 1, 2005, page 76
New York Times Book Review, April 10, 2005, page 27
Publishers Weekly, March 7, 2005, page 53
Romantic Times, April 2005, page 84

Other books by the same author:
Guardian of the Horizon, 2004
Children of the Storm, 2003
The Golden One, 2002
Lord of the Silent, 2001
He Shall Thunder in the Sky, 2000

Other books you might like:
Barbara Cleverly, *The Joe Sandilands Series*, 2001-
Laurie R. King, *The Mary Russell/Sherlock Holmes Series*, 1994-
Robin Paige, *The Kathryn Ardleigh Series*, 1994-
Michael Pearce, *The Mamur Zapt Series*, 1988-
Carol Thurston, *The Eye of Horus*, 2000

199

AUDREY PETERSON

Murder in Stratford

(Waterville, Maine: Five Star, 2005)

Story type: Historical/Elizabethan
Subject(s): Theater; Marriage; History

Major character(s): Anne Hathaway, Historical Figure, Spouse; William Shakespeare, Historical Figure, Writer
Time period(s): 16th century; 17th century
Locale(s): Stratford-on-Avon, England

Summary: As much a history of the marriage between Anne Hathaway and William Shakespeare as a detective story, this meticulously researched novel is Anne's own account of how she met, was courted by, and married Will and eventually worked to clear him of a murder charge. Shakespeare spent most of his time in London and the theatrical world there, while Anne stayed in Stratford, raising the children and seeing him only on occasional visits. On one of those, family friend Richard Quiney is killed on the grounds of Shakespeare's cottage, and a guest claims to have seen Will holding the murder weapon. The author has written two series, one featuring California English professor Claire Camden and the other about British journalist and music writer Jane Winfield in London, as well as another stand-alone mystery.

Where it's reviewed:
Booklist, March 15, 2005, page 1271
Library Journal, March 1, 2005, page 70
Mystery News, April/May 2005, page 19

Other books by the same author:
An Unmourned Death, 2002
Shroud for a Scholar, 1995 (Claire Camden series)
Death Too Soon, 1994 (Claire Camden series)
Dartmoor Burial, 1992 (Claire Camden series)
Lament for Christabel, 1991 (Jane Winfield series)

Other books you might like:
Philip Gooden, *The Nick Revill Series*, 2000-
Simon Hawke, *The Smythe/Shakespeare Series*, 2000-
Tony Hays, *Murder on the Twelfth Night*, 1993
Faye Kellerman, *The Quality of Mercy*, 1989
Leonard Tourney, *Time's Fool*, 2004

200

CAROLINE PETIT

The Fat Man's Daughter
(New York: Soho, 2005)

Story type: Historical
Subject(s): China; Antiques; History
Major character(s): Leah Kolbe, Young Woman
Time period(s): 1930s (1937)
Locale(s): Hong Kong; China

Summary: Left penniless except for a houseful of valuable antiquities upon the death of her father, a legendary Hong Kong antiques dealer known for his shady dealings, 19-year-old Leah Kolbe faces a cold and treacherous world with only her faithful amah, An-li, to protect her. She desperately needs cash to keep the house and business going, and so reluctantly accepts a proposition put to her by the mysterious Mr. Chang, which sends her on a train journey to the Japanese puppet government of Manchukuo (Manchuria), on to Nanking, and back by boat down the Yangtze River to Hong Kong. While Leah is in no way as vicious as the criminals she's forced to deal with, she was raised to be essentially amoral. Although she is repulsed by some of the personal and political atrocities

she witnesses on her journey, her chief concern is always her own survival. While it's hard to sympathize with her, her story is still a fascinating and unique view of this turbulent time and place in history. First novel.

Where it's reviewed:
Publishers Weekly, May 15, 2005, page 38

Other books you might like:
Jonathan Gash, *Jade Woman*, 1988
Mo Hayder, *The Devil of Nanking*, 2005
John P. Marquand, *Mr. Moto Is So Sorry*, 1936
James Norman, *Murder, Chop Chop*, 1942

201

CHRISTINE POULSON

Stage Fright
(New York: St. Martin's Minotaur, 2005)

Story type: Amateur Detective
Series: Cassandra James. Book 2
Subject(s): Academia; Theater; Universities and Colleges
Major character(s): Cassandra James, Professor (English), Detective—Amateur
Time period(s): 2000s
Locale(s): Cambridge, England

Summary: While on maternity leave after the birth of her first child, Cambridge professor and single mom Cassandra James becomes involved in a theatrical production of the Victorian melodrama, *East Lynne*, based on the 1860s novel by Mrs. Henry Wood. There is a great deal of tension among the cast members, culminating with the disappearance of the leading lady just before opening night. Cassandra knows it's not just a case of stage fright, for Melissa has left behind her six-month-old daughter. With a quote from a Byron poem her only clue as to her friend's whereabouts, Cassandra turns to Melissa's abusive ex-husband and old boyfriends for information.

Other books by the same author:
Murder Is Academic, 2004

Other books you might like:
Joanne Dobson, *The Karen Pelletier Series*, 1997-
Nora Kelly, *In the Shadow of King's*, 1984
Jill Paton Walsh, *The Imogen Quy Series*, 1993-
Joan Smith, *The Loretta Lawson Series*, 1987-
Veronica Stallwood, *The Kate Ivory Series*, 1993-

202

BILL PRONZINI

Nightcrawlers
(New York: Forge, 2005)

Story type: Private Detective
Series: Nameless Detective. Book 30
Subject(s): Homosexuality/Lesbianism; Violence; Fathers and Sons
Major character(s): Nameless Detective, Detective—Private; Jake Runyon, Detective—Private (former cop); Tamara Corbin, Detective—Private
Time period(s): 2000s

Locale(s): San Francisco, California

Summary: This entry in the longest-running private eye series being published (as of 2005) shows no sign of going stale, as the cast of characters has expanded to include not only Nameless' wife Kerry and adopted daughter Emily, but his new partner, Tamara Corbin, and ex-cop Jake Runyon. As ''Bill'' (his first name is finally revealed) settles into semi-retirement, Jake and Tamara take on more of the day-to-day investigations, but when they encounter a nasty gang of gay bashers (the nightcrawlers of the title) roaming the Castro District and viciously attacking gay men, Bill steps in as well. One of the victims turns out to be Jake's son's lover, and he pursues the case doggedly on his own time. The story is told from multiple viewpoints, and the three main characters grapple with domestic and other problems as well as the crimes at hand. The issue of violence against gays is compassionately explored by this veteran author and scholar of the genre, who has written a number of stand-alone mysteries as well as numerous short stories and Westerns in addition to editing many anthologies.

Where it's reviewed:
Booklist, February 1, 2005, page 947
New York Times Book Review, March 27, 2005, page 21
Publishers Weekly, February 21, 2005, page 161

Other books by the same author:
Scenarios, 2003 (short stories)
Spook, 2002
Bleeders, 2001
Crazybone, 2000
Boobytrap, 1998

Other books you might like:
Earl Emerson, *The Thomas Black Series*, 1985-
Loren D. Estleman, *The Amos Walker Series*, 1980-
Joe Gores, *The DKA Series*, 1972-
Stephen Greenleaf, *The John Marshall Tanner Series*, 1979-
Jeremiah Healy, *The John Francis Cuddy Series*, 1984-

203

ANN PURSER

Weeping on Wednesday
(New York: Berkley, 2005)

Story type: Amateur Detective; Traditional
Series: Lois Meade. Book 3
Subject(s): Small Town Life; Secrets
Major character(s): Lois Meade, Businesswoman (owner of housecleaning agency), Detective—Amateur
Time period(s): 2000s
Locale(s): Long Farnden, England

Summary: Lois Meade, a contented wife, mother of three, and owner of her own housecleaning agency, doesn't have the time or inclination to do any detecting. She's tried it before, at the behest of her old friend Inspector Hunter Cowgill, and it's only led to trouble and put her family in danger. Besides, she's just training a new employee, Enid Abraham, who lives in seclusion at Carthanger Mill with her mysterious family. After Lois spies a body in the millstream and her husband starts getting poison pen letters about an affair Lois is suppos-

edly having, she finally agrees to help Cowgill in the investigation of these events. The premise may be a bit preposterous, but the story is eminently readable and Lois is an appealing protagonist. Originally published in 2004 in England in hardcover.

Other books by the same author:
Terror on Tuesday, 2004
Murder on Monday, 2003

Other books you might like:
M.C. Beaton, *The Agatha Raisin Series*, 1992-
Simon Brett, *The Carol Seddon Series*, 2000-
Jeanne M. Dams, *The Dorothy Martin Series*, 1995-
Patricia Harwin, *The Far Wychwood Series*, 2004
Hazel Holt, *The Mrs. Malory Series*, 1989-

204

IAN RANKIN

Fleshmarket Alley
(New York: Little, Brown, 2005)

Story type: Police Procedural
Series: Inspector John Rebus. Book 17
Subject(s): Crime and Criminals; Racism; Refugees
Major character(s): John Rebus, Detective—Police (detective inspector); Siobhan Clarke, Detective—Police (detective sergeant)
Time period(s): 2000s
Locale(s): Edinburgh, Scotland

Summary: As hardened as he's become after years of dealing with criminals and lowlifes, Inspector John Rebus (who is nearing retirement) is horrified by his newest case. The death of an illegal Kurdish immigrant in a racially troubled Edinburgh public housing project leads Rebus into a bleak world of people-smuggling, slavery, and an unfeeling bureaucracy ill-equipped to deal with the problem of refugees seeking asylum. His associate, Siobhan Clarke, is investigating the disappearance of a woman whose sister, a rape victim, committed suicide. Eventually the two cases intersect when two skeletons are found in a pub on Fleshmarket Close (the original English title of the book).

Where it's reviewed:
Booklist, December 1, 2004, page 619
Entertainment Weekly, February 4, 2005, page 137
Library Journal, January 2005, page 85
New York Times Book Review, February 6, 2005, page 25
Publishers Weekly, January 10, 2005, page 41

Other books by the same author:
A Question of Blood, 2004
Resurrection Men, 2003
A Good Hanging, 2002 (short stories)
The Falls, 2001
Set in Darkness, 2000

Other books you might like:
Ken Bruen, *The White Trilogy*, 2003
John Harvey, *The Charlie Resnick Series*, 1989-1998
Bill James, *The Colin Harpur Series*, 1985-
Quintin Jardine, *The Robert Skinner Series*, 1993-
Denise Mina, *The Garnethill Trilogy*, 1999-2002

205

RICHARD RAYNER

The Devil's Wind

(New York: HarperCollins, 2005)

Story type: Historical
Subject(s): Organized Crime; Crime and Criminals; Politics
Major character(s): Maurice Valentine, Architect; Mallory Walker, Young Woman
Time period(s): 1950s (1956)
Locale(s): Las Vegas, Nevada; Los Angeles, California

Summary: Maurice Valentine is a very successful Los Angeles architect who got where he is through talent, hard work, ruthless ambition, and a very rich wife who's also the daughter of a senator. His work frequently takes him to Las Vegas, where he designs casinos along the burgeoning Strip and mock tract houses in the desert to be blown up in monthly A-bomb tests. Then he risks everything when he falls in love with Mallory Walker, a beautiful heiress and budding architect who first offers Valentine a commission and then seduces him. He falls for her in a big way, even though what he learns about her could eventually destroy him. When she is apparently murdered, he does what he can to find out what happened and becomes caught in a web involving the Mafia, crooked politicians, and all the crime Las Vegas can offer. First mystery.

Where it's reviewed:
Library Journal, January 2005, page 100
Mystery News, February/March 2005, page 23
Mystery Scene, Winter 2005, page 71
Publishers Weekly, January 10, 2005, page 39

Other books by the same author:
The Cloud Sketcher, 2000 (historical fiction)

Other books you might like:
Andrew Bergman, *Tender Is LeVine*, 2001
Max Allan Collins, *The Neon Mirage*, 1988
James Ellroy, *The Cold Six Thousand*, 2001
Charles Fleming, *The Ivory Coast*, 2002
Bill Moody, *Death of a Tenor Man*, 1995

206

KATHY REICHS

Cross Bones

(New York: Scribner, 2005)

Story type: Psychological Suspense
Series: Tempe Brennan. Book 8
Subject(s): Ancient History; Archaeology; Anthropology
Major character(s): Temperance Brennan, Anthropologist (forensic); Andrew Ryan, Detective—Homicide
Time period(s): 2000s
Locale(s): Montreal, Quebec, Canada; Jerusalem, Israel

Summary: Tempe Brennan is called to examine the body of an Orthodox Jew who was found shot to death in his Montreal office, and after she has performed the autopsy, she's handed a photograph by a strange man and told that it will help explain his murder. The photo shows a skeleton from a 1963 archaeological dig in Israel, and the victim turns out to be a black market antiquities dealer. To pursue this connection, Tempe flies to Israel where she and Detective Andrew Ryan learn of an ossuary at Masada and a tomb that may have contained the remains of Jesus' family. In fact, it may contain proof that he didn't die on the cross but lived to marry, have children, and die of old age. The plot, based on recent archaeological findings, is an absorbing blend of fact and supposition.

Where it's reviewed:
Publishers Weekly, May 9, 2005, page 43

Other books by the same author:
Monday Mourning, 2004
Bare Bones, 2003
Grave Secrets, 2002
Fatal Voyage, 2001
Deadly Decisions, 2000

Other books you might like:
Patricia Cornwell, *The Kay Scarpetta Series*, 1990-
D.J. Donaldson, *The Andy Brouchard Series*, 1988-
Linda Fairstein, *The Alexandra Cooper Series*, 1996-
Tess Gerritsen, *The Jane Rizzoli Series*, 2001-
Anna Salter, *The Michael Stone Series*, 1997-

207

CYNTHIA RIGGS

The Paperwhite Narcissus

(New York: St. Martin's Minotaur, 2005)

Story type: Amateur Detective
Series: Victoria Trumbull. Book 5
Subject(s): Small Town Life; Journalism; Aging
Major character(s): Victoria Trumbull, Journalist (newspaper columnist), Aged Person
Time period(s): 2000s
Locale(s): West Tisbury, Massachusetts (Martha's Vineyard)

Summary: At 92, Victoria Trumbull is sharper than many people half her age. She handles her job as columnist for *The Island Enquirer* with aplomb, but her editor decides the newspaper needs a young look and cancels her weekly column. In retaliation, she signs on with the West Tisbury *Grackle*, a small newsletter that she intends to turn into a competitor to her former newspaper. Her first big story concerns the murder of an unpopular developer whose severed body is found in two locations. In the meantime, her former editor has been receiving a series of fake obituaries naming him as the deceased. Knowing that Victoria is probably the only person on the island who can solve this mystery, he turns to her for help. Steeped in the geography and atmosphere of the island, the book is the next best thing to a visit to Martha's Vineyard.

Where it's reviewed:
Library Journal, May 1, 2005, page 66
Publishers Weekly, March 7, 2005, page 53

Other books by the same author:
Jack in the Pulpit, 2004
The Cemetery Yew, 2003
The Cranefly Orchid Murders, 2002

Deadly Nightshade, 2001

Other books you might like:
Philip R. Craig, *The J.W. Jackson Series*, 1989-
Francine Mathews, *The Merry Folger Series*, 1994-
Stefanie Matteson, *The Charlotte Graham Series*, 1990-
David Osborn, *Murder on Martha's Vineyard*, 1989
Katherine Hall Page, *The Body in the Lighthouse*, 2003

208

RICK RIORDAN

Mission Road

(New York: Bantam, 2005)

Story type: Private Detective
Series: Tres Navarre. Book 6
Subject(s): Friendship; Organized Crime; Mexican Americans
Major character(s): Jackson "Tres" Navarre, Detective—Private, Professor (former)
Time period(s): 2000s; 1980s
Locale(s): San Antonio, Texas

Summary: The past intersects with the present when Tres' boyhood friend, Ralph Arguello, comes to him for help after the San Antonio police finger him for the murder of his wife, cold case detective Ana DeLeon. The cops think Ralph, a reformed criminal, killed Ana because she was about to name him as the chief suspect in the murder of Frank White, a mobster's son who was Ralph's friend in high school. Ralph insists he's been set up, and the two friends search the city for the real killer while evading the police. The action alternates between the present and the 1980s, when Ana's mother Lucia was one of San Antonio's first female cops. The author has also written a stand-alone thriller, *Cold Spring* (2003).

Where it's reviewed:
Publishers Weekly, May 16, 2005, page 40

Other books by the same author:
Southtown, 2004
The Devil Went Down to Austin, 2001
The Last King of Texas, 2000
Widower's Two-Step, 1999
Big Red Tequila, 1997

Other books you might like:
Jay Brandon, *Local Rules*, 1998
Harlan Coben, *The Myron Bolitar Series*, 1995-
Robert Crais, *The Elvis Cole Series*, 1987-
Bill Crider, *The Truman Smith Series*, 1991-
Robert B. Parker, *The Spenser Series*, 1973-

209

JOHN MADDOX ROBERTS

SPQR IX: The Princess and the Pirates

(New York: St. Martin's Minotaur, 2005)

Story type: Historical/Ancient Rome
Series: SPQR. Book IX
Subject(s): Roman Empire; Ancient History; Pirates
Major character(s): Decius Caecilius Metellus, Detective—Amateur

Time period(s): 1st century B.C. (70 B.C.)
Locale(s): Cyprus; Rome, Roman Empire

Summary: With his two years as aedile (a glorified public works inspector) over, Decius is ready to run for the office of praetor, but his father thinks he still needs more military experience and so obtains for him a naval command in the Mediterranean, where a new wave of piracy needs to be stopped. Decius and his men make landfall on the island of Cyprus, where a 16-year-old Cleopatra is visiting on behalf of her father. Even as he is making plans for glory at sea, his host Silvanus, the ruler of the island, is murdered and Decius is obligated to find his murderer, hoping desperately that it isn't Cleopatra.

Where it's reviewed:
Publishers Weekly, May 23, 2005, page 62

Other books by the same author:
SPQR VIII: The River God's Vengeance, 2004
SPQR VII: The Tribune's Curse, 2003
SPQR VI: Nobody Loves a Centurion, 2001
SPQR V: Saturnalia, 1999
SPQR IV: Temple of the Muses, 1992

Other books you might like:
Ron Burns, *Roman Shadows*, 1992
Lindsey Davis, *The Marcus Didius Falco Series*, 1989-
Joan O'Hagan, *A Roman Death*, 1988
Steven Saylor, *The Judgment of Caesar*, 2004
Marilyn Todd, *The Claudia Seferius Series*, 1995-

210

PETER ROBINSON

Strange Affair

(New York: William Morrow, 2005)

Story type: Police Procedural
Series: Inspector Alan Banks. Book 15
Subject(s): Brothers; Secrets; Missing Persons
Major character(s): Alan Banks, Police Officer (detective inspector); Annie Cabbot, Police Officer (detective inspector)
Time period(s): 2000s
Locale(s): England

Summary: Living in a rented flat since his home was destroyed by a serial arsonist (*Playing with Fire*), Alan Banks is struggling with depression and trying to put his life back together when he gets a call from his estranged younger brother, Roy, claiming his life is in danger. Alan rushes to London to find that Roy has disappeared, and he starts interviewing his brother's friends, including a former fiancee, to determine what has happened. Back in Eastvale, Annie Cabbot, Alan's colleague and former lover, discovers Alan's address on the body of a young woman found murdered in her car, and when she and Alan meet, they find the murder victim's name in Roy's address book. Determining how the crimes are linked leads them into an underworld of forced prostitution and other social evils. The author, whose many awards include the Anthony, Canada's Arthur Ellis, and France's Grand Prix, continues to grow with each book in this outstanding series.

Where it's reviewed:
Library Journal, February 1, 2005, page 58
Mystery Scene, Winter 2005, page 76
New York Times Book Review, February 20, 2005, page 21
Publishers Weekly, January 17, 2005, page 35
Romantic Times, March 2005, page 86

Other books by the same author:
Playing with Fire, 2004
Close to Home, 2003
Aftermath, 2001
Cold Is the Grave, 2000
In a Dry Season, 1999

Other books you might like:
Stephen Booth, *The Ben Cooper/Diane Fry Series*, 2000-
Deborah Crombie, *The Duncan Kincaid/Gemma James Series*, 1993-
Reginald Hill, *The Dalziel/Pascoe Series*, 1970-
Ian Rankin, *The Inspector John Rebus Series*, 1987-
Ruth Rendell, *The Inspector Wexford Series*, 1964-

211

KELLEY ROOS (Pseudonym of Audrey Kelley Roos and William Roos)

The Frightened Stiff

(Lyons, Colorado: Rue Morgue Press, 2005)

Story type: Amateur Detective; Humor
Series: Jeff & Haila Troy. Book 3
Subject(s): Neighbors and Neighborhoods; Marriage
Major character(s): Haila Troy, Actress, Detective—Amateur; Jeff Troy, Photographer, Detective—Amateur
Time period(s): 1940s (ca. 1942)
Locale(s): New York, New York (Greenwich Village)

Summary: Haila Troy is thrilled to be moving into a charming garden apartment in an old brownstone in the Village, even if their furniture is late arriving and the locks on the doors don't work. Jeff is equally delighted, especially after he realizes that it used to be a favorite speakeasy he frequented in his bachelor days. When Haila overhears a patron in the neighborhood bar arrange a rendezvous at their apartment that same night, and when a naked body is found in their garden the next morning (after having been drowned in their bathtub), she begins to be alarmed. While the cops do their best work, Jeff and Haila turn detective to speed things up, quickly learning that just about every tenant in the building could be the killer. Originally published in 1942.

Other books by the same author:
Ghost of a Chance, 1947
There Was a Crooked Man, 1945
Sailor, Take Warning!, 1944
If the Shroud Fits, 1941
Made Up to Kill, 1940 (reprinted in 2005)

Other books you might like:
Delano Ames, *The Jane & Dagobert Brown Series*, 1948-1959
Frances Crane, *The Pat & Jean Abbot Series*, 1941-1962
Dashiell Hammett, *The Thin Man*, 1934

Frances Lockridge, *The Mrs. & Mrs. North Series*, 1940-1963
Richard Lockridge, co-author
Margaret Scherf, *The Henry & Emily Bryce Series*, 1949-1963

212

P.B. RYAN

Death on Beacon Hill

(New York: Berkley, 2005)

Story type: Historical/Victorian America; Amateur Detective
Series: Nell Sweeney. Book 3
Subject(s): Social Classes; Irish Americans; Blackmail
Major character(s): Nell Sweeney, Governess, Detective—Amateur
Time period(s): 1860s (1869)
Locale(s): Boston, Massachusetts

Summary: As governess to the wealthy, aristocratic Hewitt family, Irish immigrant Nell Sweeney occupies a peculiar social position in post-Civil War Boston society. Her own shadowy past was put behind her when her employer, kindly Violet Hewitt, took her under her wing. The bond between the two women was strengthened when Nell helped her employer locate her son William, missing since the Civil War. Now one of the Hewitt servants seeks Nell's aid in clearing the name of his young niece Fiona, maid to the notorious actress Virginia Kimball. Fiona is suspected of having murdered her employer while trying to steal her diamonds, but she was shot to death while in the act, apparently by a dying Mrs. Kimball, and so is unable to speak for herself. Nell quickly discovers that Mrs. Kimball was blackmailing any number of Boston's most prominent citizens and that there are many men with motives far more plausible than poor Fiona's for wanting to see the actress dead.

Other books by the same author:
Murder in a Mill Town, 2004
Still Life with Murder, 2003

Other books you might like:
Rhys Bowen, *The Molly Murphy Series*, 2001-
Jeanne M. Dams, *The Hilda Johansson Series*, 1999-
Mark Graham, *The Wilton McCleary Series*, 1998-
Anna MacLean, *The Louisa May Alcott Series*, 2004-
Cynthia Peale, *The Caroline Ames Series*, 2000-

213

JOHN SANDFORD (Pseudonym of John Case)

Broken Prey

(New York: Putnam, 2005)

Story type: Police Procedural
Series: Lucas Davenport. Book 16
Subject(s): Serial Killers; Law Enforcement; Rock Music
Major character(s): Lucas Davenport, Police Officer (investigator for state)
Time period(s): 2000s
Locale(s): Minneapolis, Minnesota; St. Paul, Minnesota

Summary: Davenport, who's lately been doing special jobs for the Minnesota governor, here packs his family off to London and with his partner, Detective Sloan, dives into a juicy case involving a psychopathic serial killer, which he claims isn't as rare a phenomenon as the public believes. A recently released sex offender is the first suspect, but he doesn't seem smart enough to be their man, who not only has a taste for mutilating his victims but seems to enjoy playing games with his pursuers. A slight but amusing side story has Davenport trying to pick the 100 best rock songs for his newly acquired iPod, which provides brief but welcome moments of comic relief from the unrelenting suspense. Lucas' final song list is included.

Where it's reviewed:
Entertainment Weekly, May 13, 2005, page 92
New York Times Book Review, May 29, 2005, page 14
Publishers Weekly, April 11, 2005, page 15

Other books by the same author:
Hidden Prey, 2004
Naked Prey, 2003
Mortal Prey, 2002
Chosen Prey, 2001
Easy Prey, 2000

Other books you might like:
Michael Connelly, *The Harry Bosch Series*, 1992-
Jeffery Deaver, *The Lincoln Rhyme Series*, 1997-
Chuck Logan, *The Phil Broker Series*, 1997-
James Patterson, *The Alex Cross Series*, 1993-
Ridley Pearson, *The Lou Boldt Series*, 1988-

214

C.J. SANSOM

Dark Fire

(New York: Viking, 2005)

Story type: Historical/Renaissance
Series: Matthew Shardlake. Book 2
Subject(s): Religion; Alchemy; Social Conditions
Major character(s): Matthew Shardlake, Lawyer, Handicapped (hunchback)
Time period(s): 16th century (1540)
Locale(s): London, England

Summary: Shardlake, a sharp-witted lawyer who was turned down for the priesthood because of his deformity, has been engaged to defend a friend's young niece who is accused of murder. She refuses to speak, despite threats of torture, and under English law she will be crushed to death unless she makes some sort of plea. Then Henry VIII's fearsome vicar general, Lord Thomas Cromwell, offers a temporary stay of execution if Shardlake will undertake a delicate mission for him, calculated to return him to the king's favor. He is ordered to find the formula for a new liquid weapon of mass destruction called Greek Fire, but before he can meet with the alchemists responsible, they are murdered. The author pays great attention to social and economic conditions in the great city of London, as well as to the roles that religion and the law play in the lives of its citizens.

Where it's reviewed:
Booklist, November 15, 2004, page 566
Publishers Weekly, November 15, 2004, page 40

Other books by the same author:
Dissolution, 2003

Other books you might like:
Iris Collier, *Day of Wrath*, 2002
Jane Feather, *The Widow's Kiss*, 2002
Karen Harper, *The Poyson Garden*, 1999
Jeremy Potter, *A Trail of Blood*, 1970
Sheila Radley, *New Blood from Old Bones*, 1998

215

WALTER SATTERTHWAIT

Cavalcade

(New York: St. Martin's Minotaur, 2005)

Story type: Historical/Roaring Twenties; Private Detective
Series: Phil Beaumont/Jane Turner. Book 3
Subject(s): Nazis; Anti-Semitism; Political Movements
Major character(s): Phil Beaumont, Detective—Private (Pinkerton operative); Jane Turner, Detective—Private (Pinkerton operative)
Time period(s): 1920s (1923)
Locale(s): Berlin, Germany; Bayreuth, Germany; Munich, Germany

Summary: Pinkerton agents Phil Beaumont and Jane Turner are assigned to investigate an assassination attempt on a rising young politician who's taken control of the German Nationalist Socialist Workers' Party. From Berlin to Bayreuth to Munich, they interview witnesses and suspects and finally the Fuhrer himself, peeling away layers of treachery and fear and revealing a sinister new order that they little realized existed. Through the observant eyes of Phil and Jane, this chilling time and place are brought into sharp focus. The story is told partly from Phil's point of view and partly from Jane's. Phil is laconic, cynical, and realistic; Jane is girlish, naive, and surprisingly unshockable. Satterthwait uses these contrasting viewpoints masterfully to paint a picture the reader won't soon forget of a world beginning to go horribly wrong. The author has also written other mysteries set in the past using real-life historical characters (Oscar Wilde, Lizzie Borden), as well as a contemporary series about Santa Fe private detective Joshua Croft.

Where it's reviewed:
Publishers Weekly, January 3, 2005, page 39

Other books by the same author:
Masquerade, 1998
Escapade, 1995

Other books you might like:
Jon Cleary, *City of Fading Light*, 1985
Max Allan Collins, *The Hindenburg Murders*, 2000
Jeffery Deaver, *Garden of Beasts*, 2004
Kristine Kathryn Rusch, *Hitler's Angel*, 1998
Darwin L. Teilhet, *The Talking Sparrow Murders*, 1934 reprinted in 1985

216

STEVEN SAYLOR

A Gladiator Dies Only Once

(New York: St. Martin's Minotaur, 2005)

Story type: Collection; Historical/Ancient Rome
Series: Roma Sub Rosa. Book 11
Subject(s): Short Stories; Roman Empire; Ancient History
Major character(s): Gordianus the Finder, Detective—Private
Time period(s): 1st century B.C.
Locale(s): Roman Empire

Summary: In his second collection of short stories featuring Gordianus the Finder, the author fills in some of the gaps in the detective's early years, between 77 and 64 B.C. Topics and historical figures not dealt with at any length in the novels, such as gladiators and chariot races and Sempronia and Lucullus, figure in some of the stories. Some deal with familiar public figures such as Cicero and Archimedes, while others have a more domestic setting and shed light on Gordianus' relationship with Bethesda, the Jewish/Egyptian slave who went on to be his concubine and eventually his wife. Most of the nine stories take place in Rome, but Spain, Sicily, and other parts of Italy also provide settings. The author has also written a stand-alone mystery set in 1885 Texas, *A Twist at the End* (2000), featuring the writer known as O Henry.

Where it's reviewed:
Library Journal, May 1, 2005, page 66
Publishers Weekly, May 2, 2005, page 179

Other books by the same author:
The Judgment of Caesar, 2004
A Mist of Prophecies, 2002
Last Seen in Massilia, 2000
Rubicon, 1999
The House of the Vestals, 1997 (short stories)

Other books you might like:
Mike Ashley, *The Mammoth Book of Roman Whodunnits*, 2003
  editor
Ron Burns, *Roman Shadows*, 1992
Lindsey Davis, *The Marcus Didius Falco Series*, 1989-
Joan O'Hagan, *A Roman Death*, 1988
John Maddox Roberts, *The SPQR Series*, 1990-

217

MARGARET SCHERF

The Green Plaid Pants

(Lyons, Colorado: Rue Morgue Press, 2005)

Story type: Amateur Detective; Humor
Series: Henry & Emily Bryce. Book 2
Subject(s): Antiques; Marriage
Major character(s): Emily Murdock Bryce, Interior Decorator, Detective—Amateur; Henry Bryce, Interior Decorator, Detective—Amateur
Time period(s): 1950s (ca. 1950)
Locale(s): New York, New York

Summary: Emily and Henry Bryce own an interior decorating store in Manhattan which specializes in refinishing old furniture. They've been married a little over two years now, and things are getting a bit dull until they travel to England for a decorating job. They return to New York with an entire entourage of eccentric Brits, as well as a pair of Bonnie Prince Charlie's trousers. Then one of their English friends gets murdered, Emily gets knocked on the head when she dabbles in detection, and Henry is nearly poisoned. First published in 1951, it's a lighthearted comedy of manners and the second in a four-book series. The author also wrote a series about a small-town Montana Episcopal minister, Martin Buell, another about pathologist Grace Severance, and a number of stand-alone mysteries, all with a light comic touch.

Other books by the same author:
The Diplomat and the Gold Piano, 1965
Glass on the Stairs, 1954
The Gun in Daniel Webster's Bust, 1949

Other books you might like:
Delano Ames, *The Jane & Dagobert Brown Series*, 1948-1959
Frances Crane, *The Pat & Jean Abbot Series*, 1941-1962
Dashiell Hammett, *The Thin Man*, 1934
Frances Lockridge, *The Mrs. & Mrs. North Series*, 1940-1963
  Richard Lockridge, co-author
Kelley Roos, *The Jeff & Haila Troy Series*, 1940-1966

218

LISA SCOTTOLINE

Devil's Corner

(New York: HarperCollins, 2005)

Story type: Legal
Subject(s): Law; Gangs; Drugs
Major character(s): Vicki Allegretti, Lawyer (assistant U.S. attorney)
Time period(s): 2000s
Locale(s): Philadelphia, Pennsylvania

Summary: The author's first stand-alone thriller is based on one of the biggest crack cocaine busts in Philadelphia history and features a young assistant U.S. attorney, Vicki Allegretti, an Italian-American who grew up in one of the city's better neighborhoods. She joins forces with a beautiful black woman, Reheema Bristow, who was raised in Devil's Corner, a decaying neighborhood overrun by drugs and gangs. It's also where Vicki's father grew up. Initially a suspect in the case, Reheema wins Vicki's trust and they set out to salvage what they can of Devil's Corner. Each has a personal stake in the case: Vicki's partner and Reheema's mother were both killed during the course of the investigation. The author has also written a very successful Philadelphia-based series featuring various members of the all-female law firm of Rosato & Associates.

Where it's reviewed:
Publishers Weekly, March 28, 2005, page 53

Other books by the same author:
Killer Smile, 2004
Dead Ringer, 2003

Courting Trouble, 2002
The Vendetta Defense, 2001
Moment of Truth, 2000

Other books you might like:
Alafair Burke, *Judgment Calls*, 2003
Rose Connors, *The Marty Nickerson Series*, 2002-
Perri O'Shaughnessy, *The Nina Reilly Series*, 1995-
Marianne Wesson, *The Cinda Hayes Series*, 1998-
Kate Wilhelm, *The Barbara Holloway Series*, 1991-

219

MAGGIE SEFTON (Pseudonym of Margaret Aunon)

Knit One, Kill Two

(New York: Berkley, 2005)

Story type: Amateur Detective
Series: Kelly Flynn. Book 1
Subject(s): Crafts; Hobbies
Major character(s): Kelly Flynn, Accountant, Detective—Amateur
Time period(s): 2000s
Locale(s): Fort Connor, Colorado (thinly disguised Fort Collins)

Summary: When her beloved Aunt Helen dies, Kelly returns to her childhood home in Colorado to attend her funeral, taking a break from her boring corporate life in Washington, D.C. Although the police think that Helen died as the result of a burglary gone wrong, their verdict doesn't answer some questions Kelly has. For example, why did Helen borrow $20,000 shortly before she died? And why is her cherished heirloom quilt missing? With the help of some of her aunt's friends from the local knitting shop, Kelly unravels the mystery, finds an absorbing new hobby, and reconnects with her past. A recipe and a knitting pattern are included. First novel.

Other books you might like:
Susan Wittig Albert, *The China Bayles Series*, 1992-
Maggie Bruce, *Murder Most Crafty*, 2005
  editor
Monica Ferris, *The Betsy Devonshire Series*, 1999-
Mary Kruger, *Died in the Wool*, 2005
Tim Myers, *The Harrison Black Series*, 2004-

220

JOHN SHANNON

Dangerous Games

(New York: Carroll & Graf, 2005)

Story type: Private Detective
Series: Jack Liffey. Book 8
Subject(s): Crime and Criminals; Fathers and Daughters; Runaways
Major character(s): Jack Liffey, Detective—Private
Time period(s): 2000s
Locale(s): Los Angeles, California

Summary: Jack's girlfriend, police sergeant Gloria Martinez, wants him to help her find her lovely young niece Luisa. A naive teenager, Luisa has left her tiny Paiute reservation to seek fame in the underground adult movie industry in the San Fernando Valley. What she discovers instead is a sordid, cruel world in which she's abused in worse ways than she was at home, but she finds an unlikely savior in the person of the Rastafarian thug Terror Pennycooke, whose rough exterior hides a gentle and caring heart as romantic as Luisa's. Meanwhile, a random drive-by shooting apparently intended for Jack leaves his strong-willed teenage daughter Maeve severely wounded. Jack goes after the young Latino gangster Thumb Estrada with vengeance in mind, only to find himself reluctantly taking the boy under his wing. In fact, the story is filled with such unlikely and arresting alliances, which are explored in satisfying depth. It's is another first-rate effort from an author who always deals sensitively and informatively with Southern California's multicultural society.

Other books by the same author:
Terminal Island, 2004
City of Strangers, 2003
Streets on Fire, 2002
The Orange Curtain, 2001
The Poison Sky, 2000

Other books you might like:
Michael Connelly, *The Harry Bosch Series*, 1992-
Denise Hamilton, *The Eve Diamond Series*, 2001-
T. Jefferson Parker, *California Girl*, 2004
Nina Revoyr, *Southland*, 2003
John Straley, *The Cecil Younger Series*, 1992-

221

SHARON SHORT

Death in the Cards

(New York: Avon, 2005)

Story type: Amateur Detective; Humor
Series: Josie Toadfern. Book 3
Subject(s): Small Town Life; Fairs
Major character(s): Josie Toadfern, Businesswoman (laundromat owner), Detective—Amateur
Time period(s): 2000s
Locale(s): Paradise, Ohio

Summary: Josie Toadfern, owner of a laundromat and an expert on stain removal, has rented the apartment over her business to a couple who own the local New Age bookshop and Tarot card reading room. The town is filled with all manner of psychics, from fortune tellers to healers to dream interpreters, all setting up for the Paradise Psychic Fair, an event that has an evangelist church pastor up in arms. When Josie is unlucky enough to stumble over a dead body, she doesn't expect that her discovery will put her into real danger.

Where it's reviewed:
Mystery Scene, Spring 2005, page 63

Other books by the same author:
Death by Deep Dish Pie, 2004
Death of a Domestic Diva, 2003

Other books you might like:
Monica Ferris, *The Betsy Devonshire Series*, 1999-
Joanne Fluke, *The Hannah Swenson Series*, 2000-
Yasmine Galenorn, *The Emerald O'Brien Series*, 2003-

Dolores Johnson, *The Mandy Dyer Series*, 1997-
Denise Swanson, *The Scumble River Series*, 2000-

222

DANIEL SILVA

Prince of Fire

(New York: Putnam, 2005)

Story type: Espionage
Series: Gabriel Allon. Book 5
Subject(s): Terrorism; Middle East; Politics
Major character(s): Gabriel Allon, Spy (Israeli), Art Historian (art restorer)
Time period(s): 2000s
Locale(s): Venice, Italy; Rome, Italy; Israel

Summary: Israeli intelligence officer Gabriel Allon, whose true passion in life is art restoration, is called from Venice to Israel to search for a group of terrorists who have bombed the Israeli embassy in Rome, killing numerous staff and civilians. The elusive leader of the group is a French archaeologist whose father was killed by the Israelis and who became a Palestinian agent. Allon's search takes him throughout the Middle East, France, and England before the book's conclusion. An aging, reluctant spy whose chance at happiness has been destroyed by terrorists, Allon is compelled to see this assignment through, as the mastermind he's searching for may be the same man who's responsible for the death of his son and the maiming, both physically and mentally, of his wife. The author has also written two thrillers featuring CIA agent Michael Osbourne.

Where it's reviewed:
Library Journal, February 15, 2005, page 121
Publishers Weekly, January 24, 2005, page 221

Other books by the same author:
A Death in Vienna, 2004
The Confessor, 2003
The English Assassin, 2002
The Kill Artist, 2001

Other books you might like:
John Altman, *The Watchmen*, 2004
Lionel Davidson, *The Menorah Men*, 1966
Joseph Finder, *The Zero Hour*, 1996
Alan Furst, *Blood of Victory*, 2002
Robert Wilson, *The Company of Strangers*, 2001

223

DAVID SKIBBINS

Eight of Swords

(New York: St. Martin's Minotaur, 2005)

Story type: Amateur Detective
Subject(s): Kidnapping; Extrasensory Perception
Major character(s): Warren Ritter, Fugitive, Detective—Amateur
Time period(s): 2000s
Locale(s): Berkeley, California

Summary: Warren Ritter (not his real name) reads tarot cards for a living on Berkeley's Telegraph Avenue, one of the last outposts of the counterculture, known to locals as "the open ward." Well, he doesn't really make his living at it, but it gives him a cover and a place to hang out. He's really a fugitive member of the Weather Underground, on the lam from the FBI for the last 30 years, with a number of forged identities and strategically placed stashes of cash, weapons, and vehicles to fall back on if the going ever gets tough. One fine day he does a reading for Heather Wellington, a slumming suburban teenager, and is chilled at what he sees. Warren doesn't really believe in the tarot, but once in a while the cards seem to take on a life of their own. Shortly thereafter Heather is kidnapped, her mother is murdered, and Warren, who is being framed for these events, turns detective to find Heather and her mom's killer. The book won the St. Martin/Malice Domestic contest for best first traditional mystery, the first time ever a man has won. If it's a little short on clues, Warren is an original, engaging character and the author exactly nails the Berkeley scene.

Where it's reviewed:
Booklist, March 1, 2005, page 1147
Library Journal, March 1, 2005, page 71
Publishers Weekly, March 14, 2005, page 48

Other books you might like:
Richard Barre, *The Wil Hardesty Series*, 1995-
Susan Dunlap, *The Jill Smith Series*, 1981-
John Shannon, *The Jack Liffey Series*, 1996-
Roger L. Simon, *The Big Fix*, 1972
John Straley, *The Cecil Younger Series*, 1992-

224

JUDITH SKILLINGS

Dangerous Curves

(New York: Avon, 2005)

Story type: Amateur Detective
Series: Rebecca Moore. Book 2
Subject(s): Automobiles; Social Conditions; Romance
Major character(s): Rebecca Moore, Store Owner (auto restoration shop), Detective—Amateur; Mick Hagan, Detective—Homicide
Time period(s): 2000s
Locale(s): Head Tide, Maryland; Washington, District of Columbia

Summary: Rebecca Moore was a reporter in the nation's capital whose investigation into a corporate crime inadvertently led to the suicide of her lover, who turned out to be the embezzler in question. In despair she fled Washington for rural Maryland, where she inherited a vintage auto restoration shop from her late uncle. Many of her employees are ex-convicts, and when the body of a young, pregnant exotic dancer is found dead in the back seat of a vintage Bentley, the police naturally suspect the ex-cons. Rebecca's reporter instincts kick in when a second young dancer is found in the Potomac, and she goes undercover at an upscale strip joint owned by a handsome Egyptian to find out what's going on. The pitiable conditions the young dancers live in and the heartless way they are exploited by the club's owner, one of

their own countrymen, set this apart from the average cozy. Rebecca's romance with ex-cop Mick Hagan continues to develop.

Where it's reviewed:
Mystery Scene, Spring 2005, page 63

Other books by the same author:
Dead End, 2004

Other books you might like:
Susan Wittig Albert, *The China Bayles Series*, 1992-
JoAnna Carl, *The Lee McKinney Series*, 2002-
Monica Ferris, *A Murderous Yarn*, 2002
Earlene Fowler, *The Benni Harper Series*, 1994-
Sarah Graves, *The Jacobia Tiptree Series*, 1998-

225

JULIA SPENCER-FLEMING

To Darkness and to Death
(New York: St. Martin's Minotaur, 2005)

Story type: Amateur Detective
Series: Clare Fergusson. Book 4
Subject(s): Small Town Life; Episcopalians; Environment
Major character(s): Clare Fergusson, Religious (Episcopal priest), Detective—Amateur; Russ Van Alstyne, Police Officer (police chief)
Time period(s): 2000s
Locale(s): Millers Kill, New York (Adirondacks)

Summary: The Rev. Clare Fergusson, a former helicopter pilot turned Episcopal priest, should be preparing for the bishop's annual visit when she's asked to join the search and rescue squad to look for a missing young woman. Millicent van der Hoeven and her siblings were on the point of selling their home and acreage to eventually become part of the local nature conservancy, a step that has angered local lumber interests. Clare once again works with her sheriff friend, the married Russ Van Alstyne, who is finding it increasingly difficult to keep their uncertain relationship from his loyal wife, although their strong moral codes have so far kept both Clare and Russ from acting on their strong attraction to one another.

Where it's reviewed:
Publishers Weekly, May 30, 2005, page 42

Other books by the same author:
Out of the Deep I Cry, 2004
A Fountain Filled with Blood, 2003
In the Bleak Midwinter, 2002

Other books you might like:
Michelle Blake, *The Lilly Connor Series*, 1999-
Kate Gallison, *The Mother Lavinia Gray Series*, 1995-
D.M. Greenwood, *The Theodora Braithwaite Series*, 1991-
Isabelle Holland, *The Claire Aldington Series*, 1983-
Cristina Sumners, *Crooked Heart*, 2002

226

PATRICIA SPRINKLE

Who Killed the Queen of Clubs?
(New York: Signet, 2005)

Story type: Amateur Detective
Series: MacLaren Yarbrough. Book 6
Subject(s): Small Town Life; American South; Aging
Major character(s): MacLaren Yarbrough, Judge, Store Owner (garden shop); Joe Riddley Yarbrough, Judge (former), Spouse (to MacLaren)
Time period(s): 2000s
Locale(s): Hopemore, Georgia

Summary: Since her husband Joe Riddley's stroke, MacLaren Yarbrough has taken over his duties as county magistrate in addition to managing their garden shop and coping with a large extended family. She worries about her old friend Edith Burkett, widowed when her pharmacist husband committed suicide and left nearly penniless because he'd spent all they had on drugs. Her children want her to sell the family pecan farm and live closer to them, but she's reluctant to do so. Then Edie is savagely murdered, and suspicion falls on Henry, the farm foreman, whose machete was indeed the murder weapon. Not believing he could be guilty, Mac sets out to find the real killer. The author also writes an Atlanta-based series featuring public relations consultant Sheila Travis.

Where it's reviewed:
Romantic Times, March 2005, page 82

Other books by the same author:
Who Let That Killer in the House?, 2003
Who Invited the Dead Man?, 2002
Who Left That Body in the Rain?, 2002
But Why Shoot the Magistrate?, 1998
When Did We Lose Harriet?, 1997

Other books you might like:
Anne George, *The Southern Sisters Series*, 1996-2001
Charlaine Harris, *The Aurora Teagarden Series*, 1990-
Margaret Maron, *The Deborah Knott Series*, 1992-
Celestine Sibley, *The Kate Kincaid Mulcay Series*, 1959-
Elizabeth Daniels Squire, *The Peaches Dann Series*, 1994-2000

227

OLEN STEINHAUER

36 Yalta Boulevard
(New York: St. Martin's Minotaur, 2005)

Story type: Psychological Suspense
Subject(s): Communism; Fathers and Sons; Memory Loss
Major character(s): Brano Sev, Amnesiac, Spy (former)
Time period(s): 1960s (1966)
Locale(s): Bobkra, Europe; Vienna, Austria

Summary: Brano Sev is an intelligence officer for an unnamed Eastern European country who may or may not have killed the wrong man while on a mission in Vienna. His punishment is to be assigned a job as a factory worker, far preferable to the prison term he might have been sentenced to. He's called up

again by his superiors to hunt down a defector who might possibly be hiding in Sven's native village of Bobkra, north of the capital, where he still has family. Sven, a victim of amnesia, doesn't even know if he's guilty of the crime he's been charged with, but he knows this is his only chance at being reinstated to his former position. A strong subplot involves Sven's father, who left the country after having been accused of collaboration after World War II. It's the third in a loosely connected series of crime novels set in the same Eastern Bloc country, detailing the rise of communism and the development of the Cold War, from a Texan who's long lived in Budapest.

Where it's reviewed:
Library Journal, April 15, 2005, page 80
Publishers Weekly, March 28, 2005, page 53

Other books by the same author:
The Confession, 2004
The Bridge of Sighs, 2003

Other books you might like:
Lionel Davidson, *The Night of Wenceslas*, 1960
Joseph Kanon, *The Prodigal Spy*, 1998
Robert Littell, *The October Circle*, 1976
Charles T. Powers, *In the Memory of the Forest*, 1997
Josef Svorecky, *The End of Lieutenant Boruvka*, 1975

228

SARAH STROHMEYER

Bubbles Betrothed

(New York: Dutton, 2005)

Story type: Amateur Detective; Humor
Series: Bubbles Yablonsky. Book 5
Subject(s): Social Classes; Journalism; Crime and Criminals
Major character(s): Bubbles Yablonsky, Journalist (aspiring), Detective—Amateur
Time period(s): 2000s
Locale(s): Lehigh, Pennsylvania

Summary: Former hairdresser turned rookie reporter Bubbles Yablonsky rushes out and buys her first business suit ever (a $30 hot-pink acetate number) just before she interviews Jill "Crazy Popeye" Simon, a homeless woman accused of murdering a beloved high school principal. As the woman is explaining what really happened, she falls over dead, and suddenly a lot of very odd people want to see Bubbles' notes. At the same time, her ex-husband wants Bubbles to help him out of his latest jam, and her major love interest, photographer Steve Stiletto, tells everyone they're engaged—but only to prevent an imminent job transfer. If Bubbles, with her big hair, flashy clothes, eccentric relatives, and Italian-American boyfriend, reminds people a lot of Janet Evanovich's Stephanie Plum—well, isn't that the idea?

Where it's reviewed:
Library Journal, March 1, 2005, page 71
People, April 11, 2005, page 53
Publishers Weekly, February 14, 2005, page 56
Romantic Times, April 2005, page 84

Other books by the same author:
Bubbles a Broad, 2004

Bubbles Ablaze, 2003
Bubbles in Trouble, 2002
Bubbles Unbound, 2001

Other books you might like:
Nancy Bartholomew, *The Sierra Lavatoni Series*, 1998-
Nancy J. Cohen, *The Marla Shore Series*, 1999-
Sophie Dunbar, *The Claire Claiborne Series*, 1993-
Janet Evanovich, *The Stephanie Plum Series*, 1994-
Harley Jane Kozak, *Dating Dead Men*, 2004

229

JAMES SWAIN

Mr. Lucky

(New York: Ballantine, 2005)

Story type: Private Detective; Humor
Series: Tony Valentine. Book 5
Subject(s): Gambling; Crime and Criminals; Small Town Life
Major character(s): Tony Valentine, Detective—Private (ex-cop); Gerry Valentine, Assistant (Tony's son)
Time period(s): 2000s
Locale(s): Slippery Rock, North Carolina; Gulfport, Mississippi; Las Vegas, Nevada

Summary: Tony Valentine is a widowed ex-cop who makes his lonely living spotting gambling scams and cheaters for the casinos. Most of the time he works long-distance, using videotapes provided by his clients and e-mailing his findings back to them. Sometimes, though, he has to get up close and personal to see what's going on, as in the case of Ricky Smith, a good ol' boy from Slippery Rock, North Carolina. Ricky in one memorable night in Las Vegas cheated death by jumping from a burning hotel into a swimming pool, borrowed 20 bucks from a retired bookkeeper, and won over $200,000 at blackjack. He went on to win equally impressive amounts at roulette and craps, and capped off the evening by cleaning the clock of legendary poker champion Tex "All In" Snyder. Tony knows that Ricky has to be cheating, but how? He goes to Slippery Rock and sends his screw-up son Gerry to Gulfport, Mississippi, to talk to Tex. Gerry's valiant efforts to stay straight and make his dad proud are both hilarious and touching, and the relationship between father and son defines the book as much as the central story. It doesn't hurt that it's also fast, funny, hugely entertaining, and of course absolutely accurate about the crooked gambling, a subject on which the author is a recognized authority.

Where it's reviewed:
Deadly Pleasures, Winter 2005, page 37
Entertainment Weekly, March 4, 2005, page 77
Publishers Weekly, February 7, 2005, page 41

Other books by the same author:
Loaded Dice, 2004
Sucker Bet, 2003
Funny Money, 2002
Grift Sense, 2001

Other books you might like:
Pete Hautman, *Drawing Dead*, 1993
Martin Hegwood, *Jackpot Bay*, 2002
Brian Hodge, *Wild Horses*, 1999

Tom Kakonis, *Shadow Counter*, 1993
Ted Thackrey, *Aces and Eights*, 1989

230

LEANN SWEENEY

A Wedding to Die For

(New York: Signet, 2005)

Story type: Private Detective; Humor
Series: Abby Rose. Book 2
Subject(s): American South; Weddings; Adoption
Major character(s): Abby Rose, Detective—Private, Heiress
Time period(s): 2000s
Locale(s): Houston, Texas; Kingston, Jamaica

Summary: Abby and her twin sister Kate live in luxury in the elegant home left to them by their wealthy father. Divorced and wondering what she should do with her life, Abby has become an adoption P.I., helping clients find their birth parents. She's drawn to this line of work in part because she herself is adopted and learned about it in a traumatic way. Not needing the money, she donates what she earns to charity. Here she's been hired by a bride who desperately wants to be reunited with her birth mother before her wedding, but Abby is unable to locate the woman and her client is horribly disappointed. When the bride's adoptive father is killed at the wedding reception, Abby decides to renew her investigation for the missing mother, a search that takes her to Jamaica and back before the mystery is resolved.

Where it's reviewed:
Mystery Scene, Winter 2005, page 64
Romantic Times, January 2005, page 85

Other books by the same author:
Pick Your Poison, 2004

Other books you might like:
Mary Kay Andrews, *Little Bitty Lies*, 2003
Carolyn Haines, *The Sarah Booth Delaney Series*, 1999-
Nancy Martin, *The Blackbird Sisters Series*, 2002-
Susan McBride, *Blue Blood*, 2004
Cathy Pickens, *Southern Fried*, 2004

231

LOU JANE TEMPLE

The Spice Box

(New York: Berkley Prime Crime, 2005)

Story type: Historical/Victorian America; Amateur Detective
Series: Bridget Heaney. Book 1
Subject(s): Irish Americans; Judaism; Food
Major character(s): Bridget Heaney, Immigrant, Cook
Time period(s): 1860s (1864)
Locale(s): New York, New York

Summary: Young Irish immigrant and former pickpocket Bridget Heaney learned to cook in an orphanage and worked in a restaurant and a boarding house after she was ''put out'' at the age of 15. Now almost 20, she's thrilled to be hired as assistant cook in the household of wealthy merchant Isaac Gold, a Sephardic Jew. On her first day on the job she finds the body of Gold's youngest son, who has been missing for several days, with two gunshot wounds through the chest. Bridget's former life on the streets qualifies her to turn detective and help her heartbroken employers find their son's killer. Period recipes included. This is the first in a new series, projected to follow a spice box handed down from generation to generation of cooks, from the author of the Heaven Lee mysteries about a contemporary Kansas City restaurateur.

Where it's reviewed:
Publishers Weekly, April 4, 2005, page 47

Other books by the same author:
Death Is Semisweet, 2002
Red Beans and Vice, 2001
The Cornbread Killer, 1999
Bread on Arrival, 1998
A Stiff Risotto, 1997

Other books you might like:
Rhys Bowen, *The Molly Murphy Series*, 2001-
J.D. Christilian, *Scarlet Women*, 1996
Paula Cohen, *Gramercy Park*, 2002
Maan Meyers, *The Lucifer Contract*, 1997
Owen Parry, *Shadows of Glory*, 2000

232

WILL THOMAS

To Kingdom Come

(New York: Touchstone, 2005)

Story type: Historical/Victorian; Private Detective
Subject(s): Terrorism; Crime and Criminals; Irish Republican Army
Major character(s): Cyrus Barker, Detective—Private; Thomas Llewelyn, Detective—Private
Time period(s): 1880s (1884)
Locale(s): London, England

Summary: Colorful London private enquiry agent Cyrus Barker and his diminutive young Welsh assistant, Thomas Llewelyn, have made a deal with Scotland Yard to infiltrate a murderous cell of the Irish Republican Brotherhood to keep London from being blown to bits by dynamiters. Barker poses as an irascible German explosives expert and Llewelyn as his hot-headed protege. The Invisibles, as the secretive cell members are known, quickly take them in on the strength of their newly acquired ability to make nitroglycerine and manufacture infernal devices. The story is lively, full of convincing historical detail, and reveals a few more tantalizing facts from Barker's mysterious past. Real-life persons of the period, such as Israel Zangwill, Charles Parnell, and William Butler Yeats, have supporting roles, but mostly it's the wonderful chemistry between Barker and Llewelyn that makes the book, like its predecessor (*Some Danger Involved*), a thorough delight. The author has written a number of Sherlock Holmes pastiches for *Ellery Queen's Mystery Magazine* and other publications.

Where it's reviewed:
Booklist, March 15, 2005, page 127
Library Journal, April 15, 2005, page 80
Publishers Weekly, April 18, 2005, page 41

Other books by the same author:
Some Danger Involved, 2004

Other books you might like:
David Dickinson, *The Lord Francis Powerscourt Series*, 2002-
Quinn Fawcett, *The Mycroft Holmes Series*, 1997-
Peter Lovesey, *The Tick of Death*, 1974
    published in Britain as *Invitation to a Dynamite Party*
Amy Myers, *The Auguste Didier Series*, 1986-
Gerald Williams, *The Dr. Mortimer Series*, 2000-

233

VICTORIA THOMPSON

Murder on Lenox Hill
(New York: Berkley Prime Crime, 2005)

Story type: Historical/Edwardian
Series: Sarah Brandt. Book 7
Subject(s): Social Conditions; Clergy; Social Classes
Major character(s): Sarah Brandt, Midwife, Widow(er); Frank Malloy, Detective—Police (sergeant)
Time period(s): 1900s
Locale(s): New York, New York

Summary: The widow of a physician who was murdered four years ago, Sarah Brandt works as a midwife, mostly among the poor, and her fierce social conscience has served to estrange her from her wealthy and socially prominent family. She has become friends with Irish police detective Frank Malloy, who is keenly aware of the social gulf between them. He's suspicious when Sarah's father wants him to reopen Thomas Brandt's murder case, especially since they both know that Dr. Brandt was not the man his widow thinks he was. At the same time Sarah is called by a wealthy family, the Lintons, to examine their mentally retarded teenage daughter, who turns out to be pregnant, although she's never been left on her own. Sarah asks Frank to help her in this delicate mission. The minister of the Lintons' church falls under suspicion, but then he is murdered from sipping poisoned wine during communion, and now Frank has a homicide on his hands.

Other books by the same author:
Murder on Marble Row, 2004
Murder on Mulberry Bend, 2003
Murder in Washington Square, 2002
Murder on Gramercy Park, 2001
Murder on Astor Place, 2000

Other books you might like:
Lauren Belfer, *City of Light*, 1999
Rhys Bowen, *The Molly Murphy Series*, 2001-
Karen Rose Cercone, *The Helen Sorby Series*, 1997-
Cynthia Peale, *Murder at Bertram's Bower*, 2001
Troy Soos, *The Marshall Webb/Rebecca Davies Series*, 2001-

234

AIMEE THURLO
DAVID THURLO, Co-Author

White Thunder
(New York: Forge, 2005)

Story type: Police Procedural
Series: Ella Clah. Book 11
Subject(s): Indian Reservations; Missing Persons; Cultural Conflict
Major character(s): Ella Clah, Police Officer (tribal), Indian (Navajo)
Time period(s): 2000s
Locale(s): Navajo Reservation, New Mexico

Summary: An FBI agent, working on a social security fraud case, has gone missing on the reservation and Ella is searching for him. Agent Thomas inadvertently interrupted a Sing, or Navajo healing ceremony, which casts suspicion on a medicine man who might be responsible for the agent's disappearance. Because tampering with a Sing is a major offense in their culture, many Navajo traditionalists on the reservation are uncooperative when Ella tries to find out what happened. She determines that the medicine man is innocent, which leaves her former colleague, FBI Agent Blalock, a primary suspect.

Where it's reviewed:
Booklist, March 25, 2005, page 1271
Publishers Weekly, March 14, 2005, page 49
Romantic Times, April 2005, page 89

Other books by the same author:
Wind Spirit, 2004
Plant Them Deep, 2003
Tracking Bear, 2003
Changing Woman, 2002
Red Mesa, 2001

Other books you might like:
Margaret Coel, *The Father John O'Malley/Vicky Holden Series*, 1995-
James D. Doss, *The Shaman Series*, 1994-
Tony Hillerman, *The Joe Leaphorn/Jim Chee Series*, 1970-
Barbara Moore, *The Wolf Whispered Death*, 1986
Susan Slater, *The Ben Pecos Series*, 1999-

235

CHARLES TODD (Pseudonym of Charles Todd and Caroline Todd)

A Cold Treachery
(New York: Bantam, 2005)

Story type: Police Procedural; Historical
Series: Ian Rutledge. Book 7
Subject(s): Mental Illness; Secrets; World War I
Major character(s): Ian Rutledge, Detective—Police, Veteran (World War I); Hamish MacLeod, Spirit, Military Personnel (executed)
Time period(s): 1910s (1919)
Locale(s): Urskdale, England (Lake District)

Summary: Ian Rutledge returned to his job as a Scotland Yard inspector at the end of World War I, but with a difference. He's haunted by his war experiences but unable to communicate his pain to others, because he hears in his head the jeering voice of a young corporal, Hamish MacLeod, whom he ordered executed for insubordination in the face of battle. His ghostly commentary is a running counterpoint to everything Rutledge says and does. Here Rutledge is sent to the north of England to investigate the wholesale slaughter of a family in the insular village of Urskdale. The local police want to blame an outsider for the crime, but Rutledge thinks the key to the crime may lie with a missing 10-year-old boy, the only family member to escape the carnage.

Where it's reviewed:
Library Journal, January 2005, page 86
New York Times Book Review, February 6, 2005, page 25
Publishers Weekly, December 6, 2004, page 46

Other books by the same author:
A Fearsome Doubt, 2002
Watchers of Time, 2001
Legacy of the Dead, 2000
Search the Dark, 1999
Wings of Fire, 1998

Other books you might like:
Rennie Airth, *River of Darkness*, 1999
Barbara Cleverly, *The Joe Sandilands Series*, 2001-
Robert Goddard, *In Pale Battalions*, 1988
Laurie R. King, *A Monstrous Regiment of Women*, 1995
Jacqueline Winspear, *Maisie Dobbs*, 2003

236

EMILY TOLL (Pseudonym of Taffy Cannon)

Keys to Death
(New York: Berkley, 2005)

Story type: Amateur Detective
Series: Lynne Montgomery. Book 4
Subject(s): Vacations; Islands; Mothers and Daughters
Major character(s): Lynne Montgomery, Travel Agent, Detective—Amateur
Time period(s): 2000s
Locale(s): Little Sister Key, Florida

Summary: When she was left a widow at the age of 52, Lynne Montgomery used the money from her late husband's insurance to buy the travel agency she was working for. Now she's taking a much-needed vacation with her daughter Jenna in the Florida Keys, visiting an old friend who's just opened a new resort. Right after they arrive, a guest is found dead on the beach, and Lynne's holiday turns into a murder investigation. The author has written a number of mysteries under her own name, including a series featuring California state bar investigator Nan Robertson.

Other books by the same author:
Fall Into Death, 2004
Murder Pans Out, 2003
Murder Will Travel, 2002

Other books you might like:
Mary Daheim, *The Judith McMonigle Flynn Series*, 1991-

Monica Ferris, *The Betsy Devonshire Series*, 1999-
Maddy Hunter, *The Emily Andrew Series*, 2003-
Joyce Lavene, *The Peggy Lee Series*, 2005-
    Jim Lavene, co-author
Tim Myers, *The Alex Winston Series*, 2001-

237

P.J. TRACY (Pseudonym of Patricia Lambrecht and Traci Lambrecht)

Dead Run
(New York: Putnam, 2005)

Story type: Psychological Suspense; Humor
Series: Monkeewrench. Book 3
Subject(s): Serial Killers; Militia Movements; Terrorism
Major character(s): Grace McBride, Computer Expert; Annie Belinsky, Computer Expert; Sharon Mueller, FBI Agent (profiler)
Time period(s): 2000s
Locale(s): Four Corners, Wisconsin; Minneapolis, Minnesota

Summary: Monkeewrench is the name of a Minneapolis software firm founded by brainy, wary Grace McBride and staffed by a group of equally gifted social misfits, including the generously proportioned, sexy Annie Belinsky. They've prospered from their gaming software and have developed a program to aid police departments having to deal with serial killers, which they're giving away free. Together with FBI profiler Sharon Mueller, Grace and Annie are driving from Minneapolis to Green Bay, Wisconsin, where a serial killer has just emerged, when their Range Rover breaks down near the tiny town of Four Corners. In fact, the town now has zero population, since a truck carrying nerve gas rolled over and destroyed all life in the area. Even worse, the town has been surrounded by a sinister paramilitary group who are intent on hunting down and destroying the three women. The men at Monkeewrench get worried when the ladies fail to arrive in Green Bay and set out to rescue them, but they're quite able to take care of themselves. There is plenty of quirky humor mixed in with the exciting plot; imagine the best qualities of Patricia Cornwell and Carl Hiaasen mixed together. The pseudonymous authors are really a mother-daughter writing team. Note: This series is best read in order.

Where it's reviewed:
Entertainment Weekly, April 22, 2005, page 67
Library Journal, April 15, 2005, page 80
Publishers Weekly, February 21, 2005, page 157
Romantic Times, April 2005, page 85

Other books by the same author:
Live Bait, 2004 (Monkeewrench. Book 2)
Monkeewrench, 2003 (Monkeewrench. Book 1)

Other books you might like:
Nevada Barr, *The Anna Pigeon Series*, 1993-
Earl Emerson, *Into the Inferno*, 2003
William Kent Krueger, *The Cork O'Connor Series*, 1998-
Theresa Monsour, *Dark House*, 2005
John Sandford, *The Lucas Davenport Series*, 1989-

238

PETER TREMAYNE (Pseudonym of Peter Berresford Ellis)

Badger's Moon

(New York: St. Martin's Minotaur, 2005)

Story type: Collection; Historical/Medieval
Series: Sister Fidelma. Book 14
Subject(s): Celts; Dark Ages; Christianity
Major character(s): Sister Fidelma, Religious (former nun), Scholar; Brother Eadulf, Religious (monk)
Time period(s): 7th century (667)
Locale(s): Ireland

Summary: Fidelma, formerly a nun but now primarily a *dalaigh*, or advocate of the ancient law courts of Ireland, has married her longtime companion Brother Eadulf, and the two now have a four-month-old son. At this time in history neither the Roman nor Celtic branches of the Catholic Church had formally embraced celibacy and it was not uncommon for those in monastic orders to marry. Fidelma and Eadulf live in a double house, in which men and women raise their children in Christ's service. Fidelma, however, is not particularly suited to domesticity, and she welcomes the opportunity to journey to Muman with Eadulf (leaving their son with a capable nurse) to investigate the murders of three young girls on consecutive full moons. There is a useful introduction explaining the role of women in Ireland, a remarkably enlightened country at that time.

Where it's reviewed:
Booklist, January 1, 2005, page 829
Library Journal, November 1, 2004, page 62
Publishers Weekly, February 21, 2005, page 161

Other books by the same author:
The Haunted Abbot, 2004
Whispers of the Dead, 2004 (short stories)
Smoke in the Wind, 2003
Our Lady of Darkness, 2002
Act of Mercy, 2001

Other books you might like:
Alys Clare, *The Abbess Helewise Series*, 1999-
Anthony Clarke, *Ordeal at Lichfield*, 1998
Margaret Frazer, *The Dame Frevisse Series*, 1992-
Sharan Newman, *Death Comes as Epiphany*, 1993
Priscilla Royal, *The Eleanor of Wynethorpe Series*, 2003-

239

ELAINE VIETS

Just Murdered

(New York: Signet, 2005)

Story type: Amateur Detective; Humor
Series: Helen Hawthorne. Book 4
Subject(s): Weddings; Work; Animals/Cats
Major character(s): Helen Hawthorne, Fugitive, Detective—Amateur
Time period(s): 2000s
Locale(s): Fort Lauderdale, Florida

Summary: On the lam since she assaulted her no-good ex-husband with a crowbar, Helen has taken a series of low-paying jobs for which she's paid in cash, settled into a retro Fort Lauderdale apartment with her six-toed cat, Thumbs, and generally managed to fly under the law enforcement radar. She doesn't miss much about her old life in St. Louis except the six-figure salary she once pulled down. Now she's working at an upscale bridal salon helping brides pick out their gowns. One day a particularly obnoxious client, a mother-of-the-bride named Kiki, is killed and Helen's fingerprints are found on the murder weapon, which is a wedding dress. To clear herself, Helen starts sifting through suspects, which include Kiki's ex-husband, her meek daughter, the groom, and all of her younger boyfriends. The author also writes a series about St. Louis reporter Francesca Vierling.

Other books by the same author:
Dying to Call You, 2004
Murder between the Covers, 2003
Shop Till You Drop, 2003

Other books you might like:
Deborah Donnelly, *The Carnegie Kincaid Series*, 2002-
Janet Evanovich, *The Stephanie Plum Series*, 1994-
Jerrilyn Farmer, *Killer Wedding*, 2000
Sparkle Hayter, *The Robin Hudson Series*, 1994-
Lora Roberts, *The Liz Sullivan Series*, 1994-

240

ANN WALDRON

Unholy Death in Princeton

(New York: Berkley, 2005)

Story type: Amateur Detective
Series: McLeod Dulaney. Book 3
Subject(s): Academia; Religion; History
Major character(s): McLeod Dulaney, Journalist, Detective—Amateur
Time period(s): 2000s
Locale(s): Princeton, New Jersey

Summary: McLeod Dulaney's annual visit to Princeton takes her to the Princeton Theological Seminary, where she is researching a book on the abolitionist preacher Elijah P. Lovejoy, who was lynched by a pro-slavery mob in Illinois in 1837. While taking a walk along the picturesque towpath, she literally stumbles across the dead body of a young man enclosed in a garment bag and is dismayed when she realizes the police suspect her of being the killer. With some help from her friends at the seminary, she manages to clear her name, but learns in the process that the institution is a hotbed of controversy and dissent over a number of contemporary theological issues. Recipes for faculty events included.

Other books by the same author:
Death of a Princeton President, 2004
The Princeton Murders, 2003

Other books you might like:
Amanda Cross, *The Kate Fansler Series*, 1964-2002
Joanne Dobson, *The Karen Pelletier Series*, 1997-
Kate Flora, *An Educated Death*, 1997
Carolyn Hart, *The Henrie O Series*, 1993-

Jane Langton, *The Homer Kelly Series*, 1964-

241

KATHRYN R. WALL

Resurrection Road

(New York: St. Martin's Minotaur, 2005)

Story type: Private Detective
Series: Bay Tanner. Book 5
Subject(s): American South; Missing Persons; Adolescence
Major character(s): Lydia Baynard Simpson "Bay" Tanner, Widow(er), Detective—Private; Erik Whiteside, Detective—Private, Computer Expert
Time period(s): 2000s
Locale(s): Hilton Head, South Carolina; St. Helena Island, South Carolina

Summary: After her husband was murdered, financial consultant Bay Tanner opened a detective agency with her father and a young computer whiz named Erik Whiteside. Now she's dissolved the partnership, she and her lover Alain Darnay have reunited, and she's hoping to put her life back together. Then Cart Anderson, a resentful teenager who wants to know the details of his father's murder, approaches Bay for the answers that he's somehow convinced she has. His questions reopen old wounds for Bay, going back to the nightmarish summer when her husband was murdered. The boy disappears and when his blood-spattered car is found on a nearby island, Bay and Alain become the police's chief suspects. She turns to Erik and a local reporter for help in finding the real killer.

Where it's reviewed:
Library Journal, May 1, 2005, page 66
Publishers Weekly, April 4, 2005, page 47

Other books by the same author:
Judas Island, 2004
Perdition House, 2003
And Not a Penny More, 2002
In for a Penny, 2001

Other books you might like:
Mary Anna Evans, *Artifacts*, 2003
Carolyn Haines, *The Sarah Booth Delaney Series*, 1999-
Charlaine Harris, *The Lily Bard Series*, 1996-
Carolyn Hart, *The Death on Demand Series*, 1987-
Kathy Hogan Trocheck, *The Callahan Garrity Series*, 1992-

242

DONALD E. WESTLAKE

Watch Your Back!

(New York: Mysterious, 2005)

Story type: Humor
Series: Dortmunder. Book 13
Subject(s): Crime and Criminals; Burglary; Organized Crime
Major character(s): John Dortmunder, Thief (burglar)
Time period(s): 2000s
Locale(s): New York, New York; Pennsylvania

Summary: No one can keep more balls in the air at one time than Donald E. Westlake when it comes to juggling the various components of the comic caper novel. His hard-luck "master" thief John Dortmunder is about to be let in on a surefire heist by Arnie Albright, a fence who's just gotten back from a Club Med (his family did an intervention and sent him there to improve his disposition). There Arnie met billionaire Manhattan art collector Preston Fareweather, who is away from his Fifth Avenue penthouse and hiding out from various ex-wives in the Caribbean. The plan to loot his apartment falters when Dortmunder and his equally hapless cohorts discover that the O.J. Bar & Grill, their habitual hangout, has been taken over by the mob. Somehow they have to take the O.J. back and cash in on Fareweather's absence, and naturally, everything will go wrong. The versatile author also writes non-series crime novels and, as Richard Stark, a much darker series about the amoral thief Parker.

Where it's reviewed:
Booklist, March 1, 2005, page 1103
Entertainment Weekly, April 15, 2005, page 88
Mystery News, April/May 2005, page 14
Publishers Weekly, March 14, 2005, page 49

Other books by the same author:
The Road to Ruin, 2004
Thieves' Dozen, 2004 (short stories)
Bad News, 2001
What's the Worst That Could Happen, 1996
Don't Ask, 1993

Other books you might like:
Lawrence Block, *The Bernie Rhodenbarr Series*, 1977-
Joe Gores, *32 Cadillacs*, 1992
Pete Hautman, *Short Money*, 1995
Elmore Leonard, *The Big Bounce*, 1969
Ross Thomas, *Out on the Rim*, 1987

243

RANDY WAYNE WHITE

Dead of Night

(New York: Putnam, 2005)

Story type: Action/Adventure
Series: Doc Ford. Book 13
Subject(s): Ecothriller; Environment; Animals
Major character(s): Marion "Doc" Ford, Scientist (marine biologist), Single Parent; Sighurdhr Tomlinson, Genius, Hippie
Time period(s): 2000s
Locale(s): Sanibel Island, Florida

Summary: Doc Ford, a marine biologist whose murky past as a CIA operative frequently comes back to haunt him, agrees to help out an old friend by looking in on her reclusive biologist brother. To his horror he discovers the man eaten alive by a particularly vicious species of parasite. Eventually it becomes evident that some insane scientist has unleashed not only these internal parasites but huge quantities of poisonous snakes, fish, spiders, and other deadly exotics, which could result in an environmental disaster of apocalyptic proportions. Ford's old friend Tomlinson is also on the scene, bemoaning his unprecedented financial success as an Internet Zen advisor, aided by Doc's Bahamian cousin Ransom.

Where it's reviewed:
Booklist, March 15, 2005, page 127
Publishers Weekly, February 28, 2005, page 42

Other books by the same author:
Tampa Burn, 2004
Everglades, 2003
Twelve Mile Limit, 2002
Shark River, 2001
Ten Thousand Islands, 2000

Other books you might like:
James W. Hall, *The Thorn Series*, 1987-
Carl Hiaasen, *Skinny Dip*, 2004
John D. MacDonald, *The Travis McGee Series*, 1964-1985
Laurence Shames, *The Key West Series*, 1992-
Les Standiford, *The John Deal Series*, 1993-

244

STEPHEN WHITE

Missing Persons

(New York: Dutton, 2005)

Story type: Psychological Suspense
Series: Alan Gregory. Book 13
Subject(s): Psychology; Ethics; Mental Illness
Major character(s): Alan Gregory, Psychologist; Sam Purdy, Detective—Homicide; Lauren Crowder, Lawyer (assistant district attorney), Spouse (to Alan)
Time period(s): 2000s
Locale(s): Boulder, Colorado; Las Vegas, Nevada

Summary: Eight years to the day since JonBenet Ramsey disappeared, Mallory Miller, who lives in the same neighborhood, goes missing. At 14, she may simply have run away from her extremely odd family, but when Alan's colleague, psychologist Diane Estevez, disappears, and her friend Hannah Grant is apparently murdered, links between all the events begin to emerge. As is often the case in this series, the complicated plot involves patient confidentiality and professional ethics, and employs a number of players, including Alan's wife, assistant district attorney Lauren Crowder, and his friend Sam Purdy, a divorced Boulder cop.

Where it's reviewed:
Booklist, December 15, 2004, page 691
Library Journal, February 1, 2005, page 72
Publishers Weekly, December 6, 2004, page 41

Other books by the same author:
Blinded, 2004
The Best Revenge, 2003
Warning Signs, 2002
The Program, 2001
Cold Case, 2000

Other books you might like:
Jonathan Kellerman, *The Alex Delaware Series*, 1985-
Sarah Lovett, *The Sylvia Strange Series*, 1995-
Philip Luber, *The Harry Kline Series*, 1994-
Howard Roughan, *The Promise of a Lie*, 2004
Marianne Wesson, *The Cinda Hayes Series*, 1998-

245

DEREK WILSON

The Nature of Rare Things

(New York: Carroll & Graf, 2005)

Story type: Amateur Detective
Series: Nathaniel Gye. Book 2
Subject(s): Paranormal; Art; Missing Persons
Major character(s): Nathaniel Gye, Professor, Paranormal Investigator
Time period(s): 2000s
Locale(s): Cambridge, England

Summary: Although Cambridge lecturer Dr. Nathaniel Gye is billed as a paranormal investigator in this series, he's really a skeptic when it comes to psychic phenomena, despite (or perhaps because of) his considerable research into the subject. When a man formerly employed by the university is accused of stealing a valuable Renaissance painting and later commits suicide, Nat attends a seance as a courtesy to the man's widow. The medium claims to be channeling the dead man, who implores Nat to prove his innocence and warns him against letting his wife Kathryn travel to Italy. Nat figures the whole thing is just a hoax, but when Kathryn disappears en route to Florence to attend a seminar on Robert and Elizabeth Barrett Browning, he rushes to find her and the missing painting. The author has also written a mystery series featuring art recovery expert Tim Lacey, as well as many works of historical nonfiction.

Where it's reviewed:
Booklist, March 1, 2005, page 1148
Library Journal, April 1, 2005, page 74
Mystery Scene, Spring 2005, page 78
Romantic Times, April 2005, page 86

Other books by the same author:
Tripletree, 2004

Other books you might like:
Roy Lewis, *The Arnold Landon Series*, 1982-
John Malcolm, *The Tim Simpson Series*, 1984-
Iain Pears, *The Jonathan Argyll Series*, 1991-
Thomas Swan, *The Jack Oxby Series*, 1990-
David Williams, *The Mark Treasure Series*, 1976-

246

ROBERT WILSON

The Vanished Hands

(Orlando, Florida: Harcourt, 2005)

Story type: Police Procedural; Psychological Suspense
Series: Javier Falcon. Book 2
Subject(s): Suicide; Secrets
Major character(s): Javier Falcon, Police Officer
Time period(s): 2000s
Locale(s): Seville, Spain

Summary: Spanish police inspector Javier Falcon is investigating what seems to be a gruesome suicide or murder/suicide pact involving a wealthy couple living in an exclusive enclave on the outskirts of Seville. The details don't add up, but

Falcon's investigations eventually lead him to the Russian Mafia, with whom the dead man's construction company had ties, and many other evils, including pedophiles, police corruption, the CIA, and even 9/11. Further complicating matters are two additional suicides and a host of arresting characters, including the dead man's neighbors. In addition to the Falcon books and two splendid historical thrillers, the author has written three *noir* mysteries set in West Africa and featuring private detective Bruce Medway.

Where it's reviewed:
Booklist, January 1, 2005, page 829
Library Journal, October 1, 2004, page 65
Publishers Weekly, November 8, 2004, page 38

Other books by the same author:
The Blind Man of Seville, 2003 (Javier Falcon. Book 1)
The Company of Strangers, 2001
A Small Death in Lisbon, 1999

Other books you might like:
Roderic Jeffries, *The Inspector Enrique Alvarez Series*, 1976-
Rebecca Pawel, *The Inspector Tejada Series*, 2003-
Arturo Perez-Reverte, *The Seville Communion*, 1998
David Serafin, *The Superintendent Luis Bernal Series*, 1979-
Manuel Vazquez Montalban, *The Pepe Carvalho Series*, 1985-

247

DON WINSLOW

The Power of the Dog

(New York: Knopf, 2005)

Story type: Action/Adventure; Psychological Suspense
Subject(s): Drugs; Crime and Criminals; Organized Crime
Major character(s): Art Keller, Government Official (DEA agent)
Time period(s): 1970s; 1990s (1999)
Locale(s): New York, New York; Tijuana, Mexico; Mexico City, Mexico

Summary: This long, ambitious crime novel introduces a large cast of characters, including DEA agent Art Keller (a rookie at the start of the book), and spans the years from the 1970s through 1999. The action, narrated in the present tense, takes place primarily in Mexico but ranges from there to Washington, D.C., to Manhattan, and to the American Southwest. The four main characters cross and re-cross each other's paths as the story, involving the international drug trade, unfolds, and the end result is a powerful indictment of the war on drugs, which the author clearly feels is not only failing to stem the influx of illegal drugs into the U.S. but is encouraging crime and costing both money and lives. The author has written other stand-alone crime novels as well as a series featuring private eye Neal Carey.

Where it's reviewed:
Booklist, March 15, 2005, page 1271
Library Journal, May 1, 2005, page 78
Publishers Weekly, April 4, 2005, page 41

Other books by the same author:
California Fire and Life, 1999
The Life and Death of Bobby Z, 1997

Way Down on the High Lonely, 1996 (Neal Carey series)
While Drowning in the Desert, 1996 (Neal Carey series)
A Long Walk Up the Waterslide, 1994 (Neal Carey series)

Other books you might like:
Lee Child, *The Jack Reacher Series*, 1997-
Michael Connelly, *The Harry Bosch Series*, 1992-
Barry Eisler, *Killing Rain*, 2005
Dennis Lehane, *Mystic River*, 2001
George P. Pelecanos, *King Suckerman*, 1997

248

VALERIE WOLZIEN

Death in Duplicate

(New York: Fawcett, 2005)

Story type: Amateur Detective
Series: Susan Henshaw. Book 16
Subject(s): Grandparents; Twins; Animals/Dogs
Major character(s): Susan Henshaw, Housewife, Detective—Amateur
Time period(s): 2000s
Locale(s): Hancock, Connecticut

Summary: Susan Henshaw is thrilled to have become the grandmother of twins, and even more thrilled when her daughter and son-in-law ask to move in temporarily until they can find a proper apartment in New York, where Stephen has just gotten a job. The only catch, if there is one, is that they're bringing their giant bullmastiffs with them. Then there's the nanny, who's been engaged for six months and is, to Susan's mind, superfluous, but she's a present from Stephen's parents. Then Susan gets some disturbing news from a neighbor: the nanny looks suspiciously like a woman suspected of several murders in a nursing home. The author also writes a series about contractor Josie Pigeon and her all-woman construction crew.

Where it's reviewed:
Romantic Times, March 2005, page 88

Other books by the same author:
Death in a Beach Chair, 2004
An Anniversary to Die For, 2002
Death at a Discount, 2000
The Student Body, 1999
Weddings Are Murder, 1998

Other books you might like:
Joyce Christmas, *The Betty Trenka Series*, 1993-
Jill Churchill, *The Jane Jeffry Series*, 1989-
Lee Harris, *The Christine Bennett Series*, 1992-
Jonnie Jacobs, *The Kate Austen Series*, 1994-
Leslie Meier, *The Lucy Stone Series*, 1993-

249

NANCY MEANS WRIGHT

Mad Cow Nightmare

(New York: St. Martin's Minotaur, 2005)

Story type: Amateur Detective
Series: Ruth Wilmarth. Book 5

Subject(s): Rural Life; Farm Life; Animals/Cows
Major character(s): Ruth Wilmarth, Farmer, Detective—
Amateur
Time period(s): 2000s
Locale(s): Branbury, Vermont

Summary: When Ruth's lover invites his cousin Darren to help out on her Vermont farm, neither expected him to bring his large extended family of Irish Travellers (also known as Tinkers and often mistaken for gypsies) with him. One of them, Ritchie, is soon found strangled in a nearby swamp and his girlfriend, Nola, who is suspected of harboring the human form of mad cow disease, disappears. The authorities want to slaughter two of Ruth's newly purchased calves and quarantine the rest of her herd because of their possible exposure to the disease. Ruth is beside herself at the possibility she may lose everything she owns and has fought so hard to keep. She became a hardscrabble farmer when her husband walked out

on her some years earlier, and it's only the support of family and friends that keeps her grounded during this latest crisis.

Where it's reviewed:
Library Journal, April 1, 2005, page 74
Publishers Weekly, March 21, 2005, page 38

Other books by the same author:
Stolen Honey, 2002
Poison Apples, 2000
Harvest of Bones, 1998
Mad Season, 1996

Other books you might like:
Judy Clemens, *Till the Cows Come Home*, 2004
B.J. Oliphant, *The Shirley McClintock Series*, 1990-1997
M.K. Preston, *The Chantalene Morrell Series*, 2001-
Rebecca Tope, *A Death to Record*, 2003
Susan Wade, *Walking Rain*, 1996

Romance Fiction in Review
by
Kristin Ramsdell

"Romance has been elegantly defined as the offspring of fiction and love."
—Benjamin Disraeli

"Romance Fiction: Have We Got a Story for You!"
—Strategic Committee on Image, Romance Writers of America

And despite a few shakeups in the industry and a softening of certain elements of the market, the stories of romance do continue to flow unabated and in increasingly diverse directions.

A Few Preliminary Statistics

While the official compilation of 2004 statistics from the Romance Writers of America (RWA) will not be released until later and is unavailable as of this writing, some preliminary figures for the publishing industry as a whole have been released. News from the industry was mixed. On the one hand, Bowker's annual book tally showed the number of books published in the U.S. rising from 171,000 to 195,000 in 2004 for more than a 12% increase, with adult fiction titles rising by a whopping 43% to 25,184. ["Cranking It Out," *Publishers Weekly*, 252 (30 May 2005).] Unfortunately, the revenue generated by total book sales for 2004 increased only slightly, according to the Association of American Publishers (AAP) which reported total sales of $23.7 billion, up 1.3% for the year. ["Industry Sales Inch Ahead," *Publishers Weekly*, 252 (7 March 2005).] According to Bowker (which has the sales figures listed as an increase of 1.9%), the discrepancy is caused by the rapidly increasing number of small presses and self-publishers, because the larger houses have not increased their title output significantly. Last year, revenue growth was driven largely by an increase in adult hardcovers (6.3%) and, not surprisingly given the current assessment push, standardized tests (12.4%). Children's hardcovers, book clubs, and mass market paperbacks took major hits, down 16.7%, 8.9%, and

8.9%, respectively. The tumble by the mass market sector is of particular concern to the romance industry because, while the number of trade and hardcover romance titles is increasing, the vast majority of romances are still released as mass market titles. While these general numbers are certain to be reflected to some extent in the forthcoming romance figures, until all data is in and the romance statistics have been tabulated, we won't have a true picture of where we stand. Stay tuned for the annual romance statistics update in volume one of the 2006 edition of *What Do I Read Next?*

A Mid-Year Perspective

So far, the romance genre has had a busy year; and even though we're only half way through 2005 as of this writing, enough has been happening that a quick overview is in order.

As always, when it comes to time periods, the present takes precedence over the past and Contemporary Romances of all types continue to outsell Historical by a wide margin. This is not to say, however, that Historicals are on their way out; they aren't, even though their numbers have been declining lately. Most likely this is simply another nadir in the cycle of the genre, and while the younger readership is certainly focusing on the hip, sassy chick lit-style Contemporaries that are flooding the market, the appeal of the Historical is still there. As one perceptive bookseller says, "They. . .think history is dry. But if you can hand sell them a good one, they're hooked." [Dyer, Lucinda. "Romance: In Its Own Time." *Publishers Weekly*, 252 (13 June 2005): 20-24.] Unfortunately, while the Regency-set Historicals continue to attract readers, the traditional Regency is doing less well.

Paranormals of all types continue to shine, and vampires of all flavors (Susan Squires' darkly erotic *The Companion* to MaryJanice Davidson's funny *Undead and Unappreciated*) combine with psychics (*Shadow Haven* by Emily LaForge), ghosts (*Black Rose* by Nora Roberts), faeries of all types (*Master of the Moon* by Angela Knight), witches

(*The Divine Circle of Ladies Making Mischief* by Delores Stewart Riccio), and assorted other-worldly individuals ensure the amazing diversity of characters and types. Futuristics are growing in popularity and Susan Kearney's *The Challenge* and *Unmasked* by C.J. Barry are only two of the current crop.

Romantic Suspense, as always, is popular; and its mystery elements are often found in many other subgenres. Interestingly, psychics and even werewolves and vampires can be found as characters within the subgenre (e.g., Rebecca York's *Crimson Moon*). Multicultural Romance, especially that focused on African Americans, continues to be strong, and characters of various ethnic backgrounds are often found routinely within non-ethnically oriented romances. The same is true of gay and lesbian characters. Inspirationals continue to soar, as do all things religious, according to the latest industry statistics; and on the opposite side of the coin, by some standards, the super sexy romances of both the Historical and Contemporary varieties are off the charts and rising.

Although often defined by their subgenres, romances are not easily pigeonholed and continue to be incredibly diverse. Various styles, themes, and topics span all genres, reinforcing the fact that romance truly does offer something to everyone.

Humor has been increasing in popularity for a number of years and while there are some romances without a trace, many are adding a sense of fun. Susan Andersen's *Skintight* and Suzanne Simmons' *Goodnight, Sweetheart* are only two current examples.

The sensuality levels of the genre continue to rise, and although there are specific lines and imprints that feature steamier romances, many other romances feature stories that are just as hot. There is no one subgenre that has a monopoly, and romances of all types, Contemporaries, Historicals, and all of the various Alternative Realities sub-subgenres, have their share of hot love stories. Readers who enjoy humor might also be interested that Kensington plans a new line of humorous erotica.

Although much attention has been paid to the young, urban reader via the chick lit stories, there is a growing trend to focus on older characters. Of particular interest is Harlequin's new Next line launched recently, which features older heroines on their "next" journey in life, and their planned Epic line which would follow a romance over time.

Finally, romances linked by character, family, setting, or theme, have exploded with an impact felt across all subgenres. While not new—trilogies, sagas, and continuity series have been around for years—suddenly every author seems to be writing books that are related in some way. Whether linked formally (e.g., Claire Delacroix's Jewels of Kinfairlie series, Jasmine Cresswell's Melody Beecham series, Nora Roberts' In the Garden trilogy, or Christine Feehan's Drake Sisters series) or simply through books that reprise characters from earlier books (e.g., Suzanne Brockmann's *Breaking Point*), these books are increasing and they seem to be popular with readers. This seems to be a trend rather than a flash in the pan, but only time will tell.

Romance in Review

Romance continues to be regularly reviewed in print in the quarterly romance column (with occasional additional minicolumns) in *Library Journal*, the "Forecasts" section of *Publishers Weekly*, *Booklist*, and in a number of newspapers throughout the country. In addition, many of these reviews are picked up by various indexing services, such as EbscoHosts' Academic Search Premier, InfoTrac's Expanded Academic ASAP, or bookseller's Web sites, such as Amazon.com. and Barnes & Noble, and reprinted or posted to their Web sites. Nevertheless, the most comprehensive coverage still is provided by the genre-specific publications, such as *Romantic Times Bookclub Magazine*, *Rendezvous*, and *Affaire de Coeur*. Online romance review sites are becoming increasingly popular; and while most of them, like any Web source, need to be viewed with a critical eye, they are certainly worth checking out. All about Romance (www .likesbooks.com), A Romance Review (www.aromance review.com/news/), Romance Reviews Today (www .romrevtoday.com), The Romance Reader (www .theromancereader.com), and Romance in Color (www .romanceincolor.com) are only several of the many currently online. Finally, there are the listservs. RRA-L (Romance Readers Anonymous) was one of the first lists (est. 1992), and it remains one of the primary forums for romance readers to discuss the genre and share their views and recommendations. It also has a Web site (http://www.toad.net/~ dolma/), which, among other things, lists the RRA-L Award winners from their establishment in 1994 to the present and provides links to RRA-L's archives. Fiction-L is another list of interest to readers and librarians that, while not specifically devoted to romance, does focus on the genre on a regular basis. For more information see their Web site (www .webrary.org/rs/flbklistmenu.html).

Romance News of Interest

Serious scholarship focusing on the romance genre has always been in short supply. RWA provides a research grant that is to be awarded for the serious study of the romance genre. In 2005 the RWA committee charged with the responsibility to screen applicants and make the award, chose its first recipient, Jayashree Kamble, a doctoral student at the University of Minnesota. The program has been approved for another year.

Publishers have been busy this year announcing changes to various lines, most likely driven by the plummeting statistics that have been reported recently. Harlequin, hit particularly hard it by a drop in North American sales, is doing major renovation work on its offerings, including the following: Flipside will cease publication,

Temptation and Harlequin Historicals will only be offered overseas and through the North American direct mail program, Intimate Moments will drop to four from six books a month, Harlequin American will stop acquiring for several months, and Blaze will increase by two titles a month. Next year, the sweet Harlequin and Silhouette lines will cease publication and a new, six-book line similar but with a somewhat different personality will take their places. Also of interest, Kensington has announced both the discontinuation of its Zebra Regency line and its intention to begin acquiring for a line of humorous erotica. The demise of Zebra's Regency line leaves only Signet publishing traditional Regencies, and there are serious doubts about that line's future.

Each year, the Romance Writers of America holds its Annual Conference in July. In 2005 the members gathered to celebrate RWA's silver anniversary, quite appropriately, in Reno, Nevada, the Silver State. Romance writers, editors, librarians, and booksellers gathered to connect, share ideas, learn from each other, and further their careers in the four-day conference that began with the annual Literacy for Life book-signing event, which was open to the public and earned $58,116.34 for local and national literacy programs and ended with the Rita and Golden Heart Awards ceremony which rewards writing excellence in the genre. Workshops, luncheons, editor/agent appointments, and meetings with fellow writers are all on the agenda for the conference. Among the featured speakers this year were Debbie Macomber and Susan Elizabeth Phillips.

As usual, the conference was preceded by the annual Booksellers and Librarians Day Pre-Conference. Created and organized by best-selling author Cathie Linz, this event is now in its seventh year and is one of the highlights of the conference. Focusing on local librarians and booksellers, this day-long event featured presentations by some of the stars of the genre, including authors Nora Roberts, Susan Elizabeth Phillips, Suzanne Brockmann, Jennifer Greene, Linda Howard, Jayne Ann Krentz, and Maggie Osborne; editors Monique Patterson, Anna Genoese, and Beth de Guzman; and librarians John Charles and Joanne Hamilton-Selway. Of particular note: Hamilton-Selway was honored as RWA's 2005 Librarian of the Year as a librarian who goes ''above and beyond in their support of the romance genre.'' She is Head of Collection Development at Scottsdale Public Library in Scottsdale, Arizona.

Future Trends

While it's always risky to try to predict the future, there have been plenty of clues so far this year as to where the genre might be headed. Linked stories, increasingly popular for a number of years, are on a major roll that is likely to continue for some time. Inspirational Romances will continue strong, mirroring the increase in popularity of the overall Christian fiction market. Contemporaries will continue to outpace Historicals, and the traditional Regency will continue its decline, perhaps even losing its last dedicated line. Humor will continue to be a major draw in all subgenres and will include everything from a subtle sense of fun to off-the-wall slapstick comedy—and everything in between. Stories across the board will continue to ratchet up the sexual heat as new erotica-focused publishing houses and lines appear and existing romance lines incorporate steamier sex. All things paranormal should be strong in the near future, although, given the past history of the type, this will likely peak at some point. Multicultural Romance will continue to thrive through ethnically-focused lines (e.g., BET's Arabesque) and multicultural romances published by traditional houses. In addition, characters will become generally more diverse, reflecting the changing cultural, ethnic, age, and sexual realities of the country and the romance readership. Although much of this has already taken place, publishers will continue to monitor sales and adjust their lines accordingly. Finally, with genre-blending working its fuzzy magic and writers increasingly pushing at the boundaries and taking the genre in new directions, Romance will continue to evolve in unexpected ways. This is currently generating a major discussion within the professional writers' ranks about the definition of a romance. Stay tuned for the next half of what has already been a most interesting year.

Recommendations for Romance

Reading tastes vary greatly. What makes a book appeal to one person may make another reject it. By the same token, two people may like the same book for totally different reasons. Obviously, reading is a highly subjective and personal undertaking. For this reason, the recommended readings attached to each entry have tried to cast as broad a net as was reasonably possible. Suggested titles have been chosen on the basis of similarity to the main entry in one or more of the following areas: historical time period, geographic setting, theme, character types, plot pattern or premise, writing style, or overall mood or ''feel.'' All suggestions may not appeal to the same person, but it is to be hoped that at least one would appeal to most.

Because romance reading tastes do vary so widely and readers (and writers) often apply vastly differing criteria in determining what makes a romance good, bad, or exceptional, I cannot claim that the following list of recommendations consists solely of the ''best'' romance novels of the year. (In fact many of these received no awards or special recognition at all.) It is simply a selection of books that the romance contributors, John Charles and Shelley Mosley, and I found particularly interesting; perhaps some of these will appeal to you, too.

Simply Unforgettable by Mary Balogh

The Butterfly Garden by Annette Blair

Something about Emmaline by Elizabeth Boyle

My Surrender by Connie Brockway

Measure of a Man by Adrianne Byrd

The Perfect Family by Carla Cassidy

Mr. Impossible by Loretta Chase

Oceans of Fire by Christine Feehan

The Seduction of an English Scoundrel by Jillian Hunter

To Tame a Wolf by Susan Krinard

Heartbreak Hotel by Jill Marie Landis

To Love a Thief by Julie Anne Long

Sweetgrass by Mary Alice Monroe

Sexy Lexy by Kate Moore

Jigsaw by Kathleen Nance

The Beauty of Bond Street by Jacqueline Navin

Every Waking Moment by Brenda Novak

Tangled Lies by Patricia Potter

Lie by Moonlight by Amanda Quick

Much Ado about Magic by Patricia Rice

Endless Chain by Emilie Richards

A Lady of Talent by Evelyn Richardson

Lord of the Isles by Amanda Scott

Goodnight, Sweetheart by Suzanne Simmons

Table for Five by Susan Wiggs

For Further Reference

Review Journals

Booklist, Library Journal, and to a lesser extent *Publishers Weekly,* continue their coverage of the romance genre. *Library Journal* publishes a quarterly romance review column—January, April 15, August, and November 15, with occasional additional mini-columns; *Booklist* has a separate romance fiction category in each issue, as do the other genres; and *Publishers Weekly* has some romance reviewers who are generally, though unfortunately not always, conversant with the genre. Though some reviews appear in these publications, most romance reviews still appear in sources—both print and online—that specialize in the romance genre. Several of the more important of these sources are listed below.

Affaire de Coeur (www.affairedecoeur.com) includes reviews, articles, and information on the world of romance ficction, in general. 3976 Oak Hill Road, Oakland, CA 94605-4931; phone, (510) 569-5675; fax, (510) 632-8868. Subscriptions, Monthly, $35 a year (U.S. First Class Rates); $65 for 2 years (U.S. First Class Rates); $30 a year (U.S. Third Class Rates); $55 for 2 years (U.S. Third Class Rates); $65 a year (Canadian Rates); $6 single copy U.S.

All about Romance (www.likesbooks.com) contains selected, graded, and sometimes hostile reviews.

Amazon.com (www.amazon.com) includes some published reviews, as well as readers' comments. Quite comprehensive.

Barnes and Noble (www.barnesandnoble.com) includes some published reviews, as well as readers' comments.

Rendezvous: A Monthly Review of Contemporary and Historical Romances, Mysteries, and Women's Fiction (www.rendezvousreviews.com/)includes reviews of most romances published each month. Published by Love Designers Writers' Club, Inc., 1507 Burnham Avenue, Calumet City, IL 60409; phone, (708) 862-9797. Subscriptions, Monthly, $45 a year; $24 for 6 months; $4 single copy.

Romance in Color (www.romanceincolor.com) focuses on African-American romance and, in addition to other features, includes ranked reviews by the RIC staff reviewers.

The Romance Reader (www.theromancereader.com) has a good selection of ranked, sometimes personally harsh reviews.

Romance Reviews Today (www.romrevtoday.com) has a comprehensive selection of reviews.

Romantic Times Book Club (www.romantictimes.com) includes reviews of most romances published each month, articles, and information about the world of romance fiction. Also includes miscellaneous news and reviews of books in other genres and mainstream women's fiction. Note: Name changed from *Romantic Times* midyear in 2002. Published by *Romantic Times* Publishing Group, 55 Bergen Street, Brooklyn Heights, NY 11201; phone, (718) 237-1097; fax, (718) 624-4231. Subscriptions, Monthly, $29.95 for 1 year (Fourth Class U.S. Rates); $59.90 for 2 years (Fourth Class U.S. Rates); $54 for 1 year (First Class U.S. Rates); $108 for 2 years (First Class U.S. Rates); $65 for 1 year (Canadian and Mexican Rates); $130 for 2 years (Canadian and Mexican Rates); $65 for 1 year (International Rates); $130 for 2 years (International Rates); $99 for 1 year (International Airmail Rates); $198 for 2 years (International Airmail Rates).

Book Suppliers/Web Sites/Book Clubs

In addition to going to the general Web sites of online book suppliers like Amazon.com and traditional bookstores such as Borders and Barnes & Noble, readers can now order books directly from some individual publishers' Web sites. Many of these Web sites also feature reviews, information on any subscription book clubs the publisher has, and ways for readers to connect with each other. Services vary from Web site to Web site; several of the more popular are listed below.

Publishers

Avalon Books. www.avalonbooks.com/

BET Books (BET/Arabesque). www.bet.com/Books/

Five Star. www.galegroup.com/fivestar/

HarperCollins/Avon Books. www.harpercollins.com/hc/features/romance/

Dorchester Publishing (Leisure and Love Spell). http://www.dorchesterpub.com/. See Web site for book club information.

Harlequin/Silhouette/MIRA/Red Dress Ink/Steeple Hill/LUNA/HQN/. eharlequin.com

Kensington Books (Zebra, Dafina, Brava, Strapless). www.kensingtonbooks.com. See Web site for book club information.

Book Suppliers

Amazon.com. www.amazon.com

Barnes & Noble. www.barnesandnoble.com

Borders (teamed with Amazon). www.borders.com

Book Clubs and Mail Order Services

Harlequin Book Club. Provides books in the Harlequin and Silhouette series on a monthly subscription basis. Write, phone, or check the Web site for series descriptions and price information. http://www.bookclubdeals.com/harle quinbookclub.html; P.O. Box 5190, Buffalo, NY 14240-5190; or http://www.bookclubdeals.com/harlequinbookclub.html; P.O. Box 615, Fort Erie, Ontario L2A 5X3.

Rhapsody: The Romance Lover's Book Club. Offered through Booksonline.com, a direct marketer created through a partnership between Doubleday Direct, Inc. and Book-of-the-Month Club Holdings LLC, Rhapsody provides romances from a variety of sources on a subscription basis. Check the Web site, phone, or write for more information. http://www.rhapsodybookclub.com

Conferences

Numerous conferences are held each year for writers and readers of romance fiction. Two of the more important national ones are listed below. For a more complete listing, particularly of regional or local conferences designed primarily for romance writers, consult the *Romance Writers' Report*, a monthly publication of The Romance Writers of America.

Annual RT Book Lovers Convention is sponsored by *Romantic Times Book Club Magazine*. The 22nd Annual RT Book Lovers Convention was held on April 27-May 1, 2005, in St. Louis, Missouri (This organization also sponsors a number of romance-related tours for readers and writers.) The 23rd Annual Book Lovers Convention is scheduled for May 16-21, 2006, in Daytona Beach, Florida. Note: This event will celebrate *Romantic Times Book Club Magazine*'s 25th anniversary.

RWA Annual Conference is sponsored by Romance Writers of America and usually held in July. The 2005 Conference was held July 27-30 in Reno, Nevada. The 2006 Conference is scheduled for July 26-29 in Atlanta, Georgia.

Romance Titles

250

CHERRY ADAIR
JILL SHALVIS, Co-Author
JULIE ELIZABETH LETO, Co-Author

Dare Me
(New York: Signet Eclipse, 2005)

Story type: Contemporary; Romantic Suspense
Subject(s): Suspense; Adventure and Adventurers
Time period(s): 2000s

Summary: Action-packed romantic suspense, risky adventure, and lusty passion link this trio of daring novellas by some of the genre's hottest authors. Included are ''Playing for Keeps,'' Cherry Adair's gripping story of an flight attendant who saves the life of the young son of the president of a small South American country and is targeted for murder for her efforts; ''Nothing to Lose,'' a tale of two people looking for the same killer who find love in the process by Jill Shalvis; and ''Dare to Desire,'' Julie Elizabeth Leto's compelling thriller of blackmail, international terrorism, and passion.

Where it's reviewed:
Rendezvous, February 2005, page 20
Romantic Times, March 2005, page 100

Other books you might like:
Suzanne Brockmann, *Flashpoint*, 2004
Jasmine Cresswell, *The Disappearance*, 1999
Alison Kent, *The Samms Agenda*, 2004
    Smithson Group 5. Book 3
Alison Kent, *The Shaughnessey Accord*, 2004
    Smithson Group 5. Book 2
Christina Skye, *Going Overboard*, 2001

251

KYLIE ADAMS (Pseudonym of Jon Salem)

First Kiss
(New York: Signet, 2005)

Story type: Contemporary; Humor
Series: Bridesmaid Chronicles. Book 2
Subject(s): Weddings; Scandal; Family Relations
Major character(s): Kiki Sonntag Douglas, Actress (unemployed); Fabrizio Tomba, Hotel Owner
Time period(s): 2000s
Locale(s): New York, New York

Summary: When fast-living, newly divorced, unemployed actress and former beauty queen Kiki Douglas finds herself the subject of a tabloid scandal and suddenly the most hated woman in Manhattan, she goes to ground in the newest, trendiest hotel, Hotel Affair. It's not easy to avoid the press, but the hotel's owner, handsome Fab Tomba agrees to help; and as he gets to know Kiki, he begins to realize she's not quite the shallow woman everyone thinks her to be. Fast-paced with a chick lit feel.

Where it's reviewed:
Romantic Times, July 2005, page 107

Other books by the same author:
Fly Me to the Moon, 2001

Other books you might like:
Alesia Holliday, *American Idle*, 2004
    celebrity humor
Karen Kendall, *First Dance*, 2005
    Bridesmaid Chronicles. Book 3
Karen Kendall, *First Date*, 2005
    Bridesmaid Chronicles. Book 1
Julie Kenner, *First Love*, 2005
    Bridesmaid Chronicles. Book 4
Lisa Plumley, *Perfect Together*, 2003
    celebrity humor

252

CARRIE ALEXANDER
PAMELA BRITTON, Co-Author
SUSAN DONOVAN, Co-Author
LORA LEIGH, Co-Author

Honk If You Love Real Men
(New York: St. Martin's Griffin, 2005)

Story type: Contemporary; Anthology
Subject(s): Sexual Behavior; Seduction
Time period(s): 2000s
Locale(s): United States

Summary: Handsome, usually take-charge men are the focus of this anthology of occasionally unconventional, sexually explicit short stories by four of the genre's best-selling writers. Included are ''Naughty Girl,'' Carrie Alexander's no-holds-barred story of a woman who uses her car to get the attention of a savvy road construction worker; ''Wanted: One Hot-Blooded Man,'' Pamela Britton's tale of a woman who tries to use her first love to cure her fear of sex and ends up finding love, as well; ''Mercy Me,'' Susan Donovan's story of a disillusioned screenwriter who finds her muse—and love—in the mountains; and ''Reno's Chance,'' Lora Leigh's story of a woman who finally finds love with her best friend's hunky older brother.

Other books you might like:
Suzanne Forster, *All through the Night*, 2001
    erotic anthology
Lori Foster, *Bad Boys on Board*, 2003
    erotic anthology
Lori Foster, *Bad Boys to Go*, 2003
    erotic anthology
Janet Maynard, *Wildest Dreams*, 2003
    erotic anthology
Shannon McKenna, *Bad Boys Next Exit*, 2004
    erotic anthology

253

REGAN ALLEN (Pseudonym of Regina Lundgren)

The Pleasure Garden
(New York: Zebra, 2005)

Story type: Historical/Regency
Subject(s): Legends; Mystery; Mythology
Major character(s): Angelica Pruitt, Governess, Scholar; Jason Kitterage, Gentleman, Businessman (rare artifacts dealer)
Time period(s): 1810s
Locale(s): London, England

Summary: Reluctantly agreeing to attend a party at Vauxhall given by her current pupil and employer, courtesan Cicely Bryant, gently bred scholar and teacher Angelica Pruitt is not about to become any man's mistress. However, when she meets Jason Kitterage, a world traveler and dealer in rare artifacts, she is intrigued—especially when he claims to have found the mythical Mask of Aphrodite, a piece that gives the wearer great power over others. Mystery, danger, and passion

are all part of this intricately plotted story that is filled with good Regency detail. Allen writes Regency romances as Regina Scott.

Where it's reviewed:
Romantic Times, April 2005, page 46

Other books you might like:
Jacqueline Navin, *The Beauty of Bond Street*, 2005
    Mayfair Brides. Book 3
Jacqueline Navin, *The Heiress of Hyde Park*, 2004
    Mayfair Brides. Book 2
Joan Overfield, *Exquisite*, 1998
Amanda Quick, *With This Ring*, 1998
    more humorous
Debbie Raleigh, *How to Marry a Duke*, 2005
    anthology; contains story by Allen

254

SUSAN ANDERSEN

Skintight
(Don Mills, Ontario: MIRA, 2005)

Story type: Contemporary; Humor
Subject(s): Humor; Gambling; Crime and Criminals
Major character(s): Treena McCall, Dancer (Vegas showgirl), Widow(er); Jax Gallagher, Gambler (professional), Genius (mathematics)
Time period(s): 2000s
Locale(s): Las Vegas, Nevada

Summary: Las Vegas showgirl Treena McCall marries a wealthy, older man, then uses his fortune, as well as her own savings, to pay for his medical care. Jax Gallagher, her late husband's estranged son, thinks Treena's a money-grubbing opportunist, but she has something he needs. A professional gambler, Jax has lost a priceless antique autographed baseball to an Elvis-impersonating mobster, and only Treena knows its location. This emotion-filled, suspenseful story is augmented by heavy doses of humor, particularly the secondary romance between a retired librarian who's found her inner sex goddess and the man who's glad she has.

Other books by the same author:
Hot and Bothered, 2004
Getting Lucky, 2003
Head over Heels, 2002
All Shook Up, 2001
Baby, Don't Go, 2000

Other books you might like:
Kylie Adams, *Fly Me to the Moon*, 2001
Tess Hudson, *Double Down*, 2005
Connie Lane, *Guilty Little Secrets*, 2003
Lisa Plumley, *Josie Day Is Coming Home*, 2005
Sarah Strohmeyer, *Bubbles a Broad*, 2004

255

AMANDA ASHLEY (Pseudonym of Madeline Baker)

Night's Kiss

(New York: Zebra, 2005)

Story type: Contemporary; Paranormal
Series: Vampire
Subject(s): Vampires
Major character(s): Brenna Flanagan, Time Traveler, Witch; Roshan DeLongpre, Vampire
Time period(s): 2000s; 17th century (1692)
Locale(s): United States

Summary: Jaded and weary of his dark life, vampire Roshan DeLongpre gets new incentive when he notices the uncanny resemblance of a witch burned in 1692 to his late beloved wife. Determined to rescue Brenna from the stake, he goes back in time to bring her into his world—and into his life. Powerful evil forces lurk and threaten their safety and happiness in this lively, sensual vampire tale.

Where it's reviewed:
Romantic Times, February 2005, page 108

Other books by the same author:
A Whisper of Eternity, 2004
After Sundown, 2003
Midnight Embrace, 2002
Shades of Gray, 1998
A Darker Dream, 1997

Other books you might like:
Christine Feehan, *Dark Secret*, 2005
Laurell K. Hamilton, *Bite*, 2005
    vampire anthology
Sherrilyn Kenyon, *Fantasy Lover*, 2002
Maggie Shayne, *Twilight Hunger*, 2002

256

JENNIFER ASHLEY

The Care and Feeding of Pirates

(New York: Leisure, 2005)

Story type: Historical/Regency
Subject(s): Pirates; Seduction
Major character(s): Honoria Ardmore, Gentlewoman; Christopher Raine, Pirate, Sea Captain
Time period(s): 1810s (1813)
Locale(s): England; *Starcrosse*, At Sea

Summary: The night before he is scheduled to be executed, Honoria Ardmore marries pirate Christopher Raine in a Charleston prison cell. Honoria never expected to see her new husband again, and thus she is a bit surprised when Christopher turns up in London four years later looking for his wife. In order to get rid of Christopher, Honoria agrees to accompany him on his latest trip across the Atlantic. What she doesn't know is Christopher is determined that by the end of the voyage Honoria will once again be his wife.

Where it's reviewed:
Booklist, February 1, 2005, page 948

Romantic Times, February 2005, page 36

Other books by the same author:
The Pirate Hunter, 2004
The Pirate Next Door, 2003
Perils of the Heart, 2002

Other books you might like:
Pamela Britton, *Seduced*, 2003
Kresley Cole, *The Captain of All Pleasures*, 2002
Claudia Dain, *Tell Me Lies*, 2000
Sabrina Jeffries, *The Pirate Lord*, 1998
Malia Martin, *Pride and Prudence*, 2002

257

SAM BAKER

Fashion Victim

(New York: Ballantine, 2005)

Story type: Romantic Suspense; Contemporary
Subject(s): Models, Fashion; Murder; Suspense
Major character(s): Annie Anderson, Journalist (investigative reporter); Chris Mahoney, Advertising (executive)
Time period(s): 2000s
Locale(s): New York, New York; London, England; Milan, Italy

Summary: When Annie Anderson begins her secret investigation of the fashion industry, she doesn't expect to be right next to celebrity designer Mark Mailer when he is shot to death. Compelled to find out what's going on, Annie follows the fashion shows from New York City to London to Milan. Danger, suspense, and an unexpected love with advertising executive Chris Mahoney make Annie's journey a memorable one. This is the author's debut novel.

Where it's reviewed:
Library Journal, April 1, 2005, page 83

Other books you might like:
Sheryl J. Anderson, *Killer Heels*, 2004
Jane Blackwood, *A Hard Man Is Good to Find*, 2004
Connie Lane, *Dirty Little Lies*, 2004
Sarah Mason, *Playing James*, 2004
Jane Moore, *The Ex-Files*, 2004

258

KATHLEEN BALDWIN

Cut from the Same Cloth

(New York: Zebra, 2005)

Story type: Regency
Subject(s): Clothes; Courtship; Espionage
Major character(s): Elizabeth Hampton, Gentlewoman; Valen Ransley, Nobleman (Lord St. Cleve)
Time period(s): 1810s
Locale(s): London, England

Summary: Elizabeth Hampton's plan to repair her family's fortunes by finding a wealthy nobleman to wed are being ruined by Valen Ransley, Lord St. Cleve. She had been using her unique sense of fashion to draw the interest of several

suitors. However, when Valen shows up at a society soiree in a ridiculous suit composed of the same fabric as her gown, Elizabeth fears she will quickly become the laughingstock of the *ton*. Elizabeth vows that Valen is not going to ruin her stylish reputation only to discover that when it comes to a certain infuriatingly handsome nobleman, romance never looked more fashionable.

Where it's reviewed:
Romantic Times, March 2005, page 125

Other books by the same author:
Mistaken Kiss, 2005
Lady Fiasco, 2004

Other books you might like:
Laurie Bishop, *The Best Laid Plans*, 2003
Kate Huntington, *The Captain's Courtship*, 1999
Valerie King, *A Rogue's Revenge*, 2004
Joy Reed, *Lord Yates and the Yankee*, 2003
Nonnie St. George, *Courting Trouble*, 2004

259

KATHLEEN BALDWIN

Mistaken Kiss
(New York: Zebra, 2005)

Story type: Regency
Subject(s): Courtship
Major character(s): Wilhemina "Willa" Linnet, Gentlewoman; Alexander Braeburn, Gentleman
Time period(s): 1810s
Locale(s): England

Summary: Before she will agree to marry Daniel Braeburn, Willa Linnet wants to kiss him first to see if any hint of passion might lurk beneath Daniel's dull, boring facade. The only problem is that a very near-sighted Willa mistakes Alexander Braeburn for his brother, and she kisses him instead. One kiss with Alexander is enough to convince Willa he is the only man for her, but now Willa must find some way to let Daniel know she prefers his brother!

Where it's reviewed:
Romantic Times, January 2005, page 106

Other books by the same author:
Lady Fiasco, 2004

Other books you might like:
Mary Balogh, *The Plumed Bonnet*, 2003
Kate Huntington, *Town Bronze*, 2003
Martha Kirkland, *The Marrying Season*, 1995
Joy Reed, *Lord Desmond's Destiny*, 2002
Regina Scott, *Lord Borin's Secret Love*, 2002

260

KATHLEEN BALDWIN
MONA GEDNEY, Co-Author
LISA NOELI, Co-Author

Waltz with a Rogue
(New York: Zebra, 2005)

Story type: Anthology; Regency
Subject(s): Courtship; Dancing
Time period(s): 1810s
Locale(s): England

Summary: The seductive pleasures of the waltz lead to romance in these three Regency novellas. In Kathleen Baldwin's "The Highwayman Came Waltzing," Elizabeth Claegburn is certain that if Lord Ryerton discovers the true identity of the highwayman he seeks, he won't be quite as pleased to be waltzing with her. "The Rebel and the Rogue" by Mona Gedney has Vivian Woodruff desperately seeking a husband other than the one chosen for her by her stepfather. When she shares a waltz with infamous rake Anthony Mallory, Vivian thinks she may just have found her man. Pretending to be a dancing master gives Neville Dunsleigh terrific opportunities to investigate ladies as potential brides; but it only takes one waltz with Penelope Spencer to convince Neville he never wants to dance with anyone else ever again in Lisa Noeli's "Dance with Me."

Where it's reviewed:
Romantic Times, March 2005, page 125

Other books you might like:
Janice Bennett, *Notorious and Noble*, 1999
Lynn Collum, *My Favorite Rogue*, 2004
Shannon Donnelly, *With This Ring*, 2004
Alice Holden, *On Bended Knee*, 2003
Lynn Kerstan, *A June Betrothal*, 1993

261

MARY BALOGH

Simply Unforgettable
(New York: Delacorte, 2005)

Story type: Historical/Regency
Series: Simply. Book 1
Subject(s): Courtship; Marriage; Conduct of Life
Major character(s): Frances Allard, Spinster, Teacher; Lucius Marshall, Nobleman (Viscount Sinclair)
Time period(s): 19th century
Locale(s): England

Summary: When a surprisingly vicious snowstorm strands Frances Allard and Lucius Marshall together in a remote country inn, the stage is set for a romantic interlude that, in spite of their intentions to the contrary, becomes a lasting relationship that neither had expected. A classic historical plot pattern (different social classes) is enhanced by Balogh's deft handling of the intricacies of the period and well-developed characters. First in a projected quartet.

Where it's reviewed:
Romantic Times, April 2005, page 44

Romance

Other books by the same author:
Slightly Dangerous, 2004
Slightly Sinful, 2004
Slightly Married, 2003
Slightly Scandalous, 2003
Slightly Wicked, 2003

Other books you might like:
Connie Brockway, *My Seduction*, 2004
Karen Hawkins, *Confessions of a Scoundrel*, 2003
Brenda Hiatt, *Rogue's Honor*, 2001
Stephanie Laurens, *A Rake's Vow*, 1998
Johanna Lindsey, *The Heir*, 2000

262

BLAIR BANCROFT (Pseudonym of Grace Ann Kone)

The Lady and the Cit

(New York: Signet, 2005)

Story type: Regency
Subject(s): Marriage; Politics
Major character(s): Aurelia Trevor, Heiress; Thomas Lanning, Businessman
Time period(s): 1800s
Locale(s): England

Summary: If she wants to keep her beloved family estate, Pevensey Park, out of her greedy uncle's clutches, Aurelia Trevor must immediately find a man willing to marry her. After rejecting several potential suitors, Aurelia reluctantly settles upon London cit Thomas Lanning as her best choice. Even though their marriage starts out as a business contract, as Aurelia and Thomas get to know one another better, their relationship with each other begins to resemble a love match instead.

Where it's reviewed:
Romantic Times, February 2005, page 26

Other books by the same author:
A Season for Love, 2004
The Harem Bride, 2004
The Indifferent Earl, 2003
The Major Meets His Match, 2003

Other books you might like:
Rita Boucher, *The Poet and the Paragon*, 2003
Susannah Carleton, *The Marriage Campaign*, 2003
Carla Kelly, *With This Ring*, 1997
Donna Simpson, *Lord Pierson Reforms*, 2004
Rhonda Woodward, *Moonlight and Mischief*, 2004

263

NINA BANGS

Wicked Nights

(New York: Berkley Sensation, 2005)

Story type: Contemporary/Fantasy; Paranormal
Series: Castle of Dark Dreams. Book 1
Subject(s): Vampires; Paranormal; Amusement Parks

Major character(s): Donna Nolan, Radio Personality (talk show host); Eric McNair, Vampire; Sparkle Stardust, Mythical Creature (cosmic troublemaker), Matchmaker
Time period(s): 2000s
Locale(s): Galveston, Texas

Summary: Radio talk show host Donna Nolan comes to Galveston to check out a caller's stories about erotic happenings at the Castle of Dark Dreams in an adult amusement park. She ends up having the adventure of her life and finds love with a vampire in the process. This is the first in a series featuring three non-humans who pass themselves off as brothers who run the castle. A mischievous cosmic matchmaker named Sparkle Stardust livens things up in this sizzling, sexy fantasy that features a wide variety of supernatural characters.

Where it's reviewed:
Romantic Times, April 2005, page 108

Other books by the same author:
Night Bites, 2005
Master of Ecstasy, 2004
From Boardwalk with Love, 2003
Night Games, 2002
An Original Sin, 1999

Other books you might like:
Amanda Ashley, *Night's Kiss*, 2005
Christine Feehan, *Dark Melody*, 2003
Sherrilyn Kenyon, *Night Play*, 2004
   Dark Hunter series
Sherrilyn Kenyon, *Stroke of Midnight*, 2004
   paranormal anthology
Angela Knight, *Master of the Night*, 2004

264

C.J. BARRY

Unmasked

(New York: Love Spell, 2005)

Story type: Futuristic
Subject(s): Pirates; Space Travel; Slavery
Major character(s): Torrie Masters, Spaceship Captain (aka Sheri Maullet), Businesswoman (family shipping company); Qaade Deter, Spaceship Captain, Pirate (Ghost Rider)
Time period(s): Indeterminate Future
Locale(s): Outer Space

Summary: Starship captain Torrie Masters has part of her medical cargo stolen by the infamous Ghost Rider of the Dead Zone on her maiden voyage. She then sets off in pursuit and ends up captured by thugs and rescued from a life of slavery by the very man she was hunting. Qaade Deter is no simple space pirate; he is on a mission to rescue as many slaves as possible, restore their memories, and send them off to new lives—a goal that puts him in direct conflict with the interests of many within the galaxy. When an insane villain sets out to destroy Qaade and his freedom network, the resulting action draws Torrie into an adventure and a romance she never expected. Fast-paced and sensual.

Where it's reviewed:
Romantic Times, June 2005, page 135

Other books by the same author:
Unleashed, 2004
Unearthed, 2003
Unraveled, 2003

Other books you might like:
Anne Avery, *All's Fair*, 1994
Justine Davis, *The Sky Pirate*, 1995
Amanda Glass, *Shield's Lady*, 1989
   Amanda Glass is a pseudonym for Jayne Anne Krentz
Susan Grant, *The Star Prince*, 2001
   Vash. Book 2
Susan Krinard, *Kinsman's Oath*, 2004

265

BEVERLY BARTON (Pseudonym of Beverly Beaver)

Killing Her Softly

(New York: Zebra, 2005)

Story type: Contemporary; Romantic Suspense
Subject(s): Murder; Serial Killers
Major character(s): Annabelle Austin Vanderley, Socialite, Philanthropist (manages family's funds); Quinn Cortez, Lawyer (criminal)
Time period(s): 2000s
Locale(s): Memphis, Tennessee; Mississippi

Summary: Prime suspect in the murder of one of his former lovers, attorney Quinn Cortez seeks to hire crack defense attorney Griffin Powell. When Annabelle Vanderley, cousin of the murdered woman, wants to hire the same attorney, they agree to work together to find the truth. A sick, twisted killer, mounting circumstantial evidence, and a growing romantic relationship between Quinn and Annabelle add to this chilling tale of romantic suspense.

Where it's reviewed:
Romantic Times, July 2005, page 94

Other books by the same author:
The Last to Die, 2004
The Fifth Victim, 2003
What She Doesn't Know, 2002
After Dark, 2000
Keeping Annie Safe, 1999

Other books you might like:
Linda Howard, *Kill and Tell*, 1998
Lisa Jackson, *The Night Before*, 2003
Hunter Morgan, *The Other Twin*, 2003
Hunter Morgan, *What She Can't See*, 2005
Karen Young, *Someone Knows*, 2002

266

LOUISE BERGIN

The Winter Duke

(New York: Signet, 2005)

Story type: Regency
Subject(s): Art; Courtship
Major character(s): Lydia Grenville, Gentlewoman; John Penhope, Nobleman (Duke of Winterbourne)

Time period(s): 1800s (1804)
Locale(s): Essex, England

Summary: While out sketching in the woods one morning, Lydia Grenville meets a handsome stranger whom she mistakes for the Duke of Winterbourne's new secretary. More comfortable as a scholar than with his new responsibilities as a duke, John Penhope does nothing to correct Lydia's misconceptions, but instead encourages her innocent flirting. When the truth about his real identity comes out, and everyone in the neighborhood learns just whom Lydia has been meeting and kissing in the woods, the scandal not only threatens to destroy Lydia's reputation but also her love for John.

Where it's reviewed:
Romantic Times, April 2005, page 67

Other books by the same author:
A Worthy Opponent, 2004
The Spinster and the Wastrel, 2004

Other books you might like:
Blair Bancroft, *The Indifferent Earl*, 2003
Susannah Carleton, *A Scandalous Journey*, 2002
Victoria Hinshaw, *The Fontainebleau Fan*, 2002
Amanda McCabe, *Lady Rogue*, 2002
Rhonda Woodward, *Moonlight and Mischief*, 2004

267

ANNETTE BLAIR

The Butterfly Garden

(Waterville, Maine: Five Star, 2005)

Story type: Historical/Americana
Subject(s): Amish; Healing; Anger
Major character(s): Sara Lapp, Midwife, Spinster; Adam Zuckerman, Widow(er), Single Parent
Time period(s): 1880s (1883)
Locale(s): Walnut Creek, Ohio

Summary: Surprised and puzzled when Adam Zuckerman wants her to take charge of his four daughters, including newborn Hannah, immediately after the death of his wife, Abby, spinster and fledgling midwife Sara Lapp reluctantly agrees and takes them home with her. However, Sara knows that the crusty widower needs his children around him, and when Adam gets drunk, falls off a ladder, and injures himself so badly that he can't care for himself, Sara moves back with the girls to care for him, resulting in a situation that can only end one way, according to the Amish elders, marriage. A father struggling with anger issues, a woman who believes in him, and four charming little girls combine in an emotionally rich, heartwarming story that focuses more on the cultural details of Amish life than the religious aspects. Sensual.

Other books by the same author:
A Christmas Baby, 2004
An Unmistakable Rogue, 2003
An Unforgettable Rogue, 2002
Thee I Love, 1999 (Amish life)

Other books you might like:
Catherine Anderson, *Simply Love*, 1997
Robin Lee Hatcher, *Promise Me Spring*, 1991

Stef Ann Holm, *Weeping Angel*, 1996
  heartwarming, more humorous
Stephanie Mittman, *The Marriage Bed*, 1996
Pamela Morsi, *Simple Jess*, 1996

268

MEREDITH BOND (Pseudonym of Merry Banerji)

Love of My Life

(New York: Zebra, 2005)

Story type: Historical/Regency
Series: Merry Men. Book 3
Subject(s): Social Classes; Social Issues; Romance
Major character(s): Cassandra Renwick, Gentlewoman (baronet's daughter); Julian Ritchie, Businessman
Time period(s): 19th century
Locale(s): England; Calcutta, India

Summary: Fleeing a humiliating rejection at the hands of a cruel young lord, Cassandra heads for Calcutta to stay with her parents, hoping for a less restrictive environment. Unfortunately, Calcutta society is worse, and when Cassie is attracted to the handsome son of an English nobleman and a high-born Indian woman, she discovers just how prejudiced people can be. Social class and racial issues are front and center in this unusual romance.

Where it's reviewed:
Library Journal, April 15, 2005, page 68

Other books by the same author:
Miss Seton's Sonata, 2004 (Merry Men. Book 1)
Wooing Miss Whately, 2004 (Merry Men. Book 2)

Other books you might like:
Mary Balogh, *One Night for Love*, 1999
  class issues
Alyssa Deane, *Once and Always*, 2000
  more serious
Candice Hern, *Once a Gentleman*, 2004
  class issues
Brenda Hiatt, *Rogue's Honor*, 2001
  class issues
Mary Jo Putney, *Veils of Silk*, 1992
  colonial India

269

STEPHANIE BOND (Pseudonym of Stephanie Bond Hauck)

My Favorite Mistake

(Toronto: Harlequin, 2005)

Story type: Contemporary
Subject(s): Marriage
Major character(s): Denise Cooke, Businesswoman (financial planner); Redford DeMoss, Military Personnel (former Marine sergeant), Horse Trainer
Time period(s): 2000s
Locale(s): New York, New York

Summary: Prompted by way too much liquor and way too much physical chemistry, Denise Cooke marries U.S. Marine Sergeant Redford DeMoss in Las Vegas just before Redford ships out on overseas duty. Once Denise gets back to New York and realizes just what she has done, she and Redford agree to annul their brief marriage. Now three years later the IRS wants to audit them, and Denise is about to be reunited with Redford. One thing Denise is certain about though: no matter how much she might still dream about her sexy ex, she isn't about to repeat the same mistake twice by marrying him again!

Where it's reviewed:
Romantic Times, February 2005, page 115

Other books by the same author:
Cover Me, 2004
Party Crashers, 2004
Whole Lotta Trouble, 2004
Kill the Competition, 2003
I Think I Love You, 2002

Other books you might like:
Jamie Denton, *Rules of Engagement*, 2003
Kristin Hardy, *Slippery When Wet*, 2003
Alison Kent, *Bound to Happen*, 2002
Joanne Rock, *Her Final Fling*, 2004
Cathy Yardley, *Working It*, 2003

270

ELIZABETH BOYLE

Something about Emmaline

(New York: Avon, 2005)

Story type: Historical/Regency
Subject(s): Identity, Concealed; Marriage
Major character(s): Emmaline Denford, Noblewoman (Lady Sedgwick); Alexander Denford, Nobleman (Baron Sedgwick)
Time period(s): 1800s (1801)
Locale(s): England

Summary: To avoid being trapped in marriage, Alexander Denford, Baron Sedgwick, comes up with the perfect plan: he invents a wife for himself. For five years Alexander's little deception works perfectly, but suddenly he begins receiving bills charged by a ''Lady Sedgwick.'' When Alexander arrives in London to investigate matters, he finds a very real ''wife'' waiting for him!

Where it's reviewed:
Booklist, February 1, 2005, page 948
Romantic Times, February 2005, page 33

Other books by the same author:
It Takes a Hero, 2004
Stealing the Bride, 2003
One Night of Passion, 2002
Once Tempted, 2001
No Marriage of Convenience, 2000

Other books you might like:
Jacquie D'Alessandro, *Love and the Single Heiress*, 2001
Suzanne Enoch, *A Matter of Scandal*, 2001
Candice Hern, *Her Scandalous Affair*, 2004
Eloisa James, *Duchess in Love*, 2002
Diane Perkins, *The Improper Wife*, 2004

271

BARBARA BRETTON

Someone Like You

(New York: Berkley, 2005)

Story type: Contemporary/Mainstream
Subject(s): Sisters; Family Relations; Guilt
Major character(s): Catherine Doyle, Artisan (weaves custom sweaters); Joely Doyle, Genius, Scientist (biomedical engineer)
Time period(s): 2000s
Locale(s): Idle Point, Maine; Bel Air, Maryland; Loch Craig, Scotland

Summary: Being on the cover of *Rolling Stone* doesn't make a couple good parents, and folk singers Mark and Mimi Doyle prove this over and over. Even after Mark leaves Mimi, she spends the next 30 years drinking and obsessing over him. The Doyles' daughters, Catherine and Joely, basically raise themselves. The brilliant Joely graduates from MIT and moves to Scotland. Catherine, the creative one, raises sheep and makes custom sweaters from their wool. When Mimi has a stroke and burns down her house, Joely comes home to help Catherine care for her. Family relations are explored in-depth in this beautifully written story of love and commitment.

Other books by the same author:
Girls of Summer, 2003
Shore Lights, 2003
A Soft Place to Fall, 2001
At Last, 2000
The Day We Met, 1999

Other books you might like:
Barbara Freethy, *Summer Secrets*, 2003
Mary Alice Monroe, *Sweetgrass*, 2005
Pamela Morsi, *Suburban Renewal*, 2004
LaVyrle Spencer, *Home Song*, 1995
Susan Wiggs, *Table for Five*, 2005

272

TERRI BRISBIN

The King's Mistress

(Toronto: Harlequin, 2005)

Story type: Historical/Medieval
Subject(s): Marriage
Major character(s): Marguerite of Alencon, Noblewoman; Orrick of Silloth, Nobleman
Time period(s): 12th century (1177-1178)
Locale(s): France; England

Summary: Marguerite of Alencon had planned on a long career as King Henry's royal mistress, but when Henry finds another beautiful woman to play his favorite, Marguerite is given a new role: wife of Orrick of Silloth. While Orrick is less than pleased with the idea of wedding the king's cast-off mistress, he still tries to win over his new bride. Furious at first with her loss of status, Marguerite snubs her new husband's attempts to win her affections, but as she gets to know

Orrick better, Marguerite suddenly finds the idea of being married to him much more palatable.

Where it's reviewed:
Booklist, December 15, 2004, page 714
Romantic Times, January 2005, page 36

Other books by the same author:
The Countess Bride, 2004
The Norman's Bride, 2004
The Dumont Bride, 2002
The Queen's Man, 2000
A Matter of Time, 1999

Other books you might like:
Shari Anton, *The Ideal Husband*, 2000
Glynnis Campbell, *My Champion*, 2000
Madeline Hunter, *By Arrangement*, 2000
Betina Krahn, *The Wife Test*, 2003
Tina St. John, *Lady of Valor*, 2000

273

PAMELA BRITTON

Dangerous Curves

(Don Mills, Ontario: Harlequin, 2005)

Story type: Romantic Suspense; Contemporary
Subject(s): Murder; Suspense; Sports/Auto Racing
Major character(s): Cece Blackwell, FBI Agent; Blain Sanders, Sports Figure (NASCAR driver), Crime Suspect
Time period(s): 2000s
Locale(s): San Francisco, California; Las Vegas, Nevada

Summary: NASCAR superstar Blain Sanders, now the team owner, is the prime suspect in the "accident" that killed his best friend, a fellow race car driver. FBI agent Cece Blackwell has been assigned to the case, not that she's happy about it. She and Blain have a history going all the way back to high school. The killer is relentless, and soon, Blain, himself, is a target. There's lots of adventure and suspense as the two former rivals find love at the race track.

Where it's reviewed:
Romantic Times, February 2005, page 105

Other books by the same author:
Scandal, 2004
Tempted, 2004
Cowboy Lessons, 2003
Seduced, 2003
Enchanted by Your Kisses, 2001

Other books you might like:
Catherine George, *The Right Choice*, 2001
Patricia Hagan, *Race to the Altar*, 2001
Bobby Hutchinson, *Intensive Caring*, 2001
Roxanne St. Claire, *Dangerous Curves*, 2005
    NASCAR driver
Kathryn Shay, *Trust in Me*, 2003
    NASCAR driver

274

SUZANNE BROCKMANN

Breaking Point

(New York: Ballantine, 2005)

Story type: Contemporary; Romantic Suspense
Subject(s): Kidnapping; Crime and Criminals; Terrorism
Major character(s): Gina Vitagliano, Captive (hostage); Max Bhagat, FBI Agent (negotiator)
Time period(s): 2000s
Locale(s): United States; Germany; Indonesia

Summary: When Gina Vitagliano is listed as a victim in a Hamburg cafe bombing, Max Bhagat heads to Germany to claim the body, only to find it isn't Gina and that she seems to be missing. Gina has been kidnapped and Max needs to find a former U.S. special agent named Jones to win her release. Of course, Max has a few plans of his own, and everything is not always as it seems in this hard-hitting, rip-roaring adventure that sweeps its characters from place to exotic place as the intricate, cleverly crafted plot unfolds. The book makes use of time and place flashbacks, and reprises characters from Brockmann's earlier novels.

Other books by the same author:
Flashpoint, 2004
Hot Target, 2004
Gone Too Far, 2003
Into the Night, 2002
Unsung Hero, 2000

Other books you might like:
Jasmine Cresswell, *Final Justice*, 2005
Christine Feehan, *Mind Game*, 2004
    paranormal elements
Christine Feehan, *Shadow Game*, 2003
    paranormal elements
Heather Graham, *On the Edge*, 2003
    adventurous anthology
Lindsay McKenna, *First Born*, 2004

275

CONNIE BROCKWAY

My Surrender

(New York: Pocket, 2005)

Story type: Historical/Regency
Series: Rose Hunters Trilogy. Book 3
Subject(s): Spies; Identity, Concealed
Major character(s): Charlotte Nash, Spy, Gentlewoman; Dand Ross, Spy
Time period(s): 1800s (1804)
Locale(s): England

Summary: Charlotte Nash, last of the three Nash sisters, is determined to continue her late father's secret agent work and find the man responsible for his death. When one of her risky forays catches the attention of Rose Hunter Dand Ross, a man sworn to protect the Nash sisters after their father's death, they realize they may be after the same villain, Comte Jean St. Lyon. They agree to join forces in a bold masquerade that will

put their lives in danger before they achieve their goals. This fast-paced, enjoyable adventure concludes the trilogy in fine style.

Where it's reviewed:
Romantic Times, May 2005, page 43

Other books by the same author:
My Pleasure, 2004 (Rose Hunters Trilogy. Book 2)
My Seduction, 2004 (Rose Hunters Trilogy. Book 1)
Bridal Favors, 2002
Once upon a Pillow, 2002
Bridal Season, 2001

Other books you might like:
Celeste Bradley, *The Pretender*, 2003
Elizabeth Elliott, *Scoundrel*, 1996
Jane Feather, *Velvet*, 1994
Lynn Kerstan, *The Silver Lion*, 2003
Elizabeth Thornton, *Dangerous to Hold*, 1996

276

DIXIE BROWNING

Her Fifth Husband?

(New York: Silhouette, 2005)

Story type: Contemporary; Humor
Series: Divas Who Dish. Book 3
Subject(s): Humor; Babies; Marriage
Major character(s): Sasha Lasiter, Interior Decorator; Jake Smith, Detective—Private, Single Parent
Time period(s): 2000s
Locale(s): Muddy Landing, North Carolina

Summary: Born Sally June Parrish, daughter of a tobacco farmer turned preacher, Sasha Combs Cassidy Boone Lasiter has been married—and divorced—four times. As a member of Muddy Landing's matchmaking trio, "Divas Who Dish," she's always ready to help people find their perfect mates. Sasha has sworn off men forever, until she meets Jake Smith, private investigator. Things get complicated when Jake's teenage son's girlfriend has a baby and Jake winds up taking care of it. Humor and pathos pave the way to Sasha's fifth trip to the altar.

Where it's reviewed:
Romantic Times, March 2005, page 116

Other books by the same author:
Her Man Upstairs, 2005 (Divas Who Dish. Book 2)
Her Passionate Plan B, 2005 (Divas Who Dish. Book 1)
Driven to Distraction, 2004
Beckett's Convenient Bride, 2003
Social Graces, 2003

Other books you might like:
Rochelle Alers, *Beyond Business*, 2005
Heidi Betts, *Bought by a Millionaire*, 2005
Robyn Carr, *Down by the River*, 2003
Susan Meier, *The Baby Bequest*, 2000
Isabel Sharpe, *Follow That Baby!*, 2001

277

DIXIE BROWNING

Her Man Upstairs

(New York: Silhouette, 2005)

Story type: Contemporary; Humor
Series: Divas Who Dish. Book 2
Subject(s): Humor; Trust; Small Town Life
Major character(s): Marty Owens, Store Owner (bookstore); Cole Stevens, Contractor
Time period(s): 2000s
Locale(s): Muddy Landing, North Carolina

Summary: Setting a pie on fire isn't the best way to meet a man; but even though unplanned, this was Cole Stevens' introduction to Marty Owens. Now an independent contractor after his split with his crooked father-in-law and divorce from a not much better wife, Marty's house remodel is supposed to be just another job for Cole. Marty, who lost one husband and divorced another, has lost her storefront, and has to convert the first floor of her house into a bookstore. A very big dog with an attitude and a mysterious stalker add to the excitement as Marty and Cole find that the thing they need to build the most is their relationship. Score another win for Muddy Landing's matchmaking trio, ''Divas Who Dish.''

Where it's reviewed:
Romantic Times, February 2005, page 120

Other books by the same author:
Her Fifth Husband?, 2005 (Divas Who Dish. Book 3)
Her Passionate Plan B, 2005 (Divas Who Dish. Book 1)
Driven to Distraction, 2004
Beckett's Convenient Bride, 2003
Social Graces, 2003

Other books you might like:
Wendy Etherington, *My Place or Yours?*, 2002
Joan Hohl, *A Man Apart*, 2005
Cait London, *Total Package*, 2005
Kasey Michaels, *Love to Love You, Baby*, 2001
Julie Ortolon, *Dear Cupid*, 2001

278

DIXIE BROWNING

Her Passionate Plan B

(New York: Silhouette, 2005)

Story type: Contemporary; Humor
Series: Divas Who Dish. Book 1
Subject(s): Humor; Genealogy; Grief
Major character(s): Daisy Hunter, Nurse (geriatric); Kell Magee, Sports Figure (former baseball star)
Time period(s): 2000s
Locale(s): Muddy Landing, North Carolina

Summary: When Muddy Landing, North Carolina's official matchmaking trio, ''Divas Who Dish,'' decide that a man and a woman belong together, watch out! Their latest project is uniting geriatric nurse Daisy Hunter and former baseball star Kell Magee, the man claiming to be the long-lost nephew of Daisy's favorite patient, Harvey Snow, who has just died. Daisy's one of the Divas, and she's all set to marry Egbert, her dependable, modest, mild-mannered accountant, even if he's not quite ready to commit. This humorous, heartwarming story about a man looking for his roots and finding love is the first in a trilogy.

Where it's reviewed:
Romantic Times, January 2005, page 98

Other books by the same author:
Her Fifth Husband?, 2005 (Divas Who Dish. Book 3)
Her Man Upstairs, 2005 (Divas Who Dish. Book 2)
Driven to Distraction, 2004
Beckett's Convenient Bride, 2003
Social Graces, 2003

Other books you might like:
Margaret Allison, *A Single Demand*, 2005
Sue Civil-Brown, *Catching Kelly*, 2000
Kathie DeNosky, *A Rare Sensation*, 2005
Susan Elizabeth Phillips, *Heaven, Texas*, 1995
Emilie Rose, *Breathless Passion*, 2005

279

GEMMA BRUCE

Who's Been Sleeping in My Bed?

(New York: Brava, 2005)

Story type: Contemporary; Romantic Suspense
Series: Wicked Women Whodunit
Subject(s): Mystery; Murder
Major character(s): Hannah Harrington-Scott, Detective—Private (aka Nan Scott); Geena Cole, Detective—Private; Delia Petrocelli, Detective—Private
Time period(s): 2000s
Locale(s): New York

Summary: Friends and debutantes as ''bad girl'' teenagers, Nan, Geena, and Delia link up together as private detectives at Women-Tek. Humor, sassy dialogue, and sizzling sensuality highlight each of the three stories (one focusing on each woman) in this explicitly sexy collection. Part of the Wicked Women Whodunit series, titles included are ''Wicked Widow,'' ''Man with a Past,'' and ''Love Bites.''

Where it's reviewed:
Romantic Times, July 2005, page 96

Other books you might like:
Susanna Carr, *Confessions of a Wicked Woman*, 2005
MaryJanice Davidson, *How to Be a Wicked Woman*, 2004
  erotic anthology
MaryJanice Davidson, *Wicked Women Whodunit*, 2005
  erotic mystery anthology
Tina Donahue, *Wicked Women on Top*, 2005
  erotic mystery anthology
Lori Foster, *Bad Boys on Board*, 2003
  erotic anthology

280

WANDA E. BRUNSTETTER

The Storekeeper's Daughter

(Uhrichsville, Ohio: Barbour, 2005)

Story type: Contemporary; Inspirational
Series: Daughters of Lancaster County. Book 1
Subject(s): Amish; Healing; Religious Life
Major character(s): Naomi Fisher, Young Woman (Amish), Clerk (family general store); Caleb Hoffmeir, Businessman (buggy maker)
Time period(s): 2000s
Locale(s): Pennsylvania

Summary: Saddled with the responsibility of her seven younger brothers and sisters after her mother's accidental death, Naomi Fisher tries her best to look after the family and help her father in the family's general store. Her grief-stricken father depends on her far too much and restricts her social life unbearably, not even allowing her to be courted by an eligible young man. The breaking point comes when her one-year-old brother is kidnapped and things begin to fall apart. Blaming herself and filled with guilt and unhappiness, Naomi leaves the community with an English friend, determined to find happiness in the outside world. Eventually, she returns, but it takes much soul-searching and signs from God to make sure it all works out in the end. Intriguing Amish cultural detail; heavily religious.

Other books you might like:
Annette Blair, *The Butterfly Garden*, 2005
   historical Amish
Annette Blair, *Thee I Love*, 1999
Sharon De Vita, *The Marriage Promise*, 2000
Beverly Lewis, *The Crossroad*, 1999
   contemporary Amish
Jessamyn West, *The Friendly Persuasion*, 1945
   classic Amish tale

281

ANN BURTON

Abigail's Story

(New York: Signet, 2005)

Story type: Historical/Pre-history; Inspirational
Series: Women of the Bible. Book 1
Subject(s): Marriage; War; Biblical Fiction
Major character(s): Abigail of Carmel, Young Woman, Biblical Figure; David, Shepherd, Biblical Figure
Time period(s): Indeterminate Past
Locale(s): Judea

Summary: Wed to a loutish man she cannot stand in order to save her family from financial ruin, Abigail of Carmel accepts her fate, determined to be a good wife. Her brutal husband, Nabal, sends her off to the country to take care of his flocks. As she comes to love the country and its people, including the heroic David, she also begins to realize that she has another purpose in life to fulfill. This romantic, fictionalized account

of the Biblical Abigail will especially appeal to inspirational readers.

Other books by the same author:
Rahab's Story, 2005

Other books you might like:
Anita Diamant, *The Red Tent*, 1997
Marjorie Holmes, *Two from Galilee*, 1997
   classic Biblical tale
Gladys Malvern, *Behold Your Queen*, 1951
   the story of Esther
Francine Rivers, *Unveiled*, 2000
   the story of Tamar
Sheri Cobb South, *The Cobra and the Lily*, 2002
   ancient Egypt

282

RACHEL BUTLER

The Assassin

(New York: Dell, 2005)

Story type: Contemporary; Romantic Suspense
Subject(s): Murder; Crime and Criminals
Major character(s): Selena McCaffrey, Martial Arts Expert, Criminal (would-be assassin); Tony Ceola, Detective—Homicide
Time period(s): 2000s
Locale(s): Tulsa, Oklahoma

Summary: Sent by crime boss William Davis, the man to whom she owes everything, to kill Detective Tony Ceola, Selena McCaffrey finds herself attracted to her quarry, with potentially disastrous results. Fast-paced action and beautifully developed, memorable characters, especially a deadly, biracial heroine who can take care of herself, are highlights.

Where it's reviewed:
Romantic Times, June 2005, page 116

Other books by the same author:
Deep Cover, 2005

Other books you might like:
Suzanne Brockmann, *Over the Edge*, 2001
Christine Feehan, *Mind Game*, 2004
   strong heroine
Tess Gerritsen, *The Apprentice*, 2002
   strong heroine
Karen Robards, *Bait*, 2005
Maureen Tan, *A Perfect Cover*, 2004

283

ADRIANNE BYRD

Measure of a Man

(Washington, D.C.: BET, 2005)

Story type: Contemporary; Multicultural
Subject(s): African Americans; Homosexuality/Lesbianism; Humor

Romance

Major character(s): Peyton Garner, Agent (art agent); Trey ''Lincoln'' Carver, Fire Fighter, Artist (amateur sculptor); Flex Adams, Fire Fighter, Homosexual
Time period(s): 2000s
Locale(s): San Jose, California

Summary: When art agent Peyton Garner and fire fighter and closet sculptor Trey ''Lincoln'' Carver develop a relationship, Peyton has no idea that her Trey and her gay fire fighter brother's colleague Lincoln (whom she mistakenly thinks is his new boyfriend) are the same person. In an effort to calm his five sisters' concerns about his ailing love life, Flex Adams allows them to think Lincoln is his new love interest, unwittingly setting the stage for a series of hilarious events as the family gathers for a wedding. This funny, heartwarming comedy of errors deals nicely with some gay issues and is first in a projected series about the Adams siblings.

Where it's reviewed:
Library Journal, January 2005, page 90
Romantic Times, January 2005, page 111

Other books by the same author:
Deadly Double, 2005
If You Dare, 2004
Unforgettable, 2004
Comfort of a Man, 2003
Say You Love Me, 2000

Other books you might like:
Suzanne Brockmann, *Hot Target*, 2004
    gay issues subplot
Robyn Carr, *The Wedding Party*, 2001
    family, humor, and weddings
Sandra Kitt, *Family Affairs*, 1999
Cathie Linz, *The Marine Meets His Match*, 2004
    humor
Kasey Michaels, *Bachelor on the Prowl*, 2001

284

LAURA CALDWELL

Look Closely

(Don Mills, Ontario: MIRA, 2005)

Story type: Contemporary; Romantic Suspense
Subject(s): Family Relations; Secrets; Murder
Major character(s): Hailey Sutter, Lawyer; Ty Manning, Innkeeper (bed-and-breakfast owner)
Time period(s): 2000s
Locale(s): New York, New York; Chicago, Illinois

Summary: When corporate attorney Hailey Sutter receives an anonymous letter suggesting that her mother's death years earlier might not have been an accident, she begins a quest for the truth that is not at all what she had expected. Blackmail, old family secrets, and some corporate intrigue are all part of this intricately plotted story that is more mystery than romance.

Other books by the same author:
A Clean Slate, 2003
Burning the Map, 2002

Other books you might like:
Jasmine Cresswell, *Secret Sins*, 1997
Christina Dodd, *Close to You*, 2005
    Prescott Siblings. Book 3
Patricia Potter, *The Perfect Family*, 2001
Patricia Potter, *Twisted Shadows*, 2003
Antoinette Stockenberg, *Keepsake*, 1999

285

CANDACE CAMP

An Unexpected Pleasure

(Don Mills, Ontario: HQN, 2005)

Story type: Historical/Victorian; Paranormal
Subject(s): Murder; Dreams and Nightmares; Identity, Concealed
Major character(s): Megan Mulcahey, Journalist (newspaper reporter), Tutor (fake); Theo Moreland, Adventurer, Nobleman (Lord Raine)
Time period(s): 1870s (1879)
Locale(s): New York, New York; London, England

Summary: American newspaper reporter Megan Mulcahey goes undercover as a tutor in London to gather evidence concerning her brother's murder. Her prime suspect, Theo Moreland, Lord Raine, seems like a decent fellow, and his house, complete with relatives of all ages, is filled with love and laughter. Although her young charges have scared away other tutors with their enthusiastic pranks and precocity, Megan finds them quite charming. Something isn't right. If Theo is a cold-blooded killer, as another witness on that ill-fated jungle treasure hunt claims, he's a master actor. The ''Mad Morelands'' have yet another adventure, and this one is just as exciting and humorous as the others.

Other books by the same author:
Beyond Compare, 2004
Winterset, 2004
Mesmerized, 2003
Secrets of the Heart, 2003 (Heart. Book 3)
The Hidden Heart, 2002 (Heart. Book 2)

Other books you might like:
Jo Ann Ferguson, *Her Only Hero*, 2000
Jill Marie Landis, *The Orchid Hunter*, 2000
Glenna McReynolds, *River of Eden*, 2002
Madeleine E. Robins, *Point of Honour*, 2003
Nan Ryan, *The Seduction of Ellen*, 2001

286

ROBYN CARR

Runaway Mistress

(Don Mills, Ontario: MIRA, 2005)

Story type: Romantic Suspense; Contemporary
Subject(s): Identity, Concealed; Crime and Criminals; Small Town Life
Major character(s): Jennifer Chaise, Prostitute (professional mistress), Runaway; Alex Nichols, Police Officer
Time period(s): 2000s

Locale(s): Fort Lauderdale, Florida; Boulder City, Nevada; Las Vegas, Nevada

Summary: Jennifer Chaise is a polished, professional, high-paid mistress. Her current companion, wealthy high-roller Nick Noble, takes her to Las Vegas to show her a good time, but trouble follows when Nick's wife shows up, too. Angry because of his spouse's accusations, he kills her. Jennifer sees the bloody body and hears Nick tell his goons to take care of her, too, so she flees to Boulder City, Nevada. She changes her appearance from a head-turning beauty to a homeless punk look by shaving her hair and eyebrows. Once disguised, she takes a job at a local greasy spoon. Las Vegas cop Alex Nichols feels a strange attraction to the bald waitress the small town has taken in, but Jennifer knows that even he is no match for Nick and his men. That is, if Alex knew who she really was, and why she was hiding.

Where it's reviewed:
Booklist, May 15, 2005, page 1640
Romantic Times, June 2005, page 89

Other books by the same author:
Blue Skies, 2004
Down by the River, 2003 (Grace Valley. Book 3)
Just over the Mountain, 2002 (Grace Valley. Book 2)
The Wedding Party, 2001
Deep in the Valley, 2000 (Grace Valley. Book 1)

Other books you might like:
Sharon De Vita, *Anything for Her Family*, 2002
Marie Ferrarella, *An Uncommon Hero*, 2001
Patricia Forsythe, *The Runaway Princess*, 2001
Lori Foster, *When Bruce Met Cyn. . .*, 2004
Karen Young, *Somebody Knows*, 2002

287

KATHRYN CASKIE

Lady in Waiting

(New York: Warner, 2005)

Story type: Historical/Regency
Subject(s): Business Enterprises; Identity, Concealed
Major character(s): Jenny Penny, Servant (lady's maid), Imposter ("Lady Genevieve"); Callum Campbell, Nobleman (Viscount Argyll)
Time period(s): 1810s (1817-1818)
Locale(s): Bath, England

Summary: When lady's maid Jenny Penny is caught "trying out" a most magnificent carriage by its owner, Callum Campbell, she escapes by pretending to be Lady Genevieve d'en Bas. Jenny never expects to see the sexy Scotsman again, but upon arriving home, Jenny is shocked to discover her employers, the Featherton sisters, entertaining their old family friend: Callum. Much to her surprise, the matchmaking Feathertons help Jenny continue to masquerade as Lady Genevieve, but at some point Jenny knows she is going to have to figure out a way to tell Callum he is falling in love with a maid!

Where it's reviewed:
Booklist, December 1, 2004, page 640
Publishers Weekly, November 29, 2004, page 28
Romantic Times, January 2005, page 31

Other books by the same author:
Rules of Engagement, 2004

Other books you might like:
Rexanne Becnel, *The Matchmaker*, 2002
Katherine Greyle, *Miss Woodley's Experiment*, 2002
Sabrina Jeffries, *A Notorious Love*, 2001
Rebecca Hagan Lee, *Hardly a Husband*, 2004
Teresa Medeiros, *A Kiss to Remember*, 2001

288

CARLA CASSIDY (Pseudonym of Carla Bracale)

The Perfect Family

(New York: Signet Eclipse, 2005)

Story type: Contemporary; Romantic Suspense
Subject(s): Suspense; Grief; Change
Major character(s): Marissa Jamison, Widow(er), Single Parent; Alex Kincaid, Architect
Time period(s): 2000s
Locale(s): Cass Creek, Missouri (suburb of Kansas City)

Summary: Finally emerging from the nightmare of her fire fighter husband's death, Marissa Jamison's life is beginning to come back into focus; her shop is doing well, her children are beginning to adjust, and an old boyfriend has just moved back to town. Someone out there, though, has decided that Marissa and her children will be his perfect family, and he is determined to claim his due. Now as the bodies start appearing—tied up in red bows as gifts to Marissa—along with roses and silent phone calls, Marissa's life takes on a nightmarish quality, as she, Alex, and a pair of exceptional police officers race against time to identify the killer and stop him before he adds Marissa and her children to his list of victims.

Where it's reviewed:
Library Journal, January 2005, page 91
Romantic Times, March 2005, page 101

Other books by the same author:
Rules of Engagement, 2004
Dead Certain, 2003 (Cherokee Corners. Book 2)
Trace Evidence, 2003 (Cherokee Corners. Book 3)
More than Meets the Eye, 2002
Just One Kiss, 2001

Other books you might like:
Beverly Barton, *The Fifth Victim*, 2003
Beverly Barton, *Whitelaw's Wedding*, 2001
Karen Rose, *Have You Seen Her?*, 2004
Karen Rose, *I'm Watching You*, 2004
Tina Wainscott, *The Unforgivable*, 2001
  especially chilling

289

P.C. CAST

Goddess of Light

(New York: Berkley Sensation, 2005)

Story type: Contemporary/Fantasy; Fantasy
Series: Goddess Summoning. Book 4
Subject(s): Mythology

Major character(s): Pamela Gray, Interior Decorator (owns design firm); Apollo, Deity (Greek)
Time period(s): 2000s
Locale(s): Las Vegas, Nevada

Summary: Interior designer Pamela Gray is in Las Vegas to redo the house of a noted fantasy author; Apollo is there at the insistence of his sister, Artemis, who thinks he needs to get on with his life after being rejected by Persephone. When Pamela inadvertently completes a magical incantation that forces Artemis to grant her wish for romance with a true godlike man, Apollo is the man for the job. There is mischief afoot, however, and when the gods decide to meddle in the mortal world, things don't always work out as planned. Love, romance, issues of self-esteem, and a bit of treachery add to the mix in this installment of Cast's Goddess Summoning series.

Where it's reviewed:
Rendezvous, March 2005, page 32
Romantic Times, April 2005, page 108

Other books by the same author:
Goddess of Spring, 2004 (Goddess Summoning. Book 3)
Goddess of the Sea, 2003 (Goddess Summoning. Book 2)
Goddess by Mistake, 2001 (Goddess Summoning. Book 1)

Other books you might like:
Alicia Fields, *Love Underground*, 2005
Karen Harbaugh, *Cupid's Kiss*, 1999
    god's meddle Regency-style
Deborah Smith, *Alice at Heart*, 2002
    Waterlilies. Book 1
Evelyn Vaughn, *A.K.A. Goddess*, 2004

290

LAURA CASTORO

A New Lu

(Don Mills, Ontario: Red Dress Ink, 2005)

Story type: Contemporary
Subject(s): Pregnancy; Change; Conduct of Life
Major character(s): Tallulah "Lu" Nichols, Journalist (magazine columnist); William Templeton, Doctor
Time period(s): 2000s
Locale(s): Upper Montclair, New Jersey; New York

Summary: Newly and amicably divorced, getting ready to marry off her daughter, and about to undertake a total makeover and write about it in her magazine column, almost 50-year-old Lu is stunned to discover she is pregnant—a totally unexpected result of a parting weekend with her ex-husband. How Lu deals with this life-changing event is heartwarming, poignant, and hilarious; and the fact that the doctor hero is not only sexy but can cook, too, is a definite plus. Brave, sassy, and irrepressible.

Where it's reviewed:
Romantic Times, March 2005, page 65

Other books by the same author:
Crossing the Line, 2002

Other books you might like:
Carly Alexander, *The Eggnog Chronicles*, 2004
Lynn Messina, *Fashionistas*, 2003

Lynn Messina, *Mim Warner's Lost Her Cool*, 2005
Lisa Plumley, *My Best Friend's Wedding*, 2005
    another unmarried mother
Heather Swain, *Luscious Lemon*, 2004
    independent, pregnant heroine

291

JANET CHAPMAN

The Dangerous Protector

(New York: Pocket Star, 2005)

Story type: Contemporary
Series: Foster Sisters. Book 2
Subject(s): Pollution; Environmental Problems; Fishing
Major character(s): Willow Foster, Lawyer (assistant attorney general); Duncan Ross, Saloon Keeper/Owner (pub owner), Nobleman (Duke of Spierhenge)
Time period(s): 2000s
Locale(s): Puffin Harbor, Maine

Summary: When assistant attorney general Willow Foster returns to Puffin Harbor to investigate some deformed lobsters that have suddenly started turning up in the traps near one of the local islands, she becomes the target of criminals who will stop at nothing to hide their illegal activities. She also has to deal with sexy, determined Duncan Ross, a man who has announced his intentions to marry her to the entire town and is not about to take no for an answer. Humor blends nicely with lively action in this sensual contemporary that is the second of two books about the Foster sisters, following *The Seductive Imposter*.

Other books by the same author:
Tempting the Highlander, 2004 (Highlander. Book 4)
The Seductive Imposter, 2004 (Foster Sisters. Book 1)
Charming the Highlander, 2003 (Highlander. Book 1)
Loving the Highlander, 2003 (Highlander. Book 2)
Wedding the Highlander, 2003 (Highlander. Book 3)

Other books you might like:
Jeanette Baker, *Chesapeake Tide*, 2004
    pollution, small towns
Jill Barnett, *Carried Away*, 2002
    Maine ambience, Scottish twist
Marcia Evanick, *Christmas on Conrad Street*, 2002
Curtiss Ann Matlock, *At the Corner of Love and Heartache*, 2002
    reunions, humor, small towns
Nora Roberts, *Chesapeake Blue*, 2002

292

LORETTA CHASE (Pseudonym of Loretta Chekani)

Mr. Impossible

(New York: Berkley Sensation, 2005)

Story type: Historical/Regency
Series: Carsington Family. Book 2
Subject(s): Egyptian Antiquities; Adventure and Adventurers; Self-Esteem

Major character(s): Daphne Pembroke, Gentlewoman, Scholar (hieroglyphic expert); Rupert Carsington, Nobleman (son of the Earl of Hargate)
Time period(s): 1820s (1821)
Locale(s): Egypt

Summary: Widowed Daphne Pembroke's brother Miles is kidnapped because he is thought to have discovered the secret to translating Egyptian hieroglyphics. Daphne, the real scholar in the family, heads off in search of him, taking with her Rupert Carsington, a noted noble hellion who has been exiled to Egypt by his family. Various villains vie for possession of an ancient papyrus, chop off the heads of their enemies, and engage in all kinds of dastardly deeds in this fast-paced, often humorous story that sweeps its protagonists along the Nile and in and out of ancient ruins with expert flair. Sensual and well-written. Follows *Miss Wonderful*.

Where it's reviewed:
Romantic Times, March 2005, page 30

Other books by the same author:
Miss Wonderful, 2004
The Last Hellion, 1998
Lord of Scoundrels, 1995
Captives of the Night, 1994
Lion's Daughter, 1992

Other books you might like:
Connie Brockway, *As You Desire*, 1997
Hilary Fields, *Marrying Jezebel*, 1997
Constance O'Banyon, *Desert Song*, 1995
Elizabeth Peters, *The Crocodile on the Sandbank*, 1975
    classic Egyptian adventure
Amanda Quick, *Slightly Shady*, 2001
    funny, fast-paced, sensual

293

MAUREEN CHILD

The Tempting Mrs. Reilly
(New York: Silhouette, 2005)

Story type: Contemporary; Humor
Series: Three-Way Wager. Book 1
Subject(s): Seduction; Humor; Military Life
Major character(s): Tina Reilly, Real Estate Agent, Divorced Person; Brian Reilly, Military Personnel, Divorced Person
Time period(s): 2000s
Locale(s): Baywater, South Carolina

Summary: Father Liam Reilly bets his triplet siblings that they can't go three months without sex. If they fail, they have to make a hefty contribution to the church roofing fund. Brian Reilly knows it will be tough, but he hasn't counted on his ex-wife, Tina, coming back to town with seduction on her mind. For reasons of his own, Brian divorced her five years earlier, but his feelings for her never really died. Tina is a woman on a mission. She wants to have a baby, and she wants Brian to be the father. She just doesn't want him to know about it. Two stubborn people who never should have parted are given a little shove by several matchmakers, including an unorthodox priest who isn't above using a non-clerical approach to get them back together.

Where it's reviewed:
Romantic Times, May 2005, page 129

Other books by the same author:
A Crazy Kind of Love, 2005
Society-Page Seduction, 2005
Whatever Reilly Wants. . ., 2005 (Three-Way Wager. Book 2)
The Last Reilly Standing, 2005 (Three-Way Wager. Book 3)
Lost in Sensation, 2004

Other books you might like:
Heidi Betts, *Blame It on the Blackout*, 2005
Suzanne Brockmann, *The Admiral's Bride*, 1999
Susan Crosby, *Secrets of Paternity*, 2005
Sara Orwig, *Estate Affair*, 2005
Emilie Rose, *Scandalous Passion*, 2005

294

JAN COFFEY (Pseudonym of Nikoo K. McGoldrick and James A. McGoldrick)

Five in a Row
(Don Mills, Ontario: MIRA, 2005)

Story type: Contemporary; Romantic Suspense
Subject(s): Accidents; Computers; Terrorism
Major character(s): Emily Doyle, Computer Expert (security expert), Single Parent (teenage son); Ben Colter, Insurance Investigator
Time period(s): 2000s
Locale(s): Connecticut

Summary: When five seemingly unrelated car crashes lead to computer security expert Emily Doyle, it attracts the attention of Ben Colter, an insurance investigator. An obsessed computer geek has claimed Emily as his own, and he is taking control of people's automobiles to prove a point, with deadly results. Tense and riveting.

Other books by the same author:
Fourth Victim, 2004
Triple Threat, 2003
Twice Burned, 2002
Trust Me Once, 2001

Other books you might like:
Carla Cassidy, *The Perfect Family*, 2005
Jacey Ford, *Dangerous Curves*, 2004
Merline Lovelace, *Call of Duty*, 1998
Kathleen Nance, *Jigsaw*, 2005
Karen Rose, *I'm Watching You*, 2004

295

LYNN COLLUM (Pseudonym of Jerry Lynn Smith)

The Captain
(New York: Zebra, 2005)

Story type: Regency
Subject(s): Marriage; Reunions
Major character(s): Jacinda Blanchett, Gentlewoman; Andrew Morrow, Sea Captain, Gentleman
Time period(s): 1800s (1806); 1810s (1814)
Locale(s): England

Summary: Betrothed to young Jacinda Blanchett in order to save his father from ruin, teenager Andrew Morrow escapes and runs away to join the Navy and seek his fortune. Jacinda's father is murdered soon after and fearing for her life, Jacinda ends up on the London streets, posing as a boy. Years later, Jacinda and Andrew are reunited in a bizarre sequence of events, and although Drew doesn't see through Jacinda's disguise for some time, the marriage that was planned years earlier eventually takes place. An adventurous Regency filled with humor, lively action, and a bit of suspense.

Where it's reviewed:
Romantic Times, April 2005, page 67

Other books by the same author:
When the Slipper Fits, 2003
A Kiss at Midnight, 2002
The Valentine Charm, 2001
The Wedding Charm, 2001
The Christmas Charm, 2000

Other books you might like:
Mona Gedney, *Lady Diana's Daring Deed*, 2000
Emily Hendrickson, *Miss Cheney's Charade*, 2004
  cross-dressing heroine
Judith A. Lansdowne, *Shall We Dance?*, 2000
  an imposter hero
Johanna Lindsey, *A Loving Scoundrel*, 2004
  more sensual
Evelyn Richardson, *Lady Alex's Gamble*, 1995
  cross-dressing heroine

296

KRISTINA COOK (Pseudonym of Kristina Cook Hort)

Unveiled

(New York: Zebra, 2005)

Story type: Historical/Regency; Historical/Georgian
Subject(s): Marriage; Mental Illness; Secrets
Major character(s): Jane Rosemoor, Gentlewoman, Spinster (by choice); Hayden Moreland, Nobleman (Earl of Westfield), Guardian (of Madeline); Madeline Moreland, Bastard Daughter (of Hayden's brother), Ward
Time period(s): 1820s (1824); 1810s (1810)
Locale(s): Essex, England; Derbyshire, England

Summary: Overhearing that madness afflicts the women in her family and gets worse after childbearing, 12-year-old Jane Rosemoor vowed never to marry—a promise she has kept successfully for 14 years. Then she meets the arrogant, devastatingly attractive Earl of Westfield, a man with a similar aversion to marriage but in serious need of a wife to help raise his young ward, and the battle begins. Light, lively, and sexy, this story explores some serious issues with humor and sensitivity.

Other books by the same author:
Unlaced, 2004

Other books you might like:
Loretta Chase, *Lord of Scoundrels*, 1995
Sabrina Jeffries, *In the Prince's Bed*, 2004
Lisa Kleypas, *Secrets of a Summer Night*, 2004
  Victorian setting

Stephanie Laurens, *On a Wild Night*, 2002
Julia Quinn, *Romancing Mr. Bridgerton*, 2002

297

JASMINE CRESSWELL

Final Justice

(Don Mills, Ontario: MIRA, 2005)

Story type: Contemporary; Romantic Suspense
Series: Melody Beecham. Book 3
Subject(s): Murder; Suspense; Revenge
Major character(s): Melody Beecham, Spy (secret agent); Nikolai Anwar, Spy (secret agent)
Time period(s): 2000s
Locale(s): United States; Mexico

Summary: Any number of people could want special agent Melody Beecham dead, but when it becomes obvious that someone really does want to kill her, the problem is to figure out just who that someone might be. With her partner and lover Nick Anwar, Melody is once again thrown into a fast-paced adventure of violence and danger as the pair track down the slippery killer.

Other books by the same author:
Decoy, 2004 (Melody Beecham. Book 1)
Full Pursuit, 2004 (Melody Beecham. Book 2)
The Conspiracy, 2001
The Inheritance, 2000
The Refuge, 2000

Other books you might like:
Suzanne Brockmann, *Bodyguard*, 1999
Suzanne Brockmann, *Breaking Point*, 2005
Christiane Heggan, *Scent of a Killer*, 2004
Caridad Pineiro, *Darkness Calls*, 2004
Meryl Sawyer, *Lady Killer*, 2004

298

MILLIE CRISWELL

No Strings Attached

(Don Mills, Ontario: HQN, 2005)

Story type: Contemporary
Subject(s): Romance; Friendship
Major character(s): Samantha Brady, Writer (aspiring novelist); Jack Turner, Real Estate Agent, Landlord (apartment buildings)
Time period(s): 2000s
Locale(s): New York, New York

Summary: Best friends since childhood, Jack and Samantha have platonically shared a New York apartment for six years. Then, when their rental car breaks down and they are forced to spend the night together in a motel, too much Jack Daniels and a game of spin the bottle take their relationship to a new level and things are never the same between them again. Humor and lively action counterbalance the more serious issues of commitment, family, and love.

Where it's reviewed:
Romantic Times, July 2005, page 108

Other books by the same author:
Mad about Mia, 2004 (Little Italy. Book 4)
The Trials of Angela, 2002 (Little Italy. Book 3)
The Trouble with Mary, 2001 (Little Italy. Book 1)
What to Do about Annie?, 2001 (Little Italy. Book 2)
The Marrying Man, 2000

Other books you might like:
Carly Alexander, *The Eggnog Chronicles*, 2004
Trisha Alexander, *Falling for an Older Man*, 2000
Sue Civil-Brown, *Carried Away*, 1997
Sheila Rabe, *A Prince of a Guy*, 2003
Heather Swain, *Luscious Lemon*, 2004

299

SHEILA CURRAN

Diana Lively Is Falling Down

(New York: Berkley, 2005)

Story type: Humor; Contemporary
Subject(s): Humor; Amusement Parks; Moving, Household
Major character(s): Diana Lively, Architect, Parent (three children); Wally Gold, Wealthy (ammunition manufacturing), Widow(er)
Time period(s): 2000s
Locale(s): Oxford, England; Phoenix, Arizona

Summary: Diana Lively's husband, Ted, is a world-class jerk. He pinches pennies where his family is concerned, then squanders them on his young mistress. He uses every opportunity to put down Diana and the children. However, he is Oxford's expert on the Arthurian legend, and wealthy Wally ''The Ammo King'' Gold wants to build an amusement park in Arizona in honor of his late Anglophile wife with that theme. A hefty donation from Wally to Oxford University assures the Lively family's relocation. As Diana looks for the snakes, spiders, and scorpions she's sure roam the mean streets of Phoenix, she finds something unexpected— romance. Excellent writing and a nice blend of humor and pathos make this story of culture shock turned international love a wonderful one.

Other books you might like:
Barbara Freethy, *Love Will Find a Way*, 2002
Kathy Love, *Wanting Something More*, 2005
Curtiss Ann Matlock, *Driving Lessons*, 2000
Susan Elizabeth Phillips, *Honey Moon*, 1993
Lisa Plumley, *Josie Day Is Coming Home*, 2005

300

JANET DAILEY

Lone Star Calder

(New York: Kensington, 2005)

Story type: Contemporary
Series: Calder. Book 9
Subject(s): Ranch Life; Family Saga
Major character(s): Dallas Garner, Student—College, Waiter/Waitress; Quint Echohawk, Rancher, Government Official (former Treasury agent)

Time period(s): 2000s
Locale(s): Montana; Texas

Summary: Sent from Montana to see what the problems are at the family's Cee Bar Ranch in Texas, Quint Echohawk finds expected danger from greedy Max Rutledge, who will stop at nothing to get the land he wants. He also finds unexpected love in the form of Dallas Garner, fiery daughter of the one man who is on Quint's side.

Other books by the same author:
Calder Promise, 2004 (Calder. Book 8)
Shifting Calder Wind, 2003 (Calder. Book 7)
Green Calder Grass, 2002 (Calder. Book 6)
Calder Pride, 1999 (Calder. Book 5)
This Calder Sky, 1981 (Calder. Book 1)

Other books you might like:
Kathleen Eagle, *The Last True Cowboy*, 1998
Fiona Hood-Stewart, *Silent Wishes*, 2003
Curtiss Ann Matlock, *If Wishes Were Horses*, 1998
Nora Roberts, *Montana Sky*, 1996
Alexandra Thorne, *Lawless*, 1994

301

MARYJANICE DAVIDSON

Undead and Unappreciated

(New York: Berkley Sensation, 2005)

Story type: Contemporary/Fantasy; Paranormal
Series: Undead. Book 3
Subject(s): Vampires; Humor
Major character(s): Betsy Taylor, Vampire, Ruler (Queen of the Vampires); Eric Sinclair, Vampire, Ruler (King of the Vampires)
Time period(s): 2000s
Locale(s): Minneapolis, Minnesota; St. Paul, Minnesota

Summary: This sassy addition to the trials and tribulations of Vampire Queen Betsy Taylor takes Betsy on a quest to find a half sister she never knew about. Her half sister is not only the Devil's child (he possessed Betsy's stepmother's body during the pregnancy), but according to the *Book of the Dead*, she is supposed to rule the world. Naturally, Betsy needs to find her to check things out. Short chapters keep the pace quick in this funny, trendy story.

Where it's reviewed:
Romantic Times, July 2005, page 109

Other books by the same author:
The Royal Treatment, 2004
Undead and Unemployed, 2004 (Undead. Book 2)
Undead and Unwed, 2004 (Undead. Book 1)
By Any Other Name, 1998

Other books you might like:
Laurell K. Hamilton, *Incubus Dreams*, 2004
  Anita Blake Vampire Hunter series
Charlaine Harris, *Dead Until Dark*, 2001
Lynsay Sands, *Love Bites*, 2004
Lynsay Sands, *Single White Vampire*, 2003
Lynsay Sands, *Tall, Dark, and Hungry*, 2004

302

MARYJANICE DAVIDSON
AMY GARVEY, Co-Author
JENNIFER APODACA, Co-Author
NANCY J. COHEN, Co-Author

Wicked Women Whodunit

(New York: Brava, 2005)

Story type: Contemporary; Romantic Suspense
Subject(s): Murder; Suspense; Sexual Behavior
Time period(s): 2000s
Locale(s): United States

Summary: Murder, mystery, and sex are front and center in this anthology of novellas that puts new sizzle in romantic suspense. Included are ''Ten Little Idiots,'' an Agatha Christie-inspired tale of passion and mystery by MaryJanice Davidson; ''Single White Dead Guy,'' Amy Garvey's chilly story of death in the backwoods; ''Fast Boys,'' a story of life (and death) in NASCAR's fastlane by Jennifer Apodaca; and ''Three Men and a Body,'' Nancy J. Cohen's trendy tale of the world of reality shows and what someone will do to win. Graphic sex.

Where it's reviewed:
Romantic Times, March 2005, page 99

Other books you might like:
Jaid Black, *One Dark Night*, 2004
    erotic thriller
Alison Kent, *The Samms Agenda*, 2004
    passion and intrigue
Shannon McKenna, *Standing in the Shadows*, 2003
    dark erotic mystery
Nancy Warren, *Drive Me Crazy*, 2004

303

JUSTINE DAVIS (Pseudonym of Janice Davis Smith)

Second-Chance Hero

(New York: Silhouette, 2005)

Story type: Contemporary; Romantic Suspense
Subject(s): Construction; Crime and Criminals; Parent and Child
Major character(s): Grace O'Conner, Businesswoman (construction project manager); John Draven, Security Officer (chief of security); Marilyn ''Marly'' O'Conner, Teenager
Time period(s): 2000s
Locale(s): Belize

Summary: When John Draven, Redstone Inc.'s Chief of Security, arrives in Belize to investigate the sabotage threatening the airstrip Redstone is building there, he never expects the construction project manager would be Grace O'Conner. The last time John saw Grace he was pulling her injured body out of an earthquake site in Turkey, and he is pretty certain he is the last person Grace would ever want to see again. As the incidents of sabotage continue, John realizes he is being given another chance to protect Grace, and he isn't about to let anyone or anything hurt her again.

Where it's reviewed:
Romantic Times, March 2005, page 117

Other books by the same author:
In His Sights, 2004
Midnight Seduction, 2004
Proof, 2004
One of These Nights, 2003
Avenging Angel, 2002

Other books you might like:
Suzanne Brockmann, *Night Watch*, 2003
Melissa James, *Her Galahad*, 2002
Virginia Kantra, *All a Man Can Ask*, 2003
Susan Vaughan, *Guarding Laura*, 2004
Ruth Wind, *Born Brave*, 2001

304

GERALYN DAWSON (Pseudonym of Geralyn Dawson Williams)

Her Bodyguard

(Don Mills, Ontario: HQN, 2005)

Story type: Historical/American West
Series: Bad Luck Brides
Subject(s): Humor; Love; Legends
Major character(s): Mari McBride, Store Owner (sweet shop); Luke Garrett, Saloon Keeper/Owner (wealthy), Outlaw (former)
Time period(s): 1890s (1890)
Locale(s): Fort Worth, Texas

Summary: Although Mari McBride doesn't believe in fortune telling and magic, when a strange Scottish seeress tells her and her two sisters, Emma and Kat, (the McBride Menaces) that they are the chosen ones to end the Curse of the Clan McBride, she can't help but wonder, just a bit, if there is something to it. She knows it's true when things start to fall apart as one of her sisters disappears with the brother of the highly attractive and dangerous Luke Garrett and the pair of them set off on a lively chase to find them. Fast-paced action, sexual tension, and just plain fun are hallmarks of Dawson's stories.

Where it's reviewed:
Romantic Times, June 2005, page 54

Other books by the same author:
The Bad Luck Wedding Night, 2001
Simmer All Night, 1999
The Bad Luck Wedding Cake, 1998
The Wedding Ransom, 1998
The Bad Luck Wedding Dress, 1996

Other books you might like:
Lori Copeland, *Marrying Walker McKay*, 2000
Millie Criswell, *Sweet Laurel*, 1996
Susan Kay Law, *The Bad Man's Bride*, 2001
Pamela Morsi, *Garters*, 1992
Pamela Morsi, *Sealed with a Kiss*, 1998

305

CLAIRE DELACROIX

The Beauty Bride

(New York: Warner, 2005)

Story type: Historical/Medieval; Historical/Fantasy
Series: Jewels of Kinfairlie. Book 1
Subject(s): Marriage
Major character(s): Lady Madeline Lammergeier, Noble-woman; Rhys FitzHenry, Warrior
Time period(s): 15th century (1421)
Locale(s): Scotland

Summary: Frustrated by mounting debts and the need to see his five sisters suitably wed, the new Laird of Kinfairlie auctions off the hand of the eldest, Lady Madeline, to her shock and dismay. Madeline is no biddable miss, and when Rhys FitzHenry, a hardened warrior charged with treason, makes the winning bid, she flees before the nuptials can take place, with unexpected results. A wicked, mischievous fairy complicates things as she tangles the lives of the characters in this fascinating tale that is the first in a projected series.

Where it's reviewed:
Rendezvous, December 2004, page 20
Romantic Times, January 2005, page 37

Other books by the same author:
The Rose Red Bride, 2005 (Jewels of Kinfairlie. Book 2)

Other books you might like:
Shari Anton, *The Conqueror*, 2000
    Knights of the Black Rose. Book 2
Catherine Coulter, *The Penwyth Curse*, 2003
Samantha James, *A Promise Given*, 1998
Johanna Lindsey, *Joining*, 1999
Anne Stuart, *Lord of Danger*, 1997
    darker

306

CHRISTINA DODD

Close to You

(New York: Pocket Star, 2005)

Story type: Contemporary; Romantic Suspense
Series: Prescott Siblings. Book 3
Subject(s): Scandal; Brothers and Sisters; Orphans
Major character(s): Kate Montgomery, Journalist (television); Teague Ramos, Security Officer (security expert)
Time period(s): 2000s
Locale(s): Austin, Texas

Summary: When TV journalist Kate Montgomery ends up with a plum job covering the political beat in Austin, Texas, she has no idea as to her real identity or the reason she has been given the job. Someone dangerous wants her nearby; and when she finds herself being stalked, the TV studio hires attractive security expert Teague Ramos to protect her. While her life may be a little safer, her heart is definitely in jeopardy. This fast-paced thriller solves the mystery of the Prescott siblings' separation and nicely ties up the loose ends from the

previous volumes in this trilogy, in addition to providing a satisfactory stand-alone love story.

Where it's reviewed:
Romantic Times, April 2005, page 113

Other books by the same author:
Almost Like Being in Love, 2004 (Prescott Siblings. Book 2)
Just the Way You Are, 2003 (Prescott Siblings. Book 1)
Scandalous Again, 2003 (Changing Places. Book 1)
One Kiss from You, 2003 (Changing Places. Book 2)
Rules of Attraction, 2001 (Governess Brides. Book 3)

Other books you might like:
Mary Lynn Baxter, *His Touch*, 2003
    bodyguards, politics
Jasmine Cresswell, *Secret Sins*, 1997
    lies, adoption, chilling story
Dee Davis, *Dark of the Night*, 2002
Andrea Kane, *No Way Out*, 2002
Dinah McCall, *Bloodlines*, 2005
    family issues, deadly secrets

307

TINA DONAHUE (Pseudonym of Darlene Zambruski)

Take My Breath Away

(New York: Kensington, 2005)

Story type: Contemporary
Subject(s): Islands; Writing; Survival
Major character(s): Ariel Leigh, Consultant, Adventurer; Cole Ryder, Writer, Military Personnel (former)
Time period(s): 2000s
Locale(s): Isla de Delicia, Tropical Island

Summary: Ariel Leigh, adventurer and helicopter pilot, has been asked by her rich uncle to fly to his private island and consult on a movie script. Cole Ryder, ex-Marine turned scriptwriter, disagrees with Ariel's changes, which include the sex of the main character. To prove the realism of her edits, the two of them go out into the jungle and follow the survival script. They know they can survive a capricious Mother Nature, but neither one of them knows if they'll survive her uncle's reverse psychology matchmaking.

Where it's reviewed:
Booklist, April 15, 2005, page 1436
Romantic Times, May 2005, page 113

Other books by the same author:
Wicked Women on Top, 2005 (anthology)
Irish Eyes, 2002 (anthology)

Other books you might like:
Beverly Brandt, *True North*, 2003
Lori Foster, *Unexpected*, 2003
Connie Lane, *Dirty Little Lies*, 2004
Lori Wilde, *Mission: Irresistible*, 2005
Sherryl Woods, *Along Came Trouble*, 2002

308

TINA DONAHUE
JEN NICHOLAS, Co-Author
JORDAN SUMMERS, Co-Author

Wicked Women on Top

(New York: Brava, 2005)

Story type: Contemporary
Subject(s): Sexual Behavior; Success
Time period(s): 2000s
Locale(s): United States

Summary: In these three super sexy novellas, the heroines know that the place for any woman, wicked or not, is on top. Included are ''Let the Games Begin,'' Tina Donahue's racy tale of a brainy teenager who grew up in a most amazing way and is out to get the man she wants, Las Vegas style; ''Not Another Fairy Tale,'' Jen Nicholas' funny story of a romance writer who needs a happy ending; and ''Private Investigations,'' Jordan Summers' lively tale of an inept PI who ends up being caught by the man she's always wanted. Graphic sex.

Where it's reviewed:
Romantic Times, February 2005, page 103

Other books you might like:
MaryJanice Davidson, *Wicked Women Whodunit*, 2005
    erotic anthology
Suzanne Forster, *All through the Night*, 2001
    erotic anthology
Lori Foster, *Bad Boys on Board*, 2003
    erotic anthology
Erin McCarthy, *Bad Boys over Easy*, 2005
Shannon McKenna, *Bad Boys Next Exit*, 2004
    erotic anthology

309

SHANNON DRAKE (Pseudonym of Heather Graham Pozzessere)

Wicked

(Don Mills, Ontario: HQN, 2005)

Story type: Historical/Victorian; Gothic
Subject(s): Identity, Concealed; Trust; Murder
Major character(s): Camille Montgomery, Scholar (Egyptology), Museum Curator (assistant, British Museum); Brian Stirling, Nobleman (Earl of Carlyle), Scholar (Egyptology)
Time period(s): 19th century
Locale(s): England

Summary: Camille Montgomery goes to Carlyle Castle to retrieve her irresponsible guardian who was injured while trespassing on the castle grounds. The Earl of Carlyle, a reclusive man who wears a beast-like leather mask, sees his opportunity to use her and her position at the British Museum to discover the identity of the people who killed his parents years earlier on a archaeological dig in Egypt. They strike a bargain—he won't prosecute her guardian, if she will cooperate and help him re-enter society and the archaeological world

once again. Romance follows, but so does deadly danger, in this dark Beauty and the Beast tale with a gothic touch.

Where it's reviewed:
Romantic Times, April 2005, page 45

Other books by the same author:
When We Touch, 2004
The Awakening, 2003
The Lion in Glory, 2003
Knight Triumphant, 2002
Realm of Shadows, 2002

Other books you might like:
Gabriella Anderson, *Yours Always*, 2004
    Victorian mystery
Susan Carroll, *The Bride Finder*, 1998
    Beauty and the Beast theme
Lynn Kerstan, *The Golden Leopard*, 2002
JoAnn Power, *Treasures*, 1996
Susan Sizemore, *The Price of Passion*, 2001

310

LAURA DREWRY

Here Comes the Bride

(New York: Zebra, 2005)

Story type: Historical/American West
Subject(s): Ranch Life; American West
Major character(s): Tess Kinley, Gentlewoman (Bostonian), Runaway; Gabriel Calloway, Rancher
Time period(s): 1880s (1885)
Locale(s): Porter Creek, Montana (El Cielo Ranch)

Summary: When a bizarre set of circumstances lands idealistic, gently raised Tess Kinley in a bed on Gabe Calloway's Montana ranch, she is determined to convince him that she needs to stay and fulfill her dreams of living a real life, instead of the superficial one facing her in Boston. Gabe, of course, sees things differently, but he can't help but being attracted to the fiery Tess. Funny, sensual, and sassy.

Where it's reviewed:
Romantic Times, May 2005, page 43

Other books you might like:
Millie Criswell, *The Marrying Man*, 2000
Millie Criswell, *True Love*, 1999
Maureen McKade, *A Dime Novel Hero*, 1998
Maggie Osborne, *The Brides of Bowie Stone*, 1994
Lisa Plumley, *The Outlaw*, 1999

311

CASSIE EDWARDS

Silver Feather

(New York: Signet, 2005)

Story type: Historical/American West; Multicultural
Subject(s): Cultural Conflict; Racism; Native Americans
Major character(s): Diana Turner, Imposter (disguised as a man), Driver (stagecoach); Silver Feather, Indian (Choctaw)

Time period(s): 1810s (1814); 1820s (1825)
Locale(s): Mississippi Valley

Summary: As a young girl, Diana falls in love with Silver Feather, a Choctaw boy, but when his family is brutally murdered, Silver Feather leaves to avoid being killed himself. Years later, Diana has become a stagecoach driver, posing as a man, and ends up being captured by Silver Feather during a holdup. The results are predictably romantic.

Other books by the same author:
Proud Eagle, 2004
Wind Walker, 2004
Night Wolf, 2003
White Fire, 1997
Wild Splendor, 1993

Other books you might like:
Madeline Baker, *Lakota Legacy*, 2003
    anthology
Michael Blake, *Dances with Wolves*, 1988
Genell Dellin, *Cherokee Warriors: The Loner*, 2003
Kathleen Harrington, *Cherish the Dream*, 1990
Karen Kay, *Soaring Eagle's Embrace*, 2003

312

JANET EVANOVICH
CHARLOTTE HUGHES, Co-Author

Full Bloom

(New York: St. Martin's Paperbacks, 2005)

Story type: Contemporary; Humor
Subject(s): Humor; Identity, Concealed; Ghosts
Major character(s): Annie Fortenberry, Innkeeper, Widow(er); Wes Bridges, Investigator, Imposter
Time period(s): 2000s
Locale(s): Beaumont, South Carolina

Summary: Wes Bridges has been hired by Charles Fortenberry's mother to look into his disappearance. Posing as a photographer, he checks into the Peach Tree Bread and Breakfast, which happens to be owned by Annie Fortenberry, Charles' wife. Things heat up when Charles' body is found in the garden, but Wes knows in his heart that Annie's not the murderer, and the guilty party could be anyone from the resident psychic to the aging ballerina. Murder, mayhem, and madcap merriment fill the pages of this entertaining novel.

Where it's reviewed:
Booklist, March 15, 2005, page 1272
Romantic Times, April 2005, page 99

Other books by the same author:
Full Blast, 2004
Full Speed, 2003
Full Tilt, 2003
Full House, 2002

Other books you might like:
Emily Carmichael, *Diamond in the Ruff*, 1999
Rachel Gibson, *Truly, Madly Yours*, 1999
Pam McCutcheon, *Her Favorite Husband*, 2004
Lisa Plumley, *Reconsidering Riley*, 2002
Pat White, *Got a Hold on You*, 2003

313

CHRISTINE FEEHAN

Dark Secret

(New York: Jove, 2005)

Story type: Contemporary/Fantasy; Gothic
Series: Dark
Subject(s): Vampires; Paranormal; Family Relations
Major character(s): Colby Jansen, Rancher, Guardian (of her stepsiblings); Rafael De La Cruz, Vampire
Time period(s): 2000s
Locale(s): United States

Summary: Determined to save the family ranch and provide a home for her stepbrother and sister, Colby is furious when the wealthy Chevez family tries to get custody of the children. After all, they had disowned their brother, the children's father, years earlier when he married against their will. The Chevezes have enlisted Carpathian aid in the form of Rafael De La Cruz and his brother, and Colby has her work cut out for her—especially once Rafael sees Colby and realizes that she is to be his lifemate. This entry in Feehan's Dark series of Carpathian vampire tales is the second in an internal five story set about the South American brothers.

Where it's reviewed:
Library Journal, January 2005, page 91
Romantic Times, February 2005, page 110

Other books by the same author:
Dark Melody, 2003 (Dark series)
Dark Symphony, 2003 (Dark series)
Dark Guardian, 2002 (Dark series)
Dark Fire, 2001 (Dark series)
The Scarletti Curse, 2001

Other books you might like:
Amanda Ashley, *After Sundown*, 2003
Amanda Ashley, *Night's Kiss*, 2005
Wendy Haley, *This Dark Paradise*, 1994
Sherrilyn Kenyon, *Fantasy Lover*, 2002

314

CHRISTINE FEEHAN

Oceans of Fire

(New York: Jove, 2005)

Story type: Contemporary/Fantasy; Paranormal
Series: Drake Sisters. Book 2
Subject(s): Magic; Paranormal; Animals/Dolphins
Major character(s): Abigail Drake, Scientist (marine biologist), Witch; Aleksandr Volstov, Police Officer (Interpol agent)
Time period(s): 2000s
Locale(s): Sea Haven, California

Summary: Returning from a swim with the dolphins she has been studying, marine biologist Abigail Drake witnesses a murder. She then comes face to face with Interpol agent Aleksandr Volstov, the man whose partner has just been killed and the man Abbey has been trying to get over for four years. Fast-paced action involving stolen Russian antiquities

and the Russian Mafia drive the plot of this intense, but magically romantic, thriller that sees the third Drake sister find love, purpose, and healing as she and Alek finally come to terms with the past. Follows ''Magic in the Wind,'' a short story originally published in the anthology *Lover Beware*, and *The Twilight Before Christmas*.

Where it's reviewed:
Romantic Times, June 2005, page 133

Other books by the same author:
Mind Game, 2004 (Ghostwalker. Book 2)
Wild Rain, 2004
Lover Beware, 2003 (anthology with linked story)
Shadow Game, 2003 (Ghostwalker. Book 1)
The Twilight before Christmas, 2003 (Drake Sisters. Book 1)

Other books you might like:
Mary Jo Putney, *Kiss of Fate*, 2004
    another gifted family
Patricia Rice, *The Magic Series*, 2000-
    family of gifted women
Nora Roberts, *Dance upon the Air*, 2001
    witches and magic
Nora Roberts, *Face the Fire*, 2002
    witches and magic
Deborah Smith, *Alice at Heart*, 2002
    merfolk, magic, and the sea

315

JO ANN FERGUSON
CYNTHIA BAILEY PRATT, Co-Author
VALERIE KING, Co-Author

Valentine Kittens
(New York: Zebra, 2005)

Story type: Anthology; Regency
Subject(s): Animals/Cats; Holidays
Time period(s): 1800s
Locale(s): England

Summary: Mischievous kittens play matchmaker in this charming collection of three Regency novellas. In Jo Ann Ferguson's ''Belling the Kitten,'' Jason Farraday is hoping to escape his memories of war in the quiet countryside, but instead he finds his solitude interrupted by Amaris Woodward and a litter of spirited kittens. While trying to find good homes for some kittens, Anne Cassington encounters Lord Marecham, the mysterious stranger Anne kissed just a few weeks before in ''A Tangle of Kittens'' by Valerie King. A birthday present in the form of a stray kitten helps give a married couple bored with their relationship another chance at a happily ever after ending in Cynthia Pratt's ''The Birthday Kitten.''

Where it's reviewed:
Romantic Times, January 2005, page 106

Other books by the same author:
A Valentine Waltz, 2004

Other books you might like:
Janice Bennett, *Summer Kittens*, 2002
Shannon Donnelly, *My Sweet Valentine*, 2002

Pamela Tanner Girard, *A Valentine Bouquet*, 1997
Victoria Hinshaw, *My Only Valentine*, 2003

316

JO ANN FERGUSON
ALICE HOLDEN, Co-Author
MELYNDA BETH SKINNER, Co-Author

Wedding Day Kittens
(New York: Zebra, 2005)

Story type: Regency; Anthology
Subject(s): Weddings; Animals/Cats
Time period(s): 1810s
Locale(s): England

Summary: This light, charming trilogy of novellas by three popular Regency authors focuses on cats and kittens, and the roles they play in the romantic, matrimonial doings of three delightful couples. ''Something Old, Something Mew'' is Jo Ann Ferguson's heartwarming tale of a noble lord who reconnects with his former tutor's daughter while home for his sister's wedding. Alice Holden's lively tale ''The Perfect Bride'' concerns a reluctant groom who almost marries the wrong woman. ''Up to Scratch'' by Melynda Beth Skinner is a paranormal tale of an unlikely pair whose companion cats take matters into their own hands to get their owners together.

Where it's reviewed:
Romantic Times, May 2005, page 30

Other books you might like:
Donna Bell, *Magical Kittens*, 2000
    Regency anthology
Janice Bennett, *Autumn Kittens*, 2001
    Regency anthology
Cindy Holbrook, *The Missing Grooms*, 2001
Miranda Jarrett, *Starlight*, 2000
    magic and kittens, Georgian-style
Judith A. Lansdowne, *Stocking Stuffers*, 2000
    a Christmas kitten

317

ALICIA FIELDS

Love Underground
(New York: Signet Eclipse, 2005)

Story type: Historical/Pre-history; Historical/Fantasy
Series: Goddesses. Book 1
Subject(s): Mythology
Major character(s): Persephone, Deity (goddess); Hades, Deity (god of the underworld)
Time period(s): Indeterminate Past
Locale(s): Greece; Hell

Summary: Beautiful Persephone leads a sheltered life because most of the young men are kept at bay by her formidable mother, the goddess Demeter. However, when Persephone is kidnapped by Hades and taken to the lower realms, she learns about seduction, romance, and, eventually, love.

Other books by the same author:
Fatal Attraction: Aphrodite's Tale, 2005 (The Goddesses. Book 2)

Other books you might like:
Marilyn Campbell, *Stolen Dreams*, 1994
　　science fiction with a mythical twist
P.C. Cast, *Goddess of Spring*, 2004
　　Goddess Summoning. Book 3
P.C. Cast, *Goddess of the Sea*, 2003
　　Goddess Summoning. Book 2
Deborah Smith, *Alice at Heart*, 2002
　　Waterlilies. Book 1
Evelyn Vaughn, *A.K.A. Goddess*, 2004

318

LORI FOSTER

Jamie
(New York: Zebra, 2005)

Story type: Contemporary; Paranormal
Series: Visitation. Book 5
Subject(s): Psychic Powers; Hermits; Extrasensory Perception
Major character(s): Faith Owen, Single Parent; Jamie Creed, Psychic, Recluse
Time period(s): 2000s
Locale(s): Visitation, North Carolina

Summary: Jamie Creed is a hermit. His exile is self-imposed—his life as a psychic has shown him that it's dangerous to get close to people. Faith Owen is the single mother of a psychic child. She knows she has to hook up with Jamie to protect her daughter. Evil forces are at work that want Jamie for his abilities, and, whether he likes it or not, he needs his friends in Visitation for help.

Other books by the same author:
Just a Hint—Clint, 2004 (Visitation. Book 4)
The Secret Life of Bryan, 2004 (Visitation. Book 2)
When Bruce Met Cyn..., 2004 (Visitation. Book 3)
Say No to Joe?, 2003 (Visitation. Book 1)
Unexpected, 2003

Other books you might like:
Sandra Hill, *Love Potion*, 1995
Linda Howard, *Dream Man*, 1995
Jayne Ann Krentz, *Absolutely, Positively*, 1996
Dolores Stewart Riccio, *Circle of Five*, 2003
Christina Skye, *The Perfect Gift*, 1999

319

LORI FOSTER
DONNA KAUFFMAN, Co-Author
JILL SHALVIS, Co-Author

Men of Courage II
(Toronto: Harlequin, 2005)

Story type: Contemporary
Subject(s): Disasters
Time period(s): 2000s
Locale(s): Ohio

Summary: This trio of fast-paced, sensual stories focuses on the effects of a tornado on the lives of three courageous heroes (a military officer, a storm chaser, and a rescue expert) and the women who love them. Included are ''An Honorable Man'' by Lori Foster, ''Blown Away'' by Donna Kauffman, and ''Perilous Waters'' by Jill Shalvis.

Where it's reviewed:
Romantic Times, February 2005, page 97

Other books you might like:
Georgia Bockoven, *Disguised Blessing*, 2004
　　tragedy and relationships
Suzanne Brockmann, *Over the Edge*, 2001
　　military adventure
Amy J. Fetzer, *Tell It to the Marines*, 2004
Cathie Linz, *Her Millionnaire Marine*, 2004

320

LORI FOSTER
LUCY MONROE, Co-Author
DIANNE CASTELL, Co-Author

Star Quality
(New York: Brava, 2005)

Story type: Contemporary/Fantasy; Anthology
Subject(s): Magic; Romance; Fantasy
Time period(s): 2000s
Locale(s): Delicious, Ohio

Summary: Linked by the magical effects of the moon and set in the small town of Delicious, Ohio, this lively trilogy of sexually explicit stories includes ''Once in a Blue Moon,'' Lori Foster's erotic romp featuring a hero who, courtesy of a blue moon, reads the sexy thoughts of a very proper bookstore owner and decides to make them a reality; ''Moon Magnetism,'' Lucy Monroe's funny story of a woman who becomes magnetic during the full moon and wreaks havoc on all things electronic, to the fascination of her technology-oriented boss; and ''Moonstruck,'' Dianne Castell's story of a hero and heroine who are brought together by blue moon magic and then wonder just where it will all lead.

Where it's reviewed:
Rendezvous, April 2005, page 17
Romantic Times, May 2005, page 120

Other books you might like:
Dianne Castell, *A Cowboy and a Kiss*, 2004
Sherrilyn Kenyon, *What Dreams May Come*, 2005
　　magical anthology
Erin McCarthy, *Bad Boys over Easy*, 2005
　　humor, magic, and sex
Lucy Monroe, *Come Up and See Me Sometime*, 2005
Nora Roberts, *Moon Shadows*, 2004
　　fantasy anthology

321

AMY GARVEY

Murder in the Hamptons

(New York: Brava, 2005)

Story type: Contemporary; Romantic Suspense
Series: Wicked Women Whodunit
Subject(s): Murder; Mystery
Major character(s): Maggie Harding, Interior Decorator; Tyler Brody, Hotel Owner
Time period(s): 2000s
Locale(s): Long Island, New York (the Hamptons)

Summary: When interior designer Maggie Harding runs into the sexy guy she'd had a weekend fling with in Florida five years ago at a posh party in the Hamptons, the stage is set for a sizzling reunion—and then someone ends up dead and things take a more sinister turn. Hollywood celebrities, upscale lifestyles, and hot sex are part of this fast-paced romance that is part of the Wicked Women Whodunit series.

Where it's reviewed:
Romantic Times, June 2005, page 125

Other books you might like:
Gemma Bruce, *Who's Been Sleeping in My Bed?*, 2005
Susanna Carr, *Confessions of a Wicked Woman*, 2005
MaryJanice Davidson, *How to Be a Wicked Woman*, 2004
    erotic anthology
MaryJanice Davidson, *Wicked Women Whodunit*, 2005
    erotic mystery anthology
Tina Donahue, *Wicked Women on Top*, 2005
    erotic mystery anthology

322

MELANIE GEORGE

Naughty or Nice

(New York: Pocket, 2004)

Story type: Historical; Holiday Themes
Series: Pleasure Seekers. Book 2
Subject(s): Christmas; Identity, Concealed
Major character(s): Lady Francine ''Fancy'' Fitz Hugh, Noblewoman, Ward; Lucien Kendall, Nobleman, Guardian
Time period(s): 19th century
Locale(s): Cornwall, England (Moors End); London, England

Summary: Lucien Kendall arrives in Cornwall to assume the guardianship of the sister of one of his officers who was killed. He is stunned to find that his ward, Lady Francine Fitz Hugh, bears a remarkable resemblance to a young thief he encountered—and who knocked him out and also escaped a later more amorous encounter—on his way to her home. Naturally, Fancy had a reason for her disguise—she was looking for evidence to save her friend from a forced marriage; and although Lucien is not looking forward to being the hellion's guardian, he is eventually drawn into Fancy's plans—and, in the process, is attracted to her, as well. There's lots of sex and adventure in this, the second in George's Pleasure Seekers series.

Where it's reviewed:
Romantic Times, December 2004, page 37

Other books by the same author:
The Pleasure Seekers, 2003 (Pleasure Seekers. Book 1)
The Art of Seduction, 2002
The Mating Game, 2002
The Devil's Due, 2001
The Handsome Devil, 2001

Other books you might like:
Connie Brockway, *All through the Night*, 1997
Emma Holly, *Beyond Innocence*, 2001
    highly sensual
Nicole Jordan, *The Seduction*, 2000
Stephanie Laurens, *A Rake's Vow*, 1998
    Cynster. Book 2
Amanda Quick, *Mistress*, 1994

323

PATRICIA GRASSO

Seducing the Prince

(New York: Zebra, 2005)

Story type: Historical/Regency
Subject(s): Scandal; Seduction; Murder
Major character(s): Regina Bradford, Noblewoman (Countess of Langley), Writer (would-be novelist); Viktor Kazanov, Royalty (prince)
Time period(s): 1820s (1821)
Locale(s): London, England

Summary: Trapped in unhappy marriages, Regina Bradford and Viktor Kazanov become friends; and although they might wish it, they know that is all they will ever be. However, when their respective spouses are caught together and then are both murdered, it is Viktor who is accused and must stand trial. More than simple jealousy is at work, and it isn't long before Viktor and Regina realize that something far more dangerous is in the mix and that Regina may be a target as well. Sensual.

Where it's reviewed:
Romantic Times, April 2005, page 47

Other books by the same author:
To Catch a Countess, 2004 (Douglas Sisters. Book 3)
To Love a Princess, 2004
To Charm a Prince, 2003 (Douglas Sisters. Book 2)
To Tame an Angel, 2002 (Douglas Sisters. Book 1)
Violets in the Snow, 1998

Other books you might like:
Jane Ashford, *Bride to Be*, 1999
Adrienne Basso, *To Protect an Heiress*, 2002
Stephanie Laurens, *All about Love*, 2002
Stephanie Laurens, *A Secret Love*, 2000
Kat Martin, *Silk and Steel*, 2000
    greedy relatives

324

SHIRLEY HAILSTOCK

You Made Me Love You
(New York: Dafina, 2005)

Story type: Contemporary; Multicultural
Subject(s): African Americans; Federal Witness Security Program; Secrets
Major character(s): Rachel Wells, Young Woman; Samuel Hairston, Police Officer (police chief), Lawyer
Time period(s): 2000s
Locale(s): Lake Como, New York

Summary: Whisked into the Federal Witness Protection Program at the age of 17 when her father testifies against a mob boss, Rachel Wells returns home to Lake Como to regain her real life after the deaths of her parents and the criminals involved. Rachel doesn't realize that she is being set up. As she tries to come to terms with her past and start a new life— one that seems to involve the local police chief, in spite of her intentions to the contrary—the danger, in the form of an avenging grandson, comes closer with each day. Passion, suspense, and danger enhance a story that will appeal far beyond its target African-American audience.

Where it's reviewed:
Romantic Times, April 2005, page 102

Other books by the same author:
More than Gold, 2000
Opposites Attract, 1999
Mirror Image, 1998
White Diamonds, 1996 (reprinted in 2001)
Whispers of Love, 1994

Other books you might like:
Rochelle Alers, *Just Before Dawn*, 2000
Rochelle Alers, *No Compromise*, 2002
Dinah McCall, *Tallchief*, 1997
   more FWPP aftermath
Sharon Sala, *Dark Water*, 2002
Tracey Tillis, *Nightwatcher*, 1995

325

LORI HANDELAND

Dark Moon
(New York: St. Martin's Paperbacks, 2005)

Story type: Contemporary/Fantasy; Paranormal
Series: Moon. Book 3
Subject(s): Werewolves; Mystery
Major character(s): Elise Hanover, Scientist (virologist), Werewolf; Dominic "Nic" Franklin, FBI Agent, Lawyer
Time period(s): 2000s
Locale(s): Montana; Fairhaven, Wisconsin

Summary: Virologist and werewolf, Dr. Elise Hanover is determined to find a cure for the condition that afflicts her and many others, lycanthropy. However, when her college love, FBI agent Nic Franklin suddenly appears in her Montana laboratory with questions about mysteriously missing persons, Elise is torn between her need to keep her secret hidden and the realization that she still loves Nic. Then a suspicious explosion destroys her lab and research, along with the precious antidote she needs during each full moon. Before long Elise realizes that not only is her life in danger, but her heart is at risk, as well. Chilling, sexy, and laced with Objibwe lore and occasional humor.

Where it's reviewed:
Romantic Times, July 2005, page 108

Other books by the same author:
Hunter's Moon, 2005 (Moon. Book 2)
Blue Moon, 2004 (Moon. Book 1)
The Husband Quest, 2004
Dreams of an Eagle, 1998
Full Moon Dreams, 1996

Other books you might like:
Christine Feehan, *Oceans of Fire*, 2005
   witches
Sherrilyn Kenyon, *Stroke of Midnight*, 2004
   paranormal anthology
Susan Krinard, *Prince of Shadows*, 1996
   werewolves
Rebecca York, *Witching Moon*, 2003
   werewolves

326

KAREN HARPER

Dark Angel
(Don Mills, Ontario: MIRA, 2005)

Story type: Contemporary; Romantic Suspense
Series: Maplecreek. Book 3
Subject(s): Amish; Genetic Disease; Genetic Research
Major character(s): Leah Kurtz, Teacher (former), Single Parent (of an adopted baby); Mark Morelli, Doctor (pediatrician), Scientist (geneticist)
Time period(s): 2000s
Locale(s): Maplecreek, Ohio

Summary: When Leah Kurtz agrees to adopt the infant daughter of her best friend who is dying of a genetic disease that afflicts the Amish, her life changes rather wonderfully. However, when she agrees to help pediatrician Mark Morelli, an English doctor who has come to Maplecreek to research some of the genetic diseases that affect the Amish, her life changes in ways she never expected. Danger, greed, and kidnapping are part of this chilling tale.

Where it's reviewed:
Romantic Times, June 2005, page 121

Other books by the same author:
Dark Harvest, 2004 (Maplecreek. Book 2)
The Baby Farm, 1999
The Empty Cradle, 1998
Dark Road Home, 1996 (Maplecreek. Book 1)
Wings of the Morning, 1993

Other books you might like:
Annette Blair, *The Butterfly Garden*, 2005
   historical Amish
Annette Blair, *Thee I Love*, 1999

Wanda E. Brunstetter, *The Storekeeper's Daughter*, 2005
more religious
Tami Hoag, *Still Waters*, 1992
Jodi Picoult, *Plain Truth*, 2001

327

MELINDA RUCKER HAYNES

Essence of Trust

(Waterville, Maine: Five Star, 2005)

Story type: Contemporary/Fantasy; Paranormal
Subject(s): Good and Evil; Trust; Fantasy
Major character(s): Rian Farsante, Psychic (healer), Psychologist; Jonathan Spencer, Psychic; Ian Stoddard, Psychic (spymaster)
Time period(s): 2000s
Locale(s): United States

Summary: When her godson Marty's parents are attacked and left for dead and the boy is abducted by a power-driven psychic, Rian Farsante reluctantly joins forces with her former lover, Jonathan Spencer, to rescue Marty. Violent, fast-paced action highlights this story that combines Egyptian mythology, a pair of powerful swords, and supernatural abilities with compelling romance and an intriguing plot.

Other books by the same author:
Breach of Trust, 2004
Eternal Trust, 2003
Ghostly Acts, 2001
A Wing and a Kiss, 2000
The Haunting of Josh Weston, 2000

Other books you might like:
Jill Jones, *Circle of the Lily*, 1998
Maggie Shayne, *Destiny*, 2001
Maggie Shayne, *Infinity*, 1999
Patricia Simpson, *The Dark Lord*, 2004
Anne Stuart, *Moon-Rise*, 1996

328

EMILY HENDRICKSON (Pseudonym of Doris Emily Hendrickson)

My Lady Faire

(New York: Signet, 2005)

Story type: Regency
Subject(s): Artists and Art; Children; Fairies
Major character(s): Claudia Fairfax, Gentlewoman, Widow(er); Noel Clifford, Nobleman (Lord Hawke)
Time period(s): 1810s (1817-1818)
Locale(s): England

Summary: While Lady Claudia Fairfax might have to share guardianship of her young stepson Edward with Noel Clifford, Lord Hawke, it doesn't mean she always agrees with the bossy nobleman as to what is best for the child. So when Noel tries to convince Claudia to accept the wisdom of his plans for Edward, she takes special delight in doing her best to thwart him. Then much to Claudia's surprise she discovers not only

has Noel been planning Edward's life, he has some ideas about her future as well!

Where it's reviewed:
Booklist, March 15, 2005, page 1272
Romantic Times, March 2005, page 125

Other books by the same author:
Tabitha's Tangle, 2004
The Madcap Heiress, 2004
Drusilla's Downfall, 2003
Pursuing Priscilla, 2003
Lord Nick's Folly, 2002

Other books you might like:
Louise Bergin, *A Worthy Opponent*, 2004
Sandra Heath, *Lavender Blue*, 2003
Valerie King, *A Rogue's Deception*, 2002
Barbara Metzger, *An Enchanted Affair*, 1996
Patricia Oliver, *The Lady in Gray*, 1999

329

PATTI CALLAHAN HENRY

Where the River Runs

(New York: Penguin, 2005)

Story type: Contemporary/Mainstream
Subject(s): Guilt; Self-Acceptance; Secrets
Major character(s): Meridy McFadden Dresden, Volunteer (curriculum development); Beau Dresden, Lawyer
Time period(s): 2000s
Locale(s): Atlanta, Georgia; Seaboro, Georgia; Buckhead, Georgia

Summary: Meridy McFadden Dresden's attorney husband, Beau, is busy on a big case, and her son is away at college, so she finds herself with too much free time. When the private school where Meridy's a board member asks her to develop a curriculum on the Gullah, she agrees to go back to her hometown of Seaboro to do the research. Her interviews with her former housekeeper, a Gullah, soon turn into lessons in life, and Meridy knows she has to face the horrible secret of her youth. Beautifully written, this emotionally riveting story is one to savor.

Other books by the same author:
Losing the Moon, 2004 (debut novel)

Other books you might like:
Patricia Gaffney, *Flight Lessons*, 2002
Cassandra King, *The Sunday Wife*, 2002
Mary Alice Monroe, *Skyward*, 2003
also about the Gullah
Kathryn Shay, *After the Fire*, 2003
Susan Wiggs, *The Ocean between Us*, 2004

330

SANDRA HILL

The Red-Hot Cajun

(New York: Warner, 2005)

Story type: Humor; Contemporary

Romance

Series: Cajun. Book 4
Subject(s): Humor; Environmental Problems; Child Abuse
Major character(s): Valerie Breaux, Television Personality, Captive; Rene LeDeux, Lobbyist (former), Environmentalist
Time period(s): 2000s
Locale(s): Bayou Black, Louisiana

Summary: When former environmental lobbyist Rene LeDeux's tree-hugging, aging hippie friends kidnap television celebrity Valerie ''Ice'' Breaux, it's up to him to fix the problem. Bayou bubba Tante Lulu sees Valerie as Rene's soulmate, and with a little help from St. Jude, begins some serious matchmaking. Despite the humor and outrageous cast of characters, the serious subtexts of child abuse and wetlands ecology come though loud and clear.

Where it's reviewed:
Booklist, April 1, 2005, page 1349
Romantic Times, February 2005, page 100

Other books by the same author:
A Tale of Two Vikings, 2004 (Vikings Series 1. Book 7)
The Cajun Cowboy, 2004 (Cajun. Book 3)
Wet and Wild, 2004 (Vikings Series 2. Book 4)
Tall, Dark, and Cajun, 2003 (Cajun. Book 2)
The Very Virile Viking, 2003 (Vikings Series 2. Book 3)

Other books you might like:
Susan Donovan, *Public Displays of Affection*, 2004
Shirley Jump, *The Bride Wore Chocolate*, 2004
Julia London, *Beauty Queen*, 2004
Kathy Love, *Getting What You Want*, 2004
Pat White, *Got a Hold on You*, 2003

331

COLBY HODGE (Pseudonym of Cindy Holby)

Stargazer

(New York: Love Spell, 2005)

Story type: Futuristic; Paranormal
Subject(s): War; Politics; Secrets
Major character(s): Lilly, Royalty (princess), Telepath; Shaun Phoenix, Fugitive, Telepath
Time period(s): Indeterminate Future
Locale(s): Spaceship; Planet—Imaginary (various)

Summary: A woman of noble blood and a condemned prisoner, who are both descended from the telepathic Circe ''witches,'' are forced to to work together in this fast-paced, cleverly crafted story of interplanetary conflict. Psychic powers, political intrigue, and romance are all part of this futuristic debut by an experienced author in other romance subgenres.

Where it's reviewed:
Romantic Times, April 2005, page 108

Other books you might like:
Anne Avery, *Far Star*, 1995
Justine Davis, *Lord of the Storm*, 1994
Justine Davis, *The Sky Pirate*, 1995
Susan Krinard, *Kinsman's Oath*, 2004
Susan Krinard, *Star-Crossed*, 1995

332

FRANCES HOUSDEN

Stranded with a Stranger

(New York: Silhouette, 2005)

Story type: Contemporary; Romantic Suspense
Subject(s): Mountaineering; Sisters
Major character(s): Chelsea Tedman, Linguist; Kurt Jellic, Guide (mountain)
Time period(s): 2000s
Locale(s): Nepal

Summary: Chelsea Tedman believes her sister Atlanta's accidental death while climbing Mount Everest was anything but an accident. In order to retrieve the key her sister carried that can prove their cousin is guilty of embezzling funds from their family company, Chelsea needs a guide to take her up Everest to the place where Atlanta was last seen. The best man for the job is Kurt Jellic, but convincing Kurt to take her to the location proves to be just as difficult for Chelsea as trying to convince herself she isn't interested in Kurt as anything but a guide.

Where it's reviewed:
Romantic Times, March 2005, page 118

Other books by the same author:
Shadows of the Past, 2004
Heartbreak Hero, 2003
Love under Fire, 2002
The Man for Maggie, 2001

Other books you might like:
Cherry Adair, *On Thin Ice*, 2004
Suzanne Brockmann, *Identity: Unknown*, 2000
Linda Howard, *Cry No More*, 2003
Jayne Ann Krentz, *Deep Waters*, 1997
Nora Roberts, *Northern Lights*, 2004

333

HANNAH HOWELL

Highland Conqueror

(New York: Zebra, 2005)

Story type: Historical/Renaissance
Subject(s): Marriage; Greed
Major character(s): Lady Jolene Gerard, Noblewoman; Sigimor Cameron, Warrior (Highlander)
Time period(s): 15th century (1473)
Locale(s): England; Scotland

Summary: When her brother Peter is killed by his greedy kinsman, Lady Jolene knows she must get her young nephew, heir to Drumwich Castle, to safety. She bargains with Sigimor Cameron, a Highlander who had come to help Peter and ended up imprisoned, to help her. Fast-paced adventure, passion, and lively action add to Howell's Highland romance.

Where it's reviewed:
Romantic Times, March 2005, page 33

Other books by the same author:
Highland Warrior, 2004 (Wild Hearts of Scotland. Book 3)

Highland Angel, 2003 (Wild Hearts of Scotland. Book 1)
Highland Groom, 2003 (Wild Hearts of Scotland. Book 2)
Highland Bride, 2002
Highland Hearts, 2002

Other books you might like:
Connie Brockway, *McClairen's Isle: The Passionate One*, 1999
Arnette Lamb, *The Chieftain*, 1996
Ruth Ryan Langan, *The Highlander*, 1994
Patricia Potter, *The Starfinder*, 1998
Amanda Scott, *The Secret Clan: Abducted Heiress*, 1999

334

TESS HUDSON (Pseudonym of Erica Orloff)

Double Down

(Don Mills, Ontario: MIRA, 2005)

Story type: Contemporary; Humor
Subject(s): Humor; Gambling; Sports/Football
Major character(s): Skye McNally, Gambler, Addict (gambling); Mark Shannon, Sports Figure (football player)
Time period(s): 2000s
Locale(s): Las Vegas, Nevada; New York, New York

Summary: Skye McNally, raised by a bookie father, is a compulsive gambler. She attends Gamblers Anonymous meetings with her guardian angel sponsor, T.D. Russell, but has yet to earn her 30-day coin. She lives in Las Vegas, not a good place for a person addicted to gambling. One day, Skye leaves the city, and somewhere in the Nevada desert, meets AWOL NFL star Mark Shannon. It's almost love at first sight, but the footbal commissioner will do anything to break them up. Anything. Full of humorous moments, this book also deals with serious addictions.

Other books you might like:
Kylie Adams, *Fly Me to the Moon*, 2001
Dave Barry, *Tricky Business*, 2002
Katherine Garbera, *Let It Ride*, 2004
Sarah Strohmeyer, *Bubbles a Broad*, 2004
James Swain, *Loaded Dice*, 2004

335

JILLIAN HUNTER (Pseudonym of Maria Hoag)

The Love Affair of an English Lord

(New York: Ivy, 2005)

Story type: Historical/Regency
Series: Boscastle Trilogy. Book 2
Subject(s): Marriage; Scandal; Mystery
Major character(s): Lady Chloe Boscastle, Noblewoman; Dominic Breckland, Nobleman (Viscount Stratfield)
Time period(s): 1810s (1814)
Locale(s): England

Summary: Banished to the country when she is caught kissing a young man in a London park, the bright, slightly wild Lady Chloe Boscastle is prepared for an uneventful few months. That all changes when she discovers the notorious Stratfield Ghost hiding in her closet, wounded, but very much alive.

Having survived the stabbing two weeks ago that was thought to have killed him, Dominic Breckland is determined to find out who wants him dead, and being thought dead is critical to his goal. Can he convince Chloe to keep his secret? Romance, passion, and just plain fun are part of this enjoyable Regency romp.

Where it's reviewed:
Romantic Times, June 2005, page 59

Other books by the same author:
The Seduction of an English Scoundrel, 2005 (Boscastle Trilogy. Book 1)
The Wedding Night of an English Rogue, 2005 (Boscastle Trilogy. Book 3)
Abandon, 2001
Indiscretion, 2000
Delight, 1999

Other books you might like:
Mary Balogh, *Thief of Dreams*, 1998
Jo Beverley, *Secrets of the Night*, 1999
Malloren Chronicles. Book 4
Jo Beverley, *Tempting Fortune*, 1995
Christina Dodd, *A Knight to Remember*, 1997
earlier time period
Suzanne Enoch, *Meet Me at Midnight*, 2000

336

JILLIAN HUNTER (Pseudonym of Maria Hoag)

The Seduction of an English Scoundrel

(New York: Ivy, 2005)

Story type: Historical/Regency
Series: Boscastle Trilogy. Book 1
Subject(s): Marriage; Seduction; Scandal
Major character(s): Lady Jane Welsham, Noblewoman (daughter of an earl); Grayson Boscastle, Nobleman (Marquess of Sedgecroft)
Time period(s): 1810s (1814)
Locale(s): England

Summary: When her long-time friend and fiance, Sir Nigel Boscastle, leaves her standing at the altar, Lady Jane Welsham may be socially ruined but she is thrilled that their joint plan to assure their separate happinesses (his to marry the governess he loves; hers to be free of arranged marriages) has actually succeeded. Her relief is short lived because Grayson Boscastle, the disreputable Marquess of Sedgecroft and head of the Boscastle family, is determined to save the lady's reputation and his family's honor by courting her himself. Of course, his aim to redeem her in the eyes of society soon takes a seductive bent and then the fun begins. Sexy, funny, and cleverly plotted, this is the first in the Boscastle Trilogy.

Where it's reviewed:
Romantic Times, May 2005, page 39

Other books by the same author:
The Love Affair of an English Lord, 2005 (Boscastle Trilogy. Book 2)
The Wedding Night of an English Rogue, 2005 (Boscastle Trilogy. Book 3)
Abandon, 2001

Indiscretion, 2000
Delight, 1999

Other books you might like:
Jo Beverley, *Devilish*, 2000
Nicole Byrd, *Lady in Waiting*, 2002
Christina Dodd, *Scandalous Again*, 2003
Edith Layton, *The Chance*, 2000
Laura Parker, *Notorious*, 2003

337

JILLIAN HUNTER (Pseudonym of Maria Hoag)

The Wedding Night of an English Rogue
(New York: Ivy, 2005)

Story type: Historical/Regency
Series: Boscastle Trilogy. Book 3
Subject(s): Revenge; Spies
Major character(s): Lady Julia Hepworth Whitby, Widow(er), Noblewoman; Lord Heath Boscastle, Military Personnel (lieutenant colonel), Nobleman
Time period(s): 1810s (1814)
Locale(s): England

Summary: When Russell Althorne asks Heath Boscastle to protect his fiancee, Julia Whitby, while he goes in search of a ruthless assassin, he has no idea that Heath and Julia share a brief, but passionate past. Heath owes his life to Russell and can't refuse; and as Heath works to keep Julia safe, the romance between them flares out of control, complicating an already dangerous, difficult situation. An action-packed conclusion to Hunter's Boscastle Trilogy.

Where it's reviewed:
Romantic Times, July 2005, page 31

Other books by the same author:
The Love Affair of an English Lord, 2005 (Boscastle Trilogy. Book 2)
The Seduction of an English Scoundrel, 2005 (Boscastle Trilogy. Book 1)
Abandon, 2001
Indiscretion, 2000
Delight, 1999

Other books you might like:
Jo Beverley, *Secrets of the Night*, 1999
Jo Beverley, *Something Wicked*, 1997
Connie Brockway, *Promise Me Heaven*, 1994
Jo Goodman, *Everything I Wanted*, 2003
Stephanie Laurens, *The Lady Chosen*, 2003

338

MADELINE HUNTER

Lord of Sin
(New York: Bantam, 2005)

Story type: Historical
Subject(s): Art; Inheritance
Major character(s): Bride Cameron, Noblewoman (daughter of an earl); Ewan McLean, Nobleman (Earl of Lyndale)
Time period(s): 19th century

Locale(s): England

Summary: The new Earl of Lyndale, Ewan McLean, has no intention of changing his leisurely ways; but first, he must honor his late uncle's last wishes and see to the welfare of Bride Cameron and her younger sisters. All Bride wants is to be left alone to continue her art engraving business, a fact that intrigues Ewan no end and sets the pace for this lively, passionate romance with more than enough secrets and plot twists to keep things interesting.

Where it's reviewed:
Romantic Times, May 2005, page 44

Other books by the same author:
Lord of a Thousand Nights, 2002
Stealing Heaven, 2002
By Design, 2001
By Arrangement, 2000
By Possession, 2000

Other books you might like:
Melanie George, *Naughty or Nice*, 2004
Sabrina Jeffries, *In the Prince's Bed*, 2004
Sabrina Jeffries, *To Pleasure a Prince*, 2005
Lisa Kleypas, *Secrets of a Summer Night*, 2004
Susan Sizemore, *On a Long Ago Night*, 2000

339

BRENDA JACKSON
JOYLYNN JOSSEL, Co-Author
KAYLA PERRIN, Co-Author
TAMARA SNEED, Co-Author

An All Night Man
(New York: St. Martin's Griffin, 2005)

Story type: Contemporary; Multicultural
Subject(s): African Americans; Romance
Time period(s): 2000s
Locale(s): United States

Summary: This sensual, diverse anthology by some of the genre's favorite authors features African-American heroes and heroines who share a night (in various circumstances) and find unexpected love in the process. Included are ''The Hunter'' by Brenda Jackson, ''Just Wanna Love Ya'' by Joylynn Jossel, ''Never Satisfied'' by Kayla Perrin, and ''Fantasy Man'' by Tamara Sneed.

Where it's reviewed:
Romantic Times, February 2005, page 97

Other books by the same author:
The Best Man, 2003

Other books you might like:
Rochelle Alers, *Island Magic*, 2000 anthology
Carmen Green, *Wine and Roses*, 1999 anthology
Kayla Perrin, *If You Want Me*, 2001
Kayla Perrin, *In an Instant*, 2003

340

HOLLY JACOBS (Pseudonym of Holly Fuhrman)

Pickup Lines

(New York: Avalon, 2005)

Story type: Contemporary; Humor
Subject(s): Humor; Contests; Radio Broadcasting
Major character(s): Mary Rosenthal, Teacher; Ethan Westbrook, Businessman (family pharmacy business)
Time period(s): 2000s
Locale(s): Erie, Pennsylvania

Summary: Radio WLVH, a.k.a. Love Handles, is having a contest, and the prize is a truck. The catch is that the two contestants have to sit in the cab of the truck until one of them gives up. Mary Rosenthal needs a new vehicle since her old car has given up the ghost and she can't afford a new one on a teacher's salary. Ethan Westbrook doesn't need a truck—his family owns a chain of pharmacies. Neither of them is willing to say uncle, and soon, a simple contest becomes a battle of the sexes.

Where it's reviewed:
Booklist, April 1, 2005, page 1349

Other books by the same author:
Once upon a Prince, 2005
Once upon a Princess, 2005
Be My Baby, 2004
Found and Lost, 2004
Dad Today, Groom Tomorrow, 2003

Other books you might like:
Barbara Daly, *You Call This Romance?*, 2002
Rita Herron, *Marry Me, Maddie?*, 2001
Sharon Sala, *Amber by Night*, 2003
Deborah Shelley, *My Favorite Flavor*, 2000
Sherryl Woods, *Ask Anyone*, 2002

341

ELOISA JAMES (Pseudonym of Mary Bly)

Much Ado about You

(New York: Avon, 2005)

Story type: Historical/Regency
Subject(s): Courtship; Sisters
Major character(s): Teresa "Tess" Essex, Gentlewoman; Lucius Felton, Gentleman
Time period(s): 1810s (1816)
Locale(s): England

Summary: Immediately after meeting their new guardian, Rafe Jourdain, Tess Essex knew she would have to take matters into her own hands if she and her three sisters were to have any hope of securing good matches for themselves. Tess begins her matrimonial campaign by encouraging the romantic attentions of Rafe's handsome, titled, and socially connected friend, Garret Langham, the Earl of Mayne. The only problem with Tess' little scheme is that she never expected to meet Rafe's other friend, the sexy and so very improper Lucius Felton.

Where it's reviewed:
Booklist, December 1, 2004, page 640
Publishers Weekly, December 20, 2004, page 42
Romantic Times, January 2005, page 29

Other books by the same author:
A Wild Pursuit, 2004
Your Wicked Ways, 2004
Fool for Love, 2003
Duchess in Love, 2002
Enchanting Pleasures, 2001

Other books you might like:
Mary Balogh, *Slightly Sinful*, 2004
Loretta Chase, *Miss Wonderful*, 2004
Christina Dodd, *One Kiss from You*, 2003
Stephanie Laurens, *The Perfect Lover*, 2003
Amanda Quick, *Seduction*, 1990

342

SABRINA JEFFRIES (Pseudonym of Deborah Gonzales)

One Night with a Prince

(New York: Pocket Star, 2005)

Story type: Historical/Regency
Series: Royal Brotherhood. Book 3
Subject(s): Revenge; Scandal; Seduction
Major character(s): Lady Christabel Sims, Noblewoman (Marchioness of Haversham), Widow(er); Gavin Byrne, Businessman (owner of a gaming club), Bastard Son (of the Prince of Wales)
Time period(s): 1810s (1815)
Locale(s): England

Summary: Shocked and puzzled when he receives word that the prince regent will grant him a barony if he helps Lady Christabel, the Marchioness of Haversham, retrieve some family letters sold by her late husband to pay a gambling debt, wealthy gaming club owner Gavin Byrne agrees. He plans to use the situation to avenge himself and his mother on the father who refused to acknowledge him, the prince regent, himself. The plan, of course, involves much togetherness on the part of Christabel and Byrne, including a pretend romantic relationship that eventually becomes real. Politics, intrigue, and passion set the tone of this lively, funny, adventure that is the third volume of Jeffries' Royal Brotherhood series.

Other books by the same author:
To Pleasure a Prince, 2005 (Royal Brotherhood. Book 2)
In the Prince's Bed, 2004 (Royal Brotherhood. Book 1)
Dance of Seduction, 2003
A Notorious Love, 2001
A Dangerous Lord, 2000

Other books you might like:
Jo Beverley, *Tempting Fortune*, 1995
    Malloren Chronicles. Book 2
Celeste Bradley, *The Pretender*, 2003
Lisa Kleypas, *Lady Sophia's Lover*, 2002
Stephanie Laurens, *A Secret Love*, 2000
    Cynster. Book 5
Amanda Quick, *Mistress*, 1994

343

SABRINA JEFFRIES (Pseudonym of Deborah Gonzales)

To Pleasure a Prince

(New York: Pocket Star, 2005)

Story type: Historical/Regency
Series: Royal Brotherhood. Book 2
Subject(s): Courtship; Scandal
Major character(s): Lady Regina Tremaine, Noblewoman (daughter and sister of a duke); Marcus North, Nobleman (Viscount Draker), Bastard Son (of the Prince of Wales)
Time period(s): 1810s (1814)
Locale(s): England

Summary: When Lady Regina arrives at Castlemaine, the home of the reclusive, scarred ''Dragon Viscount,'' Marcus North, Viscount Draker, her one goal is to convince him to agree to let her brother Simon, the Duke of Foxmoor, court Draker's half sister, Louisa. Draker is suspicious of Simon's motives, and when he finally does agree to let Simon and Louisa court for one month, he only does it on the condition that Regina allows him to court her. This classic Beauty and the Beast tale is the second in Jeffries' Royal Brotherhood series about three bastard sons of George, Prince of Wales, later King George IV. Sensual, humorous, and fast-paced.

Where it's reviewed:
Romantic Times, March 2005, page 35

Other books by the same author:
One Night with a Prince, 2005 (Royal Brotherhood. Book 3)
In the Prince's Bed, 2004 (Royal Brotherhood. Book 1)
Dance of Seduction, 2003
A Notorious Love, 2001
A Dangerous Lord, 2000

Other books you might like:
Gabriella Anderson, *Forever Yours*, 2003
   gentler
Nicole Byrd, *Beauty in Black*, 2004
   Beauty and the Beast elements
Susan Carroll, *The Bride Finder*, 1998
   St. Leger. Book 1; Beauty and the Beast elements
Susan Carroll, *Midnight Bride*, 2001
   paranormal aspects
Mary Jo Putney, *Thunder and Roses*, 1993
   Beauty and the Beast elements

344

TRISH JENSEN

Without a Clue

(Toronto: Harlequin, 2005)

Story type: Humor; Contemporary
Subject(s): Humor; Actors and Actresses; Games/Literary
Major character(s): Meg Renshaw, Bride (jilted), Tour Guide (murder mystery events); Matt Rossi, Wealthy (real estate)
Time period(s): 2000s
Locale(s): Charleston, South Carolina

Summary: The bad news is Meg Renshaw was jilted at the altar. The good news is she's free to be the special events coordinator for Big Adventures Travel. Her specialty, murder mystery weekends, have proven to be popular, and she's found the perfect place to hold this one—a sumptuous Southern mansion. Matt Rossi is coming home after a business coup that will make him even wealthier. Much to his surprise, his house has been turned into a location for interactive theater, and he's been hired to play the corpse. Chaotic fun, unexpected situations, and slapstick comedy fill the pages of this laugh-aloud tour de force.

Where it's reviewed:
Romantic Times, February 2005, page 116

Other books by the same author:
Phi Beta Bimbo, 2005
Stuck with You, 2001
Against His Will, 2000
The Harder They Fall, 1997

Other books you might like:
Elizabeth Bevarly, *First Comes Love*, 2000
Barbara Daly, *You Call This Romance?*, 2002
Mary Leo, *A Pinch of Cool*, 2005
Hailey North, *Opposites Attract*, 2003
Nikki Rivers, *Random Acts of Fashion*, 2005

345

SUSAN JOHNSON

Hot Spot

(New York: Berkley Sensation, 2005)

Story type: Contemporary
Subject(s): Difference; Sexual Behavior; Popular Culture
Major character(s): Stella Scott, Store Owner (comic book-store); Danny Rees, Collector (comic books)
Time period(s): 2000s
Locale(s): Stillwater, Minnesota

Summary: Comic bookstore owner Stella Scott and comic book collector Danny Rees find passion and, eventually, love in spite of their different backgrounds. Explicit sex and steamy sensuality are Johnson's trademarks.

Where it's reviewed:
Rendezvous, May 2005, page 28
Romantic Times, June 2005, page 142

Other books by the same author:
Not Just for Tonight, 2005 (anthology)
Hot Legs, 2004
Pure Silk, 2004
Force of Nature, 2003
Seduction in Mind, 2001

Other books you might like:
Suzanne Forster, *All through the Night*, 2001
   erotic anthology
Lori Foster, *Perfect for the Beach*, 2004
   erotic anthology
Lori Foster, *Too Much Temptation*, 2002
Donna Kauffman, *Walk on the Wild Side*, 2001
Bertrice Small, *Fascinated*, 2000
   erotic anthology

346

SUSAN JOHNSON
KATHERINE O'NEAL, Co-Author
DIANE WHITESIDE, Co-Author

Not Just for Tonight

(New York: Brava, 2005)

Story type: Historical; Anthology
Subject(s): Sexual Behavior; Seduction

Summary: Loosely linked by the idea of ongoing relationships, these historical novellas feature steamy passion and explicit sex. Included are "American Beauty," veteran writer Susan Johnson's tale of an American horse expert who finds love with an English lord; "Dr. Yes," Katherine O'Neal's exotic story of sex and danger with a South American flair; and "The Seduction of Mrs. Rutledge," a sizzling story of childhood friends who marry for convenience and find passion, as well, by Diane Whiteside.

Other books by the same author:
Strangers in the Night, 2004 (erotic anthology)

Other books you might like:
Katherine O'Neal, *My One and Only*, 2000
Bertrice Small, *Delighted*, 2002
    erotic anthology
Bertrice Small, *The Dragon Lord's Daughters*, 2004
Shelley Thacker, *Into the Sunset*, 1999
Diane Whiteside, *The Irish Devil*, 2004

347

LINDA WINSTEAD JONES

The Moon Witch

(New York: Berkley Sensation, 2005)

Story type: Fantasy; Paranormal
Series: Sisters of the Sun. Book 2
Subject(s): Werewolves; Witches and Witchcraft; Magic
Major character(s): Juliet Fyne, Witch, Captive; Ryn of Anwyn, Werewolf (shapeshifter), Kidnapper
Time period(s): Indeterminate
Locale(s): Columbyana, Fictional Country

Summary: Juliet Fyne is a witch, but all of her magic, even combined with that of her two sisters, can't save her from the clutches of the evil emperor. As the imperial forces take her to their nefarious ruler, Juliet is captured again, this time by Ryn, a man who becomes a wolf at night. Ryn claims that she's his lifemate. Unfortunately, because of an old family curse, any mate of Juliet's, shapeshifter or not, will die by the age of 30. This is the second book in the series, and like the first, ends with a cliffhanger. Magic, adventure, and the paranormal make this an exciting romantic series. Set in the 366th Year of the Reign of the Beckyts.

Other books by the same author:
One Major Distraction, 2005
Truly, Madly, Dangerously, 2005
A Touch of the Beast, 2004
Running Scared, 2004
The Sun Witch, 2004

Other books you might like:
Christine Feehan, *Wild Rain*, 2004
Susan Krinard, *To Catch a Wolf*, 2003
Gena Showalter, *Awaken Me Darkly*, 2005
Susan Squires, *The Companion*, 2005
Rebecca York, *Witching Moon*, 2003

348

LINDA WINSTEAD JONES

Truly, Madly, Dangerously

(New York: Silhouette, 2005)

Story type: Contemporary; Romantic Suspense
Subject(s): Family; Murder; Small Town Life
Major character(s): Sadie Mae Harlow, Detective—Private; Truman McCain, Police Officer (deputy)
Time period(s): 2000s
Locale(s): Garth, Alabama

Summary: Sadie Harlow would never have come home if she thought she would have to face Truman McCain again; but because her aunt needs her, Sadie reluctantly returns to Garth to help out at the family motel and cafe. When Sadie stumbles across a dead body while cleaning one of the motel's rooms, Truman, who inspired one of the most romantically humiliating moments in Sadie's teenage life, turns out to be the deputy assigned to investigate the crime. Now even though all Sadie wants to do is find the killer and get out of town, Truman isn't about to let her get away from him again.

Where it's reviewed:
Romantic Times, February 2005, page 120

Other books by the same author:
Fever, 2004
The Sun Witch, 2004
Clint's Wild Ride, 2003
On Dean's Watch, 2003
Wilder Days, 2003

Other books you might like:
Kylie Brant, *An Irresistible Man*, 2003
Justine Davis, *One of These Nights*, 2003
Linda Howard, *Open Season*, 2001
Virginia Kantra, *All a Man Can Be*, 2003
Vickie Taylor, *The Renegade Steals a Lady*, 2001

349

BRENDA JOYCE

Deadly Illusions

(Don Mills, Ontario: MIRA, 2005)

Story type: Historical; Romantic Suspense
Series: Francesca Cahill. Book 7
Subject(s): Serial Killers; Murder
Major character(s): Francesca Cahill, Detective—Amateur, Fiance(e) (of Calder); Rick Bragg, Police Officer (police commissioner); Calder Hart, Wealthy
Time period(s): 1900s (1902)
Locale(s): New York, New York

Summary: A crazed killer nicknamed "The Slasher" is preying on beautiful, young Irishwomen in a poor area of Manhattan, and, once again, amateur sleuth Francesca Cahill is involved up to her eyeballs. Of course, this doesn't set too well with her wealthy fiance, Calder Hart, who is also the brother of sexy Police Commissioner Rick Bragg, Francesca's partner in crime detection. However, the fiery Francesca is not about to let the Slasher kill any more women, especially when her friends' lives are at stake. Fast-paced adventure, passion, and fascinating interpersonal relationships add to this addition to Joyce's turn-of-the-century New York series.

Where it's reviewed:
Romantic Times, February 2005, page 42

Other books by the same author:
Deadly Caress, 2003 (Francesca Cahill. Book 5)
Deadly Promise, 2003 (Francesca Cahill. Book 6)
Deadly Affairs, 2002 (Francesca Cahill. Book 3)
Deadly Desire, 2002 (Francesca Cahill. Book 4)
Deadly Love, 2001 (Francesca Cahill. Book 1)

Other books you might like:
Laura Lee Guhrke, *Breathless*, 1990
    historical romantic suspense
Elizabeth Kary, *Midnight Lace*, 1990
Linda Francis Lee, *Nightingale's Gate*, 2001
    Victorian Boston suspense
Lisa Manuel, *Mostly Mayhem*, 2004
    Regency serial killer
Carla Simpson, *Seductive Caress*, 1992
    Victorian serial killer

350

ELISE JUSKA
TARA MCCARTHY, Co-Author
PAMELA RIBON, Co-Author
HEATHER SWAIN, Co-Author
LISA TUCKER, Co-Author

Cold Feet
(New York: Downtown, 2005)

Story type: Contemporary; Anthology
Subject(s): Weddings; Marriage
Time period(s): 2000s
Locale(s): United States

Summary: Five very different but equally modern and trendy novellas from some of Downtown Press' more popular writers make up this lively anthology that focuses on weddings, marriage, and commitment and will appeal to the chick lit crowd. A couple sort out their feelings when confined to a hotel room after a car accident in "Perfect Weather for Driving" by Elise Juska; a surfing instructor must choose between love and romance or playing it safe in "Losing California" by Tara McCarthy; a bride-to-be who's always done the right thing decides to live on the wild side in "Sara King Goes Bad" by Pamela Ribon; a bomb blast on the subway line her fiance rides causes a young web designer to focus on what's really important in Heather Swain's "The Happiest Day of Your Life;" and a pair of agoraphobics who meet online

overcome their fears and find love in "Emily & Jules" by Lisa Tucker.

Where it's reviewed:
Romantic Times, May 2005, page 100

Other books you might like:
Carly Alexander, *The Eggnog Chronicles*, 2004
Gila Berkowitz, *The Brides*, 1992
Melissa Nathan, *The Waitress*, 2005
Lori Soard, *The Lipstick Diaries*, 2004
Heather Swain, *Luscious Lemon*, 2004

351

VIRGINIA KANTRA (Pseudonym of Virginia Kantra Ritchey)

Stolen Memory
(New York: Silhouette, 2005)

Story type: Contemporary; Romantic Suspense
Subject(s): Family; Memory Loss; Murder
Major character(s): Laura Baker, Detective—Police; Simon Ford, Businessman, Inventor
Time period(s): 2000s
Locale(s): Eden, Illinois

Summary: Late one night thieves break into reclusive inventor Simon Ford's lab, stealing half a million dollars in cultured rubies and leaving Simon with no memory of what happened. Now Simon not only doesn't know who he is, he doesn't know whom he can trust. One person Simon does trust is Laura Baker, the police detective assigned to the case. Simon convinces Laura the only way for her to investigate the crime is by pretending to be romantically involved with him; but Laura knows pretending to like Simon could prove to be dangerous for both of them.

Where it's reviewed:
Romantic Times, February 2005, page 120

Other books by the same author:
Guilty Secrets, 2004
All a Man Can Ask, 2003
All a Man Can Be, 2003
Her Beautiful Assassin, 2003
All a Man Can Do, 2002

Other books you might like:
Kylie Brant, *Undercover Lover*, 2000
Suzanne Brockmann, *Identity: Unknown*, 2000
Amanda Stevens, *Nighttime Guardian*, 2001
Susan Vaughan, *Dangerous Attraction*, 2001
Joanna Wayne, *As Darkness Fell*, 2004

352

SUSAN KEARNEY

The Challenge
(New York: Tor Romance, 2005)

Story type: Futuristic; Paranormal
Subject(s): Psychic Powers; Time Travel; Science Fiction

Major character(s): Tessa Camen, Martial Arts Expert (presidential protection agent), Time Traveler; Kahn, Alien (from the planet Rystan)
Time period(s): 2000s; 24th century (2324)
Locale(s): Space Station; Earth

Summary: Pulled from the present into the future milleseconds before a bullet would have killed her, special agent Tessa Camen isn't about to believe she has traveled through time or that she is her planet's choice and only chance to take "The Challenge" and save Earth and humanity. However, a quick visit to the Earth of the future convinces her that it really is true; now it is up to the sexy alien Kahn to help her quickly develop her latent psi abilities—using a technique that involves sexual frustration—so she can win. Sexy, funny, and full of fast-paced adventure.

Where it's reviewed:
Romantic Times, February 2005, page 106

Other books by the same author:
On the Edge, 2005
The Dare, 2005 (sequel to *The Challenge*)
Enslaved, 2002
Hidden Hearts, 2001
The Hidden Years, 2001

Other books you might like:
Megan Sybil Baker, *An Accidental Goddess*, 2004
   another time traveling heroine
Justine Davis, *Lord of the Storm*, 1994
Susan Grant, *The Legend of Banzai Maguire*, 1994
   2176. Book 1
Susan Krinard, *Kinsman's Oath*, 2004
   more challenges, less sensual
Patti O'Shea, *The Power of Two*, 2004
   2176. Book 4

353

KAREN KENDALL (Pseudonym of Karen Moser)

First Dance

(New York: Signet, 2005)

Story type: Contemporary; Humor
Series: Bridesmaid Chronicles. Book 3
Subject(s): Weddings
Major character(s): Vivien Shelton, Lawyer (divorce), Animal Lover (rescues greyhounds); J.B. Anglin, Lawyer, Divorced Person
Time period(s): 2000s
Locale(s): New York, New York; Fredericksburg, Texas

Summary: The last thing hot shot New York divorce attorney Viv Shelton wants to do is be a bridesmaid in a wedding, especially when it probably will mean running into the groom's family lawyer, J.B. Anglin, a drop-dead gorgeous man she did battle with three years ago and has never quite forgotten. J.B. has never forgotten either—especially the one night they spent together—and when their paths cross once again before the wedding, the fireworks are bound to start. Lively, funny, and sassy.

Other books by the same author:
First Date, 2005 (Bridesmaid Chronicles. Book 1)

Other books you might like:
Adrianne Byrd, *Measure of a Man*, 2005
   humor/family/weddings
Robyn Carr, *The Wedding Party*, 2001
Susan Mallery, *Falling for Gracie*, 2005
Kasey Michaels, *This Can't Be Love*, 2004
Suzanne Simmons, *Sweetheart, Indiana*, 2004

354

KAREN KENDALL (Pseudonym of Karen Moser)

First Date

(New York: Signet, 2005)

Story type: Contemporary; Humor
Series: Bridesmaid Chronicles. Book 1
Subject(s): Weddings; Illness; Family Relations
Major character(s): Sydney Spinelli, Accountant; Alex Kimball, Wealthy (venture capitalist)
Time period(s): 2000s
Locale(s): Fredericksburg, Texas; South River, New Jersey

Summary: When Sydney Spinelli gets a glowing e-mail from her not-always-sensible sister saying that she is going to marry an amazing man she has only known for a month, Syd heads for Texas, determined to stop the wedding. Alex Kimball, the groom's best friend, proves to be a major distraction, and before long, she realizes that sister Julia is not the only one who has found a Texan to love. Heartwarming, sometimes slapstick humor is a nice foil for the more serious issue of Alzheimer's disease in this lively story that is the first of a quartet of linked romances.

Where it's reviewed:
Library Journal, April 15, 2005, page 70

Other books by the same author:
First Dance, 2005
Unzipped, 2005
Who's on Top?, 2005
Someone Like Him, 2003
To Catch a Kiss, 2001

Other books you might like:
Susan Andersen, *Baby, Don't Go*, 2000
Millie Criswell, *What to Do about Annie?*, 2001
Rachel Gibson, *Truly, Madly Yours*, 1999
Kasey Michaels, *This Can't Be Love*, 2004
Suzanne Simmons, *Sweetheart, Indiana*, 2004

355

BETH KENDRICK (Pseudonym of Beth Macias)

Exes and Ohs

(New York: Downtown, 2005)

Story type: Contemporary
Subject(s): Children; Dating (Social Customs); Friendship
Major character(s): Gwen Traynor, Psychologist (child), Student—Graduate; Alex Coughlin, Businessman (financial analyst)
Time period(s): 2000s
Locale(s): Los Angeles, California; Las Vegas, Nevada

Summary: Six months after her fiance dumped her right before their wedding, psychologist Gwen Traynor is finally ready to give dating another try, and sexy, successful Alex Coughlin seems like perfect potential boyfriend material. Her newest patient is Leo and she meets his gorgeous soap opera actress mother Harmony St. James, and discovers that not only is Harmony Alex's crazy ex-girlfriend, but Leo might be the child Alex never knew he had. Now just as Gwen has found the one man who can tempt her into giving romance another chance, she may end up having to convince Alex he belongs with another woman!

Where it's reviewed:
Booklist, February 15, 2005, page 1061
Romantic Times, April 2005, page 55

Other books by the same author:
My Favorite Mistake, 2004

Other books you might like:
Lisa Cach, *Dating Without Novocaine*, 2002
Stephanie Doyle, *One True Love*, 2003
Donna Kauffman, *Dear Prince Charming*, 2004
Melissa Senate, *See Jane Date*, 2001
Cathy Yardley, *L.A. Woman*, 2002

356

ALISON KENT

The McKenzie Artifact

(New York: Brava, 2005)

Story type: Contemporary; Romantic Suspense
Series: Smithson Group 5. Book 5
Subject(s): Spies; Adventure and Adventurers
Major character(s): Stella Banks, Detective—Private; Eli McKenzie, Spy (Smithson Group), Detective (undercover)
Time period(s): 2000s
Locale(s): Texas; Mexico

Summary: Back in Mexico after recovering from being poisoned, Smithson Group 5 agent Eli McKenzie is determined to shut down evil Spectra IT's white slavery ring. The problem is that PI Stella Banks has gotten herself imprisoned in the compound he's out to destroy and he knows he's going to have to rescue her, as well as the young girls before he can finish his mission. Explicitly sexy and action-oriented.

Where it's reviewed:
Romantic Times, February 2005, page 97

Other books by the same author:
The Beach Alibi, 2005 (Smithson Group 5. Book 4)
Indiscreet, 2004
The Samms Agenda, 2004 (Smithson Group 5. Book 3)
The Bane Affair, 2004 (Smithson Group 5. Book 1)
The Shaughnessey Accord, 2004 (Smithson Group 5. Book 2)

Other books you might like:
Nina Bangs, *From Boardwalk with Love*, 2003
  B.L.I.S.S. Book 1
Lisa Cach, *Dr. Yes*, 2003
  B.L.I.S.S. Book 2
MaryJanice Davidson, *Wicked Women Whodunit*, 2005

Shannon McKenna, *Standing in the Shadows*, 2003
  sexy adventure
Lynsay Sands, *The Loving Daylights*, 2003
  sexy spies with humor

357

SHERRILYN KENYON
MELANIE GEORGE, Co-Author
JAID BLACK, Co-Author

Tie Me Up, Tie Me Down

(New York: Pocket, 2005)

Story type: Contemporary; Anthology
Subject(s): Erotica; Sexual Behavior
Time period(s): 2000s

Summary: Loosely linked by the theme of bondage and/or captivity, this diverse trio of erotic novellas features fast-paced adventure and graphic sex. A heroine goes undercover as a dominatrix in order to catch a terrorist in Sherrilyn Kenyon's ''Captivated by You;'' a bride is kidnapped just before her wedding by a former lover in Melanie George's ''Promise Me Forever;'' and a heroine discovers the hidden colony of New Sweden after she survives a chopper crash in the Arctic and finds love in the arms of a Viking hero in Jaid Black's ''Hunter's Right.''

Where it's reviewed:
Romantic Times, February 2005, page 47

Other books you might like:
Jaid Black, *One Dark Night*, 2004
Lori Foster, *Bad Boys on Board*, 2003
  erotic anthology
Melanie George, *The Mating Game*, 2002
Susan Johnson, *Hot Legs*, 2004
Shannon McKenna, *Return to Me*, 2004

358

SHERRILYN KENYON
REBECCA YORK, Co-Author
ROBIN D. OWENS, Co-Author

What Dreams May Come

(New York: Berkley Sensation, 2005)

Story type: Contemporary/Fantasy; Fantasy
Subject(s): Magic; Romance; Fantasy
Locale(s): United States

Summary: Linked together by threads of magic and fantasy, this trilogy of diverse novellas is enchanting and sensual. Included are ''Knightly Dreams,'' Sherrilyn Kenyon's story in which an old-fashioned hero springs to life from the pages of a romance novel; ''Shattered Dreams,'' Rebecca York's tale of a man who answers his former lover's psychic distress call with romantic results; and ''Road to Adventure,'' Robin D. Owens' charming story of two people who are given a second chance at love, literally. Magical and delightful.

Other books by the same author:
Fantasy Lover, 2002

Other books you might like:
Robin D. Owens, *Heart Duel*, 2004
Nora Roberts, *Moon Shadows*, 2004
    fantasy anthology
Rebecca York, *Gypsy Magic*, 2002
Rebecca York, *Phantom Lover*, 2003

359

VALERIE KING (Pseudonym of Valerie Bosna)

Garden of Dreams

(New York: Zebra, 2005)

Story type: Regency
Subject(s): Family; Gardens and Gardening; Secrets
Major character(s): Lucinda Stiles, Gentlewoman; Robert Sandifort, Nobleman
Time period(s): 1810s (1817)
Locale(s): Hampshire, England; London, England

Summary: It has been three years since Lucy Stiles last visited the Sandifort family, and she is shocked by how much things have changed since then. The estate's beautiful gardens, and even the Sandiforts themselves, seemed to be in desperate need of repair. When Lucy offers her help, Robert Sandifort lets her know in no uncertain terms that her ''meddling'' is not welcome. Lucy never could resist a challenge though, and she is determined to restore both the gardens and the Sandifort family to their once happy states.

Where it's reviewed:
Booklist, May 1, 2005, page 1574
Romantic Times, May 2005, page 30

Other books by the same author:
A Rogue's Revenge, 2004
An Adventurous Lady, 2004
A Daring Courtship, 2003
A Rogue's Wager, 2003
My Darling Coquette, 2003

Other books you might like:
Catherine Blair, *Athena's Conquest*, 2001
Shannon Donnelly, *A Proper Mistress*, 2003
Kate Huntington, *Lady Diana's Darlings*, 2000
Martha Kirkland, *His Lordship's Swan*, 2001
Laura Paquet, *Lord Langdon's Tutor*, 2000

360

ANGELA KNIGHT

Master of the Moon

(New York: Berkley Sensation, 2005)

Story type: Contemporary/Fantasy; Paranormal
Subject(s): Magic; Werewolves; Fantasy
Major character(s): Diana London, Werewolf (shapeshifter), Government Official (city manager); Llyr Galatyn, Ruler (King of Cachamwri Sidhe), Mythical Creature (Sidhe or fairy)
Time period(s): 2000s
Locale(s): Veradale, South Carolina; Mageverse Earth, Mythical Place

Summary: When the quiet town of Veradale begins to experience strange murders, city manager and part-time cop Diana London, with her supernatural abilities, realizes that the killer is not human and is something far more dangerous. Knowing that Earth is in danger, King Llyr Galatyn leaves his faerie realm and comes to offer help—and to get to know the woman who has been haunting his dreams, Diana, herself. Sensual, passionate, and magical. Follows *Master of the Night*.

Where it's reviewed:
Romantic Times, May 2005, page 118

Other books by the same author:
Jane's Warlord, 2004
Master of the Night, 2004
The Forever Kiss, 2004

Other books you might like:
Sherrilyn Kenyon, *Seize the Night*, 2004
Susan Krinard, *The Forest Lord*, 2002
Susan Krinard, *Prince of Shadows*, 1996
M.J. Putney, *Stolen Magic*, 2005
Mary Jo Putney, *Kiss of Fate*, 2004

361

JACKIE KRAMER

Warrior's Heart

(Waterville, Maine: Five Star, 2005)

Story type: Contemporary
Subject(s): Animals/Ostriches; Ranch Life; Abuse
Major character(s): Victoria Culver, Widow(er), Rancher; Jacob Lone Wolf, Rancher, Indian (Osage)
Time period(s): 2000s
Locale(s): Capston, Oklahoma

Summary: Imprisoned for a crime he didn't commit, Jake Lone Wolf is now out on parole, determined to see his young daughter, Audrey. However, Audrey has been adopted by his late brother-in-law and is now in the care of the widowed Vicki Culver—a woman who needs help on her ostrich ranch and is in the market for a hired hand. A heartwarming story about two wounded people who find love when they least expect it.

Other books you might like:
Harper Allen, *The Night in Question*, 2002
Virginia Kantra, *All a Man Can Be*, 2003
Curtiss Ann Matlock, *Driving Lessons*, 2000
Dinah McCall, *Jackson Rule*, 2002
Anne Stuart, *Still Lake*, 2002

362

SUSAN KRINARD

To Tame a Wolf

(Don Mills, Ontario: HQN, 2005)

Story type: Paranormal; Historical/American West
Subject(s): Werewolves; Treasure, Buried; Redemption
Major character(s): Tally Bernard, Young Woman; Sim Kavanaugh, Werewolf, Orphan

Time period(s): 1860s (1866); 1880s (1881)
Locale(s): Hat Rock, Texas; Tombstone, Arizona

Summary: When Tally Bernard's brother goes missing, she hires Sim Kavanaugh to find him—on the condition that she accompany Sim on his search through the Arizona desert. Once on the trail, Tally makes the startling discovery that her companion becomes a wolf at night. An entertaining tale of the American West where the good guys are the so-called monsters and the bad guys are the humans.

Where it's reviewed:
Booklist, May 15, 2005, page 1641
Romantic Times, May 2005, page 44

Other books by the same author:
Kinsman's Oath, 2004 (futuristic)
To Catch a Wolf, 2003
The Forest Lord, 2002 (fantasy)
Secret of the Wolf, 2001 (Forster. Book 3)
Once a Wolf, 2000 (Forster. Book 2)

Other books you might like:
Laura Marie Altom, *Sleep Tight*, 2004
Linda Winstead Jones, *The Moon Witch*, 2005
Kathleen Kane, *Catch a Fallen Cowboy*, 2000
    western paranormal
Sherrilyn Kenyon, *Night Pleasures*, 2002
Susan King, *Taming the Heiress*, 2003

363

JENNIFER LABRECQUE

Really Hot

(Toronto: Harlequin, 2005)

Story type: Contemporary
Subject(s): Dating (Social Customs); Television
Major character(s): Portia Tomlinson, Producer (television program); Rourke O'Malley, Banker (investment)
Time period(s): 2000s
Locale(s): Los Angeles, California; Boston, Massachusetts

Summary: Working in Hollywood has given Portia Tomlinson her fill of sweet-talking pretty boys, which is exactly what Rourke O'Malley, star of reality television's hottest new dating show, appears to be. Fortunately for Portia, the associate producer of the show, all she has to do is work with Rourke, not date him. With 12 beautiful, wealthy women from whom to choose, Rourke should not have any trouble finding the right woman for him, but much to Portia's surprise, that woman turns out to be her.

Where it's reviewed:
Romantic Times, February 2005, page 118

Other books by the same author:
Better than Chocolate, 2004
Barely Behaving, 2003
Barely Decent, 2002
Barely Mistaken, 2002
Jingle Bell Bride?, 2001

Other books you might like:
Stephanie Bond, *Two Sexy*, 2004
Samantha Connolly, *I Will Survive*, 2004

Julie Kenner, *Stolen Kisses*, 2004
Vicki Lewis Thompson, *Truly, Madly, Deeply*, 2002
Wendy Wax, *7 Days and 7 Nights*, 2003

364

PAMELA LABUD

Spirited Away

(New York: Zebra, 2005)

Story type: Historical/Regency; Paranormal
Subject(s): Ghosts; Revenge; Magic
Major character(s): Lady Arianna Halverson, Noblewoman, Psychic; William Markham, Sea Captain (merchant), Spirit (ghost)
Time period(s): 1810s
Locale(s): England

Summary: Hanged for a crime he did not commit, merchant captain William Markham vows vengeance on the evil villain, Richard Barrons, who set him up and his spirit will not rest until he makes this happen. William needs help and it comes in the form of Lady Arianna Halverson, a lovely psychic who counsels the dead and helps them move on. When her magical amulet allows him to regain his physical form, William is determined to carry out his plans against Barrons; but when he realizes that Barrons is drawing Arianna into his deadly web, he has even more reason to want the greedy, murdering opportunist out of the way.

Where it's reviewed:
Rendezvous, April 2005, page 32
Romantic Times, April 2005, page 44

Other books you might like:
Lynn Kerstan, *Gwen's Christmas Ghost*, 1995
    Alicia Rasley, co-author
Patricia Simpson, *Whisper of Midnight*, 1991
Antoinette Stockenberg, *Emily's Ghost*, 1992
Gayle Wilson, *Her Dearest Sin*, 2002
    not paranormal

365

EMILY LAFORGE (Pseudonym of Jill Jones)

Shadow Haven

(New York: Pocket, 2005)

Story type: Contemporary/Fantasy; Gothic
Subject(s): Secrets; Paranormal; Psychic Powers
Major character(s): Gabriella Deveaux, Widow(er), Psychic; Jarrod Landry, Lawyer; Michaela Colquitt, Child
Time period(s): 2000s
Locale(s): Bayou Teche, Louisiana (Shadow Haven)

Summary: Returning to her beloved Shadow Haven with her young daughter after her husband's death, Gabriella Deveaux is faced with both the tasks of renovating her ancestral home (which her husband, Charles, had let fall apart) and fending off a custody suit from her in-laws for her daughter, Michaela. With the help of Jarrod Landry, an attorney for her in-laws who had also, surprisingly, urged her not to marry Charles years earlier, she manages to sort things out. It isn't until she

finally realizes she must come to terms with and accept her family's psychic heritage that the real evil can be overcome. A chilling contemporary paranormal gothic.

Where it's reviewed:
Romantic Times, April 2005, page 115

Other books by the same author:
Beneath the Raven's Moon, 2003

Other books you might like:
Ginna Gray, *Pale Moon Rising*, 2004
Kay Hooper, *Amanda*, 1995
Kay Hooper, *Haunting Rachel*, 1998
Jill Jones, *Circle of the Lily*, 1998
    paranormal touches
Diane Tyrrel, *On Winding Hill Road*, 2005

366

JILL MARIE LANDIS

Heartbreak Hotel

(New York: Ballantine, 2005)

Story type: Contemporary/Fantasy
Series: Twilight Cove Trilogy. Book 3
Subject(s): Ghosts; Hotels and Motels; Trust
Major character(s): Tracy Potter, Widow(er), Hotel Owner; Wade MacAllister, Writer, Biker
Time period(s): 2000s
Locale(s): Twilight Cove, California

Summary: Stunned when her husband's sudden death leaves her without resources, Tracy Potter decides to use the only asset she has, an old derelict hotel in Twilight Cove; so she moves in with her young son and gets to work. Her first guest turns out to be a writer who has lost his inspiration. However, when the ghost of the fisherman who used to live in the hotel seems to want his story told, Wade is writing once more. An optimistic heroine, a wounded hero, a memorable young boy, and a touch of magic add to this heartwarming story that nicely concludes the Twilight Cove Trilogy.

Where it's reviewed:
Library Journal, April 15, 2005, page 68
Romantic Times, May 2005, page 95

Other books by the same author:
Heat Wave, 2004 (Twilight Cove Trilogy. Book 2)
Lover's Lane, 2003 (Twilight Cove Trilogy. Book 1)
Magnolia Creek, 2002
Summer Moon, 2001
The Orchid Hunter, 2000

Other books you might like:
Catherine Anderson, *Only by Your Touch*, 2003
Kristin Hannah, *On Mystic Lake*, 1999
Kate Moore, *Sexy Lexy*, 2005
Alexandra Raife, *Belonging*, 1999
Antoinette Stockenberg, *A Charmed Place*, 1998

367

ANN LAWRENCE

Do You Believe?

(New York: Tor, 2005)

Story type: Contemporary/Fantasy; Paranormal
Subject(s): Good and Evil; Art; Religion
Major character(s): Rose Early, Photographer; V.F. "Vic" Drummond, Writer (novelist)
Time period(s): 2000s
Locale(s): Marleton Village, England (in the Cotswolds)

Summary: Rose Early goes to Marleton Village in the Cotswolds to see why her photojournalist sister isn't responding to her e-mail. She finds Joan missing, a chilling notation in the margin of a horror novel, and a crusty, but appealing author who eventually joins forces with her to solve the mystery. Ancient evil, religious artifacts, and secret societies are at the heart of this complex story that is all the more sinister because of its idyllic Cotswolds setting.

Where it's reviewed:
Library Journal, April 15, 2005, page 70
Romantic Times, May 2005, page 118

Other books by the same author:
Lord of the Keep, 2003

Other books you might like:
Marion Zimmer Bradley, *Gravelight*, 1997
Jill Jones, *Circle of the Lily*, 1998
Meagan McKinney, *Still of the Night*, 2001
Patricia Simpson, *The Dark Lord*, 2004
Anne Stuart, *The Widow*, 2001
    not paranormal

368

JADE LEE

Hungry Tigress

(New York: Leisure, 2005)

Story type: Historical/Victorian; Historical/Exotic
Subject(s): China; Sexual Behavior; Rebellions, Revolts, and Uprisings
Major character(s): Joanna Crane, Gentlewoman; Zou Tun, Religious (pretend Shaolin monk), Nobleman (Mandarin)
Time period(s): 1890s (1897)
Locale(s): China

Summary: When restless, idealistic Joanna Crane leaves her safe Shanghai environment to join the Boxer Rebellion, she is saved from her own folly by a Manchurian prince disguised as a Shaolin monk. She guesses his secret and Zou Tun cannot risk her telling anyone, so instead of returning her home, he has no choice but to take her to a place where she will be safe, the realm of the Tigress Shi Po. However, the Tigress has plans, and instead of allowing Zou Tun to leave, she blackmails him into staying and learning—with Joanna as his partner. Erotic passion in an exotic setting.

Where it's reviewed:
Romantic Times, June 2005, page 65

Other books by the same author:
White Tigress, 2005
Devil's Bargain, 2004

Other books you might like:
Susan Johnson, *Taboo*, 1997
   explicit sex
Susanna Leigh, *Jade Dawn*, 1993
Mary Jo Putney, *The Bartered Bride*, 2002
   exotic
Robin Schone, *The Lady's Tutor*, 1999
   explicit sex
Bertrice Small, *The Love Slave*, 1995

369

REBECCA HAGAN LEE

Truly a Wife

(New York: Berkley Sensation, 2005)

Story type: Historical/Regency
Series: Free Fellows League. Book 4
Subject(s): Spies; Marriage; Memory Loss
Major character(s): Miranda St. Germaine, Noblewoman (Marchioness of St. Germaine); Daniel Sussex, Nobleman (Duke of Sussex)
Time period(s): 1810s
Locale(s): England

Summary: Although wounded while on a secret mission for the country as a new member of the Free Fellows League, Daniel, Duke of Sussex, knows he must make an appearance at his mother's ball. When he ends up bleeding all over Miranda, his long-time friend and estranged love, she fakes a nosebleed and they escape to get Daniel some medical attention. Aware of the damage to Miranda's reputation, Daniel insists they drop by the archbishop first and get married. The only problem is that when Daniel recovers, he doesn't remember their marriage! Charming, romantic, and very much in keeping with the earlier volume s in the series.

Where it's reviewed:
Romantic Times, April 2005, page 43

Other books by the same author:
Hardly a Husband, 2004 (Free Fellows League. Book 3)
Merely the Groom, 2004 (Free Fellows League. Book 2)
Barely a Bride, 2003 (Free Fellows League. Book 1)
Always a Lady, 2002
Hint of Heather, 2000

Other books you might like:
Mary Balogh, *Simply Unforgettable*, 2005
Christina Dodd, *That Scandalous Evening*, 1998
Karen Hawkins, *A Belated Bride*, 2001
Stephanie Laurens, *All about Passion*, 2001
Gayle Wilson, *Lady Sarah's Son*, 1999

370

JO LEIGH (Pseudonym of Jolie Kramer)

A Lick and a Promise

(Toronto: Harlequin, 2005)

Story type: Contemporary
Subject(s): Change; Food; Seduction
Major character(s): Margot Janowitz, Artist (food stylist); Daniel Houghton III, Architect, Neighbor
Time period(s): 2000s
Locale(s): New York, New York

Summary: There is nothing Margot Janowitz likes better than a new project, and when Daniel Houghton III moves into her apartment building, he becomes her latest fix-up challenge. Margot just knows there is a sexy man lurking beneath Daniel's boring, conservative exterior, and she is determined to bring him out. The only flaw in Margot's plan is that the new and improved Daniel isn't interested in just a temporary fling with her; he wants a real relationship with Margot!

Where it's reviewed:
Romantic Times, January 2005, page 94

Other books by the same author:
Arm Candy, 2004
Christmas Stalking, 2004
The One Who Got Away, 2004
The Trouble with Twins, 2004
Truth or Dare, 2003

Other books you might like:
Carrie Alexander, *The Chocolate Seduction*, 2003
Kristin Hardy, *Scoring*, 2003
Dorien Kelly, *Hot Nights in Ballymuir*, 2004
Julie Elizabeth Leto, *Just Watch Me*, 2002
Joanne Rock, *Girl Gone Wild*, 2004

371

MARY LENNOX (Pseudonym of Mary Glazer)

My Lord Beast

(Waterville, Maine: Five Star, 2005)

Story type: Historical/Victorian
Subject(s): Inheritance; Revenge
Major character(s): Lilias Merrit, Gentlewoman, Companion (nurse); Aubrey Drelincorte, Nobleman (Earl of Breme), Invalid (malaria)
Time period(s): 1840s (1842-1843)
Locale(s): India; England

Summary: Home from India suffering from both malaria and facial scars, Aubrey Drelincorte's reputation as a beast who murdered his wife while in India precedes him. Although his memory of the events are fuzzy and the threat of having to stand trial for murder still hangs over his head, he is determined that the title will not pass to his cousin, the man who was having an affair with his wife—so he must marry and produce an heir as soon as he can. The problem, of course is his reputation and physical appearance. Enter Lilias Merrit, an intrepid young woman escaping from an unwanted marriage to a brutal farmer and seeking employment as a companion

and nurse to the earl. Caring and friendship soon turn to love, in this lively, nicely-plotted Beauty and the Beast tale that has its share of danger and suspense.

Other books you might like:
Susan Carroll, *The Bride Finder*, 1998
Shannon Drake, *Wicked*, 2005
    similar themes
Lynn Kerstan, *The Golden Leopard*, 2002
Lynn Kerstan, *The Silver Lion*, 2003
Mary Jo Putney, *Thunder and Roses*, 1993

372
MARY LEO

A Pinch of Cool
(Toronto: Harlequin, 2005)

Story type: Contemporary; Humor
Subject(s): Cooks and Cooking; Family; Television Programs
Major character(s): Mya Strano, Consultant (trend-spotter); Eric Baldini, Filmmaker, Student—Graduate
Time period(s): 2000s
Locale(s): Los Angeles, California; Las Vegas, Nevada

Summary: When slipping ratings threaten her mother's network cooking show, trend-spotter and style guru extraordinaire Mya Strano knows exactly what to do: give the show a new look. Mya arrives home to discover that not only is her childhood friend and tormentor Eric Baldini staying with her mom, but that he has his own ideas about how to change the show as well. At first Mya refuses to let Eric influence her plans one bit, but somehow whenever the totally unhip but surprisingly sexy Eric is around, Mya finds herself losing her own cool!

Where it's reviewed:
Romantic Times, March 2005, page 113

Other books by the same author:
For Better or Cursed, 2004
Stick Shift, 2004

Other books you might like:
Carrie Alexander, *The Chocolate Seduction*, 2003
Samantha Connolly, *I Will Survive*, 2004
Barbara Dunlop, *Out of Order*, 2004
Tanya Michaels, *Not Quite as Advertised*, 2004
Molly O'Keefe, *Pencil Him In*, 2004

373
JULIE ANNE LONG

To Love a Thief
(New York: Warner Forever, 2005)

Story type: Historical/Regency
Subject(s): Courtship; Jealousy; Marriage
Major character(s): Lily Masters, Thief (pickpocket); Gideon Cole, Lawyer (barrister)
Time period(s): 1810s
Locale(s): London, England

Summary: Working as a pickpocket to take care of her young sister and herself, Lily Masters is as skillful as they come. When she gets caught trying to steal a watch, she is stunned when the same man she tried to steal from the day before, Gideon Cole, rescues her by impulsively buying her freedom. Gideon has a goal in mind—marriage to the lovely Lady Constance in order to further his career; and, when he realizes that the lovely Lily also has the manners of a lady, he plans to use Lily to make Constance jealous. Naturally, things end up a bit differently than Gideon had planned in this story with a Pygmalion twist. Lively, funny, and sensual.

Where it's reviewed:
Romantic Times, April 2005, page 44

Other books you might like:
Mary Balogh, *Promise of Spring*, 1990
    traditional Regency
Deborah Hale, *The Wedding Wager*, 2001
    a twist on Pygmalion
Georgette Heyer, *These Old Shades*, 1999
    classic Georgian era story
Judith Ivory, *The Proposition*, 1999
Judith A. Lansdowne, *A Devilish Dilemma*, 1998
    traditional Regency

374
SASHA LORD (Pseudonym of Rebecca Saria)

Across a Wild Sea
(New York: Signet Eclipse, 2005)

Story type: Historical/Medieval; Historical/Fantasy
Series: Wild Trilogy. Book 3
Subject(s): Animals/Horses; Blindness; Change
Major character(s): Alannah, Handicapped (blind), Telepath (communicates with horses); Xanthier O'Bannon, Sea Captain, Nobleman
Time period(s): Indeterminate Past
Locale(s): Scotland

Summary: When a freak storm casts him ashore on a remote island, Captain Xanthier O'Bannon, exiled and estranged from his family, is rescued by the lovely Alannah, a blind woman who has a rare ability to communicate with the wild horses that roam the island. Alannah's past is shrouded in mystery, and as Xanthier begins to put the pieces of the puzzle together, he realizes that he and Alannah must leave the island if she is to learn who she really is—and if he is to be reconciled with his family. Concludes Lord's Wild Trilogy and ties up a number of loose ends from *In a Wild Wood*. Highly sensual.

Where it's reviewed:
Library Journal, January 2005, page 91
Romantic Times, February 2005, page 36

Other books by the same author:
In a Wild Wood, 2004 (Wild Trilogy. Book 2)
Under a Wild Sky, 2004 (Wild Trilogy. Book 1)

Other books you might like:
Katherine Deauxville, *Eyes of Love*, 1996
    a touch of magic

Emma Holly, *Hunting Midnight*, 2003
  highly sensual
Janet Lynnford, *Shetland Summer*, 2002
  gentler
Susan Plunkett, *Untamed Time*, 1999
Susan Squires, *Danelaw*, 2003
  another telepathic heroine

375

KATHY LOVE

Wanting Something More

(New York: Kensington, 2005)

Story type: Contemporary; Romantic Suspense
Series: Stepp Sisters. Book 3
Subject(s): Small Town Life; Models, Fashion; Sisters
Major character(s): Marty Stepp, Model; Nate Peck, Police Officer, Crime Victim (vicious attack)
Time period(s): 2000s
Locale(s): Millbrook, Maine; New York, New York (Manhattan)

Summary: The three Stepp sisters were outcasts. Dirt poor, each of them had something the in-crowd could make fun of—brains, weight, or height. Marty, at six-feet-tall, was considered "the freakiest of the ugly Stepp sisters." To impress his friends, Nate Peck takes a dare that he'll kiss Marty in front of everyone at the prom. He follows through, and Marty is humiliated. Now Marty is a supermodel, one of the town's few celebrities. Nate is a police officer, a changed man since a near-death experience. However, the blows to his head by an unknown assailant have affected his memory, and he doesn't remember the cruel prank he played at the prom. More importantly, Nate can't understand why Marty hates him when her family likes him so much. An emotional look at how high school experiences affect people years later.

Other books by the same author:
Fangs for the Memories, 2005
Getting What You Want, 2004 (Stepp Sisters. Book 1)
Wanting What You Get, 2004 (Stepp Sisters. Book 2)

Other books you might like:
Lori Foster, *The Secret Life of Bryan*, 2004
Lorraine Heath, *Hard Lovin' Man*, 2003
Connie Lane, *Dirty Little Lies*, 2004
Lisa Plumley, *Josie Day Is Coming Home*, 2005
LaVyrle Spencer, *Small Town Girl*, 1998

376

MERLINE LOVELACE

The First Mistake

(Don Mills, Ontario: MIRA, 2005)

Story type: Contemporary; Romantic Suspense
Series: Cleo North. Book 1
Subject(s): Murder; Movie Industry; Terrorism
Major character(s): Cleo North, Consultant, Military Personnel (former special agent); Jack Donovan, Military Personnel (major)

Time period(s): 2000s
Locale(s): Santa Fe, New Mexico; Las Vegas, Nevada

Summary: After a botched assignment that ended in a murder-suicide, Cleo North, formerly with the Air Force Office of Special Investigations, has resigned her position to become a bodyguard to celebrities. Her current assignment is protecting a movie star playing a less-than-virgin Mary in a controversial film from a homicidal stalker. Major Jack Donovan is at the same Santa Fe film festival as Cleo, but he's there to check out a North Korean technology that could be used against America. Jack and Cleo rediscover romance, but whether or not they'll live to enjoy it is the question of the day.

Where it's reviewed:
Romantic Times, April 2005, page 114

Other books by the same author:
One of the Boys, 2005
The Last Bullet, 2005
The Middle Sin, 2005
A Man of His Word, 2004
Untamed, 2004

Other books you might like:
Suzanne Brockmann, *Flashpoint*, 2004
Lori Foster, *Unexpected*, 2003
Vicki Hinze, *Acts of Honor*, 1999
Rachel Lee, *After I Dream*, 2000
Patricia Potter, *Broken Honor*, 2002

377

MERLINE LOVELACE

The Last Bullet

(Don Mills, Ontario: MIRA, 2005)

Story type: Contemporary; Romantic Suspense
Series: Cleo North. Book 3
Subject(s): Murder; Mystery; World War II
Major character(s): Cleo North, Consultant (security & investigations), Military Personnel (ex-USAF investigator); Jack Donovan, Military Personnel (Air Force major)
Time period(s): 2000s
Locale(s): United States; England

Summary: Although no longer part of the Air Force, independent security consultant Cleo North is recruited by the USAF Office of Special Investigations to solve the mystery around the murder of a USAF captain stationed in England. Of course, the fact that she will be working with her sometimes lover Jack Donovan, special agent with OSI, adds to the attraction, and together the pair head to England to find the answers. Heart-stopping danger and sizzling sensuality highlight this well-plotted tale of romantic suspense.

Where it's reviewed:
Romantic Times, June 2005, page 117

Other books by the same author:
One of the Boys, 2005
The First Mistake, 2005 (Cleo North. Book 1)
The Middle Sin, 2005 (Cleo North. Book 2)
A Man of His Word, 2004
Untamed, 2004

Romance

Other books you might like:
Suzanne Brockmann, *Breaking Point*, 2005
Suzanne Brockmann, *Into the Night*, 2002
Jasmine Cresswell, *Decoy*, 2004
    Melody Beecham. Book 1
Jasmine Cresswell, *Final Justice*, 2005
    Melody Beecham. Book 3
Vicki Hinze, *Duplicity*, 1999

378

MERLINE LOVELACE

The Middle Sin

(Don Mills, Ontario: MIRA, 2005)

Story type: Contemporary; Romantic Suspense
Series: Cleo North. Book 2
Subject(s): Terrorism; Missing Persons; Suspense
Major character(s): Cleo North, Consultant, Military Personnel (former special agent); Jack Donovan, Military Personnel (USAF special agent)
Time period(s): 2000s
Locale(s): United States; Malta

Summary: The missing woman P.I. Cleo North is hired to find turns out to have some connection to a case that Major Jack Donovan is working on. Cleo and Jack, once again, join forces to solve a mystery. The investigation takes them to Malta and involves them in a race against time to stop a terrorist plot. Nuclear threats, passion, and fast-paced action are part of this, the second in Lovelace's Cleo North trilogy.

Where it's reviewed:
Rendezvous, April 2005, page 41

Other books by the same author:
One of the Boys, 2005
The First Mistake, 2005 (Cleo North. Book 1)
The Last Bullet, 2005 (Cleo North. Book 3)
A Man of His Word, 2004
Untamed, 2004

Other books you might like:
Suzanne Brockmann, *Breaking Point*, 2005
Jasmine Cresswell, *Final Justice*, 2005
    Melody Beecham. Book 3
Jasmine Cresswell, *Full Pursuit*, 2004
    Melody Beecham. Book 2
Eileen Wilks, *Night of No Return*, 2000
Ruth Wind, *Born Brave*, 2001

379

KATIE MACALISTER (Pseudonym of Marthe Arends)

Hard Day's Knight

(New York: Signet, 2005)

Story type: Contemporary; Humor
Subject(s): Competition; Fairs; Knights and Knighthood
Major character(s): Pepper Marsh, Computer Expert (software engineer), Unemployed; Walker McPhail, Knight (former jouster)
Time period(s): 2000s

Locale(s): Ontario, Canada

Summary: Pepper Marsh only agreed to attend a Renaissance Fair with her cousin because she thought she might actually have a chance to meet a real knight rather than the techno-geeks she is used to dating. On the very first day of the fair, Pepper's wish comes true when Walker McPhail rides up out of nowhere and rescues Pepper just before she is about to be trampled by a horse. When Pepper later discovers that her sexy hero has given up professional jousting, she vows to return the favor by rescuing Walker from his past.

Where it's reviewed:
Booklist, January 1, 2005, page 831
Romantic Times, January 2005, page 110

Other books by the same author:
Sex and the Single Vampire, 2004
The Corset Diaries, 2004
The Trouble with Harry, 2004
You Slay Me, 2004
Men in Kilts, 2003

Other books you might like:
Patti Berg, *And Then He Kissed Me*, 2003
Katherine Deauxville, *The Last Male Virgin*, 2002
Rachel Gibson, *True Confessions*, 2001
Karen Kendall, *Someone Like Him*, 2003
Suzanne MacPherson, *Talk of the Town*, 2003

380

DEBBIE MACOMBER

A Good Yarn

(Don Mills, Ontario: MIRA, 2005)

Story type: Contemporary/Mainstream
Subject(s): Crafts; Friendship; Healing
Major character(s): Elise Beaumont, Librarian (retired); Bethanne Hamilton, Divorced Person; Courtney Pulanski, Teenager, Orphan
Time period(s): 2000s
Locale(s): Seattle, Washington

Summary: When her initial knitting class is a success, yarn shop owner Lydia Hoffman offers another, and ends up providing friendship, help, and healing—as well as knitting advice—to a diverse trio of women, each suffering from a loss of some kind. Elise is a retired librarian with family and financial problems on her mind; Bethanne is a divorcee looking for new directions; and Courtney is an adolescent with depression and weight problems whose mother has recently died. This sequel to *The Shop on Blossom Street*, is heart-warming and charming, and has the added bonus of a knitting pattern for socks.

Where it's reviewed:
Rendezvous, April 2005, page 27
Romantic Times, May 2005, page 96

Other books by the same author:
The Shop on Blossom Street, 2004
311 Pelican Court, 2003 (Cedar Cove Chronicles. Book 3)
The Christmas Bride, 2003
204 Rosewood Lane, 2002 (Cedar Cove Chronicles. Book 2)

16 Lighthouse Road, 2001 (Cedar Cove Chronicles. Book 1)

Other books you might like:
Patricia Gaffney, *Saving Graces*, 1999
Kristin Hannah, *Summer Island*, 2001
Mary Alice Monroe, *The Book Club*, 1999
Constance O'Day-Flannery, *Seasons*, 1995
Jean Stone, *First Loves*, 1995

381

SUSAN MALLERY (Pseudonym of Susan Macias Redmond)

Falling for Gracie

(Toronto: Harlequin, 2005)

Story type: Contemporary; Humor
Subject(s): Weddings; Family Relations; Revenge
Major character(s): Gracie Landon, Baker (celebrity wedding cakes); Riley Whitefield, Political Figure (mayoral candidate), Wealthy
Time period(s): 2000s
Locale(s): Los Lobos, California

Summary: Fourteen-year-old Gracie Landon was consumed by her obsession with 18-year-old Riley Whitefield, so much so that she sabotaged his dates and stalked him. Everyone in Los Lobos, California, knew about it because the newspaper accounts of her escapades came to be known as the "Gracie Chronicles." Exiled from the town in shame by her mother, Gracie, now baker to the stars, is back in town to make a wedding cake for her sister's wedding. Her brother-in-law is a campaign manager for Riley's mayoral bid, and his indiscretion has forced Gracie to hook up with Riley to investigate the affair. Humor and poignancy make a nice blend as Gracie tries to break free of her past.

Where it's reviewed:
Booklist, February 15, 2005, page 1068
Romantic Times, March 2005, page 91

Other books by the same author:
The Sheik and the Bride Who Said No, 2005
There's Always Plan B, 2005
Expecting!, 2004
Sheik's Kidnapped Bride, 2004
Someone Like You, 2004

Other books you might like:
Mary Kay Andrews, *Hissy Fit*, 2004
Shirley Jump, *The Bride Wore Chocolate*, 2004
Ann Kline, *The Ride to Dinah's Wedding*, 2004
Kathy Love, *Getting What You Want*, 2004
Lisa Plumley, *Josie Day Is Coming Home*, 2005

382

LISA MANUEL

Mostly a Lady

(New York: Zebra, 2005)

Story type: Historical/Regency
Subject(s): Identity, Concealed; Secrets
Major character(s): Eliza Kent, Widow(er), Imposter; Dylan Fergusson, Gentleman, Businessman (family investments)

Time period(s): 1820s
Locale(s): England

Summary: Recently widowed and penniless, Eliza Kent sees no point in living. However, when a carriage accident results in a young widowed gentlewoman dying in her arms, Eliza seizes the chance at a new life and assumes the identity of the dead woman, Elizabeth Mendoza de Leone. When she is rescued by Scotsman Dylan Fergusson and he takes her to stay with his sister, Eliza is certain her masquerade will be discovered and her chance at happiness destroyed. Mysteries, villains, and romance abound in this lively story of a heroine who learns that living someone else's life can be dangerous indeed.

Other books by the same author:
Mostly Married, 2004 (Mostly. Book 1)
Mostly Mayhem, 2004 (Mostly. Book 2)

Other books you might like:
Celeste Bradley, *The Pretender*, 2003
Liz Carlyle, *A Woman Scorned*, 2000
Catherine Coulter, *The Deception*, 1998
Christina Dodd, *Scandalous Again*, 2003
Mary Jo Putney, *One Perfect Rose*, 1997

383

KAT MARTIN

The Bride's Necklace

(Don Mills, Ontario: MIRA, 2005)

Story type: Historical/Regency
Series: Necklace Trilogy. Book 1
Subject(s): Abuse; Marriage
Major character(s): Victoria Temple Whiting, Noblewoman, Runaway (from stepfather); Cordell Easton, Nobleman (Earl of Brant); Claire Marion Whiting, Noblewoman
Time period(s): 1800s (1804)
Locale(s): England

Summary: Her odious stepfather's attempted attack on her beautiful, innocent sister, Claire, is the last straw; so Victoria knocks him out with the bed warmer, takes a family heirloom necklace, and heads for London in search of a job. As luck would have it, the Earl of Brant is in the market for a new mistress, as well as a new housekeeper, so when when Claire and Victoria appear at his door, he hires them on the spot. His unspoken plans to take Claire as a mistress go gradually awry as Cord realizes how childlike she really is, and he begins to contemplate his other option, the smart, no-nonsense, Victoria. Her stepfather's unexpected arrival forces a showdown and Cord quickly realizes that he must marry Tory if he wants to keep them safe. Complex plotting, simmering sensuality, and a lively pace add interest to this story that features mystery, legendary curses, and a wonderfully diverse group of characters. First in a projected trilogy.

Where it's reviewed:
Library Journal, January 2005, page 92
Romantic Times, January 2005, page 32

Other books by the same author:
Desert Heat, 2004
Midnight Sun, 2003

Fanning the Flame, 2002
The Fire Inside, 2002
Hot Rain, 2002

Other books you might like:
Mary Balogh, *More than a Mistress*, 2000
Liz Carlyle, *A Deal with the Devil*, 2004
Liz Carlyle, *A Woman of Virtue*, 2000
Christina Kingston, *Ride the Wind Home*, 2003
Stephanie Laurens, *The Lady Chosen*, 2003

384

DINAH MCCALL (Pseudonym of Sharon Sala)

Bloodlines

(Don Mills, Ontario: MIRA, 2005)

Story type: Contemporary; Romantic Suspense
Subject(s): Kidnapping; Memory Loss; Murder
Major character(s): Olivia Sealy, Amnesiac, Wealthy; Trey
    Bonney, Detective—Police
Time period(s): 2000s
Locale(s): Texas

Summary: When the skeleton of a two-year old girl is found
during the renovation of an old cabin on Lake Texoma, a
physical deformity immediately links the case to the 25-year-
old kidnapping and ransoming of Olivia Sealy. Although
Olivia's grandfather swears she is his grandchild, Livvy begins to question her total lack of memory about the kidnapping, and she begins to wonder if she really is who she has
always thought she was. Romantic complications come in the
form of her high school love, detective Trey Bonney, and
more frightening ones come from a killer who is determined
to keep his secrets at all costs. Fast-paced, tense action marks
this emotionally involving tale of romantic suspense.

Where it's reviewed:
Rendezvous, April 2005, page 42
Romantic Times, April 2005, page 115

Other books by the same author:
The Perfect Lie, 2003
White Mountain, 2002
Storm Warning, 2001
The Return, 2000
Tallchief, 1997

Other books you might like:
Christina Dodd, *Close to You*, 2005
Kay Hooper, *Whisper of Evil*, 2002
Cait London, *Leaving Lonely Town*, 2000
    childhood kidnapping mystery
Nora Roberts, *Birthright*, 2003
    another childhood kidnapping
Ruth Wind, *In the Midnight Rain*, 2000

385

ERIN MCCARTHY
JEN NICHOLAS, Co-Author
JORDAN SUMMERS, Co-Author

Bad Boys over Easy

(New York: Brava, 2005)

Story type: Contemporary
Subject(s): Sexual Behavior; Erotica; Relationships
Time period(s): 2000s
Locale(s): United States

Summary: This trio of steamy, upbeat novellas includes
''Fuzzy Logic,'' Erin McCarthy's funny tale of a Pleasure
Party consultant, a logical chemist, and a mail mix-up; ''The
Cupid Curse,'' Jen Nicholas' magical story of a heroine
named Valentine who appeals to Cupid and gets unexpected
results; and ''Mesmerized,'' Jordan Summers' unusual story
of a hypnotist and a reporter who will do just about anything
for an interview. Explicit sex.

Other books you might like:
Suzanne Forster, *All through the Night*, 2001
    erotic anthology
Lori Foster, *Bad Boys in Black Tie*, 2003
    erotic anthology
Lori Foster, *Bad Boys to Go*, 2003
Lori Foster, *I Love Bad Boys*, 2002
    erotic anthology
Susan Johnson, *Hot Pink*, 2001
    erotic romance

386

SHARON MCCLELLAN

The Midas Trap

(New York: Silhouette, 2005)

Story type: Contemporary; Romantic Suspense
Subject(s): Mythology; Treasure
Major character(s): Veronica Bright, Archaeologist; Simon
    Owens, Archaeologist
Time period(s): 2000s
Locale(s): Italy; Istanbul, Turkey; Greece

Summary: Archaeologist Veronica Bright believes many of
the world's myths and legends have a basis in fact, but her
unconventional views earned her the scorn of the professional
archaeological community, including Simon Owens. Now Simon wants Veronica's help in locating the legendary Midas
Stone. Working with Simon would be one way for Veronica
to redeem her professional status, but it would also mean
learning to think of Simon as a business partner only and not
as the man whose kiss Veronica can't forget.

Where it's reviewed:
Romantic Times, April 2005, page 124

Other books you might like:
Melissa James, *Can You Forget?*, 2004
Jenna Mills, *The Perfect Target*, 2003
Vickie Taylor, *The Renegade Steals a Lady*, 2001
Evelyn Vaughn, *A.K.A. Goddess*, 2004

387

DOROTHY MCFALLS

The Marriage List

(New York: Signet, 2005)

Story type: Regency
Subject(s): Courtship; Family
Major character(s): Margaret "May" Sheffers, Gentlewoman; Radford Evers, Nobleman (Viscount Evers)
Time period(s): 1810s (1813)
Locale(s): Bath, England; Widcombe, England

Summary: A war injury helps convince Radford, Viscount Evers, that it is time to get married. After giving the matter considerable thought, Radford comes up with a list of qualities he requires in a wife. All it takes is one meeting with the exasperating, infuriating, and all too tempting May Sheffers for Radford to realize that May doesn't have even one of qualities he is looking for in a wife, but that for her he just might be willing to throw his list out!

Where it's reviewed:
Romantic Times, May 2005, page 30

Other books you might like:
Susannah Carleton, *The Marriage Campaign*, 2003
Diane Farr, *Falling for Chloe*, 2000
April Kihlstrom, *An Outrageous Proposal*, 1998
Teresa McCarthy, *The Rejected Suitor*, 2004
Donna Simpson, *Lord Pierson Reforms*, 2004

388

PATRICIA MCLINN

Least Likely Wedding

(New York: Silhouette, 2005)

Story type: Contemporary
Subject(s): Family; Small Town Life
Major character(s): Kay Aaronson, Director; Rob Dalton, Businessman (financial analyst)
Time period(s): 2000s
Locale(s): Tobias, Wisconsin

Summary: Director Kay Aaronson can't believe her luck when she finds the perfect location to shoot her new music video in her grandmother's hometown of Tobias, but then her luck changes when her tempermental lead actor walks off the set. In desperation, Kay latches upon Rob Dalton, a financial analyst who has come home to Tobias to do some thinking about a problem at work, as a replacement. Kay doesn't mind teaching the acting challenged Rob exactly how he needs to kiss his leading lady; Kay just never expects to want to continue with the lessons after the shoot is over!

Where it's reviewed:
Booklist, April 15, 2005, page 1437
Romantic Times, April 2005, page 128

Other books by the same author:
The Unexpected Wedding Guest, 2003
Wedding of the Century, 2003
The Runaway Bride, 2002

Match Made in Wyoming, 2001
My Heart Remembers, 2001

Other books you might like:
Patricia Coughlin, *The Cupcake Queen*, 2002
Jennifer Greene, *Wild in the Moment*, 2004
Holly Jacobs, *Do You Hear What I Hear?*, 2001
Cathie Linz, *The Marine Meets His Match*, 2004
Ruth Wind, *Beautiful Stranger*, 2000

389

MARY ALICE MONROE (Pseudonym of Mary Alice Kruesi)

Sweetgrass

(Don Mills, Ontario: MIRA, 2005)

Story type: Contemporary/Mainstream
Subject(s): Conservation; Grief; Healing
Major character(s): Mary June Blakely, Spouse, Parent; Preston Blakely, Spouse, Patient
Time period(s): 2000s
Locale(s): South Carolina (Sweetgrass, a plantation)

Summary: When domineering patriarch Preston Blakely has a stroke, the world tips on its side for his family. Suddenly, his beloved Sweetgrass, the family plantation for eight generations, is at risk. His estranged son, Morgan, returns home from Montana to help run the place, while Preston's emotionally jaded sister tries to take advantage of his condition to sell Sweetgrass. Preston's eloquent silence during his recovery makes his wife, Mary June, reevaluate their life together. A powerful prodigal son parable of grief, healing, and the importance of family.

Other books by the same author:
Skyward, 2003
The Beach House, 2002
The Four Seasons, 2001
The Book Club, 1999
Girl in the Mirror, 1998

Other books you might like:
Barbara Bretton, *Shore Lights*, 2003
Patricia Gaffney, *Flight Lessons*, 2002
Patti Callahan Henry, *Where the River Runs*, 2005
Barbara Samuel, *A Piece of Heaven*, 2003
Kathryn Shay, *Promises to Keep*, 2002

390

KATE MOORE

Sexy Lexy

(New York: Love Spell, 2005)

Story type: Contemporary
Subject(s): Identity, Concealed; Privacy; Sexuality
Major character(s): Alexandra "Lexy" Clark, Physical Fitness Expert, Innkeeper; Sam Worth, Architect, Carpenter
Time period(s): 2000s
Locale(s): Drake's Point, California; Hollywood, California

Summary: Fleeing the unwanted public attention her best-selling book, *Workout Sex*, has generated, physical fitness expert Lexy Clark heads for a tiny secluded town on the

Romance

northern California coast and her new life as the owner of an inn. Romance blossoms between Lexy and the man she thinks is a local carpenter, but Sam Worth has issues similar to Lexy's, if only they knew it. Secrets, self-concept, and self-worth are all issues in this well-written, funny, touching story, the first contemporary romance by an experienced historical and Regency writer.

Where it's reviewed:
Library Journal, April 15, 2005, page 68
Romantic Times, April 2005, page 100

Other books by the same author:
A Prince Among Men, 1997
An Improper Widow, 1996
Winterburn's Rose, 1996
The Mercenary Major, 1994
Sweet Bargain, 1993

Other books you might like:
Suzanne Judson, *Harper's Wood*, 2000
   fleeing heroine/less humor
Jayne Ann Krentz, *Deep Waters*, 1997
Alexandra Raife, *Belonging*, 1999
   fleeing heroine/Scotland
Nora Roberts, *Jewels of the Sun*, 1999
   fleeing heroine/Ireland
Suzanne Simmons, *Sweetheart, Indiana*, 2004

391

MARGARET MOORE (Pseudonym of Margaret Wilkins)

Lord of Dunkeathe
(Don Mills, Ontario: HQN, 2005)

Story type: Historical/Medieval
Subject(s): Marriage; Competition; Middle Ages
Major character(s): Lady Riona Mac Gordon, Noblewoman (Scottish), Impoverished; Sir Nicholas of Dunkeathe, Nobleman (Norman)
Time period(s): 13th century (1240)
Locale(s): Scotland

Summary: Word gets out that Sir Nicholas of Dunkeathe, a Norman recently gifted with a large estate, is looking for a wife. In an unusual move, Nicholas is welcoming potential brides to his castle so he can choose from among them, and Riona Mac Gordon knows it is her duty to her impoverished family to go. Although Riona can't hold a candle to the other women when it comes to wealth or social standing, Nicholas is attracted to her from the beginning. The problem, of course, is money. Sensual.

Where it's reviewed:
Romantic Times, February 2005, page 40

Other books by the same author:
In the King's Service, 2003
Kiss Me Quick, 2003
All My Desire, 2002
Gwyneth and the Thief, 2002
His Forbidden Kiss, 2001

Other books you might like:
Jill Barnett, *Wicked*, 1999
   humorous treatment
Jillian Hart, *Malcolm's Honor*, 2000
Lynn Kurland, *This Is All I Ask*, 1997
Johanna Lindsey, *Joining*, 1999
Karyn Monk, *The Rose and the Warrior*, 2000

392

HUNTER MORGAN (Pseudonym of Colleen Faulkner)

What She Can't See
(New York: Zebra, 2005)

Story type: Contemporary; Romantic Suspense
Subject(s): Serial Killers; Murder
Major character(s): M.K. Shaughnessy, FBI Agent (special agent); Adam Thomas, FBI Agent (special agent)
Time period(s): 2000s
Locale(s): Maryland (Baltimore area)

Summary: When a politician's son is one of four Chesapeake Bay College students killed in what appears to be an accident, the FBI is brought in to check things out. Special Agent M.K. Shaughnessy has a feeling this isn't just an accident, but convincing the agent she is assigned to work with, Adam Thomas, isn't so easy. However, as the bodies begin to pile up, it becomes clear that they have a serial killer on their hands; now the problem is to find him before he kills another student. Romance combines with suspense in this chilling novel.

Where it's reviewed:
Romantic Times, May 2005, page 89

Other books you might like:
Margaret Allison, *The Last Curve*, 1999
Beverly Barton, *Killing Her Softly*, 2005
Suzanne Brockmann, *Get Lucky*, 2000
Karen Robards, *Wait Until Dark*, 2001
   anthology
Nora Roberts, *Carnal Innocence*, 1992

393

PAMELA MORSI

By Summer's End
(Don Mills, Ontario: MIRA, 2005)

Story type: Contemporary
Subject(s): Cancer; Family Relations
Major character(s): Dawn Leland, Parent, Patient (cancer); Del Tegge Jr., Scientist (environmental), Activist (environmental); Dakota Leland, Teenager, Narrator
Time period(s): 2000s
Locale(s): Knoxville, Tennessee

Summary: When she develops cancer, Dawn Leland does what she swore she would never do and takes her two teenage daughters back to Knoxville to stay with her estranged former in-laws. Still blaming Dawn for her son's hasty marriage and accidental death, Sophrona Leland is not in a forgiving mood; but as everyone begins to deal with the situation, love begins

to work its magic. Romance blossoms quietly in this story charmingly told through the insightful, honest eyes of the young narrator.

Where it's reviewed:
Rendezvous, February 2005, page 33
Romantic Times, February 2005, page 62

Other books by the same author:
Suburban Renewal, 2004
Letting Go, 2003
Doing Good, 2002
Here Comes the Bride, 2000
Sealed with a Kiss, 1998

Other books you might like:
Kathleen Eagle, *The Last Good Man*, 2000
Ginna Gray, *The Prodigal Daughter*, 2000
Kristin Hannah, *Between Sisters*, 2003
Kristin Hannah, *Summer Island*, 2001
Kathleen Gilles Seidel, *Please Remember This*, 2002

394

CINDI MYERS

Detour Ahead
(Toronto: Harlequin, 2005)

Story type: Contemporary; Humor
Subject(s): Travel
Major character(s): Marlee Jones, Advertising; Craig Brinkman, Cook
Time period(s): 2000s
Locale(s): Washington, District of Columbia; San Diego, California

Summary: To get to her best friend's wedding, Marlee Jones, who was born without a good sense of direction, hitches a ride with Craig Brinkman, the best man, thinking that a cross-country road trip could be fun. Marlee quickly learns that the ever efficient Craig has a different kind of trip in mind once she discovers he has plans for every minute of their trip on his master schedule. Now Marlee is determined to prove to Craig that the best things in life, and love, are the surprise detours that come up along the way.

Where it's reviewed:
Romantic Times, March 2005, page 112

Other books by the same author:
Good, Bad. . .Better, 2005
Life According to Lucy, 2004
Taking It All Off, 2004
What Phoebe Wants, 2004
Rumor Has It, 2004

Other books you might like:
Stephanie Bond, *It Takes a Rebel*, 2000
Stephanie Doyle, *One True Love*, 2003
Kristin Gabriel, *Dangerously Irresistible*, 2001
Holly Jacobs, *I Waxed My Legs for This?*, 2001
Mary Leo, *Stick Shift*, 2004

395

KATHLEEN NANCE

Jigsaw
(New York: Leisure, 2005)

Story type: Contemporary; Romantic Suspense
Subject(s): Murder; Mystery; Artificial Intelligence
Major character(s): Isabella Quintera, Professor, Computer Expert (artificial intelligence); Daniel Champlain, Government Official (national security agent)
Time period(s): 2000s
Locale(s): Michigan

Summary: Computer expert (and jigsaw puzzle creator) Bella Quintera is run off an icy Michigan road, only to be rescued by the one man she doesn't want to see, government security agent Daniel Champlain, her former lover and the man who destroyed her father. Nevertheless, the attraction is still there, even though Bella doesn't trust him. However, she may have no choice, because she has become a target of a dangerous group that will stop at nothing to get what it wants. An artificial intelligence named Fran adds some humor to this chilling tale involving international hackers, national security, and some very nasty villains.

Other books you might like:
Christine Feehan, *Shadow Game*, 2003
    chilling research
Jacey Ford, *Dangerous Curves*, 2004
Iris Johansen, *Long After Midnight*, 1997
    pursued heroine
Merline Lovelace, *Call of Duty*, 1998

396

SOPHIA NASH (Pseudonym of Sophia Nash Ours)

Lord Will and Her Grace
(New York: Signet, 2005)

Story type: Regency
Subject(s): Secrets; Seduction
Major character(s): Sophie Somerset, Gentlewoman, Heiress; William Barclay, Gentleman, Rake
Time period(s): 1810s
Locale(s): Yorkshire, England; Burnham-by-the-Sea, England

Summary: Still smarting from the shredding her reputation received from London's busiest gossips, Miss Sophie Somerset arrives in quiet little Burnham-by-the-Sea hoping for a brief vacation before she must continue on with the arduous task of finding a nobleman to wed. When Sophie unexpectedly meets William Barclay in the seaside town and he offers to teach her the art of attracting an aristocratic husband, it seems like the solution to all her problems. Little does Sophie realize she isn't getting lessons in love from a harmless dandy, but rather from a rake well versed in the art of seduction.

Where it's reviewed:
Booklist, March 15, 2005, page 1274
Romantic Times, April 2005, page 67

Romance

Other books by the same author:
A Passionate Endeavor, 2004
A Secret Passion, 2004

Other books you might like:
Jessica Benson, *Lord Stanhope's Proposal*, 2000
Candice Hern, *A Garden Folly*, 1997
Emma Jensen, *Best Laid Schemes*, 1998
Laura Matthews, *A Rival Heir*, 2002
Joy Reed, *Mr. Jeffries and the Jilt*, 2003

397

JACQUELINE NAVIN

The Beauty of Bond Street

(New York: Berkley Sensation, 2005)

Story type: Historical/Regency
Series: Mayfair Brides. Book 3
Subject(s): Marriage; Honesty; Identity, Concealed
Major character(s): Sophie Kent, Imposter, Gentlewoman; Gideon Hayworth, Nobleman (Earl of Ashford); Lady May Hayworth, Noblewoman (daughter of an earl)
Time period(s): 1810s (1814)
Locale(s): London, England

Summary: Although she had dearly loved her actress/courtesan mother and the two women she had called her aunts, Sophie has no wish to follow in their footsteps. Now, with the death of Aunt Millicent, Sophie is on her own. When she finds a letter among her aunt's things from Lady May Hayworth asking about a child that Millicent had borne to Lady May's late brother, Sophie seizes the opportunity and presents herself to Lady May as the missing girl. Sophie's plans to marry well and lead a respectable life take an interesting turn when Lady May's wounded rakehell brother-in-law moves in to recover. Their mutual attraction cannot be denied, but lies and secrets must be dealt with before they can find happiness. A lively, heartwarming story with some serious issues.

Where it's reviewed:
Romantic Times, June 2005, page 54

Other books by the same author:
The Heiress of Hyde Park, 2004 (Mayfair Brides. Book 2)
The Princess of Park Lane, 2003 (Mayfair Brides. Book 1)
The Bliss, 2002
Meet Me at Midnight, 2001
The Sleeping Beauty, 2001

Other books you might like:
Mary Balogh, *The Secret Pearl*, 1997
Mary Chase Comstock, *Fortune's Mistress*, 1996
Betina Krahn, *The Perfect Mistress*, 1995
Julia Quinn, *Everything and the Moon*, 1997
Gayle Wilson, *Lady Sarah's Son*, 1999

398

LISA NOELI

The Passionate Miss Prudence

(New York: Zebra, 2005)

Story type: Regency

Subject(s): Books and Reading; Libraries
Major character(s): Prudence Reese, Gentlewoman; Alwyn Purcell, Architect, Nobleman
Time period(s): 1810s (1815)
Locale(s): London, England

Summary: When her eccentric cousin Lady Agatha Purcell decides to build a library for the ladies of London, Prudence Reese quickly finds herself drafted into helping with the project. While sorting through the dreary lot of dull donations the library has received, Prudence finds some scandalous sketches tucked in one of the volumes. She is almost positive the drawings belong to Lord Alwyn Purcell, Lady Agatha's second son and the architect of the library, but Alwyn insists the only thing he is guilty of is falling for Prudence's charms.

Where it's reviewed:
Romantic Times, January 2005, page 106

Other books by the same author:
The Beautiful Miss Mousey, 2004

Other books you might like:
Emma Jensen, *A Grand Design*, 2001
Barbara Metzger, *Miss Westlake's Windfall*, 2001
Laura Paquet, *Mr. MacAlister Sets His Cap*, 2003
Joy Reed, *The Baron and the Bluestocking*, 2002
Nonnie St. George, *The Ideal Bride*, 2003

399

LISA NOELI

A Summer's Day

(New York: Zebra, 2005)

Story type: Regency
Subject(s): Animals/Cats; Children; Courtship
Major character(s): Emma Snow, Governess; William Kent, Nobleman
Time period(s): 1810s
Locale(s): Devon, England; London, England

Summary: While Lord William Kent enjoys having his young nephew Charles, his niece Caroline, and even their cat Nefret stay with him, their constant misadventures mean his summer is anything but quiet. Fortunately, the children's temporary governess, the lovely Miss Emma Snow, seems quite capable of taking care of both the children and their feline companion. The more William gets to know Emma, the more delightful he finds her to be, but if he intends on courting Emma he will have to work fast before the summer is over and Emma is gone.

Where it's reviewed:
Romantic Times, March 2005, page 125

Other books by the same author:
The Passionate Miss Prudence, 2005
The Beautiful Miss Mousey, 2004

Other books you might like:
Mary Blayney, *The Captain's Mermaid*, 2004
Candice Hern, *The Best Intentions*, 1999
Julia Parks, *His Saving Grace*, 2002
Joy Reed, *Lord Desmond's Destiny*, 2002
Donna Simpson, *Lord St. Claire's Angel*, 1999

400

BRENDA NOVAK

Every Waking Moment

(Don Mills, Ontario: HQN, 2005)

Story type: Contemporary; Romantic Suspense
Subject(s): Abuse; Runaways; Diabetes
Major character(s): Vanessa Beacon, Runaway, Parent; Preston Holman, Stock Broker, Avenger; Dominick Rodriguez, Child (diabetic)
Time period(s): 2000s
Locale(s): San Diego, California; Nevada; Iowa

Summary: Unwilling to put up with her lover's increasingly abusive, restrictive treatment any longer, Vanessa Beacon dons a new identity and escapes with her young diabetic son. Her plans go awry when her car is spotted and she is forced to ask a stranger for help. Preston Holman is on a journey to confront the man responsible for his son's death, and the last thing he needs is a woman and a child, especially one who reminds him of his son, to slow him down. Nevertheless, he agrees, and as they make their way across the country, they find healing and love, even as they are pursued by some seriously bad characters and see their share of violent action. The day-to-day details of living with a diabetic child are omnipresent but not overwhelming. Sensual.

Other books by the same author:
Stranger in Town, 2005
Cold Feet, 2004
A Husband of Her Own, 2003
Sanctuary, 2003
Taking the Heat, 2003

Other books you might like:
Jasmine Cresswell, *No Sin Too Great*, 1996
  pursuit, romance, and a new life
Ginna Gray, *The Witness*, 2001
  another fleeing heroine
Dinah McCall, *Storm Warning*, 2001
Mary Alice Monroe, *Skyward*, 2003
  another child diabetic/not romantic suspense
Karen Rose, *Have You Seen Her?*, 2004
  suspense and children

401

BRENDA NOVAK

Stranger in Town

(Toronto: Harlequin, 2005)

Story type: Contemporary; Romantic Suspense
Subject(s): Sports/Football; Schools/High Schools; Healing
Major character(s): Hannah Price, Single Parent, Photographer (studio owner); Gabriel Holbrook, Handicapped (paraplegic), Sports Figure (former pro football star)
Time period(s): 2000s
Locale(s): Dundee, Idaho

Summary: Three years after his professional football career was shattered when a car crash left him unable to walk, Gabe Holbrook reluctantly allows himself to be drawn back into the life of his small hometown when he agrees to coach the high school football team after the longtime coach suddenly dies. His budding star quarterback is the son of Hannah Price, the woman who caused his accident; and their growing attraction for each other forces them to rethink what is really important to them. Exceptionally well-rendered small town ambiance, a pair of realistic children, a lovable dog, and some classic secondary characters add to this heartwarming, lively romance.

Other books by the same author:
Every Waking Moment, 2005
Cold Feet, 2004
A Husband of Her Own, 2003
Sanctuary, 2003
Taking the Heat, 2003

Other books you might like:
Catherine Anderson, *Only by Your Touch*, 2003
  heartwarming
Catherine Anderson, *Phantom Waltz*, 1981
  a wheelchair-bound heroine
Fern Michaels, *Jingle All the Way*, 2004
  wheelchair-bound characters
Danielle Steel, *Palomino*, 1981
Pat Warren, *Bright Hopes*, 1992

402

DIANA PALMER

Before Sunrise

(Don Mills, Ontario: HQN, 2005)

Story type: Multicultural; Romantic Suspense
Subject(s): Native Americans; Murder; Suspense
Major character(s): Phoebe Keller, Archaeologist, Museum Curator; Jeremiah Cortez, FBI Agent, Single Parent
Time period(s): 2000s
Locale(s): Chenocetah, North Carolina (Cherokee reservation)

Summary: Archaeologist Phoebe Margaret Keller is sure that Jeremiah Cortez, a Choctaw, loves her, until she gets a newspaper clipping telling of his marriage to another woman. A devastated Phoebe becomes the curator of a museum on the Cherokee reservation in Chenocetah, North Carolina. One day, she gets a call about the ancient remains of a Neanderthal that's been found in the caves near where a major development is being built. Soon there's another body, and this one is recent. Jeremiah, now a widower and member of the FBI's newly-formed Indian Country Crime Unit, is sent to investigate. Phoebe, too, has become a target, and there's no way he's leaving her alone. Even as danger closes in, old flames start to rekindle. Full of information about the Cherokee culture, this is one book that educates as it entertains.

Other books by the same author:
Renegade, 2004
Lawless, 2003
A Man of Means, 2002
Desperado, 2002
Texas Ranger, 2001

Other books you might like:
Laura Baker, *Raven*, 2001

Kathleen Eagle, *The Night Remembers*, 1996
Nora Roberts, *Pride of Jared MacKade*, 1995
Aimee Thurlo, *Black Raven's Pride*, 2000
Sheri Whitefeather, *A Kept Woman*, 2004

403

JULIA PARKS (Pseudonym of Donna Bell)

Marriage Minded

(New York: Zebra, 2005)

Story type: Regency
Subject(s): Marriage; Honesty
Major character(s): Lady Elizabeth Winters, Noblewoman, Heiress; Gideon Sparks, Sea Captain
Time period(s): 1810s
Locale(s): England

Summary: Beautiful, titled, and wealthy, Lady Elizabeth Winters has rejected more suitors than she can count. She is not about to marry a man she can't love—or doesn't find interesting. Her family, however, wants to get her settled. When her grandmother asks her cousin Avery to help find a new suitor, he brings home dashing Gideon Sparks, an American sea captain who had saved Avery's life, with deceptive, but romantic results. Light, lively, and enjoyable.

Where it's reviewed:
Romantic Times, April 2005, page 67

Other books by the same author:
Fortune's Fools, 2004
To Marry an Heiress, 2003
A Gift for a Rogue, 2002
His Saving Grace, 2002
The Devil and Miss Webster, 2001

Other books you might like:
Donna Bell, *Heiress to Love*, 2000
Donna Bell, *A Tangled Web*, 2001
Martha Kirkland, *His Lordship's Swan*, 2001
Debbie Raleigh, *A Bride for Lord Challmond*, 2001
Regina Scott, *The Irredeemable Miss Renfield*, 2001

404

LISA PLUMLEY

Josie Day Is Coming Home

(New York: Kensington, 2005)

Story type: Humor; Contemporary
Subject(s): Humor; Outcasts; Small Town Life
Major character(s): Josie Day, Dancer (Las Vegas showgirl); Luke Donovan, Handyman, Heir
Time period(s): 2000s
Locale(s): Las Vegas, Nevada; Donovan's Corner, Arizona

Summary: After Las Vegas showgirl Josie Day saves the life of wealthy Tallulah Carlyle, the grateful eccentric gives Josie one of her estates. Josie moves from Las Vegas back to her old hometown of Donovan's Corner, Arizona, where the gift mansion is located. Unfortunately, rumors in the small town have circulated that Josie's a lap dancer, and no one wants to send their kids to her new dance school. In fact, no one wants

to socialize with Josie, period. Luke Donovan knows that Josie's a good person. He's the handyman—and rightful heir—of the estate. An interesting take on coming home again.

Where it's reviewed:
Booklist, February 15, 2005, page 1068
Romantic Times, April 2005, page 102

Other books by the same author:
Perfect Switch, 2004
Perfect Together, 2003
Falling for April, 2002
Reconsidering Riley, 2002
Making Over Mike, 2001

Other books you might like:
Jane Blackwood, *The Sexiest Dead Man Alive*, 2001
Millie Criswell, *What to Do about Annie?*, 2001
Susan Donovan, *Public Displays of Affection*, 2004
Shirley Jump, *The Devil Served Tortellini*, 2005
Susan Mallery, *Falling for Gracie*, 2005

405

PATRICIA POTTER

Tangle of Lies

(New York: Berkley Sensation, 2005)

Story type: Contemporary; Romantic Suspense
Subject(s): Murder; Secrets
Major character(s): Liz Connor, Businesswoman (adventure trips), Political Figure (city councilwoman); Caleb Adams, Detective—Private (former cop)
Time period(s): 2000s
Locale(s): New Mexico

Summary: When her mother is arrested for a 34-year-old armored car robbery and murder, Liz Connor is determined to get to the bottom of things. Unfortunately, her mother isn't talking, and things take a dangerous turn when her house is burned, her niece is threatened, and she is attacked in her office. Reluctantly, she enlists the aid of detective Caleb Adams to help her find some answers; answers that he badly needs, as well, but for very different reasons. Many players intertwine in this well-crafted story that pits those who want the truth to come out against those who want it kept hidden and the tension keeps rising until the end. The story takes a hard look at the effects of past actions on the present.

Other books by the same author:
Dancing with a Rogue, 2003
Twisted Shadows, 2003
Broken Honor, 2002
The Perfect Family, 2001
The Black Knave, 2000

Other books you might like:
Lynn Erickson, *The Eleventh Hour*, 1999
Lynn Erickson, *The Ripple Effect*, 1999
Christiane Heggan, *The Enemy Within*, 2000
Nora Roberts, *Carolina Moon*, 1999
Antoinette Stockenberg, *Keepsake*, 1999

406

AMANDA QUICK (Pseudonym of Jayne Ann Krentz)

Lie by Moonlight

(New York: Putnam, 2005)

Story type: Historical/Victorian; Romantic Suspense
Series: Midnight. Book 2
Subject(s): Suspense; Victorian Period; Crime and Criminals
Major character(s): Concordia Glade, Governess; Ambrose Wells, Detective—Private, Thief (gentleman)
Time period(s): 19th century
Locale(s): London, England

Summary: Concordia Glade has added explosives making and escape techniques to her curriculum to get her four orphaned students from the clutches of the nefarious crime lord, Alexander Larkin, who has plans to sell the girls to the highest bidders. Ambrose Wells, who's investigating Larkin, is surprised to see the criminal's castle and outbuildings in flames, not to mention one of his thugs dead. The biggest shock of all is finding out that these battlefield conditions were created by a ''mere'' woman and four girls. Knowing that Larkin's in a murderous rage, Wells offers the five females his protection, and insists they go with him to his townhouse. The feisty Concordia knows that she can do a pretty good job on her own, and soon, they go head-to-head over who's supposed to protect whom.

Where it's reviewed:
Booklist, April 15, 2005, page 1414

Other books by the same author:
Wait Until Midnight, 2005 (Midnight. Book 1)
The Paid Companion, 2004
Late for the Wedding, 2003 (Lake and March. Book 3)
Don't Look Back, 2002 (Lake and March. Book 2)
Slightly Shady, 2001 (Lake and March. Book 1)

Other books you might like:
Pamela Britton, *Scandal*, 2004
Suzanne Enoch, *London's Perfect Scoundrel*, 2003
Barbara Metzger, *A Perfect Gentleman*, 2004
Madeleine E. Robins, *Point of Honour*, 2003
Elizabeth Thornton, *The Marriage Trap*, 2005

407

AMANDA QUICK (Pseudonym of Jayne Ann Krentz)

Wait Until Midnight

(New York: Jove, 2005)

Story type: Historical/Victorian; Romantic Suspense
Subject(s): Suspense; Victorian Period; Murder
Major character(s): Caroline Fordyce, Writer (popular fiction), Detective—Amateur; Adam Hardesty, Wealthy, Detective—Amateur
Time period(s): 19th century (late)
Locale(s): London, England

Summary: When a noted medium is murdered and a diary is stolen, popular writer Caroline Fordyce and wealthy, enigmatic Adam Hardesty go into high gear to find the killer. Threading their way through the seamier side of Victorian London, Caroline and Adam also find time for romance and passion in this fast-paced adventure.

Where it's reviewed:
Romantic Times, February 2005, page 41

Other books by the same author:
Lie by Moonlight, 2005
The Paid Companion, 2004
Late for the Wedding, 2003 (Lake and March. Book 3)
Don't Look Back, 2002 (Lake and March. Book 2)
Slightly Shady, 2001 (Lake and March. Book 1)

Other books you might like:
Gabriella Anderson, *Yours Always*, 2004
Connie Brockway, *As You Desire*, 1997
Shannon Drake, *When We Touch*, 2004
Elizabeth Kary, *Midnight Lace*, 1990
Carla Simpson, *Seductive Caress*, 1992
    darker

408

DEBBIE RALEIGH
SANDY BLAIR, Co-Author
REGAN ALLEN, Co-Author

How to Marry a Duke

(New York: Zebra, 2005)

Story type: Anthology; Historical/Regency
Subject(s): Courtship; Marriage
Time period(s): 1800s
Locale(s): England

Summary: Three different Regency heroines find romance with three different dukes in this trio of novellas. In Debbie Raleigh's ''To Woo a Duke,'' Shevron Quinn is determined to prove that Mrs. Dobson's school for young ladies, which claims to teach its students how to marry nobility, is nothing but a sham. It turns out Shevron may have learned her lessons a bit too well when she draws the romantic attention of Lord Damon Morrow. In Sandy Blair's ''The Accidental Duchess,'' penniless governess Rachel O'Leary is looking for a place to stay when she lets herself into an empty townhouse. When the Duke of Killgory returns home unexpectedly, he is reluctant to let his new ''guest'' leave. Tess Dewood discovers it will take more than a bit of magic to convince Stephen Anthony, Duke of Longford, that she is the fairy queen he is fated to marry in Regan Allen's ''A Touch of Magic.''

Where it's reviewed:
Library Journal, January 2005, page 92
Romantic Times, February 2005, page 39

Other books you might like:
Celeste Bradley, *My Scandalous Bride*, 2004
Christina Dodd, *Scottish Brides*, 1999
Lisa Kleypas, *Where's My Hero*, 2003
Allison Lane, *Wedding Belles*, 2004
Patricia Rice, *A Wedding Bouquet*, 1996

409

DEBBIE RALEIGH

Miss Frazer's Adventure

(New York: Zebra, 2005)

Story type: Regency
Subject(s): Adventure and Adventurers; Courtship
Major character(s): Katherine Frazer, Gentlewoman; Lucius Jonathan Duval, Nobleman (Earl of Calfied)
Time period(s): 1810s
Locale(s): Kent, England; London, England; Brighton, England

Summary: After her fiance, Lucius Duval, jilts her at the altar, a humiliated Kate Frazer decides from that moment on she is going to stop worrying about what everyone else thinks is proper and do what she wants in life. The first thing Kate does is adopt a new name as she sets out to explore the many delights of London. When Lucius finally tracks her down, he finds he not only must get her to forgive him for missing their wedding, he must also find some way to convince Kate to marry him again!

Where it's reviewed:
Romantic Times, February 2005, page 26

Other books by the same author:
A Scandalous Marriage, 2003
My Lord Eternity, 2003
My Lord Immortality, 2003
My Lord Vampire, 2003
A Convenient Marriage, 2002

Other books you might like:
Jessica Benson, *Much Obliged*, 2001
Candice Hern, *Miss Lacey's Last Fling*, 2001
Sophia Nash, *A Secret Passion*, 2004
Laura Paquet, *Miss Scott Meets Her Match*, 2002
Jeanne Savery, *An Independent Lady*, 2003

410

DOLORES STEWART RICCIO

The Divine Circle of Ladies Making Mischief

(New York: Kensington, 2005)

Story type: Paranormal; Humor
Series: Circle. Book 3
Subject(s): Murder; Humor; Wicca
Major character(s): Cassandra Shipton, Businesswoman (herbal cosmetics), Fiance(e); Joe Ulysses, Activist (Greenpeace), Fiance(e)
Time period(s): 2000s
Locale(s): Plymouth, Massachusetts

Summary: Cassandra Shipton wants her fiance, Joe Ulysses, to take a break in his Greenpeace activities long enough for them to get married. In the meantime, she and her coven of intrepid Wiccan sleuths, headed by a branch librarian, are investigating, in their own bumbling fashion, the sudden outbreak of deaths at a local nursing home. This is a great mix of humor, romance, suspense, and, of course, magic.

Where it's reviewed:
Booklist, February 15, 2005, page 1066
Romantic Times, May 2005, page 99

Other books by the same author:
Charmed Circle, 2003 (Circle. Book 2)
Circle of Five, 2003 (Circle. Book 1)
Spirit, 2001

Other books you might like:
Jill Barnett, *Bewitching*, 1993
Kay Hooper, *Wizard of Seattle*, 1993
Jayne Ann Krentz, *Absolutely, Positively*, 1996
Teresa Medeiros, *Breath of Magic*, 1996
    time-traveling witch
Nora Roberts, *Heaven and Earth*, 2001

411

PATRICIA RICE

Much Ado about Magic

(New York: Signet Eclipse, 2005)

Story type: Historical/Georgian; Historical/Fantasy
Series: Magic. Book 5
Subject(s): Magic; Artists and Art; Scandal
Major character(s): Lady Lucinda Malcolm Pembroke, Noblewoman, Artist (painter); Sir Trevelyan Rochester, Sea Captain, Bastard Son
Time period(s): 1750s (1755)
Locale(s): England

Summary: Shocked and angered to see himself immortalized in a painting that has everyone thinking he murdered his cousin, Sir Trevelyan Rochester sets out in search of the artist, the magically gifted Lady Lucinda whose paintings are said to predict the future. Lucinda is in hiding to escape the notoriety. Although Trev does find her, it takes him some time to penetrate her disguise, but by then they have fallen in love. A charming, magical tale with several unexpected twists.

Other books by the same author:
This Magic Moment, 2004 (Magic. Book 4)
The Trouble with Magic, 2003 (Magic. Book 3)
Must Be Magic, 2002 (Magic. Book 2)
All a Woman Wants, 2001
Merely Magic, 2000 (Magic. Book 1)

Other books you might like:
Susan Carroll, *The Bride Finder*, 1998
Kimberly Cates, *Magic*, 1998
M.J. Putney, *Stolen Magic*, 2005
Mary Jo Putney, *Kiss of Magic*, 2004
Evelyn Richardson, *A Lady of Talent*, 2005
    artistic heroine/Regency

412

EMILIE RICHARDS (Pseudonym of Emilie Richards McGee)

Endless Chain

(Don Mills, Ontario: MIRA, 2005)

Story type: Contemporary/Mainstream
Series: Shenandoah Album. Book 2
Subject(s): Small Town Life; Politics; Secrets
Major character(s): Elisa Martinez, Refugee (aka Alicia Santos), Maintenance Worker (church sexton); Sam Kincade, Religious (pastor), Activist (social activist)
Time period(s): 2000s
Locale(s): Toms Brook, Virginia

Summary: Running from the authorities and fearing extradition back to Guatemala where she is wanted for political reasons, Elisa Martinez comes to rural Virginia and accepts a position as church sexton and finds love in the arms of the young pastor—a love that she knows can never be. Social conflicts, church politics, and an exceptionally well-conceived setting (including the newsy Quilting Bee minutes) add to this story that nicely continues Richards' Shenandoah Valley series.

Where it's reviewed:
Library Journal, June 1, 2005, page 121
Romantic Times, July 2005, page 48

Other books by the same author:
Wedding Ring, 2004 (Shenandoah Valley. Book 1)
Prospect Street, 2002
Whiskey Island, 2000
Rising Tides, 1997
Iron Lace, 1996

Other books you might like:
Suzanne Judson, *Harper's Wood*, 2000
   an escaping heroine
Jan Karon, *At Home in Mitford*, 1994
   first Mitford novel
Jan Karon, *Light from Heaven*, 2005
   final Mitford book
Jan Karon, *A Light in the Window*, 1995
Debbie Macomber, *16 Lighthouse Road*, 2001
   small town series

413

EVELYN RICHARDSON (Pseudonym of Cynthia Johnson)

A Lady of Talent

(New York: Signet, 2005)

Story type: Regency
Subject(s): Marriage; Artists and Art; Identity, Concealed
Major character(s): Lady Cecilia Manners, Noblewoman (daughter of a marquess), Artist (portrait); Sebastian, Nobleman (Earl of Charrington)
Time period(s): 1810s
Locale(s): London, England

Summary: When Sebastian, Earl of Charrington, and his bride-to-be, Miss Barbara Wyatt, select C.A. Manners to paint the lady's portrait, they are startled to find that the artist is not only a woman, but also the daughter of a marquess. Sebastian is surprised for another reason: Cecilia Manners is the painter of the self-portrait he has had hanging on his wall and to whose paintings he has been drawn for years. As the painting progresses, so do the various relationships, and by the end of this charming, well-written story, all the characters are appropriately realigned.

Where it's reviewed:
Romantic Times, February 2005, page 26

Other books by the same author:
A Foreign Affair, 2003
Fortune's Lady, 2002
Lord Harry's Daughter, 2001
My Lady Nightingale, 1999
The Reluctant Heiress, 1996

Other books you might like:
June Calvin, *Isabella's Rake*, 1997
   artist heroine
Jo Ann Ferguson, *A Model Marriage*, 1998
Candice Hern, *Once a Scoundrel*, 2003
   talented, independent heroine
Carla Kelly, *Mrs. Drew Plays Her Hand*, 1994
   well-written/thoughtful
Martha Kirkland, *The Artful Heir*, 1998

414

NIKKI RIVERS (Pseudonym of Sharon Edwin)

Random Acts of Fashion

(Toronto: Harlequin, 2005)

Story type: Humor; Contemporary
Subject(s): Humor; Small Town Life; Fashion Design
Major character(s): Gillian Caine, Store Owner (clothing store), Accident Victim (broken arm); Lukas McCoy, Contractor
Time period(s): 2000s
Locale(s): Timber Bay, Michigan

Summary: Haute couture in Timber Bay, Michigan, is flannel shirts and blue jeans, but Gillian Caine, transplanted New Yorker, is sure that her new clothing store will bring the locals to their fashion senses. Lukas McCoy interrupts Gillian's store preparations by breaking her arm during a freak accident. The judge orders Lukas to help her get the store ready, but a contractor in a woman's wear boutique has a lot in common with a bull in a china shop.

Where it's reviewed:
Romantic Times, February 2005, page 116

Other books by the same author:
Crime and Engagement, 2005
Finding Mr. Perfect, 2004
A Snowball's Chance, 2001
For Better, for Bachelor, 1999
Her Prince Charming, 1998

Other books you might like:
Barbara Daly, *Home Improvement*, 1999
Rachel Gibson, *Truly, Madly Yours*, 1999
Cathy McDavid, *Real Men Sell Bras*, 2003

Deborah Shelley, *Talk about Love*, 1999
Sharon Swan, *Cowboys and Cradles*, 2002

415

KAREN ROBARDS

Bait

(New York: Signet, 2005)

Story type: Contemporary; Romantic Suspense
Subject(s): Serial Killers; Murder
Major character(s): Maddie Fitzgerald, Advertising (executive); Sam McCabe, FBI Agent
Time period(s): 2000s
Locale(s): New Orleans, Louisiana

Summary: Although Maddie Fitzgerald believes she was a victim of a random attack, FBI Agent Sam McCabe thinks that she was targeted by a serial killer—and he also knows that she is lucky to be alive. The only way to trap the killer is to use the rather unwilling Maddie as bait, a tactic dangerous in more ways than one. A chilling, well-plotted story of murder, suspense, and secrets with romance and a dash of humor to add a tantalizing touch.

Other books by the same author:
Superstition, 2005
The Beachcomber, 2003
Whispers at Midnight, 2003
Ghost Moon, 2000
Hunter's Moon, 1996

Other books you might like:
Margaret Allison, *The Last Curve*, 1999
Beverly Barton, *Killing Her Softly*, 2005
Julie Garwood, *Murder List*, 2005
Lisa Jackson, *The Morning After*, 2004
Hunter Morgan, *What She Can't See*, 2005

416

J.D. ROBB (Pseudonym of Nora Roberts)

Origin in Death

(New York: Putnam, 2005)

Story type: Romantic Suspense; Futuristic
Series: Eve Dallas. Book 21
Subject(s): Murder; Secrets
Major character(s): Eve Dallas, Detective—Homicide (lieutenant), Spouse (of Roarke); Roarke, Businessman, Wealthy
Time period(s): 2050s (2059)
Locale(s): New York, New York

Summary: When a renowned cosmetic surgeon is murdered in his office and then his son, also a doctor, is murdered the same way, Lieutenant Eve Dallas knows there has to be something more to this than simply a dissatisfied patient. What she finally uncovers, with a little help from Roarke, is more horrifying than she had dreamed. The search for perfection and scientific advances come together in chilling ways in this installment of Robb's suspenseful, still quite romantic, series.

Where it's reviewed:
Romantic Times, July 2005, page 93

Other books by the same author:
Survivor in Death, 2005
Imitation in Death, 2003
Purity in Death, 2002
Seduction in Death, 2001
Conspiracy in Death, 1999

Other books you might like:
Beverly Barton, *Killing Her Softly*, 2005
Suzanne Forster, *Angel Face*, 2001
Linda Howard, *Now You See Her*, 1998
Lisa Jackson, *The Morning After*, 2004
Helen R. Myers, *Come Sundown*, 1998

417

NORA ROBERTS

Black Rose

(New York: Jove, 2005)

Story type: Contemporary/Fantasy; Paranormal
Series: In the Garden Trilogy. Book 2
Subject(s): Gardens and Gardening; Ghosts
Major character(s): Rosalind Harper, Businesswoman (nursery owner); Mitchell Carnagie, Genealogist
Time period(s): 2000s
Locale(s): Memphis, Tennessee

Summary: When take charge, marriage-shy Roz Harper decides to hire genealogist Mitch Carnagie to research the background of their ghost, Amelia, she unexpectedly ends up falling in love, to the violent wrath of Amelia and the cheers of the rest of her household. A slimy ex-husband and some small-minded women try to make Roz's life difficult, but in her typical fashion she puts them in their places and gets on with her life. Exceptionally appealing secondary characters reprise their roles in this second book in the In the Garden Trilogy.

Other books by the same author:
Red Lily, 2005 (In the Garden Trilogy. Book 3)
Blue Dahlia, 2004 (In the Garden Trilogy. Book 1)
Face the Fire, 2002 (Three Sisters Island Trilogy. Book 3)
Dance upon the Air, 2001 (Three Sisters Island Trilogy. Book 1)
Heaven and Earth, 2001 (Three Sisters Island Trilogy. Book 2)

Other books you might like:
Emily Carmichael, *A Ghost for Maggie*, 1999
Jill Marie Landis, *Heartbreak Hotel*, 2005
    a seafaring ghost
Jennifer Malin, *Eternally Yours*, 2002
Marilyn Pappano, *First Kiss*, 2002
Antoinette Stockenberg, *Dream a Little Dream*, 1997
    ghosts

418

ANN ROBINS (Pseudonym of Alice Duncan)

A Perfect Wedding

(New York: Zebra, 2005)

Story type: Historical/American West Coast
Subject(s): Crime and Criminals; Fear; Singing
Major character(s): Marjorie MacTavish, Secretary; Jason Abernathy, Doctor
Time period(s): 1910s (1912; 1915)
Locale(s): R.M.S. Titanic, At Sea; San Francisco, California

Summary: Determined to conquer her fears and start taking new chances in life, Marjorie MacTavish auditions for a part in her church's production of a Gilbert and Sullivan operetta. Much to her surprise, Marjorie lands one of the leading roles. However, one of her other co-stars is none other than Jason Abernathy, who delights in tormenting her with his flirtatious teasing. After losing her beloved fiance several years earlier, Marjorie never expected to experience love again, but fate it seems is giving Marjorie another chance with Jason.

Where it's reviewed:
Booklist, April 15, 2005, page 1438
Romantic Times, April 2005, page 47

Other books by the same author:
A Perfect Romance, 2004
A Perfect Stranger, 2004

Other books you might like:
Jane Goodger, The Perfect Wife, 2000
Betina Krahn, Sweet Talking Man, 2000
Susan Kay Law, A Wedding Story, 2003
Maggie Osborne, A Stranger's Wife, 1989
Bronwyn Williams, The Paper Marriage, 2000

419

JOANNE ROCK

My Lady's Favor

(Toronto: Harlequin, 2005)

Story type: Historical/Medieval
Subject(s): Independence; Marriage
Major character(s): Elysia Rougemont, Noblewoman; Conon St. Simeon, Knight, Nobleman (Comte de Vannes)
Time period(s): 14th century (1345)
Locale(s): France; England

Summary: After her new husband, the aged Comte de Vannes, unexpectedly dies on their wedding night, Elysia Rougemont thinks she might finally regain some measure of control over her own life. Then her guardian shatters Elysia's hopes for a marriage-free future by announcing he is arranging for a tournament, the winner of which will become Elysia's next husband. The only person Elysia can turn to for help is the new Comte de Vannes, Conon St. Simeon, but Elysia never expected that Conon might turn out to be the one man she wouldn't mind marrying.

Where it's reviewed:
Booklist, May 15, 2005, page 1641

Romantic Times, June 2005, page 61

Other books by the same author:
His Wicked Ways, 2005
Silk Confessions, 2005
Date with a Diva, 2004
Her Final Fling, 2004
The Knight's Confession, 2004

Other books you might like:
Jo Beverley, Lord of Midnight, 1998
Glynnis Campbell, My Champion, 2000
Madeline Hunter, By Arrangement, 2000
Linda Needham, Her Secret Guardian, 1998
Anne Stuart, Hidden Honor, 2004

420

ROSEMARIE SANTINI

Sex & Sensibility

(New York: Saint, 2005)

Story type: Contemporary
Subject(s): Sexual Behavior; Dating (Social Customs); Conduct of Life
Major character(s): Lizzie Parsons, Writer (freelance), Critic (film); Harry Archer, Editor (editor-in-chief)
Time period(s): 2000s
Locale(s): New York, New York

Summary: Acknowledged Jane Austen addict and film critic Lizzie Parsons tries to reconcile her fast-paced, modern, and very sexy reality with her dreams of the more genteel world of the early 19th century as she looks for love with funny, frustrating, and ultimately successful results. Chick lit with a historical twist.

Other books by the same author:
The Disenchanted Diva, 1987 (Rick & Rosie mysteries)
A Swell Style of Murder, 1985 (Rick & Rosie mysteries)

Other books you might like:
Jane Austen, Sense and Sensibility, 1811
   the original classic
Helen Fielding, Bridget Jones's Diary, 1996
Alesia Holliday, American Idle, 2004
Melissa Nathan, Pride, Prejudice, and Jasmine Field, 2001

421

AMANDA SCOTT (Pseudonym of Lynne Scott-Drennan)

Lord of the Isles

(New York: Warner Forever, 2005)

Story type: Historical/Medieval
Subject(s): Marriage
Major character(s): Lady Cristina Macleod, Noblewoman (laird's daughter); Hector Reaganach, Laird (of Lochbuie)
Time period(s): 14th century (1370)
Locale(s): Highlands, Scotland; Western Isles, Scotland

Summary: Even though she knows that Hector Reaganach wants to marry her younger sister, Mariota, Cristina Macleod is literally blackmailed into marrying him by her stubborn

father—and then she must deal with an angry husband for whom she is beginning to care. Hector, of course, eventually realizes that Cristina is twice the woman her superficial sister is, but it does take a bit of doing. Action-filled and sensual, this book follows *Highland Princess*, the story of Hector's twin brother, Lachlan.

Where it's reviewed:
Rendezvous, April 2005, page 23
Romantic Times, May 2005, page 43

Other books by the same author:
Highland Princess, 2004
The Hidden Heiress, 2002 (Secret Clan. Book 2)
Border Storm, 2001
The Secret Clan: Abducted Heiress, 2001 (Secret Clan. Book 1)
Highland Fling, 1995

Other books you might like:
Shana Abe, *The Truelove Bride*, 1999
Julie Garwood, *Saving Grace*, 1993
Samantha James, *A Promise Given*, 1998
Stephanie Laurens, *All about Passion*, 2001
  more trickery
Lyn Stone, *The Highland Wife*, 2001

422

LEANNE SHAWLER

Dangerous to Know

(New York: Zebra, 2005)

Story type: Regency
Subject(s): Scandal; Conduct of Life; Identity, Concealed
Major character(s): Elisabeth Stockwell, Gentlewoman; Lord Henry Langdon, Nobleman, Rake
Time period(s): 1810s
Locale(s): England

Summary: When Miss Elisabeth Stockwell finds a badly wounded man in her stable, she has no choice but to take him to the house and nurse him back to health. She knows he's a gentleman, but has no idea that he is the wicked Lord Henry Langdon who, according to gossip, had dueled over the wife of a family friend. Hidden identities, secrecy, and honor are all part of this traditional debut Regency that is both suspenseful and romantic.

Where it's reviewed:
Romantic Times, April 2005, page 67

Other books you might like:
Gail Eastwood, *The Captain's Dilemma*, 1995
Jean R. Ewing, *Valor's Reward*, 1996
Kate Huntington, *A Rogue for Christmas*, 2001
Allison Lane, *A Bird in Hand*, 1999
Regina Scott, *Utterly Devoted*, 2002

423

KATHRYN SHAY (Pseudonym of Mary Catharine Schaefer)

Nothing More to Lose

(New York: Berkley, 2005)

Story type: Contemporary; Romantic Suspense
Subject(s): Small Town Life; Guilt; Depression
Major character(s): Lisel Loring, Actress; Ian Woodward, Fire Fighter, Handicapped
Time period(s): 2000s
Locale(s): Hidden Cove, New York

Summary: New York firefighter Ian Woodward left the tragic horrors of 9/11 with survivor's guilt and a permanent disability. His depression goes on hold when actress Lisel Loring befriends him. She wants more than friendship, but Ian decides he doesn't want to burden her with someone in a wheelchair, so he moves back to Hidden Cove. However, a crazed fan is stalking Lisel, and now she's in Hidden Cove, too. Self-acceptance comes hard in this poignant tale as Ian comes to realize that he is still worthy of love.

Where it's reviewed:
Booklist, February 1, 2005, page 950
Romantic Times, February 2005, page 104

Other books by the same author:
Our Two Sons, 2005
On the Line, 2004
The Unknown, 2004
After the Fire, 2003
Against the Odds, 2003

Other books you might like:
Jessica Bird, *Leaping Hearts*, 2002
Lori Foster, *Jamie*, 2005
Dee Holmes, *Coming Home*, 2003
Mary Alice Monroe, *Sweetgrass*, 2005
Barbara Samuel, *A Piece of Heaven*, 2003

424

E.C. SHEEDY

Killing Bliss

(New York: Zebra, 2005)

Story type: Contemporary; Romantic Suspense
Subject(s): Murder; Secrets
Major character(s): Addy Michaels, Businesswoman (resort owner); Cade Harding, Professor (of criminalistics), Police Officer (former)
Time period(s): 2000s
Locale(s): Washington

Summary: Reluctantly drawn into the 15-year-old unsolved murder of Belle Bliss when his aunt seeks his help in locating her young grandson who disappeared from Belle's care the night of the killing, Cade Harding, academic and criminal profiling expert, sets out to find some answers. In particular, he is looking for the three teenagers, especially Addelene Wartenski, who were also at Belle's but fled the night of the murder. Someone else is on their trail, too, and his mission is far more deadly. A dark, chilling tale of romantic suspense

filled with conflicted, badly wounded characters, some of whom finally get it together.

Where it's reviewed:
Romantic Times, January 2005, page 86

Other books by the same author:
Room 33, 2004
Perfect Evil, 2003

Other books you might like:
Beverly Barton, *After Dark*, 2000
Suzanne Forster, *While She Was Sleeping*, 2003
Cait London, *With Her Last Breath*, 2003
Erica Spindler, *Shocking Pink*, 1998
   another tale of past sins
Anne Stuart, *Black Ice*, 2002

425

SANDI KAHN SHELTON

What Comes After Crazy

(New York: Shaye Areheart, 2005)

Story type: Contemporary; Humor
Subject(s): Humor; Family Relations; Mothers and Daughters
Major character(s): Masden ''Maz'' Lombard, Single Parent; Dan Briggs, Doctor (naturopath)
Time period(s): 2000s
Locale(s): New Haven, Connecticut

Summary: Health food store baker Masden ''Maz'' Lombard longs for normalcy. Her ''criminally weird'' mother, Madame Lucille, Fortune-Teller to the Stars, a serial bride, is getting married for the sixth time. Maz's husband went to Santa Fe to earn money for a few months, and never came back. Her daughters are weird, too. Hope is perpetually hostile, and Abbie insists on going to school with her slip over her dress. All Maz wants is a regular life. . .and naturopath Dr. Dan Briggs. A wild, wacky, and wonderful debut novel.

Where it's reviewed:
Library Journal, February 15, 2005, page 121

Other books you might like:
Meg Cabot, *Boy Meets Girl*, 2001
Sue Civil-Brown, *Next Stop, Paradise*, 2001
Donna Kauffman, *The Big, Bad Wolf Tells All*, 2003
Sheri McInnis, *Devil May Care*, 2003
Jane Moore, *The Ex-Files*, 2004

426

GENA SHOWALTER

Awaken Me Darkly

(New York: Downtown, 2005)

Story type: Paranormal; Futuristic
Series: Alien Huntress. Book 1
Subject(s): Aliens; Murder; Future
Major character(s): Mia Snow, Warrior (alien hunter), Detective—Police (New Chicago Police Dept.); Kyrin en Arr, Alien (Arcadian)
Time period(s): Indeterminate Future

Locale(s): Chicago, Illinois

Summary: Detective Mia Snow has a license to kill aliens, and she uses it liberally. After all, aliens killed her brother. Not all extraterrestrials who live on Earth are bad, but as head of the New Chicago Police Department's Alien Investigation and Removal Agency, Mia suspects them all. Unfortunately, a prime suspect in a series of murders, an Arcadian named Kyrin en Arr, is also her latest love interest. An exciting beginning to the Alien Huntress series.

Other books by the same author:
The Pleasure Slave, 2005
The Stone Prince, 2004

Other books you might like:
Linda Winstead Jones, *The Moon Witch*, 2005
Sherrilyn Kenyon, *Night Pleasures*, 2002
Susan Krinard, *Kinsman's Oath*, 2004
J.D. Robb, *Imitation in Death*, 2003
Susan Squires, *The Companion*, 2005

427

GENA SHOWALTER

The Pleasure Slave

(Don Mills, Ontario: HQN, 2005)

Story type: Contemporary; Fantasy
Subject(s): Magic; Seduction
Major character(s): Julia Anderson, Antiques Dealer; Tristan ar Malik, Warrior
Time period(s): 2000s
Locale(s): Santa Fe, New Mexico; Imperia, Fictional Country

Summary: Antiques dealer Julia Anderson knew the battered jewelry box she bought at a local flea market was special; she just never expected it would contain a man whose sole job was to cater to her every whim. At first Julia has no intention of availing herself of Tristan's ''services,'' but Julia finally decides that Tristan might be of some use after all, if he can teach Julia how to tempt her next door neighbor into finally asking her for a date. Even though Tristan is bound to do whatever his new mistress commands, he is determined that he is going to be the only man in her life!

Where it's reviewed:
Romantic Times, February 2005, page 106

Other books by the same author:
The Stone Prince, 2004

Other books you might like:
Annette Blair, *The Kitchen Witch*, 2004
P.C. Cast, *Goddess of Spring*, 2004
Kristine Grayson, *Utterly Charming*, 2000
Sherrilyn Kenyon, *Fantasy Lover*, 2002
Jenna McKnight, *A Greek God at the Ladies' Club*, 2003

SUZANNE SIMMONS (Pseudonym of Suzanne Simmons Guntrum)

Goodnight, Sweetheart

(New York: Berkley Sensation, 2005)

Story type: Contemporary; Humor
Series: Sweetheart, Indiana. Book 2
Subject(s): Reunions; Small Town Life
Major character(s): Sydney Marie St. John, Businesswoman (finance expert), Unemployed; Eric Law, Lawyer
Time period(s): 2000s
Locale(s): Sweetheart, Indiana

Summary: Fired from her high-powered job because she discovered some accounting irregularities in the firm's books, Sydney St. John heads home to Sweetheart, Indiana, to recuperate from the experience and visit her Aunt Minerva. When she runs into her high school love, attorney Eric Law and he doesn't even recognize her, things become interesting and eventually more romantic. Mystery, humor, and lively action abound in this funny romp that follows *Sweetheart, Indiana.*

Where it's reviewed:
Romantic Times, April 2005, page 100

Other books by the same author:
Sweetheart, Indiana, 2004
Lip Service, 2001
Lady's Man, 1999
No Ordinary Man, 1998
Paradise Man, 1997

Other books you might like:
Jennifer Crusie, *Welcome to Temptation*, 2000
Susan Donovan, *He Loves Lucy*, 2005
Lorraine Heath, *Hard Lovin' Man*, 2003
Shirley Jump, *The Bride Wore Chocolate*, 2004
Gina Wilkins, *Seductively Yours*, 2000

429

SUSAN SIZEMORE

I Hunger for You

(New York: Pocket Star, 2005)

Story type: Contemporary/Fantasy; Paranormal
Series: Vampire. Book 3
Subject(s): Vampires; Difference
Major character(s): Caramia ''Mia'' Luchese, Writer (travel/extreme sports articles); Colin Foxe, Vampire, Police Officer (SWAT team leader)
Time period(s): 2000s
Locale(s): Los Angeles, California

Summary: Involved in a passionate affair, SWAT team leader and vampire Colin Foxe and wealthy vampire hunter Mia Luchese have no idea of the other's true nature. When a particularly vicious vampire group, the Tribe, senses Colin's interest in Mia and begins to target her, the two eventually share their secrets and then must figure out how to deal with their ancient inherent enmities and their own knowledge that they are destined to be together. Passionate and fast-paced.

Where it's reviewed:
Rendezvous, March 2005, page 32
Romantic Times, April 2005, page 106

Other books by the same author:
I Thirst for You, 2004 (Vampire. Book 2)
Captured Innocence, 2003
I Burn for You, 2003 (Vampire. Book 1)
The Price of Passion, 2001
On a Long Ago Night, 2000

Other books you might like:
Amanda Ashley, *After Sundown*, 2003
Christine Feehan, *Dark Symphony*, 2003
Lori Herter, *Obsession*, 1991
Jaye Roycraft, *Afterimage*, 2002
Maggie Shayne, *Born in Twilight*, 1997

430

JENNIFER SKULLY (Pseudonym of Jennifer Skullestad)

Sex and the Serial Killer

(Don Mills, Ontario: HQN, 2005)

Story type: Contemporary; Humor
Subject(s): Change; Murder; Small Town Life
Major character(s): Roberta Jones Spivey, Waiter/Waitress; Nick Angel, Artist
Time period(s): 2000s
Locale(s): San Francisco, California; Cottonmouth, California

Summary: After her husband Warren walks out on her for his old high school sweetheart, Roberta Jones Spivey decides it is time for a change. With a new look and a new name, Bobbie Jones traces Warren to Cottonmouth, where she decides to show Warren that lots of other men still find her desirable. Despite what she hears about her new neighbor, artist Nick Angel, Bobbie is almost certain there is nothing to the rumors about Nick being a serial killer. Besides which, even if they are the tiniest bit true, dark, dangerous, and sexy Nick is just the kind of bad boy the new and improved Bobbie would date!

Where it's reviewed:
Romantic Times, January 2005, page 110

Other books you might like:
Jennifer Crusie, *Tell Me Lies*, 1998
Linda Howard, *Mr. Perfect*, 2000
Luanne Jones, *Sweethearts of the Twilight Lanes*, 2001
Susan Elizabeth Phillips, *Ain't She Sweet*, 2004
Deborah Smith, *Charming Grace*, 2004

431

BERTRICE SMALL

Lara

(Don Mills, Ontario: HQN, 2005)

Story type: Historical/Fantasy; Fantasy
Series: World of Hetar. Book 1
Subject(s): Fairies; Quest; Adventure and Adventurers
Major character(s): Lara, Slave, Mythical Creature (half-faerie/half-human)
Time period(s): Indeterminate Past

Locale(s): Hetar, Fictional Country

Summary: Sold by her father to become a Pleasure Woman so he can become a Crusader Knight, Lara, gentle and gifted with her faerie mother's beauty, begins a fantastic journey that sweeps her from the pleasure trader's auction block to the realm of the Forest Lords and places beyond. She learns about sex, power, and the role she is eventually destined to play. This is classic Bertrice Small with various love relationships and explicit sex, but with a fantasy twist.

Where it's reviewed:
Romantic Times, June 2005, page 53

Other books by the same author:
The Dragon Lord's Daughters, 2004
Until You, 2003
Intrigued, 2001
A Memory of Love, 2000
Skye O'Malley, 1980 (classic sweet/savage)

Other books you might like:
Emma Holly, *Hunting Midnight*, 2003
    highly sensual/fantasy
Susan Johnson, *Sinful*, 1993
Sasha Lord, *In a Wild Wood*, 2004
Laura Parker, *Risque*, 1996
Robin Schone, *The Lady's Tutor*, 1999

432

HAYWOOD SMITH

The Red Hat Club Rides Again

(New York: St Martin's Press, 2005)

Story type: Contemporary; Humor
Series: Red Hat Club. Book 2
Subject(s): Friendship; Kidnapping; Plastic Surgery
Major character(s): Georgia, Narrator; Teeny, Wealthy
Time period(s): 2000s
Locale(s): Atlanta, Georgia; Buckhead, Georgia

Summary: The 50-something steel magnolias of the Red Hat Club are at it again. Between such adventures as kidnapping a drug-addicted friend and having group plastic surgery on a luxury liner, Georgia rediscovers the love of her husband, and Diane hooks up with a childhood flame on the Internet. Middle age was never so exciting.

Where it's reviewed:
Library Journal, March 1, 2005, page 80

Other books by the same author:
The Red Hat Club, 2003 (Red Hat Club. Book 1)
Queen Bee of Mimosa Branch, 2002
Border Lord, 2001
Highland Princess, 2000
Dangerous Gifts, 1999

Other books you might like:
Laurie Graham, *The Future Homemakers of America*, 2004
Francis Ray, *Like the First Time*, 2004
Dolores Stewart Riccio, *Circle of Five*, 2003
Alisa Valdes-Rodriguez, *The Dirty Girls Social Club*, 2003
Rebecca Wells, *Ya-Yas in Bloom*, 2005

433

SUSAN SQUIRES

The Companion

(New York: St Martin's Paperbacks, 2005)

Story type: Paranormal; Historical/Regency
Subject(s): Vampires; Slavery; Erotica
Major character(s): Elizabeth Rochewell, Archaeologist; Ian Rufford, Vampire, Slave
Time period(s): 1810s (1818)
Locale(s): Sahara Desert, Africa; London, England

Summary: After being the much tortured sex slave of a vampire queen in the Sahara Desert, Ian Rufford's only wish is death. Elizabeth Rochewell loves the desert, especially going out on digs with her archaeologist father. Now, her father's dead, and propriety demands that she return to London. There's something odd about Elizabeth's shipmate, but she's drawn to him, even though his kisses have a real bite to them. A darkly erotic novel.

Where it's reviewed:
Booklist, April 1, 2005, page 1350
Romantic Times, May 2005, page 44

Other books by the same author:
Danelaw, 2003
Body Electric, 2002
Sacrament, 2002
Danegeld, 2001

Other books you might like:
Amanda Ashley, *A Whisper of Eternity*, 2004
Christine Feehan, *Dark Melody*, 2003
Maggie Shayne, *Twilight Hunger*, 2002
Susan Sizemore, *I Burn for You*, 2003
Chelsea Quinn Yarbro, *Writ in Blood*, 1997

434

AMANDA STEVENS (Pseudonym of Marilyn Medlock Amman)

Intimate Knowledge

(Toronto: Harlequin, 2005)

Story type: Contemporary; Romantic Suspense
Series: Matchmaker's Underground. Book 2
Subject(s): Drugs; Museums; Smuggling
Major character(s): Penelope Moon, Museum Curator (assistant); Simon Decker, Accountant, Government Official
Time period(s): 2000s
Locale(s): Houston, Texas; Dallas, Texas; Manzanillo, Mexico

Summary: While on a business trip in Mexico, assistant museum curator Penelope Moon thinks she sees her fiance Simon on the deck of a yacht. Of course, Penelope knows this is impossible since for the last few weeks Simon has been in a nursing facility in Dallas unable to wake up from a coma. When Penelope finds herself caught up in a dangerous scheme to smuggle drugs into the United States, she quickly learns that Simon is not the man she thought, but she also discovers he will do whatever it takes to protect her.

Where it's reviewed:
Romantic Times, February 2005, page 116

Other books by the same author:
Just Past Midnight, 2004
Secret Passage, 2004
Silent Storm, 2004
Unauthorized Passion, 2004
His Mysterious Ways, 2003

Other books you might like:
Jean Barrett, *Private Investigations*, 2003
Julie Miller, *The Rookie*, 2003
Ann Voss Peterson, *Accessory to Marriage*, 2002
Gayle Wilson, *The Bride's Protector*, 1999
Rebecca York, *Phantom Lover*, 2003

435

JEAN STONE

Once upon a Bride

(New York: Bantam, 2005)

Story type: Contemporary
Series: Second Chances. Book 1
Subject(s): Weddings; Change
Major character(s): Jo Lyons, Businesswoman (Second Chances partner), Public Relations (former expert); Andrew Kennedy, Journalist (undercover)
Time period(s): 2000s
Locale(s): West Hope, Massachusetts (Berkshires)

Summary: Four college friends, Lily, Elaine, Jo, and Sarah, now in mid-life, become partners in a wedding-planning service for second marriages in a lively, emotionally rich story that nicely sets the stage for the volumes to come in this series. Needing a receptionist, the women hire Andrew Kennedy, ostensibly a gay father raising his young daughter, but who is really a journalist for a men's magazine and is using what he learns on the job for his column. The interesting dynamics in this story focus on middle-aged women and the struggles of starting over.

Where it's reviewed:
Romantic Times, April 2005, page 57

Other books by the same author:
Twice upon a Wedding, 2005 (Second Chances. Book 2)
Tides of the Heart, 1999
Places by the Sea, 1997
First Loves, 1995
Ivy Secrets, 1994

Other books you might like:
Kathleen Eagle, *Once upon a Wedding*, 2002
Debbie Macomber, *Three Brides, No Groom*, 1997
   school chums reunite
Pamela Morsi, *By Summer's End*, 2005
Constance O'Day-Flannery, *Seasons*, 1995
Kathleen Gilles Seidel, *Summer's End*, 1999

436

JEAN STONE

Twice upon a Wedding

(New York: Bantam, 2005)

Story type: Contemporary
Series: Second Chances. Book 2
Subject(s): Weddings; Change
Major character(s): Jo Lyons, Businesswoman (Second Chances partner), Public Relations (former expert); Andrew Kennedy, Journalist (undercover); Elaine Thomas, Businesswoman (Second Chances partner)
Time period(s): 2000s
Locale(s): West Hope, Massachusetts (Berkshires)

Summary: Nicely continuing the story of four best friends who go into partnership as wedding consultants for second marriages, Stone's *Twice upon a Wedding* takes its characters through a New Year's wedding and other major events, plus various other serious difficulties, with all the flair and charm of the first volume in the series. Although the story involves all of the primary characters, especially Elaine and Andrew, the romantic interest is really between Jo and Andrew. More women's fiction than true romance, this series has enough romance in it to appeal to the genre's fans.

Where it's reviewed:
Romantic Times, April 2005, page 57

Other books by the same author:
Once upon a Bride, 2005 (Second Chances. Book 1)
Tides of the Heart, 1999
Places by the Sea, 1997
First Loves, 1995
Ivy Secrets, 1994

Other books you might like:
Kathleen Eagle, *Once upon a Wedding*, 2002
Debbie Macomber, *16 Lighthouse Road*, 2001
   Cedar Grove Chronicles. Book 1
Debbie Macomber, *Three Brides, No Groom*, 1997
Lynn Michaels, *Mother of the Bride*, 2002
Kathleen Gilles Seidel, *Summer's End*, 1999

437

SARAH STORME

The Long Way Home

(Waterville, Maine: Five Star, 2005)

Story type: Contemporary
Subject(s): Abuse; Change; Love
Major character(s): Allison Parker Tate, Runaway (from an abusive husband); Sam Calvert, Veterinarian, Parent (teenage daughter)
Time period(s): 2000s
Locale(s): Rocky Butte, Colorado

Summary: When Allie catches her controlling, abusive husband cheating on her with his secretary, it's the last straw—and so she runs. Then her car breaks down, stranding her in Rocky Butte, Colorado, and she ends up, bizarrely, in a drinking contest with the local veterinarian that results in

Allie passing out and Sam taking her home. A troubled teen-age girl, a possessive husband, a number of charming animals, and a pair of wounded protagonists just meant to be together interact beautifully in this heartwarming romance.

Where it's reviewed:
Library Journal, January 2005, page 92

Other books by the same author:
Just Kiss Me, 2004
Wild Montana Hearts, 2003
Emily Again, 2001

Other books you might like:
Catherine Anderson, *Forever After*, 1998
    similar theme and mood
Catherine Anderson, *Only by Your Touch*, 2003
Patti Berg, *And Then He Kissed Me*, 2003
    humorous treatment
Teresa Hill, *The Edge of Heaven*, 2003
    small town/heartwarming
Jill Marie Landis, *Heat Wave*, 2004
    heartwarming

438

JANET TANNER

No Hiding Place

(Sutton, England: Severn House, 2005)

Story type: Contemporary; Romantic Suspense
Subject(s): Suspense; Crime and Criminals; Family Relations
Major character(s): Julia Wilson, Lawyer; Paul Wilson, Businessman
Time period(s): 2000s
Locale(s): London, England; Wiltshire, England

Summary: In this modern day gothic, attorney Julia Wilson finds the name of a business involved in illegal activities on a list of her husband, Paul's, contacts. After she brings this up, someone shoves her down the parking garage stairs. Paul sends her home to Wiltshire to recuperate, where Julia's housekeeper disappears, and a strange, snooping woman with no domestic skills takes her place. Just when her whole world turns sinister and forbidding, Julia finds out she's pregnant.

Where it's reviewed:
Booklist, February 15, 2005, page 1062

Other books by the same author:
Tucker's Inn, 2004
Shadows of the Past, 2003
Morwennan House, 2002
All That Glisters, 2001
Hostage to Love, 2001

Other books you might like:
Cait London, *With Her Last Breath*, 2003
Patricia Potter, *Cold Target*, 2004
Antoinette Stockenberg, *A Month at the Shore*, 2003
Janelle Taylor, *Dying to Marry*, 2004
Karen Young, *Someone Knows*, 2002

439

JANET TANNER

The Penrose Treasure

(Sutton, England: Severn House, 2005)

Story type: Gothic; Historical
Subject(s): Secrets; Treasure, Buried; Inheritance
Major character(s): Tasmin Hardy, Servant (former), Bride; Adam Penrose, Veteran, Heir
Time period(s): 18th century
Locale(s): Cornwall, England

Summary: When lady's maid Tasmin Hardy returns home to care for her critically ill mother, she finds her barely alive, the victim of a brutal attack. A silver button is the only clue to the identity of the attacker. Since Tasmin is home, her childhood friend Isobel Penrose asks her to be her companion. There's an evil secret at Penrose Manor, one that might destroy Tasmin and Adam Penrose, the man she marries. A classic Gothic with the requisite young woman in peril and a dark, brooding hero.

Other books by the same author:
No Hiding Place, 2005
Tucker's Inn, 2004
Shadows of the Past, 2003
Morwennan House, 2002
Hostage to Love, 2001

Other books you might like:
Virginia Henley, *Ravished*, 2002
Victoria Holt, *Mistress of Mellyn*, 1960
Victoria Holt, *The Spring of the Tiger*, 1979
Kathryn Smith, *Elusive Passion*, 2001
Mary Stewart, *Nine Coaches Waiting*, 1958

440

VICKIE TAYLOR (Pseudonym of Vickie Spears)

Carved in Stone

(New York: Berkley Sensation, 2005)

Story type: Contemporary/Fantasy; Paranormal
Subject(s): Fantasy; Paranormal; Revenge
Major character(s): Rachel Vandermere, Police Officer (Interpol agent), Orphan; Nathan Cross, Mythical Creature (shapeshifting gargoyle), Professor (art)
Time period(s): 2000s
Locale(s): Chicago, Illinois

Summary: Interpol agent Rachel Vandermere knows firsthand that monsters really exist—after all, her parents were killed by one. Now, while on assignment in Chicago, Rachel encounters the enigmatic Nathan Cross, a titular art professor but in reality a gargoyle immortal determined to reject his heritage, and feels a strange connection she can't explain. When the murder of Nathan's long-time friend throws them together, the stage is set for a passionate romance and an unusual tale of love and vengeance.

Where it's reviewed:
Rendezvous, May 2005, page 35
Romantic Times, June 2005, page 134

Other books you might like:
Amanda Ashley, *After Sundown*, 2003
Alice Borchardt, *Night of the Wolf*, 2000
Christine Feehan, *Dark Melody*, 2003
Christine Feehan, *The Only One*, 2003
    paranormal anthology
Jaye Roycraft, *Afterimage*, 2002

441

ELIZABETH THORNTON

The Marriage Trap
(New York: Bantam, 2005)

Story type: Historical/Regency
Subject(s): Identity, Concealed; Murder; Gambling
Major character(s): Ellie Hill, Genius (mathematical), Gambler; Jack Rigg, Nobleman (Lord Raleigh), Military Personnel (Waterloo veteran)
Time period(s): 1810s
Locale(s): Paris, France; London, England

Summary: Six months after the Battle of Waterloo, jaded war veteran Jack Rigg finds himself in his Paris hotel sheltering a magnificently lovely female gambler, whose streak of luck was so good it set off a riot. Vicar's daughter Ellie Hill is a mathematical genius, and she uses that talent to win money at the gaming tables to support her brother and herself. However, she gambles not as Ellie, but as the mysterious beauty ''Aurora.'' Ellie's presence in Jack's quarters is her only alibi against an accusation of theft, and she immediately finds herself a fallen woman. To make matters worse, her brother is falsely accused of murder. A strong, resourceful woman and a cynical, avowed bachelor enter a marriage of convenience, but find themselves in a true love match as they face Regency society—and the real killer—together.

Other books by the same author:
Shady Lady, 2004
Almost a Princess, 2003
Princess Charming, 2001
The Perfect Princess, 2001
Strangers at Dawn, 1999

Other books you might like:
Candace Camp, *An Unexpected Pleasure*, 2005
Stephanie Laurens, *A Secret Love*, 2000
Barbara Metzger, *A Perfect Gentleman*, 2004
Amanda Quick, *Lie by Moonlight*, 2005
    Victorian era
Karen Robards, *Scandalous*, 2001

442

DIANE TYRREL

On Winding Hill Road
(New York: Berkley Sensation, 2005)

Story type: Contemporary; Gothic
Subject(s): Mystery; Suspense; Secrets
Major character(s): Sarah Logan, Companion (to young girl); Gatien Defalle, Wealthy

Time period(s): 2000s
Locale(s): San Mateo Peninsula, California

Summary: Recovering from illness and needing to recoup financially, Sarah Logan comes to be a companion—actually something of a combination mother/governess—to 13-year-old May Defalle and finds mystery, love, and danger in this suspenseful story with more than a few surprises. A brooding, enigmatic hero; a savvy, but vulnerable heroine; an isolated house with a view of San Francisco Bay; deadly family secrets; and an air of mystery add up to a contemporary gothic in the tradition of early Phyllis Whitney and Barbara Michaels.

Other books by the same author:
On the Edge of the Woods, 2004

Other books you might like:
Daphne Du Maurier, *Rebecca*, 1938
    classic Gothic
Victoria Holt, *Mistress of Mellyn*, 1960
Kay Hooper, *Amanda*, 1995
Susanna Kearsley, *Season of Storms*, 2001
Phyllis Whitney, *Flaming Tree*, 1960

443

SUSAN VAUGHAN

Code Name: Fiancee
(New York: Silhouette, 2005)

Story type: Contemporary; Romantic Suspense
Subject(s): Identity, Concealed; Terrorism
Major character(s): Vanessa Wade, Government Official (federal agent); Nicholas Markos, Businessman
Time period(s): 2000s
Locale(s): Washington, District of Columbia; Chevy Chase, Maryland

Summary: Before he was killed, Nick Markos' brother embezzled ten million dollars from a dangerous group of terrorists. Now even though Nick had no idea what his brother had done, the terrorists have threatened to kill Nick's fiancee, Danielle LeBec, if he doesn't return their money. In order to catch the leader of the terrorists and protect Danielle, anti-terrorist agent Vanessa Wade has agreed to pose as Nick's fiancee. Vanessa intends on keeping things strictly professional between herself and Nick, but it is a good thing Vanessa is skilled in the art of deception since resisting Nick proves to be quite challenging.

Where it's reviewed:
Romantic Times, January 2005, page 99

Other books by the same author:
Guarding Laura, 2004
Dangerous Attraction, 2001

Other books you might like:
Suzanne Brockmann, *Night Watch*, 2003
Dee Davis, *After Twilight*, 2001
Melissa James, *Can You Forget?*, 2004
Jenna Mills, *The Perfect Target*, 2003
Margaret Watson, *Someone to Watch over Her*, 2001

444

SUE-ELLEN WELFONDER

Only for a Knight
(New York: Warner Forever, 2005)

Story type: Historical/Medieval; Gothic
Subject(s): Memory Loss; Marriage
Major character(s): Juliana Mackay, Noblewoman (niece of a laird), Amnesiac; Robbie MacKenzie, Laird (heir of clan)
Time period(s): 14th century (1344)
Locale(s): Highlands, Scotland

Summary: Reluctantly agreeing to her dying mother's wish that she repay the Black Stag clan laird Duncan MacKenzie for helping them after the death of Kenneth, her father and also Duncan's half brother, Juliana Mackay sets out for Eilean Creag Castle. When an attack along the way results in the loss of her memory and she is rescued by none other than the wild Robbie MacKenzie, home from a decade of fast-living and slated to marry a woman he's never seen, their resulting attraction for each other has far-reaching consequences. Jealousy, old animosities, and passion combine in this lively tale of medieval Scotland.

Where it's reviewed:
Romantic Times, July 2005, page 33

Other books by the same author:
Wedding for a Knight, 2004
Bride of the Beast, 2003
Master of the Highlands, 2003
Knight in My Bed, 2002
Devil in a Kilt, 2001

Other books you might like:
Juliana Garnett, *The Laird*, 2002
Hannah Howell, *Highland Warrior*, 2004
Samantha James, *A Promise Given*, 1998
Karyn Monk, *The Rose and the Warrior*, 2000
Lyn Stone, *The Highland Wife*, 2001

445

SUSAN WIGGS

Table for Five
(Don Mills, Ontario: MIRA, 2005)

Story type: Contemporary/Mainstream
Subject(s): Death; Grief; Healing
Major character(s): Lily Robinson, Teacher; Sean McGuire, Sports Figure (golfer), Guardian (for half-brother's children)
Time period(s): 2000s
Locale(s): Oregon

Summary: Lily Robinson is more than a teacher to the Holloway kids. She's their mother Crystal's best friend, the one Crystal wants to raise them if anything happens to her. Something does happen—Crystal and Derek, her ex-husband, die in a car accident. Unfortunately, the will was never changed, and Derek's half-brother, Sean, is named legal guardian. Lily refuses to give up the children; Sean won't back down, either.

Guilt, grief, and eventually, love, form the tenuous bonds of a new family in this powerful novel.

Where it's reviewed:
Booklist, April 15, 2005, page 1437
Romantic Times, April 2005, page 54

Other books by the same author:
Summer by the Sea, 2004
The Ocean between Us, 2004
A Summer Affair, 2003
Home Before Dark, 2003
Enchanted Afternoon, 2002

Other books you might like:
Roz Denny Fox, *Someone to Watch over Me*, 2002
Patti Callahan Henry, *Where the River Runs*, 2005
Mary Alice Monroe, *Skyward*, 2003
Barbara Samuel, *A Piece of Heaven*, 2003
Kathryn Shay, *Trust in Me*, 2003

446

LORI WILDE (Pseudonym of Laurie Vanzura)

Mission: Irresistible
(New York: Warner, 2005)

Story type: Romantic Suspense; Humor
Subject(s): Egyptian Antiquities; Museums; Crime and Criminals
Major character(s): Cassie Cooper, Advertising (museum marketing and events); Harrison Standish, Archaeologist, Adventurer
Time period(s): 1980s; 2000s
Locale(s): Valley of the Kings, Egypt; Dallas, Texas

Summary: The costumed museum event celebrating the arrival of a legendary amulet goes wildly awry when someone stabs the mummy and steals the ancient treasure. Cassie Cooper, who coordinated the event, knows her reputation is at stake and recruits archaeologist Harrison Standish, although he's not her favorite person in the world, to help her find it. Lots of adventure with generous dollops of humor make this lively chase a fun and exciting one.

Where it's reviewed:
Booklist, May 15, 2005, page 1642

Other books by the same author:
Shockingly Sensual, 2005
As You Like It, 2004
Gotta Have It, 2004
Charmed and Dangerous, 2004
Racing against the Clock, 2004

Other books you might like:
Jessica Bird, *Heart of Gold*, 2003
Rachel Lee, *Under Suspicion*, 2001
Diana Palmer, *Before Sunrise*, 2005
Patricia Potter, *Broken Honor*, 2002
Roxanne St. Claire, *French Twist*, 2004

Romance

447

JILL WINTERS

Just Peachy

(New York: New American Library, 2005)

Story type: Contemporary; Romantic Suspense
Subject(s): Murder; Romance; Mystery
Major character(s): Peach Kelley, Designer (of gift baskets); Adam Quinlan, Computer Expert (network administrator)
Time period(s): 2000s
Locale(s): Boston, Massachusetts

Summary: Although attracted to each other, sunny, bubbly Peach Kelley and self-absorbed Adam Quinlan aren't about to get involved. However, when one of their coworkers goes missing and they try to find out why, they realize that their feelings for each other might well be something more than a passing fancy. Light romance combines with serious murder mystery.

Where it's reviewed:
Romantic Times, May 2005, page 115

Other books by the same author:
Raspberry Crush, 2004
Blushing Pink, 2003
Plum Girl, 2002

Other books you might like:
Susan Andersen, *Baby, Don't Go*, 2000
Susan Andersen, *Head over Heels*, 2002
Jennifer Crusie, *Tell Me Lies*, 1998
Rachel Gibson, *True Confessions*, 2001
Jane Graves, *Light My Fire*, 2004

448

LINDA RANDALL WISDOM

After the Midnight Hour

(New York: Silhouette, 2005)

Story type: Romantic Suspense
Subject(s): Crime and Criminals; Ghosts; Murder
Major character(s): Rachel Bingham, Spirit; Jared Stryker, Detective—Homicide
Time period(s): 2000s
Locale(s): Sierra Vista, California

Summary: Cynical, logical homicide detective Jared Stryker is the last person in the world to believe the rumors that the ranch he recently inherited is haunted. Then he begins to suspect that Rachel Bingham, the lovely lady he finds living in his new home, just might be a ghost. After being murdered by her husband over 100 years ago, Rachel has been waiting for someone who can break the curse that binds her to the ranch. At first Jared wants to find the key that will set Rachel free until he begins to suspect that in doing so, Rachel might be gone forever.

Where it's reviewed:
Romantic Times, May 2005, page 130

Other books by the same author:
Pregnancy Countdown, 2003

Roses after Midnight, 2003
Small-Town Secrets, 2002
Two Little Secrets, 2002
Mirror, Mirror, 2001

Other books you might like:
Virginia Kantra, *All a Man Can Be*, 2003
Amanda Stevens, *Nightime Guardian*, 2001
Susan Vaughan, *Dangerous Attraction*, 2001
Joanna Wayne, *As Darkness Fell*, 2004
Rebecca York, *Phantom Lover*, 2003

449

REBECCA YORK (Pseudonym of Ruth Glick)

Crimson Moon

(New York: Berkley Sensation, 2005)

Story type: Contemporary/Fantasy; Paranormal
Series: Moon. Book 4
Subject(s): Werewolves; Environmental Problems; Pollution
Major character(s): Olivia Woodlock, Wealthy; Sam Morgan, Werewolf, Thief
Time period(s): 2000s
Locale(s): California

Summary: Left for dead after a barroom brawl, trouble-prone werewolf Johnny Marshall changes his identity and heads west as Sam Morgan, master thief and protector of the environment. When he is recruited by the daughter and son of a lumber baron he is targeting in order to recover an ancient heirloom critical to the Woodlock family's survival, his ethical dilemma is compounded by his intense attraction to Olivia Woodlock. The supernatural and the real combine in this intense tale of romantic suspense.

Where it's reviewed:
Rendezvous, January 2005, page 32
Romantic Times, January 2005, page 117

Other books by the same author:
Bedroom Therapy, 2004
Out of Nowhere, 2004
Edge of the Moon, 2003 (Moon. Book 2)
Killing Moon, 2003 (Moon. Book 1)
Witching Moon, 2003 (Moon. Book 3)

Other books you might like:
Amanda Ashley, *Midnight Pleasures*, 2003
    paranormal anthology
Lori Handeland, *Blue Moon*, 2004
    lighter
Susan Krinard, *Prince of Shadows*, 1996
Susan Krinard, *Prince of Wolves*, 1994
Rhonda Thompson, *Call of the Moon*, 2002

450

KAREN YOUNG (Pseudonym of Karen Stone)

Never Tell

(Don Mills, Ontario: MIRA, 2005)

Story type: Contemporary; Romantic Suspense
Subject(s): Suspense; Memory Loss; Accidents

Major character(s): Erica Stewart, Designer (clothing), Amnesiac (some memory loss); Hunter McCabe, Architect
Time period(s): 2000s
Locale(s): Houston, Texas

Summary: After her husband and child are killed in an accident, Erica Stewart's life revolves totally around her promising clothing design business. When she meets Hunter McCabe, things change in delightfully romantic ways. However, the fact that Erica has been unable to remember the events of the night her husband and baby were killed has been the only thing that has kept her alive and as she begins to remember the accident, her life is increasingly at risk. A riveting, fast-paced read.

Where it's reviewed:
Romantic Times, June 2005, page 121

Other books by the same author:
In Confidence, 2004
Someone Knows, 2002
Heat of the Night, 2000
Kiss and Tell, 2000
Good Girls, 1998

Other books you might like:
Beverly Barton, *After Dark*, 2000
Beverly Barton, *Keeping Annie Safe*, 1999
Laura Caldwell, *Look Closely*, 2005
Fern Michaels, *About Face*, 2003
Maggie Shayne, *Forgotten Vows*, 1994

Romance

Western Fiction in Review
by
D.R. Meredith

Last year, I said I noticed a trend toward ranchers seeking revenge on the murderers of their families. I still have no explanation for the increase in this type of Western. There have always been Westerns with revenge as a theme, but not so many. It seems that greed, sex, and money are stronger motives. There are not nearly so many "Save the Ranch" stories in which some land grabbing, power hungry individual tries to seize someone's land by sleuth or violence. There are no longer so many Westerns about bank robbers. Instead, the murder of one's family in a particularly gruesome manner is required. Perhaps that is a reflection of modern society. But I don't want to go there, because I could spend hours searching out modern issues thinly disguised as Westerns. I will merely say that in the more than eighty Westerns annotated in this volume, there are eight novels with this exact theme. Matt Braun's *The Wages of Sin* concerns the SuttonTaylor feud in Texas, which began with the killing of a husband and father. The families of both victim and killer are dragged into a vicious cycle of revenge. In *Guns of Wolf Valley* by Ralph Cotton, a gunfighter poses as a woman's dead husband to protect the widow from land grabbers. That is a "Save the Ranch" theme that has violence, yes, but it also includes greed, courage, love, and perseverance. There is some meat on the bones of that plot. In many ways it mirrors Louis L'Amour's best Western: *Hondo*. J.D. Harkleroad's *Blood Atonement* is a modern revenge tale, but an unexpected twist turns it into a story of guilt and coverup. Charles G. West uses the revenge against a family's killers in *Bloody Hills* and in *Devil's Kin*. *Death Rides a Red Horse* by Cotton Smith is another revenge story. *Riders to Moon Rock* by Andrew J. Fenady is also a revenge story about family, but it is so subtle and no one is killed until the very end. It is poignant and a bit of a tearjerker, but Fenady develops his characters so well that the reader sees tragedy coming.

I don't mean to belabor this point. Revenge against the killers of one's family is a perfectly good and very human theme. I'm just not able to explain why there have been so many in the last two years. Perhaps it reflects society's fear that it is no longer secure, that one can no longer protect one's family, and that fear, I believe, is a consequence of 9/11. But enough of hunting for explanations for what might be coincidence. Let me go on to another mini-trend that I have noticed, and that is the increasing number of books that feature Indian folklore, creation tales, and literature. There has always been a proliferation of nonfiction books about these topics, but these learned tomes approached the whole subject from an anthropological or sociological perspective. The books I have noticed present these many folktales as stories, and of course, they are. Religion, tribal history, creation tales were all taught to children through the medium of storytelling. We should return the heavy, footnoted, annotated volumes to the shelf and learn about the culture of our indigenous neighbors through stories as their children learned their culture. Those who are interested can study those tomes after they absorb the basics through stories.

There are several books in this volume that illustrate this theme. Jane Archer's *The First Fire* features stories from the original homes of four tribes. There are interesting similarities but differences also in these stories. *Moon in the Water*, although a novel written by a white man, is the story of the most famous woman warrior of the Apaches: Lozen, sister to the famous chief, Victorio. The author, Stan Gordon, is very careful to include much information about Apache culture. My own novel, *Tome of Death*, is a story of the past and present. The reader becomes more familiar with and understanding of the complexities of the Comanche society.

Another book that contrasts white and Indian culture is *Horse of the Seven Moons* by Karen Taschek. In this story, a horse is a catalyst for an Apache youth and a white girl to learn something of one another beyond the stereotypes held by each race about the other. Reading *Chinnubbie and the Owl* by Alexander Posey is an excellent way to learn about

the Muskogee Nation. These stories were written for the various Indian newspapers in the late nineteenth and very early twentieth centuries. When the editor of the volume began collecting these articles, he found only one copy for each, consisting of yellowed, crumbling newspapers. A few more years and these stories would have been lost. Deborah L. Duvall is writing, one at a time, the Grandmother stories she heard from her Cherokee grandmother. *Rabbit and the Wolves* is the most recent volume of the Grandmother stories. It is presented like a children's picture book, but after all, these stories were originally told to children. Archaeologists Kathleen O'Neal Gear and W. Michael Gear are a husband and wife writing team. *People of the Moon* is their latest entry in the First North Americans series. Readers will receive no better education into the Anasazi culture of pre-contact America than this book. The Gears' archaeological training allows them to present realistic portraits of the culture and their behavior. There are no Hollywood Indians or New Age Indians in any novel the Gears write. This is how the Anasazi lived, this is how they behaved, this is how their government is run, this is how cruel they were to one another. This is very interesting stuff.

Another work annotated in this volume is *Masterpieces of American Indian Literature* edited by Willis G. Regier. This volume is the real McCoy. This book concerns Indians of various tribes talking about themselves, and we are allowed to listen in. *Mending Skins* by Eric Gansworth is another novel that tells the modern story of an old Indian woman whose land is being seized by the government. The reader can learn a lot about this woman's life and the culture she is clinging to, although it makes no sense to many of her neighbors.

Another trend that I have noticed trying to birth itself in the last year is the modern Western. By that I mean a book with a strong Western setting that influences the plot or character, but taking place from the very late nineteenth century to the present day. The writers of these novels believe as I do that one's physical environment, particularly in the West, can influence character development and behavior. There is an almost symbiotic relationship between people in the rural West, and most of it is rural, and the land. The empty spaces definitely affect one. In Rudolfo Anaya's *Jemez Springs* the protagonist is a Hispanic detective who fights an evil spirit, and solves crimes in New Mexico. To the detective, the evil spirit is as real as the bomber he searches for. This plot would not work in Manhattan. It works very well in New Mexico with it age-old Indian culture and Hispanic folktales. Harkleroad's *Blood Atonement* is set in modern day Utah among a radical Mormon sect that secretly practices polygamy. The young man in the book is sent to prison for a murder he did not commit. He was doomed from the moment he was arrested, since the deputy sheriff and the prosecutor were both members of this radical sect, as was the young man's defense attorney and the judge. Most of the jury were also members. Our hero is

an outsider, not a Mormon, and his story will not be given credence, despite the fact that everyone in town knows just what kind of girl the victim was. The plot, the motive for the girl's murder, are Western. There are still sects that practice polygamy in isolated areas; this book would not ''work'' outside of the West.

From a radical Mormon sect to a cult in Jane Kirkpatrick's *A Land of Sheltered Promise*, the variations of plot in the modern Western is infinite. Kirkpatrick follows three generations of women and their experiences on the Big Muddy Ranch: a ranch hand's wife, a member of a radical and fraudulent cult, and the cult member's daughter who organizes a camp for children. As the story moves from the late nineteenth century to the twentieth century, one thing remains constant—Big Muddy Ranch. The Big Muddy is a working ranch in the first story; a cult headquarters in the second; and a campground for children in the third.

Return to Abo by Sharon Niederman also concerns a ranch and the characters' relationship to it. A failed journalist returns home to a tiny ranching community in New Mexico to attend the funeral of a ranch hand. She believes she hates the ranch, hates the community, but her mother is very ill, and the journalist finds herself working on the ranch. Somewhat to her surprise, she joins a group fighting a powerful land developer with political backing, seeking to buy out all the ranchers and build a community of houses set on five acres or so, like ranches in miniature. The powerful land developer is a fact of life in the West, and his influence is destroying the agricultural West and a way of life. *Galveston Rose* by Mary Powell is a different kind of book. Rose, an elderly woman with no family, is dying, but she doesn't want to be alone, so she gathers a group of eccentric individuals to whom she rents rooms in her old Victorian style home. Framing the story is Galveston, its history, its ambiance, its people. Galveston is another character. I'm not saying that this plot wouldn't work in a book set anywhere else, but it would be different. Without the background of Galveston the book doesn't work. Without New Mexico, *The Belen Hitch* doesn't work either. On the surface, the book is a rather nicely done mystery, but a more careful reading will convince one that the New Mexican setting adds to the plot, even influences it. Robert James Waller's *High Plains Tango*, another modern novel, features a man's fight against the confiscation of his land for a superhighway.

These are just a few of the trends I have observed over the past year. Whether the trend of setting modern novels in the West, and using Western themes, such as water rights and the Westerner's distaste for the practice of eminent domain, will continue I don't know. I support those modern novels as a necessary development in the field of Western writing. The modern West is full of stories to tell and we have some writers who can tell those stories with passion.

Now I must switch hats from editor to reader and select the top twenty-five Westerns preceded by my usual disclaimer. These are my favorites out of those listed in this

volume. This does not mean that I am infallible. It does not mean that my judgment is the final arbitrator of what is good and what is bad in Westerns. It does not mean you should avoid reading those books not included on my list. I have tripped over my own assertions too many times for my recommendations to be foolproof. Feel free to disagree after reading several on the list. You might feel so-and-so's book is the next Pulitzer Prize winner, and I should have included it on my list. You might be right and I might be wrong and both possibilities exist. Everyone has their own personal criteria as to what constitutes a good book, and that is why there are over 50,000 books published in the United States each year. So readers will have choices. These are mine. Happy Reading.

1. *No Holier Spot of Ground* by John Warren Smith is simply too compelling a story not to make No. 1 on my list. The book is almost mesmerizing in its power.

2. *People of the Moon* by Kathleen O'Neal Gear and W. Michael Gear is a masterpiece of storytelling. We can never meet the Anasazi face to face, but we can come close in this work.

3. *Zorro* by Isabel Allende is a thoughtful literary work that focuses on the psychological, rather than the swashbuckling nature of Zorro's character. It is fascinating to watch young Diego develop his new persona.

4. *The Undertaker's Wife* by Loren D. Estleman is more than an examination of the methods of reconstructing and burying a body. It is also the story of a marriage, and of a woman who endures not lack of love, but lack of communication. The book is graphic, but compelling, even if you do learn more than you would like about funeral practices.

5. *Camp Ford* is another page turner by Johnny D. Boggs. Based on little known facts, as so many of Boggs' books are, it is entertaining, as well as informative. It is especially fun reading for those who are real baseball fans.

6. *Devil's Domain* by Tim Champlin is interchangeable with Johnny D. Boggs' *Camp Ford*. Both are set during the Civil War, but Champlin's plot is much more dark and so is his writing. The Devil's Domain that Champlin is referring to is Andersonville Prison, an unspeakable place of horror operated by the Confederacy. Champlin does a magnificent job of dragging the reader into his Devil's Domain. Once into the story, one can't stop reading.

7. *Sons of Texas* by Elmer Kelton is the first volume of what will be a series following the fortune of a family immigrating to Texas in the 1820s. Once more I am amazed at how real Kelton's characters are. Judging by the first volume, this series will be as enjoyable as his Texas Rangers series.

8. *Six Bits a Day* by Elmer Kelton is the prequel to his famous novel, *The Good Old Boys*. If you like Hewey Calloway in the original book, you'll love him here as he tries to save his brother from a fate worse than death: marriage.

9. *Dancing with the Golden Bear* by Win Blevins is the third of the author's Rendezvous series. After surviving the trip to California, Sam Morgan and his wife don't enjoy their stay. As usual, Win Blevins has done his research. The book sparkles with descriptive narrative that vividly evokes the setting.

10. *Riders to Moon Rock* by Andrew J. Fenady is just sheer fun to read. It is a dark story but has flashes of hope.

11. *Dream West* by David Nevin is one of those old-fashioned novels with little sex, violence where and when it is needed, and lots of detail.

12. *Bad Money* by Ed Gorman has slipped off the radar, but this is an outstanding traditional Western that everyone will enjoy.

13. *Trapp's Mountain* by Robert J. Randisi is another traditional Western with an interesting story. Trapp, who is just released from prison, educates the reader on how it feels to do hard time.

14. *Honor Thy Father* by Robert A. Roripaugh is a sensitive picture of the Johnson County War through the eyes of a rancher's young son. The book offers a different perspective than we are used to.

15. *Galveston Rose* by Mary Powell is a powerful story of loneliness and what it takes to make a family.

16. *Lone Star Law* edited by Robert J. Randisi contains a series of short stories written by well-known Western authors, such as Loren D. Estleman and Elmer Kelton.

17. *An Obituary for Major Reno* by Richard S. Wheeler tells the other side of the Major Reno story at Little Bighorn.

18. *Trouble in Tombstone* by Richard S. Wheeler is a psychological study of Wyatt Earp, as he narrates the story of the gunfight at the O.K. Corral.

19. *The Only Road There Is* by Rebecca Bailey tells the story of a daughter and her eccentric mother driving to visit the daughter's brother whom she's not seen in over eighteen years. Not only is this story humorous, but it has a strong sense of place.

20. *Marshal of Medicine Lodge* by Stan Lynde is a humorous story of a deputy U.S. marshal who is great deal better and smarter than he thinks he is.

21. *Hardwater* by Steve Sherwood is another modern blend of Western and mystery genres that works on both levels.

22. *The Diezmo* by Rick Bass is a thoughtful story of a young man who learns the horrors of war.

23. *Out of Range* by C.J. Box is another blend of Western and mystery that has a strong sense of place, and in fact,

could not work in another region, so closely tied is it to Wyoming.

24. *Bent Red Moon* by Russ Hall is a strong Western with lots of action and suspense, and has a nice love story.

25. *The Belen Hitch* by Pari Noskin Taichert is a mix of humor and pathos and the dirty little secrets of a small town. The picture of a rural New Mexico town is very effective.

For More Information about Western Fiction

The Western Writers of America maintain a database of bookstores willing to stock and/or order Western titles. For information on the database, or to add your favorite bookstore to it, write to Candy Moulton, Editor, *Roundup Magazine*, Box 29 Star Route, Encampment, WY 82325.

For general information on what's happening in Western writing, subscribe to *Roundup Magazine* at the above address. *Roundup* is the official publication of the Western Writers of America and includes reviews of Western fiction and nonfiction done by yours truly. In addition, there is a series of features on Writers of the 20th Century, a section on what's doing in Hollywood by Miles Hood Swarthout, and articles on new directions in Western writing.

For the computer literate there is no source like amazon.com for finding out-of-print Westerns, or just titles by a favorite that you are missing. Remember also to periodically check for titles in your local used bookstores, estate sales, flea markets, garage sales, and your local Friends of the Library book sale. And speaking of libraries, if the title you want is in hardback, ask your local library to get it for you on interlibrary loan. Some libraries will order original paperbacks on interlibrary loan, but you will need to ask. As a last resort, contact a rare book dealer for some desired title you want, but be prepared to pay dearly. I found one of my first printing, original paperbacks, used, for $108. I didn't make a whole lot more than that when I wrote it.

Western Titles

ISABEL ALLENDE

Zorro

(New York: HarperCollins, 2005)

Story type: Historical/American West; Saga
Subject(s): Mexicans; Legends
Major character(s): Diego de la Vega, Hero; Manuel Escalante, Gentleman; Bernardo, Servant, Companion
Time period(s): 1810s (1815)
Locale(s): California; Barcelona, Spain

Summary: Born in 1795, the son of a wealthy landowner and a half Shoshone Indian, Diego de la Vega is a child of privilege, but sympathizes with the Indians and poor Mexicans who are oppressed by the Mexican government still under the control of Spain. When he and his best friend Bernardo, the son of his nurse, are sent to Barcelona for Diego's education, a famous fencing master and leader of a secret society, Manuel Escalante, notices his superb swordwork and tutors him. Escalante also recruits him into La Justicia, a secret society that opposes oppression. It is there that Diego forges the alter ego that will become famous when he returns to California: Zorro.

Where it's reviewed:
Library Journal, March 1, 2005, page 74
Publishers Weekly, February 28, 2005, page 39

Other books by the same author:
Daughter of Fortune, 1999

Other books you might like:
Rudolfo Anaya, *Serafina's Stories*, 2004
Eric Gansworth, *Mending Skins*, 2005
Eric Gansworth, *Smoke Dancing*, 2004
Frank B. Linderman, *Indian Why Stories*, 2004

RUDOLFO ANAYA

Jemez Spring

(Albuquerque: University of New Mexico Press, 2005)

Story type: Modern; Mystery
Series: Sonny Baca. Book 5
Subject(s): American West; Crime and Criminals
Major character(s): Sonny Baca, Detective—Private; Chica, Animal (dachshund); Raven, Villain, Murderer
Time period(s): 2000s
Locale(s): Albuquerque, New Mexico; Jemez Spring, New Mexico

Summary: When the governor of New Mexico is found drowned in the Bath House at Jemez Springs, Albuquerque private detective and former schoolteacher Sonny Baca is called in to investigate. Accompanied by his inseparable companion, Chica, a dachshund that Sonny swears can dream, the private eye descends on Jemez Springs and is soon up to his neck in evil. There is a bomb planted near the Los Alamos National Laboratories, a top secret government establishment that will not react well to an explosion. Rather, it may react by making that area of New Mexico uninhabitable. Sonny must not only try to catch Raven, the ultimate villain in the vein of Sherlock Holmes' Dr. Moriarity, whom he suspects of planting the bomb, but also fight off various ghosts and sorcerers as well as land developers and politicians. Anaya's mysteries are heavy on both setting and magic.

Where it's reviewed:
Roundup Magazine, August 2005, page 32

Other books by the same author:
Tortuga, 2004
My Land Sings, 2001
Shaman Winter, 1999 (Sonny Baca. Book 4)
Zia Summer, 1995 (Sonny Baca. Book 2)
Bless Me, Ultima, 1972

Other books you might like:
Steven F. Havill, *Convenient Disposal*, 2004
   Posados County. Book 12
Tony Hillerman, *Skeleton Man*, 2004
   Joe Leaphorn/Jim Chee. Book 17
Frank B. Linderman, *Indian Why Stories*, 2004
Lisa Sandlin, *In the River Province*, 2004
Jose Skinner, *Flight and Other Stories*, 2001

453

JANE ARCHER

The First Fire

(Dallas: Taylor, 2005)

Story type: Historical/American West; Indian Culture
Subject(s): Short Stories; Indians of North America; Religious Traditions
Time period(s): Indeterminate Past
Locale(s): United States

Summary: Archer retells folk tales that originated in the Smoky Mountains of the Cherokees; the woodlands of the Great Lakes, home of the Kickapoo; the High Plains of the West where the Kiowa lived; and the pueblos of the Southwest from where the Tigua came. Humorous tales, tragic tales, stories of creation, and stories of prophesy provide a portrait of both the variation and the similarity of Indian culture in different regions of what became the United States.

Where it's reviewed:
Roundup Magazine, August 2005, page 32

Other books by the same author:
100% Me Journal (Potter Style), 2005
Flower Journal, 2005
Let Not Your Flight Be in Winter, 2002
Texas Indian Myths and Legends, 2000
Maverick Moon, 1997

Other books you might like:
Rudolfo Anaya, *Serafina's Stories*, 2004
Eric Gansworth, *Mending Skins*, 2005
Eric Gansworth, *Smoke Dancing*, 2004
Frank B. Linderman, *Indian Why Stories*, 2004

454

DARRELL ARNOLD, Editor

Good Medicine

(La Veta, Colorado: Range Writer, 2005)

Story type: Modern; Anthology
Subject(s): Cowboys/Cowgirls; Humor; Short Stories
Time period(s): 20th century (1950s-1990s)
Locale(s): West

Summary: Pure humor is the hallmark of these cowboy stories originally published by *Cowboy Magazine*. In ''The Ranch Women's Code of the West,'' Sally Harper Bates lists the rules that a rancher or cowboy's wife must follow if she wants to retain her sanity. In ''Ice Ball Rodeo,'' Sam Dawson explains how to survive sharing a line shack with a spooked horse during a hail storm. ''Wild West in Georgia'' describes a cowboy going toe to toe with a Black Brangus steer who objects to being manhandled into a feedlot. One of the funniest stories is ''The Race,'' in which the author describes how to get on your horse and away before the bull, cow, or big yearling into whose body you just injected antibiotics runs you down and stomps you flat. Whether or not a person has ever worked cattle, ridden a horse, or fixed a fence, these tales will tickle the funny bone.

Where it's reviewed:
Roundup Magazine, August 2005, page 32

Other books you might like:
Frank Bonham, *The Phantom Bandit*, 2004
B.M. Bower, *The Terror*, 2003
Dan Cushman, *No Gold on Boothill*, 2001
T.T. Flynn, *Reunion at Cottonwood Station*, 2004
Les Savage Jr., *Gambler's Row*, 2002

455

REBECCA BAILEY

The Only Road There Is

(Huntsville: Texas Review Press, 2005)

Story type: Modern; Saga
Subject(s): American West; Humor
Major character(s): Brenda Marlene Simpkins, Care Giver (for her elderly mother); Mauda Belle Simpkins, Aged Person (Brenda's 80-year-old mother); Dennis Ishman Simpkins, Relative (Marlene's brother)
Time period(s): 2000s
Locale(s): Cooke City, Montana

Summary: Brenda Marlene Simpkins calls herself a variety of flower child names such as Starflower Jade-Eagle or her current favorite, Cerise Cloudmist. Her mother, Mauda Belle Simpkins, calls her Brenda Marlene, and her brother, Dennis Ishman Simpkins, calls her Pooh. Brenda calls herself by such hippy-sounding names to disguise the fact that she is an authentic hillbilly from Kentucky who grew up eating squirrel and wearing jammies made from feed sacks. Dennis pretends to be a mountain man by living in a shack in Montana and hunting his own food. When Brenda decides to take her mother to visit Dennis, whom she hasn't seen in 13 years, she soon wishes she had stayed in Kentucky. She feels obligated to get her mother away from the computer, where Mauda has a collection of friends in chat rooms and buys obsolete cereal and lipstick on the Web. Upon reaching Cooke City, Montana, Brenda realizes that the man calling himself Dennis is not Dennis at all. Dennis has always been a trial to her from birth, and nothing has changed. Now she has to discover what happened to her real brother in this humorous tale of the new West.

Where it's reviewed:
Roundup Magazine, August 2005, page 34

Other books by the same author:
Wild Kentucky Garden, 1998

Other books you might like:
Sandra Dallas, *The Chili Queen*, 2002
Ken Hodgson, *Surviving Wisdom*, 2003
Joe R. Lansdale, *The Magic Wagon*, 2001

Michael Little, *Queen of the Rodeo*, 2001
Clay Reynolds, *The Vigil*, 2001

456

RICK BASS

The Diezmo

(Boston: Houghton Mifflin, 2005)

Story type: Historical/American West; Man Alone
Subject(s): Mexicans; War
Major character(s): James Alexander, Military Personnel (member of a Texas militia), Teenager (16-year-old)
Time period(s): 1840s (1842)
Locale(s): LaGrange, Texas; Mexico

Summary: In 1842, when the Republic of Texas is only a few years old, and feelings against Mexico are still running high, a group of Texas Militia stop in LaGrange, Texas, seeking recruits to join in a march into Mexico in search of Mexicans who attacked San Antonio. Sixteen-year-old James Alexander joints the militia in a fever of patriotism and desire for justice. Marching into Mexico, the group is captured by the Mexican Army. They escape but the hot, waterless desert of Mexico almost defeats them. Weak, thirsty, and unable to fight, they are captured again. This time they are imprisoned in the infamous Castle of Perve. The story has a gritty realism and scenes of violence that alternate with descriptions of the beauty of the land.

Where it's reviewed:
Publishers Weekly, March 21, 2005, page 35

Other books by the same author:
Where the Sea Used to Be, 1998
The Sky, the Stars, the Wilderness, 1997

Other books you might like:
Jane Candia Coleman, *Moving On*, 1999
T.T. Flynn, *Night of the Comanche Moon*, 1995
Jovita Gonzales, *Caballero*, 1996
    Eve Raleigh, co-author
Jeff Shaara, *Gone for Soldiers*, 2000
Norman Zollinger, *Chapultepec*, 1995

457

WIN BLEVINS

Dancing with the Golden Bear

(New York: Forge, 2005)

Story type: Mountain Man; Man Alone
Series: Rendezvous. Book 3
Subject(s): American West; Gold Discoveries
Major character(s): Sam Morgan, Mountain Man; Jedediah Smith, Mountain Man, Explorer; Meadowlark, Spouse (of Sam Morgan), Indian (Crow)
Time period(s): 1820s (1826)
Locale(s): West; Los Angeles, California

Summary: Jedediah Smith, the greatest of the mountain men, if the most private, proposes to lead an expedition west hunting for better beaver trapping with the final destination actually California although he tells no one but Sam Morgan and his young Crow wife, Meadowlark. They must cross the Colorado River, then travel across the Mojave Desert. Staggering into Pueblo de los Angeles, suffering from lack of food and water, they find the Mexican government suspicious of them. After a knife fight in which two prominent citizens' sons are killed, the brigade flees back to the desert. When Meadowlark becomes ill, Sam takes her to Monterey where he learns that life is like a golden bear: it's beautiful but it bites.

Where it's reviewed:
Roundup Magazine, August 2005, page 32

Other books by the same author:
Give Your Heart to the Hawks, 2005
Beauty for Ashes, 2004 (Rendezvous. Book 2)
So Wild a Dream, 2003 (Rendezvous. Book 1)
RavenShadow, 2002
The Rock Child, 2001

Other books you might like:
Frederic Bean, *The Red River*, 1998
Don Coldsmith, *South Wind*, 1998
W. Michael Gear, *Coyote Summer*, 1997
W. Michael Gear, *The Morning River*, 1996
Richard S. Wheeler, *Rendezvous*, 1997
    Skye's West. Book 9

458

JOHNNY D. BOGGS

Camp Ford

(Waterville, Maine: Five Star, 2005)

Story type: Traditional; Historical/American Civil War
Subject(s): Sports/Baseball; Prisoners of War
Major character(s): Win MacNaughton, Military Personnel (Union Army soldier); Mike Peabody, Sidekick (of Win MacNaughton); Connel McGee, Military Personnel (Union Army captain)
Time period(s): 1860s (1863); 1940s (1946)
Locale(s): Camp Ford, Texas; St. Louis, Missouri

Summary: Ninety-nine-year-old Win MacNaughton is invited to the World Series in 1946 in St. Louis because he has spent his whole life in the business of baseball. From the time he saw his first baseball game when he was 11, Win has been an avid player, umpire, manager, and fan. The sports writers always ask him who were the best of all the teams he'd seen. He always tells the truth: Mr. Lincoln's Hirelings and the Ford City Gallinippers. Everyone thinks he is senile and never prints his opinion, so Win sits down with a Big Chief tablet and a pencil to tell the story of moving to Texas because his father wanted to establish an Abolitionist colony. From there young Win enlists in the Union Army under the command of Captain Connel McGee, and meets up again with his childhood friend, Mike Peabody. Win and all of General Banks' army that didn't outrun the Rebels are captured and sent to Camp Ford, the largest prisoner of war camp west of the Mississippi. There they organize a baseball game as cover for an escape attempt, except winning the game becomes the more important goal. Based on research into baseball games

played during the Civil War, *Camp Ford* is both humorous and tragic.

Where it's reviewed:
Roundup Magazine, August 2005, page 33

Other books by the same author:
Dark Voyage of the Mittie Stephens, 2004
East of the Border, 2004
Purgatoire, 2003
The Big Fifty, 2003
The Despoilers, 2002

Other books you might like:
G.G. Boyer, *Custer, Terry, and Me*, 2004
Tim Champlin, *Raiders of the Western & Atlantic*, 2002
Ed Gorman, *The Blue and the Gray Undercover*, 2001
Randall Beth Platt, *The 1898 Base-Ball Fe-As-Ko*, 2000
Joseph A. West, *Me and Johnny Blue*, 2000

459

B.M. BOWER

Law on the Flying U
(Waterville, Maine: Five Star, 2005)

Story type: Ranch Life; Collection
Subject(s): American West; Humor; Short Stories
Time period(s): 19th century (post-Civil War)
Locale(s): West

Summary: B.M. Bower was the first woman Western author who was able to support herself by writing. Her most well-known works are those set on the Flying U Ranch, where a group of eccentric cowboys work for the Old Man, J.G. Whitmore, who is eccentric himself. The majority of the stories in this collection possess Bower's hallmark humor. An example is "The Intervention of Almighty Voice," in which a scheming widow decides the Old Man is husband material. In "On the Middle Guard," a new-fangled automobile suddenly appears on a cattle herd's best bedding ground. Other stories are not so humorous. In "The Outlaw," a young cowboy kills in self-defense but is still convicted and sent to prison. A wonderful collection of short stories.

Where it's reviewed:
Roundup Magazine, October 2005, page 34

Other books by the same author:
The Terror, 2003
The Lonesome Land, 1912
Chip, of the Flying U, 1906

Other books you might like:
Max Brand, *The Lost Valley*, 2002
Ralph M. Flores, *The Horse in the Kitchen*, 2004
John Jakes, *The Funeral of Tanner Moody*, 2004
   Elmer Kelton, Robert J. Randisi, and others, co-authors
Annie Proulx, *Bad Dirt*, 2004
Cherry Wilson, *The Throwback*, 2002

460

C.J. BOX

Out of Range
(New York: Putnam, 2005)

Story type: Modern; Mystery
Series: Joe Pickett. Book 5
Subject(s): Crime and Criminals; Law Enforcement
Major character(s): Joe Pickett, Game Warden (for state of Wyoming); Will Jensen, Game Warden (for state of Wyoming), Friend (of Joe Pickett); Marybeth Pickett, Spouse (of Joe Pickett)
Time period(s): 2000s
Locale(s): Saddlestring, Wyoming; Jackson Hole, Wyoming

Summary: Game Warden Joe Pickett is happy working out of Saddlestring, Wyoming. The town is small and generally peaceful with certain notable exceptions. He is ordered to take a temporary assignment in Jackson Hole when his co-worker and friend, Will Jensen, dies as an apparent suicide. Joe is not thrilled by his new post. Jackson Hole is too full of rich celebrities and wealthy socialites, all of them from somewhere else besides Wyoming. He immediately finds himself the target of various political groups: animal rights activists, environment extremists, and just plain hunters. All want him to endorse their position on a building project. Joe refuses, and his pickup truck is set on fire. That convinces Joe that Will's supposed suicide was actually murder, because Will had also been recalcitrant in the face of pressure groups. If Joe didn't have enough worries, his wife, Marybeth, is being difficult about his absence and the family budget. A wonderful Western mystery with pickups and cell phones instead of horses and .45s.

Where it's reviewed:
Library Journal, May 1, 2005, page 67

Other books by the same author:
Trophy Hunt, 2004 (Joe Pickett. Book 4)
Winterkill, 2003 (Joe Pickett. Book 3)
Savage Run, 2002 (Joe Pickett. Book 2)
Open Season, 2001 (Joe Pickett. Book 1)

Other books you might like:
Frederic Bean, *Murder at the Spirit Cave*, 1999
Margaret Coel, *Killing Raven*, 2003
James D. Doss, *Dead Soul*, 2003
   Charlie Moon. Book 8
Tony Hillerman, *The Sinister Pig*, 2003
Michael McGarrity, *Slow Kill*, 2004
   Kevin Kerney. Book 9

461

MAX BRAND

Bad Man's Gulch
(Waterville, Maine: Five Star, 2005)

Story type: Traditional; Collection
Subject(s): Ranch Life; Feuds; Short Stories
Time period(s): 19th century (post-Civil War)
Locale(s): Tennessee

Summary: Three of Max Brand's finest long short stories present three different pictures of a Western man. In "The Adopted Son" Lazy Purdue flees a shooting in Texas and rides the rails to Tennessee, to the home he was driven from by his family. He joins a blood feud on the side of his family's enemy, and finds a way to end the feud once and for all. In "Billy Angel, Trouble Lover" a wounded young man fleeing a posse finds refuge and redemption in the person of a kind woman. "Bad Man's Gulch" is the story of a reformed gunfighter, who takes up his guns again to protect a helpless woman and her elderly father.

Where it's reviewed:
Roundup Magazine, August 2005, page 34

Other books by the same author:
Trouble's Messenger, 2005
Hawks and Eagles, 2004
The Golden Cat, 2004
Mountain Storms, 2004
Peter Blue, 2003

Other books you might like:
Giff Cheshire, *Comanche Prairie*, 2003
Bennett Fisher, *Gila City*, 2003
Steve Frazee, *Nights of Terror*, 2003
Louis L'Amour, *The Collected Short Stories of Louis L'Amour: The Frontier Stories*, 2003
Lewis B. Patten, *Guns of Vengeance*, 2003

462
LYLE BRANDT

Rebel Gun
(New York: Berkley, 2005)

Story type: Traditional; Chase
Subject(s): Indians of North America; Crime and Criminals; Revolutions
Major character(s): Matthew Price, Drifter; Gray Wolf, Indian (Apache); Cesar Zapata de Leon, Revolutionary
Time period(s): 19th century (post-Civil War)
Locale(s): Pequeno, Mexico; Chihuahua Desert, Mexico

Summary: While riding through a tiny village, Matthew Price sees a poster advertising the hanging of Gray Wolf the next day. He steals the padre's robe and breaks Gray Wolf out of the Mexican jail disguised as a priest. Matt also frees the Apache's cell mates: a common thief and the infamous Mexican revolutionary, Cesar Zapata de Leon. The thief is killed almost immediately, but Matt and his companions escape. The posse soon catches up, but Matt kills the eight men in the posse. Without a gun Cesar can only watch, but what he sees convinces him that Matt would be an asset to the revolution. Matt has no intention of joining a ragged band of Mexican peasants fighting a well-supplied army, but after he notices a poster with his face on it, he decides Mexican peasant revolutionaries sound better than a firing squad.

Where it's reviewed:
Roundup Magazine, October 2005, page 34

Other books by the same author:
Justice Gun, 2003
Gun, 2002

Other books you might like:
Robert J. Conley, *The Gunfighter*, 2001
Thomas Eidson, *The Missing*, 2003
Stephen Overholser, *Track of a Killer*, 2003
Cotton Smith, *Sons of Thunder*, 2003
Richard S. Wheeler, *The Bounty Trail*, 2004

463
MATT BRAUN

Dakota
(New York: St. Martin's Paperbacks, 2005)

Story type: Traditional; Ranch Life
Subject(s): Crime and Criminals; American West
Major character(s): Theodore Roosevelt, Historical Figure, Rancher; Bill Merrifield, Cowboy, Rancher (ranch foreman); Marquis de Mores, Rancher
Time period(s): 1880s (1884-1885)
Locale(s): Medora, North Dakota; New York, New York

Summary: After his mother and wife die on the same day in 1884, Theodore Roosevelt, overcome with grief, leaves New York and settles on a ranch near the town of Medora in present day North Dakota. He becomes part of the community and is elected to represent Dakota at a meeting of cattlemen in Montana that is focusing on the problem of cattle rustling. Rustlers are stealing hundreds of cattle and horses from ranchers every year, and the committee even considers forming a vigilante group. This proposal causes Roosevelt to walk out and return to Medora. He organizes a cattlemen's association, and defeats the Marquis de Mores for the presidency of the group. Everyone knows that the marquis is hand in glove with the rustlers, although no one can prove it. A corrupt brand inspector in Mores' pocket charges one of Teddy's men with rustling, and Teddy, fed up with Mores' crooked ways, challenges him to a duel with shotguns. After humiliating Mores and getting rid of the rustlers, Teddy returns to the east and enters politics again.

Where it's reviewed:
Roundup Magazine, September 2005, page 33

Other books by the same author:
Black Gold, 2004
Crossfire, 2004
Highbinders, 2004
The Wages of Sin, 2004
Judas Tree, 2003

Other books you might like:
Ralph Cotton, *Hell's Riders*, 2004
James Rhodes, *Hardscrabble Valley*, 2003
Dusty Richards, *Deuces Wild*, 2004
Cotton Smith, *Winter Kill*, 2004
Charles G. West, *Bloody Hills*, 2004

464

MATT BRAUN

The Wages of Sin

(New York: St. Martin's Paperbacks, 2004)

Story type: Traditional; Revenge
Subject(s): Crime and Criminals; Law Enforcement; American West
Major character(s): Ash Tallman, Detective—Private (Pinkerton agent); Vivian Valentine, Detective—Private (Pinkerton agent); Pitkin Taylor, Rancher
Time period(s): 1860s (1869)
Locale(s): Cuero, Texas

Summary: The Civil War has been over for four years, but hatreds between Yankee and Confederate sympathizers burn as hot as ever in Cuero, Texas. The feud between the Suttons and the Taylors threatens to destroy the town and the county. In desperation, the governor calls the Pinkerton Detective Agency. Ash Tallman soon appears in the county, a harmless drifter whose secret skills with a gun will tame any town. His partner, Vivian Valentine, poses as an Evangelical Christian missionary out to make peace in the town. Peace is a long way away after the Suttons murder old Pitkin Taylor in his own front yard. Then, too, the Taylors being cousins of John Wesley Hardin, who hates Yankees more than he hates sin, doesn't much encourage peace either. A book of blazing action based on an actual Texas feud.

Where it's reviewed:
Roundup Magazine, August 2005, page 33

Other books by the same author:
Hangman's Creek, 2002
The Wild Ones, 2002
Kinch Riley, 2000
Shadow Killers, 2000
You Know My Name, 1999

Other books you might like:
Ralph Cotton, *Hell's Riders*, 2004
James Rhodes, *Hardscrabble Valley*, 2003
Dusty Richards, *Deuces Wild*, 2004
Cotton Smith, *Winter Kill*, 2004
Charles G. West, *Bloody Hills*, 2004

465

MATT BRAUN

Windward West

(New York: St. Martin's Paperbacks, 2005)

Story type: Traditional; Quest
Subject(s): Crime and Criminals; Indians of North America; Railroads
Major character(s): Virgil Brannock, Businessman (owns a railroad); Clint Brannock, Military Personnel (army scout), Frontiersman (Indian fighter); Earl Brannock, Adoptee (adopted into the Comanches)
Time period(s): 1870s (1873)
Locale(s): Palo Duro Canyon, Texas; Llano Estacada, Texas

Summary: The three Brannock brothers are alike in their fierce independence and determination to make their own way, but very different in how they choose to fulfill their dreams. Virgil Brannock is determined to build a railroad empire. Clint Brannock enjoys his own company and is an army scout for Colonel Mackenzie, whose assignment is to break the back of the Kiowa and Comanche tribes. Earl Brannock, the youngest of the brothers and the one who chooses a path that brings him into a deadly confrontation with his brothers, joins the Comanches and vows to follow their way of honor. The three brothers' paths will cross in blood, gunfire, and greed.

Where it's reviewed:
Roundup Magazine, August 2005, page 34

Other books by the same author:
The Wages of Sin, 2004
Hangman's Creek, 2002 (Luke Starbuck. Book 1)
The Wild Ones, 2002
Kinch Riley, 2000
Shadow Killers, 2000

Other books you might like:
James Carlos Blake, *Under the Skin*, 2003
Henry Chappell, *Blood Kin*, 2004
Henry Chappell, *The Callings*, 2002
Elmer Kelton, *The Buckskin Line*, 1999
    Texas Rangers. Book 1
Richard S. Wheeler, *Vengeance Valley*, 2004

466

K. CELESTE BRYAN

Moon of the Sleeping Bear

(Bedford, Indiana: JoNa Books, 2005)

Story type: Historical/American West; Saga
Subject(s): American West; Pioneers
Major character(s): Wynter McCain, Twin (of Sage); Sage Denzer, Twin (kidnapped at birth); Lucette Denzer, Midwife (delivered Wynter and Sage), Kidnapper (steals Sage at birth)
Time period(s): 1840s (1843); 1860s (1861-1865)
Locale(s): New Olm, Minnesota

Summary: Lucette Denzer is a midwife who is hired to attend at the birth of Clarissa McCain's baby. She delivers twin girls after Clarissa suffers a lengthy labor. The first baby is believed stillborn, but the second baby is healthy and named Wynter. That night, the first infant awakes from a coma in the guest cabin where Lucette stays. Lonely and with no family, Lucette keeps the baby, naming her Sage and passing off Sage as her granddaughter. The two girls grow to maturity in ignorance of one another, Wynter in North Carolina and Sage in the woods of Minnesota. At the beginning of the Civil War, Wynter arrives in Minnesota to stay with her aunt. A brief love affair with Dax Oliver before he enlists in the Union army leaves her pregnant and married to Dax's brother, Cord. Sage is also married—to a Winnibago Indian she saved from death. During the Sioux uprising in Minnesota, Wynter is kidnapped after her relatives are murdered. Dax and Sage's husband rescue Wynter, but Cord has disappeared during a futile search for her. The first half of this story paints an

accurate picture of the potions and medicines made by pioneer women healers, as well as the harsh circumstances in which early pioneers lived. Obviously there must be a sequel planned, because the story ends in a cliff-hanger.

Where it's reviewed:
Roundup Magazine, August 2005, page 34

Other books you might like:
Thomas Eidson, *The Missing*, 2003
Evan Hunter, *The Chisholms*, 2004
Jane Kirkpatrick, *Hold Tight the Thread*, 2004
    Tender Ties. Book 3
Al Lacy, *One More Sunrise*, 2004
    Joanna Lacy, co-author
Stephen Overholser, *Chasing Destiny*, 2005

467

TOM CALHOUN

Showdown in Austin

(New York: Jove, 2005)

Story type: Traditional; Man Alone
Series: Bounty Hunter. Book 2
Subject(s): Crime and Criminals; American West
Major character(s): J.T. Law, Bounty Hunter; Sara Gibbons, Spouse (of judge), Girlfriend (J.T. Law's former); Tom Ellsworth, Outlaw (sentenced to be hanged)
Time period(s): 19th century (post-Civil War)
Locale(s): St. Joseph, Missouri

Summary: After leaving Missouri with the reputation of a man always in trouble, J.T. Law becomes a bounty hunter. He is exhausted after his last manhunt, but rides to Austin anyway when his friend, Captain Covington of the Texas Rangers, calls him. J.T.'s old sweetheart, Sara Woodall, now Gibbons, is in trouble. Her father, who always hated J.T., hires him to find his missing son-in-law, Oliver Gibbons, a judge in St. Joseph, Missouri, and to protect Sara and her two children. J.T. would rather go to Hell than Missouri, but for Sara he will. Talking to Sara he learns her husband's life was threatened if he didn't take a bribe and free five murderers scheduled to be hanged. Gibbons took the bribe, sentenced the five men to death, then went missing. Sara believes one of the jailed men, Tom Ellsworth, is responsible for the bribe and Gibbons' disappearance. Some prominent citizen of St. Joseph is backing Ellsworth's play, but Sara doesn't know who. The mystery man plus eight or so members of Ellsworth's gang are still free and will be gunning for J.T. The bounty hunter isn't concerned. Eight to one aren't bad odds if you're J.T. Law.

Where it's reviewed:
Roundup Magazine, November 2005, page 34

Other books by the same author:
Texas Tracker, 2004

Other books you might like:
James Carlos Blake, *Under the Skin*, 2003
Henry Chappell, *Blood Kin*, 2004
Henry Chappell, *The Callings*, 2002
Elmer Kelton, *The Buckskin Line*, 1999
    Texas Rangers. Book 1

Richard S. Wheeler, *Vengeance Valley*, 2004

468

TIM CHAMPLIN

Devil's Domain

(Waterville, Maine: Five Star, 2005)

Story type: Historical/American Civil War; Saga
Subject(s): Prisoners of War; War; Diseases
Major character(s): John Mulroy, Military Personnel (Union Army sergeant), Prisoner (in Andersonville Prison); Cal Blackwood, Military Personnel (Confederate guard at prison); Captain Henri Wirz, Military Personnel (commander of prison), Historical Figure
Time period(s): 1860s (1862)
Locale(s): Andersonville, Georgia

Summary: Sergeant John Mulroy, a farmer from western Iowa and a volunteer in the Union Army, is captured with his men and sent to the infamous Andersonville Prison in Georgia. The commander or military warden of the prison, Captain Henri Wirz, is a bitter, mentally unstable German volunteer in the Confederate Army. A bone in his arm, broken by a bullet early in the war, has never healed, leaving him in constant pain and contributing to his cruelty. Conditions inside the prison are appalling, and prisoners die at the rate of a thousand men a week from gangrene, cholera, dysentery, diphtheria, pneumonia, starvation, beatings by the guards and other prisoners, and other causes too numerous to list. Mulroy is determined to escape. He would rather be shot trying to escape than slowly starve to death or die of some filthy disease. He finds an ally in Cal Blackwood, a Confederate guard, who has his own reasons for escaping Andersonville and the Confederate army. The only question is can he trust the enemy?

Where it's reviewed:
Roundup Magazine, August 2005, page 35

Other books by the same author:
Fire Bell in the Night, 2004
White Lights Roar, 2003
By Flare of Northern Lights, 2002
Raiders of the Western & Atlantic, 2002
A Trail to Wounded Knee, 2001

Other books you might like:
Johnny D. Boggs, *Camp Ford*, 2005
Loren D. Estleman, *Black Powder, White Smoke*, 2002
Fred Grove, *The Spring of Valor*, 2003
C. Jack Lewis, *Mojave*, 2004
Gary Warlick, *Rancho Vermejo*, 2002

469

RALPH COTTON

Guns of Wolf Valley

(New York: Signet, 2005)

Story type: Historical/American West; Man Alone
Subject(s): Crime and Criminals

Major character(s): Callie Mosely, Spouse (of Sloane Mosely); CC Ellis, Gunfighter; Malcom Jessup, Religious (preacher), Banker
Time period(s): 19th century (post-Civil War)
Locale(s): Paradise, West

Summary: Callie Mosely and her young son Dillard have been pretending for a year that her husband, Sloan Mosely, is still present on their small place. Sloan Mosely is a shootist of wide reputation, and as long as the Reverend Malcom Jessup believes he is alive, the religious fanatic will not force Callie into his community family as one of his wives. Callie fears that Jessup will learn that Sloan has not been home for a year. When Dillard finds CC Ellis, wounded after his fight will wolf hunters, he brings him home for his mother to care for. CC guesses that Callie is alone and offers to pretend to be Sloan to protect her and Dillard. Their relationship is in name only, at least at first. Then Callie begins to wonder how CC knows so much about her and Dillard, and why he knows so much about Sloane. A traditional Western with non-stop action.

Where it's reviewed:
Roundup Magazine, August 2005, page 36

Other books by the same author:
Between Hell and Texas, 2004
Dead Man's Canyon, 2004
Gunman's Song, 2004
Hell's Riders, 2004
Blood Rock, 2001

Other books you might like:
Ralph Compton, *Nowhere, Texas*, 2004
Richard Curtis, *Blood Cut*, 2003
T.A. Mort, *Showdown at Verity*, 2004
Charles G. West, *Bloody Hills*, 2004
Richard S. Wheeler, *The Bounty Trail*, 2004

470

RALPH COTTON

Killing Plain

(New York: Signet, 2005)

Story type: Historical/American West; Chase
Subject(s): American West; Crime and Criminals; Law Enforcement
Major character(s): Sam Burrack, Lawman (Arizona Ranger); Hadley Jones, Lawman (Arizona Ranger); Lonzo Greer, Outlaw (leader of the Black Moon gang)
Time period(s): 19th century (post-Civil War)
Locale(s): Cottonwood, Arizona; Barstow, Arizona

Summary: Arizona Ranger Sam Burrack has never had a partner before, but Hadley Jones seems like a smart enough youngster. The two men take charge of three prisoners in Cottonwood, including Stone Eddie Deaks, a well-known gunslinger. Sam and Hadley are on their way to Marshal Springs to clean out McAllister and his cohorts who have murdered the sheriff. While they are there, Lonzo Greer and his Black Moon gang take over the town of Barstow, looting and killing anyone who gets in their way. Stone Eddie Deaks is set free for lack of witnesses to his last murder, but Sam figures Deaks will end up at the end of a rope the minute he

leaves alive a witness to one of his killings. Sam doesn't realize that Deaks' next target is him until he sees the sun glint off the outlaw's gun barrel. Sam is knocked off a cliff by the bullet, but his silver hat band saves his life. When he recovers he goes after Deaks, and this time the gunslinger will be the one receiving the bullet. Deaks' death brings the Black Moon gang gunning for Sam, but he doesn't back down to anyone.

Where it's reviewed:
Roundup Magazine, November 2005, page 35

Other books by the same author:
Dead Man's Canyon, 2004
Gunman's Song, 2004
Hell's Riders, 2004
Blood Money, 2002
Blood Rock, 2001

Other books you might like:
Thomas Eidson, *The Missing*, 2003
John Holt, *Hunted*, 2003
Robert J. Horton, *The Hanging X*, 2003
Grey Judson, *Down to Marrowbone*, 2000
Stephen Overholser, *Chasing Destiny*, 2005

471

RALPH COTTON

The Law in Somos Santos

(New York: Signet, 2005)

Story type: Traditional; Man Alone
Subject(s): Crime and Criminals; American West; Law Enforcement
Major character(s): Cray Dawson, Lawman (sheriff); Hooney Carter, Lawman (Dawson's deputy); Odell Clarkson, Outlaw
Time period(s): 19th century (post-Civil War)
Locale(s): Somos Santos, Texas

Summary: Cray Dawson has a good reputation with a gun, so when the citizens of Somos Santos ask him to get rid of the town's corrupt sheriff and clean up the riff-raff around town, he does. Then he agrees to be the town sheriff for three months until Somos Santos can hire a permanent lawman. No one applies for the job so Cray agrees to be formally sworn in as sheriff. When he takes on the three baddies that come to town to kill him, he has no way of knowing that the one who got away would run into Odell Clarkson's gang. Odell is not worried about Cray Dawson and his two-bit deputy, Hooney Carter, but forewarned is forearmed, and Odell plans to ride into Somos Santos with guns blazing and take care of Cray Dawson. Then the town will be his.

Where it's reviewed:
Roundup Magazine, November 2005, page 35

Other books by the same author:
Killing Plain, 2005
Gunman's Song, 2004
Hell's Riders, 2004
Blood Money, 2002
Blood Rock, 2001

Other books you might like:
Johnny D. Boggs, *Camp Ford*, 2005
Loren D. Estleman, *Black Powder, White Smoke*, 2002
Fred Grove, *The Spring of Valor*, 2003
C. Jack Lewis, *Mojave*, 2004
Gary Warlick, *Rancho Vermejo*, 2002

472

C.K. CRIGGER

The Winning Hand

(Lake Forest, California: Behler, 2005)

Story type: Historical/American West; Chase
Subject(s): Crime and Criminals; Animals/Horses
Major character(s): Caroline Pruett, Heiress (to bankrupt horse ranch); Micah Sutton, Rancher; King, Animal (thoroughbred stallion)
Time period(s): 1890s (1893)
Locale(s): West

Summary: Caroline Pruett is left destitue because her senile grandmother lost everything due to some bad business decisions before her death. A thoroughbred stallion named King is the only thing Caroline manages to save from her grandmother's creditors. Desperate, she wagers everything in a poker game, and loses her horse to Micah Sutton. Unwilling to lose King, Caroline ambushes Micah on the trail and steals the horse, accidentally shooting Micah in the process. After checking to make sure that he is not badly hurt, she rides away on King. When the owner of a cabin where she stops for the night tries to rape her, Caroline escapes when King breaks the man's arm, but not before she herself is seriously wounded. Micah, who has been pursuing her, catches up to her and saves her life. He has decided to press charges for horse stealing, but then someone else starts shooting at them. King has become a target for horse thieves, and Micah finds himself allied with Caroline in a fight to protect the stallion.

Where it's reviewed:
Roundup Magazine, September 2005, page 36

Other books you might like:
Ralph Compton, *Nowhere, Texas*, 2004
Richard Curtis, *Blood Cut*, 2003
T.A. Mort, *Showdown at Verity*, 2004
Charles G. West, *Bloody Hills*, 2004
Richard S. Wheeler, *The Bounty Trail*, 2004

473

DAN CUSHMAN

White Water Trail

(Waterville, Maine: Five Star, 2005)

Story type: Traditional; Collection
Subject(s): American West; Short Stories
Time period(s): 19th century (post-Civil War)
Locale(s): West

Summary: A trio of short novels showcases Cushman's ear for dialogue and his sense of place. In *The Phantom Herds of Furnace Flat*, murder takes center stage. In *Boothill Loves a*

Pilgrim, a timid Chicago bookkeeper inherits a ranch in Montana Territory. On the train west he hires a gunfighter as his foreman. *White Water Trail* is the story of Tim Calloway's return to Alaska and his father's salmon business, where he finds a rival has established a monopoly and is squeezing his father out.

Where it's reviewed:
Roundup Magazine, November 2005, page 35

Other books by the same author:
Outcasts of the Storm, 2004
The Return of Comanche John, 2003
The Adventures of Comanche John, 2002
No Gold on Boothill, 2001
The Pecos Kid Returns, 2000

Other books you might like:
Steve Frazee, *Voices in the Hill*, 2002
Ed Gorman, *The Long Ride Back*, 2004
Ed Gorman, *Texas Rangers*, 2004
    Martin H. Greenberg, co-editor
Louis L'Amour, *Bowdrie*, 1983
Les Savage Jr., *The Devil's Corral*, 2003

474

TRACY DAUGHERTY

Late in the Standoff

(Dallas: Southern Methodist University Press, 2005)

Story type: Modern; Collection
Subject(s): Indians of North America; Short Stories; American West
Time period(s): 2000s
Locale(s): Texas

Summary: Daugherty illuminates the social and cultural forces that shape intimate behavior in this literate collection of short stories. Among them is ''The Standoff,'' in which a grandfather bonds with his grandson on a trip to Oklahoma to settle ''an Indian dispute'' in a small town. In ''Cotton Flat Road,'' a brother discovers the secret life led by his sister in the small oil town where they grew up. Each story is a gem and each in its own way is a family story. Daugherty is a literary writer who chooses to set all his work in the modern West.

Where it's reviewed:
Roundup Magazine, November 2005, page 35

Other books by the same author:
Axeman's Jazz, 2003
Five Shades of Shadow, 2003
It Takes a Worried Man, 2002
The Boy Orator, 1999
The Woman in the Oil Field, 1996

Other books you might like:
Sandra Babb, *Where Names Are Unknown*, 2004
Patrick Dearen, *When the Sky Rained Dust*, 2004
Ralph M. Flores, *The Horse in the Kitchen*, 2004
Elmer Kelton, *The Time It Never Rained*, 1973
Giles Tippette, *Southwest of Heaven*, 1999

475

PETER DAWSON

Forgotten Destiny

(New York: Leisure, 2005)

Story type: Traditional; Collection
Subject(s): Money; Short Stories
Time period(s): 19th century (post-Civil War)
Locale(s): West

Summary: Three of Dawson's best short novels are published for the first time in book form. In *Forgotten Destiny*, a man is on his way to his best friend's house to help him avoid foreclosure when he is robbed of all the money he carries. He is left for dead and doesn't remember who he is, or that he is bringing help to a friend. *Brand of Luck* concerns land grabbers, while *Death Brings in the Opir* is about a dishonest county commission that tries to force a mine owner to close his mine.

Where it's reviewed:
Roundup Magazine, September 2005, page 35

Other books by the same author:
Rattlesnake Mesa, 2002
Ghost Brand of the Wishbones, 1997

Other books you might like:
Phyllis de la Garza, *Silk and Sagebrush*, 2004
T.T. Flynn, *Reunion at Cottonwood Station*, 2004
Steve Frazee, *Voices in the Hill*, 2002
Ed Gorman, *The Long Ride Back*, 2004
W.W. Lee, *Rustler's Venom*, 1990

476

PETER DAWSON

Showdown at Anchor

(Waterville, Maine: Five Star, 2005)

Story type: Traditional; Collection
Subject(s): Crime and Criminals; American West; Short Stories
Time period(s): 19th century (post-Civil War)
Locale(s): West

Summary: The theme of this fine collection by Peter Dawson, featuring stylish writing and strong characters, is conflict in capital letters. There is no man against nature in these stories; it is man against man. In ''A Tinhorn Takes a Tank Town,'' the conflict is High-Card Stevens against a crooked gambler, a game that involves murder and power. In ''Unwanted Gold,'' it is brother against brother, while in ''Hell for Homesteaders,'' two cowboys who file on newly opened reservation land confront the greed of large ranchers.

Where it's reviewed:
Roundup Magazine, November 2005, page 36

Other books by the same author:
Phantom Raiders, 2003
Forgotten Destiny, 2002
Lone Rider from Texas, 2001
Claiming of the Deerfoot, 2000

Ghost of the Chinook, 2000

Other books you might like:
Phyllis de la Garza, *Silk and Sagebrush*, 2004
T.T. Flynn, *Reunion at Cottonwood Station*, 2004
Ed Gorman, *The Long Ride Back*, 2004
Louis L'Amour, *Bowdrie*, 1983
Les Savage Jr., *The Devil's Corral*, 2003

477

PHIL DUNLAP

The Death of Desert Belle

(New York: Avalon, 2004)

Story type: Traditional; Chase
Subject(s): American West; Crime and Criminals; Law Enforcement
Major character(s): Piedmont Kelly, Lawman (marshal); Ben Satterfield, Lawman (deputy sheriff); Zebulan A. Pooder, Drifter
Time period(s): 19th century (post-Civil War)
Locale(s): Desert Belle, Arizona

Summary: When the jail at Desert Belle, Arizona, explodes, everyone believes that the Bishop brothers are crushed in the wreckage, but their bodies are so disfigured it is hard to be sure. Deputy Sheriff Ben Satterfield is suspicious, believing the explosion is just too convenient and the bodies just a little too mangled to have been buried under debris. Marshal Piedmont Kelly isn't certain about the explosion either, so he rides to Desert Belle to investigate. Meanwhile, Zebulan A. Pooder, who looks like a pig farmer and smells like one, too, shoots a member of the Bishop gang in self-defense. When he discovers his victim's identity, he and his friend Blue leave town on the run. The Bishop gang isn't through with Pooder and Blue, and when the two cross paths with Marshal Kelly, a partnership between two runaway teenagers and a lawman seems a good way to protect themselves and the good folk of Desert Belle.

Where it's reviewed:
Roundup Magazine, August 2005, page 35

Other books by the same author:
Call of the Gun, 2005

Other books you might like:
Ralph Compton, *Vengeance Rider*, 2004
Cameron Judd, *Bad Night at Dry Creek*, 2004
John D. Nesbitt, *West of Rock River*, 2004
Robert J. Randisi, *Backshooter*, 2004
Richard S. Wheeler, *The Bounty Trail*, 2004

478

DEBORAH L. DUVALL

Rabbit and the Wolves

(Albuquerque: University of New Mexico Press, 2005)

Story type: Traditional; Indian Culture
Series: Grandmother Stories. Book 6
Subject(s): Indians of North America; Folk Tales

Major character(s): Ji-Stu, Animal (rabbit); Wa-Ya, Animal (wolf); Redbird, Animal (redbird)
Time period(s): Indeterminate Past
Locale(s): West

Summary: Ji-Stu the rabbit runs into his friend Wa-Ya the wolf on his way home from a dance. Ji-Stu asks Wa-Ya to tell him the story of Redbird whose singing the rabbit envies. Wa-Ya tells Ji-Stu of Redbird who did a favor for a wolf named Black Eye. Black Eye told Redbird where a brilliant paint could be found, which Redbird uses to paint himself. Ever since Redbird has been red. Ji-Stu finds the red paint, but it doesn't give him a beautiful singing voice. Distracted, he doesn't notice the pack of wolves who have surrounded him, planning to have him for dinner. Will the trickster rabbit manage to escape with his life? A wonderful Cherokee folk-tale that is reminiscent of one of Aesop's fables.

Where it's reviewed:
Roundup Magazine, November 2005, page 36

Other books by the same author:
Rabbit Goes Duck Hunting, 2004 (Grandmother Stories. Book 5)
Rabbit and the Bears, 2004 (Grandmother Stories. Book 4)
How Medicine Came to the People, 2003 (Grandmother Stories. Book 2)
How Rabbit Lost His Tail, 2003 (Grandmother Stories. Book 3)
The Great Ball Game of the Birds and Animals, 2002 (Grandmother Stories. Book 1)

Other books you might like:
Rudolfo Anaya, *Serafina's Stories*, 2004
Patrick Dearen, *Comanche Peace Pipe*, 2001
Patrick Dearen, *Hidden Treasure of the Chisos*, 2001
James Rice, *Victor Lopez at the Alamo*, 2001
Melinda Rice, *Fire on the Hillside*, 2001

479

LOREN D. ESTLEMAN

The Undertaker's Wife

(New York: Forge, 2005)

Story type: Historical/American West; Saga
Subject(s): Money; Suicide
Major character(s): Richard Connable, Undertaker; Lucy Connable, Spouse (of Richard); Victoria Connable, Child (Lucy's daughter)
Time period(s): 1860s (1861-1869); 1890s (1899)
Locale(s): Buffalo, New York; San Francisco, California; Virginia City, Nevada

Summary: When a railroad baron is found dead in his private car with a recently fired revolver in his hand, it is assumed that he committed suicide. A business acquaintance, John C. Broughty, realizes the economic damage to markets all over the world if word should reach the public that the railroad baron had killed himself. Panic will ensue as everyone will believe that financial reversals were the reason. Broughty knows there is only one way to prevent a financial panic: hire Richard Connable. Richard is an undertaker, but one with an unusual gift: he can restore and reconstruct a corpse to such a

degree that only microscopic examination would reveal his handiwork. After Richard leaves for New York to secretly patch the bullet hole in the millionaire's head, his wife, Lucy, visits his former funeral parlor to make the arrangements for her own death which the doctor has informed her is imminent. When she returns home she reviews her life as an undertaker's wife, including the birth of her daughter, Victoria Connable, fathered by another man during a time Richard left her behind. Her reminiscences are a history of the West, from San Francisco to Virginia City, Abilene, Kansas, and Tucson. This is a most unusual novel about a profession seldom discussed, and the personalities of the men and their families who prepare the dead for burial.

Where it's reviewed:
Roundup Magazine, August 2005, page 35

Other books by the same author:
Little Black Dress, 2005
Retro, 2004 (Amos Walker. Book 17)
Poison Blonde, 2003 (Amos Walker. Book 16)
Port Hazard, 2003 (Page Murdock. Book 5)
Black Powder, White Smoke, 2002

Other books you might like:
Johnny D. Boggs, *East of the Border*, 2004
Tim Champlin, *The Last Campaign*, 1996
Ed Gorman, *Branded*, 2004
Stephen Overholser, *Chasing Destiny*, 2005
Frank Roderus, *Judgment Day*, 2004

480

ANDREW J. FENADY

Riders to Moon Rock

(New York: Leisure, 2005)

Story type: Traditional; Man Alone
Subject(s): American West; Crime and Criminals; Indians of North America
Major character(s): Shannon Glennshannon, Orphan (adopted by the Kiowa); Hadley Glennshannon, Relative (son of the elder Glennshannon), Heir (to ranching empire); Heather Glennshannon, Relative (daughter of elder Glennshannon)
Time period(s): 19th century (1847-1870)
Locale(s): Gilead, Texas

Summary: Shannon Glennshannon grows up among the Kiowa, but after his adopted Kiowa father is killed, he is taken and renamed by a man who gives Shannon his own name and raises him as his own son. The elder Glennshannon's biological son, Hadley, hates Shannon because of his Indian upbringing and because Shannon is everything Hadley is not: strong, handsome, and intelligent. When Glennshannon dies, Hadley forces Shannon to live in the stables. Shannon suffers in silence because he is in love with Heather Glennshannon, Hadley's sister. When the Civil War breaks out, Shannon joins the Union Army, since he despises everything the Confederacy stands for, especially Texans like Hadley. After the war, Shannon returns as a colonel and a gentleman. He buys the mortgage on the Glennshannon ranch, relegating Hadley to a back bedroom. Now he has everything he ever wanted, except Heather, who is married to another man.

Western

Where it's reviewed:
Roundup Magazine, November 2005, page 35

Other books by the same author:
Claws of the Eagle, 2004
There Came a Stranger, 2004
Double Eagles, 2002
The Runaways, 1994

Other books you might like:
Dave Austin, *Man on the Border*, 2004
Frederic Bean, *Law of the Gun*, 1993
Stan Lynde, *Saving Miss Julie*, 2004
Stephen Overholser, *Chasing Destiny*, 2005
Frank Roderus, *Judgment Day*, 2004

481

E. LEE FISHER

Pendencia Creek

(Baltimore: Publish America, 2004)

Story type: Traditional; Man Alone
Subject(s): Crime and Criminals; Law Enforcement; American West
Major character(s): John King Fisher, Rancher, Historical Figure; Leander McNelly, Lawman (Texas Ranger captain), Historical Figure; Sarah Vivian Fisher, Spouse (of King Fisher), Historical Figure
Time period(s): 19th century (1854-1884)
Locale(s): Goliad, Texas; Eagle Pass, Texas; San Antonio, Texas

Summary: Based on the life of his grandfather's first cousin, E. Lee Fisher's biographical novel tells the story of John King Fisher, always called King, from his birth in 1854 until his murder by gunfighter Ben Thompson in 1884. Abused both physically and emotionally as a child until the death of his mentally disturbed stepmother when he was 14, King Fisher grew up to befriend and offer sanctuary to some of the worst outlaws and thugs in Texas. He was feared by almost everyone because of his skill with a gun, but was also given complete loyalty by those who loved him or considered themselves his friends. Unfortunately, other than his family and his wife Sarah Vivian Fisher, most who gave him loyalty were outlaws. Captain Leander McNelly of the Texas Rangers considered King Fisher one of the worst men in Texas, and spent his career, until illness forced him into retirement at 32, trying to send Fisher to jail, if not to Hell at the end of a rope. Despite his upbringing and his preference for friends outside the law, Fisher was in many ways a good man. This is a fascinating look at a real outlaw who lacked the widespread publicity allotted to Billy the Kid or John Wesley Hardin, but was more interesting and complex a character than either.

Where it's reviewed:
Roundup Magazine, August 2005, page 35

Other books you might like:
Frederic Bean, *Law of the Gun*, 1993
J. Lee Butts, *A Bad Day to Die*, 2004
Dick Clason, *The Deputy and the Devil's Eye*, 2004
Ed Gorman, *Branded*, 2004
Mackey Murdock, *Blood for Brother*, 2004

482

T.T. FLYNN

Noose of Fate

(Waterville, Maine: Five Star, 2005)

Story type: Traditional; Collection
Subject(s): Crime and Criminals
Time period(s): 19th century (post-Civil War)
Locale(s): West

Summary: Among Flynn's many Westerns one stands out: *The Man from Laramie*. These four novellas are just as good in their own way. "Brothers of the Damned" is the best of the four. In it a young man riding shotgun on a gold shipment fails to fire on one of the bandits attempting to rob it because he recognizes his younger brother. In "The Fighting Breed," two partners buy a ranch. If they can whip the rustlers they may keep it. These are stories full of suspense, violence, and great characters.

Where it's reviewed:
Roundup Magazine, November 2005, page 36

Other books by the same author:
Reunion at Cottonwood Station, 2004
Hell's Canon, 2002
Rawhide, 2002
The Devil's Lode, 1999
Night of the Comanche Moon, 1995

Other books you might like:
B.M. Bower, *The Terror*, 2003
Max Brand, *Flaming Fortune*, 2003
John Holt, *Hunted*, 2003
Wayne D. Overholser, *Wild Horse River*, 2003
Les Savage Jr., *Trail of the Silver Saddle*, 2005

483

STEVE FRAZEE

Four Graves West

(Waterville, Maine: Five Star, 2005)

Story type: Traditional; Collection
Subject(s): American West; Crime and Criminals; Short Stories
Time period(s): 19th century (post-Civil War)
Locale(s): West

Summary: This duo of novellas feature excellent dialogue, complex plots, and wonderful characters. In "Mormon Forge," a sheriff tries to prevent a blood feud, but his opinion doesn't count with the two feuding ranching families. It counts even less when the daughter of one of the families reveals that the sheriff is her lover. "Four Graves West" finds a drought on the land. The only water is on the Wagon Wheel Ranch, where the owner doesn't carry a gun and doesn't want his sons to either. When the other ranchers attack the Wagon Wheel to force the owner to share his water, the owner must compromise his position or die.

Where it's reviewed:
Roundup Magazine, November 2005, page 37

Other books by the same author:
Tower of Rocks, 2004
Nights of Terror, 2003
Voices in the Hill, 2002
Ghost Mine, 2000
Hidden Gold, 1997

Other books you might like:
Frank Bonham, *The Phantom Bandit*, 2004
Louis L'Amour, *Bowdrie*, 1983
Dale L. Walker, *Westward*, 2004
Richard S. Wheeler, *Valley of Vengeance*, 2004

484

STEVE FRAZEE

Tower of Rocks

(New York: Leisure, 2005)

Story type: Traditional; Collection
Subject(s): Short Stories; American West
Time period(s): 19th century (post-Civil War)
Locale(s): West

Summary: Frazee utilizes his historical research to create a strong sense of place and accuracy in the details of human behavior. In "Death Rides This Trail," the Breslin family are traveling by covered wagon in search of a better life when Mrs. Breslin dies. It is all the family can do to continue and leave her in an unmarked grave. In "Tower of Rocks," a former Confederate captain receives a note about a mission that will pay well—if he survives the attempt.

Where it's reviewed:
Roundup Magazine, November 2005, page 37

Other books by the same author:
Four Graves West, 2005
Nights of Terror, 2003
Voices in the Hill, 2002
Ghost Mine, 2000
Hidden Gold, 1997

Other books you might like:
Max Brand, *Jokers Extra Wild*, 2002
Walt Coburn, *Coffin Ranch*, 2002
T.T. Flynn, *The Devil's Lode*, 1999
Wayne D. Overholser, *Wheels Roll West*, 2002
Cherry Wilson, *The Throwback*, 2002

485

ERIC GANSWORTH

Mending Skins

(Lincoln: University of Nebraska Press, 2005)

Story type: Traditional; Indian Culture
Subject(s): Indians of North America
Major character(s): Shirley Mounter, Indian (Tuscarora); Annie Boans, Indian (Shirley's daughter), Art Historian; Dougie Boans, Indian (Annie's husband)
Time period(s): 20th century (1957-1999); 2000s
Locale(s): Niagara Falls, New York; Tuscarora Reservation, New York

Summary: While her daughter, art historian Annie Boans, is giving the keynote address at the Seventh Annual Conference of the Society for Protection and Reclamation of Indian Images, Shirley Mounter is recalling her life, beginning with the loss of her land when New York state confiscated it to build a power plant. Forced to move to an apartment in Niagara Falls, Shirley takes what little money her lying, womanizing, alcoholic husband tells her he got from the state for her property and plans what to do with the rest of her life. Shirley usually tries not to think of her loss, but she and her son-in-law, Annie's husband Dougie Boans, share the sadness of the dispossessed. Shirley is a feisty character who looks life in the face and finds it pock-marked.

Where it's reviewed:
Publishers Weekly, February 21, 2005, page 158
Roundup Magazine, August 2005, page 36

Other books by the same author:
Smoke Dancing, 2004
Nickel Eclipse: Iroquois Moon, 2000
Indian Summers, 1998

Other books you might like:
Rudolfo Anaya, *Serafina's Stories*, 2004
Tim Champlin, *The Last Campaign*, 1996
Craig Johnson, *The Cold Dish*, 2005
Frank B. Linderman, *Indian Why Stories*, 2004
D.R. Meredith, *Tome of Death*, 2005

486

KATHLEEN O'NEAL GEAR
W. MICHAEL GEAR, Co-Author

People of the Moon

(New York: Forge, 2005)

Story type: Historical/American West; Indian Culture
Series: First North Americans. Book 13
Subject(s): Indians of North America; Pre-Columbian History; Mysticism
Major character(s): Young Ripple, Indian (People of the Moon); Leather Hand, Indian (Chaco Anasazi), Chieftain (war chief); Mountain Witch, Indian (People of the Moon), Shaman
Time period(s): Indeterminate Past
Locale(s): Aztec, New Mexico; Pueblo Bonito, New Mexico; Chimney Rock, Colorado

Summary: The Chaco Anasazi rule most of what is now New Mexico and southern Colorado with arrogance and brutality. When they conquer the People of the Moon, they take every tenth person and work them to death building roads. They are hated among all their subject people. Young Ripple is of the People of the Moon, but he never considers himself special in any way. When Cold Bringing Woman, the goddess of winter, appears to him and orders him to seek the Mountain Witch who can read the portents and knows the future, and to prepare to lead his people against the Chaco Anasazi, Young Ripple is disbelieving. The ring of frozen earth persuades him that he has indeed become a Dreamer, one who dreams the gods and obeys their instructions. As Young Ripple seeks out the Mountain Witch and prepares his people for war, Leather

Hand, war chief of the Chaco Anasazi, hears the rumors of rebellion and prepares his warriors for battle. The war between the People of the Moon and the Chaco Anasazi, according to archaeological evidence, was brutal almost beyond believing, rivaling anything Alexander or the Romans or the Spanish Inquisition committed. A beautifully written fictional account of actual happenings in prehistoric America.

Where it's reviewed:
Roundup Magazine, September 2005, page 34

Other books by the same author:
People of the Raven, 2004 (First North Americans. Book 12)
People of the Owl, 2003 (First North Americans. Book 11)
People of the Masks, 1998 (First North Americans. Book 10)
People of the Mist, 1998 (First North Americans. Book 9)
People of the Silence, 1997 (First North Americans. Book 8)

Other books you might like:
Margaret Allan, *Keeper of the Stone*, 1994
Margaret Allan, *The Last Mammoth*, 1995
Robert J. Conley, *Crazy Snake*, 1994
Robert J. Conley, *The Peace Chief*, 1998
Robert J. Conley, *War Woman*, 1997

487

PHILLIP GESSERT

The Cold Trail

(Cottondale, Alabama: St. John Press, 2005)

Story type: Historical/American West; Man Alone
Subject(s): Frontier and Pioneer Life
Major character(s): Harliss Avery, Gunfighter; Ben Avery, Relative (brother of Harliss), Businessman; Ben Avery Jr., Runaway (nephew of Harliss)
Time period(s): 1870s (1878)
Locale(s): St. Louis, Missouri; West

Summary: Harliss Avery leaves St. Louis as a teenager to go west. There he becomes a cowboy, then a hired gun. He fights on the side of ranchers against homesteaders, a job that makes him sick. He tries every way possible to get himself killed, but still lives. He returns to St. Louis to learn that his nephew, Ben Avery, Jr., has been missing since he was very young, younger even than Harliss when he went west. His brother is dying of heart failure and wants to see Ben again. Harliss agrees to find the youngster. It will be his last task before resuming his quest for his own death.

Where it's reviewed:
Roundup Magazine, November 2005, page 36

Other books you might like:
Johnny D. Boggs, *Purgatoire*, 2003
Tom Franklin, *Hell at the Breech*, 2003
Hiram King, *Broken Rank*, 2001
P.G. Nagle, *Red River*, 2003
Edwin Shrake, *The Borderland*, 2000

488

STAN GORDON

Moon in the Water

(Waterville, Maine: Five Star, 2005)

Story type: Historical/American West; Indian Culture
Subject(s): Indians of North America
Major character(s): Lozen, Indian (female Apache warrior), Relative (Victorio's sister); Gray Wolf, Indian (Seneca); Victorio, Chieftain (of the Apaches), Relative (Lozen's brother)
Time period(s): 19th century (post-Civil War)
Locale(s): Arizona

Summary: Lozen is an Apache maiden, the sister of one of the Apaches' most famous warriors. She is more skilled at fighting than are her male peers, so she is accepted as a warrior, the equal to any man. She is also a skilled healer. She falls in love with a stranger who stumbles into her village. Gray Wolf is a Seneca, a chief with much experience fighting the White Eyes. Lozen makes him her own, but one night he leaves her, for what destination she does not know. The novel follows Lozen through her life, and details the travails of the Apache nation as they are taken to a reservation where they die by the hundreds from smallpox and other diseases. The novel presents a chilling picture of two cultures in conflict, with neither understanding the other, but is definitely a one-sided picture of the times.

Where it's reviewed:
Roundup Magazine, August 2005, page 35

Other books you might like:
Win Blevins, *So Wild a Dream*, 2003
Emerson Hough, *The Covered Wagon*, 2000
Jane Kirkpatrick, *All Together in One Place*, 2000
 Kinship and Courage. Book 1
Jane Kirkpatrick, *No Eye Can See*, 2001
 Kinship and Courage. Book 2
Robert J. Randisi, *Lancaster's Orphans*, 2004

489

ED GORMAN

Bad Money

(New York: Berkley, 2005)

Story type: Traditional; Man Alone
Series: Dev Mallory. Book 1
Subject(s): Crime and Criminals; American West
Major character(s): Dev Mallory, Government Official (Secret Service agent), Investigator (for the U.S. Treasury); Henry Juvenal Cummings, Printer; Cora Mallory, Spouse (of Dev Mallory)
Time period(s): 1880s (1887)
Locale(s): Washington, Oregon; Denver, Colorado

Summary: No one can put out a better book than Ed Gorman, with great characters to identify with, strong plots that don't fall apart under scrutiny, and a You-Are-There sense of place. Book 1 of his new series about Dev Mallory, a Secret Service agent, is a case in point. Dev is sent to Denver to learn who

killed another Secret Service agent who was investigating a counterfeiting ring whose money is almost indistinguishable from the real thing. President Grover Cleveland wants the man responsible caught and the ring broken up before all that bad money ruins the economy. In Denver, Dev soon learns the name of a former Engraving and Printing worker who was skilled enough to make plates almost identical to the U.S. Mint's. The question is why Henry Juvenal Cummings, a heretofore staid government employee, suddenly joined the ranks of criminals. Even worse for Dev is the discovery that his wife, Cora Mallory, is a bigamist. A wonderful book with more twists than a sidewinder.

Where it's reviewed:
Roundup Magazine, November 2005, page 37

Other books by the same author:
Branded, 2004
Texas Rangers, 2004 (editor)
The Long Ride Back, 2004
Gun Truth, 2003
Night of Shadows, 2002

Other books you might like:
Tim Champlin, *Fire Bell in the Night*, 2004
Tim Champlin, *A Trail to Wounded Knee*, 2001
Stephen Overholser, *Track of a Killer*, 2003
Gladys Smith, *Deliverance Valley*, 2003
Joseph A. West, *Me and Johnny Blue*, 2000

490

LOREN ZANE GREY

Ambush for Lassiter
(New York: Leisure, 2005)

Story type: Traditional; Revenge
Subject(s): American West; Crime and Criminals
Major character(s): Lassiter, Drifter; Craig Moran, Foreman (of ranch), Murderer; Meager Joplin, Guard (at Rimshaw Prison), Murderer (hired to kill)
Time period(s): 19th century (post-Civil War)
Locale(s): Hopeville, Texas

Summary: Lassiter and his friend Timmie Borling are in Rimshaw Prison serving 25 years for a murder they didn't commit. A dance hall girl representing an anonymous friend of the pair leaves money for them to bribe the head guard, Meager Joplin, to let them escape. Borling is shot by Joplin and Lassiter is captured and five more years are added to his sentence. Joplin is fired by the warden, then rides to Hopeville to confront Craig Moran for a little blackmail money. Moran is the foreman of Borling's ranch now, and had provided the bribe money. A homesteader confesses to murdering the man Lassiter and Borling were accused of killing, then kills himself. Lassiter is pardoned, but warned not to go after Joplin or anyone he suspects of arranging Borling's murder. Lassiter is silent but he intends to bring Joplin to justice, as well as whoever hired him. If justice equals vengeance, that's fine with Lassiter.

Where it's reviewed:
Roundup Magazine, November 2005, page 37

Other books by the same author:
Lassiter, 2004

Other books you might like:
Ralph Cotton, *Between Hell and Texas*, 2004
Zane Grey, *The Maverick Queen*, 2004
Martin Marcus, *Freedom Land*, 2003
John D. Nesbitt, *West of Rock River*, 2004
Richard S. Wheeler, *Vengeance Valley*, 2004

491

FRED GROVE

The Vanishing Raiders
(Waterville, Maine: Five Star, 2005)

Story type: Traditional; Collection
Subject(s): American West; Short Stories
Time period(s): 19th century (post-Civil War)
Locale(s): West

Summary: Nine of Grove's short stories illustrate the scope of both his subjects and his writing skills. ''The Hangrope Ghost,'' the first short story Grove ever published, as well as ''Catch Your Killer'' carry his trademark wry humor. ''Crow Bait'' features quarter horse racing, a subject that he later wrote about in two novels that both won Spur Awards. ''War Path'' is a more serious story in which a U.S. Army officer distrusts his Kiowa scout. ''A Matter of Blood'' tells the story of a Tarahumari Indian prostitute who takes revenge against a zealous informant. ''The Vanishing Raiders,'' a story Grove wrote for this collection, is a gritty realistic one about old Fort Belknap. This is a superb series of stories that every Western fan will enjoy.

Where it's reviewed:
Roundup Magazine, August 2005, page 36

Other books by the same author:
A Soldier Returns, 2004
The Spring of Valor, 2003
The Years of Fear, 2002
Red River Stage, 2001
Destiny Valley, 2000

Other books you might like:
Debra Magpie Earling, *Perma Red*, 2002
Ricardo L. Garcia, *Brother Bill's Bait Bites Back and Other Tales from the Raton*, 2004
Stephen Overholser, *Shadow Valley Rising*, 2001
Tess Pendergrass, *Colorado Twilight*, 2001
Jon Tuska, *Stories of the Golden West. Book Four*, 2004 editor

492

RUSS HALL

Bent Red Moon
(Waterville, Maine: Five Star, 2005)

Story type: Traditional; Indian Wars
Subject(s): Crime and Criminals; Veterans; American West
Major character(s): Mick Dixon, Orphan, Teenager; Syd, Orphan; Bob Pattie, Prospector (for gold), Outlaw

Western

Time period(s): 1870s (1872)
Locale(s): Mason, Texas

Summary: Mick Dixon, a 17-year-old orphan, is searching for his uncle, Bill Hinton, when he runs into Syd, half Mexican and half Anglo, and an orphan herself. Syd is also looking for Bill Hinton, but she intends to kill him when she finds him. Hinton abused her and murdered her mother when Syd was seven. Mick and Syd ride the hill country of Texas searching for Hinton and trying to stay out of reach of the Comanches and Kiowa. Mick goes to Mason in search of medicine after Syd is clawed by a bear. He is followed out of town by Bob Pattie, who seems to know more about Mick than he should. Is he Mick's uncle? Mick doesn't know, but he hopes not, since there is something not quite right about Pattie. Mick learns how right he is when Pattie ties him to a tree and abducts Syd. If not for a freed slave and ex-Buffalo Soldier named Harlan, Mick would have died. Instead he and Harlan ride after Syd. Mick was a Cheyenne captive during his childhood and he knows something about tracking down an enemy—and what to do when he catches him.

Where it's reviewed:
Roundup Magazine, November 2005, page 37

Other books by the same author:
No Murder Before Its Time, 2004
Blue-Eyed Indian, 1997

Other books you might like:
James Carlos Blake, *Under the Skin*, 2003
Frank Bonham, *Stage Trails West*, 2003
Henry Chappell, *Blood Kin*, 2004
Henry Chappell, *The Callings*, 2002
Elmer Kelton, *The Buckskin Line*, 1999
   Texas Rangers. Book 1

493

J.D. HARKLEROAD

Blood Atonement

(Baltimore: Publish America, 2004)

Story type: Modern; Revenge
Subject(s): American West; Crime and Criminals; Mormons
Major character(s): Hart McKeon, Fugitive, Convict (on parole); Keri Lord, Girlfriend (of Hart); Marv Thulin, Lawman (corrupt sheriff)
Time period(s): 1970s (1972); 1980s (1982)
Locale(s): Utah

Summary: Hart McKeon celebrates his 18th birthday by going to a dance after winning at bronc busting at the rodeo. When he allows himself to be seduced by Rosamond Thulin, he doesn't know she is underage and Deputy Sheriff Marv Thulin's daughter. Caught in Hart's car by the deputy, Rosamond claims Hart raped her. After being beaten by Marv Thulin, and defended by Marv's best friend and former lover of Rosamond, Hart goes to prison for ten years. On parole he finds work as a wilderness guide, and meets Keri Lord with whom he falls in love. Then Rosamond's younger sister is found in Hart's cabin beaten nearly to death and raped. The girl doesn't regain consciousness, and again Marv Thulin's beats up Hart and throws him in jail. He escapes and is raiding the house of a polygamist who turns out to be his court-ordered counselor and best friend, Kemper, who shoots Hart. Shot through the lung, Hart escapes and hides out in an Anazai burial cave. Not knowing if he will live or die or be caught and sent to prison again, Hart goes over in his mind why he is deliberately being targeted by someone. A mystery and adventure story that exposes the dark side of polygamy.

Where it's reviewed:
Roundup Magazine, August 2005, page 36

Other books by the same author:
Horsethief Trail, 2004

Other books you might like:
Dave Austin, *Man on the Border*, 2004
Dick Clason, *The Ranger and the Green Derby*, 2004
Stan Lynde, *Saving Miss Julie*, 2004
Stephen Overholser, *Chasing Destiny*, 2005
Frank Roderus, *Judgment Day*, 2004

494

RAY HOGAN

The Cuchillo Plains

(Waterville, Maine: Five Star, 2005)

Story type: Traditional; Collection
Subject(s): Crime and Criminals
Time period(s): 19th century (post-Civil War)
Locale(s): West

Summary: Two short novels revolve around a man unjustly accused of a crime. In "Lawless Strip," a young ranch hand entrusted with money with which to buy cattle is robbed. He sets out in pursuit of the men, but discovers that his employer has charged him with the crime. The outlaws' trail leads to the Strip commonly known as No Man's Land because no state, territory, or the federal government claims it. As a result there is no law except for what a man makes for himself. Hogan's second short novel also involves an unjust accusation. "The Cuchillo Plains" features a young rancher who witnesses a murder and chases the murderer, only to find himself the accused.

Where it's reviewed:
Roundup Magazine, August 2005, page 36

Other books by the same author:
Truth at Gunpoint, 2004
Valley of the Wandering River, 2003
Drifter's End, 2002
The Red Eagle, 2001
Stonebreaker's Ridge, 2000

Other books you might like:
B.M. Bower, *The Terror*, 2003
Max Brand, *Flaming Fortune*, 2003
John Holt, *Hunted*, 2003
Wayne D. Overholser, *Wild Horse River*, 2003
Les Savage Jr., *Trail of the Silver Saddle*, 2005

495

ROBERT E. HOWARD

The End of the Trail

(Lincoln: University of Nebraska Press, 2005)

Story type: Traditional; Collection
Subject(s): American West; Crime and Criminals
Time period(s): 19th century (post-Civil War)
Locale(s): Texas

Summary: Better known as the creator of Conan the Barbarian, Kull of ancient Atlantis, and Solomon Kane in Africa, Robert Howard's first love was writing Westerns. In fact, in the last months of his life before committing suicide at age 30, he had turned toward writing about the West instead of his fantastical lands of Conan and Kull. This collection features Western stories that he wrote beginning in 1929, until his death in 1936. His Westerns were unlike any written in his lifetime, being grim, with often graphic violence and less than happy endings. ''Gunman's Debt'' is bleak in outlook, and has a violent ending. ''The Devil's Joker'' and ''Knife, Bullet and Noose'' are about outlaws, reflecting Howard's fascination with gunfighters such Billy the Kid and John Wesley Hardin. For stories that were written nearly 70 years ago, Howard's reveal the realism and psychological insight of recent Western fiction.

Where it's reviewed:
Roundup Magazine, August 2005, page 37

Other books by the same author:
Boxing Stories, 2005
Bran Mak Morn: The Last King, 2005
Lord of Samarcand and Other Adventure Tales of the Old Orient, 2005
The Black Stranger and Other American Tales, 2005
Shadow Kingdoms, 2004

Other books you might like:
Frank Bonham, *The Phantom Bandit*, 2004
T.T. Flynn, *Reunion at Cottonwood Station*, 2004
Steve Frazee, *Voices in the Hill*, 2002
Will Henry, *Blind Canon*, 2005
Louis L'Amour, *Bowdrie*, 1983

496

ROBERT E. HOWARD

The Riot at Bucksnort and Other Western Tales

(Lincoln: University of Nebraska Press, 2005)

Story type: Traditional; Collection
Subject(s): Short Stories; American West; Humor
Time period(s): 19th century (post-Civil War)
Locale(s): Texas

Summary: The 16 stories in this collection are less grim than those in *The End of the Trail*; in fact, they are humorous stories in the vein of Bret Harte and Mark Twain. All the stories feature Breckinridge Elkins, Pike Bearfield, and Buckner J. Grimes, three misfits who blunder into confusion in search of riches. Sometimes they aren't sure what they are searching for. They are the champions of mischance and the masters of inducing catastrophe into any situation. First introduced in ''Mountain Man,'' Breckinridge is a physical giant capable of great deeds in the manner of Pecos Bill whom Howard admitted basing the character on. Pike Bearfield first appears in ''A Gent from the Pecos.'' The Pike stories are always written in the form of letters or newspaper articles, while the stories featuring Grimes are more stylistically like the Elkins stories. Grimes is not a physical giant and he is smarter, at least, smart enough to occasionally win out over his enemies. These are hysterically funny tales that will induce sore ribs from laughter.

Where it's reviewed:
Roundup Magazine, August 2005, page 37

Other books by the same author:
Boxing Stories, 2005
Bran Mak Morn: The Last King, 2005
Lord of Samarcand and Other Adventure Tales of the Old Orient, 2005
The Black Stranger and Other American Tales, 2005
Shadow Kingdoms, 2004

Other books you might like:
Max Brand, *Jokers Extra Wild*, 2002
Walt Coburn, *Coffin Ranch*, 2002
T.T. Flynn, *The Devil's Lode*, 1999
Wayne D. Overholser, *Wheels Roll West*, 2002
Cherry Wilson, *The Throwback*, 2002

497

WILLIAM W. JOHNSTONE

Revenge of Eagles

(New York: Pinnacle, 2005)

Story type: Traditional; Revenge
Series: Falcon MacCallister. Book 10
Subject(s): American West
Major character(s): Falcon MacCallister, Gunfighter, Mine Owner; Fargo Ford, Outlaw; Keytano, Indian (Apache), Chieftain
Time period(s): 19th century (post-Civil War)
Locale(s): Oro Blanco, Arizona

Summary: Falcon MacCallister is waiting to catch the stage to Oro Blanco to check out the mine he bought from Doc Holliday, when six men led by Fargo Ford try to rob the express office. The sheriff and his deputies hold them off with Falcon's help. Fargo and his men are jailed and the stage leaves with Falcon, a mother and her son, a drummer, and an Indian girl returning home from school in the east. Fargo and his gang break out of jail and ambush the stage, killing two people, one of them the Indian girl. Unfortunately for southern Arizona the girl is the daughter of Chief Keytano. The settlers expect the Apache led by Keytano to ride off the reservation to make war in vengeance for his daughter. Falcon knows he must find Fargo and his men before Arizona is awash with blood.

Where it's reviewed:
Roundup Magazine, November 2005, page 37

Other books by the same author:
Destiny of Eagles, 2004 (Falcon MacCallister. Book 8)
Cry of Eagles, 2002 (Falcon MacCallister. Book 7)
Song of Eagles, 2000 (Falcon MacCallister. Book 6)
Rage of Eagles, 1998 (Falcon MacCallister. Book 5)
Scream of Eagles, 1996 (Falcon MacCallister. Book 4)

Other books you might like:
Elizabeth Black, *Buffalo Spirits*, 2003
Robert J. Conley, *The Gunfighter*, 2001
Ralph Cotton, *Dead Man's Canyon*, 2004
Ralph Cotton, *Gunman's Song*, 2004
Stephen Overholser, *Track of a Killer*, 2003

498

CAMERON JUDD

The Treasure of Jericho Mountain

(New York: Leisure, 2005)

Story type: Traditional; Man Alone
Subject(s): American West; Crime and Criminals; Gold Discoveries
Major character(s): Jeremy Prine, Drifter; Priscilla Tate, Young Woman (an outlaw's daughter); Thomas Stuart, Relative (of Bob Stuart)
Time period(s): 19th century (post-Civil War)
Locale(s): Dawson, Colorado

Summary: Drifter Jeremy Prine has nothing better to do, so he agrees to a meeting with Thomas Stuart, the son of an old Confederate officer of his. Two other members of his old unit are also present at the meeting. Stuart tells them the story of a thief who died at his father's house after giving the elder Stuart a map to an abandoned mine where a million dollars in stolen cash is hidden. The thief wants the money returned to the government, and there is a reward of $250,000 for its recovery. The four men agree to find the money and split the reward four ways. It seems like the easiest $50,000 Jeremy will ever make, but there is one catch. The thief had killed the other members of his gang, planning to keep all the money for himself. The daughter of one of the dead men, Priscilla Tate, has hired a bunch of gunfighters to help her track down Prine, Stuart, and the others and steal the map. This may not be such easy money after all.

Where it's reviewed:
Roundup Magazine, November 2005, page 37

Other books by the same author:
Bad Night at Dry Creek, 2004
Beggar's Gulch, 2004
War at Fire Creek, 2004
Overmountain Men, 2003
Shootout in Dodge City, 2003

Other books you might like:
Will Cade, *Henry Kidd, Outlaw*, 2003
Jason Manning, *The Outlaw Trail*, 2003
Stephen Overholser, *Track of a Killer*, 2003
Ford Pendleton, *Gunmaster*, 2003
Cotton Smith, *The Thirteenth Bullet*, 2004

499

ELMER KELTON

Six Bits a Day

(New York: Forge, 2005)

Story type: Traditional; Ranch Life
Subject(s): American West; Animals/Cows
Major character(s): Hewey Calloway, Cowboy; Walter Calloway, Cowboy (brother of Hewey); C.C. Tarpley, Rancher, Employer (of Hewey and Walter)
Time period(s): 1880s (1889)
Locale(s): Texas

Summary: In a prequel to one of his most famous Westerns, *The Good Old Boys*, Kelton recounts the early days of Hewey Calloway, a footloose and fancy-free cowboy who works for C.C. Tarpley for six bits, or 75 cents, a day. Hewey is worried sick about his brother, Walter Calloway, who has fallen in love, a sad state of affairs to Hewey's mind. Walter wants to get married. Worse than that, he wants to settle down and farm. Farm! What a terrible end for a Calloway. Hewey doesn't plan to let his brother ruin his life, so he talks Walter into accompanying him on a cattle drive for Tarpley. Once Walter gets back in the saddle and behind a cow, he'll be cured of wanting to farm. That things don't quite work out the way he planned isn't Hewey's fault. Trouble just happens to him, but that's no reason for Walter to turn against cowboying. A wonderful, humorous story by one of the masters of Western writing.

Where it's reviewed:
Roundup Magazine, September 2005, page 37

Other books by the same author:
Sons of Texas, 2005
Texas Vendetta, 2004 (Texas Rangers. Book 5)
Ranger's Trail, 2002 (Texas Rangers. Book 4)
The Way of the Coyote, 2001 (Texas Rangers. Book 2)
Badger Boy, 2000 (Texas Rangers. Book 3)

Other books you might like:
Tim Champlin, *Fire Bell in the Night*, 2004
Ralph Cotton, *Dead Man's Canyon*, 2004
Louis L'Amour, *Hondo*, 2004
Clay Reynolds, *The Tentmaker*, 2002
Richard S. Wheeler, *The Bounty Trail*, 2004

500

ELMER KELTON

Sons of Texas

(New York: Forge, 2005)

Story type: Historical/American West; Saga
Subject(s): Animals/Horses; Frontier and Pioneer Life
Major character(s): Mordecai Lewis, Frontiersman, Horse Trainer; Michael Lewis, Frontiersman (Mordecai's son); Andrew Lewis, Frontiersman (Mordecai's son)
Time period(s): 1810s (1816); 1820s (1821)
Locale(s): Tennessee; Texas

Summary: The first volume in an unnamed trilogy, *Sons of Texas* introduces the Lewis family, father Mordecai Lewis

and his sons, Michael and Andrew. Along with their older brother Joseph and younger siblings, Michael and Andrew try to keep the family in food while Mordecai wanders the frontier that constantly moves farther west. When Mordecai returns home, he announces that he and some backwoods friends plan to go to Spanish Texas to round up a herd of wild mustangs to bring back to Tennessee to sell. This time Michael and Andrew accompany their father, but tragedy strikes. An officer in the Spanish army kills Mordecai for being on Spanish land. Michael and Andrew, along with those of Mordecai's friends still alive, flee Texas back to Tennessee. Five years later Michael and Andrew re-enter Texas to join Stephen F. Austin and his group of settlers. Austin has little regard for these backwoods brothers from Tennessee, and the same Spanish officer who murdered their father dogs their path. As usual, Kelton has created characters living exciting lives, in an adventure as big as Texas.

Where it's reviewed:
Roundup Magazine, August 2005, page 36

Other books by the same author:
Jericho's Road, 2004 (The Texas Rangers. Book 6)
Texas Vendetta, 2004 (The Texas Rangers. Book 5)
Lone Star Rising, 2003
Ranger's Trail, 2002 (The Texas Rangers. Book 4)
The Way of the Coyote, 2001 (The Texas Rangers. Book 3)

Other books you might like:
Johnny D. Boggs, *Purgatoire*, 2003
Tom Franklin, *Hell at the Breech*, 2003
Hiram King, *Broken Rank*, 2001
P.G. Nagle, *Red River*, 2003
Edwin Shrake, *The Borderland*, 2000

501

JANE KIRKPATRICK

A Land of Sheltered Promise

(Colorado Springs, Colorado: WaterBrook, 2005)

Story type: Ranch Life; Saga
Subject(s): Cults; American West; Family Life
Major character(s): Eva Cora Thompson Bruner, Rancher (owns the Big Muddy Ranch); Cora Swensen, Parent (of a daughter in a cult); Charity Swensen, Child (Cora's granddaughter), Abuse Victim (neglected in the commune)
Time period(s): 20th century (1901-1997)
Locale(s): Oregon

Summary: Three generations of women experience life-changing events on a place called Big Muddy Ranch. In 1901, Eva Cora Thompson Bruner lives through her husband's trial for murder. When he is found guilty and sentenced to prison for life, she must raise their daughter by herself and build a future for the two of them. In 1984, Cora Swensen arrives at the Big Muddy, now a commune called Rancho Rajneeshpuram, and her daughter, Rachel, and granddaughter, Charity, live inside. Rachel is totally convinced that the commune and its East Indian leaders will bring her happiness and enlightenment, even when she learns that her telephone and apartment are bugged and that the commune ordered the spread of salmonella at a local cafe. Finally, Cora agrees to

release Rachel's trust fund in exchange for the right to take Charity back East and raise her. In 1997, Charity returns to the ruins of the commune and begins a Christian camp for neglected children.

Where it's reviewed:
Roundup Magazine, August 2005, page 37

Other books by the same author:
Hold Tight the Thread, 2004 (Tender Ties. Book 3)
Every Fixed Star, 2003 (Tender Ties. Book 2)
A Name of Her Own, 2002 (Tender Ties. Book 1)
No Eye Can See, 2001 (Kinship and Courage. Book 2)
What Once We Loved, 2001 (Kinship and Courage. Book 3)

Other books you might like:
Patrick Dearen, *When the Sky Rained Dust*, 2004
Diane Glancy, *Designs of the Night Sky*, 2002
Elmer Kelton, *Cloudy in the West*, 1997
Gladys Smith, *Deliverance Valley*, 2003
Jeanne Williams, *The Underground River*, 2004
 Beneath the Burning Ground. Book 1

502

STAN LYNDE

Marshal of Medicine Lodge

(Lincoln, Nebraska: iUniverse, 2005)

Story type: Traditional; Man Alone
Series: Merlin Fanshaw. Book 1
Subject(s): Law Enforcement; Crime and Criminals
Major character(s): Merlin Fanshaw, Lawman (deputy U.S. marshal); Chance Ridgeway, Lawman (U.S. marshal); Jefferson Brown, Lawman (marshal)
Time period(s): 1880s (1886)
Locale(s): Medicine Lodge, Montana; Crow Reservation, Montana; Dry Creek, Montana

Summary: Deputy U.S. Marshal Merlin Fanshaw, acting as deputy undersheriff to Glenn Murdoch in Dry Creek, Montana, is bored. By the time the thaw hits in April of 1886, Dry Creek is so peaceful that a man is likely to fall asleep over his cribbage board, so Merlin isn't sorry to get a telegram from his boss, U.S. Marshal Chance Ridgeway. Only Fort Custer, a few farmers, a few big ranchers, and Medicine Lodge are located along the Bighorn River. The farmers, the ranchers, and Medicine Lodge are on Crow Indian land. The Crow are starving for lack of promised rations, so the braves steal a cow or two every now and then. The ranchers and farmers grumble a bit and steal some Crow horses. The two thefts offset each other, so all in all, the Crow and the white settlers get along peacefully. Then a young renegade named Archie Young Bull leads a gang of ne'er-do-well warriors, and starts breaking into homes, stealing more than just a cow or two, accosting settlers, until finally, they beat up the town marshal of Medicine Lodge and burn the jail. The town council hires a former soldier named Jefferson Brown to handle the situation, and he needs some help. Fanshaw packs his bedroll and rides for Medicine Lodge and the most trouble of his young life.

Where it's reviewed:
Roundup Magazine, August 2005, page 37

Other books by the same author:
Saving Miss Julie, 2004
Vigilante Moon, 2003
Careless Creek, 1999
The Bodacious Kid, 1996

Other books you might like:
Ralph Cotton, *Between Hell and Texas*, 2004
Zane Grey, *The Maverick Queen*, 2004
Martin Marcus, *Freedom Land*, 2003
John D. Nesbitt, *West of Rock River*, 2004
Dan O'Brien, *The Indian Agent*, 2004

503

WILLIAM COLT MACDONALD

Powder Smoke

(Waterville, Maine: Five Star, 2005)

Story type: Traditional; Collection
Subject(s): Crime and Criminals; Family Life; American West
Time period(s): 19th century (post-Civil War)
Locale(s): West

Summary: Two novellas by William Colt MacDonald both explore the different routes revenge may take. In the first, a small rancher loses his ranch to the greed of a rancher baron. In turn, the small rancher kidnaps his enemy's son, planning to raise the infant to be an outlaw, then turn him loose on his father. The second novella deals with a young man accused of murdering his own brother because his gun is found at the scene of the crime. The rancher for whom the young man worked decides the best way to avenge the victim and save his younger brother is to find the real murderer.

Where it's reviewed:
Roundup Magazine, August 2005, page 37

Other books by the same author:
Riddle of Ramrod Ridge, 2005
Boomtown Buccaneers, 2004
Rebel Ranger, 2004
The Red Raider, 2004
Stir Up the Dust, 2004

Other books you might like:
Frank Bonham, *Stage Trails West*, 2003
Max Brand, *Flaming Fortune*, 2003
Max Brand, *Jokers Extra Wild*, 2002
Will Henry, *Blind Canon*, 2005
Les Savage Jr., *Trail of the Silver Saddle*, 2005

504

WILLIAM COLT MACDONALD

The Red Raider

(New York: Leisure, 2005)

Story type: Traditional; Indian Wars
Subject(s): American West; Indians of North America; Short Stories
Time period(s): 19th century (post-Civil War)
Locale(s): West

Summary: Two novellas that are among MacDonald's best both tell of murder, each from a different perspective. In "Gun Fog," a young cowboy loses more than he has in a poker game. He agree to work for a rancher for free until he pays off his debt, but he doesn't agree to be framed for murder. In "The Red Raider," a father rides out to avenge his son's death. What he doesn't know is that a band of Apaches wait for him over the next hill.

Where it's reviewed:
Roundup Magazine, November 2005, page 37

Other books by the same author:
Galloping Ghost, 2004
King of Crazy River, 2004
Rebel Ranger, 2004
Phantom Pass, 2003
Action at Arcanum, 2002

Other books you might like:
Lyle Brandt, *Justice Gun*, 2003
J. Lee Butts, *Brotherhood of Blood*, 2004
Ralph Cotton, *Gunman's Song*, 2004
Ford Pendleton, *Gunmaster*, 2003
Jory Sherman, *Texas Dust*, 2004

505

JOHN D. NESBITT

Rancho Alegre

(New York: Leisure, 2005)

Story type: Traditional; Man Alone
Subject(s): American West
Major character(s): Jimmy Clevis, Cowboy; Matthew Tull, Rancher (heir to ranch); Raymond Bowden, Heir—Lost, Bastard Son (of Lawrence Tull)
Time period(s): 19th century (post-Civil War)
Locale(s): Paloma Springs, Colorado

Summary: Jimmy Clevis is out of a job and broke when he hears that Lawrence Tull wants to talk to him. He wants Jimmy to find his illegitimate son, who may be named Raymond Bowden, and arrange for Tull to meet the son he's never seen. It sounds easy enough: ride to Paloma Springs, find this young man, and convince him to see Tull. Like most jobs that sound simple and promise a big payoff, this one isn't so easy and he has to be alive to spend a payoff. There are lies, deceit, even murder surrounding him. What Jimmy wants to know is how much does Lawrence Tull's legitimate son, Matthew Tull, have to do with the mess he's ridden into without knowing it?

Where it's reviewed:
Roundup Magazine, September 2005, page 38

Other books by the same author:
West of Rock River, 2004
Black Hat Butte, 2003
Red Wind Crossing, 2003
Man from Wolf River, 2001
North of Cheyenne, 2000

Other books you might like:
Peter Brandvold, *Once Late With a .38*, 2003

Tim Champlin, *White Lights Roar*, 2003
Jane Candia Coleman, *Lost River*, 2003
Tom Franklin, *Hell at the Breech*, 2003
Bobby R. Woodall, *Clearwater*, 2003

506

DAVID NEVIN

Dream West

(New York: Forge, 2005)

Story type: Historical/Americana; Saga
Subject(s): American West; Family Life
Major character(s): John Charles Fremont, Historical Figure, Explorer; Jessie Benton Fremont, Spouse (of John), Historical Figure; Kit Carson, Guide (for Fremont), Historical Figure
Time period(s): 19th century (1840-1890)
Locale(s): Washington, District of Columbia; West

Summary: The story of explorer, governor, and senator John Charles Fremont and his wife, Jessie Benton Fremont, *Dream West* is a beautifully written and compelling book. Famous figures such as Abraham Lincoln, Kit Carson, and Ulysses S. Grant, are all characters in this historical novel. The most exciting parts of the book are Fremont's expeditions, told in detail that evokes the images of the wild, untamed country that he so loved. Nevin doesn't shy away from describing Fremont's less endearing traits: his pride, his ambition, his poor judgment, but that only makes a historical figure more human, more a person one can identify with. This is truly a novel that catches the spirit of the 19th century in America.

Where it's reviewed:
Roundup Magazine, November 2005, page 37

Other books by the same author:
Meriwether, 2005
Treason, 2001
Eagle's Cry, 2000
1812, 1996

Other books you might like:
Stephen Harrigan, *The Gates of the Alamo*, 2000
Elmer Kelton, *Sons of Texas*, 2005
Robert Lewis Taylor, *The Travels of Jamie McPheeters*, 1992
Norman Zollinger, *Chapultepec*, 1995
Norman Zollinger, *Meridian*, 1997

507

THOM NICHOLSON

Ride the Red Sun Down

(New York: Signet, 2005)

Story type: Traditional; Revenge
Subject(s): American West; Crime and Criminals
Major character(s): Martin Keller, Bounty Hunter (hunts for his family's killer); Al Hulett, Murderer (killed Keller's family); Caroline Thompson, Widow(er)
Time period(s): 1870s (1875)
Locale(s): Cimarron, New Mexico

Summary: Martin Keller becomes a bounty hunter when Al Hulett murders his wife and son. He swears to hunt down the murderer and shoot him for resisting arrest. It is what the man deserves and what he will get. When Keller is wounded, he stays in Cimarron, New Mexico, while he recovers. He meets Caroline Thompson, and for the first time since his wife and son died, he feels interest in a woman. Caroline tells him how her husband was shot in the back, and Keller makes a vow that he will hunt down her husband's murderer. Never does he dream that his family's killer might also be Caroline's husband's murderer.

Where it's reviewed:
Roundup Magazine, November 2005, page 38

Other books you might like:
Max Brand, *Tales of the Wild West*, 2000
Ed Gorman, *The Blue and the Gray Undercover*, 2001
   editor
T.V. Olsen, *Loud Hand*, 2001
Wayne D. Overholser, *Chumley's Gold*, 2001
Jon Tuska, *Stories of the Golden West. Book Two*, 2001
   editor

508

SHARON NIEDERMAN

Return to Abo

(Albuquerque: University of New Mexico Press, 2005)

Story type: Ranch Life; Modern
Subject(s): American West; Ranch Life
Major character(s): Maggie Chilton, Journalist, Rancher; Lucy Chilton, Rancher, Parent (Maggie's mother); Roger Dawson, Boyfriend (former), Political Figure (mayor)
Time period(s): 2000s
Locale(s): Monte Alto, New Mexico

Summary: When Maggie Chilton writes a story about a young woman who escaped domestic violence, and the woman is murdered by her estranged boyfriend shortly after the feature appears in the San Francisco paper Maggie works for, Maggie is distraught and unable to write, so the paper fires her. Her mother, Lucy Chilton, calls her back to Monte Alto, the rural New Mexico ranching community where Maggie grew up, for the funeral of a longtime ranch hand. Maggie notices her mother is ill, but Lucy refuses to admit it. Maggie hardly arrives back in San Francisco before Lucy capitulates and asks her daughter to come home. Maggie knows how to run a ranch and how to survive in a small town, but both ranching and small towns have changed in the 20 years she has been gone. Monte Alto is a dying community even though Mayor Roger Dawson tries to keep it alive. A rich Texas land developer wants to buy Chilton Ranch and the rest of the family ranches around Monte Alto. Maggie and her neighbors must decide if they want to face the economic uncertainty of ranching or sell up. A wonderful save the ranch story set in the modern West.

Where it's reviewed:
Roundup Magazine, August 2005, page 37

Other books you might like:
Elizabeth Black, *Buffalo Spirits*, 2003

Western

K. Follis Cheatham, *Kansas Dancer*, 2002
Sandra Dallas, *The Chili Queen*, 2002
Diane Glancy, *Signs in the Night Sky*, 2002
Gladys Smith, *Deliverance Valley*, 2003

509

WAYNE D. OVERHOLSER

Twin Rocks

(Waterville, Maine: Five Star, 2005)

Story type: Traditional; Collection
Subject(s): American West; Crime and Criminals
Time period(s): 19th century (post-Civil War)
Locale(s): West

Summary: Two fine novellas by Spur Award-winning author Wayne D. Overholser focus on character and the psychology of human beings. In ''Trouble at Gold Plume,'' a former lawman is out to avenge his sister's death, caused by the dishonest actions of her husband. Played out against the background of a booming gold camp, the brother confronts a crooked syndicate he is sure is hiding his brother-in-law. In the title story, a young man loses his fiancee because his older sister is controlling the family ranch until he turns 25. Complications arise when a crooked banker weighs in on the young man's future inheritance.

Where it's reviewed:
Roundup Magazine, November 2005, page 39

Other books by the same author:
The Law at Miles City, 2004
Wild Horse River, 2003
Wheels Roll West, 2002
Gateway House, 2001
Rainbow Rider, 2001

Other books you might like:
Peter Brandvold, *Staring Down the Devil*, 2004
Ralph Compton, *The Palo Duro Trail*, 2004
Cameron Judd, *Bad Night at Dry Creek*, 2004
L.J. Martin, *McKeog's Mountain*, 2004
John D. Nesbitt, *Man from Wolf River*, 2001

510

LAURAN PAINE

Holding the Ace Card

(Waterville, Maine: Five Star, 2005)

Story type: Traditional; Ranch Life
Subject(s): American West; Crime and Criminals
Time period(s): 19th century (post-Civil War)
Locale(s): West

Summary: Two novellas by prolific Western novelist Lauran Paine focus on ranch life and the range wars that sometimes occurred between large ranchers and small ones, or between ranchers and farmers. In ''Terror Trail,'' a large rancher rustles some of small rancher Reno Balfor's cattle, setting off a range war where the winner is the last man standing. ''Holding the Ace Card'' finds gunfighter Lou Bellanger hired by the mother he hasn't seen since he was a very young child, to fight

for her small ranch against a greedy neighboring rancher who wants her land and water rights.

Where it's reviewed:
Roundup Magazine, August 2005, page 37

Other books by the same author:
Guns in Oregon, 2004
Rain Valley, 2004
Gathering Storm, 2003
Night of the Comancheros, 2003
Guns in the Desert, 2002

Other books you might like:
Cameron Judd, *Beggar's Gulch*, 2004
Noel M. Loomis, *Cheyenne War Cry*, 2003
Stan Lynde, *The Bodacious Kid*, 1996
Wolf MacKenna, *The Hellraisers*, 2004
Cotton Smith, *The Thirteenth Bullet*, 2004

511

LEWIS B. PATTEN

Sundown

(Waterville, Maine: Five Star, 2005)

Story type: Traditional; Collection
Subject(s): American West; Short Stories
Time period(s): 19th century (post-Civil War)
Locale(s): West

Summary: The first novella in this collection concerns a young Confederate veteran who comes home to find his father dead and his ranch sold for back taxes to a carpetbagger. The sheriff advises the young man to move on, but he rides to his former home to ask for a job. He is beaten senseless instead. The local doctor patches him up and suggests a diabolical plan for revenge. In the second novella, ''Sundown,'' a rancher is battling rustlers whom he suspects are being led by a local homesteader who never grows anything, but always has gold to spend. The problem is the rancher is in love with the homesteader's wife, making it difficult to turn in her husband to the sheriff.

Where it's reviewed:
Roundup Magazine, September 2005, page 39

Other books by the same author:
Back Trail, 2004
Guns of Vengeance, 2003
Blood on the Grass, 2002
Ride the Red Trail, 2001
The Woman at Ox-Yoke, 2000

Other books you might like:
Frank Bonham, *Stage Trails West*, 2003
Ricardo L. Garcia, *Brother Bill's Bait Bites Back and Other Tales from the Raton*, 2004
Ed Gorman, *The Long Ride Back*, 2004
Lisa Sandlin, *In the River Province*, 2004
Jon Tuska, *Stories of the Golden West. Book Four*, 2003 editor

512

PETE PETERSON

The Relentless Gun

(New York: Avalon, 2004)

Story type: Traditional; Revenge
Subject(s): American West; Crime and Criminals
Major character(s): Jack Dancer, Farmer, Teenager (17-year-old); Cash McCabe, Bully (son of a rich carpetbagger); John Dancer, Gunfighter (Jack's uncle)
Time period(s): 19th century (post-Civil War)
Locale(s): Buffalo Springs, Texas

Summary: Seventeen-year-old Jack Dancer, a farmer's son in worn, too small overalls, just wants to have a beer and a game of billiards with a pretty saloon girl. Instead, he finds himself pushed into a gunfight with Cash McCabe, using a borrowed gun. He flees town after besting McCabe, believing he killed the young bully. He knows the McCabe brothers, sons of the richest carpetbagger in North Texas, will be after him with guns blazing. The McCabes first take vengeance on Jack's family, leaving his mother and brother for dead, then begin trailing Jack to add him to the number of dead. Jack runs into his uncle, John Dancer, the best gunman in Texas, and the two plot revenge on the loutish McCabe brothers.

Where it's reviewed:
Roundup Magazine, August 2005, page 37

Other books by the same author:
Reckoning at Raindance, 2005
Cowboy Years, 2004
The Relentless Gun, 2004

Other books you might like:
Lyle Brandt, *Justice Gun*, 2003
J. Lee Butts, *Brotherhood of Blood*, 2004
Ralph Cotton, *Gunman's Song*, 2004
Ford Pendleton, *Gunmaster*, 2003
Jory Sherman, *Texas Dust*, 2004

513

ALEXANDER POSEY

Chinnubbie and the Owl

(Lincoln: University of Nebraska Press, 2005)

Story type: Collection; Indian Culture
Subject(s): American West; Indians of North America; Short Stories
Time period(s): Indeterminate Past
Locale(s): West

Summary: Nine stories, five orations, and nine works of oral tradition are the first works ever collected in book form by the Muscogee poet, journalist, and humorist who died in 1908 at the age of 34. Posey was the most famous American Indian writer of his time. Most of the stories, orations, and works of oral tradition were written for Oklahoma Territorial newspapers and magazines and exist in clippings in a few archives. These are wonderful accounts of the trickster theme, orations that define Posey's political stance, and works of oral tradition that reveal his Muscogee cultural roots.

Where it's reviewed:
Roundup Magazine, August 2005, page 38

Other books by the same author:
Fus Fixico Letters, 2002

Other books you might like:
Sherman Alexie, *Ten Little Indians*, 2003
James D. Doss, *Dead Soul*, 2003
Terry Gamble, *The Water Dancers*, 2003
Garth Murphy, *The Indian Lover*, 2002
James Willard Schultz, *Blackfeet Tales from Opikuna's World*, 2003

514

MARY POWELL

Galveston Rose

(Fort Worth: Texas Christian University Press, 2005)

Story type: Modern; Saga
Subject(s): American West; Family Life
Major character(s): Rose Parrish, Wealthy, Aged Person; J.J. Broussard, Businessman (owns charter boat business), Consultant (advises Rose on investments); Jessie Martin, Student (in medical school)
Time period(s): 2000s
Locale(s): Galveston, Texas

Summary: Rose Parrish is old, ill, widowed, and childless. She lives in a mansion on Galveston Island just off the Texas coast. What does a lonely woman in her terminal years do? She creates her own family by befriending a group of eccentric people, also without families. First is J.J. Broussard, raised wealthy but now dependent on a charter boat service for his living until he meets Rose who asks him to handle some risky investments from which they both make a fortune. Then there is Jessie Martin to whom Rose rents a bedroom in her mansion, giving Galveston gossips much to talk about. Jessie is a medical student and the son Rose never had. Then there is Dooley Thomas who rescues endangered dolphins while searching for his family. While Galveston believes these peculiar people are taking advantage of Rose, it is Rose who influences them. Galveston is brought to life and almost becomes a character in this wonderful book about love and family in the modern West.

Where it's reviewed:
Roundup Magazine, August 2005, page 37

Other books by the same author:
Auslander, 2001

Other books you might like:
James Carlos Blake, *Under the Skin*, 2003
Matt Braun, *The Overlords*, 2002
Louise Erdrich, *The Master Butchers Singing Club*, 2003
Joe R. Lansdale, *The Big Blow*, 2000
P.G. Nagle, *Galveston*, 2002

Western

515

BILL PRONZINI

Quincannon's Game

(Waterville, Maine: Five Star, 2005)

Story type: Collection; Mystery
Subject(s): Crime and Criminals; American West
Major character(s): John Quincannon, Detective—Private (former Secret Service agent); Sabina Carpenter, Detective—Private (Quincannon's partner)
Time period(s): 19th century (post-Civil War)
Locale(s): West

Summary: John Quincannon is one of Pronzini's best characters, on a par with his Nameless Detective in his mysteries. A former Secret Service agent, Quincannon partners up with Sabina Carpenter to open a detective agency. Together the two have rousing adventures solving crimes even the Pinkertons won't touch. In this collection, Quincannon and Sherlock Holmes team up to solve a string of burglaries and a locked room mystery. In another story, Quincannon and Sabina attend a seance to expose the medium as a fraud, and find murder instead. A delightful read for the Western fan.

Where it's reviewed:
Roundup Magazine, September 2005, page 39

Other books by the same author:
Burgade's Crossing, 2005
All the Long Years, 2003
Blue Lonesome, 1999

Other books you might like:
T.T. Flynn, *The Devil's Lode*, 1999
Ed Gorman, *The Long Ride Back*, 2004
Clinton McKinzie, *Crossing the Line*, 2004
Annie Proulx, *Bad Dirt*, 2004
Marcus Stevens, *Useful Girl*, 2004

516

ROBERT J. RANDISI, Editor

Lone Star Law

(New York: Pocket, 2005)

Story type: Traditional; Anthology
Subject(s): American West; Crime and Criminals; Short Stories
Time period(s): 19th century (post-Civil War)
Locale(s): West

Summary: This anthology of short stories about the Texas Rangers features some of the finest Western writers, including Elmer Kelton, Troy D. Smith, Louis L'Amour, Peter Brandvold, and Ed Gorman.

Where it's reviewed:
Roundup Magazine, August 2005, page 38

Other books by the same author:
Backshooter, 2004
Boot Hill, 2002 (editor)
White Hats, 2002 (editor)
Tin Star, 2000 (editor)

The Ghost with Blue Eyes, 1999

Other books you might like:
Max Brand, *Tales of the Wild West*, 2000
Ed Gorman, *The Blue and the Gray Undercover*, 2001
 editor
T.V. Olsen, *Loud Hand*, 2001
Wayne D. Overholser, *Chumley's Gold*, 2001
Jon Tuska, *Stories of the Golden West. Book Two*, 2001
 editor

517

ROBERT J. RANDISI

Trapp's Mountain

(New York: Leisure, 2005)

Story type: Traditional; Man Alone
Subject(s): American West; Crime and Criminals
Major character(s): John Henry Trapp, Convict; Wendell Fry, Drifter, Gunfighter
Time period(s): 19th century (1846-1871)
Locale(s): Texas

Summary: John Henry Trapp, a mountain man of tremendous height and muscle, returns to his camp to find his squaw burned to death along with everything he owns. He tracks down the two murderers and kills them both. With the money and influence of one of the killers' fathers, Trapp gets 25 years in Huntsville Prison in Texas. The other inmates soon learn to leave him alone. He makes one friend, a gambler who teaches him how to cheat at poker. When he walks out, now 64-years-old, he and a kid named Wendell Fry kill two men who try to kill Trapp. They become partners and friends, but never seem to get any closer to Trapp's mountain. Someone is always chasing them, testing them. When they are captured by the Comanches, they meet another captive. The three escape together, but the newcomer is only thinking about turning in Fry for the $10,000 price on his head. Another action-packed thriller from Randisi.

Where it's reviewed:
Roundup Magazine, November 2005, page 38

Other books by the same author:
Vengeance Creek, 2005 (The Sons of Daniel Shane. Book 2)
Backshooter, 2004
Lancaster's Orphans, 2004
Leaving Epitaph, 2004 (The Sons of Daniel Shane. Book 1)
Turnback Creek, 2004 (Widowmaker. Book 2)

Other books you might like:
Ralph Cotton, *Hell's Riders*, 2004
J.T. Edson, *Cold Deck, Hot Lead*, 2004
T.A. Mort, *Showdown at Verity*, 2004
Charles G. West, *Devil's Kin*, 2005

518

WILLIS G. REGIER, Editor

Masterpieces of American Indian Literature

(Lincoln: University of Nebraska Press, 2005)

Story type: Indian Culture; Anthology
Subject(s): American West; Indians of North America
Time period(s): Indeterminate Past
Locale(s): West

Summary: Five works by American Indians, some famous, some not, are collected together to reveal their culture. These works discuss identity, family, community, caste, gender, nature, the future, the past, solitude, duty, trust, betrayal, leadership, war, and apocalypse. The works are *The Life of Kah-ge-ga-gah-bowh* by George Copway, a Canadian Ojibwe; *The Soul of the Indian* by Charles Eastman, a discussion of Indian religious life before the white man; *American Indian Stories* by Zitkala-Sa, a famous Sioux writer; *Coyote Stories* by Mourning Dove, tells the tales of the trickster rabbit; and *Black Elk Speaks* as told through John G. Neihardt, the story of a Lakota holy man.

Where it's reviewed:
Roundup Magazine, November 2005, page 38

Other books you might like:
D.L. Birchfield, *Field of Honor*, 2004
James Lee Burke, *In the Moon of Red Ponies*, 2004
Louise Erdrich, *Four Souls*, 2004
Frank B. Linderman, *Indian Why Stories*, 2004
Billy Moore, *Little Brother Real Snake*, 2004

519

FRANK RODERUS

The Wrangler

(New York: Berkley, 2005)

Story type: Traditional; Ranch Life
Subject(s): American West; Family Life
Major character(s): John Chandler, Cowboy, Veteran (of Confederate Army); Eddie Mannet, Cowboy; Catherine Wolbrough, Rancher, Widow(er)
Time period(s): 19th century (post-Civil War)
Locale(s): West

Summary: John Chandler is an out-of-work cowboy, a Confederate veteran, and a homely man with a birthmark on his cheek and a crooked nose. He knows widowed ranch owner Catherine Wolbrough didn't hire him for his looks; she hired him to round up lost cattle she can sell, so she can move back east. Chandler knows how to punch cows and he doesn't need Eddie Mannet telling him how. Mannet was hired the same time Chandler was, but acts like he's foreman and boss over Chandler and the other hands. When Mannet isn't trying to boss everyone else, he is sparking the widow. When that doesn't work, Mannet isn't above using deadlier means. That brings back Chandler's love of lost causes, and sticking his nose in on the side of the widow could turn out to be a worse lost cause than the Confederacy.

Where it's reviewed:
Roundup Magazine, November 2005, page 38

Other books by the same author:
Charlie and the Sir, 2005
Billy Ray and the Good News, 2004
Judgment Day, 2004
Lewisville Flats, 2002

Other books you might like:
Jane Candia Coleman, *Lost River*, 2003
Ed Gorman, *Night of Shadows*, 2002
Stephen Overholser, *Chasing Destiny*, 2005
Glendon Swarthout, *The Shootist*, 1998
Joseph A. West, *Donovan's Dove*, 2004

520

ROBERT A. RORIPAUGH

Honor Thy Father

(New York: HarperCollins, 2004)

Story type: Traditional; Ranch Life
Subject(s): American West; Crime and Criminals
Major character(s): Ira Tyrrell, Rancher, Student—Boarding School; Mart Tyrrell, Rancher; Karr, Rancher, Political Figure (state senator)
Time period(s): 1880s (1889)
Locale(s): Bothwell, Wyoming

Summary: Originally published in 1968 and out of print for years, *Honor Thy Father* is a literary Western in the vein of *Shane* or *Lonesome Dove*. The famous Johnson County War in Wyoming is narrated by Mart Tyrrell when he is an old man, long after the events have passed into history. It is a thoughtful look at the events and mind-set of both ranchers and homesteaders that led to one of the bloodiest range wars in the history of the West. Mart's father, Martin Tyrrell, and his close friend, Senator Karr, a rancher and state senator, are determined to control the open range, and drive homesteaders and small ranchers out of business by preventing them from gathering and selling their cattle if they failed to join the Cattlemen's Association, which will refuse them membership even if they apply. Ira Tyrrell, Mart's older brother, is on the opposite side of the conflict. He believes that the cattlemen can no long expect to control the land and the markets, and should not behave like outlaws in an effort to hold onto free range. When Senator Karr orders Martin Tyrrell's most loyal friend killed on false charges, Ira begs his father to refute the charges. His father refuses and the line is drawn between the two men. This is probably one of the best novels about the Johnson County War, and makes plain the conflicting loyalties among the two sides.

Where it's reviewed:
Roundup Magazine, June 2005, page 38

Other books by the same author:
A Fever for Living, 1962

Other books you might like:
Peter Brandvold, *Staring Down the Devil*, 2004
Ralph Compton, *The Palo Duro Trail*, 2004
Cameron Judd, *Bad Night at Dry Creek*, 2004
L.J. Martin, *McKeog's Mountain*, 2004

Western

John D. Nesbitt, *Man from Wolf River*, 2001

521

HAROLD G. ROSS

Comanche Crossing

(Manhattan, Kansas: Harold G. Ross, 2005)

Story type: Traditional; Man Alone
Subject(s): American West
Major character(s): James Shannon, Farmer, Sailor (shanghaied); Aguila, Chieftain (Apache), Friend (of James Shannon); Elizabeth Shannon, Young Woman (James' sister), Captive (of the Apache)
Time period(s): 19th century (1855-1894)
Locale(s): West

Summary: The Shannon family comes to America in 1855. Within a few years, they purchase a ranch and cattle, for a bargain price, on Comanche Creek in West Texas. On a trip to New Orleans, James Shannon is shanghaied and is forced to spend a year at sea. He escapes during a mutiny, with the captain's horde of gemstones. Although he meets a girl named Suzette in New Orleans, he still feels he has to return to the ranch. His homecoming is not a happy one: the ranch has been burned to the ground; his parents have been massacred; and his sister, Elizabeth, has been kidnapped by the Apache. The ranch turns out to be located in Apache country, and the area is subject to Comanche raids as well, finally explaining why the land was so cheap to begin with. James manages to rescue his sister, becoming friends with Aguila, an Apache chieftain, in the process. He lives a long, though often dangerous life, which Ross relates, along with a deep feeling for the land on which James lives.

Where it's reviewed:
Roundup Magazine, November 2005, page 38

Other books by the same author:
Uncharted Journey, 2004
The Emerald Prairie, 2003
Horizons West, 2002
Brannick, 2001

Other books you might like:
James Carlos Blake, *Wildwood Boys*, 2000
Tim Champlin, *Raiders of the Western & Atlantic*, 2002
Lisa Sandlin, *In the River Province*, 2004
Les Savage Jr., *Trail of the Silver Saddle*, 2005

522

LES SAVAGE JR.

The Beast in Canada Diablo

(New York: Leisure, 2005)

Story type: Traditional; Collection
Subject(s): American West; Short Stories
Time period(s): 19th century (post-Civil War)
Locale(s): West

Summary: Three long short stories by the master of the psychological Western are restored to their original length for this publication. The title story, "The Beast in Canada Diablo," is the most frightening and the most suspenseful. A giant catlike creature identical to that described in Mexican myth is prowling the brasada country of south Texas, killing men and animals alike. Three rustlers can choose to enter the dense underbrush where it hides, or face the noose. They chose the brasada. In "The Brand of Senorita Scorpion," Savage introduces the adventurous woman Elgera Douglas, who became one of his most popular characters. In "Queen of the Long Rifles," Bateau Severn falls in love with Mira, the daughter of another mountain man, and takes her along when he is fleeing a man determined to control all the free trappers beginning with Severn.

Where it's reviewed:
Roundup Magazine, August 2005, page 38

Other books by the same author:
Trail of the Silver Saddle, 2005
The Devil's Corral, 2003
West of Laramie, 2003
The Cavan Breed, 2001
The Shadow in Renegade Basin, 2001

Other books you might like:
Frank Bonham, *Stage Trails West*, 2003
Ricardo L. Garcia, *Brother Bill's Bait Bites Back and Other Tales from the Raton*, 2004
Ed Gorman, *The Long Ride Back*, 2004
Lisa Sandlin, *In the River Province*, 2004
Jon Tuska, *Stories of the Golden West. Book Four*, 2003 editor

523

STEVE SHERWOOD

Hardwater

(Huntsville: Texas Review Press, 2005)

Story type: Modern; Chase
Subject(s): Crime and Criminals; American West; Serial Killers
Major character(s): Peter Hoback, Publisher (owns newspaper), Detective—Amateur; Gil Iverson, Lawman (deputy sheriff), Friend (of Peter); Goldie Gudmundsen, Truck Driver, Lover (of Peter)
Time period(s): 2000s
Locale(s): Hardwater, Wyoming

Summary: After Peter Hoback's wife is murdered, he spends three months tracking down the killer, finally turning him in to the police. After that, he and his baby son, Bart, drift until they arrive in Hardwater, Wyoming, where the newspaper's publisher has just fired his editor. Peter takes the job and he and Bart settle in, buying an old Victorian three-story house, and renting its third floor apartment to Goldie Gudmundsen, a beautiful blonde truck driver, who is Peter's lover when she's in town. Life is good, with camping and fishing in the nearby mountains, and visits with his friends on the Shoshone and Arapaho Reservation. Then a modern day drifter tells Peter about stumbling on a deserted cabin with three scalped bodies arranged in a triangle. Peter checks out the man's story, and calls the sheriff, who sends his deputy, Gil Iverson, to the scene. Gil is Peter's best friend in Hardwater, but that doesn't

Western

mean much when Peter is intent on writing about the mass murder and the figure of a man in a wolf mask in the trees near the cabin. Sheriff Spiker is afraid that if Peter mentions the figure, it will trigger a war between the whites in Hardwater and the Indians on the reservation. Sensitive about murder, Peter decides to track down the killer himself, regardless of whether the man is white or Indian. Most of all Peter will protect his family in the expectation of violence erupting between the town and the reservation.

Where it's reviewed:
Roundup Magazine, August 2005, page 38

Other books you might like:
Patrick Dearen, *When the Sky Rained Dust*, 2004
Fred Harris, *Following the Harvest*, 2004
Clinton McKinzie, *Crossing the Line*, 2004
Annie Proulx, *Bad Dirt*, 2004
Marcus Stevens, *Useful Girl*, 2004

524

COTTON SMITH

Death Rides a Red Horse

(New York: Leisure, 2005)

Story type: Traditional; Revenge
Subject(s): American West; Crime and Criminals
Major character(s): Cole Kerry, Rancher (with his brothers); Ethan Kerry, Rancher, Handicapped (blind); Victorio Gee, Outlaw, Murderer
Time period(s): 19th century (post-Civil War)
Locale(s): Uvalde, Texas

Summary: Cole and Ethan Kerry and their families ride into Uvalde, Texas, for supplies and run into Victorio Gee's gang in the general story. Cole breaks up a raid on the town, but unfortunately the gang kidnaps his wife as they escape. Cole goes after them, but is shot in the back. Now it is up to his older brother, Ethan, to rescue Cole's wife, and do whatever is necessary to stay alive. Ethan swears he will succeed even if he is blind.

Where it's reviewed:
Roundup Magazine, August 2005, page 38

Other books by the same author:
The 13th Bullet, 2004
Winter Kill, 2004
Sons of Thunder, 2003
Spirit Rider, 2003
Brothers of the Gun, 2002

Other books you might like:
Ralph Cotton, *Hell's Riders*, 2004
J.T. Edson, *Cold Deck, Hot Lead*, 2004
T.A. Mort, *Showdown at Verity*, 2004
Charles G. West, *Devil's Kin*, 2005

525

JOHN WARREN SMITH

No Holier Spot of Ground

(Huntsville: Texas Review Press, 2004)

Story type: Traditional; Family Saga
Subject(s): American West; Cowboys/Cowgirls
Major character(s): John Stephen Smith, Plantation Owner; Robert Smith, Cousin (of John Stephen), Plantation Owner (owns Smith's Landing); George Elliott Hunter, Saloon Keeper/Owner (owns Hunter's Tavern)
Time period(s): 19th century (1835-1869)
Locale(s): Cincinnati, Texas

Summary: This family saga novelizes the story of author John Warren Smith's family on their cotton plantation on the Trinity River in Texas in the mid-19th century. In the course of researching the family history, Smith discovers a number of events he would have rather not known, including the abuse of slaves, an insane son hidden away, tragic deaths, and quarrels among siblings and half-siblings that tore the family apart. Joseph Stephen Smith and his best friend and cousin, Robert Smith, establish neighboring plantations called Harvest Home and Smith's Landing, respectively. Their story involves much of the history of Texas from 1835-1869, especially the love of the land by early Texas settlers. The author does not shy away from painful or controversial subjects, including racial mixing, adultery, land grabs, murder, and the rise of the Ku Klux Klan.

Where it's reviewed:
Roundup Magazine, August 2005, page 38

Other books you might like:
Sandra Babb, *Where Names Are Unknown*, 2004
Louise Erdrich, *Four Souls*, 2004
Zane Grey, *Riders of the Purple Sage*, 2005
Evan Hunter, *The Chisholms*, 2004
Louis L'Amour, *Hondo*, 2004

526

PARI NOSKIN TAICHERT

The Belen Hitch

(Albuquerque: University of New Mexico Press, 2005)

Story type: Modern; Mystery
Subject(s): American West; Crime and Criminals
Major character(s): Sasha Solomon, Advertising (public relations person), Detective—Amateur; Lydia Herndon, Aged Person; Rita Woodson, Nurse
Time period(s): 2000s
Locale(s): Belen, New Mexico

Summary: Sasha Solomon, public relations consultant and amateur sleuth, takes a job in Belen, New Mexico, a small town without much going for it. She is supposed to work up a publicity campaign for the abandoned Harvey House, one of the old restaurants that served train passengers in the 19th century. A group of train enthusiasts wants to turn Harvey House into a bed-and-breakfast and reopen the restaurant; an artists' group wants to turn it into a museum showcasing the

blasphemous art of the late Phillipa Petty. Interviewing people on both sides of the issue, Sasha realizes that nobody has anything good to say about the recently deceased Phillipa, and comes to believe that the woman may have been murdered. Sasha's mother was a close friend of Phillipa, but is unable to shed much light on the situation, as she is suffering from a form of dementia.

Where it's reviewed:
Roundup Magazine, November 2005, page 39

Other books by the same author:
The Clovis Incident, 2004

Other books you might like:
Frederic Bean, *Murder at the Spirit Cave*, 1999
James D. Doss, *The Witch's Tongue*, 2004
J.A. Jance, *Exit Wounds*, 2004
Michael McGarrity, *Slow Kill*, 2004
D.R. Meredith, *Tome of Death*, 2005

527

KAREN TASCHEK

Horse of Seven Moons

(Albuquerque: University of New Mexico Press, 2005)

Story type: Traditional; Indian Culture
Subject(s): Animals/Horses; Indians of North America
Major character(s): Bin-daa-dee-nin, Indian (Mescalero Apache), Teenager (16-year-old); Sarah Chilton, Teenager (14-year-old), Animal Lover; Moon Dancer, Animal (pinto horse)
Time period(s): 1880s (1881)
Locale(s): Silver City, New Mexico

Summary: Bin-daa-dee-nin has lived off the reservation since the death of Victorio six months before. One night he finds a beautiful black and white pinto horse, the most beautiful horse he has ever seen. He trains the horse, but then loses him when the U.S. Calvary attacks the Apache camp one night. Not far away, young Sarah Chilton, fresh from Fort Smith, Arkansas, still doesn't feel at home on her father's ranch in New Mexico. On a bright moonlit night, she hears a noise and finds a beautiful black and white pinto. She names him Moon Dancer and teaches him how to jump. Then the Apaches raid the ranch and Bin-daa-dee-nin regains his horse. The horse keeps running away from one to the other and back again, and each wonders at what new tricks the horse knows. A wonderful story written for teens that can be enjoyed by adults.

Where it's reviewed:
Roundup Magazine, August 2005, page 38

Other books you might like:
Robert J. Avrech, *The Hebrew Kid and the Apache Maiden*, 2005
   The Hebrew Kid. Book 1
Tony Hillerman, *The Sinister Pig*, 2003
Frank B. Linderman, *Indian Why Stories*, 2004
Kent Nelson, *Land That Moves, Land That Stands Still*, 2003

528

JON TUSKA, Editor

Stories of the Golden West. Book Six

(Waterville, Maine: Five Star, 2005)

Story type: Traditional; Anthology
Series: Stories of the Golden West
Subject(s): American West; Short Stories
Time period(s): 19th century (post-Civil War)
Locale(s): West

Summary: Three short novels appear in this anthology edited by Jon Tuska. The first, "Thirsty Acres" by L.P. Holmes, concerns a prolonged period of drought, and a rancher taking advantage of the fact. "Hell for Sale" by Tom W. Blackburn finds Russ Cameron ordered to buy the Harpoon Ranch from Burt Orr. Unfortunately, Orr won't sell. "Proud Rider" by Harvey Fergusson concerns a young Navajo boy named Juan who gentles a wild stallion, Diablo.

Where it's reviewed:
Roundup Magazine, August 2005, page 38

Other books by the same author:
Stories of the Golden West. Book Five, 2004
Stories of the Golden West. Book Four, 2003
Stories of the Golden West. Book Three, 2002
Stories of the Golden West. Book Two, 2001
Stories of the Golden West. Book One, 2000

Other books you might like:
Max Brand, *Flaming Fortune*, 2003
Max Brand, *Jokers Extra Wild*, 2002
Lisa Sandlin, *In the River Province*, 2004
Les Savage Jr., *Trail of the Silver Saddle*, 2005

529

ROBERT JAMES WALLER

High Plains Tango

(New York: Shaye Areheart, 2005)

Story type: Modern; Man Alone
Subject(s): American West; Crime and Criminals
Major character(s): Carlisle McMillan, Carpenter; Susanna Benteen, Friend (of the Sioux); Gally Deveraux, Abuse Victim (battered wife), Widow(er)
Time period(s): 2000s
Locale(s): Salamander, South Dakota

Summary: After failing to find his father, the famous photographer of *Bridges of Madison County*, Carlisle McMillan, Stanford graduate and master carpenter, decides to settle in Salamander, South Dakota, a tiny isolated town near the Sioux reservation. He buys an abandoned house that he restores and settles down to rusticate on the High Plains and to enjoy the beauty of Gally Deveraux, a widow now that her brutal husband is dead. However, it is Susanna Benteen, a mysterious woman who lives with the Sioux, who Carlisle has his eye on. He could happily live out his life enjoying friendship and a little more from both women—until a certain corrupt developer tries to seize Carlisle's property for a highway. Carlisle fights the seizure while Susanna and the Sioux

watch. This very good modern Western echoes the problems many Westerners face.

Where it's reviewed:
Library Journal, June 15, 2005, page 62
Publishers Weekly, March 21, 2005, page 34

Other books by the same author:
A Thousand Country Roads, 2000
Puerta Vallarta Squeeze, 1996
Border Music, 1995
Images, 1994
Old Songs in a New Cafe, 1994

Other books you might like:
C.J. Box, *Out of Range*, 2005
 Joe Pickett. Book 4
C.J. Box, *Trophy Hunt*, 2004
 Joe Pickett. Book 3
James D. Doss, *The Witch's Tongue*, 2004
 Charlie Moon. Book 9
Michael McGarrity, *Slow Kill*, 2004
D.R. Meredith, *Murder by Deception*, 2004
 John Lloyd Branson. Book 2

530

CHARLES G. WEST

Bloody Hills
(New York: Signet, 2004)

Story type: Traditional; Revenge
Subject(s): American West; Crime and Criminals
Major character(s): Billy Ray Blevins, Outlaw, Murderer; Clay Culver, Scout (for the U.S. Army); Rachael Andrews, Spouse (wife of murdered schoolmaster), Employer (of Clay Culver)
Time period(s): 1870s (1875)
Locale(s): Dry Folk, South Dakota; Black Hills, South Dakota

Summary: Billy Ray Blevins is a short, skinny kid who is a deadly shot and likes to engage in gunfights because he discovers that he likes to kill. He first kills a young cowboy over a wager; then he kills the schoolmaster after forcibly fondling his wife; then he kills the sheriff when the lawman tries to arrest him. He rides out of town toward the Black Hills ahead of a posse, planning to hide out until he decides where to go. Rachael Andrews doesn't intend to let Billy Ray get away with her husband's murder, so she teams up with Deputy Sheriff Lon Fortson to hunt down Billy Ray. They quickly learn that they can't track a pair of muddy bootprints across a clean kitchen floor, so they hire army scout Clay Culver to help them. There is an obstacle though. The Sioux are on the warpath and trailing the three. None have any doubts about what will happen to them if the Sioux catch them. In the meantime, Billy Ray joins up with an old reprobate named Henry who also doesn't lose any sleep over killing someone. The pair capture Rachel and rape her. Rachel manages to steal Billy Ray's gun and kills both men, but her mental state is unsettled. Clay Culver, when he finds her, believes she will never recover from her ordeal. Of course, it probably doesn't matter because the Sioux will kill them anyway.

Where it's reviewed:
Roundup Magazine, June 2005, page 39

Other books by the same author:
Devil's Kin, 2005
Hangman's Song, 2005
Evil Breed, 2003
Hero's Stand, 2003
Savage Cry, 2002

Other books you might like:
James Carlos Blake, *Under the Skin*, 2003
Peter Brandvold, *Riding with the Devil's Mistress*, 2003
Stan Lynde, *Saving Miss Julie*, 2004
John D. Nesbitt, *Red Wind Crossing*, 2003
Frank Roderus, *Old Marsden*, 1999

531

CHARLES G. WEST

Devil's Kin
(New York: Signet, 2005)

Story type: Traditional; Revenge
Subject(s): American West; Crime and Criminals
Major character(s): Jordan Gray, Rancher; Jed Ramey, Lawman (deputy U.S. marshal); Johnny Spratte, Lawman (deputy sheriff), Outlaw (joins gang of killers)
Time period(s): 19th century (post-Civil War)
Locale(s): Oklahoma; Fort Smith, Arkansas

Summary: Leach, Snake, and Roach ride into Jordan Gray's homestead, murder his wife and son, and burn his cabin. Jordan buries his dead family after returning from riding with a posse looking for these same killers. Jordan reports the crime to the sheriff who frets about rounding up another posse. The sheriff's deputy, Johnny Spratte, was consorting with three rough-looking strangers the night before, and Jordan remembers that it was Spratte who led the posse in the wrong direction, and who insisted the outlaws had left the territory. Jordan deduces that Spratte has thrown in with the killers for whatever reason, and rides back to his cabin to pick up the trail from there. Meanwhile, the three outlaws and Johnny Spratte rob the bank in Fort Smith and kill two people. U.S. Deputy Marshal Jed Ramey, reputed to be the meanest lawman in Arkansas and the Indian Nations, rounds up a posse to chase down the killers. With poor descriptions from eye witnesses, Jordan is arrested. He escapes, takes the lawmen's rifles and horses, and heads for Indian Territory after Johnny and his partners. Now he faces death on all sides, from both Johnny and Jed.

Where it's reviewed:
Roundup Magazine, June 2005, page 39

Other books by the same author:
Hangman's Song, 2005
Bloody Hills, 2004
Evil Breed, 2003
Hero's Stand, 2003
Savage Cry, 2002

Other books you might like:
Ed Gorman, *Night of Shadows*, 2002
Stephen Overholser, *Chasing Destiny*, 2005

Bill Pronzini, *Borgade's Crossing*, 2004
Jory Sherman, *Bloody River*, 2005
Gary Svee, *Vengeance Peacemaker*, 2003

532

CHARLES G. WEST

Hangman's Song

(New York: Signet, 2005)

Story type: Traditional; Revenge
Subject(s): American West; Crime and Criminals
Major character(s): Nathaniel Rix, Religious (traveling preacher), Murderer; Jordan Gray, Rancher
Time period(s): 19th century (post-Civil War)
Locale(s): West

Summary: Jordan Gray is a widower whose wife and son were murdered and their cabin burned. Although he has no proof, he believes that the barbarous Rix family did it. Nathaniel Rix can deny it any way he wants, but Jordan knows he is right. He has heard stories of Preacher Rix using his gun on people, dispatching them to Heaven with a bullet to the head, but it doesn't matter. Jordan is coming after them even if he risks losing his life in the process.

Where it's reviewed:
Roundup Magazine, November 2005, page 39

Other books by the same author:
Devil's Kin, 2005
Hangman's Song, 2005
Evil Breed, 2003
Hero's Stand, 2003
Savage Cry, 2002

Other books you might like:
James Carlos Blake, *Under the Skin*, 2003
Peter Brandvold, *Riding with the Devil's Mistress*, 2003
Stan Lynde, *Saving Miss Julie*, 2004
John D. Nesbitt, *Red Wind Crossing*, 2003
Frank Roderus, *Old Marsden*, 1999

533

JOSEPH A. WEST

Gunsmoke: The Last Dog Soldier

(New York: Signet, 2005)

Story type: Traditional; Indian Wars
Subject(s): Law Enforcement; Indians of North America
Major character(s): Matt Dillon, Lawman (marshal of Dodge City); Abbey McKenna, Farmer; Iron Hawk, Indian (Cheyenne), Warrior
Time period(s): 19th century (post-Civil War)
Locale(s): Dodge City, Kansas

Summary: Marshal Matt Dillon of Dodge City is suspicious of Abbey McKenna and her brother Abe. They never seem to do much planting, but always have plenty of cash. Their cattle herd includes cows with a dozen or more different brands, and Abbey McKenna can't seem to lay her hands on the bills of sale. Then the body of the previous owner is discovered in a shallow grave. The McKennas had told everyone that the owner had sold them his place then gone back east. If Dillon's day hadn't been bad enough, when he gets back to Dodge he finds Iron Hawk, a local Cheyenne, busting up a saloon. The next day, Dillon learns that Iron Hawk is the last of the famous warrior clan called Dog Soldiers. When Iron Hawk's father is killed, he blames the McKennas and swears revenge. Now Marshal Dillon has the McKennas on one hand and an angry bunch of Cheyenne on the other. This book is a fun trip into the past where Kitty, Festus, and the doctor get together for an encore.

Where it's reviewed:
Roundup Magazine, November 2005, page 39

Other books by the same author:
Johnny Blue and the Texas Rangers, 2004 (Johnny Blue. Book 3)
Johnny Blue and the Hanging Judge, 2001 (Johnny Blue. Book 2)
Me and Johnny Blue, 2000 (Johnny Blue. Book 1)

Other books you might like:
Matt Braun, *Doc Holliday*, 1997
Tim Champlin, *A Trail to Wounded Knee*, 2001
Ralph Cotton, *Hell's Riders*, 2004
Ernest Haycox, *Bugles in the Afternoon*, 2003
Will Henry, *From Where the Sun Now Stands*, 2000

534

RICHARD S. WHEELER

An Obituary for Major Reno

(New York: Forge, 2004)

Story type: Saga; Indian Wars
Subject(s): Military Life; Indians of North America
Major character(s): Marcus Reno, Military Personnel (major), Historical Figure; George Armstrong Custer, Military Personnel (colonel), Historical Figure; Joseph Richler, Journalist (newspaper reporter)
Time period(s): 1870s (1876); 1880s (1889)
Locale(s): Valley of the Little Bighorn, Montana; Washington, District of Columbia

Summary: Major Marcus Reno is dying of cancer in 1889. Thirteen years before, in the Valley of the Little BigHorn he was the legendary Colonel George Armstrong Custer's senior officer. When Custer and half his command were massacred on that hot, dry hillside by the Little Bighorn River, Major Reno was blamed for failing to come to Custer's aid. Reno feels his honor has been besmirched and wants the black mark against him erased. He arranges for a last newspaper interview with the *New York Herald*, hoping that reporter Joseph Richler will tell his side of Custer's last battle. Unable to talk because his tongue has been butchered by his doctors in a futile effort to save his life from the cancer that is ravaging his throat and mouth, Reno writes his answers to Richler's questions. Surprisingly, Richler not only finds himself liking the dour, bitter Reno, but also believing him. Finally, with just minutes to live, Reno exacts a promise from Richler that the journalist will investigate Reno's story and clear his name.

Where it's reviewed:
Publishers Weekly, December 6, 2004, page 45

Roundup Magazine, August 2005, page 39

Other books by the same author:
The Bounty Trail, 2004
Trouble in Tombstone, 2004
Vengeance Valley, 2004
The Deliverance, 2003
The Exile, 2003

Other books you might like:
G.G. Boyer, *Custer, Terry, and Me*, 2004
Tim Champlin, *A Trail to Wounded Knee*, 2001
Keith Coplin, *Crofton's Fire*, 2004
Ernest Haycox, *Bugles in the Afternoon*, 2003
Will Henry, *From Where the Sun Now Stands*, 2000

535

RICHARD S. WHEELER

Trouble in Tombstone

(New York: Signet, 2004)

Story type: Traditional; Man Alone
Subject(s): American West; Crime and Criminals
Major character(s): Wyatt Earp, Lawman (in Tombstone), Historical Figure; John Henry "Doc" Holliday, Dentist (former), Historical Figure; John Behan, Lawman (sheriff), Friend (of the Cowboys gang)
Time period(s): 1880s (1881)
Locale(s): Tombstone, Arizona

Summary: This is not just another book about the shootout at the O.K. Corral, but rather a psychological profile of the parties involved, especially the Earp brothers, John Behan, Doc Holliday, and even the entire population of Tombstone. The Earps arrive in Tombstone hoping to make their fortunes, and soon have their fingers in several moneymaking pies. They are also lawmen, and Virgil assumes the position of marshal after the previous lawman is gunned down. The Earps try to break the Cowboys hold on Tombstone, but they are outnumbered 20-1. The infamous gunfight finally errupts, followed by Morgan Earp's murder and Virgil's disabling arm wound. After the deaths of all his Tombstone contemporaries, Wyatt, as a old man, puzzles over the events of his younger days, finally concluding that he did not understand the politics of the town. This is a deeper study of Wyatt Earp than has ever been done before, plus it has all the rip-snorting action of the best Western novels.

Where it's reviewed:
Roundup Magazine, June 2005, page 39

Other books by the same author:
An Obituary for Major Reno, 2004
The Bounty Trail, 2004
Restitution, 2003
The Exile, 2003
Going Home, 2000

Other books you might like:
Matt Braun, *Wyatt Earp*, 1994
Bill Brooks, *Law for Hire: Saving Masterson*, 2004
    Law for Hire. Book 3
Richard Jensen, *Ride the Wild Trail*, 2003
Preston Lewis, *Mix-Up at the O.K. Corral*, 1996

Nelson Nye, *Gunfight at the O.K. Corral*, 2003

536

JEANNE WILLIAMS

The Trampled Field

(Waterville, Maine: Five Star, 2005)

Story type: Historical/American West; Saga
Series: Beneath the Burning Ground. Book 3
Subject(s): Civil War
Major character(s): Christy Ware, Heroine, Farmer (runs the family farm); Melissa Jardine Ware, Spouse (wife of Christy's brother); Lafe Ballard, Bully (threatens Christy with rape)
Time period(s): 1860s (1861)
Locale(s): Kansas

Summary: The war is less than eight months old and already Jonathan Ware, Christy Ware's father, has been killed by guerrillas. Melissa Jardine Ware, Christy's sister-in-law, has seen her parents die and all but two of her slaves driven off. All her family is dead except her careless brother and her husband, Charlie Ware, and both of them are in the Confederate army, risking their lives everyday. Melissa gives birth to her infant son soon after her parents die. Christy, besides losing her father, has also been threatened with rape by Lafe Ballard who rides with William Quantrill. Still, after Christy leads her family to a hidden valley occupied only by an old Osage Indian woman, she returns to the Ware family farm to tend to the land, and defend it if necessary. She is pregnant with Dan O'Brien's child and is determined that something remain for her family and her baby after the war is over. This is the conclusion of the trilogy about the Ware family's experiences in Kansas before and during the Civil War.

Where it's reviewed:
Roundup Magazine, August 2005, page 39

Other books by the same author:
Hidden Valley, 2004 (Beneath the Burning Ground. Book 1)
The Underground River, 2004 (Beneath the Burning Ground. Book 2)
Wind River, 1997
Home Station, 1996
The Unplowed Sky, 1994

Other books you might like:
Irene Bennett Brown, *Haven*, 2004
Irene Bennett Brown, *Long Road Turning*, 2000
    Women of Paragon Springs. Book 1
Jane Candia Coleman, *Tombstone Travesty*, 2004
Jane Kirkpatrick, *Every Fixed Star*, 2003
    Tender Ties. Book 2
Gladys Smith, *Deliverance Valley*, 2003

537

JAMES C. WORK

Riders of Deathwater Valley

(Waterville, Maine: Five Star, 2005)

Story type: Traditional; Man Alone

Subject(s): American West; Crime and Criminals
Major character(s): Link Lochlin, Cowboy; Gwen Pendragon, Spouse (of ranch owner); Flynt Malin, Murderer, Outlaw (leader of the rustlers)
Time period(s): 19th century (post-Civil War)
Locale(s): Colorado

Summary: Flynt Malin and his gang of rustlers are wreaking havoc on Art Pendragon's Keystone Ranch, as well as on the herds of his neighbors. The ranchers have a meeting to discuss their strategy, and while they are meeting, Malin and his gang raid a picnic of women and children sponsored by Gwen Pendragon, Art's wife. All are taken prisoner. Link Lochlin, a rider for the Keystone Ranch, who has secretly been in love with Gwen Pendragon since he first met her, returns to the ranch from a trip and learns what happened. Link won't wait for Art and the other ranchers to make plans. He's going after Gwen. Malin will sell the women and children into slavery, but he will have something special in mind for Gwen. Link doesn't intend to give Malin a chance, even if it kills him.

Where it's reviewed:
Roundup Magazine, November 2005, page 40

Other books by the same author:
A Title to Murder, 2004
The Dead Ride Alone, 2004
Ride to Banshee Canon, 2002
Ride West to Dawn, 2001
The Tobermory Manuscript, 2000

Other books you might like:
Frederic Bean, *Murder at the Spirit Cave*, 1999
Margaret Coel, *The Shadow Dancer*, 2002
    Father John O'Malley/Vickie Holden. Book 8
Elizabeth Dearl, *Twice Dead*, 2001
    Taylor Madison. Book 2
James D. Doss, *The Witch's Tongue*, 2004
    Charlie Moon. Book 9
D.R. Meredith, *Tome of Death*, 2005
    Megan Clark. Book 4

Fantastic Animals
by
Don D'Ammassa

Although fantasy novels have been around for much longer than science fiction, they were generally considered a subset of that genre during most of the twentieth century and have only recently emerged as a separate category. The rising popularity of fantasy has resulted in literally hundreds of new titles per year, but for the most part, fantasy remains a very conservative corner of the literary world. The vast majority of new books are simply variations of stories already told, and they in turn are based in large part upon legends and myths gathered from various parts of the world. They are also dominated by several distinctive plots and plot elements: castles, wizards, stolen thrones, quests, magical swords, and other elements which strike a resonant chord with readers.

One very common element in fantasy fiction is the presence of animals as characters rather than just a part of the setting. There are three general methods in which animals are incorporated into fantasy fiction. The first, and most common, involves mythical creatures like dragons, unicorns, hippogriffs, basilisks, and the like. The second makes use of real animals, such as cats, dogs, horses, and rabbits, given either an elevated level of intelligence or some other magical attribute, usually with few if any human characters. Sometimes this is for satiric purposes—using animals as representatives for humans in order to poke fun at or exaggerate some trait of our own civilization. Frequently, the author makes a genuine effort to create a society appropriate for the specific animal that is the subject of the story. Finally, we have comparatively realistic depictions of everyday animals, dogs, cats, and so forth, in a contemporary setting.

The most common animal to appear in fantasy fiction is by far some form of dragon, usually in the European mode, although occasionally derived from other myth systems. In some instances, the dragon is an intelligent being with various human attributes, a culture, and perhaps even the ability to speak, but in the vast majority of cases, it is portrayed either as a powerful ally rather than the dangerous menace more common in motion pictures. In *Joust* (2003) and several sequels by Mercedes Lackey, for example, dragons are trained to cooperate with humans much like dogs and horses, and are used as instruments of war when the need arises. This is a very common theme in fantasy, and has even spilled over into science fiction in Anne McCaffrey's long running Pern series, with rationalized dragonlike creatures on an alien world entering into a virtually symbiotic relationship with human colonists.

One of the more interesting variations of the use of the dragon is a series of nine novels by Gordon R. Dickson, which began with *The Dragon and the George* (1976) and concluded with *The Dragon and the Fair Maid of Kent* (2000). In the opening volume, a human hero's personality is magically transported into the body of a dragon, in which form he rescues the woman he loves. Dickson mixes humor and light adventure in a variety of historical settings, giving his protagonist the ability to shift back and forth between human and dragon form. The concept of the weredragon is handled very differently in a trilogy by Lawrence Watt-Evans consisting of *Dragon Weather* (1999), *The Dragon Society* (2001), and *Dragon Venom* (2003). The malevolent dragons in this series appear to be simple animals until the revelation that they have a symbiotic relationship with a minority of humans who protect them and are literally born out of the bodies of their allies.

The Bazil Broketail series by Christopher Rowley is one of the best examples of the intelligent dragon story, opening with *Bazil Broketail* (1992) and concluding with the seventh volume, *Dragon Ultimate* (1999). Rowley's dragons are allied with humanity against a host of evil wizards. Irene Radford also portrays dragons as protectors of humanity in her two Dragon Nimbus sequences, starting with *The Glass Dragon* (1994) and concluding with the seventh book, *The Renegade Dragon* (1999). The dragon in Barbara Hambly's *Dragonsbane* (1985) is initially believed to be evil, but proves itself an ally in the sequel, *Dragonshadow* (1999).

If the dragon's nature is portrayed as spanning a wide spectrum from good to evil, the unicorn is almost invariably associated with goodness, purity, and virginity. The most famous unicorn novel is undoubtedly *The Last Unicorn* (1968) by Peter S. Beagle, in which a unicorn, believing herself to be the last of her kind, travels with a testy woman and an unreliable wizard to determine whether or not she is in fact alone. Michael Bishop's *Unicorn Mountain* (1988) has unicorns appearing in contemporary Georgia, fleeing a mysterious plague that threatens them in their own reality. An unusual unicorn becomes the pivotal plot element in *The Particolored Unicorn* (1987) by Jon Decles. Robin Wayne Bailey turned the conventions regarding both dragons and unicorns around in a trilogy consisting of *Brothers of the Dragon* (1992), *Flames of the Dragon* (1993), and *Triumph of the Dragon* (1995). Two brothers from our world are transported into what appears to be a typical fantasy realm, this one torn by a war with dragons on one side and unicorns on the other. They are initially fooled into believing that the dragons are evil, but soon discover otherwise.

Talking animals were for many years associated almost exclusively with children's literature, rarely rising to a level where adults would find them rewarding. Kenneth Grahame's *The Wind in the Willows* (1908) and the Cowardly Lion in the Oz books were notable exceptions, and they also appear occasionally for satiric purposes, as in George Orwell's *Animal Farm* (1945). Richard Adams altered that perception with *Watership Down* (1972), his best-selling novel cast in the form of an epic fantasy. Although all of the characters are rabbits living in a rabbitlike environment, he imbued them with human characteristics so that readers could identify with them. This innovation attracted the attention of many other writers, whose works met with varying degrees of success. William Horwood's *Dunction Wood* (1980) and its five sequels describe the struggles for survival of a group of moles. Horwood also wrote two sequels to *The Wind in the Willows*, *The Willows in Winter* (1993), and *Toad Triumphant* (1996). Clare Bell's Ratha books, starting with *Ratha's Creature* (1983), are set within a colony of feral cats. Tad Williams also reached best-seller status with *Tailchaser's Song* (1985), which also involves cats, and Walter Wangerin, Jr. invoked an entire farmyard for *The Book of the Dun Cow* (1978) and its sequel, *The Book of Sorrows* (1985).

The trend rapidly lost steam during the 1990s, although a few titles continued to appear. Most notable among these are *The Foxes of First Dark* (1989, also published as *Hunter's Moon: A Story of Foxes*, *Midnight Sun: A Story of Wolves* (1990), and *Frost Dancers: A Story of Hares* (1992), all by Garry Kilworth; *The Wild Road* (1997) and *The Golden Cat* (1998), both by M. John Harrison and Jane Johnson, writing together as Gabriel King; and most recently *One for Sorrow, Two for Joy* (2002) by Clive Woodall, the last of which involves birds. Mary Stanton also used the form with horses in *The Heavenly Horse from the*

Outermost West (1988) and its sequel, *Piper at the Gate* (1989). Straddling the gap between traditional talking animal stories and the more modern type is Brian Jacques, whose Redwall series, which was launched with *Redwall* (1986) and has now been extended to almost twenty volumes. Jacques ignores the human world entirely and concentrates on mice, ferrets, badgers, and other animals, but they live very much like human beings and their animal natures are more idiosyncratic than authentic.

The third category of animal oriented fantasy uses much more realistic portrayals of familiar animals, usually in a contemporary setting. The most common of these by far is the cat, and there has even been a series of original anthologies starting with *Catfantastic* (1989) edited by Andre Norton and Martin H. Greenberg, which ran to five volumes by 1999. At one extreme are those stories in which cats are actually magical beings, intelligent and concealing secrets. In *The Book of Night with Moon* (1997) and its sequel, *To Visit the Queen* (1999), by Diane Duane, for example, cats are the secret guardians of portals which allow travel from one reality to another. The protagonist of P.N. Elrod's *The Adventures of Myhr* (2003) is the magical offspring of human and feline forebears. Christopher Stasheff also created an intelligent cat as protagonist of *The Feline Wizard* (2000).

The cats in *Majyk by Accident* (1993) by Esther Friesner are not quite as smart, but when a cat from our world strays into an alternate reality, it becomes the focus of great magical power. Before the story ends, the cat has in fact become an intelligent being, who takes a more active role in two sequels, *Magic by Hook or Crook* (1994) and *Majyk by Design* (1994). In Robert Westall's *The Cats of Seroster* (1984), the cats have their own magical kingdom, and prove instrumental in reversing an injustice among humans. *Cat House* (1989) by Michael Peak is more ambiguous, with cats gathering in tribes and exhibiting some traits of an intelligent species. Shirley Rousseau Murphy created perhaps the most interesting feline character for her Joe Grey series of detective stories. The cat in question gains the power of speech and becomes a witness to murder in the first book, *Cat on the Edge* (1996), and subsequently returned in three sequels.

Dogs are not nearly as popular. Part of the pituitary gland of a criminal is implanted in a dog in Mikhail Bulgakov's *Heart of a Dog* (1968), and the animal acquires part of the donor's personality. James Herbert took an excursion from his usual horror fare to write *Fluke* (1977), in which a murdered man is reincarnated in the body of a dog and must solve the mystery of his own death. Similarly a business executive wakes up one morning to discover he has been transformed into a dog in Jerry Carroll's satiric *Top Dog* (1996). He then views the world from a very different perspective. In *Dogsbody* (1975) by Diana Wynne Jones, a supernatural being is sent to Earth in the form of a pet dog, which impedes his ability to accomplish his mission. The canine characters in *Dogland* (1997) are more ordinary. A

family attempting to create a tourist attraction, with dogs as its theme, is hampered by local prejudice.

Other animals have appeared as major characters in fantasy on a less frequent basis. A horse is changed into the form of a woman in *Dun Lady's Jess* (1996) by Doranna Durgin. She then seeks to find her owner and to reconcile the conflicting aspects of her own personality. Durgin later added two sequels, *Changespell* (1997) and *Changespell Legacy* (2002). Horses were created by the gods to watch over humanity in Jean Rabe's *The Finest Creation* (2004), the first in a series. Horses are viewed with distrust in a trilogy by Constance Ash consisting of *The Horse Girl* (1988), *The Stalking Horse* (1990), and *The Stallion Queen* (1992), in which they are believed to be the familiars of evil sorcerers. Michael Peak's *Catamount* describes the efforts of a puma and an eagle to avert a disaster when a warning comes from the god who watches over animals.

The popularity of animals as characters in fantasy has persisted and is clearly not a passing fad. A likely contributing factor is that fantasy lets the author speculate about them in ways impossible in other forms of literature. People who are fond of animals can, at least metaphorically, take a look inside the minds of dogs and cats and other animals, and indulge the common urge to anthropomorphize their behavior. It, is perhaps somewhat disappointing, however, that most fantasy writers to date have chosen to portray their intelligent animals simply as differently enabled human characters.

Recommended Titles

Entries for the following books are included in this volume.

The Hallowed Hunt by Lois McMaster Bujold

The Tyranny of the Night by Glen Cook

The Iron Tree by Cecilia Dart-Thornton

The House of Storms by Ian R. MacLeod

Od Magic by Patricia A. McKillip

Alector's Choice by L.E. Modesitt, Jr.

Three Hands for Scorpio by Andre Norton

A Princess of Roumania by Paul Park

The Secret Atlas by Michael Stackpole

A Rumor of Gems by Ellen Steiber

The Hidden Family by Charles Stross

Fantasy Titles

538

LYNN ABBEY

Down Time

(New York: Ace, 2005)

Story type: Contemporary; Time Travel
Series: Emma Merrigan. Book 4
Subject(s): Time Travel; Secrets
Major character(s): Emma Merrigan, Time Traveler, Vacationer; Eleanor Graves, Vacationer, Time Traveler
Time period(s): 2000s; Indeterminate Past
Locale(s): Caribbean

Summary: Emma Merrigan and her mother, Eleanor, are both taking a Caribbean cruise, during which they hope to patch up their personal differences. They also hope to refrain from their shared talent, which enables them to travel mentally through time. Unfortunately, Emma senses that another of the passengers is suffering from an ancient curse and is compelled to investigate.

Other books by the same author:
Taking Time, 2004
Sanctuary, 2002
Behind Time, 2001
Out of Time, 2000
Jerlayne, 1999

Other books you might like:
Elaine Bergstrom, *The Door through Washington Square*, 1998
John Dickson Carr, *Fear Is the Same*, 1956
Charles Dickinson, *A Shortcut in Time*, 2002
Jack Finney, *Time and Again*, 1970
Terence M. Green, *Shadow of Ashland*, 2000

539

FIONA AVERY

The Crown Rose

(Amherst, New York: Pyr, 2005)

Story type: Historical; Light Fantasy
Subject(s): Immortality; Secrets
Major character(s): Isabelle, Noblewoman; Louis IX, Ruler (King of France), Historical Figure; Jean Adaret Benariel, Traveler
Time period(s): 13th century
Locale(s): France

Summary: Isabelle was the sister of King Louis IX of France. She has ambivalent feelings about her role as the king's sister, but on several occasions during her lifetime she has an encounter with a mysterious figure who appears to be hundreds of years old, and whose intercession changes her life repeatedly. First novel.

Other books you might like:
Gael Baudino, *Maze of Moonlight*, 1993
Ann Chamberlin, *The Merlin of Oak Wood*, 2001
Thomas Harlan, *The Shadow of Ararat*, 1999
Michele Hauf, *Seraphim*, 2004
Gail Van Asten, *Charlemagne's Champion*, 1990

540

KEITH BAKER

The City of Towers

(Renton, Washington: Wizards of the Coast, 2005)

Story type: Sword and Sorcery; Mystery
Series: Dreaming Dark. Book 1
Subject(s): Magic; Military Life
Major character(s): Daine, Military Personnel; Pierce, Military Personnel; Saerath, Military Personnel
Time period(s): Indeterminate
Locale(s): Eberron, Fictional Country

Summary: Four soldiers, survivors of a series of protracted magical wars, finally decide to immigrate to a new part of the world. Weary of war, they are resigned to careers as soldiers. However, they are unprepared for what they discover in the fabled city of towers, where they hope to find employment. Someone is killing people, not openly on the field of battle, but rather by stealth. First novel.

Other books you might like:
Glen Cook, *Soldiers Live*, 2000
Simon R. Green, *Winner Takes All*, 1991
Richard A. Knaak, *The Citadel*, 2000
Stan Nicholls, *Orcs*, 2004
John Maddox Roberts, *Murder in Tarsis*, 1996

541

R. SCOTT BAKKER

The Warrior-Prophet

(Woodstock, New York: Overlook, 2005)

Story type: Sword and Sorcery; Magic Conflict
Series: Prince of Nothing Trilogy. Book 2
Subject(s): Magic; Quest
Major character(s): Anasurimbor Kellhus, Religious; Drusas Achamian, Sorcerer; Ikurei Conphas, Military Personnel
Time period(s): Indeterminate
Locale(s): Alternate Universe

Summary: As a great war with religious undertones moves inexorably toward apocalypse, a religious professional seeks to gain mastery of magical powers which will help turn the tide of battle. At the same time, he is searching for the secret of his own origin, and the identity of his mysterious father.

Where it's reviewed:
Publishers Weekly, December 6, 2004, page 48

Other books by the same author:
The Darkness That Comes Before, 2004

Other books you might like:
Stephen R. Donaldson, *The Runes of the Earth*, 2004
George R.R. Martin, *A Clash of Kings*, 1999
L.E. Modesitt Jr., *The Order War*, 1995
Michael Moorcock, *Corum*, 1997
R.A. Salvatore, *Bastion of Darkness*, 2000

542

HILARI BELL

Rise of a Hero

(New York: Hyperion, 2005)

Story type: Young Adult; Magic Conflict
Series: Farsala. Book 2
Subject(s): Magic
Major character(s): Jiaan, Teenager; Kavi, Teenager; Soraya, Teenager, Spy
Time period(s): Indeterminate
Locale(s): Farsala, Fictional Country; Hrum, Fictional Country

Summary: The nations of Farsala and Hrum have gone to war. The former believe themselves invincible, but three young people are among the few who realize that defeat is entirely possible. Each in their own way contributes, through planning, spying, or force of arms, and their combined effort will change the course of the war.

Other books by the same author:
Fall of a Kingdom, 2003
A Matter of Profit, 2001
Navohar, 2000
Songs of Power, 2000

Other books you might like:
L. Sprague de Camp, *The Goblin Tower*, 1968
Robert Jordan, *From the Two Rivers*, 2002
Mercedes Lackey, *Joust*, 2003
L.E. Modesitt Jr., *Legacies*, 2002
Lawrence Watt-Evans, *Touched by the Gods*, 1997

543

CURT BENJAMIN

Lords of Grass and Thunder

(New York: DAW, 2005)

Story type: Sword and Sorcery; Magic Conflict
Subject(s): Magic
Major character(s): Tayyichiut, Royalty (prince); Mergen-Khan, Ruler; Qutula, Warrior
Time period(s): Indeterminate
Locale(s): Alternate Universe

Summary: Prince Tayy returns from the wars as a hero, honored by his people and more self-confident. Although he is too young to assume the throne, his uncle is the caretaker and seems content to allow the boy to rule when he is old enough. Unfortunately, one of Tayy's cousins is less willing to let that happen. This novel is set in the same world as the author's Seven Brothers trilogy.

Where it's reviewed:
Library Journal, April 15, 2005, page 78
Publishers Weekly, March 7, 2005, page 54

Other books by the same author:
The Gates of Heaven, 2003
The Prince of Dreams, 2002
The Prince of Shadows, 2001

Other books you might like:
Storm Constantine, *The Way of Light*, 2001
Elaine Cunningham, *Wind Walker*, 2002
Dave Duncan, *Impossible Odds*, 2002
David Gemmell, *Ravenheart*, 2001
R.A. Salvatore, *The Demon Apostle*, 1989

544

ANNE BISHOP

Dreams Made Flesh

(New York: Ace, 2005)

Story type: Sword and Sorcery; Alternate World

Series: Black Jewels. Book 5
Subject(s): Magic; Women
Major character(s): Jaenelle, Witch; Lucivar, Warlord; Saetan, Ruler
Time period(s): Indeterminate
Locale(s): Alternate Universe

Summary: Jaenelle is the most powerful witch of all time, but that doesn't make her the supreme power in her world. She threads her way among three larger than life characters, Saetan, Lucivar, and Daemon, falls in love with one of them, and nearly loses everything in the process.

Where it's reviewed:
Chronicle, February 2005, page 33
Library Journal, January 2005, page 102
Locus, February 2005, page 27
Publishers Weekly, December 20, 2004, page 41

Other books by the same author:
Shadows and Light, 2002
The Pillars of the World, 2001
Queen of the Darkness, 2000
The Invisible Ring, 2000
Heir to the Shadows, 1999

Other books you might like:
Steven Brust, *To Reign in Hell*, 1984
C.J. Cherryh, *The Legions of Hell*, 1987
Edward Lee, *Infernal Angel*, 2003
Janet Morris, *The Little Helliad*, 1988
   Chris Morris, co-author
Meredith Pierce, *Darkangel*, 1982

545

DAMIEN BRODERICK

Godplayers

(New York: Thunder's Mouth, 2005)

Story type: Alternate World; Contemporary
Subject(s): Alternate History
Major character(s): August Seebeck, Traveler, Worker; Lune Sagara, Spy, Entertainer; Tansy, Aged Person (August's aunt)
Time period(s): 2000s
Locale(s): United States; Alternate Universe

Summary: August Seebeck is startled when his elderly Aunt Tansy tells him that dead bodies have been appearing and disappearing in her apartment. He is even more startled when he sees one of them himself. In due course, he discovers that there are gateways between realities and that some people move freely from one plane of existence to another, and that he is fated to become one of them.

Where it's reviewed:
Locus, May 2005, page 15
Publishers Weekly, April 4, 2005, page 48

Other books by the same author:
The Sea's Furthest End, 1993
The Dark between the Stars, 1991
The Dreaming Dragons, 1990
The Black Grail, 1986

The Judas Mandala, 1982

Other books you might like:
John Gregory Betancourt, *The Dawn of Amber*, 2002
Kenneth Bulmer, *The Hunters of Jundagai*, 1971
Garfield Reeves-Stevens, *Shifter*, 1990
   Judith Reeves-Stevens, co-author
Charles Stross, *The Family Trade*, 2004
Roger Zelazny, *Nine Princes in Amber*, 1970

546

SIMON BROWN

Empire's Daughter

(New York: DAW, 2005)

Story type: Sword and Sorcery; Magic Conflict
Series: Chronicles of Kydan. Book 1
Subject(s): Magic; Princes and Princesses
Major character(s): Maddyn Kevleren, Royalty (exiled prince); Yunara Kevleren, Sorceress, Noblewoman (duchess); Kadburn, Noblewoman
Time period(s): Indeterminate
Locale(s): Hamilay, Fictional Country

Summary: Prince Maddyn Kevleren is one of the few members of his family who cannot draw upon magical resources. When he offends his cousin, Duchess Yunara, who is the most powerful sorceress in the land, he is in so much danger that he volunteers to undertake a perilous mission to a foreign country just to get away from her.

Other books by the same author:
Sovereign, 2004
Fire and Sword, 2002
Inheritance, 2001

Other books you might like:
Dave Duncan, *The Jaguar Knights*, 2004
Phyllis Eisenstein, *Born to Exile*, 1978
Kate Jacoby, *The Exile's Return*, 1998
Jennifer Roberson, *Sword-Sworn*, 2002
R.A. Salvatore, *Exile*, 1990

547

LOIS MCMASTER BUJOLD

The Hallowed Hunt

(New York: Eos, 2005)

Story type: Mystery; Alternate World
Series: Chalion. Book 3
Subject(s): Princes and Princesses; Wizards
Major character(s): Lord Ingrey kin Wolfcliff, Nobleman; Ijada dy Castos, Noblewoman, Prisoner; Hallana, Sorceress
Time period(s): Indeterminate
Locale(s): Alternate Universe

Summary: Lord Ingrey is sent to escort a prisoner back to court after she is found in the bedroom of a prince, who was murdered while performing a forbidden magical rite. Ingrey is convinced that the woman is innocent, but someone doesn't

want them to return successfully. Inexplicable impulses almost cause Ingrey to murder her himself.

Where it's reviewed:
Locus, March 2005, page 27

Other books by the same author:
Paladin of Souls, 2003
The Curse of Chalion, 2001
Cetaganda, 1998
Mirror Dance, 1994
The Spirit Ring, 1992

Other books you might like:
Diane Duane, *Stealing the Elf-King's Roses*, 2002
Dave Duncan, *Sir Stalwart*, 1999
David Eddings, *The Redemption of Althalus*, 2000
    Leigh Eddings, co-author
Melisa Michaels, *Cold Iron*, 1997
John Maddox Roberts, *Murder in Tarsis*, 1996

548

JIM BUTCHER

Academ's Fury

(New York: Ace, 2005)

Story type: Sword and Sorcery; Magic Conflict
Series: Codex Alera. Book 2
Subject(s): Magic; Quest
Major character(s): Tavi, Teenager, Spy; Amara, Spy; Doroga, Warrior
Time period(s): Indeterminate
Locale(s): Alera, Fictional Country

Summary: In a world where forces of nature can manifest themselves physically, a young boy begins the process of training as a spy for the throne. An attack from another nation causes considerable unrest and the possibility of a civil war, aggravated by the awakening of a supernatural creature.

Other books by the same author:
Dead Beat, 2005
Blood Rites, 2004
Furies of Calderon, 2004
Death Masks, 2003
Storm Front, 2000

Other books you might like:
Barbara Hambly, *The Rainbow Abyss*, 1991
Naomi Kritzer, *Freedom's Apprentice*, 2005
Mercedes Lackey, *The Fire Rose*, 1995
L.E. Modesitt Jr., *Darknesses*, 2003
Lawrence Watt-Evans, *Dragon Weather*, 1999

549

RICHARD LEE BYERS

The Rite

(Renton, Washington: Wizards of the Coast, 2005)

Story type: Magic Conflict; Sword and Sorcery
Series: Year of Rogue Dragons. Book 2
Subject(s): Magic

Major character(s): Dorn Graybrook, Warrior; Raryn Snowstealer, Warrior; Pavel Shemov, Warrior
Time period(s): Indeterminate
Locale(s): Faerun, Fictional Country

Summary: Humans and dragons lived in comparative peace for many generations, but now there is a contagious madness affecting the dragons. Unless they release their rage, they endanger their own souls. The violence that ensues causes human dragon hunters to redouble their efforts.

Other books by the same author:
The Rage, 2004
Joy Ride, 2003
The Black Bouquet, 2003
Warlock Games, 1993
Fright Line, 1989

Other books you might like:
Robin Wayne Bailey, *Brothers of the Dragon*, 1993
Wayland Drew, *Dragonslayer*, 1981
Elizabeth Kerner, *Lesser Kindred*, 2000
Dennis L. McKiernan, *Dragon Doom*, 1990
Lawrence Watt-Evans, *Dragon Weather*, 1999

550

BARBARA CAMPBELL

Heartwood

(New York: DAW, 2005)

Story type: Magic Conflict; Legend
Subject(s): Magic; Quest
Major character(s): Darak, Hunter; Tinnean, Teenager, Apprentice; Oak-Lord, Deity
Time period(s): Indeterminate
Locale(s): Alternate Universe

Summary: Already unhappy when his younger brother apprentices himself to the worship of one of the two deities recognized by his people, Darak is even more distressed when his brother and the Oak-Lord himself are magically spirited away and imprisoned. He sets out into a mystical forest to rescue both of them. First novel.

Other books you might like:
Carol Berg, *Revelation*, 2001
Anne Bishop, *Heir to the Shadows*, 1999
Elizabeth Haydon, *Prophecy*, 2000
Paul Hazel, *The Wealdwife's Tale*, 1993
Juliet Marillier, *Daughter of the Forest*, 2000

551

STEVE CASH

The Meq

(New York: Del Rey, 2005)

Story type: Historical; Quest
Subject(s): Immortality; Secrets
Major character(s): Zianno Zezen, Mythical Creature (Meq); Fleur-du-Mal, Mythical Creature (Meq), Criminal; Opari, Mythical Creature (Meq)
Time period(s): 19th century; 20th century

Locale(s): United States; Europe

Summary: When he reaches 12 years of age, Zianno Zezen discovers that he is a Meq and not a human. The Meq live secretly among us, but they stop aging when they are 12 and don't start again until they meet their destined mate. Over the decades that follow, Zianno searches for his lover and battles a renegade Meq turned assassin. First novel.

Where it's reviewed:
Booklist, December 15, 2004, page 715
Library Journal, January 2005, page 103
Locus, March 2005, page 20
Publishers Weekly, November 22, 2004, page 42

Other books you might like:
Sara Douglass, *The Nameless Day*, 2000
Philip Pullman, *The Amber Spyglass*, 2000
Wen Spencer, *Bitter Waters*, 2003
A.E. van Vogt, *Slan*, 1940
Chelsea Quinn Yarbro, *The Angry Angel*, 1998

552

P.C. CAST

Elphame's Choice
(New York: LUNA, 2005)

Story type: Romance; Light Fantasy
Subject(s): Secrets
Major character(s): Elphame, Religious; Cuchulainn, Teenager; Lochlan, Young Man
Time period(s): Indeterminate
Locale(s): Partholon, Fictional Country

Summary: Although this novel is set in the fictional country of Partholon, it draws heavily on Irish folklore. Elphame is a young woman who was marked by the goddess at an early age. This distinction has made it difficult for her to have normal relationships with those around her, and certainly never a romance. Her journey to a distant castle changes that, exposing her to adventure, as well as love.

Other books by the same author:
Goddess of Spring, 2004
Goddess of the Sea, 2003
Goddess by Mistake, 2001

Other books you might like:
Catherine Asaro, *The Charmed Sphere*, 2004
Gail Dayton, *The Compass Rose*, 2005
Laura Gilman, *Staying Dead*, 2004
Mercedes Lackey, *The Fairy Godmother*, 2004
Jennifer Macaire, *The Secret of Shabaz*, 2004

553

DAN CHERNENKO

The Scepter's Return
(New York: Roc, 2005)

Story type: Quest; Magic Conflict
Series: Scepter of Mercy. Book 3
Subject(s): Magic; Quest

Major character(s): Lanus, Ruler (king); Grus, Ruler (king); Banished One, Deity
Time period(s): Indeterminate
Locale(s): Avornis, Alternate Universe

Summary: King Lanus and King Grus put aside their differences to cooperate in their quest to retrieve a magical sword that could bring peace to the land. Unfortunately, a sleeping god has awakened and is not happy with their efforts. He plans to seize control of both their kingdoms and see that the sword is not raised against its own power.

Where it's reviewed:
Publishers Weekly, February 14, 2005, page 58

Other books by the same author:
The Chernagor Pirates, 2004
The Bastard King, 2003

Other books you might like:
Mark Garland, *Sword of the Prophets*, 1997
David Gemmell, *The Last Sword of Power*, 1996
Ann Marston, *Broken Blade*, 1997
Andrew J. Offutt, *The Ironlords*, 1979
R.A. Salvatore, *Immortalis*, 2003

554

JAMES CLEMENS

Shadowfall
(New York: Roc, 2005)

Story type: Magic Conflict; Mystery
Series: Godslayer Chronicles. Book 1
Subject(s): Secrets; Magic
Major character(s): Tylar de Noche, Knight, Fugitive; Dart, Teenager; Rogger, Criminal
Time period(s): Indeterminate
Locale(s): Myrillia, Fictional Country

Summary: The land of Myrillia has long been protected by several gods and goddesses. When a disabled knight witnesses a fatal assault on one of them by a mysterious supernatural entity, he is granted a cure for his wounds in return for his kindness. However, others believe that he killed the goddess in order to force her to heal him, and he becomes a fugitive, determined to make the truth known.

Other books by the same author:
Wit'ch Star, 2002
Wit'ch Gate, 2001
Wit'ch War, 2000
Wit'ch Storm, 1999

Other books you might like:
David Eddings, *The Shining Ones*, 1993
David Gemmell, *The Jerusalem Man*, 1988
Simon R. Green, *The God Killer*, 1991
Jean Rabe, *Downfall*, 2000
R.A. Salvatore, *The Demon Awakens*, 1997

Fantasy

555

DAVID B. COE

Bonds of Vengeance

(New York: Tor, 2005)

Story type: Sword and Sorcery; Magic Conflict
Series: Winds of the Forelands. Book 3
Subject(s): Magic; Secrets
Major character(s): Keziah, Government Official; Grinsa, Wizard; Lord Tavis, Nobleman
Time period(s): Indeterminate
Locale(s): Forelands, Alternate Universe

Summary: The world of the Forelands is divided into two classes, one which dominates the government, the other which makes up much of the population. Although the former have not been particularly repressive, there is growing resentment of them, which has been building quickly toward open rebellion and warfare. The protagonist is one of several who seek to find a more peaceful compromise.

Other books by the same author:
Seeds of Betrayal, 2003
Rules of Ascension, 2002
Eagle-Sage, 2000
The Outlanders, 1998
Children of Amarid, 1997

Other books you might like:
James Barclay, *Demonstorm*, 2004
Storm Constantine, *The Wraiths of Will and Pleasure*, 2003
Maggie Furey, *Echo of Eternity*, 2003
R.A. Salvatore, *Transcendence*, 2002
Freda Warrington, *The Sapphire Throne*, 2000

556

LOREN L. COLEMAN

Blood of Wolves

(New York: Ace, 2005)

Story type: Sword and Sorcery; Magic Conflict
Series: Hyborian Adventures. Book 1
Subject(s): Quest; Magic
Major character(s): Kern, Warrior; Grimnir, Warrior; Daol, Warrior
Time period(s): Indeterminate Past
Locale(s): Cimmeria, Fictional Country

Summary: This is the first of a series of novels set against the same background as the Conan series by Robert E. Howard. Kern, a young warrior, is given the task of dealing with Grimnir, an outlaw and leader of a band of fierce raiders pillaging the outlying regions of Cimmeria. Although Kern feels inadequate to the task, he perseveres.

Other books by the same author:
The Sword of Sedition, 2005
Call to Arms, 2003
Endgame, 2002
Patriots and Tyrants, 2001
Into the Maelstrom, 1999

Other books you might like:
Poul Anderson, *Conan the Rebel*, 1980
Robert E. Howard, *The Bloody Crown of Conan*, 2004
Robert Jordan, *Conan the Victorious*, 1984
Andrew J. Offutt, *King Dragon*, 1980
Karl Edward Wagner, *The Road of Kings*, 1979

557

GLEN COOK

The Tyranny of the Night

(New York: Tor, 2005)

Story type: Sword and Sorcery; Mystery
Series: Instrumentalities of Night. Book 1
Subject(s): Secrets; Magic
Major character(s): Else, Warrior; Bronte Doneto, Diplomat; Gordimer, Government Official
Time period(s): Indeterminate
Locale(s): Andoray, Fictional Country

Summary: Else, a warrior who should not have survived an encounter with a superhuman being, managed to do so. This marks him as a man to watch in a world where two powerful nations with very different belief systems are involved in serious espionage, possibly in preparation for open warfare.

Other books by the same author:
Angry Lead Skies, 2002
Soldiers Live, 2000
Faded Steel Heat, 1999
She Is the Darkness, 1997
Bleak Seasons, 1996

Other books you might like:
Steven Brust, *Orca*, 1996
Dan Chernenko, *The Bastard King*, 2003
David Gemmell, *Stormrider*, 2002
Andrew J. Offutt, *Deathknight*, 1990
R.A. Salvatore, *The Highwayman*, 2004

558

BEN COUNTER

Crimson Tears

(Nottingham, England: Black Library, 2005)

Story type: Science Fiction; Military
Series: Warhammer
Subject(s): Magic
Major character(s): Xarius, Military Personnel; Reinez, Military Personnel; Sarpedon, Alien
Time period(s): Indeterminate Future
Locale(s): Outer Space

Summary: *Crimson Tears* is an uneasy blend of science fiction and fantasy. A group of battle-hardened space marines is pitted against supernatural demons who exist in outer space and who manipulate both humans and aliens to advance their own evil plans for the universe. Most of the novel involves battle sequences and military life.

Other books by the same author:
Grey Knights, 2004

The Bleeding Chalice, 2003
Soul Drinker, 2002

Other books you might like:
Dan Abnett, *Ravenor Returned*, 2005
Jonathan Green, *Iron Hands*, 2004
Sandy Mitchell, *For the Emperor*, 2003
Gordon Rennie, *Zavant*, 2002
Gav Thorpe, *Angels of Darkness*, 2003

559

A.C. CRISPIN

Storms of Destiny
(New York: Eos, 2005)

Story type: Sword and Sorcery; Magic Conflict
Series: Exiles of Boq'urain. Book 1
Subject(s): Magic; Quest
Major character(s): Jezzil, Warrior; Thia, Religious; Khith, Scholar
Time period(s): Indeterminate
Locale(s): Alternate Universe

Summary: When their country is threatened with invasion, various unlikely characters come together to meet the challenge. They include a priestess who has lost her faith, a soldier disenchanted with the army, a non-human scholar alienated from his own people, and others, none of whom quite seem to fit in where they are expected.

Other books by the same author:
Rebel Dawn, 1998
Alien Resurrection, 1997
The Paradise Snare, 1997
Sarek, 1995
The Eyes of the Beholder, 1990

Other books you might like:
Jo Clayton, *Wild Magic*, 1991
Clayton Emery, *Sword Play*, 1996
Sharon Green, *Convergence*, 1996
Mercedes Lackey, *Storm Rising*, 1995
Andre Norton, *Moon Called*, 1982

560

CECILIA DART-THORNTON

The Iron Tree
(New York: Tor, 2005)

Story type: Quest; Mystery
Series: Crowthistle Chronicles. Book 1
Subject(s): Quest; Magic
Major character(s): Jarred, Traveler; Lilith Heronswood Hawksburn, Worker; Eolacha Kingfisher Arrowgrass, Aged Person
Time period(s): Indeterminate
Locale(s): Alternate Universe

Summary: Jarred grew up without ever knowing his father or much of anything about him, and that mystery has influenced his life ever since. Now an adult, he sets out to find his destiny, and promptly encounters a fascinating young woman

who will change his life forever. The opening volume hints at more mysteries that will presumably be solved in subsequent titles.

Other books by the same author:
The Battle of Evernight, 2003
The Lady of the Sorrows, 2002
The Ill-Made Knight, 2001

Other books you might like:
Paul Hazel, *Yearwood*, 1980
Sarah A. Hoyt, *Any Man So Daring*, 2003
L.E. Modesitt Jr., *Legacies*, 2002
Sharon Shinn, *Mystic and Rider*, 2005
Lawrence Watt-Evans, *Dragon Weather*, 1999

561

GAIL DAYTON

The Compass Rose
(New York: LUNA, 2005)

Story type: Sword and Sorcery; Romance
Subject(s): Magic
Major character(s): Kallista Varyl, Sorceress, Military Personnel; Torchay, Bodyguard, Military Personnel; Stone, Military Personnel
Time period(s): Indeterminate
Locale(s): Adara, Fictional Country

Summary: Kallista has been granted extraordinary powers by the gods and her ability to manipulate magic is so great that she is a danger even to her companions. As war looms, she hopes to use her gift to unlock the secrets of a powerful magic. However, she must overcome several obstacles, and fall hopelessly in love, before that can be accomplished. First novel.

Other books you might like:
Caitlin Brennan, *The Mountain's Call*, 2004
Lois McMaster Bujold, *The Hallowed Hunt*, 2005
P.C. Cast, *Elphame's Choice*, 2005
Deborah Hale, *The Wizard's Ward*, 2004
Sarah Zettel, *In Camelot's Shadow*, 2004

562

JOHN DICKINSON

The Widow and the King
(New York: David Fickling, 2005)

Story type: Young Adult; Sword and Sorcery
Subject(s): Magic; Secrets
Major character(s): Sophia, Teenager; Ambrose, Teenager, Nobleman; Undercraft, Mythical Creature
Time period(s): Indeterminate
Locale(s): Alternate Universe

Summary: A young boy, son of a dead but unpopular king, seeks the aid of a woman with magical powers to protect him from the supernatural enemies of his family. When she is unable to defeat his enemies, his fate seems certain. However, her young daughter proves to have previously unsuspected resources. This is the sequel to *The Cup of the World*.

Fantasy

Other books by the same author:
The Cup of the World, 2004

Other books you might like:
Diana Wynne Jones, *The Merlin Conspiracy*, 2003
Katherine Langrish, *Troll Fell*, 2003
L.E. Modesitt Jr., *Legacies*, 2002
E. Rose Sabin, *A School for Sorcery*, 2002
Lawrence Watt-Evans, *Dragon Weather*, 1999

563

CORY DOCTOROW

Someone Comes to Town, Someone Leaves Town

(New York: Tor, 2005)

Story type: Literary; Satire
Subject(s): Humor
Major character(s): Alan, Businessman; Natalie, Student; Davey, Child
Time period(s): 2000s
Locale(s): Toronto, Ontario, Canada

Summary: This is a surreal novel in which Alan, a businessman whose siblings are dolls, moves into a new home. He discovers first, that his next door neighbor has wings that grow back whenever she cuts them off and second, that the brother he killed many years before has somehow survived and is just as nasty as ever.

Where it's reviewed:
Locus, March 2005, page 19

Other books by the same author:
Eastern Standard Tribe, 2004
A Place So Foreign and Eight More, 2003
Down and Out in the Magic Kingdom, 2003

Other books you might like:
Steven Aylett, *Only an Alligator*, 2002
James P. Blaylock, *The Paper Grail*, 1991
Paul Di Filippo, *Ciphers*, 1997
Steve Erickson, *Our Ecstatic Days*, 2005
Lance Olsen, *Sewing Shut My Eyes*, 2000

564

SARA DOUGLASS

Darkwitch Rising

(New York: Tor, 2005)

Story type: Historical; Magic Conflict
Series: Troy Game. Book 3
Subject(s): Secrets; Reincarnation
Major character(s): Charles II, Historical Figure, Ruler (king); Noah Banks, Reincarnated Person; Jane Orr, Prostitute, Reincarnated Person
Time period(s): Indeterminate Past
Locale(s): England, Alternate Universe

Summary: In a magical alternate version of historical England, Charles II is on the throne. A variety of individuals, not all of them completely mortal, have been reincarnated and become

instrumental in the resolution of a major civil war in the British Isles. This is a complex novel with many characters.

Other books by the same author:
Gods' Concubine, 2004
Hades' Daughter, 2003
Threshold, 2003
The Nameless Day, 2000
Sinner, 1987

Other books you might like:
Lynn Abbey, *Unicorn and Dragon*, 1987
Robert Holdstock, *The Iron Grail*, 2002
Sarah A. Hoyt, *Any Man So Daring*, 2003
Brian Stableford, *The Werewolves of London*, 1990
Judith Tarr, *The House of War*, 2003

565

SARA DOUGLASS

The Wounded Hawk

(New York: Tor, 2005)

Story type: Historical; Magic Conflict
Series: Crucible. Book 2
Subject(s): Magic; Legends
Major character(s): Thomas Neville, Religious; Robert Courtenay, Landowner; Margaret Neville, Housewife
Time period(s): 14th century (1379-1380)
Locale(s): Europe

Summary: In the aftermath of the Black Plague, Europe is torn by a series of wars. Thomas Neville, a priest, is puzzled by the resurgence of evil until he discovers that Hell has sent several of its agents to physically interact with humans, each capable of changing shape and assuming alternate identities. He is reluctantly cast in the role of hunter, searching for and destroying Hell's minions.

Where it's reviewed:
Booklist, January 1, 2005, page 833
Chronicle, February 2005, page 31
Publishers Weekly, December 20, 2004, page 41

Other books by the same author:
Gods' Concubine, 2004
Beyond the Hanging Wall, 2003
Hades' Daughter, 2003
The Nameless Day, 2000
Battleaxe, 1998

Other books you might like:
Gael Baudino, *Maze of Moonlight*, 1993
Ann Chamberlin, *The Merlin of Oak Wood*, 2001
Thomas Harlan, *The Gate of Fire*, 2000
Michele Hauf, *Seraphim*, 2004
Chelsea Quinn Yarbro, *The Angry Angel*, 1998

566

STEVE ERICKSON

Our Ecstatic Days

(New York: Simon & Schuster, 2005)

Story type: Mystical; Literary
Subject(s): Secrets
Major character(s): Kristin Blumenthal, Businesswoman; Kirk Blumenthal, Baby
Time period(s): 21st century (2004-2031)
Locale(s): Los Angeles, California

Summary: When a mysterious lake magically appears in the middle of Los Angeles, the event is particularly disturbing to Kristin Blumenthal, who believes it poses a danger for her infant son Kirk. Their lives are caught up in a chain of miraculous events in this mystical, often stream of consciousness novel that at times verges on the surreal.

Where it's reviewed:
Booklist, January 1, 2005, page 813
Library Journal, December 2004, page 99
Locus, February 2005, page 22
Publishers Weekly, January 31, 2005, page 51

Other books by the same author:
The Sea Came in at Midnight, 1999
Amnesiascope, 1996
Arc d'X, 1993
Tours of the Black Clock, 1989
Days between Stations, 1985

Other books you might like:
Steven Aylett, *Dummyland*, 2002
James P. Blaylock, *All the Bells of Earth*, 1995
Paul Di Filippo, *The Steampunk Trilogy*, 1996
Cory Doctorow, *Someone Comes to Town, Someone Leaves Town*, 2005
Madeleine E. Robins, *The Stone War*, 1999

567

STEVEN ERIKSON

Deadhouse Gates

(New York: Tor, 2005)

Story type: Magic Conflict; Alternate World
Series: Malazan. Book 2
Subject(s): Magic
Major character(s): Sha'ik, Religious, Rebel; Icarium, Traveler; Duiker, Historian
Time period(s): Indeterminate
Locale(s): Alternate Universe

Summary: The people of the Seven Cities have chafed under their present rulers for generations, but now a charismatic religious leader has called for a rebellion, the fulfillment of a long-standing prophecy. The violence escalates quickly, however, and no one is capable of controlling it. A very large cast of characters results in a complex narrative.

Where it's reviewed:
Library Journal, February 15, 2005, page 122

Other books by the same author:
Gardens of the Moon, 2004
The Healthy Dead, 2003
Blood Follows, 2002

Other books you might like:
David Farland, *Wizardborn*, 2001
Raymond E. Feist, *Krondor: Tear of the Gods*, 2001
L.E. Modesitt Jr., *Shadowsinger*, 2002
Lawrence Watt-Evans, *Touched by the Gods*, 1997
Janny Wurts, *Shadowfane*, 1988

568

JENNIFER FALLON

Harshini

(New York: Tor, 2005)

Story type: Sword and Sorcery; Magic Conflict
Series: Hythrun Chronicles. Book 3
Subject(s): Quest; Magic
Major character(s): Tarja Tenragen, Nobleman, Fugitive; Damin Wolfblade, Military Personnel; R'Shiel, Religious
Time period(s): Indeterminate
Locale(s): Medalon, Fictional Country

Summary: The defenders of Medalon have not been able to prevent their enemies from overrunning the country. Now fugitives, they seek the help of a legendary warrior and his followers, while elsewhere a young woman finally comes to terms with her destiny. The various factions and separate story lines finally converge for a climactic battle sequence.

Where it's reviewed:
Publishers Weekly, May 9, 2005, page 51

Other books by the same author:
Medalon, 2004
Treason Keep, 2004
Lord of the Shadows, 2003
Eye of the Labyrinth, 2002
The Lion of Senet, 2002

Other books you might like:
Raymond E. Feist, *Krondor, the Betrayal*, 1999
Maggie Furey, *Echo of Eternity*, 2003
Mercedes Lackey, *Exile's Valor*, 2003
George R.R. Martin, *A Storm of Swords*, 2000
Angus Wells, *Yesterday's Kings*, 2001

569

S.L. FARRELL

Heir of Stone

(New York: DAW, 2005)

Story type: Magic Conflict; Political
Series: Cloudmages. Book 4
Subject(s): Magic; Legends
Major character(s): Sevei Geraghty, Sorceress; Kayne Gerachtyent, Warlock; Doyle Mac Ard, Rebel
Time period(s): Indeterminate
Locale(s): Alternate Universe

Summary: The magical power of the master stone has been passed down through generations, and Sevei Geraghty and her brother are conforming to family tradition by learning the magical arts and using them to aid their people. Unfortunately, their uncle Doyle has more personal ambitions, and uses force in his efforts to seize the throne.

Where it's reviewed:
Booklist, January 1, 2005, page 833
Publishers Weekly, December 20, 2004, page 41

Other books by the same author:
Mage of Clouds, 2004
Holder of Lightnings, 2003

Other books you might like:
Risa Aratyr, *Hunter of the Light*, 1995
Kenneth Flint, *Legends Reborn*, 1992
Casey Flynn, *Most Ancient Song*, 1991
Gregory Frost, *Tain*, 1986
Juliet Marillier, *Daughter of the Forest*, 2000

570

CHARLES COLEMAN FINLAY

The Prodigal Troll

(Amherst, New York: Pyr, 2005)

Story type: Humor; Quest
Subject(s): Quest; Legends
Major character(s): Claye, Child; Lady Portia, Noblewoman; Windy, Mythical Creature (troll)
Time period(s): Indeterminate
Locale(s): Alternate Universe

Summary: When invaders threaten to overthrow a king, he sends his young son Claye off to safety with a single knight. Through mischance, the child ends up alone and is raised by trolls. Although he eventually returns to human society, his upbringing makes it very difficult for him to adjust to his own kind and hampers his efforts to regain his birthright. First fantasy novel.

Where it's reviewed:
Publishers Weekly, April 11, 2005, page 38

Other books you might like:
Gordon R. Dickson, *The Dragon, the Earl, and the Troll*, 1994
Rose Estes, *Troll Taken*, 1993
L.E. Modesitt Jr., *Legacies*, 2002
Stan Nicholls, *Orcs*, 2004
Lawrence Watt-Evans, *Blood of a Dragon*, 1991

571

JUDE FISHER

The Rose of the World

(New York: DAW, 2005)

Story type: Magic Conflict; Quest
Series: Fool's Gold. Book 3
Subject(s): Magic

Major character(s): Rosa Eldi, Mythical Creature, Amnesiac; Bete, Animal (cat); Rahe, Wizard
Time period(s): Indeterminate
Locale(s): Istria, Fictional Country; Eyra, Fictional Country

Summary: A wizard seeks to gain power over the world by capturing certain supernatural forces, but one of them escapes in the form of a woman, although she has no memory. Her powers are so great that she is dangerous even when she intends no harm. However, she is also in danger because the wizard wants to recapture her.

Where it's reviewed:
Publishers Weekly, January 17, 2005, page 39

Other books by the same author:
Wild Magic, 2003
Sorcery Rising, 2002

Other books you might like:
Sara Douglass, *Enchanter*, 2001
David Gemmell, *Stormrider*, 2002
Sean Russell, *The One Kingdom*, 2001
R.A. Salvatore, *Mortalis*, 2001
Lawrence Watt-Evans, *Night of Madness*, 2000

572

DAVE FREER

A Mankind Witch

(New York: Baen, 2005)

Story type: Historical; Sword and Sorcery
Subject(s): Magic
Major character(s): Jarl Cair, Wanderer; Erik Hakkonsen, Warrior; Signy, Royalty (princess)
Time period(s): 16th century (1538)
Locale(s): Europe

Summary: A wandering adventurer has a series of experiences involving evil magic, villainous plots, a beautiful princess, and a variety of captures and escapes. The settings are predominantly Norse and the plot depends primarily on overt action as he develops his own abilities and uses magic, as well as mundane weapons, to defeat his enemies.

Other books by the same author:
The Forlorn, 1999

Other books you might like:
Poul Anderson, *The Broken Sword*, 1954
Linda Evans, *Sleipnir*, 1994
Harry Harrison, *One King's Way*, 1995
Juliet Marillier, *Foxmask*, 2004
Lars Walker, *Wolf Time*, 1999

573

ISABEL GLASS

The Divided Crown

(New York: Tor, 2005)

Story type: Sword and Sorcery; Magic Conflict
Subject(s): Quest; Magic

Major character(s): Jerret, Ruler (king); Lady Angarred Hashan, Noblewoman; Mathewar, Wizard
Time period(s): Indeterminate
Locale(s): Alternate Universe

Summary: King Jerret has been installed on the throne, even though he is too young to be at ease dealing with court intrigues. There is a conspiracy aimed at removing him from power. However, the few people who might be able to help him have been made to feel unwelcome near the throne, particularly Lady Angarred and her husband, a wizard. This is the sequel to *Daughter of Exile*.

Other books by the same author:
Daughter of Exile, 2004

Other books you might like:
Dave Duncan, *Sky of Swords*, 2000
Doranna Durgin, *Seer's Blood*, 2000
Mindy L. Klasky, *The Glasswright's Apprentice*, 2001
Diana L. Paxson, *The Sea Star*, 1988
Jo Walton, *The King's Peace*, 2000

574

TERRY GOODKIND

Chainfire

(New York: Tor, 2005)

Story type: Sword and Sorcery; Magic Conflict
Series: Sword of Truth. Book 10
Subject(s): Magic; Quest
Major character(s): Richard Rahl, Wizard; Kahlan Rahl, Religious; Nicci, Healer
Time period(s): Indeterminate
Locale(s): Alternate Universe

Summary: After recovering from a near fatal wound, Richard Rahl discovers that his wife Kahlan is missing. Even more perplexing is the fact that absolutely no one has ever heard of her and everyone believes that he is suffering from some form of delusion caused by his injuries.

Other books by the same author:
Naked Empire, 2003
The Pillars of Creation, 2001
Faith of the Fallen, 2000
Soul of the Fire, 1999
Temple of the Winds, 1997

Other books you might like:
James Barclay, *Noonshade*, 2000
David Feintuch, *The Still*, 1997
Robert Jordan, *Winter's Heart*, 2000
George R.R. Martin, *A Game of Thrones*, 1996
L.E. Modesitt Jr., *Alector's Choice*, 2005

575

LAURELL K. HAMILTON

A Stroke of Midnight

(New York: Ballantine, 2005)

Story type: Alternate World; Mystery

Series: Meredith Gentry. Book 5
Subject(s): Secrets; Elves
Major character(s): Meredith Gentry, Detective—Private; Mistral, Mythical Creature (elf); Cel, Mythical Creature (elf), Prisoner
Time period(s): Indeterminate
Locale(s): Alternate Universe

Summary: Meredith Gentry is still reluctant to recognize that she is partly elvish, preferring to continue her career as a private detective in an alternate version of this world. Unfortunately, her jealous cousin is still plotting her death, despite his imprisonment, and other complications in her life are making it difficult to balance the two sides of her nature.

Where it's reviewed:
Publishers Weekly, April 25, 2005, page 19

Other books by the same author:
Incubus Dreams, 2004
Seduced by Moonlight, 2004
Cerulean Sins, 2003
Narcissus in Chains, 2001
Burnt Offerings, 1998

Other books you might like:
Glen Cook, *Sweet Silver Blues*, 1987
Diane Duane, *Stealing the Elf-King's Roses*, 2002
Randall Garrett, *Lord Darcy*, 2002
Michael Reaves, *Darkworld Detective*, 1982
Mike Resnick, *Stalking the Unicorn*, 1987

576

VICTORIA HANLEY

The Light of the Oracle

(New York: David Fickling, 2005)

Story type: Young Adult; Magic Conflict
Subject(s): Magic; Secrets
Major character(s): Bryn, Teenager; Kiran, Horse Trainer, Teenager; Renchard, Religious
Time period(s): Indeterminate
Locale(s): Sorana, Fictional Country

Summary: A young girl is subject to visions which make the others in her village distrust her, and only the local priest seems able to tolerate her presence. Eventually she leaves, searching for a better place, and finds herself in the middle of a magical conflict, with her only ally a young horse trainer with remarkable talents of his own.

Other books by the same author:
The Healer's Keep, 2004
The Seer and the Sword, 2002

Other books you might like:
Emily Drake, *The Magickers*, 2001
Diana Wynne Jones, *The Dark Lord of Derkholm*, 1998
Andre Norton, *The Warding of Witch World*, 1996
E. Rose Sabin, *When the Beast Ravens*, 2005
Jane Yolen, *The Sword of the Rightful King*, 2003

Fantasy

577

NARELLE M. HARRIS

Witch Honour

(Waterville, Maine: Five Star, 2005)

Story type: Science Fiction; Magic Conflict
Subject(s): Magic; Space Colonies
Major character(s): Magda, Witch; Tephes, Witch; Zuleika Tallan, Witch
Time period(s): Indeterminate Future
Locale(s): Tunston, Planet—Imaginary

Summary: In the distant future, a woman from Earth moves to the planet Tunston, one of the worlds upon which magic actually works. There she gets involved when a powerful witch deposes the planet's king and rules in his stead, despite the opposition of most of the population. This first novel is an uneasy but sometimes amusing blend of science fiction and fantasy themes.

Where it's reviewed:
Library Journal, January 2005, page 102

Other books you might like:
David Alexander, *Fane*, 1981
Piers Anthony, *Faith of Tarot*, 1980
Jayne Castle, *After Dark*, 2000
Christopher Stasheff, *The Warlock Insane*, 1989
Lawrence Watt-Evans, *Out of This World*, 1994

578

MICHELE HAUF

Gossamyr

(New York: Luna, 2005)

Story type: Romance; Magic Conflict
Subject(s): Fairies; Magic
Major character(s): Gossamyr de Wintershinn, Mythical Creature (fairy); Red Lady, Mythical Creature; Jean Cesar Ulrich Villon III, Warrior
Time period(s): Indeterminate Past
Locale(s): Europe; Faerie, Mythical Place

Summary: Gossamyr, half human, half fairy, moves between the magical world of the fairies and Earth. Having vowed to defeat the Red Lady, an evil creature currently residing in Paris, Gossamyr sets off to confront her. Along the way, she acquires the dubious help of Ulrich, with whom she will eventually become romantically involved.

Other books by the same author:
Seraphim, 2004

Other books you might like:
Catherine Asaro, *The Charmed Sphere*, 2004
Caitlin Brennan, *The Mountain's Call*, 2004
Deborah Hale, *The Wizard's Ward*, 2004
Mercedes Lackey, *The Fairy Godmother*, 2004
Robin D. Owens, *Guardian of Honor*, 2005

579

AMANDA HEMINGWAY

The Greenstone Grail

(New York: Del Rey, 2005)

Story type: Contemporary; Young Adult
Series: Nathan Ward. Book 1
Subject(s): Magic; Secrets
Major character(s): Nathan Ward, Teenager; Hazel Bagot, Teenager; Bartlemy, Recluse
Time period(s): 2000s
Locale(s): England

Summary: Nathan Ward is raised in a remote part of England after his mother mysteriously seeks shelter with Bartlemy, a reclusive and mysterious man. As Nathan grows older, he and his friends discover that he is the focus of a secret involving a magical artifact brought from another world. First fantasy novel.

Where it's reviewed:
Library Journal, February 15, 2005, page 122
Publishers Weekly, January 3, 2005, page 40

Other books you might like:
Emma Bull, *War for the Oaks*, 1987
Alan Garner, *The Weirdstone of Brisingamen*, 1960
Andre Norton, *The Gate of the Cat*, 1987
James Stoddard, *The High House*, 1999
Vivian Vande Velde, *The Changeling Prince*, 1998

580

BARB HENDEE
J.C. HENDEE, Co-Author

Sister of the Dead

(New York: Roc, 2005)

Story type: Sword and Sorcery; Horror
Series: Noble Dead. Book 3
Subject(s): Magic; Quest; Vampires
Major character(s): Magiere, Vampire; Lessel, Mythical Creature (elf); Wynn Hygeohrt, Apprentice
Time period(s): Indeterminate
Locale(s): The Far Lands, Alternate Universe

Summary: Magiere is specially bred, half-human, half-vampire, her role in life to hunt down and slay vampires using that portion of her nature that allows her to mimic their skills. Accompanied by her half-elf friend and an enthusiastic apprentice, she helps raise a curse on a small village, battling a very powerful evil in the process.

Where it's reviewed:
Chronicle, February 2005, page 35

Other books by the same author:
Thief of Lives, 2004 (J.C. Hendee, co-author)
Dhampir, 2003 (J.C. Hendee, co-author)

Other books you might like:
Steven Brust, *Taltos*, 1988
Christie Golden, *Vampire of the Mists*, 1991
Tanith Lee, *Sabella*, 1980

Meredith Pierce, *Darkangel*, 1982
Chelsea Quinn Yarbro, *Dark Light*, 1999

581

MARY H. HERBERT

Return of the Exile

(Renton, Washington: Wizards of the Coast, 2005)

Story type: Magic Conflict; Sword and Sorcery
Series: Linsha. Book 3
Subject(s): Magic; Secrets
Major character(s): Linsha Majere, Prisoner, Noblewoman;
Sir Liam Ehrling, Knight; Lanther Darthassian, Warrior
Time period(s): Indeterminate
Locale(s): Ansalon, Fictional Country

Summary: Linsha Majere, taken as a prize of war by the
invaders from Tarmak, is now to be married against her will to
one of their war leaders. Her efforts to escape her fate seem
doomed until she discovers that there are some among her
enemies who might be willing to champion her cause.

Other books by the same author:
Dragon's Bluff, 2001
The Clandestine Circle, 2000
Legacy of Steel, 1998
City of Sorcerors, 1994
Dark Horse, 1990

Other books you might like:
Lynn Abbey, *Daughter of the Bright Moon*, 1979
Lois McMaster Bujold, *The Hallowed Hunt*, 2005
Stephen R. Donaldson, *The Mirror of Her Dreams*, 1986
Dave Duncan, *Sky of Swords*, 2000
Mary Mackey, *The Last Warrior Queen*, 1983

582

TRACY HICKMAN
LAURA HICKMAN, Co-Author

Mystic Quest

(New York: Warner, 2005)

Story type: Magic Conflict; Sword and Sorcery
Series: Bronze Canticles. Book 2
Subject(s): Magic; Quest
Major character(s): Galen Arvad, Leader; Caelith Arvad,
Nobleman; Berkita, Religious
Time period(s): Indeterminate
Locale(s): Alternate Universe

Summary: Although the evil menace that threatened the world
was defeated in *Mystic Warrior*, there are plenty of new
villains to make the future just as uncertain for the protagonists. Two brothers struggle to protect their clan from magical
enemies, and learn to deal with their changing roles among
their own people.

Where it's reviewed:
Publishers Weekly, March 21, 2005, page 40

Other books by the same author:
Mystic Warrior, 2005 (Laura Hickman, co-author)

Requiem of Stars, 1996
The Immortals, 1996

Other books you might like:
Maggie Furey, *Echo of Eternity*, 2003
David Gemmell, *The Knights of Dark Renown*, 1993
Sean McMullen, *Glass Dragons*, 2004
Michael Moorcock, *Count Brass*, 1981
R.A. Salvatore, *The Two Swords*, 2004

583

ROBERT E. HOWARD

The Black Stranger and Other American Tales

(Lincoln: University of Nebraska Press, 2005)

Story type: Collection
Subject(s): Short Stories

Summary: This volume collects 15 of the author's best stories,
mostly fantasy and a few horror, with settings primarily in the
New World. The tales involve the discovery of lost civilizations, ancient curses, supernatural entities, and lingering ma-
gics. The stories were all originally published during the
1930s and most of them are considered among the author's
very best.

Where it's reviewed:
Publishers Weekly, March 28, 2005, page 62

Other books by the same author:
The Bloody Crown of Conan, 2004
The Savage Tales of Solomon Kane, 2004
Eons of the Night, 1996
Trails in Darkness, 1996
Cthulhu, 1988

Other books you might like:
Simon R. Green, *Haven of Lost Souls*, 1999
Fritz Leiber, *Farewell to Lankhmar*, 1998
Michael Moorcock, *The Champion of Garathorm*, 1973
Andrew J. Offutt, *Deathknight*, 1990
Karl Edward Wagner, *The Book of Kane*, 1985

584

ROBERT E. HOWARD
GARY GIANNI, Illustrator

Bran Mak Morn: The Last King

(New York: Del Rey, 2005)

Story type: Collection
Subject(s): Short Stories
Major character(s): Bran Mak Morn, Ruler

Summary: This volume collects all of Howard's stories and
poems about Bran Mak Morn, a legendary figure from ancient
days in the British Isles. Story fragments, notes, and alternate
versions are also included. The stories involve Druidic magic
and high adventure and tend to be darker in tone than most of
Howard's other fantasy.

Other books by the same author:
The Bloody Crown of Conan, 2004

The Savage Tales of Solomon Kane, 2004
The Hour of the Dragon, 2001
Eons of the Night, 1996
Kull, 1985

Other books you might like:
Kenneth Flint, *The Dark Druid*, 1987
Gregory Frost, *Tain*, 1986
Robert Jordan, *Conan the Magnificent*, 1984
Andrew J. Offutt, *The Undying Wizard*, 1976
Karl Edward Wagner, *Legion from the Shadows*, 1976

585

KERRIE HUGHES, Editor
MARTIN H. GREENBERG, Co-Editor

Maiden, Matron, Crone

(New York: DAW, 2005)

Story type: Anthology
Subject(s): Short Stories; Mythology

Summary: This collection of 13 original fantasy stories illustrates the three stages of the triple goddess, youth, maturity, and old age. Contributors include Charles De Lint, Tanya Huff, Jane Lindskold, Fiona Patton, and Michelle West. The stories are generally serious in tone and make use of settings varying from the contemporary world to fantasy realms.

Other books you might like:
Charles De Lint, *Tapping the Dream Tree*, 2002
Tanya Huff, *Smoke and Shadows*, 2004
Jane Lindskold, *The Buried Pyramid*, 2004
Fiona Patton, *The Golden Sword*, 2001
Michelle West, *The Sun Sword*, 2004

586

TONY JOHNSTON

The Spoon in the Bathroom Wall

(Orlando, Florida: Harcourt, 2005)

Story type: Young Adult; Contemporary
Subject(s): Magic
Major character(s): Martha Snapdragon, Child; Luther Snapdragon, Maintenance Worker; Dr. Klunk, Principal
Time period(s): 2000s
Locale(s): United States

Summary: Martha Snapdragon is not happy about the current situation at school. The other children are making fun of her, and the teachers aren't much better. When she spots a carved inscription that seems to have appeared magically, she dismisses its statement that something magical is coming, but other signs occur later, convincing her the warning is genuine.

Other books you might like:
John Bellairs, *The Mansion in the Mist*, 1992
Bruce Coville, *Odder than Ever*, 1999
E. Rose Sabin, *A School for Sorcery*, 2002
Vivian Vande Velde, *Curses Inc.*, 1997
Jane Yolen, *The Bagpiper's Ghost*, 2002

587

MARVIN KAYE, Editor

The Fair Folk

(New York: Science Fiction Book Club, 2005)

Story type: Anthology
Subject(s): Short Stories; Elves

Summary: Elves are the subjects of the tales in this collection of never before published stories, with contributions from Patricia A. McKillip, Tanith Lee, Megan Lindholm, Kim Newman, Craig Shaw Gardner, Midori Snyder, and Jane Yolen. Most of the stories involve encounters with magical creatures in this world, with a few set in a completely magical alternate world.

Where it's reviewed:
Locus, April 2005, page 31

Other books by the same author:
Fantastique, 1992
The Ghosts of Night and Morning, 1987
The Amorous Umbrella, 1981
The Possession of Immanuel Kant, 1981
The Incredible Umbrella, 1980

Other books you might like:
Craig Shaw Gardner, *A Disagreement with Death*, 1989
Tanith Lee, *The White Serpent*, 1988
Megan Lindholm, *Cloven Hooves*, 1991
Patricia A. McKillip, *A Song for Basilisk*, 1998
Midori Snyder, *Beldan's Fire*, 1993

588

SYLVIA KELSO

Everran's Bane

(Waterville, Maine: Five Star, 2005)

Story type: Adventure; Quest
Subject(s): Magic
Major character(s): Beryx, Ruler (king); Harman, Musician; Ragnor, Sailor
Time period(s): Indeterminate
Locale(s): Everran, Fictional Country

Summary: The kingdom of Everran is beset by a powerful dragon who apparently cannot be defeated by conventional kings. The king and a musician travel to neighboring realms to seek help primarily in the form of information about why the dragon has chosen Everran as its target. The two have a number of episodic adventures before learning the truth. First novel.

Other books you might like:
Mark Acres, *Dragonspawn*, 1994
Robin Wayne Bailey, *Brothers of the Dragon*, 1993
Carol Dennis, *Dragon's Pawn*, 1987
Mercedes Lackey, *Joust*, 2003
Andre Norton, *Dragon Blade*, 2005
    Sasha Miller, co-author

589

NAOMI KRITZER

Freedom's Apprentice

(New York: Bantam, 2005)

Story type: Sword and Sorcery; Magic Conflict
Series: Lauria. Book 2
Subject(s): Magic
Major character(s): Lauria, Spy, Sorceress; Tamar, Warrior; Phoibe, Sorceress
Time period(s): Indeterminate
Locale(s): Alternate Universe

Summary: Lauria has learned that what she believed about the rulers of her people was false. She has now returned from her espionage assignment outside her own borders with a new mission: to free as many of her people as possible. To accomplish this, she decides to apprentice herself to a sorceress and gain more power to influence others.

Where it's reviewed:
Publishers Weekly, April 18, 2005, page 49

Other books by the same author:
Freedom's Gate, 2004
Turning the Storm, 2003
Fires of the Faithful, 2002

Other books you might like:
Suzy McKee Charnas, *The Conqueror's Child*, 1999
Barbara Hambly, *The Witches of Wenshar*, 1987
Mary H. Herbert, *Return of the Exile*, 2005
Paula Volsky, *The Sorcerer's Lady*, 1986
Lawrence Watt-Evans, *The Book of Silence*, 1984

590

MERCEDES LACKEY
ROBERTA GELLIS, Co-Author

Ill Met by Moonlight

(New York: Baen, 2005)

Story type: Historical; Light Fantasy
Subject(s): Elves; Secrets
Major character(s): Pasgen Silverhair, Mythical Creature (elf); Elizabeth I, Historical Figure, Ruler; Lady Rhoslyn, Mythical Creature (elf)
Time period(s): 16th century
Locale(s): England

Summary: Elizabeth is destined to assume the throne of England when she grows up, but there are dark supernatural forces determined to see that she does not live that long. Her old protectors are gone, so Pasgen Silverhair, an elf, finds himself caught up in a secret behind the scenes battle in the courts of England. This is the sequel to *This Scepter'd Isle*.

Other books by the same author:
Alta, 2004
Exile's Valor, 2003
Joust, 2003
The Gates of Sleep, 2002
Take a Thief, 2001

Other books you might like:
Fiona Avery, *The Crown Rose*, 2005
Michael G. Coney, *King of the Scepter'd Isle*, 1990
Sara Douglass, *Hades' Daughter*, 2003
Sarah A. Hoyt, *Ill Met by Moonlight*, 2001
Judith Tarr, *Rite of Conquest*, 2004

591

MERCEDES LACKEY

Sanctuary

(New York: DAW, 2005)

Story type: Sword and Sorcery; Magic Conflict
Series: Dragon Jousters. Book 3
Subject(s): Secrets; Magic
Major character(s): Kiron, Warrior; Avatre, Mythical Creature (dragon); Nofret-te-en, Ruler (queen)
Time period(s): Indeterminate
Locale(s): Alta, Fictional Country

Summary: After finding a new home in Alta, Kiron has used his talents for taming and riding dragons to help form a military unit of dragon riders to serve his new homeland. Unfortunately, things are not entirely peaceful in Alta, and a nefarious plot against the royal family is underway. Kiron is able to rescue the beleaguered queen and carry her off to a legendary, remote city where they can regroup.

Where it's reviewed:
Publishers Weekly, April 18, 2005, page 48

Other books by the same author:
Alta, 2004
Exile's Valor, 2003
Joust, 2003
Take a Thief, 2001
Fiddler's Fair, 1998

Other books you might like:
Mark Acres, *Dragon War*, 1994
Joanne Bertin, *Dragon and Phoenix*, 1999
Barbara Hambly, *Dragonsbane*, 1985
Jean Rabe, *The Dawning of a New Age*, 1996
Irene Radford, *The Dragon's Touchstone*, 1997

592

GLENDA LARKE

The Aware

(New York: Ace, 2005)

Story type: Sword and Sorcery; Magic Conflict
Series: Isles of Glory. Book 1
Subject(s): Secrets
Major character(s): Blaze, Outcast, Spy; Niamor, Spy; Syrsylv Duthrick, Government Official
Time period(s): Indeterminate
Locale(s): Gorthan Spit, Fictional Country

Summary: Blaze is an outcast with no rights of citizenship to any of the individual islands in the Isles of Glory. She works as a spy for one of the more powerful groups, hoping to eventually be rewarded by a grant of citizenship. Her current

Fantasy (side tab)

mission is on a remote island where there is suspicion that evil magic may be underway. This novel was previously published in Australia in 2003.

Other books you might like:
Gayle Greeno, *Sunderlies Seeking*, 1998
Anne Kelleher, *Silver's Edge*, 2004
Naomi Kritzer, *Freedom's Gate*, 2004
Jennifer Roberson, *Sword Born*, 1998
Jo Walton, *The King's Peace*, 2000

593

RACHEL LEE

The Hidden Queen
(New York: Eos, 2005)

Story type: Romance; Quest
Subject(s): Quest; Magic
Major character(s): Anghara Kir Hama, Sorceress; Sif Kir Hama, Nobleman; Feor, Warrior, Bodyguard
Time period(s): Indeterminate
Locale(s): Kheldrin, Fictional Country; Roisinan, Fictional Country

Summary: When her half brother arranges the murder of her parents, Anghara Kir Hama is deprived of her throne and her homeland, and goes into exile with a handful of her closest supporters. There she develops her latent magical talents in preparation for a return and a confrontation, and finds love in the process. This is the first half of a novel that concludes in *Changer of Days*.

Other books by the same author:
Changer of Days, 2005
The Secrets of Jin-Shei, 2004

Other books you might like:
Lynn Abbey, *Jerlayne*, 1999
Phyllis Eisenstein, *Born to Exile*, 1978
Anne Kelleher, *Silver's Edge*, 2004
Elizabeth Ann Scarborough, *Bronwyn's Bane*, 1983
Jo Walton, *The King's Name*, 2001

594

RACHEL LEE

Shadows of Myth
(New York: LUNA, 2005)

Story type: Romance; Magic Conflict
Subject(s): Quest
Major character(s): Archer Blackcloak, Warrior; Sara Deepwell, Witch; Tess Birdsong, Amnesiac
Time period(s): Indeterminate
Locale(s): Alternate Universe

Summary: A mysterious band of assassins uses secrecy and magic to protect themselves and their sinister plans from outside intervention. Archer Blackcloak gathers together a very unlikely group to oppose them, including an amnesiac, a witch, and a warrior. In the course of their efforts, he also discovers his true love. First fantasy novel.

Other books by the same author:
Wildcard, 2005
Nighthawk, 2004
After I Dream, 2000
An Officer and a Gentleman, 1990

Other books you might like:
Catherine Asaro, *The Charmed Sphere*, 2004
Jessica Bryan, *Across a Wine Dark Sea*, 1991
David Gemmell, *The White Wolf*, 2003
Mercedes Lackey, *The Gates of Sleep*, 2002
Jennifer Macaire, *The Secret of Shabaz*, 2004

595

HOLLY LISLE

Talyn
(New York: Tor, 2005)

Story type: Sword and Sorcery; Magic Conflict
Subject(s): Magic
Major character(s): Talyn, Military Personnel; Skirmig, Diplomat; Pada, Military Personnel
Time period(s): Indeterminate
Locale(s): Korre, Fictional Country

Summary: In another reality, two nations have been long engaged in a brutal war of magic. At last a third power intervenes, negotiating a peace that is applied unevenly but which seems to be working. Professional soldier Talyn is uncertain about her future in a peaceful world. When she becomes romantically involved with a foreign diplomat, she uncovers an insidious plot threatening both nations.

Other books by the same author:
Gods Old and Dark, 2004
The Wreck of Heaven, 2003
Diplomacy of Wolves, 1998
Minerva Wakes, 1994
Bones of the Past, 1993

Other books you might like:
Storm Constantine, *The Crown of Silence*, 2001
David Farland, *The Lair of Bones*, 2003
David Gemmell, *The Dark Prince*, 1991
Robin Hobb, *Fool's Fate*, 2004
Jane Lindskold, *The Dragon of Despair*, 2003

596

EDWARD S. LOUIS

Odysseus on the Rhine
(Waterville, Maine: Five Star, 2005)

Story type: Historical; Legend
Subject(s): Legends; Quest
Major character(s): Odysseus, Nobleman, Traveler; Philoctetes, Traveler, Warrior; Diomedes, Traveler
Time period(s): Indeterminate Past
Locale(s): Germany

Summary: This is a sequel to Homer's *The Odyssey*, set after Odysseus' wife Penelope has died. Restless, he lets his old friend Diomedes talk him into taking a journey of exploration

up the Rhine River, during which he has various adventures and meets a number of friends, and enemies. First fantasy novel.

Other books you might like:
Patrick Adkins, *Lord of the Crooked Paths*, 1987
Robert Graves, *Hercules, My Shipmate*, 1945
Robert Holdstock, *Celtika*, 2001
Richard Purtill, *The Mirror of Helen*, 1983
Thomas Burnett Swann, *Green Phoenix*, 1972

597

IAN R. MACLEOD

The House of Storms

(New York: Ace, 2005)

Story type: Alternate World; Quest
Series: Light Ages. Book 2
Subject(s): Secrets; Alternate History
Major character(s): Alice Meynell, Worker (telegrapher); Ralph Meynell, Patient; Marion Price, Servant
Time period(s): Indeterminate
Locale(s): Alternate Universe

Summary: In an alternate version of Victorian England where magic works, Alice Meynell takes her ailing son to a remote area, supposedly for a vacation. She actually plans to appeal to a magical power rumored to exist in that region. Her simple quest becomes much more complicated when she finally communicates her desires.

Where it's reviewed:
Locus, February 2005, page 25
Publishers Weekly, April 11, 2005, page 38

Other books by the same author:
Breathmoss and Other Exhalations, 2004
The Light Ages, 2003
The Great Wheel, 1997
Voyages by Starlight, 1996

Other books you might like:
James P. Blaylock, *Homunculus*, 1986
Esther Friesner, *Druid's Blood*, 1988
Barbara Hambly, *Bride of the Rat God*, 1994
K.W. Jeter, *Infernal Devices*, 1987
Brian Stableford, *The Werewolves of London*, 1990

598

JULIET MARILLIER

The Dark Mirror

(New York: Tor, 2005)

Story type: Sword and Sorcery; Magic Conflict
Series: Bridei Chronicles. Book 1
Subject(s): Magic; Fairies
Major character(s): Bridei, Nobleman; Broichan, Religious (druid); Tuala, Foundling
Time period(s): Indeterminate
Locale(s): Alternate Universe

Summary: Bridei, the son of a noble family, is being raised under the tutelage of Broichan, a druid. When a foundling child is left with them, Bridei becomes increasingly attached to the girl, who they name Tuala. The two grow up together and become ever closer, but there is a hidden danger hovering over both of them.

Other books by the same author:
Wolfskin, 2003
Child of the Prophecy, 2002
Daughter of the Forest, 2000
Son of the Shadows, 2000

Other books you might like:
Sara Douglass, *Enchanter*, 2001
Jennifer Fallon, *Medalon*, 2004
David Farland, *Wizardborn*, 2001
Elizabeth Haydon, *Rhapsody*, 1999
Jo Walton, *The King's Peace*, 2000

599

JULIAN MAY

Ironcrown Moon

(New York: Ace, 2005)

Story type: Sword and Sorcery; Magic Conflict
Series: Boreal Moon. Book 2
Subject(s): Magic
Major character(s): Sir Deveron Austrey, Nobleman; Conrig, Ruler (king); Beynor, Royalty (prince)
Time period(s): Indeterminate
Locale(s): Alternate Universe

Summary: King Conrig has begun extending his control over neighboring countries, even when they do not threaten him, but a series of sudden reversals has him worried. A woman he thought dead has reappeared with her son, who might be true heir to the throne. Even worse, a cache of magical artifacts has been stolen by his enemies for use against him.

Other books by the same author:
Conqueror's Moon, 2003
The Orion Arm, 1999
The Perseus Spur, 1999
Sky Trillium, 1997
The Diamond Mask, 1994

Other books you might like:
R. Scott Bakker, *The Warrior-Prophet*, 2005
Dan Chernenko, *The Scepter's Return*, 2005
Sara Douglass, *The Wounded Hawk*, 2005
Juliet Marillier, *Daughter of the Forest*, 2000
L.E. Modesitt Jr., *Ordermaster*, 2005

600

SCOTT MCGOUGH

Heretic Betrayers

(Renton, Washington: Wizards of the Coast, 2005)

Story type: Sword and Sorcery; Magic Conflict
Series: Kamigawa Cycle. Book 2
Subject(s): Magic

Major character(s): Toshi Umezawa, Warrior; Michiko, Royalty (princess); Yamagushi Hidetsugu, Warrior
Time period(s): Indeterminate
Locale(s): Kamigawa, Fictional Country

Summary: Toshi Umezawa, a warrior who finds himself in the employment of a royal princess, is still under obligation to those who helped him out of various difficulties in *Outlaws: Champions of Kanizawa*, the previous book in this series. Now he treads a delicate path between his own desires and the requirements of those to whom he is bound. The setting is an alternate, magical version of ancient Japan.

Other books by the same author:
Outlaws: Champions of Kanizawa, 2004
Champion's Trial, 2003
Emperor's Fist, 2003
Assassin's Blade, 2002
Chainer's Torment, 2002

Other books you might like:
Edward Bolme, *The Steel Throne*, 2002
Stan Brown, *The Crab*, 2001
Jessica Amanda Salmonson, *The Golden Naginata*, 1982
Ree Soesbee, *Wind of Honor*, 1982
Stephen Sullivan, *The Scorpion*, 2000

601

FIONA MCINTOSH

Blood and Memory

(New York: Eos, 2005)

Story type: Sword and Sorcery; Magic Conflict
Series: Quickening. Book 2
Subject(s): Magic
Major character(s): Wyl Thirsk, Military Personnel; Celimus, Ruler (king); Valentyna, Ruler (queen)
Time period(s): Indeterminate
Locale(s): Morgravia, Fictional Country

Summary: Wyl Thirsk is still trying to successfully raise a rebellion against the evil King Celimus in this second book in the Quickening series. His efforts are hampered by a curse which has trapped him in another man's body, so his most pressing task is to find the witch responsible for his more immediate affliction.

Other books by the same author:
Myrren's Gift, 2005

Other books you might like:
Chris Bunch, *The Empire Stone*, 2000
Dan Chernenko, *The Scepter's Return*, 2005
Raymond E. Feist, *King of Foxes*, 2004
David Gemmell, *The White Wolf*, 2003
Barbara Hambly, *The Magicians of Night*, 1991

602

FIONA MCINTOSH

Myrren's Gift

(New York: Eos, 2005)

Story type: Magic Conflict; Political
Series: Quickening. Book 1
Subject(s): Magic; Military Life
Major character(s): Wyl Thirsk, Military Personnel; Celimus, Ruler (king); Myrren, Witch
Time period(s): Indeterminate
Locale(s): Morgravia, Fictional Country

Summary: Wyl grows up as a playmate of Celimus, a willful boy who becomes a cruel and sadistic ruler. Eventually, his excesses convince Wyl that his loyalties should lie elsewhere, and he uses a magical gift provided by a dying witch to help organize resistance against the despotic king. This is the opening volume in a series and is the author's first novel.

Where it's reviewed:
Chronicle, February 2005, page 33
Library Journal, January 2005, page 103
Publishers Weekly, January 10, 2005, page 43

Other books you might like:
Chris Bunch, *The Demon King*, 1998
David Feintuch, *The King*, 2002
Raymond E. Feist, *Rage of a Demon King*, 1997
Barbara Hambly, *Icefalcon's Quest*, 1998
George R.R. Martin, *A Storm of Swords*, 2000

603

DENNIS L. MCKIERNAN

Once upon a Summer Day

(New York: Roc, 2005)

Story type: Alternate World; Quest
Subject(s): Fairies; Quest
Major character(s): Borel, Royalty (prince); Flic, Traveler
Time period(s): Indeterminate
Locale(s): Faery, Mythical Place

Summary: Prince Borel is troubled by dreams in which a young woman appeals to him for help. Convinced that she is real, he sets off on a perilous, episodic quest across the mythical land of Faery in an attempt to find and rescue her, encountering various parties both friendly and unfriendly along the way. This novel is related to *Once upon a Winter's Night*.

Other books by the same author:
Red Slippers, 2004
Once upon a Winter's Night, 2001
Silver Wolf, Black Falcon, 2000
Into the Fire, 1998
Into the Forge, 1997

Other books you might like:
Diane Duane, *Stealing the Elf-King's Roses*, 2002
Dunsany, *The King of Elfland's Daughter*, 1924
Paul Hazel, *The Wealdwife's Tale*, 1993

Sarah A. Hoyt, *Any Man So Daring*, 2003
Sylvia Townsend Warner, *Kingdoms of Elfin*, 1977

604

PATRICIA A. MCKILLIP

Od Magic

(New York: Ace, 2005)

Story type: Light Fantasy; Magic Conflict
Subject(s): Magic; Secrets
Major character(s): Brendan Vetch, Gardener; Od, Wizard; Mistral, Noblewoman
Time period(s): Indeterminate
Locale(s): Numis, Fictional Country

Summary: Brendan Vetch is a gardener who has a special talent for growing things. When the wizard Od summons him for a new job, he believes that it is simply to make use of his talent to improve the gardens. Od has an ulterior motive, however, for he knows that Brendan's magical talent actually is more significant and could affect the outcome of a major power struggle.

Where it's reviewed:
Publishers Weekly, May 2, 2005, page 181

Other books by the same author:
Alphabet of Thorn, 2004
In the Forest of Serre, 2003
Ombria in Shadow, 2002
The Book of Atrix Wolfe, 1998
The House on Parchment Street, 1973

Other books you might like:
Jeffrey Ford, *The Physiognomy*, 1997
Ursula K. Le Guin, *The Beginning Place*, 1980
Robin McKinley, *Deerskin*, 1993
Mel Odom, *The Destruction of the Books*, 2004
Tad Williams, *Caliban's Hour*, 1994

605

CLIFF MCNISH

The Silver Child

(Minneapolis: Carolrhoda, 2005)

Story type: Young Adult; Psychic Powers
Series: Silver Sequence. Book 1
Subject(s): Psychic Powers
Major character(s): Milo, Teenager; Walter, Teenager; Helen, Teenager, Telepath
Time period(s): 2000s
Locale(s): England

Summary: Six children all mysteriously develop what might be construed as superpowers, although in many cases their function is unclear. One is a giant, one reads minds, one heals, two begin to walk on all fours, and the last changes colors. They are also attracted to a run-down area where they instinctively know their enemy awaits them.

Other books by the same author:
The Scent of Magic, 2001

The Wizard's Promise, 2001
Doomspell, 2000

Other books you might like:
K.A. Applegate, *Predator*, 1996
Adam-Troy Castro, *The Gathering of the Sinister Six*, 1999
Arthur Byron Cover, *Born in Fire*, 2002
Greg Cox, *Search and Destroy*, 1999
Dave Smeds, *Law of the Jungle*, 1998

606

O.R. MELLING

The Hunter's Moon

(New York: Amulet, 2005)

Story type: Young Adult; Contemporary
Series: Chronicles of Faerie. Book 1
Subject(s): Fairies; Magic
Major character(s): Gwen Woods, Teenager, Tourist; Findabhair, Teenager, Cousin (Gwen's); Mattie O'Shea, Worker
Time period(s): 2000s
Locale(s): Ireland

Summary: Vacationing in Ireland, Gwen Woods is visiting her cousin Findabhair when the other girl disappears, apparently kidnapped by the king of the fairies, who wants her to be his bride. Gwen finds friends among the local people and is eventually able to rescue her cousin, but only after a series of low-key adventures.

Other books by the same author:
The Book of Dreams, 2003
The Light Bearer's Daughter, 2001
The Druid's Tune, 1983

Other books you might like:
Margaret J. Anderson, *The Druid's Gift*, 1999
Esther Friesner, *Elf Defense*, 1988
Alan Garner, *The Moon of Gomrath*, 1963
Mollie Hunter, *The Walking Stones*, 1970
Sarban, *Ringstones and Other Curious Tales*, 1951

607

L.E. MODESITT JR.

Alector's Choice

(New York: Tor, 2005)

Story type: Magic Conflict; Sword and Sorcery
Series: Corean Chronicles. Book 4
Subject(s): Magic; Secrets
Major character(s): Dainyl, Military Personnel; Mykel, Military Personnel; Rachlya, Young Woman
Time period(s): Indeterminate
Locale(s): Corus, Fictional Country

Summary: Although this is the fourth in the series, it takes place a thousand years before the events in the previous novels. The world of Corus is being prepared for the mass migration of an entire people from an alternate reality, and power struggles and conspiracies reach even into the heart of the army.

Other books by the same author:
Flash, 2004
Scepters, 2004 (Corean Chronicles. Book 3)
Darknesses, 2003 (Corean Chronicles. Book 2)
Legacies, 2002 (Corean Chronicles. Book 1)
Shadowsinger, 2002

Other books you might like:
Curt Benjamin, *The Prince of Dreams*, 2002
Glen Cook, *Bleak Seasons*, 1996
Raymond E. Feist, *A Darkness at Sethanon*, 1986
Robin Hobb, *Assassin's Quest*, 1997
Mercedes Lackey, *The White Gryphon*, 1995

608

L.E. MODESITT JR.

Ordermaster

(New York: Tor, 2005)

Story type: Sword and Sorcery; Magic Conflict
Series: Recluce. Book 13
Subject(s): Magic; Secrets
Major character(s): Kharl, Artisan (cooper); Hagen, Government Official; Lord Ghrant, Nobleman
Time period(s): Indeterminate
Locale(s): Recluce, Fictional Country; Nordla, Fictional Country

Summary: A humble man with magical talents is reluctantly forced out of retirement when a group of rebellious aristocrats menace the throne, and now he has a new task. He must travel to a weaker neighboring state and help prepare them to resist the expansion of a powerful enemy.

Where it's reviewed:
Chronicle, February 2005, page 31

Other books by the same author:
Flash, 2004
Scepters, 2004
Darknesses, 2003
Legacies, 2002
The Shadow Sorceress, 2001

Other books you might like:
Neal Barrett Jr., *The Treachery of Kings*, 2001
Dave Duncan, *Lord of the Fire Lands*, 2000
Robert Jordan, *Winter's Heart*, 2000
George R.R. Martin, *A Clash of Kings*, 1999
Lawrence Watt-Evans, *Touched by the Gods*, 1997

609

JONATHAN MOELLER

Demonsouled

(Waterville, Maine: Five Star, 2005)

Story type: Sword and Sorcery; Magic Conflict
Subject(s): Magic
Major character(s): Mazael Cravenlock, Nobleman; Gerald Roland, Nobleman; Silar, Religious
Time period(s): Indeterminate
Locale(s): Alternate Universe

Summary: When Mazael Cravenlock returns to his home castle after a long absence, he finds himself caught up in a web of political machinations, kidnappings, magic, and court intrigues. With a long-time friend, he rescues his sister, and convinces his brother not to engage in a fruitless rebellion without being prepared for the consequences. First fantasy novel.

Other books you might like:
Steven Brust, *The Lord of Castle Black*, 2003
Lois McMaster Bujold, *Paladin of Souls*, 2003
Peter Garrison, *The Magic Dead*, 2000
Marie Jakober, *The Black Chalice*, 2000
Janny Wurts, *Peril's Gate*, 2002

610

JOHN MOORE

The Unhandsome Prince

(New York: Ace, 2005)

Story type: Humor; Quest
Subject(s): Humor
Major character(s): Caroline, Young Woman; Hal, Royalty (prince); Emily, Young Woman
Time period(s): Indeterminate
Locale(s): Melinower, Fictional Country

Summary: When Prince Hal is turned into a frog after trying to steal from a sorceress, several young women try unsuccessfully to find him so that they can kiss him, turn him back into a prince, and live happily ever after. Only Caroline perseveres until she finally finds him, but she is disappointed with the results. Hal is not a particularly good catch.

Other books by the same author:
Heroics for Beginners, 2004
Slay and Rescue, 1993

Other books you might like:
Piers Anthony, *Currant Events*, 2004
John DeChancie, *Castle Dreams*, 1992
Esther Friesner, *Majyk by Accident*, 1993
John Morressey, *The Questing of Kedrigern*, 1987
Terry Pratchett, *Feet of Clay*, 1996

611

ANDRE NORTON
LYN MCCONCHIE, Co-Author

The Duke's Ballad

(New York: Tor, 2005)

Story type: Sword and Sorcery; Magic Conflict
Series: Witch World. Book 25
Subject(s): Secrets; Magic
Major character(s): Aisling, Witch; Kirion, Warlock; Keelan, Teenager
Time period(s): Indeterminate
Locale(s): Kars, Fictional Country

Summary: Aisling and her younger brother have been in exile from Kars, thanks to the evil sorcery of their older brother, Kirion. Aisling has developed her powers and secretly re-

turns, hoping to set things right, but her abilities still may not be a match for Kirion.

Where it's reviewed:
Booklist, January 1, 2005, page 834
Chronicle, February 2005, page 31
Publishers Weekly, December 20, 2004, page 41

Other books by the same author:
The Lost Lands of Witch World, 2004
Janus, 2003
Warlock, 2002
Ciara's Song, 1998 (Lyn McConchie, co-author)
The Key of the Keplian, 1995 (Lyn McConchie, co-author)

Other books you might like:
Raymond E. Feist, *Exile's Return*, 2004
Simon R. Green, *Beyond the Blue Moon*, 2000
Ann Logston, *The Exile*, 1999
Melanie Rawn, *Exiles*, 1995
Jennifer Roberson, *Sword-Sworn*, 2002

| 612 |

ANDRE NORTON

Three Hands for Scorpio

(New York: Tor, 2005)

Story type: Adventure; Magic Conflict
Subject(s): Mental Telepathy
Major character(s): Tamara Scorpys, Prisoner, Telepath; Sabina Scorpys, Prisoner, Telepath; Desmond Scorpys, Prisoner, Telepath
Time period(s): Indeterminate
Locale(s): Alternate Universe

Summary: The three Scorpys siblings are kidnapped by enemies from across the border as part of a political struggle. Although they are abandoned to die, they find an odd but helpful friend. In the process of making their escape, they discover an even darker menace, one which has implications beyond its effect on their own lives.

Other books by the same author:
The Solar Queen, 2003
Warlock, 2002
A Scent of Magic, 1998
Wizards' Worlds, 1990
The Magic Books, 1988

Other books you might like:
Lois McMaster Bujold, *The Spirit Ring*, 1992
Stephen R. Donaldson, *The Mirror of Her Dreams*, 1986
Dave Duncan, *Sky of Swords*, 2000
Mercedes Lackey, *Alta*, 2004
Nancy Springer, *The Golden Swan*, 1983

| 613 |

MEL ODOM

Lord of the Libraries

(New York: Tor, 2005)

Story type: Magic Conflict; Sword and Sorcery

Series: Edgewick Lamplighter. Book 3
Subject(s): Secrets; Quest; Libraries
Major character(s): Edgewick Lamplighter, Librarian; Jugh, Librarian; Craugh, Wizard
Time period(s): Indeterminate
Locale(s): Alternate Universe

Summary: Edgewick Lamplighter and his apprentice, Jugh, are charged with overseeing a library filled with books that contain the secrets of powerful magic. Although they have been successful in keeping this knowledge from falling into the wrong hands, they suspect that another library exists, one in the possession of evil forces, and decide to do something about it.

Where it's reviewed:
Publishers Weekly, May 2, 2005, page 181

Other books by the same author:
Hunters of the Dark Sea, 2004
The Destruction of the Books, 2004
Cursed, 2003
Crossings, 2002
The Black Road, 2002

Other books you might like:
Barbara Hambly, *The Dog Wizard*, 1993
Nancy Kress, *The White Pipes*, 1985
Patricia A. McKillip, *Alphabet of Thorn*, 2004
Andre Norton, *Three Hands for Scorpio*, 2005
Lawrence Watt-Evans, *With a Single Spell*, 1987

| 614 |

ROBIN D. OWENS

Guardian of Honor

(New York: Luna, 2005)

Story type: Romance; Alternate World
Subject(s): Alternate History; Magic
Major character(s): Alexa Fitzwalter, Lawyer; Bastien, Nobleman; Reynardus, Wizard
Time period(s): 2000s
Locale(s): United States; Alternate Universe

Summary: Lawyer Alexa Fitzwalter discovers other worlds exist parallel to this one. She crosses over to one in which magic works, the subject of a mysterious conspiracy, where she is put under the protection of Bastien, a resident of that reality. As she and Bastien fall in love, sinister forces plot a darker fate for the intruder.

Other books by the same author:
Heart Choice, 2005
Heart Duel, 2004
Heart Thief, 2003

Other books you might like:
Robin Wayne Bailey, *Brothers of the Dragon*, 1993
Laurell K. Hamilton, *Seduced by Moonlight*, 2004
Garfield Reeves-Stevens, *Shifter*, 1990
    Judith Reeves-Stevens, co-author
Mickey Zucker Reichert, *The Beasts of Barakhai*, 2001
Roger Zelazny, *The Blood of Amber*, 1986

615

PAUL PARK

A Princess of Roumania

(New York: Tor, 2005)

Story type: Alternate History; Magic Conflict
Subject(s): Alternate History; Secrets
Major character(s): Miranda Popescu, Noblewoman, Fugitive; Aegypta Schenck, Sorceress; Baroness Ceaucescu, Noblewoman
Time period(s): 2000s
Locale(s): Romania; Alternate Universe

Summary: Miranda Popescu lives in this world, but is actually from an alternate reality where magic works. She has been sent here for protection from the magical attacks of an enemy in an alternate history in which one of the leading nations of Europe is Roumania. With two friends, she returns to her own reality to find out the truth and confront those who wish her harm.

Where it's reviewed:
Locus, May 2005, page 23

Other books by the same author:
If Lions Could Speak and Other Stories, 2002
Celestis, 1995
The Cult of Loving Kindness, 1991
Sugar Rain, 1989
Soldiers of Paradise, 1987

Other books you might like:
Esther Friesner, *Child of the Eagle*, 1996
Thomas Harlan, *The Shadow of Ararat*, 1999
Robin D. Owens, *Guardian of Honor*, 2005
Garfield Reeves-Stevens, *Nightshifter*, 1991
   Judith Reeves-Stevens, co-author
Roger Zelazny, *Trumps of Doom*, 1985

616

CHRIS PIERSON

Blades of the Tiger

(Renton, Washington: Wizards of the Coast, 2005)

Story type: Sword and Sorcery; Magic Conflict
Series: Taladas. Book 1
Subject(s): Magic
Major character(s): Shedara, Mythical Creature (elf); Chovuk Tegin, Leader; Forlo, Warrior
Time period(s): Indeterminate
Locale(s): Taladas, Fictional Country

Summary: Taladas is a land from which magic has long been absent. People have adjusted to their new life and no longer are prepared to deal with the complexities and dangers that magic entails. When that force returns, it causes considerable upheaval. An elf, who wishes to conceal her nature from humans, has a series of adventures as she travels across the newly transformed landscape.

Other books by the same author:
Sacred Fire, 2003

Divine Hammer, 2002
Chosen of the Gods, 2001
Dezra's Quest, 1999
Spirit of the Wind, 1998

Other books you might like:
Dan Abnett, *Xenos*, 2001
Jonathan Green, *Magestorm*, 2004
Andrew J. Offutt, *Shadowspawn*, 1987
Jean Rabe, *Downfall*, 2000
Gav Thorpe, *The Blades of Chaos*, 2003

617

IRENE RADFORD

Guardian of the Freedom

(New York: DAW, 2005)

Story type: Historical; Mystery
Series: Merlin's Descendants. Book 5
Subject(s): Magic; Secrets
Major character(s): Drake Kirkwood, Nobleman, Magician; Georgina Kirkwood, Spy; Dr. Milton Marlowe, Magician
Time period(s): 18th century
Locale(s): England

Summary: Drake Kirkwood, head of a secret society that uses magic to help protect England, has bad health and his closest allies are scattered around the world. He is forced to become dependent upon his cousin, Dr. Milton Marlowe, who is less trustworthy than he seems. A crisis is coming, because the American colonists are slowly moving toward open revolt, but the society is unable to react quickly.

Where it's reviewed:
Booklist, March 15, 2005, page 12
Library Journal, April 15, 2005, page 79
Publishers Weekly, March 14, 2005, page 50

Other books by the same author:
The Dragon Circle, 2004
Guardian of the Promise, 2003
The Hidden Dragon, 2002
Guardian of the Trust, 2001
Guardian of the Vision, 2001

Other books you might like:
Joan Aiken, *Black Hearts in Battersea*, 1964
James P. Blaylock, *Homunculus*, 1986
Barbara Hambly, *Bride of the Rat God*, 1994
J. Gregory Keyes, *Newton's Cannon*, 1998
Brian Stableford, *The Angel of Pain*, 1991

618

KEN RAND

Fairy BrewHaHa at the Lucky Nickel Saloon

(Waterville, Maine: Five Star, 2005)

Story type: Historical; Humor
Subject(s): Humor; Fairies; Saloons

Major character(s): Tom Dooley, Worker; Tom Murphy, Entertainer; Mick, Saloon Keeper/Owner
Time period(s): 19th century
Locale(s): Wyoming

Summary: The Lucky Nickel Saloon in Wyoming Territory has a loyal corps of regular customers, but things get more interesting when a group of fairies shows up, demanding their favorite drink, which Mick the barkeeper created by accident years in the past. Unfortunately, he doesn't know how to make a fresh supply, and the fairies are not amused. First novel.

Other books you might like:
Piers Anthony, *Currant Events*, 2004
Emma Bull, *War for the Oaks*, 1987
Brett Davis, *The Faery Convention*, 1995
John DeChancie, *Castle for Rent*, 1989
Esther Friesner, *Gnome Man's Land*, 1991

619

JOHN RINGO

Against the Tide
(New York: Baen, 2005)

Story type: Military; Magic Conflict
Subject(s): Magic; Military Life
Major character(s): Edmund Talbot, Military Personnel; Megan Travante, Spy; Herzer Herrick, Military Personnel
Time period(s): Indeterminate
Locale(s): Alternate Universe

Summary: This unusual blend of science fiction and fantasy is set after the collapse of a technological civilization, not necessarily ours. Warfare erupts between two coalitions of states, using magical weapons and dragons and throwing a number of unprepared people into battle.

Other books by the same author:
The Emerald Sea, 2004
Hell's Faire, 2003
There Will Be Dragons, 2003
When the Devil Dances, 2002
Gust Front, 2001

Other books you might like:
Dan Abnett, *Riders of the Dead*, 2003
Glen Cook, *Soldiers Live*, 2000
China Mieville, *The Iron Council*, 2004
Stan Nicholls, *Orcs*, 2004
Harry Turtledove, *Out of Darkness*, 2004

620

E. ROSE SABIN

When the Beast Ravens
(New York: Tor, 2005)

Story type: Young Adult; Mystery
Series: School for Sorcery. Book 3
Subject(s): Coming-of-Age; Magicians; Schools
Major character(s): Gray Becq, Student; Rehanne Zalos, Student; Miryam Vedreaux, Administrator, Teacher

Time period(s): Indeterminate
Locale(s): Mythical Place

Summary: Gray Becq returns to the school for the magically gifted after coming back from another reality where demons exist. Within a few days, accidents begin to happen to his fellow students, to each of which he has some connection, suggesting that perhaps he was changed by his experience, or followed back by a demonic power.

Where it's reviewed:
Booklist, January 1, 2005, page 835

Other books by the same author:
A Perilous Power, 2004
A School for Sorcery, 2002

Other books you might like:
Diana Wynne Jones, *A Sudden Wild Magic*, 1992
Philip Pullman, *The Amber Spyglass*, 2000
J.K. Rowling, *Harry Potter and the Sorcerer's Stone*, 1998
Patricia Wrede, *Sorcery and Cecilia*, 1988
    Caroline Steverner, co-author
Mary Frances Zambreno, *Journeyman Wizard*, 1994

621

BRANDON SANDERSON

Elantris
(New York: Tor, 2005)

Story type: Magic Conflict; Quest
Subject(s): Secrets; Magic
Major character(s): Sarene, Royalty (princess); Raodon, Royalty (prince); Hrathen, Religious
Time period(s): Indeterminate
Locale(s): Arelon, Fictional Country

Summary: Princess Sarene journeys to a neighboring country for a marriage of state, but when she arrives is told that her husband-to-be has died. Suddenly legally a widow, she decides to exert her efforts to oppose a cult of religious fanatics, unaware of the fact that her betrothed is still alive and secretly laboring to free an entire hidden underclass. First fantasy novel.

Where it's reviewed:
Publishers Weekly, April 18, 2005, page 48

Other books you might like:
Peter Garrison, *The Sorcerer's Gun*, 1999
Mary Gentle, *Rats and Gargoyles*, 1990
China Mieville, *Perdido Street Station*, 2001
R.A. Salvatore, *Ascendance*, 2001
Lawrence Watt-Evans, *The Unwilling Warlord*, 1989

622

E. SEDIA

According to Crow
(Waterville, Maine: Five Star, 2005)

Story type: Sword and Sorcery; Magic Conflict
Subject(s): Magic; Quest

Fantasy

Major character(s): Josiah, Traveler, Orphan; Caleb, Religious; Crow, Traveler
Time period(s): Indeterminate
Locale(s): Mer, Fictional Country; Sium, Fictional Country

Summary: In the aftermath of a devastating magical war, resentment and racial prejudice make life difficult for Josiah, a young orphaned boy. As soon as he is old enough to leave, he sets off to discover the truth about his family, accompanied by a mysterious religious figure named Crow and two friends. Their adventures take them into a neighboring country, where they adjust to a very different culture and discover the truth about Josiah's father. First fantasy novel.

Other books you might like:
Jude Fisher, *Sorcery Rising*, 2002
Maggie Furey, *The Spirit of Stone*, 2001
Andre Norton, *Zarsthor's Bane*, 1978
Jennifer Roberson, *Sword Dancer*, 1986
Freda Warrington, *The Sapphire Throne*, 2000

623

SHARON SHINN

Mystic and Rider

(New York: Ace, 2005)

Story type: Magic Conflict; Quest
Subject(s): Quest; Secrets
Major character(s): Senneth, Religious; Kirra, Healer; Tayse, Military Personnel
Time period(s): Indeterminate
Locale(s): Gillengaria, Fictional Country

Summary: The King of Gillengaria has recently ordered that the practice of magic no longer be prohibited. His people are increasingly restive, believing that he has fallen under the influence of his new queen, who has magical powers. The king sends a group of people headed by a seer to discover how serious the problem is, but there are dissensions even among this small party.

Where it's reviewed:
Publishers Weekly, February 7, 2005, page 46

Other books by the same author:
Angel Seeker, 2004
Angelika, 2003
Jenna Starborn, 2002
Summers at Castle Auburn, 2001
Heart of Gold, 2000

Other books you might like:
Joanne Bertin, *The Last Dragonlord*, 1998
Louise Cooper, *The Sleep of Stone*, 1991
Patricia A. McKillip, *Riddle-Master*, 1999
Jennifer Roberson, *The Shapechanger's Song*, 2001
Sheri S. Tepper, *The Song of Mavin Manyshaped*, 1985

624

MICHAEL A. STACKPOLE

Perchance to Dream and Other Stories

(Waterville, Maine: Five Star, 2005)

Story type: Collection
Subject(s): Short Stories

Summary: These 16 stories, all reprints except for one original to the collection, were published between 1990 and 2005. The subject matter ranges from sword and sorcery adventure to murder mysteries in fantasy settings to stories of heroes with unusual powers. The predominant tone is action, with occasional humorous diversions.

Other books by the same author:
A Secret Atlas, 2005
The Grand Crusade, 2003
When Dragons Rage, 2002
Fortress Draconis, 2001
Onslaught, 2000

Other books you might like:
Lynn Abbey, *Cinnabar Shadows*, 1995
David Gemmell, *The Midnight Falcon*, 1999
Richard A. Knaak, *The Janus Mask*, 1995
Andrew J. Offutt, *Deathknight*, 1990
R.A. Salvatore, *The Highwayman*, 2004

625

MICHAEL A. STACKPOLE

A Secret Atlas

(New York: Bantam, 2005)

Story type: Adventure; Mystery
Subject(s): Secrets; Magic
Major character(s): Keles Anturasi, Cartographer, Explorer; Jorim Anturasi, Cartographer, Explorer; Nirati Anturasi, Businesswoman
Time period(s): Indeterminate
Locale(s): Tir, Alternate Universe

Summary: Two brothers, Keles and Jorim Anturasi, are mapmakers by trade. In the land of Tir, mapmakers have to do their work firsthand, so they are off on a series of adventures in a remote part of their world to chart the last unknown territories. Their long absence causes difficulties at home, which their sister Nirati must deal with herself.

Where it's reviewed:
Library Journal, February 15, 2005, page 123
Publishers Weekly, February 7, 2005, page 47

Other books by the same author:
The Grand Crusade, 2003
The Ghost War, 2002
When Dragons Rage, 2002
Fortress Draconis, 2001
Onslaught, 2000

Other books you might like:
David Gemmell, *The Midnight Falcon*, 1999
Simon R. Green, *Beyond the Blue Moon*, 2000

China Mieville, *The Scar*, 2002
Jennifer Roberson, *Sword-Sworn*, 2002
Lawrence Watt-Evans, *Taking Flight*, 1993

626

CHRISTOPHER STASHEFF

Saint Vidicon to the Rescue

(New York: Ace, 2005)

Story type: Humor; Contemporary
Subject(s): Humor; Computers
Major character(s): Tony Ricci, Computer Expert; Vidicon, Religious; Sandra Clavier, Computer Expert, Business-woman
Time period(s): 2000s
Locale(s): United States

Summary: Tony Ricci is hired to find out why a company's computers keep coughing up religious tracts. His investigation leads to the discovery of Saint Vidicon, whose job is to help people in trouble because of Finagle's Law. This is a lightly humorous contemporary romp that mixes computers and magic.

Other books by the same author:
Sage, 1996
Quicksilver's Knight, 1995
Shaman, 1995
M'Lady Witch, 1994
We Open on Venus, 1994

Other books you might like:
Piers Anthony, *Blue Adept*, 1981
Margaret Balle, *No Earthly Sunne*, 1994
John DeChancie, *MagicNet*, 1993
Esther Friesner, *The Sherwood Game*, 1995
Katherine Kurtz, *Saint Patrick's Gargoyle*, 2001

627

ELLEN STEIBER

A Rumor of Gems

(New York: Tor, 2005)

Story type: Contemporary; Mystery
Subject(s): Magic; Secrets
Major character(s): Lucinda de Francesco, Worker; Sebastian Keane, Antiques Dealer; Michael Fortunato, Child
Time period(s): 2000s
Locale(s): Fictional Country

Summary: In a town supposedly somewhere in the contemporary world, the sudden appearance of magical gems has a disruptive impact on nearly everyone. Some of those affected are a woman who has no wish to become involved with magic, a child who may be acting under the influence of evil spirits, and an antiques dealer who may be more than he appears.

Where it's reviewed:
Publishers Weekly, May 9, 2005, page 51

Other books by the same author:
Haunted, 2000
Grotesque, 1998
Empathy, 1997
Eve, 1997
Squeeze, 1996

Other books you might like:
Mark Anthony, *The Dark Remains*, 2001
Jeffrey Barlough, *Strange Cargo*, 2004
Tanya Huff, *The Second Summoning*, 2001
Ian R. MacLeod, *The House of Storms*, 2005
James Stoddard, *The High House*, 1999

628

CHARLES STROSS

The Hidden Family

(New York: Tor, 2005)

Story type: Alternate Universe; Science Fiction
Series: Merchant Princes. Book 2
Subject(s): Magic; Alternate History
Major character(s): Miriam Fletcher, Businesswoman; Lady Olga, Noblewoman; Matthias, Secretary
Time period(s): 2000s
Locale(s): Boston, Massachusetts; Alternate Universe

Summary: Miriam Fletcher has the ability to move from one alternate reality to another, and has established herself with her quasi-relatives in another world. She seeks to employ modern business techniques from this world in order to increase the wealth of her extended family, but in doing so finds herself having a series of exciting adventures.

Where it's reviewed:
Locus, April 2005, page 27
Publishers Weekly, April 25, 2005, page 43

Other books by the same author:
Iron Sunrise, 2004
The Atrocity Archives, 2004
The Family Trade, 2004
Singularity Sky, 2003

Other books you might like:
John Gregory Betancourt, *The Dawn of Amber*, 2002
Kenneth Bulmer, *The Wizards of Senchuria*, 1969
H. Beam Piper, *Lord Kalvan of Otherwhen*, 1965
Garfield Reeves-Stevens, *Shifter*, 1990
    Judith Reeves-Stevens, co-author
Roger Zelazny, *Nine Princes in Amber*, 1970

629

ELDON THOMPSON

The Crimson Sword

(New York: William Morrow, 2005)

Story type: Magic Conflict; Quest
Series: Legend of Asahiel. Book 1
Subject(s): Quest; Secrets
Major character(s): Jarom, Bodyguard; Allion, Warrior; Spithaera, Ruler

Time period(s): Indeterminate
Locale(s): Alson, Alternate Universe

Summary: The assassination of the king precipitates a major crisis. Jarom is assigned the task of seeking out and recovering a magical sword, which could be instrumental in restoring order and defeating the forces of evil. Unfortunately, he has little hope of succeeding, even before he discovers that a demonic queen has wakened from an age-old sleep. First fantasy novel.

Other books you might like:
R. Scott Bakker, *The Darkness That Comes Before*, 2004
Steven Erikson, *Gardens of the Moon*, 2004
Raymond E. Feist, *Rage of a Demon King*, 1997
L.E. Modesitt Jr., *Darknesses*, 2003
R.A. Salvatore, *Mortalis*, 2001

630

JULES WATSON

The White Mare

(Woodstock, New York: Overlook, 2005)

Story type: Historical; Magic Conflict
Series: Dalriada. Book 1
Subject(s): Legends; Magic
Major character(s): Rhiann, Religious, Royalty; Eremon, Expatriate, Royalty; Drust, Nobleman
Time period(s): 1st century (79)
Locale(s): Scotland

Summary: The Romans have subjugated most of the British Isles, but the Scots remain fiercely independent. Their fate may be determined by the unlikely alliance between Rhiann, a priestess, and Eremon, an exiled prince seeking to reclaim his lost throne. First novel.

Where it's reviewed:
Library Journal, February 15, 2005, page 123
Publishers Weekly, February 7, 2005, page 46

Other books you might like:
Poul Anderson, *Dahut*, 1988
Marion Zimmer Bradley, *The Forest House*, 1993
Kenneth Flint, *Cromm*, 1990
Juliet Marillier, *Daughter of the Forest*, 2000
Diana L. Paxson, *Ancestors of Avalon*, 2004

631

C.L. WERNER

Witch Finder

(Nottingham, England: Black Library, 2005)

Story type: Sword and Sorcery; Magic Conflict
Series: Warhammer
Subject(s): Magic
Major character(s): Mathias Thulman, Vampire Hunter; Streng, Servant; Sibbechai, Vampire
Time period(s): Indeterminate
Locale(s): Wurtbad, Fictional Country

Summary: A witch hunter and his assistant have taken to tracking down vampires as well, but now a powerful vampire has returned the honor, pursuing them as they travel into a remote region to battle another supernatural menace. The forces of evil mean to overthrow the existing order and spread their own power across the world.

Other books by the same author:
Blood of the Dragon, 2004
Witch Hunter, 2004
Blood Money, 2003
Blood and Steel, 2003

Other books you might like:
Mark Acres, *Dark Divide*, 1994
Jo Clayton, *Drinker of Souls*, 1986
Oliver Johnson, *The Forging of the Shadows*, 1996
Richard A. Knaak, *Ruby Flames*, 1999
Meredith Pierce, *Darkangel*, 1982

632

PAUL WITCOVER

Tumbling After

(New York: Eos, 2005)

Story type: Contemporary; Magic Conflict
Subject(s): Magic; Legends
Major character(s): Jack Doone, Child; Jilly Doone, Child; Kestrel, Mythical Creature (Aerie)
Time period(s): 2000s
Locale(s): Virginia

Summary: Two children from our world, brother and sister, share secrets known to no others. They are thrust into a pivotal role when Kestrel, a non-human creature from another magical reality, is called upon to fight a new threat against humanity, and discovers that the children are essential to his victory. Despite its child characters, this unusually intense novel is not for young adults.

Where it's reviewed:
Locus, February 2005, page 21
Publishers Weekly, January 17, 2005, page 39

Other books by the same author:
Waking Beauty, 1997

Other books you might like:
Emma Bull, *War for the Oaks*, 1987
Esther Friesner, *Sphynxes Wild*, 1989
Alan Garner, *The Weirdstone of Brisingamen*, 1960
Will Shetterly, *NeverNever*, 1993
James Stoddard, *The False House*, 2000

633

CLIVE WOODALL

One for Sorrow, Two for Joy

(New York: Ace, 2005)

Story type: Light Fantasy; Young Adult
Subject(s): Fantasy; Magic

Major character(s): Slyekin, Animal (bird); Kirrick, Animal (bird); Traska, Animal (bird)
Time period(s): Indeterminate
Locale(s): Birddom, Alternate Universe

Summary: The setting is a world where birds are intelligent and humans don't exist. Slyekin and his magpies and crows have launched a war of extermination against the other bird species, and it appears that no force can possibly save the rest of the world. Kirrick, a young robin who survives an attack on his people, goes on a perilous journey to find salvation. First novel.

Where it's reviewed:
Library Journal, December 2004, page 105
Publishers Weekly, December 20, 2004, page 41

Other books you might like:
Richard Adams, *Watership Down*, 1972
Steven Bauer, *Satyrday*, 1980
Michael Fessier, *Clovis*, 1948
Brian Jacques, *Taggerung*, 2001
Gabriel King, *The Golden Cat*, 1999

634

JOHN WRIGHT

Mists of Everness
(New York: Tor, 2005)

Story type: Magic Conflict; Quest
Series: War of the Dreaming. Book 2
Subject(s): Secrets; Quest
Major character(s): Galen Waylock, Sorcerer; Azrael de Gray, Wizard; Raven Ravenson, Warrior
Time period(s): 2000s
Locale(s): United States

Summary: Although Galen Waylock, who guards the gateway that protects humanity from the dream world, appears to have been killed, his friends are prepared to carry on the fight against evil without him. Wizard Azrael de Gray plots to regain the power he feels should be his, and gathers his own followers.

Where it's reviewed:
Locus, March 2005, page 23
Publishers Weekly, February 21, 2005, page 162

Other books by the same author:
The Last Guardians of Everness, 2004
The Golden Transcendence, 2003
The Phoenix Exultant, 2003
The Golden Age, 2002

Other books you might like:
John Gregory Betancourt, *The Dawn of Amber*, 2002
James P. Blaylock, *The Land of Dreams*, 1987
Charles De Lint, *Yarrow*, 1986
Jody Lynn Nye, *Waking in Dreamland*, 1998
Roger Zelazny, *Nine Princes in Amber*, 1970

635

JANE YOLEN
ADAM STEMPLE, Co-Author

Pay the Piper
(New York: Starscape, 2005)

Story type: Contemporary; Young Adult
Subject(s): Legends; Fairy Tales
Major character(s): Calcephony, Teenager; Gingras, Musician; Josee, Teenager
Time period(s): 2000s
Locale(s): Massachusetts

Summary: This is a modernized retelling of the story of the Pied Piper of Hamelin, who lures children away when their parents refuse to pay what they owe him. In this book, several teenagers become more interested than usual in a musical group that is giving a concert in their town.

Other books by the same author:
The Sword of the Rightful King, 2003
The Bagpiper's Ghost, 2002
Not One Damsel in Distress, 2000
The Pictish Child, 1999
Merlin, 1997

Other books you might like:
Sarah Ash, *Songspinners*, 1996
Charles De Lint, *The Harp of the Grey Rose*, 1985
Christie Golden, *Instrument of Fate*, 1996
Andrea Shettle, *Flute Song Magic*, 1990
Nancy Springer, *Metal Angel*, 1994

636

MARLY YOUMANS

Ingledove
(New York: Farrar, Straus and Giroux, 2005)

Story type: Young Adult; Quest
Subject(s): Quest
Major character(s): Ingledove, Teenager; Lang, Teenager
Time period(s): Indeterminate Past
Locale(s): Atlantis, Mythical Place

Summary: This unusual variation of the story of Atlantis has two young people from this world traveling across a mystical barrier into a lost world partially based on Cherokee mythology. Lang is seduced by the magic of a beautiful singer and his sister, Ingledove, must brave the unknown in order to save him. The novel is loosely related to *The Curse of the Raven Mocker*.

Other books by the same author:
The Curse of the Raven Mocker, 2003

Other books you might like:
Piers Anthony, *Mercycle*, 1991
K.A. Applegate, *Understanding the Unknown*, 2000
Jane Gaskell, *Strange Evil*, 1957
Stephen R. Lawhead, *Taliesin*, 1987
H. Warner Munn, *The Ship from Atlantis*, 1967

Fantasy

637

SARAH ZETTEL

For Camelot's Honor

(New York: LUNA, 2005)

Story type: Romance; Legend

Subject(s): Arthurian Legends; Magic

Major character(s): Elen, Sorceress; Morgaine, Sorceress; Sir Geraint, Knight

Time period(s): Indeterminate Past

Locale(s): England

Summary: Elen has been using her magical powers to search for the people who killed her family. She is opposed by Morgaine, the most powerful sorceress in the world.

Morgaine uses trickery to make it appear that Elen is a traitor to Camelot. Elen is forced to clear her name with only the assistance of the knight, Sir Geraint.

Other books by the same author:

In Camelot's Shadow, 2004

The Firebird's Vengeance, 2004

The Usurper's Crown, 2003

The Sorcerer's Treason, 2002

Playing God, 1998

Other books you might like:

Vera Chapman, *The Green Knight*, 1975

Carey James, *King and Raven*, 1995

Ian McDowell, *Mordred's Curse*, 1996

Susan Shwartz, *The Grail of Hearts*, 1992

Judith Tarr, *Kingdom of the Grail*, 2000

The Literary Legacy of Arkham House
by
Stefan Dziemianowicz

It may be hard for modern readers who have grown accustomed to the omnipresence of Stephen King novels in bookstores and regular appearances by Dean Koontz, Anne Rice, and Laurell K. Hamilton on the bestseller lists to accept that there was once a time when horror fiction was considered a risky undertaking for trade publication in America. The truth is, the mass popularity of horror fiction is a relatively recent phenomenon. For most of the twentieth century horror was, like most other genre fiction, considered a niche interest, and its publication limited to pulp fiction magazines and their digest-sized successors. Notwithstanding a history that extends back to the late eighteenth century, when the Gothic novel filtered out as its own subgenre of popular fiction, horror wasn't taken seriously by most publishers until long after other genres developed in its wake—mystery, science fiction—were ubiquitous in the publishing marketplace. In contrast to England, where books of supernatural fiction were regular parts of the mix of publisher book lines and not treated any differently than other forms of popular fiction, United States publishers were more discriminating—which is to say snobbish. Hardcover books of horror fiction appeared infrequently from large publishing houses, and almost never if the author was known primarily as a horror writer.

It comes as no surprise, then, that the first publisher in America to treat horror fiction seriously, and develop a horror book line, was Arkham House, a small press with a special interest in promoting horror fiction. Its founders, August Derleth and Donald Wandrei, were both writers of horror fiction, very well connected with the pulp horror, fantasy, and science fiction communities. Arkham House came into being in 1939, and its continued existence in the twenty-first century make it the longest-lived specialty press publisher devoted to horror, fantasy, and science fiction. The firm is also arguably one of the most influential publishers of modern fantastic fiction, since it proved to the publishing world that the niche market for horror fiction was large enough to support an ambitious schedule of hardcover publication of horror fiction.

Arkham House's history is virtually synonymous with the literary legacy of H.P. Lovecraft, whose fiction, which appeared predominantly in the pulp fiction magazine, *Weird Tales*, gave a modern cosmic twist to the tale of Gothic horror. Lovecraft influenced a generation of writers, many of whom wrote works inspired by his vision and became his colleagues and correspondents, among them Derleth and Wandrei. After Lovecraft's death in 1937, the two proposed a volume that would preserve his best fiction for posterity. When they were unsuccessful selling the book to trade publishers, they decided to finance their own publishing house for the sole purpose of putting Lovecraft's fiction and correspondence between hardcovers. They named their new imprint after the imaginary Massachusetts town with a sinister pedigree that served as the setting for many of Lovecraft's tales. The firm was established in Derleth's home town of Sauk City, Wisconsin (where it is still located today), far outside the New York publishing community, and it was funded in large part by money Derleth had made as a writer of popular regional and historical fiction (to which his horror fiction was a tiny adjunct).

The first Arkham House book, the Lovecraft omnibus *The Outsider and Others* (11939), is generally acknowledged as a literary landmark of horror publishing. It collected nearly two-thirds of Lovecraft's known fiction between hardcovers and became the source book from which standard editions and eventual paperback reprints of Lovecraft were carved. At the time, however, it was a white elephant, overpriced for its market, and because it took years to sell through its 1217- copy print run it would appear that trade publishers were vindicated in their belief that horror was an unremunerative market of diminishing returns.

In 1941 Derleth shifted Arkham House's publishing agenda with its second book—not a Lovecraft volume, but *Someone in the Dark*, Derleth's own first collection of

supernatural fiction. Some critics accused Derleth of vanity publishing, but the book sold well and it proved a cost-effective way for Derleth to subsidize the venture. Over the years, Derleth would keep the Arkham House stocklist active with regular and well-timed infusions of his own writing.

The decision to change Arkham House from a press devoted exclusively to Lovecraft to a publisher of other writers was one of the more important for weird fiction publishing in the twentieth century. Derleth became the sole publisher for all intents and purposes after Wandrei was inducted into military service in the early 1940s. He began issuing collections of stories by his contemporaries in the weird fiction magazines under the Arkham House imprint, rescuing a significant amount of modern weird fiction from the same oblivion that would claim much pulp fiction in other genres that never spawned an enterprising book publisher. His example may have inspired the specialty presses for science fiction, which emerged toward the end of the 1940s.

The decade of the 1940s was the most vital and important in Arkham House's history. Thirty-seven books appeared—nine in 1946 alone—many of them first books for their authors, and the titles read like a Who's Who of modern weird fiction: Clark Ashton Smith's *Out of Space and Time* (1942) and *Lost Worlds* (1944), Henry S. Whitehead's *Jumbee and Other Uncanny Tales* (1944) and *West India Light* (1946), Donald Wandrei's *The Eye and the Finger* (1944), Robert Bloch's *The Opener of the Way* (1945), Frank Belknap Long's *The Hounds of Tindalos* (1946), Robert E. Howard's *SkullFace and Others* (1946), Ray Bradbury's *Dark Carnival* (1947), Fritz Leiber's *Night's Black Agents* (1947), and Carl Jacobi's *Revelations in Black* (1947). Print runs for the books eventually topped 2000 copies, and in some instances 3000 copies—no small feat for a small publisher facing wartime paper shortages. What's more, the books were reviewed in prestigious periodicals such as *The New York Times Book Review*, often by equally prestigious writers (Eudora Welty, for example, reviewed an Arkham House volume of Henry S. Whitehead's fiction), which seemingly gave lie to publisher perception that horror fiction was beneath serious literary consideration.

The scope of Arkham House's publishing program expanded by the end of the decade. In 1947 Derleth published Evangeline Walton's *Witch House* the first of a projected program of novel-length works. Tepid sales suggested that, in contrast to trade publishing, readers of fantasy fiction were more interested in short stories. In 1947 Derleth also edited *Dark of the Moon*, the first of several volumes of macabre verse. In the years to come Arkham House would publish significant collections of poetry by Lovecraft, Smith, Long, Wandrei, Stanley McNail, L. Sprague de Camp, and Joseph Payne Brennan. In 1948 Derleth launched the *Arkham Sampler*, a magazine that would run eight issues and be instrumental in promoting fiction and nonfiction by

Arkham House writers. With the publication of A.E. van Vogt's *Slan* in 1947, Derleth signaled his intention to tap the equally vast science fiction market of the time, but curtailed these ambitions shortly after the explosion of science fiction small press publishing began at the same time. (Some of the science fiction projects Derleth relinquished eventually were published, in slightly altered form, by the speciality science fiction houses that emerged in the years after World War II. Prime Press, Gnome Press, Fantasy Press, Shasta, and FPCI all took their cue from Arkham House, and their contributions are recognized today as the cornerstone of modern science fiction publishing.) Derleth also invented the Mycroft and Moran imprint in 1947 to bring out mystery fiction starting with his own Conan Doyle pastiches in *In Re: Sherlock Holmes*, but much of the fiction that eventually appeared under this imprint had enough supernaturalism that it was indistinguishable from regular Arkham house fare.

With the publication of J. Sheridan Le Fanu's *Green Tea and Other Ghost Stories* in 1945, Derleth indicated an interest in bringing readers works of classic horror fiction by British writers whom most American readers would be largely unfamiliar with. In years to come, Arkham House would publish books by Cynthia Asquith, Algernon Blackwood, H. Russell Wakefield, Arthur Machen, A.E. Coppard, John Metcalfe, and William Hope Hodgson, whose *The House on the Borderland and Other Novels* (1946) and *Carnacki the Ghost-Finder* (1947) were instrumental for reviving interest in a neglected writer whose fiction is recognized today as an important bridge between the Victorian and modern weird tale.

The most auspicious event of this interval was the publication in 1946 of *The Lurker at the Threshold*, billed as a collaborative novel by Lovecraft and Derleth. Derleth claimed to have completed a fragment left by Lovecraft, but the bulk of the text was his own. Volumes of similar "posthumous collaborations" would appear—*The Survivor and Others* (1957), *The Dark Brotherhood and Others* (1966) and *The Shuttered Room* (1959) and the all-inclusive *The Watchers out of Time and Others* (1974)—most of the stories suggested, at best, by a line or phrase jotted by Lovecraft in his commonplace book. Clearly, Derleth recognized that Lovecraft was Arkham House's drawing card, and with the finite body of Lovecraft's work that could be published, something had to be done to sustain his salability. Derleth dutifully farmed these stories out when he could for initial publication in *Weird Tales* and other magazines to keep Lovecraft's name and Arkham House's prospects alive. These stories are also where one sees the origins of the Cthulhu Mythos—the controversial framework Derleth imposed on the work of Lovecraft and his colleagues and which would ultimately inspire a mountain of pastiches by other writers that today dwarfs Lovecraft's total output.

The fulminant growth of the 1940s was replaced by retrenchment in the 1950s. The emergence between 1945 and 1948 of a number of presses specializing in science

fiction meant that Arkham House was not the only specialty publisher in town. These presses tended to mine sources that Derleth stayed away from, but some occasionally poached on his territory with works of weird and supernatural fiction, and they doubtless competed for reader attention. Arkham House published only half as many books as it had the decade before, many of them by Derleth and a significant number of diminutive books of poetry, possibly subsidized by their authors. The book of greatest note from this period is *Nine Horrors and a Dream* (1958) by Joseph Payne Brennan, one of the last writers nurtured in *Weird Tales*.

The publishing house reclaimed some ground in the 1960s, a decade distinguished for several trends. In 1962 Derleth published an anthology of all new weird fiction, *Dark Mind, Dark Heart*. Nearly two decades before, Derleth had published a series of anthologies with trade publisher Pellegrini and Cudahy, including *Sleep No More*, *Who Knocks?*, *The Night Side*, and *The Sleeping and the Dead*—which had showcased reprints of Arkham House writers in volumes sold in a trade market. This new anthology featured all new fiction and would prove the first of four anthologies—including *Over the Edge*, *Travellers by Night*, and *Dark Things*—Derleth would assemble before his death. More important, the 1960s were the decade that saw the consolidation of Arkham House's Lovecraft focus. The standard editions of Lovecraft began appearing in 1963 with *The Dunwich Horror and Others*. It would be joined by *At the Mountains of Madness and Other Novels* (1964) and *Dagon and Other Macabre Tales* (1965) to become the uniform edition of Lovecraft's fiction still in print today. Also, Lovecraft's long-projected collected letters began appearing in 1965, ultimately growing to five volumes published through 1976.

Arkham House published in 1964 *The Inhabitant of the Lake and Less Welcome Tenants*, a collection of Lovecraft pastiches by Ramsey Campbell, who had made his first professional sale to the *Dark Mind, Dark Heart* anthology. This proved an auspicious publishing event in several regards. Derleth had become increasingly proprietary over the years of the of Lovecraftian elements in horror fiction, to the extent that he openly discouraged writers from borrowing from Lovecraft's Cthulhu mythology without seeking permission from Arkham House. The publication of Campbell's volume was a preemptive strike against such unsanctioned referencing of Lovecraft, with Derleth essentially appointing a new writer to carry on the Lovecraft tradition. With the publication of his *Tales of the Cthulhu Mythos* compilation in 1969, Derleth formally anointed contributors Campbell, Brian Lumley, Colin Wilson, and James Wade as new writers in the Lovecraft tradition to whom the torch was passed.

This infusion of new blood was important for the publisher. By the 1970s, Arkham House was still predominantly publishing writers from the pulp markets that had entertained a previous generation. The appearance of

Lumley's first collection, *The Caller of the Black*, in 1971, and most significantly Ramsey Campbell's breakthrough collection *Demons by Daylight*, recognized as a cornerstone of modern horror fiction, ensured that Arkham House would continue to be relevant to a new generation of weird fiction readers. Derleth's death in 1971, however, and ensuing legal wrangles with co-founder Donald Wandrei pitched Arkham House into a chaotic situation for several years that changed with the induction of James Turner in 1975 as the new editor. Turner dutifully sustained the Lovecraft backlist and oversaw such traditional Arkham House projects as S.T. Joshi's reissue of the revised corrected text of Lovecraft's standard works between 1984 and 1986. However, under Turner, Arkham House's publications shifted increasingly toward science fiction, a controversial change. The quality of Turner's choices were indisputable: James Tiptree, Jr., John Kessel, Joanna Russ, James Blaylock, Ian Macleod, J.G. Ballard, and in the case of Lucius Shepard and Michael Shea, authors who effectively wrote science fiction faithful to the horror tradition. To some extent, Turner's decision also reflected the rampant competition in the horror field from the profusion of specialty presses that arose during horror's boom years in the 1980s (thanks, ironically, to the tradition and standards Arkham House had helped to create), whereas science fiction had few. Arguably, Turner was consistent in following Derleth's ambition to publish the best in contemporary fantasy fiction, even if that included science fiction.

With Turner's departure in 1999, Arkham House returned squarely to the supernatural field, with the retrospective volume *Arkham's Masters of Horror* edited by Peter Ruber and collections of fiction by Nelson Bond and Derleth upholding its pulp ties, and new novels by Fred Durbin and John Harvey indicating its willingness to introduce new authors. Arkham House is no longer the distinguished or exclusive publisher it once was, but merely another player in a supernatural fiction market dominated by specialty presses. Yet it is safe to say without Arkham House, the horror publishing market as it stands today would not exist.

Readers who want to know more about Arkham House and its legacy should consult Sheldon Jaffery's *The Arkham House Companion*, (Starmont House, 1989), a revision of his previous *Horrors and Unpleasantries* (Popular Press, 1982), and S.T. Joshi's *Sixty Years of Arkham House* (Arkham House, 1999), which incorporates most of the text of Derleth's earlier *Thirty Years of Arkham House* (Arkham House, 1969). Also of interest are the extensive biographical notes in *Arkham's Masters of Horror* (Arkham House, 1999), much of whose information is drawn from correspondence with writers in the Arkham House publisher's files.

Recommended Titles

Entries for the following books are included in this volume.

John Connolly, *Nocturnes*

Fritz Leiber, *Horrible Imaginings*

H.P. Lovecraft, *Tales*

Lee Martinez, *Gil's All Fright Diner*

Tom Piccirilli, *November Mourns*

Lucius Shepard, *Eternity and Other Stories*

Lisa Tuttle, *The Mysteries*

Horror Titles

638

NANCY ATHERTON

Aunt Dimity and the Next of Kin
(New York: Viking, 2005)

Story type: Mystery
Series: Aunt Dimity. Book 10
Subject(s): Family Relations; Mystery
Major character(s): Lori Shepherd, Volunteer, Detective—Amateur; Elizabeth Beacham, Aged Person; Dimity Westwood, Spirit
Time period(s): 2000s
Locale(s): Finch, England

Summary: While volunteering at the local hospital, Lori befriends Elizabeth, a solitary patient who is terminally ill with cancer. Upon Elizabeth's death, Lori discovers the woman was wealthy and once well connected with a wide network of friends. When her efforts to track down Elizabeth's missing brother are thwarted by the lawyer representing the estate, Lori enlists the help of Aunt Dimity, a deceased family friend who communicates with her through writing in a magic journal, to help her get to the bottom of Elizabeth's secret life and the intrigue surrounding her death.

Other books by the same author:
Aunt Dimity, Snowbound, 2004
Aunt Dimity Takes a Holiday, 2003
Aunt Dimity, Detective, 2001
Aunt Dimity Beats the Devil, 2000
Aunt Dimity's Christmas, 1999

Other books you might like:
Yasmine Galenorn, *Ghost of a Chance*, 2003
Alice Kimberly, *The Ghost and Mrs. McClure*, 2004
Graham Masterton, *Rook*, 1996
Thorne Smith, *Topper*, 1926
L.L. Thrasher, *Charlie's Bones*, 1998

639

L.A. BANKS

The Bitten
(New York: St. Martin's Griffin, 2004)

Story type: Vampire Story
Series: Vampire Huntress Legend. Book 4
Subject(s): Romance; Supernatural; Vampires
Major character(s): Damali Richards, Musician, Vampire Hunter; Carlos Rivera, Vampire; Berkfield, Detective—Police
Time period(s): 2000s
Locale(s): Beverly Hills, California; Sydney, Australia

Summary: Damali and her vampire lover Carlos help suppress a vampire uprising in Brazil, but one of the vampire insurgents manages to steal a Key, or vial containing the blood of Jesus Christ. The couple hasten to Australia for a showdown with the thief, for it has been foretold that spilling the blood will open the Sixth Seal chronicled in the biblical Book of Revelations, unleashing Armageddon. Fourth book in a series in which Damali, a hip-hop performer, and her band double as vampire hunters.

Where it's reviewed:
Publishers Weekly, December 13, 2004, page 49

Other books by the same author:
The Forbidden, 2005
The Awakening, 2004
The Hunted, 2004
Minion, 2003

Other books you might like:
Nancy Collins, *Midnight Blue*, 1995
Christopher Golden, *Immortal*, 1999
    Nancy Holder, co-author
Laurell K. Hamilton, *Guilty Pleasures*, 1993
Mel Odom, *Blade*, 1998
John Steakley, *Vampire$*, 1990

640

L.A. BANKS

The Forbidden

(New York: St. Martin's Griffin, 2005)

Story type: Vampire Story
Series: Vampire Huntress Legend. Book 5
Subject(s): Demons; Supernatural; Vampires
Major character(s): Damali Richards, Musician, Vampire Hunter; Carlos Rivera, Vampire; Lilith, Demon
Time period(s): 2000s
Locale(s): Los Angeles, California; Sydney, Australia

Summary: Plans to impregnate vampire hunter Damali Richards with the seed of a vampire and give birth to the anti-Christ have failed, and now Damali's lover Carlos, who had been manipulated into impregnating her by the Chairman of the Vampire Council, is resurrected from his ashes as a normal human being. Dissatisfied with this state of affairs, the Devil dispatches Lilith from the seventh circle of Hell to hunt down Carlos and find Damali. At the very least, Lilith hopes to steal the fertilized egg that Damali miscarried and provide a surrogate womb for it herself.

Other books by the same author:
The Damned, 2006
The Bitten, 2005
The Awakening, 2004
The Hunted, 2004
Minion, 2003

Other books you might like:
Peter Atkins, *Morningstar*, 1993
Nancy Collins, *Sunglasses After Dark*, 1989
Laurell K. Hamilton, *Incubus Dreams*, 2004
Susan Sizemore, *Laws of the Blood*, 2000
John Steakley, *Vampire$*, 1990

641

CARRIE BEBRIS

Suspense and Sensibility

(New York: Forge, 2005)

Story type: Occult
Series: Mr. & Mrs. Darcy. Book 2
Subject(s): Mystery; Occult; Supernatural
Major character(s): Elizabeth Bennet Darcy, Gentlewoman, Spouse; Fitzwilliam Darcy, Gentleman, Spouse; Harry Dashwood, Young Man
Time period(s): 1810s (1813)
Locale(s): London, England

Summary: Shortly after Elizabeth's sister Kitty becomes engaged to young Harry Dashwood, Harry begins to show increasingly erratic and unspeakable behavior. Elizabeth and her husband, Mr. Darcy, investigate and discover that Harry has recently returned from his family home bringing with him a mirror which played a role in rituals of the Hellfire Club, which several of his father's friends were members of. In order to save Harry, Elizabeth and Darcy must confront supernatural evil. Second book in a series featuring characters from the novels of Jane Austen and their involvement in mysteries with a macabre edge.

Other books by the same author:
Pride and Prescience, 2004
Pool of Radiance, 2001
Bloodspawn, 2000
Hogunmark, 1999
The Ruins of Myth Drannor, 1993

Other books you might like:
Jane Austen, *Pride and Prejudice*, 1813
Emmanuel Carrere, *Gothic Romance*, 1990
William Hjortsberg, *Nevermore*, 1994
Stephen Marlowe, *The Lighthouse at the End of the World*, 1995
Tim Powers, *The Stress of Her Regard*, 1989

642

E.F. BENSON

Sea Mist

(Ashcroft, British Columbia: Ash-Tree Press, 2005)

Story type: Collection
Series: Collected Spook Stories. Book 5
Subject(s): Horror; Short Stories; Supernatural

Summary: This book consists of 17 stories of horror and the supernatural by a writer whose work is considered a bridge between the classic Jamesian ghost story and the modern horror tale. The contents all were published in the years 1927-1940 and include ''Monkeys,'' in which vengeful simian spirits attack a pathologist known for his animal experimentation; ''The Hanging of Alfred Wadham,'' in which the ghost of a wrongly executed man haunts those responsible for his death; and ''The Wishing-Well,'' a tale of spell and counterspell in which a woman uses folk magic to curse the object of her unrequited love. Edited by Jack Adrian, who also includes several essays by Benson on ghost story writing and writers, this is the fifth volume in a series that reprints all of the author's short weird tales in the order of their publication.

Other books by the same author:
The Face, 2003
Mrs. Amworth, 2001
The Passenger, 1999
The Terror by Night, 1998
The Collected Ghost Stories of E.F. Benson, 1992

Other books you might like:
Algernon Blackwood, *Ancient Sorceries and Other Weird Stories*, 2002
A.M. Burrage, *Warning Whispers*, 1988
William Fryer Harvey, *Midnight Tales*, 1946
M.R. James, *The Best Ghost Stories of M.R. James*, 1944
H. Russell Wakefield, *They Return at Evening*, 1928

643

DAVID BISHOP

Suffer the Children

(Nottingham, England: Black Flame, 2005)

Story type: Occult
Series: Nightmare on Elm Street. Book 1
Subject(s): Dreams and Nightmares; Supernatural; Teen Relationships
Major character(s): Alex Corwin, Teenager; Peter O'Mahoney, Teenager; Chris Harris, Teenager
Time period(s): 2000s
Locale(s): Springwood, Ohio

Summary: Six high school students take part in an experiment to test an anti-insomnia drug, unaware that its creation has been engineered from beyond the grave by Freddy Krueger, a former child molester who was burned to death by his community but whose existence is perpetuated unnaturally through the nightmares of his child victims. Once asleep, the teenagers become unwilling agents in Freddy's scheme to terrify the town. First in a series of books to be based on Wes Craven's 1984 film *Nightmare on Elm Street*.

Other books by the same author:
The Strangelove Gambit, 2005
Bad Moon Rising, 2004

Other books you might like:
Jeffrey Cooper, *The Nightmares on Elm Street: Parts 1, 2 and 3: The Continuing Story*, 1987
Ray Garton, *The Nightmares on Elm Street: Parts 4 and 5*, 1989
Martin H. Greenberg, *Nightmares on Elm Street: Freddy Krueger's Seven Sweetest Dreams*, 1991
Tim Waggoner, *Dreamspawn*, 2005

644

ALGERNON BLACKWOOD

The Empty House and Other Ghost Stories

(Holicong, Pennsylvania: Wildside, 2005)

Story type: Collection; Ghost Story
Subject(s): Horror; Short Stories; Ghosts

Summary: Presented here are eight ghostly tales by a prominent writer of horror fiction of the early 20th century. Included are "The Haunted Island," about an explorer who sees a ghostly premonition of his own death; "Keeping His Promise," about a friend who visits a student from the afterlife; and the title story, about a house haunted by the ghost of a murderer. Reprint of a landmark first collection of ghost stories first published in England in 1906.

Other books by the same author:
The Best Ghost Stories of Algernon Blackwood, 1973
The Doll and One Other, 1946
Tongues of Fire and Other Sketches, 1924
Incredible Adventures, 1914
The Listener and Other Stories, 1907

Other books you might like:
E.F. Benson, *The Room in the Tower*, 1912
M.R. James, *Ghost Stories of an Antiquary*, 1904
J. Sheridan Le Fanu, *Green Tea and Other Ghost Stories*, 1945
Oliver Onions, *The Collected Ghost Stories of Oliver Onions*, 1971
Sarban, *Ringstones and Other Curious Tales*, 1951

645

ROBERT BLOCH

The Fear Planet and Other Unusual Destinations

(Burton, Michigan: Subterranean, 2005)

Story type: Collection; Science Fiction
Series: Reader's Bloch
Subject(s): Horror; Science Fiction; Short Stories

Summary: This collection of 20 stories of science fiction, several with a horrific edge, are by a writer whose specialty was weird fiction and who is best known as the author of the novel *Psycho*. Selections include the title story, about an unfortunate mission to a planet populated by ravenous plants; "The Phantom from the Film," in which a monster from a horror film achieves independent life and goes on a rampage; and "The End of Science Fiction," a play on ideas and themes from the horror tales of H.P. Lovecraft set at a science fiction convention. Edited and introduced by Stefan Dziemianowicz with a cover design by Gahan Wilson. Published as a signed limited edition hardcover.

Other books by the same author:
Bitter Ends, 1988
Final Reckonings, 1988
Last Rites, 1988
The Best of Robert Bloch, 1977
Fear Today, Gone Tomorrow, 1971

Other books you might like:
Jerome Bixby, *Space by the Tail*, 1964
Anthony Boucher, *The Compleat Werewolf and Other Stories of Fantasy and Science Fiction*, 1969
Ray Bradbury, *The Golden Apples of the Sun*, 1953
Fredric Brown, *From These Ashes*, 2000
Henry Kuttner, *The Best of Henry Kuttner*, 1975

646

JEFFREY B. BURTON

Shadow Play

(Clifton, Virginia: Pocol, 2005)

Story type: Collection
Subject(s): Horror; Short Stories; Supernatural

Summary: This first book collects 20 short tales of horror and suspense by an author who publishes predominantly with the small press. Seven stories are original to the book. Contents include "Shadow Play," in which a man recounts how since childhood shadow figures only he can see act on his murderous will, and "Eykiltimac Stump Acres," in which the ram-

Horror

blings of an Alzheimer's disease victim are clues to horrible revelations of his criminal past.

Other books you might like:
Gary A. Braunbeck, *Things Left Behind*, 1991
Janet Fox, *A Witch's Dozen*, 2003
Brian Keene, *Fear of Gravity*, 2004
Kurt Newton, *The House Spider and Other Strange Visitors*, 1999
Shane Ryan Staley, *I'll Be Damned*, 2001

647

JIM BUTCHER

Dead Beat

(New York: Penguin, 2005)

Story type: Vampire Story
Series: Dresden Files. Book 7
Subject(s): Occult; Supernatural; Vampires
Major character(s): Harry Dresden, Detective—Private; Karrin Murphy, Police Officer; Mavra, Vampire
Time period(s): 2000s
Locale(s): Chicago, Illinois

Summary: To help his girlfriend, Karrin, who is being blackmailed by the vampire Mavra, psychic detective Harry Dresden agrees to provide Mavra with the Word of Kemmler, a necromantic spell of extraordinary power. The spell, alas, has a reputation well-known to the occult community, and as Halloween approaches Harry finds himself in hot competition with six other necromancers who hope grab the spell, and its powers, for themselves. In this series, Dresden, a wizard leading the Special Investigations unit of the Chicago Police Department, protects mortals from supernatural invasions from the occult dimension.

Other books by the same author:
Blood Rites, 2004
Death Masks, 2003
Summer Knight, 2002
Grave Peril, 2001
Fool Moon, 2000

Other books you might like:
P.N. Elrod, *Bloodlist*, 1990
Charles L. Grant, *Goblins*, 1995
Laurell K. Hamilton, *The Laughing Corpse*, 1994
Charlaine Harris, *Dead as a Doornail*, 2005
Tanya Huff, *Smoke and Mirrors*, 2005

648

PAT CADIGAN

Jason X

(Nottingham, England: Black Flame, 2005)

Story type: Science Fiction; Serial Killer
Series: Jason X
Subject(s): Horror; Scientific Experiments; Serial Killers
Major character(s): Jason Voorhees, Serial Killer; Rowan LaFontaine, Scientist; Braithwaite Lowe, Professor
Time period(s): 25th century (2455)

Locale(s): Amherst, New Hampshire

Summary: An experiment to cryogenically freeze indestructible serial killer Jason Vorhees accidentally traps a scientist inside the preservation chamber with him. More than four centuries later, when most of the earth's population has moved off-planet onto artificially constructed living units in space, a research team stumbles upon the intact laboratory and thaws Jason and the scientist out. As Jason starts his killing rampage once more, the scientist and the research team struggle desperately to find a way to neutralize him before he eliminates all of them aboard their spaceship. A novelization of the script for a film in the *Friday the Thirteenth* series, written by Todd Farmer and based on characters created by Victor Miller.

Other books by the same author:
Jason X: The Experiment, 2005
Cellular, 2004
Upgrade/Sensuous Cindy, 2004
Avatar, 1999
Lost in Space: Promised Land, 1999

Other books you might like:
Alan Dean Foster, *Alien*, 1979
Simon Hawke, *Friday the Thirteenth: Jason Lives*, 1986
Simon Hawke, *Friday the Thirteenth. Volume 1*, 1987
Alex Johnson, *Jason X: Death Moon*, 2005
Eric Morse, *Friday the Thirteenth: The Carnival*, 1994

649

PAT CADIGAN

Jason X: The Experiment

(Nottingham, England: Black Flame, 2005)

Story type: Science Fiction; Serial Killer
Series: Jason X
Subject(s): Horror; Scientific Experiments; Serial Killers
Major character(s): Lynne Bowes, Journalist; Timothy Olsen, Scientist; Jason Voorhees, Serial Killer
Time period(s): 25th century
Locale(s): Earth II, Planet—Imaginary

Summary: Killing machine Jason Voorhees was thought to have been destroyed in an explosion in outer space, but a fragment of his remains falls to Earth II and the nanobots previously implanted in his body set about reconstructing him. When the military begins studying him as a potential weapon, Jason escapes into subterranean tunnels beneath the laboratory and embarks on his serial killing spree once more. A novelization of the script for a film in the *Friday the Thirteenth* series, written by Todd Farmer and based on characters created by Victor Miller.

Other books by the same author:
Jason X, 2005
Cellular, 2004
Upgrade/Sensuous Cindy, 2004
Avatar, 1999
Lost in Space: Promised Land, 1999

Other books you might like:
Alan Dean Foster, *Alien*, 1979
Simon Hawke, *Friday the Thirteenth: Jason Lives*, 1986

Simon Hawke, *Friday the Thirteenth. Volume 1*, 1987
Alex Johnson, *Jason X: Death Moon*, 2005
Eric Morse, *Friday the Thirteenth: The Carnival*, 1994

650

DOUGLAS CLEGG

The Abandoned

(New York: Leisure, 2005)

Story type: Haunted House
Subject(s): Horror; Small Town Life; Supernatural
Major character(s): Ronnie Pond, Teenager; Kazi Vrabec, Child; Sam Pratt, Teenager
Time period(s): 2000s
Locale(s): Watch Point, New York

Summary: Harrow Academy, a haunted former school for boys, has been abandoned for years since an attempt to exorcise its ghosts. When a mysterious night watchman comes to town to reopen the school, the townsfolk in Watch Point find themselves troubled by horrible nightmares that suggest Harrow's malignant influence is leaking out. Something must be done to prevent those bad dreams from becoming worse realities. Fourth novel set at the Harrow Academy.

Other books by the same author:
Afterlife, 2004
The Attraction, 2004
Nightmare House, 2003
The Infinite, 2001
Mischief, 2000

Other books you might like:
Tom Elliott, *The Dwelling*, 1989
Bentley Little, *House*, 1997
Richard Matheson, *Hell House*, 1971
Peter Straub, *Floating Dragon*, 1982
T.M. Wright, *The School*, 1990

651

JOHN CONNOLLY

The Black Angel

(New York: Atria, 2005)

Story type: Reanimated Dead
Subject(s): Cults; Horror; Suspense
Major character(s): Charlie Parker, Detective—Private; Rachel, Psychologist; Louis, Criminal (assassin)
Time period(s): 2000s
Locale(s): Portland, Maine; New York, New York

Summary: Private eye Charlie Parker often takes cases with supernatural overtones. His latest involves the cousin of his hit man confidante, Louis, a prostitute who recently disappeared. When Parker discovers she was involved with the theft of an ancient manuscript that divulged the whereabouts of the statue of a fallen angel, he speculates that she was done away with by the Believers, a creepy cult who believe themselves to be fallen angels.

Other books by the same author:
Bad Men, 2003

The White Road, 2002
The Killing Kind, 2001
Dark Hollow, 2000
Every Dead Thing, 1999

Other books you might like:
Dan Brown, *The Da Vinci Code*, 2003
Graham Masterton, *The Doorkeepers*, 2001
Douglas Preston, *Brimstone*, 2004
    Lincoln Child, co-author
Stephen Woodworth, *With Red Hands*, 2005

652

JOHN CONNOLLY

Nocturnes

(New York: Atria, 2004)

Story type: Collection
Subject(s): Horror; Short Stories; Supernatural

Summary: This first collection of modern horror stories in the classic tradition is from a writer best known as a crime novelist. ''The Cancer Cowboy Rides'' is the story of a man who can spread cancer through his handshake. ''Miss Froom, Vampire'' tells of a female vampire who hides her true nature behind the facade of a kindly old spinster. ''Mr. Pettinger's Demon'' tells of a demonic creature that lives beneath a church. The novella ''The Reflecting Eye'' features the author's series character, private detective Charlie Parker, investigating a house haunted by the legacy of the child killer who once lived there. Originally published in the UK in 2004.

Other books by the same author:
Bad Men, 2003
The White Road, 2002
The Killing Kind, 2001
Dark Hollow, 2000
Every Dead Thing, 1999

Other books you might like:
Robert Aickman, *Cold Hand in Mine*, 1975
Ramsey Campbell, *Alone with the Horrors*, 1993
Joyce Carol Oates, *Haunted: Tales of the Grotesque*, 1994
Peter Straub, *Houses Without Doors*, 1990
Lisa Tuttle, *Ghosts and Other Lovers*, 2001

653

JOHN MICHAEL CURLOVICH

The Blood of Kings

(Boston: Alyson, 2005)

Story type: Vampire Story
Subject(s): Homosexuality/Lesbianism; Supernatural; Vampires
Major character(s): Jamie Dunn, Student, Homosexual; Danilo Semenkaru, Professor (Egyptologist), Immortal
Time period(s): 2000s
Locale(s): Pittsburgh, Pennsylvania; Paris, France

Summary: On the rebound from a break-up with his lover, Jamie falls hard for Danilo Semenkaru, who teaches a class on Egyptology and who reciprocates Jamie's amorous feelings.

Shortly after several deaths on campus in which student victims are found drained of their blood, Jamie travels with Danilo to Paris, where he is perplexed to see a figure in an exhibition of ancient Egyptian artifacts who bears a striking resemblance to the professor. Danilo explains that he is descended from a bloodline of immortal kings who must prey on others in order to survive, and he offers Jamie the choice of returning to the world of mortals, or joining him in his culture of death and immortality. The author also writes horror novels as Michael Paine, but this is the first book published under his given name.

Other books you might like:
John Peyton Cooke, *Out for Blood*, 1991
Scott Edelman, *The Gift*, 1990
Anne Rice, *The Vampire Lestat*, 1985
Michael Schiefelbein, *The Vampire Thrall*, 2003

654

MARYJANICE DAVIDSON

Derik's Bane

(New York: Berkley Sensation, 2005)

Story type: Werewolf Story
Series: Wyndham Werewolf Tales
Subject(s): Humor; Romance; Werewolves
Major character(s): Derik Gardner, Cook, Werewolf; Sara Gunn, Nurse, Witch
Time period(s): 2000s
Locale(s): Monterey, California; Salem, Massachusetts

Summary: In this screwball paranormal romance, Derik, a werewolf newly turned alpha, is charged by his pack to travel to California and "take care of" Sara Gunn, a nurse unaware that she is the reincarnation of Arthurian witch Morgan Le Fay. Derik bungles his task, but he and Sara fall in love, and the two are given a new duty to perform together: to travel to Massachusetts and dispose of Arthur's Chosen, who are plotting Sara's death so that the legendary King Arthur can return.

Other books by the same author:
Undead and Unemployed, 2004
Undead and Unwed, 2004

Other books you might like:
Peter S. Beagle, *Lila the Werewolf*, 1969
Michael Cadnum, *St. Peter's Wolf*, 1991
Dennis Danvers, *Wilderness*, 1991
Cheri Scotch, *The Werewolf's Touch*, 1993
Jane Toombs, *Under the Shadow*, 1992

655

HARLAN ELLISON

Strange Wine

(New York: iBooks, 2005)

Story type: Collection
Subject(s): Fantasy; Short Stories; Supernatural

Summary: Ellison's 15 stories span the horror, fantasy, mystery, and science fiction genres. The title story is a tale of fantastically displaced identity. "Croatoan" is a dark fantasy

in which a man's search for an unborn child in the sewer systems under New York City reflects his allegorical quest to come to terms with his own responsibilities. "Killing Bernstein" is a hard-boiled crime story. Originally published in 1978.

Other books by the same author:
Slippage, 1998
Angry Candy, 1988
Stalking the Nightmare, 1982
Shatterday, 1980
Deathbird Stories, 1975

Other books you might like:
Graham Joyce, *Partial Eclipse and Other Stories*, 2003
Fritz Leiber, *Shadows with Eyes*, 1962
Dan Simmons, *Prayers to Broken Stones*, 1990
Michael Marshall Smith, *More Tomorrow and Other Stories*, 2003
Gene Wolfe, *Innocents Aboard*, 2004

656

JOHN FARRIS

Phantom Nights

(New York: Tor, 2005)

Story type: Ghost Story
Subject(s): Children; Race Relations; Supernatural
Major character(s): Alex Gambier, Child, Handicapped (mute); Mally Shaw, Nurse; Leland Howard, Political Figure
Time period(s): 1950s (1952)
Locale(s): Night Shade, Tennessee

Summary: Believing that his father revealed to black nurse Mally Shaw that he was an embezzler and thief, southern aristocrat and political hopeful Leland Howard abducts and kills her to ensure her silence. Mally, however, only days before, had befriended mute Alex Gambier, and through Alex Mally's ghost schemes for justice and revenge.

Where it's reviewed:
Publishers Weekly, January 10, 2005, page 44

Other books by the same author:
The Fury and the Power, 2003
Solar Eclipse, 1999
The Fury and the Terror, 1999
Soon She Will Be Gone, 1997
Dragonfly, 1995

Other books you might like:
Jack Cady, *The Well*, 1980
Stephen King, *Bag of Bones*, 1998
Joe R. Lansdale, *The Bottoms*, 2000
Robert R. McCammon, *Boy's Life*, 1991
Craig Spector, *Underground*, 2005

657

CHRISTA FAUST

Burned/One Night at Mercy

(New York: Black Flame, 2005)

Story type: Collection
Series: Twilight Zone
Subject(s): Horror; Short Stories; Supernatural

Summary: This volume contains novelizations of two stories dramatized on the revived ''Twilight Zone'' television series originally created by Rod Serling. ''Burned'' tells of the reanimated essences of two children who burned to death and seek to avenge themselves against the person who started the fire. In ''One Night at Mercy,'' death takes a holiday when the Grim Reaper checks into a hospital and asks a physician's advice because he's tired of collecting souls.

Other books by the same author:
Dreamspawn, 2005
Hoodtown, 2004
Control Freak, 1998

Other books you might like:
Pat Cadigan, *Upgrade/Sensuous Cindy*, 2004
Jay Russell, *Memphis/The Pool Guy*, 2004
Jay Slater, *Sunrise/Into the Light*, 2004
K.C. Winters, *Chosen/The Placebo Effect*, 2005

658

CHRISTA FAUST

Dreamspawn

(Nottingham, England: Black Flame, 2005)

Story type: Occult
Series: Nightmare on Elm Street
Subject(s): Dreams and Nightmares; Supernatural; Teen Relationships
Major character(s): Jane DeHaan, Teenager; Lola Cole, Teenager; Amber Dunn, Teenager
Time period(s): 2000s
Locale(s): Springwood, California

Summary: Newly transferred to Hemingway High School, Jane finds herself an outsider among her cruel and superficial peers. When she joins the Petticoat Mafia, an informal gang of other teen misfits, she isn't aware their collective despair will summon Freddy Krueger, a demonic being who infiltrates the dreams of teenagers, and who, for an unspeakable price, will lay waste to the whole school for them. This is part of a series of books based on Wes Craven's 1984 film *Nightmare on Elm Street*.

Other books by the same author:
Burned/One Night at Mercy, 2005
Hoodtown, 2004
Control Freak, 1998

Other books you might like:
Jeffrey Cooper, *The Nightmares on Elm Street: Parts 1, 2 and 3: The Continuing Story*, 1987

Ray Garton, *The Nightmares on Elm Street: Parts 4 and 5*, 1989
Martin H. Greenberg, *Nightmares on Elm Street: Freddy Krueger's Seven Sweetest Dreams*, 1991
Stephen King, *Carrie*, 1974
Tim Waggoner, *Dreamspawn*, 2005

659

YASMINE GALENORN

Murder under a Mystic Moon

(New York: Berkley Prime Crime, 2005)

Story type: Mystery
Series: Chintz 'n China Mysteries. Book 3
Subject(s): Legends; Mystery; Monsters
Major character(s): Emerald O'Brien, Psychic, Store Owner (tea shop); Anna Murray, Police Officer
Time period(s): 2000s
Locale(s): Chiqetaw, Washington

Summary: Emerald O'Brien, proprietor of the Chintz 'n China tea shop, is consulted by her friend Jimbo to investigate the death of a biker buddy found mutilated in the woods outside of town. The police have blamed a local cougar for the killing but Emerald, who possesses psychic sensitivity, knows the town is a paranormally charged location. She entertains the idea that the legendary Klakatat monster is the culprit, even as her investigations increasingly suggest that a more human murderer may have been responsible.

Other books by the same author:
Legend of the Jade Dragon, 2004
Ghost of a Chance, 2003
Embracing the Moon, 1998

Other books you might like:
Susan Wittig Albert, *Dead Man's Bones*, 2005
Cleo Coyle, *Through the Grinder*, 2004
Catherine Dain, *Darkness at the Door*, 2001
Rosemary Edghill, *Bell, Book and Murder*, 1998
Douglas Preston, *Still Life with Crows*, 2003
    Lincoln Child, co-author

660

STEPHEN GALLAGHER

The Spirit Box

(Burton, Michigan: Subterranean, 2005)

Story type: Psychological Suspense; Wild Talents
Subject(s): Crime and Criminals; Drugs; Scientific Experiments
Major character(s): John Bishop, Businessman; Rachel Young, Maintenance Worker; Cyrus Behan, Maintenance Worker
Time period(s): 2000s
Locale(s): Charlotte, North Carolina

Summary: While grieving over the death of his teenage daughter from a drug overdose, John Bishop investigates the theft of several experimental drugs from the research facility where he works. Guilt compels John to search meticulously for the

Horror

thieves, since the drugs were apparently smuggled out by body packing, and there is no telling what kind of effect they might have were they to open up in a person's digestive tract. Indeed, John can't disregard his belief that his daughter is trying to contact him from beyond the grave as a result of one of the thieves developing uncanny powers through exposure to the drugs.

Other books by the same author:
White Bizango, 2002
Red Red Robin, 1995
Nightmare, with Angel, 1992
The Boat House, 1991
Rain, 1990

Other books you might like:
Douglas Clegg, *Dark of the Eye*, 1994
Mary K. Hanner, *Rapid Growth*, 1993
Brian Hodge, *Nightlife*, 1991
K.W. Jeter, *Dark Seeker*, 1987
Peter Straub, *Floating Dragon*, 1982

661

CHRISTOPHER GOLDEN

Wildwood Road

(New York: Bantam/Spectra, 2005)

Story type: Child-in-Peril; Occult
Subject(s): Children; Marriage; Supernatural
Major character(s): Michael Dansky, Advertising; Jillian Dansky, Paralegal; Teddy Polito, Advertising
Time period(s): 2000s
Locale(s): Andover, Massachusetts

Summary: Returning home from a Halloween masquerade party, Michael and Jillian give a lift to a young girl who leaves them on the steps of a seemingly abandoned house with the injunction to "come find me." Thereafter, Michael finds himself obsessed by the image of the girl, but unable to find the house again. The peculiar experience begins to exert a malign influence on Jillian and on their marriage, suggesting to Michael that a supernatural menace has entered into their lives, and that it can only be exorcised by finding the house once more and getting to the bottom of its mystery.

Other books by the same author:
The Boys Are Back in Town, 2004
The Ferryman, 2002
Straight On 'Til Morning, 2001
Strangewood, 1999
Of Saints and Shadows, 1994

Other books you might like:
Dennis Etchison, *Shadow Man*, 1992
Patrick Gates, *Grimm Memorials*, 1990
Samuel M. Key, *From a Whisper to a Scream*, 1992
J.N. Williamson, *The Black School*, 1989
T.M. Wright, *Little Boy Lost*, 1992

662

T.M. GRAY

Ghosts of Eden

(Waterville, Maine: Five Star, 2005)

Story type: Ancient Evil Unleashed; Haunted House
Subject(s): Folklore; Haunted Houses; Horror
Major character(s): Saxon Faraday, Patient; Clem, Teenager, Handicapped (mentally challenged); Moses, Aged Person
Time period(s): 1940s (1947)
Locale(s): Mount Desert Island, Maine

Summary: Saxon Faraday returns to Roquefort Manor five years after she was committed to an insane asylum for having killed her abusive father in cold blood and attempting to take her own life. Haunted by the Serpent, a malignant influence that has destroyed the lives of generations of women who have lived there, the house immediately begins manifesting supernatural horrors that challenge Saxon's assumptions regarding her sanity. With the help of a mentally deficient teenage neighbor and his teacher, Saxon sorts out the real from the imagined horrors as part of her quest to exorcise the house's evil.

Other books by the same author:
The Ravenous, 2004
Feast of Faust, 2003

Other books you might like:
Stephen King, *Bag of Bones*, 1998
Joseph Nassise, *Riverwatch*, 2001
Dan Simmons, *A Winter Haunting*, 2002
Bernard Taylor, *Sweetheart, Sweetheart*, 1977
Lisa Tuttle, *Familiar Spirit*, 1983

663

SIMON R. GREEN

Hex and the City

(New York: Ace, 2005)

Story type: Occult; Mystery
Series: Nightside. Book 4
Subject(s): Mothers and Sons; Quest; Supernatural
Major character(s): John Taylor, Detective—Private; Pretty Poison, Mercenary; Lilith, Supernatural Being
Time period(s): 2000s
Locale(s): London, England

Summary: John Taylor's latest client, Lady Luck, hires him for the unusual task of finding out why and how the Nightside came into being. The Nightside is an alternate side of London where it is perpetually gloomy, magic works, and humans and supernatural beings mix uneasily. John, who has an uncanny talent for being able to find things, realizes that by solving the mystery of the Nightside, he will also solve the mystery of his origins. The mother he never knew was herself a resident of the Nightside who married his mortal father, and then returned to Nightside and obscurity shortly after giving birth to him.

Other books by the same author:
Nightingale's Lament, 2004

Agents of Light and Darkness, 2003
Something from the Nightside, 2003

Other books you might like:
Christopher Fowler, *Roofworld*, 1988
Graham Masterton, *The Doorkeepers*, 2001
J. Michael Straczynski, *OtherSyde*, 1990
Lisa Tuttle, *The Mysteries*, 2005
Tim Waggoner, *Like Death*, 2005

664

LAURELL K. HAMILTON
CHARLAINE HARRIS, Co-Author
MARYJANICE DAVIDSON, Co-Author
ANGELA KNIGHT, Co-Author
VICKIE TAYLOR, Co-Author

Bite
(New York: Jove, 2005)

Story type: Anthology; Vampire Story
Subject(s): Short Stories; Supernatural; Vampires

Summary: These five tales of paranormal romance all involve vampires. Laurell K. Hamilton contributes a story featuring her popular series character Anita Blake, Vampire Hunter, and Charlaine Harris' story features Sookie Stackhouse, the heroine of her romantic vampire comedy series. Angela Knight's "Galahad" tells of a benevolent vampire knight's quest with the help of his witch lover to eradicate an evil vampire cult. Vickie Taylor's bloodlust concerns a romance between a vampire and microbiologist that leads to transformations of vampire biology and, by extension, the entire vampire subculture. MaryJanice Davidson presents the story of a vampire vet who seeks the help of a mortal to stop a rogue vampire.

Other books by the same author:
Cravings, 2004 (MaryJanice Davidson, Eileen Wilks, and Rebecca York, co-authors)

Other books you might like:
Poppy Z. Brite, *Love in Vein II*, 1996
  editor
Poppy Z. Brite, *Love in Vein*, 1994
  editor
Christine Feehan, *Hot Blooded*, 2004
  Maggie Shayne, Emma Holly, and Angela Knight, co-authors
Greg Herren, *Midnight Thirsts*, 2004
  Michael Thomas Ford, Timothy Ridge, and Sean Wolfe, co-authors

665

M.A. HARPER

The Year of Past Things
(Orlando, Florida: Harcourt, 2005)

Story type: Ghost Story
Subject(s): Family Relations; Marriage; Supernatural

Major character(s): Phil Randazzo, Cook, Spouse (of Michelle); Michelle Wickham, Professor, Spouse (of Phil); Cam Savoie, Teenager
Time period(s): 2000s
Locale(s): New Orleans, Louisiana

Summary: Strange manifestations and noises around the house are clues that the ghost of Adrien Paul Savoie, a musician killed in a car accident, has come back to haunt his wife, Michelle, and her new husband, Phil. When Adrien's ghost leaves a message saying that he is "not going to let her be hurt again," Michelle re-examines her difficult first marriage, and also her occasionally problematic relations with Phil and her two children, as she tries to puzzle out the meaning of Adrien's intentions.

Where it's reviewed:
Publishers Weekly, December 13, 2004, page 50

Other books by the same author:
The Worst Day of My Life, So Far, 2001

Other books you might like:
Ramsey Campbell, *The Influence*, 1988
Robert Girardi, *Madeleine's Ghost*, 1995
Rick Hautala, *Beyond the Shroud*, 1995
Peter Straub, *lost boy lost girl*, 2003
Michael Upchurch, *Passive Intruder*, 1995

666

ALEXA HAYES

Vampire Beach
(New York: iBooks, 2005)

Story type: Vampire Story
Subject(s): Romance; Supernatural; Vampires
Major character(s): Alexandra Hart, Store Owner; Rafe O'Neill, Businessman, Vampire
Time period(s): 2000s
Locale(s): Santa del Sol, California

Summary: Vampire Rafe O'Neill moves to Santa del Sol to further his business interests as a nightclub owner and set up a compound that will provide safe haven for him and his vampire entourage. His only difficulty is Alexandra, owner of a shop on the boardwalk, who refuses to sell him the property he covets for his endeavors. Respecting the tenacity in Alexandra that resembles his own, Rafe soon becomes her lover.

Other books you might like:
Laurell K. Hamilton, *Guilty Pleasures*, 1993
Charlaine Harris, *Dead Until Dark*, 2001
Brent Monahan, *Blood of the Covenant*, 1995
Susan Sizemore, *I Hunger for You*, 2005
Karen E. Taylor, *Blood Secrets*, 1994

667

BARB HENDEE
J.C. HENDEE, Co-Author

Sister of the Dead

(New York: Roc, 2005)

Story type: Vampire Story
Series: Noble Dead. Book 3
Subject(s): Fantasy; Quest; Vampires
Major character(s): Magiere, Vampire; Leesil, Mythical Creature; Welstiel Massing, Warrior
Time period(s): Indeterminate
Locale(s): Chemestuk, Fictional City

Summary: Magiere, a dhampir born of a mortal woman and vampire father, travels with her entourage of supernatural comrades to the city of her birth, where she hopes to find the truth about her mysterious origins. Dhampirs by their nature are mortal enemies of vampires, and Magiere's quest to understand why her father would knowingly sire her is complicated by pursuers with indecipherable motives who attempt to thwart her along the way.

Other books by the same author:
Thief of Lives, 2004
Dhampir, 2003

Other books you might like:
Elaine Bergstrom, *Baroness of Blood*, 1995
P.N. Elrod, *I, Strahd*, 1993
Christie Golden, *The Enemy Within*, 1993
Laurell K. Hamilton, *Death of a Darklord*, 1995
J. Robert King, *Carnival of Fear*, 1993

668

WILLIAM HOPE HODGSON

The Dream of X and Other Fantastic Visions

(Portland, Oregon: Night Shade, 2005)

Story type: Collection
Series: Collected Fiction of William Hope Hodgson
Subject(s): Horror; Short Stories; Supernatural

Summary: This collection consists of 23 stories of horror and the supernatural, six of which are abridgements or shorter versions of longer, better-known works by an author of visionary cosmic horror fiction. "The Dream of X" is a shortened version of the dark fantasy romance *The Night Land*. There are also shorter versions of *The Ghost Pirates* and the psychic sleuth story *Carnacki the Ghost Finder*. Included as well is the story "Eloi, Eloi, Lama Sabachthani," in which a man tries to recreate scientifically the darkness that purportedly fell upon the world at the moment of Christ's death. Introduction by Jeremy Lassen.

Other books by the same author:
The Night Land and Other Romances, 2005
The House on the Borderland and Other Mysterious Places, 2004

The Boats of the Glen Carrig and Other Nautical Adventures, 2002
Deep Waters, 1967
Carnacki the Ghost-Finder, 1947

Other books you might like:
Algernon Blackwood, *Tales of Algernon Blackwood*, 1939
H.P. Lovecraft, *Tales*, 2005
Arthur Machen, *The Great God Pan and The Inmost Light*, 1894
Adrian Ross, *The Hole of the Pit*, 1914
Clark Ashton Smith, *Out of Space and Time*, 1942

669

WILLIAM HOPE HODGSON

The Night Land and Other Romances

(Portland, Oregon: Night Shade, 2005)

Story type: Collection
Series: Collected Fiction of William Hope Hodgson. Book 4
Subject(s): Horror; Short Stories; Supernatural

Summary: One novel and six shorter stories represent the works of a British writer from the early 20th century whose tales of horror and fantasy have a unique cosmic scope. The title story is a quasi-science fiction tale set a million years in the future in a world where the sun has died and humanity lives inside pyramidal strongholds menaced by evil monsters without. The main plot concerns an attempt on the part of one young man to travel from his pyramid, the Great Redoubt, to another, in response to a call for help. With an introduction by Jeremy Lassen, this is the fourth volume in a series collecting all of the author's known published work.

Other books by the same author:
The Dream of X and Other Fantastic Visions, 2005
The House on the Borderland and Other Mysterious Places, 2004
The Boats of the Glen Carrig and Other Nautical Adventures, 2002
Terrors of the Sea, 1996
Deep Waters, 1967

Other books you might like:
Algernon Blackwood, *Tales of Algernon Blackwood*, 1939
Thomas Ligotti, *The Nightmare Factory*, 1996
H.P. Lovecraft, *Tales*, 2005
Adrian Ross, *The Hole of the Pit*, 1914
Clark Ashton Smith, *Out of Space and Time*, 1942

670

ROBERT E. HOWARD

The Black Stranger and Other American Tales

(Lincoln: University of Nebraska Press, 2005)

Story type: Collection
Subject(s): Horror; Short Stories; Supernatural
Locale(s): United States

Summary: This collection of horror stories with American settings is by a prolific contributor to the pulp magazines of the early 20th century whose brief career as a professional writer lasted less than 10 years. Howard, a native Texan, wrote mostly fantasy and adventure fiction, but his distinctive body of horror fiction often featured themes drawn from folklore and cultural issues of the southern and southwestern states, including ''Pigeons from Hell,'' about a house haunted by the malignant influence of a voodoo practitioner who once lived there, and ''Black Canaan,'' about a sorcerer slave in the Louisiana bayous with the power to transform his enemies into horrible monsters. Steven Tompkins' introduction presents these stories as examples of early 20th century regionalist writing.

Other books by the same author:
The Moon of Skulls, 2005 (The Weird Works of Robert E. Howard. Volume 2)
Eons of the Night, 1996
The Dark Man and Others, 1963
Skull-Face and Other Stories, 1946

Other books you might like:
Hugh B. Cave, *Murgunstrumm and Others*, 1977
H.P. Lovecraft, *Tales*, 2005
E. Hoffman Price, *Far Lands and Other Days*, 1975
Karl Edward Wagner, *The Book of Kane*, 1985
Manly Wade Wellman, *Worse Things Waiting*, 1973

671

ROBERT E. HOWARD

The Moon of Skulls

(Doylestown, Pennsylvania: Wildside, 2005)

Story type: Collection
Series: Weird Works of Robert E. Howard. Volume 2
Subject(s): Horror; Short Stories; Supernatural

Summary: This is the second volume of a series of books collecting the weird fiction of Robert E. Howard, an American writer of the pulp era best known as the creator of the sword-and-sorcery saga of Conan the Barbarian. Many of Howard's stories feature swashbuckling heroic characters, including his tales of Puritan mercenary Solomon Kane, a 16th-century adventurer whose travels frequently bring him into contact with the supernatural, as in the title story and ''The Hills of the Dead,'' each concerned with vampire races in the wilds of Africa. The nine stories also include the short novel ''Skull-Face,'' about a mummy-like survivor from Atlantis, who has lived into the modern age and employs supernatural powers in his schemes for world domination. Introduction by Mark Finn.

Other books by the same author:
The Black Stranger and Other American Tales, 2005
Beyond the Borders, 1996
Eons of the Night, 1996
Trails in Darkness, 1996

Other books you might like:
Hugh B. Cave, *Murgunstrumm and Others*, 1977
Fritz Leiber, *Heroes and Horrors*, 1984
E. Hoffman Price, *Far Lands and Other Days*, 1975

Karl Edward Wagner, *The Book of Kane*, 1985
Manly Wade Wellman, *Worse Things Waiting*, 1973

672

TANYA HUFF

Smoke and Mirrors

(New York: Ace, 2005)

Story type: Haunted House
Subject(s): Ghosts; Supernatural; Television
Major character(s): Tony Foster, Filmmaker; Henry Fitzroy, Vampire; Lee Nicholas, Actor
Time period(s): 2000s
Locale(s): Vancouver, British Columbia, Canada

Summary: When they shoot on location at Caulfield House, the cast of the popular vampire detective show ''Darkest Knight'' know that the house has a reputation for being haunted. What they don't know is that the house will trap them, and try to incorporate them into its endlessly replaying scenes of murder and suicide in order to increase its supernatural powers. This series is spun off from the author's tales of vampire Henry Fitzroy whose protege, Tony, discovers he has wizardly powers while working as a production assistant on the set of a supernatural television program.

Other books by the same author:
Smoke and Shadows, 2004
Blood Debt, 1997
Blood Pact, 1993
Blood Lines, 1992
Blood Trail, 1992

Other books you might like:
Clive Barker, *Cold Heart Canyon*, 2001
Jim Butcher, *Blood Rites*, 2004
David Darke, *Horrorshow*, 1994
John Douglas, *The Late Show*, 1994
Joe R. Lansdale, *The Drive-In*, 1988

673

JEMIAH JEFFERSON

Fiend

(New York: Leisure, 2005)

Story type: Vampire Story
Subject(s): Horror; Supernatural; Vampires
Major character(s): Orfeo Ricari, Vampire; Jadzia Vilma Kopernik, Vampire
Time period(s): 1980s
Locale(s): Paris, France

Summary: Young Orfeo travels to Paris from his home in Italy in the early 19th century, filled with romance and the silly notion that he will gain a personal audience with Lord Byron. Instead, Orfeo is rendered destitute and compelled to work for a mysterious mistress, a vampire who turns him into one of her own kind and initiates him into debaucheries of the flesh and blood which he gleefully relates.

Other books by the same author:
Wounds, 2002

Voice of the Blood, 2001

Other books you might like:
Mara McCuniff, *The Vampire Memoirs*, 1991
    Traci Briery, co-author
Anne Rice, *Interview with the Vampire*, 1976
Michael Romkey, *I, Vampire*, 1990
T. Lucien Wright, *Thirst of the Vampire*, 1992
Chelsea Quinn Yarbro, *Hotel Transylvania*, 1978

674

STEPHEN JONES, Editor

Don't Turn Out the Light

(Harrogate, England: PS Publishing, 2005)

Story type: Anthology
Subject(s): Horror; Short Stories; Supernatural

Summary: Jones' anthology contains 18 stories of horror and the supernatural, a number original to the book. Included are Ray Bradbury's ''Fever Dream,'' in which a young boy's illness manifests as a form of supernatural possession; Richard Matheson's ''Dance of the Dead,'' set in a postapocalyptic world where radiation poisoning has created bizarre and horrifying life forms; and Hugh B. Cave's weird menace tale ''The Cult of the White Ape.'' Other contributors include Charles L. Grant, David J. Schow, Roberta Lannes, Richard Christian Matheson, Basil Copper, and Terry Lamsley.

Other books by the same author:
By Moonlight Only, 2003
Keep Out the Night, 2002
Dark Detectives, 1999
White of the Moon, 1999
Dark of the Night, 1997

Other books you might like:
Richard Chizmar, *Subterranean Gallery*, 1999
    William Schafer, co-editor
Peter Crowther, *Narrow Houses*, 1992
    editor
Ellen Datlow, *The Dark*, 2003
    editor
Elizabeth Monteleone, *Borderlands 5*, 2003
    Thomas Monteleone, co-editor
Barbara Roden, *Acquainted with the Night*, 2004
    Christopher Roden, co-editor

675

BRIAN KEENE

City of the Dead

(New York: Leisure, 2005)

Story type: Reanimated Dead
Subject(s): Fathers and Sons; Horror; Supernatural
Major character(s): Jim Thurmond, Parent; Thomas Martin, Religious; Darren Ramsey, Businessman
Time period(s): 2000s
Locale(s): Bloomington, New Jersey

Summary: Jim Thurmond and his friends rescue Jim's son, Danny, from a house besieged by zombies and flee to Ramsey Towers, a seemingly impregnable fortress built by a businessman to withstand terrorist attacks. Soon enough, however, defenses are breached, and the humans find their fortress in danger of becoming their tomb. This is a sequel to *The Rising* (2004), whose premise is that the newly dead are being used as vessels for extradimensional monsters, who kill relentlessly with the intent of increasing their numbers.

Other books by the same author:
Terminal, 2005
The Rising, 2003

Other books you might like:
Hugh B. Cave, *Isle of the Whisperers*, 1999
James Lowder, *The Book of All Flesh*, 2001
    editor
John Russo, *Night of the Living Dead*, 1974
Al Sarrantonio, *Skeletons*, 1992
John Skipp, *Book of the Dead*, 1989
    Craig Spector, co-editor

676

BRIAN KEENE

Terminal

(New York: Bantam, 2005)

Story type: Wild Talents
Subject(s): Psychic Powers; Robbers and Outlaws; Supernatural
Major character(s): Tommy O'Brien, Worker, Thief; John, Worker; Benjy, Child
Time period(s): 2000s
Locale(s): Hanover, Pennsylvania

Summary: When he's diagnosed with terminal cancer, Tommy O'Brien decides to go out in a blaze of glory by robbing a local bank. Only after his plans fail and hostages are taken does Tommy realize that a young boy among the hostages can heal by the laying on of hands, and that Tommy's future may depend on ensuring the boy lives through his showdown with the police.

Other books by the same author:
City of the Dead, 2005
Fear of Gravity, 2004
The Rising, 2003

Other books you might like:
John Byrne, *Whipping Boy*, 1992
Stephen King, *Desperation*, 1996
Robert R. McCammon, *Mystery Walk*, 1983
Yvonne Navarro, *Deadrush*, 1995
F. Paul Wilson, *The Touch*, 1987

677

JULIE KENNER

Carpe Demon

(New York: Berkley, 2005)

Story type: Occult

Subject(s): Demons; Humor; Supernatural
Major character(s): Kate Connor, Housewife; Stuart Connor, Lawyer; Laura Dupont, Housewife
Time period(s): 2000s
Locale(s): San Diablo, California

Summary: Kate, a Vatican-trained demonkiller with a lengthy resume of kills, has turned her back on her past career and become an ordinary homemaker in her Southern California suburb. When the demon Goramesh arrives in town, stirring up trouble and inciting other demons to make her life miserable, Kate must find a delicate way to resume her demonslaying without revealing her past to her oblivious husband.

Other books by the same author:
Aphrodite's Flame, 2004
The Givenchy Code, 2004
The Spy Who Loves Me, 2004
Aphrodite's Passion, 2002
Nobody but You, 2002

Other books you might like:
MaryJanice Davidson, *Derik's Bane*, 2005
Charlaine Harris, *Dead as a Doornail*, 2005
Kim Harrison, *Dead Witch Walking*, 2004
Sherrilyn Kenyon, *Seize the Night*, 2004
Christopher Moore, *Practical Demonkeeping*, 1991

678

JACK KETCHUM

The Girl Next Door

(New York: Leisure, 2005)

Story type: Psychological Suspense
Subject(s): Abuse; Suspense
Major character(s): David Moran, Child; Meg Loughlin, Teenager; Ruth Chandler, Parent
Time period(s): 1950s (1958)
Locale(s): New Jersey

Summary: After a car crash kills their parents, Meg Loughlin and her crippled sister Susan move in with their aunt, Ruth Chandler, and her three sons. As presented through the eyes of next-door neighbor David Moran, who befriends Meg, Ruth is a psychologically unbalanced woman, unhinged by estrangement from her husband, who begins severely disciplining the girls, eventually imprisoning them and encouraging her sons to inflict the worst depravities on them. This is a fictionalized treatment of a true crime story that occurred in Indiana in the 1950s. Reprint of a novel first published in 1989.

Other books by the same author:
The Crossings, 2004
The Lost, 2000
Ladies Night, 1997
Red, 1995
She Wakes, 1989

Other books you might like:
V.C. Andrews, *Flowers in the Attic*, 1979
John Fowles, *The Collector*, 1963
Dean R. Koontz, *Intensity*, 1995
Richard Laymon, *The Woods Are Dark*, 1981

Billie Sue Mosiman, *Night Cruise*, 1992

679

HIDEYUKI KIKUCHI
YOSHITAKA AMANO, Illustrator

Vampire Hunter D

(Milwaukie, Oregon: DH Press, 2005)

Story type: Vampire Story
Series: Vampire Hunter D
Subject(s): Horror; Supernatural; Vampires
Major character(s): Doris Lang, Young Woman; Vampire Hunter D, Vampire Hunter; Magnus Lee, Vampire
Time period(s): Indeterminate Future
Locale(s): Ransylva, Fictional City

Summary: In a post-apocalyptic future where vampires have taken over the world, Doris Lang, one of the few surviving humans, is bitten by the evil vampire Count Magnus Lee. Her only hope for avoiding an inevitable conversion to vampirism is Vampire Hunter D, a genetically manipulated vampire killer, who must fight Magnus Lee to the death. Novelization of an animated film.

Other books by the same author:
Raiser of Gales, 2005

Other books you might like:
Brian W. Aldiss, *Dracula Unbound*, 1991
Kim Newman, *Anno Dracula*, 1993
Lucius Shepard, *The Golden*, 1993
Brian Stableford, *The Empire of Fear*, 1988
F. Paul Wilson, *Midnight Mass*, 2004

680

H.R. KNIGHT

What Rough Beast

(New York: Leisure, 2005)

Story type: Occult
Subject(s): Horror; Psychic Powers; Supernatural
Major character(s): Arthur Conan Doyle, Writer, Historical Figure; Harry Houdini, Magician, Historical Figure; Maximillian Cairo, Psychic
Time period(s): 1900s (1903)
Locale(s): London, England

Summary: Sir Arthur Conan Doyle and Harry Houdini team up to debunk the seances held by spirit medium Maximillian Cairo, but one in which Cairo has promised to call down Dionysus, the god of inspiration and violence, proves genuine. When Houdini interrupts the proceedings, Dionysus is accidentally unleashed upon London, goading people to creative acts of madness and violence that threaten to overwhelm the city.

Other books you might like:
Kevin J. Anderson, *The League of Extraordinary Gentlemen*, 2003
Mark Frost, *The List of 7*, 1992
William Hjortsberg, *Nevermore*, 1994

Horror

Daniel Stashower, *The Adventure of the Ectoplasmic Man*, 1985

Thomas Wheeler, *The Arcanum*, 2004

681

DEAN R. KOONTZ

KEVIN J. ANDERSON, Co-Author

Dean Koontz's Frankenstein. Book 1: Prodigal Son

(New York: Bantam, 2005)

Story type: Reanimated Dead; Serial Killer
Series: Dean Koontz's Frankenstein. Book 1
Subject(s): Crime and Criminals; Horror; Scientific Experiments
Major character(s): Victor Helios, Scientist; Carson O'Connor, Detective—Police; Michael Maddison, Detective—Police
Time period(s): 2000s
Locale(s): New Orleans, Louisiana

Summary: Victor Frankenstein has lived into the 21st century, and as Victor Helios is busily crafting reanimated members of the New Race, whom he will use to kill and replace ordinary mortals. When one of the New Race (who mingle unobtrusively with the citizens of New Orleans) develops his own psychotic schemes and turns serial killer, it alerts not only the local constabulary, but Deucalion, the original Frankenstein monster. Deucalion recognizes the handiwork of his creator and travels from Tibet to put a stop to Helios' nightmarish plan. First novel in a series based on a scuttled cable television series that Koontz had partially scripted.

Where it's reviewed:
Publishers Weekly, January 17, 2005, page 40

Other books you might like:
C. Dean Andersson, *I Am Frankenstein*, 1996
Martin H. Greenberg, *Frankenstein: The Monster Wakes*, 1993
    editor
Byron Preiss, *The Ultimate Frankenstein*, 1991
    John Betancourt, co-editor
Mary Shelley, *Frankenstein*, 1818

682

DEAN R. KOONTZ

Velocity

(New York: Bantam, 2005)

Story type: Psychological Suspense; Mystery
Subject(s): Murder; Mystery; Serial Killers
Major character(s): Billy Miles, Saloon Keeper/Owner; Lanny Olson, Police Officer; Steve Zillis, Saloon Keeper/Owner
Time period(s): 2000s
Locale(s): Vineyard Hills, California

Summary: Billy Miles dismisses an anonymous note sent to him from someone who threatens to kill one of two people whom he has never met, but whom the writer demands he choose between. When one of the persons named later turns up dead, Billy becomes caught up in a cat-and-mouse game in which the note writer escalates the stakes of the murder game with promises of more killings and threats against Billy and his loved ones. Billy must search through associations and relationships in his own life to determine the identity and motive of the killer.

Other books by the same author:
Life Expectancy, 2004
The Taking, 2004
The Face, 2003
By the Light of the Moon, 2002
One Door Away from Heaven, 2001

Other books you might like:
Giles Blunt, *Cold Eye*, 1988
Ramsey Campbell, *The Count of Eleven*, 1991
Thomas Harris, *Red Dragon*, 1981
Douglas Preston, *Brimstone*, 2004
    Lincoln Child, co-author
Michael Slade, *Cutthroat*, 1992

683

MICHAEL LAIMO

The Demonologist

(New York: Leisure, 2005)

Story type: Occult
Subject(s): Demons; Music and Musicians; Horror
Major character(s): Bevand Mathers, Musician; Kristin Mathers, Young Woman; Thomas Danto, Religious
Time period(s): 2000s
Locale(s): Los Angeles, California

Summary: Plagued by voices in his head and blackout periods during which he cannot account for his actions, musician Bev Mathers seeks professional help. To his absolute incredulity, he discovers that he is serving as a vessel for a demon, which in turn is being cultivated by an even greater demonic entity that hopes to absorb it and become an insuperable evil power. To stop this infernal scheme, Bev must find some way to exorcise the demon inside him, even though it may have been responsible for all his success and all he holds dear in life.

Other books by the same author:
Deep in the Darkness, 2004
Sleepwalker, 2004
Atmosphere, 2002
Demons, Freaks and Other Abnormalities, 1999

Other books you might like:
Ray Garton, *Crucifax*, 1988
Clifford Mohr, *Requiem*, 1992
Jeffrey Sackett, *Candlemas Eve*, 1988
John Skipp, *The Scream*, 1988
    Craig Spector, co-author
Fred Mustard Stewart, *The Mephisto Waltz*, 1969

684

MARGO LANAGAN

Black Juice

(New York: Eos, 2005)

Story type: Collection; Young Adult
Subject(s): Fantasy; Short Stories; Supernatural

Summary: Lanagan's ten stories interweave myth and fable as part of their supernaturalism. ''Singing My Sister Down'' is a grim but poignant account of a family's vigil for their child on the eve of her execution by a peculiarly nasty means. In ''Yowlinin,'' a young girl's warnings about an approaching plague go unheeded by her village. ''Red Nose Day'' concerns a pair of assassins who specifically target clowns as their victims. Although marketed as a young adult volume in the United States, this book was an adult trade publication in England in 2004.

Other books by the same author:
Wild Game, 1998
The Best Thing, 1995

Other books you might like:
Janet Fox, *A Witch's Dozen*, 2003
Tanith Lee, *Dreams of Dark and Light*, 1986
Frances Oliver, *Dancing on Air*, 2004
Jessica Amanda Salmonson, *The Dark Tales*, 2002
James Tiptree Jr., *Tales of the Quintana Roo*, 1986

685

STEPHEN LAWS

Fear Me

(New York: Leisure, 2005)

Story type: Vampire Story
Subject(s): Horror; Supernatural; Vampires
Major character(s): Paul Shapiro, Young Man; Gideon, Vampire; Bernice Adams, Television Personality
Time period(s): 1990s
Locale(s): London, England

Summary: In this variation on the traditional vampire theme, vampires perpetuate their life by siring children with mortal women and then transferring their personalities into whomever emerges the sole victor in their progeny's struggle for dominance and survival. Gideon, a sexually voracious vampire, has initiated his own next generation of offspring when he is unexpectedly killed, changing the stakes of the game for his discarnate soul, which is now determined to secure a body at any cost. Originally published in 1993 as *Gideon.*

Other books by the same author:
Chasm, 1998
Somewhere South of Midnight, 1996
Daemonic, 1995
Macabre, 1994
Darkfall, 1992

Other books you might like:
Poppy Z. Brite, *Lot Souls*, 1992

Nancy Collins, *Sunglasses After Dark*, 1989
Brent Monahan, *The Book of Common Dread*, 1993
Whitley Streiber, *The Hunger*, 1981

686

RICHARD LAYMON

Resurrection Dreams

(New York: Leisure, 2005)

Story type: Reanimated Dead
Subject(s): Horror; Schools/High Schools; Scientific Experiments
Major character(s): Vicki Chandler, Doctor; Melvin Dobbs, Worker; Ace, Store Owner
Time period(s): 1980s
Locale(s): Ellsworth, California

Summary: Ten years ago, oddball teenager Melvin Dobbs was institutionalized after trying to reanimate a dead student with a car battery as part of a school science experiment. Now Melvin is out of the hospital, and hopeful of pursuing a romance with Vicki, his unrequited high school love, who has just returned to town to start her medical practice. What Vicki doesn't know is that Melvin has become more successful at creating zombies and that he will stop at nothing to have her for his own. Originally published in 1989.

Other books by the same author:
The Glory Bus, 2005
The Hearse, 2004
Amara, 2002
Night in the Lonesome October, 2001
No Sanctuary, 2001

Other books you might like:
Randall Boyll, *Mongster*, 1991
Daniel Gower, *The Orpheus Process*, 1992
Stephen King, *Pet Sematary*, 1983
Dean R. Koontz, *Dean Koontz's Frankenstein. Book 1: Prodigal Son*, 2005
    Kevin J. Anderson, co-author
Del Stone Jr., *Dead Heat*, 1996

687

J. SHERIDAN LE FANU

Mr. Justice Harbottle and Others

(Ashcroft, British Columbia: Ash-Tree Press, 2005)

Story type: Collection
Subject(s): Horror; Short Stories; Supernatural

Summary: Twelve tales of ghosts and hauntings by an influential 19th-century Irish writer are contained in this book. Included are ''Carmilla,'' a vampire story generally believed to have influenced Bram Stoker's *Dracula*; the title tale, about an evil magistrate judged by a ghostly tribunal; and ''The Familiar,'' about a man pursued by a shadowy wraith for a crime he committed. Edited and with an introduction and bibliography by James Rockhill, this is the third and final volume collecting the author's complete weird fiction.

Other books by the same author:
The Haunted Baronet and Others, 2003
Schalken the Painter and Others, 2002
Ghost Stories and Mysteries, 1975
Best Ghost Stories, 1964
Green Tea and Other Ghost Stories, 1945

Other books you might like:
Rhoda Broughton, *Twilight Stories*, 1947
Henry Ferris, *A Night with Mephistopheles*, 1997
M.R. James, *Ghost Stories of an Antiquary*, 1904
Fitz-James O'Brien, *The Supernatural Tales of Fitz-James O'Brien*, 1988
Edgar Allan Poe, *Complete Tales and Poems*, 1938

688

TIM LEBBON

Desolation

(New York: Leisure, 2005)

Story type: Psychological Suspense
Subject(s): Fathers and Sons; Horror; Scientific Experiments
Major character(s): Cain, Young Man; Magenta, Entertainer; Peter, Landlord
Time period(s): 2000s
Locale(s): Tall Stennington, England

Summary: The victim of his father's bizarre experiments in sensory deprivation to bring out his undeveloped powers of Pure Sight, Cain is newly released from Afresh, a special institution. Determined to start a new life of his own, Cain moves to an apartment on Endless Crescent, home to a number of weird people. Through Cain's eyes, the world appears a distorted vision of reality, shaped by his peculiar childhood and ultimately related to the contents of a mysterious trunk that he brings with him to his new residence. An allegorical dark fantasy novel.

Other books by the same author:
Changing of Faces, 2003
Until She Sleeps, 2002
Face, 2001
The Nature of Balance, 2001
Mesmer, 1997

Other books you might like:
Robert Bloch, *Psycho*, 1959
Patrick McGrath, *Spider*, 1990
T.L. Parkinson, *The Man Upstairs*, 1991
Roland Topor, *The Tenant*, 1966

689

TIM LEBBON

Pieces of Hate

(Escanaba, Michigan: Necessary Evil, 2005)

Story type: Occult
Series: Assassin. Book 2
Subject(s): Demons; Horror; Supernatural
Major character(s): Gabriel, Sailor; Sparks, Religious; Captain Parker, Sailor

Time period(s): 19th century
Locale(s): Port Royal, England

Summary: Gabriel's quest to find Temple, the demonic entity who slaughtered his family and who brings death and destruction wherever he goes, is hampered by the discovery that Temple can assume human form and even masquerade as a close confidante. This is the second novel in an allegorical series concerned with the battle between good and evil.

Other books by the same author:
Desolation, 2005
Dead Man's Hand, 2004
Changing of Faces, 2003
Until She Sleeps, 2002
Face, 2001

Other books you might like:
Mark Chadbourn, *The Eternal*, 1996
Nancy Collins, *Lynch*, 1998
Joe R. Lansdale, *Dead in the West*, 1986
Rodman Philbrick, *Coffins*, 2002

690

DEBORAH LEBLANC

Grave Intent

(New York: Leisure, 2005)

Story type: Curse; Occult
Subject(s): Customs; Gypsies; Supernatural
Major character(s): Janet Savoy, Store Owner; Michael Savoy, Undertaker; Ellie Savoy, Child
Time period(s): 2000s
Locale(s): Brusley, Louisiana

Summary: During the viewing of the body of Thalia Stevenson at the Savoy Funeral Home, a special engraved coin the corpse is holding disappears. Janet and Michael Savoy are informed by Thalia's father, Ephraim, that Thalia has gypsy blood, and the coin, her birthright since infancy, is a token to pay for her entrance to "the other side." If the coin is not found before the rising of the second sun, someone in the Savoy family will die horribly as supernatural retribution.

Other books by the same author:
Family Inheritance, 2004

Other books you might like:
John Farris, *All Heads Turn When the Hunt Goes By*, 1977
Christopher Golden, *The Ferryman*, 2002
Brian Hodge, *Oasis*, 1989
A.R. Morlan, *The Amulet*, 1991
Robert Weinberg, *The Devil's Auction*, 1988

691

EDWARD LEE

Flesh Gothic

(New York: Leisure, 2005)

Story type: Occult
Subject(s): Horror; Sexual Behavior; Supernatural

Major character(s): Elizabeth Bennet Westmore, Detective—
  Private; Alexander Nyvysk, Religious; Mack Colmes, Se-
  curity Officer
Time period(s): 2000s
Locale(s): St. Petersburg, Florida

Summary: Hildreth House, the private mansion of porn
magnate Arthur Hildreth, is the site of a recent mass murder of
porn stars, after which Hildreth disappeared. Although it is
commonly believed that Hildreth did away with himself, his
widow, Vivica, believes otherwise and hires Westmore to
keep tabs on a crew of psychics she has hired to investigate
the supposedly haunted house. Unknown to Westmore,
Hildreth believed in the paranormal power of sexuality and
the house is a huge storage battery that draws on the sexual
energy of those inside it, channeling it for occult purposes.
Originally published as a specialty press hardcover in 2004.

Other books by the same author:
The Messenger, 2004
Infernal Angel, 2003
Monstrosity, 2002
City Infernal, 2001
Stickmen, 1999

Other books you might like:
Poppy Z. Brite, *Drawing Blood*, 1993
Tom Elliott, *The Dwelling*, 1989
Richard Matheson, *Hell House*, 1971
Al Sarrantonio, *House Haunted*, 1991
Chet Williamson, *Soulstorm*, 1986

692

FRITZ LEIBER

Horrible Imaginings
(Seattle: Midnight House, 2005)

Story type: Collection
Subject(s): Horror; Short Stories; Supernatural

Summary: These 15 horror and dark fantasy stories are by an
author who began writing for the pulp fiction magazines of the
1940s, and whose literate, highly regarded work dominated
horror and fantasy fiction for most of the second half of the
20th century. The book includes several modern updates of
classic horror themes, including ''The Girl with the Hungry
Eyes,'' in which a vampiric model feeds on the desires and
tastes of society through her presence in advertising images,
and ''The Automatic Pistol,'' which likens a gangster's relationship with his firearm to that of a witch and her familiar.
The title story is an urban horror tale concerning a haunted
apartment building. Included as well is a blend of science
fiction and Lovecraftian horror, ''Diary in the Snow,'' and the
previously unpublished story ''Skinny's Wonderful.'' With
an introduction by editor John Pelan.

Other books by the same author:
Day Dark, Night Bright, 2002
Smoke Ghost and Other Apparitions, 2002
The Black Gondolier and Other Stories, 2001
The Leiber Chronicles, 1990
Night's Black Agents, 1947

Other books you might like:
Charles Beaumont, *The Hunger and Other Stories*, 1957
Ramsey Campbell, *Dark Companions*, 1982
Ted Klein, *Dark Gods*, 1985
Kim Newman, *The Original Dr. Shade and Other Stories*,
  1994
Peter Straub, *Magic Terror*, 2001

693

H.P. LOVECRAFT

Tales
(New York: Library of America, 2005)

Story type: Collection
Subject(s): Horror; Short Stories; Supernatural

Summary: This collection of 22 stories of horror and the
supernatural is by a writer of the American pulp era who is
generally recognized as the most important American writer
of supernatural fiction since Edgar Allan Poe. The selections
range in theme and approach from the gothic horrors of ''The
Rats in the Walls,'' about a family home haunted nightly by
the scurrying of rats only the owner can hear, and ''Herbert
West—Reanimator,'' a variation on the theme of
Frankenstein, to the cosmic horrors of ''The Call of
Cthulhu,'' which proposes a race of extradimensional monsters with designs on the earth and the science fiction of ''The
Colour out of Space,'' in which a malignant influence that
comes to Earth in a meteorite despoils farmland in rural
Massachusetts and creates gruesome mutations in the local
flora and fauna. Edited and with an introduction by Peter
Straub.

Where it's reviewed:
Locus, March 2005, page 15
Publishers Weekly, January 3, 2005, page 40

Other books by the same author:
The Dreams in the Witch House and Other Weird Stories,
  2004
The Call of Cthulhu and Other Weird Stories, 1999
Dagon and Other Macabre Tales, 1965
At the Mountains of Madness and Other Novels, 1964
The Dunwich Horror and Others, 1963

Other books you might like:
Algernon Blackwood, *Ancient Sorceries and Other Weird
  Stories*, 2002
August Derleth, *Someone in the Dark*, 1944
Frank Belknap Long, *The Hounds of Tindalos*, 1946
Edgar Allan Poe, *Poetry and Tales*, 1984
Clark Ashton Smith, *Out of Space and Time*, 1942

694

TIM LUCAS

The Book of Renfield
(New York: Touchstone, 2005)

Story type: Vampire Story
Subject(s): Horror; Supernatural; Vampires

Major character(s): Renfield, Patient, Mentally Ill Person; John L. Seward, Doctor; Madame Iorga, Housekeeper
Time period(s): 19th century
Locale(s): London, England

Summary: This novel, which serves as a prequel to Bram Stoker's vampire classic *Dracula*, presents the life story of Renfield, the madman incarcerated at the insane asylum next to Carfax Abbey where Dracula took up residence in England. Renfield relates the sad Dickensian history of his loveless childhood, and presents his manipulation by Dracula and his minions as the twisted culminarion of his lifelong search for love and affection.

Other books by the same author:
Throat Sprockets, 1994

Other books you might like:
Jeanne Kalogridis, *Children of the Vampire*, 1995
Marie Kiraly, *Mina*, 1994
Fred Saberhagen, *The Dracula Tape*, 1975
Bram Stoker, *Dracula*, 1897
Chelsea Quinn Yarbro, *The Angry Angel*, 1998

695

ROGER LUCKHURST, Editor

Late Victorian Gothic Tales
(London: Oxford, 2005)

Story type: Anthology
Subject(s): Short Stories

Summary: These 12 classic stories were chosen by the editor as representative of the persistence of the Gothic sensibility in late-19th- and early-20th-century English and continental fiction. Contents include Rudyard Kipling's tale of bestial transformation, "The Mark of the Beast;" Sir Arthur Conan Doyle's account of a reanimated Egyptian mummy, "Lot 249;" and Arthur Machen's story of a femme fatale of non-human origin, "The Great God Pan." Other authors in the book include Oscar Wilde, Vernon Lee, Jean Lorrain, Henry James, and M.P. Shiel.

Other books you might like:
Christopher Baldick, *The Oxford Book of Gothic Tales*, 1992
  editor
E.F. Bleiler, *A Treasury of Victorian Ghost Stories*, 1981
  editor
Michael Cox, *Victorian Ghost Stories*, 1991
  editor
Peter Haining, *Great Tales of Terror from Europe and America*, 1972
  editor
Joyce Carol Oates, *American Gothic Tales*, 1996
  editor

696

ARTHUR MACHEN

The Bowmen and Other Legends of the War
(Holicong, Pennsylvania: Wildside, 2005)

Story type: Collection
Subject(s): Short Stories; Supernatural; War

Summary: This book contains five stories of World War I, and wartime adventures shaped by supernatural incidents. The title story evokes the popular legend of the Angel of Mons in its account of ghostly bowmen who help the British win a battle. "The Soldier's Rest" and "The Monstrance" both concern the intervention of angels and figures from Great Britain's historical past in English war victories. Retitling of a volume first published in 1915.

Other books by the same author:
Ritual: And Other Stories, 1997
Tales of Horror and the Supernatural, 1948
The Cosy Room: And Other Stories, 1936
The House of Souls, 1906
The Three Impostors, 1894

Other books you might like:
Algernon Blackwood, *The Best Ghost Stories of Algernon Blackwood*, 1973
Chaz Brenchley, *The Keys to D'Esperance*, 1998
A.M. Burrage, *Someone in the Room*, 1997
Simon Clark, *Exorcising Angels*, 2003
  Tim Lebbon, co-author
Oliver Onions, *The Collected Ghost Stories of Oliver Onions*, 1971

697

JEFF MARRIOTTE

Boogeyman
(New York: Pocket Star, 2004)

Story type: Occult
Subject(s): Fear; Horror; Supernatural
Major character(s): Tim Jensen, Editor; Kate Houghton, Young Woman; Jessica Brittan, Artist
Time period(s): 2000s
Locale(s): Danville

Summary: As a young child, Tim saw his father snatched away by the archetypal boogeyman living in his closet. The family has maintained ever since that Tim's dad abandoned them, which leads Tim to question whether his father was really abducted by the monster, or whether he imagined the boogeyman into existence to justify the emotional trauma caused by his dad's absence. Years later, when his mother dies, Tim returns to his home to settle the estate, and that entails poking into his closet one more time to determine whether the boogeyman exists or not. Novelization of a screenplay by Eric Kripke, Juliet Snowdon, and Stiles White, based on a story by Eric Kripke. The film was directed by Stephen Kay.

Other books by the same author:
The Shield: Spotlight, 2004
The Slab, 2003
Desperadoes: Quiet of the Grave, 2002
Desperadoes: A Moment's Sunlight, 1998

Other books you might like:
Gary Brandner, *Cameron's Closet*, 1986
Christopher Golden, *Strangewood*, 1999
Charles L. Grant, *In a Dark Dream*, 1988
Michael Paine, *Steel Ghosts*, 2005
David B. Silva, *The Disappeared*, 1995

698

A. LEE MARTINEZ

Gil's All Fright Diner

(New York: Tor, 2005)

Story type: Ancient Evil Unleashed
Subject(s): Humor; Supernatural; Vampires
Major character(s): Earl, Vampire; Duke, Werewolf; Tammy, Teenager
Time period(s): 2000s
Locale(s): Rockwood County

Summary: Earl, a vampire, and Duke, a werewolf, come to the assistance of Loretta, manager of Gil's All Night Diner, whose establishment has been under siege from the walking dead for more than five years. The two discover that the diner is situated on a focal point of cosmic power, and that Tammy, a rambunctious local teenager determined to become Queen of the Universe, is hoping to drive Loretta out of business so that she can use the location to summon Lovecraftian Elder Gods. This comic horror tale is a first novel.

Other books you might like:
David Barbour, *Shadows Bend*, 2000
   Richard Raleigh, co-author
Christopher Moore, *Practical Demonkeeping*, 1991
William Browning Spencer, *Resume with Monsters*, 1995
Richard L. Tierney, *The House of the Toad*, 1993

699

GRAHAM MASTERTON

Unspeakable

(New York: Pocket Star, 2005)

Story type: Occult; Child-in-Peril
Subject(s): Deafness; Folklore; Kidnapping
Major character(s): Holly Summers, Social Worker, Handicapped (deaf); Elliott Joseph, Unemployed; Mickey "Slim" Kavanagh, Police Officer
Time period(s): 2000s
Locale(s): Portland, Oregon

Summary: When deaf social welfare officer Holly Summers turns in Elliott Joseph for abusing his wife and child, Joseph, who is of Native American descent and who believes his son was possessed by the malignant spirit of Raven, puts a curse on Holly. Shortly thereafter, Holly's life turns miserable, and her young daughter Daisy is kidnapped, leading her to wonder if there is actual merit to the supernatural curse.

Where it's reviewed:
Publishers Weekly, January 10, 2005, page 44

Other books by the same author:
Holy Terror, 2004
Innocent Blood, 2004
The Devil in Gray, 2004
A Terrible Beauty, 2003
Genius, 2003

Other books you might like:
Muriel Gray, *Trickster*, 1994
T. Chris Martindale, *Demon Dance*, 1991
Catherine Montrose, *Wendigo Border*, 1995
Jessica Palmer, *Shadow Dance*, 1994

700

RICHARD MATHESON

Collected Stories. Volume 2

(Colorado Springs, Colorado: Gauntlet, 2005)

Story type: Collection
Series: Richard Matheson: Collected Stories. Volume 2
Subject(s): Horror; Science Fiction; Short Stories

Summary: These 29 stories of horror, fantasy, and science fiction are from a writer whose tendency to focus on the dark side of ordinary experience made him one of the most influential writers of horror fiction in the post-World War II era. "Slaughter House" is a haunted house story; "Trespass" presents the quirky behavior of a woman during her pregnancy as proof that she carries the offspring of an alien being; "The Funeral" is a comic macabre story about a supernatural being who tries to arrange a funeral for himself and the rowdy monsters who attend. Edited and with an introduction by Stanley Wiater, the book also includes appreciations of Matheson from Jack Finney and George Clayton Johnson.

Other books by the same author:
Richard Matheson's Darker Places, 2005
Unrealized Dreams, 2004
Duel, 2002
Offbeat: Uncollected Stories, 2002
Nightmare at 20,000 Feet, 2000

Other books you might like:
Charles Beaumont, *Selected Stories*, 1988
Robert Bloch, *The Fear Planet and Other Unusual Destinations*, 2005
Ray Bradbury, *Bradbury Stories: 100 of His Most Celebrated Tales*, 2003
Fritz Leiber, *The Leiber Chronicles*, 1990
William F. Nolan, *Night Shapes*, 1995

Horror

701

RICHARD MATHESON

Woman

(Colorado Springs, Colorado: Gauntlet, 2005)

Story type: Wild Talents
Subject(s): Men; Supernatural; Women
Major character(s): David Harper, Psychologist; Liz Harper, Producer (television); Ganine Woodbury, Young Woman
Time period(s): 2000s
Locale(s): Los Angeles, California

Summary: Ganine Woodbury, a pathetic but persistent young woman, seeks help from radio psychologist David Harper on the night David and his television producer wife, Liz, host a party for their Hollywood friends. In the days that follow, all who attended the party are subject to inexplicable healings and health problems which lead David to suspect that Ganine, the one common denominator in their lives, is possessed of uncanny supernatural powers that express themselves in response to manifestations of the age-old battle of the sexes.

Other books by the same author:
Come Fygures, Come Shadowes, 2003
Hunted Past Reason, 2002
Camp Pleasant, 2001
Hunger and Thirst, 2000
Passion Play, 2000

Other books you might like:
Shirley Jackson, *We Have Always Lived in the Castle*, 1962
Jack Ketchum, *Ladies Night*, 1997
Stephen King, *Rose Madder*, 1995
Kate Pullinger, *Where Does Kissing End?*, 1995
Lisa Tuttle, *Pillow Friend*, 1996

702

JONATHAN MOELLER

Demonsouled

(Waterville, Maine: Five Star, 2005)

Story type: Occult
Subject(s): Demons; Horror; Supernatural
Major character(s): Mazael Cravenlock, Nobleman; Gerald Roland, Nobleman; Richard Mandragon, Nobleman
Time period(s): Indeterminate
Locale(s): Fictional Country

Summary: Returning home to his family castle after a 15-year absence, Mazael Cravenlock finds the building vulnerable to supernatural incursions, including the Grim Marches, a siege conducted by the living dead. Richard partners with agents of good to reverse the family fortunes, but is hindered by nightmares and experiences that seem out of character. Eventually, he learns that he is demonsouled, possessed by an ancient demon who is part of his lineage, and that his life will be a neverending struggle to suppress the dark side he harbors. First novel.

Other books you might like:
Laurell K. Hamilton, *Death of a Darklord*, 1995
Trystam Kith, *A Cold Summer Night*, 2004

Lucius Shepard, *The Golden*, 1993
Chet Williamson, *Murder in Cormyr*, 1996
David Niall Wilson, *To Sift through Bitter Ashes*, 1997

703

THOMAS F. MONTELEONE

Horn of Plenty

(Fork, Maryland: Borderlands, 2005)

Story type: Vampire Story
Series: Dark Voices. Book 1
Subject(s): Horror; Music and Musicians; Supernatural
Major character(s): George Thurston, Musician; Roland Blades, Musician; Satchel Ross, Musician
Time period(s): 2000s
Locale(s): Kansas City, Kansas

Summary: At a small jazz club in Kansas City, the trumpeter of the George Thurston Quintet finds an abandoned trumpet that plays uncommonly magnificent music. As the band's career flourishes, the trumpeter grows increasingly sickly and gaunt, suggesting that the instrument is vampirically draining vitality from him. This short story chapbook is accompanied by a CD of the author reading it aloud.

Other books by the same author:
A Little Brown Book of Bizarre Stories, 2004
Fearful Symmetries, 2004
Rough Beasts and Other Mutations, 2003
Dark Stars and Other Illuminations, 1981

Other books you might like:
Nancy Collins, *Tempter*, 1991
Jeff Gelb, *Shock Rock*, 1992
  editor
Jeff Gelb, *Shock Rock II*, 1994
  editor
Paul J. McAuley, *In Dreams*, 1986
  Kim Newman, co-editor

704

JAMES A. MOORE

Rabid Growth

(New York: Leisure, 2005)

Story type: Occult
Subject(s): Brothers and Sisters; Cults; Supernatural
Major character(s): Christopher Corin, Young Man; Brittany Corin, Young Woman; Jerry Murphy, Young Man
Time period(s): 2000s
Locale(s): United States

Summary: Chris Corin and his friends have survived the weird events chronicled in *Possessions* (2004), including a weird cult's scheme to use them as fodder for extradimensional demons with a foothold in this world. However, their problems persist: Chris is pursued around town by the resurrected corpses of the dead, and his friend Jerry is being infested with strange tumors related to his contact with supernatural entities. The key to their salvation may be dreams in which Chris

hears talk of The Western Key, an amulet with occult forces that was responsible for their previous adventures.

Other books by the same author:
Possessions, 2004
Serenity Falls, 2003
Fireworks, 2001
Under the Overtree, 2000

Other books you might like:
Poppy Z. Brite, *Drawing Blood*, 1993
Tananarive Due, *The Good House*, 2003
Edward Lee, *Flesh Gothic*, 2005
Robert Wayne McCoy, *The King of Ice Cream*, 2004
Brian Smith, *House of Blood*, 2004

705

JILL MORROW

The Open Channel

(New York: Pocket, 2005)

Story type: Occult
Subject(s): Demons; Faith; Supernatural
Major character(s): Katerina Piretti, Lawyer; Stephen Carmichael, Restaurateur; Julia Carmichael, Teenager
Time period(s): 2000s
Locale(s): Baltimore, Maryland

Summary: Kat and Stephen thought they had vanquished the demon Asteroth in their previous adventure, chronicled in *The Angel Cafe* (2004), but when their daughter Julia begins having troubled dreams about 14th-century England, they realize that Asteroth is still alive, having possessed the body of a medieval Englishman. With the help of their religiously devout Aunt Francesca, Kat and Stephen once again wrestle with Asteroth, who is using his human guise to seduce a convent novitiate in order to return to the 21st century and prevent the prophesied Child of Light.

Other books by the same author:
The Angel Cafe, 2004

Other books you might like:
William Peter Blatty, *The Exorcist*, 1971
M.A. Harper, *The Year of Past Things*, 2005
John Saul, *Midnight Voices*, 2002
Eileen Wilks, *Tempting Danger*, 2004

706

STEVE NILES

Savage Membrane

(New York: iBooks, 2005)

Story type: Mystery; Occult
Series: Monster Hunter
Subject(s): Detection; Mystery; Supernatural
Major character(s): Cal McDonald, Detective—Private; Mo'lock, Supernatural Being (ghoul); Jefferson Blout, Police Officer
Time period(s): 2000s
Locale(s): Washington, District of Columbia

Summary: Hard-boiled detective Cal McDonald, formerly of the Washington, D.C., police force, is consulted on a bizarre case in which corpses are turning up in quantity with their brains removed. Cal, who is sensitive to the occult world and supernatural beings who coexist anonymously with human beings, realizes that the clues to solving the crimes are tied up with evidence from an earlier case involving a sociopath who absorbed brains remotely, and whom Cal has already killed. First published in 2002. The author is best known for his work on the comic *30 Days of Night*.

Other books by the same author:
Guns, Drugs, and Monsters, 2002

Other books you might like:
P.N. Elrod, *Fire in the Blood*, 1992
Stephen Gallagher, *Valley of Lights*, 1987
Tanya Huff, *Blood Trail*, 1991
Richard Jaccoma, *The Werewolf's Tale*, 1989
Dan Vining, *The Quick*, 2004

707

MICHAEL PAINE (Pseudonym of John Michael Curlovich)

Steel Ghosts

(New York: Berkley, 2005)

Story type: Occult
Subject(s): Horror; Industry and Trade; Small Town Life
Major character(s): Tom Kruvener, Producer; Ruth Fawcett, Baker; Bill Vicosz, Religious
Time period(s): 2000s
Locale(s): Steadbridge, Pennsylvania

Summary: Although haunted by visions of ghostly individuals at the steel mill where his father died when he was a child, Tom Kruvener returns to his hometown of Steadbridge as an adult, hoping he can incorporate the mill and the town into the low-budget horror film he is helping to produce. Tom's plans are supposed to rejuvenate the dying town, but all he succeeds in doing is reanimating the ghosts in the steel mill who, emboldened by his activities, begin killing off people in the town with fiery deaths.

Other books by the same author:
The Colors of Hell, 1990
Owl Light, 1989
Cities of the Dead, 1988

Other books you might like:
Douglas Clegg, *The Children's Hour*, 1995
Charles L. Grant, *Something Stirs*, 1991
Stephen King, *Needful Things*, 1990
Alan Ryan, *The Kill*, 1982
David J. Searls, *Yellow Moon*, 1994

708

FRANK PERETTI

Monster

(Nashville: WestBow, 2005)

Story type: Nature in Revolt
Subject(s): Camps and Camping; Monsters

Major character(s): Reed Shelton, Police Officer (deputy); Rebecca Shelton, Spouse (of Reed); Michael Capella, Doctor
Time period(s): 2000s
Locale(s): Idaho (Tall Pine Resort)

Summary: On a weekend camping trip meant to toughen her up and quell her anxieties, Rebecca Shelton is abducted by a beast of the forest that brings her back to its lair. As Rebecca's husband, Reed, organizes a manhunt to save his wife, clues to her abductor point increasingly to a Bigfoot-type creature whose very existence challenges everyone's concepts of biology. The writer is best-known as an author of Christian fiction, and this book offers subtle commentary on generally accepted ideas regarding evolution.

Other books by the same author:
The Visitation, 1999
The Oath, 1995
Piercing the Darkness, 1989
This Present Darkness, 1986

Other books you might like:
Rick Hautala, *The Mountain King*, 1996
Dean R. Koontz, *Watchers*, 1987
Jay Kumar, *Dark Woods*, 2003
Edward Lee, *Monstrosity*, 2002
Peter Tremayne, *Snowbeast!*, 1992

709

TOM PICCIRILLI

November Mourns

(New York: Bantam, 2005)

Story type: Occult
Subject(s): Country Life; Horror; Supernatural
Major character(s): Shad Jenkins, Convict; Dave Fox, Police Officer; Preacher Dudlow, Religious
Time period(s): 2000s
Locale(s): Moon Run Hollow, Appalachians

Summary: Newly released from prison, Shad Jenkins sets out to learn the truth about the fate of his younger sister, who was found dead on a mountain road, with a smile on her face and no signs of foul play. In the mountains above Moon Run Hollow, Shad encounters a variety of Appalachian grotesques, including moonshiners, fundamentalist cultists, and inbred families, none of whom shed light on the mystery but all of whose strangeness contributes to Shad's understanding of the many weird things possible in their remote part of the world.

Other books by the same author:
A Choir of Ill Children, 2003
A Lower Deep, 2001
Night Class, 2000
Hexes, 1999
Dark Father, 1990

Other books you might like:
Jack Cady, *The Hauntings of Hood Canal*, 2003
Victor Heck, *A Darkness Inbred*, 2000
Edward Lee, *Creekers*, 1994
Robert R. McCammon, *Usher's Passing*, 1984

Michael McDowell, *The Amulet*, 1982

710

ROBERT M. PRICE, Editor

Tales out of Dunwich

(New York: Hippocampus, 2005)

Story type: Anthology
Subject(s): Horror; Short Stories; Supernatural

Summary: These ten stories were chosen by the editor for their bearing on Dunwich, a fictional New England town created by H.P. Lovecraft as a locus of occult horrors. Contents include Jack Williamson's "Mark of the Monster," a shudder pulp story of weird scientific experiments, and *The Thing in the Woods*, a werewolf novel by Harper Williams that may have influenced Lovecraft to write his well-known tale "The Dunwich Horror."

Other books by the same author:
The Tsathoggua Cycle, 2002
Acolytes of Cthulhu, 2000
Tales of the Lovecraft Mythos, 2000
Tales out of Innsmouth, 1998
The Ithaqua Cycle, 1998

Other books you might like:
David Scott Aniolowski, *Made in Goatswood*, 1995
  editor
David Scott Aniolowski, *Singers of Strange Songs*, 1997
  editor
Edward P. Berglund, *Disciples of Cthulhu*, 1976
  editor
August Derleth, *Tales of the Cthulhu Mythos*, 1969
  editor
Stephen Jones, *Shadows over Innsmouth*, 1994

711

CHERIE PRIEST

Four and Twenty Blackbirds

(New York: Tor, 2005)

Story type: Occult
Subject(s): Horror; Family Problems; Supernatural
Major character(s): Eden Moore, Young Woman; Eliza DuFresne, Aged Person; David Copeland, Photographer
Time period(s): 2000s
Locale(s): Chattanooga, Tennessee

Summary: Since childhood, Eden has had visions of female ghosts and experienced supernatural phenomena which, although frightening, ultimately prove protective. When her mad half brother tries repeatedly to murder her, in the belief that she is the reincarnation of a malevolent ancestor, Eden investigates her past, trying to uncover the identity of her unknown father and the mother who died before she knew her. Her investigations uncover a sordid family history extending back more than a century and including a sorcerer forebear who may be trying to resurrect himself from the dead through her agency. First novel.

Other books you might like:
Poppy Z. Brite, *Drawing Blood*, 1993
Jack Cady, *The Well*, 1980
Robert R. McCammon, *Usher's Passing*, 1984
Michael McDowell, *Cold Moon over Babylon*, 1980
Craig Spector, *Underground*, 2005

712

ANDREW RAMAGE, Editor

Forgotten Gems from the Twilight Zone. Volume 1

(Boalsberg, Pennsylvania: Bear Manor Media, 2005)

Story type: Anthology
Subject(s): Horror; Television; Supernatural

Summary: These five scripts by diverse hands served as teleplays for Rod Serling's original "Twilight Zone" television series. Included are William Idleson's "Long Distance Call," in which a young boy receives calls from his dead grandmother on his toy telephone; "Dead Man's Shoes" by Ocee Rich, in which the supernaturally possessed shoes of a murdered man compel whoever puts them on to seek his murderer; and "The Chaser," Robert Presnell, Jr.'s adaptation of John Collier's tale of a love potion that works better than anyone could have anticipated. The editor provides comprehensive notes and commentary on the scripts and their writers.

Other books by the same author:
Forgotten Gems from the Twilight Zone. Volume 2, 2005

Other books you might like:
Charles Beaumont, *The Twilight Zone Scripts of Charles Beaumont. Volume 1*, 2004
Earl Hamner, *The Twilight Zone Scripts of Earl Hamner*, 2003
George Clayton Johnson, *Writing for the Twilight Zone*, 1980
Richard Matheson, *Richard Matheson's The Twilight Zone Scripts*, 1998
Rod Serling, *As Timeless as Infinity: The Complete Twilight Zone Scripts of Rod Serling. Volume 1*, 2004

713

ANDREW RAMAGE, Editor

Forgotten Gems from the Twilight Zone. Volume 2

(Boalsberg, Pennsylvania: Bear Manor Media, 2005)

Story type: Anthology
Subject(s): Horror; Television; Supernatural

Summary: Five scripts written for Rod Serling's original television program, "The Twilight Zone," include Martin M. Goldsmith's "What's in the Box," in which a man discovers that his newly repaired television set now shows embarrassing and incriminating scenes from his own life; Reginald Rose's "The Incredible World of Horace Ford," in which a toy manufacturer discovers he can slip back into to the nostalgic world of his childhood and experience all of its pleasures and

its pain; and Martin M. Goldsmith's "The Encounter," in which a haunted samurai sword drives two men to revive the racial prejudices of soldiers from World War II. Also included is "Dreamflight," a script for the program written by William F. Nolan and George Clayton Johnson that was never filmed. With extensive notes and commentary by the editor.

Other books by the same author:
Forgotten Gems from the Twilight Zone. Volume 1, 2005

Other books you might like:
Charles Beaumont, *The Twilight Zone Scripts of Charles Beaumont. Volume 1*, 2004
Earl Hamner, *The Twilight Zone Scripts of Earl Hamner*, 2003
George Clayton Johnson, *Writing for the Twilight Zone*, 1980
Richard Matheson, *Richard Matheson's The Twilight Zone Scripts*, 1998
Rod Serling, *As Timeless as Infinity: The Complete Twilight Zone Scripts of Rod Serling. Volume 1*, 2004

714

EVIE RHODES

Expired

(New York: DaFina, 2005)

Story type: Serial Killer; Occult
Subject(s): Allegories; Horror; Supernatural
Major character(s): Tracie Burlingame, Hairdresser (beautician); Dre Burlingame, Child; Michael Burlingame, Child
Time period(s): 2000s
Locale(s): New York, New York

Summary: A serial killer is stalking Harlem, and taking the lives of youths who represent the best and brightest of the black culture. Tracie Burlingame, a single mother of four, finds her faith and maternal instincts sorely tested when the killer targets two of her children, one of whom is skilled at basketball and the other artistically inclined. This parable of the urban black experience, which is infused with a strong inspirational and religious sensibility, is a first novel for this writer, who is better known as a singer.

Other books you might like:
Steve Barnes, *Charisma*, 2002
Bertice Berry, *The Haunting of Hip Hop*, 2001
Tananarive Due, *The Good House*, 2003
Robert Fleming, *Havoc After Dark*, 2004
Brandon Massey, *Dark Corner*, 2004

715

NATASHA RHODES

Dead Reckoning

(Nottingham, England: Black Flame, 2005)

Story type: Occult
Series: Final Destination
Subject(s): Fate; Horror; Supernatural
Major character(s): Jess Golden, Musician; Jamie, Musician; Eric, Teenager

Horror

Time period(s): 2000s
Locale(s): Los Angeles, California

Summary: Moments before she is kicked out of Club Kitty, Jess Golden has a premonition that the club will be destroyed by an explosive fire that will kill everyone in it. Afterwards, the handful of patrons who survived with Jess begin dying under mysterious circumstances, proof that they were supposed to have perished in the club and that fate is intervening supernaturally to force the outcome that should have been. This novel was suggested by the plot of the film *Final Destination* (2000).

Other books by the same author:
Blade: Trinity, 2004

Other books you might like:
Tananarive Due, *The Between*, 1995
David McIntee, *Destination Zero*, 2005
James Swallow, *The Butterfly Effect*, 2004
Bernard Taylor, *Charmed Life*, 1991

716

TONY RICHARDS

Ghost Dance

(Carmarthenshire, Wales: Sarob, 2005)

Story type: Collection
Subject(s): Horror; Short Stories; Supernatural

Summary: The eight short stories and novellas in this collection are by a contemporary British writer whose work has been appearing in horror and weird fiction publications for three decades. "Under the Ice" concerns a man accidentally resurrected from the dead to compete with his brother for the hand of a loved one. "Lightning Dogs" tells of spectral dogs who haunt the London subway. "Beyond the Western Walls" is a futuristic blend of science fiction and fantasy about grotesque scientific experiments uncovered in a secret compound in the Nicaraguan jungle. With an introduction by Graham Joyce. Published as a limited edition hardcover.

Other books by the same author:
Postcards from Terri, 2004
Hot Blood, 1996
Night Feast, 1995
Harvest Bride, 1986

Other books you might like:
Simon Clark, *Salt Snake and Other Bloody Cuts*, 1998
Steve Duffy, *The Night Comes On*, 1998
Paul Finch, *After Shocks*, 2001
Graham Joyce, *Partial Eclipse and Other Stories*, 2003
Tim Lebbon, *As the Sun Goes Down*, 2000

717

AL SARRANTONIO

A Little Yellow Book of Fevered Stories

(Fork, Maryland: Borderlands, 2005)

Story type: Collection
Subject(s): Horror; Short Stories; Supernatural

Summary: Sarrantonio presents eight stories of horror and dark fantasy, many written in the lyrical style of Ray Bradbury. Contents include "Pumpkin Head," about the nasty revenge of a boy upon his taunting schoolmates; "The Ropy Thing," in which a monster partly fashioned from imagination overruns the world; and "Father Dear," a bizarre memoir of a child's macabre relationship with his father. This is part of the publisher's series of short books of short stories with similar titles.

Other books by the same author:
Hallows Eve, 2004
Hornets and Others, 2004
Orangefield, 2002
Toybox, 2000
House Haunted, 1991

Other books you might like:
Gary A. Braunbeck, *A Little Orange Book of Odd Stories*, 2004
Joe R. Lansdale, *A Little Green Book of Monster Stories*, 2003
John Maclay, *A Little Red Book of Vampire Stories*, 2003
Thomas F. Monteleone, *A Little Brown Book of Bizarre Stories*, 2004
David B. Silva, *A Little White Book of Lies*, 2005

718

ROD SERLING

As Timeless as Infinity: The Complete Twilight Zone Scripts of Rod Serling. Volume 3

(Colorado Springs, Colorado: Gauntlet, 2005)

Story type: Collection
Series: Complete Twilight Zone Scripts of Rod Serling. Volume 3
Subject(s): Horror; Supernatural; Television Programs

Summary: Rod Serling's television program, "The Twilight Zone," which ran initially from 1959 to 1964, had an enormous impact on modern horror fiction, film, and television. Included in these nine scripts are "Time Enough at Last," the ironic tale of a book lover who is the sole survivor of nuclear armageddon; "The Four of Us Are Dying," about a man with a malleable personality who takes the imprint of whomever people want to see him as; and "One for the Angels," about a sidewalk salesman who uses his talents to cheat Death incarnate of a soul. Edited and with extensive notes by Tony Albarella, this is published as a limited edition hardcover.

Other books by the same author:
As Timeless as Infinity: The Complete Twilight Zone Scripts of Rod Serling. Volume 2, 2005
As Timeless as Infinity: The Complete Twilight Zone Scripts of Rod Serling. Volume 1, 2004
The Twilight Zone: Complete Stories, 1980
Night Gallery 2, 1972
Night Gallery, 1971

Other books you might like:
Charles Beaumont, *The Twilight Zone Scripts of Charles Beaumont. Volume 1*, 2004

Earl Hamner, *The Twilight Zone Scripts of Earl Hamner*, 2003

George Clayton Johnson, *Writing for the Twilight Zone*, 1980

Richard Matheson, *Richard Matheson's Kolchak Scripts*, 2003

Richard Matheson, *Richard Matheson's The Twilight Zone Scripts*, 1998

719

ROD SERLING

As Timeless as Infinity: The Complete Twilight Zone Scripts of Rod Serling. Volume 2

(Colorado Springs, Colorado: Gauntlet, 2005)

Story type: Collection

Series: Complete Twilight Zone Scripts of Rod Serling. Volume 2

Subject(s): Horror; Supernatural; Television Programs

Summary: This book contains nine scripts by Rod Serling, whose television program, "The Twilight Zone," which ran initially from 1959 to 1964, had an enormous impact on modern horror fiction, film, and television. Included are "Walking Distance," in which a man's nostalgia for the past transports him back in time to meet the child he once was; "Judgment Night," in which a U-boat captain finds himself a passenger on a ship doomed repeatedly to be sunk by the German navy; and "I Am the Night—Color Me Black," in which the hatred of a small town's citizens on the eve of a criminal's execution manifests as unchanging nightfall that engulfs the town. Edited and with extensive notes by Tony Albarella, this is published as a limited edition hardcover.

Other books by the same author:

As Timeless as Infinity: The Complete Twilight Zone Scripts of Rod Serling. Volume 3, 2005

As Timeless as Infinity: The Complete Twilight Zone Scripts of Rod Serling. Volume 1, 2004

The Twilight Zone: Complete Stories, 1980

Night Gallery 2, 1972

Night Gallery, 1971

Other books you might like:

Charles Beaumont, *The Twilight Zone Scripts of Charles Beaumont. Volume 1*, 2004

Earl Hamner, *The Twilight Zone Scripts of Earl Hamner*, 2003

George Clayton Johnson, *Writing for the Twilight Zone*, 1980

Richard Matheson, *Richard Matheson's Kolchak Scripts*, 2003

Richard Matheson, *Richard Matheson's The Twilight Zone Scripts*, 1998

720

MARY SHELLEY

Transformation

(London: Hesperus, 2005)

Story type: Collection

Subject(s): Horror; Short Stories; Supernatural

Summary: These three tales of Gothic horror are by the author of *Frankenstein*. "The Mortal Immortal" concerns a man who, after 300 years of life, seeks an end to the immortality that has become his curse. "Transformation" tells of an exchange of souls between a handsome young man and a deformed, demonic dwarf. "The Evil Eye" involves the kidnapping of a child by a man shunned for his supposed evil powers.

Other books by the same author:

The Mortal Immortal, 1996

Collected Tales and Stories, 1969

The Last Man, 1826

Frankenstein, 1818

Other books you might like:

Catherine Crowe, *Ghosts and Family Legends*, 2005

Elizabeth Gaskell, *Mrs. Gaskell's Tales of Mystery and Horror*, 1978

Margaret Oliphant, *Stories of the Seen and Unseen*, 1889

Mrs. J.H. Riddell, *The Collected Ghost Stories of Mrs. J.H. Riddell*, 1977

721

LUCIUS SHEPARD

Eternity and Other Stories

(New York: Thunder's Mouth, 2005)

Story type: Collection

Subject(s): Horror; Short Stories; Supernatural

Summary: These nine stories, most of novella-length, are set in exotic locales that heighten their sense of the strange and outre. In "Eternity and Afterward," a Russian detective confronts a demonic underworld kingpin to save his girlfriend. "Only Partly Here" is a ghost story of loss and longing set in the ruins of the World Trade Center disaster. In "Crocodile Rock," supernaturally endowed humans shapeshift into crocodiles as an expression of their predatory natures.

Other books by the same author:

Trujillo, 2004

Two Trains Running, 2004

Beast of the Heartland, 1999

The Ends of the Earth, 1991

The Jaguar Hunter, 1987

Other books you might like:

Harlan Ellison, *Slippage*, 1998

Elizabeth Hand, *Bibliomancy*, 2003

Graham Joyce, *Partial Eclipse and Other Stories*, 2003

Dan Simmons, *Lovedeath*, 1993

Michael Marshall Smith, *More Tomorrow and Other Stories*, 2003

Horror

722

M.P. SHIEL

The House of Sounds and Others

(New York: Hippocampus, 2005)

Story type: Collection
Subject(s): Horror; Short Stories; Supernatural

Summary: This collection of tales is from a writer of florid, Poesque horror tales in the late 19th and early 20th centuries. Selections include ''Huguenin's Wife,'' in which a woman's soul transmigrates into the body of a mythical animal after her death; ''Xelucha'' and ''The Bride,'' both of which concern amorous advances from beyond the grave; and the title story, about an eccentric and doomed family household. Also included is the full novel *The Purple Cloud*, an epic disaster novel in which poison gases kill most life on earth and leaves civilization to be rebuilt. Edited and with an introduction by S.T. Joshi, as part of the publisher's series of books recommended by H.P. Lovecraft.

Other books by the same author:
Xelucha and Others, 1975
The Best Short Stories of M.P. Shiel, 1948
Here Comes the Lady, 1928
The Pale Ape and Other Pulses, 1911
Shapes in the Fire, 1896

Other books you might like:
R. Murray Gilchrist, *The Stone Dragon and Other Tragic Romances*, 1998
Arthur Machen, *The White People and Other Tales*, 2003
Vincent O'Sullivan, *Master of the Fallen Years*, 1990
Barry Pain, *Stories in the Dark*, 1901
Edgar Allan Poe, *Complete Tales and Poems*, 1938

723

JOHN SHIRLEY

Cellars

(Akron, Ohio: Infrapress, 2005)

Story type: Occult
Subject(s): City and Town Life; Horror; Supernatural
Major character(s): Carl Lanyard, Journalist; Madelaine Springer, Psychic; Cyril Gribner, Police Officer
Time period(s): 1980s
Locale(s): New York, New York

Summary: Journalist Carl Lanyard, a writer on true occult subjects, discovers a thriving cult of Ahriman practicing secretly in Manhattan and paying obeisance to a monster of Persian mythology that both feeds on and sustains the misery driving the city. Reprint of a novel first published in 1982.

Other books by the same author:
Crawlers, 2003
Spider Moon, 2002
The View from Hell, 2001
Demons, 2000
In Darkness Waiting, 1988

Other books you might like:
Fritz Leiber, *Our Lady of Darkness*, 1977
Thomas F. Monteleone, *Night Train*, 1984
David J. Schow, *The Shaft*, 1990
Chet Williamson, *Lowland Rider*, 1988

724

JOHN SHIRLEY

Constantine

(New York: Pocket Star, 2005)

Story type: Occult; Ancient Evil Unleashed
Subject(s): Good and Evil; Hell; Supernatural
Major character(s): John Constantine, Detective—Private; Angela Dodson, Police Officer; Balthazar, Demon
Time period(s): 2000s
Locale(s): Los Angeles, California

Summary: John Constantine, a private detective with the paranormal power to see angels and demons who walk the earth in human form, spends his life exorcising demons and agents of Satan as atonement for a suicide attempt years before that has virtually damned him to Hell upon his death. When he agrees to help Angela Dodson investigate the inexplicable (apparent) suicide of her twin sister, he uncovers an infernal plot involving the recovery of the awesomely powerful occult talisman, the Spear of Destiny, and its employment to help bring the son of Satan to Earth. Novelization of a screenplay by Kevin Brodbin and Frank Cappello. The story, by Brodbin, is adapted from the Hellblazer graphic novel series. The script was filmed by director Francis Lawrence for Warner Brothers.

Other books by the same author:
Crawlers, 2003
Spider Moon, 2002
And the Angel with Television Eyes, 2001
The View from Hell, 2001
Demons, 2000

Other books you might like:
Jim Butcher, *Blood Rites*, 2004
Laurell K. Hamilton, *Guilty Pleasures*, 1993
James Herbert, *The Spear*, 1978
Robert Morgan, *The Things That Are Not There*, 1992
Yvonne Navarro, *Hellboy*, 2004

725

JOHN SHIRLEY

In Darkness Waiting

(Akron, Ohio: Infrapress, 2005)

Story type: Science Fiction
Subject(s): Horror; Scientific Experiments; Violence
Major character(s): Perry Strandman, Researcher; Arthur Rofocale, Doctor; Lois Rutherford, Teenager
Time period(s): 2000s
Locale(s): Jasper, Oregon

Summary: Dr. Arthur Rofocale's experiments in Empathy Suppression Syndrome help liberate from a test subject a

Gray Pilot, a creature of pure violent impulse that represents the inherent tendency of mankind toward wanton cruelty and violence. Although millennia of civilization have helped humans to suppress their Gray Pilots, this one flits about the small town of Jasper, stinging victims and inciting them to random acts of senseless violence. First published in 1988 and updated slightly by the author.

Where it's reviewed:
Publishers Weekly, January 24, 2005, page 226

Other books by the same author:
Constantine, 2005
Crawlers, 2003
Spider Moon, 2002
And the Angel with Television Eyes, 2001
The View from Hell, 2001

Other books you might like:
Simon Clark, *Blood Crazy*, 1995
Michael Crichton, *The Terminal Man*, 1972
David Cronenberg, *The Brood*, 1979
Michael Green, *The Jim Jams*, 1994
David J. Searls, *Yellow Moon*, 1994

726
DAVID B. SILVA

A Little White Book of Lies
(Fork, Maryland: Borderlands, 2005)

Story type: Collection
Subject(s): Horror; Short Stories; Supernatural

Summary: Five stories by Silva, a writer of poignant and haunting horror fiction, are collected here. ''Brothers'' concerns a young boy so attached to his brother that he resurrects him after his death through the power of his imagination. In ''The Hollow,'' a young boy befriends a monster living in the hole beneath a tree on the outskirts of his town. ''Where the Past Lay Buried'' is an imaginary world fantasy written in homage to the fiction of fantasist Clark Ashton Smith. This is part of the publisher's series of short books of short stories with similar titles.

Other books by the same author:
All the Lonely People, 2003
The Many, 2003
Through Shattered Glass, 2001
The Disappeared, 1995
The Presence, 1994

Other books you might like:
Gary A. Braunbeck, *A Little Orange Book of Odd Stories*, 2004
Joe R. Lansdale, *A Little Green Book of Monster Stories*, 2003
John Maclay, *A Little Red Book of Vampire Stories*, 2003
Thomas F. Monteleone, *A Little Brown Book of Bizarre Stories*, 2004
Al Sarrantonio, *A Little Yellow Book of Fevered Stories*, 2005

727
SUSAN SIZEMORE

I Hunger for You
(New York: Pocket Star, 2005)

Story type: Vampire Story
Subject(s): Romance; Supernatural; Vampires
Major character(s): Caramia ''Mia'' Luchese, Writer; Colin Foxe, Vampire, Police Officer; Laurent, Vampire
Time period(s): 2000s
Locale(s): Los Angeles, California

Summary: Colin Foxe, who heads a S.W.A.T. for the Los Angeles Police Department, falls in love with Mia Luchese when he rescues her during a hostage situation. Their love is complicated by the fact that Colin is a vampire, and Mia the descendant of a vampire-hunting family. Worse yet, Colin is being watched by members of rival vampire gangs who will use any vulnerability they detect in him to their advantage.

Other books by the same author:
I Thirst for You, 2004
Heroes, 2003
I Burn for You, 2003
Deceptions, 2002
Companions, 2001

Other books you might like:
Mick Farren, *The Time of Feasting*, 1996
Laurell K. Hamilton, *Guilty Pleasures*, 1993
Tanya Huff, *Blood Trail*, 1992
Brent Monahan, *The Book of Common Dread*, 1993
Karen E. Taylor, *Blood Ties*, 2005

728
CRAIG SPECTOR

Underground
(New York: Tor, 2005)

Story type: Occult
Subject(s): Horror; Slavery; Supernatural
Major character(s): Josh Custis, Wealthy; Caroline Tabb Connolly, Real Estate Agent; Justin Van Slyke, Prisoner
Time period(s): 2000s; 1980s
Locale(s): Stilson Beach, Virginia

Summary: Josh Custis, the youngest son of an established Virginia family with political ambitions and roots reaching back to the antebellum South, reconvenes the Underground, a group of friends who were renegades in high school before they went on to their boring middle-aged, middle-class lives. Years before, at Josh's family home, a party with Underground members opened the portal to an occult dimension accessed through a magic mirror, which resulted in the loss of their friend Mia. Mia has lived in the world on the other side of the mirror—a world that has entrapped the souls of all those killed in blood sacrifices the Custis family has made for political gain over the centuries—and Josh is determined to save her and Justin, who recently entered that world himself searching for Mia. To do so, Josh and the Underground will have to overcome the lethargy of their sell-out lives and enter

Horror

the world on the far side of the mirror before the next blood sacrifice can be made.

Other books by the same author:
To Bury the Dead, 2000

Other books you might like:
Poppy Z. Brite, *Drawing Blood*, 1993
Tananarive Due, *The Good House*, 2003
Tom Elliott, *The Dwelling*, 1989
Caitlin Kiernan, *Silk*, 1998
Stephen King, *It*, 1986

729

BRIAN STABLEFORD

Kiss the Goat

(Canton, Ohio: Prime, 2005)

Story type: Ghost Story
Subject(s): Ghosts
Major character(s): Kit Miner, Driver; Stephen Carraway, Student; Rose Selavy, Prostitute, Spirit (ghost)
Time period(s): 2000s
Locale(s): Reading, England

Summary: Bus driver Kit Miner discovers that the inexpensive boarding room where she stays is haunted by the ghost of Rose Selavy, a former prostitute who died on its premises. With the help of student and sometime lover Stephen, Kit digs into Rose's past in the hope of discovering why Rose is so persistent in her attentions to Kit, and why others among the dear departed are beginning to manifest to her exclusively.

Other books by the same author:
Sheena and Other Gothic Tales, 2005
The Hunger and Ecstasy of Vampires, 1996
Young Blood, 1992
The Werewolves of London, 1990
The Empire of Fear, 1988

Other books you might like:
Jonathan Aycliffe, *Naomi's Room*, 1991
Poppy Z. Brite, *Drawing Blood*, 1993
Ramsey Campbell, *The Influence*, 1988
John Harwood, *The Ghost Writer*, 2004
Peter Straub, *Mrs. God*, 1990

730

ROBERT LOUIS STEVENSON

The Suicide Club and Other Dark Adventures

(East Sussex, England: Tartarus, 2005)

Story type: Collection
Subject(s): Horror; Short Stories; Supernatural

Summary: This collection contains 31 stories of mystery and horror, including a reprint of the short novel ''The Strange Case of Dr. Jekyll and Mr. Hyde.'' Also included are ''The Body-Snatcher,'' about the grim business and fates of a team of grave robbers; ''Thrawn Janet,'' a tale of witchcraft; and ''The Isle of Voices,'' a tale of occult adventures in the South

Sea islands. Published as a limited edition hardcover, the book contains an introduction by Mark Valentine.

Other books by the same author:
Tales and Fantasies, 1905
Island Nights' Entertainments, 1893
The Merry Men and Other Tales and Fables, 1887
New Arabian Nights, 1882

Other books you might like:
Ambrose Bierce, *Ghost and Horror Stories*, 1964
Robert W. Chambers, *The King in Yellow*, 1895
Ralph Adams Cram, *Black Spirits and White*, 2004
Francis Marion Crawford, *For the Blood Is the Life and Other Stories*, 1996
W.C. Morrow, *The Monster Maker and Other Stories*, 2000

731

THOMAS TESSIER

Finishing Touches

(New York: Leisure, 2005)

Story type: Erotic Horror; Psychological Suspense
Subject(s): Doctors; Horror; Sexuality
Major character(s): Tom Sutherland, Doctor; Roger Nordhagen, Doctor; Lina Ravinal, Assistant
Time period(s): 1980s
Locale(s): London, England

Summary: Newly graduated from medical school in the United States, Tom Sutherland becomes a protege of Roger Nordhagen, a London physician with unorthodox beliefs and practices. Under Nordhagen's Mephistophlean influence, Sutherland becomes a lover to Lina, Nordhagen's assistant, and is drawn into a world of perverse sexuality that culminates in the discovery of gruesome experiments Nordhagen conducts secretly in the basement beneath his practice. Reprint of a novel first published in 1986.

Other books by the same author:
Fogheart, 1997
Phantom, 1982
Shockwaves, 1982
The Nightwalker, 1980
The Fates, 1978

Other books you might like:
Jonathan Aycliffe, *Naomi's Room*, 1991
Robin Cook, *Coma*, 1977
K.W. Jeter, *Dr. Adder*, 1984
David J. Skal, *Antibodies*, 1988
F. Paul Wilson, *Sibs*, 1991

732

LISA TUTTLE

The Mysteries

(New York: Random House, 2005)

Story type: Occult
Subject(s): Folklore; Missing Persons; Supernatural
Major character(s): Ian Kennedy, Detective—Private; Perri Lensky, Young Woman; Hugh Bell-Rivers, Filmmaker

Time period(s): 2000s
Locale(s): London, England; Scotland

Summary: Private detective Ian Kennedy is a specialist in missing persons cases, owing to the emotional impact of his own father's abandonment of their family when Ian was a child. His latest case, the two-year-old disappearance of Perri Lensky, begins routinely enough. However, the more thoroughly Ian interviews those who knew her, and the more he reads of her personal writings from before she vanished, the more parallels he sees between Perri's case and the Celtic legends of the *sidhe*, faerie folk who seduce mortals into the Otherworld from which only they can choose to leave.

Where it's reviewed:
Publishers Weekly, January 17, 2005, page 38

Other books by the same author:
My Death, 2004
Pillow Friend, 1996
Lost Futures, 1992
Gabriel, 1987
Familiar Spirit, 1983

Other books you might like:
Jonathan Carroll, *Sleeping in Flame*, 1988
Elaine Cunningham, *Shadows in the Darkness*, 2004
Chris Curry, *Panic*, 1994
Charles De Lint, *The Little Country*, 1991
Elizabeth Hand, *Mortal Love*, 2004

733

TIM WAGGONER

Like Death

(New York: Leisure, 2005)

Story type: Occult; Child-in-Peril
Subject(s): Horror
Major character(s): Scott Raymond, Journalist; Miranda Tanner, Teenager; Laura Foster, Teacher
Time period(s): 2000s
Locale(s): Ash Creek, Ohio

Summary: As a young boy, Scott was emotionally and psychologically disturbed when he witnessed his family's brutal slaying. Now a crime reporter recently moved to Ash Creek to be with his own estranged family, Scott investigates the mystery of Miranda Tanner, a six-year-old girl who disappeared almost a decade before. Scott's investigations bring him into contact with a teenage girl also named Miranda, who seems to have unusual knowledge of the case, and who introduces him to the Shadow, a world hidden beneath the surface of normal reality that can shape the world's events.

Other books by the same author:
Dreamspawn, 2005
Protege, 2005
Necropolis, 2004
The Harmony Society, 2003
Dying for It, 2001

Other books you might like:
Graham Masterton, *The Doorkeepers*, 2001
Mark Morris, *Toady*, 1989

Craig Spector, *Underground*, 2005
J. Michael Straczynski, *OtherSyde*, 1990
Lisa Tuttle, *The Mysteries*, 2005

734

H. RUSSELL WAKEFIELD

They Return at Evening

(Ashcroft, British Columbia: Ash-Tree Press, 2005)

Story type: Collection
Subject(s): Horror; Short Stories; Supernatural

Summary: *They Return at Evening* provides ten tales of ghosts and the supernatural by a leading British writer of horror fiction in the first half of the 20th century. Stories include "He Cometh and He Passeth By," about a Satanist (modeled on real-life occultist Aleister Crowley) who kills his enemies with sympathetic magic. "The Red Lodge" concerns a house haunted by the ghost of a drowning victim while "The Seventeenth Hole at Duncaster" tells of a haunted golf course. This book was first published in England in 1928 and is one of the most highly regarded ghost story collections of the pre-World War II era. Introduction by Barbara Roden.

Other books by the same author:
Strayers from Sheol, 1961
The Clock Strikes Twelve, 1940
A Ghostly Company, 1935
Ghost Stories, 1932
Imagine a Man in a Box, 1931

Other books you might like:
E.F. Benson, *Sea Mist*, 2005
Andrew Caldecott, *Fires Burn Blue*, 1948
M.R. James, *Ghost Stories of an Antiquary*, 1904
Margery Lawrence, *The Floating Cafe: And Other Stories*, 1936
L.A. Lewis, *Tales of the Grotesque*, 1934

735

MANLY WADE WELLMAN

Strangers on the Heights

(Portland, Oregon: Night Shade, 2005)

Story type: Collection; Science Fiction
Series: Lost Wellman
Subject(s): Horror; Aliens; Short Stories

Summary: These two stories were first published in science fiction pulp magazines in the 1930s and 1940s. The title tale concerns an extraterrestrial race who adopt the form of occult monsters. They then present themselves as servants of black magic to prey on the fears of superstitious earthmen and compel them to serve their interest in taking over the planet. "Nuisance Value" is yet another story of alien invasion, concerning extraterrestrials from a cold planet hampered in their efforts to take over Earth by temperate climates.

Other books by the same author:
Giants of Eternity, 2005
Owls Hoot in the Daytime and Other Omens, 2002
Sin's Doorway and Other Ominous Entrances, 2002

Fearful Rock and Other Precarious Locales, 2001
The Devil Is Not Mocked and Other Warnings, 2001

Other books you might like:
Robert A. Heinlein, *The Unpleasant Profession of Jonathan Hoag*, 1959
C.L. Moore, *Shambleau*, 1953
Lewis Padgett, *A Gnome There Was and Other Tales of Science Fiction and Fantasy*, 1950
Theodore Sturgeon, *Without Sorcery*, 1948
Jack Williamson, *Spider Island*, 2001

736

CONRAD WILLIAMS

London Revenant

(Portland, Oregon: Night Shade, 2005)

Story type: Serial Killer
Subject(s): City and Town Life; Horror; Serial Killers
Major character(s): Adam Buckley, Worker; Nuala Deuel, Young Woman; Iain Wild, Guard
Time period(s): 2000s
Locale(s): London, England

Summary: Two plotlines converge in this urban *noir* novel. In one, a secret community of people who live in the tunnels of the London underground seek out a renegade who has gone topside and is causing unwanted attention by pushing people to their deaths under subway trains. In the other, Adam, a narcoleptic vulnerable to hypnogogic visions, falls in with a group of friends whose obsession with the subway serial killer is drawing him increasingly to the dark underbelly of London, and especially to the subway system, where he makes a stunning revelation about his personal identity. First published in the United Kingdom in 2004.

Other books by the same author:
Game, 2004
Use Once Then Destroy, 2004
Nearly People, 2001
Head Injuries, 1998

Other books you might like:
Christopher Fowler, *Roofworld*, 1988
Simon R. Green, *Something from the Nightside*, 2003
Graham Masterton, *The Doorkeepers*, 2001
John Maxim, *Platforms*, 1980
Chet Williamson, *Lowland Rider*, 1988

737

K.C. WINTERS

Chosen/The Placebo Effect

(New York: Black Flame, 2005)

Story type: Collection
Series: Twilight Zone

Subject(s): Horror; Television; Supernatural

Summary: This volume novelizes two episodes from the first season of the revived television program, "The Twilight Zone." In "Chosen," a man who mistakes an unusually persistent pair of prosletyzers for evangelists discovers they are actually angels seeking his help to prevent the apocalypse. "The Placebo Effect" concerns a hypochondriac whose unusual ability to manifest diseases produces a plague that could wipe out civilization.

Other books you might like:
Pat Cadigan, *Upgrade/Sensuous Cindy*, 2004
Christa Faust, *Burned/One Night at Mercy*, 2005
Jay Russell, *Memphis/The Pool Guy*, 2004
Rod Serling, *Rod Serling's The Twilight Zone*, 1963
Paul A. Woods, *Into the Light/Sunrise*, 2004

738

STEPHEN WOODWORTH

With Red Hands

(New York: Dell, 2005)

Story type: Wild Talents
Subject(s): Crime and Criminals; Murder; Supernatural
Major character(s): Natalie Lindstrom, Psychic; Inez Mendoza, Lawyer; George, Spy
Time period(s): 2000s
Locale(s): Los Angeles, California

Summary: This is a sequel to *Through Violet Eyes*, which introduced the Violets, a race of violet-eyed humans who can channel the dead and who have thus become instrumental courtroom tools for murder cases where guilt and innocence are not clear. Natalie Lindstrom is a Violet who has retired from the North American Afterlife Communication Corps and who is trying to keep her young daughter Callie out of their hands to save her from the anguish she has known because of her profession. Natalie gets involved in a high-profile murder case being adjudicated with the help of another Violet whom she thinks is falsifying information. She discovers that the influence being channeled may be related to "the Thresher," a serial killer who was executed years before, but whose channeling drove her mother mad and who may still be killing from beyond the grave.

Where it's reviewed:
Publishers Weekly, November 29, 2004, page 28

Other books by the same author:
In Golden Blood, 2006
Through Violet Eyes, 2004

Other books you might like:
P.N. Elrod, *Bloodlist*, 1990
Thomas Harris, *Red Dragon*, 1981
Brian Lumley, *Necroscope*, 1986
Graham Masterton, *Unspeakable*, 2005
Dan Vining, *The Quick*, 2004

Strange Powers of the Mind
by
Don D'Ammassa

One of the most pervasive plot elements in science fiction is the potential development of new powers of the human mind, either through spontaneous mutation, genetic manipulation, or in some cases by means of an artificial device to enhance latent abilities. These abilities fall loosely into the realm of parapsychology and are generally referred to as ESP (extrasensory perception), psi powers, or psychic powers. The most commonly found psi power is telepathy, the ability to read the thoughts of others, followed by teleportation—the ability to move oneself from one location to another through non-physical means, telekinesis or psychokinesis—the ability to move or affect physical objects solely through mental influence, and a handful of less common talents. Many of these same abilities can be found in horror or fantasy fiction and are often described as having a supernatural or magical source, and in some cases individual works of fiction are ambiguous and open to more than one interpretation. Stephen King's first novel, *Carrie* (1974), for example, leaves open the question of whether Carrie White's telekinesis is simply a freakish natural ability or derives from an unknown supernatural source.

Telepathy in science fiction generally takes two forms. The first, and less common, is simply the ability to look into the minds of others and read their thoughts. The second assumes that humanity, or a subset thereof, will eventually develop the ability to pass information back and forth mentally, sometimes with aliens or animals, as well as other humans. In the vast majority of cases, telepathy and telepaths are subsidiary plot elements, either introduced to advance a plot point, or as part of a general background designed to signify a sharp departure from the present day. A comparative handful of novels have concentrated on the phenomenon of telepathy itself, and either its effects on society at large or upon the individual so gifted, or in some cases, so cursed.

One of the most interesting and most enduring novels to explore the consequences of telepathy is *The Demolisheed Man* (1953) by Alfred Bester. Bester speculates that the appearance of reliable telepaths in the near future might lead to the creation of a special police force which would employ telepaths to determine the truth in criminal investigations. The novel is set in the form of a reverse mystery, told in part from the viewpoint of an ingenious murderer who discovers a way to commit a seemingly perfect murder even though his thoughts are subject to scrutiny by the police. Lee Killough partially reversed this device in *The Deadly Silents* (1981), in which non-telepathic human investigators are called upon to solve a murder on an alien world, all of whose citizens are telepathic, to solve a crime impenetrable to the natives, who have never developed the tools since they believed it impossible for any individual to conceal such a secret. John Brunner similarly considered the possibility that telepaths might serve as expert diagnosticians in the psychiatric profession in *The Whole Man* (1964, also published as *Telepathist*) because of their ability to eavesdrop on the dreams of disturbed patients and effect a cure. This device was later used in the motion pictures *Dreamscape* (1983) and *The Cell* (2000).

Robert A. Heinlein suggested a different possibility in *Time for the Stars* (1956). Only identical twins can function as telepaths in his future, a comparative rarity that helps humanity overcome a significant problem. Although it is possible to launch spaceships on very long voyages to the stars, the only way to stay in close communication is by splitting a pair of telepathic twins, placing one aboard the ship while the other remains on Earth. Even this proves to be of limited utility, however, since time operates at different rates depending on the ship's acceleration, the disparity in ages between the twins grows rapidly wider. Andre Norton suggested another possible use in *Daybreak 2250 A.D.* (1954, also published as *Star Man's Son*, a post apocalyptic novel in which the young protagonist is able to better his chances for survival by linking himself telepathically to a handful of animals, enabling him to influence their behavior. Norton would use this same device repeatedly in her later science fiction and fantasy, most nota-

bly in *The Beast Master* (1959). Other writers have adapted that device for their own purposes, as in *Rider at the Gate* (1995) by C.J. Cherryh.

Several novels have concentrated on the individual telepath, rather than society at large. In *The Hollow Man* (1992), the protagonist's telepathy has been suppressed through the influence of his wife. Following her death, he discovers that he is unable to control his power, and it has caused him to acquire knowledge about the identity of a vicious killer. *The Journal of Nicholas the American* (1986) examines a subtler form of telepathy, an enhanced form of empathy that allows one individual to directly experience the emotions of another. The empathic hero isolates himself from the rest of the world in self defense until an encounter with a fatally ill woman changes his perspective. Similarly thoughtful and even more impressively written is *Dying Inside* (1972) by Robert Silverberg, in which a lonely man conceals the existence of his telepathic powers, which he considers a curse, but who perversely feels a great sense of loss when he realizes his extrasensory talent is lessening and will eventually disappear entirely. *Telepath* (1962, also published as *Silent Speakers*) by Arthur Sellings takes a more positive tone, suggesting that the ability to read minds might improve one's lot in life.

Other writers have attempted to describe how a society of telepaths might function, or how the experience might actually feel. The best of the latter is *And Chaos Died* (1970), wherein a space traveler is stranded on a planet whose inhabitants have developed telepathy and other mental powers. A.E. van Vogt suggested in *Slan* (1946) that telepaths would more likely be feared than accepted, forcing them to conceal themselves from ordinary humanity. This pessimistic viewpoint has been in common use in the genre ever since. Isolated individuals with telepathic powers would almost certainly conceal their differences, as in *Wild Talent* (1954, also published as *The Man from Tomorrow*), and possibly with malevolent intentions, as in *Waiting* (1999) by Frank M. Robinson.

The second most commonly used psi power in science fiction is telekinesis or psychokinesis, sometimes simply called PK, the ability to influence physical objects remotely. This is the power that Stephen King's Carrie White uses to lock the doors and confine her tormentors before taking her own life by literally collapsing a house in upon herself. Perhaps the most interesting depiction of telekinesis is that found in three related books by Larry Niven, *The Long Arm of Gil Hamilton* (1976), *The Patchwork Girl* (1980), and *Flatlander* (1995). Gil Hamilton can touch objects with his mind, but the ability is so difficult for him to accept that he must visualize an invisible third arm to focus his talent, which limits the range across which he can operate. Hamilton solves a variety of mysteries in the novel and two short story collections that chronicle his career.

Several novels have focused on the emergence of reliable telekinesis in one or more individuals. That premise is used to launch an elaborate chase sequence with various groups, usually including a more or less malevolent government agency, seeking to capture and exploit the protagonist. Perhaps the best known of these is *The Fury* (1976) by John Farris, who has recently added two sequels, moving the series from science fiction to fantasy. S. Andrew Swann, writing as Steven Krane, provides a more rationalized variation in *Teek* (1999), as does Louis Charbonneau in *The Sensitives* (1968). Colonists on a new planet are horrified to discover that all of their children have developed telekinesis in *A Coming of Age* (1984) by Timothy Zahn, while one telekinetic in *The Hidden Ones* (1988) by Gwyneth Jones uses her powers to help deal with an environmental crisis. Quentin Thomas, the lawyer protagonist of *The Venetian Court* (1982) and *Lunar Justice* (1991) by Charles L. Harness, uses his telekinetic abilities to aid him in the development of his legal cases. Telekinesis is also a significant plot element in Philip K. Dick's *Dr. Bloodmoney* (1965). Randall Garrett and Laurence Janifer treated the theme humorously in *The Impossibles* (1963), published under the pseudonym Mark Phillips.

A less popular psi power is teleportation, although it is often achieved through artificial means, most often referred to as matter transmission. Teleportation is the transfer, usually instantaneous, of an object or a person from one place to another without the object passing through the intervening space. This differentiates it from telekinesis or levitation, the ability to defy the force of gravity. The best known application of the artificial form is the transporter beams in the television series ''Star Trek,'' but the most famous single work of fiction involving mental teleportation is Alfred Bester's *The Stars My Destination* (1957, also published as *Tiger! Tiger!*). Gully Foyle, a petty criminal abandoned to die in space, spontaneously develops the ability to teleport (called ''jaunting'' in the novel) in order to save himself. A more upbeat view of teleportation can be found in *Jumper* (1992) by Stephen Gould and its sequel, *Reflex* (2004), both of which suggest that even possession of such an extraordinary power cannot ensure an individual's safety.

A few authors have suggested that an entire gamut of psi powers might appear simultaneously, either in one individual or in a small group. One of the earliest and best of these is *Jack of Eagles* (1952, also published as *ESPer*) by James Blish, in which the protagonist is able to read minds and has precognition, the ability to foresee the future. However, he unwisely calls attention to himself by ostentatiously using his talents to acquire great wealth. Frequently the emergence of multiple psi powers is the result of a nuclear war or related incident, as in *The Children of the Atom* (1954) by Wilmar Shiras or *Re-Birth* (1955, also published as *The Chrysalids*) by John Wyndham. Multiple extraordinary powers are also common to the various novels tied in to superhero comic book and graphic novel series, but there is rarely any attempt to provide a rational basis for their existence.

Another unusual power is pyrolysis, or the ability to start fires through force of will. Stephen King's *Firestarter*

(1980) is the best example. The hero of *The Shores of Kansas* (1976) by Rob Chilson has the ability to transport himself back and forth in time and escapes notoriety by taking refuge in prehistory. Charles Eric Maine suggested a similar power in *Timeliner* (1955), but in this case travel is involuntary and it is only the personality, not the body, which moves through time, displacing other personalities to lodge in their bodies.

Another psi power which verges on the supernatural is the ability to occupy and control another person's body, akin to demonic possession. In *Carrion Comfort* (1989) by Dan Simmons, a small minority of the human race gains this ability and engages in vicarious battles, using innocent people as their puppets. Similar situations arise in *A Plague of Pythons* (1965, revised as *Demon in the Skull*), *The Power* (1956) by Frank M. Robinson, and elsewhere, although more commonly a machine of some sort is involved in the process.

The possibility that we are not making complete use of the human brain is one that has fascinated people both as a literary device and in the real world. Dozens of nonfiction books have appeared speculating about such possibilities, sometimes more wildly improbable than even science fiction authors have suggested. There has been some experimental evidence suggesting the possibility that there might be a kernel of truth hidden there, but as yet these various hypotheses remain unproven. Until we know for certain, the area remains a fertile one for fictional speculation.

Recommended Titles

Entries for the following books are included in this volume.

Sunborn by Gregory Benford

Mercury by Ben Bova

Destroyer by C.J. Cherryh

Live! From Planet Earth by George Alec Effinger

Metallic Love by Tanith Lee

Homecalling and Other Stories by Judith Merril

Century Rain by Alastair Reynolds

The Seven Hills by John Maddox Roberts

The Man Who Lost the Sea by Theodore Sturgeon

Mammoth by John Varley

Spin by Robert Charles Wilson

For More Information about Fantastic Fiction by Neil Barron

Hundreds of books about fantastic literature, film, and illustration have been published since the 1940s, such as J.O. Bailey's *Pilgrims through Space and Time* (1947), adapted from his 1934 doctoral dissertation. The publishers have ranged from university presses to fan publishers such as Borgo and Starmont, both defunct, and Wildside Press, ac-

tive as a print-on-demand fan publisher. One of the most recent entrants (since 2003) is the Austin, Texas- based MonkeyBrain Books (www.monkeybrainbooks.com), distributed by NBN. Their audience is fans, students and, to some degree, academics. Several of their books are reviewed below.

Michael Moorcock is one of Britain's more versatile writers, having written both SF and fantasy as well as traditional fiction. His decidedly heterodox work investigating religious faith, *Behold the Man* (Allison & Busby, 1969), may be his best single work. In 1987 Gollancz published his *Wizardry and Wild Romance: A Study of Epic Fantasy*, and MonkeyBrain Books issued a revised edition in 2004. The main body is unchanged. The short list of sources has been slightly updated, his foreward revised, and several of his reprinted book reviews (called ''appendices'') are new, including a new introduction by China Mieville and a new afterword by Jeff VanderMeer. Moorcock's study reflects his somewhat polemical views, vigorously expressed. It's not meant to be a systematic, balanced survey like, say, Eric Rabkin's *The Fantastic in Literature* (Princeton University Press, 1976) or C.N. Manlove's *The Impulse of Fantasy Literature* (Kent State University Press, 1983). He devotes his initial chapter to selected Gothic tales, with other chapters discussing the exotic landscapes (''dreamscenery'') of many fantasies; heroes and heroines in classical and modern works; wit and humor (Mervyn Peake and Terry Pratchett's works are praised); a large part of the chapter titled ''Epic Pooh'' is dismissive of the moral conservatism of A.A. Milne, J.R.R. Tolkien, and Richard Adams. The books reviewed are usually not dated; several reviews are reprinted from *The Guardian*. VanderMeer's afterword provides a useful and fair assessment of this study, noting that Moorcock modestly omits his own epic fantasies from discussion. Larger public libraries, especially those with many fantasy enthusiasts, should consider this very personal survey.

Lou Anders is the editorial director of Pyr, a recently established SF imprint of Prometheus Books, and has written many articles, with a heavy emphasis on film and TV (www.louanders.com provides more details). His latest edited book, *Projections: Science Fiction in Literature & Film* (MonkeyBrain Books, 2004), assembles twenty-nine recent essays by SF authors and critics, seven of them original, the balance reprints, along with brief profiles of all contributors. Some essays favor films—*Star Wars*, the *Matrix* trilogy, *THX 1138*, *Blade Runner*, *X-Men*, scientists in SF films, and a revised version of James Gunn's valuable historical survey, ''The Tinsel Screen.'' More essays analyze printed SF, from Edgar Rice Burroughs to Mervyn Peake (a perceptive view by Michael Moorcock) to David Brin (a hard SF writer) on Tolkien, on to contemporary writers like Robert Sawyer. With its wide coverage and broad appeal, this is a good choice for public libraries with a knowledgeable SF reader base.

The League of Extraordinary Gentlemen is a graphic novel, written by Alan Moore, illustrated by Kevin O'Neill and published by DC Comics (volume 1 in 2002, volume 2 in 2003). It converted Victorian characters to superheroes, including Minna Murray from Bram Stoker's *Dracula*, Robert Louis Stevenson's Jekyll and Hyde, Jules Verne's Captain Nemo, etc. The popular film based on the books received a mixed reception. Jess Nevins wrote "unofficial companions" to the books. That for volume 1 is titled *Heroes and Monsters* (MonkeyBrain, 2003). Volume 2 is titled *A Blazing World* (MonkeyBrain, 2004). Both are similar in content and both explain the many references the graphic novels make to Victorian literature and popular culture. The Nevins' companions include an introduction by Moore, an author foreward, and interviews with O'Neill and Moore. Most of the companions are detailed annotations to the text of the two novels, keyed page by page, panel by panel. The annotations refer to hundreds of literary sources, some standard, many relatively obscure. Nevins drew on the enthusiasm and knowledge of dozens of people who read his Web site. The original graphic novel set was very favorably reviewed and probably was bought by many libraries, especially after the film was released. If interest is still strong, public libraries should consider acquiring the two (admittedly esoteric) companions.

The British TV series "Doctor Who," which told 159 multiple-episode stories over 26 years (1963-1989) under the guidance of several producers, was notoriously careless about "continuity," "the agreed upon collective mythology of consistent details that paint the reality of a fictional world," in the words of Paul Cornell, Martin Day, and Keith Topping, authors of *The Discontinuity Guide* (MonkeyBrain, 2004). With incredible erudition they examine the continuity issues and "roots" (references to literature, films and other TV) for each Who story, as well as providing credits for writers and directors but not actors and noting "goofs" and "fluffs" (common in this cheaply produced series), along with especially good or poor dialogue and examples of "technobabble." The authors give a terse critical appraisal of each story but not a synopsis; readers are assumed to be familiar with the series. The guide is not indexed.

Special effects are usually thought of only in connection with motion pictures, but they long predate the cinema in the form of fireworks, automatons and various types of image projections, all briefly discussed in the first of eight chapters of *Special Effects: An Oral History; Interviews with 37 Masters Spanning 100 Years* (Abrams, 2005) by Pascal Pinteau, a journalist, screenwriter and, special effects designer. Chapters 1 and 2 discuss the early work of Georges Melies, Mack Sennett, Cecil B. De Mille, Fritz Lang's *Metropolis*, Willis O'Brien's *King Kong* and technical developments like the traveling matte and optical printer. Interspersed with the more general text are interviews of figures important in the development of special effects,

beginning with Ray Harryhausen and his stop motion animation, and including Martin Bower (*Alien*), Mark Coulier (*Harry Potter*), John Dykstra and Joe Viskocil (*Star Wars*), and Gene Rizzardi (*Titanic*). The cover illustration is from John Winston's *Terminator 3*, one of 1,136 illustrations, 982 in color. Most examples are from SF and fantasy films, old and new, including television. The prose is generally well translated from the 2003 French original but is sometimes a bit technical or not very detailed. A chapter is devoted to theme parks featuring special effects, not only Disney creations, in the U.S. and abroad, and an appendix provides more details on visiting such sites. A chapter profiles about 150 DVDs that feature notable special effects. This is mainly a book for browsing. Not as colorful, though very well-illustrated is the more straightforward work of Richard Rickett, *Special Effects: The History and Techniques* (Watson-Guptill, 2000). Also good, if growing dated, is Christopher Finch's *Special Effects: Creating Movie Magic* (Abbeville, 1984). In spite of its limitations, Pinteau is a reasonably priced, current and knowledgeable guide, generally recommended to most libraries.

Who directed *American Graffiti* (1973, five Oscars) and *Star Wars* (1977, 8 Oscar nominations, including best picture) and was the executive producer for the Steven Spielberg adventures, *Raiders of the Lost Ark* (1981) and its two sequels? George Lucas is the answer and he is the subject of *The Cinema of George Lucas* by Marcus Hearn (Abrams, 2005). Hearn drew on new and unpublished older interviews, production histories and other sources, many of them in the Lucasfilm archives on Skywalker ranch north of San Francisco. Lucas' interest in SF goes back to his prize-winning student short film produced at the University of Southern California's film school, *THX1138*, expanded in 1971 as a feature film, which he also directed. *American Graffiti* is based on his years growing up in Modesto in California's central valley. The latter film was both a critical and popular success. Lucas has long been associated with the series of *Star Wars* films, though now more as a producer and general film business consultant than as a director. This is easily the most detailed and authoritative guide to the films and life of Lucas.

As I stated in volume 1 of the 2005 edition of *What Do I Read Next?*, Ray Bradbury is among the best known of SF writers, but most of his fiction is clearly not SF. He largely escaped from the SF ghetto by about 1950 and during the past half century has attracted a general audience not limited to SF fans. His first book, 1947's *Dark Carnival* published by Arkham House, assembled some of his best stories, all tinged with horror. The book that most closely links him to SF is the series of linked stories making up *The Martian Chronicles*, which has continued to sell steadily in various editions since it was originally published by Doubleday in 1950. But the stories are set on a poet's world haunted by memories, nostalgia, and sorrow, far removed from the exotic playground envisioned by Edgar Rice Burroughs in his

Barsoom (Mars) tales, and even farther removed from the hard SF depictions of Mars, such as the trio of novels by Kim Stanley Robinson. His other well-known work, *Fahrenheit 451* (Ballantine, 1953), is a dystopian view of America from the McCarthy period, with few elements from SF. The range of his fiction is best seen in two major, non-overlapping collections, *The Stories of Ray Bradbury* (Knopf, 1980) and *Bradbury Stories* (William Morrow, 2003), which assemble close to 200 tales from both the pulps and more prestigious magazines, the so-called ''slicks'' (in contrast to the rough pages of the pulps).

Now 84 and in declining health, it's not surprising that he's been the subject of an increasing number of books. The latest is an admiring and presumably authorized biography, *The Bradbury Chronicles: The Life of Ray Bradbury* (William Morrow, 2005) by Sam Weller, a journalist and former *Publishers Weekly* correspondent who now teaches at Chicago's Columbia College, including a course devoted to Bradbury. Like his subject, Weller grew up in northern Illinois (Bradbury was born in Waukegan) and effectively shows the heavy influence on his writings of his early years, before his family's move to Los Angeles in the depression 1930s. Weller's biography is based on extensive interviews with his subject, his recently-deceased wife of many years, his longtime agent, friends, and many others, all of whose help is acknowledged in a chapter and in notes.

In readable, somewhat chatty prose, Weller explores how Bradbury drew on his early years for almost all his writings—fiction, poetry, children's books, essays—and effectively shows how his strong determination to become a successful writer overcame an unpromising background. Weller also chronicles Bradbury's involvement in radio, TV, film, including staged versions based on his works. This is not a work of literary criticism in any academic sense. Weller's familiarity with SF is obviously limited, but he does provide a useful and detailed context for much of Bradbury's fiction and other writings, awards, and activities, and Bradbury fans will especially enjoy the many anecdotes and ''inside'' information. Weller admires his subject, but he acknowledges some frailties, such as marital infidelity and ''an insatiable appetite for sweets.'' Critical biographies and literary studies will certainly be published after Bradbury dies, but this is a useful beginning and should have wide appeal to Bradbury fans, as well as introducing him to readers suspicious of ''that Buck Rogers stuff.''

Necrology

This section highlights selected figures associated with fantastic literature, illustration or film who have died since the previous fall. The most detailed obituaries, often accompanied by appreciations, are found in the monthly news magazine, *Locus*. Additional details may often be found in standard reference works.

Frank Kelly Freas (1922-2 January 2005) was one of the best-known and most admired illustrators, whose career spanned more than fifty years. His work appeared in *Astounding* (now *Analog*) from 1953 through 2001, as well as in other magazines, on book covers, etc. His work was collected in *Frank Kelly Freas* (1971), *The Art of Science Fiction* (1977), *A Separate Star* (1984), and *Frank Kelly Freas: As He Sees It* (2000). He was nominated for the Hugo award for illustration twenty-five times and won ten times, among many other awards. He may be best known for a cover drawing on *Mad* magazine of its mascot, Alfred E. Newman (''What? Me Worry?'').

Will Eisner (1917-3 January 2005) died in Fort Lauderdale, Florida. He is best known for his newspaper comic, *The Spirit*, which began in the 1940s. This detective adventure comic (or ''sequential art'' as he preferred to call it) had a hero with no superpowers. World War II service interrupted his comic work, to which he returned, producing weekly installments until 1952. He taught cartooning at the School of Visual Arts in NYC and authored two standard works, *Comics and Sequential Art* (1985) and *Graphic Storytelling* (1996). In 2004 a major overview of his work was published, *The Will Eisner Companion* by N.C. Christopher Crouch and Stephen Weiner. Forthcoming in late 2005 is an authorized biography, *Will Eisner: A Spirited Life* by Bob Andleman.

Jack L. Chalker (1944-11 February 2005) died in Baltimore. A fan from his early years, he founded a fanzine and in 1961 Mirage Press, which is best known for its nonfiction works, most notably *The Index to the Science Fantasy Publishers* (1966, revised 1979, greatly enlarged 1991). The first of his more than forty SF novels were published in the 1970s, most part of series, of which the best known is the Well of Souls series (10 volumes, 1977-2000). Most of his short fiction was collected in *Dance Band on the Titanic* (1988).

Andre Norton (1912-17 March 2005) died at her home in Tennessee. Born Alice Mary Norton in Cleveland, she wrote more than 130 books, beginning her professional career as a writer of books for children. She used the pen name, Andre Norton, because she expected to be writing for young boys. In 1934 she legally changed her name to Andre Alice Norton. She was a children's librarian at Cleveland Public Library, 1932-1940, worked elsewhere for several years, and returned to Cleveland's library, where she remained until 1950. Her first SF novel was for young adults, *Star Man's Son, 2250 AD* (1952). Another YA novel, *Operation Time Search* (1967), is one of her best works. Most of her fantasy and SF are part of series, notably the popular science fantasy Witch World series. She also wrote almost twenty non-fantasy/SF books, beginning with *The Prince Commands*, published in 1934 when she was 22. Her final solo novel, *Three Hands for Scorpio*, was published in April 2005, and a collaboration with

Jean Rabe, *Return to Quag Keep*, is to be available in early 2006. She was the first woman to receive the Grand Master of Fantasy award from the SFWA (SF and Fantasy Writers of America) in 1977, and won the SFWA's Nebula Grand Master award in 1984. The SFWA recently created the Andre Norton award for YA novels, with the first award to be given in 2006.

Science Fiction Titles

739

DAN ABNETT

Ravenor Returned

(Nottingham, England: Black Library, 2005)

Story type: Space Opera; Espionage Thriller
Series: Warhammer
Subject(s): Space Colonies
Major character(s): Gideon Ravenor, Spy; Zael, Teenager; Carl Thonius, Spy
Time period(s): Indeterminate Future
Locale(s): Eustis Majoris, Planet—Imaginary

Summary: Gideon Ravenor and his elite group of agents have been presumed dead, but they are very much alive and active. This time they investigate rumors originating on the planet Eustis. They uncover an intricate plot against the human interstellar empire in time to prevent it from being effective.

Other books by the same author:
Ravenor, 2004
Traitor General, 2004
Sabbat Martyr, 2003
Straight Silver, 2002
The Guns of Tanith, 2002

Other books you might like:
Poul Anderson, *Mayday Orbit*, 1961
Ben Counter, *Crimson Tears*, 2005
Matthew Farrer, *Legacy*, 2004
Simon Spurrier, *Fire Warrior*, 2003
Ian Watson, *Harlequin*, 2004

740

KEVIN J. ANDERSON

Scattered Suns

(New York: Aspect, 2005)

Story type: Space Opera; Military
Series: Saga of Seven Suns. Book 4

Subject(s): Space Travel; Aliens
Major character(s): Basic Wenceslas, Ruler; Jora'h, Leader; Lev Stromo, Military Personnel (admiral)
Time period(s): Indeterminate Future
Locale(s): Outer Space

Summary: A war continues to rage through the galaxy, pulling more and more worlds into the conflict. The alliance that includes humanity has additional problems, because the human government is growing ever more repressive and totalitarian and their chief allies are in danger of splitting in a civil war.

Other books by the same author:
Horizon Storms, 2004
Captain Nemo, 2002
The Hidden Empire, 2002
Hopscotch, 2002
Antibodies, 1997

Other books you might like:
Lois McMaster Bujold, *Barrayar*, 1991
Peter Hamilton, *Pandora's Star*, 2004
Frank Herbert, *Chapterhouse: Dune*, 1985
Dan Simmons, *The Hyperion Omnibus*, 2004
Joan D. Vinge, *The Summer Queen*, 1991

741

M.T. ANDERSON

Whales on Stilts

(Orlando, Florida: Harcourt, 2005)

Story type: Young Adult; Humor
Subject(s): Humor; Technology
Major character(s): Lily Gefelty, Teenager; Jasper Dash, Teenager; Katie Morgan, Teenager
Time period(s): 2000s
Locale(s): United States

Summary: A group of teenage heroes discover a plot by a mad scientist to rule the world. He intends to equip whales so that they can move on land, then arm them with laser weapons and

use them as an army of conquest. This is a broad farce but amusingly told, poking fun at old-time science fiction adventure stories from the pulp era.

Other books by the same author:
The Game of Sunken Places, 2004
Thirsty, 2003
Feed, 2002

Other books you might like:
Kevin J. Anderson, *Sky Captain and the World of Tomorrow*, 2004
Eoin Colfer, *Artemis Fowl*, 2001
Bruce Coville, *Aliens Ate My Homework*, 1993
Isidore Haiblum, *Specterworld*, 1991
Daniel Pinkwater, *The Snarkout Boys and the Avocado of Death*, 1982

742

CHRISTOPHER ANVIL

Interstellar Patrol II: The Federation of Humanity

(New York: Baen, 2005)

Story type: Collection
Subject(s): Short Stories

Summary: The late Christopher Anvil was a very prolific short story writer during the 1960s and 1970s and many of his stories were loosely set in the same future history of the human race. This second collection includes 22 short stories plus one full-length novel. Predominantly action stories, usually involving the solution of some technical problem, they are often lightly humorous as well.

Other books by the same author:
Interstellar Patrol, 2003
Pandora's Legions, 2002
The Steel, the Mist, and the Blazing Sun, 1980
Strangers in Paradise, 1969
The Day the Machines Stopped, 1964

Other books you might like:
Poul Anderson, *The Space Folk*, 1989
Gordon R. Dickson, *In the Bone*, 1987
Mack Reynolds, *The Best of Mack Reynolds*, 1976
Eric Frank Russell, *Entities*, 2001
Robert Sheckley, *The People Trap*, 1968

743

NEAL ASHER

Cowl

(New York: Tor, 2005)

Story type: Time Travel; Horror
Subject(s): Time Travel
Major character(s): Tack, Police Officer (government assassin), Time Traveler; Cowl, Time Traveler, Fugitive; Polly, Young Woman
Time period(s): Indeterminate Future; Indeterminate Past
Locale(s): Outer Space; Earth

Summary: In the far distant future, an interstellar war ends with one group escaping through time. The most dangerous of the fugitives is Cowl, who hides in the past and uses organic time machines to seek out and trap its prey. Tack is a government assassin marked for destruction who becomes bait in a trap to end Cowl's depredations.

Other books by the same author:
Gridlinked, 2003
The Skinner, 2002
The Engineer, 1998

Other books you might like:
Brian W. Aldiss, *Dracula Unbound*, 1991
Stephen Baxter, *Timelike Infinity*, 1993
Gregory Benford, *Cosm*, 1998
Dan Simmons, *Hyperion*, 1989
A.E. van Vogt, *Universe Maker*, 1953

744

MIKE ASHLEY, Editor
ERIC BROWN, Co-Editor

The Mammoth Book of New Jules Verne Adventures

(New York: Carroll & Graf, 2005)

Story type: Anthology
Subject(s): Short Stories

Summary: This collection includes 23 original stories, each emulating in some fashion the work of Jules Verne, either using Verne's characters or situations, or creating new ones in the style he popularized. The contributors include Ian Watson, Stephen Baxter, Richard A. Lupoff, Paul Di Filippo, and many others. The tone is almost always one of light adventure, sometimes with liberal doses of humor.

Other books by the same author:
The Merriest Knight, 2001
The Mammoth Book of Comic Fantasy, 1998
The Chronicles of the Holy Grail, 1996
The Merlin Chronicles, 1995
The Camelot Chronicles, 1992

Other books you might like:
Kevin J. Anderson, *Captain Nemo*, 2002
Jeff Rollins, *Subterranean*, 1999
John Taine, *The Greatest Adventure*, 1929
Jules Verne, *Off on a Comet*, 1877
John Wyndham, *The Secret People*, 1935

745

PIERCE ASKEGREN

Fall Girl

(New York: Ace, 2005)

Story type: Espionage Thriller; Hard Science Fiction
Subject(s): Space Travel
Major character(s): Erik Morrison, Businessman; Enola Hasbro, Journalist; Sarrah Chrysler, Businesswoman
Time period(s): Indeterminate Future

Locale(s): Moon (Earth's)

Summary: The discovery of an alien artifact on the moon has provided a new form of technology, making it possible to build a ship that can leave the solar system. While construction is underway, entrepreneur Erik Morrison discovers that there are power groups on Earth violently opposed to the project, and willing to commit murder to see it halted.

Other books by the same author:
Human Resource, 2005
Countdown to Chaos, 1998
Thunderbolts, 1998

Other books you might like:
John DeChancie, *Starrigger*, 1983
Dean McLaughlin, *The Man Who Wanted Stars*, 1965
Frederik Pohl, *Gateway*, 1978
Robert Silverberg, *Across a Billion Years*, 1969
George Zebrowski, *Stranger Suns*, 1991

746

PIERCE ASKEGREN

Human Resource

(New York: Ace, 2005)

Story type: Mystery; Space Colony
Series: Inconstant Moon. Book 1
Subject(s): Secrets; Space Exploration
Major character(s): Erik Morrison, Businessman; Wendy Scheer, Computer Expert; Juanita Garcia, Businesswoman
Time period(s): Indeterminate Future
Locale(s): Moon (Earth's)

Summary: Erik Morrison isn't thrilled with his latest assignment, which is to conduct an audit of EnTek's operation on the moon. He is even less thrilled when mysterious circumstances hamper his efforts, eventually leading him to discover that there is a much more serious problem than just low profits and some minor unexplained losses.

Other books by the same author:
Countdown to Chaos, 1998
Thunderbolts, 1998
Sabotage, 1997 (David Fingeroth, co-author)
Wreckage, 1997 (Eric Fein, co-author)

Other books you might like:
Ben Bova, *Colony*, 1978
Nancy Holder, *The Six Families*, 1998
Allen Steele, *Clarke County, Space*, 1990
E.C. Tubb, *Moon Base*, 1963
John Varley, *Steel Beach*, 1992

747

PAUL L. BATES

Imprint

(Waterville, Maine: Five Star, 2005)

Story type: Dystopian; Mystery
Subject(s): Utopia/Dystopia

Major character(s): Wyatt Weston, Worker; Rachel Void, Young Woman; Victor Crist, Businessman
Time period(s): Indeterminate Future
Locale(s): Earth

Summary: Wyatt Weston wakes up one day to discover that his girlfriend is missing and that he is the only one who remembers her, and that one of his arms is missing. Technology is advanced enough to reconstruct his arm, but he continues to search for information about his girlfriend, arousing the attention of a secretive government agency. First novel.

Other books you might like:
Mark Adlard, *Volteface*, 1972
John Brunner, *Shockwave Rider*, 1975
Fritz Leiber, *You're All Alone*, 1972
Mack Reynolds, *The Cosmic Eye*, 1969
A.E. van Vogt, *The Mind Cage*, 1957

748

STEPHEN BAXTER
ARTHUR C. CLARKE, Co-Author

Sunstorm

(New York: Del Rey, 2005)

Story type: Hard Science Fiction; Disaster
Series: Time Odyssey. Book 2
Subject(s): Disasters; Space Travel
Major character(s): Bisesa Dutt, Military Personnel; Mikhail Martynov, Scientist; Siobhan McGorran, Scientist (astronomer)
Time period(s): 2030s (2037)
Locale(s): United States; England; Outer Space

Summary: Various people from different walks of life find their circumstances radically changed when an unusual disturbance in the sun's corona indicates the potential for a disaster. Humanity must hasten the development of a space umbrella.

Other books by the same author:
Exultant, 2004
Coalescent, 2003
Evolution, 2002
Longtusk, 2001
Moonseed, 1998

Other books you might like:
Greg Bear, *Anvil of Stars*, 1992
Ben Bova, *When the Sky Burned*, 1973
Richard A. Lupoff, *Sun's End*, 1984
Charles Sheffield, *Starfire*, 1999
Roger Zelazny, *Flare*, 1992
   Thomas T. Thomas, co-author

749

ELIZABETH BEAR

Hammered

(New York: Bantam, 2005)

Story type: Dystopian; Medical
Subject(s): Scientific Experiments; Futuristic Fiction

Science Fiction

Major character(s): Jenny Casey, Fugitive; Razorface, Criminal; Elspeth Dunsany, Scientist, Prisoner
Time period(s): 2060s (2062)
Locale(s): Connecticut; Canada

Summary: Jenny Casey, on the run from the authorities in Canada, is hiding in Connecticut. She becomes an increased object of interest for a group planning a highly advanced scientific experiment for which she is the perfect subject. Her fugitive status also puts her on the edge of dangerous criminal activity. First novel.

Where it's reviewed:
Chronicle, February 2005, page 33
Locus, February 2005, page 23

Other books you might like:
Brian W. Aldiss, *Enemies of the System*, 1978
John Brunner, *Shockwave Rider*, 1975
Louise Marley, *The Maquisarde*, 2002
Mack Reynolds, *The Cosmic Eye*, 1969
Fred Saberhagen, *Love Conquers All*, 1974

750

GREGORY BENFORD

The Sunborn
(New York: Aspect, 2005)

Story type: Hard Science Fiction; Space Opera
Subject(s): Space Exploration; Technology
Major character(s): Shanna Axelrod, Spaceship Captain; Viktor, Spaceman; Julia, Spacewoman
Time period(s): Indeterminate Future
Locale(s): *High Flyer*, Spaceship; *Prosperina*, Spaceship

Summary: Two separate expeditions are sent into the outer reaches of the solar system to conduct research beyond the orbit of Pluto. One is captained by an ambitious individual who wishes to transcend the discoveries of earlier space heroes, the very same people who are in charge of the other ship. A crisis forces them to work cooperatively instead of competitively.

Where it's reviewed:
Locus, March 2005, page 15

Other books by the same author:
Beyond Infinity, 2004
Cosm, 1998
Furious Gulf, 1994
In Alien Flesh, 1986
Artifact, 1985

Other books you might like:
William Barton, *Iris*, 1990
   Michael Capobianco, co-author
James Blish, *They Shall Have Stars*, 1957
Arthur C. Clarke, *3001: The Final Odyssey*, 1997
Rick Gauger, *Charon's Ark*, 1987
Frederik Pohl, *Mining the Oort*, 1992

751

BEN BOVA

Mercury
(New York: Tor, 2005)

Story type: Hard Science Fiction; Space Colony
Subject(s): Space Travel; Technology
Major character(s): Saito Yamagata, Businessman; Victor Molina, Scientist; Elliot Danvers, Religious
Time period(s): Indeterminate Future
Locale(s): Mercury

Summary: Although the planet Mercury is too inhospitable to provide a home for normal colonists, it is a perfect place to build a system that will provide inexpensive energy to Earth. The development of that project is complicated by natural difficulties, internal conflicts, a religious fanatic, and a bitter saboteur.

Other books by the same author:
Powersat, 2005
Tales of the Grand Tour, 2004
The Silent War, 2004
Saturn, 2003
The Rock Rats, 2002

Other books you might like:
Isaac Asimov, *Lucky Starr and the Big Sun of Mercury*, 1956
David Brin, *Sundiver*, 1980
Paul Cook, *Fortress on the Sun*, 1997
E.C. Tubb, *The Hell Planet*, 1954
George Zebrowski, *Sun Spacer*, 1984

752

BEN BOVA

Powersat
(New York: Tor, 2005)

Story type: Hard Science Fiction; Espionage Thriller
Subject(s): Physics; Space Travel
Major character(s): Dan Randolph, Businessman; Asim al-Bashir, Criminal; Jane Thornton, Government Official
Time period(s): Indeterminate Future
Locale(s): Outer Space; Earth

Summary: Dan Randolph wants to establish a system of power generating satellites in orbit around the Earth. However, there are various groups who oppose his efforts, for either political or financial reasons. Some people are ready to resort to violence to prevent him from achieving his goals, even though they would benefit humanity as a whole.

Where it's reviewed:
Chronicle, February 2005, page 30
Library Journal, January 2005, page 103
Publishers Weekly, December 13, 2004, page 50

Other books by the same author:
Tales of the Grand Tour, 2004
The Silent War, 2004
Saturn, 2003
Jupiter, 2000

Venus, 2000

Other books you might like:
Arthur C. Clarke, *Islands in the Sky*, 1952
Howard Hendrix, *Standing Wave*, 1998
Allen Steele, *Orbital Decay*, 1989
Jeff Sutton, *Spacehive*, 1960
Michael Swanwick, *Vacuum Flowers*, 1987

753

TERRY BRAMLETT

Formidable Enemy

(Waterville, Maine: Five Star, 2005)

Story type: Mystery; Political
Subject(s): Aliens
Major character(s): Roger Stimson, Nurse; Dingo, Alien; Kristen Windham, Teenager
Time period(s): Indeterminate Future
Locale(s): United States

Summary: The protagonist is a professional nurse who was formerly an agent of the government during what might have turned into a devastating war against an alien race. When an alien refugee informs him that there is a plot to assassinate the American president in an effort to provoke a new war, he decides to help expose the plan before it can be consummated. First novel.

Other books you might like:
Poul Anderson, *Ensign Flandry*, 1966
Joe Haldeman, *The Coming*, 2000
Keith Laumer, *End as a Hero*, 1985
Maxine McArthur, *Time Future*, 2001
Robert J. Sawyer, *Illegal Alien*, 1998

754

ERIC BROWN

The Fall of Tartarus

(London: Gollancz, 2005)

Story type: Collection
Subject(s): Short Stories
Locale(s): Tartarus, Planet—Imaginary

Summary: The eight stories in this collection were all previously published between 1995 and 2000. All are set on the planet Tartarus, where humanity is scattered over literally thousands of islands and despite a nominal theocracy, scores of different cults and belief systems exist. There are also rumors that an apocalyptic event will take place there, and numerous travelers have arrived to see if it happens.

Other books by the same author:
Approaching Omega, 2005
Bengal Station, 2004
New York Dreams, 2004
New York Nights, 2000
Penumbra, 1999

Other books you might like:
Michael Bishop, *Stolen Faces*, 1977

John Brunner, *The Altar on Asconel*, 1965
L. Sprague de Camp, *The Continent Makers and Other Tales of the Viagens*, 1953
Joseph Green, *The Loafers of Refuge*, 1965
Frank Herbert, *Dune*, 1965

755

ORSON SCOTT CARD

Shadow of the Giant

(New York: Tor, 2005)

Story type: Political; Space Colony
Series: Ender. Book 5
Subject(s): Aliens; Space Colonies
Major character(s): Peter Wiggins, Political Figure; Bean, Genius; Petra Arkanian, Political Figure
Time period(s): Indeterminate Future
Locale(s): Earth; Outer Space

Summary: This is the fifth volume in a series of novels that parallels events in the main Ender series. Despite having saved the world and become its political leader, Ender and his friends discover that they have made so many enemies in the process that their only chance of leading a happy life is to emigrate from Earth and settle on another world.

Where it's reviewed:
Booklist, March 1, 2005, page 1101
Library Journal, April 15, 2005, page 78
Locus, April 2005, page 49
Publishers Weekly, February 21, 2005, page 162

Other books by the same author:
The Crystal City, 2003
Shadow Puppets, 2002
Enchantment, 1999
Ender's Shadow, 1999
Pastwatch, 1996

Other books you might like:
Poul Anderson, *Harvest the Fire*, 1995
Joe Haldeman, *Forever Free*, 1999
Robert A. Heinlein, *Beyond This Horizon*, 1942
Andre Norton, *The Stars Are Ours*, 1954
Frederik Pohl, *Jem*, 1979

756

C.J. CHERRYH

Destroyer

(New York: DAW, 2005)

Story type: Space Colony; Space Opera
Series: Foreigner. Book 7
Subject(s): Aliens; Space Colonies
Major character(s): Bren Cameron, Government Official, Spaceman; Banichi, Alien; Jago, Alien
Time period(s): Indeterminate Future
Locale(s): Outer Space; Mospheira, Planet—Imaginary

Summary: The involuntary colonists on Mospheira have progressed from almost complete isolation from the native aliens to a limited form of interaction and cooperation in their

Science Fiction

spacefaring efforts. By doing so, they become enmeshed in Mospheiran clan politics. First in a third series of three novels set against this background.

Where it's reviewed:
Locus, February 2005, page 71

Other books by the same author:
Explorer, 2002
Defender, 2001
Hammerfall, 2001
Finity's End, 1997
Tripoint, 1994

Other books you might like:
Michael Bishop, *Stolen Faces*, 1977
Doris Egan, *The Complete Ivory*, 2001
Lisanne Norman, *Fire Margins*, 1996
Andre Norton, *The Beast Master*, 1959
Mike Resnick, *Paradise*, 1989

757

RICHARD COX

The God Particle
(New York: Del Rey, 2005)

Story type: Religious; Hard Science Fiction
Subject(s): Scientific Experiments; Psychic Powers
Major character(s): Steve Keeley, Businessman; Mike McNair, Scientist; Kelly Smith, Journalist
Time period(s): 2000s
Locale(s): United States; Switzerland

Summary: Mike McNair is engaged in a series of scientific experiments that turn up startling results, suggesting that what humans think of as ''God'' might actually have a physical basis, subject to manipulation by the power of the will. Simultaneously, an accident leaves a businessman with unusual mental abilities that might be another aspect of the same revelation.

Where it's reviewed:
Publishers Weekly, March 14, 2005, page 252

Other books you might like:
Karel Capek, *The Absolute at Large*, 1927
Victor Koman, *The Jehovah Contract*, 1984
James Morrow, *Only Begotten Daughter*, 1990
Jamil Nasir, *Distance Haze*, 2000
Ian Watson, *God's World*, 1979

758

PETER CROWTHER, Editor

Constellations
(New York: DAW, 2005)

Story type: Anthology
Subject(s): Short Stories

Summary: This collection of 15 previously unpublished short stories involve humanity's future in outer space. The contributors include Brian W. Aldiss, Stephen Baxter, Alastair Reynolds, Paul J. McAuley, and Ian Watson. Although the stories are generally adventurous or speculative, they have a very high literary quality as well.

Where it's reviewed:
Locus, February 2005, page 25

Other books by the same author:
Darkness, Darkness, 2002
Lonesome Roads, 1999
The Hand That Feeds, 1997 (James Lovegrove, co-author)
Escardy Gap, 1996 (James Lovegrove, co-author)

Other books you might like:
Brian W. Aldiss, *Seasons in Flight*, 1985
Stephen Baxter, *Flux*, 1993
Paul J. McAuley, *White Devils*, 2004
Alastair Reynolds, *Chasm City*, 2001
Ian Watson, *The Inquisition War*, 2004

759

JULIE E. CZERNEDA

Migration
(New York: DAW, 2005)

Story type: Hard Science Fiction; Space Opera
Series: Species Imperative. Book 2
Subject(s): Aliens; Secrets
Major character(s): MacKenzie Connor, Scientist; Emily Mamani, Scientist; Nikolai Trojanowski, Government Official
Time period(s): Indeterminate Future
Locale(s): Earth; Outer Space

Summary: A team of human scientists has become involuntarily involved in an interstellar conflict that appears to be a straightforward case of one aggressive race attacking another. As they become more familiar with the situation, they realize that this is an oversimplification, as the aggressors may be acting under the duress of a biological imperative.

Where it's reviewed:
Publishers Weekly, April 25, 2005, page 43

Other books by the same author:
Survival, 2004
Hidden in Sight, 2003
To Trade the Stars, 2002
Changing Vision, 2000
The Beholder's Eye, 1998

Other books you might like:
John Brunner, *The Dramaturges of Yan*, 1972
C.J. Cherryh, *Foreigner*, 1994
Alan Dean Foster, *Dirge*, 2000
Maxine McArthur, *Time Future*, 2001
S.L. Viehl, *Bladedancer*, 2003

760

JACK DANN, Editor

Nebula Awards Showcase 2005
(New York: Roc, 2005)

Story type: Anthology

Subject(s): Short Stories

Summary: This volume in an annual series presents the best short stories of the previous year, plus various articles about the state of the field. The contributors to this volume include Cory Doctorow, Charles L. Harness, Robert Silverberg, China Mieville, Lucius Shepard, Harlan Ellison, and others.

Where it's reviewed:
Locus, February 2005, page 17

Other books by the same author:
Visitations, 2003
Jubilee, 2001
The Memory Cathedral, 1995
The Man Who Melted, 1984
Junction, 1981

Other books you might like:
Cory Doctorow, *Eastern Standard Tribe*, 2004
Harlan Ellison, *Dreams with Sharp Teeth*, 1991
Charles L. Harness, *An Ornament to His Profession*, 1998
Barry N. Malzberg, *In the Stone House*, 2000
Lucius Shepard, *Louisiana Breakdown*, 2003

761

L. SPRAGUE DE CAMP

Years in the Making

(Framingham, Massachusetts: NESFA, 2005)

Story type: Collection; Time Travel
Subject(s): Short Stories; Time Travel

Summary: This retrospective collection of all the time travel stories written by the late L. Sprague de Camp includes his complete novel, *Lest Darkness Fall*, about a modern day man who tries to introduce technology into ancient Rome. Many of the stories are genre classics, including ''A Gun for Dinosaur'' and ''The Gnarly Man.''

Other books by the same author:
Aristotle and the Gun, 2003
The Rivers of Time, 1993
The Venom Trees of Sunga, 1992
The Swords of Zinjaban, 1991
The Unbeheaded King, 1983

Other books you might like:
Poul Anderson, *The Guardians of Time*, 1960
Andre Norton, *The Time Traders*, 1958
Fred Saberhagen, *The Masks of the Sun*, 1979
Robert Silverberg, *Hawksbill Station*, 1968
Michael Swanwick, *Bones of the Earth*, 2002

762

PAUL DI FILIPPO

The Emperor of Gondwanaland and Other Stories

(New York: Thunder's Mouth, 2005)

Story type: Collection
Subject(s): Short Stories

Summary: These 18 stories, all previously published, are from one of the more interesting stylists in contemporary SF. Ranging from serious to humorous, satiric to speculative, there are stories of biotechnology, alternate histories, and high-tech transformations of human society.

Other books by the same author:
Little Doors, 2002
Strange Trades, 2001
Lost Pages, 1998
Fractal Paisleys, 1997
The Steampunk Trilogy, 1996

Other books you might like:
J.G. Ballard, *War Fever*, 1990
Michael Bishop, *Brighten to Incandescence*, 2003
Joanna Russ, *The Zanzibar Cat*, 1983
James Tiptree Jr., *Star Songs of an Old Primate*, 1978
Gene Wolfe, *Starwater Strains*, 2005

763

GARDNER DOZOIS, Editor

The Best of the Best

(New York: St Martin's Press, 2005)

Story type: Anthology
Subject(s): Short Stories

Summary: Gardner Dozois has been editing a best of the year anthology for 20 years. Now he selects the outstanding stories from those earlier volumes in a single new collection. Among the many authors represented are Lucius Shepard, Robert Silverberg, Connie Willis, Gene Wolfe, Charles Stross, and Ted Chiang.

Where it's reviewed:
Locus, January 2005, page 17

Other books by the same author:
Strange Days, 2001
Geodesic Dreams, 1992
Strangers, 1978
The Visible Man, 1977
Nightmare Blue, 1975 (George Alec Effinger, co-author)

Other books you might like:
Lucius Shepard, *Two Trains Running*, 2004
Robert Silverberg, *Beyond the Safe Zone*, 1986
Charles Stross, *The Atrocity Archives*, 2004
Connie Willis, *Impossible Things*, 1994
Gene Wolfe, *Innocents Aboard*, 2004

764

GARDNER DOZOIS, Editor

The Year's Best Science Fiction: Twenty-Second Annual Collection

(New York: St Martin's Press, 2005)

Story type: Anthology
Subject(s): Short Stories

Summary: This is the largest and most comprehensive of the best of the year collections, including 28 stories from 2004,

plus the usual summations and list of honorable mentions. The contributors this time include Nancy Kress, Terry Bisson, Kage Baker, Vernor Vinge, William Sanders, Robert Reed, and Paul Di Filippo. The summation covers various aspects of the field, including films and the state of the publishing business.

Other books by the same author:
Strange Days, 2001
Geodesic Dreams, 1992
Strangers, 1978
The Visible Man, 1977
Nightmare Blue, 1975 (George Alec Effinger, co-author)

Other books you might like:
Kage Baker, *Black Projects, White Knights*, 2002
Paul Di Filippo, *Little Doors*, 2002
Nancy Kress, *Nothing Human*, 2003
Robert Reed, *The Well of Stars*, 2005
William Sanders, *Are We Having Fun Yet?*, 2002

765

DAVID DRAKE

The Way to Glory

(New York: Baen, 2005)

Story type: Space Opera; Military
Series: Lieutenant Leary. Book 4
Subject(s): Military Life; Space Travel
Major character(s): Daniel Leary, Military Personnel (lieutenant); Adele Mundy, Military Personnel, Spy; Paolo Zileri, Military Personnel
Time period(s): Indeterminate Future
Locale(s): Outer Space; Cinnabar, Planet—Imaginary

Summary: A devastating interstellar war has begun to destabilize the government of the planet of Cinnabar and has also put pressure on the space navy. Leary, a brilliant but unorthodox officer, finds himself under the command of a brutal and possibly insane commander just as he becomes involved with an apparent murder and possible espionage case.

Other books by the same author:
Master of the Cauldron, 2004
Grimmer than Hell, 2003
The Far Side of the Stars, 2003
Paying the Piper, 2002
The Butcher's Bill, 1998

Other books you might like:
John Dalmas, *The Regiment*, 1987
David Feintuch, *Prisoner's Hope*, 1995
Gordon Kendall, *White Wing*, 1985
John Ringo, *In the Looking Glass*, 2005
Mark Shepherd, *Kris Longknife, Mutineer*, 2004

766

JEANNE DUPRAU

The People of Sparks

(New York: Random House, 2005)

Story type: Young Adult; Future Shock

Subject(s): Post Nuclear Holocaust; Environmental Problems
Major character(s): Lina, Teenager; Doon, Teenager; Torren, Teenager
Time period(s): Indeterminate Future
Locale(s): Earth

Summary: In this sequel to *The City of Embers*, a group of teenagers begin to adjust to life on the surface of the Earth after discovering that adults were lying to them about the necessity of remaining in underground shelters. As they expand onto the surface, differences of opinion about their future begin to fragment the new society.

Other books by the same author:
The City of Embers, 2003

Other books you might like:
Michael G. Coney, *The Hero of Downways*, 1973
Paul Cook, *Duende Meadow*, 1985
Philip K. Dick, *The Penultimate Truth*, 1964
Suzanne Martel, *The City under Ground*, 1964
Andre Norton, *Outside*, 1974

767

GEORGE ALEC EFFINGER

Live! From Planet Earth

(Urbana, Illinois: Golden Gryphon, 2005)

Story type: Collection
Subject(s): Short Stories

Summary: The late George Alec Effinger wrote a large body of quirky, understated short stories. This retrospective collection of more than 20 stories was chosen by a number of his fellow writers, each of whom wrote an introduction to the work they selected. They include two Hugo nominated stories and are generally of exceptionally high quality.

Other books by the same author:
Idle Pleasures, 1993
The Exile Kiss, 1991
A Fire in the Sun, 1990
Look Away, 1990
When Gravity Fails, 1986

Other books you might like:
Avram Davidson, *The Avram Davidson Treasury*, 1998
Paul Di Filippo, *The Steampunk Trilogy*, 1996
Pamela Sargent, *Thumbprints*, 2004
Robert Sheckley, *Can You Feel Anything When I Do This?*, 1971
Howard Waldrop, *Custer's Last Jump*, 2003

768

CAROL EMSHWILLER

I Live with You

(San Francisco: Tachyon, 2005)

Story type: Collection
Subject(s): Short Stories

Summary: Carol Emshwiller has been writing offbeat science fiction stories for several decades. Some of her better work is

included in this collection of 12 stories, all published since 2000. Emshwiller tends toward the literary side of science fiction and avoids adventure centered fiction. Also included is a transcript of a speech she made at a convention.

Where it's reviewed:
Locus, May 2005, page 15
Publishers Weekly, April 25, 2005, page 44

Other books by the same author:
The Start of the End of It All, 1990
Verging on the Pertinent, 1990
Joy in Our Cause, 1974

Other books you might like:
Paul Di Filippo, *Babylon Sisters*, 2003
Damon Knight, *Off Center*, 1965
Kit Reed, *Magic Time*, 1980
Joanna Russ, *The Hidden Side of the Moon*, 1987
Lisa Tuttle, *Memories of the Body*, 1992

769

ANDREAS ESCHBACH

The Carpet Makers

(New York: Tor, 2005)

Story type: Future Shock; Space Colony
Subject(s): Space Colonies; Political Thriller
Major character(s): Moarkan, Businessman; Ostvan, Artisan; Parnag, Religious
Time period(s): Indeterminate Future
Locale(s): Planet—Imaginary

Summary: On a distant world, the emperor has always been honored by the weaving of elaborate carpets that a corps of artisans create. When outsiders arrive, they discover that the emperor is missing, and that the carpets have an even greater significance than is readily apparent. This novel originally appeared in Germany and has been translated by Doryl Jensen.

Other books you might like:
Michael Bishop, *Transfigurations*, 1979
Alan Dean Foster, *The Howling Stones*, 1997
Herbert Franke, *The Orchid Cage*, 1961
Frank Herbert, *Dune*, 1965
Frederik Pohl, *Stopping at Slowyear*, 1991

770

ERIC FLINT

The Rivers of War

(New York: Del Rey, 2005)

Story type: Alternate Universe; Political
Series: Alternate Frontier. Book 1
Subject(s): Alternate History
Major character(s): Sam Houston, Historical Figure, Military Personnel; Andrew Jackson, Historical Figure, Military Personnel; John Ross, Historical Figure
Time period(s): 1800s; 1810s (1805-1815)
Locale(s): United States

Summary: History begins to diverge from this world early in the 19th century as the various Indian nations, constantly pushed west, finally begin to form an alliance against the European invaders. Aided by escaped slaves and by a willingness to involve themselves in the political structure of the new nation to the East, they are able to form a coalition that blocks further advances into their territory, at least for the time being.

Where it's reviewed:
Publishers Weekly, April 25, 2005, page 252

Other books by the same author:
1634, 2004 (Andrew Dennis, co-author)
The Tyrant, 2002 (David Drake, co-author)
The Philosophical Strangler, 2001
1632, 2000
Mother of Demons, 1997

Other books you might like:
Michael Kurland, *The Whenabouts of Burr*, 1975
Jake Page, *Apacheria*, 1998
William Sanders, *Journey to Fusang*, 1988
Pamela Sargent, *Climb the Wind*, 1999
Martin Cruz Smith, *The Indians Won*, 1970

771

ALAN DEAN FOSTER

The Light-Years Beneath My Feet

(New York: Del Rey, 2005)

Story type: Humor; First Contact
Series: Taken. Book 2
Subject(s): Aliens; Humor
Major character(s): Marcus Walker, Businessman; George, Animal (dog); Saluu-hir-lek, Alien
Time period(s): Indeterminate Future
Locale(s): Planet—Imaginary

Summary: Marcus Walker has been abducted by aliens who wish to sell him elsewhere in the galaxy as a pet. While the ship is on one of their planets, he and George, a dog whose intelligence has been enhanced and who has the power to speak, escape their captors and try to survive in a very strange alien metropolis.

Other books by the same author:
Lost and Found, 2004
Sliding Scales, 2004
Flinx's Folly, 2003
Diuturnity's Dawn, 2002
Impossible Places, 2002

Other books you might like:
F.M. Busby, *Cage a Man*, 1973
Juanita Coulson, *Star Sister*, 1990
Brian Herbert, *The Prisoners of Arionn*, 1989
James Luceno, *A Fearful Symmetry*, 1989
Rebecca Ore, *Becoming Alien*, 1986

Science Fiction

772

GREGORY FROST

Attack of the Jazz Giants and Other Stories

(Urbana, Illinois: Golden Gryphon, 2005)

Story type: Collection
Subject(s): Short Stories

Summary: These 13 reprints and one original story include most of this author's best short stories. They vary considerably in tone, from serious to humorous, and in subject matter, ranging from satirical science fiction to atmospheric horror. ''The Girlfriends of Dorian Gray'' and the title story are particularly well done.

Other books by the same author:
Fitcher's Brides, 2002
A Pure Cold Light, 1993
Remscela, 1988
Tain, 1986
Lyrec, 1984

Other books you might like:
Anthony Boucher, *The Compleat Boucher*, 1999
L. Sprague de Camp, *Aristotle and the Gun*, 2003
Charles De Lint, *Moonlight and Vines*, 1999
Theodore Sturgeon, *The Man Who Lost the Sea*, 2005
John Wyndham, *Tales of Gooseflesh and Laughter*, 1956

773

JAMES ALAN GARDNER

Gravity Wells

(New York: Eos, 2005)

Story type: Collection
Subject(s): Short Stories

Summary: The 14 short stories in this collection include almost everything the author has had published at that length. The stories vary widely in subject matter and tone, from adventure to humor to mild satire, and take place both on Earth and in outer space. Several have been award contenders.

Other books by the same author:
Radiant, 2004
Trapped, 2002
Hunted, 2000
Vigilant, 1999
Expendable, 1997

Other books you might like:
Poul Anderson, *Going for Infinity*, 2002
Joe Haldeman, *Dealing in Futures*, 1985
John Kessel, *Meeting in Infinity*, 1992
Keith Laumer, *Future Imperfect*, 2003
Vernor Vinge, *Collected Stories*, 2001

774

SIMON R. GREEN

Deathstalker Coda

(New York: Roc, 2005)

Story type: Space Opera; Time Travel
Series: Deathstalker. Book 7
Subject(s): Time Travel; Space Travel
Major character(s): Owen Deathstalker, Nobleman, Time Traveler; Lewis Deathstalker, Nobleman, Military Personnel; Finn Durandal, Ruler
Time period(s): Indeterminate Future
Locale(s): Outer Space

Summary: Owen Deathstalker travels back through time to try to prevent the transformation that claimed the life of the woman he loves. That leaves Lewis Deathstalker to lead their forces alone against the tyrant Finn Durandal, who has usurped the throne of an interstellar empire.

Where it's reviewed:
Library Journal, December 2004, page 643
Publishers Weekly, January 3, 2005, page 41

Other books by the same author:
Deathstalker Legacy, 2002
Deathstalker Honor, 1998
Deathstalker, 1995
Ghostworld, 1993
Hellworld, 1993

Other books you might like:
Poul Anderson, *Flandry*, 1993
John Brunner, *Interstellar Empire*, 1976
Edmond Hamilton, *The Star Kings*, 1949
Frank Herbert, *Dune*, 1965
Dan Simmons, *The Rise of Endymion*, 1997

775

TARA HARPER

Wolf in the Night

(New York: Del Rey, 2005)

Story type: Space Colony; Mystical
Series: Wolfwalker. Book 7
Subject(s): Mental Telepathy; Coming-of-Age
Major character(s): Nori, Young Woman; Grey Rishte, Animal (wolf); Kittre, Businessman
Time period(s): Indeterminate Future
Locale(s): Planet—Imaginary

Summary: Nori is a young woman who has very uncertain ideas about her own future on a largely undeveloped colony world. Then she finds herself in an odd relationship with one of the intelligent, telepathic wolves native to that planet, and right in the middle of a complex web of intrigue and danger.

Other books by the same author:
Silver Moon, Black Steel, 2001
Wolf's Bane, 1997
Grayheart, 1996
Cataract, 1995

Cat Scratch Fever, 1994

Other books you might like:
Leigh Brackett, *The Hounds of Skaith*, 1974
C.J. Cherryh, *Cloud's Rider*, 1996
Andre Norton, *The Beast Master*, 1959
Jody Lynn Nye, *Taylor's Ark*, 1993
Kenneth Von Gunden, *Cry Wolf*, 1992

776

JAMES P. HOGAN

Mission to Minerva
(New York: Baen, 2005)

Story type: Hard Science Fiction; Alternate Universe
Series: Giants. Book 4
Subject(s): Aliens
Major character(s): Victor Hunt, Scientist; Porthik Eesyan, Alien (Thurien); Gregg Caldwell, Scientist
Time period(s): Indeterminate Future
Locale(s): United States; Outer Space

Summary: James Hogan returns to the multiverse of the Thurien giants for this novel. Humanity is slowly adjusting to the fact that there are multiple universes and timelines, knowledge they gained through contact with the Thuriens, who resemble giant humans. Unfortunately, a new anomaly could spell disaster for both races so a joint space mission is launched. There is considerable discussion of quantum physics and other abstruse theories.

Where it's reviewed:
Publishers Weekly, April 25, 2005, page 23

Other books by the same author:
The Anguished Dawn, 2003
Martian Knightlife, 2001
The Legend That Was Earth, 2000
Outward Bound, 1999
Bug Park, 1997

Other books you might like:
Roger MacBride Allen, *The Depths of Time*, 2000
Jack McDevitt, *Chindi*, 2002
Alastair Reynolds, *Century Rain*, 2004
Robert J. Sawyer, *Factoring Humanity*, 1998
John E. Stith, *Reckoning Infinity*, 1997

777

WALTER H. HUNT

The Dark Crusade
(New York: Tor, 2005)

Story type: Military; Space Opera
Series: Dark. Book 4
Subject(s): Military Life; Space Travel
Major character(s): Jackie Lappierre, Military Personnel; Owen Garrett, Military Personnel; Antonio St. Giles, Military Personnel
Time period(s): 25th century (2422-2424)
Locale(s): Outer Space

Summary: Humanity and the alien Zor have discovered that the war between them was engineered by a third race, and the former foes are now allies. The outcome is still in question, but one factor in the conflict is a single unconventional human military officer. His rebellious and sometimes insubordinate inclinations have beneficial results.

Other books by the same author:
The Dark Ascent, 2004
The Dark Path, 2003
The Dark Wing, 2001

Other books you might like:
Roger MacBride Allen, *Allies and Aliens*, 1995
Kevin J. Anderson, *The Hidden Empire*, 2002
Alan Dean Foster, *Dirge*, 2000
John Ringo, *Into the Looking Glass*, 2005
David Weber, *War of Honor*, 2002

778

BEN JEAPES

New World Order
(New York: David Fickling, 2005)

Story type: Young Adult; Alternate History
Subject(s): Alternate History; Aliens
Major character(s): Daniel Matthews, Teenager; Khonol Le, Military Personnel; John Donder, Worker
Time period(s): 17th century (1645)
Locale(s): England

Summary: Various characters interact in this alternate version of the 17th century. Aliens have landed on Earth and have integrated many humans into their culture, completely changing the course of human history and introducing advanced technology into the mix. When their influence affects human politics, the English Civil War takes an unexpected turn.

Other books by the same author:
The Xenocide Mission, 2002
Winged Chariot, 2000
The Ark, 1998

Other books you might like:
Poul Anderson, *The High Crusade*, 1960
John Brunner, *The Super Barbarians*, 1962
William R. Forstchen, *Men of War*, 1999
Jerry Pournelle, *Janissaries*, 1999
David Weber, *The Excalibur Alternative*, 2002

779

SUSAN KEARNEY

The Dare
(New York: Tor, 2005)

Story type: Alternate Intelligence; Techno-Thriller
Series: Dora. Book 2
Subject(s): Artificial Intelligence; Sexuality
Major character(s): Dora, Artificial Intelligence; Zical, Military Personnel
Time period(s): Indeterminate Future
Locale(s): Planet—Imaginary

Summary: Dora is an artificial intelligence who decides she is not content to remain in her original form. She fashions a body that is essentially human and transfers her personality into it. In this form she attempts and eventually succeeds in indulging her new romantic instincts with the aid of a warrior pilot whose initial hesitation makes him even more of a challenge.

Other books by the same author:
On the Edge, 2005
The Challenge, 2005
A Burning Obsession, 2004
Enslaved, 2002
Conquer the Mist, 1998

Other books you might like:
Isaac Asimov, *The Positronic Man*, 1993
   Robert Silverberg, co-author
Barrington J. Bayley, *The Soul of the Robot*, 1974
Joseph Delaney, *Valentina*, 1984
   Marc Stiegler, co-author
Esther Friesner, *The Sherwood Game*, 1995
David Gerrold, *When Harlie Was One*, 1972

780

KEITH LAUMER

Imperium

(New York: Baen, 2005)

Story type: Collection; Alternate Universe
Subject(s): Alternate History
Major character(s): Brion Bayard, Diplomat

Summary: This is an omnibus edition of the first three of a four novel series about Brion Bayard. Bayard is abducted into an alternate world in the first story, *Worlds of the Imperium*, to impersonate the version of himself who has become a repressive dictator. He defends the status quo from other dangers in the remaining two novels, *The Other Side of Time* and *Assignment in Nowhere*. The three novels were originally published during the 1960s.

Other books by the same author:
The Legions of Space, 2004
Future Imperfect, 2003
Odyssey, 2002
Retief, 2002
The Lighter Side, 2002

Other books you might like:
Fredric Brown, *What Mad Universe*, 1949
Lester Del Rey, *Infinite Worlds of Maybe*, 1966
James P. Hogan, *Paths to Otherwhere*, 1996
Robert Silverberg, *Roma Eterna*, 2003
S.M. Stirling, *The Peshawar Lancers*, 2002

781

SHARON LEE
STEVE MILLER, Co-Author

Crystal Soldier

(Atlanta: Meisha Merlin, 2005)

Story type: Space Opera; Military
Series: Great Migration. Book 1
Subject(s): Space Travel
Major character(s): M. Jela Granthor's Guard, Military Personnel; Cantra yos'Phelium, Spaceship Captain, Criminal
Time period(s): Indeterminate Future
Locale(s): Spaceship

Summary: A spaceship captain, who resorts to smuggling when legitimate trade doesn't pay the bills, teams up with a genetically enhanced soldier for a series of episodic adventures in this, the first half of a two part novel. The background is the same as for the Liadem series by the same authors.

Other books by the same author:
I Dare, 2002 (Steve Miller, co-author)
Local Custom, 2001 (Steve Miller, co-author)
Plan B, 1999 (Steve Miller, co-author)
Carpe Diem, 1989 (Steve Miller, co-author)
Agent of Change, 1988 (Steve Miller, co-author)

Other books you might like:
Poul Anderson, *The Rebel Worlds*, 1969
C.J. Cherryh, *Merchanter's Luck*, 1982
Denise Lopes Heald, *Mistwalker*, 1994
Andre Norton, *Plague Ship*, 1956
S.L. Viehl, *Endurance*, 2001

782

TANITH LEE

Metallic Love

(New York: Bantam, 2005)

Story type: Robot Fiction; Dystopian
Subject(s): Utopia/Dystopia; Future
Major character(s): Loren, Child, Orphan; Goldhawk, Robot; Verlis, Robot
Time period(s): Indeterminate Future
Locale(s): Earth

Summary: An orphan child struggling to survive in the city of a vaguely repressive future society discovers the story of a woman who fell in love with a robot. This inspires her to a new relationship with the robots around her. The book is the sequel to *The Silver Metal Lover*, which is a more detailed account of the woman who loved a machine.

Other books by the same author:
Mortal Suns, 2003
Venus Preserved, 2003
White as Snow, 2000
The Red Unicorn, 1997
The Silver Metal Lover, 1986

Other books you might like:
Barrington J. Bayley, *The Soul of the Robot*, 1974

Philip K. Dick, *We Can Build You*, 1970
Lisa Mason, *Arachne*, 1990
Charles Platt, *Free Zone*, 1989
Clifford D. Simak, *Project Pope*, 1981

783

EDWARD M. LERNER

Moonstruck

(New York: Baen, 2005)

Story type: First Contact; Mystery
Subject(s): Aliens; Secrets
Major character(s): Kyle Gustafson, Government Official;
Britt Arledge, Government Official; Harold Robeson, Political Figure (president)
Time period(s): Indeterminate Future
Locale(s): United States

Summary: Emissaries from a galactic civilization arrive on Earth in the not so distant future, offering what appears at first to be a very favorable arrangement. There are some within the American government who suspect their motives, however, and further investigation reveals, as expected, that the arrangement has a definite downside.

Other books by the same author:
Probe, 1991

Other books you might like:
Michael Bishop, *A Little Knowledge*, 1977
D.G. Compton, *Missionaries*, 1972
Philip K. Dick, *Our Friends from Frolix 8*, 1970
Sheri S. Tepper, *The Fresco*, 2000
Liz Williams, *Empire of Bones*, 2002

784

KARIN LOWACHEE

Cagebird

(New York: Aspect, 2005)

Story type: Space Opera; Espionage Thriller
Series: Warchild. Book 3
Subject(s): Space Travel; Secrets
Major character(s): Yuri Kirov, Prisoner, Criminal; Andreas Lukacs, Government Official; Bo-Sheng, Spaceship Captain
Time period(s): Indeterminate Future
Locale(s): Outer Space; Spaceship

Summary: Yuri Kirov was captured after living for several years as a space pirate and spy. He is offered a chance to leave prison, but only if he agrees to act as an undercover agent for the government of an interstellar alliance. His subsequent reluctant efforts redeem his character, as well as save his life.

Other books by the same author:
Burndive, 2003
Warchild, 2002

Other books you might like:
C.J. Cherryh, *Chanur's Venture*, 1984
Julie E. Czerneda, *The Beholder's Eye*, 1998

Harry Harrison, *The Stainless Steel Rat*, 1961
S.L. Viehl, *Eternity Row*, 2002
Timothy Zahn, *Spinneret*, 1985

785

ANNE MCCAFFREY
ELIZABETH ANN SCARBOROUGH, Co-Author

First Warning

(New York: Eos, 2005)

Story type: Space Opera; Medical
Series: Acorna's Children. Book 1
Subject(s): Space Travel
Major character(s): Khoriilya, Spacewoman; Aari, Spaceman;
Hap Hellstrom, Student
Time period(s): Indeterminate Future
Locale(s): Outer Space

Summary: Stumbling across a derelict spaceship, two space travelers uncover a secret that might help them solve a problem that menaces the entire human race. A mysterious plague has been spreading from planet to planet, and the authorities are unable to find a cure. This is the opening volume of a trilogy featuring the child of the protagonist of the Acorna series.

Other books by the same author:
A Gift of Dragons, 2002
Freedom's Ransom, 2002
Pegasus in Space, 2000
Dragonseye, 1999
Nimisha's Ship, 1999

Other books you might like:
John Boyd, *The Organ Bank Farm*, 1970
Marion Zimmer Bradley, *The Planet Savers*, 1962
Octavia Butler, *Clay's Ark*, 1984
Andre Norton, *Plague Ship*, 1956
Steve Perry, *The Tularemia Gambit*, 1981

786

TODD MCCAFFREY

Dragonsblood

(New York: Del Rey, 2005)

Story type: Space Colony; Disaster
Series: Pern. Book 1
Subject(s): Space Colonies; Disasters
Major character(s): Lorana, Young Woman; Wind Blossom, Scientist; M'Tal, Government Official
Time period(s): Indeterminate Future
Locale(s): Pern, Planet—Imaginary

Summary: This is the author's first solo novel set in the universe created by his mother, Anne McCaffrey, although he collaborated with her on one previous novel. The dragons of Pern are rapidly dying out, and the key to their preservation lies with one unlikely young woman, and an ancient song that holds a key to their origin.

Where it's reviewed:
Booklist, November 1, 2004, page 444

Library Journal, December 2004, page 104
Publishers Weekly, November 8, 2004, page 40

Other books you might like:
Jeffrey A. Carver, *Dragon Rigger*, 1993
Chris Cymri, *Dragons Can Only Rust*, 1995
Marjorie Kellogg, *The Book of Air*, 2003
Anne McCaffrey, *Dragonflight*, 1968
Irene Radford, *The Hidden Dragon*, 2002

787

WIL MCCARTHY

To Crush the Moon
(New York: Bantam, 2005)

Story type: Space Opera; Immortality
Series: Queendom. Book 4
Subject(s): Disasters; Immortality
Major character(s): Conrad Mursk, Spaceman; Bruno de Towaji, Immortal; Xiomara Li Wing, Spaceship Captain
Time period(s): Indeterminate Future
Locale(s): Earth; Outer Space

Summary: After attempts to colonize another planet fail, a group of near immortals returns to Earth, many of them in suspended animation. During the interval since their departure, Earth has become hopelessly overcrowded and a fanatical religious cult is threatening to destabilize civilization beyond the point where it can support an advanced technology.

Other books by the same author:
Lost in Transmission, 2004
The Wellstone, 2003
The Collapsium, 2000
Bloom, 1998
Flies from Amber, 1995

Other books you might like:
Roger MacBride Allen, *The Depths of Time*, 2000
Poul Anderson, *Starfarers*, 1998
Alexander Jablokov, *Nimbus*, 1993
Keith Laumer, *Star Colony*, 1981
Frederik Pohl, *The Other End of Time*, 1996

788

JOHN MEANEY

Paradox
(Amherst, New York: Pyr, 2005)

Story type: Mystery; Space Colony
Series: Nulapeiron. Book 1
Subject(s): Space Colonies; Quest
Major character(s): Tom Corcorigan, Worker; Zhao-ji, Orphan; Karyn, Worker
Time period(s): 35th century (3404)
Locale(s): Nulapeiron, Fictional Country

Summary: Tom Corcorigan is not happy with the situation in the underground city of Nulapeiron. The government, which is effectively controlled by the precognitive Oracles, have punished him unjustly and he seeks revenge, aided by a

mysterious legacy. This novel was previously published in England in 2001 and is the first in a trilogy.

Other books by the same author:
Resolution, 2004
Context, 2003
To Hold Infinity, 1998

Other books you might like:
Paul Cook, *The Alejandra Variations*, 1984
Philip K. Dick, *The Penultimate Truth*, 1964
Michael Frayn, *A Very Private Life*, 1968
Mike McQuay, *Lifekeeper*, 1980
Tim Powers, *The Skies Discrowned*, 1976

789

R.M. MELUCH

The Myriad
(New York: DAW, 2005)

Story type: Space Opera; Military
Series: Tour of the Merrimack. Book 1
Subject(s): Military Life; Space Colonies
Major character(s): John Farragut, Spaceship Captain, Military Personnel; Kerry Blue, Military Personnel (sergeant); Augustus, Consultant, Military Personnel (colonel)
Time period(s): Indeterminate Future
Locale(s): *U.S. Merrimack*, Spaceship; Outer Space

Summary: In the middle of an interstellar war with a mysterious alien race, a military ship on a reconnaissance mission stumbles across a cluster of colony worlds who appear to have escaped the attention of the aliens. However, they have evolved into a society that is very secretive. This is the author's first new book in more than a decade.

Where it's reviewed:
Analog, May 2005, page 134
Chronicle, February 2005, page 32

Other books by the same author:
The Queen's Squadron, 1992
Chicago Red, 1990
War Birds, 1989
Jerusalem Fire, 1985
Wind Child, 1982

Other books you might like:
Lois McMaster Bujold, *The Warrior's Apprentice*, 1986
William C. Dietz, *Freehold*, 1987
Peter Hamilton, *Fallen Dragon*, 2002
Frederik Pohl, *Stopping at Slowyear*, 1991
Diann Thornley, *Ganwold's Child*, 1995

790

JUDITH MERRIL

Homecalling and Other Stories
(Framingham, Massachusetts: NESFA, 2005)

Story type: Collection
Subject(s): Short Stories

Summary: Although Judith Merril was known primarily as an anthologist and critic of science fiction, she also produced 25 short stories of her own and several others collaboratively. This volume collects all of the former into one volume, stories originally published between 1941 and the 1970s. Her work was much more character driven than most of her contemporaries and includes several well-known tales, including ''That Only a Mother'' and ''Daughters of Earth.''

Other books by the same author:
The Best of Judith Merril, 1976
Survival Ship and Other Stories, 1973
Daughters of Earth, 1968
Out of Bounds, 1960
The Tomorrow People, 1960

Other books you might like:
Cyril M. Kornbluth, *His Share of Glory*, 1997
Kit Reed, *Thinner than Thou*, 2004
Pamela Sargent, *Thumbprints*, 2004
Theodore Sturgeon, *The Man Who Lost the Sea*, 2005
James Tiptree Jr., *Meet Me at Infinity*, 2000

791

ROBERT A. METZGER

Cusp

(New York: Ace, 2004)

Story type: Post-Disaster; Hard Science Fiction
Subject(s): Computers; Disasters
Major character(s): Christina Olmos, Computer Expert; Xavier Olmos, Computer Expert; Simon Ryan, Cyborg
Time period(s): 2050s (2051)
Locale(s): Earth

Summary: A solar flare has changed the Earth utterly, leaving civilization in ruins and two rings around the planet, permanently affecting the world's climate. In the aftermath, a group of scientists develop an unusually sophisticated computer and consider trying to alter the sun to change things back, but they are opposed by various people, some of whom fear they will make things even worse.

Where it's reviewed:
Chronicle, February 2005, page 32

Other books by the same author:
Picoverse, 2001
Quad World, 1991

Other books you might like:
Greg Bear, *The Forge of God*, 1987
James Blish, *And All the Stars a Stage*, 1971
Ben Bova, *When the Sky Burned*, 1973
Richard A. Lupoff, *Sun's End*, 1984
Charles Sheffield, *Starfire*, 1999

792

RICHARD MORGAN

Woken Furies

(London: Gollancz, 2005)

Story type: Dystopian; Political
Series: Takeshi Kovacs. Book 3
Subject(s): Secrets
Major character(s): Takeshi Kovacs, Adventurer; Quellcrist Falconer, Fugitive; Virginia Vidaura, Young Woman
Time period(s): Indeterminate Future
Locale(s): Harlan's World, Planet—Imaginary

Summary: When Takeshi Kovacs is restored to life after two centuries, he finds human society much altered. There is an alternate version of himself running around, searching for a fugitive who may be connected to the rise of a new religious cult. As he adjusts to his new surroundings, Kovacs begins to suspect that his benefactors have ulterior motives.

Other books by the same author:
Market Forces, 2004
Broken Angels, 2003
Altered Carbon, 2002

Other books you might like:
Alexander Besher, *Mir*, 1998
David Brin, *The Kiln People*, 2002
Mike McQuay, *The Deadliest Game in Town*, 1982
Alastair Reynolds, *Century Rain*, 2004
Bruce Sterling, *Distraction*, 1998

793

WALTER MOSLEY

47

(New York: Little, Brown, 2005)

Story type: Young Adult; Immortality
Subject(s): Immortality; Legends
Major character(s): 47, Slave; Tall John, Immortal
Time period(s): 19th century; 20th century
Locale(s): United States

Summary: This young adult novel mixes fantasy themes with science fiction. 47 is the name of a young slave whose life is transformed when he meets Tall John, an immortal who has various unusual powers, perhaps natural in origin, perhaps magical. The encounter forces 47 to participate in a secret battle hidden from the rest of the world.

Other books by the same author:
Little Scarlet, 2004
Blue Light, 2001
Futureland, 2001

Other books you might like:
Roger MacBride Allen, *Orphan of Creation*, 1988
John Barnes, *Sin of Origin*, 1988
Michael Bishop, *Ancient of Days*, 1985
Nalo Hopkinson, *The Brown Girl in the Ring*, 1998
John Jakes, *Black in Time*, 1970

794

DOUGLAS NILES

The War of the Worlds: New Millennium
(New York: Tor, 2005)

Story type: Invasion of Earth; Disaster
Subject(s): Aliens; Mars
Major character(s): Mark Devane, Writer; Alexandra Devane, Scientist; Duke Hayes, Military Personnel
Time period(s): 2000s
Locale(s): United States

Summary: This is an attempt to update H.G. Wells' *The War of the Worlds* by moving the time of the invasion forward to the present day and upgrading the technology. The adventures of a very varied group of characters are followed as Martians begin landing all around the world, although the action in this case all takes place in the United States.

Other books by the same author:
The Wizards' Conclave, 2004
The Goddess Worldweaver, 2003
Winterheim, 2003
The Golden Orb, 2002
The Puppet King, 1999

Other books you might like:
John Christopher, *The White Mountains*, 1967
Murray Leinster, *Creatures of the Abyss*, 1961
Larry Niven, *Footfall*, 1985
   Jerry Pournelle, co-author
H.G. Wells, *The War of the Worlds*, 1898
John Wyndham, *Out of the Deeps*, 1953

795

LARRY NIVEN
BRENDA COOPER, Co-Author

Building Harlequin's Moon
(New York: Tor, 2005)

Story type: Hard Science Fiction; Space Colony
Subject(s): Space Colonies; Technology
Major character(s): Gabrielle, Scientist; Rachel Vanowen, Slave; Ursula, Slave
Time period(s): Indeterminate Future
Locale(s): Selene, Planet—Imaginary

Summary: Efforts to colonize another world go awry when the starship arrives in the wrong system. The crew is forced to transform a small world into a temporary home while they refit and prepare to resume their voyage, hoping to arrive at their goal this time. Their efforts are complicated by the fact that their workers are virtually enslaved.

Other books by the same author:
Ringworld's Children, 2004
Scatterbrain, 2003
Rainbow Mars, 1999
Destiny's Road, 1997
Flatlander, 1995

Other books you might like:
Poul Anderson, *The Boat of a Million Years*, 1989
Lois McMaster Bujold, *Falling Free*, 1988
Keith Laumer, *Star Colony*, 1981
Laura J. Mixon, *Burning the Ice*, 2002
Allen Steele, *Coyote*, 2002

796

WILLIAM F. NOLAN

Wild Galaxy
(Urbana, Illinois: Golden Gryphon, 2005)

Story type: Collection
Subject(s): Short Stories

Summary: Although William F. Nolan has become better known in recent years for his supernatural stories, he is also the author of a significant amount of science fiction, including the novel, *Logan's Run*, written with George Clayton Johnson. This collection reprints 19 of his short stories published from the 1950s to the present.

Other books by the same author:
Helltracks, 1991
Look Out for Space, 1985
Alien Horizons, 1974
Logan's Run, 1967 (George Clayton Johnson, co-author)
Impact 20, 1963

Other books you might like:
Gordon R. Dickson, *In the Bone*, 1987
Keith Laumer, *Future Imperfect*, 2003
Murray Leinster, *First Contacts*, 1998
Alan E. Nourse, *Psi-High and Others*, 1967
Robert Sheckley, *The Robot Who Looked Like Me*, 1982

797

JERRY OLTION

Anywhere but Here
(New York: Tor, 2005)

Story type: Dystopian; Techno-Thriller
Subject(s): Secrets; Political Thriller
Major character(s): Trent Stinson, Spaceman, Rebel; Donna Stinson, Spacewoman, Rebel
Time period(s): Indeterminate Future
Locale(s): United States; Outer Space

Summary: In a future where the United States has become the overwhelmingly dominant power on Earth, and where that power has led to despotism, the discovery of a cheap interstellar drive system promises to provide freedom among the stars. When it becomes evident that the government intends to extend its control beyond the solar system, two people decide that it is time to use that technology to change things back home. This is the sequel to *The Getaway Special*.

Where it's reviewed:
Publishers Weekly, January 17, 2005, page 39

Other books by the same author:
The Getaway Special, 2001

Abandon in Place, 2000
Where Sea Meets Sky, 1998
Alliance, 1990
Frame of Reference, 1987

Other books you might like:
Joe Haldeman, *Forever Free*, 1999
Larry Niven, *The Legacy of Heorot*, 1987
    Jerry Pournelle, co-author
Allen Steele, *Coyote Rising*, 2004
Jack Williamson, *The Silicon Dagger*, 1999
George Zebrowski, *Brute Orbits*, 1998

798

JAMES PATTERSON

Maximum Ride: The Angel Experiment
(New York: Little, Brown, 2005)

Story type: Young Adult; Mystery
Subject(s): Genetic Engineering
Major character(s): Angel, Teenager, Genetically Altered Being; Nudge, Teenager, Genetically Altered Being; Fang, Teenager, Genetically Altered Being
Time period(s): Indeterminate Future
Locale(s): United States

Summary: A half dozen teenagers whose DNA was manipulated to make them partially birds and therefore able to fly, have a series of adventures as they travel across a future United States. They try to keep out of the reach of powerful forces who wish to exploit their special talents. The story is an exciting adventure, although the scientific background is implausible. This is the author's first venture into fantastic fiction.

Where it's reviewed:
Publishers Weekly, March 21, 2005, page 52
School Library Journal, February 1, 2005, page 918

Other books you might like:
John Brunner, *Children of Thunder*, 1989
Tom DeHaven, *Freaks Amour*, 1979
Karen Ripley, *The Tenth Class*, 1991
Michael Swanwick, *In the Drift*, 1985
A.E. van Vogt, *Slan*, 1940

799

ROBERT REED

The Well of Stars
(New York: Tor, 2005)

Story type: Space Opera; Disaster
Series: Marrow. Book 2
Subject(s): Space Travel; Disasters
Major character(s): Mir, Spaceship Captain; Washen, Spacewoman; Pamir, Spaceman
Time period(s): Indeterminate Future
Locale(s): Spaceship; Outer Space

Summary: The *Great Ship* is a vessel so large that it contains an entire planet and a variety of different civilizations. The captains discover that they are headed directly into an anom-

aly in space and attempt to gather intelligence, but are unable to do so before they find themselves immersed in their greatest danger yet.

Where it's reviewed:
Locus, February 2005, page 25

Other books by the same author:
Marrow, 2000
The Dragons of Springplace, 1999
Beneath the Gated Sky, 1997
An Exaltation of Larks, 1995
The Remarkables, 1992

Other books you might like:
Brian W. Aldiss, *Non-Stop*, 1958
Greg Bear, *Eon*, 1985
Jack L. Chalker, *Midnight in the Well of Souls*, 1977
Arthur C. Clarke, *Rendezvous with Rama*, 1973
Larry Niven, *Ringworld's Children*, 2004

800

MIKE RESNICK, Editor

I, Alien
(New York: DAW, 2005)

Story type: Anthology
Subject(s): Short Stories; Aliens

Summary: These more than two dozen original short stories all involve some sort of intelligent alien life form. The tales vary from problem stories to humor to adventure to suspense. Contributors include John DeChancie, Kay Kenyon, Kristine Kathryn Rusch, William Sanders, and Robert J. Sawyer.

Other books by the same author:
The Return of Santiago, 2003
Outpost, 2001
A Hunger in the Soul, 1998
Kirinyaga, 1998
The Widowmaker, 1996

Other books you might like:
John DeChancie, *Paradox Alley*, 1987
Kay Kenyon, *Maximum Ice*, 2002
Kristine Kathryn Rusch, *Buried Deep*, 2005
William Sanders, *The Wild Blue and the Gray*, 1991
Robert J. Sawyer, *Relativity*, 2005

801

ALASTAIR REYNOLDS

Century Rain
(London: Gollancz, 2004)

Story type: Post-Holocaust; Hard Science Fiction
Subject(s): Alternate History; Disasters
Major character(s): Verity Auger, Archaeologist; Floyd, Detective—Private; Andre Custine, Detective—Private
Time period(s): 22nd century
Locale(s): Outer Space; Alternate Universe

Summary: Earth has been rendered uninhabitable by nanotechnology that got out of control. Elsewhere, an exact copy

of 1930s Earth has been found in an artificial sphere, complete with copies of everyone who was alive at that time. One group seeks to destroy this world, while others race desperately to save its inhabitants.

Where it's reviewed:
Locus, January 2005, page 25

Other books by the same author:
Absolution Gap, 2004
Diamond Dogs, Turquoise Days, 2003
Redemption Ark, 2002
Chasm City, 2001
Revelation Space, 2000

Other books you might like:
Albert E. Cowdrey, *Flux*, 2004
Peter Hamilton, *Pandora's Star*, 2004
Robert Reed, *Marrow*, 2000
Dan Simmons, *Ilium*, 2003
Vernor Vinge, *A Deepness in the Sky*, 1999

802

JOHN RINGO

Into the Looking Glass

(New York: Baen, 2005)

Story type: Military; Invasion of Earth
Subject(s): Aliens
Major character(s): Bob Crichton, Military Personnel; William Weaver, Scientist; Tchar, Alien
Time period(s): Indeterminate Future
Locale(s): United States

Summary: A nuclear explosion in a rural portion of Florida is initially believed to be a strike by a foreign power. Subsequent investigation reveals that it marked the opening of a gateway to another world, through which emerge deadly and inhuman creatures.

Where it's reviewed:
Publishers Weekly, May 2, 2005, page 182

Other books by the same author:
Against the Tide, 2005
The Emerald Sea, 2004
Hell's Faire, 2003
There Will Be Dragons, 2003
When the Devil Dances, 2002

Other books you might like:
Richard Fawkes, *Nature of the Beast*, 2004
David Gerrold, *A Matter for Men*, 1983
Larry Niven, *Footfall*, 1985
   Jerry Pournelle, co-author
David Sherman, *Hangfire*, 2001
   Dan Cragg, co-author
David Weber, *Bolo!*, 2005

803

CHRIS ROBERSON

Here, There, and Everywhere

(Amherst, New York: Pyr, 2005)

Story type: Humor; Time Travel
Subject(s): Time Travel; Humor
Major character(s): Roxanne Bonaventure, Time Traveler, Teenager; Nigel Grant, Student; Pol Kenaston, Police Officer
Time period(s): 2000s; Indeterminate Past
Locale(s): United States; England; Egypt

Summary: Teenager Roxanne Bonaventure has an interesting secret. Thanks to a piece of advanced technology, she can travel back and forth through time, which she does, observing various historical events and weathering problems with the time police. This is the author's first novel, and the tone is predominantly humorous.

Where it's reviewed:
Locus, March 2005, page 23
Publishers Weekly, February 14, 2005, page 57

Other books you might like:
Poul Anderson, *The Shield of Time*, 1990
Kirk Mitchell, *Never the Twain*, 1987
Andre Norton, *Operation Time Search*, 1967
Robert Silverberg, *The Time Hoppers*, 1967
Connie Willis, *To Say Nothing of the Dog*, 1998

804

JOHN MADDOX ROBERTS

The Seven Hills

(New York: Ace, 2005)

Story type: Alternate Universe; Political
Series: Rome. Book 2
Subject(s): Alternate History; Military Life
Major character(s): Marcus Cornelius Scipio, Military Personnel; Titus Norbanus, Military Personnel; Zeno, Philosopher
Time period(s): Indeterminate Past
Locale(s): Roman Empire

Summary: In the sequel to *Hannibal's Children*, the Roman nation has re-established control of the Italian peninsula after being driven out by Hannibal's armies. Now they seem poised to extend their power beyond their borders, but the rivalry between two determined military leaders threatens to dissipate their energy in internal conflicts.

Other books by the same author:
Hannibal's Children, 2002
The Enigma Variations, 1989
Window of the Mind, 1989
Cloak of Illusion, 1985
The Cingulum, 1985

Other books you might like:
John Barnes, *Caesar's Bicycle*, 1997
L. Sprague de Camp, *Lest Darkness Fall*, 1949

David Drake, *Vettus and His Friends*, 1989
Crawford Kilian, *Rogue Emperor*, 1988
Kirk Mitchell, *The New Barbarians*, 1986

805

JUSTINA ROBSON

Natural History

(New York: Bantam, 2005)

Story type: Space Opera; Space Colony
Subject(s): Space Colonies; Cyborgs
Major character(s): Zephyr Duquesne, Archaeologist; Isol, Cyborg; Corvax, Alien
Time period(s): Indeterminate Future
Locale(s): Outer Space

Summary: The cyborg starship *Isol* returns from an exploratory mission to the stars, announcing that a new planet has been found that could provide a good home for some of the population from Earth. This leads to a further expedition, but also to some unusual discoveries. *Natural History* is the author's first novel published in the United States.

Where it's reviewed:
Chronicle, February 2005, page 32

Other books by the same author:
Mappa Minds, 2003
Silver Screen, 2002

Other books you might like:
Gordon R. Dickson, *The Forever Man*, 1986
Anne McCaffrey, *The Ship Who Sang*, 1970
Jody Lynn Nye, *The Ship Errant*, 1997
Kevin O'Donnell, *Mayflies*, 1979
S.M. Stirling, *The Ship Avenged*, 1997

806

KRISTINE KATHRYN RUSCH

Buried Deep

(New York: Roc, 2005)

Story type: Mystery; Space Opera
Series: Retrieval Artist. Book 4
Subject(s): Aliens; Secrets
Major character(s): Aisha Costard, Anthropologist; Miles Flint, Detective—Private; Sharyn Scott-Olson, Police Officer
Time period(s): Indeterminate Future
Locale(s): Earth; Mars

Summary: When aliens are given permission to build a structure on Mars, they unearth the skeleton of a human woman who disappeared decades earlier. Investigators from Earth try to solve the mystery of her death, which appears to involve more than simply human motives.

Where it's reviewed:
Locus, March 2005, page 20

Other books by the same author:
Consequences, 2004
Extremes, 2003

Fantasy Life, 2003
The Retrieval Artist, 2002
The Devil's Churn, 1996

Other books you might like:
Lee Killough, *The Deadly Silents*, 1981
Maxine McArthur, *Less than Human*, 2004
Mel Odom, *Lethal Interface*, 1992
John E. Stith, *Death Tolls*, 1987
Robert Tine, *Midnight City*, 1987

807

C.J. RYAN

Dexta

(New York: Bantam, 2005)

Story type: Political; Military
Series: Dexta. Book 1
Subject(s): Space Colonies
Major character(s): Gloria VanDeen, Government Official; Vladislav Rhinehart, Government Official; Zoe Zachary, Government Official
Time period(s): Indeterminate Future
Locale(s): Mynjhino, Planet—Imaginary

Summary: Gloria VanDeen, the ex-wife of the emperor of a human interstellar empire, is sent to a distant planet in the throes of a rebellion. The strategy is at least in part to get her away from the imperial court for a while, but before her visit is over she ends up as acting governor in the middle of a major crisis. First novel.

Other books you might like:
Richard Fawkes, *Face of the Enemy*, 1999
Robert Frezza, *A Small Colonial War*, 1990
Keith Laumer, *Retief*, 2002
Donald E. McQuinn, *With Full Honors*, 1997
David Weber, *Echoes of Honor*, 1998

808

FRED SABERHAGEN

Rogue Berserker

(New York: Baen, 2005)

Story type: Space Opera; Robot Fiction
Series: Berserker. Book 14
Subject(s): Space Exploration; Brainwashing
Major character(s): Harry Silver, Spaceman; Winston Cheng, Businessman; Gianopolous, Professor
Time period(s): Indeterminate Future
Locale(s): Outer Space

Summary: Harry Silver is stranded on a remote world, looking for a new assignment aboard a starship, when he is contacted by Winston Cheng, who wants to hire his services in a very strange matter. Harry soon crosses paths with a berserker, a robot ship left over from another age, programmed to eliminate all forms of life.

Where it's reviewed:
Booklist, January 1, 2005, page 835

Other books by the same author:
Berserker Prime, 2004
A Coldness in the Blood, 2002
Vlad Tepes, 2000
Ariadne's Web, 1999
Berserker Fury, 1997

Other books you might like:
Glen Cook, *The Dragon Never Sleeps*, 1988
David Mace, *Nightrider*, 1985
Victor Norwood, *Polar Fleet*, 1985
Robert J. Sawyer, *Golden Fleece*, 1990
S.M. Stirling, *The Ship Avenged*, 1997

809

ROBERT J. SAWYER

Mindscan

(New York: Tor, 2005)

Story type: Future Shock; Immortality
Subject(s): Immortality; Technology
Major character(s): Jacob Sullivan, Financier; Karen Bessarian, Writer; Quentin Ashburn, Worker
Time period(s): 2010s (2018)
Locale(s): Earth; Moon (Earth's)

Summary: Jacob Sullivan has a potentially fatal disease, so he decides to have his personality copied into an artificial body. Unfortunately, his original self is still doomed to die, and the copy discovers that he is not accepted by friends or family as being the same person he believes himself to be. A complex legal battle follows in an attempt to define the nature of human existence.

Where it's reviewed:
Publishers Weekly, January 24, 2005, page 226

Other books by the same author:
Iterations, 2004
Humans, 2003
Hominids, 2002
Flash Forward, 1999
Foreigner, 1994

Other books you might like:
Roger MacBride Allen, *The Modular Man*, 1992
David Brin, *The Kiln People*, 2002
Dennis Danvers, *The End of Days*, 1999
Charles L. Harness, *Lunar Justice*, 1991
H. Beam Piper, *The Other Human Race*, 1964

810

ROBERT J. SAWYER

Relativity

(Deerfield, Illinois: Isfic, 2005)

Story type: Collection
Subject(s): Short Stories

Summary: This volume collects eight short stories and 27 short essays and articles, plus an autobiography and other materials. All previously published between 1990 and 2005,

the stories tend toward hard science fiction and light adventure, and most have been previously collected. Some of the included articles were originally speeches.

Other books by the same author:
Iterations, 2004
Humans, 2003
Hominids, 2002
Flash Forward, 1999
Factoring Humanity, 1998

Other books you might like:
Poul Anderson, *Kinship with the Stars*, 1991
Gordon R. Dickson, *Beginnings*, 1988
Joe Haldeman, *None So Blind*, 1996
James Tiptree Jr., *Meet Me at Infinity*, 2000
Robert Charles Wilson, *The Perseids and Other Stories*, 2000

811

JOHN SCALZI

Old Man's War

(New York: Tor, 2005)

Story type: Military; Space Opera
Subject(s): Military Life; Space Travel
Major character(s): John Perry, Aged Person, Military Personnel; Harry Wilson, Aged Person, Military Personnel; Thomas Jane, Aged Person, Military Personnel
Time period(s): Indeterminate Future
Locale(s): Outer Space

Summary: Humanity is spread so thin among the stars, thanks to a number of hostile alien races, that elderly citizens are encouraged to join the military. They serve a short tour in exchange for the right to homestead on one of the new colony worlds. This book follows the career of one such man. First novel.

Where it's reviewed:
Booklist, January 1, 2005, page 835
Chronicle, February 2005, page 30
Library Journal, January 2005, page 103
Publishers Weekly, December 6, 2004, page 47

Other books you might like:
Brian W. Aldiss, *Greybeard*, 1964
David Drake, *The Military Dimension*, 1991
Elizabeth Moon, *Once a Hero*, 1997
Diann Thornley, *Dominion's Reach*, 1997
David Weber, *War of Honor*, 2002

812

KARL SCHROEDER

Lady of Mazes

(New York: Tor, 2005)

Story type: Space Opera; Future Shock
Subject(s): Coming-of-Age
Major character(s): Livia Kodaly, Singer; Aaron Varese, Scientist; Qiingi, Religious
Time period(s): Indeterminate Future
Locale(s): Planet—Imaginary; Outer Space

Summary: Livia Kodaly lives in a society that is as close to Utopian as humans can achieve, but that tranquility is disrupted when outside forces arrive. Livia travels far from her own world seeking assistance to help restore the status quo, and discovers much about herself along the way. This novel is set in the same future as the author's previous *Ventus*.

Where it's reviewed:
Locus, March 2005, page 21

Other books by the same author:
Permanence, 2002
Ventus, 2000
The Claus Effect, 1998 (David Nickle, co-author)

Other books you might like:
David Bischoff, *Mandala*, 1983
Larry Niven, *The Ringworld Engineers*, 1980
Robert Reed, *Marrow*, 2000
Alastair Reynolds, *Revelation Space*, 2000
Bob Shaw, *Orbitsville*, 1975

813

LINNEA SINCLAIR

Finders Keepers
(New York: Bantam, 2005)

Story type: Space Opera; Military
Subject(s): Secrets; Space Travel
Major character(s): Trilby Elliot, Spaceship Captain; Rhis Vanur, Military Personnel; Jagan Grantforth, Wealthy
Time period(s): Indeterminate Future
Locale(s): Outer Space; Spaceship

Summary: When tramp spaceship captain Trilby Elliot rescues a stranded military officer from a remote world, she finds that she has gotten more than she bargained for. Not only is she trapped with him in a web of intrigue, danger, and chases across space, but despite her efforts not to, she is falling in love with her new passenger.

Other books you might like:
C.J. Cherryh, *Chanur's Homecoming*, 1987
Denise Lopes Heald, *Mistwalker*, 1994
Robert Hoskins, *To Control the Stars*, 1977
Jayne Ann Krentz, *Shield's Lady*, 1989
Timothy Zahn, *The Icarus Hunt*, 1999

814

ROLAND SMITH

Cryptid Hunters
(New York: Hyperion, 2005)

Story type: Young Adult; Adventure
Subject(s): Secrets; Animals/Prehistoric
Major character(s): Marty O'Hara, Teenager; Grace O'Hara, Teenager; Travis Wolfe, Veterinarian
Time period(s): 2000s
Locale(s): Republic of the Congo

Summary: Two teenagers are sent to live with their uncle after an accident claims their parents, but he leaves to lead an expedition to the Congo in a race to discover the existence of surviving dinosaurs. They manage to follow, despite his opposition, and are crucial in allowing him to succeed despite a problem with an unscrupulous rival.

Other books you might like:
Marc Alexander, *The Mist Lizard*, 1977
James Blish, *The Night Shapes*, 1962
L.M. Boston, *The Sea Egg*, 1967
Eleanor Cameron, *The Terrible Churnadryne*, 1959
Richard Marsten, *Danger! Dinosaurs!*, 1953

815

WEN SPENCER

A Brother's Price
(New York: Roc, 2005)

Story type: Post-Holocaust; Satire
Subject(s): Princes and Princesses
Major character(s): Jerin Whistler, Teenager; Rennsellaer, Royalty (princess); Corelle Whistler, Teenager
Time period(s): Indeterminate Future
Locale(s): Earth

Summary: In a post-apocalyptic society, the world has lost its technology and reverted to a medieval style culture, except that male children have become extremely rare and women dominate all aspects of civilization. A young boy is determined to escape an arranged marriage and find a way to be with the princess he loves, even though both families are opposed.

Other books by the same author:
Dog Warrior, 2004
Bitter Waters, 2003
Tinker, 2003
Tainted Trail, 2002
Alien Taste, 2001

Other books you might like:
Margaret Atwood, *The Handmaid's Tale*, 1985
M.J. Engh, *Rainbow Man*, 1993
Charlotte Perkins Gilman, *Herland*, 1916
Joanna Russ, *The Female Man*, 1975
N. Lee Wood, *Master of None*, 2004

816

CHARLES STROSS

Accelerando
(New York: Ace, 2005)

Story type: Collection
Subject(s): Short Stories; Technology

Summary: The loosely related stories in this collection are primarily reprints from 2001-2004. The stories chronicle the efforts by several generations of a prominent family to help the world adjust to the rapid rate of technological change. Although each story is a separate adventure, the overall theme is that technological change can help the world, but only if managed properly.

Other books by the same author:
The Hidden Family, 2005
Iron Sunrise, 2004
The Atrocity Archives, 2004
The Family Trade, 2004
Singularity Sky, 2003

Other books you might like:
Stephen Baxter, *Vacuum Diagrams*, 1997
Greg Bear, *Women in Deep Time*, 2003
Gregory Benford, *Worlds Vast and Various*, 2000
Greg Egan, *Axiomatic*, 1995
Robert J. Sawyer, *Iterations*, 2004

817

THEODORE STURGEON

The Man Who Lost the Sea

(Berkeley, California: North Atlantic, 2005)

Story type: Collection
Subject(s): Short Stories

Summary: This tenth volume in the complete short stories of Theodore Sturgeon covers the years 1958 through 1962. The 12 stories included here number several classics among them, including ''The Comedian's Children,'' ''A Touch of Strange,'' and the title story. Each story is accompanied by substantial commentary.

Other books by the same author:
And Now the News, 2003
Bright Segment, 2002
Baby Is Three, 1999
Killdozer, 1996
The Ultimate Egoist, 1994

Other books you might like:
Michael Bishop, *Brighten to Incandescence*, 2003
Avram Davidson, *Strange Seas and Shores*, 1971
Dan Simmons, *Lovedeath*, 1993
Robert Charles Wilson, *The Perseids and Other Stories*, 2000
John Wyndham, *The Infinite Moment*, 1961

818

TRAVIS S. TAYLOR

The Quantum Connection

(New York: Baen, 2005)

Story type: Future Shock; Hard Science Fiction
Series: Warp Speed. Book 2
Subject(s): Space Travel
Major character(s): Steve Montana, Computer Expert; Tabitha Ames, Spacewoman; Larry Waterford, Computer Game Player
Time period(s): 2000s
Locale(s): United States; Outer Space

Summary: The discovery of a revolutionary new propulsion system makes travel in outer space more practical and allows humans to contemplate expanding to the stars. Unfortunately, they discover that there are already alien civilizations out there, battling one another for control of worlds and unwilling to tolerate yet more competition.

Other books by the same author:
Warp Speed, 2004

Other books you might like:
Gregory Benford, *In the Ocean of Night*, 1977
Frederik Pohl, *Black Star Rising*, 1985
T.L. Sherred, *Alien Island*, 1970
Sheri S. Tepper, *After Long Silence*, 1987
Liz Williams, *Empire of Bones*, 2002

819

SHEREE THOMAS, Editor

Dark Matter: Reading the Bones

(New York: Aspect, 2005)

Story type: Anthology
Subject(s): Short Stories

Summary: This is the second in a series of anthologies spotlighting science fiction writers of African descent, some of them known within the genre and some new names. Not all of the stories deal with African-related themes. Among the contributors are Samuel R. Delany, Charles R. Saunders, Tananarive Due, and Nalo Hopkinson.

Other books by the same author:
Dark Matter: A Century of Speculative Fiction from the African Diaspora, 2000

Other books you might like:
Octavia Butler, *Blood Child*, 1995
Samuel R. Delany, *Distant Stars*, 1981
Nalo Hopkinson, *The Midnight Robber*, 2002
Ian McDonald, *Evolution's Shore*, 1995
Charles R. Saunders, *Imaro*, 1981

820

JAMES TIPTREE JR. (Pseudonym of Alice Sheldon)

Her Smoke Rose Up Forever

(San Francisco: Tachyon, 2005)

Story type: Collection
Subject(s): Short Stories

Summary: Eighteen of the best stories from the 1960s through the end of the 1970s by James Tiptree, Jr. are reprinted here. Tiptree was one of those rare writers who can integrate thoughtful concepts, complex prose, and superior storytelling talents. The stories vary considerably in tone and subject matter. One of the best has no human characters at all. Her later stories were more obviously concerned with feminist issues.

Other books by the same author:
Meet Me at Infinity, 2000
Crown of Stars, 1988
The Starry Rift, 1986
Brightness Falls from the Air, 1985
Out of the Everywhere, 1981

Other books you might like:
Michael Bishop, *Brighten to Incandescence*, 2003
Paul Di Filippo, *Little Doors*, 2002
Harlan Ellison, *The Troublemakers*, 2001
Pamela Sargent, *Thumbprints*, 2004
Gene Wolfe, *Endangered Species*, 1989

821

J.D. TOWNSEND

The Assassin's Dream

(Waterville, Maine: Five Star, 2005)

Story type: Dystopian; Post-Disaster
Subject(s): Feminism; Secrets
Major character(s): Kay Black, Government Official, Criminal (assassin); Angela Potemkin, Scientist; Mother Avalon, Government Official
Time period(s): 22nd century (2174)
Locale(s): Earth

Summary: A new plague has wiped out almost all of the males on Earth and women have created a new, repressive civilization in which dissidents are killed by government employed assassins. One of these is Kay Black, who begins to question the way things are when one of her scheduled victims reveals information previously held secret. First novel.

Other books you might like:
William F. Nolan, *Logan's Run*, 1967
    George Clayton Johnson, co-author
Joanna Russ, *The Female Man*, 1975
Pamela Sargent, *The Shore of Women*, 1986
Sheri S. Tepper, *Singer from the Sea*, 1999
Wilson Tucker, *Resurrection Days*, 1981

822

HARRY TURTLEDOVE, Editor

Alternate Generals III

(New York: Baen, 2005)

Story type: Anthology; Alternate History
Subject(s): Short Stories; Alternate History

Summary: This is the third in a series of original anthologies in which various authors explore alternate histories in which battles were decided differently than in the real world, affecting the outcome of a war and the futures of nations. Most stories involve a character who was not historically a military figure cast in the role of military leader. The contributors include Mike Resnick, Esther Friesner, Judith Tarr, and several others.

Other books by the same author:
Homeward Bound, 2005
Advance and Retreat, 2004
Days of Infamy, 2004
Conan of Venarium, 2004
Gunpowder Empire, 2003

Other books you might like:
Robert Conroy, *1901*, 1995
Alfred Coppel, *The Burning Mountain*, 1982

Harry Harrison, *The Stars and Stripes Forever*, 1998
Martin Cruz Smith, *The Indians Won*, 1970
Bill Yenne, *A Damned Fine War*, 2004

823

HARRY TURTLEDOVE, Editor
MARTIN H. GREENBERG, Co-Editor

The Best Time Travel Stories of the 20th Century

(New York: Del Rey, 2005)

Story type: Anthology; Time Travel
Subject(s): Short Stories; Time Travel

Summary: This collection of 18 time travel stories, all previously published, includes classics like ''A Gun for Dinosaur'' by L. Sprague de Camp and ''A Sound of Thunder'' by Ray Bradbury, as well as newer titles. The contributors include Nancy Kress, Robert Silverberg, R.A. Lafferty, Larry Niven, and others.

Other books by the same author:
Advance and Retreat, 2004
Days of Infamy, 2004
Out of Darkness, 2004
Return Engagement, 2004
Conan of Venarium, 2004

Other books you might like:
Isaac Asimov, *The End of Eternity*, 1955
David Gerrold, *The Man Who Folded Himself*, 1973
Robert A. Heinlein, *The Door into Summer*, 1956
Robert Silverberg, *Hawksbill Station*, 1968
Connie Willis, *Doomsday Book*, 1992

824

GORDON VAN GELDER, Editor

Fourth Planet from the Sun

(New York: Thunder's Mouth, 2005)

Story type: Anthology
Subject(s): Short Stories; Mars
Locale(s): Mars

Summary: The dozen stories in this volume, previously published in *The Magazine of Fantasy and Science Fiction*, all involve the planet Mars. The contributors include Ray Bradbury, Philip K. Dick, Roger Zelazny, and Leigh Brackett, and vary from hard science fiction to highly literary works. Several of the stories included are acknowledged classics in the field.

Where it's reviewed:
Locus, March 2005, page 29

Other books by the same author:
One Lamp, 2003
The Best from Fantasy and Science Fiction: The Fiftieth Anniversary Anthology, 1999

Other books you might like:
Leigh Brackett, *The Sword of Rhiannon*, 1953
Ray Bradbury, *The Martian Chronicles*, 1958

Science Fiction

Philip K. Dick, *Martian Timeslip*, 1964
Christopher Priest, *The Space Machine*, 1976
Kim Stanley Robinson, *The Martians*, 1998

825

JOHN VARLEY

Mammoth

(New York: Ace, 2005)

Story type: Time Travel; Hard Science Fiction
Subject(s): Cloning; Scientific Experiments
Major character(s): Howard Christian, Wealthy; Susan Morgan, Scientist; Matthew Wright, Scientist
Time period(s): 2000s
Locale(s): United States; Canada

Summary: A bored billionaire is inspired when a mammoth is discovered perfectly preserved in the ice. His original plan is to clone the creature and recreate the species, but he is even more intrigued by a second discovery: there is also a caveman wearing a wristwatch in the ice. The puzzle unravels as he recruits a team of scientists to investigate.

Where it's reviewed:
Publishers Weekly, May 9, 2005, page 51

Other books by the same author:
The John Varley Reader, 2004
Red Thunder, 2003
The Golden Globe, 1998
Steel Beach, 1992
Demon, 1984

Other books you might like:
Michael Bishop, *No Enemy but Time*, 1982
Michael Crichton, *Sphere*, 1987
L. Sprague de Camp, *The Rivers of Time*, 1993
Will Hubbell, *Cretaceous Sea*, 2002
Andre Norton, *Operation Time Search*, 1967

826

S.L. VIEHL

Afterburn

(New York: Roc, 2005)

Story type: Space Opera; Political
Series: Allied League of Worlds. Book 2
Subject(s): Space Travel
Major character(s): Burn mu Znora, Health Care Professional; Liana, Alien, Child; Onkar, Health Care Professional
Time period(s): Indeterminate Future
Locale(s): Outer Space

Summary: Following an interstellar conflict, negotiations for extended peace are to take place on a planet occupied by a water-breathing race. Unfortunately, someone attacks the party of one of the ambassadors, and a space-going medical rescue team finds themselves in the middle of a potential interstellar crisis.

Other books by the same author:
Bio Rescue, 2004

Bladedancer, 2003
Eternity Row, 2002
Endurance, 2001
Shockball, 2001

Other books you might like:
Julie E. Czerneda, *Migration*, 2005
Murray Leinster, *Med Ship*, 2002
Alan E. Nourse, *Star Surgeon*, 1959
Jody Lynn Nye, *Taylor's Ark*, 1993
James White, *Monsters and Medics*, 1977

827

PETER WATTS

Behemoth: Seppuku

(New York: Tor, 2005)

Story type: Post-Disaster; Genetic Manipulation
Series: Starfist. Book 4
Subject(s): Environmental Problems; Disasters
Major character(s): Lenie Clarke, Cyborg, Businesswoman; Lubin, Businessman
Time period(s): Indeterminate Future
Locale(s): Earth; Undersea Environment/Habitat

Summary: Lenie Clarke has come to terms with the fact that she released a devastating catastrophe which destroyed most of the surface world while she and a few influential people sheltered in an undersea habitat. Now she must make amends. This is actually the second half of the novel started in *Behemoth: B-Max* and is not a separate story.

Where it's reviewed:
Booklist, January 1, 2005, page 835
Library Journal, January 2005, page 102
Publishers Weekly, December 13, 2004, page 50

Other books by the same author:
Behemoth: B-Max, 2004
Maelstrom, 2001
Starfish, 1999

Other books you might like:
T.J. Bass, *The Godwhale*, 1974
Dean McLaughlin, *Dome World*, 1962
Allen Steele, *Oceanspace*, 2000
Wilson Tucker, *The City in the Sea*, 1951
Kenneth Von Gunden, *The Sounding Stillness*, 1993

828

DAVID WEBER

Bolo!

(New York: Baen, 2005)

Story type: Military; Collection
Series: Bolo
Subject(s): Short Stories

Summary: The bolos are oversized, high-tech military tanks used in interplanetary wars in the far future. Instead of a normal crew, they are actually integrated with a single human being, who uses the tank as he would his own body. The

concept was originated by the late Keith Laumer but other authors have expanded on the idea. This is a collection of four long stories, three published previously, set in that universe.

Other books by the same author:
Empire from the Ashes, 2003
The Excalibur Alternative, 2002
Ashes of Victory, 2000
The Apocalypse Troll, 1999
On Basilisk Station, 1993

Other books you might like:
David Drake, *The Tank Lords*, 1997
Leo Frankowski, *A Boy and His Tank*, 1999
William Keith, *Bolo Strike*, 2001
Keith Laumer, *The Compleat Bolo*, 1990
Jerry Pournelle, *Falkenberg's Legion*, 1990

829

DAVID WEBER
JOHN RINGO, Co-Author

We Few
(New York: Baen, 2005)

Story type: Military; Space Opera
Series: Prince Roger. Book 4
Subject(s): Military Life; Secrets
Major character(s): Roger MacClintock, Nobleman; Jackson Adoula, Nobleman; Nimashet Despreaux, Military Personnel
Time period(s): Indeterminate Future
Locale(s): Outer Space; Planet—Imaginary

Summary: Prince Roger MacClintock gets caught up in a mixture of interstellar conflict, espionage, treachery, and adventure in outer space in his fourth outing. Two writers who specialize in military science fiction create a society in space in which an aristocracy rules the stars and sons of the upper class are expected to fill a predestined role.

Where it's reviewed:
Locus, February 2005, page 27

Other books by the same author:
Windrider's Oath, 2004
Empire from the Ashes, 2003
The Excalibur Alternative, 2002
War of Honor, 2002
More than Honor, 1998

Other books you might like:
Lois McMaster Bujold, *Brothers in Arms*, 1989
W. Michael Gear, *Starstrike*, 1990
R.M. Meluch, *The Queen's Squadron*, 1992
Elizabeth Moon, *Once a Hero*, 1997
Joel Rosenberg, *Not for Glory*, 1988

830

T.K.F. WEISKOPF, Editor

Adventures in Far Futures
(New York: Baen, 2005)

Story type: Anthology
Subject(s): Short Stories
Time period(s): Indeterminate Future

Summary: This collection of new short stories set in the very distant future includes contributions by James P. Hogan, Gregory Benford, Dave Freer, Eric Flint, Mark L. Van Name, and others. The common thread in each story is that the future will see humanity spread to the stars rather than remain confined to a single solar system.

Other books by the same author:
Adventures in Sol System, 2004
Tomorrow Bites, 1995 (Greg Cox, co-editor)
Tomorrow Sucks, 1994 (Greg Cox, co-editor)

Other books you might like:
Gregory Benford, *Cosm*, 1998
Gordon R. Dickson, *The Chantry Guild*, 1988
Dave Freer, *The Rats, the Bats, and the Ugly*, 2004
    Eric Flint, co-author
Joe Haldeman, *Forever Free*, 1999
James P. Hogan, *The Legend That Was Earth*, 2000

831

SCOTT WESTERFELD

Uglies
(New York: Simon Pulse, 2005)

Story type: Young Adult; Dystopian
Series: Specials. Book 1
Subject(s): Utopia/Dystopia; Beauty
Major character(s): Tally Youngblood, Teenager; Cable, Doctor, Government Official; Shay, Teenager, Rebel
Time period(s): Indeterminate Future
Locale(s): Earth

Summary: In the indeterminate future, Earth has been transformed. Everyone is declared ugly at birth and, on their 16th birthday, submit to an operation which makes them ''beautiful.'' Tally has accepted this all her life, but when her friend Shay questions the system, and when she is threatened by the sinister Dr. Cable, she begins to wonder if the government has been lying to her.

Other books by the same author:
So Yesterday, 2004
The Killing of Worlds, 2003
Evolution's Darling, 1999
Fine Prey, 1998
Polymorph, 1997

Other books you might like:
Jim Aikin, *The Wall at the Edge of the World*, 1993
Ray Bradbury, *Fahrenheit 451*, 1953
William F. Nolan, *Logan's Run*, 1967
    George Clayton Johnson, co-author

Charles Oberndorf, *Testing*, 1993
Rebecca Ore, *Outlaw School*, 2000

832

STEVE WHITE

The Prometheus Project

(New York: Baen, 2005)

Story type: Invasion of Earth; Mystery
Subject(s): Aliens; Espionage
Major character(s): Devaney, Spy; Chloe Bryant, Government Official; Renata Novak, Government Official
Time period(s): 1960s (1963-1969)
Locale(s): United States

Summary: Devaney has performed a number of quasi-legal duties for the U.S. government in the past, but none of that prepares him for the fact that aliens have discovered Earth and that they are being dealt with by a secret organization. This group has concocted an elaborate hoax to prevent the visitors from understanding how divided and vulnerable the Earth really is.

Other books by the same author:
Demon's Gate, 2004
Forge of the Titans, 2003
Prince of Sunset, 1998
Legacy, 1995

Other books you might like:
Poul Anderson, *The High Crusade*, 1960
Keith Laumer, *The Monitors*, 1966
Eric Frank Russell, *Next of Kin*, 1959
Clifford D. Simak, *Time Is the Simplest Thing*, 1971
Richard Wilson, *The 30 Day Wonder*, 1960

833

EDWARD WILLETT

Lost in Translation

(Waterville, Maine: Five Star, 2005)

Story type: Psychic Powers; Political
Subject(s): Aliens; Psychic Powers
Major character(s): Jarrikk, Alien, Empath; Kathryn Bircher, Empath
Time period(s): Indeterminate Future
Locale(s): Planet—Imaginary

Summary: Humans and aliens both colonize the same distant world, which inevitably leads to conflict. When it appears that this is driving both sides toward war, two empaths—one from each culture—decide to falsify their readings in order to prevent open conflict. Both endanger their own futures by their deception.

Other books by the same author:
Spirit Singer, 2003
Soulworm, 1997

Other books you might like:
Ray Aldridge, *The Orpheus Machine*, 1992
Julie E. Czerneda, *Hidden in Sight*, 2003

Barry Longyear, *Enemy Mine*, 1985
  David Gerrold, co-author
H.M. Major, *The Alien Trace*, 1984
S.L. Viehl, *Endurance*, 2001

834

JACK WILLIAMSON

The Stonehenge Gate

(New York: Tor, 2005)

Story type: Hard Science Fiction; First Contact
Subject(s): Space Exploration
Major character(s): Will Stone, Teacher; Derek Ironcraft, Teacher; Lupe, Scientist
Time period(s): 2000s
Locale(s): New Mexico

Summary: Four friends discover an alien artifact that leads to a gateway between worlds. A variety of other worlds are visited, ranging from ones in which the entire population has been destroyed to others that still enjoy highly advanced technology. The friends have various adventures before finally finding their way back to Earth.

Other books by the same author:
Terraforming Earth, 2001
Wolves of Darkness, 1999
The Black Sun, 1997
Beachhead, 1992
The Humanoids, 1949

Other books you might like:
Greg Bear, *The Forge of God*, 1987
John DeChancie, *Red Limit Freeway*, 1984
Jack McDevitt, *Ancient Shores*, 1996
Andre Norton, *Galactic Derelict*, 1959
Frederik Pohl, *Gateway*, 1978

835

ROBERT CHARLES WILSON

Spin

(New York: Tor, 2005)

Story type: Disaster; Hard Science Fiction
Subject(s): Disasters; Aliens
Major character(s): Diane Lawton, Wealthy; Jason Lawton, Businessman, Wealthy; Tyler Dupree, Doctor
Time period(s): Indeterminate Future
Locale(s): United States; Outer Space

Summary: One day the human race discovers that the sky has been altered. The Earth has been enclosed in an artificial sphere and what appears to be the sun is actually a kind of projection. As the years pass, the initial uproar dies down but a group of government officials and entrepreneurs continue to search for a way to break out of the sphere and discover who is responsible.

Where it's reviewed:
Analog, June 2005, page 134
Locus, March 2005, page 15

Other books by the same author:
Blind Lake, 2003
The Chronoliths, 2001
Bios, 1999
Darwinia, 1998
Mysterium, 1994

Other books you might like:
Roger MacBride Allen, *The Ring of Charon*, 1990
Edmond Hamilton, *City at World's End*, 1951
Robert Reed, *Beneath the Gated Sky*, 1997
Alastair Reynolds, *Century Rain*, 2004
John E. Stith, *Manhattan Transfer*, 1993

836

GENE WOLFE

Starwater Strains

(New York: Tor, 2005)

Story type: Collection
Subject(s): Short Stories

Summary: This collection reprints 25 short stories, primarily science fiction, previously published between 1997 and 2004. Wolfe employs a highly literate style and occasional bits of humor to enliven his stories of the near future. Rarely do they involve technology, but are more concerned with the effects of change on the human characters in the stories.

Other books by the same author:
Innocents Aboard, 2004
Latro of the Mists, 2003
Return to the Whorl, 2001
On Blue's Waters, 1999
Castleview, 1990

Other books you might like:
J.G. Ballard, *The Impossible Man*, 1966
Damon Knight, *Rule Golden and Other Stories*, 1979
Theodore Sturgeon, *Bright Segment*, 2002
James Tiptree Jr., *Out of the Everywhere*, 1981
Robert Charles Wilson, *The Perseids and Other Stories*, 2000

837

SUSAN WRIGHT

Slaves Unchained

(New York: Pocket, 2005)

Story type: Space Opera; Dystopian
Series: Rose Rico. Book 3
Subject(s): Aliens; Sexual Abuse
Major character(s): Rose Rico, Rebel, Slave; G'Kaan, Alien; Ash, Genetically Altered Being
Time period(s): Indeterminate Future
Locale(s): Outer Space; Earth

Summary: Rose Rico is one of many humans sold into slavery by her own government, part of a secret pact with an alien race who desire humans for sexual purposes. She escapes along with some of her fellow slaves, with the connivance of some of the aliens, and returns to Earth intent upon ensuring the overthrow of the government.

Other books by the same author:
Slave Trade, 2003
Dark Passion, 2001
One Small Step, 2001
The Badlands, 1999
Violations, 1995

Other books you might like:
Donald Barr, *Space Relations*, 1960
J.F. Bone, *The Lani People*, 1961
John Cleve, *Star Slaver*, 1983
Sharon Green, *Gateway to Xanadu*, 1985
Elizabeth Lynn, *The Sardonyx Net*, 1981

838

JANE YOLEN, Editor
PATRICK NIELSEN HAYDEN, Co-Editor

The Year's Best Science Fiction and Fantasy for Teens: First Annual Collection

(New York: Tor, 2005)

Story type: Anthology; Young Adult
Subject(s): Short Stories

Summary: These 11 short stories published in 2004 were deemed by the editors to be the best for teenage readers. Most of the selections originally appeared in markets that are not specifically aimed at this age group. The contributors include David Gerrold, Garth Nix, S.M. Stirling, Delia Sherman, and others.

Other books by the same author:
The Sword of the Rightful King, 2003
The Bagpiper's Ghost, 2002
Not One Damsel in Distress, 2000
Sister Emily's Lightship, 2000
Merlin, 1997

Other books you might like:
Isaac Asimov, *David Starr: Space Ranger*, 1952
Bruce Coville, *Robot Trouble*, 1986
Robert A. Heinlein, *Tunnel in the Sky*, 1955
Andre Norton, *Galactic Derelict*, 1959
Jerry Pournelle, *Starswarm*, 1998

839

TIMOTHY ZAHN

Dragon and Slave

(New York: Tor, 2005)

Story type: Young Adult; Space Opera
Series: Dragonback. Book 3
Subject(s): Aliens; Space Travel
Major character(s): Jack Morgan, Teenager, Spaceman; Draycos, Alien; Virgil, Artificial Intelligence
Time period(s): Indeterminate Future
Locale(s): Brum-a-dum, Planet—Imaginary

Summary: Teenager Jack Morgan is still on the run, framed for a crime he didn't commit. He is aided by the electronically reproduced intelligence of his uncle Virgil and an alien

symbiote, Draycos, who can conceal himself by becoming a pattern on Jack's body. The secret to clearing his name may be contained in the files of an interstellar slave trader, so Jack surrenders his freedom in an attempt to get access.

Other books by the same author:
Dragon and Soldier, 2004
Survivor's Quest, 2004
The Green and the Gray, 2004

Dragon and Thief, 2003
Manta's Gift, 2002

Other books you might like:
John Barnes, *Sin of Origin*, 1988
John Brunner, *Slavers of Space*, 1960
Hal Clement, *Through the Eye of the Needle*, 1978
John Morressey, *Starbrat*, 1972
Andre Norton, *The Sioux Spaceman*, 1960

Historical Fiction in Review
by
Daniel S. Burt

For the last several years there has been a noticeable boom in historical novels in both quantity and quality. The historical novel continues to be the most represented genre on the best seller and the year's best book lists. Looking at the literary prize winners over the last five years, historical novels have been conspicuously represented. Three of the last five Pulitzer Prizes have gone to historical novels—Marilynne Robinson's *Gilead* (2005), Edward P. Jones' *The Known World* (2004), and Michael Chabon's *Adventures of Kavalier & Clay* (2001). Two of the last four National Book Awards went to historical novels—Lily Tuck's *The News from Paraguay* (2004) and Susan Sontag's *In America* (2000)—and three of the last five National Book Critics Circle Award winners were historical novels—Robinson's *Gilead* (2004), Jones' *The Known World* (2003), and Ian McEwan's *Atonement* (2002). This is an impressive record for a literary genre that is often maligned and is forever receiving premature predictions of its decline and demise. It seems that every year critics forecast that this marks the end of the boom, that the well is drying up, and history is losing its power to stimulate the imagination and spark a lively and significant narrative. After all, what possibly is left for a historical novelist to record that has not been done before since the days of Sir Walter Scott?

Has the current wave in historical novels peaked? Has the boon turned to bust? Not based on the number and quality of the fiction collected here. Are there any new historical figures, regions, or eras left to be discovered? Are there any new ways to present familiar historical material? Based on recent historical novels, the answer is an unqualified yes on all counts. Evident here are the signs of a genre's vitality: new works by established, distinguished novelists; promising first novels; and interesting second efforts. There are several launches of new series that bode well for the future, as well as intriguing new takes on familiar subjects—the Civil War, the Depression era, World War II—and fascinating rediscoveries of overlooked or forgotten histori-

cal figures and events. The novels collected here underscore the appeal of historical fiction for writer and reader alike. The power and persistence of historical fiction can be attributed to the form's ability to transport readers back in time to explore the unfamiliar intimately, while shocking with both the strange and affirming the recognizable in the distant past. Good historical novelists bring the past to life; great historical novelists bridge the gap between previous eras and our own to uncover commonality and timeless relevance.

Despite its appeal, the historical novel remains one of the most contested of literary genres. Historical novelists have been criticized both for their errors and falsification of history, as well as for indulging in historical detail work at the expense of a novel's purported main job of plot and character development. By invading the province of the historian with an intention to elucidate the past as well as to entertain, the historical novelist must serve two contradictory masters, satisfying the often opposed goals of historical and imaginative truth. Not bound by the same restrictions as the historian to report only what is known and verifiable, the historical novelist is free to look beneath the facts of history for insights, to fill in gaps in the historical record with speculation and surmise. The writer of historical fiction must satisfy *both* the impulses of the historian and the novelist that often diverge. It is not surprising that achieving the ideal balance between historical truth and imaginative invention makes success in the historical novel so difficult and elusive.

Selection Criteria

More than any other fictional genre, it is necessary to define exactly what constitutes a historical novel. All novels deal with the past, except science fiction that is set in the future, or fantasy novels set in an imagined, alternative world outside historical time. Yet not all novels are truly historical. Central to any workable definition of historical fiction is the degree to which the writer attempts not to recall the past but to recreate it. In some cases the time frame,

setting, and customs of a novel's era are merely incidental to its action and characterization. In other cases, period details function as little more than a colorful backdrop for characters and situations that could as easily be played out in a different era with little alteration. So-called historical "costume dramas" could to a greater or lesser degree work as well with a change of costume in a different place and time. The novels that we can identify as truly historical, however, attempt much more than incidental period surface details or interchangeable historical eras. What justifies a designation as a historical novel is the writer's attempt at providing an accurate and believable representation of a particular historical era. The writer of historical fiction shares with the historian a verifiable depiction of past events, lives, and customs. In historical fiction, the past itself becomes as much a subject for the novelist as the characters and action.

Most of us use the phrase "historical novel" casually, never really needing an exact definition to make ourselves understood. We just know it when we see it. This listing, however, requires a set of criteria to determine what's in and what's out. Otherwise the list has no boundaries. If the working definition of historical fiction is too loose, every novel set in a period before the present qualifies, and nearly every novel becomes a historical novel immediately upon publication. If the definition is so strict that only books set in a time before the author's birth, for example, make the cut, then countless works that critics, readers, librarians, and the authors themselves think of as historical novels would be excluded.

The challenge here, therefore, has been to fashion a definition or set of criteria flexible enough to include novels that pass what can be regarded as the litmus test for historical fiction: did the author use his or her imagination—and often quite a bit of research—to evoke another and earlier time than the author's own? Walter Scott, who is credited with "inventing" the historical novel in English during the early nineteenth century provides a useful criterion in the subtitle of *Waverley*, his initial historical novel, the story of Scottish life at the time of the Jacobite Rebellion of 1745: "'Tis Sixty Years Since." This supplies a possible formula for separating the created past from the remembered past. What is unique and distinctive about the so-called historical novel is its attempt to imagine a distant period of time before the novelist's lifetime. Scott's sixty-year span (the same, incidentally, used by Leo Tolstoy in *War and Peace*) between a novel's composition and its imagined era offers an arbitrary but useful means to distinguish between the personal and the historical past. The distance of two generations or nearly a lifetime provides a necessary span for the past to emerge as history and forces the writer to rely on more than recollection to uncover the patterns and textures of the past. I have, therefore, adopted Scott's formula but adjusted it to fifty years, including those books in which the significant portion of their plots is set in a period fifty years or more before the novel was written.

Because a rigid application of this fifty-year rule might disqualify quite a few books intended by their authors and

regarded by their readers to be historical novels, another test has been applied to books written about more recent eras: did the author use actual historical figures and events while setting out to recreate a specific, rather than a general or incidental, historical period? Although it is, of course, risky to speculate about a writer's intention, it is possible by looking at the book's approach, its use of actual historical figures, and its emphasis on a distinctive time and place that enhances the reader's knowledge of past lives, events, and customs to detect when a book conforms to what most would consider a central preoccupation of the historical novel.

I have tried to apply these criteria for the historical novel as a guide, not as an inflexible rule, and have allowed some exceptions when warranted by special circumstances. I hope I have been able to anticipate what most readers would consider historical novels, but I recognize that I may have overlooked some worthy representations of the past in the interest of dealing with a manageable list of titles. Finally, not every title in the Western, historical mystery, or historical romance genres has been included to avoid unnecessary duplication with the other sections of this book. I have included those novels that share characteristics with another genre—whether fantasy, Western, mystery, or romance—that seem to put the strongest emphasis on historical interest, detail, and accuracy.

Historical Fiction Highlights

What trends are evident in the novels collected here? A few come to mind. The historical series remains perhaps the most noteworthy of contemporary handling of the historical novel genre. While the series is the rule in historical mysteries, multivolume historical novels, with recurring characters in ongoing episodes are increasingly in vogue. Writers seem to prefer telling their stories in a multipart format, rather than in a single stand-alone volume. This is likely as much a publishing and economic decision as an artistic one, since sequels trade on a novel's hard-earned success. Catering to an audience who demands more of the same can have its drawbacks, however, and some historical fiction series seem more like franchises than fresh and innovative reading experiences. While there is something to be said for the elbow room to follow a character's development over time and through multiple situations, or to examine a period's evolution, there are also certain benefits for letting a series close naturally before it has a chance to repeat itself.

There are several initial installments of projected new series here, including one by veteran historical novelist Bernard Cornwell set in ninth-century Britain (*The Last Kingdom*), a new nautical series set during the Napoleonic War (Jay Worrall's *Sails on the Horizon*), and the first in a series on the American settling of Texas by Western veteran Elmer Kelton (*Sons of Texas*). Morgan Llywelyn offers another installment in her survey of Irish history in the twentieth century with *1972*. Conn Iggulden delivers the third of his four-volume fictional biography of Julius Caesar (*Emperor:*

The Field of Swords). James L. Nelson and David Poyer present further adventures in their series on the Civil War at sea (*Thieves of Mercy* and *That Anvil of Our Souls*). Jennifer Chiaverini supplies a new chapter in her Elm Creek Quilts series (*The Sugar Camp Quilt*), while Albert Murray adds to his multipart fictionalized autobiography with *The Magic Keys*. Several novels bring series to a close: Andrei Makine's Russian history trilogy with *The Earth and Sky of Jacques Dorme*; Newt Gingrich and William R. Forstchen's alternative version of the Civil War (*Never Call Retreat*); and regrettably by his death, the Sir John Fielding Georgian era mystery series by Bruce Alexander (*Rules of Engagement*).

Another popular trend among recent historical novels is incorporating fantasy or deliberate altering the past as part of the fictional strategy. Several books mix supernatural elements with historical events and figures. Examples are Mercedes Lackey and Roberta Gellis' *Ill Met by Moonlight*, Jules Watson's *The White Mare*, and Sara Douglass' *Darkwitch Rising*. Others offer intriguing what-if scenarios, such as Susan Swan's imagining Casanova's last affair in *What Casanova Told Me* and the survival of a Gothic novel by Byron in John Cowley's *Lord Byron's Novel*. Still others imagine an entire alternative version of history, from John Maddox Roberts' speculation about the fall of Rome to the Carthaginians in *The Seven Hills* to Eric Flint's alternate chronicle of the War of 1812 in *The Rivers of War* to Su Tong's imagining an alternative Chinese dynasty in *My Life as Emperor*. All these novels press the limits of what is conventional in historical novels, while finding new energy and angles of view by subverting and expanding the historical record with the imagination.

The novels assembled range widely across the world and the historical past with several popular stops along the way. The Civil War and World War I and II remain favorite topics, as does the Depression era, with multiple volumes looking at these years from different angles. Other novels take their readers to places and times well off the beaten track, including Tash Aw's depiction of Malaysia in the 1930s and 1940s in *The Harmony Silk Factory*; Hungary in the 1950s in Zsuzsa Banks' *The Swimmer*; the Irish Potato Famine in Maura D. Shaw's *The Keeners*; Dutch settlers in South Africa in the seventeenth century in Dan Sleigh's *Islands*; Tampa, Florida, at the time of the Spanish-American War in Catherine Chidgey's *The Transformation*; and two very different views of Palermo, Sicily, in the twelfth century under Muslim rule in Tariq Ali's *A Sultan in Palermo* and in the thirteenth century under Holy Roman Emperor Frederick II in Maria Bordihn's *The Falcon of Palermo*. Still others base their stories on actual events, such as the 1848 American expedition to the Holy Land in search of the Biblical cities of Sodom and Gommorah in C.A. Andrew Jampoler's *Sailors in the Holy Land*, John Wycliffe's struggle to produce an English translation of the Bible in Brenda Rickman Vantrease's *The Illuminator*, the Mier Expedition into Mexico during the days of the Texas

Republic in Rick Bass' *The Diezmo*, the Rape of Nanking in Mo Hayder's *The Devil of Nanking*, and the construction of the Empire State Building in Thomas Kelly's *Empire Rising*.

There are several promising debuts, including Jane Guill's *Nectar from a Stone* that deals with medieval Wales; Caroline Petit's *The Fat Man's Daughter*, about the recovery of Chinese art treasures from Japanese occupied China; E. Duke Vincent's *Mafia Summer*, about New York City gang wars in the 1950s; and Donis Casey's atmospheric Oklahoma mystery *The Old Buzzard Had It Coming*. Several authors prove that their first efforts were no flukes with worthy second efforts, including Nancy E. Turner's *Sarah's Quilt*, a sequel to the highly acclaimed *These Is My Words*; Susann Cokal's *Breath and Bones*; and Peter Quinn's much anticipated second novel, *Hour of the Cat*.

Historical Mysteries

The consistent mainstay of historical novels and the single largest subcategory of historical fiction remains historical mysteries, a genre that continues to attract a diverse group of writers who demonstrate the effectiveness of using suspense and secrets to propel readers into the historical past and sustain their interest there. Virtually every historical era has some detective work going on—from Ancient Egypt (Brad Geagley's *Year of the Hyenas*) through Ancient Rome (Albert Noyer's *The Cybelene Conspiracy*, John Maddox Roberts' *The Princess and the Pirates*, and Steven Saylor's *A Gladiator Dies Only Once*), the Middle Ages (P.C. Doherty's *The Hangman's Hymn*, John Pilkington's *The Mapmaker's Daughter*, and Kate Sedley's *The Burgundian's Tale*), and the Elizabethan period (Edward Marston's *The Malevolent Comedy*, Kathy Lynn Emerson's *Face Down Below the Banqueting House*, Karen Harper's *The Fyre Mirror*, and Philip Gooden's *An Honorable Murder*). There is sleuthing going on in the seventeenth century (Janet Gleeson's *The Serpent in the Garden* and Charles O'Brien's *Lethal Beauty*), and the Victorian period (Anne Perry's *Long Spoon Lane*, Will Thomas' *To Kingdom Come*, and Edward Marston's *The Excursion Train*). Historical mysteries also take place throughout the twentieth century: in and immediately after World War I (Michael Pearce's *Prince of Darkness* and Jonathan Rabb's *Rosa*), during the Roaring Twenties (Elizabeth Peters' *The Serpent on the Crown*, Barbara Cleverly's *The Palace Tiger*, and Walter Satterthwait's *Cavalcade*), and during World War II (Sandra Scoppettone's *This Dame for Hire* and Peter Quinn's *Hour of the Cat*). Historical figures appear as sleuth: Jane Austen in Stephanie Barron's *Jane and His Lordship's Legacy*, Ambrose Bierce in Oakley Hall's *Ambrose Bierce and the Ace of Shoots*, Beatrix Potter in Susan Wittig Albert's *Tales of Holly How*, and the irrepressible Groucho Marx in Ron Goulart's *Groucho Marx, King of the Jungle*.

Finally, the most popular fictional character in literary history, Sherlock Holmes, is featured in actual cases or variations on his history. Martin Davies' *Mrs. Hudson and*

the Spirits' Curse exploits the sleuthing skills of Holmes' housekeeper. The talented historical novelist Caleb Carr offers his version of a classic Holmes' case in *The Italian Secretary*, and Mitch Cullin imagines Holmes' last days in post-World War II in *A Single Trick of the Mind*.

Fictional Biographies

One of the most intriguing and interesting subgenres of the historical novel is fictional biography, in which a significant portion of a historical figure's actual life is recreated. Freed from some of the factual constraints of actual biographers, the fictional biographers can enter the psyches of their subjects, as well as imagine scenes and scenarios to dramatize telling exposures of their subjects. The result can shed interesting light on a familiar historical figure and bring the little-known from obscurity to prominence. Represented are the well-known, such as Julius Caesar (Conn Iggulden's *Emperor: The Field of Swords*), the lesser known—Attila the Hun in William Dietrich's *The Scourge of God* and Michael Curtis Ford's *The Sword of Attila*, pirate Anne Bonny in Christopher John Farley's *Kingston by Starlight*, Renaissance painter Raphael in Diane Haeger's *The Ruby Ring*, and Elizabethan poet and playwright Christopher Marlowe in Louise Welsh's *Tamburlaine Must Die*—and the virtually unknown, such as proto-bohemian and feminist Elsa von Freytag-Loringhoven in Rene Steinke's *Holy Skirt*, pioneering nineteenth-century physicians David Hosack in Gillen D'Arcy Wood's *Hosack's Folly* and Heinrich Hoffman in Clare Dudman's *98 Reasons for Being*, and the wives of Moses in Marek Halter's *Zipporah, Wife of Moses* and Ralph Waldo Emerson in Amy Belding Brown's *Mr. Emerson's Wife*. Other novels offer fictionalized versions of actual figures, including NAACP crusader against lynchings Walter White in Thomas Dyja's *The Moon in Our Hands*, Renaissance artist Artemisia Gentileschi in Pauline Holdstock's *A Rare and Curious Gift*, and novelist Ralph Ellison and artist Romare Bearden in Albert Murray's *The Magic Keys*.

Other novels feature intriguing cameo appearances by such historical figures as Cleopatra in John Maddox Roberts' *The Princess and the Pirate*, Ben Jonson in Philip Gooden's *An Honorable Murder*, the Big Three—Winston Churchill, Franklin Delano Roosevelt, and Josef Stalin—in Philip Kerr's *Hitler's Peace*, Major John Andre and Benedict Arnold in Lucia St. Clair Robson's *Shadow Patriots*, General Gordon and the Mahdi in Wilbur A. Smith's *The Triumph of the Sun*, Stephen F. Austin in Elmer Kelton's *Sons of Texas*, and James Monroe and James Madison in Eric Flint's *The Rivers of War*.

Oddities

Let me conclude this survey of the historical novels with a mention of the odd and the offbeat, books that impressed with their unusual subjects and perspectives. Elizabeth Aston continues her chronicle of the Darcy family from Jane Austen's *Pride and Prejudice* in *The Exploits and Adventures of Miss Alethea Darcy*. Julian Branston arranges a meeting between Cervantes and Don Quixote in *Tilting at Windmills*, while Ellen Feldman imagines the survival of Anne Frank's boyfriend in *The Boy Who Loved Anne Frank*. Grace Tiffany retells the story of the *Merchant of Venice*, and Geraldine Brooks in *March* imagines the Civil War career of the father in Louisa May Alcott's *Little Women*. Turning the historical novel into a truly multimedia experience, Rupert Holmes includes with his period mystery novel, *Swing*, a CD of vintage music that contains clues to help solve the mystery.

Finally, in the truly odd category, Wesley Stace, better known as the singer John Wesley Harding, debuts with a transgendered Dickensian tale, *Misfortune*, set in Victorian England about a foundling boy raised as a girl. Who says the historical novel cannot find something new to say?

Recommended Titles

Here are my selections of the twenty-five most accomplished and interesting historical novels for the first half of 2005:

Boris Akunin, *The Turkish Gambit*

Tariq Ali, *A Sultan in Palermo*

Isabel Allende, *Zorro*

Rick Bass, *The Diezmo*

Geraldine Brooks, *March*

Caleb Carr, *The Italian Secretary*

Bernard Cornwell, *The Last Kingdom*

Mitch Cullin, *A Single Trick of the Mind*

Frank Delaney, *Ireland*

Clare Dudman, *98 Reasons for Being*

Thomas Dyja, *The Moon in Our Hands*

Christopher John Farley, *Kingston by Starlight*

Michael Curtis Ford, *The Sword of Attila*

Elizabeth Gaffney, *Metropolis*

Conn Iggulden, *Emperor: The Field of Swords*

Thomas Kelly, *Empire Rising*

Elmore Leonard, *The Hot Kid*

Andrei Makine, *The Earth and Sky of Jacques Dorme*

Albert Murray, *The Magic Keys*

Robert B. Parker, *Appaloosa*

Arturo Perez-Reverte, *Captain Alatriste*

David Poyer, *That Anvil of Our Souls*

Peter Quinn, *Hour of the Cat*

Rene Steinke, *Holy Skirts*

Gillen D'Arcy Wood, *Hosack's Folly*

For More Information about Historical Fiction

Printed Sources

Lynda G. Adamson, *American Historical Fiction: An Annotated Guide to Novels for Adults and Young Adults.* Phoenix: Oryx Press, 1999.

Lynda G. Adamson, *World Historical Fiction: An Annotated Guide to Novels for Adults and Young Adults.* Phoenix: Oryx Press, 1999.

Daniel S. Burt, *What Historical Fiction Do I Read Next?* Detroit: Gale, Vols. 1-3, 1997-2003.

Daniel S. Burt, *The Biography Book.* Westport: Oryx/Greenwood Press, 2001.

Donald K. Hartman, *Historical Figures in Fiction.* Phoenix: Oryx Press, 1994.

Electronic Sources

The Historical Novel Society (http//www.historicalnovel society.org). Includes articles, interviews, and reviews of historical novels.

Of Ages Past: The Online Magazine of Historical Fiction (http://www.angelfire.com/il/ofagespast/). Includes novel excerpts, short stories, articles, author profiles, and reviews.

Soon's Historical Fiction Site (http://uts.cc.utexas.edu/ ~soon/histfiction/). A rich source of information on the historical novel genre, including links to more specialized sites on particular authors and types of historical fiction. 8

Historical Titles

840

BORIS AKUNIN (Pseudonym of Grigory Chkhartishvili)

The Turkish Gambit
(New York: Random House, 2005)

Story type: Mystery; Historical/Victorian
Series: Erast Fandorin. Book 3
Subject(s): Mystery and Detective Stories; Espionage
Major character(s): Erast Fandorin, Diplomat, Detective—Police; Varvara Andreevna "Varya" Suvorova, Worker (telegraphist)
Time period(s): 1870s (1877)
Locale(s): Bulgaria

Summary: Set during the Russo-Turkish War, the third Erast Fandorin mystery has the diplomat and sleuth gathering intelligence for the Russian army on the Bulgarian front. He joins forces with a midwife-turned-telegraphist Varya Suvorova to help clear her fiance of an espionage charge. Fans of a complex puzzle with colorful period background will be entertained and impatient for the next book in the series.

Where it's reviewed:
Kirkus Reviews, January 1, 2005, page 83
Library Journal, March 1, 2005, page 74
Publishers Weekly, February 21, 2005, page 161

Other books by the same author:
Murder on the Leviathan, 2004
The Winter Queen, 2003

Other books you might like:
Robert Cormier, *The Rag and Bone Shop*, 2001
Helen Dunmore, *The Siege*, 2002
Andrew Miller, *Ingenious Pain*, 1997
Jody Shields, *The Fig Eater*, 2000
Daniel Silva, *The English Assassin*, 2002
Paullina Simons, *The Bronze Horseman*, 2000

841

SUSAN WITTIG ALBERT

The Tale of Holly How
(New York: Berkley Prime Crime, 2005)

Story type: Mystery; Historical/Edwardian
Series: Cottage Tales of Beatrix Potter. Book 2
Subject(s): Mystery and Detective Stories; Authors and Writers; Rural Life
Major character(s): Beatrix Potter, Historical Figure, Writer
Time period(s): 1900s
Locale(s): Sawry, England

Summary: In Albert's second Cottage Tales mystery featuring writer Beatrix Potter as sleuth, the death of a local shepherd who seems to be a favorite of everyone sparks Potter to investigate. The novel ingeniously connects details of Potter's life and work with a fully-realized rural English setting, and an entertaining mystery puzzle.

Where it's reviewed:
Kirkus Reviews, May 15, 2005, page 564

Other books by the same author:
A Dilly of a Death, 2004
The Tale of Hill Top Farm, 2004
Indigo Dying, 2003
Bloodroot, 2001
Mistletoe Man, 2000

Other books you might like:
Irene Allen, *The Elizabeth Elliot Series*, 1992-
Carola Dunn, *Rattle His Bones*, 2000
Roma Greth, *The Hana Shaner Series*, 1988-
Robin Paige, *Death at Gallows Green*, 1995
Deborah Woodworth, *A Deadly Shaker Spring*, 1998

842

BRUCE ALEXANDER (Pseudonym of Bruce Cook)

Rules of Engagement

(New York: Putnam, 2005)

Story type: Historical/Georgian; Mystery
Series: Sir John Fielding. Book 11
Subject(s): Mystery and Detective Stories; City and Town Life; Revolutionary War
Major character(s): Sir John Fielding, Historical Figure, Judge (magistrate); Jeremy Proctor, Assistant
Time period(s): 1770s
Locale(s): London, England

Summary: Alexander, who died in 2003, provides the final Sir John Fielding mystery, completed by Alexander's wife, Judith Aller and John Shannon. The blind magistrate and real-life founder of London's police force, investigates the death of a nobleman and anti-colonist politician on the eve of the American Revolution. Fielding's faithful companion, Jeremy Proctor, turns up evidence of murder. The novel features the series' characteristic colorful period details and engaging protagonists. Alexander, Fielding, and Proctor will be missed.

Where it's reviewed:
Kirkus Reviews, January 15, 2005, page 83
Library Journal, February 1, 2005, page 56
Publishers Weekly, January 10, 2005, page 41

Other books by the same author:
The Price of Murder, 2003
An Experiment in Treason, 2002
Smuggler's Moon, 2001
The Color of Death, 2000
Death of a Colonial, 1999

Other books you might like:
T.F. Banks, *The Thief-Taker*, 2001
Stephanie Barron, *The Jane Austen Series*, 1996-
Ross King, *Domino*, 2002
Deryn Lake, *Death at St. James's Palace*, 2002
Fidelis Morgan, *The Rival Queens*, 2002

843

TARIQ ALI

A Sultan in Palermo

(New York: Verso, 2005)

Story type: Historical/Medieval
Series: Islam Quintet. Book 4
Subject(s): Middle Ages; Muslims; Kings, Queens, Rulers, etc.
Major character(s): Muhammed al-Idrisi, Cartographer, Historical Figure; Rujari, Historical Figure, Ruler (sultan)
Time period(s): 12th century (1153)
Locale(s): Palermo, Italy (Sicily)

Summary: Book four of Ali's Islam Quintet is set in the medieval city of Palermo, Sicily, which in the 12th century was a Muslim city rivaling Baghdad and Cordoba as an Islamic center. The novel treats the court world of Sultan Rujari through the perspective of historical cartographer Muhammed al-Idrisi. As Muslim rule is contested by the Normans, Idrisi is divided between his enjoyment of the pleasures of the harem and his concern for the fate of the populace. This is an intriguing chronicle of an aspect of Islamic history that most readers will be introduced to for the first time.

Other books by the same author:
The Stone Woman, 2001
The Book of Saladin, 1999
Fear of Mirrors, 1998
Shadows of the Pomegranate Tree, 1992
Redemption, 1990

Other books you might like:
Maria Bordihn, *The Falcon of Palermo*, 2005
Colin Falconer, *The Sultan's Harem*, 2004
Cecelia Holland, *Great Maria*, 1974
Amin Maalouf, *Balthasar's Odyssey*, 2002
Cesar J. Rotondi, *The Garden of Persephone*, 1982

844

JANE ALISON

Natives and Exotics

(Orlando, Florida: Harcourt, 2005)

Story type: Family Saga
Subject(s): Family Relations; Pioneers; Nature
Major character(s): Alice Forder, Young Woman; Violet Clarence, Settler; George Clarence, Settler
Time period(s): 19th century; 20th century (1820s-1970s)
Locale(s): Ecuador; Australia

Summary: Alison weaves together multiple stories ranging over two centuries in a family's history. Beginning with the experiences of young Alice Forder in Ecuador in the 1970s, the story shifts back to Alice's grandmother, Violet Clarence, in 1929, in the Australian bush, and Violet's great-great-grandfather George Clarence, one of Australia's first settlers. Linking the stories is a common fascination with the magic of nature and the universals of human nature.

Where it's reviewed:
New York Times Book Review, May 15, 2005, page 27
Publishers Weekly, April 4, 2005, page 44

Other books by the same author:
The Marriage of the Sea, 2003
The Love-Artist, 2001

Other books you might like:
Rick Bass, *The Sky, the Stars, the Wilderness*, 1997
Timothy Findley, *Pilgrim*, 1999
Mardi McConnochie, *Coldwater*, 2001
Colleen McCullough, *Morgan's Run*, 2000
Jody Shields, *The Fig Eater*, 2000

845

CONRAD ALLEN (Pseudonym of Keith Miles)

Murder on the Salsette

(New York: St. Martin's Minotaur, 2005)

Story type: Historical/Edwardian; Mystery
Series: George Porter Dillman/Genevieve Masefield. Book 6
Subject(s): Mystery and Detective Stories; Crime and Criminals; Cruise Ships
Major character(s): George Porter Dillman, Detective—Private; Genevieve Masefield, Gentlewoman, Detective—Private
Time period(s): 1900s (1909)
Locale(s): *Salsette*, At Sea

Summary: Married, sea-going sleuths George Dillman and Genevieve Masefield work undercover to foil a jewel thief aboard the *Salsette* on a four-day passage from Bombay to Aden. A shipboard murder escalates the challenges for the sleuths and reveals no end of potential suspects in this atmospheric period mystery set on one of history's great ocean liners.

Where it's reviewed:
Booklist, January 1, 2005, page 824

Other books by the same author:
Murder on the Marmora, 2004
Murder on the Caronia, 2003
Murder on the Minnesota, 2002
Murder on the Mauretania, 2000
Murder on the Lusitania, 1999

Other books you might like:
Cynthia Bass, *Maiden Voyage*, 1993
Lawrence Block, *Death Cruise*, 1999
Carolyn Hart, *Murder Walks the Plank*, 2004
Michael Kilian, *Dance on a Sinking Ship*, 1988
Susan Sussman, *Cruising for Murder*, 2000

846

ISABEL ALLENDE

Zorro

(New York: HarperCollins, 2005)

Story type: Historical/American West Coast; Historical/Napoleonic Wars
Subject(s): Adventure and Adventurers; Legends
Major character(s): Diego de la Vega, Hero; Manuel Escalante, Gentleman; Bernardo, Servant, Companion (of Zorro)
Time period(s): 1790s
Locale(s): California; Barcelona, Spain

Summary: Allende offers a realistic take on the legend of Zorro, the famous Robin Hood of 18th-century colonial California. The novel treats Diego de la Vega's upbringing in California and his relationship with his wet nurse's son, Bernardo. Diego is sent to Barcelona for his education, and his swordsmanship brings him to the attention of Manuel Escalante, the head of a secret society committed to fighting all forms of oppression. As a member of the society, Diego, as

Zorro, returns to California to reclaim his family's estate. The swashbuckling here is solidly anchored by authentic customs and period details.

Where it's reviewed:
Booklist, February 15, 2005, page 1035
Kirkus Reviews, February 15, 2005, page 187
Library Journal, March 1, 2005, page 74
Publishers Weekly, February 28, 2005, page 39

Other books by the same author:
Portrait in Sepia, 2001
Daughter of Fortune, 1999
Paula, 1995
The Infinite Plan, 1993
The House of the Spirits, 1985

Other books you might like:
Michael Dibdin, *The Dying of the Light*, 1993
Cecelia Holland, *The Bear Flag*, 1990
Johnston McCulley, *The Mark of Zorro*, 1924
Arturo Perez-Reverte, *The Fencing Master*, 1999
Isabelle Gibson Ziegler, *Nine Days of Father Serra*, 1951

847

NICK ARVIN

Articles of War

(New York: Doubleday, 2005)

Story type: Historical/World War II
Subject(s): World War II; War
Major character(s): George "Heck" Tilson, Military Personnel
Time period(s): 1940s (1944)
Locale(s): France

Summary: Arvin's first novel looks at combat in World War II from the perspective of boots on the ground, more specifically, from the perspective of a common GI, Iowa farm boy George "Heck" Tilson. Tilson lands in Normandy, loses his virginity to a French girl, and then must contend with his fears as he experiences combat for the first time. Confronting his cowardice, Tilson struggles to live up to the ideal of the American soldier as best as he can. What is so refreshing here is that Arvin does not sugarcoat either the reality of combat or the hard truth about the combatants.

Where it's reviewed:
Booklist, November 15, 2004, page 551
Kirkus Reviews, December 1, 2004, page 1099
Library Journal, January 2005, page 93
Publishers Weekly, November 1, 2004, page 40

Other books by the same author:
In the Electric Eden, 2003

Other books you might like:
Dennis Bock, *The Ash Garden*, 2001
Sebastian Faulks, *Charlotte Gray*, 1998
Robert Irwin, *Exquisite Corpse*, 1997
James McBride, *Miracle at St. Anna*, 2002
David L. Robbins, *Liberation Road*, 2005

Historical

848

ELIZABETH ASTON

The Exploits and Adventures of Miss Alethea Darcy

(New York: Simon & Schuster, 2005)

Story type: Historical/Regency
Subject(s): Family Relations; Romance
Major character(s): Alethea Darcy, Gentlewoman; Titus Manningtree, Gentleman
Time period(s): 1820s
Locale(s): England; Europe

Summary: This is Aston's second attempt to fill in the subsequent family history of the Darcys, based on Jane Austen's *Pride and Prejudice*. The focus here is on the youngest daughter of Elizabeth Bennett and Fitzwilliam Darcy, who escapes her abusive husband by disguising herself as a man on a journey to Venice. On the way she encounters Titus Manningtree, who is trying to recover a valuable painting that has gone missing. Several plot twists both block and facilitate the inevitable romance.

Where it's reviewed:
Library Journal, February 15, 2005, page 113

Other books by the same author:
Mr. Darcy's Daughters, 2003

Other books you might like:
Joan Aiken, *Eliza's Daughter*, 1994
Joan Aiken, *Jane Fairfax*, 1990
Ted Bader, *Desire and Duty*, 1997
    Marilyn Bader, co-author
Julia Barrett, *Presumption*, 1995
Emma Tennant, *Pemberley*, 1995

849

TASH AW

The Harmony Silk Factory

(New York: Riverhead, 2005)

Story type: Historical/Exotic; Historical/World War II
Subject(s): Business Enterprises
Major character(s): Johnny Lim, Businessman; Jasper Lim, Relative (son of Johnny); Snow Lim, Spouse (of Jasper)
Time period(s): 1930s; 1940s
Locale(s): Malaysia

Summary: This first novel looks at the life of Johnny Lim, the controversial owner of the Harmony Silk Factory. A Communist leader, an informer for the Japanese during the war, a black-market trader, the contradictory Johnny is viewed from the perspectives of his son, Jasper; Jasper's wife, Snow; and Jasper's best friend, Englishman Peter Wormwood. Malaysia's colorful history and rich culture are glimpsed in this novel about a protagonist who embodies the country's contradictions.

Where it's reviewed:
Kirkus Reviews, January 1, 2005, page 3
Library Journal, February 15, 2005, page 113

Publishers Weekly, February 14, 2005, page 52

Other books you might like:
Anthony Burgess, *The Long Day Wanes*, 1964
Peter Carey, *My Life as a Fake*, 2003
C.S. Godshalk, *Kalimantaan*, 1998
Rani Monika, *The Rice Mother*, 2002
Paul Theroux, *The Consul's File*, 1977

850

JANE BAILEY

Tommy Glover's Sketch of Heaven

(New York: Carroll & Graf, 2005)

Story type: Historical/World War II
Subject(s): World War II; Small Town Life; Evacuees
Major character(s): Kitty Green, Young Woman; Tommy Glover, Young Man
Time period(s): 1940s (1944)
Locale(s): Gloucestershire, England

Summary: This novel looks at the impact of World War II on two young evacuees from London, Kitty Green and her best friend Tommy Glover. Both must adjust to life in a rural village in Gloucestershire, while the villagers must adjust to them as well. Kitty interacts with American airmen, gypsies, and German POWs. This is a sweet depiction of wartime life and the disruptions it caused.

Other books by the same author:
Alyssa, 1982
A Portrait of Louise, 1980

Other books you might like:
Sheila Garrique, *All the Children Were Sent Away*, 1979
Andrew Greig, *The Clouds Above*, 2000
Mick Jackson, *Five Boys*, 2002
Penelope Lively, *Going Back*, 1975
Jill Paton Walsh, *Fireweed*, 1972

851

ZSUZSA BANK

The Swimmer

(Orlando, Florida: Harcourt, 2005)

Story type: Coming-of-Age
Subject(s): Brothers and Sisters; Family Life; Childhood
Major character(s): Kata Valencei, Young Woman; Isti Valencei, Young Man; Kalman Valencei, Parent
Time period(s): 1950s
Locale(s): Hungary

Summary: First-time novelist Bank supplies a poignant portrait of family life in Hungary during the 1950s. The novel explores the impact on Kata and Isti Valencei of the abrupt departure of their mother to the West. The act unhinges their father who becomes a vagabond, dragging his children from place to place. As the children attempt to understand their mother's decision to abandon them, their loss is registered in various emotional and physical ways. Only when their father takes his children swimming does a semblance of the former united family reemerge.

Where it's reviewed:

Booklist, December 1, 2004, page 634
Library Journal, October 15, 2004, page 52
New York Times Book Review, March 27, 2005, page 23
Publishers Weekly, October 15, 2004, page 45

Other books you might like:

Ursula Hegi, *The Vision of Emma Blau*, 2000
Andrei Makine, *Dreams of My Russian Summers*, 1997
John Reed, *A Still Small Voice*, 2000
Adam Thorpe, *Pieces of Light*, 2000
Marita Van der Vyver, *Childish Things*, 1996

852

STEPHANIE BARRON (Pseudonym of Francine Mathews)

Jane and His Lordship's Legacy

(New York: Bantam, 2005)

Story type: Historical/Regency; Mystery
Series: Jane Austen. Book 8
Subject(s): Mystery and Detective Stories
Major character(s): Jane Austen, Historical Figure, Writer
Time period(s): 1800s (1809)
Locale(s): Hampshire, England

Summary: Jane receives a bequest from the late Lord Harold Trowbridge, murdered at the end of *Jane and the Ghosts of Netley*: a chest containing his personal papers. When a laborer is found murdered, Jane takes up the investigation and seeks a connection between the secrets contained in the lord's bequest and the murder. The novel features Barron's characteristic adept impersonation of Austen's voice, period details, and biographical elements drawn from Austen's life.

Where it's reviewed:

Kirkus Reviews, January 15, 2005, page 83
Library Journal, February 1, 2005, page 57
Publishers Weekly, February 14, 2005, page 57

Other books by the same author:

Jane and the Ghosts of Netley, 2003
Jane and the Prisoner of Wool House, 2001
Jane and the Stillroom Maid, 2000
Jane and the Genius of the Place, 1999
Jane and the Wandering Eye, 1998

Other books you might like:

Bruce Alexander, *The Sir John Fielding Series*, 1994-2005
T.F. Banks, *The Thief-Taker*, 2001
Wilder Perkins, *Hoare and the Matter of Treason*, 2001
S.K. Rizzolo, *Blood for Blood*, 2003
Rosemary Stevens, *The Beau Brummell Series*, 2000-

853

SEBASTIAN BARRY

A Long Long Way

(New York: Viking, 2005)

Story type: Historical/World War I
Subject(s): World War I; War
Major character(s): Willie Dunne, Military Personnel (Irish soldier)

Time period(s): 1910s
Locale(s): Ireland; France

Summary: The novel takes up the story of the brother of the title character in Barry's earlier *Annie Dunne* in this World War I-era tale. Willie Dunne goes to fight in the trenches of France as a member of the Royal Dublin Fusiliers. On leave, he is pressed into service quelling the Easter 1916 Rising, and returns home at the war's end to find a transformed Ireland. Graphic scenes of trench warfare alternate with a knowing documentation of British-Irish history from a human vantage point.

Where it's reviewed:

Kirkus Reviews, December 15, 2004, page 1152
Publishers Weekly, January 31, 2005, page 811

Other books by the same author:

Annie Dunne, 2002
The Whereabouts of Eneas McNulty, 1998

Other books you might like:

James Carroll, *Supply of Heroes*, 1986
J.G. Farrell, *The Troubles*, 1970
Thomas Flanagan, *The End of the Hunt*, 1994
Morgan Llywelyn, *1921*, 2001
Jessica Stirling, *Shamrock Green*, 2002

854

RICK BASS

The Diezmo

(Boston: Houghton Mifflin, 2005)

Story type: Historical/American West
Subject(s): Prisoners and Prisons; War; Mexicans
Major character(s): James Alexander, Military Personnel, Teenager
Time period(s): 1840s (1842)
Locale(s): Texas; Mexico

Summary: Loosely based on the Mier Expedition, an event in the history of the Republic of Texas, this often-harrowing story chronicles the experiences of teenager James Alexander who joins a militia ordered by Sam Houston to patrol the border with Mexico in 1842. He, along with many of his comrades, is captured and imprisoned in a isolated mountain fortress whose Mexican commander enforces the *diezmo*, or arbitrary execution of one prisoner in ten. Brutally realistic, this narrative of endurance and degradation celebrates both the evil to which humans can resort and the bravery of resistance.

Where it's reviewed:

Booklist, March 1, 2005, page 1101
Kirkus Reviews, March 1, 2005, page 242
Library Journal, April 15, 2005, page 71
New York Times Book Review, May 8, 2005, page 15
Publishers Weekly, March 21, 2005, page 35

Other books by the same author:

The Hermit's Story, 2002
Where the Sea Used to Be, 1998
The Sky, the Stars, the Wilderness, 1997
Platte River, 1994

The Watch, 1989

Other books you might like:
Jim Fergus, *Wild Girl*, 2005
Stephen Harrigan, *The Gates of the Alamo*, 2000
William W. Johnstone, *Eyes of Eagles*, 1993
Jeff Long, *Empire of Bones*, 1993
Cormac McCarthy, *All the Pretty Horses*, 1992

855

HOLLY BAXTER

Tears of the Dragon

(Scottsdale, Arizona: Poisoned Pen Press, 2005)

Story type: Mystery; Historical/Depression Era
Subject(s): Mystery and Detective Stories; Crime and Criminals; Chinese Americans
Major character(s): Elodie Browne, Writer, Detective—Amateur
Time period(s): 1930s
Locale(s): Chicago, Illinois

Summary: This new historical mystery series set in Depression-era Chicago features young writer Elodie Browne who gets involved in a complex intrigue that takes her into the heart of mob-ruled Chicago and Chinese politics. This is a promising debut featuring believable dialogue, realistic characters, and authentic period details.

Where it's reviewed:
Kirkus Reviews, April 15, 2005, page 452
Library Journal, May 1, 2005, page 65
Publishers Weekly, April 4, 2005, page 46

Other books you might like:
Craig Holden, *The Jazz Bird*, 2001
Lise McClendon, *One O'Clock Jump*, 2001
Terry McMillan, *A Day Late and a Dollar Short*, 2001
Jacquelyn Mitchard, *The Deep End of the Ocean*, 1996
Scott Turow, *Pleading Guilty*, 1993

856

MARIA BORDIHN

The Falcon of Palermo

(New York: Atlantic Monthly, 2005)

Story type: Historical/Medieval
Subject(s): Middle Ages; Kings, Queens, Rulers, etc.; Biography
Major character(s): Frederick II, Historical Figure, Ruler (Holy Roman Emperor); Berard, Historical Figure, Religious (archbishop); Innocent III, Historical Figure, Religious (pope)
Time period(s): 13th century
Locale(s): Sicily, Italy

Summary: This first novel provides a fictional biography of Holy Roman Emperor Frederick II. Left after the untimely death of his parents to mingle with street urchins in 13th-century Sicily's Muslim quarter, Frederick is befriended by Pope Innocent's emissary, Archbishop Berard, and is later chosen by the pope and German princes as Holy Roman Emperor. The novel shows Frederick's rise to power, his development, and struggle to maintain control over a contentious empire. The novel is meticulously researched and historically accurate, shedding light on an important medieval figure and his era.

Where it's reviewed:
Booklist, January 1, 2005, page 811
Kirkus Reviews, December 1, 2004, page 1100
Library Journal, February 1, 2005, page 66
Publishers Weekly, January 3, 2005, page 34

Other books you might like:
Joseph Jay Deiss, *The Great Infidel*, 1963
Umberto Eco, *Baudolino*, 2002
Lisa Goldstein, *The Alchemist's Door*, 2002
Cecelia Holland, *The Antichrist*, 1970
Amin Maalouf, *Balthasar's Odyssey*, 2002

857

RHYS BOWEN (Pseudonym of Janet Quin-Harkin)

In Like Flynn

(New York: St. Martin's Minotaur, 2005)

Story type: Historical/Victorian America; Mystery
Series: Molly Murphy. Book 4
Subject(s): Mystery and Detective Stories; Irish Americans; Spiritualism
Major character(s): Molly Murphy, Immigrant (Irish), Detective—Private; Daniel Sullivan, Police Officer
Time period(s): 1900s (1902)
Locale(s): New York, New York; Peekskill, New York

Summary: Molly Murphy goes undercover at the suggestion of her erstwhile boyfriend, New York police officer Daniel Sullivan, in the home of a prominent senator whose wife is mourning the death of their kidnapped son and turning to spiritualists for solace. Molly tries to expose the spiritualists as frauds, while solving the kidnapping case. Set in the world of Ragtime, the series develops a plausible and intriguing sense of the place and the era.

Where it's reviewed:
Kirkus Reviews, February 1, 2005, page 149
Library Journal, February 1, 2005, page 57
Publishers Weekly, February 28, 2005, page 45

Other books by the same author:
Evan's Gate, 2004
Evan Only Knows, 2003
For the Love of Mike, 2003
Death of Riley, 2002
Evans to Betsy, 2002

Other books you might like:
Richard E. Crabbe, *The Empire of Shadows*, 2003
Carole Nelson Douglas, *Femme Fatale*, 2003
Thomas Fleming, *A Passionate Girl*, 2004
Christine Shea, *Moira's Crossing*, 2000
Troy Soos, *Island of Tears*, 2001

858

JOSEPH BOYDEN

Three-Day Road

(New York: Viking, 2005)

Story type: Historical/World War I
Subject(s): World War I; Indians of North America; War
Major character(s): Xavier Bird, Indian (Cree), Military Personnel; Elijah Whiskeyjack, Indian (Cree), Military Personnel
Time period(s): 1910s
Locale(s): Canada; France; Belgium

Summary: This fascinating first novel looks at the impact of World War I from the perspective of two Cree Indian friends—Xavier Bird and Elijah Whiskeyjack—who join the Canadian Army in 1915 and experience the horror and brutality of trench warfare in France and Belgium. Expert sharpshooters, the friends become snipers, and the story traces the consequences of warfare on the two men and on Cree culture at home. The novel is in part inspired by the story of Francis Pegahmagabow, the great Indian sniper of World War I.

Where it's reviewed:
Booklist, March 15, 2005, page 1763
Kirkus Reviews, February 15, 2005, page 189
Publishers Weekly, March 21, 2005, page 35

Other books by the same author:
Born with a Tooth, 2001

Other books you might like:
Pat Barker, *Regeneration*, 1991
Sebastian Faulks, *Birdsong*, 1996
Ian McEwan, *Atonement*, 2001
Jane Urquhart, *The Stone Carvers*, 2002
James Welch, *The Heartsong of Charging Elk*, 2000

859

JULIAN BRANSTON

Tilting at Windmills

(New York: Shaye Areheart, 2005)

Story type: Historical/Seventeenth Century
Subject(s): Authors and Writers; Knights and Knighthood
Major character(s): Miguel de Cervantes, Historical Figure, Writer; Old Knight, Knight
Time period(s): 17th century
Locale(s): Spain

Summary: The premise of this entertaining novel is that Miguel de Cervantes' greatest creation, the foolish, noble questing knight Don Quixote, had a true-life counterpart that the author meets and who comes to Cervantes' aid against a scheming poet. Introduced to a man known only as the Old Knight, Cervantes has the opportunity to get to know a Don Quixote in fact. The adventures that ensue provide a guided tour of life in 17th-century Spain, while paying tribute to one of the greatest novels of all time.

Where it's reviewed:
Booklist, January 1, 2005, page 811

Kirkus Reviews, December 1, 2004, page 1101
Library Journal, January 2005, page 94
Publishers Weekly, January 31, 2005, page 50

Other books by the same author:
The Eternal Quest, 2003

Other books you might like:
Frank Bruno, *A Man Called Cervantes*, 1935
Robin Chapman, *The Duchess's Diary*, 1985
John Spencer Hill, *Ghirlandaio's Daughter*, 1997
Stephen Marlowe, *The Death and Life of Miguel de Cervantes*, 1996
Arturo Perez-Reverte, *The Fencing Master*, 1999

860

GERALDINE BROOKS

March

(New York: Viking, 2004)

Story type: Historical/American Civil War
Subject(s): Civil War; Slavery; Family Life
Major character(s): John March, Religious, Military Personnel (chaplain); Marmee March, Spouse; Ralph Waldo Emerson, Historical Figure, Writer
Time period(s): 1850s; 1860s
Locale(s): Concord, Massachusetts; Washington, District of Columbia; Mississippi

Summary: Brooks' intriguing novel looks at the American Civil War from the perspective of the absent father in Louisa May Alcott's *Little Women*. Mr. March becomes a Union chaplain and is assigned as a teacher of freed slaves on a cotton plantation. The story reveals March's early life and relationship with such literary luminaries as Ralph Waldo Emerson and Henry David Thoreau and his courtship and married life with the quick-tempered Marmee. The novel alternates between the war zone and the imaginary world of *Little Women* in a productive expansion of both.

Where it's reviewed:
Kirkus Reviews, January 1, 2005, page 5
New York Times Book Review, March 27, 2005, page 11
Publishers Weekly, December 20, 2004, page 34

Other books by the same author:
Year of Wonders, 2001

Other books you might like:
Louisa May Alcott, *Little Women*, 1869
Bruce Olds, *Raising Holy Hell*, 1995
Alice Randall, *The Wind Done Gone*, 2001
Jewell Parker Rhodes, *Douglass' Women*, 2002
Margaret Walker, *Jubilee*, 1966

861

AMY BELDING BROWN

Mr. Emerson's Wife

(New York: St. Martin's Press, 2005)

Story type: Historical/Victorian America; Historical/Americana

Subject(s): Biography; Marriage; Authors and Writers
Major character(s): Lidian Jackson Emerson, Historical Figure, Spouse (of Ralph Waldo Emerson); Ralph Waldo Emerson, Historical Figure, Writer; Henry David Thoreau, Historical Figure, Writer
Time period(s): 19th century
Locale(s): Concord, Massachusetts

Summary: Brown's novel explores the married life of writer Ralph Waldo Emerson. Overshadowed by Emerson's genius and celebrity, Lidian Jackson Emerson becomes deeply disappointed by her marriage, while growing increasingly attracted to the energy and passion of Emerson's friend, Henry David Thoreau. This is an intriguing look at Emerson and his circle with factual, historical details mixing with fictional speculation.

Where it's reviewed:
Booklist, May 15, 2005, page 1646

Other books by the same author:
Strawberry Lace, 1994
Island Summer Love, 1992

Other books you might like:
Robert J. Begiebing, *The Adventures of Allegra Fullerton*, 1999
Christopher Bigsby, *Hester*, 1994
Sena Jeter Naslund, *Ahab's Wife*, 1999
Matthew Pearl, *The Dante Club*, 2003
Elizabeth Savage, *Willowwood*, 1978

862

CALEB CARR

The Italian Secretary
(New York: Carroll & Graf, 2005)

Story type: Historical/Victorian; Mystery
Subject(s): Mystery and Detective Stories; Paranormal
Major character(s): Sherlock Holmes, Detective—Private; John Watson, Doctor, Sidekick
Time period(s): 19th century
Locale(s): London, England; Edinburgh, Scotland

Summary: Carr designs an intriguing case for Sherlock Holmes that draws on the historical murder of David Rizzio, music teacher and confidant to Mary, Queen of Scots. Holmes and Watson are summoned to Edinburgh to investigate strange doings at Holyrood House, Queen Victoria's royal palace. When an architect and his foreman are killed in a manner that recalls Rizzio's death, Holmes begins to suspect that Rizzio himself may be responsible. This is a clever and atmospheric Holmes pastiche.

Where it's reviewed:
Kirkus Reviews, March 15, 2005, page 302
Library Journal, April 15, 2005, page 74
New York Times Book Review, May 22, 2005, page 15
Publishers Weekly, April 4, 2005, page 44

Other books by the same author:
Killing Time, 2000
The Angel of Darkness, 1997
The Alienist, 1994

Casing the Promised Land, 1980

Other books you might like:
Michael Chabon, *The Final Solution*, 2004
Mitch Cullin, *A Slight Trick of the Mind*, 2005
Martin Davies, *Mrs. Hudson and the Spirits' Curse*, 2005
Quinn Fawcett, *The Mycroft Holmes Series*, 1997-
Laurie R. King, *The Mary Russell/Sherlock Holmes Series*, 1994-

863

SUSAN CARROLL

The Dark Queen
(New York: Ballantine, 2005)

Story type: Historical/Fantasy; Historical/Renaissance
Subject(s): Kings, Queens, Rulers, etc.; Witches and Witchcraft
Major character(s): Ariane, Psychic; Renard, Nobleman; Catherine de Medici, Historical Figure, Royalty
Time period(s): 16th century
Locale(s): Brittany, France; Paris, France

Summary: Carroll's fantasy, set in Renaissance France during the time of Catherine de Medici, involves Ariane, the Lady of Faire Isle in Brittany, who possesses mystical power that brands her a sorceress. She comes into possession of a secret that Catherine will do everything in her power to possess, and Ariane turns to a nobleman, the Comte de Renard, to assist her in keeping it safe.

Where it's reviewed:
Kirkus Reviews, February 1, 2005, page 133

Other books by the same author:
Midnight Bride, 2001
The Night Drifter, 1999
The Bride Finder, 1998
The Painted Veil, 1995
Winterbourne, 1987

Other books you might like:
Dorothy Dunnett, *Queens' Play*, 1973
Jean Plaidy, *Madame Serpent*, 1975
Judith Merkle Riley, *The Master of All Desires*, 1999
Michaela Roessner, *The Stars Dispose*, 1997
Hugh Ross Williamson, *Paris Is Worth a Mass*, 1973

864

DONIS CASEY

The Old Buzzard Had It Coming
(Scottsdale, Arizona: Poisoned Pen Press, 2005)

Story type: Mystery; Historical/Americana
Series: Alafair Tucker. Book 1
Subject(s): Mystery and Detective Stories; Farm Life; Rural Life
Major character(s): Alafair Tucker, Detective—Amateur
Time period(s): 1910s (1912)
Locale(s): Oklahoma

Summary: This first novel, voted the best unpublished mystery in 2004 by the Oklahoma Writers' Federation, and the initial installment in a projected series, is set in Oklahoma farm country in 1912. Alafair Tucker investigates the death of the unloved Harley Day, when suspicion falls on his son who is romantically involved with Alafair's daughter. The author knows her region and successfully transports readers to the period.

Other books you might like:
Clancy Carlile, *Children of the Dust*, 1995
Robert J. Conley, *Go-Ahead Rider*, 1990
Tracy Daugherty, *The Boy Orator*, 1999
Fred Harris, *Coyote Revenge*, 2000
Elmore Leonard, *The Hot Kid*, 2005

865

MARION CHESNEY

Sick of Shadows

(New York: St. Martin's Minotaur, 2005)

Story type: Historical/Edwardian; Mystery
Series: Edwardian Murder Mystery. Book 3
Subject(s): Mystery and Detective Stories; Crime and Criminals
Major character(s): Captain Harry Cathcart, Detective—Private; Lady Rose Summer, Noblewoman, Detective—Amateur
Time period(s): 1900s
Locale(s): London, England

Summary: In the midst of the London social season, Captain Harry Cathcart and Lady Rose Summer investigate the death of a young debutante found floating in the river. Chesney, the author of both Regency romances and the Agatha Raisin and Hamish Macbeth mysteries, brings both of her interests and expertise to bear in this engaging series.

Other books by the same author:
Hasty Death, 2004
Snobbery with Violence, 2003
Milady in Love, 2002
The Duke's Diamond, 2002
My Dear Duchess, 2001

Other books you might like:
Tracy Chevalier, *Falling Angels*, 2001
David Holland, *The Devil in Bellminster*, 2002
J.P. Morrissey, *A Weekend at Blenheim*, 2002
Robin Paige, *Death in Hyde Park*, 2004
David Roberts, *Sweet Poison*, 2001

866

JENNIFER CHIAVERINI

The Sugar Camp Quilt

(New York: Simon & Schuster, 2005)

Story type: Historical/Americana
Series: Elm Creek Quilts. Book 7
Subject(s): Slavery; Quilts; Small Town Life

Major character(s): Dorothea Granger, Teacher; Jacob Granger, Farmer
Time period(s): 1840s (1849)
Locale(s): Creek's Crossing, Pennsylvania

Summary: When the Granger family loses its farm in a flood, they come to live with their harsh Uncle Jacob who asks his niece Dorothea to make him a quilt with a very specific design. When he is found dead, the family learns that Jacob's Sugar Camp is a station on the Underground Railroad, and the quilt is intended as a map to the next station. Despite the danger, the family decides to continue Jacob's work in helping escaped slaves.

Where it's reviewed:
Booklist, March 15, 2005, page 1263
Library Journal, March 1, 2005, page 76

Other books by the same author:
The Master Quilt, 2004
The Quilter's Legacy, 2003
The Cross-Country Quilt, 2002
The Runaway Quilt, 2002
Round Robin, 2000

Other books you might like:
Earlene Fowler, *Arkansas Traveler*, 2001
Jane Smiley, *The All-True Travels and Adventures of Lidie Newton*, 1998
Nancy E. Turner, *Sarah's Quilt*, 2005
Otto Whitney, *How to Make an American Quilt*, 1991
Penelope Williamson, *The Outsider*, 1996

867

CATHERINE CHIDGEY

The Transformation

(New York: Henry Holt, 2005)

Story type: Historical/Americana
Subject(s): Spanish-American War; Beauty; City and Town Life
Major character(s): Lucien Goulet, Businessman (wig maker); Marion Unger, Widow(er); Rafael Mendez, Businessman (cigar maker)
Time period(s): 1890s (1898)
Locale(s): Tampa, Florida

Summary: Chidgey's imaginative novel concerns the relationship among three characters: Lucien Goulet, a wig maker famed for his hairpiece constructions known as "transformations;" Rafael Mendez, a cigar maker, whom Goulet hires to scavenge hair for his wigs; and Detroit widow Marion Unger, whose white-blond hair becomes Goulet's obsession. The stories of these characters are related to the history of Florida and Tampa during the Spanish-American War.

Where it's reviewed:
Booklist, March 15, 2005, page 1263
Library Journal, February 1, 2005, page 66
Publishers Weekly, March 14, 2005, page 45

Other books by the same author:
The Strength of the Sun, 2002
Golden Deeds, 2001

Other books you might like:
James Carlos Blake, *Red Grass River*, 1998
Amy Ephron, *White Rose*, 1999
Elmore Leonard, *Cuba Libre*, 1998
Daniel Lynch, *Yellow*, 1992
Robert Newton Peck, *Hallapoosa*, 1998

868

BARBARA CLEVERLY

The Palace Tiger

(New York: Carroll & Graf, 2005)

Story type: Mystery; Historical/Roaring Twenties
Series: Joe Sandilands. Book 4
Subject(s): Mystery and Detective Stories
Major character(s): Joe Sandilands, Detective—Police
Time period(s): 1920s (1922)
Locale(s): Simla, India; Ranipur, India

Summary: Joe Sandilands, Scotland Yard detective, is dispatched to the Princely State of Ranipur, where a man-eating tiger is terrorizing the populace. The maharajah is dying, and the line of succession has been broken after his first son is killed in a panther-related incident and a second son dies before Joe's eyes. Who is responsible and what lies in store for Sandilands while hunting tiger?

Other books by the same author:
The Damascened Blade, 2004
Ragtime in Simla, 2003
The Last Kashmiri Rose, 2001

Other books you might like:
David Davidar, *The House of Blue Mangoes*, 2002
Timeri Murani, *The Imperial Agent*, 1989
Rebecca Ryman, *Shalimar*, 1999
Carolyn Slaughter, *A Black Englishman*, 2004
Andrew Ward, *The Blood Seed*, 1985

869

SUSANN COKAL

Breath and Bones

(Denver: Unbridled, 2005)

Story type: Historical/American West; Adventure
Subject(s): American West; Artists and Art
Major character(s): Famke Summerfugl, Orphan; Albert Castle, Artist
Time period(s): 19th century
Locale(s): Copenhagen, Denmark; Colorado; California

Summary: Cokal's second novel follows the adventures of Danish beauty Famke Summerfugl from a Copenhagen orphanage on the trail of a young painter, Albert Castle, whom she loves. She winds up marrying a polygamous Mormon and is taken in by an eccentric California inventor before a series of coincidences finally leads to her explosive reunion with Albert. It's all a bit over the top with an emphasis on the seamy and steamy side of the American West.

Where it's reviewed:
Library Journal, March 1, 2005, page 76

Publishers Weekly, March 7, 2005, page 49

Other books by the same author:
Mirabilis, 2001

Other books you might like:
Christine Balint, *Ophelia's Fan*, 2004
Adam Braver, *Divine Sarah*, 2004
E.L. Doctorow, *Ragtime*, 1975
Larry McMurtry, *Sin Killer*, 2002
Susan Sontag, *In America*, 2000

870

BERNARD CORNWELL

The Last Kingdom

(New York: HarperCollins, 2005)

Story type: Historical/Medieval
Series: Alfred the Great. Book 1
Subject(s): Kings, Queens, Rulers, etc.; Vikings
Major character(s): Alfred the Great, Historical Figure, Ruler (King of Wessex); Uhtred, Heir, Nobleman; Ragnar, Warrior (Viking)
Time period(s): 9th century
Locale(s): England

Summary: Historical adventure master Cornwell launches a new series set in Britain during the 9th century when the four Anglo-Saxon kingdoms of Northumbria, East Anglia, Mercia, and Wessex are under attack by the invading Vikings. Out of this conflict emerges one of England's greatest leaders, King Alfred the Great. Perspective on Alfred and his time comes from Uhtred, heir to an earldom, who is captured and raised as a Viking by Ragnar. Returning to Britain, Uhtred serves Alfred while plotting vengeance on the murderer of Ragnar. This is a bracing adventure narrative, solidly anchored by evident knowledge of the period, its major figures, and customs.

Where it's reviewed:
Booklist, November 15, 2004, page 531
Library Journal, December 2004, page 98
Publishers Weekly, December 6, 2004, page 41

Other books by the same author:
Sharpe's Escape, 2004
Heretic, 2003

Other books you might like:
Alfred Duggan, *The Right Line of Cedric*, 1961
Haley Elizabeth Garwood, *Swords Across the Thames*, 1999
Cecelia Holland, *The Soul Thief*, 2002
Juliet Marillier, *Foxmask*, 2004
Rebecca Tingle, *The Edge of the Sword*, 2001

871

JOHN CROWLEY

Lord Byron's Novel

(New York: William Morrow, 2005)

Story type: Historical/Regency
Subject(s): Authors and Writers

Major character(s): George Gordon Byron, Historical Figure, Writer; Alexandra Novak, Writer
Time period(s): 1810s; 21st century
Locale(s): England

Summary: Crowley imagines the survival of the ghost story Byron wrote as part of the activities for a rainy evening when Mary Shelley came up with *Frankenstein*. Byron's Gothic tale is interwoven with the efforts of Byron's daughter, Ada, to save it by translating it into a secret code, and researcher Alexandra Novak, in the present, who discovers the long-lost manuscript and tries to make sense of it.

Where it's reviewed:
Publishers Weekly, April 18, 2005, page 40

Other books by the same author:
The Translator, 2002
Daemonomania, 2000
Aegypt, 1987
Engine Summer, 1979
Beasts, 1976

Other books you might like:
Frederico Andahazi, *The Merciful Women*, 2000
Anne Edwards, *Haunted Summer*, 1972
Derek Marlowe, *A Single Summer with Lord Byron*, 1970
Frederic Prokosch, *The Missolonghi Manuscript*, 1968
Paul West, *Lord Byron's Manuscript*, 1968

872

MITCH CULLIN

A Single Trick of the Mind

(New York: Doubleday, 2005)

Story type: Mystery; Historical/World War II
Subject(s): Mystery and Detective Stories; Nuclear Warfare; Old Age
Major character(s): Sherlock Holmes, Detective—Private
Time period(s): 1940s (1947)
Locale(s): Hiroshima, Japan; Sussex, England

Summary: In a variant on the aging Sherlock Holmes' post-retirement life, Cullin imagines the great detective in 1947, frail, forgetful, but still capable of brilliant detective work. The 93-year-old Holmes travels to post-war Japan, where he sees the aftermath of the atomic bombing of Hiroshima as he works on an account of one of his earlier cases. He develops a touching relationship with his housekeeper's young son. This is an often moving account of Holmes sorting out his life before his last great mystery: his own death.

Where it's reviewed:
Booklist, February 1, 2005, page 945
Kirkus Reviews, February 1, 2005, page 133
Library Journal, April 15, 2005, page 74
New York Times Book Review, May 15, 2005, page 14
Publishers Weekly, February 14, 2005, page 50

Other books by the same author:
Undersurface, 2002
The Cosmology of Bing, 2001
Branches, 2000
Tideland, 2000

Whompyjawed, 1999

Other books you might like:
Caleb Carr, *The Italian Secretary*, 2005
Michael Chabon, *The Final Solution*, 2004
Martin Davies, *Mrs. Hudson and the Spirits' Curse*, 2005
Quinn Fawcett, *The Mycroft Holmes Series*, 1997-
Laurie R. King, *The Mary Russell/Sherlock Holmes Series*, 1994-

---

873

WILL DAVENPORT

The Sinner's Tale

(New York: Bantam, 2005)

Story type: Historical/Medieval
Subject(s): Knights and Knighthood; War
Major character(s): Sir Guy de Bryan, Knight; Beth Battock, Government Official
Time period(s): 14th century (1372); 21st century
Locale(s): England; New York, New York

Summary: Davenport weaves together a narrative set in both the 14th century and the present day. The first story concerns the circumstances surrounding Sir Guy de Bryan, a knight with a guilty conscience; while the second involves Beth Battock, a British government aide who is on the side of Britain's support of the U.S. strategy of preemptive war. If this seems a stretch: read on. Davenport skillfully cuts back and forth in time, producing an ingenious connection that spans the centuries.

Where it's reviewed:
Kirkus Reviews, February 1, 2005, page 134

Other books by the same author:
The Perfect Sinner, 2004
The Painter, 2003

Other books you might like:
Nicholas Christopher, *The Franklin Flyer*, 2002
Timothy Findley, *Pilgrim*, 1999
David E. Morse, *The Iron Bridge*, 1998
Richard Rayner, *The Cloud Sketcher*, 2000
James Runcie, *The Discovery of Chocolate*, 2001

874

MARTIN DAVIES

Mrs. Hudson and the Spirits' Curse

(New York: Berkley Prime Crime, 2005)

Story type: Mystery; Historical/Victorian
Subject(s): Mystery and Detective Stories; Crime and Criminals; Servants
Major character(s): Mrs. Emma Hudson, Housekeeper; Sherlock Holmes, Detective—Private; John Watson, Doctor, Sidekick
Time period(s): 19th century
Locale(s): London, England

Summary: BBC producer Davies' first foray into Sherlock Holmes pastiche takes the measure of the sleuthing ability of

Historical

the great detective's housekeeper, Mrs. Hudson, who assists in the investigation of a man pursued from Sumatra by assassins. The indefatigable Mrs. Hudson is ably assisted by an orphan she has rescued from the London streets. Davies wrote the novel as a birthday present to his father who often wondered what life was like for Holmes' housekeeper.

Where it's reviewed:
Kirkus Reviews, December 1, 2004, page 142
Publishers Weekly, November 8, 2004, page 39

Other books you might like:
Emily Brightwell, *The Mrs. Jeffries Series*, 1993-
Quinn Fawcett, *The Mycroft Holmes Series*, 1997-
Sydney Hosier, *The Game's Afoot, Mrs. Hudson*, 1998
Sydney Hosier, *Murder, Mrs. Hudson*, 1997
Robin Paige, *The Kathryn Ardleigh Series*, 1994-

875

FRANK DELANEY

Ireland

(New York: HarperCollins, 2005)

Story type: Coming-of-Age; Legend
Subject(s): Storytelling; Mythology; History
Major character(s): Ronan O'Mara, Historian
Time period(s): Multiple Time Periods
Locale(s): Ireland

Summary: Delaney chronicles a fictionalized history of Ireland in the many stories told by an aging, itinerant storyteller who arrives unannounced at the home of the O'Maras in 1951. He captivates the nine-year-old Ronan O'Mara with accounts of Irish myths, legends, and history. Ronan's coming of age is connected with his pursuit of the storyteller over the years and his coming to terms with the implications of the stories on his identity and understanding of his country and heritage. This is a delightful way of capturing the colorful history of Ireland, in the country's shaping myths and in the language of the oral storytelling tradition.

Where it's reviewed:
Kirkus Reviews, November 15, 2004, page 1060
Library Journal, December 2004, page 98
Publishers Weekly, December 13, 2004, page 43

Other books by the same author:
Desire and Pursuit, 1998
A Stranger in Their Midst, 1995
Telling the Pictures, 1993
The Sins of the Mothers, 1992
My Dark Rosaleen, 1989

Other books you might like:
Stephen R. Lawhead, *Patrick: Son of Ireland*, 2003
Morgan Llywelyn, *The Last Prince of Ireland*, 1992
Morgan Llywelyn, *Lion of Ireland*, 1981
Juilene Osborne-McKnight, *Bright Sword of Ireland*, 2004
Edward Rutherfurd, *The Princes of Ireland*, 2004

876

WILLIAM DIETRICH

The Scourge of God

(New York: HarperCollins, 2005)

Story type: Historical/Ancient Rome
Subject(s): War; Ancient History; Roman Empire
Major character(s): Attila the Hun, Historical Figure, Warrior; Jonas Alabanda, Scholar, Diplomat; Ilana, Slave
Time period(s): 5th century
Locale(s): Europe; Roman Empire

Summary: Dietrich dramatizes the final days of the Roman Empire and the attempt by Attila the Hun to conquer the West and dominate all of Europe in the 5th century. The story of Attila's western campaign is anchored by the experiences of Jonas Alabanda, a scribe assigned to a diplomatic mission to Attila's camp, and a Roman woman, Ilana, taken by the Huns as a slave. Both play a significant role in foiling Attila's conquest. The novel excels in its battlefield descriptions, anchored by evident research into the period and its customs.

Where it's reviewed:
Kirkus Reviews, February 1, 2005, page 134
Library Journal, February 15, 2005, page 114
Publishers Weekly, February 7, 2005, page 41

Other books by the same author:
Hadrian's Wall, 2004
Dark Winter, 2001
Getting Back, 2000

Other books you might like:
Thomas B. Costain, *The Darkness and the Dawn*, 1959
Louis De Wohl, *Throne of the World*, 1949
Michael Curtis Ford, *The Sword of Attila*, 2005
Roger Fuller, *Sign of the Pagan*, 1954
Stephen Grundy, *Attila's Treasure*, 1996

877

P.C. DOHERTY

The Hangman's Hymn

(New York: St. Martin's Minotaur, 2005)

Story type: Historical/Medieval; Mystery
Series: Canterbury Tales of Mystery and Murder. Book 5
Subject(s): Mystery and Detective Stories; Witches and Witchcraft; Middle Ages
Major character(s): Simon Cotterill, Executioner
Time period(s): 14th century
Locale(s): Kent, England (en route to Canterbury); Gloucester, England

Summary: Doherty's version of the *Canterbury Tales* has the carpenter telling the story of Simon Cotterill who comes to Gloucester and ends up joining the local hangman's crew. He becomes involved in hunting down and killing a coven of murderous witches who are terrorizing the Gloucester countryside. This is an atmospheric period tale that draws on the author's evident expert knowledge of medieval life.

Where it's reviewed:
Booklist, December 15, 2004, page 710
Kirkus Reviews, December 15, 2004, page 466
Publishers Weekly, November 15, 2004, page 44

Other books by the same author:
Corpse Candle, 2004
The Slayers of Seth, 2002
Spy in Chancery, 2001
Ghostly Murders, 1998
A Tournament of Murders, 1997

Other books you might like:
Peter Ackroyd, *The Clerkenwell Tales*, 2004
Simon Beaufort, *The Geoffrey de Mappestone Series*, 1998-
Margaret Frazer, *The Sister Frevisse Series*, 1993-
Bernard Knight, *The Crowner John Series*, 1998-
Sharan Newman, *Strong as Death*, 1996

878

SARA DOUGLASS

Darkwitch Rising

(New York: Tor, 2005)

Story type: Historical/Seventeenth Century; Historical/Fantasy
Series: Troy Game. Book 3
Subject(s): Fantasy; Magic
Major character(s): Charles II, Historical Figure, Ruler (King of England); Brutus, Ruler (King of Troy)
Time period(s): 17th century
Locale(s): England

Summary: In the third installment of the author's Troy Game historical fantasy series, Brutus, the legendary king of Troy, is now a companion of Charles II, who was once a Celtic Stagking of folklore. The working of the magical Labyrinth is interwoven with actual details of 17th-century English history, including the Great Fire of London. Readers new to Douglass' series are advised to start at the beginning rather than jumping in here.

Where it's reviewed:
Library Journal, May 15, 2005, page 111
Publishers Weekly, April 11, 2005, page 38

Other books by the same author:
The Wounded Hawk, 2005
Gods' Concubine, 2004
Hades' Daughter, 2003
Starman, 2002
The Nameless Day, 2000

Other books you might like:
Ann Benson, *The Burning Road*, 1999
Geraldine Brooks, *Year of Wonders*, 2001
Jeff Long, *Year Zero*, 2002
Maria McCann, *As Meat Loves Salt*, 2001
Steve White, *Demon's Gate*, 2004

879

CLARE DUDMAN

98 Reasons for Being

(New York: Viking, 2005)

Story type: Historical/Victorian; Medical
Subject(s): Biography; Mental Illness; Jews
Major character(s): Heinrich Hoffmann, Historical Figure, Doctor; Hannah Meyer, Young Woman
Time period(s): 1850s
Locale(s): Frankfurt, Germany

Summary: Dudman explores the life of pioneering German physician Heinrich Hoffmann, best known for his children's book, *Shockheaded Peter*. In 1850s Frankfurt, Hoffmann treats a young Jewish girl named Hannah Meyer confined to the city's insane asylum. None of the accepted methods work in getting through to Hannah, until Dr. Hoffmann resorts to simply talking with her, and she gradually begins to open up to him. Hannah's history is joined with the story of Hoffmann and the various cases with which he has dealt. This is a rich and satisfying glimpse into the past and into the lives of fascinating characters that reflect German, Jewish, and medical history.

Where it's reviewed:
Kirkus Reviews, May 1, 2005, page 493

Other books by the same author:
One Day the Ice Will Reveal All Its Dead, 2004
Wegener's Jigsaw, 2003
Edge of Danger, 1995

Other books you might like:
John Katzenbach, *The Madman's Tale*, 2004
Patrick McGrath, *Asylum*, 1997
Cynthia Ozick, *The Puttermesser Papers*, 1997
Graham Swift, *Waterland*, 1983
D.M. Thomas, *The White Hotel*, 1981

880

THOMAS DYJA

The Moon in Our Hands

(New York: Carroll & Graf, 2005)

Story type: Historical/World War II
Subject(s): Small Town Life; Rural Life; African Americans
Major character(s): Walter White, Historical Figure, Investigator
Time period(s): 1910s (1918)
Locale(s): Sibley Springs, Tennessee

Summary: Dyja's novel draws on the experiences of real-life Walter White, a light-skinned black man sent by the NAACP undercover as a white man to investigate racial violence in the South. His assignment brings him to Sibley Springs, Tennessee, where a black farmer has been tortured, castrated, and burned alive. White struggles to understand the motives of those who could have done such a thing, the South, and himself.

Historical

Where it's reviewed:
Kirkus Reviews, December 1, 2004, page 1104
Publishers Weekly, January 17, 2005, page 35

Other books by the same author:
Meet John Trow, 2002
Play for a Kingdom, 1997

Other books you might like:
Christopher Brookhouse, *Passing Game*, 2000
Tananarive Due, *The Black Rose*, 2000
Aaron Roy Even, *Bloodroot*, 2000
Jewell Parker Rhodes, *Douglass' Women*, 2002
Sharon Rolens, *Worthy's Town*, 2000

881

CLIVE EGLETON

A Dying Fall

(Sutton, England: Severn House, 2005)

Story type: Historical/World War II
Subject(s): World War II; Espionage; Nazis
Major character(s): Paul Heinrich Gerhardt, Military Personnel (German general); Michael Ashby, Military Personnel (British lieutenant colonel)
Time period(s): 1940s (1944)
Locale(s): England; Wales; Germany

Summary: Egleton's World War II-era thriller involves a plot to kill Martin Bormann and disrupt the German command in 1944. The plot is hatched by German General Paul Heinrich Gerhardt who has escaped to England after the failed assassination attempt on Adolf Hitler. His plan is dismissed by Allied command, but taken seriously by Lieutenant Colonel Michael Ashby, and the novel follows the training and execution of a mission designed to shorten the war.

Where it's reviewed:
Kirkus Reviews, January 1, 2005, page 6

Other books by the same author:
Never Surrender, 2004
A Spy's Ransom, 2003
Dead Reckoning, 2000
The Honey Trap, 2000
A Double Deception, 1992

Other books you might like:
Ken Follett, *The Key to Rebecca*, 1980
Robert Harris, *Enigma*, 1995
Jack Higgins, *The Eagle Has Flown*, 1990
Walter Satterthwait, *Cavalcade*, 2005
Daniel Silva, *The Unlikely Spy*, 1996

882

KATHY LYNN EMERSON

Face Down Below the Banqueting House

(McKinleyville, California: Perseverance, 2005)

Story type: Historical/Elizabethan; Mystery
Series: Susanna, Lady Appleton

Subject(s): Mystery and Detective Stories; Kings, Queens, Rulers, etc.
Major character(s): Lady Susanna Appleton, Herbalist, Detective—Amateur; Elizabeth I, Historical Figure, Ruler (Queen of England)
Time period(s): 16th century
Locale(s): England

Summary: On the eve of Queen Elizabeth I's visit to Susanna, Lady Appleton's home at Leigh Abbey, a suspicious death occurs in Susanna's garden. Is this part of a plot against the queen? Susanna investigates in this installment of Emerson's atmospheric Elizabethan-era mystery series.

Where it's reviewed:
Kirkus Reviews, February 1, 2005, page 150
Library Journal, March 1, 2005, page 71

Other books by the same author:
Deadlier than the Pen, 2004
Face Down Across the Western Sea, 2002
Face Down Before the Rebel Hooves, 2001
Face Down upon a Herbal, 2001
Face Down under the Wych Elm, 2000

Other books you might like:
Fiona Buckley, *The Ursula Blanchard Series*, 1997-
Karen Harper, *The Elizabeth I Series*, 1999-
Edward Marston, *The Nicholas Bracewell Series*, 1988-
Ian Morson, *The William Falconer Series*, 1994-
Sharan Newman, *The Catherine LeVendeur Series*, 1993-

883

AMY EPHRON

One Sunday Morning

(New York: William Morrow, 2005)

Story type: Historical/Roaring Twenties
Subject(s): Social Classes; Social Issues
Major character(s): Mary Nell, Young Woman; Lizzie Carswell, Young Woman; Billy Holmes, Young Man
Time period(s): 1920s (1927)
Locale(s): New York, New York; Paris, France

Summary: Ephron's historical novel is set during the Jazz Age of the 1920s in New York and Paris. Aspiring writer Mary Nell tells what happens when four women at a bridge party in New York's Gramercy Park Hotel see a beautiful young woman, Lizzie Carswell, leaving a nearby hotel with Billy Holmes, who is not her husband. This is Edith Wharton territory but with a more realistic look at the hidden, sinister side of the era's liberations.

Where it's reviewed:
Booklist, March 1, 2005, page 1140
Kirkus Reviews, February 1, 2005, page 135
Library Journal, March 15, 2005, page 70
Publishers Weekly, March 14, 2005, page 44

Other books by the same author:
White Rose, 1999
A Cup of Tea, 1997
Biodegradable Soap, 1991
Bruised Fruit, 1987

Other books you might like:
Louis Auchincloss, *East Side Story*, 2004
Elaine Bissell, *Family Fortune*, 1985
Dominick Dunne, *The Two Mrs. Grenvilles*, 1985
Suzanne Morris, *Wives and Mistresses*, 1986
Fred Mustard Stewart, *Savages in Love and War*, 2001

884

MORIS FARHI

Young Turk

(New York: Arcade, 2005)

Story type: Historical/Exotic; Coming-of-Age
Subject(s): Short Stories; Cultures and Customs; Muslims
Time period(s): 20th century (1930s-1950s)
Locale(s): Istanbul, Turkey; Salonica, Turkey

Summary: These 13 linked stories record life in and around Istanbul, Turkey, and elsewhere from the late 1930s to the mid-1950s. The stories explore what it means to be Turkish, touching on the various ethnic and religious groups—Muslim, Christian, Jewish, Greek, Armenian, Gypsy, and others—that make up the population. Of particular interest are aspects of Turkish history that are not well-known, including the fate of the Jewish city of Salonica, and the punitive tax imposed on all minority groups in 1942, when Turkey was considering aligning with Germany.

Where it's reviewed:
Kirkus Reviews, April 15, 2005, page 437

Other books by the same author:
Children of the Rainbow, 1999
Journey through the Wilderness, 1989
The Last of Days, 1983

Other books you might like:
Louis De Bernieres, *Birds Without Wings*, 2004
Carol Edgarian, *Rise the Euphrates*, 1994
Elia Kazan, *The Anatolian*, 1982
Richard Reinhardt, *The Ashes of Smyrna*, 1971
Barry Unsworth, *The Songs of the Kings*, 2003

885

CHRISTOPHER JOHN FARLEY

Kingston by Starlight

(New York: Crown, 2005)

Story type: Historical/Georgian
Subject(s): Pirates; Biography; Sea Stories
Major character(s): Anne Bonny, Historical Figure, Pirate; Calico Jack Rackam, Historical Figure, Pirate
Time period(s): 1710s
Locale(s): Ireland; Kingston, Jamaica; West Indies

Summary: Farley offers a swashbuckling tale based on the historical figure Anne Bonny. As a teenager, Anne leaves her native Ireland to seek her fortune in the West Indies disguised as a young man. She finds work on a ship commanded by Calico Jack Rackam, a pirate determined to capture the richest ship in the Caribbean, the *Madrid Galleon*, which sails from Kingston, Jamaica, laden with Cuban gold and Jamaican rum.

The novel chronicles their attempt and culminates in a trial in which secrets and identities are revealed.

Where it's reviewed:
Kirkus Reviews, April 15, 2005, page 437
Library Journal, April 1, 2005, page 85

Other books by the same author:
My Favorite War, 1996

Other books you might like:
Pamela Jekel, *Sea Star*, 1983
Morgan Llywelyn, *Grania: She-King of the Irish Seas*, 1986
Alison MacLeod, *The Changeling*, 1996
Robin Maxwell, *The Wild Irish*, 2003
James L. Nelson, *The Sweet Trade*, 2001

886

ELLEN FELDMAN

The Boy Who Loved Anne Frank

(New York: Norton, 2005)

Story type: Historical/World War II
Subject(s): World War II; Holocaust; Jews
Major character(s): Peter van Pels, Immigrant
Time period(s): 1940s; 1950s
Locale(s): United States

Summary: Feldman imagines an alternate version of the events surrounding Anne Frank in which the teenage Anne was attracted to Peter van Pels (van Daan in her famous diary). He survives and immigrates to the U.S. where he denies his Jewishness and hides his past, marrying, raising a family, and succeeding in business. The international success of the *Diary* forces him to come forward to set the record straight.

Where it's reviewed:
Kirkus Reviews, January 15, 2005, page 69
Library Journal, March 1, 2005, page 78
Publishers Weekly, March 7, 2005, page 51

Other books by the same author:
Lucy, 2003
God Bless the Child, 1998
Too Close for Comfort, 1994
Looking for Love, 1990
Conjugal Rites, 1986

Other books you might like:
Jane Gardam, *Crusoe's Daughter*, 1986
John Katzenbach, *The Shadow Man*, 1995
Barth Landor, *A Week in Winter*, 2004
Elly Welt, *Berlin Wild*, 1986
Elie Wiesel, *Twilight*, 1988

887

JIM FERGUS

Wild Girl

(New York: Hyperion, 2005)

Story type: Historical/Depression Era; Historical/American West

Historical

Subject(s): Indians of North America
Major character(s): Ned Giles, Orphan, Photographer; La Nina Bronca, Indian (Apache)
Time period(s): 1930s (1932)
Locale(s): Sierre Madre Mountains, Arizona; Mexico

Summary: Photographer Ned Giles joins the 1932 Great Apache Expedition to search for the son of a wealthy Mexican landowner kidnapped by an Apache band. The mission is complicated by a wild Apache girl, La Nina Bronca, a victim of a Mexican massacre of her tribe, who will be used as ransom.

Where it's reviewed:
Kirkus Reviews, March 15, 2005, page 304
Publishers Weekly, March 28, 2005, page 54

Other books by the same author:
One Thousand White Women, 1998

Other books you might like:
Michael Blake, *The Holy Road*, 2001
Deborah Larsen, *The White*, 2002
Cormac McCarthy, *The Crossing*, 1994
Lucia St. Clair Robson, *Ghost Warrior*, 2002
Janice Woods Windle, *Hill Country*, 1998

888

ERIC FLINT

The Rivers of War

(New York: Del Rey, 2005)

Story type: Historical/War of 1812; Alternate History
Subject(s): Alternate History; War of 1812; Indians of North America
Major character(s): James Madison, Historical Figure, Political Figure; James Monroe, Historical Figure, Political Figure; Andrew Jackson, Historical Figure, Military Personnel
Time period(s): 1810s (1814)
Locale(s): United States

Summary: In the first of a projected two-volume alternate history of the War of 1812, Flint poses the what-if scenario that the Cherokees, assisted by escaped slaves and white allies, were able to lead a united Indian front against the Americans. By altering the dynamic of the war, Flint offers an interesting variation on history to study a huge cast of historical figures, including James Monroe, James Madison, Andrew Jackson, Sam Houston, Francis Scott Key, British General Robert Ross, and Cherokee chiefs John Ross and Major Ridge.

Where it's reviewed:
Kirkus Reviews, May 1, 2005, page 518
Publishers Weekly, April 25, 2005, page 43

Other books by the same author:
1634, 2004
Crown of Slaves, 2003
This Rough Magic, 2003
The Shadow of the Lion, 2002
1632, 2000

Other books you might like:
Max Byrd, *Jackson*, 1997
Diane Glancy, *Pushing the Bear*, 1996
David Nevin, *1812*, 1996
David Nevin, *Eagle's Cry*, 2000
Lucia St. Clair Robson, *Walk in My Soul*, 1985

889

MICHAEL CURTIS FORD

The Sword of Attila

(New York: Thomas Dunne, 2005)

Story type: Historical/Ancient Rome
Subject(s): War; Roman Empire; Military Life
Major character(s): Attila the Hun, Historical Figure, Warrior; Flavius Aetius, Military Personnel (Roman commander), Historical Figure
Time period(s): 5th century (451)
Locale(s): Gaul; Ravenna, Italy

Summary: One of world history's decisive combats is the 451 Battle of Chalons, in Gaul, where more than a million Romans and Huns contested for the rule of Europe. The leaders of the armies—Attila and Flavius Aetius—are the subjects of Ford's novel. As children both were exchanged as hostages to live with the enemy. Flavius is raised in the rough wooden huts of the Huns; while Attila grows up in the Roman court. Ford presents the contrasting customs and values of both peoples before the climactic meeting on the battlefield that decides the fate of Europe.

Where it's reviewed:
Kirkus Reviews, January 15, 2005, page 70

Other books by the same author:
The Last King, 2004
Gods and Legions, 2002
The Ten Thousand, 2001

Other books you might like:
Louis De Wohl, *Throne of the World*, 1949
William Dietrich, *The Scourge of God*, 2005
Allan Massie, *The Evening of the World*, 2001
Diana L. Paxson, *The Lord of Horses*, 1996
Edith Simon, *The Twelve Pictures*, 1955

890

DAVID FRANCIS

The Great Inland Sea

(San Francisco: MacAdam/Cage, 2005)

Story type: Family Saga
Subject(s): Animals/Horses; Horse Racing
Major character(s): Day, Jockey; Callie, Jockey
Time period(s): 1940s; 1950s
Locale(s): Australia; United States

Summary: This brooding novel follows the relationship between Australian emigres—Day and Callie—who work the East Coast horse circuit. Day is haunted by the death of his mother, an Austrian Jew driven to madness by the harsh Australian conditions and an abusive husband, and the novel

provides a journey of self-discovery and the uncovering of long-buried family secrets. The author, who grew up in Australia's horse country, is particularly convincing on the details of horse training and racing, as well as the Australian elements.

Where it's reviewed:
Booklist, March 15, 2005, page 1263
Library Journal, March 15, 2005, page 70
Publishers Weekly, April 25, 2005, page 38

Other books by the same author:
Agapanthus Tango, 2001

Other books you might like:
Sara Challis, *Turning for Home*, 2003
Eleanor Dark, *Storm of Time*, 1950
Mardi McConnochie, *Coldwater*, 2001
Alex Miller, *Conditions of Faith*, 2000
Karen Roberts, *The Flower Boy*, 2000

891

ELIZABETH GAFFNEY

Metropolis

(New York: Random House, 2005)

Story type: Historical/Post-American Civil War
Subject(s): City and Town Life; Gangs
Major character(s): Frank Harris, Immigrant, Gang Member; Beatrice O'Gamhna, Gang Member
Time period(s): 19th century (post-Civil War)
Locale(s): New York, New York

Summary: Gaffney looks at the development of New York City in the post-Civil War period from the perspective of German immigrant Frank Harris, who is drawn by Beatrice O'Gamhna into the notorious Irish Whyo street gang. Harris' gang adventures and jobs laying cobblestones, working in the sewers, and especially building the Brooklyn Bridge provide the opportunity for Gaffney to document city life during the period in a highly readable, and accomplished, historical novel debut.

Where it's reviewed:
Booklist, January 1, 2005, page 814
Kirkus Reviews, January 15, 2005, page 70
Library Journal, January 2005, page 95
Publishers Weekly, December 20, 2004, page 34

Other books you might like:
Frederick Busch, *The Night Inspector*, 1999
Willa Cather, *Alexander's Bridge*, 1912
Richard E. Crabbe, *Suspension*, 2000
Louise Erdrich, *The Master Butchers Singing Club*, 2003
Pete Hamill, *Snow in August*, 1997

892

BRAD GEAGLEY

Year of the Hyenas

(New York: Simon & Schuster, 2005)

Story type: Historical/Ancient Egypt; Mystery

Subject(s): Mystery and Detective Stories; Ancient History; Egyptian Religion
Major character(s): Semerket, Detective—Police; Ramses III, Historical Figure, Ruler (pharaoh)
Time period(s): 12th century B.C. (1153 B.C.)
Locale(s): Egypt

Summary: Set during the reign of Ramses III, this police procedural has the hard-drinking Semerket, former Clerk of Investigations and Secrets, looking into the death of an elderly Theban priestess. Semerket uncovers corruption and conspiracy that threatens Ramses' reign. This fast-paced, atmospheric mystery draws on the actual facts surrounding the murder of Ramses III, the oldest documented murder case.

Where it's reviewed:
Booklist, January 1, 2005, page 826
Kirkus Reviews, December 15, 2004, page 1167
Library Journal, January 2005, page 83

Other books you might like:
P.C. Doherty, *The Anubis Slaying*, 2001
Anton Gill, *The Huy the Scribe Series*, 1991-
Lauren Haney, *A Curse of Silence*, 2000
Lee Levin, *King Tut's Private Eye*, 1996
Lynda S. Robinson, *The Lord Meren Series*, 1994-

893

MARY GENTLE

A Sundial in a Grave: 1610

(New York: Perennial, 2005)

Story type: Historical/Seventeenth Century
Subject(s): Kings, Queens, Rulers, etc.
Major character(s): Edward Fludd, Scientist (mathematician); Valentin Rochefort, Nobleman; Marie de Medici, Historical Figure, Royalty
Time period(s): 17th century (1610)
Locale(s): England; France

Summary: Gentle's inventive novel connects the story of mathematician Edward Fludd who has learned the secret of predicting the future and wants to change it by arranging the assassination of King James I, thereby changing the course of history. Meanwhile, in France, duelist and aristocrat Valentin Rochefort is blackmailed by Marie de Medici to kill Henri IV, causing him to flee to England, where he becomes Fludd's hit man. Meticulously researched, this is an entertaining period adventure with a colorful cast of characters and an odd point of view on historical figures and events.

Where it's reviewed:
Booklist, May 15, 2005, page 1646

Other books by the same author:
Carthage Ascendant, 2000
The Architect of Desire, 1991
Rats and Gargoyles, 1990
A Hawk in Silver, 1986
Golden Witchbreed, 1984

Other books you might like:
Susan Carroll, *The Dark Queen*, 2005
Susanna Clarke, *Jonathan Strange & Mr. Norrell*, 2004

Historical

Mercedes Lackey, *Ill Met by Moonlight*, 2005
Judith Merkle Riley, *The Master of All Desires*, 1999
Neal Stephenson, *The System of the World*, 2004

894

NEWT GINGRICH
WILLIAM R. FORSTCHEN, Co-Author

Never Call Retreat

(New York: St. Martin's Press, 2005)

Story type: Historical/American Civil War; Alternate History
Subject(s): Civil War; Alternate History; War
Major character(s): Robert E. Lee, Historical Figure, Military Personnel; Ulysses S. Grant, Historical Figure, Military Personnel; Abraham Lincoln, Historical Figure, Political Figure
Time period(s): 1860s
Locale(s): Washington, District of Columbia; Maryland; Virginia

Summary: Gingrich and Forstchen conclude their alternate history of the Civil War that posits a possible Confederate victory. After his great victories at Gettysburg and Union Mills, Lee attacks Washington. The city is successfully defended, but the Union army is crippled, and President Lincoln must call on General Grant to save the Union. The novel has the two great Civil War generals—Lee and Grant—locked in a series of deadly maneuvers that will decide the war.

Where it's reviewed:
Booklist, May 15, 2005, page 1613

Other books by the same author:
Grant Comes East, 2004
Gettysburg, 2003
1945, 1995

Other books you might like:
Max Byrd, *Grant*, 2000
Lamar Herrin, *The Unwritten Chronicles of Robert E. Lee*, 1989
Richard Parry, *That Fateful Lightning*, 2000
Douglas Savage, *The Court Martial of Robert E. Lee*, 1993
Jeff Shaara, *The Last Full Measure*, 1998

895

JANET GLEESON

The Serpent in the Garden

(New York: Simon & Schuster, 2005)

Story type: Historical/Georgian; Mystery
Subject(s): Mystery and Detective Stories; Crime and Criminals; Artists and Art
Major character(s): Joshua Pope, Artist (portrait painter)
Time period(s): 1760s (1765)
Locale(s): Richmond, England

Summary: Gleeson's second historical mystery puts another skilled craftsman in charge of investigating a murder in Georgian England. Portrait painter Joshua Pope is commissioned to paint the wedding portrait of a fashionable couple. The bride insists on wearing an emerald necklace in the shape of a serpent, despite its reputation of bringing bad luck. When a stranger is found dead and the necklace disappears, Joshua is the prime suspect, and he must take up the investigation. The intrigue is anchored by a detailed portrait of 18th-century English life and its art world.

Where it's reviewed:
Booklist, January 1, 2005, page 827
Kirkus Reviews, December 1, 2004, page 1106
Publishers Weekly, January 24, 2005, page 225

Other books by the same author:
The Grenadillo Box, 2002

Other books you might like:
Bruce Alexander, *The Sir John Fielding Series*, 1994-2005
T.F. Banks, *The Thief-Taker*, 2001
Stephanie Barron, *The Jane Austen Series*, 1996-
Jeffrey Ford, *The Portrait of Mrs. Charbuque*, 2002
Ciji Ware, *Wicked Company*, 1992

896

PHILIP GOODEN

An Honorable Murder

(New York: Carroll & Graf, 2005)

Story type: Historical/Seventeenth Century; Mystery
Series: Nicholas Revill. Book 6
Subject(s): Mystery and Detective Stories; Theater; Actors and Actresses
Major character(s): Nicholas Revill, Actor, Detective—Amateur; Ben Jonson, Historical Figure, Writer
Time period(s): 17th century (1604)
Locale(s): London, England

Summary: In this installment of Gooden's Elizabethan-era mystery series, featuring actor Nicholas Revill, James I is on the throne and Nick has been invited by playwright Ben Jonson to take part in a court masque. When a courtier dies during a rehearsal, it is the first of a series of sinister deaths with suspects, including Jonson himself.

Where it's reviewed:
Kirkus Reviews, February 15, 2005, page 201

Other books by the same author:
Mask of Night, 2004
Alms for Oblivion, 2003
The Pale Companion, 2002
Death of Kings, 2001
Sleep of Death, 2000

Other books you might like:
Fiona Buckley, *The Ursula Blanchard Series*, 1997-
Karen Harper, *The Elizabeth I Series*, 1999-
Simon Hawke, *The Shakespeare and Smythe Series*, 2000-
Philip Kerr, *Dark Matter*, 2002
Edward Marston, *The Nicholas Bracewell Series*, 1988-

897

RON GOULART

Groucho Marx, King of the Jungle

(New York: St. Martin's Minotaur, 2005)

Story type: Mystery; Historical/Depression Era
Series: Groucho Marx. Book 6
Subject(s): Mystery and Detective Stories; Movies; Actors and Actresses
Major character(s): Groucho Marx, Historical Figure, Actor; Frank Denby, Journalist (former crime reporter), Writer
Time period(s): 1930s (1939)
Locale(s): Los Angeles, California

Summary: Groucho Marx and his sidekick Frank Denby return to investigate the murder of the star in a series of Tarzan-like jungle B-movies. Suspicion falls on the victim's former flame who is on the lam. While tracking their prey, the sleuths discover a treasure map and evidence of blackmail, as they make a pun-filled, wisecracking tour of period Hollywood, Groucho-style.

Where it's reviewed:
Kirkus Reviews, May 15, 2005, page 565

Other books by the same author:
Groucho Marx, Secret Agent, 2002
Groucho Marx and the Broadway Murders, 2001
Elementary, My Dear Groucho, 1999
Groucho Marx, Private Eye, 1999
Groucho Marx, Master Detective, 1998

Other books you might like:
George Baxt, *The Noel Coward Murder Case*, 1992
Max Allan Collins, *Angel in Black*, 2001
Robert Lee Hall, *Murder at San Simeon*, 1988
Stuart M. Kaminsky, *To Catch a Spy*, 2002
Stuart M. Kaminsky, *You Bet Your Life*, 1978

898

POSIE GRAEME-EVANS

The Exiled

(New York: Atria, 2005)

Story type: Historical/Medieval
Subject(s): Middle Ages; Kings, Queens, Rulers, etc.
Major character(s): Anne, Businesswoman (merchant); Edward IV, Historical Figure, Ruler (King of England)
Time period(s): 15th century
Locale(s): England

Summary: This novel, set in 15th-century England, concerns the ever-resourceful Anne who raises her child in exile while supporting her household as a merchant. Anne, however, has a secret: her son is the result of a passionate affair with the king, Edward IV, and this information, in the wrong hands, could prove deadly.

Other books by the same author:
The Innocent, 2004

Other books you might like:
Peter Ackroyd, *The Clerkenwell Tales*, 2004

Norman Bogner, *The Deadliest Art*, 2001
Catherine Darby, *The Love Knot*, 1991
Philippa Gregory, *Earthly Joys*, 1998
Alan Hollinghurst, *The Folding Star*, 1994

899

KERRY GREENWOOD

Away with the Fairies

(Scottsdale, Arizona: Poisoned Pen Press, 2005)

Story type: Mystery; Historical/Roaring Twenties
Series: Phryne Fisher. Book 10
Subject(s): Mystery and Detective Stories; Crime and Criminals
Major character(s): Phryne Fisher, Detective—Private
Time period(s): 1920s (1928)
Locale(s): Melbourne, Australia

Summary: Sassy Australian Phryne Fisher returns for another case in this delightful mystery series set down under during the 1920s. Phryne takes up the case of the murder of a well-known author of fairy stories. The investigation leads her to a temporary job at the magazine that employed the victim. The intrigue here is mixed with a convincing portrait of post-war Australia and the challenges liberated women faced during the era.

Where it's reviewed:
Booklist, December 15, 2004, page 711
Kirkus Reviews, December 1, 2004, page 1120

Other books by the same author:
Murder in Montparnasse, 2004
The Castlemaine Murders, 2002
Murder on the Ballarat Train, 1993
Flying Too High, 1992
Death by Misadventure, 1991

Other books you might like:
Janet Evanovich, *Hot Six*, 2000
Elizabeth George, *In the Presence of the Enemy*, 1996
Susan Isaacs, *Long Time No See*, 2001
James Patterson, *2nd Chance*, 2002
Phyllis Whitney, *Star Flight*, 1993

900

JANE GUILL

Nectar from a Stone

(New York: Simon & Schuster, 2005)

Story type: Historical/Medieval
Subject(s): Middle Ages; Psychic Powers
Major character(s): Elise, Psychic; Gwydion, Nobleman; Annora, Servant
Time period(s): 14th century (1351)
Locale(s): Wales

Summary: In this atmospheric novel, clairvoyant Elise, and her servant, Annora, flee from the scene of a crime, where Elise has apparently killed her abusive husband in self defense. Their paths cross that of enigmatic nobleman Gwydion, who seeks to avenge the murder of his father and reclaim his

birthright. As their parallel stories intersect, Gwydion and Elise come together in a story that draws on the often eerie and foreboding landscape of Wales.

Where it's reviewed:
Kirkus Reviews, January 15, 2005, page 73
Publishers Weekly, February 14, 2005, page 53

Other books you might like:
Haley Elizabeth Garwood, *Swords Across the Thames*, 1999
Glenna McReynolds, *The Chalice and the Blade*, 1997
Sharon Kay Penman, *Here Be Dragons*, 1988
Martha Rofheart, *Glendower Country*, 1973
Anna Lee Waldo, *Circle of Stones*, 1999

901
BETH GUTCHEON

Leeway Cottage
(New York: William Morrow, 2005)

Story type: Historical/World War II
Subject(s): World War II; Music and Musicians; Resistance Movements
Major character(s): Sydney Brant, Singer; Laurus Moss, Musician (piano player)
Time period(s): 20th century
Locale(s): Maine; New York, New York; Europe

Summary: Gutcheon moves beyond the activities of a fictional Maine summer colony to tell the World War II-era story of Sydney Brant who marries Laurus Moss, a half-Jewish piano player from Copenhagen. The story of their marriage is connected with the extraordinary efforts of the Danish Resistance in their protection of the Jews.

Where it's reviewed:
Booklist, March 1, 2005, page 1265
Kirkus Reviews, February 1, 2005, page 137
New York Times Book Review, June 5, 2005, page 13
Publishers Weekly, February 28, 2005, page 40

Other books by the same author:
More than You Know, 2000
Five Fortunes, 1998
Saying Grace, 1995
Domestic Pleasures, 1991
Still Missing, 1981

Other books you might like:
Sarah Blake, *Grange House*, 2000
Nora Roberts, *Homeport*, 1998
Richard Russo, *Empire Falls*, 2001
Anne Rivers Siddons, *Colony*, 1992
LaVyrle Spencer, *That Camden Summer*, 1996

902
DIANE HAEGER

The Ruby Ring
(New York: Three Rivers, 2005)

Story type: Historical/Renaissance
Subject(s): Artists and Art; Women; Religious Life

Major character(s): Margherita Luti, Historical Figure, Lover; Raphael, Historical Figure, Artist
Time period(s): 16th century (1520)
Locale(s): Rome, Italy

Summary: Haeger dramatizes the love affair between Renaissance painter Raphael and Margherita Luti, a baker's daughter who served as Raphael's model in some of his most famous works. After Raphael's death, Margherita, to survive, decides to seek refuge in a religious order, but first she must give up the ruby ring she had worn in Raphael's scandalous nude engagement portrait. The novel brings to life the Italian Renaissance and one of the most passionate love affairs of the era.

Other books by the same author:
My Dearest Cecelia, 2003
The Secret Wife of King George IV, 2000
Beyond the Glen, 1998
Pieces of April, 1997
Courtesan, 1993

Other books you might like:
Tracy Chevalier, *Girl with a Pearl Earring*, 1999
Sarah Dunant, *The Birth of Venus*, 2003
Robert S. Elegant, *Bianca*, 1992
Pauline Holdstock, *A Rare and Curious Gift*, 2005
Susan Vreeland, *The Passion of Artemisia*, 2002

903
OAKLEY HALL

Ambrose Bierce and the Ace of Shoots
(New York: Viking, 2005)

Story type: Mystery; Historical/Victorian America
Series: Ambrose Bierce. Book 5
Subject(s): Mystery and Detective Stories
Major character(s): Ambrose Bierce, Journalist, Historical Figure; Tom Redmond, Sidekick (of Bierce)
Time period(s): 1890s
Locale(s): San Francisco, California

Summary: When the owner of a visiting Wild West Show is murdered, writer Ambrose Bierce and his companion Tom Redmond search for the killer. Their investigation takes them on a colorful tour of the more sinister side of San Francisco.

Where it's reviewed:
Kirkus Reviews, February 15, 2005, page 201
Publishers Weekly, March 7, 2005, page 53

Other books by the same author:
Ambrose Bierce and the Trey of Pearls, 2004
Ambrose Bierce and the One-Eyed Jacks, 2003
Ambrose Bierce and the Death of Kings, 2001
Ambrose Bierce and the Queen of Spades, 1998
Warlock, 1996

Other books you might like:
Dianne Day, *The Fremont Jones Series*, 1995-
Carlos Fuentes, *The Old Gringo*, 1986
Robert Lee Hall, *Murder at San Simeon*, 1988
Cecelia Holland, *Pacific Street*, 1992
Daniel Lynch, *Yellow*, 1992

904

MAREK HALTER

Zipporah, Wife of Moses

(New York: Crown, 2005)

Story type: Legend; Biblical Fiction
Series: Cannan Trilogy. Book 2
Subject(s): Ancient History; Biblical Fiction; Women
Major character(s): Zipporah, Historical Figure, Biblical Figure; Moses, Historical Figure, Biblical Figure; Jethro, Historical Figure, Religious
Time period(s): 13th century B.C.
Locale(s): Egypt; Middle East

Summary: In the second of a projected trilogy on women of the Bible, Halter looks at the life of Zipporah, a Cushite, one of the black people of Africa who is adopted by Jethro, high priest of the Midianites. She meets Moses who has fled from Egypt after killing one of the pharaoh's cruel overseers. When God reveals himself to Moses, he returns to Egypt with Zipporah, now his wife, at his side. This is an interesting angle on the story of Moses and the Exodus in which much of Moses' greatness is traced to the influence of the remarkable Zipporah.

Where it's reviewed:
Booklist, May 15, 2005, page 1648
Kirkus Reviews, May 15, 2005, page 558

Other books by the same author:
Sarah, 2004
The Wind of the Khazars, 2003
The Children of Abraham, 1990
The Book of Abraham, 1986

Other books you might like:
Anita Diamant, *The Red Tent*, 1997
India Edghill, *Queenmaker*, 2002
Angela Elwell Hunt, *The Shadow Women*, 2002
Judith Tarr, *Pillar of Fire*, 1999
Les Whitten, *Moses*, 1999

905

KAREN HARPER

The Fyre Mirror

(New York: St. Martin's Minotaur, 2005)

Story type: Historical/Elizabethan; Mystery
Series: Elizabeth I. Book 7
Subject(s): Mystery and Detective Stories
Major character(s): Elizabeth I, Historical Figure, Ruler (Queen of England); Gil Sharpe, Artist; Sir William Cecil, Historical Figure, Government Official
Time period(s): 16th century (1565)
Locale(s): London, England; Surrey, England

Summary: Harper's seventh Elizabethan-era mystery using Elizabeth herself as sleuth involves Gil Sharpe, portrait artist and friend of the queen, who becomes a suspect in the death of a fellow artist and his serving boy. The queen's investigation uncovers a sinister conspiracy that could involve one of Elizabeth's most trusted advisers. This well-researched pe-riod mystery features actual details from Elizabeth's biography and reign, and such historical figures as Sir William Cecil, the queen's secretary, and infamous alchemist Dr. John Dee.

Where it's reviewed:
Kirkus Reviews, January 15, 2005, page 86
Library Journal, February 1, 2005, page 56
Publishers Weekly, January 31, 2005, page 52

Other books by the same author:
The Queene's Christmas, 2003
The Thorne Maze, 2003
The Queene's Cure, 2002
The Twylight Tower, 2001
The Tidal Poole, 2000

Other books you might like:
Fiona Buckley, *The Ursula Blanchard Series*, 1997-
Kathy Lynn Emerson, *The Susanna, Lady Appleton Series*, 1997-
Philip Gooden, *An Honorable Murder*, 2005
Leonard Tourney, *Time's Fool*, 2004

906

TOM HARPER

The Mosaic of Shadows

(New York: St. Martin's Minotaur, 2005)

Story type: Mystery; Historical/Medieval
Subject(s): Mystery and Detective Stories; Byzantine Empire
Major character(s): Demetrios the Apokalyptor, Detective—Private
Time period(s): 11th century (1096)
Locale(s): Constantinople, Byzantine Empire

Summary: This historical mystery debut is set during the waning years of the Byzantine Empire and involves Demetrios the Apokalyptor, a widower, former mercenary, and bounty hunter with a pair of independent-minded daughters. When an assassination attempt is made on the life of the emperor, Demetrios is hired to investigate. The author provides a colorful tour of 11th-century Constantinople in the exciting company of Demetrios and a band of fierce Celts, while a Norman barbarian army lays siege. Harper, a student of medieval history at Oxford, provides a great start to a promising series.

Where it's reviewed:
Kirkus Reviews, April 1, 2005, page 388
Publishers Weekly, May 16, 2005, page 43

Other books by the same author:
Knights of the Cross, 2005

Other books you might like:
Colin Falconer, *The Sultan's Harem*, 2004
Alan Gordon, *A Death in the Venetian Quarter*, 2002
Susan Moody, *Mosaic*, 1991
Mary Reed, *The John the Eunuch Series*, 1999-
    Eric Mayer, co-author
Susan Shwartz, *Cross and Crescent*, 1997

Historical

907

MO HAYDER

The Devil of Nanking

(New York: Grove, 2005)

Story type: Historical/World War II
Subject(s): War; China; Massacres
Major character(s): Grey Hutchins, Young Woman; Shi Chongming, Professor
Time period(s): 1930s (1937); 21st century
Locale(s): Tokyo, Japan; Nanking, China

Summary: This literary thriller divides its focus between contemporary Tokyo and the 1937 massacre of Nanking in which Japanese troops conducted unspeakable atrocities against the city's populace. Englishwoman Grey Hutchins searches for film of the massacre which is in the possession of Shi Chongming, a survivor teaching at a Tokyo university. To gain it, Grey takes a job as a hostess at a night club whose mobster owner may possess the power for her to get the film from the Chinese professor. Grey's experiences alternate with Shi Chongming's harrowing 1937 diary.

Where it's reviewed:
Kirkus Reviews, February 15, 2005, page 192
Publishers Weekly, January 31, 2005, page 48

Other books by the same author:
Tokyo, 2004
The Treatment, 2001
Birdman, 1999

Other books you might like:
Stephen D. Becker, *The Last Mandarin*, 1979
William Marshall, *Shanghai*, 1979
Christopher New, *Shanghai*, 1985
Paul West, *The Tent of Orange Mist*, 1995
Zhaoyan Ye, *Nanjing 1937*, 2003

908

HOMER HICKAM

The Ambassador's Son

(New York: Thomas Dunne, 2004)

Story type: Historical/World War II
Subject(s): World War II; Sea Stories
Major character(s): Josh Thurlow, Military Personnel (Coast Guard commander); John Fitzgerald Kennedy, Historical Figure, Military Personnel; Richard Nixon, Historical Figure, Military Personnel
Time period(s): 1940s (1943)
Locale(s): Solomon Islands

Summary: Following *The Keeper's Son*, Hickam continues the story of U.S. Coast Guard Commander Josh Thurlow and his North Carolina crew. It is 1943, and Thurlow and his men are fighting the Japanese around the Pacific's Solomon Islands. Thurlow is given the mission of finding a deserter, a cousin of President Franklin D. Roosevelt. He is assisted by a young Navy lieutenant, John Fitzgerald Kennedy, who is awaiting court-martial for losing his boat, PT-109. The mismatched pair must deal with the Japanese, cannibals, and a cult leader. Into the mix appears a young but recognizable Richard Nixon.

Where it's reviewed:
Booklist, January 1, 2005, page 783
Publishers Weekly, February 7, 2005, page 41

Other books by the same author:
The Keeper's Son, 2003
Back to the Moon, 1999

Other books you might like:
Stephen W. Frey, *The Legacy*, 1998
John J. Gobbell, *A Code for Tomorrow*, 1999
James A. Michener, *Tales of the South Pacific*, 1949
David Poyer, *The Only Thing to Fear*, 1995
James Webb, *The Emperor's General*, 1999

909

ELIZABETH HICKEY

The Painted Kiss

(New York: Atria, 2005)

Story type: Historical/Victorian
Subject(s): Artists and Art; Art
Major character(s): Gustav Klimt, Historical Figure, Artist; Emilie Floege, Historical Figure, Artist
Time period(s): 19th century; 20th century
Locale(s): Vienna, Austria

Summary: Art historian Hickey's debut novel traces the relationship between artist Gustav Klimt and Emilie Floege, the woman who inspired Klimt's most famous painting, *The Kiss*. Set in fin-de-siecle Vienna, the novel dramatizes the young painter's relationship with his model, and her development as a designer.

Where it's reviewed:
Kirkus Reviews, March 1, 2005, page 249

Other books you might like:
Susan M. Dodd, *The Silent Woman*, 2001
J.D. Landis, *Longing*, 2000
Barbara Mujica, *Frida*, 2001
Max Phillips, *The Artist Wife*, 2001
Emma Tennant, *Sylvia and Ted*, 2001

910

PAULINE HOLDSTOCK

A Rare and Curious Gift

(New York: Norton, 2005)

Story type: Historical/Seventeenth Century
Subject(s): Artists and Art; Women
Major character(s): Sofonisba Fabroni, Artist (painter); Orazio Fabroni, Artist (painter), Parent; Matteo Tassi, Artist (sculptor)
Time period(s): 17th century
Locale(s): Florence, Italy

Summary: Based loosely on the life of Artemisia Gentileschi, the Florentine painter, the novel traces the development of Sofonisba Fabroni, daughter of painter Orazio Fabroni. From

assisting her father, Sofonisba grows into an accomplished artist in her own right while contending with a difficult relationship with sculptor Matteo Tassi. The catalyst to generate the novel's conflict is the arrival of a young female slave with strangely mottled skin. She becomes an object of fascination for the artists and of fear by the community. This is a vivid, at times graphic, look at the era from the intriguing angle of a woman's perspective.

Where it's reviewed:
Booklist, January 1, 2005, page 817
Kirkus Reviews, December 1, 2004, page 1107
New York Times Book Review, March 6, 2005, page 17
Publishers Weekly, November 8, 2004, page 32

Other books by the same author:
Beyond Measure, 2003
The Turning, 1996
House, 1994
The Burial Ground, 1991
The Blackbird's Song, 1990

Other books you might like:
Sarah Dunant, *The Birth of Venus*, 2003
Alexandra Lapierre, *Artemisia*, 2000
Barbara Mujica, *Frida*, 2001
Nina Schuyler, *The Painting*, 2004
Susan Vreeland, *The Passion of Artemisia*, 2002

911

LINDA HOLEMAN

The Linnet Bird

(New York: Crown, 2005)

Story type: Historical/Victorian
Subject(s): Prostitution; Indian Empire; Homosexuality/Lesbianism
Major character(s): Linny Gow, Prostitute; Somers Ingram, Spouse (of Linny), Homosexual
Time period(s): 1830s (1839)
Locale(s): Liverpool, England; Calcutta, India

Summary: This Victorian-era tale follows the adventures of Linny Gow from Liverpool where, after her mother's death, her father begins prostituting her at the age of 12. She manages to immigrate to India for a fresh start but is coerced into a loveless marriage with the abusive homosexual Somers Ingram. The novel traces Linny's rebellion and resistance to repressive customs against a colorful period backdrop of the Indian Raj.

Where it's reviewed:
Library Journal, May 1, 2005, page 74

Other books you might like:
David Davidar, *The House of Blue Mangoes*, 2002
Ruth Prawer Jhabvala, *Heat and Dust*, 1975
Susanna Moore, *One Last Look*, 2003
Rebecca Ryman, *Shalimar*, 1999
Carolyn Slaughter, *A Black Englishman*, 2004

912

RUPERT HOLMES

Swing

(New York: Random House, 2005)

Story type: Historical; Mystery
Subject(s): Mystery and Detective Stories; Music and Musicians
Major character(s): Ray Sherwood, Musician
Time period(s): 1940s (1940)
Locale(s): San Francisco, California

Summary: This innovative mystery comes equipped with a CD of original music and illustrations making it a true multimedia experience. Set during the 1940 San Francisco Golden Gate International Exposition, the mystery has jazz musician Ray Sherwood investigate when a woman falls to her death at his feet. The music on the CD, written and orchestrated by Holmes, refers to the action in the novel and contains clues to the mystery's solution. Great fun.

Where it's reviewed:
Kirkus Reviews, January 15, 2005, page 73
New York Times Book Review, March 27, 2005, page 21
Publishers Weekly, January 31, 2005, page 49

Other books by the same author:
Where the Truth Lies, 2003

Other books you might like:
Roddy Doyle, *Oh, Play That Thing*, 2004
Jack Fuller, *The Best of Jackson Payne*, 2000
Jonathan Kellerman, *A Cold Heart*, 2003
Paule Marshall, *The Fisher King*, 2000
Fay Weldon, *Leader of the Band*, 1989

913

SUZANNE HUDSON

In the Dark of the Moon

(San Francisco: MacAdam/Cage, 2005)

Story type: Historical/Depression Era; Family Saga
Subject(s): Racial Conflict; Mothers and Daughters; Family Relations
Major character(s): Elizabeth Lacey, Young Woman; Kansas Lacey, Young Woman
Time period(s): 20th century (1929-1962)
Locale(s): Georgia

Summary: Hudson's novel dramatizes racism in the South through multiple generations of a southern family. Elizabeth Lacey is impregnated and abandoned by a traveling salesman and eventually commits suicide, leaving behind a daughter, Kansas. She learns the truth about her family and their connection to local lynchings from her black nanny. This is a graphic and emotional novel that explores important issues in the South in transition towards the Civil Rights movement.

Where it's reviewed:
Library Journal, May 15, 2005, page 106

Other books by the same author:
In a Temple of Trees, 2003

Historical

Opposable Thumbs, 2001

Other books you might like:
William Cobb, *A Walk through Fire*, 1992
John Grisham, *The Chamber*, 1994
Anthony Grooms, *Bombingham*, 2001
Sena Jeter Naslund, *Four Spirits*, 2003
Lillian Eugenia Smith, *Strange Fruit*, 1944

914

CONN IGGULDEN

Emperor: The Field of Swords
(New York: Delacorte, 2005)

Story type: Historical/Ancient Rome
Series: Emperor. Book 3
Subject(s): Biography; Roman Empire; Politics
Major character(s): Julius Caesar, Historical Figure, Military Personnel; Marcus Junius Brutus, Historical Figure, Political Figure; Pompey the Great, Historical Figure, Military Personnel
Time period(s): 1st century B.C.
Locale(s): Rome, Roman Empire

Summary: In the third of a projected four-volume fictional biography of Julius Caesar, the military commander enters the dangerous arena of Roman politics. Aided by his fellow general Marcus Brutus, Caesar forms an alliance with Pompey and Crassus, and is elected consul. His campaigns against Vercingetorix in Gaul and expedition into Britain add to his glory and power. The novel ends as Caesar learns that Pompey has betrayed him, and Caesar and Brutus prepare to cross the Rubicon and march on Rome.

Where it's reviewed:
Kirkus Reviews, January 1, 2005, page 11
Publishers Weekly, February 21, 2005, page 52

Other books by the same author:
Emperor: The Death of Kings, 2004
Emperor: The Gates of Rome, 2003

Other books you might like:
Colin Falconer, *When We Were Gods*, 2000
Margaret George, *The Memoirs of Cleopatra*, 1997
Allan Massie, *Caesar*, 1994
Colleen McCullough, *Fortune's Favorites*, 1993
Thornton Wilder, *The Ides of March*, 1948

915

GRAHAM ISON

Hardcastle's Armistice
(Sutton, England: Severn House, 2004)

Story type: Historical/World War I; Mystery
Series: Hardcastle. Book 2
Subject(s): World War I; Mystery and Detective Stories
Major character(s): Ernest Hardcastle, Detective—Police
Time period(s): 1910s (1918)
Locale(s): London, England

Summary: As London celebrates the end of the Great War in 1918, Detective Inspector Ernest Hardcastle investigates the brutal murder of a prostitute and a connected case of blackmail. Hardcastle is unrelenting in his search for the truth that takes him on an impressive tour of World War I-era London.

Where it's reviewed:
Booklist, January 1, 2005, page 827
Kirkus Reviews, February 1, 2005, page 152

Other books by the same author:
Hardcastle's Spy, 2004
Whiplash, 2004
Light Fantastic, 2003
Working Girl, 2002
Division, 1997

Other books you might like:
Philippa Gregory, *The Favored Child*, 2003
Lilian Nattel, *The Singing Fire*, 2004
Anne Perry, *No Graves as Yet*, 2003
David Roberts, *The Bones of the Buried*, 2001
Charles Todd, *A Cold Treachery*, 2005

916

MARIE JAKOBER

Sons of Liberty
(New York: Forge, 2005)

Story type: Historical/American Civil War
Subject(s): Civil War; Resistance Movements; City and Town Life
Major character(s): Branden Rolfe, Military Personnel; Langdon Everett, Resistance Fighter
Time period(s): 1860s (1862)
Locale(s): Baltimore, Maryland

Summary: Canadian author Jakober continues her chronicle of neglected aspects of the American Civil War with this account of the battle for Baltimore. The Union-held city with a prominent pro-Confederate population is under the command of Branden Rolfe, a former Austrian revolutionary, now Union Provost Marshal. He must contend with a secret group of secessionists, the Sons of Liberty, led by the dedicated Langdon Everett, who musters popular support and a considerable cache of weapons and explosives. Rolfe must rely on a network of spies to penetrate the group and stop it before the city is lost.

Where it's reviewed:
Kirkus Reviews, May 15, 2005, page 559

Other books by the same author:
Only Call Us Faithful, 2002
The Black Chalice, 2000
Sandinista, 1985

Other books you might like:
Bernard Cornwell, *The Bloody Ground*, 1996
Richard Croker, *To Make Men Free*, 2004
Thomas Fleming, *A Passionate Girl*, 2004
C.X. Moreau, *Promise of Glory*, 2000
Owen Parry, *The Bold Sons of Erin*, 2003

917

ANDREW C.A. JAMPOLER

Sailors in the Holy Land

(Annapolis, Maryland: Naval Institute Press, 2004)

Story type: Historical/Exotic
Subject(s): Sea Stories; Adventure and Adventurers; Military Life
Major character(s): William Lynch, Historical Figure, Military Personnel (naval officer)
Time period(s): 1840s (1848)
Locale(s): Ottoman Empire

Summary: Jampoler, a retired naval aviator, provides a narrative account of an actual U.S. Navy expedition to the Dead Sea in search of the ruins of the cities of Sodom and Gomorrah and proof of the literal truth of the Bible. The expedition's leader is Lt. William Lynch, and the band of explorers launch two small boats on the Sea of Galilee to run the Jordan rapids to the Dead Sea. The account of the expedition comes largely from Lynch's perspective, with vivid glimpses of shipboard life during the period, as well as many key political developments of the time.

Other books you might like:
Alev Lytle Croutier, *The Palace of Tears*, 2000
Jean-Christophe Rufin, *The Abyssinian*, 1999
Jean-Christophe Rufin, *The Siege of Isfahan*, 2001
John Vernon, *The Last Canyon*, 2001
John Wilson, *North with Franklin*, 2000

918

JEFF JANODA

Saga: A Novel of Medieval Iceland

(Chicago: Academy Chicago Publishers, 2005)

Story type: Historical/Medieval
Subject(s): Middle Ages; Legends; Vikings
Major character(s): Arnkel, Chieftain; Snorri, Chieftain
Time period(s): 10th century
Locale(s): Iceland

Summary: This first novel retells the Icelandic *Saga of the People of Eyri* as a historical novel chronicling the first Viking Icelandic settlements. The story concerns the campaign of vengeance of Norse chieftain Arnkel who is determined to gain back his inheritance, putting him in bloody conflict with rival chieftain Snorri. Janoda, an expert on Norse culture, uses his research to advantage in this recreation of life in a Norse Icelandic community.

Where it's reviewed:
Booklist, May 15, 2005, page 1648

Other books you might like:
Bernard Assiniwi, *The Beothuk Saga*, 2002
Michael Crichton, *Eaters of the Dead*, 1976
Jan Fridegard, *Land of Wooden Gods*, 1989
Cecelia Holland, *The Soul Thief*, 2002
Henry Treece, *Viking's Dawn*, 1956

919

JOSEPH KANON

Alibi

(New York: Henry Holt, 2005)

Story type: Historical/World War II; Mystery
Subject(s): World War II; Mystery and Detective Stories
Major character(s): Adam Miller, Military Personnel (war crimes investigator); Claudia Grassini, Survivor; Gianni Mangioni, Doctor
Time period(s): 1940s (1946)
Locale(s): Venice, Italy

Summary: Kanon's thriller is set in post-World War II Venice as war crimes investigator Adam Miller visits his widowed mother and tries to forget the horrors he has experienced. He falls in love with Claudia Grassini, an Italian Jew with a complex history. Adam's mother has a romance as well, with Doctor Gianni Mangioni, whom Adam suspects of hiding secrets about his past, particularly during the German occupation. Adam's investigation escalates when murder occurs.

Where it's reviewed:
Kirkus Reviews, March 1, 2005, page 250

Other books by the same author:
The Good German, 2001
The Prodigal Spy, 1998
Los Alamos, 1997

Other books you might like:
Cara Black, *Murder in the Marais*, 1999
Jonathan Hull, *Losing Julia*, 2000
Helen MacInnes, *The Venetian Affair*, 1963
William Riviere, *By the Grand Canal*, 2005
Thomas Sanchez, *Day of the Bees*, 2000

920

THOMAS KELLY

Empire Rising

(New York: Farrar, Straus and Giroux, 2005)

Story type: Historical/Depression Era
Subject(s): Irish Americans; City and Town Life; Construction
Major character(s): Michael Briody, Immigrant, Worker (steelworker); Johnny Farrell, Organized Crime Figure, Lawyer; Grace Masterson, Artist
Time period(s): 1930s
Locale(s): New York, New York

Summary: The construction of the Empire State Building during the 1930s is the focus for this lively historical and cultural chronicle of life in New York City during the Depression. The wheeling-and-dealing to get the building constructed is reflected through the relationships among Johnny Farrell, a bagman for Mayor Jimmy Walker; his artist girlfriend Grace Masterson; and Irish-American steelworker Michael Briody. This fascinating novel offers glimpses of a large cast of historical figures, including Governor Franklin Delano Roosevelt, Mayor Walker, Judge Joseph Crater, and Al Smith, who is put in charge of the construction of the world's tallest building.

Historical

Where it's reviewed:
Booklist, December 15, 2004, page 708
Kirkus Reviews, November 15, 2004, page 1063
Library Journal, January 2005, page 98
New York Times Book Review, February 13, 2005, page 12
Publishers Weekly, January 17, 2005, page 34

Other books by the same author:
The Rackets, 2001
Payback, 1997

Other books you might like:
Colin Bateman, *Empire State*, 1997
Carolyn Chute, *Snow Man*, 1999
Nelson DeMille, *Cathedral*, 1981
Pietro D. Donato, *Christ in Concrete*, 1939
Pete Hamill, *Forever*, 2003

921

ELMER KELTON

Sons of Texas
(New York: Forge, 2005)

Story type: Historical/American West
Subject(s): American West; Mexicans; Frontier and Pioneer Life
Major character(s): Michael Lewis, Frontiersman; Stephen F. Austin, Historical Figure, Political Figure; Andrew Lewis, Frontiersman
Time period(s): 1810s; 1820s
Locale(s): Texas; Tennessee

Summary: Set mainly in Mexican-ruled Texas, Kelton's novel describes an excursion in 1816 of the Lewis clan of Tennessee into Texas to capture wild horses. The patriarch is killed and Michael goes home. With his brother Andrew, Michael returns to Texas with the first American settlers to gain revenge, as well as a new life for themselves. They encounter Stephen F. Austin, the leader of the new American colony in Texas. A second and third installment is slated to cover the Battle of the Alamo and the war for Texas independence.

Where it's reviewed:
Kirkus Reviews, April 15, 2005, page 440
Publishers Weekly, April 25, 2005, page 37

Other books by the same author:
Jericho's Road, 2004
Texas Vendetta, 2004
Lone Star Rising, 2003
The War of the Coyote, 2001
Badger Boy, 2000

Other books you might like:
James A. Michener, *Texas*, 1985
E.V. Thompson, *Republic: A Novel of Texas*, 1985
Guy Vanderhaeghe, *The Last Crossing*, 2004
Richard S. Wheeler, *The Deliverance*, 2003
Don Worcester, *Gone to Texas*, 1993

922

PHILIP KERR

Hitler's Peace
(New York: Putnam, 2005)

Story type: Historical/World War II; Espionage Thriller
Subject(s): World War II; Espionage
Major character(s): Willard Mayer, Spy, Professor (philosophy); Walter Schellenberger, Spy; Franklin Delano Roosevelt, Historical Figure, Political Figure
Time period(s): 1940s (1943)
Locale(s): Teheran, Iran

Summary: Kerr imagines what might have happened had Adolf Hitler put out peace feelers in 1943 and tried to split the Allies. When the Nazis learn of the secret summit in Teheran, Iran, Hitler orders a hit on the Big Three (Franklin Delano Roosevelt, Winston Churchill, and Josef Stalin). The intrigue is witnessed by OSS agent Walter Schellenberger and philosophy professor Willard Mayer, a Roosevelt adviser. The novel remains close to the historical facts and includes appearances by FDR, Hitler, Churchill, Stalin, Heinrich Himmler, Martin Bormann, Vyacheslav Molotov, and even Kim Philby, Anthony Blunt, and Evelyn Waugh.

Where it's reviewed:
Kirkus Reviews, March 15, 2005, page 308
Library Journal, April 15, 2005, page 74
Publishers Weekly, April 18, 2005, page 44

Other books by the same author:
Dark Matter, 2002
The Second Angel, 1999
A Five Year Plan, 1997
The Grid, 1995
Berlin Noir, 1993

Other books you might like:
Alan Furst, *Blood of Victory*, 2002
Christopher Reich, *The Runner*, 2000
William Riviere, *By the Grand Canal*, 2005
Daniel Silva, *The English Assassin*, 2002
Robert Wilson, *The Company of Strangers*, 2001

923

MERCEDES LACKEY
ROBERTA GELLIS, Co-Author

Ill Met by Moonlight
(New York: Baen, 2005)

Story type: Historical/Fantasy; Historical/Elizabethan
Subject(s): Kings, Queens, Rulers, etc.; Occult; Witches and Witchcraft
Major character(s): Elizabeth I, Historical Figure, Ruler; Unseleighe Sidhe, Witch; Denoriel, Witch
Time period(s): 16th century
Locale(s): England

Summary: The authors present an alternative, fantasy view of the succession of Elizabeth I to the throne in the 16th century. The evil witch queen Unseleighe Sidhe is determined to prevent Henry VIII's daughter from reaching the throne; the

good Sidhe, Denoriel, is just as determined to foil any attempt to kidnap Elizabeth and replace her with a changeling. This historical fantasy is an intriguing blend of Celtic folklore and history.

Other books by the same author:
This Scepter'd Isle, 2004

Other books you might like:
Marion Zimmer Bradley, *The Forest House*, 1993
Elizabeth Cunningham, *Daughter of the Shining Isles*, 2000
Morgan Llywelyn, *Druids*, 1991
Juilene Osborne-McKnight, *I Am of Irelaunde*, 2000
Edward Rutherfurd, *The Princes of Ireland*, 2004

924

LORNA LANDVIK

Oh My Stars

(New York: Ballantine, 2005)

Story type: Historical/Depression Era
Subject(s): Small Town Life; Music and Musicians
Major character(s): Violet Mathers, Teenager; Kjel Hedstrom, Musician; Austin Sykes, Musician
Time period(s): 1930s (1937)
Locale(s): Kentucky; North Dakota

Summary: This Depression-era story follows the improbable adventures of Violet Mathers, abandoned by her mother, abused by her father, and victim of an accident in which she loses her arm. She sets out by bus to get to the Golden Gate Bridge, from which she plans to jump, but when her bus crashes she falls in with two aspiring musicians—Kjel Hedstrom and Austin Sykes. Violet serves as the manager of their band, the Pearltones, who travel into the South for encounters with the Ku Klux Klan. The fairy-tale aspect of the ugly duckling transformed is balanced by solid period and regional reconstruction.

Where it's reviewed:
Publishers Weekly, April 4, 2005, page 45

Other books by the same author:
Angry Housewives Eating Bon Bons, 2003
Welcome to the Great Mysterious, 2000
The Tall Pine Polka, 1999
Your Oasis on Flame Lake, 1997
Patty Jane's House of Curl, 1995

Other books you might like:
Louise Erdrich, *The Beet Queen*, 1986
Aaron Roy Even, *Bloodroot*, 2000
Larry McMurtry, *Loop Group*, 2004
Susan Power, *The Grass Dancer*, 1994
Sharon Rolens, *Worthy's Town*, 2000

925

STEPHANIE LAURENS

The Truth about Love

(New York: William Morrow, 2005)

Story type: Family Saga; Historical/Regency

Series: Cynster. Book 12
Subject(s): Family Relations; Romance
Major character(s): Gerrard Debbington, Gentleman; Jacqueline Tregonning, Gentlewoman
Time period(s): 1800s
Locale(s): London, England

Summary: In this installment of Laurens' Regency-era Cynster family saga, the focus is on Gerrard Debbington who falls in love with Jacqueline Tregonning. Ensconced in Hellebore Hall, Gerrard soon must come to the defense of his new bride who is accused of being a double murderess.

Where it's reviewed:
Publishers Weekly, February 28, 2005, page 42

Other books by the same author:
The Ideal Bride, 2004
The Lady Chosen, 2003
The Perfect Lover, 2003
On a Wild Night, 2002
The Promise in a Kiss, 2001

Other books you might like:
Brian Cleeve, *Sara*, 1976
Jane Aiken Hodge, *Caterina*, 1999
Carla Kelly, *With This Ring*, 1997
Sheila Simonson, *Lady Elizabeth's Comet*, 1985
Joanna Trollope, *Eliza Standhope*, 1979

926

ELMORE LEONARD

The Hot Kid

(New York: William Morrow, 2005)

Story type: Historical/Depression Era
Subject(s): Crime and Criminals
Major character(s): Carlos Webster, Lawman; Emmet Long, Outlaw; Jack Belmont, Criminal
Time period(s): 1930s
Locale(s): Oklahoma

Summary: The title of Leonard's Depression era crime story refers to the part-Cuban, part-Indian Carlos Webster who becomes a U.S. marshal and gains notoriety by bringing bank robber Emmet Long to justice. Webster's celebrity brings him into conflict with Jack Belmont who intends to become public enemy number one. This is a perfect pitch period crime novel with a colorful cast.

Where it's reviewed:
Booklist, March 15, 2005, page 1246
Library Journal, April 15, 2005, page 74
New York Times Book Review, May 8, 2005, page 1
Publishers Weekly, March 28, 2005, page 55

Other books by the same author:
Mr. Paradise, 2004
Tishomingo Blues, 2002
Cuba Libre, 1998
Get Shorty, 1990
Glitz, 1985

Other books you might like:
James Carlos Blake, *A World of Thieves*, 2002

Historical

Edna Ferber, *Cimarron*, 1930
Barbara Kingsolver, *Pigs in Heaven*, 1993
Larry McMurtry, *Pretty Boy Floyd*, 1994
    Diana Ossama, co-author
Toni Morrison, *Paradise*, 1998

927

ANDREA LEVY

Small Island

(New York: Picador, 2005)

Story type: Historical/World War II
Subject(s): Race Relations; Family Relations
Major character(s): Gilbert Joseph, Veteran; Hortense Joseph, Spouse (of Gilbert); Queenie Bligh, Landlord
Time period(s): 1940s (1948)
Locale(s): England; Jamaica

Summary: This winner of the 2004 Whitbread Book of the Year Award and the 2004 Orange Prize (the first novel ever so honored with both awards) draws on its author's Jamaican background in a story about two couples—one English and one Jamaican—in World War II-era England. Jamaican Gilbert Joseph volunteers for the RAF, and, after marrying Hortense, a Jamaican teacher, immigrates to Britain after the war to study law. The couple's experiences in Britain and with their landlady, Queenie Bligh, and her husband Bernard, dramatize the clash of cultures and race in Britain.

Where it's reviewed:
Kirkus Reviews, February 15, 2005, page 192
Publishers Weekly, March 7, 2005, page 50

Other books by the same author:
Never Far from Nowhere, 1996

Other books you might like:
Jill Barnett, *Sentimental Journey*, 2001
Ann Howard Creel, *The Magic of Ordinary Days*, 2001
Robb Forman Dew, *The Evidence Against Her*, 2001
Jane Gardam, *The Flight of the Maidens*, 2001
Allen Morris Jones, *Last Year's River*, 2001

928

MORGAN LLYWELYN

1972

(New York: Forge, 2005)

Story type: Political
Subject(s): Irish Republican Army; Religious Conflict; Terrorism
Major character(s): Barry Halloran, Revolutionary, Photographer; Barbara Kavanagh, Singer
Time period(s): 20th century (1950-1972)
Locale(s): Ireland; Ireland, Northern

Summary: Llywelyn continues to document 20th-century Irish history with an exploration of the conflict in Northern Ireland that culminated in 1972 with Bloody Sunday in Derry. Llywelyn centers her account on the activities of Barry Halloran, the son and grandson of Irish Republicans who joins the IRA to unify the country. Barry's sobering experience with violence and the contradictions inherent in Northern Ireland takes him through a career as a photographer documenting the bloodshed, into an affair with an American singer, and into the center of the violence in Derry that shocked the world.

Where it's reviewed:
Kirkus Reviews, February 1, 2005, page 149

Other books by the same author:
1949, 2003
1921, 2001
1916, 1998
Pride of Lions, 1996
The Last Prince of Ireland, 1992

Other books you might like:
Frank Delaney, *Ireland*, 2005
Aidan Higgins, *Langrishe, Go Down*, 2004
Neil Jordan, *Shade*, 2004
Regina McBride, *The Marriage Bed*, 2004
John McGahern, *The Barracks*, 2004

929

MICHELE CLAIRE LUCAS

A High and Hidden Place

(San Francisco: HarperSanFrancisco, 2005)

Story type: Historical/World War II
Subject(s): World War II; Family Life; Massacres
Major character(s): Christine Lenoir, Journalist
Time period(s): 1940s; 1960s
Locale(s): France; United States

Summary: In the 1960s, journalist Christine Lenoir delves into her past in wartime France and learns that her parents were among the 642 men, women, and children rounded up and killed on June 10, 1944 in the French village of Oradour-sur-Glane, just outside of Limoges. Lucas' first novel alternates between Lenoir's later life during the period of Kennedy's assassination and the details of the massacre.

Where it's reviewed:
Kirkus Reviews, January 15, 2005, page 77
Library Journal, February 1, 2005, page 62

Other books you might like:
Linda D. Cirino, *Eva's Story*, 2000
James D. Forman, *Ceremonies of Innocence*, 1970
David Fraser, *The Fortunes of War*, 1985
Ian MacMillan, *Village of a Million Spirits*, 1999
Elio Romano, *A Generation of Wrath*, 1986

930

ANDREI MAKINE

The Earth and Sky of Jacques Dorme

(New York: Arcade, 2005)

Story type: Historical/World War II
Subject(s): World War II
Major character(s): Jacques Dorme, Military Personnel (French fighter pilot); Alexandra, Nurse; Unnamed Character, Narrator, Writer (of novel)

Time period(s): 1940s; 1950s
Locale(s): Stalingrad, Union of Soviet Socialist Republics

Summary: Makine closes his 20th-century Russian trilogy, preceded by *Dreams of My Russian Summers* and *Requiem for a Lost Empire* with this narrative beginning in wartime Stalingrad. Narrated by an unnamed, middle-aged protagonist, the story traces the tragic love affair between a French fighter pilot, Jacques Dorme, and a nurse named Alexandra. Jacques escapes a German POW camp and makes his way to Stalingrad, where he meets Alexandra, before being killed. Their story is interwoven with the experiences of the narrator, growing up in a Russian orphanage and his interactions with Alexandra as he later writes a novel based on Dorme's life.

Where it's reviewed:
Library Journal, February 1, 2005, page 69
Publishers Weekly, December 20, 2004, page 34

Other books by the same author:
Music of a Life, 2002
Requiem for a Lost Empire, 2001
The Crime of Olga Arbyelina, 1999
Once upon the River Love, 1998
Dreams of My Russian Summers, 1997

Other books you might like:
Dennis Bock, *The Ash Garden*, 2001
Lorenzo Carcaterra, *Street Boys*, 2002
Monique Charlesworth, *The Children's War*, 2004
David L. Robbins, *The War of the Rats*, 1999
Paullina Simons, *The Bronze Horseman*, 2000

931

EDWARD MARSTON (Pseudonym of Keith Miles)

The Excursion Train
(London: Allison & Busby, 2005)

Story type: Mystery; Historical/Victorian
Subject(s): Mystery and Detective Stories; Railroads; Crime and Criminals
Major character(s): Robert Colbeck, Detective—Police
Time period(s): 1850s (1852)
Locale(s): London, England

Summary: Marston returns with another installment of his Victorian mystery series featuring Detective Inspector Robert Colbeck, who investigates murder on an excursion train to Maidenhead bound for an illegal bare-knuckle prizefight. The solution to the grisly murder lies in the dead man's secrets that Colbeck must uncover. Rich in historical detail, the novel also features a winning cast of characters.

Where it's reviewed:
Kirkus Reviews, May 1, 2005, page 514
Library Journal, May 1, 2005, page 66

Other books by the same author:
The Frost Fair, 2004
The Railroad Detective, 2004
The Domesday Book Series, 1993-
The Nicholas Bracewell Series, 1988-

Other books you might like:
Carola Dunn, *Murder on the Flying Scotsman*, 1997

Elizabeth Howard, *A Scent of Murder*, 1987
Peter Lovesey, *The Sergeant Cribb/Constable Thackeray Series*, 1970-1978
Roberta Rogow, *The Charles Dodgson/Arthur Conan Doyle Series*, 1998-
James Wilson, *The Dark Clue*, 2001

932

EDWARD MARSTON (Pseudonym of Keith Miles)

The Malevolent Comedy
(New York: St. Martin's Minotaur, 2005)

Story type: Historical/Elizabethan; Mystery
Series: Nicholas Bracewell. Book 15
Subject(s): Mystery and Detective Stories; Theater
Major character(s): Nicholas Bracewell, Producer (theatrical), Detective—Amateur; Saul Hibbert, Writer (playwright); Edmund Hoode, Writer (playwright)
Time period(s): 16th century
Locale(s): London, England

Summary: When the resident playwright of the Elizabethan acting company, the Westfield's Men, Edmund Hoode, is hit with writer's block, the company turns to an unknown writer, Saul Hibbert, for their new work, the *Malevolent Comedy*. When it is first performed, one of the actors is poisoned, and on its next performance, a stray dog bites one of the actors. Nicholas Bracewell is convinced that someone is bent on ruining the production, and he sets out to get to the bottom of things. Marston excels at harnessing a lively story to a colorful depiction of the Elizabethan theatrical world.

Where it's reviewed:
Kirkus Reviews, June 1, 2005, page 613

Other books by the same author:
The Excursion Train, 2005
The Frost Fair, 2004
The Railroad Detective, 2004
The Domesday Book Series, 1993-
The Nicholas Bracewell Series, 1988-

Other books you might like:
Fiona Buckley, *A Pawn for a Queen*, 2002
Stephanie Cowell, *The Players*, 1997
Simon Hawke, *The Slaying of the Shrew*, 2001
Kate Sedley, *The Roger the Chapman Series*, 1991-
Leonard Tourney, *The Matthew Stock Series*, 1980-

933

PATRICK MCCORMACK

The Last Companion
(New York: Carroll & Graf, 2005)

Story type: Historical/Fantasy; Legend
Series: Albion. Book 1
Subject(s): Arthurian Legends; Legends; Knights and Knighthood
Major character(s): Budoc, Knight (former), Recluse; Vortepor of Dyfed, Warlord; Eremon, Mercenary
Time period(s): 5th century

Locale(s): England

Summary: McCormack makes his U.S. debut with the first of his Albion series set in Britain following the death of King Arthur. The story centers on a hermit, Budoc, who is actually the last of Arthur's fabled knights and the guardian of the holy relic that legitimized Arthur's rule. The warlord Vortepor of Dyfed sends Irish mercenary Eremon to find the relic to make Vortepor king of all Britain. Budoc, aided by a Saxon boy and a peasant girl, protects the relic from Eremon's attacks. Flashbacks depict events during Arthur's reign.

Where it's reviewed:
Kirkus Reviews, December 15, 2004, page 1160

Other books by the same author:
The White Phantom, 2000

Other books you might like:
Bernard Cornwell, *The Arthurian Warlord Chronicles*, 1996-1998
Parke Godwin, *Firelord*, 1980
Rosalind Miles, *The Knight of the Sacred Lake*, 2000
Jules Watson, *The White Mare*, 2005
Persia Woolley, *The Guinevere Trilogy*, 1987-1991

934

PAT MCINTOSH

The Nicholas Feast

(New York: Carroll & Graf, 2005)

Story type: Mystery; Historical/Renaissance
Series: Gil Cunningham. Book 2
Subject(s): Mystery and Detective Stories; Law; Universities and Colleges
Major character(s): Gil Cunningham, Lawyer
Time period(s): 15th century (1492)
Locale(s): Glasgow, Scotland

Summary: Gil Cunningham investigates the murder of a young actor at Glasgow University found strangled in the coalhouse. There is no end of suspects, and a wolfhound puppy named Socrates is responsible for uncovering an important clue.

Where it's reviewed:
Kirkus Reviews, May 15, 2005, page 565

Other books by the same author:
The Harper's Quine, 2004

Other books you might like:
Fiona Buckley, *A Pawn for a Queen*, 2002
Claudia Gross, *Scholarium*, 2004
Ian Morson, *The William Falconer Series*, 1994-
Robin Paige, *Death at Glamis Castle*, 2003
Ellis Peters, *The Brother Cadfael Series*, 1977-1994

935

DAN MILLMAN

The Journeys of Socrates

(San Francisco: HarperSanFrancisco, 2005)

Story type: Coming-of-Age

Subject(s): Russian Empire; Military Life; Philosophy
Major character(s): Sergei Ivanov, Military Personnel; Dmitri Zakolyev, Military Personnel
Time period(s): 19th century
Locale(s): Russia

Summary: Millman's 1980 novel, *Way of the Peaceful Warrior*, introduced the mysterious sage named Socrates. In this prequel, Millman dramatizes Socrates' early development in 19th-century Russia as the part-Jewish, part-Cossack orphan Sergei Ivanov. Sergei's coming-of-age and growing enlightenment about the way of the world takes place as he trains to become one of the czar's elite guards. When Sergei saves the life of a brutal fellow student, Dmitri Zakolyev, he makes an enemy who will play a role in Sergei's development.

Where it's reviewed:
Library Journal, April 15, 2005, page 76
Publishers Weekly, March 28, 2005, page 58

Other books by the same author:
Sacred Journey of the Peaceful Warrior, 1991
Way of the Peaceful Warrior, 1980

Other books you might like:
Henry Carlisle, *The Idealists*, 1999
    Olga Andreyev Carlisle, co-author
Emily Hanlon, *Petersburg*, 1988
Yannick Murphy, *The Sea of Trees*, 1997
Frederick Nolan, *White Nights, Red Dawn*, 1980
Karen Roberts, *The Flower Boy*, 2000

936

MARY MCGARRY MORRIS

The Lost Mother

(New York: Viking, 2005)

Story type: Historical/Depression Era
Subject(s): Family Relations; Brothers and Sisters
Major character(s): Thomas Talcott, Child; Margaret Talcott, Child; Henry Talcott, Butcher, Single Parent
Time period(s): 1930s
Locale(s): Vermont

Summary: Morris' study of a family in distress is set in Vermont during the Depression as young Thomas and Margaret Talcott are abandoned by their mother, and are forced to live with their father, Henry, an itinerant butcher, in a tent in the woods. As Henry's efforts to provide for his family fail, the children fall prey to a succession of predatory adults. It's a harrowing narrative that ably documents the impact of poverty and neglect, as well as the redemptive power of love.

Where it's reviewed:
Booklist, December 1, 2004, page 618
Kirkus Reviews, December 1, 2004, page 1110
New York Times Book Review, March 6, 2005, page 17
Publishers Weekly, January 3, 2005, page 34

Other books by the same author:
A Hole in the Universe, 2004
Fiona Range, 2000
Songs in Ordinary Time, 1995
A Dangerous Woman, 1991

Vanished, 1988

Other books you might like:
Amanda Craig, *In a Dark Wood*, 2002
Dorothy Garlock, *Mother Road*, 2003
Lori Lansens, *Rush Home Road*, 2002
Joyce Carol Oates, *Man Crazy*, 1997
Anita Shreve, *Light on the Snow*, 2004

937

KATHERINE MOSBY

Twilight

(New York: HarperCollins, 2005)

Story type: Historical/Depression Era
Subject(s): Women; Marriage
Major character(s): Lavinia Gibbs, Fiance(e); Gaston Lesseur, Banker
Time period(s): 1930s
Locale(s): New York, New York; Paris, France

Summary: Well-born Lavinia Gibbs shocks her family by breaking off her engagement and going to Paris where she begins an affair with the married French banker Gaston Lesseur. Their relationship is set against a backdrop of Paris moving ever closer to war, culminating in the German occupation. Lavinia was first introduced in Mosby's *The Season of Lillian Dawes*.

Where it's reviewed:
Library Journal, March 1, 2005, page 79
Publishers Weekly, March 14, 2005, page 42

Other books by the same author:
The Season of Lillian Dawes, 2002
Private Altars, 1995

Other books you might like:
Saul Bellow, *Ravelstein*, 2000
Francis Cottam, *The Fire Fighter*, 2002
Caroline Harvey, *The Brass Dolphin*, 1999
Marie Joseph, *The Listening Silence*, 1983
Susan Perabo, *The Broken Places*, 2001

938

ALBERT MURRAY

The Magic Keys

(New York: Pantheon, 2005)

Story type: Coming-of-Age
Subject(s): Music and Musicians; African Americans; City and Town Life
Major character(s): Scooter, Musician; Taft Edison, Writer; Roland Beasley, Artist
Time period(s): 20th century
Locale(s): New York, New York; Alabama

Summary: Musical prodigy Scooter, from Gasoline Point, Alabama, has come to New York City and is searching for his true calling. Along the way he encounters novelist Taft Edison, a fictional portrait of Ralph Ellison, and Roland Beasley,

a version of artist Romare Bearden. The novel captures with skill and grace the place, the moment, and vital characters.

Where it's reviewed:
Library Journal, May 15, 2005, page 107
New York Times Book Review, May 22, 2005, page 14

Other books by the same author:
The Seven League Boots, 1995
The Spyglass Tree, 1991
Stomping the Blues, 1976
Train Whistle Guitar, 1974
South to a Very Old Place, 1971

Other books you might like:
Gail Carson, *Dave at Night*, 1999
Pete Dexter, *Train*, 2003
Ernest J. Gaines, *A Lesson Before Dying*, 1993
Rosa Guy, *A Measure of Time*, 1983
Persia Walker, *Harlem Redux*, 2002

939

BEVERLE GRAVES MYERS

Painted Veil

(Scottsdale, Arizona: Poisoned Pen Press, 2005)

Story type: Historical/Georgian; Mystery
Series: Baroque Mystery. Book 2
Subject(s): Mystery and Detective Stories; Opera; Music and Musicians
Major character(s): Tito Amato, Singer (opera)
Time period(s): 18th century
Locale(s): Venice, Italy

Summary: In Myers' second period mystery set in the musical world of 18th-century Venice, castrato soprano Tito Amato investigates the disappearance of a scene painter. His inquiry exposes him to the dark side of Venetian life and its anti-Semitism. Myers' mystery offers an intriguing glimpse at the outsiders in that society—the castrati, Jews, and women—in a deftly handled narrative.

Where it's reviewed:
Kirkus Reviews, January 15, 2005, page 87
Publishers Weekly, February 28, 2005, page 46

Other books by the same author:
Interrupted Aria, 2004

Other books you might like:
Lawrence Goldman, *The Castrato*, 1973
John Spencer Hill, *The Last Castrato*, 1993
Ross King, *Domino*, 2002
Michele Lovric, *The Floating Book*, 2003
Jim Williams, *Scherzo*, 1999

940

JAMES L. NELSON

Thieves of Mercy

(New York: William Morrow, 2005)

Story type: Historical/American Civil War
Series: Civil War at Sea

Historical *(side margin)*

Subject(s): Civil War; Sea Stories; Military Life
Major character(s): Samuel Bowater, Military Personnel (Confederate naval officer); Wendy Atkins, Spy (accused); Mike Sullivan, Military Personnel (Confederate captain)
Time period(s): 1860s
Locale(s): Memphis, Tennessee; Norfolk, Virginia

Summary: Nelson continues the story of Confederate naval officer Samuel Bowater in this sequel to *Glory in the Name*. After the Battle of New Orleans, Bowater awaits his new command—an ironclad warship—in Memphis, having come up with riverman ''Mississippi'' Mike Sullivan. Meanwhile, Bowater's love, Wendy Atkins, tries to escape the Union army in Norfolk, Virginia, is accused of spying, is kidnapped, and is involved in the sinking of the *Merrimack*. Despite some implausibility, including Atkins' chance meeting with Abraham Lincoln, the novel is packed with authentic action.

Where it's reviewed:
Kirkus Reviews, January 15, 2005, page 78
Library Journal, February 1, 2005, page 70
Publishers Weekly, February 21, 2005, page 157

Other books by the same author:
Glory in the Name, 2003
The Blackbirder, 2001
The Sweet Trade, 2001
All the Brave Fellows, 2000
The Guardship, 2000

Other books you might like:
F. Van Wyck Mason, *Proud New Flags*, 1951
Christopher Nicole, *Iron Ships, Iron Men*, 1989
David Poyer, *A Country of Our Own*, 2003
David Poyer, *Fire on the Waters*, 2001
Willard M. Wallace, *The Raiders*, 1970

941

ALBERT NOYER

The Cybelene Conspiracy

(New Milford, Connecticut: Toby, 2005)

Story type: Mystery; Historical/Ancient Rome
Subject(s): Mystery and Detective Stories; Roman Empire
Major character(s): Getorius Asterius, Doctor; Arcadia, Religious
Time period(s): 5th century (440)
Locale(s): Ravenna, Italy

Summary: Surgeon Getorius Asterius and his wife Arcadia, an archpriest of a pagan fertility cult, investigate the death of a youth in Arcadia's church. A coded message and a Vestal Virgin lead the sleuths to a secret tunnel, the sinister temple of Cybele, and a series of deadly encounters that could change the course of western history.

Where it's reviewed:
Kirkus Reviews, April 1, 2005, page 390

Other books by the same author:
The Secundus Papyrus, 2003
The Saint's Day Deaths, 2000

Other books you might like:
Ron Burns, *Roman Shadows*, 1992

Lindsey Davis, *The Marcus Didius Falco Series*, 1989-
Mary Reed, *The John the Eunuch Series*, 1999-
   Eric Mayer, co-author
John Maddox Roberts, *The SPQR Series*, 1990-
Steven Saylor, *The Roma Sub Rosa Series*, 1991-

942

CHARLES O'BRIEN

Lethal Beauty

(Sutton, England: Severn House, 2005)

Story type: Mystery; Historical/Georgian
Series: Anne Cartier. Book 4
Subject(s): Mystery and Detective Stories; Artists and Art
Major character(s): Anne Cartier, Teacher, Detective—Amateur; Paul de Saint-Martin, Spouse (of Anne), Detective—Police
Time period(s): 1780s (1787)
Locale(s): Paris, France

Summary: Anne Cartier, a teacher of the deaf, and her husband Paul de Saint-Martin of the French police investigate the shocking death of a womanizing artist after his portrait of a noblewoman was replaced by a skull.

Where it's reviewed:
Kirkus Reviews, April 15, 2005, page 455
Publishers Weekly, May 16, 2005, page 44

Other books by the same author:
Noble Blood, 2004
Black Gold, 2002
Mute Witness, 2001

Other books you might like:
T.F. Banks, *The Thief-Taker*, 2001
Stephanie Barron, *The Jane Austen Series*, 1996-
Kathryn Davis, *Versailles*, 2002
S.K. Rizzolo, *The Rose in the Wheel*, 2002
Rosemary Stevens, *The Beau Brummell Series*, 2000-

943

SCOTT ODEN

Men of Bronze

(Palm Beach, Florida: Medallion, 2005)

Story type: Historical/Ancient Egypt
Subject(s): Ancient History; War
Major character(s): Hasdrabal Barca, Military Personnel; Jauharah, Slave
Time period(s): 6th century B.C. (526 B.C.)
Locale(s): Egypt; Palestine

Summary: This novel looks at Ancient Egypt as it struggles to survive a crippling war with the Persians. The Egyptian warrior champion is Hasdrabal Barca who must contend with the defection of one of Egypt's most celebrated generals and is sustained by the spirit of an Arabian slave girl, Jauharah. His mettle will be tested in the final conflict that will seal the fate of the pharaohs.

Where it's reviewed:
Publishers Weekly, April 25, 2005, page 37

Other books you might like:
Paula Gedge, *House of Illusions*, 1996
Steven Pressfield, *Gates of Fire*, 1998
Wilbur A. Smith, *River God*, 1994
Judith Tarr, *Lord of the Two Lands*, 1993
Gene Wolfe, *Soldier of the Mist*, 1986

944

ROBERT B. PARKER

Appaloosa

(New York: Putnam, 2005)

Story type: Historical/American West
Subject(s): American West; Law Enforcement
Major character(s): Virgil Cole, Lawman; Everett Hitch, Lawman; Randall Bragg, Rancher
Time period(s): 19th century
Locale(s): Appaloosa, West

Summary: Parker's second western, following *Gunman's Rhapsody*, is set in the mining/ranching town of Appaloosa and tells the story of lawmen Virgil Cole and Everett Hitch who take on corrupt rancher Randall Bragg. They manage to arrest Bragg and gain his conviction for murder, but a jail escape and chase are just two of the twists in this thoroughly entertaining western that abides by the traditions of the form but with an impressive freshness.

Where it's reviewed:
Kirkus Reviews, March 15, 2005, page 310
Library Journal, May 15, 2005, page 108
Publishers Weekly, March 28, 2005, page 53

Other books by the same author:
Gunman's Rhapsody, 2001
Paper Doll, 1993
Double Deuce, 1992
Pastime, 1991
Valediction, 1984

Other books you might like:
Randy Lee Eickhoff, *The Fourth Horseman*, 1998
Loren D. Estleman, *Bloody Season*, 1988
Bruce Olds, *Bucking the Tiger*, 2001
Leslie Scott, *Tombstone Showdown*, 1957
Paul West, *O.K.: The Corral, the Earps, and Doc Holliday*, 2000

945

OWEN PARRY

Rebels of Babylon

(New York: William Morrow, 2005)

Story type: Historical/American Civil War; Mystery
Series: Abel Jones. Book 6
Subject(s): Mystery and Detective Stories; Civil War
Major character(s): Abel Jones, Military Personnel (Union major), Spy
Time period(s): 1860s (1863)

Locale(s): New Orleans, Louisiana

Summary: Occupied New Orleans during the Civil War is the setting for this installment of Parry's well-crafted mystery series featuring secret agent Major Abel Jones. The case involves the murder of a Yankee heiress, but the real point is a thrilling series of confrontations with the exotic dangers New Orleans has in store for the down-to-earth Jones, including voodoo priestesses, smugglers, newly freed slaves, and vengeful former masters. This is suspense with a very high standard of historical accuracy and authenticity.

Where it's reviewed:
Kirkus Reviews, January 1, 2005, page 16
Publishers Weekly, February 28, 2005, page 42

Other books by the same author:
The Bold Sons of Erin, 2003
Honor's Kingdom, 2002
Call Each River Jordan, 2001
Shadows of Glory, 2000
Faded Coat of Blue, 1999

Other books you might like:
Thomas Fleming, *When This Cruel War Is Over*, 2001
Barbara Hambly, *Die upon a Kiss*, 2001
Michael Kilian, *The Ironclad Alibi*, 2002
Ann McMillan, *Civil Blood*, 2001
Miriam Grace Monfredo, *Brothers of Cain*, 2001

946

ALEXANDER PARSONS

In the Shadow of the Sun

(New York: Doubleday, 2005)

Story type: Historical/World War II
Subject(s): World War II; Ranch Life; Family Life
Major character(s): Ross Strickland, Rancher; Baylis Strickland, Rancher; Jack Strickland, Military Personnel
Time period(s): 1940s
Locale(s): New Mexico

Summary: Parsons looks at the consequences of World War II on a New Mexico ranching family. The story focuses on the extended Strickland family, including ranchers Ross and his brother Baylis. Ross' son, Jack, enlists in the army, is reported dead, and participates in the Bataan Death March. Meanwhile, the Stricklands receive an eviction notice because their land is being commandeered as a test site for the atomic bomb. This is an interesting look at the war on the homefront that connects a solid family story with the details surrounding the development of the atomic bomb.

Where it's reviewed:
Booklist, March 1, 2005, page 1143
Kirkus Reviews, February 1, 2005, page 143
Library Journal, February 15, 2005, page 120
Publishers Weekly, March 14, 2005, page 43

Other books by the same author:
Leaving Disneyland, 2001

Other books you might like:
Martin Booth, *Hiroshima Joe*, 1985
Richard Bradford, *Red Sky at Morning*, 1968

Historical

Tess Uriza Holthe, *When the Elephants Dance*, 2002
Joseph Kanon, *Los Alamos*, 1997
Leslie Silko, *Ceremony*, 1977

947

MICHAEL PEARCE

The Point in the Market

(Scottsdale, Arizona: Poisoned Pen Press, 2005)

Story type: Mystery; Historical/World War I
Series: Mamur Zapt. Book 15
Subject(s): Mystery and Detective Stories; World War I
Major character(s): Gareth Owen, Government Official; Zeinab, Spouse (of Gareth)
Time period(s): 1910s (1914)
Locale(s): Cairo, Egypt

Summary: Cairo during World War I is the setting for this installment of Pearce's period mystery featuring the head of the Secret Police, or Mamur Zapt, Gareth Owen. He has married his longtime lover, Zeinab, the Pasha's daughter, and both must deal with the ensuing cultural conflict. On the professional side, Owen contends with a commotion in Cairo's camel market as the tensions surrounding English rule in Egypt are exposed by the war.

Where it's reviewed:
Kirkus Reviews, March 1, 2005, page 263

Other books by the same author:
A Cold Touch of Ice, 2004
A Dead Man in Trieste, 2004
The Face in the Cemetery, 2004
The Fig Tree Murder, 2003
The Snake Catcher's Daughter, 2003

Other books you might like:
Olivia Manning, *The Danger Tree*, 1977
Glenn Meades, *The Sands of Sakkara*, 1999
Elizabeth Peters, *The Amelia Peabody Series*, 1975-
Robert Sole, *The Photographer's Wife*, 1999
David Stevens, *The Waters of Babylon*, 2000

948

IAIN PEARS

The Portrait

(New York: Riverhead, 2005)

Story type: Historical/Edwardian
Subject(s): Artists and Art
Major character(s): Henry MacAlpine, Artist; William Naysmith, Writer (art critic)
Time period(s): 20th century (early)
Locale(s): London, England; Brittany, France

Summary: Pears, the author of complex historical thrillers, simplifies matters here in the dramatic monologue of portrait painter Henry McAlpine during the early years of the 20th century. MacAlpine, self-exiled on an island off the coast of Brittany, lures British art critic William Naysmith to visit, and the novel slowly uncovers their careers and relationships.

Rich in period and regional atmosphere, the story is a satisfyingly complex psychological thriller.

Where it's reviewed:
Booklist, February 1, 2005, page 918
Kirkus Reviews, February 1, 2005, page 144
Library Journal, March 1, 2005, page 80
New York Times Book Review, May 22, 2005, page 24
Publishers Weekly, January 17, 2005, page 33

Other books by the same author:
The Dream of Scipio, 2002
The Immaculate Deception, 2000
An Instance of the Fingerpost, 1998
Death and Restoration, 1996
The Last Judgement, 1993

Other books you might like:
Jeffrey Ford, *The Portrait of Mrs. Charbuque*, 2002
Janet Gleeson, *The Serpent in the Garden*, 2003
John Lanchester, *The Debt to Pleasure*, 1996
Helen MacInnes, *Assignment in Brittany*, 1942
Deborah Moggach, *Tulip Fever*, 1999

949

SHARON KAY PENMAN

Prince of Darkness

(New York: Putnam, 2005)

Story type: Historical/Medieval; Mystery
Series: Justin de Quincy. Book 4
Subject(s): Mystery and Detective Stories; Middle Ages; Kings, Queens, Rulers, etc.
Major character(s): Justin de Quincy, Agent, Bastard Son; John, Historical Figure, Royalty; Eleanor of Aquitaine, Historical Figure, Royalty
Time period(s): 12th century (1193)
Locale(s): England; France

Summary: Eleanor of Aquitaine's secret agent, Justin de Quincy, comes to the aid of his sworn enemy, Prince John, to find a forged document threatening violence on Richard the Lionheart and endangering the queen Justin serves. The case takes him to France and adventures on Mont-Saint-Michel, a dungeon in Brittany, and a cemetery in Paris to foil a conspiracy that could change history.

Where it's reviewed:
Kirkus Reviews, February 15, 2005, page 202
Library Journal, December 2004, page 96
Publishers Weekly, March 7, 2005, page 54

Other books by the same author:
Dragon's Lair, 2003
Time and Chance, 2002
Cruel as the Grave, 1998
The Queen's Man, 1996
When Christ and His Saints Slept, 1995

Other books you might like:
Simon Beaufort, *The Bishop's Brood*, 2003
P.C. Doherty, *The Hugh Corbett Series*, 1986-
C.L. Grace, *The Kathryn Swinbrooke Series*, 1993-
Ian Morson, *The William Falconer Series*, 1994-

Sharan Newman, *The Catherine LeVendeur Series*, 1993-

950

ARTURO PEREZ-REVERTE

Captain Alatriste
(New York: Putnam, 2005)

Story type: Historical/Seventeenth Century; Adventure
Series: Captain Alatriste. Book 1
Subject(s): Adventure and Adventurers
Major character(s): Diego Alatriste y Tenorio, Veteran, Military Personnel (captain)
Time period(s): 17th century
Locale(s): Madrid, Spain

Summary: Perez-Reverte launches a historical novel series featuring swordsman Captain Diego Alatriste y Tenorio, who, after being wounded in the Thirty Years' War, is forced to retire from the army. He is employed in Madrid as a sword-for-hire. Hired to intimidate visiting Englishmen, Captain Alatriste gets involved in a complex intrigue of the powerful in Spain's Golden Age. The swashbuckling here is firmly anchored in authentic period detail.

Where it's reviewed:
Kirkus Reviews, April 1, 2005, page 379
Library Journal, April 1, 2005, page 88
Publishers Weekly, April 25, 2005, page 39

Other books by the same author:
The Queen of the South, 2004
The Nautical Chart, 2001
The Fencing Master, 1999
The Seville Communion, 1998
The Club Dumas, 1996

Other books you might like:
Francoise d'Aubigne Chandernagor, *The King's Way*, 1984
Nicholas Griffin, *The House of Sight and Shadow*, 2001
Andrew Miller, *Ingenious Pain*, 1997
Jean-Christophe Rufin, *The Abyssinian*, 1999
Wilbur A. Smith, *Birds of Prey*, 1997

951

ANNE PERRY

Long Spoon Lane
(New York: Ballantine, 2005)

Story type: Historical/Victorian; Mystery
Series: Thomas and Charlotte Pitt. Book 24
Subject(s): Mystery and Detective Stories; Terrorism
Major character(s): Thomas Pitt, Police Officer (inspector); Charlotte Pitt, Socialite, Spouse (of Thomas)
Time period(s): 1890s
Locale(s): London, England

Summary: Husband and wife sleuths Thomas and Charlotte Pitt investigate anarchist bombings, which lead to grimy Long Spoon Lane where the body of a well-connected lord is discovered. The question raised about how much police power can be used for homeland security has a distinctly modern relevance.

Where it's reviewed:
Booklist, December 15, 2004, page 691
Kirkus Reviews, March 1, 2005, page 264
Publishers Weekly, February 14, 2005, page 57

Other books by the same author:
A Christmas Visitor, 2004
Shoulder the Sky, 2004
No Graves as Yet, 2003
Seven Dials, 2003
Southampton Row, 2002
The Whitechapel Conspiracy, 2001

Other books you might like:
Peter Ackroyd, *The Trial of Elizabeth Cree*, 1995
Agatha Christie, *The Seven Dials Mystery*, 1957
Laurie R. King, *The Mary Russell/Sherlock Holmes Series*, 1994-
Gillian Linscott, *The Nell Bray Series*, 1991-
Sarah Waters, *Fingersmith*, 2002

952

ELIZABETH PETERS (Pseudonym of Barbara Mertz)

The Serpent on the Crown
(New York: William Morrow, 2005)

Story type: Historical/Roaring Twenties; Mystery
Series: Amelia Peabody. Book 17
Subject(s): Mystery and Detective Stories; Egyptian Antiquities; Archaeology
Major character(s): Amelia Peabody, Archaeologist, Detective—Amateur; Radcliffe Emerson, Archaeologist, Spouse (of Amelia)
Time period(s): 1920s (1922)
Locale(s): Luxor, Egypt

Summary: Archaeologists Amelia Peabody and her husband Radcliffe Emerson have resumed their excavations in the Valley of the Kings. They get involved with a widow in possession of a golden statue of a king, which she claims is cursed, and must be returned to the tomb from which it was stolen, or more people will die. Amelia and her clan take up the investigation to uncover the secrets of the statue's origin and the murders that follow in its wake.

Where it's reviewed:
Kirkus Reviews, February 15, 2005, page 202
Library Journal, December 2004, page 96
Publishers Weekly, March 7, 2005, page 53

Other books by the same author:
Guardian of the Horizon, 2004
Children of the Storm, 2003
The Golden One, 2002
Lord of the Silent, 2001
He Shall Thunder in the Sky, 2000

Other books you might like:
David Freeman, *One of Us*, 1977
Sara Hylton, *In the Shadow of the Nile*, 1994
Penelope Lively, *Moon Tiger*, 1988
Barbara Michaels, *Be Buried in the Rain*, 1985
Michael Pearce, *The Mamur Zapt Series*, 1988-

Historical

953

AUDREY PETERSON

Murder in Stratford

(Waterville, Maine: Five Star, 2005)

Story type: Historical/Seventeenth Century; Mystery
Subject(s): Mystery and Detective Stories; Authors and Writers
Major character(s): Anne Hathaway, Historical Figure, Spouse (of Shakespeare); William Shakespeare, Historical Figure, Writer
Time period(s): 16th century; 17th century
Locale(s): Stratford-on-Avon, England

Summary: Peterson supplies a period mystery that employs Shakespeare's widow, Anne Hathaway, as sleuth. Anne narrates her side of the story in her relationship with her illustrious husband—how they met, courted, and married—as well as their relationship to a man who was killed in the Bard's backyard. Anne uses her considerable intellectual skills to solve the baffling case.

Where it's reviewed:
Kirkus Reviews, February 1, 2005, page 153
Library Journal, March 1, 2005, page 70

Other books by the same author:
An Unmourned Death, 2002
Death Too Soon, 1994
Dartmoor Burial, 1992
Elegy in a Country Graveyard, 1990
The Nocturne Murder, 1987

Other books you might like:
Simon Hawke, *The Mystery of Errors*, 2000
Faye Kellerman, *The Quality of Mercy*, 1989
Robert Nye, *Mrs. Shakespeare*, 2000
Grace Tiffany, *Will*, 2004
Leonard Tourney, *Time's Fool*, 2004

954

CAROLINE PETIT

The Fat Man's Daughter

(New York: Soho, 2005)

Story type: Historical/Exotic
Subject(s): China; Art
Major character(s): Leah Kolbe, Young Woman
Time period(s): 1930s (1937)
Locale(s): Hong Kong; China

Summary: Leah Kolbe, a young woman of American and Russian descent, is pressed into service reclaiming imperial Chinese treasures from the Japanese-controlled region of Manchukuo. Using a backdrop of the rape of Nanking, the novel plunges into the shady underworld of ancient art dealing.

Where it's reviewed:
Publishers Weekly, May 16, 2005, page 38

Other books you might like:
Stephen J. Cannell, *Riding the Snake*, 1998

Mo Hayder, *The Devil of Nanking*, 2005
Shirley Hazzard, *The Great Fire*, 2003
John Lanchester, *Fragrant Harbor*, 2002
James Stewart Thayer, *The Golden Swan*, 2002

955

JOHN PILKINGTON

The Mapmaker's Daughter

(Sutton, England: Severn House, 2005)

Story type: Historical/Elizabethan; Mystery
Series: Thomas the Falconer. Book 4
Subject(s): Mystery and Detective Stories; Animals/Falcons
Major character(s): Thomas Finbow, Animal Trainer (falconer); Sir Robert Vicary, Nobleman
Time period(s): 16th century (1580s)
Locale(s): England

Summary: Pilkington's fourth Thomas the Falconer mystery involves the investigation into the death of a laborer found in a burned-out barn. It is learned that the man died before the fire started. Several other murders follow, and Thomas begins to penetrate a complex conspiracy involving revenge. The mystery is rich in period details and authentic in its delivery of convincing dialogue and customs of 16th-century English life.

Where it's reviewed:
Booklist, January 1, 2005, page 828
Publishers Weekly, February 28, 2005, page 45

Other books by the same author:
Reap a Wicked Harvest, 2004
The Ramage Hawk, 2004
The Ruinous Wind, 2004
The Ruffler's Child, 2002

Other books you might like:
Fiona Buckley, *The Ursula Blanchard Series*, 1997-
Philip Gooden, *Mask of Night*, 2004
Karen Harper, *The Elizabeth I Series*, 1999-
Simon Hawke, *The Shakespeare and Smythe Series*, 2000-
Edward Marston, *The Nicholas Bracewell Series*, 1988-

956

J. MARK POWELL
L.D. MEAGHER, Co-Author

The Curse of Cain

(New York: Forge, 2005)

Story type: Historical/American Civil War; Alternate History
Subject(s): Civil War; Conspiracies; Espionage
Major character(s): Jack Tanner, Spy (Confederate); Basil Tarleton, Spy (Confederate); John Wilkes Booth, Historical Figure, Actor
Time period(s): 1860s (1865)
Locale(s): Washington, District of Columbia

Summary: CNN writers Powell and Meagher offer an alternate version of the Lincoln assassination in this historical thriller. John Wilkes Booth plays second fiddle here to hired assassin Basil Tarleton, who is pursued by Confederate secret agent

Jack Tanner. The authors provide enough twists and turns to produce a page-turner with a colorful background derived from historical details of wartime Washington and the actual facts of the Lincoln assassination.

Where it's reviewed:
Kirkus Reviews, February 1, 2005, page 145

Other books you might like:
Richard Adicks, *A Court of Owls*, 1989
Ardyth Kennelly, *The Spur*, 1951
Benjamin King, *A Bullet for Lincoln*, 1993
Thomas Mallon, *Henry and Clara*, 1994
David Robertson, *Booth*, 1998

▮957▮

DAVID POYER

That Anvil of Our Souls
(New York: Simon & Schuster, 2005)

Story type: Historical/American Civil War
Series: Civil War at Sea. Book 3
Subject(s): Sea Stories; Civil War; Military Life
Major character(s): Ker Claiborne, Military Personnel (Confederate naval officer); Catherine Claiborne, Spouse (of Ker); Theodorus Hubbard, Engineer
Time period(s): 1860s (1862)
Locale(s): Norfolk, Virginia; Richmond, Virginia; New York, New York

Summary: In the third volume of Poyer's Civil War at Sea series, the first great naval battle between ironclads—the *Monitor* versus the *Merrimack*—is chronicled from the perspective of Confederate officer Ker Claiborne, his wife Catherine, and Theodorus Hubbard, the engineer for the Union's experimental new fighting machine. This is an authentic account of Civil War action that integrates a believable fictional story into historical events and circumstances.

Where it's reviewed:
Booklist, May 15, 2005, page 1649
Kirkus Reviews, April 15, 2005, page 445

Other books by the same author:
A Country of Our Own, 2003
Black Storm, 2002
Fire on the Waters, 2001
China Sea, 2000
Thunder on the Mountain, 1999

Other books you might like:
Clarence B. Kelland, *The Monitor Affair*, 1960
Robert N. Macomber, *At the Edge of Honor*, 2002
F. Van Wyck Mason, *Armored Giants*, 1980
James L. Nelson, *Glory in the Name*, 2003
Christopher Nicole, *Iron Ships, Iron Men*, 1989

▮958▮

PETER QUINN

Hour of the Cat
(Woodstock, New York: Overlook, 2005)

Story type: Historical/World War II; Mystery
Subject(s): Mystery and Detective Stories; World War II; City and Town Life
Major character(s): Fintan Dunne, Detective—Private; Wilfredo Grillo, Immigrant
Time period(s): 1930s (1938)
Locale(s): New York, New York

Summary: Quinn's second novel is set in New York City on the eve of World War II as private eye Fintan Dunne seeks to clear Cuban immigrant Wilfredo Grillo of a murder charge. Dunne's investigation takes him on a tour of NYC from Hell's Kitchen to the Bronx and City Hall. The novel is full of atmospheric period detail that captures the mood of the nation on the brink of war.

Where it's reviewed:
Publishers Weekly, May 9, 2005, page 46

Other books by the same author:
Banished Children of Eve, 1994

Other books you might like:
James Carlos Blake, *A World of Thieves*, 2002
William Diehl, *Eureka*, 2002
Lise McClendon, *Sweet and Lowdown*, 2002
Philip Roth, *The Plot Against America*, 2004
Rene Steinke, *Holy Skirts*, 2005

▮959▮

THOMAS QUINN

The Lion of St. Mark
(New York: St. Martin's Press, 2005)

Story type: Historical/Renaissance; Adventure
Series: Venetians. Book 1
Subject(s): Adventure and Adventurers; Business; Muslims
Major character(s): Antonio Ziani, Adventurer, Businessman; Giovanni Soranzo, Businessman
Time period(s): 15th century
Locale(s): Venice, Italy; Mediterranean

Summary: Quinn debuts with the first book in a projected series set in late-Renaissance Venice with an emphasis on its take-no-prisoners, cutthroat business ethics. The focus is on adventurer Antonio Ziani and his rival Giovanni Soranzo as they battle each other and the Turks for control of the Mediterranean trade. This is a fast-moving adventure that draws on a solid sense of history.

Where it's reviewed:
Kirkus Reviews, April 1, 2005, page 382

Other books you might like:
Robert S. Elegant, *Bianca*, 1992
Erica Jong, *Shylock's Daughter*, 1987
Frances Sherwood, *The Book of Splendor*, 2002

Historical

Armin Shimerman, *The Merchant Prince*, 2001
  Michael Scott, co-author
Grace Tiffany, *The Turquoise Ring*, 2005

960

JONATHAN RABB

Rosa

(New York: Crown, 2005)

Story type: Historical/World War I; Mystery
Subject(s): Mystery and Detective Stories
Major character(s): Nikolai Hoffner, Detective—Police
Time period(s): 1910s (1919)
Locale(s): Berlin, Germany

Summary: Set during the political chaos and violence following Germany's defeat in World War I, Rabb's mystery is derived in part from the actual murder of revolutionary Rosa Luxemburg. The founder of the first German Communist Party, Luxemburg was found drowned in a Berlin canal in 1919. Here, Berlin Detective-Inspector Nikolai Hoffner investigates a series of murders of women, each with the same markings cut into their backs. When Rosa Luxemburg's corpse is discovered with the same markings, the case takes an ominous turn. The intrigue here is mixed with considerable documentation of the political and economic chaos in Berlin following Germany's defeat.

Where it's reviewed:
Booklist, December 1, 2004, page 619
Kirkus Reviews, January 15, 2005, page 87
Library Journal, February 15, 2005, page 124
Publishers Weekly, February 7, 2005, page 41

Other books by the same author:
The Book of Q, 2001
The Overseer, 1998

Other books you might like:
Jeffery Deaver, *Garden of Beasts*, 2004
Alfred Doblin, *Karl and Rosa*, 1983
Alfred Doblin, *November 1918*, 1983
Michael Pye, *The Pieces of Berlin*, 2003
Robert Wilson, *The Company of Strangers*, 2001

961

RICHARD RAYNER

The Devil's Wind

(New York: HarperCollins, 2005)

Story type: Historical/Americana; Mystery
Subject(s): City and Town Life; Crime and Criminals; Mystery and Detective Stories
Major character(s): Maurice Valentine, Architect; Mallory Walker, Young Woman; Paul Mantilini, Organized Crime Figure
Time period(s): 1950s
Locale(s): Las Vegas, Nevada

Summary: Rayner looks at Las Vegas in the 1950s, mixing actual Vegas history, such as the development of the city's first integrated casino, the unsolved murder of a black saxo-

phone player, and the impact of the nuclear tests conducted in the nearby Nevada desert, with the story of architect Maurice Valentine who investigates the murder of the mysterious Mallory Walker. Valentine's investigation touches on the underworld empire of crime boss and casino owner Paul Mantilini. This is an atmospheric crime novel, animated by a believable portrait of newly-minted, old-time Las Vegas.

Where it's reviewed:
Library Journal, January 2005, page 100
Publishers Weekly, January 10, 2005, page 39

Other books by the same author:
The Cloud Sketcher, 2000
Murder Book, 1997

Other books you might like:
William Bernhardt, *Dark Eye*, 2005
William Diehl, *Eureka*, 2002
Charles Fleming, *The Ivory Coast*, 2002
Stephen Hunter, *Hot Springs*, 2000
Bill Moody, *Death of a Tenor Man*, 1995

962

WILLIAM RIVIERE

By the Grand Canal

(New York: Grove, 2005)

Story type: Historical/Roaring Twenties; Historical/World War I
Subject(s): World War I
Major character(s): Hugh Thurne, Diplomat; Violet Mancroft, Widow(er)
Time period(s): 1910s (1919)
Locale(s): Venice, Italy

Summary: Riviere sets his story in Venice in the aftermath of World War I for an atmospheric and moving dramatization of the emotional and psychological consequence of the debacle. Hugh Thurne is a British diplomat who arrives in Venice following the armistice talks to pick up his shattered life. He is soon involved with other casualties of the conflict, including old friends Giacomo and Valentina Venier and Violet Mancroft, the widow of his best friend killed in the war, in the effort of burying the past and making peace with it.

Where it's reviewed:
Booklist, January 1, 2005, page 822
Kirkus Reviews, December 1, 2004, page 1112
Library Journal, February 1, 2005, page 70
Publishers Weekly, January 3, 2005, page 33

Other books by the same author:
Kate Caterina, 2001
Echoes of War, 1997
Borneo Fire, 1995

Other books you might like:
Pat Barker, *The Regeneration Trilogy*, 1991-1995
Sebastian Faulks, *Birdsong*, 1996
Mark Helperin, *A Soldier of the Great War*, 1991
Jonathan Hull, *Losing Julia*, 2000
Helen MacInnes, *The Venetian Affair*, 1963

963

JOHN MADDOX ROBERTS

The Seven Hills
(New York: Ace, 2005)

Story type: Historical/Ancient Rome; Alternate History
Subject(s): Roman Empire; Alternate History
Major character(s): Marcus Cornelius Scipio, Military Personnel (Roman commander); Titus Norbanus, Military Personnel (Roman commander)
Time period(s): Indeterminate
Locale(s): Roman Empire; Mediterranean

Summary: Roberts continues his fascinating what-if scenario: What if Rome fell to Hannibal's forces and was forced to rise again? In this installment, Roman commander Marcus Scipio must contend with the ambitions of Titus Norbanus and his legions. Norbanus plans to conquer Carthage and become the emperor of the Second Roman Empire, and Marcus Scipio is the only one strong enough to stand in his way.

Other books by the same author:
The River God's Vengeance, 2004
The Tribune's Curse, 2003
Hannibal's Children, 2002
Nobody Loves a Centurion, 2001
Saturnalia, 1999

Other books you might like:
Gillian Bradshaw, *Cleopatra's Heir*, 2002
Bryher, *The Coin of Carthage*, 1963
David Anthony Durham, *Pride of Carthage*, 2005
Ross Leckie, *Hannibal*, 1996
Harry Turtledove, *Thessalonica*, 1997

964

JOHN MADDOX ROBERTS

SPQR IX: The Princess and the Pirates
(New York: St. Martin's Minotaur, 2005)

Story type: Historical/Ancient Rome; Mystery
Series: SPQR. IX
Subject(s): Mystery and Detective Stories; Roman Empire; Pirates
Major character(s): Decius Caecilius Metellus, Detective—Amateur; Hermes, Slave, Companion (of Decius); Cleopatra, Historical Figure, Ruler (Queen of Egypt)
Time period(s): 1st century B.C.
Locale(s): Rome, Roman Empire; Cyprus

Summary: Decius Caecilius Metellus and his slave companion Hermes take on a mission to stop piracy in the Mediterranean. They travel to the island of Cyprus where the island's ruler is murdered, and the pair take up the investigation as suspicion falls on a young Cleopatra. The mystery draws on the historical enmity among Rome, Greece, and Egypt during the period.

Where it's reviewed:
Kirkus Reviews, May 1, 2005, page 514
Publishers Weekly, May 23, 2005, page 62

Other books by the same author:
SPQR VIII: The River God's Vengeance, 2003
The Tribune's Curse, 2003
Nobody Loves a Centurion, 2001
Saturnalia, 1999
The Sacrilege, 1992

Other books you might like:
Lindsey Davis, *The Marcus Didius Falco Series*, 1989-
Colin Falconer, *When We Were Gods*, 2000
Conn Iggulden, *Emperor: The Gates of Rome*, 2003
Steven Saylor, *The Roma Sub Rosa Series*, 1991-
Marilyn Todd, *Second Act*, 2003

965

LUCIA ST. CLAIR ROBSON

Shadow Patriots
(New York: Forge, 2005)

Story type: Historical/American Revolution; Historical/Colonial America
Subject(s): Revolutionary War; Espionage
Major character(s): Kate Darby, Spy; John Andre, Military Personnel (major), Historical Figure; Benedict Arnold, Military Personnel, Historical Figure
Time period(s): 1770s (1776)
Locale(s): New York, New York, American Colonies

Summary: Robson shows the shady, secret side of the American Revolution as a Quaker from a Loyalist family—Kate Darby—takes up the rebel cause as a spy while attracting the attention of British spymaster Major John Andre. Such historical figures as General William Howe, Benedict Arnold, Alexander Hamilton, and George Washington make appearances in this believable drama that is anchored by a solid grasp of colonial American history.

Where it's reviewed:
Kirkus Reviews, March 15, 2005, page 311

Other books by the same author:
Ghost Warrior, 2002
Fearless, 1998
Mary's Land, 1995
The Tokaido Road, 1990
Ride the Wind, 1982

Other books you might like:
Thomas Fleming, *Remember the Morning*, 1997
Ken Follett, *A Place Called Freedom*, 1995
Conrad Richter, *The Free Man*, 1943
Jeff Shaara, *The Glorious Cause*, 2002
Jeff Shaara, *Rise to Rebellion*, 2001

966

WALTER SATTERTHWAIT

Cavalcade
(New York: St. Martin's Minotaur, 2005)

Story type: Historical/Roaring Twenties; Mystery
Series: Phil Beaumont/Jane Turner. Book 3
Subject(s): Mystery and Detective Stories; Nazis

Historical

Major character(s): Jane Turner, Detective—Private (Pinkerton agent); Phil Beaumont, Detective—Private (Pinkerton agent); Adolf Hitler, Historical Figure, Political Figure
Time period(s): 1920s (1923)
Locale(s): Berlin, Germany

Summary: Pinkerton agents Jane Turner and Phil Beaumont travel to Germany in 1923 to investigate a failed attempt on the life of a young Adolf Hitler. They find themselves in the middle of Nazi party intrigue and become targets themselves. The novel offers a knowing tour of Berlin in the 1920s, with appearances by historical figures, including Hitler himself, Rudolf Hess, and Ernst (Putzi) Hanfstaengl.

Where it's reviewed:
Kirkus Reviews, December 1, 2004, page 1123
Publishers Weekly, January 3, 2005, page 39

Other books by the same author:
Masquerade, 1998 (Jane Turner/Phil Beaumont. Book 2)
Accustomed to the Dark, 1996
Escapade, 1995 (Jane Turner/Phil Beaumont. Book 1)
At Ease with the Dead, 1990
Miss Lizzie, 1989

Other books you might like:
Clive Egleton, *A Dying Fall*, 2005
Ken Follett, *Jackdaws*, 2001
Jack Higgins, *The Eagle Has Flown*, 1990
James Stewart Thayer, *Five Past Midnight*, 1997
Paul West, *The Very Rich Hours of Count von Stauffenberg*, 1980

967

STEVEN SAYLOR

A Gladiator Dies Only Once

(New York: St. Martin's Minotaur, 2005)

Story type: Historical/Ancient Rome; Mystery
Series: Roma Sub Rosa
Subject(s): Mystery and Detective Stories; Ancient History; Short Stories
Major character(s): Gordianus the Finder, Detective—Private; Marcus Tullius Cicero, Historical Figure, Political Figure
Time period(s): 1st century B.C.
Locale(s): Roman Empire

Summary: This collection of mysteries covers the early days of Ancient Roman sleuth Gordianus the Finder. Each of the nine stories present intriguing puzzles, as well as a knowing look at daily life at the time of the Roman Republic. Fans of the series get a glimpse of Gordianus' early influences, including his connection with orator Cicero. The volume includes a chronology and historical notes.

Where it's reviewed:
Library Journal, May 1, 2005, page 66
Publishers Weekly, May 2, 2005, page 179

Other books by the same author:
The Judgment of Caesar, 2004
Have You Seen Dawn?, 2003
A Mist of Prophecies, 2002

A Twist at the End, 2000
Last Seen in Massilia, 2000

Other books you might like:
Gillian Bradshaw, *Cleopatra's Heir*, 2002
Ron Burns, *Roman Shadows*, 1992
Lindsey Davis, *The Marcus Didius Falco Series*, 1989-
Colleen McCullough, *The Master of Rome Series*, 1990-2002
John Maddox Roberts, *The SPQR Series*, 1990-

968

SANDRA SCOPPETTONE

This Dame for Hire

(New York: Ballantine, 2005)

Story type: Mystery; Historical/World War II
Subject(s): Mystery and Detective Stories; Crime and Criminals; World War II
Major character(s): Faye Quick, Detective—Private
Time period(s): 1940s (1943)
Locale(s): New York, New York

Summary: Veteran mystery writer Scoppettone introduces a new sleuth, Faye Quick, in a mystery set in World War II-era New York City. Faye literally falls into her first murder case when she trips over a young woman's body on a Greenwich Village sidewalk. Her detective work provides a knowing and authentic portrait of wartime NYC.

Where it's reviewed:
Kirkus Reviews, May 1, 2005, page 515

Other books by the same author:
Gonna Take a Homicidal Journey, 1998
Let's Face the Music and Die, 1996
I'll Be Leaving You Always, 1993
Everything You Have Is Mine, 1991
Play Murder, 1985

Other books you might like:
Rhys Bowen, *Death of Riley*, 2002
Carol Higgins Clark, *Fleeced*, 2001
John Dunning, *Two O'Clock, Eastern Wartime*, 2001
Lise McClendon, *Sweet and Lowdown*, 2002
Peter Quinn, *Hour of the Cat*, 2005

969

KATE SEDLEY

The Burgundian's Tale

(Sutton, England: Severn House, 2005)

Story type: Historical/Medieval; Mystery
Series: Roger the Chapman. Book 14
Subject(s): Mystery and Detective Stories; Middle Ages
Major character(s): Roger the Chapman, Peddler, Detective—Amateur
Time period(s): 15th century
Locale(s): Bristol, England; London, England

Summary: Roger the Chapman is summoned to London to look into the murder of the son of a lady-in-waiting to the Duchess of Burgundy. Roger's investigation takes him into

the household of the powerful Duke of Gloucester and along the mean streets of 15th-century London. The intrigue and a colorful cast of characters are enhanced by deft period touches that bring the era and its customs to life.

Where it's reviewed:
Booklist, March 15, 2005, page 1271
Kirkus Reviews, May 15, 2005, page 567

Other books by the same author:
Nine Men Dancing, 2003
The Lammas Feast, 2002
The Saint John Fern, 2002
The Goldsmith's Daughter, 2001
The Weaver's Inheritance, 2001

Other books you might like:
Margaret Frazer, *The Sister Frevisse Series*, 1993-
C.L. Grace, *A Feast of Poisons*, 2004
Edward Marston, *The Domesday Book Series*, 1993-
Ian Morson, *The William Falconer Series*, 1994-
Leonard Tourney, *The Matthew Stock Series*, 1980-

970
LISA SEE

Snow Flower and the Secret Fan
(New York: Random House, 2005)

Story type: Historical/Exotic
Subject(s): China; Women; Cultures and Customs
Major character(s): Lily Lu, Young Woman; Snow Flower, Young Woman
Time period(s): 19th century
Locale(s): China

Summary: In this novel See uses the history and relationship of two friends—Lily Lu and Snow Flower—to dramatize the rigid code of conduct for women in 19th-century China. Beginning with an account of foot binding, the novel looks at the process of arranged marriages, and the various restrictions on women's lives. This is a vivid portrait of family and village life in China at the time, as well as a moving account of the struggles of women and the power of friendship.

Where it's reviewed:
Kirkus Reviews, April 15, 2005, page 447
Publishers Weekly, April 18, 2005, page 40

Other books by the same author:
Dragon Bones, 2003
The Interior, 1999
Flower Net, 1997
On Gold Mountain, 1995

Other books you might like:
Kathryn Harrison, *The Binding Chair*, 2000
Jeanne Larsen, *Manchu Palaces*, 1996
Bette Bao Lord, *Spring Moon*, 1981
Ruthanne Lum McCunn, *The Moon Pearl*, 2000
Amy Tan, *The Kitchen God's Wife*, 1991

971
MAURA D. SHAW

The Keeners
(Palm Beach, Florida: Medallion, 2004)

Story type: Historical/Victorian
Subject(s): Irish Potato Famine; Rural Life; Famine Victims
Major character(s): Margaret Meehan, Immigrant; Edward Speke, Landowner; Tom Riordan, Immigrant
Time period(s): 1840s
Locale(s): Clare, Ireland; Troy, New York

Summary: Shaw treats the horror of the Irish potato famine in the 1840s from the perspective of young Margaret Meehan of County Clare whose family is beset by an evil English land agent, Edward Speke. Relief from the famine only comes when Margaret and Tom Riordan immigrate to America to work in the factories of Troy, New York. Margaret keeps her connection to her homeland through the traditions she learns from Nuala Lynch, a keener, or professional mourner.

Where it's reviewed:
Publishers Weekly, February 7, 2005, page 40

Other books you might like:
Charles L. Grant, *In the Mood*, 1998
Regina McBride, *The Marriage Bed*, 2004
Nuala O'Faolain, *My Dream of You*, 2001
Liam O'Flaherty, *Famine*, 1937
Alice Taylor, *The Woman of the House*, 1999

972
DAN SLEIGH

Islands
(Orlando, Florida: Harcourt, 2005)

Story type: Historical/Seventeenth Century
Subject(s): Frontier and Pioneer Life; Africans
Major character(s): Autshumao, Warrior (Hottentot); Pieternella, Young Woman
Time period(s): 17th century
Locale(s): Africa

Summary: First-time novelist and Afrikaans archivist Sleigh chronicles the first 50 years of Dutch settlement in southern Africa in the 17th century. The emphasis here is not on the colonial leaders but unsung figures, such as Hottentot leader Autshumao, who first helps the Dutch and then leads a rebellion against them, and the mixed-race Pieternella. The novel interestingly traces the roots of racism to these early years. American readers may feel a bit adrift at all the many references to unfamiliar events, but the novel repays effort by shedding light on a complex and compelling region and period.

Where it's reviewed:
Booklist, January 1, 2005, page 823
Kirkus Reviews, December 1, 2004, page 142
Library Journal, January 2005, page 100

Other books you might like:
Giles Foden, *Ladysmith*, 2000

Historical

Ann Harries, *Manly Pursuits*, 1999
Legson Kayira, *Jingala*, 1969
Anne Landsman, *The Devil's Chimney*, 1997
Wilbur A. Smith, *Rage*, 1967

973

WILBUR A. SMITH

The Triumph of the Sun

(New York: St. Martin's Press, 2005)

Story type: Historical/Victorian; Adventure
Subject(s): War; Africa
Major character(s): Charles George Gordon, Historical Figure, Military Personnel (British general); Mohammed Ahmed Mahdi, Historical Figure, Religious
Time period(s): 1880s (1881)
Locale(s): Khartoum, Sudan

Summary: Smith, a master of African adventures, treats the events of the Siege of Khartoum. In 1881, the Madhi, or the "Expected One," leads a rebellion against British control of Sudan that eventually captures Khartoum and takes the life of British General Charles George Gordon. The author weaves around the historical details of the siege, the fictional adventures of members of the Courtney and Ballantyne families that are featured in his other books.

Where it's reviewed:
Booklist, May 15, 2005, page 1613
Kirkus Reviews, April 15, 2005, page 448

Other books by the same author:
The Blue Horizon, 2003
Warlock, 2001
Monsoon, 1999
River God, 1994
Power of the Sword, 1986

Other books you might like:
David W. Ball, *Empires of Sand*, 1999
Chloe Gartner, *Drums of Khartoum*, 1967
Robert Maugham, *The Last Encounter*, 1972
Jean-Christophe Rufin, *The Abyssinian*, 1999
Robert Sole, *The Photographer's Wife*, 1999

974

WESLEY STACE

Misfortune

(New York: Little, Brown, 2005)

Story type: Historical/Victorian
Subject(s): Sexuality; Gender Roles
Major character(s): Rose Old, Foundling; Lord Geoffroy Loveall, Nobleman
Time period(s): 19th century
Locale(s): England

Summary: Stace, who is best known as the musician John Wesley Harding, debuts with a transgendered Dickensian tale of a boy raised as a girl in 19th-century England. Rose Old is a foundling who is adopted by Lord Geoffroy Loveall, who brings him up as a replacement for his beloved sister who has

died. What happens to Rose, particularly when his secret becomes known, fills a crowded canvas with many plot twists, as Rose must make sense of his gender identity and where he fits in Victorian society.

Where it's reviewed:
Booklist, February 15, 2005, page 1037
Library Journal, February 1, 2005, page 71
Publishers Weekly, January 31, 2005, page 47

Other books you might like:
Donald H. Akenson, *At Face Value*, 1990
Emma Donoghue, *Slammerkin*, 2001
David Ebershoff, *The Danish Girl*, 2000
Alison MacLeod, *The Changeling*, 1996
Sarah Waters, *Tipping the Velvet*, 1999

975

RENE STEINKE

Holy Skirts

(New York: William Morrow, 2005)

Story type: Historical/World War I
Subject(s): Biography; Artists and Art
Major character(s): Elsa von Freytag-Loringhoven, Historical Figure; Marcel Duchamp, Historical Figure, Artist
Time period(s): 20th century
Locale(s): Germany; New York, New York

Summary: Steinke offers a fictionalized account of a proto-bohemian and feminist, Baroness Elsa von Freytag-Loringhoven who flees poverty in Berlin in 1904 to enter high society. Becoming an artist's model and friend of Marcel Duchamp, Elsa eventually reaches New York where her outlandish behavior and outfits make her a stand-out in the Greenwich Village bohemian community. Partially factual, partially invented, this is a lively portrait of a one-of-a-kind individual.

Where it's reviewed:
Publishers Weekly, January 3, 2005, page 33

Other books by the same author:
The Fires, 1999

Other books you might like:
Don DeLillo, *The Body Artist*, 2001
Gail Godwin, *Violet Clay*, 1978
Annette Meyers, *Murder Me Now*, 2001
Elizabeth Savage, *Willowwood*, 1978
Tom Savage, *Valentine*, 1996

976

PHILIPPA STOCKLEY

A Factory of Cunning

(Orlando, Florida: Harcourt, 2005)

Story type: Historical/Georgian
Subject(s): Social Classes; Sexuality; Women
Major character(s): Mrs. Fox, Noblewoman; Victoire, Servant
Time period(s): 1780s (1784)
Locale(s): London, England

Summary: This inventive novel provides a continuation of Pierre-Ambroise-Francois Choderlos de Laclos' classic 1782 French novel, *Les Liaisons Dangeureuses*, as an exiled French aristocrat works her wiles in London in 1784. Calling herself Mrs. Fox, she sets out, along with her equally heartless servant Victoire, to establish herself in English society, while taking advantage of the weaknesses of others. An epistolary novel, the story makes full use of authentic period details and customs.

Where it's reviewed:
Library Journal, March 1, 2005, page 81
Publishers Weekly, February 7, 2005, page 38

Other books by the same author:
The Edge of Pleasure, 2002

Other books you might like:
Emma Donoghue, *Slammerkin*, 2001
Diana Gabaldon, *Lord John and the Private Matter*, 2003
Karleen Koen, *Through a Glass Darkly*, 1986
David Liss, *A Conspiracy of Paper*, 2000
Wesley Stace, *Misfortune*, 2005

977

TONG SU

My Life as Emperor

(New York: Hyperion East, 2005)

Story type: Historical/Exotic; Political
Subject(s): China; Kings, Queens, Rulers, etc.; Politics
Major character(s): Duanbai, Ruler; Swallow, Servant
Time period(s): Indeterminate
Locale(s): China

Summary: Set in the fictional Xie Empire of China, the novel imagines the rule of the boy-emperor Duanbai, who comes to the throne at the age of 14 and must contend with court intrigue and brutal political battles. Duanbai's childish whims and unrestrained power lead to violence, self-indulgence, and cruelty, and only the young court eunuch Swallow manages to provoke humanity, genuine affection, and trust from the emperor. This is an often fascinating portrait of power that corrupts as it plays out along the corridors of the imperial Chinese court.

Where it's reviewed:
Booklist, January 1, 2005, page 823
Kirkus Reviews, December 15, 2004, page 1163
Library Journal, January 2005, page 71
Publishers Weekly, January 31, 2005, page 50

Other books by the same author:
Rice, 1995
Raise the Red Lantern, 1993

Other books you might like:
Lisa Huang Fleischman, *Dream of the Walled City*, 2000
Muriel Molland Jernigan, *Forbidden City*, 1954
Rui Li, *Silver City*, 1997
Anchee Min, *Empress Orchid*, 2004
Indu Sundaresan, *The Twentieth Wife*, 2003

978

SUSAN SWAN

What Casanova Told Me

(New York: Bloomsbury, 2005)

Story type: Historical/Georgian
Subject(s): Lovers; Biography; Diaries
Major character(s): Luce Adams, Researcher (archivist); Giovanni Giacomo Casanova, Historical Figure, Adventurer; Asked For Adams, Historical Figure
Time period(s): 2000s; 1790s
Locale(s): Venice, Italy; Athens, Greece; Istanbul, Turkey

Summary: Swan imagines the legendary Casanova's last great love as the spirited, independent daughter of a cousin of President John Adams—Asked For Adams—who disappeared while in Venice with her father in 1797. Her diary, recovered by a descendent in the present, Luce Adams, records that Asked For left with the aging Casanova and traveled with him throughout the Mediterranean. Their story alternates with that of Luce and the secret surrounding her mother. Joining the two narratives is the presiding spirit of Casanova and his passionate philosophy.

Where it's reviewed:
Booklist, May 15, 2005, page 1649
Kirkus Reviews, April 15, 2005, page 449
Publishers Weekly, May 2, 2005, page 75

Other books by the same author:
The Wives of Bath, 1993
The Last of the Golden Girls, 1991
The Biggest Modern Woman of the World, 1986

Other books you might like:
Richard Aldington, *The Romance of Casanova*, 1946
Andrei Codrescu, *Casanova in Bohemia*, 2002
John Crowley, *Lord Byron's Novel*, 2005
Andrew Miller, *Casanova in Love*, 1998
Arthur Snitzler, *Casanova's Homecoming*, 1930

979

SHIRLEY TALLMAN

The Russian Hill Murders

(New York: St. Martin's Minotaur, 2005)

Story type: Mystery; Historical/Victorian America
Series: Sarah Woolson. Book 2
Subject(s): Mystery and Detective Stories; Law; Women
Major character(s): Sarah Woolson, Lawyer
Time period(s): 1880s (1880)
Locale(s): San Francisco, California

Summary: The second outing for attorney Sarah Woolson as a sleuth in 19th-century San Francisco finds her balancing several clients—a shipping magnate, a Chinese cook, and an Irish immigrant widow. Each presents interesting challenges for the novice attorney, while exposing the racism, sexism, and classism of the period.

Where it's reviewed:
Kirkus Reviews, June 1, 2005, page 615

Historical

Other books by the same author:
Murder on Nob Hill, 2004

Other books you might like:
James Dalessandro, *1906*, 2004
Dianne Day, *The Fremont Jones Series*, 1995-
Oakley Hall, *Ambrose Bierce and the Ace of Shoots*, 2005
Marian J.A. Jackson, *The Abigail Danforth Series*, 1990-
Victoria Thompson, *Murder on Lenox Hill*, 2005

980

LOU JANE TEMPLE

The Spice Box

(New York: Berkley Prime Crime, 2005)

Story type: Mystery; Historical/American Civil War
Subject(s): Mystery and Detective Stories; Food
Major character(s): Bridget Heaney, Immigrant (Irish), Cook
Time period(s): 1860s
Locale(s): New York, New York

Summary: In the first of a projected mystery series set in various kitchens through history, Temple introduces Bridget Heaney, an Irish immigrant in Civil War-era New York City. After she goes to work as a cook in a wealthy merchant's home, Bridget discovers the body of the family's missing youngest son inside a dough box, and sets out to find the killer. The mystery includes several period recipes.

Where it's reviewed:
Kirkus Reviews, April 1, 2005, page 391
Publishers Weekly, April 4, 2005, page 47

Other books by the same author:
Death Is Semisweet, 2002
Red Beans and Vice, 2001
The Cornbread Killer, 1999
Bread on Arrival, 1998
Revenge of the Barbeque Queens, 1997

Other books you might like:
Rhys Bowen, *Murphy's Law*, 2001
Joanne Harris, *Five Quarters of the Orange*, 2001
Nina Kildham, *How to Cook a Tart*, 2002
G.A. McKevett, *Death by Chocolate*, 2003
Nancy Pickard, *The Blue Corn Murders*, 1998

981

WILL THOMAS

To Kingdom Come

(New York: Touchstone, 2005)

Story type: Historical/Victorian; Mystery
Subject(s): Mystery and Detective Stories
Major character(s): Thomas Llewelyn, Detective—Private; Cyrus Barker, Detective—Private
Time period(s): 1880s (1884)
Locale(s): London, England; Liverpool, England; Paris, France

Summary: In Thomas' second installment of his Victorian-era mystery series featuring Thomas Llewelyn, apprentice to

Scottish master detective Cyrus Barker, the sleuths take on the Irish Fenian dynamiting campaign to force Home Rule. They attempt to infiltrate the group that is responsible for bombing Scotland Yard and threatens to do worse. This is an atmospheric mystery mixing fact and fiction.

Where it's reviewed:
Booklist, March 15, 2005, page 127
Kirkus Reviews, May 1, 2005, page 516
Library Journal, April 15, 2005, page 80
Publishers Weekly, April 18, 2005, page 41

Other books by the same author:
Some Danger Involved, 2004

Other books you might like:
David Dickinson, *Death & the Jubilee*, 2003
Michel Faber, *The Crimson and the White*, 2002
Thomas Fleming, *Hours of Gladness*, 1999
James Hynes, *The Wild Colonial Boy*, 1990
Peter Maas, *Father and Son*, 1989

982

VICTORIA THOMPSON

Murder on Lenox Hill

(New York: Berkley Prime Crime, 2005)

Story type: Mystery
Series: Sarah Brandt. Book 7
Subject(s): Mystery and Detective Stories; City and Town Life
Major character(s): Sarah Brandt, Midwife, Widow(er); Frank Malloy, Detective—Police
Time period(s): 1890s
Locale(s): New York, New York

Summary: Sarah Brandt, a midwife working in the tenements of turn-of-the-century New York City, investigates the pregnancy of a teenage daughter of a wealthy family. When one of the suspects is poisoned, things turn deadly, and Sarah and her friend, Detective Sergeant Malloy, have their hands full in this atmospheric period mystery.

Where it's reviewed:
Publishers Weekly, May 3, 2005, page 175

Other books by the same author:
Murder on Marble Row, 2004
Murder on Mulberry Bend, 2003
Murder on Washington Square, 2002
Murder in Gramercy Park, 2001
Murder in St. Mark's Place, 2000

Other books you might like:
Jon Boorstin, *The Newsboys' Lodging House*, 2003
Rhys Bowen, *The Molly Murphy Series*, 2001-
Dianne Day, *The Fremont Jones Series*, 1995-
Cynthia Peale, *The White Crow*, 2002
Troy Soos, *Island of Tears*, 2001

983

GRACE TIFFANY

The Turquoise Ring

(New York: Berkley, 2005)

Story type: Historical/Renaissance
Subject(s): Jews; Women; Anti-Semitism
Major character(s): Shiloh ben Gozan, Businessman; Jessica ben Gozan, Young Woman; Portia, Gentlewoman, Heiress
Time period(s): 16th century (1568)
Locale(s): Venice, Italy

Summary: The author supplies an intriguing retelling of Shakespeare's *The Merchant of Venice*, chronicling the affairs of Shiloh ben Gozan, who flees the Spanish Inquisition to Venice with his baby daughter, Jessica. Shiloh's oddly made turquoise ring is connected with the various women in his life, including his daughter; Leah, Shiloh's first love; Nerissa, a maidservant; Xanthe, a Spanish refugee; and Portia, a rich heiress. Tiffany, a professor of Shakespeare and Renaissance drama, provides a solid and authentic period background.

Other books by the same author:
Will, 2004
My Father Had a Daughter, 2003

Other books you might like:
Robert S. Elegant, *Bianca*, 1992
Erica Jong, *Shylock's Daughter*, 1987
Thomas Quinn, *The Lion of St. Mark*, 2005
Frances Sherwood, *The Book of Splendor*, 2002
Armin Shimerman, *The Merchant Prince*, 2001
    Michael Scott, co-author

984

CHARLES TODD

A Cold Treachery

(New York: Bantam, 2005)

Story type: Historical/World War I; Mystery
Series: Inspector Ian Rutledge. Book 7
Subject(s): World War I; Mystery and Detective Stories; Small Town Life
Major character(s): Ian Rutledge, Detective—Police (Scotland Yard inspector), Veteran (World War I); Hamish MacLeod, Spirit, Military Personnel (corporal)
Time period(s): 1910s (1919)
Locale(s): Lake District, England

Summary: Todd sends Scotland Yard Inspector Ian Rutledge, a battered World War I veteran haunted by the ghost of Hamish MacLeod, the soldier he had ordered executed, to England's Lake District to investigate the murders of a sheep-farming family. While most of the locals are inclined to blame the atrocity on an outsider, Rutledge suspects that the murderer is close at hand and the motive lies in a family secret. Rutledge continues to wrestle with his demons in this atmospheric period mystery.

Where it's reviewed:
Kirkus Reviews, December 15, 2004, page 1170

Library Journal, January 2005, page 86
New York Times Book Review, February 6, 2005, page 25
Publishers Weekly, December 6, 2004, page 46

Other books by the same author:
The Murder Stone, 2003
A Fearsome Doubt, 2002
Watchers of Time, 2001
Legacy of the Dead, 2000
Wings of Fire, 1998

Other books you might like:
Philippa Gregory, *The Favored Child*, 2003
Anna Jacobs, *Our Lizzie*, 2003
Lilian Nattel, *The Singing Fire*, 2004
Anne Perry, *No Graves as Yet*, 2003
David Roberts, *The Bones of the Buried*, 2001

985

PETER TREMAYNE (Pseudonym of Peter Berresford Ellis)

Badger's Moon

(New York: St. Martin's Minotaur, 2005)

Story type: Historical/Medieval; Mystery
Series: Sister Fidelma. Book 13
Subject(s): Mystery and Detective Stories; Religious Life
Major character(s): Sister Fidelma, Religious (nun), Scholar (legal); Brother Eadulf, Religious (monk)
Time period(s): 7th century (667)
Locale(s): Ireland

Summary: In this thirteenth book in the series, Sister Fidelma is now married to her devoted companion Brother Eadulf and the mother of a newborn son. She journeys to a village beset by a series of grisly murders on consecutive full moons, the "badger's moon." Sister Fidelma must work quickly to restore order in the village and solve the mystery before the next full moon comes.

Where it's reviewed:
Booklist, January 1, 2005, page 829
Library Journal, November 1, 2004, page 62
Publishers Weekly, February 21, 2005, page 161

Other books by the same author:
The Haunted Abbot, 2004
Our Lady of Darkness, 2002
Act of Mercy, 2001
The Man Who Vanished, 2001
Valley of the Shadow, 2000

Other books you might like:
Cecelia Holland, *The Kings in Winter*, 1968
Kate Horsly, *Confessions of a Pagan Nun*, 2001
Stephen R. Lawhead, *Patrick: Son of Ireland*, 2003
Morgan Llywelyn, *Pride of Lions*, 1996
Edward Rutherfurd, *The Princes of Ireland*, 2004

986

DAWN CLIFTON TRIPP

The Season of Open Water

(New York: Random House, 2005)

Story type: Historical/Roaring Twenties
Subject(s): Prohibition Era; Family Relations; Brothers and Sisters
Major character(s): Luce Weld, Worker (icehouse); Bridge Weld, Young Woman; Noel Dowd, Fisherman
Time period(s): 1920s
Locale(s): Massachusetts

Summary: Set in coastal Massachusetts, Tripp's second novel looks at the impact of Prohibition on a family. The story centers on brother and sister Luce and Bridge Weld and their grandfather Noel Dowd, a former whaler. Bridge has an affair with a World War I veteran, while the promise of easy money lures Luce into liquor smuggling. The risk involved begins to split the family. Tripp's research and attention to period detail is impressive.

Where it's reviewed:
Booklist, May 15, 2005, page 1650
Kirkus Reviews, May 1, 2005, page 506
Library Journal, April 15, 2005, page 81
Publishers Weekly, May 2, 2005, page 175

Other books by the same author:
Moon Tide, 2003

Other books you might like:
Louise Erdrich, *The Master Butchers Singing Club*, 2003
Tim Gautreaux, *The Clearing*, 2003
Jonathan Hull, *Losing Julia*, 2000
Marianne Wiggins, *Evidence of Things Unseen*, 2003
Jacqueline Winspear, *Maisie Dobbs*, 2003

987

NANCY E. TURNER

Sarah's Quilt

(New York: St. Martin's Press, 2005)

Story type: Historical/American West
Subject(s): Frontier and Pioneer Life; Women; Ranch Life
Major character(s): Sarah Agnes Prine, Widow(er)
Time period(s): 1900s (1906)
Locale(s): Arizona

Summary: In the sequel to the much admired *These Is My Words*, Turner continues the story of Sarah Agnes Prine, based on the life of the author's great-grandmother. The novel follows Sarah's challenges in the year 1906 on a cattle ranch in the Arizona Territory. A widow, Sarah must contend both with physical hardships and family crises. This is not an idealized look at frontier life and a resilient frontierswoman, but a gritty and realistic account that achieves authenticity.

Where it's reviewed:
Booklist, March 1, 2005, page 1139
Publishers Weekly, April 18, 2005, page 44

Other books by the same author:
The Water and the Blood, 2001
These Is My Words, 1999

Other books you might like:
Molly Gloss, *The Jump-Off Creek*, 1989
Deborah Larsen, *The White*, 2002
Larry McMurtry, *Buffalo Girls*, 1990
Jane Smiley, *The All-True Travels and Adventures of Lidie Newton*, 1998
Penelope Williamson, *Heart of the West*, 1995

988

LUIS ALBERTO URREA

The Hummingbird's Daughter

(New York: Little, Brown, 2005)

Story type: Historical/Post-American Civil War
Subject(s): Saints; Religious Life; Mexicans
Major character(s): Don Tomas Urrea, Rancher; Teresita, Heroine, Healer
Time period(s): 1880s (1889)
Locale(s): Mexico

Summary: The novel explores the impact when 16-year-old Teresita, the illegitimate daughter of the wealthy and powerful rancher Don Tomas Urrea, wakes from a dream and discovers she has risen from the dead with a power to heal. Set against a period background of the guerrilla violence of post-Civil War southwestern border disputes and the civil war brewing in Mexico, this is an intriguing mix of Western fairy story, magic realism, hagiography, and Indian legend.

Where it's reviewed:
Kirkus Reviews, April 15, 2005, page 450
Publishers Weekly, April 18, 2005, page 44

Other books by the same author:
In Search of Snow, 1994

Other books you might like:
Isabel Allende, *The House of the Spirits*, 1985
Louise Erdrich, *The Last Report on the Miracle at Little No Horse*, 2001
Montserrat Fontes, *Dreams of the Centaur*, 1996
Gabriel Garcia Marquez, *One Hundred Years of Solitude*, 1970
Norman Zollinger, *Chapultepec*, 1995

989

BRENDA RICKMAN VANTREASE

The Illuminator

(New York: St. Martin's Press, 2005)

Story type: Historical/Medieval
Subject(s): Middle Ages; Religious Conflict
Major character(s): Lady Kathryn, Noblewoman; Finn, Artist (illuminator), Widow(er); John Wycliffe, Historical Figure, Religious
Time period(s): 14th century
Locale(s): East Anglia, England

Summary: This first novel mixes a medieval love story with the details surrounding the religious controversies of 14th-century England and the attempt of John Wycliffe to produce an English translation of the Bible. Recent widow Lady Kathryn takes in illuminator Finn, who is secretly at work on Wycliffe's heretical project. As the two fall in love, Finn's past and his present activities begin to break their world apart. The novel's romance is balanced by accurate period depictions and appearances by such historical figures as Wycliffe, Julian of Norwich, John Ball, and Henry Despenser.

Where it's reviewed:
Kirkus Reviews, January 15, 2005, page 78
Library Journal, March 1, 2005, page 81
Publishers Weekly, February 7, 2005, page 41

Other books you might like:
Jennifer Lang, *The Peacock and the Pearl*, 1992
Judith Merkle Riley, *A Vision of Light*, 1989
Stephen J. Rivele, *A Booke of Days*, 1997
Anya Seton, *Katherine*, 1954
Barry Unsworth, *Morality Play*, 1995

990

E. DUKE VINCENT

Mafia Summer

(New York: Bloomsbury, 2005)

Story type: Urban
Subject(s): Crime and Criminals; Organized Crime; Friendship
Major character(s): Vinny Vesta, Gang Member; Sidney Butcher, Young Man
Time period(s): 1950s (1950)
Locale(s): New York, New York

Summary: Set during the summer of 1950 and the actual mob war between gangster Frank Costello and Vito Genovese, this debut crime novel concerns the young gang leader Vinny Vesta and his relationship with his Jewish neighbor Sidney Butcher. The two unlikely friends' adventures are set in the context of the gang war that decided the fate of the Mafia in the U.S.

Where it's reviewed:
Publishers Weekly, May 9, 2005, page 42

Other books you might like:
Jimmy Breslin, *The Gang That Couldn't Shoot Straight*, 1969
Joe Connelly, *Bring Out the Dead*, 1998
Jeffery Deaver, *Hell's Kitchen*, 2001
Mario Puzo, *The Last Don*, 1996
Mario Puzo, *Omerta*, 2000

991

JULES WATSON

The White Mare

(Woodstock, New York: Overlook, 2005)

Story type: Historical/Fantasy
Subject(s): Druids

Major character(s): Rhiann, Religious (priestess), Royalty (princess); Eremon, Expatriate, Royalty (Irish prince)
Time period(s): 1st century (79)
Locale(s): Scotland

Summary: This debut novel blends history and fantasy to dramatize Scotland's resistance to the Roman invasion of Britain. As the Scottish tribes squabble among themselves, priestess and princess Rhiann is forced to make a distasteful political marriage to help unify the Scots against the Roman threat. Things grow even more complicated with the arrival of Eremon, a fugitive Irish prince who further tests Rhiann. The novel pays attention to historical detail, anchoring the fantasy elements in fact.

Where it's reviewed:
Library Journal, February 15, 2005, page 123
Publishers Weekly, February 7, 2005, page 46

Other books you might like:
Marion Zimmer Bradley, *Lady of Avalon*, 1997
Gillian Bradshaw, *Islands of Ghosts*, 1998
Patrick McCormack, *The Last Companion*, 2005
Manda Scott, *Dreaming the Eagle*, 2003
Jack Whyte, *The Skystone*, 1996

992

LOUISE WELSH

Tamburlaine Must Die

(New York: Canongate, 2005)

Story type: Historical/Elizabethan
Subject(s): Authors and Writers; Biography
Major character(s): Christopher Marlowe, Historical Figure, Writer; Blaize, Actor
Time period(s): 16th century (1593)
Locale(s): London, England

Summary: This thriller takes the form of Elizabethan poet, playwright, and spy Christopher Marlowe's own account of his activities on the eve of his mysterious death at the tavern in Deptford. Here Marlowe is at work on a new play when he is summoned by the queen's Privy Council to track down a man masquerading as Marlowe's most famous character, the tyrannical monster Tamburlaine. Assisted by a down-on-his-luck actor named Blaize, Marlowe embarks on a frantic tour of Elizabethan London's seamier side.

Where it's reviewed:
Kirkus Reviews, December 1, 2004, page 1115
Library Journal, December 2004, page 106
Publishers Weekly, January 17, 2005, page 35

Other books by the same author:
The Cutting Room, 2002

Other books you might like:
Anthony Burgess, *A Dead Man in Deptford*, 1995
Bruce Cook, *Young Will*, 2004
Judith Cook, *The Slicing Edge of Death*, 1993
George Garrett, *Entered from the Sun*, 1990
Leslie Silbert, *The Intelligencer*, 2004

Historical

993

GILLEN D'ARCY WOOD

Hosack's Folly

(New York: Other Press, 2005)

Story type: Historical/Post-American Revolution
Subject(s): Medicine; Yellow Fever; Biography
Major character(s): David Hosack, Historical Figure, Doctor; Eamonn Casey, Publisher; John Laidlaw, Businessman
Time period(s): 1820s
Locale(s): New York, New York

Summary: This accomplished first historical novel dramatizes a yellow fever epidemic in New York City during the 1820s. At the center of the drama is the historical physician David Hosack, who attended Alexander Hamilton after his duel with Aaron Burr and founded Bellevue Hospital. Hosack believes the fever is being spread by incoming ships and calls for a quarantine of New York harbor, provoking various conflicts of interest and contention with greedy merchants and corrupt politicians. Meanwhile, Eamonn Casey, newspaper publisher, and John Laidlaw, a Wall Street tycoon, join forces to save the city by constructing the Croton Aqueduct, reputedly the biggest public work program since the Roman Empire.

Where it's reviewed:
Kirkus Reviews, February 1, 2005, page 147
Library Journal, April 1, 2005, page 90
Publishers Weekly, February 14, 2005, page 52

Other books you might like:
Kevin Baker, *Paradise Alley*, 2002
Frederick Busch, *The Night Inspector*, 1999
Peter Quinn, *Banished Children of Eve*, 1994
Josh Russell, *Yellow Jack*, 1999
William Safire, *Scandalmonger*, 2000

994

JAY WORRALL

Sails on the Horizon

(New York: Random House, 2005)

Story type: Historical/Napoleonic Wars
Subject(s): Sea Stories; Military Life; War
Major character(s): Charles Edgemont, Military Personnel (British naval officer); Penelope Brown, Gentlewoman
Time period(s): 1790s (1797)
Locale(s): *Argonaut*, At Sea; *Louisa*, At Sea; England

Summary: Worrall launches a nautical adventure series featuring British naval officer Charles Edgemont who tests his mettle in engagements with the French and the Spanish. In his first battle, Edgemont must take over command for his mortally wounded captain. His success brings him advancement and a fortune with which to pursue the Quaker Penelope Brown on land, with their courtship interrupted when Edgemont is called back to sea to take on an old nemesis.

Where it's reviewed:
Booklist, March 15, 2005, page 1268
Kirkus Reviews, February 1, 2005, page 148
Publishers Weekly, March 28, 2005, page 58

Other books you might like:
Joan Druett, *A Watery Grave*, 2004
Dewey Lambdin, *Havoc's Sword*, 2003
Jan Needle, *The Spithead Nymph*, 2004
Edwin Thomas, *The Blighted Cliffs*, 2004
Richard Woodman, *A King's Cutter*, 2001

995

JOHN WRAY

Canaan's Tongue

(New York: Knopf, 2005)

Story type: Historical/American Civil War
Subject(s): Civil War; Slavery; Crime and Criminals
Major character(s): Virgil Ball, Gang Member; Thaddeus Morelle, Gang Member
Time period(s): 1850s; 1860s
Locale(s): United States

Summary: Wray's novel is based on the actual slave stealer John Murrell, known as "The Redeemer," and his "Mystic Clan" gang who traded in stolen slaves. The story centers on the relationship between gang member Virgil Ball and gang leader Thaddeus Morelle. Ball rises to the gang's inner circle, but is deeply conflicted about his involvement in the "Trade," of dealing slaves and struggles to break free of Morelle's influence and the consequences of their crimes.

Where it's reviewed:
Booklist, May 15, 2005, page 1650
Kirkus Reviews, April 15, 2005, page 451
Library Journal, May 1, 2005, page 78

Other books by the same author:
The Right Hand of Sleep, 2001

Other books you might like:
Russell Banks, *Cloudsplitter*, 1997
Desmond Barry, *The Chivalry of Crime*, 2000
Susan M. Dodd, *Mamaw*, 1988
Kevin McColley, *The Other Side*, 2000
Bruce Olds, *Raising Holy Hell*, 1995

996

TAMAR YELLIN

The Genizah at the House of Shepher

(New Milford, Connecticut: Toby, 2005)

Story type: Family Saga
Subject(s): Family Relations; Bible; Jews
Major character(s): Shulamit Shepher, Scholar (biblical)
Time period(s): 19th century; 20th century
Locale(s): Jerusalem, Israel

Summary: This debut novel uses the discovery of a mysterious, handwritten volume of the Bible to explore a family's history and relationship with Jerusalem over several generations. Shulamit Shepher is a biblical scholar who journeys from her home in England to her family's small bungalow in Jerusalem when she receives her great-grandfather's book called the Codex. In attempting to unravel the book's origin

and meaning, Shulamit reconstructs her family and Jerusalem's complex history over more than a century.

Where it's reviewed:
Kirkus Reviews, January 15, 2005, page 82
Library Journal, March 1, 2005, page 81
Publishers Weekly, February 7, 2005, page 38

Other books you might like:
Cecelia Holland, *Jerusalem*, 1996
Kanan Makiya, *The Rock*, 2001
Joel Rosenberg, *The Last Days*, 2003
Elie Wiesel, *A Beggar in Jerusalem*, 1970
Amy Wilentz, *Martyrs' Crossing*, 2001

Historical

Inspirational Fiction in Review
by
Melissa Hudak

Surprisingly, nearly twenty percent of the books discussed in this volume's section on inspirational fiction are titles by new authors. Among them are some promising new voices, following traditional paths in the inspirational fiction market, such as historical fiction and romance. However, some of the new authors have chosen to follow different paths into areas little discussed in inspirational fiction. Many of the books have violence levels seldom seen before in this genre. Others give new twists to common topics.

Among the more traditional offerings of the new authors are books by Deeanne Gist and Cecelia Dowdy. Gist's book, *A Bride Most Begrudging*, is a historical romance set in colonial America. While nothing groundbreaking, the book does have a charmingly spunky heroine to enliven the oft-used plots of kidnapped heroine and marriage of convenience turning to true love. The colonial setting is also fairly rare in inspirational historical novels. Overall, this is a very nice first effort that should please most readers. It will be good to hear from Gist again.

Cecelia Dowdy also takes on some tried and true situations in her debut novel, *First Mates*. Rainy Jackson and Winston Michaels meet on a cruise they are taking in an attempt to recover from emotional traumas. Rainy is upset over a broken relationship and Winston is mourning the death of his twin sister. The two hit it off and find some common ground in their mutual love of God, but their pasts keep coming back to haunt them. Winston is still struggling with an alcohol problem he developed after his sister's death and Rainy is finding it hard to trust any man after her fiancee's bad treatment of her. Of course, this is a romance novel so readers know it will end well, but the charm of this book is in the journey the two lead characters take to their inevitable happy conclusion. Well-developed characters are still fairly rare in inspirational fiction, and Rainy and Winston both emerge as real people, rather than cardboard stereotypes.

One stereotype that is hugely popular in mainstream fiction is the single gal looking for love, usually while obsessing over her weight, thanks to Helen Fielding's phenomenally popular Bridget Jones books. The writers who came along in the wake of the Bridget Jones phenomenon not only spawned an entire new subgenre in mainstream fiction (''chick lit''), but also crossed over into inspirational fiction. Not too long ago, a slew of authors wrote books in which their vaguely Bridget Jones-like heroines looked for love with the right (Christian) man. Some writers were more successful than others, but the experiment went well enough for a few debut writers to take their shot at this subgenre recently.

In Kissing Adrien, Siri L. Mitchell tells the story of Claire Le Noyer, a woman bordering the edge of 30 who is caught in the dual rut of boring job and complacent boyfriend. Then Claire suddenly finds herself in Paris, flirting with handsome family friend Adrien and trying to forget the boy back home. Another heroine juggling two men in a glamorous setting is Emily Hinton, the lead character in the debut novel by the writing team of Anne Dayton and May Vanderbilt. In *Emily Ever After*, the setting is Manhattan. Sweet and wholesome Emily loves the big city and her career in publishing, but vows to remain true to her small town roots. Almost immediately Emily meets a great guy, handsome, charming, and as devout a Christian as Emily is. Or is he? That is the question Emily must answer, as her new beau's faith seems to be on the shaky side, something that is quite a contrast to the faith of Jacob, the boy back home who carries a torch for Emily. A third author debuting into inspirational chick lit is Laura Jensen Walker. The heroine of *Dreaming in Black and White* is the sadly single Phoebe Grant, who suffers through bad dates while dreaming of the type of romances found in old movies. Phoebe, like the heroines of *Kissing Adrien* and *Emily Ever After* is in the big city, but life reverses soon find her back in her tiny hometown, and desperately wanting out. While Phoebe, Emily,

and Claire are all characters seen before in inspirational fiction, as well as mainstream fiction, their devout faith does give their look at life as single women a new twist. That alone makes these three debut novels ones to check out as they take chick lit into areas mainstream literature shies away from. Theses titles may not be groundbreaking, but all three are certainly fun, fluffy entertainment. Walker's novel is especially funny, with the hapless Phoebe a special delight as she moans over bad dates and moons over the romances in old-time movies.

Definitely not fun or fluffy is a new trend in inspirational fiction towards more graphic depictions of life, including overt portrayals of violent criminal acts. In an article published in the March 28, 2005 issue of *Publishers Weekly*, Marcia Ford took a look at the recent trend of ''gritty, unsanitized novels. . .finding a home in the Christian market.'' Ford looks at many books by established authors like Melody Carlson and Lisa Samson, but also focuses in on debut novelists like Creston Mapes.

Mapes' first novel is *Dark Star*, the story of a famous rock musician named Everett Lester. With his band DeathStroke, Everett lives a hedonistic life that includes sex, drugs, and booze, but it isn't enough to make him happy. Everett realizes he is going nowhere fast, but can't figure out how to get off his road to destruction. Eventually, Everett winds up in really big trouble, accused of the murder of his psychic. Help, in a spiritual form, comes from letters Everett receives from a devout woman in Kansas. Creston Mapes doesn't back away from a true portrayal of Everett's lifestyle—what he does seems very realistic and isn't sugarcoated in any way. When Everett does finally realize Christianity may have what he is looking for, his reversal is more dramatic simply because of what he has been through.

Another dramatic conversion comes in *Forgiving Solomon Long* by Chris Well. This book is very dark and doesn't shy away from depictions of violence. The title character, Solomon Long, is a hit man sent to Kansas City to rid the town of do-gooders getting in the way of the local mob. He has a list of people to deal with, the first of whom is a minister who forgives Solomon with his last words. Shaken, the once seemingly unredeemable hit man is forced to confront his horrible childhood and how it has affected his life. Although some of the other characters in the book are fairly superficial, Solomon is a frighteningly real portrayal of a man most people would consider irredeemable, but is actually a man who could be saved.

Though not violent, another title by a new author that dabbles in areas previously left almost untouched by inspirational fiction authors is by Alison Strobel. *Worlds Collide* is about the fairy tale marriage of movie star Jack Harrington and his ''nobody'' wife Grace. An interview with celebrity biographer Jada Eastman is set up to allow Jack and Grace to talk about their marriage. Surprisingly, the resulting interview reveals the ghosts from both Jack and Grace's past, including alcohol use and promiscuous sex. As Jack and Grace talk to Jada, they reveal how they battled through their troubles and found faith in God. However, that faith is not the usual ''all- problems solved'' faith found in some inspirational fiction books. Though devout Christians, the couple still has problems, and realistic ones at that. They are just more hopeful of eventually working through their difficulties and moving on with their lives together because they have a shared faith in God.

Another character facing problems is Dylan Foster in Melanie Wells' debut novel *When the Day of Evil Comes*. Dylan, a professor of psychology, is living a perfectly normal and somewhat boring life when she is suddenly catapulted into a world where evil reigns supreme. After an encounter with a strange man at a faculty picnic, Dylan becomes the target of an evil campaign of psychological torture at the hands of her assailant. Reluctant to act, Dylan soon becomes forced into a fight for her emotional, spiritual, and physical lives. Suspense titles are still fairly rare in inspirational fiction and this is a surprisingly good one, especially from a first-time author.

Another rarity in inspirational fiction is books with a military theme or setting, but two new authors have chosen this arena for their debuts. Donna Fleisher takes on the aftereffects of war in her novel *Wounded Healer*. Making the book of special interest is the fact that the two main characters are female soldiers, both veterans of Operation Desert Storm. The war has ended and Erin and Chris have gone on with their lives, but the bond they developed while serving in army keeps them close, so much so that when Chris begins having serious problems, Erin doesn't hesitate in rushing to her side to help her. The book does a good job of presenting the bonds that can exist between those who serve together in war zones, though it does tend to veer into sentimentality at times.

Another recent debut novel with a military theme is Don Brown's *Treason*, which combines a military setting with a legal plotline. *Treason* is set in the world of JAG, the office of the Judge Advocate General, the Navy's legal service. The lead character is a young lawyer who must prosecute a group of Islamic clerics who have infiltrated the Navy's chaplain service to incite sailors to commit acts of terrorism. While the book does rely heavily on cliched situations, such as the young and inexperienced lawyer taking on the renowned one and the female rival turned trusted partner, it is still a decent enough legal thriller to entertain most readers.

Although many of the newcomers to inspirational fiction wrote solid debuts, few made my list of best titles. Among them is a book by Vanessa Del Fabbro, who takes an unflinching look at racism in South Africa in *The Road to Home*, along with titles by Cecelia Dowdy, Creston Mapes, and Laura Jensen Walker. Otherwise, the books that proved most impressive were those by veterans of the genre, including the always reliable Francine Rivers and Lisa Samson. Samson, especially, continues to improve with each book as she takes unflinching looks at contemporary American life.

Recommended Titles

Kacy Barnett-Gramckow, *A Crown in the Stars*

Lawana Blackwell, *A Table by the Window*

Stephen Bly, *Memories of a Dirt Road Town*

Phil Callaway, *Wonders Never Cease*

Mindy Starns Clark, *The Trouble with Tulip*

Colleen Coble, *Black Sands*

Brandilyn Collins, *Dead of Night*

Lori Copeland, *The Drifter*

Vanessa Del Fabbro, *The Road to Home*

Cecelia Dowdy, *First Mates*

Alton Gansky, *Director's Cut*

Robin Lee Hatcher, *Veterans Way*

Roxanne Henke, *Always Jan*

Kathy Herman, *Eye of the Beholder*

Neta Jackson, *The Yada Yada Prayer Group Gets Real*

Karen Kingsbury, *A Thousand Tomorrows*

Creston Mapes, *Dark Star*

Charles Martin, *Wrapped in Rain*

Lorena McCourtney, *In Plain Sight*

Elizabeth Musser, *The Dwelling Place*

Bette Nordberg, *Detours*

Francine Rivers, *The Warrior*

Lisa Samson, *Club Sandwich*

Laura Jensen Walker, *Dreaming in Black and White*

Lori Wick, *Moonlight on the Millpond*

Inspirational Titles

RICK ACKER

Dead Man's Rule

(Grand Rapids, Michigan: Kregel, 2005)

Story type: Mystery; Legal
Subject(s): Law; Legal Thriller; Organized Crime
Major character(s): Ben Corbin, Lawyer
Time period(s): 2000s
Locale(s): Chicago, Illinois

Summary: Ben Corbin, an up-and-coming attorney, takes on a famous lawyer in a case that should be simple: the dispute over the ownership of a safety deposit box. The defendant in the case is Mikhail Ivanovsky, a famous scientist. When Dr. Ivanovsky turns up dead, Ben finds himself in the middle of a conspiracy that may involve a Chechen gang. This is author Rick Acker's first novel for adults; he has also written books for children.

Other books you might like:
James Scott Bell, *Blind Justice*, 2000
Joseph H. Hilley, *Sober Justice*, 2004
Craig Parshall, *The Chambers of Justice Series*, 2002-
Randy Singer, *Dying Declaration*, 2004
Robert Whitlow, *The Santee Series*, 2003-

DAVID AIKMAN

Qi

(Nashville: Broadman & Holman, 2005)

Story type: Mystery
Series: Richard Ireton. Book 1
Subject(s): Missing Persons; Politics
Major character(s): Richard Ireton, Journalist (foreign correspondent)
Time period(s): 2000s
Locale(s): Hong Kong; China

Summary: Foreign correspondent Richard Ireton begins to look into the disappearance of an American named McHale, who dropped out of sight near Hong Kong. Ireton begins to suspect that a cult known as Qigong is somehow responsible. He manages to track McHale to an underground church house in the Guangdong province of China. It may, however, be too late to help McHale escape from people who view him as the enemy.

Other books by the same author:
When the Almond Tree Blossoms, 1993

Other books you might like:
Randy Alcorn, *Safely Home*, 2001
T. Davis Bunn, *The Great Divide*, 2000
John Dalton, *Heaven Lake*, 2004
C. Hope Flinchbaugh, *Daughter of China*, 2002
Marilyn Kok, *Stillpoint*, 1996
Debbie Wilson, *Tiger in the Shadows*, 2004

999

HANNAH ALEXANDER (Pseudonym of Cheryl Hodde and Melvin Hodde)

Last Resort

(New York: Steeple Hill, 2005)

Story type: Romantic Suspense
Subject(s): Missing Persons
Major character(s): Noelle Cooper, Relative (aunt); Nathan Trask, Friend (of Noelle)
Time period(s): 2000s
Locale(s): Hideaway, Missouri

Summary: Twelve-year-old Clarissa Cooper is missing and it is feared she has been abducted. Clarissa's Aunt Noelle rushes to Hideaway, Missouri, to help look for her niece and as the search intensifies, Noelle finds strength from her childhood friend, Nathan Trask. Nathan, like so many in the small Missouri town, is desperate to find Clarissa, but he feels a special pain because of his feelings for Noelle.

Other books by the same author:
Safe Haven, 2004
Hideaway, 2003
Urgent Care, 2003
The Crystal Cavern, 2003
Necessary Measures, 2002

Other books you might like:
Colleen Coble, *Without a Trace*, 2003
Wanda L. Dyson, *Abduction*, 2003
Catherine Palmer, *Fatal Harvest*, 2003
Lois Richer, *The Camp Hope Series*, 2004-
Susan Warren, *Escape to Morning*, 2005

1000

KAREN BALL

Shattered Justice

(Sisters, Oregon: Multnomah, 2005)

Story type: Contemporary
Series: Family Honor. Book 1
Subject(s): Crime and Criminals; Small Town Life
Major character(s): Avidan ''Dan'' Justice, Police Officer (sheriff's deputy); Shelby Wilson, Social Worker
Time period(s): 2000s
Locale(s): Sanctuary, Oregon

Summary: Life in the small town of Sanctuary, Oregon, may seem slow to some, but to sheriff's deputy Dan Justice the town's pace gives him a chance to recover from the loss of his wife and raise their children in peace. Shelby Wilson, a local woman who works with troubled teens, enlists Dan's help in attempting to get through to a boy named Jayce. As Shelby and Dan work together to help Jayce, they begin to realize they might have a future together.

Other books by the same author:
A Test of Faith, 2004
The Breaking Point, 2003
Wilderness, 1999
Reunion, 1996

Other books you might like:
Terri Blackstock, *The Cape Refuge Series*, 2002-
Colleen Coble, *The Rock Harbor Series*, 2003-
Felicia Mason, *Sweet Devotion*, 2004
Kathi Mills-Macias, *The Toni Matthews Series*, 2001-
Patricia H. Rushford, *The Angel Delaney Series*, 2004-

1001

KACY BARNETT-GRAMCKOW

A Crown in the Stars

(Chicago: Moody, 2005)

Story type: Biblical Fiction
Series: Genesis Trilogy. Book 3
Subject(s): Biblical Fiction
Major character(s): Shoshannah, Captive
Time period(s): Indeterminate Past
Locale(s): Babylon

Summary: Through her own carelessness, Shoshannah finds herself trapped in the city of Babel, the home of her ancestors' enemies. The city itself is in turmoil after the death of Nimr-Rada, who was killed by Shoshannah's relatives. A great tower has been built in honor of their former leader, and the residents of Babel continue to add to it in honor of their king. As Shoshannah attempts to survive in the foreign city, she desperately hopes that her beloved Kaleb will save her before it is too late.

Other books by the same author:
He Who Lifts the Skies, 2004
The Heavens Before, 2004

Other books you might like:
Tracy Groot, *The Brother's Keeper*, 2003
Angela Elwell Hunt, *The Shadow Women*, 2002
Thom Lemmons, *The Daughters of Faith Series*, 1999-
Gilbert Morris, *The Lions of Judah Series*, 2002-
Francine Rivers, *The Lineage of Grace Series*, 2000-

1002

JAMES SCOTT BELL

Glimpses of Paradise

(Minneapolis: Bethany House, 2005)

Story type: Historical/Roaring Twenties
Subject(s): Actors and Actresses; Movie Industry; Murder
Major character(s): Zee Miller, Actress; Doyle Lawrence, Veteran (World War I)
Time period(s): 1920s
Locale(s): Los Angeles, California

Summary: Zee Miller, a minister's daughter, dreams of becoming a famous movie star. Her sweetheart, Doyle Lawrence, has had his life mapped out for him by his wealthy attorney father, who wants his son to follow in his footsteps and become a lawyer. Then World War I breaks out and changes all of their carefully made plans. Doyle enters the military and is sent to France. Disillusioned by war, he no longer feels compelled to do what his father wishes. Taking to life on the road, Doyle drifts to Los Angeles. Coincidentally, Zee is also in Los Angeles attempting to break into the film industry. When she is arrested for murder, the childhood sweethearts find their lives colliding once again.

Other books by the same author:
Sins of the Fathers, 2005
A Certain Truth, 2004
Breach of Promise, 2004
A Greater Glory, 2003
A Higher Justice, 2003

Other books you might like:
Jack Cavanaugh, *The Allies*, 1997
Linda Chaikin, *Valiant Hearts*, 1998
Gilbert Morris, *The Heavenly Fugitive*, 2002
Diane Noble, *The California Chronicles*, 1999-
Tracie Peterson, *The Desert Roses Series*, 2002-

| 1003 |

JAMES SCOTT BELL

Sins of the Fathers

(Grand Rapids, Michigan: Zondervan, 2005)

Story type: Legal
Subject(s): Violence
Major character(s): Lindy Field, Lawyer
Time period(s): 2000s
Locale(s): Los Angeles, California

Summary: When a 13-year-old boy opens fire at a baseball game, six people are left dead, five of them children. Lindy Field, who specializes in defending juveniles, agrees to defend the boy. Public opinion is against the teenager, and the assistant district attorney sees a chance to gain support for a political career by convicting him quickly and harshly. Lindy desperately wants to help her young client, but he refuses to speak to her or to do anything to help himself.

Other books by the same author:
Glimpses of Paradise, 2005
A Certain Truth, 2004
Breach of Promise, 2004
A Greater Glory, 2003
A Higher Justice, 2003

Other books you might like:
Chuck Chitwood, *The Trial of Job*, 2000
Dee Henderson, *The Healer*, 2002
Kathi Mills-Macias, *The Price*, 2002
Craig Parshall, *The Chambers of Justice Series*, 2002-
Robert Whitlow, *The Sacrifice*, 2002

| 1004 |

MONTRE BIBLE

Heaven Sent

(New York: Warner, 2005)

Story type: Fantasy
Subject(s): Angels; Supernatural
Major character(s): Andrew Turner, Angel, Teenager
Time period(s): 2000s
Locale(s): Heaven, Texas

Summary: Andrew Turner is just an average teenager, concerned about normal teenage things, like grades and girls. Then his mother becomes ill and dies. Soon Andrew realizes that he is anything but an average teenager; in fact, he has great supernatural powers. When his father suddenly returns, along with a brother Andrew didn't know existed, Andrew is left dazed and confused by the sudden changes in his life. He decides to use his supernatural gifts for the glory of God. First novel.

Where it's reviewed:
Library Journal, April 1, 2005, page 80

Other books you might like:
Joan Brady, *God on a Harley*, 1995
Jack Cavanaugh, *Postmarked Heaven*, 2002
Roger Elwood, *The Angelwalk Series*, 1989-

Joseph F. Girzone, *The Joshua Series*, 1987-
D. Brian Shafer, *Chronicles of the Host*, 2002

| 1005 |

KRISTIN BILLERBECK

With This Ring, I'm Confused

(Nashville: WestBow, 2005)

Story type: Romance
Series: Ashley Stockingdale. Book 3
Subject(s): Weddings
Major character(s): Ashley Stockingdale, Lawyer (patent attorney)
Time period(s): 2000s
Locale(s): Silicon Valley, California

Summary: Ashley Stockingdale has finally found the man of her dreams—maybe. She is engaged to marry handsome Dr. Kevin Novak. With the wedding plans under way, Ashley gets a surprise when Kevin's sister Emily shows up in California, determined to make certain the wedding is elegant enough to do justice to their important Southern family. When Kevin takes off for an interview in Philadelphia, Ashley finds herself battling Emily's demands on her own. Then Seth Greenwood, an old boyfriend, begins working at Ashley's place of employment and she begins to wonder if she chose the right man to marry.

Other books by the same author:
She's All That, 2005
San Francisco, 2004
What a Girl Wants, 2004
She's Out of Control, 2004
An Unbreakable Hope, 2003

Other books you might like:
Judy Baer, *The Whitney Chronicles*, 2004
Lori Copeland, *Mother of Prevention*, 2005
Penny Culliford, *The Theodora Series*, 2004-
Anne Dayton, *Emily Ever After*, 2005
Robin Jones Gunn, *The Sisterchicks Series*, 2003-

| 1006 |

LAWANA BLACKWELL

A Table by the Window

(Minneapolis: Bethany House, 2005)

Story type: Contemporary
Subject(s): Family Problems; Inheritance
Major character(s): Carley Reed, Teacher, Heiress
Time period(s): 2000s
Locale(s): San Francisco, California; Tallulah, Mississippi

Summary: Carley Reed had a troubled childhood, but has settled into a quiet and unemotional life as a schoolteacher in San Francisco. When a private investigator shows up on her doorstep to inform her that her grandmother has died, leaving her money and a home in Mississippi, Carley faces some mixed emotions. Moving south might reopen the wounds caused by her abusive parents, but the inheritance will free her to make changes in her life. The charm of the small town of

Tallulah soon convinces Carley she can make a new life for herself in the South, but when a murderer strikes Carley begins to wonder if she was better off in San Francisco.

Other books by the same author:
Leading Lady, 2004
Like a River Glorious, 2004
Measures of Grace, 2004
Catherine's Heart, 2002
Maiden of Mayfair, 2000

Other books you might like:
Brandilyn Collins, *Color the Sidewalk for Me*, 2002
Linda Hall, *Margaret's Peace*, 1998
Catherine Palmer, *The Happy Room*, 2002
Francine Rivers, *Leota's Garden*, 1999
Penelope J. Stokes, *The Amethyst Heart*, 2000
Johanna Verweerd, *The Winter Garden*, 2001

STEPHEN BLY

Memories of a Dirt Road Town

(Nashville: Broadman & Holman, 2005)

Story type: Contemporary
Series: Horse Dreams. Book 1
Subject(s): Infidelity; Marriage; Mothers and Daughters
Major character(s): Donna Woodstone, Teacher
Time period(s): 2000s
Locale(s): Illinois; Wyoming

Summary: When Donna Woodstone learns of her husband's infidelity, she divorces him without revealing her reasons to their daughter Marla. Donna soon regrets her hasty decision, but before she can attempt a reconciliation, her husband dies suddenly. Shattered by both the death and by Marla's refusal to listen to her, Donna decides to go to Wyoming for some time alone since she fondly remembers time spent as a child in the peaceful wilderness. After renting a cabin and settling in, Donna begins the process of healing.

Other books by the same author:
Courage and Compromise, 2003
Paperback Writer, 2003
The Next Roundup, 2003
Reason and Riots, 2003
Friends and Enemies, 2002

Other books you might like:
Deborah Bedford, *A Rose by the Door*, 2001
Terri Blackstock, *Seaside*, 2001
Lorena McCourtney, *Whirlpool*, 2002
Dawn Ringling, *Jumping in Sunset*, 2003
Francine Rivers, *Leota's Garden*, 1999
Penelope J. Stokes, *The Amethyst Heart*, 2000

1008

DON BROWN

Treason

(Grand Rapids, Michigan: Zondervan, 2005)

Story type: Legal

Series: Naval Justice. Book 1
Subject(s): Legal Thriller; Military Life; Muslims
Major character(s): Zack Brewer, Military Personnel (naval lieutenant), Lawyer; Diane Colcernian, Military Personnel (JAG lieutenant), Lawyer
Time period(s): 2000s
Locale(s): United States

Summary: A group of radical Islamic chaplains serving in the U.S. Naval Chaplain Corps has been accused of treason. Although not long out of law school, Navy lieutenant Zack Brewer is assigned the high profile case. Assisting him as he serves as prosecutor is his long-time nemesis Diane Colcernian, a JAG lawyer. They have a fight on their hands, since the defense is led by famous defense attorney Wells Levinson, a man who rarely loses a case. First novel.

Other books you might like:
James Scott Bell, *Blind Justice*, 2000
Chuck Chitwood, *The Trial of Job*, 2000
Dee Henderson, *The Uncommon Heroes Series*, 2000-
Craig Parshall, *The Chambers of Justice Series*, 2002-
Robert Whitlow, *The Santee Series*, 2003-

1009

WANDA E. BRUNSTETTER

The Storekeeper's Daughter

(Uhrichsville, Ohio: Barbour, 2005)

Story type: Contemporary
Subject(s): Amish; Fathers and Daughters; Missing Persons
Major character(s): Naomi Fisher, Young Woman, Clerk; Caleb Hoffmeir, Businessman (buggy maker)
Time period(s): 2000s
Locale(s): Pennsylvania

Summary: After her mother dies suddenly, Naomi Fisher finds herself taking on many extra chores. Not only is she taking care of her seven young siblings, but her strict Amish father also expects her to take care of the house, the cooking, and help in the family store. He also refuses to allow Naomi to court, though she is very interested in local boy Caleb Hoffmeir. When Naomi's baby brother disappears from the yard while she is supposed to be watching him, Naomi begins to wonder if she can continue to juggle all the duties that have been handed to her.

Other books by the same author:
Going Home, 2004
Kelly's Chance, 2004
Clowning Around, 2003
Lancaster Brides, 2002
Plain and Fancy, 2002

Other books you might like:
Carrie Bender, *The Dora's Diary Series*, 1999-
Mary Christner Borntrager, *The Ellie's People Series*, 1988-
Dudley J. Delffs, *The Father Grif Series*, 1998-
Beverly Lewis, *The Heritage of Lancaster County Series*, 1997-
Gayle Roper, *The Document*, 1998

1010

LYNN BULOCK

Love the Sinner

(New York: Steeple Hill, 2005)

Story type: Mystery
Subject(s): Murder
Major character(s): Gracie Lee Harris, Student—Graduate
Time period(s): 2000s
Locale(s): Rancho Conejo, California

Summary: Gracie Lee Harris falls hard for the very charming Dennis Peete and relocates from Missouri to California to be with him. Gracie soon learns Dennis isn't all that great. Not only has he squandered his mother's life savings and his daughter's college fund, he also lives a precarious existence as a con man. When Dennis is involved in a car accident that leaves him in a coma, the pressure of living with her mother-in-law gets to Gracie. In desperation, she turns for help to a Christian women's group. At her first meeting, Gracie gets yet another shock when a pregnant woman shows off a picture of her baby's father and it turns out to be Dennis. Little wonder that when Dennis turns up dead in his hospital bed, it's murder and not natural causes. Now Gracie is a suspect in Dennis' death and must clear herself, but is afraid that one of the other women in Dennis' life might be the killer.

Other books by the same author:
Protecting Holly, 2004
Harbor of His Arms, 2003
Change of the Heart, 2002
The Prodigal's Return, 2001
Walls of Jericho, 2001

Other books you might like:
Ron Benrey, *The Pippa Hunnechurch Series*, 2001-
Ellen Edwards Kennedy, *Irregardless of Murder*, 2001
Lorena McCourtney, *The Ivy Malone Series*, 2004-
Gayle Roper, *The Amhearst Mystery Series*, 1997-
Audrey Stallsmith, *The Thyme Will Tell Series*, 1998-

1011

PHIL CALLAWAY

Wonders Never Cease

(Eugene, Oregon: Harvest House, 2005)

Story type: Contemporary
Subject(s): Small Town Life
Major character(s): Terry Anderson, Teenager
Time period(s): 2000s
Locale(s): Grace, Montana

Summary: High school senior Terry Anderson wants nothing more than to get out of Grace, Montana. Small town life is fine for some people but not for him. Then Terry finds a dead body. Grace is the type of town where nobody locks their doors and crime is virtually unknown. As gossip starts to fly, suspicion soon settles on Terry and his family.

Other books by the same author:
Growing Up on the Edge of the World, 2004

Other books you might like:
Charlene Ann Baumbich, *The Dearest Dorothy Series*, 2004-
Mary Carlson, *The Whispering Pines Series*, 1999-
Kathy Herman, *The Baxter Series*, 2001-
Sally John, *The Other Way Home Series*, 2002-
Vinita Hampton Wright, *Velma Still Cooks in Leeway*, 2000

1012

JACK CAVANAUGH

Dear Enemy

(Minneapolis: Bethany House, 2005)

Story type: Historical/World War II
Subject(s): Prisoners of War; World War II
Major character(s): Annie Rawlings, Nurse
Time period(s): 1940s
Locale(s): Germany

Summary: Annie Rawlings is a nurse and has seen the suffering caused by war firsthand. She blames the enemy, the Germans, and sees nothing good in them. Then Annie is captured behind enemy lines and has her first close-up encounter with the Germans as something other than "The Enemy." She meets a wounded German soldier named Karl and begins to realize that the Germans are just people, like her and other Americans. When Karl and Annie are separated, she tries desperately to track him down.

Other books by the same author:
Above All Earthly Powers, 2004
Beyond the Sacred Page, 2003
His Watchful Eye, 2002
Postmarked Heaven, 2002
While Mortals Sleep, 2001

Other books you might like:
Elyse Larson, *The Women of Valor Series*, 2000-
Jane Peart, *Courageous Bride*, 1998
Judith Pella, *The Daughters of Fortune Series*, 2002-
Penelope J. Stokes, *The Faith on the Homefront Series*, 1996-
Ken Wales, *Sea of Glory*, 2001
Wilma Wall, *Forbidden*, 2004

1013

JACK CAVANAUGH
JERRY KUIPER, Co-Author

Death Watch

(Grand Rapids, Michigan: Zondervan, 2005)

Story type: Mystery
Subject(s): News; Suspense
Major character(s): Sydney St. James, Journalist (television news reporter); Hunz Vonner, Journalist (news anchor)
Time period(s): 2000s
Locale(s): Los Angeles, California

Summary: Television reporter Sydney St. James finds a mysterious note at the scene of a fatal accident. The note told the victim that they had 48 hours to live. Soon Sydney learns of other notes, and other deaths. Could somebody be stalking people and eliminating them? Or is there something even

more sinister afoot? Teaming up with famous news anchor Hunz Vonner, Sydney vows to get to the truth. Author Jack Cavanaugh has written numerous titles, but this is his co-author's first novel, and their first book together.

Other books you might like:
Athol Dickson, *The Garr Reed Series*, 1996-
Alton Gansky, *The Ridgeline Series*, 1998-
Clay Jacobsen, *Circle of Seven*, 2000
Patricia H. Rushford, *The Angel Delaney Series*, 2004-
Susan Wales, *The Chase*, 2004

1014

MINDY STARNS CLARK

The Trouble with Tulip

(Eugene, Oregon: Harvest House, 2005)

Story type: Mystery
Series: Smart Chick Mystery. Book 1
Subject(s): Murder
Major character(s): Josephine Tulip, Detective—Amateur, Writer (advice columnist); Danny Watkins, Photographer
Time period(s): 2000s
Locale(s): United States

Summary: Josephine Tulip is a chemist who has turned her scientific knowledge into a lucrative job as a helpful hints columnist. Her best friend is Danny Watkins, a photographer who dreams of the day his work will appear in the best magazines, but settles for taking pictures of babies and weddings. Danny also struggles with his romantic feelings for Josephine, feelings that are not reciprocated. Love takes a back seat when Josephine's neighbor is accused of murder. Knowing the police are wrong, Josephine decides to take matters into her own hands and find the real killer.

Other books by the same author:
A Quarter for a Kiss, 2004
The Buck Stops Here, 2004
A Dime a Dozen, 2003
Don't Take Any Wooden Nickels, 2003
A Penny for Your Thoughts, 2002

Other books you might like:
Ron Benrey, *The Royal Tunbridge Wells Series*, 2004-
Lynn Bulock, *Love the Sinner*, 2005
Mary-Jane Deeb, *Murder on the Riviera*, 2004
Tim Downs, *The Bug Man Series*, 2003-
Gilbert Morris, *The Dani Ross Series*, 2000-

1015

COLLEEN COBLE

Black Sands

(Nashville: WestBow, 2005)

Story type: Romantic Suspense
Series: Aloha Reef. Book 2
Subject(s): Family Relations
Major character(s): Leilani Silva, Researcher
Time period(s): 2000s
Locale(s): Hawaii

Summary: Leilani Silva has nursed a secret love for Mano Ohano for ages, but he scarcely notices the quiet woman who helps her father with his volcano research. Then Mano accidentally kills his best friend Kale, Leilani's brother. As Leilani's world collapses around her, Mano begins to suspect that Kale is not dead at all. When another Silva sibling turns up missing, Leilani reluctantly turns to Mano for help in learning what is going on in her family.

Other books by the same author:
Distant Echoes, 2005
Beyond a Doubt, 2004
The Cattle Baron's Wife, 2004
Into the Deep, 2004
Without a Trace, 2003

Other books you might like:
Lori Copeland, *Stranded in Paradise*, 2002
Robin Jones Gunn, *Whispers*, 1995
Catherine Palmer, *Sunrise Song*, 2003
Lauraine Snelling, *Hawaiian Sunrise*, 1999
Lori Wick, *Bamboo and Lace*, 2001

1016

JAMES R. COGGINS

Mountaintop Drive

(Chicago: Moody, 2005)

Story type: Mystery
Series: John Smyth. Book 3
Subject(s): Mountain Life
Major character(s): John Smyth, Editor (magazine)
Time period(s): 2000s
Locale(s): Abbotsford, British Columbia, Canada

Summary: John Smyth and his wife Ruby travel to Abbotsford, British Columbia, to attend a church convention. To their delight, they are staying at a beautiful mountaintop house. When a woman is murdered at the house next door, John finds himself drawn into another murder investigation which involves escaped prisoners and troubled teens.

Other books by the same author:
Desolation Highway, 2004
Who's Grace?, 2004

Other books you might like:
Mindy Starns Clark, *The Million Dollar Mysteries Series*, 2002-
Dudley J. Delffs, *The Father Grif Series*, 1998-
Tim Downs, *The Bug Man Series*, 2003-
Kathi Mills-Macias, *The Toni Matthews Series*, 2001-
Sally S. Wright, *The Ben Reese Series*, 1997-

1017

BRANDILYN COLLINS

Dead of Night

(Grand Rapids, Michigan: Zondervan, 2005)

Story type: Mystery
Series: Hidden Faces. Book 3
Subject(s): Artists and Art; Serial Killers

Major character(s): Annie Kingston, Artist (forensic)
Time period(s): 2000s
Locale(s): Redding, California

Summary: A serial killer is terrorizing the area of Redding, California. Forensic artist Annie Kingston is brought in to help in the identification of some of the victims. When the sixth victim is found right in Annie's neighborhood, she begins to wonder if she is going to be the killer's next target.

Other books by the same author:
Brink of Death, 2004
Stain of Guilt, 2004
Capture the Wind for Me, 2003
Color the Sidewalk for Me, 2002
Dread Champion, 2002

Other books you might like:
Colleen Coble, *The Rock Harbor Series*, 2003-
Athol Dickson, *The Garr Reed Series*, 1996-
Alton Gansky, *The Ridgeline Series*, 1998-
Kathi Mills-Macias, *The Toni Matthews Series*, 2001-
Patricia H. Rushford, *The Angel Delaney Series*, 2004-

1018

LORI COPELAND

The Drifter

(Wheaton, Illinois: Tyndale House, 2005)

Story type: Historical/American West
Series: Men of the Saddle. Book 2
Subject(s): American West; Pioneers
Major character(s): Beau Claxton, Cowboy, Drifter; Charity Burk, Settler, Widow(er)
Time period(s): 1860s
Locale(s): Kansas

Summary: Beau Claxton, a cowboy who enjoys the life of an aimless drifter, is found unconscious by widowed homesteader Charity Burk. After nursing Beau back to health, Charity begins to believe he might make a good second husband, however, Beau doesn't agree with her. He finds Charity attractive and charming, but Beau realizes his restless way of life doesn't make him good marriage material.

Other books by the same author:
Mother of Prevention, 2005
A Case of Nosy Neighbors, 2004
The Peacemaker, 2004
Case of Crooked Letters, 2004
Patience, 2004

Other books you might like:
Stephen Bly, *The Code of the West Series*, 1994-
Catherine Palmer, *The Town Called Hope Series*, 1997-
Tracie Peterson, *The Heirs of Montana Series*, 2004-
Lauraine Snelling, *The Red River of the North Series*, 1996-
Stephanie Grace Whitson, *The Keepsake Legacies Series*, 1998-

1019

LORI COPELAND

Mother of Prevention

(New York: Steeple Hill, 2005)

Story type: Romance
Subject(s): Widows/Widowers
Major character(s): Kate Madison, Widow(er)
Time period(s): 2000s
Locale(s): San Francisco, California

Summary: Kate Madison's life is sent into a tailspin when her firefighter husband is killed in the line of duty. Wanting a new start, Kate packs up and moves from Oklahoma to California with her two daughters. New friends help Kate cope with her loss, mother-in-law problems, and her brand new life as a single parent, but she soon learns that humor is the best way of coping with her changed circumstances.

Other books by the same author:
The Drifter, 2005
A Case of Nosy Neighbors, 2004
The Peacemaker, 2004
Case of Crooked Letters, 2004
Patience, 2004

Other books you might like:
Terri Blackstock, *The Second Chances Series*, 1996-
Ray Blackston, *Flabbergasted*, 2003
Robin Jones Gunn, *The Sisterchicks Series*, 2003-
Neta Jackson, *The Yada Yada Prayer Group Series*, 2003-
Annie Jones, *The Route 66 Series*, 1999-
Debra White Smith, *The Seven Sisters Series*, 2000-

1020

LYN COTE

Chloe

(New York: Warner Faith, 2005)

Story type: Historical/Roaring Twenties
Series: Women of Ivy Manor. Book 1
Subject(s): Money; Politics
Major character(s): Chloe Kimball, Model
Time period(s): 1920s
Locale(s): Washington, District of Columbia

Summary: Chloe Kimball should be a happy young woman. Not only is she beautiful and wealthy, but her family is politically prominent in Washington, D.C. Chloe would trade it all for the love and affection of her parents though. After meeting a young man deemed unacceptable by her parents, she breaks away from her family and elopes. Left to make her own way in the world, Chloe finds work as a model. When circumstances force her back home, she finds herself unwilling to go back to the way things used to be and obey her father's wishes.

Other books by the same author:
His Saving Grace, 2004
Loving Constance, 2004
Testing His Patience, 2004
Summer's End, 2003

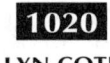

Inspirational

The Preacher's Daughter, 2003

Other books you might like:
James Scott Bell, *Glimpses of Paradise*, 2005
Gilbert Morris, *The Pilgrim Song*, 2003
Jane Peart, *The Senator's Bride*, 1994
Tracie Peterson, *The Desert Roses Series*, 2002-
Michael Phillips, *The Heathersleigh Hall Series*, 1998-

1021

ANNE DAYTON
MAY VANDERBILT, Co-Author

Emily Ever After

(New York: Random House, 2005)

Story type: Contemporary; Humor
Subject(s): Careers; City and Town Life; Publishing
Major character(s): Emily Hinton, Editor
Time period(s): 2000s
Locale(s): New York, New York

Summary: Emily Hinton dreams of escaping from her drab small town and going to New York City. The day finally arrives when she lands a job at a publishing house in Manhattan. Emily soon makes friends at her workplace and begins a flirtation with a handsome man named Bennett. She soon realizes that what Bennett wants from life may not mesh with her morals. Then one of her old boyfriends comes to town and Emily grows even more conflicted. First novel.

Other books you might like:
Judy Baer, *The Whitney Chronicles*, 2004
Kristin Billerbeck, *The Ashley Stockingdale Series*, 2004-
Lori Copeland, *Mother of Prevention*, 2005
Penny Culliford, *The Theodora Series*, 2004-
Robin Jones Gunn, *The Sisterchicks Series*, 2003-
Neta Jackson, *The Yada Yada Prayer Group Series*, 2003-

1022

VANESSA DEL FABBRO

The Road to Home

(New York: Steeple Hill, 2005)

Story type: Contemporary
Subject(s): AIDS (Disease); Race Relations
Major character(s): Monica Brunetti, Journalist
Time period(s): 2000s
Locale(s): Soweto, South Africa

Summary: Journalist Monica Brunetti is carjacked, shot, and left for dead. Monica awakens a few days after the incident to learn that she is in a hospital in Soweto, a city in South Africa populated solely by blacks. Monica wants to be transferred to a white hospital, but her condition forbids it. At first horrified by her situation, Monica soon grows to know the women in the beds near her. One is a woman with AIDS and another has tuberculosis. As Monica learns their stories, she begins to realize how narrow her life is and she resolves to change. First novel.

Where it's reviewed:
Library Journal, April 1, 2005, page 78

Publishers Weekly, March 28, 2005, page S15

Other books you might like:
Linda Chaikin, *Endangered*, 1997
Anne De Graaf, *Into the Nevernight*, 2003
Bette Nordberg, *A Season of Grace*, 2004
Catherine Palmer, *Sunrise Song*, 2003
Karen Rispin, *African Skies*, 2000
Gayle Roper, *Spring Rain*, 2001

1023

TRACI DEPREE

Aprons on a Clothesline

(Colorado Springs, Colorado: WaterBrook, 2005)

Story type: Contemporary
Series: Lake Emily. Book 3
Subject(s): Aging; Small Town Life
Major character(s): Virginia Morgan, Aged Person
Time period(s): 2000s
Locale(s): Lake Emily, Minnesota

Summary: After Virginia Morgan suffers a stroke, she feels useless. Virginia has spent her life taking care of others as a wife, mother, and grandmother. Now she is the one who has to be taken care of, and Virginia isn't sure she cares for the situation. Meanwhile, other residents of the small town of Lake Emily, Minnesota, go about their business, adjusting to the problems life throws at them.

Other books by the same author:
Dandelions in a Jelly Jar, 2004
A Can of Peas, 2003

Other books you might like:
Charlene Ann Baumbich, *The Dearest Dorothy Series*, 2004-
Lori Copeland, *The Heavenly Daze Series*, 2001-
Philip Gulley, *The Harmony Series*, 2000-
Sally John, *The Other Way Home Series*, 2002-
Jan Karon, *The Mitford Series*, 1994-

1024

CECELIA DOWDY

First Mates

(New York: Steeple Hill, 2005)

Story type: Romance
Subject(s): Cruise Ships; Grief; Travel
Major character(s): Rainy Jackson, Tourist; Winston Michaels, Tourist
Time period(s): 2000s
Locale(s): At Sea; Caribbean

Summary: Rainy Jackson almost has to be forced by concerned friends and family to take a cruise. After breaking up with her unfaithful fiance, Rainy had nearly worked herself to the point of a breakdown. Her loved ones are convinced she needs time away from her problems to get her life in order. Once aboard the cruise ship, Rainy is determined to make a new start. Things start looking up when she meets handsome Winston Michaels. Winston is also taking the cruise to have some time away from his troubles. In his case, he is grieving

over the death of his twin sister. Together, the two lonely people become friends and may become more. First novel.

Other books you might like:
Melody Carlson, *Awakening Heart*, 1998
Peggy Darty, *Getaways*, 2000
Elaine Schulte, *Voyage*, 1996
Debra White Smith, *To Rome with Love*, 2001
Linda Windsor, *It Had to Be You*, 2001

1025

SHARON DUNN

Cow Crimes and the Mustang Menace

(Grand Rapids, Michigan: Kregel, 2005)

Story type: Mystery
Series: Ruby Taylor. Book 3
Subject(s): Crime and Criminals
Major character(s): Ruby Taylor, Detective—Amateur
Time period(s): 2000s
Locale(s): Eagleton, Montana

Summary: Eagleton, Montana, is suffering through a rash of bizarre thefts. In each case, the possession that means the most to the victim is stolen. In one case it is a cat, in another a prize-winning bull. Even a 1965 Mustang is targeted. Ruby Taylor thinks she might know what is going on, but she can't get anybody to listen to her. Miffed, Ruby sets off on her own to solve the mystery, only to be confronted with the mysterious death of an outsider.

Other books by the same author:
Sassy Cinderella and the Vigilant Vigilante, 2004
Romance Rustlers and Thunderbird Thieves, 2003

Other books you might like:
Ron Benrey, *The Pippa Hunnechurch Series*, 2001-
Mindy Starns Clark, *The Million Dollar Mysteries Series*, 2002-
Colleen Coble, *The Rock Harbor Series*, 2003-
Lorena McCourtney, *The Ivy Malone Series*, 2004-
Audrey Stallsmith, *The Thyme Will Tell Series*, 1998-

1026

WANDA L. DYSON

Intimidation

(Uhrichsville, Ohio: Barbour, 2005)

Story type: Mystery
Subject(s): Kidnapping
Major character(s): Donnie Bevere, FBI Agent; J.J. Johnson, Detective—Police; Zoe Shefford, Psychic
Time period(s): 2000s
Locale(s): United States

Summary: FBI agent Donnie Bevere is horrified when his wife is kidnapped. Making matters worse is the fact that the FBI refuses to help Donnie track his wife down due to concerns over national security. In desperation, Donnie turns to J.J. Johnson and Zoe Shefford for help. Unfortunately, the terrorists behind the plot have no intention of letting their only bargaining chip—Donnie's wife—go free.

Other books by the same author:
Obsession, 2004
Abduction, 2003

Other books you might like:
James Scott Bell, *The Nephilim Seed*, 2001
Terri Blackstock, *Southern Storm*, 2003
Ted Dekker, *Thunder of Heaven*, 2002
Dee Henderson, *The Rescuer*, 2003
Kathy Herman, *Eye of the Beholder*, 2005

1027

CHERIE PARIS EDWARDS

Plenty Good Room

(New York: Warner, 2005)

Story type: Contemporary
Subject(s): Foster Children; Foster Parents; Runaways
Major character(s): Tamara Britton, Social Worker, Foster Parent
Time period(s): 2000s
Locale(s): Springfield, Illinois

Summary: Tamara Britton works for the Care for Kids Agency's child protective unit, helping parents and children who are in a state of crisis. Tamara's own troubled childhood encourages her to fight to save the children who come under her jurisdiction. Then she meets 14-year-old runaway Sienna, who lives by her own rules. With nowhere else to place Sienna, Tamara agrees to take the girl into her own home temporarily. The two clash immediately, with Sienna refusing to abide by Tamara's rules. When Tamara's suppressed memories of her abusive childhood surface, she is forced to confront her own demons, while helping Sienna fight hers as well. First novel.

Where it's reviewed:
Publishers Weekly, March 14, 2005, page 46

Other books you might like:
Angela Benson, *The Genesis House Series*, 2000-
Venise Berry, *Colored Sugar Water*, 2002
Michele Andrea Bowen, *Church Folk*, 2001
Sharon Ewell Foster, *Ain't No River*, 2001
Felicia Mason, *Testimony*, 2002

1028

DONNA FLEISHER

Wounded Healer

(Grand Rapids, Michigan: Zondervan, 2005)

Story type: Contemporary
Series: Homeland Heroes. Book 1
Subject(s): Veterans
Major character(s): Erin Grayson, Veteran (Desert Storm); Chris McIntyre, Veteran (Desert Storm)
Time period(s): 2000s
Locale(s): Colorado

Summary: During their time serving in Desert Storm, soldiers Erin Grayson and Chris McIntyre became good friends, helping each other through all the bad times. Then a secret from

Inspirational

Chris' past emerges that tears the two friends apart. Years later, Chris is still on the run from her past, certain that nothing can save her. Erin knows better, and goes to Chris' side to give her a reason to live. First novel.

Other books you might like:

G. Roger Corey, *Eden Springs*, 1999
Robin Lee Hatcher, *Beyond the Shadows*, 2004
Dee Henderson, *The Uncommon Heroes Series*, 2000-
Alan Maki, *Written on Her Heart*, 2002
Debra White Smith, *The Seven Sisters Series*, 2000-

1029

ANN H. GABHART

The Scent of Lilacs

(Grand Rapids, Michigan: Fleming H. Revell, 2005)

Story type: Contemporary
Subject(s): Clergy; Fathers and Daughters
Major character(s): Jocie Brooke, Teenager
Time period(s): 1960s (1964)
Locale(s): Hollyhill, Kentucky

Summary: Life in the small town of Hollyhill, Kentucky, in 1964 seems tranquil, but the residents have troubles just like people living in big cities. Teenager Jocie Brooke is struggling to understand her family. Her father is a local minister and pillar of the community, but he is tormented by his broken marriage and frustrated by his difficulties in raising a daughter alone. When Jocie begins to dig into her family's past to find answers to questions her father refuses to answer, she unearths secrets that might best have been left uncovered.

Other books by the same author:

The Look of Eagles, 1986
A Chance Hero, 1985
A Heart Divided, 1980
A Forbidden Yearning, 1978

Other books you might like:

Cliff Coon, *The Mending String*, 2004
Robin Lee Hatcher, *Patterns of Love*, 2001
Patricia Hickman, *The Touch*, 2002
Nicholas Sparks, *A Walk to Remember*, 1999
Brad Whittington, *Welcome to Fred*, 2003

1030

ALTON GANSKY

Before Another Dies

(Grand Rapids, Michigan: Zondervan, 2005)

Story type: Mystery
Series: Madison Glenn. Book 2
Subject(s): Politics; Serial Killers
Major character(s): Madison ''Maddy'' Glenn, Political Figure (mayor)
Time period(s): 2000s
Locale(s): Santa Rita, California

Summary: Maddy Glenn has been happily serving as the mayor of Santa Rita for some time, but she believes she can do more on a higher level and so decides to run for Congress.

As Maddy's campaign kicks into gear, she faces an unexpected challenge when three murders in three days rock the town of Santa Rita. Is there a serial killer on the loose and are the deaths somehow related to Maddy's campaign?

Other books by the same author:

Submerged, 2005
Beneath the Ice, 2004
The Incumbent, 2004
A Treasure Deep, 2003
Out of Time, 2003

Other books you might like:

T. Davis Bunn, *Drummer in the Dark*, 2001
Angela Elwell Hunt, *The Justice*, 2001
Clay Jacobsen, *Circle of Seven*, 2000
Shane Johnson, *A Form of Godliness*, 2004
Bob Larson, *The Senator's Agenda*, 1995

1031

ALTON GANSKY

Director's Cut

(Grand Rapids, Michigan: Zondervan, 2005)

Story type: Mystery
Series: Madison Glenn. Book 3
Subject(s): Movie Industry; Politics
Major character(s): Madison ''Maddy'' Glenn, Political Figure (mayor); Catherine Anderson, Actress
Time period(s): 2000s
Locale(s): Santa Rita, California

Summary: Maddy Glenn, the mayor of Santa Rita, California, is gearing up for what promises to be a tough campaign for a seat in Congress. When Maddy's actress cousin Catherine Anderson turns up in Santa Rita, the campaign takes a back seat to Catherine's trouble. In town to star in a local dinner theatre production, Catherine is shocked when the body of her chauffeur is discovered floating in her swimming pool. As the police investigate and Catherine finds herself in the middle of a growing scandal, a mysterious script is delivered to her home. Soon Catherine realizes she has become the target of a murderous stalker.

Other books by the same author:

Before Another Dies, 2005
Submerged, 2005
Beneath the Ice, 2004
The Incumbent, 2004
A Treasure Deep, 2003

Other books you might like:

Mary-Jane Deeb, *Murder on the Riviera*, 2004
Karen Kingsbury, *Fame*, 2005
Josh McDowell, *Vote of Intolerance*, 1997
Gilbert Morris, *All That Glitters*, 1999
Sally S. Wright, *The Ben Reese Series*, 1997-

1032

ALTON GANSKY

Submerged

(Uhrichsville, Ohio: Barbour, 2005)

Story type: Mystery
Series: Perry Sachs. Book 3
Subject(s): Fathers and Sons; Secrets
Major character(s): Perry Sachs, Engineer
Time period(s): 2000s
Locale(s): United States

Summary: As Perry Sachs' father lies dying from an unknown illness, he begins muttering mysterious numbers and names, and a year—1974. Believing the mysterious words are somehow connected with his father's illness, Perry resolves to track down their meanings. He digs into his father's past and learns of his involvement in a mysterious project that took place in Nevada in 1974. Two other people involved in that project have died from the same mysterious illness as Perry's father. A secret cavern may hold the truth to why the men are dying, but it may be too late for Perry to save his father, or even save himself.

Other books by the same author:
Before Another Dies, 2005
Beneath the Ice, 2004
The Incumbent, 2004
A Treasure Deep, 2003
Out of Time, 2003

Other books you might like:
Paul T. McHenry, *Code Name Antidote*, 2000
Tom Morrisey, *Deep Blue*, 2005
Oliver North, *The Peter Newman Series*, 2002-
Michael Phillips, *The Rift in Time Series*, 1997-
Kel Richards, *Dark Storm*, 2004

1033

SHARON K. GILBERT

Winds of Evil

(New Kensington, Pennsylvania: Whitaker House, 2005)

Story type: Fantasy
Series: Laodicea Chronicles. Book 1
Subject(s): Missing Persons; Supernatural
Major character(s): Katherine Adamson, Writer
Time period(s): 2000s
Locale(s): Eden, Indiana

Summary: Writer Katherine Adamson returns to her hometown of Eden, Indiana, to settle her aunt's estate. Having looked back fondly on the town, Katherine is shocked to learn of several horrifying events that have shaken it in recent months. A series of town leaders have been subjected to blackmail, with one committing suicide. Unusual babies are being born. Two teenagers have disappeared. Strange lights appear over the countryside. What is happening in Eden? Could all the mysterious happenings be the result of aliens? Or is it something even more sinister? Katherine teams up

with a local newspaper editor to find out. This book was originally published privately in 2004. First novel.

Other books you might like:
Shaunti Feldhahn, *The Veritas Conflict*, 2001
Angela Elwell Hunt, *The Immortal*, 2000
Kathleen Morgan, *The Guardians of Gadiel Series*, 2005-
Nancy Moser, *The Mustard Seed Series*, 1998-
Linda Wichman, *Legend of the Emerald Rose*, 2005

1034

DEEANNE GIST

A Bride Most Begrudging

(Minneapolis: Bethany House, 2005)

Story type: Historical
Subject(s): Kidnapping; Servants
Major character(s): Constance Morrow, Noblewoman (daughter of an earl); Drew O'Connor, Farmer (tobacco)
Time period(s): 17th century
Locale(s): Virginia, American Colonies; At Sea

Summary: Lady Constance Morrow boards a ship transporting prisoners to the American colonies in order to say good-bye to her beloved uncle. The crew realizes the beautiful young woman might earn them some extra money and they imprison her with other detainees. When her uncle dies before they reach the colonies, Lady Constance is on her own. She is bound over to a tobacco farmer, who promptly loses her in a card game to Drew O'Connor. Drew is in mourning and wants nothing romantic from Constance—just a maid and companion for his sister. Not taking Constance's claims of kidnapping seriously, Drew is dismayed when she shows little aptitude for cooking or cleaning. Soon, however, the two begin to fall in love. First novel.

Other books you might like:
Dianna Crawford, *The Frontier Women Series*, 2000-
J.M. Hochstetler, *The Let Freedom Ring Series*, 2004-
Gilbert Morris, *The Liberty Bell Series*, 1995-
Janette Oke, *The Song of Acadia Series*, 1999-
Marlo M. Schalesky, *The Freedom's Shadow Series*, 2000-

1035

TRICIA GOYER

Dawn of a Thousand Nights

(Chicago: Moody, 2005)

Story type: Historical/World War II
Subject(s): Airplanes; World War II
Major character(s): Daniel Lukens, Military Personnel (Army Air Corps), Prisoner (prisoner-of-war); Libby Conners, Pilot
Time period(s): 1940s
Locale(s): Hawaii; Philippines

Summary: Daniel Lukens loves flying and being a member of the Army Air Corps. He also loves female pilot Libby Conners whom he meets while stationed in Hawaii, but when Daniel is transferred to the Philippines, their romance seems threatened. Then Pearl Harbor is bombed and their personal

Inspirational

problems are thrust aside due to more global concerns. Already in the Armed Forces, Daniel quickly finds himself in combat situations and becomes one of the soldiers to endure the Bataan Death March. Libby joins the Women's Auxiliary Ferrying Squadron to do her bit for the war effort, but finds herself facing other challenges due to a new man in her life and a freak accident.

Other books by the same author:
Night Song, 2004
From Dust and Ashes, 2003

Other books you might like:
Elyse Larson, *The Women of Valor Series*, 2000-
Jane Peart, *Courageous Bride*, 1998
Judith Pella, *The Daughters of Fortune Series*, 2002-
Lori Wick, *Every Storm*, 2004
Robert L. Wise, *The Narrow Door at Colditz*, 2004

1036
IRENE HANNON

The Best Gift
(New York: Steeple Hill, 2005)

Story type: Romance
Subject(s): Books and Reading
Major character(s): A.J. Williams, Store Owner (bookstore); Blake Sullivan, Businessman (manager of bookstore)
Time period(s): 2000s
Locale(s): St. Louis, Missouri

Summary: Blake Sullivan has worked at the Turning Leaves bookstore for years, turning it into a thriving business when Jo, the owner, becomes ill and dies. To his dismay, Jo doesn't leave the bookstore to him, but instead wills it to her flighty niece A.J. Jo thought her niece needed an anchor in her life, and hoped that anchor will be the bookstore. Blake and A.J. do not get along at first, but soon begin to believe that Jo may have been right in throwing them together when they fall in love.

Other books by the same author:
Crossroads, 2003
Never Say Goodbye, 2002
The Way Home, 2000
It Had to Be You, 1999
One Special Christmas, 1999

Other books you might like:
Dorothy Clark, *Beauty for Ashes*, 2004
Dana Corbit, *An Honest Life*, 2003
Valerie Hansen, *Blessings of the Heart*, 2003
Mae Nunn, *Sealed with a Kiss*, 2005
Marta Perry, *Promise Forever*, 2003

1037
NEESA HART

Necessary Evils
(Wheaton, Illinois: Tyndale House, 2005)

Story type: End of the World
Series: End of State. Book 3

Subject(s): End-Times
Major character(s): Brad Benton, Political Figure (White House chief of staff)
Time period(s): Indeterminate Future
Locale(s): Washington, District of Columbia

Summary: Millions of people around the world have mysteriously disappeared. Among them is press secretary George Romero. White House Chief of Staff Brad Benton assumes Romero's disappearance is no different from all of the others. When Brad receives evidence that Romero may actually have been murdered, he begins to investigate only to find himself the target of a murder plot. This series is related to the popular Left Behind series by Jerry B. Jenkins and Tim LaHaye, with the same events shown through a political angle.

Other books by the same author:
Impeachable Offense, 2004
Want Ad Wedding, 2004
End of State, 2003
Her Passionate Pirate, 2001
You Made Me Love You, 2000

Other books you might like:
Ken Abraham, *The Prodigal Project Series*, 2003-
Andrei Codrescu, *Messiah*, 1999
Tim F. LaHaye, *The Left Behind Series*, 1995-
  Jerry B. Jenkins, co-author
Mel Odom, *The Apocalypse Series*, 2003-
Robert L. Wise, *The Tribulation Survival Series*, 2004-

1038
ROBIN LEE HATCHER

Veterans Way
(Grand Rapids, Michigan: Fleming H. Revell, 2005)

Story type: Contemporary
Series: Hart's Crossing. Book 2
Subject(s): Widows/Widowers
Major character(s): Jimmy Scott, Widow(er); Stephanie Watson, Widow(er)
Time period(s): 2000s
Locale(s): Hart's Crossing, Idaho

Summary: When he left Hart's Crossing at the age of 18 to join the Army, Jimmy Scott left behind his high school sweetheart Stephanie. Jimmy thought they were too young to marry. The years have passed and now both Jimmy and Stephanie are widowed. After being away for over 50 years, Jimmy returns home to learn that there are still sparks with Stephanie. As the two reminisce over old times, they begin to wonder if they might still have a chance at romance.

Other books by the same author:
The Victory Club, 2005
Beyond the Shadows, 2004
Legacy Lane, 2004
Catching Katie, 2003
Promised to Me, 2003

Other books you might like:
Kristen Heitzmann, *The Still of Night*, 2003
Roxanne Henke, *Finding Ruth*, 2003
David Lewis, *Coming Home*, 2004

Alan Maki, *Written on Her Heart*, 2002
Janette Oke, *The Matchmakers*, 1997
Jane Peart, *Autumn Encore*, 1985

1039

ROXANNE HENKE

Always Jan

(Eugene, Oregon: Harvest House, 2005)

Story type: Contemporary
Series: Coming Home to Brewster. Book 4
Subject(s): Aging
Major character(s): Jan Jordan, Spouse, Parent
Time period(s): 2000s
Locale(s): Brewster, North Dakota

Summary: Jan Jordan is facing another birthday, and she isn't happy about it. Jan had always been the "pretty one" in the family, so aging is not going well for her. Not liking what she sees in the mirror, Jan decides to take action. Plastic surgery may not restore her youth, but it might at least slow down what Jan believes is unacceptable: her descent into middle age.

Other books by the same author:
Becoming Olivia, 2004
Finding Ruth, 2003
After Anne, 2002

Other books you might like:
Terri Blackstock, *The Second Chances Series*, 1996-
Mary Carlson, *The Whispering Pines Series*, 1999-
Robin Jones Gunn, *The Glenbrooke Series*, 1995-
Beverly LaHaye, *The Seasons Series*, 1999-
Debra White Smith, *The Seven Sisters Series*, 2000-

1040

KATHY HERMAN

Eye of the Beholder

(Sisters, Oregon: Multnomah, 2005)

Story type: Mystery
Series: Seaport Suspense. Book 2
Subject(s): Terrorism
Major character(s): Guy Jones, Lawyer; Ellen Jones, Spouse (of Guy)
Time period(s): 2000s
Locale(s): Seaport, Oregon

Summary: Terrorism becomes more than a vague threat to the small town of Seaport when a boat containing explosives is found in its port. Five local Arabic men are arrested and it is suspected that a terrorist cell is operating somewhere nearby. Ellen Jones is as horrified at the developments as anybody else in Seaport, but she refuses to give up her friendship with an Iranian-American woman. This displeases Ellen's husband, who is concerned that the friendship will reflect badly on him and hurt his career. When the FBI begins investigating Ellen, her marriage to Guy begins to fall apart.

Other books by the same author:
A Shred of Evidence, 2005

Poor Mrs. Rigsby, 2004
A Fine Line, 2003
High Stakes, 2003
Day of Reckoning, 2002

Other books you might like:
Dee Henderson, *True Honor*, 2002
Karen Kingsbury, *One Tuesday Morning*, 2003
Lorena McCourtney, *Whirlpool*, 2002
Michael Phillips, *King's Crossroads*, 2003
Dawn Ringling, *Jumping in Sunset*, 2003

1041

PATRICIA HICKMAN

Whisper Town

(New York: Warner Faith, 2005)

Story type: Contemporary
Series: Millwood Hollow. Book 3
Subject(s): Depression (Economic); Orphans; Racism
Major character(s): Jeb Nubey, Religious (minister)
Time period(s): 1930s
Locale(s): Nazareth, Arkansas

Summary: Jeb Nubey, the fugitive turned preacher and "father" of three orphaned children, has settled into the town of Nazareth, Arkansas. The oldest of his brood is now a teenager and as Jeb copes with the typical problems of raising a daughter of that age, he is confronted with another problem when an infant is left on his doorstep. The baby is black, something that does not matter in the least to Jeb. To others in the small Southern town, Jeb's intention of caring for the baby does not sit easily and Jeb soon finds himself in the middle of growing racial tensions.

Other books by the same author:
Nazareth's Song, 2004
Fallen Angels, 2003
Sandpebbles, 2002
The Touch, 2002
Katrina's Wings, 2000

Other books you might like:
Sharon Ewell Foster, *Passing by Samaria*, 2000
Robin Lee Hatcher, *The Shepherd's Voice*, 2000
Bonnie Leon, *The Sowers Trilogy*, 1998-
Gary E. Parker, *The Blue Ridge Legacy Series*, 2001-
Lance Wubbels, *The Gentle Hills Series*, 1994-

1042

LIZ CURTIS HIGGS

Whence Came a Prince

(Colorado Springs, Colorado: WaterBrook, 2005)

Story type: Historical
Series: Lowlands of Scotland. Book 3
Subject(s): Brothers; Family Problems; Sibling Rivalry
Major character(s): Jamie McKie, Heir (potential)
Time period(s): 1780s
Locale(s): Scotland

Inspirational

Summary: Jamie McKie returns to his ancestral home of Glentrool to confront the family members that are keeping him from his rightful inheritance: his evil uncle Lachlan, his brother Evan, and his father Alec. Jamie must also come to terms with the two women in his life. Leana is the mother of his son Ian, but her sister Rose is expecting his second child. Somehow, Jamie must find the courage to make decisions that will affect the lives of many people.

Other books by the same author:
Fair Is the Rose, 2004
Thorn in My Heart, 2003
Bookends, 2000
Mixed Signals, 1999

Other books you might like:
B.J. Hoff, *The Song of Erin Series*, 1997-
Angela Elwell Hunt, *The Heirs of Cahira O'Connor Series*, 1998-
Grace Johnson, *The Scottish Shores Series*, 1997-
Kathleen Morgan, *Embrace the Dawn*, 2002
Bodie Thoene, *The Galway Chronicles*, 1997-

1043

DENISE HILDRETH

Savannah Comes Undone

(Nashville: WestBow, 2005)

Story type: Contemporary
Series: Savannah. Book 2
Subject(s): Mothers and Daughters
Major character(s): Savannah Phillips, Writer
Time period(s): 2000s
Locale(s): Savannah, Georgia

Summary: Savannah Phillips is settling into a new job and a new apartment when her always controversial mother makes another big splash by chaining herself to a monument that is causing controversy in the women's hometown. Not wanting to get involved in her mother's life yet again, Savannah does her best to ignore the situation. While that proves impossible, Savannah soon has other complications invading her life, including an old flame that refuses to be rekindled and a couple of other new men in her life.

Other books by the same author:
Savannah from Savannah, 2004

Other books you might like:
Ginny Aiken, *The Bellamy's Blossoms Series*, 2000-
Judy Baer, *The Whitney Chronicles*, 2004
Charlene Ann Baumbich, *The Dearest Dorothy Series*, 2004-
Anne Dayton, *Emily Ever After*, 2005
Annie Jones, *Deep Dixie*, 1999

1044

PATTI ANN HILL

Always Green

(Minneapolis: Bethany House, 2005)

Story type: Contemporary
Series: Garden Gates. Book 2

Subject(s): Drought; Gardens and Gardening; Widows/Widowers
Major character(s): Mibby Garrett, Landscaper, Widow(er)
Time period(s): 2000s
Locale(s): Colorado

Summary: Mibby Garrett is still adjusting to the sudden death of her husband, but is beginning to realize that life will go on. There are constant reminders of that truth as Mibby, a garden designer, faces a drought that threatens to ruin her business. Mibby is also worried about her son Ky, who is going through adolescence without a father figure in his life. To make matters worse, Mibby's mother and sister drop in for a visit.

Other books by the same author:
Like a Watered Garden, 2005

Other books you might like:
Lori Copeland, *Mother of Prevention*, 2005
Paige Lee Elliston, *Changes of Heart*, 2005
Leslie Gould, *Garden of Dreams*, 2003
Patricia Hickman, *Sandpebbles*, 2002
Marta Perry, *A Mother's Wish*, 2002

1045

JOSEPH H. HILLEY

Double Take

(Colorado Springs, Colorado: RiverOak, 2005)

Story type: Mystery
Series: Mike Connelly. Book 2
Subject(s): Alcoholism
Major character(s): Mike Connelly, Lawyer
Time period(s): 2000s
Locale(s): Mobile, Alabama

Summary: After becoming a Christian, lawyer Mike Connelly has given up drinking and parted ways with his stripper girlfriend. Unfortunately, the fact that he turned over a new leaf has done little to help Mike's career. When a police officer suspected in a bombing death turns to Mike for help, he agrees to take the case even though it takes him into the seedy world of dogfights, bars, and strip clubs.

Other books by the same author:
Sober Justice, 2004

Other books you might like:
Rick Acker, *Dead Man's Rule*, 2005
James Scott Bell, *Blind Justice*, 2000
Chuck Chitwood, *The Trial of Job*, 2000
Kathi Mills-Macias, *The Toni Matthews Series*, 2001-
Craig Parshall, *The Chambers of Justice Series*, 2002-

1046

DOUGLAS HIRT

Flight to Eden

(Colorado Springs, Colorado: RiverOak, 2005)

Story type: Fantasy
Subject(s): Ancient History; Good and Evil
Major character(s): Rhone, Prehistoric Human

Time period(s): Indeterminate Past
Locale(s): Cradleland, Fictional Country

Summary: Civilization is evolving in the world known as the Cradleland, the place where the descendents of Seth live. Satan has caused the fall of man and now wants to take over earth. The humans, among them Rhone, intend to fight Satan and honor their creator. Hearing of a prophecy declaring that a savior intended to save the humans will be born from God and a human, Satan decides to make certain the prophecy does not come true.

Other books by the same author:
Ketcham's Land, 2002
A Good Town, 2001
The Wrong Man, 2000
Shadow Road, 1999
Deadwood, 1998

Other books you might like:
Randy Alcorn, *Lord Foulgrin's Letters*, 2000
Roger Elwood, *The Angelwalk Series*, 1989-
Shaunti Feldhahn, *The Veritas Conflict*, 2001
Nancy Moser, *The Mustard Seed Series*, 1998-
Kathy Tyers, *The Firebird Trilogy*, 1999-

1047

ANGELA ELWELL HUNT

Unspoken

(Nashville: WestBow, 2005)

Story type: Contemporary
Subject(s): Animals/Monkeys; Zoos
Major character(s): Glee Granger, Scientist; Sema, Animal (gorilla)
Time period(s): 2000s
Locale(s): Clearwater, Florida

Summary: Scientist Glee Granger raised Sema, a Western Lowland gorilla from birth and the two share a special bond. Not only can they communicate through sign language, but Glee is trying to teach Sema to read. When the director of the zoo that owns Sema learns of the animal's talents, he is thrilled because her "tricks" would be a great draw for his zoo. Reluctantly, Glee agrees to return Sema to the zoo. When a near-death experience has Sema communicating with a "shiny man" who talks about God, Glee begins to question her own lack of faith.

Where it's reviewed:
Publishers Weekly, April 4, 2005, page 44

Other books by the same author:
The Awakening, 2004
The Debt, 2004
The Canopy, 2003
The Pearl, 2003
The Shadow Women, 2002

Other books you might like:
Mary Carlson, *The Whispering Pines Series*, 1999-
Colleen Coble, *The Rock Harbor Series*, 2003-
Margaret Daley, *A Family for Tory*, 2004
Robin Jones Gunn, *The Glenbrooke Series*, 1995-

Marta Perry, *Hero in Her Heart*, 2004

1048

DIANN HUNT

Hot Flashes and Cold Cream

(Nashville: WestBow, 2005)

Story type: Contemporary
Subject(s): Women
Major character(s): Maggie Hayden, Spouse
Time period(s): 2000s
Locale(s): United States

Summary: Maggie Hayden receives a vicious shock when a former classmate doesn't recognize her because she has changed so drastically. Maggie had just been going along in a rut and hadn't realized just how drab her life had become. Forced to take notice, Maggie soon realizes that her children are grown, her husband is distant, and her life is empty. Now she just has to figure out what to do to give her life meaning.

Other books by the same author:
Hearts under Construction, 2005
Prayers, Paws, and Providence, 2005
A Whale of a Marriage, 2004
Basket of Secrets, 2004
We Have This Moment, 2004

Other books you might like:
Terri Blackstock, *The Second Chances Series*, 1996-
Lori Copeland, *Mother of Prevention*, 2005
Robin Jones Gunn, *The Sisterchicks Series*, 2003-
Neta Jackson, *The Yada Yada Prayer Group Series*, 2003-
Debra White Smith, *The Austen Series*, 2004-

1049

DENISE HUNTER

Saving Grace

(West Monroe, Louisiana: Howard, 2005)

Story type: Contemporary
Series: New Heights. Book 2
Subject(s): Pregnancy; Single Parent Families
Major character(s): Natalie Coombs, Counselor (crisis pregnancy center)
Time period(s): 2000s
Locale(s): Jackson Hole, Wyoming

Summary: Natalie Coombs is a divorced mother of two sons. Her job at a crisis pregnancy center gives her a feeling of fulfillment and she does her best to help every young woman who comes through the doors looking for advice and assistance. When a new teenaged client desperately needs help, Natalie oversteps her bounds to try to get the girl the aid she needs. Unfortunately, things go horribly wrong and Natalie soon finds herself the target of a mysterious attacker.

Other books by the same author:
Mending Places, 2004

Other books you might like:
Sylvia Bambola, *Tears in a Bottle*, 2001

Inspirational

William Cutrer, *False Positive*, 2002
Beverly LaHaye, *Showers in Season*, 2000
Diane Noble, *The Last Storyteller*, 2004
Dawn Ringling, *Jumping in Sunset*, 2003

1050

NETA JACKSON

The Yada Yada Prayer Group Gets Real

(Nashville: Integrity, 2005)

Story type: Contemporary
Series: Yada Yada Prayer Group. Book 3
Subject(s): Friendship; Prayer
Major character(s): Jodi Baxter, Spouse, Parent; Leslie "Stu" Stuart, Neighbor
Time period(s): 2000s
Locale(s): Chicago, Illinois

Summary: Jodi Baxter faces a crisis when her upstairs neighbors move out and Leslie "Stu" Stuart, who is definitely not amongst her friends, moves in. With Stu living right upstairs, Jodi's peaceful life is turned upside down. However, there is also a possibility of good coming from the situation. Stu has always kept secrets about herself and with her new physical closeness to Jodi, it is possible that the two might finally be able to put the past behind them and become friends.

Other books by the same author:
The Yada Yada Prayer Group Gets Down, 2004
The Yada Yada Prayer Group, 2003

Other books you might like:
Terri Blackstock, *The Second Chances Series*, 1996-
Robin Jones Gunn, *The Glenbrooke Series*, 1995-
Robin Jones Gunn, *The Sisterchicks Series*, 2003-
Beverly LaHaye, *The Seasons Series*, 1999-
Lisa Samson, *The Church Ladies*, 2001
Debra White Smith, *The Seven Sisters Series*, 2000-

1051

MELANIE M. JESCHKE

Expectations

(Eugene, Oregon: Harvest House, 2005)

Story type: Contemporary
Series: Oxford Chronicles. Book 2
Subject(s): Universities and Colleges
Major character(s): Kate MacKenzie, Spouse; David MacKenzie, Spouse, Professor
Time period(s): 1960s
Locale(s): Oxford, England; Paris, France

Summary: Kate MacKenzie has recently learned that she is pregnant. She is ambivalent about her expected child since she is newly married and had hoped to have some time alone with her husband before they took on the responsibility of parenthood. Her husband David is thrilled with the news, however. Coupled with his news that he has a new position as visiting lecturer at the American University in Paris, David believes the couple is starting their marriage extremely well. Unfortunately, the MacKenzies have some problems ahead.

Other books by the same author:
Inklings, 2004

Other books you might like:
Donna Fletcher Crow, *The Cambridge Chronicles*, 1994-
Robin Jones Gunn, *The Christy and Todd the College Years Series*, 2000-
Jim Kraus, *The Circle of Destiny Series*, 2000-
Lauraine Snelling, *The Return to Red River Series*, 2001-
Brad Whittington, *The Fred Series*, 2003-

1052

JO KADLECEK

The Sound of My Voice

(Colorado Springs, Colorado: WaterBrook, 2005)

Story type: Contemporary
Subject(s): Clergy; Fathers and Daughters
Major character(s): Jordan Riddle, Writer (aspiring playwright), Waiter/Waitress; Peter Riddle, Religious (assistant pastor)
Time period(s): 2000s
Locale(s): New York, New York; Jackson, Mississippi

Summary: Jordan Riddle waits tables to pay the bills while she waits for her big break as an aspiring playwright. Although living in New York City, she still embraces the faith she found as a young girl growing up as a minister's daughter in Mississippi. Her father is still the assistant pastor at a Baptist church and he shares his daughter's deep devotion to God. However, in spite of their shared faith, father and daughter have never gotten along well. After five years of silence, the two must now face their past difficulties and see if they can move past them. First novel.

Other books you might like:
Terri Blackstock, *Seaside*, 2001
Cliff Coon, *The Mending String*, 2004
Ann H. Gabhart, *The Scent of Lilacs*, 2005
Gilbert Morris, *All That Glitters*, 1999
Catherine Palmer, *The Happy Room*, 2002

1053

L.A. KELLY (Pseudonym of Leisha Kelly)

Tahn

(Grand Rapids, Michigan: Fleming H. Revell, 2005)

Story type: Historical
Subject(s): Kidnapping; Middle Ages; Orphans
Major character(s): Tahn Dorn, Criminal; Netta, Captive
Time period(s): Indeterminate Past
Locale(s): Fictional Country

Summary: In an unnamed medieval world, Tahn Dorn has grown up under the tutelage of an evil man named Samis. Seeing no alternative than to obey Samis, Tahn does as he is ordered. Told to kidnap the beautiful Netta from her room one night, Tahn allows her to save her loved ones by letting her scream, alerting them to the fact that their castle is on fire. Breaking away from Samis, Tahn hides Netta in a cave and manages to help eight of Samis' new young criminal trainees

get away as well. As Netta cares for the young children, she begins to see the good in Tahn, little realizing that he is the man who killed her husband. Author L.A. Kelly writes other novels under the name Leisha Kelly.

Where it's reviewed:
Publishers Weekly, January 3, 2005, page 37

Other books you might like:
DeAnna Dodson, *In Honor Bound*, 1997
Angela Elwell Hunt, *The Heirs of Cahira O'Connor Series*, 1998-
Kathleen Morgan, *Embrace the Dawn*, 2002
Francine Rivers, *The Mark of the Lion Series*, 1993-
T.M. Williams, *The Seven Kingdoms Series*, 1999-

1054

KAREN KINGSBURY

Fame

(Wheaton, Illinois: Tyndale House, 2005)

Story type: Contemporary
Series: Firstborn. Book 1
Subject(s): Actors and Actresses
Major character(s): Dayne Matthews, Actor; Katy Hart, Actress
Time period(s): 2000s
Locale(s): Bloomington, Indiana; Los Angeles, California

Summary: Dayne Matthews is one of the hottest actors in America. He has everything he has ever wanted, including fame and more money than he could ever spend in one lifetime. Something is missing from his life though. On a visit to Bloomington, Indiana, Dayne meets a young actress named Katy Hart. Thinking Katy might be what he needs in his life, Dayne convinces the producer of his new movie to hire her for a role.

Other books by the same author:
Beyond Tuesday Morning, 2004
Oceans Apart, 2004
Sarah's Song, 2004
Maggie's Miracle, 2003
One Tuesday Morning, 2003

Other books you might like:
James Scott Bell, *Breach of Promise*, 2004
Robin Jones Gunn, *Waterfalls*, 2004
Gilbert Morris, *All That Glitters*, 1999
Tracie Peterson, *A Slender Thread*, 2000
Alison Strobel, *Worlds Collide*, 2005

1055

KAREN KINGSBURY

A Thousand Tomorrows

(New York: Center Street, 2005)

Story type: Contemporary
Subject(s): Animals/Bulls; Illness; Rodeos
Major character(s): Cody Gunner, Rodeo Rider (bull rider); Ali Daniels, Rodeo Rider (cowgirl)
Time period(s): 2000s

Locale(s): United States

Summary: When bull rider Cody Gunner was only eight years old, his father abandoned his family because he could not cope with his son Carl's Down's syndrome. As a result of this betrayal, Cody has never put much faith into the ideas of true love or marriage. Then he meets spirited Ali Daniels, a cowgirl in the rodeo Cody is traveling with. Ali comes from a close-knit and loving family and is more than willing to fall in love and share her life with somebody. She has a secret though. Ali has cystic fibrosis and has a shortened lifespan, something she is worsening by her choice of career. Once Cody learns the truth about Ali's condition, he must decide whether to take off as his father did, or stand by the woman he has grown to love.

Where it's reviewed:
Library Journal, April 1, 2005, page 79

Other books by the same author:
Fame, 2005
Hannah's Hope, 2005
Beyond Tuesday Morning, 2004
Oceans Apart, 2004
Sarah's Song, 2004

Other books you might like:
Sharon Baldacci, *A Sundog Moment*, 2004
Roxanne Henke, *After Anne*, 2002
Beverly LaHaye, *Season of Blessing*, 2002
Beverly Lewis, *The Sunroom*, 1998
Janette Oke, *Dana's Valley*, 2001

1056

AL LACY
JOANNA LACY, Co-Author

The Forbidden Hills

(Sisters, Oregon: Multnomah, 2005)

Story type: Historical/American West
Series: Dreams of Gold. Book 2
Subject(s): Gold Discoveries
Major character(s): Jim Bannon, Farmer, Prospector
Time period(s): 1870s
Locale(s): Wyoming; West

Summary: Jim Bannon desperately wants to marry his long-time love Alyssa McGuire, but her father refuses to allow his daughter to marry a mere farmer. When rumors of a Gold Rush in the Dakota Territories prove to be true, Jim decides to leave his farm and become a prospector. Indian uprisings and difficult conditions conspire against Jim, however, and he must return home with less than he left with. How can he ever win Alyssa?

Other books by the same author:
Wings of Riches, 2005
Beloved Physician, 2004
One More Sunrise, 2004
The Heart Remembers, 2004
Whispers in the Wind, 2003

Other books you might like:
Lisa Tawn Bergren, *The Northern Lights Series*, 1998-

Inspirational

Stephen Bly, *Fool's Gold*, 2000
Jim Kraus, *The Price*, 2000
Gilbert Morris, *The Yukon Queen*, 1995
Bodie Thoene, *Winds of Promise*, 1997

1057

MINNIE LAMBERTH

Life with Strings Attached

(Brewster, Massachusetts: Paraclete, 2005)

Story type: Contemporary
Subject(s): Children; Women's Rights
Major character(s): Hannah Hayes, Child
Time period(s): 1970s (1972)
Locale(s): Wellton, Alabama

Summary: It is 1972 in the small town of Wellton, Alabama, and Hannah Hayes is seven years old. She lives with her father Martin, who works for the local sock factory, and has a beagle dog named Pumpkin. Hannah also has a deep faith in God and firmly believes that someday she will be a minister. Hannah's friends mock her dreams. After all, women just can't preach, can they? Hannah is determined to prove them wrong and her first test comes when Pumpkin disappears and Hannah must learn about forgiveness. First novel.

Where it's reviewed:
Library Journal, February 1, 2005, page 60

Other books you might like:
W. Dale Cramer, *Sutter's Cross*, 2003
Linda Dorrell, *True Believers*, 2001
Lisa Samson, *The Church Ladies*, 2001
Augusta Trobaugh, *Praise Jerusalem*, 1997
Brad Whittington, *The Fred Series*, 2003-

1058

BONNIE LEON

For the Love of the Land

(Grand Rapids, Michigan: Fleming H. Revell, 2005)

Story type: Historical
Series: Queensland Chronicles. Book 2
Subject(s): Drought; Pioneers
Major character(s): Rebecca Thornton, Spouse
Time period(s): 1870s
Locale(s): Queensland, Australia

Summary: Rebecca Thornton has been in Australia for a year and she continues to find life in the Outback challenging. Life in genteel Boston in no way prepared her for life on a cattle station. Things become worse when a drought hits Thornton Creek and Douloo Station suffers the consequences. Still, Rebecca has some good things to anticipate. Her Aunt Mildred is visiting, bringing news from home. Rebecca is also expecting her first child.

Other books by the same author:
The Heart of Thornton Creek, 2005
Home at Last, 2002
Worthy of Riches, 2002
Valley of Promises, 2001

A Sacred Place, 2000

Other books you might like:
Ray Blackston, *Lost in Rooville*, 2005
Lawana Blackwell, *The Gresham Chronicles*, 1998-
Linda Chaikin, *The East of the Sun Series*, 2003-
Michael Phillips, *The Russians Series*, 1991-
Lori Wick, *The English Garden Series*, 2002-

1059

BONNIE LEON

The Heart of Thornton Creek

(Grand Rapids, Michigan: Fleming H. Revell, 2005)

Story type: Historical
Series: Queensland Chronicles. Book 1
Subject(s): Fathers and Sons; Pioneers
Major character(s): Rebecca Thornton, Spouse
Time period(s): 1870s
Locale(s): Queensland, Australia

Summary: Life in Boston has always been too constricting for Rebecca Williams, so when her father dies leaving her penniless, she decides to make some changes. When she meets Australian Daniel Thornton, Rebecca agrees to marry him and immigrate to Australia. Life on a cattle station is rugged, but Rebecca believes she made the right choice, even though she doesn't love Daniel. Her main problem is the coldness between her husband and his father. Bertram Thornton controls the ranch and, through it, attempts to maintain control over his son.

Where it's reviewed:
Library Journal, February 1, 2005, page 62

Other books by the same author:
For the Love of the Land, 2005
Home at Last, 2002
Worthy of Riches, 2002
Valley of Promises, 2001
A Sacred Place, 2000

Other books you might like:
Ray Blackston, *Lost in Rooville*, 2005
Lawana Blackwell, *The Gresham Chronicles*, 1998-
Linda Chaikin, *The East of the Sun Series*, 2003-
Michael Phillips, *The Russians Series*, 1991-
Lori Wick, *The English Garden Series*, 2002-

1060

ROBERT LIPARULO

Comes a Horseman

(Nashville: WestBow, 2005)

Story type: Mystery
Subject(s): Serial Killers
Major character(s): Brady Moore, FBI Agent; Alicia Wagner, FBI Agent
Time period(s): 2000s
Locale(s): Colorado; Jerusalem, Israel; Vatican City

Summary: A team of FBI agents begins to investigate a series of grisly murders known as the Pelletier Killings. It is soon learned that a series of ancient prophecies link the victims together. As Brady Moore and Alicia Wagner come close to solving the case, they find themselves becoming the target of the killer. They refuse to back down, however, and soon follow clues that lead them to the Italian ambassador to Israel, a charismatic and powerful man who just may be plotting to take over the world. Author Robert Liparulo co-wrote a novel with Maurice Rawlings called *DeathStrand* in 2000. This is his first solo novel.

Other books you might like:
Alton Gansky, *The J.D. Stanton Series*, 1999-
T.L. Higley, *Marduk's Tablet*, 2003
Kel Richards, *Dark Storm*, 2004
Jefferson Scott, *The Operation Firebrand Series*, 2002-
Frank Simon, *Veiled Threats*, 1996

1061

CRESTON MAPES

Dark Star

(Sisters, Oregon: Multnomah, 2005)

Story type: Contemporary
Subject(s): Music and Musicians; Rock Music; Trials
Major character(s): Everett Lester, Musician (rock star); Karen Bayliss, Young Woman
Time period(s): 2000s
Locale(s): Miami-Dade County, Florida

Summary: With his band DeathStroke gaining in popularity, musician Everett Lester should be on top of the world, but a drug problem keeps him from enjoying his fame. Then his psychic dies in the middle of a session and Everett finds himself accused of murder. The trial becomes a media circus, but in the midst of the craziness Lester begins receiving letters from a fan named Karen Bayliss that give him hope for the future. First novel.

Other books you might like:
Brandilyn Collins, *Dread Champion*, 2002
Karen Kingsbury, *Fame*, 2005
Diane Noble, *Heart of Glass*, 2002
Jacquelin Thomas, *Singsation*, 2001
Robert Whitlow, *The Trial*, 2001

1062

CHARLES MARTIN

The Second Chance

(Nashville: WestBow, 2005)

Story type: Contemporary
Subject(s): Clergy; Religion
Major character(s): Ethan Jenkins, Religious (minister); Jake Sanders, Religious (minister)
Time period(s): 2000s
Locale(s): United States

Summary: Ethan Jenkins and Jake Sanders are both ministers, but they are very different men with very different congrega-tions. Ethan is white and heads a wealthy suburban church. Jake is African-American and serves in the inner city. Ethan's church members have problems, but they are nothing like those encountered by Jake's congregation. When Ethan and Jake meet and begin to work together, both their lives are changed forever.

Other books by the same author:
Wrapped in Rain, 2005
The Dead Don't Dance, 2004

Other books you might like:
Angela Benson, *The Genesis House Series*, 2000-
Michele Andrea Bowen, *Church Folk*, 2001
Linda Dorrell, *True Believers*, 2001
Paul Nigro, *Bethesda*, 2003
Lisa Samson, *The Church Ladies*, 2001

1063

CHARLES MARTIN

Wrapped in Rain

(Nashville: WestBow, 2005)

Story type: Contemporary
Subject(s): Brothers; Mentally Handicapped
Major character(s): Tucker Rain, Journalist (photojournalist); Matthew "Mutt" Mason, Mentally Ill Person
Time period(s): 2000s
Locale(s): Alabama

Summary: Alabama businessman Rex Mason was too busy making money to pay attention to his two young sons, so he hired nanny Ella Rain to care for his boys. Ella loved the children as if they were her own and she became their only source of strength. After her death, Mutt Mason descended into mental illness. Not knowing how to cope with his brother, Tucker committed Mutt to a mental institution, changed his name to Tucker Rain in honor of Ella, and took off for a globetrotting career as a photojournalist. When Mutt escapes from the mental institution, Tucker must return home and confront the demons from his childhood.

Where it's reviewed:
Library Journal, February 1, 2005, page 64
Publishers Weekly, February 7, 2005, page 44

Other books by the same author:
The Dead Don't Dance, 2004

Other books you might like:
Joseph Bentz, *A Son Comes Home*, 1999
Lawana Blackwell, *A Table by the Window*, 2005
Cliff Coon, *The Mending String*, 2004
Bette Nordberg, *A Season of Grace*, 2004
Catherine Palmer, *The Happy Room*, 2002

1064

GAIL GAYMER MARTIN

Loving Promises

(New York: Steeple Hill, 2005)

Story type: Romance

Subject(s): Accidents; Illness; Single Parent Families
Major character(s): Bev Miller, Widow(er), Single Parent; Dale Levin, Businessman
Time period(s): 2000s
Locale(s): Loving, Michigan

Summary: Bev Miller has been raising her children alone since her husband's death in a motorcycle accident. She thinks she is doing a pretty good job at being both mother and father to her kids, but she isn't thrilled when her son Michael runs a shopping cart into Dale Levin's car. There is no damage, but Dale doesn't think Michael is all that great a kid. In spite of this inauspicious start, Bev and Dale soon grow to care for one another. Unfortunately, Dale's parents had a picture-perfect marriage, one that is now near its end as Dale's mother lies dying. Unable to face the pain his father is going through watching his mother suffer, Dale decides commitment is something he is just unwilling to do, no matter how much he loves Bev.

Other books by the same author:
Adam's Promise, 2004
Loving Care, 2004
Out on a Limb, 2004
Loving Ways, 2003
The Christmas Kite, 2003

Other books you might like:
Irene Brand, *Song of Her Heart*, 2003
Cathleen Connors, *A Home of Her Own*, 2002
Lori Copeland, *Mother of Prevention*, 2005
Valerie Hansen, *The Perfect Couple*, 2000
Marta Perry, *A Mother's Wish*, 2002

1065

LORENA MCCOURTNEY

In Plain Sight

(Grand Rapids, Michigan: Fleming H. Revell, 2005)

Story type: Mystery
Series: Ivy Malone. Book 2
Subject(s): Old Age; Organized Crime
Major character(s): Ivy Malone, Detective—Amateur
Time period(s): 2000s
Locale(s): Ozarks

Summary: After amateur detective Ivy Malone's evidence gets his brother convicted of murder, Drake Braxton vows revenge. When there's a mysterious fire at her home, Ivy realizes that Braxton is serious and her life is in danger. She decides to leave her hometown in Missouri until things cool down and heads off for the Ozarks. Taking a housekeeping job to keep herself busy, Ivy soon finds herself deep in another mystery.

Other books by the same author:
Invisible, 2004
Undertow, 2003
Riptide, 2002
Whirlpool, 2002
Searching for Stardust, 1999

Other books you might like:
Ron Benrey, *The Pippa Hunnechurch Series*, 2001-

Ellen Edwards Kennedy, *Irregardless of Murder*, 2001
Gilbert Morris, *The Dani Ross Series*, 2000-
Radine Trees Nehring, *A Valley to Die For*, 2002
Patricia H. Rushford, *The Helen Bradley Series*, 1997-

1066

PAUL MCCUSKER

A Season of Shadows

(Grand Rapids, Michigan: Zondervan, 2005)

Story type: Historical/World War II
Subject(s): Spies; World War II
Major character(s): Julie Harris, Spy, Widow(er)
Time period(s): 1940s
Locale(s): London, England

Summary: After her husband's unexpected death leads to a nasty scandal, Julie Harris abandons her socialite life in Washington, D.C., and moves to London. Supposedly Julie has taken a position as an aide in the U.S. Embassy; in reality, she is working undercover. Her mission is to infiltrate an anti-fascist group that is somehow related to her husband's downfall.

Other books by the same author:
The Mill House, 2004
The Faded Flower, 2001
Epiphany, 1998
Catacombs, 1997

Other books you might like:
Linda Chaikin, *Friday's Child*, 2001
Lyn Cote, *Bette*, 2005
J.M. Hochstetler, *Daughter of Liberty*, 2004
Elyse Larson, *So Shall We Stand*, 2001
Judith Pella, *The Daughters of Fortune Series*, 2002-

1067

DIANN MILLS

When the Lion Roars

(Colorado Springs, Colorado: RiverOak, 2005)

Story type: Contemporary
Subject(s): Kidnapping; Slavery
Major character(s): Larson Kerr, Doctor
Time period(s): 2000s
Locale(s): Sudan

Summary: Larson Kerr, a doctor, works hard to save the suffering people of Sudan. The work seems thankless at times, but Kerr realizes it is necessary. When a young American girl is kidnapped, Kerr teams up with an Arab man, who is a devout Christian and a leader of the rebel army, in order to save him.

Other books by the same author:
Compassion's Charm, 2004
Footsteps, 2004
Texas Charm, 2004
Kiowa Husband, 2004
The Turncoat, 2003

Other books you might like:

Linda Chaikin, *Endangered*, 1997
Anne De Graaf, *Into the Nevernight*, 2003
Angela Elwell Hunt, *The Canopy*, 2003
Catherine Palmer, *A Touch of Betrayal*, 2000
Karen Rispin, *African Skies*, 2000

1068
SIRI L. MITCHELL

Kissing Adrien

(Eugene, Oregon: Harvest House, 2005)

Story type: Romance
Subject(s): Inheritance
Major character(s): Claire Le Noyer, Accountant
Time period(s): 2000s
Locale(s): Paris, France

Summary: Non-nonsense Claire Le Noyer reluctantly agrees to travel to Paris to oversee the renovation of an apartment building her parents have inherited. The romance and allure of Paris mean nothing to Claire. She just wants to get the job finished and return home to her job as an accountant and her tentative romance with her associate pastor. Then Claire is reunited with her childhood crush Adrien, who has grown even more handsome and dashing over the years. With Adrien anxious to show her around Paris, Claire suddenly realizes the city may have charms after all. First novel.

Other books you might like:

Cecelia Dowdy, *First Mates*, 2005
Doris Elaine Fell, *Always in September*, 1994
Robin Jones Gunn, *The Sisterchicks Series*, 2003-
Debra White Smith, *To Rome with Love*, 2001
Linda Windsor, *It Had to Be You*, 2001

1069
GILBERT MORRIS

The Gypsy Moon

(Minneapolis: Bethany House, 2005)

Story type: Historical/World War II; Family Saga
Series: House of Winslow. Book 35
Subject(s): Jews; Underground Resistance Movements
Major character(s): Gabrielle Winslow, Resistance Fighter
Time period(s): 1940s
Locale(s): Netherlands; Germany

Summary: Gabrielle Winslow joins the underground movement in Holland, hoping to save the Jews from Hitler's wrath. As Gabrielle courageously undertakes her duties smuggling people to safety, she is horrified to learn that the commander of the local occupation forces is none other than Erik Reader. She had not only known Erik earlier in Germany, but she had almost married him. When Gabrielle learns that her uncle is in danger, she is determined to travel to Nazi Germany to save him. Accompanied by an OSS agent, Gabrielle undertakes the perilous journey.

Other books by the same author:

Charade, 2005

The Eyes of Texas, 2005
The Virtuous Woman, 2005
Till Shiloh Comes, 2005
The Silent Harp, 2004

Other books you might like:

T. Davis Bunn, *The Rendezvous with Destiny Series*, 1993-
Jack Cavanaugh, *The American Family Portrait Series*, 1994-
Elyse Larson, *The Women of Valor Series*, 2000-
Jane Peart, *The Brides of Montclair Series*, 1989-
Michael Phillips, *The Secret of the Rose Series*, 1993-
Noreen Riols, *The House of Annanbrae Series*, 1994-

1070
GILBERT MORRIS

The Homeplace

(Grand Rapids, Michigan: Zondervan, 2005)

Story type: Historical
Series: Singing River. Book 1
Subject(s): Family Problems; Rural Life
Major character(s): Lanie Belle Freeman, Teenager
Time period(s): 1920s
Locale(s): Fairhope, Arkansas

Summary: Things are going well for the Freeman family. A fifth child is on the way, and Mr. Freeman is starting a new business. Then tragedy strikes: Mrs. Freeman dies in childbirth, and her husband is falsely accused of murder and sent to prison. Left on her own to care for her younger siblings, 14-year-old Lanie Belle Freeman puts her own dreams aside to try and keep her family together.

Other books by the same author:

By Way of the Wilderness, 2005
The Gypsy Moon, 2005
Till Shiloh Comes, 2005
The Eyes of Texas, 2005
Charade, 2005

Other books you might like:

Lynn Austin, *Hidden Places*, 2001
Robin Lee Hatcher, *The Shepherd's Voice*, 2000
Bonnie Leon, *The Sowers Trilogy*, 1998-
Lorena McCourtney, *Escape*, 1996
Calvin Miller, *Snow*, 1998
Ann Tatlock, *A Room of My Own*, 1998

1071
ELIZABETH MUSSER

The Dwelling Place

(Minneapolis: Bethany House, 2005)

Story type: Contemporary
Subject(s): Illness; Mothers and Daughters
Major character(s): Ellie Bartholomew, Care Giver
Time period(s): 2000s
Locale(s): Atlanta, Georgia; Scotland

Summary: Ellie Bartholomew has always felt like a misfit in her family. Everybody is successful and talented, but Ellie drifts along working as a server in a restaurant after a stint in

rehab. Then her mother's battle with cancer takes a turn for the worse and Ellie is drafted into caring for her. Ellie had always blamed her mother, Mary Swan Middleton, a famous artist, for causing the accident that left her disfigured. As Mary's condition worsens, she insists she must go to Scotland. The journey allows the two women to come to grips with their pasts, and gives them the strength to move on. Sequel to *The Swan House*.

Where it's reviewed:
Publishers Weekly, March 7, 2005, page 52

Other books by the same author:
The Swan House, 2001
Two Testaments, 1997
Two Crosses, 1996

Other books you might like:
Deborah Bedford, *A Rose by the Door*, 2001
Terri Blackstock, *Seaside*, 2001
Tracie Peterson, *A Slender Thread*, 2000
Francine Rivers, *Leota's Garden*, 1999
Johanna Verweerd, *The Winter Garden*, 2001

1072
BILL MYERS

The Presence
(Grand Rapids, Michigan: Zondervan, 2005)

Story type: Horror
Series: Soul Tracker. Book 2
Subject(s): Psychic Powers; Supernatural
Major character(s): David Kauffman, Writer
Time period(s): 2000s
Locale(s): United States

Summary: Still shaken by the death of his daughter, David Kauffman journeys to a remote mountain lodge where a seance is to be held. David hopes to prove the psychic involved is phony. Once David arrives, he realizes he is in over his head. Soon a power known as The Presence threatens to overtake all those in attendance. David wants desperately to escape, but is held captive by the person in charge of the experiment, the same person who is responsible for his daughter's death.

Other books by the same author:
Soul Tracker, 2004
The Bloodstone Chronicles, 2003
The Wager, 2003
The Face of God, 2002
When the Last Leaf Falls, 2001

Other books you might like:
Montre Bible, *Heaven Sent*, 2005
Karen Hancock, *Arena*, 2002
Nancy Moser, *The Mustard Seed Series*, 1998-
Frank Peretti, *Monster*, 2005
Eric Wilson, *Expiration Date*, 2005

1073
MARK MYNHEIR

The Rolling Thunder
(Sisters, Oregon: Multnomah, 2005)

Story type: Mystery
Series: Truth Chasers. Book 1
Subject(s): Missing Persons
Major character(s): John Russell, Detective—Police
Time period(s): 2000s
Locale(s): Florida

Summary: John Russell, a detective with the Florida Department of Law Enforcement, is assigned to the high-profile case of Dylan Jacobs, a missing boy. As John attempts to find Dylan, he struggles with his tempestuous relationship with his own father, who desperately wants John to forgive him for his past digressions. As this is something John is unwilling to do, the two remain at a standstill in their relationship. First novel.

Other books you might like:
Terri Blackstock, *Southern Storm*, 2003
T. Davis Bunn, *Elixir*, 2004
Alton Gansky, *Vanished*, 2000
Linda Hall, *Chat Room*, 2003
Cindy McCormick Martinusen, *Blue Night*, 2001

1074
BETTE NORDBERG

Detours
(Eugene, Oregon: Harvest House, 2005)

Story type: Contemporary
Subject(s): Accidents; Child Custody
Major character(s): Callie O'Brian, Businesswoman (upholstery business owner), Restaurateur (coffee shop)
Time period(s): 2000s
Locale(s): Washington

Summary: Callie O'Brian is a busy woman trying to run two small businesses when she receives some bad news. Her best friend Celia has been in a serious auto accident and is hospitalized. Celia's four-year-old son Keeshan needs somebody to take care of him. Reluctantly, Celia agrees to take on the responsibility. Then a man named Marcus Jefferson appears, claiming to be the boy's uncle. He wants to take over Keeshan's care. Since Celia had never mentioned any family, Callie begins to wonder why Marcus would appear so suddenly, and if he has ulterior motives in wanting Keeshan.

Other books by the same author:
A Season of Grace, 2004
Thin Air, 2002
Pacific Hope, 2000
Serenity Bay, 2000

Other books you might like:
Deborah Bedford, *If I Had You*, 2004
Vonette Z. Bright, *The Sister Circle*, 2003
W. Dale Cramer, *Bad Ground*, 2004
Jane Orcutt, *The Living Stone*, 2000
Gayle Roper, *Summer Shadows*, 2002

1075

MAE NUNN

Sealed with a Kiss

(New York: Steeple Hill, 2005)

Story type: Romance
Subject(s): Inheritance
Major character(s): Tara Elliott, Heiress; Sam Kennesaw, Heir
Time period(s): 2000s
Locale(s): Beardsly, Texas

Summary: When her grandmother's will is read, Tara Elliott cannot believe what she is hearing. She has inherited part of the family office building. The other new co-owner is Sam Kennesaw, the man who broke her heart years before. Now Tara is expected to work alongside the man she still views with suspicion. At first, the two can't agree on anything, but as time passes, they begin to wonder if they might not have a future together after all.

Other books by the same author:
Hearts in Bloom, 2004

Other books you might like:
Cecelia Dowdy, *First Mates*, 2005
Irene Hannon, *The Best Gift*, 2005
Arlene James, *To Heal a Heart*, 2005
Pat Marr, *Man of Her Dreams*, 2005
Marta Perry, *Unlikely Hero*, 2005

1076

CATHERINE PALMER

Sweet Violet

(Wheaton, Illinois: Tyndale House, 2005)

Story type: Historical/Regency
Series: English Ivy. Book 3
Subject(s): Missionaries; Runaways
Major character(s): Violet Rosse, Runaway; Edmund Sherbourne, Religious (missionary)
Time period(s): 1810s
Locale(s): India

Summary: Violet Rosse loves her life in India, and has no wish to live anywhere else. When she learns that her father not only intends to send her away to England but has also arranged a marriage for her, she takes action and runs away. Her annoyed father bribes missionary Edmund Sherbourne to bring Violet back in exchange for a church in Calcutta. Edmund finds Violet fairly easily, but soon learns that bringing her back home will be very difficult indeed.

Other books by the same author:
Fatal Harvest, 2003
Love's Proof, 2003
Sunrise Song, 2003
Wild Heather, 2003
English Ivy, 2002

Other books you might like:
Lawana Blackwell, *The Tales of London Series*, 2001-
Linda Chaikin, *The Royal Pavilions Series*, 1993-

Donna Fletcher Crow, *The Cambridge Chronicles*, 1994-
B.J. Hoff, *The American Anthem Series*, 2002-
Tracie Peterson, *The Bells of Lowell Series*, 2003-
Lori Wick, *The English Garden Series*, 2002-

1077

BETH PATTILLO

Heavens to Betsy

(Colorado Springs, Colorado: WaterBrook, 2005)

Story type: Romance
Subject(s): Clergy
Major character(s): Betsy Blessing, Religious (minister); David Swenson, Religious (minister)
Time period(s): 2000s
Locale(s): Nashville, Tennessee

Summary: Being a minister is not easy, but it is especially difficult for Betsy Blessing. Not only does she have to deal with the parishioners who aren't thrilled with a female minister, she also has to cope with those who see a single woman as somebody to be paired off with any available man, including ex-cons. Betsy herself is fairly certain of what she wants in a man, and she is very certain that she does not want to marry another minister. So when she begins to have romantic thoughts about her long-time friend and fellow minister David Swenson, Betsy is confused. Maybe a two-minister family would work.

Other books by the same author:
Princess Charming, 2003

Other books you might like:
Kristin Billerbeck, *The Ashley Stockingdale Series*, 2004-
Robin Jones Gunn, *The Glenbrooke Series*, 1995-
Shari MacDonald, *The Salinger Sisters Series*, 1998-
Kate Welsh, *Home to Safe Harbor*, 2003
Bonnie K. Winn, *A Family All Her Own*, 2001

1078

FRANK PERETTI

Monster

(Nashville: WestBow, 2005)

Story type: Horror
Subject(s): Monsters; Supernatural; Wilderness
Major character(s): Reed Shelton, Police Officer
Time period(s): 2000s
Locale(s): Idaho

Summary: Policeman Reed Shelton and his wife Beck are on a wilderness hike when they are attacked by a strange monster. Reed manages to escape and a full-scale search is soon underway for Beck. At first it appears as if the couple had been attacked by the mysterious creatures known as Sasquatch, or Bigfoot. Soon though, Reed learns that a local group of researchers have been experimenting with DNA and the monsters might actually be chimpanzees that have been altered genetically into hideous and evil creatures.

Where it's reviewed:
Booklist, March 15, 2005, page 1247

Inspirational

Entertainment Weekly, April 22, 2005, page 67
Library Journal, April 1, 2005, page 80
Publishers Weekly, March 28, 2005, page 58

Other books by the same author:
The Visitation, 1999
The Oath, 1995
Prophet, 1992
Piercing the Darkness, 1989
Tilly, 1988

Other books you might like:
Sigmund Brouwer, *The Double Helix*, 1995
Michael Cordy, *The Miracle Strain*, 1997
Alton Gansky, *Submerged*, 2005
W.G. Griffiths, *Driven*, 2002
Harry Lee Kraus, *Fated Genes*, 1996
Bill Myers, *Blood of Heaven*, 1996

1079
TERRI REED

A Sheltering Love
(New York: Steeple Hill, 2005)

Story type: Romance
Subject(s): Runaways
Major character(s): Claire Wilcox, Social Worker (shelter for teenage runaways); Nick Andrews, Handyman
Time period(s): 2000s
Locale(s): Oregon

Summary: A former runaway, Claire Wilcox has devoted her life to helping teenagers who have taken to life on the streets. Her shelter has become the only home many teens know, and Claire is determined to help as many people as she can. When a mysterious stranger saves her life, she impulsively invites him to stay at the shelter and do some handyman work. As Claire begins to know Nick Andrews a little better, she senses a great man behind his tough facade.

Other books by the same author:
Love Comes Home, 2004

Other books you might like:
Nan Corbitt Allen, *Asylum*, 2004
Lynn Bulock, *Change of the Heart*, 2002
Melody Carlson, *Everything I Long For*, 2000
Valerie Hansen, *The Troublesome Angel*, 2000
Patricia Sprinkle, *When Did We Lose Harriet?*, 1997

1080
LOIS RICHER

Shadowed Secrets
(Wheaton, Illinois: Tyndale House, 2005)

Story type: Mystery; Romance
Series: Camp Hope. Book 3
Subject(s): Crime and Criminals; Fathers and Daughters
Major character(s): Angie Grant, Fugitive; Rick Mercer, Police Officer
Time period(s): 2000s
Locale(s): Canada

Summary: Angie Grant survived a troubled childhood, with a father who was a thief and often spent time in jail. Angie has no intention of ever returning to her hometown and the bad memories it holds. That all changes when Angie meets six-year-old Kelly, who is the only witness to a murder. Although Angie works for the witness protection program, she realizes Kelly is in grave danger and decides to take matters into her own hands. She flees to her old home, taking Kelly with her. Once there, police officer Rick Mercer, a longtime friend, helps her. As the two fight for Kelly, they begin to rekindle their lost love.

Other books by the same author:
A Time to Remember, 2004
Dangerous Sanctuary, 2004
Heaven's Kiss, 2004
Forgotten Justice, 2004
Inner Harbor, 2003

Other books you might like:
Dee Henderson, *The Protector*, 2001
Susan Meissner, *A Window to the World*, 2005
Deborah Raney, *A Scarlet Cord*, 2003
Travis Thrasher, *Gun Lake*, 2004
Linda Windsor, *Along Came Jones*, 2003

1081
FRANCINE RIVERS

The Warrior
(Wheaton, Illinois: Tyndale House, 2005)

Story type: Biblical Fiction
Series: Sons of Encouragement. Book 2
Subject(s): Bible; Biblical Fiction; Spies
Major character(s): Caleb, Slave
Time period(s): Indeterminate Past
Locale(s): Middle East

Summary: Caleb, a slave, works in the fields of the pharaoh. He and many fellow slaves flee the horrors of their life and escape to the outskirts of Canaan. Their leader Moses sends 12 scouts to check out the land ahead. Ten of the scouts return and say the journey ahead is impossible. The other two, Caleb and Joshua, say that God will make certain of the safety of the Hebrew nation. It is this situation that sets the Hebrews wandering in the desert for 40 years because they did not believe Caleb and Joshua, and did not have faith in God.

Where it's reviewed:
Library Journal, February 1, 2005, page 62

Other books by the same author:
The Priest, 2004
And the Shofar Blew, 2003
A Voice in the Wind, 2002
As Sure as the Dawn, 2002
An Echo in the Darkness, 2002

Other books you might like:
Gene Edwards, *The First Century Diaries Series*, 1998-
Tracy Groot, *The Brother's Keeper*, 2003
Thom Lemmons, *The Daughters of Faith Series*, 1999-
Gilbert Morris, *The Lions of Judah Series*, 2002-
Robert L. Wise, *The People of the Covenant Series*, 1991-

1082

PATRICIA H. RUSHFORD

As Good as Dead

(Grand Rapids, Michigan: Fleming H. Revell, 2005)

Story type: Mystery
Series: Angel Delaney. Book 3
Subject(s): Brothers and Sisters; Missing Persons
Major character(s): Angel Delaney, Detective—Private
Time period(s): 2000s
Locale(s): United States

Summary: Angel Delaney's father dies, and she is devastated. Her grief for her father brings back the loss she felt when her brother disappeared six years earlier. Although a talented private investigator, Angel has never found so much as a trace of what became of Luke. Then a close family friend is injured and it appears as if Luke might somehow be involved in the incident. Angel must decide whether she truly wants to find out what her brother has been doing while missing.

Other books by the same author:
Deadly Aim, 2004
Dying to Kill, 2004
Sins of the Mother, 2003
When Shadows Fall, 2000
A Haunting Refrain, 1998

Other books you might like:
Mindy Starns Clark, *The Million Dollar Mysteries Series*, 2002-
Colleen Coble, *The Rock Harbor Series*, 2003-
Tim Downs, *The Bug Man Series*, 2003-
Kathi Mills-Macias, *The Toni Matthews Series*, 2001-
Gilbert Morris, *The Dani Ross Series*, 2000-

1083

PATRICIA H. RUSHFORD
HARRISON JAMES, Co-Author

Terminal 9

(Nashville: Integrity, 2005)

Story type: Mystery
Series: McAllister Files. Book 3
Subject(s): Railroads; Retirement
Major character(s): Antonio McAllister, Police Officer; Dana Bennett, Police Officer
Time period(s): 2000s
Locale(s): Oregon

Summary: Police officer Antonio "Mac" McAllister has a new partner, Dana Bennett, and a new case. The pair is assigned to investigate the mysterious death of an elderly retired railroad worker who was hit by a train. The case seems straightforward enough, but as Mac and Dana dig deeper, they begin to unearth clues that suggest the death was not an accident, but murder.

Other books by the same author:
Deadfall, 2004
Secrets, Lies & Alibis, 2003

Other books you might like:
Colleen Coble, *The Rock Harbor Series*, 2003-
Athol Dickson, *The Garr Reed Series*, 1996-
Tim Downs, *The Bug Man Series*, 2003-
Robert Funderburk, *The Dylan St. John Series*, 1996-
Kathi Mills-Macias, *The Toni Matthews Series*, 2001-

1084

LISA SAMSON

Club Sandwich

(Colorado Springs, Colorado: WaterBrook, 2005)

Story type: Contemporary
Subject(s): Family Problems; Mothers and Daughters
Major character(s): Ivy Schneider, Writer (newspaper columnist)
Time period(s): 2000s
Locale(s): Baltimore, Maryland

Summary: Ivy Schneider is juggling many responsibilities and is finding it harder and harder to cope. Her husband is often out of town, so the care of their three children is usually her responsibility. Her mother needs to get to and from dialysis treatment. Ivy writes a newspaper column and helps out in the family restaurant. Near collapse, Ivy desperately takes out an ad in the local paper asking for anybody else in the "sandwich generation"—those people who care for their children and their parents—to contact her. To her surprise, some do and they form "Club Sandwich", a support group to people trying to care for everybody in their lives.

Where it's reviewed:
Publishers Weekly, May 2, 2005, page 178

Other books by the same author:
Tiger Lillie, 2004
Songbird, 2003
The Living End, 2003
Women's Intuition, 2002
The Church Ladies, 2001

Other books you might like:
Sylvia Bambola, *The Gloria Bickford Series*, 2004-
Vonette Z. Bright, *The Sister Circle Series*, 2003-
Mary Carlson, *The Whispering Pines Series*, 1999-
Roxanne Henke, *The Coming Home to Brewster Series*, 2002-
Neta Jackson, *The Yada Yada Prayer Group Series*, 2003-

1085

ANNA SCHMIDT

Love Next Door

(New York: Steeple Hill, 2005)

Story type: Romance
Subject(s): Camps and Camping
Major character(s): Pete Fleming, Police Officer; Amanda Hunter, Counselor (camp)
Time period(s): 2000s
Locale(s): United States

Summary: After being shot in the line of duty, police officer Pete Fleming has lost the nerve that made him a great cop.

Ordered to take some time off and recoup, Pete reluctantly rents a lakeside property for some forced leisure time. His neighbor turns out to be Camp Good News, a children's camp run by widowed Amanda Hunter. As Pete is drawn into the lives of the campers, he is also drawn to Amanda, who is still mourning the loss of her husband and child, who both drowned in the same accident nearly two years previously. As Pete and Amanda attempt to save the run-down camp, they begin to realize they may also help each other recover from their emotional wounds.

Other books by the same author:
The Doctor's Miracle, 2001
A Mother for Amanda, 2000
Caroline and the Preacher, 1999
Give and Take, 1987

Other books you might like:
Irene Brand, *To Love and Honor*, 1999
Lyn Cote, *Winter's Secret*, 2002
Robin Lee Hatcher, *Whispers from Yesterday*, 1999
Leona Karr, *Rocky Mountain Miracle*, 2001
Carol Steward, *Her Kind of Hero*, 1999

1086

DEBRA WHITE SMITH

Central Park

(Eugene, Oregon: Harvest House, 2005)

Story type: Romance
Series: Austen. Book 3
Subject(s): Money; Wealth
Major character(s): Francine Ponce, Relative (unwanted); Ethan Summers, Religious (minister)
Time period(s): 2000s
Locale(s): New York, New York

Summary: Sent to live with her wealthy uncle and aunt as a child, Francine Ponce grows up unloved and unwanted. Her only solace is Ethan, the foster son of Francine's aunt and uncle. The two grow close and when Ethan goes to Paris on a missionary trip, Francine realizes she is in love with him. Unfortunately, when Ethan returns he brings brother and sister Carrie and Hugh Casper with him. Not only is Ethan besotted with the beautiful Carrie, but Francine's relatives are determined that she make a match with Hugh.

Other books by the same author:
First Impressions, 2004
Reason and Romance, 2004
Let's Begin Again, 2003
The Key, 2003
For Your Heart Only, 2002

Other books you might like:
Robin Jones Gunn, *The Glenbrooke Series*, 1995-
Barbara Jean Hicks, *The Once upon a Dream Series*, 1998-
Annie Jones, *The Route 66 Series*, 1999-
Shari MacDonald, *The Salinger Sisters Series*, 1998-
Suzy Pizzuti, *The Halo Hattie's Boarding House Series*, 1998-

1087

CAROL STEWARD

Journey to Forever

(New York: Steeple Hill, 2005)

Story type: Romance
Subject(s): Radio
Major character(s): Nikki Post, Journalist; Colin Wright, Radio Personality
Time period(s): 2000s
Locale(s): West

Summary: Nikki Post isn't thrilled at her new assignment—following radio personality Colin Wright on an eight-day, 300 mile trip throughout the western United States. Once she meets Colin, though, her feelings change. She had expected an irreverent, bad-mannered jock, not the thoughtful and generous man she is confronted with. As the two journey from New Mexico to Wyoming, they gain a new appreciation for one another and begin to fall in love.

Other books by the same author:
Finding Amy, 2004
Finding Her Home, 2004
This Time Forever, 2002
Courting Katarina, 2001
Second Time Around, 2000

Other books you might like:
Shelley Bates, *Grounds to Believe*, 2004
Jillian Hart, *Heart and Soul*, 2004
Marta Perry, *Hunter's Bride*, 2001
Janet Tronstad, *A Hero for Dry Creek*, 2003
Kate Welsh, *Her Perfect Match*, 2003

1088

ALISON STROBEL

Worlds Collide

(Colorado Springs, Colorado: WaterBrook, 2005)

Story type: Contemporary
Subject(s): Actors and Actresses
Major character(s): Jack Harrington, Actor; Grace Harrington, Teacher; Jada Eastman, Writer (celebrity biographer)
Time period(s): 2000s
Locale(s): Los Angeles, California

Summary: Famous actor Jack Harrington meets teacher Grace Winslowe when their cars collide, and he is instantly attracted to the beautiful young woman. Though Grace is a devout Christian and Jack is a non-believer who is into partying, the two soon marry. The Cinderella story attracts the attention of the tabloid press, as well as the attention of celebrity biographer Jada Eastman. Jada wants to write about their story and the couple agrees to have her live with them for six months. Soon Jack and Grace begin wondering if Jada's biography will bring them closer or tear them apart. First novel.

Where it's reviewed:
Publishers Weekly, February 1, 2005, page 159

Other books you might like:

James Scott Bell, *Breach of Promise*, 2004
Robin Jones Gunn, *Waterfalls*, 2004
Karen Kingsbury, *Fame*, 2005
Gilbert Morris, *All That Glitters*, 1999
Tracie Peterson, *A Slender Thread*, 2000

1089

LAURA JENSEN WALKER

Dreaming in Black and White

(Nashville: WestBow, 2005)

Story type: Contemporary; Humor
Subject(s): Weight Control; Writing
Major character(s): Phoebe Grant, Journalist (obituary writer)
Time period(s): 2000s
Locale(s): United States

Summary: Life has somehow gone awry for Phoebe Grant. She had dreamed of a fabulous career in journalism, living in a great apartment with a string of men begging her to marry them. Phoebe does have a job at a newspaper. Granted, it is writing obituaries but you have to start somewhere. She does have a great apartment, although it needs a little work, but Phoebe intends to get that done someday. The string of men, however, has proved elusive. Even one man would make Phoebe happy, but her dates tend to be more horrific than romantic. Then even Phoebe's small grasps at her dream disappear. She loses her job and her mother breaks both arms and needs her daughter's help. Even worse, Phoebe's best friend signs her up for an online dating service without telling her. First novel.

Where it's reviewed:
Publishers Weekly, February 7, 2005, page 39

Other books you might like:

Judy Baer, *The Whitney Chronicles*, 2004
Kristin Billerbeck, *The Ashley Stockingdale Series*, 2004-
Penny Culliford, *The Theodora Series*, 2004-
Anne Dayton, *Emily Ever After*, 2005
Robin Jones Gunn, *The Sisterchicks Series*, 2003-

1090

CHRIS WELL

Forgiving Solomon Long

(Eugene, Oregon: Harvest House, 2005)

Story type: Mystery
Subject(s): Murder; Organized Crime
Major character(s): Tom Griggs, Police Officer; Frank "Fat Cat" Catalano, Organized Crime Figure (mobster); Solomon Long, Criminal (hit man)
Time period(s): 2000s
Locale(s): Kansas City, Missouri

Summary: A group of business owners and clergy have finally had enough of the crime in Kansas City. When the people band together to shut down organized crime, the mob brings in hit man Solomon Long to kill those they view as their most dangerous enemies. When one of Solomon Long's victims

uses his last breath to forgive his killer, the hit man develops a conscience. First novel.

Where it's reviewed:
Publishers Weekly, November 22, 2004, page 39

Other books you might like:

Karen Ball, *Shattered Justice*, 2005
James Scott Bell, *Final Witness*, 1999
Tim Downs, *The Bug Man Series*, 2003-
Joseph H. Hilley, *The Mike Connelly Series*, 2004-
Creston Mapes, *Dark Star*, 2005

1091

MELANIE WELLS

When the Day of Evil Comes

(Sisters, Oregon: Multnomah, 2005)

Story type: Mystery
Subject(s): Psychological Thriller
Major character(s): Dylan Foster, Professor (psychology)
Time period(s): 2000s
Locale(s): United States

Summary: An encounter with a strange man at a faculty picnic leads psychology professor Dylan Foster into a living nightmare. Her carefully planned life begins to crumble around her as strange things begin to happen, but when her mother's engagement ring is delivered to her house, Dylan realizes she is fighting true evil. The ring was buried with her mother, and should still be on her mother's finger. Somebody taking the trouble to be so devious not only terrifies Dylan, but makes her wonder if she is strong enough to find out the truth as to who is behind her psychological torture. First novel.

Other books you might like:

Angela Elwell Hunt, *The Truth Teller*, 1999
Gilbert Morris, *Through a Glass Darkly*, 1999
Bill Myers, *Blood of Heaven*, 1996
Lisa Samson, *The Living End*, 2003
Travis Thrasher, *The Second Thief*, 2003

1092

LINDA J. WHITE

Bloody Point

(Colorado Springs, Colorado: RiverOak, 2005)

Story type: Mystery
Subject(s): Boats and Boating; Widows/Widowers
Major character(s): Cassie McKenna, Widow(er), FBI Agent
Time period(s): 2000s
Locale(s): Chesapeake Bay, Maryland

Summary: Torn apart by her FBI agent husband's death, Cassie McKenna retreats to the solitude of her boat moored on Chesapeake Bay. Cassie is also a FBI agent though, and the agency needs her help. Her ex-partner Jake Tucker visits, hoping to enlist Cassie's help in a case involving national security. Soon Cassie's peaceful life is gone and she is deep in another investigation. First novel.

Inspirational

Other books you might like:
Mindy Starns Clark, *The Million Dollar Mysteries Series*, 2002-
Colleen Coble, *The Rock Harbor Series*, 2003-
Rene Gutteridge, *The Splitting Storm*, 2004
Dee Henderson, *The O'Malley Series*, 2001-
Patricia H. Rushford, *The Angel Delaney Series*, 2004-

1093

STEPHANIE GRACE WHITSON

A Garden in Paris

(Minneapolis: Bethany House, 2005)

Story type: Contemporary
Subject(s): Mothers and Daughters; Widows/Widowers
Major character(s): Mary Davis, Widow(er)
Time period(s): 2000s
Locale(s): Omaha, Nebraska; Paris, France

Summary: Mary Davis spent most of her adult life as the trophy wife of a powerful and distant man. With his death, she finds herself adrift with no purpose left in her life. Mary's relationship with her daughter Liz, always a difficult one, is growing even more tenuous. She always regretted walking away from her true love, Jean-Marc, and decides to attempt to reunite with him in Paris. Liz, regretting a bitter argument she had with her mother, impulsively decides to follow Mary to France.

Where it's reviewed:
Library Journal, April 1, 2005, page 78
Publishers Weekly, March 14, 2005, page 46

Other books by the same author:
Footprints on the Horizon, 2005
Watchers on the Hill, 2004
Secrets on the Wind, 2003
Heart of the Sandhills, 2002
Edge of the Wilderness, 2001

Other books you might like:
Lynn Austin, *Eve's Daughters*, 1999
Robin Jones Gunn, *Gardenias for Breakfast*, 2005
Beverly Lewis, *The Sunroom*, 1998
Gayle Roper, *Summer Shadows*, 2002
Johanna Verweerd, *The Winter Garden*, 2001

1094

LORI WICK

Moonlight on the Millpond

(Eugene, Oregon: Harvest House, 2005)

Story type: Historical
Series: Tucker Mills. Book 1
Subject(s): Brothers and Sisters
Major character(s): Jace Randall, Worker (sawmill)
Time period(s): 1830s
Locale(s): Tucker Mills, Massachusetts

Summary: Jace Randall's Uncle Woody asks him to come to Tucker Mills and help him run his sawmill. He agrees and devotes himself to his work. Then Jace meets Maddie, the niece of the local storekeeper and is soon smitten. Gossip soon separates the couple, with the gossip led by Jace's sister Eden. Eden soon realizes the trouble she has caused and repents, but it may be too late for Jace and Maddie to rekindle their romance.

Other books by the same author:
Every Storm, 2004
The Pursuit, 2003
The Visitor, 2003
The Proposal, 2002
The Rescue, 2002

Other books you might like:
Louise M. Gouge, *The Ahab Series*, 2004-
B.J. Hoff, *The American Anthem Series*, 2002-
Sara Mitchell, *The Sinclair Legacy Series*, 2001-
Delia Parr, *The Trinity Series*, 2002-
Tracie Peterson, *The Bells of Lowell Series*, 2003-

1095

ERIC WILSON

Expiration Date

(Colorado Springs, Colorado: WaterBrook, 2005)

Story type: Mystery
Subject(s): Serial Killers; Supernatural; Psychic Powers
Major character(s): Clay Ryker, Businessman (failed), Psychic
Time period(s): 2000s
Locale(s): Junction City, Oregon

Summary: Once on the fast-track to success, Clay Ryker has seen his world crumble around him. With his marriage and his business both failures, Clay returns to his hometown to try to start again. Soon strange things begin happening to Clay. He discovers that when he touches people, he can feel the date of their death on their skin. As more and more people die around Clay, he struggles to find answers that may lie deep in the past.

Other books by the same author:
Dark to Mortal Eyes, 2004

Other books you might like:
Dean Briggs, *The Most Important Little Boy in the World*, 2001
Brandilyn Collins, *The Chelsea Adams Series*, 2001-
Angela Elwell Hunt, *The Immortal*, 2000
Nancy Moser, *The Mustard Seed Series*, 1998-
Frank Peretti, *Monster*, 2005

1096

LINDA WINDSOR

Fiesta Moon

(Nashville: WestBow, 2005)

Story type: Romance
Series: Moonstruck. Book 2
Subject(s): Alcoholism; Orphans
Major character(s): Mark Madison, Engineer (construction); Corinne Diaz, Assistant (at orphanage)

Time period(s): 2000s
Locale(s): Mexico

Summary: Mark Madison is arrested for the third time for driving while under the influence and that is enough for his brother Blaine. To both punish Mark and to straighten him out, Blaine arranges for Mark to go to Mexico and convert a rundown hovel into an orphanage. When Mark meets the assistant at the orphanage, Corinne Diaz, he is happy to know he will have a pretty girl for company. Corinne, though, is not interested in the shiftless Mark.

Other books by the same author:
Paper Moon, 2005
Along Came Jones, 2003
Deirdre, 2002
It Had to Be You, 2001
Riona, 2001

Other books you might like:
Linda Chaikin, *Endangered*, 1997
Cecelia Dowdy, *First Mates*, 2005
Barbara Jean Hicks, *China Doll*, 1998
Karen Rispin, *African Skies*, 2000
Debra White Smith, *The Awakening*, 2000

1097

BONNIE K. WINN

Protected Hearts
(New York: Steeple Hill, 2005)

Story type: Romance

Subject(s): Trust
Major character(s): Emma Duvere, Widow(er); Seth McAllister, Businessman
Time period(s): 2000s
Locale(s): Rosewood, Texas

Summary: When her husband and child are murdered, Emma barely has time to realize what has happened before the Witness Protection Program sends her off to Rosewood, Texas, to hide. The small town and its people give Emma the strength she needs to go on with her life. When handsome stranger Seth McAllister moves to town, also coping with the loss of his child, the two grieving people find comfort with each other. Then Emma learns the killer is on her trail, and she might have to flee again.

Other books by the same author:
For the Sake of His Child, 2004
Promise of Grace, 2003
Vanished, 2003
Family Ties, 2002
Family Found, 2001

Other books you might like:
Gena Dalton, *Stranger at the Crossroads*, 2002
Athol Dickson, *Whom Shall I Fear?*, 1996
Dee Henderson, *Danger in the Shadows*, 1999
Deborah Raney, *A Scarlet Cord*, 2003
Cheryl Wolverton, *In Search of a Hero*, 2002

Inspirational

Popular Fiction in Review
by
Tom Barton

Each generation has their benchmarks, those seminal moments that contribute to their collective memory. Such events in the twentieth century include the Great Depression, the attack on Pearl Harbor, and the assassinations of President John F. Kennedy and Dr. Martin Luther King, Jr. In the twenty-first century, the terrorist attack on the World Trade Center on September 11, 2001 falls into this category.

While the historical record keeps track of the facts associated with these events, the stories people tell about such events define them in a personal way and make them understandable. Subsequently, these stories find their way into popular fiction. Aside from what happened, people remember where they were, who they were with, what they were doing, and the impact it had on their lives and the lives of their loved ones, family and friends. Now in 2005, it would seem that writers of popular fiction are beginning to tackle 9/11. Several titles in this edition deal with the tragedy. I think it's safe to say that we can expect more books on this subject in the future.

In *Extremely Loud & Incredibly Close* by Jonathan Safran Foer, a nine-year-old boy tries to make sense of his life, after his father perishes in the attack on the World Trade Center. Although this is only his second novel, Foer has some experience interpreting large events. His first novel, *Everything Is Illuminated*, follows a young man as he travels back to the Ukraine in an effort to trace his family's history, which includes his grandfather's escape from the Holocaust. The main character in *Writing on the Wall* by Lynne Sharon Schwartz faces an emotional meltdown after the terrorist attack triggers some old and unresolved memories associated with the death of her twin sister and her father. Schwartz, who is also known for her short stories, has a knack for developing characters seeking self-knowledge and understanding in the face of events out of their control. After the terrorist attack, despite efforts to the contrary, the changes in the world were subtle but irrevocable. Take for example the main character in

The Good Priest's Son by Reynolds Price. When his transatlantic flight is diverted to Nova Scotia, the man decides to visit his elderly father in North Carolina, rather than face the aftermath in New York City. However, he finds his father, a retired Episcopal priest, has been injured and now needs a caretaker. Later, when the character returns to New York, he will deal with the destruction of his residence, his own health, and face his estranged daughter. Ian McEwan provides a slightly different perspective in his novel *Saturday*, which is set in London and deals with European perceptions of changes caused by the terrorist attack in New York City. We follow a neurosurgeon for a day as he faces dangers both imagined and brutally real. You may remember McEwan won the Booker Prize for his 2001 novel *Atonement*.

Changes in attitude tend to produce actions with real consequences. While this seems apparent, *Maps for Lost Lovers* by Nadeem Aslam, *Towelhead* by Alicia Erian, and *Bangkok Tattoo* by John Burdett illustrate the case in point. Aslam's work deals with the effects on a Muslim community in England, after an unmarried couple is murdered for having lived together. Sexuality and adolescence are key ingredients in Erian's work about a teenage girl with a Christian-Muslim heritage. Things get real interesting when her Irish mother ships her off to live with her Arab father in Texas. The story is set in the early 1990s at the time of the first Gulf War. A detective with an existential philosophy is the main character in Burdett's work. The detective finds himself hard pressed to track down the murderer of a CIA agent when his girlfriend, who works in his mother's brothel, becomes the prime suspect.

While cultural attitudes differ, angst, alienation, and disillusionment are subjects that transcend national borders. In her collection, *Give Me*, Irina Denezhkina gives us a peek into the lives of her youthful characters and the difficulties they face in modern Russia. The work is a bestseller in Russia. Angst and aimlessness in modern Poland are subjects touched upon in *Snow White and Russian Red* by Dorota Maslowska.

Conspiracies abound as youthful characters are battered by a stagnant economy, American consumerism, and a Russian black market. Disillusionment takes a slightly different tack as children are forced to deal with an aging parent in *A Short History of Tractors in Ukrainian* by Marina Lewycka. The story is set in an immigrant community in England. There a retired widower plans to marry a much younger woman from the old country, but his daughters are outraged and scandalized by his behavior. In *Sudden Rain* by the late Maritta Wolff, readers follow middle-class couples struggling with their insecurities and disillusionments in 1970s suburbia. Although Wolff wrote this book more than thirty years ago, it remained unpublished until now, after the author's husband found it hidden in his refrigerator. Insight can be one product of disillusionment or so it would seem in Philip Caputo's latest work, *Acts of Faith*. The story puts readers on the ground in Africa as cultural, social, and religious tensions set in motion by the modern world collide with the good intentions of aid workers. Caputo, you may remember, put readers on the ground in the Vietnam War with his first novel, *A Rumor of War* in 1977.

While the main character in Jodi Compton's latest work *Sympathy between Humans* isn't particularly worried about death, a gung-ho prosecutor would like to send her to jail. The fact that she is a Minneapolis police detective gives the prosecutor an added incentive. Unlike Dennis Lehane and Robert B. Parker, who live in the city (Boston) they write about, Compton lives in California. While her descriptions of Minneapolis ring true, she only lived there briefly. George Pelecanos not only sets his stories in Washington, D.C., but he grew up there, too. His 2004 novel *Hard Revolution* is a realistic portrayal of the 1968 riots that occurred in the city after the assassination of Dr. Martin Luther King. Pelecanos' has a reputation for hard-boiled reality with working-class characters. His latest work *Drama City* follows an overworked parole officer, who tries to help her clients, while sorting out her own personal difficulties.

It's fair to say that parole and prison can add complications to people's lives but that's only the tip of the iceberg. What about relatives and loved ones left behind? Their lives also become complicated. Take for instance the plight of an African-American teenager, Natasha. She is the main character in *Upstate* by Kalisha Buckhanon. After her true love, Antonio, is sent to prison for murder, Natasha is on her own. Despite putting herself through college, she continually communicates with Antonio. Another author with a flair for nitty-gritty realism is Mo Hayder. Her experience as a teacher, filmmaker, and hostess in Japan may very well have helped provide insight for her latest book, *The Devil of Nanking*. The story's main character is a woman who believes a documentary, which explicitly shows torture and murder, will provide the key to her own emotional problems. The woman travels to Japan to ask the filmmaker for his help. When he refuses, she becomes a hostess to support herself, while developing a plan to see the film.

Dogs, man's best friend, has been, and continues to be, a perennial favorite popular fiction. Although their approach is different, two novels with dogs at t mentioning, *Wild Dogs* by Helen Humphreys and *Dog* by Michelle Her Humphreys' novel, the characters are brought together because for one reason or lost their pets. While in Herman's story, the main character's life of quiet des change for the better when she adopts a puppy.

Alternative history, or the what if game, has been getting more attention lately, since Philip Roth tossed his hat into the ring with *The Plot Against America* (2004). The story imagines what might have happened if Charles Lindbergh became president and kept the United States out of World War II. While it takes a slightly different tack, *Hitler's Peace* by Philip Kerr involves a conspiracy hatched at the height of World War II. The story revolves around a plot to assassinate one of the Allied leaders, British Prime Minister Winston Churchill, American President Franklin Delano Roosevelt, or Soviet Premier Josef Stalin. If successful, Hitler believes the Allied coalition will dissolve and Germany will be able to negotiate a peace treaty and avoid defeat. On a more personal level, *The Boy Who Loved Anne Frank* by Ellen Feldman imagines what would have happened if the boy, who Anne Frank said she loved, had survived World War II. Would the boy be able to put his nightmares from the war behind him? Or would the emotional and physical devastation of the Holocaust catch up with him?

While not exactly alternative history, taking minor characters from the historical record and existing works of fiction and giving them their own story has found a place in popular fiction. Many readers will remember Jim, the character from Mark Twain's *The Adventures of Huckleberry Finn*. In *My Jim* by Nancy Rawles, we learn more about Jim's life as told by the woman he left behind. Then there is John March, a minor character in Louisa May Alcott's *Little Women*. However, in *March* by Geraldine Brooks, John takes center stage and becomes the main character. Mary Todd Lincoln, Abraham Lincoln's wife, is the main character in *The Emancipator's Wife* by Barbara Hambly. The author paints a sympathetic portrait of Mrs. Lincoln by interpreting events from her perspective.

Speaking of history, William T. Vollmann's recent work *Europe Central* abandons North America to concentrate on World War II and the conflict between the Russians and the Germans. Vollmann's last work also had a historical flavor, dealing with the first English colony in the New World, Jamestown. Although Elizabeth Gaffney's debut novel *Metropolis* isn't about Colonial Virginia, it is pure Americana. Set in New York City just after the Civil War, the story deals with the construction of the Brooklyn Bridge and the city's social and political forces, which helped and hindered the project. Gaffney, who is known for her short fiction, lives in New York and teaches at New York University. Another work based on the historical record, *Hosack's*

Folly by Gillen D'Arcy Wood is also set in New York City. It follows the struggle between public health officials and a corrupt establishment during the yellow fever epidemic of 1824.

Although Luis Alberto Urrea's latest work *The Hummingbird's Daughter* takes place shortly after the Civil War, it is set in the border area between Mexico and Texas. The story follows a young Native American woman and draws heavily on magical realism. Another novel set in the border country between Mexico and Texas, *The Diezmo*, by Rick Bass is a coming-of-age story. When a young Texan sets out on a Mexican adventure, he winds up in a brutal jail, after his companions pillage a poor village. Although set in a more modern West, *Music of the Mill* by Luis J. Rodriguez follows a Mexican immigrant family in Los Angeles. The family struggles to reconcile their dreams with the harsh reality of modern society. Speaking of family history, Nicole Krauss, who is known for her poetry, used her own family's experience in her debut novel *The History of Love*. The story is about a desperate author who lives in poverty in Europe and is unaware that his book has been published in South America. Did I mention Krauss is married to Jonathan Safran Foer?

Strong women taking responsibility for their own lives is another noticeable trend. Take for instance Arlene Fleet, the main character in *Gods in Alabama* by Joshilyn Jackson. The book's tone is humorous but the subjects are quite serious. Reluctantly, Arlene returns to her home town in Alabama, some ten years after she graduated from high school. She left pledging never to return. She had good reason for making the pledge, considering she disposed of Jim Beverly's body. However, the past has a way of catching up and Arlene must face it. In *Emilie's Voice* by Susanne Dunlap, the main character is a common young woman with a sweet singing voice. Emilie dreams of becoming a lady. She gets more than she bargained for when members of the nobility use her to win favor at the French Royal Court of Louis XIV. The main character in *Breath and Bones* by Susann Cokal makes surviving an art form. She grows up in an orphanage, rejects farm work, and moves to the city. There she becomes an artist's model and a mistress. When her lover goes to America, she sets off to find him. Subsequently, her adventures include an American brothel, Mormon polygamy, labor violence, and a California millionaire.

Dance provides a young woman with a bridge between her mixed Cuban-Japanese heritage and the modern world in *Mambo Peligroso* by Patricia Chao. Political intrigue adds a plot twist courtesy of the woman's cousin. In *The Mermaid Chair* by Sue Monk Kidd, Jessie, the main character, leaves her family to tend to her eccentric mother. In the process, Jessie falls in love with a monk and reawakens her own artistic nature, that has been repressed for many years.

When all is said and done, I think it is fair to say this is a good time to be a reader of popular fiction.

Recommended Titles

Maps for Lost Lovers by Nadeem Aslam

Upstate by Kalisha Buckhanon

Bangkok Tattoo by John Burdett

Acts of Faith by Philip Caputo

Mambo Peligroso by Patricia Chao

Breath and Bones by Susann Cokal

Sympathy between Humans by Jodi Compton

Towelhead by Alicia Erian

Extremely Loud & Incredibly Close by Jonathan Safran Foer

Metropolis by Elizabeth Gaffney

The Sad Truth about Happiness by Anne Giardini

The Devil of Nanking by Mo Hayder

Dog by Michelle Herman

Gods in Alabama by Joshilyn Jackson

The Mermaid Chair by Sue Monk Kidd

The Historian by Elizabeth Kostova

The History of Love by Nicole Krauss

A Short History of Tractors in Ukrainian by Marina Lewycka

Saturday by Ian McEwan

Shadow Family by Miyuki Miyabe

He Drown She in the Sea by Shani Mootoo

Drama City by George P. Pelecanos

The Good Priest's Son by Reynolds Price

Writing on the Wall by Lynne Sharon Schwartz

The Illuminator by Brenda Rickman Vantrease

Popular Fiction Titles

1098

PETER ABRAHAMS

Oblivion
(New York: William Morrow, 2005)

Story type: Mystery
Subject(s): Missing Persons; Psychological; Memory Loss
Major character(s): Nick Petrov, Detective—Private; Amanda Rummel, Teenager (missing person); Liza, Prostitute
Time period(s): 2000s
Locale(s): United States

Summary: Abrahams takes a hard look at identity and the role memory plays in defining who we are. The main character, Nick Petrov, is a very successful private detective with near-celebrity status. When he is hired by Liza to find her teenage daughter, Amanda Rummel, Petrov has a funny feeling. Something tells him that Liza, a high-priced call girl, is hiding something. Three days into the investigation, his gut feeling is validated. Then, he wakes up two weeks later in a hospital, suffering from a brain trauma and unable to remember anything about those weeks. The only way he can find out what happened is to retrace the steps of his investigation and find Amanda.

Where it's reviewed:
Chicago Tribune Books, April 17, 2005, page 3
Kirkus Reviews, December 15, 2004, page 1115
Library Journal, February 15, 2005, page 113
New Yorker, April 4, 2005, page 94

Other books by the same author:
Down the Rabbit Hole, 2005
Their Wildest Dreams, 2003
Crying Wolf, 2000
Lights Out, 1994
Revolution No. 9, 1992

Other books you might like:
Benjamin Anastas, *The Faithful Narrative of a Pastor's Disappearance*, 2001
Paul Auster, *The Book of Illusions*, 2002

Frederick Busch, *A Memory of War*, 2003
Catherine Bush, *Claire's Head*, 2004
Joy Fielding, *Lost*, 2003

1099

SIMONETTA AGNELLO HORNBY

The Almond Picker
(New York: Farrar, Straus and Giroux, 2005)

Story type: Romance; Family Saga
Subject(s): Mystery; Servants; Identity
Major character(s): Maria Rosalia "Mennulara" Inzerillo, Servant
Time period(s): 1960s
Locale(s): Sicily, Italy

Summary: A bestseller in Italy, the book revolves around the identity of a servant, Mennulara. The story is set in Sicily and opens when Mennulara is dead. As a young woman, she goes to work for a prominent family. She works hard and becomes administrator of the family's property. Rumors flourish that she has become wealthy. When the family gathers to hear a reading of her will, her instructions send them on a quest. Subsequently, Mennulara's story unfolds and her identity is revealed. Translated from the Italian by Alastair McEwan.

Where it's reviewed:
Booklist, January 1, 2005, page 819
Kirkus Reviews, January 1, 2005, page 10
Library Journal, January 2005, page 97

Other books you might like:
Gioia Diliberto, *I Am Madame X*, 2003
Jennifer Haigh, *Baker Towers*, 2005
Marilynne Robinson, *Gilead*, 2004
Bart Schneider, *Beautiful Inez*, 2005
Anne Tyler, *Ladder of Years*, 1996

1100

CECILIA AHERN

Rosie Dunne

(New York: Hyperion, 2005)

Story type: Humor; Romance
Subject(s): Relationships; Irish Americans; Growing Up
Major character(s): Rosie Dunne, Friend (of Alex); Alex Stewart, Friend (of Rosie)
Time period(s): 20th century; 21st century
Locale(s): Dublin, Ireland; Boston, Massachusetts

Summary: Ahern's novel is a romance that uses e-mail, instant messages, letters, and notes. As children in Dublin, Rosie loves Alex. When his family moves to Boston, Rosie and Alex vow to keep in touch. In high school, they make plans to meet at her prom, but their plans fall through and she goes with someone else. Subsequently, she gets pregnant and decides to have the child. This means she won't be going to college in the U.S. and hanging around with Alex. Meanwhile, life goes on but in the end love conquers all.

Where it's reviewed:
Booklist, January 1, 2005, page 811
Library Journal, January 2005, page 93
Publishers Weekly, January 3, 2005, page 34

Other books by the same author:
P.S. I Love You, 2004

Other books you might like:
Maeve Binchy, *Circle of Friends*, 1990
Judy Blume, *Wifey*, 1978
Eric Jerome Dickey, *Drive Me Crazy*, 2004
Jane Green, *To Have and to Hold*, 2004
Terry McMillan, *The Interruption of Everything*, 2005

1101

BORIS AKUNIN (Pseudonym of Grigory Chkhartishvili)

The Turkish Gambit

(New York: Random House, 2005)

Story type: Historical/Victorian; Mystery
Series: Erast Fandorin. Book 3
Subject(s): Spies; Communication; Russians
Major character(s): Erast Fandorin, Diplomat, Detective— Police; Varvara Andreevna "Varya" Suvorova, Worker; Petya, Young Man, Fiance(e) (of Varya)
Time period(s): 1870s (1877)
Locale(s): Bulgaria

Summary: The incomparable Russian detective Erast Fandorin returns, this time collecting information to help the Russian army in a war against the Ottoman Empire. Along the way, Erast meets Varya, a lively beauty, who attracts a colorful entourage of noblemen, soldiers, and other hangers-on, who are interested in making love to her. Varya, however, has more serious concerns. She is searching for her fiance, Petya, a cryptographer, who is in hiding. After a secret message brought a military reverse to the army, Petya was blamed. Varya sets out to clear him and Erast decides to help. Translated from the Russian by Andrew Bromfield.

Where it's reviewed:
Booklist, February 1, 2005, page 944
Kirkus Reviews, January 15, 2005, page 83
Library Journal, March 1, 2005, page 74

Other books by the same author:
Murder on the Leviathan, 2004
The Winter Queen, 2003

Other books you might like:
Tom Bradby, *The White Russian*, 2003
Dan Brown, *The Da Vinci Code*, 2003
John Burdett, *Bangkok 8*, 2003
Nelson DeMille, *Night Fall*, 2004
Martin Cruz Smith, *Wolves Eat Dogs*, 2004

1102

DANIEL ALARCON

War by Candlelight

(New York: HarperCollins, 2005)

Story type: Collection
Subject(s): Short Stories; Political Movements; Violence

Summary: Alarcon's debut collection of nine short stories deals with disasters both natural and man-made. The title story concerns a man killed after he joins the guerrillas in the jungle. In "Flood," the government destroys a prison when the inmates riot. Social protest in Peru is the backdrop in "City of Clowns" as a reporter tries to understand his father and his father's second family. In "Lima, Peru, July 28, 1979," a man hunts black dogs. Other stories include "Absence," "A Strong Good Man," "The Visitor," "Third Avenue Suicide," and "A Science for Being Alone."

Where it's reviewed:
Booklist, February 15, 2005, page 1058
Kirkus Reviews, January 1, 2005, page 3
Library Journal, February 1, 2005, page 72
Publishers Weekly, February 21, 2005, page 155

Other books you might like:
Steve Almond, *The Evil B.B. Chow and Other Stories*, 2005
Percival Everett, *Damned If I Do*, 2004
Robert Ford, *The Student Conductor*, 2003
Francine Prose, *The Peaceable Kingdom*, 1993
John Edgar Wideman, *God's Gym*, 2005

1103

JANE ALISON

Natives and Exotics

(Orlando, Florida: Harcourt, 2005)

Story type: Historical; Domestic
Subject(s): Ecology; Pioneers; Women
Major character(s): Alice Forder, Young Woman (Violet's granddaughter); Violet, Grandparent (Alice's grandmother), Pioneer (in Australia); George, Grandparent (Violet's grandfather), Gardener
Time period(s): 19th century; 20th century (1820s-1980s)
Locale(s): Ecuador; Australia; Azores

Summary: The march of progress, immigration, and the environment are examined in this family saga that follows characters from three different time periods. In the 1980s, Alice, a sensitive young woman, lives with her diplomat parents in Quito, Ecuador, where she marvels at the natural wonders of the country and questions the efficacy of modernization. In 1929, Alice's grandmother, Violet, struggles to clear land in Australia. In 1822, George, Alice and Violet's ancestor, leaves social turmoil in his native Scotland, to immigrate to the Azores. He plants citrus fruits there, which ultimately destroy the soil. In 1836, he moves to Australia.

Where it's reviewed:
Kirkus Reviews, March 15, 2005, page 301
Publishers Weekly, April 4, 2005, page 44

Other books by the same author:
The Marriage of the Sea, 2003
The Love-Artist, 2001

Other books you might like:
Rick Bass, *The Sky, the Stars, the Wilderness*, 1997
Andre Dubus III, *House of Sand and Fog*, 1999
Louise Erdrich, *The Master Butchers Singing Club*, 2003
Elizabeth Gaffney, *Metropolis*, 2005
Amitav Ghosh, *The Hungry Tide*, 2005

1104

ISABEL ALLENDE

Zorro

(New York: HarperCollins, 2005)

Story type: Historical; Legend
Subject(s): Heroes and Heroines; Identity, Concealed; Resistance Movements
Major character(s): Diego de la Vega, Hero; Bernardo, Servant, Companion
Time period(s): 18th century
Locale(s): California; Barcelona, Spain

Summary: Diego de la Vega grows up in California when it still belongs to Spain. His father comes from the Spanish aristocracy, while his mother is an Indian. Diego's mixed blood isn't an issue until he is sent to Barcelona to be educated. Social sanctions bar Diego from the woman he loves. After learning from a master, Diego becomes skillful with a sword. He joins an underground revolutionary group and becomes Zorro.

Where it's reviewed:
Booklist, February 15, 2005, page 1035
Kirkus Reviews, February 15, 2005, page 187
Library Journal, March 1, 2005, page 74
Publishers Weekly, February 28, 2005, page 39

Other books by the same author:
Portrait in Sepia, 2001
Daughter of Fortune, 1999
The Infinite Plan, 1993
The Stories of Eva Luna, 1991
Eva Luna, 1988

Other books you might like:
Madison Smartt Bell, *Master of the Crossroads*, 2000

Bernard Cornwell, *The Last Kingdom*, 2005
Michael Crichton, *Eaters of the Dead*, 1976
Larry McMurtry, *Lonesome Dove*, 1985
William T. Vollmann, *Argall*, 2001

1105

STEVE ALMOND

The Evil B.B. Chow and Other Stories

(Chapel Hill, North Carolina: Algonquin, 2005)

Story type: Collection; Adult
Subject(s): Short Stories; Sexual Behavior; Relationships
Time period(s): 2000s
Locale(s): United States

Summary: Almond's second collection offers 12 short stories, which look at life in modern society, using a lens heavily laced with humor. Relationships and sexual behavior are at the heart of most of the stories. In ''Appropriate Sex,'' the teacher of a writer's workshop is seduced by a student. In the title story, ''The Evil B.B. Chow,'' a magazine editor is attracted to an inept and immature medical student. A friend talks about kinky sex practices involving an artificial eye in ''Skull.'' An unlikely couple meet on a successful blind date in ''A Happy Dream.'' A friend reluctantly agrees to read an unpublished manuscript in ''Larsen's Novel.'' The other stories included are ''The Soul Molecule,'' ''I Am as I Am,'' ''Lincoln Arisen,'' ''The Idea of Michael Jackson's Dick,'' ''The Problem of Human Consumption,'' ''Wired for Life,'' and ''Summer, as in Love.''

Where it's reviewed:
Booklist, February 15, 2005, page 1058
Kirkus Reviews, January 15, 2005, page 63
Library Journal, March 1, 2005, page 81
Publishers Weekly, February 14, 2005, page 51

Other books by the same author:
My Life in Heavy Metal, 2002

Other books you might like:
Daniel Alarcon, *War by Candlelight*, 2005
A.S. Byatt, *The Matisse Stories*, 1993
Amy Hempel, *The Dog of the Marriage*, 2005
Antonya Nelson, *In the Land of Men*, 1992
Joyce Carol Oates, *Rape*, 2004

1106

STEVE AMICK

The Lake, the River and the Other Lake

(New York: Knopf, 2005)

Story type: Psychological; Humor
Subject(s): Identity; City and Town Life; Summer
Major character(s): Roger Drinkwater, Veteran (Vietnam War), Indian; Janey Struska, Police Officer (sheriff)
Time period(s): 2000s (2001)
Locale(s): Weneshkeen, Michigan

Summary: Amick's debut novel, set in an upscale Michigan resort, follows a group of diverse characters who follow their own agendas and interact with each other during the summer

of 2001. One of the story lines pits a Native American against a bunch of affluent and immature jet-skiers. Vietnam veteran Roger Drinkwater swims across the lake each morning. Thanks to the jet-skiers, Roger's morning swim has been turned into a dangerous adventure. He has a plan to stop the jet-skiers, but there is one complication, Sheriff Janey Struska. She is smart and good-looking, and Roger would like to stay on her good side.

Where it's reviewed:
Kirkus Reviews, February 15, 2005, page 187
Library Journal, April 1, 2005, page 83
Publishers Weekly, March 14, 2005, page 43

Other books you might like:
Margaret Atwood, *Lady Oracle*, 1976
Catherine Bush, *Claire's Head*, 2004
Dan Chaon, *You Remind Me of Me*, 2004
Linda Howard, *White Lies*, 1988
Heidi Julavits, *The Effect of Living Backwards*, 2003

NICK ARVIN

Articles of War
(New York: Doubleday, 2005)

Story type: Historical/World War II
Subject(s): War; Refugees; Coming-of-Age
Major character(s): George "Heck" Tilson, Military Personnel (U.S. Army)
Time period(s): 1940s (1944)
Locale(s): France

Summary: George "Heck" Tilson, 18, grows up on an Iowa farm. He is soft-spoken, never cusses, and is likable. Most people agree that he has the makings of a good citizen. Although this assessment might be true in a civilized society, a different yardstick is used during wartime. Complications set in after George enlists in the army and is sent to Normandy. There, in the heat of combat, George learns that he is a coward. The story revolves around the struggle with his inner demons, while he attempts to be the good soldier everyone expects him to be.

Where it's reviewed:
Booklist, November 15, 2004, page 551
Kirkus Reviews, December 2004, page 1099
Library Journal, January 2005, page 93
Publishers Weekly, November 1, 2004, page 40

Other books by the same author:
In the Electric Eden, 2003

Other books you might like:
Dennis Bock, *The Ash Garden*, 2001
Joseph Conrad, *Lord Jim*, 1900
Alan Furst, *Kingdom of Shadows*, 2001
A.E.W. Mason, *The Four Feathers*, 1902
Martin Cruz Smith, *Wolves Eat Dogs*, 2004

1108

NADEEM ASLAM

Maps for Lost Lovers
(New York: Knopf, 2005)

Story type: Domestic; Psychological
Subject(s): Women; Muslims; Religion
Major character(s): Chanda, Crime Victim (murdered); Shamas, Spouse (Kaukab's husband), Immigrant (from Pakistan); Kaukab, Spouse (Shamas' wife), Immigrant (from Pakistan)
Time period(s): 2000s
Locale(s): England

Summary: This story examines the tragic consequences resulting from the collision of a traditional cultural view with the modern world. An unmarried couple, Jagnu and Chanda, live in an English town. One day they disappear. Several months later, shock waves rock the Pakistani community when police find their bodies. Subsequently, Chanda's brothers are arrested for the double murder. The impact of the murders takes its toll on relatives and others in this Islamic community. Kaukab and her husband Shamas, who is Jagnu's brother, have their world view shattered. Kaukab struggles mightily to maintain her faith.

Where it's reviewed:
Kirkus Reviews, March 1, 2005, page 241
Library Journal, April 1, 2005, page 83
Publishers Weekly, March 7, 2005, page 47

Other books by the same author:
Season of the Rainbirds, 1993

Other books you might like:
Monica Ali, *Brick Lane*, 2003
Chitra Banerjee Divakaruni, *The Vine of Desire*, 2002
Ruth Prawer Jhabvala, *Heat and Dust*, 1975
Reynolds Price, *Noble Norfleet*, 2002
Donna Tartt, *The Little Friend*, 2002

1109

TASH AW

The Harmony Silk Factory
(New York: Riverhead, 2005)

Story type: Historical/World War II; Psychological
Subject(s): Chinese; Family Saga; Relationships
Major character(s): Johnny Lim, Businessman; Snow Lim, Spouse (Johnny's wife); Jasper Lim, Relative (Johnny's son)
Time period(s): 1930s; 1940s (1939-1945)
Locale(s): Malaysia

Summary: Johnny, a Chinese peasant who becomes a successful businessman, is seen from three differing perspectives. His upper class wife, Snow, who dies in childbirth, is seen in the pages of a diary she leaves behind. She does not have a high regard for her husband because of his low birth; she is unfaithful to him and plans to leave him. Johnny's alienated son Jasper believes his father is a murderous drug dealer, a Communist, and a collaborator with the Japanese during World

War II. In fact, Jasper refuses to see any redeeming characteristics whatsoever in his father. Peter, an English friend of Johnny, sees him as a vulnerable human being from a low class background, although Peter admits his view of Johnny was colored by his being in love with Snow.

Where it's reviewed:
Kirkus Reviews, January 1, 2005, page 3
Library Journal, February 15, 2005, page 113
Publishers Weekly, February 14, 2005, page 52

Other books you might like:
Simonetta Agnello Hornby, *The Almond Picker*, 2005
Peter Carey, *My Life as a Fake*, 2003
Kazuo Ishiguro, *When We Were Orphans*, 2000
Nora Okja Keller, *Fox Girl*, 2002
Martin Cruz Smith, *December 6*, 2002

SAM BAKER

Fashion Victim

(New York: Ballantine, 2005)

Story type: Mystery
Subject(s): Women; Journalism; Fashion Design
Major character(s): Annie Anderson, Journalist (fashion writer); Mark Miller, Designer (fashion), Crime Victim (murdered); Patty Lang, Model, Girlfriend (of Mark)
Time period(s): 2000s
Locale(s): New York, New York; London, England; Paris, France

Summary: Baker offers a debut novel that gives an insider's view of the fashion industry that is long on nuts and bolts and short on glamour. The main character is Annie Anderson, who left a job as an investigative reporter to get away from the stress. She takes a job with a premier fashion magazine. While covering a fashion show, Annie gets invited to an after show party. A gunman shows up, terrorizes everyone at the party before shooting the young designer to death. The episode awakens Annie's investigative skills and she sets out to get the story. She knows she's on track when her own life is threatened.

Where it's reviewed:
Kirkus Reviews, March 15, 2005, page 318
Library Journal, April 1, 2005, page 83

Other books you might like:
Alice Adams, *Almost Perfect*, 1993
Barbara Taylor Bradford, *Dangerous to Know*, 1995
John Grisham, *The Pelican Brief*, 1992
Plum Sykes, *Bergdorf Blondes*, 2004
Lauren Weisberger, *The Devil Wears Prada*, 2003

MELISSA BANK

The Wonder Spot

(New York: Viking, 2005)

Story type: Domestic; Coming-of-Age
Subject(s): Jews; Adolescence; Women

Major character(s): Sophie Applebaum, Heroine; Jack Applebaum, Relative (Sophie's older brother); Robert Applebaum, Relative (Sophie's younger brother)
Time period(s): 2000s
Locale(s): Philadelphia, Pennsylvania (suburban)

Summary: A middle child in a Jewish family, Sophie Applebaum has to struggle to establish her own identity. She grows up in suburban Philadelphia with a critical mother; a quiet father; an easygoing, devious older brother, Jack; and a conventional younger brother, Robert. She goes to college, gets a job, and develops a network of women friends, while searching for Mr. Right. Meanwhile, Robert marries an aggressive orthodox woman. Jack gives up womanizing to marry a woman from a well-to-do family. Sophie's father dies and her grandmother becomes senile. Other characters and plenty of humor keep things lively.

Where it's reviewed:
Booklist, March 15, 2005, page 1245
Kirkus Reviews, March 1, 2005, page 241
Library Journal, April 15, 2005, page 71
Publishers Weekly, March 14, 2005, page 42

Other books by the same author:
The Girls' Guide to Hunting and Fishing, 1999

Other books you might like:
Alicia Erian, *Towelhead*, 2005
Gale Zoe Garnett, *Visible Amazement*, 1999
Alice Hoffman, *Property of*, 1977
Sue Monk Kidd, *The Secret Life of Bees*, 2002
Alice McDermott, *Child of My Heart*, 2002

1112

RICK BASS

The Diezmo

(Boston: Houghton Mifflin, 2005)

Story type: Historical/American West; Adventure
Subject(s): War; Prisoners of War; Politics
Major character(s): James Alexander, Military Personnel, Teenager; James Shepherd, Friend (of Alexander), Teenager
Time period(s): 1840s (1842)
Locale(s): Texas; Mexico

Summary: In 1842, Sam Houston sends a ragtag group composed mostly of teenagers to patrol the border with Mexico. James Alexander is a teenager looking for adventure, so he joins up. The group, long on energy and short on maturity, crosses the border, and spreads death and destruction. After some savage fighting, the Mexican army captures them; some escape but are soon recaptured and sent to a notorious Mexican prison. Subsequently, the prisoners are tortured, terrorized, and made to participate in an exercise called the *Diezmo*, which marks every tenth man to be shot.

Where it's reviewed:
Booklist, March 1, 2005, page 1101
Kirkus Reviews, March 1, 2005, page 242
Library Journal, April 15, 2005, page 71
Publishers Weekly, March 21, 2005, page 35

Popular Fiction

Other books by the same author:
The Hermit's Story, 2002
Where the Sea Used to Be, 1998
In the Loyal Mountains, 1995
Platte River, 1994
The Watch, 1989

Other books you might like:
Barry Gifford, *The Sinaloa Story*, 1998
Ray Gonzalez, *The Ghost of John Wayne and Other Stories*, 2001
Elmer Kelton, *Jericho's Road*, 2004
Cormac McCarthy, *Blood Meridian*, 1992
Larry McMurtry, *Comanche Moon*, 1997

1113
ANN BEATTIE
Follies
(New York: Simon & Schuster, 2005)

Story type: Collection; Domestic
Subject(s): Short Stories; Aging; Family Relations
Locale(s): United States

Summary: Ann Beattie's collection consists of ten short stories and one novella. Known for her keen powers of observation, Beattie shines her skills on the relationship between adult children and aging parents. In the novella "Flechette Follies," a minor car crash sets in motion waves that have severe consequences. A series of events causes a woman to keep postponing a road trip in "Apology for a Journey Not Taken." An old man, who can't be nice to his own daughter, manages to make nice with his niece and nephew in "That Last Odd Day in L.A." The other stories are "Find and Replace," "Duchais," "Tending Something," "Mostre," "The Garden Game," "The Rabbit Hole as Likely Explanation," and "Just Going Out."

Where it's reviewed:
Booklist, February 1, 2005, page 916
Kirkus Reviews, February 15, 2005, page 188
Library Journal, March 15, 2005, page 77
New York Times, April 26, 2005, page B1
Publishers Weekly, March 14, 2005, page 43

Other books by the same author:
The Doctor's House, 2002
Perfect Recall, 2001
Park City, 1998
What Was Mine, 1991
Picturing Will, 1989

Other books you might like:
Robert Olen Butler, *Had a Good Time*, 2004
Nadine Gordimer, *Loot and Other Stories*, 2003
Antonya Nelson, *Female Trouble*, 2002
Joyce Carol Oates, *Small Avalanches and Other Stories*, 2003
ZZ Packer, *Drinking Coffee Elsewhere*, 2003

1114
MIRANDA BEVERLY-WHITTEMORE
The Effects of Light
(New York: Warner, 2005)

Story type: Psychological
Subject(s): Women; Grief; Photography
Major character(s): Kate Scott, Professor (of history); Prudence Wolfe, Relative (Kate's sister); Ruth Handel, Photographer
Time period(s): 2000s
Locale(s): East Coast; Pacific Northwest

Summary: When Myla Wolfe and her sister Prudence were children, they posed nude for photographer Ruth Handel. The photos created quite a scandal when they became public more than 20 years ago. Now, Pru is dead and Myla has been living under the name of Kate Scott, teaching history in a liberal arts college. Coincidental events cause Kate to return to the Pacific Northwest, where she grew up with her sister. She is intent on reclaiming her identity, but to do that she must face her childhood ghosts.

Where it's reviewed:
Booklist, November 15, 2004, page 551
Kirkus Reviews, December 15, 2004, page 1153
Library Journal, December 2004, page 97
Publishers Weekly, November 22, 2004, page 36

Other books you might like:
Barbara Taylor Bradford, *Where You Belong*, 2000
Mary Higgins Clark, *Moonlight Becomes You*, 1996
Kathryn Harrison, *Exposure*, 1993
Helen Humphreys, *Afterimage*, 2000
Susanna Moore, *In the Cut*, 1995

1115
JOAN BRADY
Bleedout
(New York: Simon & Schuster, 2005)

Story type: Mystery
Subject(s): Crime and Criminals; Law; Murder
Major character(s): Hugh Freyl, Lawyer, Friend (of David); David Marion, Convict (ex-con); Stephanie Willis, Assistant (Hugh's)
Time period(s): 2000s
Locale(s): Springfield, Illinois

Summary: Hugh Freyl runs a successful law firm in Springfield, Illinois. To achieve success, Hugh had to overcome blindness and other personal difficulties. When he befriends convicted criminal David Marion, Hugh sets out to rehabilitate him. Most of Hugh's friends believe he has gone too far. When someone beats Hugh to death, his friends' reservations appear to be justified. David is the prime suspect. To save himself, David must catch the killer. He receives help from Hugh's personal assistant Stephanie Willis. Together, David and Stephanie peel back layers of secrecy, revealing an underworld of corruption, greed, and murder.

Where it's reviewed:
Kirkus Reviews, December 1, 2004, page 1100
Library Journal, March 15, 2005, page 68
Publishers Weekly, March 7, 2005, page 50

Other books by the same author:
Joyride, 2003
The Emigre, 1999
Death Comes for Peter Pan, 1996
Theory of War, 1993
The Imposter, 1979

Other books you might like:
Stephen J. Cannell, *The Viking Funeral*, 2002
Michael Connelly, *City of Bones*, 2002
Michael Crichton, *Rising Sun*, 1992
James Ellroy, *L.A. Noir*, 1998
George V. Higgins, *A Change of Gravity*, 1997

1116

SONNY BREWER

The Poet of Tolstoy Park

(New York: Ballantine, 2005)

Story type: Contemporary/Mainstream
Subject(s): Spirituality; Illness; Death
Major character(s): Henry Stuart, Aged Person, Professor (retired)
Time period(s): 1920s (1925)
Locale(s): Nampa, Idaho; Fairhope, Alabama

Summary: When retired professor Henry Stuart contracts a terminal illness, he decides to leave his home in Idaho and move to an ideal community in Alabama. His family and friends try unsuccessfully to talk him out of his plan. When he arrives in Alabama, Henry builds a home and only eats what he can grow. Then, drawing on his knowledge of Leo Tolstoy, Henry David Thoreau, and Black Elk, Henry prepares to meet his death. While he waits, he survives natural disasters and snake bite and undergoes a spiritual conversion that allows hin to reach out to his neighbors.

Where it's reviewed:
Kirkus Reviews, December 15, 2004, page 1153
Library Journal, December 2004, page 97

Other books you might like:
Larry Brown, *Big Bad Love*, 1991
Tom Franklin, *Poachers*, 1999
William Gay, *I Hate to See That Evening Sun Go Down*, 2002
John Grisham, *The Last Juror*, 2004
George Minot, *The Blue Bowl*, 2004

1117

GERALDINE BROOKS

March

(New York: Viking, 2004)

Story type: Historical/American Civil War; Domestic
Subject(s): Fathers and Daughters; War; Secrets
Major character(s): John March, Religious, Military Personnel (Union chaplain); Marmee March, Spouse (John's wife)

Time period(s): 1860s (1861-1865)
Locale(s): Concord, Massachusetts

Summary: Brooks imagines what happened to John March, the absent father in Louisa May Alcott's novel *Little Women*. The first part of the story is narrated by John, and the second by his wife Marmee. John, a Union chaplain, has been assigned to a cotton plantation where he attempts to minister to the freed slaves who work there. While the narrative provides the true version of his experience, namely his horror at the soldiers' treatment of the freed slaves, his letters to his family are upbeat and hopeful. During a rebel attack on the plantation, John is wounded and sent to a hospital to recover. Marmee gives an unvarnished version of her feelings toward John, revealing things he has concealed.

Where it's reviewed:
Booklist, February 1, 2005, page 938
Chicago Tribune Books, March 6, 2005, page 1
Kirkus Reviews, January 1, 2005, page 5
Publishers Weekly, December 20, 2004, page 34

Other books by the same author:
Year of Wonder, 2001

Other books you might like:
Louisa May Alcott, *Little Women*, 1869
Andre Dubus III, *House of Sand and Fog*, 1999
Charles Frazier, *Cold Mountain*, 1997
Paulette Jiles, *Enemy Women*, 2002
Jeffrey Lent, *In the Fall*, 2000

1118

KALISHA BUCKHANON

Upstate

(New York: St. Martin's Press, 2005)

Story type: Coming-of-Age; Romance
Subject(s): African Americans; Prisoners and Prisons; Fathers
Major character(s): Antonio, Teenager, Criminal (killed his father); Natasha, Teenager, Girlfriend (of Antonio)
Time period(s): 2000s
Locale(s): New York, New York (Harlem)

Summary: Two African-American teenagers come to terms with the adult world and their relationship. Natasha graduates from high school, but Antonio is sent to prison for killing his own father. The two lovers communicate via letters, but Antonio, who has become embittered, tries to control Natasha's life. She resists, continues her education, and eventually goes to law school. Predictably, they grow apart. Although the book's tone generally favors Natasha, some events put Antonio in a favorable light.

Where it's reviewed:
Booklist, January 15, 2004, page 707
Library Journal, January 2005, page 94

Other books you might like:
Erskine Caldwell, *Southways*, 1938
Bebe Moore Campbell, *What You Owe Me*, 2001
Stanley Crouch, *Don't the Moon Look Lonesome*, 2000
Eric Jerome Dickey, *Friends and Lovers*, 1997
Alice Walker, *The Color Purple*, 1982

Popular Fiction

1119

JUDY BUDNITZ

Nice Big American Baby

(New York: Knopf, 2005)

Story type: Collection
Subject(s): Utopia/Dystopia; Short Stories; Environmental Problems
Time period(s): 2000s
Locale(s): United States

Summary: While utopian visions portray an ideal society, Budnitz's collection of 12 short stories takes the opposite point of view. Despite situations that are fantastic and eccentric, the narrators are skillful at presenting their points-of-view as not only conventional but normal. Stories included are ''Where We Come From,'' ''The Kindest Cut: Sales,'' ''Miracle,'' ''Saving Face,'' and ''Motherland.'' Budnitz won an O. Henry Award in 1991 for *I Told You So.*

Where it's reviewed:
Booklist, February 1, 2005, page 938
Kirkus Reviews, December 1, 2004, page 1101
New York Times Book Review, February 20, 2005, page 8
Publishers Weekly, December 6, 2004, page 41

Other books by the same author:
If I Told You Once, 1999
Flying Leap, 1998

Other books you might like:
Margaret Atwood, *Oryx and Crake*, 2003
A.S. Byatt, *The Matisse Stories*, 1993
Haruki Murakami, *After the Quake*, 2002
Richard Russo, *The Whore's Child and Other Stories*, 2002
Nick Sagan, *Edenborn*, 2004
Joy Williams, *The Quick and the Dead*, 2000

1120

JOHN BURDETT

Bangkok Tattoo

(New York: Knopf, 2005)

Story type: Mystery
Series: Sonchai Jitpleecheep. Book 2
Subject(s): Police Procedural; Prostitution; Violence
Major character(s): Sonchai Jitpleecheep, Detective—Police; Colonel Vikorn, Detective—Police (Sonchai's boss), Businessman (operates a brothel); Chanya, Prostitute (works for Vikorn)
Time period(s): 2000s
Locale(s): Bangkok, Thailand

Summary: Once again, Burdett depicts the mysterious and exotic world of modern day Bangkok, where Royal Police Detective Sonchai Jitpleecheep tracks down murderers. This time out, the story revolves around the brutal death of CIA agent Mitch Turner. The prime suspect is a bar girl, Chanya. Two things complicate matters. Chanya works for The Old Boys Club, a brothel owned by Colonel Vikorn and Sonchai's mother. Sonchai also is in love with Chanya. As the investiga-tion progresses, Sonchai will deal with corrupt officials and a wide variety of gangsters.

Where it's reviewed:
Kirkus Reviews, April 1, 2005, page 368
Publishers Weekly, April 25, 2005, page 40

Other books by the same author:
Bangkok 8, 2003

Other books you might like:
Julianna Baggott, *The Madam*, 2003
Lois Battle, *Storyville*, 1993
Paul Theroux, *Half Moon Street*, 1984
Betsy Tobin, *Bone House*, 2000
William T. Vollmann, *The Royal Family*, 2000

1121

KEVIN CANTY

Winslow in Love

(New York: Nan A. Talese/Doubleday, 2005)

Story type: Contemporary/Mainstream
Subject(s): Teachers; Psychological; Romance
Major character(s): Richard Winslow, Writer (poet), Professor (teaches poetry); Erika Jones, Student—College
Time period(s): 2000s
Locale(s): Athens, Montana

Summary: Richard Winslow was a promising poet with a bright future but that was 18 years ago. Now, he suffers from writer's block, too much alcohol, a dwindling bank account, and a wife who is about to leave him. When a small liberal arts college offers him a hefty salary to teach a class for one semester, Richard packs up and heads to Montana. There he meets a brilliant student with more problems than he could imagine. Her name is Erika Jones and she has an unhealthy taste for scotch whiskey and razor blades. After many conversations over glasses of scotch, the two embark upon a road trip. A tenuous relationship between them blooms and Richard becomes reconnected to life.

Where it's reviewed:
Booklist, December 1, 2004, page 634
Kirkus Reviews, December 1, 2004, page 1102
Library Journal, December 2004, page 98
Publishers Weekly, November 8, 2004, page 32

Other books by the same author:
Honeymoon and Other Stories, 2001
Nine Below Zero, 1999
Into the Great Wide Open, 1996
A Stranger in This World, 1994

Other books you might like:
Saul Bellow, *Herzog*, 1964
Willa Cather, *The Professor's House*, 1925
John Cheever, *Falconer*, 1977
Don DeLillo, *White Noise*, 1985
David Galef, *Flesh*, 1995

1122

PHILIP CAPUTO

Acts of Faith

(New York: Knopf, 2005)

Story type: Psychological; Political
Subject(s): Human Rights; Conspiracies; Violence
Major character(s): Douglas Braithwaite, Adventurer (gun-runner), Businessman (air charter service); Fitzhugh Martin, Businessman (Douglas' partner); Quinette, Activist (human rights worker)
Time period(s): 2000s
Locale(s): Lokichokio, Kenya; Sudan

Summary: Caputo paints an interesting portrait of the political struggle taking place in Sudan between the government in the north and the tribes in the southern part of the country. The north is Arab and Muslim and the south black African and Christian. Two partners, Douglas Braithwaite and Fitzhugh Martin, operate a charter service that flies humanitarian aid into the war torn country. Complications set in when a human rights worker, a woman named Quinette, arrives with funds to buy freedom for people sold into slavery. Later, she marries a rebel commander while Doug and Fitzhugh begin running guns. The author delves into the complexities that face average people, relief workers, and others who find themselves in the middle of a tragic situation.

Where it's reviewed:
Booklist, February 1, 2005, page 916
Library Journal, February 15, 2005, page 114

Other books by the same author:
The Voyage, 1999
Equation for Evil, 1996
Indian Country, 1987
Horn of Africa, 1980
A Rumor of War, 1977

Other books you might like:
Gil Courtemanche, *A Sunday at the Pool in Kigali*, 2003
    Patricia Claxton, translator
Doris Lessing, *Proper Marriage*, 1954
Ian McEwan, *The Comfort of Strangers*, 1981
Michael Ondaatje, *Anil's Ghost*, 2000
Francine Prose, *A Changed Man*, 2005

1123

MATTHEW CARNAHAN

Sex with the Serpent Girl

(New York: Villard, 2005)

Story type: Coming-of-Age
Subject(s): Circus; Drugs; Cheating
Major character(s): Bailey Quinn, Criminal (robbed his employer), Student—College (drop-out); Sissy, Addict (ex-junkie); Eelie, Entertainer (serpent girl)
Time period(s): 2000s
Locale(s): Los Angeles, California; Boise, Idaho

Summary: Bailey Quinn, a college drop-out, wakes up in the desert with no pants and no memory. After coming down from a peyote high, Bailey eventually remembers that some buddies had double-crossed him. They robbed a circus where Bailey worked, after Bailey obtained inside information from the Serpent Girl, a woman with flipper-like limbs, by sleeping with her. Bailey sets out to recover the money from his former friends.

Where it's reviewed:
Kirkus Reviews, December 15, 2004, page 1154
People, March 21, 2005, page 60
Publishers Weekly, January 24, 2005, page 220

Other books you might like:
Eric Garcia, *Matchstick Men*, 2002
Jennifer Haigh, *Mrs. Kimble*, 2003
Larry Heinemann, *Cooler by the Lake*, 1992
Joyce Carol Oates, *My Heart Laid Bare*, 1998
Richard Schmitt, *The Aerialist*, 2000

1124

PATRICIA CHAO

Mambo Peligroso

(New York: HarperCollins, 2005)

Story type: Arts; Ethnic
Subject(s): Women; Cuban Americans; Suspense
Major character(s): Catalina Ortiz Midori, Student (of dance); El Tuerto, Teacher (of dance); Wendy Cardoza, Dancer, Friend (of Catalina)
Time period(s): 2000s
Locale(s): New York, New York; Miami, Florida; Havana, Cuba

Summary: Chao's second novel follows a woman as she attempts to connect with her cultural heritage through dance and music. When Catalina Ortiz Midori, 32, enters a dance studio in New York City, she is searching for self-expression but gets more than just mambo lessons. Catalina, a Cuban-Japanese, has trouble speaking Spanish, but in the presence of El Tuerto, the one-eyed dance master, and Wendy, an incredible dancer, she feels very comfortable. She throws herself into dancing and begins an adventure that will take her to Miami and finally to Cuba. Along the way, her cousin will involve Catalina and Wendy, unbeknownst to them, in an anti-Castro plot.

Where it's reviewed:
Kirkus Reviews, March 1, 2005, page 244
Library Journal, April 15, 2005, page 71

Other books by the same author:
Monkey King, 1997

Other books you might like:
Frederick Forsyth, *The Phantom of Manhattan*, 1999
Oscar Hijuelos, *The Mambo Kings Play Songs of Love*, 1989
Ana Menendez, *Loving Che*, 2003
Anthony Powell, *The Fisher King*, 1986
Martin Cruz Smith, *Havana Bay*, 1999

Popular Fiction

1125
MARY HIGGINS CLARK

No Place Like Home
(New York: Simon & Schuster, 2005)

Story type: Psychological Suspense
Subject(s): Children; Violence; Death
Major character(s): Liza ''Celia'' Barton, Spouse (married twice), Parent (Jack's mother); Laurence Foster, Spouse (Celia's first husband), Parent (Jack's father); Alex Nolan, Spouse (Celia's second husband)
Time period(s): 2000s
Locale(s): Mendham, New Jersey; New York, New York

Summary: When she was ten, Liza Barton shot and killed her mother. Her stepfather testified against her but the court decided the shooting was an accident. Subsequently, Liza was adopted and changed her name to Celia. Later, as an interior designer in Manhattan, she meets Laurence. They get married and have a child, Jack. When Laurence is on his deathbed, Celia promises him never to reveal her true identity in order to protect Jack. Later, she meets and falls in love with Alex and gets married. Life is good until Alex surprises her, buying her childhood house in Mendham, New Jersey. On the day they move, someone spray paints her lawn with ''Little Lizzie's Place, beware.''

Where it's reviewed:
Publishers Weekly, March 28, 2005, page 56

Other books by the same author:
Nighttime Is My Time, 2004
The Second Time Around, 2003
Daddy's Little Girl, 2002
On the Street Where You Live, 2001
Before I Say Good-Bye, 2000

Other books you might like:
Anita Brookner, *Undue Influence*, 1999
James Lee Burke, *Purple Cane Road*, 2000
Nicholas Delbanco, *The Vagabonds*, 2004
Molly Giles, *Iron Shoes*, 2000
Frances Mayes, *Swan*, 2002

1126
PEARL CLEAGE

Babylon Sisters
(New York: Ballantine, 2005)

Story type: Domestic
Subject(s): Mothers and Daughters; Secrets; Emigration and Immigration
Major character(s): Catherine Sanderson, Single Parent (Phoebe's mother); Phoebe Sanderson, Teenager
Time period(s): 2000s
Locale(s): Atlanta, Georgia

Summary: Cleage deals with women negotiating and surviving in a less than friendly world. Cat Sanderson is a single mother who has struggled to raise her daughter Phoebe. Cat has kept the identity of Phoebe's father a secret for good reason. But although he did her wrong, Cat still loves him.

Now, Phoebe is 17 and adamant about finding out her father's identity. While the mother-daughter struggle escalates, Cat must deal with Ezola Mandeville, a man determined to build an empire on prostitution. He wants Cat to help him trick immigrants into becoming prostitutes. Street smarts and ingenuity are on Cat's side.

Where it's reviewed:
Kirkus Reviews, January 15, 2005, page 67
Library Journal, February 1, 2005, page 66

Other books by the same author:
Some Things I Never Thought I'd Do, 2003
I Wish I Had a Red Dress, 2001
What Looks Like Crazy on an Ordinary Day, 1997
Deals with the Devil, 1993
The Brass Bed and Other Stories, 1991

Other books you might like:
Barbara Taylor Bradford, *Unexpected Blessings*, 2005
Nicholas Delbanco, *The Vagabonds*, 2004
Eric Jerome Dickey, *Drive Me Crazy*, 2004
Sue Monk Kidd, *The Secret Life of Bees*, 2002
Danielle Steel, *Answered Prayers*, 2002

1127
HARLAN COBEN

The Innocent
(New York: Dutton, 2005)

Story type: Mystery; Psychological Suspense
Subject(s): Marriage; Legal Thriller; Murder
Major character(s): Matt Hunter, Paralegal, Spouse (Olivia's husband); Olivia Hunter, Businesswoman; Loren Muse, Detective—Homicide
Time period(s): 2000s
Locale(s): New Jersey

Summary: When he was in college, Matt Hunter tried to break up a fistfight. While doing this, he accidentally killed another man and subsequently served four years in prison. He was released five years ago. Now, he has a good job and a beautiful wife, Olivia, who is pregnant. Matt's riding high but then things start to unravel. When Olivia goes on a business trip, Matt starts getting calls on his digital cell phone showing brief videos of Olivia in a hotel room with another man. Things get worse when a nun is murdered. Evidence implicates Matt and an aggressive district attorney intends to convict him of the murder.

Where it's reviewed:
Booklist, March 1, 2005, page 1101
Kirkus Reviews, March 1, 2005, page 244
Publishers Weekly, March 7, 2005, page 50

Other books by the same author:
Just One Look, 2004
No Second Chance, 2003
Gone for Good, 2002
Tell No One, 2001
Darkest Fear, 2000

Other books you might like:
Richard Barre, *Wind on the River*, 2004

Sandra Brown, *Unspeakable*, 1998
James Lee Burke, *Two for Texas*, 1989
Susan Choi, *American Woman*, 2003
Janet Evanovich, *Three to Get Deadly*, 1997

1128

SUSANN COKAL

Breath and Bones

(Denver: Unbridled, 2005)

Story type: Romance; Adult
Subject(s): Women; Emigration and Immigration; Models
Major character(s): Famke, Model (poses nude); Albert, Artist, Lover (of Famke)
Time period(s): 19th century
Locale(s): Copenhagen, Denmark; Denver, Colorado; California

Summary: Cokal's epic tale follows a young woman, who has a talent for converting disadvantages into opportunities. Famke grows up in an orphanage, where she learns about pleasure. When she leaves the orphanage, her friends want her to do farm work. Instead, she goes to Copenhagen and becomes an artist's model for Albert, an English painter. She truly enjoys the work and becomes his mistress. When Albert leaves her to make his fortune in America, she decides to follow him. Her subsequent bawdy adventures include becoming the third wife of a Mormon in Utah; checking into a TB sanitarium, where the prescribed care provides sexual pleasure; and working as a nude model in a wax museum.

Where it's reviewed:
Kirkus Reviews, February 15, 2005, page 189
Library Journal, March 1, 2005, page 76
Publishers Weekly, March 7, 2005, page 49

Other books by the same author:
Mirabilis, 2001

Other books you might like:
Geraldine Brooks, *Year of Wonder*, 2001
Tracy Chevalier, *Girl with a Pearl Earring*, 1999
Larry McMurtry, *By Sorrow's River*, 2003
Jill Nelson, *Sexual Healing*, 2003
John Updike, *Seek My Face*, 2002

1129

JODI COMPTON

Sympathy between Humans

(New York: Delacorte, 2005)

Story type: Mystery
Series: Sarah Pribek. Book 2
Subject(s): Missing Persons; Police Procedural; Family Problems
Major character(s): Sarah Pribek, Detective—Police; Aidan Hennessy, Teenager (missing person); Cicero Ruiz, Handicapped (paraplegic), Doctor (unlicensed)
Time period(s): 2000s
Locale(s): Minneapolis, Minnesota

Summary: Minneapolis Police Detective Sarah Pribek returns in a sequel to *The 37th Hour* (2004). Previously, her husband was sent to prison and her ex-partner went into hiding, after Royce Stewart, a rapist and a murderer, was himself murdered. Now, Sarah is trying to put that behind her by throwing herself into police work. Fortunately, there's plenty for her to do. Unfortunately, an aggressive district attorney isn't totally convinced that the Stewart case is closed. The DA is hard at work to pin the crime on Sarah. Meanwhile, she keeps her head down and continues working, searching for a missing teenager, tracking an unlicensed doctor, saving a drowning child, and playing decoy for the vice squad.

Where it's reviewed:
Booklist, February 1, 2005, page 944
Kirkus Reviews, January 15, 2005, page 84
Library Journal, February 15, 2005, page 114
Publishers Weekly, February 14, 2005, page 54

Other books by the same author:
The 37th Hour, 2004

Other books you might like:
Nevada Barr, *Deep South*, 2000
Patricia Cornwell, *Southern Cross*, 1998
Barbara D'Amato, *Good Cop, Bad Cop*, 1998
Tess Gerritsen, *The Sinner*, 2003

1130

BERNARD CORNWELL

The Last Kingdom

(New York: HarperCollins, 2005)

Story type: Historical/Medieval; Political
Subject(s): Vikings; Conquest; Loyalty
Major character(s): Uhtred, Heir, Nobleman; Ragnar, Warrior; Alfred the Great, Historical Figure, Ruler (King of Wessex)
Time period(s): 9th century (871-899)
Locale(s): England

Summary: Cornwell leaves his very successful Richard Sharpe series for a first millennium historical adventure. In the ninth century, the Vikings sweep across England murdering and looting as they go. Nothing can stand up to the Vikings, until they reach the Kingdom of Wessex. The story is a prequel to the final showdown between the pagan Viking warriors and the Christian Anglo-Saxons led by King Alfred the Great. Uhtred, a Saxon by birth, captured by the Vikings as a child and trained in the art of war, grows into a fierce warrior. Now, he must choose between his distaste for Christianity and his love of Viking ways.

Where it's reviewed:
Booklist, November 15, 2004, page 531
Kirkus Reviews, November 1, 2004, page 1022
Library Journal, December 2004, page 98
Publishers Weekly, December 6, 2004, page 41

Other books by the same author:
Heretic, 2003
Gallows Thief, 2002
Vagabond, 2002
The Archer's Tale, 2001

Popular Fiction

Excalibur, 1998

Other books you might like:
Isabel Allende, *Zorro*, 2005
Michael Crichton, *Eaters of the Dead*, 1976
Jude Deveraux, *The Conquest*, 1991
William T. Vollmann, *The Ice-Shirt*, 1990
T.H. White, *The Once and Future King*, 1958

1131

MITCH CULLIN

A Slight Trick of the Mind

(New York: Nan A. Talese, 2005)

Story type: Mystery
Subject(s): Aging; Relationships; Memory
Major character(s): Sherlock Holmes, Detective—Private; Roger Munro, Assistant (to Holmes)
Time period(s): 1940s (1947)
Locale(s): Sussex, England

Summary: The year is 1947, World War II has just ended and Sherlock Holmes, 93, lives in secluded retirement. While still active by most people's standards, his short-term memory isn't what it used to be. However, there is nothing wrong with his long-term memory. This he demonstrates when it comes to a case involving a woman who played a glass harmonica and when he recalls his recent trip to occupied Japan, where he visited the devastated city of Hiroshima. Although Holmes still writes in his journal, his passion is raising bees. He shares his skillful knowledge of bees with his eager, young assistant Roger Munro, the son of Holmes' housekeeper.

Where it's reviewed:
Booklist, February 1, 2005, page 945
Kirkus Reviews, February 1, 2005, page 133
Library Journal, April 15, 2005, page 74
Publishers Weekly, February 14, 2005, page 50

Other books by the same author:
Undersurface, 2002
From the Place in the Valley Deep in the Forest, 2001
The Cosmology of Bing, 2001
Branches, 2000
Tideland, 2000

Other books you might like:
Caleb Carr, *The Italian Secretary*, 2005
Michael Chabon, *The Final Solution*, 2004
Ed Dee, *The Con Man's Daughter*, 2003
Mo Hayder, *The Devil of Nanking*, 2005
Elmore Leonard, *Mr. Paradise*, 2004

1132

KATHARINE DAVIES

The Madness of Love

(New York: Random House, 2005)

Story type: Psychological; Romance
Subject(s): Grief; Identity, Concealed; Relationships
Major character(s): Valentina, Twin, Gardener (works for Leo); Leo, Landowner; Melody, Young Woman

Time period(s): 2000s
Locale(s): London, England; Illerwick, England

Summary: This debut novel is a light-hearted romantic comedy that draws on the structure of William Shakespeare's *Twelfth Night*. Passion, love, and relationships encounter difficulties; some are generated by the characters and others are generated by circumstances, and they often keep people from making meaningful connections. Valentina is heartbroken after her twin brother abandons her for an adventure. Retreating to the countryside, she becomes a gardener for Leo. He has his heart set on Melody and he thinks he can win her affection with a flourishing garden. However, Melody couldn't care less about Leo. Meanwhile, Valentina falls for Leo and the story develops from there.

Where it's reviewed:
Kirkus Reviews, December 15, 2004, page 1154
New York Times Book Review, January 30, 2005, page 14
Publishers Weekly, December 13, 2004, page 46

Other books you might like:
Kate Atkinson, *Case Histories*, 2004
Elizabeth Berg, *Open House*, 2000
Sue Miller, *Lost in the Forest*, 2005
Danielle Steel, *Safe Harbour*, 2003
Adriana Trigiani, *The Queen of the Big Time*, 2004

1133

MARGRIET DE MOOR

The Kreutzer Sonata

(New York: Arcade, 2005)

Story type: Contemporary
Subject(s): Jealousy; Music and Musicians; Relationships
Major character(s): Unnamed Character, Narrator; Marius van Vlooten, Critic (music), Spouse (Suzanna's husband); Suzanna Flier, Musician
Time period(s): 2000s
Locale(s): Amsterdam, Netherlands

Summary: After listening to Beethoven, Leo Tolstoy was inspired to write a story about love, jealousy, and murder. De Moor's work appears to follow this formula. An unnamed narrator meets a blind music critic during an airport layover. The narrator introduces the critic to a young violinist. The critic and the violinist marry but the marriage has problems. Marius, the critic, is insanely jealous of the casual relationships he fears his wife has with her fellow musicians. In fact, only the critic's blindness prevents him from murdering his wife. The story unfolds as the critic and the narrator meet while traveling to various music concerts. The work was translated by Susan Massotty.

Where it's reviewed:
Booklist, January 1, 2005, page 813
Kirkus Reviews, November 15, 2004, page 1060
Library Journal, February 1, 2005, page 67
Publishers Weekly, January 10, 2005, page 38

Other books by the same author:
Duke of Egypt, 2001
First Gray, Then White, Then Blue, 2001
The Virtuoso, 2000

Other books you might like:
Madison Smartt Bell, *Anything Goes*, 2002
Stephanie Cowell, *Marrying Mozart*, 2004
Janice Galloway, *Clara*, 2002
J.D. Landis, *Longing*, 2000
Bonnie Marson, *Sleeping with Schubert*, 2004

1134

IRINA DENEZHKINA

Give Me

(New York: Simon & Schuster, 2005)

Story type: Collection
Subject(s): Short Stories; Russians; Modern Life
Locale(s): Russia

Summary: A bestseller in Russia, Denezhkina's collection of 11 short stories has been translated into 12 languages. Her stories provide a glimpse into the lives of young people as they struggle to make sense of life in the modern world. Viewed through the hazy veil of youthful concerns, which include drugs, sex, and alcohol, the stories appear to tap a universal chord. Characters are typically self-centered, bored with politics, and enthusiastic about music and celebrities. A young woman in the title story has simultaneous love affairs; none are serious. Another story, ''Remote Feelings,'' concerns two university students attempting to connect with each other via love notes. Yet another, ''Lyokha the Rottweiler,'' deals with a suicidal teen who is saved by a fat security guard and his dog. The other stories are ''Valerochka,'' ''Song for Lovers,'' ''Vasya and the Green Men,'' ''My Beautiful Ann,'' ''Postscript,'' ''Death in the Chat Room,'' ''You and Me,'' and ''Isupov.'' Translated from the Russian by Andrew Bromfield.

Where it's reviewed:
Booklist, January 1, 2005, page 813
Kirkus Reviews, December 1, 2004, page 1103
Library Journal, January 2005, page 94
New York Times Book Review, April 3, 2005, page 21
Publishers Weekly, January 10, 2005, page 38

Other books you might like:
Amy Hempel, *The Dog of the Marriage*, 2005
Rod Liddle, *Too Beautiful for You*, 2004
Emily Raboteau, *The Professor's Daughter*, 2005
Curtis Sittenfeld, *Prep*, 2005
Darcey Steinke, *Milk*, 2005

1135

WILLIAM DIETRICH

The Scourge of God

(New York: HarperCollins, 2005)

Story type: Historical/Ancient Rome
Subject(s): Roman Empire; War; Biography
Major character(s): Attila, Ruler (King of the Huns), Historical Figure; Jonas Alabanda, Scholar (held hostage), Diplomat; Ilana, Slave (held hostage)
Time period(s): 5th century (450)

Locale(s): Roman Empire; Gaul

Summary: The story follows the events surrounding the face-off between Attila the Hun and the Roman Empire. Attila is on the verge of conquering Rome and taking possession of the western part of the empire. Valentinian III, the emperor, has been put in a difficult position by his sister Honoria, who has been imprisoned for her part in a scandal. She appeals to Attila for help. He interprets her request as a marriage proposal and demands half the empire as dowry. There is a Roman plot to assassinate Attila. A team of diplomats, including a scribe named Jonas, is held hostage by Attila when the assassination plan is uncovered. Jonas develops a plan to escape, but complications develop when he meets and falls in love with a slave girl, Ilana, and he vows not to leave without her.

Where it's reviewed:
Booklist, March 1, 2005, page 1140
Kirkus Reviews, February 1, 2005, page 134
Library Journal, February 15, 2005, page 114
Publishers Weekly, February 7, 2005, page 41

Other books by the same author:
Hadrian's Wall, 2004
Dark Winter, 2001
Getting Back, 2000
Ice Reich, 1998

Other books you might like:
Madison Smartt Bell, *Master of the Crossroads*, 2000
Bernard Cornwell, *The Last Kingdom*, 2005
Thomas B. Costain, *The Darkness and the Dawn*, 1959
Michael Crichton, *Eaters of the Dead*, 1976
Colleen McCullough, *The October Horse*, 2002

1136

JOHN DUFRESNE

Johnny Too Bad

(New York: Norton, 2005)

Story type: Collection
Subject(s): Animals/Dogs; Relationships; Murder
Time period(s): 2000s
Locale(s): Florida

Summary: John Dufresne has a reputation for taking mundane details from everyday life and making them into the fulcrum that defines existence. This collection contains a novella and 17 short stories. The novella follows Johnny and his dog Spot, who provides many challenges for his master. The dog steals toys, breaks up parties, and bites people.

Where it's reviewed:
Kirkus Reviews, January 15, 2005, page 69
Library Journal, January 2005, page 104
Publishers Weekly, November 29, 2004, page 21

Other books by the same author:
Deep in the Shade of Paradise, 2002
Love Warps the Mind a Little, 1997
Louisiana Power & Light, 1994
The Way That Water Enters Stone, 1991

Other books you might like:
Louis Auchincloss, *The Atonement*, 1997
Richard Bausch, *The Stories of Richard Bausch*, 2003
E.L. Doctorow, *Sweet Land Stories*, 2004
Andre Dubus, *We Don't Live Here Anymore*, 1984
Joyce Carol Oates, *I Am No One You Know*, 2004

1137

SUSANNE DUNLAP

Emilie's Voice

(New York: Touchstone, 2005)

Story type: Historical; Romance
Subject(s): Women; Music and Musicians; Singing
Major character(s): Emilie Jolicoeur, Teenager, Singer; Marc-Antoine Charpentier, Composer, Historical Figure; Jean-Baptiste Lully, Composer (for the king)
Time period(s): 17th century (1680s-1690s)
Locale(s): Paris, France; Versailles, France

Summary: This debut novel uses historical details and music to paint a vivid picture of social life and politics at the court of French King Louis XIV. When composer Marc-Antoine Charpentier hears teenager Emilie's untrained voice, he is enchanted. He talks her father, a simple man, into letting her become his pupil and takes Emilie to the house of his patroness. There amid the privileges of nobility, Emilie dreams of becoming a lady. When members of the royal court hear her sing, they plot to use the child as a pawn to obtain favor with the king and to discredit his current mistress. The plan is to deliver Emilie to the king's bed, after he hears her sing. However, some surprising twists occur that foil the plan, including a duel and several abductions of Emilie.

Where it's reviewed:
Kirkus Reviews, February 15, 2005, page 190
Library Journal, April 1, 2005, page 83

Other books you might like:
Stephanie Cowell, *Marrying Mozart*, 2004
Janice Galloway, *Clara*, 2002
Ian McEwan, *Amsterdam*, 1999
Ann Patchett, *Bel Canto*, 2001
Salman Rushdie, *The Ground Beneath Her Feet*, 1999

1138

THU HUONG DUONG

No Man's Land

(New York: Hyperion, 2005)

Story type: Historical
Subject(s): Vietnamese; Chinese; War
Major character(s): Mein, Spouse (two husbands), Parent (of a son); Bon, Spouse (Mein's first husband), Veteran (Vietnam War); Hoan, Spouse (Mein's second husband), Parent (of Mein's son)
Time period(s): 1970s (1979)
Locale(s): Vietnam

Summary: Duong's novel looks at the effects of war on ordinary people in a village in the mountains of central Viet-

nam. Mein's husband, Bon, goes to fight in the Vietnam War and is reported dead. Mein marries Hoan and has a child with him. Fourteen years later, Bon shows up alive. Although she would rather stay with Hoan, Mein feels obligated to return to Bon, who is poor and disabled. Flashbacks reveal both Bon and Hoan's wartime experiences, as well as the reasons for Mein's choices, which are heavily influenced by social pressures in the village.

Where it's reviewed:
Kirkus Reviews, February 15, 2005, page 196
Library Journal, April 1, 2005, page 86
Publishers Weekly, March 7, 2005, page 50

Other books by the same author:
Beyond Illusions, 2002
Memories of Pure Spring, 2000
Paradise of the Blind, 1993

Other books you might like:
Graham Greene, *The Quiet American*, 1955
William Hart, *Never Fade Away*, 2002
Mo Hayder, *The Devil of Nanking*, 2005
Thi Diem Thuy Le, *The Gangster We Are All Looking For*, 2003
Nina Vida, *Goodbye, Saigon*, 1994

1139

UMBERTO ECO

The Mysterious Flame of Queen Loana

(Orlando, Florida: Harcourt, 2005)

Story type: Contemporary/Mainstream
Subject(s): Memory Loss; History; Relationships
Major character(s): Yambo, Antiquarian (bookseller); Paola, Spouse (Yambo's wife), Psychologist
Time period(s): 20th century
Locale(s): Milan, Italy; Turin, Italy

Summary: Yambo, who is in his late 60s, is blessed with a remarkable memory. He can recall plots and poetry unfailingly, a useful trait for a book dealer in Milan, Italy. Then, after suffering a heart attack, he loses his personal memory. He can't remember his own name and he doesn't recognize his wife or daughter. He goes back to the family home in the hills near Turin in hopes of restoring his memory. There in the attic he searches through boxes of pictures and personal memorabilia, retracing things that created the 20th century from major events, such as World War II to popular culture icons, such as Flash Gordon.

Where it's reviewed:
Booklist, March 1, 2005, page 1102
Kirkus Reviews, February 15, 2005, page 190
Library Journal, April 1, 2005, page 85

Other books by the same author:
Baudolino, 2002
The Island of the Day Before, 1995
Foucault's Pendulum, 1989
The Name of the Rose, 1984

Other books you might like:
Dan Brown, *The Da Vinci Code*, 2003

Ian Caldwell, *The Rule of Four*, 2004
   Dustin Thomason, co-author
Thomas B. Costain, *The Silver Chalice*, 1952
Robert Littell, *The Amateur*, 2003
Anne Rice, *Christ the Lord*, 2005

1140

AMY EPHRON

One Sunday Morning
(New York: William Morrow, 2005)

Story type: Historical/Roaring Twenties; Psychological
Subject(s): Relationships; Friendship; Secrets
Major character(s): Lizzie Carswell, Young Woman; Billy Holmes, Young Man; Mary Nell, Young Woman
Time period(s): 1920s (1925)
Locale(s): New York, New York

Summary: Ephron presents an insider's view of the lives of New York's upper class. Scandal ensues when Billy Holmes is seen leaving the Gramercy Hotel with Lizzie Carswell following the celebration of his engagement to Clara Hart. Mary Nell is sure she knows what really happened, but public perception of events often clashes with the facts.

Where it's reviewed:
Kirkus Reviews, February 1, 2005, page 135
Library Journal, March 15, 2005, page 70
Publishers Weekly, March 14, 2005, page 44

Other books by the same author:
White Rose, 1999
A Cup of Tea, 1997
Biodegradable Soap, 1991
Bruised Fruit, 1987

Other books you might like:
Louis Auchincloss, *East Side Story*, 2004
Megan Chance, *An Inconvenient Wife*, 2004
Dominick Dunne, *The Two Mrs. Grenvilles*, 1985
John O'Hara, *From the Terrace*, 1958
Jessica Shattuck, *The Hazards of Good Breeding*, 2003

1141

ALICIA ERIAN

Towelhead
(New York: Simon & Schuster, 2005)

Story type: Coming-of-Age; Domestic
Subject(s): Assimilation; Adolescence; Divorce
Major character(s): Jasira, Teenager, Narrator; Rifat, Parent (Jasira's father); Mr. Vuoso, Neighbor
Time period(s): 1990s
Locale(s): New York; Houston, Texas

Summary: When teenager Jasira develops a womanly figure, her Irish mother's solution is simple: she ships Jasira off to Texas to live with her Lebanese-born father. There Jasira lands in a new school amid a climate of anti-Arab feelings. However, the change of scenery doesn't stop her hormonal development. As her body changes, she must deal with her father's repressive attitudes, about the body in general, and specifically, a woman's sexuality. Mr. Vuoso, a next-door neighbor, adds some complications with a pseudosophisticated *Playboy* enlightened mentality. The author provides an interesting take on problems associated with assimilation into a new culture when faced with the sexual development of one's children.

Where it's reviewed:
Kirkus Reviews, January 15, 2005, page 69
Library Journal, February 15, 2005, page 114

Other books by the same author:
The Brutal Language of Love, 2001

Other books you might like:
Monica Ali, *Brick Lane*, 2003
Edwidge Danticat, *The Dew Breaker*, 2004
Chitra Banerjee Divakaruni, *Arranged Marriage*, 1995
Jhumpa Lahiri, *The Namesake*, 2003
Omar Tyree, *Leslie*, 2002

1142

ELLEN FELDMAN

The Boy Who Loved Anne Frank
(New York: Norton, 2005)

Story type: Historical/World War II; Alternate History
Subject(s): Holocaust; Autobiography; Refugees
Major character(s): Anne Frank, Historical Figure, Holocaust Victim; Peter van Pels, Immigrant
Time period(s): 1940s; 1950s (1945-1952)
Locale(s): Amsterdam, Netherlands; New York, New York

Summary: Feldman's novel plays the "what if" game. The author imagines that Peter van Pels, the boy Anne Frank said she loved in her diary, survived the Holocaust. Peter travels to the United States, marries, and becomes a successful businessman, seeming to have moved on with his life. Despite his experiences during World War II, he has suppressed his memories to build a new life. Then, it all seems to come apart for Peter when the diary Anne wrote is published, and his memories begin to haunt him.

Where it's reviewed:
Booklist, February 15, 2005, page 1060
Chicago Tribune Books, May 8, 2005, page 3
Kirkus Reviews, January 15, 2005, page 69
Library Journal, March 1, 2005, page 78
Publishers Weekly, March 7, 2005, page 51

Other books by the same author:
Lucy, 2003
God Bless the Child, 1998
Rearview Mirror, 1996
Too Close for Comfort, 1994
Looking for Love, 1990

Other books you might like:
Saul Bellow, *Mr. Sammler's Planet*, 1970
Gwen Edelman, *War Story*, 2001
Philip Kerr, *Hitler's Peace*, 2005
Francine Prose, *A Changed Man*, 2005
William Styron, *Sophie's Choice*, 1979

1143

JULIAN FELLOWES

Snobs

(New York: St. Martin's Press, 2005)

Story type: Humor; Satire

Subject(s): Television; Actors and Actresses; Social Classes

Major character(s): Edith Lavery, Fiance(e) (of Charles); Charles Broughton, Heir (of the Marquess of Uckfield), Nobleman; Googie Broughton, Parent (Charles' mother), Noblewoman (Marchioness of Uckfield)

Time period(s): 2000s

Locale(s): England

Summary: Successful screenwriter Fellowes aims his rapier-like wit at England's social class structure in this comedy of manners. Edith is the daughter of a successful businessman and a social climbing mother. While staying at Broughton Hall as a paying guest, Edith meets young Charles, who happens to be single and the Earl of Broughton. Charles falls under the spell of Edith's beauty. When he proposes marriage, Edith accepts. Although Charles has no doubts about Edith, his mother, Lady Uckfield, does. She wonders if the fetching young Edith is more interested in the family title than in her son and her fears appear to be warranted when a television crew arrives to film a period drama. Is Edith more attracted to the drama's leading man?

Where it's reviewed:

Booklist, January 1, 2005, page 814
Kirkus Reviews, December 15, 2004, page 1156
Library Journal, January 2005, page 95
Publishers Weekly, January 17, 2005, page 34

Other books you might like:

Louis Auchincloss, *Her Infinite Variety*, 2000
Isabel Colegate, *The Shooting Party*, 1980
E.L. Doctorow, *Ragtime*, 1975
Viktor Pelevin, *Homo Zapiens*, 2002
Gore Vidal, *The Golden Age*, 2000

1144

LINDA FERRI

Enchantments

(New York: Knopf, 2005)

Story type: Family Saga; Coming-of-Age

Subject(s): Biography; Childhood; Family Relations

Major character(s): Unnamed Character, Narrator, Child

Time period(s): 1960s

Locale(s): Paris, France; New York, New York

Summary: Ferri, co-author of the screenplay *The Son's Room*, is an established writer in Italy. This is her first novel translated into English. Written as a fictional memoir in 25 short chapters, the story follows an upper-class Italian girl as she grows up. The family lives in Paris where the children stage plays in their home, travel to the family farm, and visit the United States. She doesn't know how good life is, until, suddenly, she's grown up. Translated from the Italian by John Casey and Maria Sanminiateli.

Where it's reviewed:

Booklist, February 1, 2005, page 940
Kirkus Reviews, December 1, 2004, page 1105
New York Times Book Review, March 20, 2005, page 13
Publishers Weekly, January 10, 2005, page 37

Other books you might like:

Carmen Boullosa, *Leaving Tabasco*, 2001
Sandra Cisneros, *The House on Mango Street*, 1991
John Grisham, *A Painted House*, 2001
Jean Harfenist, *A Brief History of the Flood*, 2002
Laura Moriarty, *The Center of Everything*, 2003

1145

JOSEPH FINDER

Company Man

(New York: St. Martin's Press, 2005)

Story type: Psychological Suspense

Subject(s): Single Parent Families; Stalking; Business

Major character(s): Nick Conover, Businessman (furniture company); Eddie Rinaldi, Security Officer (head of security); Audrey Rhimes, Detective—Homicide

Time period(s): 2000s

Locale(s): Michigan

Summary: Just when life should become easier for Nick Conover, everything starts to come unglued. His beloved wife dies suddenly, leaving Nick with a troubled teenage son and a young daughter to raise. As difficult as the task might be normally, life at his plant makes things more complicated. Declining sales force the company to lay off several thousand workers to keep from going broke. Predictably, the workers are unhappy. Some start a harassment campaign aimed at Nick and his family. His house is broken into and his walls are covered with graffiti. Nick and his security chief, Eddie Rinaldi, put together a plan to thwart the intruders. The plan works but complications set in when Nick catches and kills an intruder, then in a lapse of judgment, hides the body. Meanwhile, Nick suspects that his board of directors is planning to sell his company out from under him. As he deals with corporate politics, a police investigation moves closer and closer to implicating Nick in the death of the intruder.

Where it's reviewed:

Booklist, March 15, 2005, page 1246
Kirkus Reviews, February 1, 2005, page 136
Library Journal, March 15, 2005, page 70
Publishers Weekly, February 28, 2005, page 41

Other books by the same author:

Paranoia, 2004
High Crimes, 1998
The Zero Hour, 1996
Extraordinary Powers, 1994
The Moscow Club, 1991

Other books you might like:

Sallie Bissell, *In the Forest of Harm*, 2001
Sandra Brown, *The Crush*, 2002
Mary Higgins Clark, *On the Street Where You Live*, 2001
Sarah Dunant, *Transgressions*, 1997
Dean R. Koontz, *The Face*, 2003

1146

JONATHAN SAFRAN FOER

Extremely Loud & Incredibly Close

(Boston: Houghton Mifflin, 2005)

Story type: Contemporary/Mainstream
Subject(s): Fathers and Sons; Terrorism; Quest
Major character(s): Oskar Schell, Child, Crime Victim (father murdered)
Time period(s): 2000s (2001)
Locale(s): New York, New York

Summary: Oskar Schell is nine-years-old when his father is killed at the World Trade Center on September 11, 2001. Oskar is extremely intelligent and a precocious child. When he finds a key owned by his father, Oskar sets out on a quest to find the lock the key fits. His travels take him from Manhattan to the Bronx and Coney Island. On his journey, he learns about World War II and the bombings that destroyed Dresden, Germany, and Hiroshima, Japan. A cast of colorful characters, who are survivors in their own way, adds to the story.

Where it's reviewed:
Kirkus Reviews, January 1, 2005, page 8
Library Journal, March 1, 2005, page 78
Publishers Weekly, January 31, 2005, page 46

Other books by the same author:
Everything Is Illuminated, 2002

Other books you might like:
Tom Clancy, *The Bear and the Dragon*, 2000
Kazuo Ishiguro, *Never Let Me Go*, 2005
Ha Jin, *War Trash*, 2004
John Le Carre, *Absolute Friends*, 2003
Ian McEwan, *Saturday*, 2005

1147

ELIZABETH GAFFNEY

Metropolis

(New York: Random House, 2005)

Story type: Historical/Post-American Civil War
Subject(s): Construction; Arson; Emigration and Immigration
Major character(s): Frank Harris, Immigrant (from Germany), Gang Member; Beatrice O'Gamhna, Gang Member (the Whyos); Johnny Dolan, Gang Member (leader of Whyos)
Time period(s): 1860s (1868)
Locale(s): New York, New York

Summary: In this epic story depicting the sociopolitical forces at work just after the Civil War, the author draws heavily on Herbert Asbury's classic nonfiction work, *The Gangs of New York*. The story follows a German immigrant as he struggles to make a life for himself in the New World. After he is kidnapped by Irish immigrant Beatrice O'Gamhna, at her direction, he adopts the name Frank Harris and joins the notorious Whyo street gang. The gang is run by Johnny Dolan, who does the bidding of his ruthless mother, Meg. Before all is said and done, Frank Harris will find work on the city's sewer system, the construction of the Brooklyn Bridge,

and various road and street projects. He will also be accused of arson and murder.

Where it's reviewed:
Booklist, January 1, 2005, page 814
Kirkus Reviews, January 15, 2005, page 70
Library Journal, January 2005, page 95
Publishers Weekly, December 20, 2004, page 34

Other books you might like:
Kevin Baker, *Paradise Alley*, 2002
Madison Smartt Bell, *Ten Indians*, 1996
Philip Caputo, *Acts of Faith*, 2005
E.L. Doctorow, *Ragtime*, 1975
Pete Hamill, *Forever*, 2003

1148

LISA GARDNER

Alone

(New York: Bantam, 2005)

Story type: Mystery
Subject(s): Psychological Thriller; Serial Killers; Family Relations
Major character(s): Bobby Dodge, Police Officer (a police sniper); Jimmy Gagnon, Wealthy, Spouse (Catherine's husband); Catherine Gagnon, Abuse Victim, Parent
Time period(s): 2000s
Locale(s): Boston, Massachusetts

Summary: State trooper Bobby Dodge, a quiet confident man, is a skilled marksman assigned to the state's special unit that deals with hostage situations. Catherine Gagnon is an uncommonly beautiful woman, who as a child was kidnapped, raped, and left for dead. Bobby meets Catherine one night when her husband Jimmy barricades their home and holds her and their child hostage at gunpoint. As Bobby observes the situation through the sniper scope on his rifle, Catherine is wrapped around her terrified toddler, while Jimmy stands over them pointing a gun. When Jimmy's trigger finger tightens, Bobby kills him with one shot. The hostages are unharmed and deadly force appears to be justified. Questions then arise as to whether or not Catherine manipulated her hapless husband into a situation that resulted in his death. Did Bobby help?

Where it's reviewed:
Booklist, December 1, 2004, page 639
Kirkus Reviews, November 1, 2004, page 1030
Library Journal, December 2004, page 100
Publishers Weekly, December 6, 2004, page 45

Other books by the same author:
The Killing Hour, 2003
The Survivors Club, 2002
The Next Accident, 2001
The Third Victim, 2001

Other books you might like:
A.S. Byatt, *Babel Tower*, 1996
Tess Gerritsen, *The Apprentice*, 2002
George V. Higgins, *Bomber's Law*, 1993
Dennis Lehane, *Mystic River*, 2001
Laura Lippman, *The Last Place*, 2002

1149

ANNE GIARDINI

The Sad Truth about Happiness
(New York: Fourth Estate, 2005)

Story type: Contemporary/Mainstream
Subject(s): Women; Relationships; Quest
Major character(s): Maggie Selgrin, Health Care Professional (medical technician); Lucy Selgrin, Relative (Maggie's sister); Rebecca, Roommate (Maggie's), Businesswoman (designs questionnaires)
Time period(s): 2000s
Locale(s): Vancouver, British Columbia, Canada

Summary: Thirty-something Maggie is between relationships. Her roommate Rebecca has designed a questionnaire. If a person answers the questions truthfully, Rebecca believes she can determine the day the person will die. When Maggie fills out the form, she says she is unhappy. According to the questionnaire, Maggie has three months to live, unless she can become happy. This sets Maggie in motion. She scrambles to become happy and in the process learns something about life and, more importantly, herself. This is Giardini's debut novel.

Where it's reviewed:
Booklist, April 1, 2005, page 1341
Kirkus Reviews, March 15, 2005, page 305
Library Journal, April 15, 2005, page 72
Publishers Weekly, April 4, 2005, page 42

Other books you might like:
T. Coraghessan Boyle, *Drop City*, 2003
Lisa Carey, *The Mermaids Singing*, 1998
Anna Quindlen, *Blessings*, 2002
Marilynne Robinson, *Gilead*, 2004
Carol Shields, *Unless*, 2002

1150

PIP GRANGER

Trouble in Paradise
(Scottsdale, Arizona: Poisoned Pen Press, 2005)

Story type: Family Saga; Historical
Subject(s): Family Relations; Aunts and Uncles; Marriage
Major character(s): Zelda Fluck, Spouse (Charlie's wife); Zinnia Makepeace, Healer; Tony, Young Man, Singer
Time period(s): 1940s (1946)
Locale(s): London, England

Summary: This book, which is set in a London East End working-class neighborhood called Hackney, is a prequel to *Not All Tarts Are Apple*. Although everyone is relieved that World War II is over, it hasn't ended hard times for the people living in Hackney. Zelda Fluck is anxious about her husband Charlie's return since he has a history of abusing her and she has no reason to believe he's turned over a new leaf. She's also concerned about her nephew Tony, who has the potential for a singing career. Tony is a good lad but he's taken to hanging around with the wrong crowd. Zelda turns to Zinnia, a psychic, for help. Zinnia has connections and she knows a singing coach who could help get Tony on the right path.

Where it's reviewed:
Booklist, December 15, 2004, page 711
Kirkus Reviews, December 1, 2004, page 1120
Publishers Weekly, December 20, 2004, page 40

Other books by the same author:
The Widow Ginger, 2003
Not All Tarts Are Apple, 2002

Other books you might like:
Stephen J. Cannell, *King Con*, 1997
Eric Jerome Dickey, *Thieves Paradise*, 2002
Eric Garcia, *Matchstick Men*, 2002
Jennifer Haigh, *Mrs. Kimble*, 2003
Sandra Newman, *The Only Good Thing Anyone Has Ever Done*, 2003

1151

JANE GREEN

The Other Woman
(New York: Viking, 2005)

Story type: Domestic
Subject(s): Interpersonal Relations; Women; Marriage
Major character(s): Ellie Black, Spouse (Dan's wife); Dan Cooper, Spouse (Ellie's husband), Relative (Linda Cooper's son); Linda Cooper, Parent (Dan's mother)
Time period(s): 2000s
Locale(s): London, England

Summary: Ellie Black loves Dan Cooper, the man of her dreams. When he proposes, his family welcomes her with open arms, but difficulties soon arise in the form of Linda Cooper, Dan's mother, an extremely meddlesome woman. She interferes in the wedding plans, then plants herself firmly in the young couple's lives, relentlessly playing Dan against Ellie. When Ellie gives birth to a son, it seems obvious that the marriage is about to come apart. Then Linda is involved in a traffic accident with the baby in the car, and both women are forced to come to terms with each other.

Where it's reviewed:
Library Journal, April 1, 2005, page 85
Publishers Weekly, March 28, 2005, page 56

Other books by the same author:
To Have and to Hold, 2004
Babyville, 2003
Straight Talking, 2003
Bookends, 2000
Mr. Maybe, 1999

Other books you might like:
Elizabeth Berg, *What We Keep*, 1998
Helen Fielding, *Bridget Jones's Diary*, 1996
Nick Hornby, *High Fidelity*, 1995
Lee Smith, *The Last Girls*, 2002
Jennifer Weiner, *Good in Bed*, 2001

1152

SETH GREENLAND

Bones

(New York: Bloomsbury, 2005)

Story type: Humor
Subject(s): Satire; Comedians; Television Programs
Major character(s): Frank Bones, Entertainer (stand-up comic); Lloyd Melnick, Writer (comedy)
Time period(s): 2000s
Locale(s): Hollywood, California

Summary: This is a humorous satire with a behind-the-scenes look at how success is acquired. The story follows stand-up comic Frank Bones, who had everything going for him until the night he handled a heckler by shooting real bullets. Since then, Frank's career opportunities have been severely limited. Then he is offered a role, playing an Eskimo on television. Meanwhile, comedy writer Lloyd Melnick has the most successful sitcom on television. When Lloyd was starting out, Frank helped him. Now, Frank wants him to return the favor. Frank has an idea for a show and he wants Lloyd to write it. When Lloyd turns Frank down, it sets in motion an adventure that includes a Humvee crashing into Lloyd's living room and a madcap chase to Mexico and back.

Where it's reviewed:
Booklist, February 1, 2005, page 941
Kirkus Reviews, January 15, 2005, page 72
Library Journal, February 15, 2005, page 116
New York Times, March 17, 2005, page B8
Publishers Weekly, January 31, 2005, page 49

Other books you might like:
Paul Auster, *The Book of Illusions*, 2002
Elmore Leonard, *Get Shorty*, 1990
Elizabeth McCracken, *Niagara Falls All over Again*, 2001
Harold Robbins, *Tycoon*, 1997
Jerry Stahl, *I, Fatty*, 2004

1153

JOHN GRISHAM

The Broker

(New York: Doubleday, 2005)

Story type: Political
Subject(s): Suspense; Legal Thriller; Crime and Criminals
Major character(s): Joel Blackman, Criminal, Convict
Time period(s): 2000s
Locale(s): Washington, District of Columbia; Italy

Summary: Joel Blackman was a notorious political power broker, doing business in everything, including security secrets. Subsequently, he was arrested, convicted, and sentenced to 20 years in prison. With 14 years left on his prison sentence, Blackman gets a presidential pardon. The CIA then hustles him out of the country and sets him up in Italy. Meanwhile, the CIA reveals his address to various foreign governments which at one time did business with him. They apparently want to see who will try to assassinate him.

Where it's reviewed:
New York Times, January 10, 2005, page B1
People, January 17, 2005, page 55
Publishers Weekly, January 10, 2005, page 39

Other books by the same author:
The Last Juror, 2004
Bleachers, 2003
The King of Torts, 2003
The Summons, 2002
A Painted House, 2001

Other books you might like:
Larry Brown, *Father and Son*, 1996
James Lee Burke, *The Lost Get-Back Boogie*, 1986
Ed Dee, *The Con Man's Daughter*, 2003
Sue Grafton, *R Is for Ricochet*, 2004
John Katzenbach, *Just Cause*, 1992

1154

KEVIN GUILFOILE

Cast of Shadows

(New York: Knopf, 2005)

Story type: Psychological
Subject(s): Fathers and Daughters; Murder; Cloning
Major character(s): Davis Moore, Doctor (fertility specialist), Parent; Justin Finn, Child, Clone
Time period(s): 2000s
Locale(s): Chicago, Illinois

Summary: Davis Moore, a doctor specializing in cloning, is a man on a mission that starts when his daughter is raped and murdered. Now, Moore is determined to bring her killer to justice. Due to the fact that there were no witnesses to the crimes and almost no clues, the police have run into a dead end. When a sample of the killer's DNA falls into Moore's hands, it gives him the opportunity he's looking for and he clones a child from the killer's genetic material. Once the child grows up, Moore hopes the cloned child's looks will help identify the killer.

Where it's reviewed:
Kirkus Reviews, January 15, 2005, page 73
Library Journal, March 1, 2005, page 78
Publishers Weekly, January 31, 2005, page 48

Other books you might like:
Harlan Coben, *No Second Chance*, 2003
Tess Gerritsen, *Harvest*, 1996
Reynolds Price, *Noble Norfleet*, 2002
Alice Sebold, *The Lovely Bones*, 2002
Donna Tartt, *The Little Friend*, 2002

1155

OAKLEY HALL

Ambrose Bierce and the Ace of Shoots

(New York: Viking, 2005)

Story type: Historical; Americana
Series: Ambrose Bierce. Book 5
Subject(s): Journalism; Mystery; Crime and Criminals

Major character(s): Ambrose Bierce, Journalist, Historical Figure; Tom Redmond, Sidekick; Oz Bird, Criminal (robs trains)
Time period(s): 1890s (1892)
Locale(s): San Francisco, California

Summary: Col. Studely's wild west show has come to town just as the notorious criminal Oz Bird has been released from prison. Bird is looking to settle a few scores. While Bird was in jail, his wife dumped him for Studely. Then, there's Arliff K. Potter, a railroad executive who hired Bird and then double-crossed him. When Studely and Potter turn up dead, everyone says Bird is the killer. However, Ambrose Bierce has his doubts and with his colleague Tom Redmond sets out to find the real killer. The story's details bring the period to life.

Where it's reviewed:
Booklist, March 15, 2005, page 1269
Chicago Tribune Books, April 17, 2005, page 3
Kirkus Reviews, February 15, 2005, page 201
Publishers Weekly, March 7, 2005, page 53

Other books by the same author:
Ambrose Bierce and the Trey of Pearls, 2004
Ambrose Bierce and the One-Eyed Jacks, 2003
Ambrose Bierce and the Death of Kings, 2001
Ambrose Bierce and the Queen of Spades, 1998

Other books you might like:
Alice Adams, *Almost Perfect*, 1993
Boris Akunin, *Murder on the Leviathan*, 2004
Joan Didion, *The Last Thing He Wanted*, 1996
Larry McMurtry, *By Sorrow's River*, 2003
Robert B. Parker, *Appaloosa*, 2005

1156

BARBARA HAMBLY

The Emancipator's Wife

(New York: Bantam, 2005)

Story type: Historical; Domestic
Subject(s): Women; Marriage; Presidents
Major character(s): Mary Todd Lincoln, Historical Figure; Abraham Lincoln, Historical Figure, Political Figure
Time period(s): 19th century (1839-1882)
Locale(s): Washington, District of Columbia; Springfield, Illinois; Lexington, Kentucky

Summary: While most historians agree that Abraham Lincoln was one of America's greatest presidents, opinions differ on his wife, Mary Todd Lincoln. Raised like a Southern aristocrat, Mary was intelligent, well-informed about the political issues of the day, as well as socially adroit. She had many suitors including Stephen Douglas, Lincoln's arch political rival. To the surprise of many, she chose the homespun Lincoln for a husband, who promptly broke off their engagement. The novel follows Mary through her and Lincoln's stormy courtship and domestic struggles, his political successes, and assassination, to her battles with depression and addiction, and betrayal at the hands of family and friends.

Where it's reviewed:
Booklist, December 1, 2004, page 618
Kirkus Reviews, December 15, 2004, page 1156

Library Journal, January 2005, page 97
Publishers Weekly, January 10, 2005, page 38

Other books by the same author:
Dead Water, 2004
Days of the Dead, 2003
Dragonstar, 2002
Wet Grave, 2002
Die upon a Kiss, 2001

Other books you might like:
Sandra Brown, *Exclusive*, 1996
Mary Higgins Clark, *Mount Vernon Love Story*, 2002
Joan Didion, *Democracy*, 1984
Ellen Feldman, *Lucy*, 2003
Irving Stone, *The President's Lady*, 1951

1157

DENISE HAMILTON

Savage Garden

(New York: Scribner, 2005)

Story type: Mystery
Series: Eve Diamond. Book 4
Subject(s): Murder; Actors and Actresses; Social Classes
Major character(s): Eve Diamond, Journalist, Detective—Amateur; Silvio Aguilar, Boyfriend (of Eve)
Time period(s): 2000s
Locale(s): Los Angeles, California

Summary: Eve Diamond, star reporter of the *Los Angeles Times*, accompanies her boyfriend Silvio to the theater. When the play's leading lady is a no-show, Silvio sets out to find her. Eve smells a good story and tags along. They find the poor woman murdered at the bottom of a cliff. As it turns out, the woman left numerous broken hearts in her wake. This, of course, provides police with a long and lengthy list of suspects with a motive for murder. Unfortunately, Silvio's name is on the list.

Where it's reviewed:
Booklist, February 15, 2005, page 1064
Library Journal, March 1, 2005, page 72

Other books by the same author:
Last Lullaby, 2004
Sugar Skull, 2003
The Jasmine Trade, 2001

Other books you might like:
Sandra Brown, *Standoff*, 2000
Joan Didion, *The Last Thing He Wanted*, 1996
James Patterson, *Mary, Mary*, 2005
Jerry Stahl, *I, Fatty*, 2004
Kate White, *Til Death Do Us Part*, 2004

1158

JOHN HASKELL

American Purgatorio

(New York: Farrar, Straus and Giroux, 2005)

Story type: Psychological Suspense; Quest

Subject(s): Missing Persons; Grief; Mystery
Major character(s): Unnamed Character, Narrator (unreliable), Spouse (Anne's husband); Anne, Young Woman
Time period(s): 2000s
Locale(s): New York, New York; San Diego, California

Summary: The author uses an unnamed, unreliable narrator to tell the story, which features chapters named after the seven deadly sins. One day a happily married man stops at a convenience store, leaving his wife in the car. He's gone for only a moment, but when he returns, both his wife and their car are gone, vanishing without a trace. The only clue is a map with various cities circled. The man sets out on a cross-country quest looking for his wife. On his journey, he encounters various strangers, some helpful, others not.

Where it's reviewed:
Booklist, November 15, 2004, page 553
Kirkus Reviews, October 15, 2004, page 978
Library Journal, December 2004, page 100
New York Times Book Review, January 30, 2005, page 14
Publishers Weekly, October 25, 2004, page 25

Other books by the same author:
I Am Not Jackson Pollock, 2003

Other books you might like:
Benjamin Anastas, *The Faithful Narrative of a Pastor's Disappearance*, 2001
Margaret Atwood, *Surfacing*, 1972
Paul Auster, *The Book of Illusions*, 2002
Anita Brookner, *Fraud*, 1992
Catherine Bush, *Claire's Head*, 2004

1159

MO HAYDER

The Devil of Nanking
(New York: Grove, 2005)

Story type: Historical/World War II; Adult
Subject(s): Massacres; Suspense; Sexual Behavior
Major character(s): Grey Hutchins, Young Woman; Shi Chongming, Professor; Fuyuki, Organized Crime Figure (retired)
Time period(s): 2000s
Locale(s): Tokyo, Japan

Summary: This novel was originally published in England under the title *Tokyo*. Grey Hutchins, a young Englishwoman, becomes obsessed with a film about atrocities committed by the Japanese in Nanking during World War II. She travels to Japan, when she learns that Shi Chongming, a survivor of Nanking, has a copy of the film. However, he will have nothing to do with her. To make a living, Grey takes a job as a hostess in a high class bar. There she meets an old gangster, who has a connection to Shi. He offers to help her, but, of course, he has a price.

Where it's reviewed:
Booklist, February 15, 2005, page 1064
Kirkus Reviews, February 15, 2005, page 191
Library Journal, April 1, 2005, page 86
Publishers Weekly, January 31, 2005, page 48

Other books by the same author:
The Treatment, 2001
Birdman, 1999

Other books you might like:
Kazuo Ishiguro, *When We Were Orphans*, 2000
Taiyi Lin, *War Tide*, 1943
William Marshall, *Shanghai*, 1979
Shouhua Qi, *When the Purple Mountain Burns*, 2005
Martin Cruz Smith, *December 6*, 2002

1160

AMY HEMPEL

The Dog of the Marriage
(New York: Scribner, 2005)

Story type: Collection
Subject(s): Marriage; Relationships; Short Stories
Time period(s): 2000s
Locale(s): United States

Summary: This is an edgy collection of nine short stories of varying length with female narrators. The stories are "Beach Town," "Jesus Is Waiting," "The Uninvited," "Reference 3884758485," "What Were the White Things?," "The Dog of the Marriage," "The Afterlife; Memoir," and "Offertory." The title story revolves around two women, a dog trainer and one of her clients. The husband of the dog trainer leaves her and her client's husband dies in a traffic accident while chasing the couple's dog.

Where it's reviewed:
Booklist, January 1, 2005, page 820
Kirkus Reviews, December 1, 2004, page 1106
Library Journal, February 1, 2005, page 73
Publishers Weekly, February 14, 2005, page 52

Other books by the same author:
Tumble Home, 1997
At the Gates of the Animal Kingdom, 1990
Reasons to Live, 1985

Other books you might like:
Richard Bausch, *The Stories of Richard Bausch*, 2003
Tom Franklin, *Poachers*, 1999
Ellen Gilchrist, *The Age of Miracles*, 1995
Joyce Carol Oates, *I Am No One You Know*, 2004
Francine Prose, *The Peaceable Kingdom*, 1993

1161

JUDITH RYAN HENDRICKS

The Baker's Apprentice
(New York: William Morrow, 2005)

Story type: Psychological
Subject(s): Women; Divorce; Relationships
Major character(s): Wynter Morrison, Baker; Mac, Boyfriend (Wynter's)
Time period(s): 2000s
Locale(s): Seattle, Washington; Alaska

Summary: This is a sequel to Hendricks' 2001 novel *Bread Alone*. Wyn Morrison is happily baking bread and enjoying a budding relationship with Mac in Seattle. When a literary agent expresses interest in his unfinished novel, Mac decides to head up to Alaska to finish it. Meanwhile, complications set in that threaten the existence of the bakery. Wyn must draw on an inner strength that she didn't know she had in order to save her bakery and her relationship with Mac.

Where it's reviewed:
Booklist, November 15, 2004, page 561
Kirkus Reviews, December 1, 2004, page 1107
Library Journal, February 1, 2005, page 68

Other books by the same author:
Isabel's Daughter, 2003
Bread Alone, 2001

Other books you might like:
Elizabeth Berg, *Open House*, 2000
Kate Bridges, *The Midwife's Secret*, 2003
Margaret Drabble, *The Seven Sisters*, 2002
Louise Erdrich, *Tales of Burning Love*, 1996
Ellen Gilchrist, *Sarah Conley*, 1997

1162

MICHELLE HERMAN

Dog

(San Francisco: MacAdam/Cage, 2005)

Story type: Psychological
Subject(s): Animals/Dogs; Relationships; Teachers
Major character(s): Jill Rosen, Professor (of poetry); Phil, Animal (Jill's dog)
Time period(s): 2000s
Locale(s): Midwest

Summary: Jill Rosen, aka J.T. Rosen, is a professor at a small Midwestern college who received tenure because of her potential as a poet. However, after six years, her potential hasn't been realized and she has become more and more isolated from both faculty and students alike. In fact, her existence has turned into one of quiet desperation. Then, one day she adopts a puppy and names it Phil, after her first boyfriend. As she becomes involved in the care and feeding of Phil, her life begins to turn around.

Where it's reviewed:
Kirkus Reviews, January 1, 2005, page 10
Library Journal, February 1, 2005, page 68
Publishers Weekly, January 31, 2005, page 49

Other books by the same author:
Missing, 1990

Other books you might like:
Russell Banks, *The Darling*, 2004
Mark Haddon, *The Curious Incident of the Dog in the Night-Time*, 2003
Jim Harrison, *Wolf*, 1971
Yann Martel, *Life of Pi*, 2001
Jill McCorkle, *Creatures of Habit*, 2001

1163

ALICE HOFFMAN

The Ice Queen

(New York: Little, Brown, 2005)

Story type: Psychological; Romance
Subject(s): Women; Near-Death Experience; Libraries
Major character(s): Unnamed Character, Narrator, Librarian (reference); Lazarus Jones, Survivor (of lightning)
Time period(s): 2000s
Locale(s): New Jersey; Florida

Summary: As an eight-year-old, the unnamed narrator wishes her mother would disappear. When her mother dies in a car crash that very night, she becomes emotionally remote in order to cope with her guilt. Now, in her late 30s, the narrator is struck by lightning. The shock literally removes her emotional insulation and her feelings return to her. Subsequently, she seeks out Lazarus Jones, a man who also was struck by lightning but came back from the dead after some 40 minutes. The narrator reasons that a wish couldn't kill a man like him.

Where it's reviewed:
Booklist, March 15, 2005, page 1246
Kirkus Reviews, March 1, 2005, page 249
Library Journal, April 15, 2005, page 73
Publishers Weekly, March 21, 2005, page 37

Other books by the same author:
The Probable Future, 2003
Blue Diary, 2001
The River King, 2000
White Horses, 1999
Here on Earth, 1997

Other books you might like:
Peter Carey, *Bliss*, 1981
Jude Deveraux, *The Summerhouse*, 2001
Ursula Hegi, *Stones from the River*, 1994
Elizabeth McCracken, *The Giant's House*, 1996
T.R. Pearson, *Gospel Hour*, 1991

1164

RUPERT HOLMES

Swing

(New York: Random House, 2005)

Story type: Historical; Mystery
Subject(s): Music and Musicians; Women; Secrets
Major character(s): Ray Sherwood, Musician (saxophone player); Gail Prentice, Composer, Student—College
Time period(s): 1940s (1940)
Locale(s): San Francisco, California

Summary: Ray Sherwood, a musician and an arranger with the Jack Donovan Orchestra, is approached by Gail Prentice, a college coed, for help. She wants him to arrange the music for a composition called "Swing around the Sun." The work is scheduled to be played at the upcoming Golden Gate Exposition, which is to be held on Treasure Island in San Francisco Bay. Ray, who is smitten by Gail's beauty, has an uneasy feeling about her. Subsequently, Ray witnesses the suicide

plunge of a young woman, who it turns out has a connection to Gail. As events speed toward a resolution, he's in for more surprises. A CD featuring the music from the story is included with the book.

Where it's reviewed:
Chicago Tribune Books, April 17, 2005, page 3
Kirkus Reviews, January 15, 2005, page 73
Library Journal, March 15, 2005, page 78
New York Times, March 19, 2005, page B11
Publishers Weekly, January 31, 2005, page 49

Other books by the same author:
Where the Truth Lies, 2003
Accomplice, 1991

Other books you might like:
Sherman Alexie, *Reservation Blues*, 1995
Jimmy Buffett, *Where Is Joe Merchant*, 1992
Jane Campion, *Piano*, 1994
   Kate Pullinger, co-author
David Corbett, *Done for a Dime*, 2003
Michael Ondaatje, *Coming through Slaughter*, 1976

1165

MARYA HORNBACHER

The Center of Winter
(New York: HarperCollins, 2005)

Story type: Psychological
Subject(s): Family Relations; Grief; Suicide
Major character(s): Claire Schiller, Single Parent (of Esau and Katie); Esau Schiller, Child (12-year-old); Katie Schiller, Child (6-year-old)
Time period(s): 2000s
Locale(s): Motley, Minnesota

Summary: In the middle of winter, Arnold Schiller gives in to depression and kills himself. His self-indulgent act devastates his family, especially his wife and their two children. His wife Claire is determined to put her own grief aside in order to save her children, something easier said than done. Esau, 12, has apparently inherited his father's dark disposition and is well-known in the state's psychiatric hospitals, where he has been treated. Although Katie, 6, doesn't have the same problems as her brother, she has her own issues, concerning a love-hate relationship with her father.

Where it's reviewed:
Booklist, January 1, 2005, page 819
Kirkus Reviews, December 15, 2004, page 1157
Library Journal, January 2005, page 97
Publishers Weekly, January 17, 2005, page 36

Other books you might like:
Robert Boswell, *Century's Son*, 2002
Ellen Gilchrist, *The Anna Papers*, 1988
John Grisham, *The Client*, 1993
Goldberry Long, *Juniper Tree Burning*, 2001
John O'Hara, *Appointment in Samarra*, 1934

1166

NICK HORNBY

A Long Way Down
(New York: Riverhead, 2005)

Story type: Contemporary/Mainstream
Subject(s): Depression; Relationships; Women
Major character(s): Martin, Television Personality, Convict (ex-con); Maureen, Single Parent; Jess, Young Woman
Time period(s): 2000s (2003)
Locale(s): London, England

Summary: Four characters meet coincidently on a London rooftop on New Year's Eve. Topper's House is known for attracting those interested in killing themselves by jumping off the roof. Each of the four feels justified in committing suicide. Martin destroyed his career as a television personality and his marriage when he was sent to prison for sleeping with an underage girl. Maureen, a single parent, has been worn down by taking care of her disabled child. Jess is a politician's daughter and JJ is a rock'n'roll musician. They survive the night and agree to keep in touch with each other.

Where it's reviewed:
Booklist, March 15, 2005, page 1246
Kirkus Reviews, March 1, 2005, page 249
Library Journal, April 15, 2005, page 73
Publishers Weekly, April 4, 2005, page 41

Other books by the same author:
How to Be Good, 2001
About a Boy, 1998
High Fidelity, 1995

Other books you might like:
Judy Blume, *Summer Sisters*, 1998
Larry Brown, *Father and Son*, 1996
Catherine Bush, *The Rules of Engagement*, 2000
Michael Chabon, *Wonder Boys*, 1995
Joyce Carol Oates, *The Falls*, 2004

1167

PAM HOUSTON

Sight Hound
(New York: Norton, 2005)

Story type: Romance; Psychological
Subject(s): Animals/Dogs; Human Behavior; Veterinarians
Major character(s): Rae, Writer (playwright); Dante, Animal (Rae's dog); Stanley, Animal (Rae's cat)
Time period(s): 2000s
Locale(s): Colorado

Summary: The bond between humans and their animals is a safe harbor on the stormy sea of life. The story revolves around the internal monologues of both human and animal characters. At issue is the emotionally fragile playwright Rae. Her dog Dante, an Irish wolfhound, is dying of cancer. Dante tries to comfort Rae by quoting philosophy. Rae has had bad experiences with relationships and Dante is worried his death will push her over the edge. A supporting cast includes Rose,

a younger dog; Stanley a cat; two veterinarians; Howard, an actor; a housekeeper; and Rae's therapist.

Where it's reviewed:
Booklist, November 15, 2004, page 553
Kirkus Reviews, November 1, 2004, page 1024
Library Journal, January 2005, page 98
People, February 7, 2005, page 52

Other books by the same author:
A Little More about Me, 1999
Waltzing the Cat, 1998
Cowboys Are My Weakness, 1992

Other books you might like:
John Berger, *King*, 1999
Mark Haddon, *The Curious Incident of the Dog in the Night-Time*, 2003
Jim Harrison, *Wolf*, 1971
Helen Humphreys, *Wild Dogs*, 2005
Carolyn Parkhurst, *The Dogs of Babel*, 2003

1168

DALLAS HUDGENS

Drive Like Hell
(New York: Scribner, 2005)

Story type: Coming-of-Age
Subject(s): Men; Adolescence; Psychological
Major character(s): Luke Fulmer, Teenager; Claudia Fulmer, Parent (Luke's mother); Nick Fulmer, Landscaper (Luke's brother), Drug Dealer
Time period(s): 1970s (1979)
Locale(s): Georgia

Summary: Although he learned to drive at the age of ten, Luke Fulmer has to wait until he is 16 to get a driver's license. However, he only has his license briefly; a judge revokes it after Luke borrows a neighbor's car without permission and crashes it into a tree. Expecting more trouble from her teenage son, his mother Claudia ships Luke out to live with his older brother Nick, who has a landscaping business. Luke learns a few things from his brother but not the kind of lessons taught in Sunday school. Nick's business is a front for a flourishing cocaine trade. Somehow, Luke survives the summer, finds love, and reconnects with his father who has been absent for a decade. On the surface things sound hopeless but in fact they are not serious. This is a funny story.

Where it's reviewed:
Booklist, November 15, 2004, page 553
Kirkus Reviews, December 1, 2004, page 1108
Library Journal, December 2004, page 100
Publishers Weekly, November 1, 2004, page 40

Other books you might like:
Jonathan Ames, *Wake Up, Sir!*, 2004
Madison Smartt Bell, *Anything Goes*, 2002
James Lee Burke, *The Lost Get-Back Boogie*, 1986
Michael Chabon, *The Amazing Adventures of Kavalier & Clay*, 2000
Ken Wells, *Junior's Leg*, 2002

1169

HELEN HUMPHREYS

Wild Dogs
(New York: Norton, 2005)

Story type: Romance
Subject(s): Animals/Dogs; Wilderness; Women
Major character(s): Alice, Young Woman (lost her dog); Malcolm, Scientist (lost his dog); Lily, Young Woman (lost her dog)
Time period(s): 2000s
Locale(s): Canada

Summary: A group of people gathers each day at the edge of the woods. They are united by the fact that all of them have lost a dog or dogs. The animals wandered into the woods under varying circumstances and became wild, and all the owners hope to retrieve their lost pets. Relationships develop among the different members of the group, and in the end, each will have to revise his or her view of love and nature.

Where it's reviewed:
Booklist, March 1, 2005, page 1142
Kirkus Reviews, February 1, 2005, page 138
Library Journal, March 15, 2005, page 71
Publishers Weekly, March 14, 2005, page 45

Other books by the same author:
The Lost Garden, 2002
Afterimage, 2000
Leaving Earth, 1998

Other books you might like:
Jim Harrison, *Wolf*, 1971
Jack London, *The Call of the Wild*, 1903
Yann Martel, *Life of Pi*, 2001
Cormac McCarthy, *The Crossing*, 1994
Jill McCorkle, *Creatures of Habit*, 2001

1170

GREG ILES

Blood Memory
(New York: Scribner, 2005)

Story type: Mystery
Subject(s): Serial Killers; Doctors; Women
Major character(s): Catherine Ferry, Scientist (forensic odontologist); Sean Regan, Lover (of Cat)
Time period(s): 2000s
Locale(s): New Orleans, Louisiana; Natchez, Mississippi

Summary: A serial killer is on the loose in New Orleans, Natchez, and the Mississippi delta. As the bodies begin piling up, the killer leaves unusual bites on the victims. Police summon Cat Ferry, an expert in teeth marks. When Cat discovers she is pregnant by her married lover, she retreats to her ancestral home. There she is haunted by the memory of her father, who was murdered when she was a child. As she grapples with her childhood nightmare, the serial killer appears to have followed her. Could the killer be connected to her father's murder?

Where it's reviewed:
Booklist, December 1, 2004, page 61
Chicago Tribune Books, February 20, 2005, page 2
Library Journal, February 15, 2005, page 119
Publishers Weekly, January 3, 2005, page 33

Other books by the same author:
The Footprints of God, 2003
Sleep No More, 2002
Dead Sleep, 2001
24 Hours, 2000
The Quiet Game, 1999

Other books you might like:
David Baldacci, *Hour Game*, 2004
Pat Barker, *Blow Your House Down*, 1984
Sandra Brown, *Charade*, 1994
Nelson DeMille, *The Lion's Game*, 2000
James Ellroy, *Blood on the Moon*, 2005

1171

KAZUO ISHIGURO

Never Let Me Go

(New York: Knopf, 2005)

Story type: Psychological; Science Fiction
Subject(s): Women; Cloning; Transplants
Major character(s): Kathy, Narrator, Clone; Tommy, Clone; Ruth, Clone
Time period(s): 1990s
Locale(s): England

Summary: Kazuo Ishiguro offers an offbeat story that examines human identity. At the center of the story is Hailsham, a boarding school in the English countryside. The school professes to develop a higher sensibility in its students, who never venture into the real world. Noble as this sounds, there is a dark secret behind this approach. Students begin to get wind of it when they graduate. For one thing, they find that the real world fails to live up to the ideals they were taught. However, this turns out to be a minor point. The students discover they are clones who have been created to become organ donors.

Where it's reviewed:
Booklist, January 1, 2005, page 783
Kirkus Reviews, January 1, 2005, page 11
Library Journal, January 2005, page 98

Other books by the same author:
When We Were Orphans, 2000
The Unconsoled, 1995
The Remains of the Day, 1989 (Booker Prize winner)
An Artist of the Floating World, 1986
A Pale View of Hills, 1982

Other books you might like:
Robin Cook, *Shock*, 2001
Michael Crichton, *The Lost World*, 1995
John Irving, *The Fourth Hand*, 2001
Ira Levin, *The Stepford Wives*, 1972
Danielle Steel, *The Klone and I*, 1998

1172

JOSHILYN JACKSON

Gods in Alabama

(New York: Warner, 2005)

Story type: Humor; Coming-of-Age
Subject(s): Sports/Football; Women; Interracial Dating
Major character(s): Arlene Fleet, Murderer; Jim Beverly, Crime Victim (murdered), Student—High School; Rose Mae Lolley, Girlfriend (of Jim)
Time period(s): 1980s; 1990s (1985-1997)
Locale(s): Chicago, Illinois; Possett, Alabama

Summary: In her debut novel set in a small town in Alabama, Jackson mixes murder, oaths, and rape, heavily seasoned with humor. High school student Jim Beverly is murdered but his body is never recovered. Another high school student, Arlene Fleet, promises God that she will leave town and mend her ways. Ten years later, Jim's old girlfriend, Rose Mae, shows up in Chicago on Arlene's doorstep. It becomes obvious to Arlene that she will have to return to Alabama in order to remain above suspicion.

Where it's reviewed:
Kirkus Reviews, February 1, 2005, page 139
Library Journal, March 1, 2005, page 78
Publishers Weekly, February 28, 2005, page 41

Other books you might like:
Don DeLillo, *End Zone*, 1972
Eric Jerome Dickey, *Milk in My Coffee*, 1998
Peter Gent, *North Dallas Forty*, 1973
John Grisham, *Bleachers*, 2003
Tom Wolfe, *I Am Charlotte Simmons*, 2004

1173

MADELEINE JACOB

The Mommy Fund

(New York: Plume, 2005)

Story type: Domestic
Subject(s): Friendship; Mothers; Shopping
Major character(s): Kate Thompson, Parent, Housewife; Dani Strauss, Parent, Divorced Person
Time period(s): 2000s
Locale(s): New York, New York

Summary: This is a fairy tale for modern day mothers, specifically those who stay at home and those who are stressed out from juggling childcare and work. Although Kate Thompson is devoted to her children, a part of her wishes for just a tiny bit more intellectual challenge. She does volunteer work, but she longs for something with a little more substance. Kate's friend Dani Strauss desires relief from the stress in her life. Dani is a single mom juggling work, childcare, and asking for help from her ex-husband. One day good fortune strikes when Kate receives $1 million from a benefactor connected with her volunteer work. Immediately, Kate and Dani are off on a dream shopping trip. Subsequently, the two women decide to set up a fund for overworked and underappreciated women like themselves.

Popular Fiction

Where it's reviewed:
Booklist, January 1, 2005, page 819
Library Journal, Febuary 1, 2005, page 68

Other books you might like:
Julianna Baggott, *The Madam*, 2003
Ann Beattie, *My Life, Starring Dara Falcon*, 1997
Barbara Taylor Bradford, *The Triumph of Katie Byrne*, 2001
Jill A. Davis, *Girls' Poker Night*, 2002
Meg Wolitzer, *This Is Your Life*, 1988

1174

PHILLIP JENNINGS

Nam-A-Rama

(New York: Forge, 2005)

Story type: Satire
Subject(s): Vietnam War; Political Movements; Secrets
Major character(s): Armstrong, Military Personnel (Marine), Pilot; Gearhardt, Military Personnel (Marine), Pilot; Ho Chi Minh, Historical Figure, Political Figure
Time period(s): 1960s; 1970s (1961-1975)
Locale(s): Washington, District of Columbia; Vietnam, South; Vietnam, North

Summary: This debut novel about the Vietnam War follows along the beaten path of Joseph Heller's World War II story *Catch-22*. While war is brutal, in a gallows humor way it can be funny, too. In other words, don't think serious; think absurdities; laugh at them, and don't stop laughing. The story here is loosely organized around two Marine officers, Armstrong and Gearhardt. In addition to flying missions for the CIA, they have secret orders to assassinate North Vietnam's Ho Chi Minh and/or General Giapp. The exact nature of the orders and/or how they are supposed to be carried out are vague at best. Nevertheless, the two make it to Hanoi and they meet Ho Chi Minh but instead of assassinating him, they wind up getting drunk with him.

Where it's reviewed:
Booklist, February 1, 2005, page 941
Kirkus Reviews, December 15, 2004, page 1157

Other books you might like:
Robert Olen Butler, *The Alleys of Eden*, 1981
Nelson DeMille, *Up Country*, 2002
Winston Groom, *Forrest Gump*, 1986
Joseph Heller, *Catch-22*, 1961
Robert Stone, *Dog Soldiers*, 1974

1175

TAYARI JONES

The Untelling

(New York: Warner, 2005)

Story type: Psychological
Subject(s): Women; Secrets; Pregnancy
Major character(s): Aria Jackson, Teacher; Keisha Evers, Teenager, Single Parent; Dwayne, Boyfriend (of Aria)
Time period(s): 2000s
Locale(s): Atlanta, Georgia

Summary: Fifteen years ago, a car accident killed Aria Jackson's father and her baby sister, despite her best efforts to save them. Since then, Aria and her mother have had to deal with guilt. Their relationship with each other has suffered as a result. Aria works at a literacy center, where she meets and befriends teenager Keisha Evers, who is pregnant with her second child. Aria herself believes she is pregnant, but soon discovers she isn't and never will be. She must wrestle with this news in light of the fact her fiance desperately wants a child.

Where it's reviewed:
Booklist, March 15, 2005, page 1265
Kirkus Reviews, January 15, 2005, page 75
Library Journal, March 15, 2005, page 72
Publishers Weekly, February 28, 2005, page 40

Other books by the same author:
Leaving Atlanta, 2002

Other books you might like:
Robert Boswell, *Century's Son*, 2002
Gwendolyn Brooks, *Maud Martha*, 1953
Pearl Cleage, *What Looks Like Crazy on an Ordinary Day*, 1997
Ellen Douglas, *A Lifetime Burning*, 1982
Suzan-Lori Parks, *Getting Mother's Body*, 2003

1176

JOSEPH KANON

Alibi

(New York: Henry Holt, 2005)

Story type: Historical; Mystery
Subject(s): World War II; Mothers and Sons; Revenge
Major character(s): Adam Miller, Military Personnel (U.S. Army); Grace Miller, Parent (Adam's mother); Claudia Grassini, Survivor
Time period(s): 1940s (1945)
Locale(s): Venice, Italy

Summary: Kanon's thriller mixes love and hope with large amounts of secrets and danger. American Adam Miller is on leave from the U.S. Army in post-World War II Venice. His mother, Grace, a wealthy widow, has just arrived and plans on making her home in the Italian city. Grace introduces her son to the city's social niceties, which Adam finds a welcome relief from his usual chores of investigating Nazi war crimes. When his mother introduces him to Gianni Maglione, Adam is pleasant, despite his initial reservations. He is much more interested in Claudia Grassini and they begin a love affair. Complications set in when Claudia meets Maglione. As it turns out, Claudia is Jewish and she barely escaped Nazi persecution. She accuses Maglione of sending her father to a German extermination camp.

Where it's reviewed:
Booklist, March 1, 2005, page 1102
Kirkus Reviews, March 1, 2005, page 250
Library Journal, March 15, 2005, page 72
Publishers Weekly, March 14, 2005, page 46

Other books by the same author:
The Good German, 2001

The Prodigal Spy, 1998
Los Alamos, 1997

Other books you might like:
Ted Bell, *Assassin*, 2004
David Benioff, *The 25th Hour*, 2000
Marilyn Campbell, *Pretty Maids in a Row*, 1994
Bernard Cornwell, *Vagabond*, 2002
Louise Erdrich, *Four Souls*, 2004

1177

THOMAS KELLY

Empire Rising

(New York: Farrar, Straus and Giroux, 2005)

Story type: Political; Historical/Depression Era
Subject(s): Construction; Emigration and Immigration; Irish Americans
Major character(s): Michael Briody, Immigrant, Worker; Grace Masterson, Artist; Johnny Farrell, Organized Crime Figure, Lawyer
Time period(s): 1930s
Locale(s): New York, New York

Summary: Set in New York City in the 1930s amid the Depression, the story is organized around the construction of the Empire State Building, known at the time as the eighth wonder of the world. Irish immigrant Michael Briody vacillates between making a life for himself in the U.S. and raising money, to buy arms for the Republican cause in Ireland. Along the way, Michael meets Grace Masterson. The two seem right for each other, but their budding relationship is outright dangerous. Although ostensibly an artist, Grace is also Johnny Farrell's mistress and Johnny, Mayor Jimmy Walker's connection to the underworld, is not a man to be crossed. All of this plays out against the social and political struggles of the time. Governor Franklin Delano Roosevelt struggles against Tammany Hall for political dominance, the city struggles to become a world class metropolis and its people struggle to survive a woeful economy.

Where it's reviewed:
Booklist, December 15, 2004, page 708
Chicago Tribune Books, February 6, 2005, page 1
Kirkus Reviews, November 15, 2004, page 1063
Library Journal, January 2005, page 98

Other books by the same author:
The Rackets, 2001
Payback, 1997

Other books you might like:
Jimmy Breslin, *World Without End, Amen*, 1973
Nelson DeMille, *Cathedral*, 1981
James T. Farrell, *Studs Lonigan*, 1935
Pete Hamill, *Forever*, 2003
William Kennedy, *Roscoe*, 2002

1178

PHILIP KERR

Hitler's Peace

(New York: Putnam, 2005)

Story type: Historical/World War II; Alternate History
Subject(s): Nazis; Conspiracies; Suspense
Major character(s): Willard Mayer, Spy (American), Professor; Franklin Delano Roosevelt, Historical Figure, Political Figure (U.S. president); Winston Churchill, Historical Figure, Political Figure (British prime minister)
Time period(s): 1940s (1943)
Locale(s): Washington, District of Columbia; Teheran, Iran

Summary: Kerr's work focuses on World War II and plays the what-if game. In 1943, Hitler's Germany is at war with the Allied Powers of England, the United States, and the Soviet Union. The tide has turned against Nazi Germany and everyone knows it. Unless the Allied Powers can be split, Germany will lose. The Nazis need one or more of the Allied Powers to drop out of the war. To accomplish this, Adolf Hitler needs a peace treaty with one of the Allies. To make this happen, Hitler plans the assassination of an Allied leader. They—British Prime Minister Winston Churchill, American President Franklin Delano Roosevelt, and Russian Premier Josef Stalin—are planning to meet in Teheran. There the Nazis attempt to implement their plan.

Where it's reviewed:
Booklist, April 1, 2005, page 1325
Kirkus Reviews, March 15, 2005, page 308
Library Journal, April 15, 2005, page 74
Publishers Weekly, April 18, 2005, page 44

Other books by the same author:
The Akhenaten Adventure, 2004
Dark Matter, 2002
The Second Angel, 1999
The Shot, 1999
A Five Year Plan, 1997

Other books you might like:
Frederick Forsyth, *The Day of the Jackal*, 1971
Alan Furst, *Dark Voyage*, 2004
Jack Higgins, *The Eagle Has Landed*, 1975
Greg Iles, *Black Cross*, 1995
Philip Roth, *The Plot Against America*, 2004

1179

SUE MONK KIDD

The Mermaid Chair

(New York: Viking, 2005)

Story type: Romance; Religious
Subject(s): Marriage; Women; Monks
Major character(s): Jessie Sullivan, Parent (of a daughter); Nelle, Aged Person (Jessie's mother), Mentally Ill Person (cut off a finger); Thomas, Religious (Benedictine monk), Friend (of Jessie)
Time period(s): 2000s
Locale(s): Egret Island, South Carolina

Summary: When her mother cuts off a finger, Jessie Sullivan, 43, feels obligated to help. She leaves her husband and child in Atlanta and travels to her childhood home on Egret Island. While she attempts to discover what caused her mother's accident, Jessie must confront the guilt she feels about her father's death in a boating accident when she was a child. Complications set in when Jessie meets Brother Thomas, who lives in a Benedictine monastery. Jessie becomes overwhelmed by passion. She begins to question her marriage and in the process she awakens her artistic self, which she has managed to keep repressed.

Where it's reviewed:
Booklist, February 15, 2005, page 1036
Kirkus Reviews, January 1, 2005, page 140
Publishers Weekly, February 21, 2005, page 155

Other books by the same author:
The Secret Life of Bees, 2002

Other books you might like:
Rachel Basch, *The Passion of Reverend Nash*, 2003
Dan Brown, *The Da Vinci Code*, 2003
William X. Kienzle, *The Rosary Murders*, 1979
Marilynne Robinson, *Gilead*, 2004
Adriana Trigiani, *Notes from the Villa Di Crespi*, 2005

1180

CASSANDRA KING

The Same Sweet Girls

(New York: Hyperion, 2005)

Story type: Psychological; Domestic
Subject(s): Women; Friendship; Reunions
Major character(s): Corrine Cooper, Artist; Julia Dupont, Spouse (politician's wife); Lanier Brewer, Friend (of Julia and Corrine)
Time period(s): 2000s
Locale(s): South

Summary: King's novel examines the friendship of six women, who meet at a small liberal arts college in Alabama. For the next 30 years, they keep up with each other through regular group meetings. Now in their 50s, they reflect on their choices, their decisions, and the impact each had on their lives. For example, Corrine Cooper married her therapist, Lanier Brewer's infidelity has about wrecked her marriage, Julia Dupont married a politician, and Astor Deveaux flirts but remains faithful to her husband. Corrine, Lanier, and Julia take turns narrating the story.

Where it's reviewed:
Booklist, November 1, 2004, page 504
Publishers Weekly, November 22, 2004, page 38

Other books by the same author:
The Sunday Wife, 2002
Making Waves in Zion, 1995

Other books you might like:
Ellen Douglas, *Can't Quit You, Baby*, 1988
Kaye Gibbons, *On the Occasion of My Last Afternoon*, 1998
Ellen Gilchrist, *Light Can Be Both Wave and Particle*, 1989
Lee Smith, *The Last Girls*, 2002

Elizabeth Spencer, *The Southern Woman*, 2001

1181

DAVE KING

The Ha-Ha

(New York: Little, Brown, 2005)

Story type: Psychological
Subject(s): Vietnam War; Friendship; Veterans
Major character(s): Howard Kapostash, Veteran; Sylvia, Parent (Ryan's mother); Ryan, Child
Time period(s): 2000s
Locale(s): United States

Summary: After suffering a head wound during the Vietnam War, Howard Kapostash has been mentally challenged, unable to write or speak coherently. Middle-aged Howie lives a life of quiet desperation. This all changes when a former girlfriend asks Howie for help. Sylvia wants to enter a drug treatment program and needs someone to take care of her nine-year-old son, Ryan. Howie agrees and his life begins to blossom as he progresses from a confused and overwhelmed adult to a caring and competent one because of minding the child.

Where it's reviewed:
Booklist, December 1, 2004, page 637
Kirkus Reviews, September 1, 2004, page 825
Library Journal, November 1, 2004, page 75
New York Times Book Review, January 23, 2005, page 25

Other books you might like:
Robert Bausch, *On the Way Home*, 1982
Madison Smartt Bell, *Soldier's Joy*, 1989
Sydney Blair, *Buffalo*, 1991
Robert Olen Butler, *The Deep Green Sea*, 1997
Percival Everett, *Walk Me to the Distance*, 1985

1182

DEAN R. KOONTZ

Velocity

(New York: Bantam, 2005)

Story type: Psychological Suspense
Subject(s): Serial Killers; Good and Evil; Mystery
Major character(s): Bill Wile, Saloon Keeper/Owner (bartender); Lanny Olson, Police Officer
Time period(s): 2000s
Locale(s): Napa County, California

Summary: One night after work, bartender Bill Wile finds a note under his windshield wiper that gives him a hard choice. If he goes to the police, an old woman will die but if he doesn't, a teacher will die. Bill thinks the note is a joke but the next day a teacher is found murdered. Then, Bill gets another note with an ultimatum and a deadline. Two other lives hang in the balance. There are more notes, with more ultimatums, and the body count begins to climb. The killer becomes more and more involved in Bill's life, forcing him to face up to some painful memories before confronting the killer.

Where it's reviewed:
Publishers Weekly, April 25, 2005, page 39

Other books by the same author:
Life Expectancy, 2004
Odd Thomas, 2004
The Taking, 2004
The Face, 2003
One Door Away from Heaven, 2001

Other books you might like:
Patricia Cornwell, *Blow Fly*, 2003
John Fowles, *The Collector*, 1963
Patricia Highsmith, *The Boy Who Followed Ripley*, 1980
Joyce Carol Oates, *The Rise of Life on Earth*, 1991
James Siegel, *Detour*, 2005

1183

ELIZABETH KOSTOVA

The Historian

(New York: Little, Brown, 2005)

Story type: Horror
Subject(s): Occult; Vampires; Legends
Major character(s): Paul, Diplomat, Parent (of a teenage girl); Bartholomew Rossi, Professor (Paul's mentor), Scholar (of Drakulya legend); Helen Rossi, Scholar (of Drakulya legend)
Time period(s): 1970s (1972)
Locale(s): Amsterdam, Netherlands

Summary: Kostova's debut novel puts an interesting spin on the Dracula story. In 1972 Amsterdam, a teenage girl finds a book in her father's library containing letters dating back to the 1930s. When she presses her father, Paul, about them, he tells her about his mentor, Professor Rossi, who not only believed in the truth of the ''Drakulya'' legend, but that the infamous vampire was still alive, and set out to prove it. After Rossi's disappearance, Paul and Rossi's daughter, Helen, set out to find him. The teenager compares the notes in the book with what her father tells her, and becomes curious about the discrepancies. Meanwhile, in the background, Drakulya looms.

Where it's reviewed:
Publishers Weekly, April 11, 2005, page 31

Other books you might like:
Susanna Clarke, *Jonathan Strange & Mr. Norrell*, 2004
Jon Fasman, *The Geographer's Library*, 2005
Arthur Phillips, *The Egyptologist*, 2004
Anne Rice, *Interview with the Vampire*, 1976
Bram Stoker, *Dracula*, 1897

1184

NICOLE KRAUSS

The History of Love

(New York: Norton, 2005)

Story type: Romance; Psychological
Subject(s): Authors and Writers; Emigration and Immigration; Books and Reading

Major character(s): Leo Gursky, Aged Person, Writer; Alma Singer, Teenager; Charlotte Singer, Parent (Alma's mother), Linguist (translator)
Time period(s): 2000s
Locale(s): New York, New York

Summary: Leo Gursky is an old man living a desperate life in a Polish village. In his youth, Leo wrote a book that was published in South America, although Leo doesn't know this. Fourteen-year-old Alma Singer lives in New York, where she is mainly occupied in looking after her eccentric brother Bird, who thinks he's the Messiah. Alma was named for a character in Leo's book, and wants to meet him. When a stranger asks Charlotte, Alma's mother, to translate the book into English, it sets some surprising events into motion. In writing the book, Krauss drew on her own family's experiences.

Where it's reviewed:
Booklist, March 15, 2005, page 1265
Kirkus Reviews, February 15, 2005, page 191
Library Journal, April 15, 2005, page 74
New York Times Book Review, May 1, 2005, page 19
Publishers Weekly, February 21, 2005, page 154

Other books by the same author:
Man Walks into a Room, 2002

Other books you might like:
Elizabeth Berg, *Never Change*, 2001
Cassandra King, *The Sunday Wife*, 2002
Audrey Niffenegger, *The Time Traveler's Wife*, 2003
James Patterson, *The Lake House*, 2003
Nicholas Sparks, *The Wedding*, 2003

1185

MARK KURLANSKY

Boogaloo on Second Avenue

(New York: Ballantine, 2005)

Story type: Contemporary/Mainstream
Subject(s): Emigration and Immigration; Modern Life; Relationships
Major character(s): Nathan Seltzer, Store Owner (copy shop); Karoline, Baker (pastry chef)
Time period(s): 1980s
Locale(s): New York, New York (Manhattan)

Summary: Kurlansky, a journalist with experience covering foreign affairs, sets his first novel in Manhattan. Experiencing a mid-life crisis, Nathan Seltzer seldom leaves the neighborhood. A cast of unforgettable characters, who speak several different languages, knock up against each other, as they pursue their own interests. Meanwhile, the old neighborhood is under pressure from the forces of gentrification. Nathan, a copy shop owner, must fight a larger chain to stay in business. He also worries about criticism for dating Karoline because his uncle, a Holocaust survivor, thinks her relatives were Nazis.

Where it's reviewed:
Booklist, December 15, 2004, page 691
Kirkus Reviews, January 15, 2005, page 75
Library Journal, February 1, 2005, page 69

Other books by the same author:
The White Man in the Tree and Other Stories, 2000

Other books you might like:
Anita Brookner, *Family and Friends*, 1985
Andre Dubus III, *House of Sand and Fog*, 1999
Rohinton Mistry, *Family Matters*, 2001
Henry Roth, *Call It Sleep*, 1934
Manil Suri, *The Death of Vishnu*, 2001

1186

ELMORE LEONARD

The Hot Kid

(New York: William Morrow, 2005)

Story type: Mystery
Subject(s): Law Enforcement; Crime and Criminals; Violence
Major character(s): Carlos Webster, Lawman (U.S. marshal); Jack Belmont, Criminal; Tony Antonelli, Journalist
Time period(s): 1920s; 1930s (1927-1934)
Locale(s): Oklahoma; Kansas City, Kansas

Summary: Leonard's novel follows two characters, a marshal and a man interested in becoming a public enemy. U.S. Marshal Carlos Webster has a reputation as being ''the hot kid'' and he has eight notches on his gun to prove it. Jack Belmont, son of a wealthy oil baron, has it in his head that the only way he can make his mark is through crime. Belmont and Webster are on a collision course. They meet, tangle, and live to tangle, again. Their encounters are bloody and brutal but not too serious, thanks to Leonard's tone and humor.

Where it's reviewed:
Booklist, March 15, 2005, page 1246
Kirkus Reviews, February 15, 2005, page 192
Library Journal, April 15, 2005, page 74
Publishers Weekly, March 28, 2005, page 55

Other books by the same author:
Tishomingo Blues, 2002
Pagan Babies, 2000
Be Cool, 1999
Get Shorty, 1990
City Primeval, 1980

Other books you might like:
Michael Connelly, *The Narrows*, 2004
Tom Franklin, *Hell at the Breech*, 2003
John Grisham, *The Broker*, 2005
Dennis Lehane, *Shutter Island*, 2003
Robert Stone, *Dog Soldiers*, 1974

1187

ANDREA LEVY

Small Island

(New York: Picador, 2005)

Story type: Historical/World War II
Subject(s): Emigration and Immigration; Race Relations; Jamaicans

Major character(s): Hortense Joseph, Spouse (Gilbert's wife); Gilbert Joseph, Veteran (of WWII); Queenie, Landlord, Friend (of Hortense and Gilbert)
Time period(s): 1940s (1948)
Locale(s): London, England

Summary: Although this is Levy's fourth novel, it is her first published in the U.S. When originally published in 2004 in the United Kingdom, the book won the Orange Prize and was Whitbread Book of the Year. The story revolves around four characters and their interactions with each other and society as a whole. Hortense arrives in London from Jamaica to make a life with her husband Gilbert, who has just returned from service in World War II. They encounter difficulty because of their race. Their landlady, Queenie, who grew up in the English countryside, befriends the Josephs, despite social pressures.

Where it's reviewed:
Kirkus Reviews, February 15, 2005, page 192
Publishers Weekly, March 7, 2005, page 50

Other books you might like:
Elizabeth Gaffney, *Metropolis*, 2005
Pete Hamill, *Forever*, 2003
Shirley Hazzard, *The Great Fire*, 2003
Ian McEwan, *Atonement*, 2001
Philip Roth, *The Human Stain*, 2000

1188

MARINA LEWYCKA

A Short History of Tractors in Ukrainian

(New York: Penguin, 2005)

Story type: Domestic; Psychological
Subject(s): Sisters; Emigration and Immigration; Parent and Child
Major character(s): Nadezhda Vera, Young Woman (Kolya's daughter); Vera Mayovskyj, Young Woman (Kolya's daughter); Kolya Mayovskyj, Widow(er), Engineer (retired)
Time period(s): 2000s (2004)
Locale(s): England

Summary: Kolya, a Ukrainian expatriate and a retired engineer, is living in an English village just outside of London. Depressed over the death of his wife, Kolya visits a Ukrainian social club and hooks up with Valentina, who is 50 years his junior. His daughters Nadezhda and Vera are floored when he tells them about his plans to marry Valentina. The two sisters put aside their personal grudges with each other and team up to protect their father from himself. Meanwhile, Kolya occupies his time writing a history of the tractor.

Where it's reviewed:
Booklist, January 1, 2005, page 820
Kirkus Reviews, December 1, 2004, page 1108
Publishers Weekly, January 17, 2005, page 33

Other books you might like:
Alicia Erian, *Towelhead*, 2005
Jhumpa Lahiri, *The Namesake*, 2003
Rohinton Mistry, *Family Matters*, 2001
Mary Helen Stefaniak, *The Turk and My Mother*, 2004

Irene Zabytko, *When Luba Leaves Home*, 2003

1189

BENILDE LITTLE

Who Does She Think She Is?

(New York: Simon & Schuster, 2005)

Story type: Family Saga; Contemporary/Mainstream
Subject(s): Mothers and Daughters; Marriage; African Americans
Major character(s): Aisha Branch, Young Woman (Camille's daughter); Camille Branch, Social Worker; Geneva Branch, Grandparent (Aisha's grandmother)
Time period(s): 2000s
Locale(s): United States

Summary: Little's family saga follows three strong African-American women, Aisha Branch, her mother Camille, and her grandmother Geneva. Aisha is planning her wedding and nothing less than spectacular will satisfy her. Her gown alone has a $7,000 price tag and that's just the beginning. Don't even mention that her fiance is a white boy. Despite the uproar she creates, Aisha is the one thing Camille and Geneva agree on—they both adore the girl. In her 70s, Geneva is a prim and proper woman who didn't agree with Camille's decision to become a single parent, nor did she approve when Camille started wearing dreadlocks to work.

Where it's reviewed:
Kirkus Reviews, February 15, 2005, page 193
Library Journal, April 1, 2005, page 86

Other books by the same author:
Acting Out, 2003
The Itch, 1998
Good Hair, 1996

Other books you might like:
Margaret Drabble, *The Red Queen*, 2004
Terry McMillan, *How Stella Got Her Groove Back*, 1996
Toni Morrison, *Sula*, 1974
Alice Randall, *Pushkin and the Queen of Spades*, 2004
Susan Straight, *I Been in Sorrow's Kitchen and Licked Out All the Pots*, 1992

1190

ERIC B. MARTIN

Winners

(San Francisco: MacAdam/Cage, 2005)

Story type: Contemporary/Mainstream
Subject(s): Sports/Basketball; Missing Persons; Loneliness
Major character(s): Shane McCarthy, Chimneysweep; Lou McCarthy, Spouse (Shane's wife), Businesswoman; Debra, Parent (Sam's mother)
Time period(s): 1990s (1999)
Locale(s): San Francisco, California

Summary: Loneliness is the driving force in this story set in San Francisco just before the air exited the dot.com bubble. College educated and underemployed, Shane McCarthy is a 30-something married man, trying to fight off middle age.

Shane's solution is to play basketball with a group of like-minded men. Meanwhile, his wife Lou has her sights set on making a fortune in the stock market. When Sam, a basketball regular disappears, Shane sets out to find him. As it turns out, Sam comes from a very rough neighborhood where disputes are settled with violence. Shane meets Debra, Sam's mother, and the story unfolds from there.

Where it's reviewed:
Kirkus Reviews, December 1, 2004, page 1109
Library Journal, December 2004, page 101
Publishers Weekly, November 8, 2004, page 32

Other books by the same author:
Luck, 2000

Other books you might like:
Alice Adams, *A Southern Exposure*, 1995
Paul Auster, *The Book of Illusions*, 2002
Saul Bellow, *Mr. Sammler's Planet*, 1970
Elizabeth Berg, *The Year of Pleasures*, 2005
E.L. Doctorow, *City of God*, 2000

1191

DORATA MASLOWSKA

Snow White and Russian Red

(New York: Black Cat, 2005)

Story type: Contemporary/Mainstream
Subject(s): Modern Life; Relationships; Drugs
Major character(s): Andrzej ''Nails'' Robakoski, Young Man; Magda, Girlfriend (Nails' ex); Angela, Girlfriend (of Nails)
Time period(s): 2000s
Locale(s): Poland

Summary: While Maslowska's novel was an international bestseller, this is the first U.S. edition. The story deals with the aimlessness of youth culture in post-Communist society. Andrzej ''Nails'' Robakoski attempts to assuage his dispair with narcotics. He's unemployed and lives with his parents. His girlfriend Magda dumps him and he finds solace, or attempts to find it, with Angela, Natasha, and Ala. In his spare time, he spins endless conspiracy theories about the Polish economy, American consumerism, and the Russian black market. The author makes good use of stream of consciousness. Translated to English by Benjamin Paloff.

Where it's reviewed:
Kirkus Reviews, December 15, 2004, page 1159
Library Journal, January 2005, page 94
New York Times Book Review, May 1, 2005, page 18
Publishers Weekly, February 7, 2005, page 40

Other books you might like:
David Benioff, *The 25th Hour*, 2000
Eric Bogosian, *Mall*, 2000
John Cheever, *Falconer*, 1977
Nick McDonell, *Twelve*, 2002
Irvine Welsh, *Trainspotting*, 1994

1192

CRIS MAZZA

Disability

(Tallahassee, Florida: Fiction Collection Two, 2005)

Story type: Gay/Lesbian Fiction
Subject(s): Physically Handicapped; Homosexuality/Lesbianism; Hospitals
Major character(s): Teri, Health Care Professional (nurse's aide), Parent; Cleo, Health Care Professional (nurse's aide), Lesbian
Time period(s): 2000s
Locale(s): United States

Summary: The story follows Cleo and Teri as they deal with difficulty in the workplace and in their personal lives. Both are nurse's aides in a state hospital for the severely disabled. The two women are making minimum wage but it is their work that determines how much money the hospital will get from the state. As it turns out, the state will only fund treatment that will improve a patient's condition. The problem is their patients have little chance of improving. This forces the hospital management to pressure Teri and Cleo into engaging in a charade. Meanwhile, Teri faces an emotional challenge as she tries to make amends with her estranged daughter. Cleo, a lesbian, also faces personal problems of her own as her relationship with another woman turns sour.

Where it's reviewed:
Library Journal, April 1, 2005, page 87

Other books by the same author:
Homeland, 2004
Girl Beside Him, 2001
Dog People, 1997
Former Virgin, 1997
Your Name Here, 1995

Other books you might like:
Stacey D'Erasmo, *A Seahorse Year*, 2004
Dean R. Koontz, *One Door Away from Heaven*, 2001
Tim Parks, *Goodness*, 1991
Pamela Shepherd, *Zach at Risk*, 2004
Nicholas Sparks, *The Rescue*, 2000

1193

ALEXANDER MCCALL SMITH

In the Company of Cheerful Ladies

(New York: Pantheon, 2005)

Story type: Mystery
Series: No. 1 Ladies' Detective Agency. Book 6
Subject(s): Women; Africa; Secrets
Major character(s): Precious Ramotswe, Detective—Private; Grace Makutsi, Detective—Private (Precious' assistant); J.L.B. Matekoni, Spouse (Precious' husband)
Time period(s): 2000s
Locale(s): Botswana

Summary: In this installment of McCall Smith's charming detective series, Precious must face a secret from her past. Precious' husband Mr. J.L.B. Matekoni, operator of Tlokweng Road Speedy Motors, must face difficulties of his own when his apprentice up and elopes with a rich woman. Meanwhile, Mma Makutsi signs up for dance lessons but is assigned an unsuitable partner.

Where it's reviewed:
Booklist, February 1, 2005, page 917
Kirkus Reviews, March 15, 2005, page 320
Library Journal, May 1, 2005, page 69
Publishers Weekly, February 14, 2005, page 51

Other books by the same author:
The Full Cupboard of Life, 2003
The Kalahari Typing School for Men, 2002
Morality for Beautiful Girls, 2001
Tears of the Giraffe, 2000
The No. 1 Ladies' Detective Agency, 1998

Other books you might like:
Margaret Atwood, *Alias Grace*, 1996
Agatha Christie, *The Secret Adversary*, 1922
Yann Martel, *Life of Pi*, 2001
Donna Tartt, *The Little Friend*, 2002
Robert Traver, *Anatomy of a Murder*, 1958

1194

IAN MCEWAN

Saturday

(New York: Nan A. Talese, 2005)

Story type: Political; Psychological Suspense
Subject(s): Crime and Criminals; Accidents; Political Movements
Major character(s): Henry Perowne, Doctor (neurosurgeon), Parent (two children)
Time period(s): 2000s (2003)
Locale(s): London, England

Summary: McEwan's novel examines how aspects of the modern world have changed since the attacks in New York City and Washington D.C. on September 11, 2001. Set two years later in London, the story follows Henry Perowne, a neurosurgeon, on his day off, a Saturday. Henry's inner dialogues drive the narrative. There is tension in the air because of the impending war with Iraq. A peace demonstration attracts thousands and helps increase everyone's anxiety. Then, Henry has a minor traffic accident and the driver of the other car is a hoodlum. The situation turns dangerous and Henry will have to draw heavily on his inner strength to survive.

Where it's reviewed:
Booklist, February 15, 2005, page 1036
Kirkus Reviews, January 15, 2005, page 78
New York Times Book Review, March 20, 2005, page 1
Publishers Weekly, January 31, 2005, page 48

Other books by the same author:
Atonement, 2001
Amsterdam, 1999
Enduring Love, 1998
Black Dogs, 1992
The Innocent, 1990

Other books you might like:
Saul Bellow, *Herzog*, 1964
Thomas Berger, *Vital Parts*, 1982
Nelson DeMille, *Night Fall*, 2004
Michael Dibdin, *Thanksgiving*, 2001
Jonathan Safran Foer, *Extremely Loud & Incredibly Close*, 2005

1195

PABLO MEDINA

The Cigar Roller

(New York: Grove, 2005)

Story type: Psychological; Domestic
Subject(s): Cuban Americans; Hospitals; Illness
Major character(s): Amadeo Terra, Patient (stroke victim); Julia Terra, Spouse (Amadeo's wife); Albertico Terra, Relative (Amadeo's son)
Time period(s): 2000s
Locale(s): Tampa, Florida

Summary: After suffering a stroke, Amadeo Terra is confined to a hospital bed, unable to talk or do anything for himself. His wife and youngest son are dead; the rest of his family has better things to do than visit him. His only human contacts are a nurse who bullies him, an orderly who ignores him, and a nun who annoys him. A Cuban immigrant, he made his money in the cigar business and was never one to deny himself any of the pleasures of the flesh. Now he is reduced to fantasizing about the nun who visits him, and is forced to examine his life.

Where it's reviewed:
Booklist, January 1, 2005, page 820
Kirkus Reviews, December 15, 2004, page 1160
Library Journal, January 2005, page 99
Publishers Weekly, January 31, 2005, page 48

Other books by the same author:
The Return of Felix Nogara, 2000
The Floating Island, 1999
The Marks of Birth, 1994
Arching into the Afterlife, 1991
Exiled Memories, 1990

Other books you might like:
Cristina Garcia, *Monkey Hunting*, 2003
Oscar Hijuelos, *The Mambo Kings Play Songs of Love*, 1989
Liz Jensen, *The Ninth Life of Louis Drax*, 2004
Ana Menendez, *In Cuba I Was a German Shepherd*, 2001
Ann Packer, *The Dive from Clausen's Pier*, 2002

1196

JUDITH MICHAEL

The Real Mother

(New York: William Morrow, 2005)

Story type: Family Saga
Subject(s): Family Problems; Modern Life; Sibling Rivalry

Major character(s): Sara Elliot, Businesswoman, Guardian (raising her siblings); Mack Elliot, Relative (Sara's brother); Reuben Lister, Businessman, Boyfriend (Sara's)
Time period(s): 2000s
Locale(s): Chicago, Illinois; New York, New York

Summary: The story explores the problems adults face in attempting to raise children. Sara Elliot has a choice: pursue her own career goals or return home to care for three younger siblings. She chooses the latter. At first, the adjustment is hard but doable. Younger brother Doug, and teenage sisters Carrie and Abby are very cooperative. Then older brother Mack shows up and becomes a divisive force, undermining Sara's authority. When things are almost unmanageable, she meets Reuben, an out-of-town client. Their business dealings soon develop into a relationship that gives each of them strength to deal with the challenges they face.

Where it's reviewed:
Booklist, November 15, 2004, page 532
Kirkus Reviews, January 1, 2005, page 14
Library Journal, February 1, 2005, page 69
Publishers Weekly, January 10, 2005, page 37

Other books by the same author:
A Certain Smile, 1999
Acts of Love, 1997
A Tangled Web, 1994
Pot of Gold, 1993
Sleeping Beauty, 1991

Other books you might like:
Elizabeth Berg, *Say When*, 2003
Sandra Cisneros, *Caramelo*, 2002
Stuart Dybek, *Childhood and Other Neighborhoods*, 1980
Adam Langer, *Crossing California*, 2004
Mary Helen Stefaniak, *The Turk and My Mother*, 2004

1197

ADRIENNE MILLER

The Coast of Akron

(New York: Farrar, Straus and Giroux, 2005)

Story type: Domestic
Subject(s): Family Relations; Family Problems; Secrets
Major character(s): Lowell Haven, Artist, Divorced Person; Merit Haven, Relative (Lowell's daughter); Jenny Haven, Parent (Merit's mother), Divorced Person (Lowell's ex-wife)
Time period(s): 2000s
Locale(s): Akron, Ohio; London, England

Summary: Miller puts humor to good use in a debut novel about a dysfunctional family. Lowell Haven, the family patriarch, is a painter with an international reputation. He also has a few character flaws such as womanizing and lying. However, his problem is he isn't painting. His artistic block concerns his estranged daughter, Merit, who has run away from home. Plans are in the works to lure her back home with a lavish party that includes the glitterati. Problems develop from the guest list and events come to a head at a costume party.

Popular Fiction

Where it's reviewed:
Kirkus Reviews, March 1, 2005, page 253
Library Journal, April 1, 2005, page 87
Publishers Weekly, March 7, 2005, page 47

Other books you might like:
Eleanor Bailey, *Marlene Dietrich Lived Here*, 2002
Beryl Bainbridge, *Winter Garden*, 1980
Tracy Chevalier, *The Lady and the Unicorn*, 2003
Kazuo Ishiguro, *An Artist of the Floating World*, 1986
John Updike, *Seek My Face*, 2002

1198

SUE MILLER

Lost in the Forest

(New York: Knopf, 2005)

Story type: Domestic; Psychological
Subject(s): Grief; Widows/Widowers; Accidents
Major character(s): Eva, Spouse (of John), Parent (Daisy's mother); John, Businessman, Accident Victim; Mark, Divorced Person (Eva's ex-husband)
Time period(s): 2000s
Locale(s): California

Summary: Eva and Mark have an ideal marriage until it shatters when Eva discovers Mark's infidelity. They divorce and she gets custody of their two daughters. Eva puts her life back together when she marries John. They have a child and life is glorious for five years until John dies suddenly. Life comes apart at the seams for Eva. However, she is an adult and perhaps will find her way again. The prospect for her daughters is less optimistic. Daisy, Eva's middle daughter, is seduced by an older man. Before things spin totally out of control, Mark returns and tries to help.

Where it's reviewed:
Booklist, February 1, 2005, page 917
Library Journal, February 15, 2005, page 119
Publishers Weekly, February 14, 2005, page 50

Other books by the same author:
The World Below, 2001
While I Was Gone, 1999
The Distinguished Guest, 1995
For Love, 1993
The Good Mother, 1986

Other books you might like:
James Agee, *A Death in the Family*, 1957
David Baldacci, *Wish You Well*, 2000
Percival Everett, *My Existing Condition*, 2004
Peggy Rambach, *Fighting Gravity*, 2001
Nicholas Sparks, *A Bend in the Road*, 2001

1199

J. MILLIGAN

Jack Fish

(New York: Soho, 2005)

Story type: Contemporary/Mainstream; Humor
Subject(s): Fantasy; Science Fiction; Satire

Major character(s): Jack Fish, Spy (aquaman from Atlantis); Victor Sargasso, Criminal
Time period(s): 2000s
Locale(s): New York, New York

Summary: Milligan's debut novel gives readers a fresh look at New York City from the perspective of Jack Fish, an aquaman, a creature that breathes in both water and air. Jack is from Atlantis, an underwater city located in the Atlantic Ocean just off the New Jersey coast. He's on an assignment—to assassinate Victor Sargasso. However, this is Jack's first job and unexpected things happen to him. The first difficulty is breathing. No one told him the transition from water to air would be so difficult. While searching for assistance, Jack discovers the Maltese, deadly enemies, who want to kill him. Despite these difficulties, Jack finds a couple of worthwhile things: sex and hamburgers.

Where it's reviewed:
New York Times Book Review, January 23, 2005, page 23
Publishers Weekly, January 10, 2005, page 40

Other books you might like:
Anthony Bourdain, *Gone Bamboo*, 1997
David Bowker, *I Love My Smith & Wesson*, 2004
Bill Fitzhugh, *Pest Control*, 1997
Jane Heller, *Princess Charming*, 1997
Kurt Vonnegut, *Slaughterhouse-Five*, 1969

1200

MIYUKI MIYABE

Shadow Family

(New York: Kodansha America, 2005)

Story type: Mystery
Subject(s): Internet; Murder; Psychological
Major character(s): Etsuro Takegami, Police Officer (desk sergeant); Chikako Ishizu, Detective—Police
Time period(s): 2000s
Locale(s): Tokyo, Japan

Summary: Internet chat rooms are at the center of this intriguing story. When an office worker and his teenage mistress are brutally murdered, police discover evidence on the victim's computer connecting the victims to a fantasy family. The family members regularly meet in an Internet chat room. As the investigation proceeds, the office worker's daughter complains that she is being stalked. Police devise a scheme to foil the stalker and bring the murderer to justice. All the members of the shadow family are brought in for questioning. While they are interrogated, they are observed by the victim's daughter through a two-way mirror.

Where it's reviewed:
Booklist, January 1, 2005, page 828
Kirkus Reviews, December 1, 2004, page 1122
Library Journal, February 15, 2005, page 124
Publishers Weekly, January 17, 2005, page 38

Other books by the same author:
All She Was Worth, 1996

Other books you might like:
Sylvia Brownrigg, *The Metaphysical Touch*, 1999

John Burdett, *Bangkok 8*, 2003
Richard Dooling, *Bet Your Life*, 2003
Kazuo Ishiguro, *When We Were Orphans*, 2000
William T. Vollmann, *The Royal Family*, 2000

1201

SHANI MOOTOO

He Drown She in the Sea

(New York: Grove, 2005)

Story type: Psychological Suspense; Romance
Subject(s): Friendship; Emigration and Immigration; Islands
Major character(s): Harry, Lover (of Rose); Rose, Lover (of Harry)
Time period(s): 1930s; 1940s (1939-1945)
Locale(s): Caribbean; Vancouver, British Columbia, Canada

Summary: This is a love story that begins during World War II on a tiny Caribbean island. Harry, a native teenager, meets Rose, a teenage girl. They fall deeply in love but there are complications. Aside from racial issues, Harry's mother works for Rose's family. When Rose's family discovers her relationship with Harry, they send Harry and his mother away. As the years pass, Rose marries and has a child. Meanwhile, Harry moves to Canada where he becomes a successful businessman but remains single. On a visit to Canada, Rose looks up Harry. This sets in motion a series of events that Rose fully intends to use to rekindle their relationship.

Where it's reviewed:
Library Journal, April 15, 2005, page 76
Publishers Weekly, April 4, 2005, page 44

Other books by the same author:
The Predicament of Or, 2001
Cereus Blooms at Night, 1996

Other books you might like:
Margaret Atwood, *Bodily Harm*, 1981
Austin Clarke, *The Polished Hoe*, 2002
Edwidge Danticat, *The Dew Breaker*, 2004
Joan Didion, *The Last Thing He Wanted*, 1996
Zadie Smith, *White Teeth*, 2000

1202

MARY MCGARRY MORRIS

The Lost Mother

(New York: Viking, 2005)

Story type: Historical/Depression Era; Domestic
Subject(s): Psychological; Orphans; Depression (Economic)
Major character(s): Henry Talcott, Butcher, Single Parent (of Thomas and Margaret); Thomas Talcott, Child; Margaret Talcott, Child
Time period(s): 1930s
Locale(s): Vermont

Summary: This is a story of hard times during the Depression, with struggling adults and neglected children. After his wife abandons him, Henry Talcott and his two children, Thomas and Margaret, live in a tent in the woods. As Henry travels from town to town looking for work as a butcher, the children

pretty much raise themselves. Although circumstances conspire to beat down their father, the children develop a determination to survive. Some characters set out to take advantage of the children, while others offer kindness and sustenance.

Where it's reviewed:
Booklist, December 1, 2004, page 618
Chicago Tribune Books, February 13, 2005, page 3
Kirkus Reviews, December 1, 2004, page 1110
Publishers Weekly, January 3, 2005, page 34

Other books by the same author:
A Hole in the Universe, 2004
Fiona Range, 2000
Songs in Ordinary Time, 1995
A Dangerous Woman, 1991
Vanished, 1988

Other books you might like:
Bridgett M. Davis, *Shifting through Neutral*, 2004
Nicholas Delbanco, *The Vagabonds*, 2004
Leif Enger, *Peace Like a River*, 2001
Jerzy Kosinski, *The Painted Bird*, 1965
Jeffrey Lent, *In the Fall*, 2000

1203

HARUKI MURAKAMI

Kafka on the Shore

(New York: Knopf, 2005)

Story type: Contemporary/Mainstream
Subject(s): Quest; Fantasy; Fate
Major character(s): Kafka Tamura, Teenager; Satoru Nakata, Friend (of Kafka), Aged Person
Time period(s): 2000s
Locale(s): Tokyo, Japan; Takamatsu, Japan

Summary: Murakami's epic tale revolves around two characters, Kafka Tamura, a teenager, and Satoru Nakata, a mentally challenged elderly man. Both run away from their homes, but for different reasons. Kafka searches for his mother and sister. Will he fall victim to the Oedipal myth? Nakata can't talk to people, but he can talk to cats. Did his government make him that way? The two friends see some amazing things, while meeting a colorful cast of characters.

Where it's reviewed:
Booklist, November 15, 2004, page 532
Chicago Tribune Books, January 16, 2005, page 4
Kirkus Reviews, December 1, 2004, page 1110
New York Times, January 31, 2005, page B10
Publishers Weekly, December 6, 2004, page 42

Other books by the same author:
After the Quake, 2002
The Sputnik Sweetheart, 2001
Norwegian Wood, 2000
The Wind-Up Bird Chronicle, 1997
The Elephant Vanishes, 1993

Other books you might like:
Vasily Aksyonov, *The Winter's Hero*, 1996
Jean Auel, *The Mammoth Hunters*, 1985
Michael Blake, *Dances with Wolves*, 1988

Popular Fiction

Gabriel Garcia Marquez, *One Hundred Years of Solitude*, 1970

Joyce Carol Oates, *My Heart Laid Bare*, 1998

1204
WILLIAM NICHOLSON

The Society of Others
(New York: Nan A. Talese, 2005)

Story type: Psychological
Subject(s): Men; Murder; Terror
Major character(s): Unnamed Character, Narrator, Teenager
Time period(s): 2000s
Locale(s): Europe

Summary: Nicholson, who co-wrote the script for the Academy Award-winning movie *Gladiator*, offers an edgy psychological story with an existential twist. A nameless teenager hits the road, hitchhiking across Europe searching for meaning. His destination is determined by the first truck that comes along. The driver fancies himself a philosopher and the ride is promising. However, when they cross into an unnamed country in Eastern Europe, a band of thugs stops the truck. The narrator is forced to watch as the gang first tortures and then murders the driver for carrying books of a political nature that somehow threatened the country's current regime. Now, the narrator must figure out a way to get away from the thugs and their repressive country.

Where it's reviewed:
Booklist, January 1, 2005, page 821
Kirkus Reviews, October 15, 2004, page 981
Library Journal, November 1, 2004, page 76
New York Times Book Review, February 13, 2005, page 13
Publishers Weekly, January 17, 2005, page 36

Other books by the same author:
Firesong, 2002
Slaves of the Mastery, 2001
The Wind Singer, 2000
The Seventh Level, 1979

Other books you might like:
David Baldacci, *Hour Game*, 2004
Pat Barker, *Blow Your House Down*, 1984
Ray Bradbury, *Death Is a Lonely Business*, 1985
Patricia Cornwell, *All That Remains*, 1992
Robert Ludlum, *The Sigma Protocol*, 2001

1205
STEWART O'NAN

The Good Wife
(New York: Farrar, Straus and Giroux, 2005)

Story type: Psychological; Domestic
Subject(s): Mothers and Sons; Prisoner's Families; Marriage
Major character(s): Patty Dickerson, Parent, Spouse (Tommy's wife); Tommy Dickerson, Criminal
Time period(s): 2000s
Locale(s): New York

Summary: Patty Dickerson is pregnant when her husband Tommy and a friend are arrested for burglarizing an elderly woman's house. During the crime, the woman died and her house burned to the ground. Tommy is sentenced to 28 years in prison and Patty struggles to raise her son alone and stay true to her husband. Despite pressure from family and friends to divorce Tommy, Patty stands by her man.

Where it's reviewed:
Booklist, February 15, 2005, page 1036
Kirkus Reviews, January 15, 2005, page 79
Library Journal, March 1, 2005, page 80

Other books by the same author:
The Night Country, 2003
Wish You Were Here, 2002
Everyday People, 2001
A Prayer for Dying, 1999
The Speed Queen, 1997

Other books you might like:
Robert Bausch, *The Gypsy Man*, 2002
David Anthony Durham, *Walk through Darkness*, 2002
Barry Gifford, *Wyoming*, 2000
Jacquelyn Mitchard, *The Most Wanted*, 1998
Alice Walker, *Now Is the Time to Open Your Heart*, 2004

1206
SHARON OWENS

The Tea House of Mulberry Street
(New York: Putnam, 2005)

Story type: Domestic
Subject(s): Marriage; Love; Restaurants
Major character(s): Penny Stanley, Businesswoman, Spouse (Daniel's wife); Daniel Stanley, Businessman
Time period(s): 2000s
Locale(s): Belfast, Ireland, Northern

Summary: At Muldoon's teahouse in Belfast, the locals gather to chitchat while enjoying the house specialty, cherry cheesecake. A cast of colorful characters includes a starving artist who writes love letters to her favorite movie star, a businessman who secretly yearns for a florist, a wife worried her husband is having an affair, and an editor who is searching for her childhood sweetheart. The happy life of the proprietors, Daniel and Penny Stanley, as well as their 17-year marriage, is threatened by a secret from Daniel's past.

Where it's reviewed:
Booklist, January 1, 2005, page 822
Kirkus Reviews, January 1, 2005, page 15
Publishers Weekly, January 17, 2005, page 34

Other books by the same author:
The Ballroom on Magnolia Street, 2004

Other books you might like:
Alice Adams, *After the War*, 2000
Margaret Atwood, *Life Before Man*, 1979
Charles Baxter, *Saul and Patsy*, 2003
Ann Beattie, *Another You*, 1995
Maeve Binchy, *Quentins*, 2002

1207

CHUCK PALAHNIUK

Haunted

(New York: Doubleday, 2005)

Story type: Collection
Subject(s): Short Stories; Horror; Prisoners and Prisons
Time period(s): 2000s
Locale(s): United States

Summary: Some 23 short stories are linked together to form this novel, which is a combination of satire laced with a reality television premise. The characters are recruited with an ad for a writer's retreat. They are urged to abandon the distractions of the real world and to tap into the creative force that will produce a masterpiece. However, what they find is isolation and deprivation, in short a nightmare. Each would-be writer believes their situation to be unique and tells a story that is sure to make them the main character in the book or movie they believe is bound to be made from this experience. This leads to some very extreme behavior as the would-be writers resort to starving themselves, self-mutilation, abnormal sex, and so forth.

Where it's reviewed:
Booklist, March 1, 2005, page 1102
Kirkus Reviews, February 1, 2005, page 143
Library Journal, May 1, 2005, page 75
Publishers Weekly, February 21, 2005, page 154

Other books by the same author:
Diary, 2003
Lullaby, 2002
Choke, 2001
Survivor, 1999
Fight Club, 1996

Other books you might like:
Susan Choi, *American Woman*, 2003
Tananarive Due, *The Good House*, 2003
Dean R. Koontz, *By the Light of the Moon*, 2002
J.D. Landis, *The Taking*, 2003
Louise Murphy, *The True Story of Hansel and Gretel*, 2003

1208

BARBARA PARKER

Suspicion of Rage

(New York: Dutton, 2005)

Story type: Mystery; Psychological Suspense
Series: Anthony Quintana. Book 7
Subject(s): Marriage; Cuban Americans; Women
Major character(s): Gail Connor, Lawyer; Anthony Quintana, Lawyer; Ramiro Vega, Relative (Anthony's brother-in-law)
Time period(s): 2000s
Locale(s): Miami, Florida; Cuba

Summary: Cuban American Anthony Quintana and his wife Gail are planning a trip to Cuba to celebrate their marriage. Complications set in when a Cuban exile leader wants help with a man who wishes to defect. Anthony doubts the man really wants to leave Cuba and would prefer not to get involved. However, if he doesn't help, life could be difficult when he returns to the United States. Things get really complicated when Cuban officials threaten Anthony's family if he doesn't tell them who wants to defect. Then there's a 22-year-old assassin who intends to use Quintana's daughter against him.

Where it's reviewed:
Booklist, February 15, 2005, page 1066
Kirkus Reviews, January 1, 2005, page 15
Library Journal, February 15, 2005, page 120

Other books by the same author:
Suspicion of Madness, 2003
Suspicion of Vengeance, 2001
Suspicion of Malice, 2000
Suspicion of Betrayal, 1999
Suspicion of Deceit, 1998

Other books you might like:
Alex Abella, *The Killing of the Saints*, 1991
Julia Alvarez, *In the Name of Salome*, 2000
Bill Granger, *The New York Yanquis*, 1995
Oscar Hijuelos, *The Mambo Kings Play Songs of Love*, 1989
Pablo Medina, *The Cigar Roller*, 2005

1209

ROBERT B. PARKER

Appaloosa

(New York: Putnam, 2005)

Story type: Historical/American West
Subject(s): Violence; Frontier and Pioneer Life; Law Enforcement
Major character(s): Virgil Cole, Lawman (marshal); Everett Hitch, Lawman (deputy); Randall Bragg, Rancher
Time period(s): 1880s
Locale(s): Appaloosa, West

Summary: In this work, Parker takes a break from urban New England, turns back the clock, and heads to the wild west. Virgil Cole and Everett Hitch are town tamers. Folks hire them to bring law and order to boomtowns in the west and after cleaning up a town, they move on to the next one. Cole and Hitch are called into the little town of Appaloosa after the town marshal and his deputy are gunned down. The two men immediately establish a ruthless policy of making cowboys check their guns when they come to town. Those who disobey do it at their own risk. The problem shifts from drunken cowboys to Randall Bragg, a respected rancher, who is orchestrating evil deeds for his own ends.

Where it's reviewed:
Kirkus Reviews, March 15, 2005, page 310
Publishers Weekly, March 28, 2005, page 53

Other books by the same author:
Cold Service, 2005
Double Play, 2004
Melancholy Baby, 2004
Gunman's Rhapsody, 2001
Hugger Mugger, 2000

Popular Fiction

Other books you might like:
Oakley Hall, *Ambrose Bierce and the Ace of Shoots*, 2005
Elmer Kelton, *The Far Canyon*, 1994
Elmore Leonard, *Hombre*, 1989
Cormac McCarthy, *Cities of the Plain*, 1998
Larry McMurtry, *Lonesome Dove*, 1985

1210

T.R. PEARSON

Glad News of the Natural World

(New York: Simon & Schuster, 2005)

Story type: Contemporary/Mainstream
Subject(s): City and Town Life; Parent and Child; Humor
Major character(s): Louis Benfield, Maintenance Worker
Time period(s): 2000s
Locale(s): New York, New York; Neely, North Carolina

Summary: Louis Benfield, who first appeared as a young man in Pearson's *A Short History of a Small Place* (1985), returns 20 years older in this sequel. Although he manages brief trips home to Neely, North Carolina, Louis now lives in New York City, where his father got him a job at an insurance company. Although Louis doesn't tell his parents, the company fired him. He flat out refuses to accept defeat, surviving by making deliveries and repairing small appliances. When his parents are killed in a car crash, Louis handles it with stellar courage. Pearson keeps the story interesting with humor and a cast of colorful characters.

Where it's reviewed:
Booklist, March 15, 2005, page 1267
Kirkus Reviews, March 1, 2005, page 255
Library Journal, April 1, 2005, page 88
Publishers Weekly, March 28, 2005, page 55

Other books by the same author:
True Cross, 2003
Polar, 2002
Blue Ridge, 2000
Cry Me a River, 1993
Call and Response, 1989

Other books you might like:
Wiliam Boyd, *Stars and Bars*, 1984
Arthur Bradford, *Dogwalker*, 2001
Sonny Brewer, *The Poet of Tolstoy Park*, 2005
John Irving, *The World According to Garp*, 1978
Thomas McGuane, *Something to Be Desired*, 1984

1211

GEORGE P. PELECANOS

Drama City

(New York: Little, Brown, 2005)

Story type: Psychological; Mystery
Subject(s): Revenge; Drugs; Crime and Criminals
Major character(s): Lorenzo Brown, Convict (just released); Rachel Lopez, Parole Officer
Time period(s): 2000s
Locale(s): Washington, District of Columbia

Summary: Lorenzo Brown is an ex-convict determined to go straight. He has a job working for the Humane Society and his parole officer, Rachel Lopez, is trying to help him. However, life on the streets is both unpredictable and violent. Drug dealers, gang bangers, hardened criminals, and those on the way to becoming hardened criminals rub shoulders with each other, sometimes with lethal results. As luck would have it, Brown and Lopez are about to get ensnared in a whirlwind, when a petty dispute ignites a murder-revenge scenario.

Where it's reviewed:
Booklist, February 15, 2005, page 1037
Kirkus Reviews, January 15, 2005, page 79
New York Times, March 10, 2005, page B1
Publishers Weekly, February 21, 2005, page 158

Other books by the same author:
Hard Revolution, 2004
Soul Circus, 2003
Hell to Pay, 2002
Right as Rain, 2001
Shame the Devil, 2000

Other books you might like:
Madison Smartt Bell, *Straight Cut*, 1986
David Benioff, *The 25th Hour*, 2000
Mark Haddon, *The Curious Incident of the Dog in the Night-Time*, 2003
George V. Higgins, *Defending Billy Ryan*, 1992
Julie Parsons, *Eager to Please*, 2000

1212

ARTURO PEREZ-REVERTE

Captain Alatriste

(New York: Putnam, 2005)

Story type: Historical; Mystery
Series: Captain Alatriste. Book 1
Subject(s): Conspiracies; Politics; Responsibility
Major character(s): Diego Alatriste y Tenorio, Veteran, Military Personnel; Inigo Balboa, Narrator; Fray Emilio Bocanegra, Religious
Time period(s): 17th century (1620)
Locale(s): Madrid, Spain

Summary: Captain Diego Alatriste y Tenorio is famous for his prowess with a sword. Although Diego is a man of honor, he is also a hired killer. He accepts a contract from anonymous persons to kill two Englishmen. While he has no trouble defeating the Englishmen in a sword fight, something about them convinces Diego to spare their lives. When his employers learn of his action, his own life is threatened. A young man in his service, Inigo Balboa narrates the story and helps Diego escape from the wrath of his enemies, including influential political and religious figures. This is the first book of a proposed five-book series.

Where it's reviewed:
Kirkus Reviews, April 1, 2005, page 381
Library Journal, April 1, 2005, page 88

Other books by the same author:
The Queen of the South, 2004
The Nautical Chart, 2001

The Fencing Master, 1999
The Club Dumas, 1996
The Flanders Panel, 1994

Other books you might like:
Isabel Allende, *Zorro*, 2005
Jim Harrison, *Legends of the Fall*, 1979
William T. Vollmann, *Argall*, 2001
Robert James Waller, *Border Music*, 1995
Randy Wayne White, *Dead of Night*, 2005

1213

REYNOLDS PRICE

The Good Priest's Son
(New York: Scribner, 2005)

Story type: Psychological; Domestic
Subject(s): Terrorism; Fathers and Sons; Clergy
Major character(s): Mabry Kincaid, Artisan (art restorer); Tasker Kincaid, Religious (retired priest), Parent (Mabry's father); Audrey Thornton, Care Giver (of Tasker), Student—Graduate (divinity)
Time period(s): 2000s (2001)
Locale(s): New York, New York; North Carolina

Summary: When disaster strikes on September 11, 2001, Mabry Kincaid is crossing the Atlantic Ocean on his way to New York. His flight is diverted to Nova Scotia for a couple of days. Mabry despairs at the thought of dealing with the destruction of his loft, which is located near the World Trade Center, so he goes back to North Carolina to visit his elderly father, a retired Episcopal priest. He finds an African-American divinity student, Audrey Thornton, caring for his father. Mabry becomes friends with Audrey and also reconciles some difficult issues from his past with both his friends and his father. Upon returning to New York, he deals with the destruction of his personal property and his relationship with his daughter.

Where it's reviewed:
Booklist, April 15, 2005, page 1414
Kirkus Reviews, March 15, 2005, page 311
Library Journal, May 1, 2005, page 76
Publishers Weekly, April 11, 2005, page 31

Other books by the same author:
Noble Norfleet, 2002
A Great Circle, 2001
The Honest Account of a Memorable Life, 1994
Kate Vaiden, 1986
Mustian, 1983

Other books you might like:
Willa Cather, *The Song of the Lark*, 1937
Jonathan Safran Foer, *Extremely Loud & Incredibly Close*, 2005
Ian McEwan, *Saturday*, 2005
Marilynne Robinson, *Gilead*, 2004
Nicholas Sparks, *A Walk to Remember*, 1999

1214

FRANCINE PROSE

A Changed Man
(New York: HarperCollins, 2005)

Story type: Psychological; Domestic
Subject(s): Human Rights; Neo-Nazis; Adolescence
Major character(s): Vincent Nolan, Volunteer; Meyer Maslow, Holocaust Victim (survivor), Businessman (runs non-profit agency); Bonnie Kalen, Single Parent (two children), Businesswoman (fundraiser)
Time period(s): 2000s
Locale(s): New York, New York

Summary: Vincent Nolan, a man with neo-Nazi tendencies, runs off with a truck, cash, and drugs that belong to members of an Aryan movement. They become angry but don't go to the police, but rather they set out to punish Vincent. His imaginative solution is to volunteer to help Meyer Maslow and his international human rights organization. After Vincent charms Meyer, his fundraiser Bonnie Kalen offers Vincent a place to stay. When the media gets wind of the tattooed, skinhead working with Meyer Maslow, Vincent's conversion makes him a celebrity of the day. While satirical in nature, the author raises some interesting questions that include personal change and individual motivation.

Where it's reviewed:
Booklist, December 1, 2004, page 619
Kirkus Reviews, January 1, 2005, page 17
Library Journal, January 2005, page 100
Publishers Weekly, December 20, 2004, page 34

Other books by the same author:
After, 2003
Blue Angel, 2000
The Peaceable Kingdom, 1993
Women and Children First, 1988
Bigfoot Dreams, 1986

Other books you might like:
Saul Bellow, *Mr. Sammler's Planet*, 1970
Philip Caputo, *Acts of Faith*, 2005
Gwen Edelman, *War Story*, 2001
Michael Ondaatje, *Anil's Ghost*, 2000
Philip Roth, *The Plot Against America*, 2004

1215

EMILY RABOTEAU

The Professor's Daughter
(New York: Henry Holt, 2005)

Story type: Contemporary/Mainstream; Family Saga
Subject(s): Modern Life; Fathers and Daughters; Racially Mixed People
Major character(s): Emma Boudreaux, Student—College; Bernie Boudreaux, Relative (Emma's brother), Accident Victim (in a coma); Bernard Boudreaux, Parent (of Bernie and Emma), Professor
Time period(s): 2000s

Locale(s): Princeton, New Jersey; New York, New York; New Orleans, Louisiana

Summary: Emma has a black father and a white mother, but her life hasn't been difficult since Bernie, her older brother, has been able to smooth the way for her. However, Bernie goes into a coma after an accident. Now, Emma, a first year college student, must face the complexities of the world without Bernie's help. Emma learns about her family's history, society's obsession with color, and the torments of racism. She discovers how her father, who grew up in the South during segregation, overcame the obstacles he faced and the price he paid to become a successful professor at Princeton. Her journey is insightful but difficult. Although this is Raboteau's debut novel, her short fiction won a Pushcart Prize and the *Chicago Tribune's* Nelson Algren Award.

Where it's reviewed:
Chicago Tribune Books, January 23, 2005, page 1
Kirkus Reviews, December 1, 2004, page 1111

Other books you might like:
William Faulkner, *Light in August*, 1959
Nella Larsen, *Passing*, 1929
Richard Powers, *The Time of Our Singing*, 2003
Alice Randall, *The Wind Done Gone*, 2001
Jane Stevenson, *The Empress of the Last Days*, 2004

IAN RANKIN

Fleshmarket Alley

(New York: Little, Brown, 2005)

Story type: Mystery
Series: Inspector John Rebus. Book 15
Subject(s): Police Procedural; Emigration and Immigration; Murder
Major character(s): John Rebus, Detective—Police; Siobhan Clarke, Detective—Police
Time period(s): 2000s
Locale(s): Edinburgh, Scotland

Summary: Inspector John Rebus returns once again in his never ending fight to make the streets of Edinburgh safe. When the corpse of a Kurdish refugee turns up, what appears to be a simple murder case turns out to be very complicated. Rebus, of course, connects the dots with help from his friend Siobhan Clarke. She is working on a rape case in which the victim committed suicide. Links between the two cases develop when two bodies are uncovered in a pub. This directs the investigation toward the red light district, where police find an elaborate slave labor scheme.

Where it's reviewed:
Booklist, December 1, 2004, page 619
Kirkus Reviews, December 15, 2004, page 1169
Library Journal, January 2005, page 85
New York Times, February 14, 2005, page 8
Publishers Weekly, January 10, 2005, page 41

Other books by the same author:
Witch Hunt, 2004
Watchman, 2003
A Good Hanging, 2002

The Falls, 2001
Set in Darkness, 2000

Other books you might like:
Boris Akunin, *The Winter Queen*, 2003
Andre Dubus III, *House of Sand and Fog*, 1999
Alan Furst, *Dark Voyage*, 2004
John Le Carre, *Absolute Friends*, 2003
George P. Pelecanos, *The Big Blowdown*, 1996

1217

NANCY RAWLES

My Jim

(New York: Crown, 2004)

Story type: Historical
Subject(s): African Americans; Grandparents; Psychological
Major character(s): Sadie Watson, Grandparent, Slave (former); Jim, Slave, Spouse (of Sadie); Huck, Teenager, Friend (Jim's)
Time period(s): 19th century
Locale(s): South

Summary: At first glance, this is the story of Jim, the slave who escaped bondage floating down the river with Huckleberry Finn. However, this story is told by the woman he left behind, Sadie Watson. Now a free woman telling Jim's story to her granddaughter, Sadie's intent clearly is to impress the child with the importance of love and devotion. Although Sadie never wavers in her devotion to Jim, she suffers terribly because of it. Nevertheless, she refuses to give up her love.

Where it's reviewed:
Booklist, November 15, 2004, page 563
Kirkus Reviews, November 15, 2004, page 1065
New York Times Book Review, January 30, 2005, page 26
Publishers Weekly, November 29, 2004, page 22

Other books by the same author:
Crawfish Dreams, 2003
Love Like Gumbo, 1997

Other books you might like:
Hannah Crafts, *The Bondwoman's Narrative*, 2003
    Henry Louis Gates, editor
David Anthony Durham, *Walk through Darkness*, 2002
Ernest J. Gaines, *The Autobiography of Miss Jane Pittman*, 1982
Edward P. Jones, *The Known World*, 2004
Alice Randall, *The Wind Done Gone*, 2001

1218

RICHARD RAYNER

The Devil's Wind

(New York: HarperCollins, 2005)

Story type: Mystery
Subject(s): Organized Crime; Nuclear Weapons; Political Movements
Major character(s): Maurice Valentine, Architect; Mallory Walker, Young Woman; Paul Mantilini, Organized Crime Figure

Time period(s): 1950s
Locale(s): Las Vegas, Nevada

Summary: Maurice Valentine sells his soul for the good life. He marries a woman he doesn't love because she has money and social position. Squandering his talent as an architect, he designs casinos and subdivisions earmarked for destruction on a testing range for the atomic bomb. Then, one day everything gets thrown up for grabs when blonde bombshell Mallory Walker walks into his life. A love affair ensues and Mallory turns up murdered. While attempting to solve the mystery, Maurice is forced to recognize the superficial life he has constructed and to face up to the character flaws that drive him.

Where it's reviewed:
Booklist, February 1, 2005, page 947
Chicago Tribune Books, February 20, 2005, page 2
Kirkus Reviews, November 1, 2004, page 1027
Library Journal, January 2005, page 100
Publishers Weekly, January 10, 2005, page 39

Other books by the same author:
Drake's Fortune, 2002
The Cloud Sketcher, 2000
Murder Book, 1997
The Blue Suit, 1995
The Elephant, 1992

Other books you might like:
William F. Buckley Jr., *Getting It Right*, 2003
James Lee Burke, *Burning Angel*, 1982
James Ellroy, *The Cold Six Thousand*, 2001
Eric Garcia, *Matchstick Men*, 2002
John Grisham, *The Firm*, 1991

1219

CHRISTOPHER RICE

Light Before Day

(New York: Hyperion, 2005)

Story type: Contemporary/Mainstream; Gay/Lesbian Fiction
Subject(s): Alcoholism; Drugs; Authors and Writers
Major character(s): Adam Murphy, Homosexual, Journalist; James Wilton, Writer (crime novels)
Time period(s): 2000s
Locale(s): West Hollywood, California

Summary: Rice's novel follows a gay journalist as he strives to build a successful career. When Adam Murphy gets fired, he is hired by crime writer James Wilton to follow up on allegations from a porn star that a helicopter pilot is a closet gay. Then several gays turn up murdered. Could it be the work of a homophobic serial killer or is there some connection with the helicopter pilot? Adam's efforts turn up a blackmail scheme and a child porn ring.

Where it's reviewed:
Booklist, January 1, 2005, page 784
Kirkus Reviews, January 1, 2005, page 17
Library Journal, March 1, 2005, page 80
Publishers Weekly, February 14, 2005, page 54

Other books by the same author:
The Snow Garden, 2001
A Density of Souls, 2000

Other books you might like:
Reed Arvin, *The Wind in the Wheat*, 1994
Madison Smartt Bell, *Anything Goes*, 2002
Michael Chabon, *The Amazing Adventures of Kavalier & Clay*, 2000
Alan Hollinghurst, *The Line of Beauty*, 2004
Jamie O'Neill, *At Swim, Two Boys*, 2003

1220

KIMBERLA LAWSON ROBY

The Best-Kept Secret

(New York: William Morrow, 2005)

Story type: Domestic
Series: Curtis Black. Book 2
Subject(s): Marriage; African Americans; Clergy
Major character(s): Curtis Black, Religious (minister), Spouse (Charlotte's husband); Charlotte Black, Parent, Girlfriend (Aaron's); Aaron, Friend (Curtis')
Time period(s): 2000s
Locale(s): Illinois

Summary: In this sequel to *Too Much of a Good Thing* (2004), three times is not a charm for the Rev. Curtis Black. Although Curtis is determined to mend his womanizing ways and devote his life to his family and church, his third wife has other ideas. Charlotte finds the good life is much too boring for her. She's not sure that Matthew is Curtis' son, but it doesn't worry her. She is much more interested in wild sex with Aaron, Curtis' best friend. Of course, Curtis finds out, leading to unexpected consequences.

Where it's reviewed:
Booklist, February 1, 2005, page 937
Publishers Weekly, January 10, 2005, page 39

Other books by the same author:
Too Much of a Good Thing, 2004
A Taste of Reality, 2003
It's a Thin Line, 2001
Casting the First Stone, 2000
Here and Now, 1999

Other books you might like:
Benjamin Anastas, *The Faithful Narrative of a Pastor's Disappearance*, 2001
Frederick Barthelme, *Second Marriage*, 1984
Ralph Ellison, *Juneteenth*, 1999
   John F. Callahan, editor
E. Lynn Harris, *Any Way the Wind Blows*, 2001
Heather Neff, *Accident of Birth*, 2004

1221

LUIS J. RODRIGUEZ

Music of the Mill

(New York: Rayo, 2005)

Story type: Historical; Domestic

Subject(s): Mexican Americans; Children; Emigration and Immigration
Major character(s): Procopio Salcido, Immigrant, Worker (steel mill); Johnny Salcido, Worker (steel mill), Labor Organizer; Azucena Salcido, Young Woman (Johnny's daughter)
Time period(s): 20th century (1944-1999)
Locale(s): Los Angeles, California

Summary: This is a family saga of epic proportions, tracing the struggles of the Salcido family through three generations as their hopes and dreams collide with a harsh social reality. Leaving Mexico in 1944, Procopio and his future wife Eladia walk hundreds of miles, finally settling in Los Angeles. World War II is driving the booming industrial economy. Despite blatant discrimination, Procopio finds a job at a steel mill. Years later, his son Johnny gets a job at the same place. Johnny becomes a union leader and a convenient target for management's unscrupulous tactics. After the mill is closed, granddaughter Azucena narrates the story.

Where it's reviewed:
Kirkus Reviews, March 15, 2005, page 312
Library Journal, April 1, 2005, page 88

Other books you might like:
Sandra Cisneros, *Caramelo*, 2002
Alicia Erian, *Towelhead*, 2005
Jhumpa Lahiri, *The Namesake*, 2003
Mary Helen Stefaniak, *The Turk and My Mother*, 2004
Irene Zabytko, *When Luba Leaves Home*, 2003

1222

JAMES SALTER

Last Night

(New York: Knopf, 2005)

Story type: Collection; Adult
Subject(s): Relationships; Short Stories; Redemption
Time period(s): 2000s
Locale(s): United States

Summary: Salter's work collects ten short stories dealing with varying aspects of passion, which show each relationship between a man and a woman to be unique. In the title story, a man must deal with his wife's request for assisted suicide and nothing goes as planned. A man in "Comet" confronts the reality of his marriage. An unhappy woman becomes fixated on a former lover's dog in "My Lord You." Old flames meet each other coincidentally in "Palm Court" and "Bangkok" with some interesting twists. A career army man suffers at the hands of his wife in "Arlington." Other stories are "Such Fun," "Give," and "Platinum."

Where it's reviewed:
Booklist, March 1, 2005, page 1142
Chicago Tribune Books, April 17, 2005, page 4
Kirkus Reviews, February 15, 2005, page 195
Publishers Weekly, February 14, 2005, page 51

Other books by the same author:
Cassada, 2000
Dusk and Other Stories, 1988
Solo Faces, 1979

A Sport and a Pastime, 1967
The Hunters, 1956

Other books you might like:
Carolyn Banks, *Mr. Right*, 1999
Robert Olen Butler, *They Whisper*, 1994
Gwen Davis, *The Princess and the Pauper*, 1989
David Galef, *Flesh*, 1995
Barry Gifford, *Wild at Heart*, 1990

1223

LYNNE SHARON SCHWARTZ

Writing on the Wall

(New York: Counterpoint, 2005)

Story type: Contemporary/Mainstream
Subject(s): Modern Life; Terrorism; Memory
Major character(s): Renata, Scholar (public library), Twin; Claudia, Twin (Renata's sister), Parent (Gianna's mother); Gianna, Child (Renata's niece)
Time period(s): 2000s (2001)
Locale(s): New York, New York

Summary: Renata, a language expert, is forced to face unresolved emotional problems after the attack on the World Trade Center on September 11, 2001. She has repressed feelings associated with her twin sister's death, her father's death, and her mother's mental illness. Claudia, 16, died shortly after giving birth to a daughter, Gianna, who was given up for adoption. Renata's father died in a car crash less than a year later. Subsequently, her mother was institutionalized. After coming to live with Renata, Gianna disappeared. Following the terrorist attack, Renata seeks support from her social worker boyfriend and coworkers to deal with the current tragedy and her own demons from the past.

Where it's reviewed:
Kirkus Reviews, April 1, 2005, page 383
Library Journal, April 1, 2005, page 88

Other books you might like:
Ted Bell, *Assassin*, 2004
Tom Clancy, *The Sum of All Fears*, 1991
Jonathan Safran Foer, *Extremely Loud & Incredibly Close*, 2005
Ian McEwan, *Saturday*, 2005
Reynolds Price, *The Good Priest's Son*, 2005

1224

GERALD SEYMOUR

The Unknown Soldier

(Woodstock, New York: Overlook, 2005)

Story type: Action/Adventure
Subject(s): Terrorism; Psychological Thriller; Identity, Concealed
Major character(s): Caleb Hunt, Terrorist; Eddie Wroughton, Spy (British); Jed Dietrich, Spy (American)
Time period(s): 2000s
Locale(s): Guantanamo Bay, Cuba; Afghanistan; Saudi Arabia

Summary: After spending two years in an American prison camp in Cuba, Abu Kaleb convinces his captors that he is really an innocent taxi driver. In the process of being sent back to Afghanistan, Abu Kaleb escapes. When American and British intelligence realize that Kaleb is really Caleb Hunt, a terrorist mastermind for Al-Qaeda, the chase is on. As the Allies track Caleb, he attempts to join up with his terrorist cell in the middle of the Saudi Arabian desert, where he will obtain a dirty bomb, designed to deliver death and destruction to an American city.

Where it's reviewed:
Kirkus Reviews, December 15, 2004, page 1162
Library Journal, February 1, 2005, page 70
Publishers Weekly, January 10, 2005, page 37

Other books by the same author:
A Line in the Sand, 2000
Dead Ground, 1999
Killing Ground, 1997
The Heart of Danger, 1995
The Fighting Man, 1993

Other books you might like:
David Baldacci, *Hour Game*, 2004
Nelson DeMille, *Night Fall*, 2004
John Le Carre, *Absolute Friends*, 2003
Robert Littell, *The Company*, 2002
Charles McCarry, *Old Boys*, 2004

1225

SANDI KAHN SHELTON

What Comes After Crazy

(New York: Shaye Areheart, 2005)

Story type: Domestic; Romance
Subject(s): Divorce; Mothers and Daughters; Humor
Major character(s): Masden "Maz" Lombard, Single Parent (two daughters); Hope Lombard, Child; Abbie Lombard, Child
Time period(s): 2000s
Locale(s): United States

Summary: Maz Lombard longs for a quiet, normal life but it's unlikey she will get one. When Maz was growing up, her mother divided her time between telling celebrity fortunes and collecting men. Maz got tired counting new stepfathers; now she is a single mother trying to raise two daughters, while earning a living. Maz has just met an eligible man and is worried her family will scare him off. Meanwhile, Hope, who is ten, spends her time holding seances, telling fortunes, and frightening the neighborhood children.

Where it's reviewed:
Kirkus Reviews, January 1, 2005, page 19
Library Journal, February 15, 2005, page 121
Publishers Weekly, February 7, 2005, page 43

Other books you might like:
Elizabeth Berg, *Open House*, 2000
Kate Bridges, *The Midwife's Secret*, 2003
Margaret Drabble, *The Seven Sisters*, 2002
Carrie Fisher, *The Best Awful*, 2005
Jennifer Greene, *Wild in the Moonlight*, 2004

1226

CAROL SHIELDS

Collected Stories

(New York: Fourth Estate, 2005)

Story type: Collection
Subject(s): Short Stories; Authors and Writers; Modern Life
Time period(s): 2000s

Summary: Canadian writer Carol Shields, who died in 2003, is best-known for her Pulitzer Prize-winning novel *The Stone Diaries*. However, in the course of a career that spanned 30 years, she was recognized in literary circles for her short story writing, too. This volume, which is introduced by her friend and fellow Canadian Margaret Atwood, offers an opportunity to savor Shields' light touch dealing with day-to-day living and her skill at illuminating the small but defining moments in the lives of her characters. All but one of the stories ("Segue") have been previously published.

Where it's reviewed:
Booklist, December 15, 2004, page 709
Library Journal, January 2005, page 104
New York Times Book Review, February 6, 2005, page 22
Publishers Weekly, January 24, 2005, page 223

Other books by the same author:
Unless, 2002
Dressing Up for the Carnival, 2000
Larry's Party, 1997
The Stone Diaries, 1994
The Box Garden, 1977

Other books you might like:
Margaret Atwood, *Dancing Girls and Other Stories*, 1977
Bobbie Ann Mason, *Zigzagging Down a Wild Trial*, 2001
Alice Munro, *Hateship, Friendship, Courtship, Loveship, Marriage*, 2001
Annie Proulx, *Bad Dirt*, 2004
William Trevor, *A Bit on the Side*, 2004

1227

JAMES SIEGEL

Detour

(New York: Warner, 2005)

Story type: Psychological Suspense
Subject(s): Drugs; Kidnapping; Blackmail
Major character(s): Paul Breibard, Spouse (Joanna's husband), Crime Victim (kidnapped); Joanna Breibard, Captive (hostage); Miles Goldstein, Lawyer
Time period(s): 2000s
Locale(s): New York, New York; Bogata, Colombia

Summary: Paul and Joanna, an affluent American couple, are unable to have a family of their own, so they decide to adopt a child. Arrangements are made with an orphanage in Colombia. The couple flies to South America to pick up the baby, but they are kidnapped and threatened with death. To secure their freedom Paul agrees to carry drugs back to the United States. The kidnappers hold his wife hostage until he returns with the money. The plot thickens when Paul is unable to deliver the

Popular Fiction

drugs. He seeks help first from his lawyer, an Orthodox Jew, and then a Russian mobster to save his wife's life.

Where it's reviewed:
Booklist, December 15, 2004, page 640
Kirkus Reviews, December 15, 2004, page 1162
Publishers Weekly, January 10, 2005, page 36

Other books by the same author:
Derailed, 2003
Epitaph, 2001

Other books you might like:
Madison Smartt Bell, *Straight Cut*, 1986
Tom Clancy, *The Teeth of the Tiger*, 2003
John Grisham, *The Broker*, 2005
James Patterson, *Kiss the Girls*, 1995
George P. Pelecanos, *Drama City*, 2005

1228
MARISA SILVER

No Direction Home
(New York: Norton, 2005)

Story type: Domestic; Coming-of-Age
Subject(s): Relationships; Adolescence; Illegal Immigrants
Major character(s): Will Burton, Twin (Ethan's brother); Ethan Burton, Twin (Will's brother); Caroline Burton, Single Parent (husband walked out)
Time period(s): 2000s
Locale(s): Ohio; California; Mexico

Summary: Abandonment, guilt, and longing are themes in this debut novel. Frank, Caroline's husband, abandons her and their twin sons, Ethan and Will. The boys have a rare disease that will cause them to go blind. Caroline moves with the boys to her parents' home in Los Angeles. Her mother suffers from dementia and her father feels responsible. The family hires an illegal alien named Amador as a caregiver, and Caroline has an affair with him. Amador has left a family behind in Mexico, and his son, Rogelio comes looking for him. Meanwhile, Frank's illegitimate daughter Marlene comes from Ohio in hopes of finding him.

Where it's reviewed:
Kirkus Reviews, March 15, 2005, page 313
Library Journal, April 1, 2005, page 88
Publishers Weekly, March 21, 2005, page 34

Other books by the same author:
Babe in Paradise, 2001

Other books you might like:
Chimamanda Ngozi Adichie, *Purple Hibiscus*, 2003
Ann Beattie, *Love Always*, 1985
Elizabeth Berg, *True to Form*, 2002
Robert Boswell, *American Owned Love*, 1997
Larry Brown, *Fay*, 2000

1229
CURTIS SITTENFELD

Prep
(New York: Random House, 2005)

Story type: Contemporary/Mainstream; Coming-of-Age
Subject(s): Humor; Adolescence; School Life
Major character(s): Lee Fiora, Teenager, Student—High School; Cross, Lover (of Lee)
Time period(s): 2000s
Locale(s): Massachusetts; South Bend, Indiana

Summary: Sittenfeld's debut novel explores adolescence from the perspective of a teenage girl from the Midwest who gets a scholarship to an elite Eastern prep school. Lee Fiora grows up in South Bend but finds herself going to high school in Massachusetts. She is charmed by the notion of attending an ideal school where boys and girls are socialized to appreciate tradition and each other. Of course, reality doesn't live up to her expectations. She finds snooty rich kids who prefer talking to each other rather than an outsider from Indiana. By the time she reaches her senior year, Lee succeeds in carving out her own place. However, complications develop and for awhile she becomes her own worst enemy.

Where it's reviewed:
Booklist, December 15, 2004, page 709
Kirkus Reviews, November 15, 2004, page 1067
Library Journal, December 2004, page 103
New York Times Book Review, January 16, 2005, page 17
Publishers Weekly, November 1, 2004, page 41

Other books you might like:
Don DeLillo, *Cosmopolis*, 2003
Nick McDonell, *Twelve*, 2002
John O'Hara, *Appointment in Samarra*, 1934
J.D. Salinger, *The Catcher in the Rye*, 1951
Tobias Wolff, *Old School*, 2003

1230
NICHOLAS SPARKS

True Believer
(New York: Warner, 2005)

Story type: Ghost Story
Subject(s): Authors and Writers; Science; Cemeteries
Major character(s): Jeremy Marsh, Writer (science); Doris McClellan, Psychic, Grandparent (Lexie's grandmother); Lexie Darnell, Librarian
Time period(s): 2000s
Locale(s): Boone Creek, North Carolina

Summary: Sparks is back with another story about true love. Jeremy Marsh is a science writer with a penchant for exposing hoaxes. He takes an assignment to investigate lights in a cemetery in North Carolina. There he meets Lexie Darnell, a librarian whose grandmother is the town psychic. As can be expected, complications that keep Jeremy and Lexie apart develop.

Where it's reviewed:
Booklist, March 15, 2005, page 1247

Library Journal, April 15, 2005, page 79
Publishers Weekly, March 21, 2005, page 37

Other books by the same author:
The Guardian, 2003
The Wedding, 2003
A Bend in the Road, 2001
Message in a Bottle, 1998
The Notebook, 1996

Other books you might like:
John Banville, *Eclipse*, 2001
Lisa Carey, *In the Country of the Young*, 2000
R.A. Dick, *The Ghost and Mrs. Muir*, 1945
Stewart O'Nan, *The Night Country*, 2003
Alice Sebold, *The Lovely Bones*, 2002

1231

DARCEY STEINKE

Milk

(New York: Bloomsbury, 2005)

Story type: Psychological; Adult
Subject(s): Friendship; Spirituality; Sexual Behavior
Major character(s): Mary, Parent (one child); Walter, Religious (Episcopal priest), Homosexual; John, Religious (ex-monk), Boyfriend (Mary's)
Time period(s): 2000s
Locale(s): New York, New York (Brooklyn)

Summary: Steinke's work explores sexuality and spirituality in the lives of three characters: a young mother, a gay priest, and a former monk. Mary, feeling neglected, seeks support outside her marriage. John, who left the emotional support of his church, is looking for physical contact. Walter, an Episcopal priest, is Mary's friend from college. Mary and John struggle to make a connection with each other. Meanwhile, Walter mourns the loss of his gay lover.

Where it's reviewed:
Chicago Tribune Books, February 13, 2005, page 3
Kirkus Reviews, December 1, 2004, page 1114
Library Journal, February 1, 2005, page 71
Publishers Weekly, December 20, 2004, page 35

Other books by the same author:
Jesus Saves, 1997
Suicide Blonde, 1992
Up through the Water, 1989

Other books you might like:
Margaret Atwood, *Oryx and Crake*, 2003
Julian Barnes, *Love, etc.*, 2001
Frederick Barthelme, *Tracer*, 1985
Sandra Brown, *Not Even for Love*, 2003
James M. Cain, *Mildred Pierce*, 1945

1232

PHILIPPA STOCKLEY

A Factory of Cunning

(Orlando, Florida: Harcourt, 2005)

Story type: Historical/Georgian
Subject(s): Women; Scandal; Revenge
Major character(s): Mrs. Fox, Noblewoman; Urban Fine, Nobleman (Earl of Much)
Time period(s): 18th century
Locale(s): London, England; Netherlands; France

Summary: Mrs. Fox is a wheeler-dealer among the lords, ladies, dukes, and duchesses of 18th-century London. She has just arrived from continental Europe and is determined to make a lot of money and to make a place for herself, while living in style. To accomplish her goal, she needs to escape her scandalous past, which includes employment in a Dutch brothel. Also, there's an avenger who has followed her from France. Mrs. Fox is lively, manipulative, and well-versed in the art of seduction. However, this time she may very well have met her match. Greed, lust, and lunacy abound in this bird's-eye view of the amoral upper classes of the time.

Where it's reviewed:
Kirkus Reviews, January 1, 2005, page 20
Library Journal, March 1, 2005, page 81
Publishers Weekly, February 7, 2005, page 38

Other books by the same author:
The Edge of Pleasure, 2002

Other books you might like:
Isabel Colegate, *The Shooting Party*, 1980
Julian Fellowes, *Snobs*, 2005
Henry James, *The American*, 1877
D.H. Lawrence, *Lady Chatterley's Lover*, 1928
John O'Hara, *A Rage to Live*, 1949

1233

JAMES SWAIN

Mr. Lucky

(New York: Ballantine, 2005)

Story type: Mystery
Subject(s): Fathers and Sons; Gambling; Cheating
Major character(s): Tony Valentine, Detective—Private (ex-cop); Ricky Smith, Gambler
Time period(s): 2000s
Locale(s): Slippery Rock, North Carolina

Summary: Tony Valentine has a knack for spotting con men, scam artists, and cheaters. He developed his skills working the casinos as a cop in Atlantic City. However, with all his experience, Tony has never encountered the likes of Ricky Smith, alias, Mr. Lucky. Once upon a time, he was a loser. Then one day he escaped from a hotel fire and his luck turned around. Mr. Lucky wins at everything: slots, craps, blackjack, roulette, horse racing, and even the lottery. Tony, who knows no one could be that lucky, gets involved when Smith comes to Slippery Rock, North Carolina, and the local casino hires Tony to investigate him. Soon Tony's family is in harm's way

and the police are after Tony in connection with a double homicide investigation.

Where it's reviewed:
Booklist, February 1, 2005, page 948
Kirkus Reviews, January 1, 2005, page 24
Publishers Weekly, February 7, 2005, page 41

Other books by the same author:
Loaded Dice, 2004
Sucker Bet, 2003
Funny Money, 2002
Grift Sense, 2001
The Man Who Walked through Walls, 198xx

Other books you might like:
Sandra Brown, *Hello Darkness*, 2003
James Lee Burke, *Sunset Limited*, 1998
Michael Connelly, *Void Moon*, 2000
Ed McBain, *Widows*, 1991
George P. Pelecanos, *Shame the Devil*, 2000

1234

CECELIA TISHY

Now You See Her

(New York: Mysterious, 2005)

Story type: Psychological; Mystery
Subject(s): Property Rights; Haunted Houses; Divorce
Major character(s): Regina Cutter, Detective—Amateur, Divorced Person; Francis Devaney, Detective—Homicide; Henry Faiser, Convict (convicted of murder)
Time period(s): 2000s
Locale(s): Boston, Massachusetts

Summary: This is a mystery story with a paranormal twist. After her husband leaves her for a younger woman, Regina ''Reggie'' Cutter moves back to Boston to a townhouse her aunt left her. As it turns out, Reggie has also inherited her aunt's psychic skills, although she isn't able to summon these skills on demand. Nevertheless, a realtor friend asks her to cleanse an alleged haunted house. Then Boston detective Francis Devaney asks Reggie to help him on an investigation that has gone cold. Henry Faiser, an African American, has spent 13 years in jail for the murder of a politician's son. Faiser claims he is innocent and Devaney wants Reggie's help.

Where it's reviewed:
Booklist, January 1, 2005, page 829
Chicago Tribune Books, February 20, 2005, page 2
Kirkus Reviews, December 15, 2004, page 1170
Publishers Weekly, January 3, 2005, page 39

Other books by the same author:
Jealous Heart, 1997

Other books you might like:
Barbara Taylor Bradford, *Emma's Secret*, 2004
Dan Brown, *The Da Vinci Code*, 2003
Mary Higgins Clark, *Before I Say Good-Bye*, 2000
Dean R. Koontz, *By the Light of the Moon*, 2002
Nora Roberts, *Captivated*, 1993

1235

JONATHAN TROPPER

Everything Changes

(New York: Delacorte, 2005)

Story type: Psychological
Subject(s): Modern Life; Friendship; Grief
Major character(s): Zack King, Young Man; Rael, Accident Victim (killed in crash), Friend (Zack's); Norm King, Parent (Zack's father)
Time period(s): 2000s
Locale(s): New York, New York

Summary: Zack King is old before his time. When his father walks out, Zack, 3, is the oldest child. He grows up being responsible, trying to fill the vacancy his father left behind. Zack's serious life appears to have paid off. At age 32, he has his own apartment in Manhattan, a good job, and a beautiful rich fiancee. Sure enough, trouble emerges. First, Zack's best friend Rael dies in an automobile accident, leaving a wife and baby. Then, Zack's father shows up, throwing everything up for grabs with his plans to enter into the lives of the family he abandoned. Meanwhile, Zack finds himself attracted to Rael's widow. Instead of his usual approach, Zack throws caution to the winds. Soon everything in his life comes apart and he must somehow put it all back together.

Where it's reviewed:
Booklist, March 15, 2005, page 1268
Kirkus Reviews, February 15, 2005, page 197
Library Journal, April 1, 2005, page 89
Publishers Weekly, February 21, 2005, page 156

Other books by the same author:
The Book of Joe, 2004
Plan B, 2000

Other books you might like:
Jonathan Ames, *Wake Up, Sir!*, 2004
Madison Smartt Bell, *Anything Goes*, 2002
Saul Bellow, *The Adventures of Augie March*, 1953
Marshall Boswell, *Trouble with Girls*, 2003
A.S. Byatt, *The Biographer's Tale*, 2000

1236

LUIS ALBERTO URREA

The Hummingbird's Daughter

(New York: Little, Brown, 2005)

Story type: Historical/Post-American Civil War; Coming-of-Age
Subject(s): Adolescence; Near-Death Experience; Healing
Major character(s): Teresita, Heroine, Healer; Don Tomas Urrea, Rancher
Time period(s): 1870s (1873)
Locale(s): Southwest; Mexico

Summary: Urrea dips his pen into the inkwell of magic realism in a saga set in 19th-century Mexico. A young Indian girl impregnated by a rich rancher gives birth to Teresita. From an early age, she shows great promise, despite being raised in poverty. She has healing power, can read and write, ride a

horse, and play music. As a teenager, she is raped and dies. During her wake, she comes back from the dead, an act that is condemned by the government and the church. While fantastic, the story paints a realistic picture of the tumultuous border area between Mexico and the United States shortly after the U.S. Civil War.

Where it's reviewed:
Publishers Weekly, April 18, 2005, page 44

Other books by the same author:
Six Kinds of Sky, 2002
In Search of Snow, 1994

Other books you might like:
Jean Auel, *The Mammoth Hunters*, 1985
Michael Blake, *Dances with Wolves*, 1988
Laura Esquivel, *Like Water for Chocolate*, 1992
Charles Frazier, *Cold Mountain*, 1997
Gabriel Garcia Marquez, *One Hundred Years of Solitude*, 1970

1237

BRENDA RICKMAN VANTREASE

The Illuminator
(New York: St. Martin's Press, 2005)

Story type: Historical/Medieval
Subject(s): Inheritance; Widows/Widowers; Bible
Major character(s): Finn, Artist, Widow(er); Lady Kathryn, Noblewoman; John Wycliffe, Historical Figure, Religious (priest)
Time period(s): 14th century
Locale(s): Oxford, England

Summary: Retired librarian Vantrease makes her debut with a historical novel set in 14th-century England. There are no printing presses and books are very expensive. Scribes make a living copying sacred texts in Latin and Norman French, texts which aren't accessible to the common man. Finn, a scribe during the day, spends his nights copying the Bible for the heretic John Wycliffe. Subsequently, Lady Kathryn puts up Finn and his daughter in return for protection from the monastery that employs Finn. A relationship soon develops between Finn and Lady Kathryn. Complexities set in when a plot twist puts Finn and Lady Kathryn at risk.

Where it's reviewed:
Booklist, February 15, 2005, page 1062
Kirkus Reviews, January 15, 2005, page 82
Library Journal, March 1, 2005, page 81
Publishers Weekly, February 7, 2005, page 41

Other books you might like:
Simonetta Agnello Hornby, *The Almond Picker*, 2005
Dan Brown, *The Da Vinci Code*, 2003
Susanna Clarke, *Jonathan Strange & Mr. Norrell*, 2004
Susann Cokal, *Mirabilis*, 2001
Emma Donoghue, *Life Mask*, 2004

1238

WILLIAM T. VOLLMANN

Europe Central
(New York: Viking, 2005)

Story type: Historical/World War II; Post-Holocaust
Subject(s): War; Russians; Nazis
Major character(s): Dmitri Shostakovich, Composer (of classical music), Historical Figure; Kurt Gerstein, Military Personnel (SS officer), Historical Figure; Anna Akhmatova, Writer (poet), Historical Figure
Time period(s): 1930s; 1940s (1939-1945)
Locale(s): Germany; Union of Soviet Socialist Republics

Summary: After writing about the Virginia Colony of Jamestown in *Argall* (2001), Vollmann turns his attention to World War II and he doesn't take an easy road. His work focuses on the Eastern Front, specifically the war between Germany and Russia. To make this epic manageable, he mixes historical figures including Kathe Kollwitz, Dmitri Shostakovich, Kurt Gerstein, and General Friedrich Paulus with fictional characters of his own. Kollwitz is a German artist, while Shostakovich is a Russian composer. Paulus commands the German 6th Army and is defeated at the battle of Stalingrad, a turning point on the Eastern Front. Gerstein is an SS officer who attempts to get the word out about the Holocaust. There are many others who contribute to make this a tour de force for Vollmann.

Where it's reviewed:
Booklist, January 1, 2005, page 784
New York Times Book Review, April 3, 2005, page 16
Publishers Weekly, February 7, 2005, page 38

Other books by the same author:
Argall, 2001
The Royal Family, 2000
Butterfly Stories, 1993
The Rifles, 1993
The Ice-Shirt, 1990

Other books you might like:
Jonathan Safran Foer, *Extremely Loud & Incredibly Close*, 2005
Gunter Grass, *Crabwalk*, 2002
Kazuo Ishiguro, *When We Were Orphans*, 2000
Ian McEwan, *Saturday*, 2005
Philip Roth, *The Plot Against America*, 2004

1239

JESS WALTER

Citizen Vince
(New York: ReganBooks, 2005)

Story type: Mystery
Subject(s): Law Enforcement; Crime and Criminals; Politics
Major character(s): Vince Camden, Criminal (in hiding); Ray Scatieri, Murderer (contract killer)
Time period(s): 1980s (1980)
Locale(s): Spokane, Washington; New York, New York

Popular Fiction

Summary: The federal government gives Marty Hagen, a small time New York City criminal, a new identity. He becomes Vince Camden and receives a new lease on life via the federal witness protection program. The feds move Vince to Spokane, Washington, and get him a job as a manager of a donut shop. Now, for the first time in his life, Vince decides to vote. The presidential election is only a week away and Vince must choose between the incumbent, Jimmy Carter, and the challenger, Ronald Reagan. While he mulls over the pros and cons of each candidate, Vince encounters a man from his past, Ray Scatieri, a paid killer. Vince correctly assumes that the mob has sent Scatieri to kill him. If Vince is going to vote, he is going to have to get the mob to call off Scatieri.

Where it's reviewed:
Booklist, November 15, 2004, page 566
Kirkus Reviews, September 1, 2004, page 836
Library Journal, March 15, 2005, page 76
New York Times, April 18, 2005, page B6

Other books by the same author:
Land of the Blind, 2003
Over Tumbled Graves, 2001

Other books you might like:
Pete Dexter, *Train*, 2003
John Grisham, *The Broker*, 2005
Ursula Hegi, *Salt Dancers*, 1995
George V. Higgins, *At End of Day*, 2000
Patricia H. Rushford, *Secrets, Lies & Alibis*, 2003

1240

REBECCA WELLS

Ya-Yas in Bloom

(New York: HarperCollins, 2005)

Story type: Domestic
Subject(s): Grandparents; Women; Friendship
Major character(s): Vivi Abbott Walker, Friend (of Teensy); Teensy Whitman, Friend (of Caro); Caro, Friend (of Vivi, Teensy, and Necie)
Time period(s): 20th century (1930s-1990)
Locale(s): Louisiana

Summary: Wells offers another set of snapshots from the lives of four lifelong friends. The first set was in *Little Altars Everywhere* and the second set appeared in *Divine Secrets of the Ya-Ya Sisterhood*. In 1930, Teensy Whitman, 4, who has a pecan stuck in her nose, meets Vivi Abbott Walker, who has an earache, in a doctor's office. Before the year is out, Caro and Necie will round out the group. From there, the narrative bounces around to incidents in the 1960s (when they are all mothers) and in 1994 (when they are grandmothers). Humor, friendship, and an indomitable spirit drive the narrative.

Where it's reviewed:
Booklist, January 1, 2005, page 784
Kirkus Reviews, January 1, 2005, page 21
Library Journal, February 1, 2005, page 72
Publishers Weekly, February 14, 2005, page 53

Other books by the same author:
Divine Secrets of the Ya-Ya Sisterhood, 1996
Little Altars Everywhere, 1992

Other books you might like:
Ann Beattie, *My Life, Starring Dara Falcon*, 1997
Elizabeth Berg, *The Year of Pleasures*, 2005
Judy Blume, *Summer Sisters*, 1998
Fannie Flagg, *Fried Green Tomatoes at the Whistle-Stop Cafe*, 1987
Alisa Valdes-Rodriguez, *The Dirty Girls Social Club*, 2003

1241

LOUISE WENER

Goodnight Steve McQueen

(New York: Perennial, 2005)

Story type: Contemporary/Mainstream
Subject(s): Popular Culture; Relationships; Music and Musicians
Major character(s): Steve "Danny" McQueen, Musician (rock'n'roll); Alison, Girlfriend (of Danny)
Time period(s): 2000s
Locale(s): London, England

Summary: Wener draws on her experience as the lead singer for Sleeper, a British pop band, in this story that follows musician Steve "Danny" McQueen as he tries to become a rock star. Danny would rather hang around his girlfriend Alison than pursue the tedium of the music business. However, when Alison gets a temporary overseas assignment, she lays down the law, telling Danny to get legitimate work or get out. He doesn't want to lose Alison, so he looks up an old high school buddy who is with Scarface, a really hot band. They strike a deal for Danny's band to become Scarface's opening act and go on the road.

Where it's reviewed:
Booklist, January 1, 2005, page 824
Kirkus Reviews, January 1, 2005, page 21
Library Journal, January 2005, page 101

Other books by the same author:
The Perfect Play, 2003

Other books you might like:
Marshall Boswell, *Trouble with Girls*, 2003
Helen Fielding, *Bridget Jones's Diary*, 1996
Nick Hornby, *High Fidelity*, 1995
Elmore Leonard, *Be Cool*, 1999
Tim Winton, *Dirt Music*, 1995

1242

JOHN EDGAR WIDEMAN

God's Gym

(Boston: Houghton Mifflin, 2005)

Story type: Collection
Subject(s): Short Stories; African Americans; Cultures and Customs
Time period(s): 2000s
Locale(s): United States

Summary: Wideman offers ten short stories, all of which have been previously published. Most follow a stream of consciousness. Subjects explored include faith, gender, race,

friendship, family, llness, and grief. Included are ''Weight,'' which deals with the strength of a mother in a single-parent family and ''Sharing,'' which concerns a white woman and her African-American neighbors. A gun fight occurs in ''The Silence of Thelonious Monk,'' while small town racism emerges in ''Who Invented the Jump Shot.'' The complexity of dealing with someone in prison is dealt with in ''What We Cannot Speak about We Must Pass Over in Silence'' and questions about terminal illness and a dependent left behind is discussed in ''Are Dreams Faster than the Speed of Light.'' ''Sightings'' deals with memories of friends and acquaintances who have died. The other stories are ''Who Weeps When One of Us Goes Down Blues,'' ''Hunters,'' and ''Fanon.''

Where it's reviewed:
Booklist, December 1, 2004, page 619
Kirkus Reviews, December 1, 2004, page 1115
Library Journal, January 2005, page 104
New York Times Book Review, March 20, 2005, page 20
Publishers Weekly, January 10, 2005, page 36

Other books by the same author:
Two Cities, 1998
The Cattle Killing, 1996
All Stories Are True, 1993
Philadelphia Fire, 1990
Fever, 1989

Other books you might like:
James Baldwin, *Going to Meet the Man*, 1965
Bebe Moore Campbell, *Your Blues Ain't Like Mine*, 1992
Charles Waddell Chesnutt, *The Northern Stories of Charles W. Chesnutt*, 2004
    Charles Duncan, editor
Percival Everett, *Big Picture*, 1996
ZZ Packer, *Drinking Coffee Elsewhere*, 2003

1243

A.N. WILSON

My Name Is Legion
(New York: Farrar, Straus and Giroux, 2005)

Story type: Satire
Subject(s): Modern Life; Journalism; Politics
Major character(s): Vivyan Chell, Religious (Anglican monk); Lennox Mark, Publisher (of tabloid newspaper); General Bindiga, Political Figure (dictator)
Time period(s): 2000s
Locale(s): London, England; Zariya, Fictional Country

Summary: Wilson levels his sharp wit at a corrupt relationship between an African dictatorship and a London newspaper. The *Daily Legion* specializes in star-powered journalism, while neglecting serious subjects. Although Lennox Mark is the publisher, the newspaper is financially controlled by the government of Zariya. Once a British colony, Zariya is now run by a ruthless dictator, General Bindiga. When an Anglican monk, Vivyan Chell, organizes opposition to Bindiga, Mark hires Peter d'Abo to accuse the priest of pederasty. Peter is a mentally unstable young man, who doesn't know

the identity of his father. As it turns out, both Mark and Chell had a fling with the young man's mother.

Where it's reviewed:
Chicago Tribune Books, May 8, 2005, page 3
Kirkus Reviews, March 1, 2005, page 259
Publishers Weekly, March 14, 2005, page 44

Other books by the same author:
A Watch in the Night, 1996
The Vicar of Sorrows, 1993
Stray, 1989
Scandal, or, Priscilla's Kindness, 1983
Who Was Oswald Fish?, 1981

Other books you might like:
Philip Caputo, *Acts of Faith*, 2005
Richard Dooling, *White Man's Grave*, 1994
Zakes Mda, *The Heart of Redness*, 2002
John R. Powers, *The Last Catholic in America*, 1973
Francine Prose, *Hunters and Gatherers*, 1995

1244

ROBLEY WILSON

The World Still Melting
(New York: Thomas Dunne, 2005)

Story type: Domestic; Psychological Suspense
Subject(s): Marriage; Interpersonal Relations; Farm Life
Major character(s): Paul Tobler, Farmer, Crime Victim (murdered); Arlene Tobler, Spouse (Paul's wife); Harvey Riker, Neighbor (of Paul and Arlene), Murderer (of Paul)
Time period(s): 2000s
Locale(s): Iowa

Summary: Wilson examines small-time farming, contrasting its romantic connotations with its harsh reality. Paul and Arlene Tobler are determined to make it after she inherits her family's farm. In the face of falling crop prices, harsh weather conditions, and other uncertainties, they remain steadfast. Subsequently, they are drawn into a neighbor's marital dispute. Harvey Riker is upset with his wife Nancy, who is having an affair with another neighbor, Burton Stone. In a drunken rage Harvey goes after Burton but Paul intervenes and gets killed. After Harvey goes to jail, Nancy marries Burton. Although Arlene moves away, she remains friends with Nancy.

Where it's reviewed:
Booklist, December 15, 2004, page 710
Kirkus Reviews, December 1, 2004, page 1115
Library Journal, February 1, 2005, page 72

Other books by the same author:
Splendid Omens, 2004
The Book of Lost Feathers, 2001
The Victim's Daughter, 1991
Terrible Kisses, 1989
Dancing for Men, 1983

Other books you might like:
Margaret Atwood, *Oryx and Crake*, 2003
Julian Barnes, *Love, etc.*, 2001
Frederick Barthelme, *Tracer*, 1985

William Gay, *The Long Home*, 1999
Ha Jin, *Waiting*, 1999

1245

MARITTA WOLFF

Sudden Rain

(New York: Scribner, 2005)

Story type: Contemporary/Mainstream
Subject(s): Marriage; Politics; Modern Life
Major character(s): Tom Fallon, Businessman (defense industry), Spouse (Killian's husband); Killian Fallon, Housewife; Jim Holman, Engineer (defense industry)
Time period(s): 1970s
Locale(s): California

Summary: Maritta Wolff, who died in 2002, is the author of six other novels. After her death, her husband found this manuscript stashed away in a refrigerator. The book is set in Southern California suburbia in the 1970s and deals with marriage, politics, and the environment. The story, which spans four days, follows four couples. The men go off to work, while the women stay home and look after children. Love affairs, divorce, reconciliation, and parent-child relationships are facilitated by drinking, smoking, and conversation. Meanwhile, a hot Santa Ana wind mercilessly bakes the landscape.

Where it's reviewed:
Booklist, January 1, 2005, page 824
Kirkus Reviews, February 1, 2005, page 147
Library Journal, January 2005, page 102
New York Times, March 28, 2005, page B6
Publishers Weekly, February 21, 2005, page 154

Other books by the same author:
Buttonwood, 1962
The Big Nickelodeon, 1956
Back of Town, 1952
Night Shift, 1942
Whistle Stop, 1941

Other books you might like:
Alice Adams, *A Southern Exposure*, 1995
Martin Amis, *Yellow Dog*, 2003
Helen Humphreys, *Wild Dogs*, 2005
Yann Martel, *Life of Pi*, 2001
John Updike, *Memories of the Ford Administration*, 1992

1246

GILLEN D'ARCY WOOD

Hosack's Folly

(New York: Other Press, 2005)

Story type: Historical
Subject(s): Medicine; Yellow Fever; Politics
Major character(s): David Hosack, Historical Figure, Doctor (of public health); Albert Dash, Student—Graduate (of medicine); Eamonn Casey, Publisher
Time period(s): 1820s (1824)
Locale(s): New York, New York

Summary: History shows that aside from teaching at Columbia University, Dr. David Hosack was the attending physician at Alexander Hamilton's fatal duel and the founder of Bellevue Hospital. However, in the summer of 1824, when Hosack called upon New York City officials to quarantine the city's harbor in order to stave off a yellow fever outbreak, he was attacked in the press and discredited by city officials. They measured the quarantine, which would effectively shut down business, in terms of dollars and cents. Hosack measured the action in terms of public health. This is a fictionalized account of the events surrounding the yellow fever epidemic that vindicated Hosack.

Where it's reviewed:
Kirkus Reviews, February 1, 2005, page 147
Library Journal, April 1, 2005, page 90
Publishers Weekly, February 14, 2005, page 52

Other books you might like:
Geraldine Brooks, *Year of Wonders*, 2001
Elizabeth Gaffney, *Metropolis*, 2005
Pete Hamill, *Forever*, 2003
John Irving, *The Cider House Rules*, 1985
Liz Jensen, *The Ninth Life of Louis Drax*, 2004

1247

NANCY ZAFRIS

Lucky Strike

(Denver: Unbridled, 2005)

Story type: Historical; Domestic
Subject(s): Single Parent Families; Widows/Widowers; Miners and Mining
Major character(s): Jean Waterman, Widow(er), Parent (Beth and Charlie's mother); Harry Lindstrom, Salesman (of mining equipment); Miss Dazzle, Businesswoman (motel operator)
Time period(s): 1950s
Locale(s): Utah

Summary: In the 1950s, portions of the American West were inundated by people searching for uranium and the profits to be made from it, in much the same way as California was flooded with prospectors during the Gold Rush of 1849. This novel focuses on several characters who all have their own reasons for arriving in Utah, including Jean Waterman, a widow with two young children, Charlie, who has weak lungs, and Beth; Harry Lindstrom, who sells mining equipment; Jimmy Splendid, a Native American sheriff; Jo and Leonard Dawson, a couple with marital difficulties; and Miss Dazzle, who runs a motel.

Where it's reviewed:
Booklist, March 1, 2005, page 1136
Library Journal, March 15, 2005, page 77
Publishers Weekly, March 14, 2005, page 45

Other books by the same author:
The Metal Shredders, 2002
The People I Know, 1990

Other books you might like:
Alice Adams, *Medicine Men*, 1997
Margaret Atwood, *The Blind Assassin*, 2000

Kate Chopin, *At Fault*, 1890
Ruth Prawer Jhabvala, *Travelers*, 1973

Alistair MacLeod, *No Great Mischief*, 1999

Series Index

This index alphabetically lists series to which books featured in the entries belong. Beneath each series name, book titles are listed alphabetically with author names and genre codes. The genre codes are as follows: *c* Popular Fiction, *f* Fantasy, *h* Horror, *i* Inspirational, *m* Mystery, *r* Romance, *s* Science Fiction, *t* Historical, and *w* Western. Numbers refer to the entries that feature each title.

Abby Knight
Slay It with Flowers - Kate Collins   *m*   51

Abby Rose
A Wedding to Die For - Leann Sweeney   *m*   230

Abel Jones
Rebels of Babylon - Owen Parry   *t*   945
Rebels of Babylon - Owen Parry   *m*   191

Abigail Timberlake
Monet Talks - Tamar Myers   *m*   178

Acorna's Children
First Warning - Anne McCaffrey   *s*   785

Aimee Leduc
Murder in Clichy - Cara Black   *m*   21

Alafair Tucker
The Old Buzzard Had It Coming - Donis Casey   *t*   864

Alan Gregory
Missing Persons - Stephen White   *m*   244

Albion
The Last Companion - Patrick McCormack   *t*   933

Alexandra Cooper
Entombed - Linda Fairstein   *m*   83

Alfred the Great
The Last Kingdom - Bernard Cornwell   *t*   870

Alien Huntress
Awaken Me Darkly - Gena Showalter   *r*   426

Allied League of Worlds
Afterburn - S.L. Viehl   *s*   826

Aloha Reef
Black Sands - Colleen Coble   *i*   1015

Alternate Frontier
The Rivers of War - Eric Flint   *s*   770

Ambrose Bierce
Ambrose Bierce and the Ace of Shoots - Oakley Hall   *c*   1155
Ambrose Bierce and the Ace of Shoots - Oakley Hall   *t*   903
Ambrose Bierce and the Ace of Shoots - Oakley Hall   *m*   115

Amelia Peabody
The Serpent on the Crown - Elizabeth Peters   *m*   198
The Serpent on the Crown - Elizabeth Peters   *t*   952

Angel Delaney
As Good as Dead - Patricia H. Rushford   *i*   1082

Anna Pigeon
Hard Truth - Nevada Barr   *m*   13

Annabelle Archer
Better Off Wed - Laura Durham   *m*   70

Anne Cartier
Lethal Beauty - Charles O'Brien   *t*   942

Ansel Phoenix
Carnosaur Crimes - Christine Gentry   *m*   98

Anthony Quintana
Suspicion of Rage - Barbara Parker   *c*   1208

Antonio Burns
Badwater - Clinton McKinzie   *m*   171

Ashley Stockingdale
With This Ring, I'm Confused - Kristin Billerbeck   *i*   1005

Assassin
Pieces of Hate - Tim Lebbon   *h*   689

Augusta Goodnight
Too Late for Angels - Mignon F. Ballard   *m*   10

Aunt Dimity
Aunt Dimity and the Next of Kin - Nancy Atherton   *m*   9
Aunt Dimity and the Next of Kin - Nancy Atherton   *h*   638

Austen
Central Park - Debra White Smith   *i*   1086

Bad Luck Brides
Her Bodyguard - Geralyn Dawson   *r*   304

Baroque Mystery
Painted Veil - Beverle Graves Myers   *t*   939

Bay Tanner
Resurrection Road - Kathryn R. Wall   *m*   241

Bebe Bennett
It's a Mod, Mod, Mod, Mod Murder - Rosemary Martin   *m*   160

Beneath the Burning Ground
The Trampled Field - Jeanne Williams   *w*   536

Benni Harper
Delectable Mountains - Earlene Fowler   *m*   90

Berserker
Rogue Berserker - Fred Saberhagen   *s*   808

Betsy Devonshire
Embroidered Truths - Monica Ferris   *m*   85

Black Jewels
Dreams Made Flesh - Anne Bishop   *f*   544

Blackbird Sisters
Cross Your Heart and Hope to Die - Nancy Martin   *m*   159

Bolo
Bolo! - David Weber   *s*   828

Boreal Moon
Ironcrown Moon - Julian May   *f*   599

Boscastle Trilogy
The Love Affair of an English Lord - Jillian Hunter   *r*   335
The Seduction of an English Scoundrel - Jillian Hunter   *r*   336
The Wedding Night of an English Rogue - Jillian Hunter   *r*   337

Bounty Hunter
Showdown in Austin - Tom Calhoun   *w*   467

Bridei Chronicles
The Dark Mirror - Juliet Marillier   *f*   598

Bridesmaid Chronicles
First Dance - Karen Kendall   *r*   353
First Date - Karen Kendall   *r*   354
First Kiss - Kylie Adams   *r*   251

Bridget Heaney
The Spice Box - Lou Jane Temple   *m*   231

Bronze Canticles
Mystic Quest - Tracy Hickman   *f*   582

Bubbles Yablonsky
Bubbles Betrothed - Sarah Strohmeyer   *m*   228

C.W. Sughrue
The Right Madness - James Crumley   *m*   59

Cajun
The Red-Hot Cajun - Sandra Hill   *r*   330

Calder
Lone Star Calder - Janet Dailey   *r*   300

Cally Lazar
Cruel and Unusual Intuition - Claire Daniels   *m*   62

Time Period Index

This index chronologically lists the time settings in which the featured books take place. Main headings refer to a century; where no specific time is given, the headings MULTIPLE TIME PERIODS, INDETERMINATE PAST, INDETERMINATE FUTURE, and INDETERMINATE are used. The 18th through 21st centuries are broken down into decades when possible. (Note: 1800s, for example, refers to the first decade of the 19th century.) Featured titles are listed alphabetically beneath time headings, with author names and genre codes. The genre codes are as follows: *c* Popular Fiction, *f* Fantasy, *h* Horror, *i* Inspirational, *m* Mystery, *r* Romance, *s* Science Fiction, *t* Historical, and *w* Western. Numbers refer to the entries that feature each title.

455

20th CENTURY

21st CENTURY

22nd CENTURY

24th CENTURY

25th CENTURY

35th CENTURY

INDETERMINATE FUTURE

INDETERMINATE

Geographic Index

This index provides access to all featured books by geographic settings—such as countries, continents, oceans, and planets. States and provinces are indicated for the United States and Canada. Also interfiled are headings for fictional place names (Spaceships, Imaginary Planets, etc.). Sections are further broken down by city or the specific name of the imaginary locale. Book titles are listed alphabetically under headings, with author names and genre codes. The genre codes are as follows: *c* Popular Fiction, *f* Fantasy, *h* Horror, *i* Inspirational, *m* Mystery, *r* Romance, *s* Science Fiction, *t* Historical, and *w* Western. Numbers refer to the entries that feature each title.

AFGHANISTAN

The Unknown Soldier - Gerald Seymour   *c*   1224

AFRICA

Islands - Dan Sleigh   *t*   972

Sahara Desert
The Companion - Susan Squires   *r*   433

ALTERNATE UNIVERSE

Against the Tide - John Ringo   *f*   619
Century Rain - Alastair Reynolds   *s*   801
Chainfire - Terry Goodkind   *f*   574
The Dark Mirror - Juliet Marillier   *f*   598
Deadhouse Gates - Steven Erikson   *f*   567
Demonsouled - Jonathan Moeller   *f*   609
The Divided Crown - Isabel Glass   *f*   573
Dreams Made Flesh - Anne Bishop   *f*   544
Freedom's Apprentice - Naomi Kritzer   *f*   589
Godplayers - Damien Broderick   *f*   545
Guardian of Honor - Robin D. Owens   *f*   614
The Hallowed Hunt - Lois McMaster Bujold   *f*   547
Heartwood - Barbara Campbell   *f*   550
Heir of Stone - S.L. Farrell   *f*   569
The Hidden Family - Charles Stross   *f*   628
The House of Storms - Ian R. MacLeod   *f*   597
The Iron Tree - Cecilia Dart-Thornton   *f*   560
Ironcrown Moon - Julian May   *f*   599
Lord of the Libraries - Mel Odom   *f*   613
Lords of Grass and Thunder - Curt Benjamin   *f*   543
Mystic Quest - Tracy Hickman   *f*   582
A Princess of Roumania - Paul Park   *f*   615
The Prodigal Troll - Charles Coleman Finlay   *f*   570
Shadows of Myth - Rachel Lee   *f*   594
Storms of Destiny - A.C. Crispin   *f*   559
A Stroke of Midnight - Laurell K. Hamilton   *f*   575
Three Hands for Scorpio - Andre Norton   *f*   612
The Warrior-Prophet - R. Scott Bakker   *f*   541
The Widow and the King - John Dickinson   *f*   562

Alson
The Crimson Sword - Eldon Thompson   *f*   629

Avornis
The Scepter's Return - Dan Chernenko   *f*   553

Birddom
One for Sorrow, Two for Joy - Clive Woodall   *f*   633

England
Darkwitch Rising - Sara Douglass   *f*   564

The Far Lands
Sister of the Dead - Barb Hendee   *f*   580

Forelands
Bonds of Vengeance - David B. Coe   *f*   555

Tir
A Secret Atlas - Michael A. Stackpole   *f*   625

AMERICAN COLONIES

NEW YORK

New York
Shadow Patriots - Lucia St. Clair Robson   *t*   965

VIRGINIA

A Bride Most Begrudging - Deeanne Gist   *i*   1034

AT SEA

A Bride Most Begrudging - Deeanne Gist   *i*   1034
First Mates - Cecelia Dowdy   *i*   1024

Argonaut
Sails on the Horizon - Jay Worrall   *t*   994

Louisa
Sails on the Horizon - Jay Worrall   *t*   994

R.M.S. Titanic
A Perfect Wedding - Ann Robins   *r*   418

Salsette
Murder on the Salsette - Conrad Allen   *m*   5
Murder on the Salsette - Conrad Allen   *t*   845

Starcrosse
The Care and Feeding of Pirates - Jennifer Ashley   *r*   256

AUSTRALIA

The Great Inland Sea - David Francis   *t*   890
Natives and Exotics - Jane Alison   *c*   1103
Natives and Exotics - Jane Alison   *t*   844

Melbourne
Away with the Fairies - Kerry Greenwood   *m*   108
Away with the Fairies - Kerry Greenwood   *t*   899
Ruddy Gore - Kerry Greenwood   *m*   109

Queensland
For the Love of the Land - Bonnie Leon   *i*   1058
The Heart of Thornton Creek - Bonnie Leon   *i*   1059

Sydney
The Bitten - L.A. Banks   *h*   639
The Forbidden - L.A. Banks   *h*   640

AUSTRIA

Vienna
36 Yalta Boulevard - Olen Steinhauer   *m*   227
The Painted Kiss - Elizabeth Hickey   *t*   909

AZORES

Natives and Exotics - Jane Alison   *c*   1103

BABYLON

A Crown in the Stars - Kacy Barnett-Gramckow   *i*   1001

BELGIUM

Three-Day Road - Joseph Boyden   *t*   858

BELIZE

Second-Chance Hero - Justine Davis   *r*   303

BOSNIA-HERCEGOVINA

Medjugorje
The Third Secret - Steve Berry   *m*   19

BOTSWANA

In the Company of Cheerful Ladies - Alexander McCall Smith   *m*   165
In the Company of Cheerful Ladies - Alexander McCall Smith   *c*   1193

BRAZIL

Rio de Janeiro
A Window in Copacabana - Luiz Alfredo Garcia-Roza   *m*   94

Geographic Index

SWEDEN

Ystad
Before the Frost - Henning Mankell   *m*   158

SWITZERLAND

The God Particle - Richard Cox   *s*   757

THAILAND

Bangkok
Bangkok Tattoo - John Burdett   *m*   36
Bangkok Tattoo - John Burdett   *c*   1120

TROPICAL ISLAND

Isla de Delicia
Take My Breath Away - Tina Donahue   *r*   307

TURKEY

Istanbul
The Midas Trap - Sharon McClellan   *r*   386
The Ottoman Cage - Barbara Nadel   *m*   179
What Casanova Told Me - Susan Swan   *t*   978
Young Turk - Moris Farhi   *t*   884

Salonica
Young Turk - Moris Farhi   *t*   884

UNDERSEA ENVIRONMENT/ HABITAT

Behemoth: Seppuku - Peter Watts   *s*   827

UNION OF SOVIET SOCIALIST REPUBLICS

Europe Central - William T. Vollmann   *c*   1238

Stalingrad
The Earth and Sky of Jacques Dorme - Andrei
   Makine   *t*   930

UNITED STATES

47 - Walter Mosley   *s*   793
An All Night Man - Brenda Jackson   *r*   339
Anywhere but Here - Jerry Oltion   *s*   797
As Good as Dead - Patricia H. Rushford   *i*   1082
Bad Boys over Easy - Erin McCarthy   *r*   385
The Black Stranger and Other American Tales -
   Robert E. Howard   *h*   670
The Boy Who Loved Anne Frank - Ellen
   Feldman   *t*   886
Breaking Point - Suzanne Brockmann   *r*   274
Canaan's Tongue - John Wray   *t*   995
Cold Feet - Elise Juska   *r*   350
Dark Secret - Christine Feehan   *r*   313
Disability - Cris Mazza   *c*   1192
The Dog of the Marriage - Amy Hempel   *c*   1160
Dreaming in Black and White - Laura Jensen
   Walker   *i*   1089
Essence of Trust - Melinda Rucker Haynes   *r*   327
The Evil B.B. Chow and Other Stories - Steve
   Almond   *c*   1105
Final Justice - Jasmine Cresswell   *r*   297
The First Fire - Jane Archer   *w*   453
Follies - Ann Beattie   *c*   1113
Formidable Enemy - Terry Bramlett   *s*   753
The God Particle - Richard Cox   *s*   757
Godplayers - Damien Broderick   *f*   545
God's Gym - John Edgar Wideman   *c*   1242
The Great Inland Sea - David Francis   *t*   890

Guardian of Honor - Robin D. Owens   *f*   614
The Ha-Ha - Dave King   *c*   1181
Haunted - Chuck Palahniuk   *c*   1207
Here, There, and Everywhere - Chris
   Roberson   *s*   803
A High and Hidden Place - Michele Claire
   Lucas   *t*   929
Honk If You Love Real Men - Carrie
   Alexander   *r*   252
Hot Flashes and Cold Cream - Diann Hunt   *i*   1048
Intimidation - Wanda L. Dyson   *i*   1026
Into the Looking Glass - John Ringo   *s*   802
The Last Bullet - Merline Lovelace   *r*   377
Last Night - James Salter   *c*   1222
Love Next Door - Anna Schmidt   *i*   1085
Mammoth - John Varley   *s*   825
Maximum Ride: The Angel Experiment - James
   Patterson   *s*   798
The Meq - Steve Cash   *f*   551
The Middle Sin - Merline Lovelace   *r*   378
Mission to Minerva - James P. Hogan   *s*   776
Mists of Everness - John Wright   *f*   634
Moonstruck - Edward M. Lerner   *s*   783
Nice Big American Baby - Judy Budnitz   *c*   1119
Night's Kiss - Amanda Ashley   *r*   255
Oblivion - Peter Abrahams   *c*   1098
The Presence - Bill Myers   *i*   1072
The Prometheus Project - Steve White   *s*   832
The Quantum Connection - Travis S. Taylor   *s*   818
Rabid Growth - James A. Moore   *h*   704
The Rivers of War - Eric Flint   *t*   888
The Rivers of War - Eric Flint   *s*   770
Saint Vidicon to the Rescue - Christopher
   Stasheff   *f*   626
The Second Chance - Charles Martin   *i*   1062
Spin - Robert Charles Wilson   *s*   835
The Spoon in the Bathroom Wall - Tony
   Johnston   *f*   586
Submerged - Alton Gansky   *i*   1032
Sunstorm - Stephen Baxter   *s*   748
A Thousand Tomorrows - Karen Kingsbury   *i*   1055
Treason - Don Brown   *i*   1008
The Trouble with Tulip - Mindy Starns
   Clark   *i*   1014
The War of the Worlds: New Millennium - Douglas
   Niles   *s*   794
Whales on Stilts - M.T. Anderson   *s*   741
What Comes After Crazy - Sandi Kahn
   Shelton   *c*   1225
What Dreams May Come - Sherrilyn Kenyon   *r*   358
When the Day of Evil Comes - Melanie
   Wells   *i*   1091
Who Does She Think She Is? - Benilde
   Little   *c*   1189
Wicked Women on Top - Tina Donahue   *r*   308
Wicked Women Whodunit - MaryJanice
   Davidson   *r*   302

Danville
Boogeyman - Jeff Marriotte   *h*   697

Mississippi Valley
Silver Feather - Cassie Edwards   *r*   311

Rockwood County
Gil's All Fright Diner - A. Lee Martinez   *h*   698

ALABAMA

The Magic Keys - Albert Murray   *t*   938
Wrapped in Rain - Charles Martin   *i*   1063

Fairhope
The Poet of Tolstoy Park - Sonny Brewer   *c*   1116

Garth
Truly, Madly, Dangerously - Linda Winstead
   Jones   *r*   348

Mobile
Double Take - Joseph H. Hilley   *i*   1045

Possett
Gods in Alabama - Joshilyn Jackson   *c*   1172

Wellton
Life with Strings Attached - Minnie
   Lamberth   *i*   1057

ALASKA

The Baker's Apprentice - Judith Ryan
   Hendricks   *c*   1161

Five Finger Island
Murder at Five Finger Light - Sue Henry   *m*   127

APPALACHIANS

Moon Run Hollow
November Mourns - Tom Piccirilli   *h*   709

ARIZONA

Moon in the Water - Stan Gordon   *w*   488
Sarah's Quilt - Nancy E. Turner   *t*   987

Barstow
Killing Plain - Ralph Cotton   *w*   470

Cottonwood
Killing Plain - Ralph Cotton   *w*   470

Desert Belle
The Death of Desert Belle - Phil Dunlap   *w*   477

Donovan's Corner
Josie Day Is Coming Home - Lisa Plumley   *r*   404

Oro Blanco
Revenge of Eagles - William W. Johnstone   *w*   497

Phoenix
Diana Lively Is Falling Down - Sheila
   Curran   *r*   299

Sierre Madre Mountains
Wild Girl - Jim Fergus   *t*   887

Tombstone
To Tame a Wolf - Susan Krinard   *r*   362
Trouble in Tombstone - Richard S. Wheeler   *w*   535

ARKANSAS

Fairhope
The Homeplace - Gilbert Morris   *i*   1070

Farberville
The Goodbye Body - Joan Hess   *m*   128

Fort Smith
Devil's Kin - Charles G. West   *w*   531

Nazareth
Whisper Town - Patricia Hickman   *i*   1041

CALIFORNIA

Breath and Bones - Susann Cokal   *c*   1128
Breath and Bones - Susann Cokal   *t*   869
Crimson Moon - Rebecca York   *r*   449
Lost in the Forest - Sue Miller   *c*   1198
No Direction Home - Marisa Silver   *c*   1228
Sudden Rain - Maritta Wolff   *c*   1245
Zorro - Isabel Allende   *t*   846
Zorro - Isabel Allende   *w*   451
Zorro - Isabel Allende   *c*   1104

Altadena
Gasa-Gasa Girl - Naomi Hirahara   *m*   129

Berkeley
Eight of Swords - David Skibbins   *m*   223
The Nitrogen Murder - Camille Minichino   *m*   172

United States—Wisconsin

Paradise
Guns of Wolf Valley - Ralph Cotton   *w*   469

WISCONSIN

Fairhaven
Dark Moon - Lori Handeland   *r*   325

Four Corners
Dead Run - P.J. Tracy   *m*   237

Loon Lake
Dead Jitterbug - Victoria Houston   *m*   132

Tobias
Least Likely Wedding - Patricia McLinn   *r*   388

WYOMING

Fairy BrewHaHa at the Lucky Nickel Saloon - Ken
   Rand   *f*   618
The Forbidden Hills - Al Lacy   *i*   1056

Memories of a Dirt Road Town - Stephen
   Bly   *i*   1007

Badwater
Badwater - Clinton McKinzie   *m*   171

Bothwell
Honor Thy Father - Robert A. Roripaugh   *w*   520

Hardwater
Hardwater - Steve Sherwood   *w*   523

Jackson Hole
Out of Range - C.J. Box   *m*   29
Out of Range - C.J. Box   *w*   460
Saving Grace - Denise Hunter   *i*   1049

Saddlestring
Out of Range - C.J. Box   *w*   460

VATICAN CITY

Comes a Horseman - Robert Liparulo   *i*   1060
The Third Secret - Steve Berry   *m*   19

VIETNAM

No Man's Land - Thu Huong Duong   *c*   1138

VIETNAM, NORTH

Nam-A-Rama - Phillip Jennings   *c*   1174

VIETNAM, SOUTH

Nam-A-Rama - Phillip Jennings   *c*   1174

WALES

A Dying Fall - Clive Egleton   *t*   881
Nectar from a Stone - Jane Guill   *t*   900

WEST INDIES

Kingston by Starlight - Christopher John
   Farley   *t*   885

Genre Index

This index lists the books featured as main entries in *What Do I Read Next?* by genre and story type within each genre. Beneath each of the nine genres, the story types appear alphabetically, and titles appear alphabetically under story type headings. The name of the primary author, genre code and the book entry number also appear with each title. The genre codes are as follows: *c* Popular Fiction, *f* Fantasy, *h* Horror, *i* Inspirational, *m* Mystery, *r* Romance, *s* Science Fiction, *t* Historical, and *w* Western. For definitions of the story types, see the "Key to Genre Terms" following the Introduction.

FANTASY

Adventure

Everran's Bane - Sylvia Kelso *f* 588
A Secret Atlas - Michael A. Stackpole *f* 625
Three Hands for Scorpio - Andre Norton *f* 612

Alternate History

A Princess of Roumania - Paul Park *f* 615

Alternate Universe

The Hidden Family - Charles Stross *f* 628

Alternate World

Deadhouse Gates - Steven Erikson *f* 567
Dreams Made Flesh - Anne Bishop *f* 544
Godplayers - Damien Broderick *f* 545
Guardian of Honor - Robin D. Owens *f* 614
The Hallowed Hunt - Lois McMaster Bujold *f* 547
The House of Storms - Ian R. MacLeod *f* 597
Once upon a Summer Day - Dennis L. McKiernan *f* 603
A Stroke of Midnight - Laurell K. Hamilton *f* 575

Anthology

The Fair Folk - Marvin Kaye *f* 587
Maiden, Matron, Crone - Kerrie Hughes *f* 585

Collection

The Black Stranger and Other American Tales - Robert E. Howard *f* 583
Bran Mak Morn: The Last King - Robert E. Howard *f* 584
Perchance to Dream and Other Stories - Michael A. Stackpole *f* 624

Contemporary

Down Time - Lynn Abbey *f* 538
Godplayers - Damien Broderick *f* 545
The Greenstone Grail - Amanda Hemingway *f* 579
The Hunter's Moon - O.R. Melling *f* 606
Pay the Piper - Jane Yolen *f* 635
A Rumor of Gems - Ellen Steiber *f* 627
Saint Vidicon to the Rescue - Christopher Stasheff *f* 626

The Spoon in the Bathroom Wall - Tony Johnston *f* 586
Tumbling After - Paul Witcover *f* 632

Historical

The Crown Rose - Fiona Avery *f* 539
Darkwitch Rising - Sara Douglass *f* 564
Fairy BrewHaHa at the Lucky Nickel Saloon - Ken Rand *f* 618
Guardian of the Freedom - Irene Radford *f* 617
Ill Met by Moonlight - Mercedes Lackey *f* 590
A Mankind Witch - Dave Freer *f* 572
The Meq - Steve Cash *f* 551
Odysseus on the Rhine - Edward S. Louis *f* 596
The White Mare - Jules Watson *f* 630
The Wounded Hawk - Sara Douglass *f* 565

Horror

Sister of the Dead - Barb Hendee *f* 580

Humor

Fairy BrewHaHa at the Lucky Nickel Saloon - Ken Rand *f* 618
The Prodigal Troll - Charles Coleman Finlay *f* 570
Saint Vidicon to the Rescue - Christopher Stasheff *f* 626
The Unhandsome Prince - John Moore *f* 610

Legend

For Camelot's Honor - Sarah Zettel *f* 637
Heartwood - Barbara Campbell *f* 550
Odysseus on the Rhine - Edward S. Louis *f* 596

Light Fantasy

The Crown Rose - Fiona Avery *f* 539
Elphame's Choice - P.C. Cast *f* 552
Ill Met by Moonlight - Mercedes Lackey *f* 590
Od Magic - Patricia A. McKillip *f* 604
One for Sorrow, Two for Joy - Clive Woodall *f* 633

Literary

Our Ecstatic Days - Steve Erickson *f* 566
Someone Comes to Town, Someone Leaves Town - Cory Doctorow *f* 563

Magic Conflict

Academ's Fury - Jim Butcher *f* 548
According to Crow - E. Sedia *f* 622
Against the Tide - John Ringo *f* 619
Alector's Choice - L.E. Modesitt Jr. *f* 607
The Aware - Glenda Larke *f* 592
Blades of the Tiger - Chris Pierson *f* 616
Blood and Memory - Fiona McIntosh *f* 601
Blood of Wolves - Loren L. Coleman *f* 556
Bonds of Vengeance - David B. Coe *f* 555
Chainfire - Terry Goodkind *f* 574
The Crimson Sword - Eldon Thompson *f* 629
The Dark Mirror - Juliet Marillier *f* 598
Darkwitch Rising - Sara Douglass *f* 564
Deadhouse Gates - Steven Erikson *f* 567
Demonsouled - Jonathan Moeller *f* 609
The Divided Crown - Isabel Glass *f* 573
The Duke's Ballad - Andre Norton *f* 611
Elantris - Brandon Sanderson *f* 621
Empire's Daughter - Simon Brown *f* 546
Freedom's Apprentice - Naomi Kritzer *f* 589
Gossamyr - Michele Hauf *f* 578
Harshini - Jennifer Fallon *f* 568
Heartwood - Barbara Campbell *f* 550
Heir of Stone - S.L. Farrell *f* 569
Heretic Betrayers - Scott McGough *f* 600
Ironcrown Moon - Julian May *f* 599
The Light of the Oracle - Victoria Hanley *f* 576
Lord of the Libraries - Mel Odom *f* 613
Lords of Grass and Thunder - Curt Benjamin *f* 543
Mists of Everness - John Wright *f* 634
Myrren's Gift - Fiona McIntosh *f* 602
Mystic and Rider - Sharon Shinn *f* 623
Mystic Quest - Tracy Hickman *f* 582
Od Magic - Patricia A. McKillip *f* 604
Ordermaster - L.E. Modesitt Jr. *f* 608
A Princess of Roumania - Paul Park *f* 615
Return of the Exile - Mary H. Herbert *f* 581
Rise of a Hero - Hilari Bell *f* 542
The Rite - Richard Lee Byers *f* 549
The Rose of the World - Jude Fisher *f* 571
Sanctuary - Mercedes Lackey *f* 591
The Scepter's Return - Dan Chernenko *f* 553
Shadowfall - James Clemens *f* 554
Shadows of Myth - Rachel Lee *f* 594
Storms of Destiny - A.C. Crispin *f* 559
Talyn - Holly Lisle *f* 595
Three Hands for Scorpio - Andre Norton *f* 612
Tumbling After - Paul Witcover *f* 632
The Warrior-Prophet - R. Scott Bakker *f* 541
The White Mare - Jules Watson *f* 630
Witch Finder - C.L. Werner *f* 631

Genre Index

Political

Urban

HORROR

Ancient Evil Unleashed

Anthology

Child-in-Peril

Collection

Curse

Erotic Horror

Ghost Story

Haunted House

Mystery

Nature in Revolt

Occult

Psychological Suspense

Reanimated Dead

Science Fiction

Serial Killer

Vampire Story

POPULAR FICTION

Action/Adventure

ROMANCE

SCIENCE FICTION

Genre Index

WESTERN

Genre Index

Subject Index

This index lists subjects which are covered in the featured titles. Beneath each subject heading, titles are arranged alphabetically with the author names, genre codes, and entry numbers also indicated. The genre codes are as follows: *c* Popular Fiction, *f* Fantasy, *h* Horror, *i* Inspirational, *m* Mystery, *r* Romance, *s* Science Fiction, *t* Historical, and *w* Western.

Abuse

The Bride's Necklace - Kat Martin   *r*   383
Every Waking Moment - Brenda Novak   *r*   400
The Girl Next Door - Jack Ketchum   *h*   678
Hard Truth - Nevada Barr   *m*   13
The Long Way Home - Sarah Storme   *r*   437
Warrior's Heart - Jackie Kramer   *r*   361

Academia

Slaying Is Such Sweet Sorrow - Patricia Harwin   *m*   125
Stage Fright - Christine Poulson   *m*   201
Unholy Death in Princeton - Ann Waldron   *m*   240

Accidents

Detours - Bette Nordberg   *i*   1074
Five in a Row - Jan Coffey   *r*   294
Lost in the Forest - Sue Miller   *c*   1198
Loving Promises - Gail Gaymer Martin   *i*   1064
Never Tell - Karen Young   *r*   450
Saturday - Ian McEwan   *c*   1194

Actors and Actresses

Fame - Karen Kingsbury   *i*   1054
Glimpses of Paradise - James Scott Bell   *i*   1002
Groucho Marx, King of the Jungle - Ron Goulart   *t*   897
An Honorable Murder - Philip Gooden   *m*   104
An Honorable Murder - Philip Gooden   *t*   896
Love Her to Death - Linda Palmer   *m*   187
Savage Garden - Denise Hamilton   *c*   1157
Snobs - Julian Fellowes   *c*   1143
Without a Clue - Trish Jensen   *r*   344
Worlds Collide - Alison Strobel   *i*   1088

Adolescence

A Changed Man - Francine Prose   *c*   1214
Drive Like Hell - Dallas Hudgens   *c*   1168
The Headmaster's Wife - Jane Haddam   *m*   113
The Hummingbird's Daughter - Luis Alberto Urrea   *c*   1236
Murder Can Mess Up Your Mascara - Selma Eichler   *m*   72
No Direction Home - Marisa Silver   *c*   1228
Prep - Curtis Sittenfeld   *c*   1229
Resurrection Road - Kathryn R. Wall   *m*   241
To the Power of Three - Laura Lippman   *m*   153

Towelhead - Alicia Erian   *c*   1141
The Wonder Spot - Melissa Bank   *c*   1111

Adoption

Desert Blood - Alicia Gaspar de Alba   *m*   96
Shadows - Edna Buchanan   *m*   35
Son of a Gun - Randye Lordon   *m*   155
A Wedding to Die For - Leann Sweeney   *m*   230

Adventure and Adventurers

Captain Alatriste - Arturo Perez-Reverte   *t*   950
Dare Me - Cherry Adair   *r*   250
Lara - Bertrice Small   *r*   431
The Lion of St. Mark - Thomas Quinn   *t*   959
The McKenzie Artifact - Alison Kent   *r*   356
Miss Frazer's Adventure - Debbie Raleigh   *r*   409
Mr. Impossible - Loretta Chase   *r*   292
Sailors in the Holy Land - Andrew C.A. Jampoler   *t*   917
Zorro - Isabel Allende   *t*   846

Africa

In the Company of Cheerful Ladies - Alexander McCall Smith   *m*   165
In the Company of Cheerful Ladies - Alexander McCall Smith   *c*   1193
The Triumph of the Sun - Wilbur A. Smith   *t*   973

African Americans

An All Night Man - Brenda Jackson   *r*   339
The Best-Kept Secret - Kimberla Lawson Roby   *c*   1220
God's Gym - John Edgar Wideman   *c*   1242
The Magic Keys - Albert Murray   *t*   938
Measure of a Man - Adrianne Byrd   *r*   283
The Moon in Our Hands - Thomas Dyja   *t*   880
My Jim - Nancy Rawles   *c*   1217
Sex, Murder and a Double Latte - Kyra Davis   *m*   63
Tin City - David Housewright   *m*   131
Trip Wire - Charlotte Carter   *m*   42
Upstate - Kalisha Buckhanon   *c*   1118
War at Home - Kris Nelscott   *m*   180
Who Does She Think She Is? - Benilde Little   *c*   1189
You Made Me Love You - Shirley Hailstock   *r*   324

Africans

Islands - Dan Sleigh   *t*   972

Aging

Always Jan - Roxanne Henke   *i*   1039
Aprons on a Clothesline - Traci DePree   *i*   1023
Follies - Ann Beattie   *c*   1113
The Paperwhite Narcissus - Cynthia Riggs   *m*   207
A Slight Trick of the Mind - Mitch Cullin   *c*   1131
The Water Room - Christopher Fowler   *m*   89
Who Killed the Queen of Clubs? - Patricia Sprinkle   *m*   226

AIDS (Disease)

The Road to Home - Vanessa Del Fabbro   *i*   1022

Airplanes

Dawn of a Thousand Nights - Tricia Goyer   *i*   1035

Alchemy

Dark Fire - C.J. Sansom   *m*   214

Alcoholism

Double Take - Joseph H. Hilley   *i*   1045
Fiesta Moon - Linda Windsor   *i*   1096
Light Before Day - Christopher Rice   *c*   1219
The Magdalen Martyrs - Ken Bruen   *m*   34
The Right Madness - James Crumley   *m*   59

Aliens

Awaken Me Darkly - Gena Showalter   *r*   426
Buried Deep - Kristine Kathryn Rusch   *s*   806
Destroyer - C.J. Cherryh   *s*   756
Dragon and Slave - Timothy Zahn   *s*   839
Formidable Enemy - Terry Bramlett   *s*   753
I, Alien - Mike Resnick   *s*   800
Into the Looking Glass - John Ringo   *s*   802
The Light-Years Beneath My Feet - Alan Dean Foster   *s*   771
Lost in Translation - Edward Willett   *s*   833
Migration - Julie E. Czerneda   *s*   759
Mission to Minerva - James P. Hogan   *s*   776
Moonstruck - Edward M. Lerner   *s*   783
New World Order - Ben Jeapes   *s*   778
The Prometheus Project - Steve White   *s*   832

Dangerous Games - John Shannon   *m*   220
March - Geraldine Brooks   *c*   1117
The Professor's Daughter - Emily
   Raboteau   *c*   1215
The Scent of Lilacs - Ann H. Gabhart   *i*   1029
Shadowed Secrets - Lois Richer   *i*   1080
The Sound of My Voice - Jo Kadlecek   *i*   1052
The Storekeeper's Daughter - Wanda E.
   Brunstetter   *i*   1009

Fathers and Sons

36 Yalta Boulevard - Olen Steinhauer   *m*   227
City of the Dead - Brian Keene   *h*   675
Desolation - Tim Lebbon   *h*   688
Extremely Loud & Incredibly Close - Jonathan Safran
   Foer   *c*   1146
The Forgotten Man - Robert Crais   *m*   57
The Good Priest's Son - Reynolds Price   *c*   1213
The Heart of Thornton Creek - Bonnie
   Leon   *i*   1059
Mr. Lucky - James Swain   *c*   1233
Nightcrawlers - Bill Pronzini   *m*   202
Submerged - Alton Gansky   *i*   1032

Fear

Boogeyman - Jeff Marriotte   *h*   697
A Perfect Wedding - Ann Robins   *r*   418

Federal Witness Security Program

Cut and Run - Ridley Pearson   *m*   194
You Made Me Love You - Shirley Hailstock   *r*   324

Feminism

The Assassin's Dream - J.D. Townsend   *s*   821

Feuds

Bad Man's Gulch - Max Brand   *w*   461

Fires

Death Takes a Honeymoon - Deborah
   Donnelly   *m*   66
Locked Rooms - Laurie R. King   *m*   144
The Smoke Room - Earl Emerson   *m*   76

Fishing

The Dangerous Protector - Janet Chapman   *r*   291
Dead Jitterbug - Victoria Houston   *m*   132

Folk Tales

Rabbit and the Wolves - Deborah L. Duvall   *w*   478

Folklore

Ghosts of Eden - T.M. Gray   *h*   662
The Mysteries - Lisa Tuttle   *h*   732
Unspeakable - Graham Masterton   *h*   699

Food

The Body in the Snowdrift - Katherine Hall
   Page   *m*   185
Chamomile Mourning - Laura Childs   *m*   46
A Lick and a Promise - Jo Leigh   *r*   370
Murder Can Mess Up Your Mascara - Selma
   Eichler   *m*   72
No Reservations Required - Ellen Hart   *m*   124
The Spice Box - Lou Jane Temple   *m*   231
The Spice Box - Lou Jane Temple   *t*   980

Foster Children

Plenty Good Room - Cherie Paris Edwards   *i*   1027

Foster Parents

Plenty Good Room - Cherie Paris Edwards   *i*   1027

Friendship

Cold Service - Robert B. Parker   *m*   190
Everything Changes - Jonathan Tropper   *c*   1235
Exes and Ohs - Beth Kendrick   *r*   355
False Premises- Leslie Caine   *m*   38
Flesh Wounds - John Lawton   *m*   149
The Forgotten Man - Robert Crais   *m*   57
A Good Yarn - Debbie Macomber   *r*   380
The Ha-Ha - Dave King   *c*   1181
He Drown She in the Sea - Shani Mootoo   *c*   1201
Mafia Summer - E. Duke Vincent   *t*   990
Milk - Darcey Steinke   *c*   1231
Mission Road - Rick Riordan   *m*   208
The Mommy Fund - Madeleine Jacob   *c*   1173
No Strings Attached - Millie Criswell   *r*   298
One Sunday Morning - Amy Ephron   *c*   1140
The Red Hat Club Rides Again - Haywood
   Smith   *r*   432
The Right Madness - James Crumley   *m*   59
The Same Sweet Girls - Cassandra King   *c*   1180
Ten Little New Yorkers - Kinky Friedman   *m*   92
To the Power of Three - Laura Lippman   *m*   153
Tool & Die - Sarah Graves   *m*   107
Ya-Yas in Bloom - Rebecca Wells   *c*   1240
The Yada Yada Prayer Group Gets Real - Neta
   Jackson   *i*   1050

Frontier and Pioneer Life

Appaloosa - Robert B. Parker   *c*   1209
The Cold Trail - Phillip Gessert   *w*   487
Islands - Dan Sleigh   *t*   972
Sarah's Quilt - Nancy E. Turner   *t*   987
Sons of Texas - Elmer Kelton   *t*   921
Sons of Texas - Elmer Kelton   *w*   500

Future

Awaken Me Darkly - Gena Showalter   *r*   426
Metallic Love - Tanith Lee   *s*   782

Futuristic Fiction

Hammered - Elizabeth Bear   *s*   749

Gambling

Double Down - Tess Hudson   *r*   334
The Marriage Trap - Elizabeth Thornton   *r*   441
Mr. Lucky - James Swain   *c*   1233
Mr. Lucky - James Swain   *m*   229
Skintight - Susan Andersen   *r*   254

Games/Literary

Without a Clue - Trish Jensen   *r*   344

Gangs

Black Fly Season - Giles Blunt   *m*   24
Devil's Corner - Lisa Scottoline   *m*   218
Metropolis - Elizabeth Gaffney   *t*   891

Gardens and Gardening

Always Green - Patti Ann Hill   *i*   1044
Black Rose - Nora Roberts   *r*   417
Garden of Dreams - Valerie King   *r*   359

Gender Roles

Misfortune - Wesley Stace   *t*   974

Genealogy

Her Passionate Plan B - Dixie Browning   *r*   278
Thicker than Water - Rett MacPherson   *m*   157

Genetic Disease

Dark Angel - Karen Harper   *r*   326

Genetic Engineering

Maximum Ride: The Angel Experiment - James
   Patterson   *s*   798

Genetic Research

Dark Angel - Karen Harper   *r*   326

Ghosts

After the Midnight Hour - Linda Randall
   Wisdom   *r*   448
Aunt Dimity and the Next of Kin - Nancy
   Atherton   *m*   9
Black Rose - Nora Roberts   *r*   417
The Empty House and Other Ghost Stories - Algernon
   Blackwood   *h*   644
Full Bloom - Janet Evanovich   *r*   312
Heartbreak Hotel - Jill Marie Landis   *r*   366
The Italian Secretary - Caleb Carr   *m*   41
Kiss the Goat - Brian Stableford   *h*   729
Smoke and Mirrors - Tanya Huff   *h*   672
Spirited Away - Pamela Labud   *r*   364

Gold Discoveries

Dancing with the Golden Bear - Win
   Blevins   *w*   457
The Forbidden Hills - Al Lacy   *i*   1056
The Treasure of Jericho Mountain - Cameron
   Judd   *w*   498

Good and Evil

Constantine - John Shirley   *h*   724
Do You Believe? - Ann Lawrence   *r*   367
Essence of Trust - Melinda Rucker Haynes   *r*   327
Flight to Eden - Douglas Hirt   *i*   1046
Velocity - Dean R. Koontz   *c*   1182

Grandparents

Death in Duplicate - Valerie Wolzien   *m*   248
My Jim - Nancy Rawles   *c*   1217
Ya-Yas in Bloom - Rebecca Wells   *c*   1240

Greed

Highland Conqueror - Hannah Howell   *r*   333

Grief

American Purgatorio - John Haskell   *c*   1158
The Center of Winter - Marya Hornbacher   *c*   1165
The Closers - Michael Connelly   *m*   53
The Effects of Light - Miranda Beverly-
   Whittemore   *c*   1114

Identity

Identity, Concealed

Illegal Immigrants

Illness

Immortality

Independence

Indian Empire

Indian Reservations

Indians of North America

Industry and Trade

Infidelity

Inheritance

Internet

Internet

Interpersonal Relations

Interracial Dating

Irish Americans

Irish Potato Famine

Irish Republican Army

Islands

Italian Americans

Jamaicans

Japanese Americans

Jealousy

Jews

Papacy

The Third Secret - Steve Berry   *m*   19

Paranormal

Carved in Stone - Vickie Taylor   *r*   440
Cruel and Unusual Intuition - Claire Daniels   *m*   62
Dark Secret - Christine Feehan   *r*   313
The Italian Secretary - Caleb Carr   *t*   862
The Nature of Rare Things - Derek Wilson   *m*   245
Oceans of Fire - Christine Feehan   *r*   314
Shadow Haven - Emily LaForge   *r*   365
Wicked Nights - Nina Bangs   *r*   263

Parent and Child

Glad News of the Natural World - T.R. Pearson   *c*   1210
Second-Chance Hero - Justine Davis   *r*   303
A Short History of Tractors in Ukrainian - Marina Lewycka   *c*   1188

Parenthood

Unlucky for Some - Jill McGown   *m*   167

Philosophy

The Journeys of Socrates - Dan Millman   *t*   935

Phobias

The Fyre Mirror - Karen Harper   *m*   119

Photography

Digging James Dean - Robert Eversz   *m*   81
The Effects of Light - Miranda Beverly-Whittemore   *c*   1114

Physically Handicapped

Disability - Cris Mazza   *c*   1192

Physics

The Nitrogen Murder - Camille Minichino   *m*   172
Powersat - Ben Bova   *s*   752

Pioneers

The Drifter - Lori Copeland   *i*   1018
For the Love of the Land - Bonnie Leon   *i*   1058
The Heart of Thornton Creek - Bonnie Leon   *i*   1059
Moon of the Sleeping Bear - K. Celeste Bryan   *w*   466
Natives and Exotics - Jane Alison   *c*   1103
Natives and Exotics - Jane Alison   *t*   844

Pirates

The Care and Feeding of Pirates - Jennifer Ashley   *r*   256
Kingston by Starlight - Christopher John Farley   *t*   885
SPQR IX: The Princess and the Pirates - John Maddox Roberts   *t*   964
SPQR IX: The Princess and the Pirates - John Maddox Roberts   *m*   209
Unmasked - C.J. Barry   *r*   264

Plastic Surgery

The Red Hat Club Rides Again - Haywood Smith   *r*   432

Police Procedural

Bangkok Tattoo - John Burdett   *c*   1120
Fleshmarket Alley - Ian Rankin   *c*   1216
Sympathy between Humans - Jodi Compton   *c*   1129

Political Movements

Cavalcade - Walter Satterthwait   *m*   215
The Devil's Wind - Richard Rayner   *c*   1218
Nam-A-Rama - Phillip Jennings   *c*   1174
Saturday - Ian McEwan   *c*   1194
War by Candlelight - Daniel Alarcon   *c*   1102
The Watcher in the Pine - Rebecca Pawel   *m*   192

Political Prisoners

An Honorable Murder - Philip Gooden   *m*   104

Political Thriller

Anywhere but Here - Jerry Oltion   *s*   797
The Carpet Makers - Andreas Eschbach   *s*   769

Politics

Before Another Dies - Alton Gansky   *i*   1030
Captain Alatriste - Arturo Perez-Reverte   *c*   1212
Chloe - Lyn Cote   *i*   1020
Citizen Vince - Jess Walter   *c*   1239
The Devil's Wind - Richard Rayner   *m*   205
Die Like a Hero - Clyde Linsley   *m*   152
The Diezmo - Rick Bass   *c*   1112
Director's Cut - Alton Gansky   *i*   1031
Emperor: The Field of Swords - Conn Iggulden   *t*   914
Endless Chain - Emilie Richards   *r*   412
Hosack's Folly - Gillen D'Arcy Wood   *c*   1246
The James Deans - Reed Farrel Coleman   *m*   49
The Lady and the Cit - Blair Bancroft   *r*   262
Long Spoon Lane - Anne Perry   *m*   197
The Motive - John Lescroart   *m*   151
My Life as Emperor - Tong Su   *t*   977
My Name Is Legion - A.N. Wilson   *c*   1243
The Point in the Market - Michael Pearce   *m*   193
Prince of Fire - Daniel Silva   *m*   222
Qi - David Aikman   *i*   998
Stargazer - Colby Hodge   *r*   331
Sudden Rain - Maritta Wolff   *c*   1245
Suspicion of Rage - Barbara Parker   *m*   189
Three Strikes You're Dead - Robert Goldsborough   *m*   103
The Widow's Tale - Margaret Frazer   *m*   91

Pollution

Crimson Moon - Rebecca York   *r*   449
The Dangerous Protector - Janet Chapman   *r*   291

Popular Culture

Goodnight Steve McQueen - Louise Wener   *c*   1241
Hot Spot - Susan Johnson   *r*   345

Post Nuclear Holocaust

The People of Sparks - Jeanne Duprau   *s*   766

Prayer

The Yada Yada Prayer Group Gets Real - Neta Jackson   *i*   1050

Pre-Columbian History

People of the Moon - Kathleen O'Neal Gear   *w*   486

Pregnancy

A New Lu - Laura Castoro   *r*   290
Saving Grace - Denise Hunter   *i*   1049
The Untelling - Tayari Jones   *c*   1175

Prejudice

Legacy of Masks - Sallie Bissell   *m*   20
Ruddy Gore - Kerry Greenwood   *m*   109

Presidents

The Emancipator's Wife - Barbara Hambly   *c*   1156

Princes and Princesses

A Brother's Price - Wen Spencer   *s*   815
Empire's Daughter - Simon Brown   *f*   546
The Hallowed Hunt - Lois McMaster Bujold   *f*   547

Prisoners and Prisons

The Diezmo - Rick Bass   *t*   854
Haunted - Chuck Palahniuk   *c*   1207
Upstate - Kalisha Buckhanon   *c*   1118

Prisoner's Families

The Good Wife - Stewart O'Nan   *c*   1205

Prisoners of War

Camp Ford - Johnny D. Boggs   *w*   458
Dear Enemy - Jack Cavanaugh   *i*   1012
Devil's Domain - Tim Champlin   *w*   468
The Diezmo - Rick Bass   *c*   1112

Privacy

Sexy Lexy - Kate Moore   *r*   390

Prohibition Era

The Season of Open Water - Dawn Clifton Tripp   *t*   986

Property Rights

Now You See Her - Cecelia Tishy   *c*   1234

Prostitution

Bangkok Tattoo - John Burdett   *c*   1120
Bangkok Tattoo - John Burdett   *m*   36
The Linnet Bird - Linda Holeman   *t*   911

Psychic Powers

Better Read than Dead - Victoria Laurie   *m*   147
The Challenge - Susan Kearney   *r*   352
Cruel and Unusual Intuition - Claire Daniels   *m*   62
Expiration Date - Eric Wilson   *i*   1095
The God Particle - Richard Cox   *s*   757
Jamie - Lori Foster   *r*   318
Lost in Translation - Edward Willett   *s*   833
Nectar from a Stone - Jane Guill   *t*   900
The Presence - Bill Myers   *i*   1072
Shadow Haven - Emily LaForge   *r*   365
The Silver Child - Cliff McNish   *f*   605
Terminal - Brian Keene   *h*   676
What Rough Beast - H.R. Knight   *h*   680

Seduction

Self-Acceptance

Self-Esteem

Serial Killers

Servants

Sewing

Sexual Abuse

Sexual Behavior

Sexuality

Ships

Shopping

Short Stories

Character Name Index

This index alphabetically lists the major characters in each featured title. Each character name is followed by a description of the character. Citations also provide titles of the books featuring the character, listed alphabetically if there is more than one title; author names and genre codes. The genre codes are as follows: *c* Popular Fiction, *f* Fantasy, *h* Horror, *i* Inspirational, *m* Mystery, *r* Romance, *s* Science Fiction, *t* Historical, and *w* Western. Numbers refer to the entries that feature each title.

A

47 (Slave)
47 - Walter Mosley *s* 793

Aari (Spaceman)
First Warning - Anne McCaffrey *s* 785

Aaron (Friend)
The Best-Kept Secret - Kimberla Lawson Roby *c* 1220

Aaronson, Kay (Director)
Least Likely Wedding - Patricia McLinn *r* 388

Abbott, Pat (Detective—Private)
The Golden Box - Frances Crane *m* 58

Abernathy, Jason (Doctor)
A Perfect Wedding - Ann Robins *r* 418

Abigail of Carmel (Young Woman; Biblical Figure)
Abigail's Story - Ann Burton *r* 281

Ace (Store Owner)
Resurrection Dreams - Richard Laymon *h* 686

Achamian, Drusas (Sorcerer)
The Warrior-Prophet - R. Scott Bakker *f* 541

Ackroyd, Laura (Journalist)
Dead Reckoning - Patricia Hall *m* 116

Adams, Asked For (Historical Figure)
What Casanova Told Me - Susan Swan *t* 978

Adams, Bernice (Television Personality)
Fear Me - Stephen Laws *h* 685

Adams, Caleb (Detective—Private)
Tangle of Lies - Patricia Potter *r* 405

Adams, Flex (Fire Fighter; Homosexual)
Measure of a Man - Adrianne Byrd *r* 283

Adams, Luce (Researcher)
What Casanova Told Me - Susan Swan *t* 978

Adamson, Katherine (Writer)
Winds of Evil - Sharon K. Gilbert *i* 1033

Adoula, Jackson (Nobleman)
We Few - David Weber *s* 829

Aetius, Flavius (Military Personnel; Historical Figure)
The Sword of Attila - Michael Curtis Ford *t* 889

Aguila (Chieftain; Friend)
Comanche Crossing - Harold G. Ross *w* 521

Aguilar, Silvio (Boyfriend)
Savage Garden - Denise Hamilton *c* 1157

Aisling (Witch)
The Duke's Ballad - Andre Norton *f* 611

Akhmatova, Anna (Writer; Historical Figure)
Europe Central - William T. Vollmann *c* 1238

al-Bashir, Asim (Criminal)
Powersat - Ben Bova *s* 752

al-Idrisi, Muhammed (Cartographer; Historical Figure)
A Sultan in Palermo - Tariq Ali *t* 843

Alabanda, Jonas (Scholar; Diplomat)
The Scourge of God - William Dietrich *c* 1135
The Scourge of God - William Dietrich *t* 876

Alan (Businessman)
Someone Comes to Town, Someone Leaves Town - Cory Doctorow *f* 563

Alannah (Handicapped; Telepath)
Across a Wild Sea - Sasha Lord *r* 374

Alatriste y Tenorio, Diego (Veteran; Military Personnel)
Captain Alatriste - Arturo Perez-Reverte *t* 950
Captain Alatriste - Arturo Perez-Reverte *c* 1212

Albert (Artist; Lover)
Breath and Bones - Susann Cokal *c* 1128

Alexander, James (Military Personnel; Teenager)
The Diezmo - Rick Bass *c* 1112
The Diezmo - Rick Bass *t* 854
The Diezmo - Rick Bass *w* 456

Alexandra (Nurse)
The Earth and Sky of Jacques Dorme - Andrei Makine *t* 930

Alfred the Great (Historical Figure; Ruler)
The Last Kingdom - Bernard Cornwell *c* 1130
The Last Kingdom - Bernard Cornwell *t* 870

Alice (Young Woman)
Wild Dogs - Helen Humphreys *c* 1169

Alison (Girlfriend)
Goodnight Steve McQueen - Louise Wener *c* 1241

Allard, Frances (Spinster; Teacher)
Simply Unforgettable - Mary Balogh *r* 261

Allegretti, Vicki (Lawyer)
Devil's Corner - Lisa Scottoline *m* 218

Allion (Warrior)
The Crimson Sword - Eldon Thompson *f* 629

Allon, Gabriel (Spy; Art Historian)
Prince of Fire - Daniel Silva *m* 222

Amara (Spy)
Academ's Fury - Jim Butcher *f* 548

Amato, Tito (Singer)
Painted Veil - Beverle Graves Myers *m* 176
Painted Veil - Beverle Graves Myers *t* 939

Ambrose (Teenager; Nobleman)
The Widow and the King - John Dickinson *f* 562

Ames, Tabitha (Spacewoman)
The Quantum Connection - Travis S. Taylor *s* 818

Anderson, Annie (Journalist)
Fashion Victim - Sam Baker *r* 257
Fashion Victim - Sam Baker *c* 1110

Anderson, Catherine (Actress)
Director's Cut - Alton Gansky *i* 1031

Anderson, Julia (Antiques Dealer)
The Pleasure Slave - Gena Showalter *r* 427

Anderson, Terry (Teenager)
Wonders Never Cease - Phil Callaway *i* 1011

Anderson, Tom (Historical Figure; Political Figure)
Jass - David Fulmer *m* 93

Andre, John (Military Personnel; Historical Figure)
Shadow Patriots - Lucia St. Clair Robson *t* 965

Andrews, Nick (Handyman)
A Sheltering Love - Terri Reed *i* 1079

Andrews, Rachael (Spouse; Employer)
Bloody Hills - Charles G. West *w* 530

Angel (Teenager; Genetically Altered Being)
Maximum Ride: The Angel Experiment - James Patterson *s* 798

Angel, Nick (Artist)
Sex and the Serial Killer - Jennifer Skully *r* 430

Angela (Girlfriend)
Snow White and Russian Red - Dorata Maslowska *c* 1191

Anglin, J.B. (Lawyer; Divorced Person)
First Dance - Karen Kendall *r* 353

Anne (Young Woman)
American Purgatorio - John Haskell *c* 1158

Anne (Businesswoman)
The Exiled - Posie Graeme-Evans *t* 898

Annora (Servant)
Nectar from a Stone - Jane Guill *t* 900

Antonelli, Tony (Journalist)
The Hot Kid - Elmore Leonard *c* 1186

Antonio (Teenager; Criminal)
Upstate - Kalisha Buckhanon   *c*   1118

Anturasi, Jorim (Cartographer; Explorer)
A Secret Atlas - Michael A. Stackpole   *f*   625

Anturasi, Keles (Cartographer; Explorer)
A Secret Atlas - Michael A. Stackpole   *f*   625

Anturasi, Nirati (Businesswoman)
A Secret Atlas - Michael A. Stackpole   *f*   625

Anwar, Nikolai (Spy)
Final Justice - Jasmine Cresswell   *r*   297

Apollo (Deity)
Goddess of Light - P.C. Cast   *r*   289

Applebaum, Jack (Relative)
The Wonder Spot - Melissa Bank   *c*   1111

Applebaum, Robert (Relative)
The Wonder Spot - Melissa Bank   *c*   1111

Applebaum, Sophie (Heroine)
The Wonder Spot - Melissa Bank   *c*   1111

Appleton, Susanna (Herbalist; Detective—Amateur)
Face Down Below the Banqueting House - Kathy Lynn Emerson   *m*   77
Face Down Below the Banqueting House - Kathy Lynn Emerson   *t*   882

Arai, Mas (Gardener; Detective—Amateur)
Gasa-Gasa Girl - Naomi Hirahara   *m*   129

Arcadia (Religious)
The Cybelene Conspiracy - Albert Noyer   *t*   941

Archer, Annabelle (Consultant; Detective—Amateur)
Better Off Wed - Laura Durham   *m*   70

Archer, Harry (Editor)
Sex & Sensibility - Rosemarie Santini   *r*   420

Ardmore, Honoria (Gentlewoman)
The Care and Feeding of Pirates - Jennifer Ashley   *r*   256

Ariane (Psychic)
The Dark Queen - Susan Carroll   *t*   863

Arkanian, Petra (Political Figure)
Shadow of the Giant - Orson Scott Card   *s*   755

Arledge, Britt (Government Official)
Moonstruck - Edward M. Lerner   *s*   783

Armstrong (Military Personnel; Pilot)
Nam-A-Rama - Phillip Jennings   *c*   1174

Arnkel (Chieftain)
Saga: A Novel of Medieval Iceland - Jeff Janoda   *t*   918

Arnold, Benedict (Military Personnel; Historical Figure)
Shadow Patriots - Lucia St. Clair Robson   *t*   965

Arnold, Jessie (Animal Trainer; Detective—Amateur)
Murder at Five Finger Light - Sue Henry   *m*   127

Arrowgrass, Eolacha Kingfisher (Aged Person)
The Iron Tree - Cecilia Dart-Thornton   *f*   560

Arvad, Caelith (Nobleman)
Mystic Quest - Tracy Hickman   *f*   582

Arvad, Galen (Leader)
Mystic Quest - Tracy Hickman   *f*   582

Ash (Genetically Altered Being)
Slaves Unchained - Susan Wright   *s*   837

Ashburn, Quentin (Worker)
Mindscan - Robert J. Sawyer   *s*   809

Ashby, Michael (Military Personnel)
A Dying Fall - Clive Egleton   *t*   881

Asterius, Arcadia (Spouse; Sidekick)
The Cybelene Conspiracy - Albert Noyer   *m*   181

Asterius, Getorius (Doctor)
The Cybelene Conspiracy - Albert Noyer   *m*   181
The Cybelene Conspiracy - Albert Noyer   *t*   941

Atkins, Wendy (Spy)
Thieves of Mercy - James L. Nelson   *t*   940

Attila (Ruler; Historical Figure)
The Scourge of God - William Dietrich   *c*   1135

Attila the Hun (Historical Figure; Warrior)
The Scourge of God - William Dietrich   *t*   876
The Sword of Attila - Michael Curtis Ford   *t*   889

Auger, Verity (Archaeologist)
Century Rain - Alastair Reynolds   *s*   801

Augustus (Consultant; Military Personnel)
The Myriad - R.M. Meluch   *s*   789

Austen, Jane (Historical Figure; Writer)
Jane and His Lordship's Legacy - Stephanie Barron   *t*   852
Jane and His Lordship's Legacy - Stephanie Barron   *m*   14

Austin, Stephen F. (Historical Figure; Political Figure)
Sons of Texas - Elmer Kelton   *t*   921

Austrey, Deveron (Nobleman)
Ironcrown Moon - Julian May   *f*   599

Autshumao (Warrior)
Islands - Dan Sleigh   *t*   972

Avalon (Government Official)
The Assassin's Dream - J.D. Townsend   *s*   821

Avatre (Mythical Creature)
Sanctuary - Mercedes Lackey   *f*   591

Avery, Ben (Relative; Businessman)
The Cold Trail - Phillip Gessert   *w*   487

Avery, Ben Jr. (Runaway)
The Cold Trail - Phillip Gessert   *w*   487

Avery, Harliss (Gunfighter)
The Cold Trail - Phillip Gessert   *w*   487

Axelrod, Shanna (Spaceship Captain)
The Sunborn - Gregory Benford   *s*   750

B

Baca, Sonny (Detective—Private)
Jemez Spring - Rudolfo Anaya   *m*   6
Jemez Spring - Rudolfo Anaya   *w*   452

Bagot, Hazel (Teenager)
The Greenstone Grail - Amanda Hemingway   *f*   579

Baker, Laura (Detective—Police)
Stolen Memory - Virginia Kantra   *r*   351

Balboa, Inigo (Narrator)
Captain Alatriste - Arturo Perez-Reverte   *c*   1212

Baldini, Eric (Filmmaker; Student—Graduate)
A Pinch of Cool - Mary Leo   *r*   372

Ball, Virgil (Gang Member)
Canaan's Tongue - John Wray   *t*   995

Ballard, Lafe (Bully)
The Trampled Field - Jeanne Williams   *w*   536

Ballentyne, Kendra (Lawyer; Detective—Amateur)
Sit, Stay, Slay - Linda O. Johnston   *m*   137

Balthazar (Demon)
Constantine - John Shirley   *h*   724

Banichi (Alien)
Destroyer - C.J. Cherryh   *s*   756

Banished One (Deity)
The Scepter's Return - Dan Chernenko   *f*   553

Banks, Alan (Police Officer)
Strange Affair - Peter Robinson   *m*   210

Banks, Noah (Reincarnated Person)
Darkwitch Rising - Sara Douglass   *f*   564

Banks, Stella (Detective—Private)
The McKenzie Artifact - Alison Kent   *r*   356

Bannon, Jim (Farmer; Prospector)
The Forbidden Hills - Al Lacy   *i*   1056

Barclay, William (Gentleman; Rake)
Lord Will and Her Grace - Sophia Nash   *r*   396

Barker, Cyrus (Detective—Private)
To Kingdom Come - Will Thomas   *m*   232
To Kingdom Come - Will Thomas   *t*   981

Barr, Temple (Public Relations; Detective—Amateur)
Cat in a Hot Pink Pursuit - Carole Nelson Douglas   *m*   68

Bartholomew, Ellie (Care Giver)
The Dwelling Place - Elizabeth Musser   *i*   1071

Bartlemy (Recluse)
The Greenstone Grail - Amanda Hemingway   *f*   579

Barton, Liza "Celia" (Spouse; Parent)
No Place Like Home - Mary Higgins Clark   *c*   1125

Bastien (Nobleman)
Guardian of Honor - Robin D. Owens   *f*   614

Battock, Beth (Government Official)
The Sinner's Tale - Will Davenport   *t*   873

Bauer, Jane (Detective—Homicide)
Murder in Alphabet City - Lee Harris   *m*   122

Baxter, Jodi (Spouse; Parent)
The Yada Yada Prayer Group Gets Real - Neta Jackson   *i*   1050

Bayard, Brion (Diplomat)
Imperium - Keith Laumer   *s*   780

Bayles, China (Herbalist; Detective—Amateur)
Dead Man's Bones - Susan Wittig Albert   *m*   3

Bayliss, Karen (Young Woman)
Dark Star - Creston Mapes   *i*   1061

Beacham, Elizabeth (Aged Person)
Aunt Dimity and the Next of Kin - Nancy Atherton   *h*   638

Beacon, Vanessa (Runaway; Parent)
Every Waking Moment - Brenda Novak   *r*   400

Bean (Genius)
Shadow of the Giant - Orson Scott Card   *s*   755

Bean, Madeleine (Caterer; Detective—Amateur)
The Flaming Luau of Death - Jerrilyn Farmer   *m*   84

Beasley, Roland (Artist)
The Magic Keys - Albert Murray   *t*   938

Beaumont, Elise (Librarian)
A Good Yarn - Debbie Macomber   *r*   380

Beaumont, Phil (Detective—Private)
Cavalcade - Walter Satterthwait   *m*   215
Cavalcade - Walter Satterthwait   *t*   966

Becq, Gray (Student)
When the Beast Ravens - E. Rose Sabin   *f*   620

Beecham, Melody (Spy)
Final Justice - Jasmine Cresswell   *r*   297

Beede, Josiah (Lawyer; Farmer)
Die Like a Hero - Clyde Linsley   *m*   152

Begay, Joe (Veteran; Spy)
Vineyard Prey - Philip R. Craig   *m*   56

Behan, Cyrus (Maintenance Worker)
The Spirit Box - Stephen Gallagher   *h*   660

Behan, John (Lawman; Friend)
Trouble in Tombstone - Richard S. Wheeler   *w*   535

Carmichael, Julia (Teenager)
The Open Channel - Jill Morrow   *h*   705

Carmichael, Stephen (Restaurateur)
The Open Channel - Jill Morrow   *h*   705

Carnagie, Mitchell (Genealogist)
Black Rose - Nora Roberts   *r*   417

Caro (Friend)
Ya-Yas in Bloom - Rebecca Wells   *c*   1240

Caroline (Young Woman)
The Unhandsome Prince - John Moore   *f*   610

Carpenter, Sabina (Detective—Private)
Quincannon's Game - Bill Pronzini   *w*   515

Carraway, Stephen (Student)
Kiss the Goat - Brian Stableford   *h*   729

Carsington, Rupert (Nobleman)
Mr. Impossible - Loretta Chase   *r*   292

Carson, Kit (Guide; Historical Figure)
Dream West - David Nevin   *w*   506

Carswell, Lizzie (Young Woman)
One Sunday Morning - Amy Ephron   *t*   883
One Sunday Morning - Amy Ephron   *c*   1140

Carter, Hooney (Lawman)
The Law in Somos Santos - Ralph Cotton   *w*   471

Cartier, Anne (Teacher; Detective—Amateur)
Lethal Beauty - Charles O'Brien   *t*   942

Caruso, Cece (Writer; Detective—Amateur)
Not a Girl Detective - Susan Kandel   *m*   138

Carver, Trey "Lincoln" (Fire Fighter; Artist)
Measure of a Man - Adrianne Byrd   *r*   283

Casanova, Giovanni Giacomo (Historical Figure; Adventurer)
What Casanova Told Me - Susan Swan   *t*   978

Casey, Eamonn (Publisher)
Hosack's Folly - Gillen D'Arcy Wood   *c*   1246
Hosack's Folly - Gillen D'Arcy Wood   *t*   993

Casey, Jenny (Fugitive)
Hammered - Elizabeth Bear   *s*   749

Castle, Albert (Artist)
Breath and Bones - Susann Cokal   *t*   869

Catalano, Frank "Fat Cat" (Organized Crime Figure)
Forgiving Solomon Long - Chris Well   *i*   1090

Cathcart, Harry (Detective—Private)
Sick of Shadows - Marion Chesney   *m*   44
Sick of Shadows - Marion Chesney   *t*   865

Catherine de Medici (Historical Figure; Royalty)
The Dark Queen - Susan Carroll   *t*   863

Ceaucescu (Noblewoman)
A Princess of Roumania - Paul Park   *f*   615

Cecil, William (Historical Figure; Government Official)
The Fyre Mirror - Karen Harper   *t*   905

Cel (Mythical Creature; Prisoner)
A Stroke of Midnight - Laurell K. Hamilton   *f*   575

Celimus (Ruler)
Blood and Memory - Fiona McIntosh   *f*   601
Myrren's Gift - Fiona McIntosh   *f*   602

Ceola, Tony (Detective—Homicide)
The Assassin - Rachel Butler   *r*   282

Cervantes, Miguel de (Historical Figure; Writer)
Tilting at Windmills - Julian Branston   *t*   859

Chaise, Jennifer (Prostitute; Runaway)
Runaway Mistress - Robyn Carr   *r*   286

Champlain, Daniel (Government Official)
Jigsaw - Kathleen Nance   *r*   395

Chanda (Crime Victim)
Maps for Lost Lovers - Nadeem Aslam   *c*   1108

Chandler, John (Cowboy; Veteran)
The Wrangler - Frank Roderus   *w*   519

Chandler, Ruth (Parent)
The Girl Next Door - Jack Ketchum   *h*   678

Chandler, Vicki (Doctor)
Resurrection Dreams - Richard Laymon   *h*   686

Channon (Detective—Homicide)
No Corners for the Devil - Olive Etchells   *m*   79

Chanya (Prostitute)
Bangkok Tattoo - John Burdett   *c*   1120

Chapman, Mike (Detective—Homicide)
Entombed - Linda Fairstein   *m*   83

Charles II (Historical Figure; Ruler)
Darkwitch Rising - Sara Douglass   *t*   878
Darkwitch Rising - Sara Douglass   *f*   564

Charpentier, Marc-Antoine (Composer; Historical Figure)
Emilie's Voice - Susanne Dunlap   *c*   1137

Chell, Vivyan (Religious)
My Name Is Legion - A.N. Wilson   *c*   1243

Cheng, Winston (Businessman)
Rogue Berserker - Fred Saberhagen   *s*   808

Chica (Animal)
Jemez Spring - Rudolfo Anaya   *w*   452

Chilton, Lucy (Rancher; Parent)
Return to Abo - Sharon Niederman   *w*   508

Chilton, Maggie (Journalist; Rancher)
Return to Abo - Sharon Niederman   *w*   508

Chilton, Sarah (Teenager; Animal Lover)
Horse of Seven Moons - Karen Taschek   *w*   527

Christian, Howard (Wealthy)
Mammoth - John Varley   *s*   825

Chrysler, Sarrah (Businesswoman)
Fall Girl - Pierce Askegren   *s*   745

Chung, Lin (Businessman)
Away with the Fairies - Kerry Greenwood   *m*   108
Ruddy Gore - Kerry Greenwood   *m*   109

Churchill, Winston (Historical Figure; Political Figure)
Hitler's Peace - Philip Kerr   *c*   1178

Cicero, Marcus Tullius (Historical Figure; Political Figure)
A Gladiator Dies Only Once - Steven Saylor   *t*   967

Clah, Ella (Police Officer; Indian)
White Thunder - Aimee Thurlo   *m*   234

Claiborne, Catherine (Spouse)
That Anvil of Our Souls - David Poyer   *t*   957

Claiborne, Ker (Military Personnel)
That Anvil of Our Souls - David Poyer   *t*   957

Clarence, George (Settler)
Natives and Exotics - Jane Alison   *t*   844

Clarence, Violet (Settler)
Natives and Exotics - Jane Alison   *t*   844

Clark, Alexandra "Lexy" (Physical Fitness Expert; Innkeeper)
Sexy Lexy - Kate Moore   *r*   390

Clarke, Lenie (Cyborg; Businesswoman)
Behemoth: Seppuku - Peter Watts   *s*   827

Clarke, Siobhan (Detective—Police)
Fleshmarket Alley - Ian Rankin   *c*   1216
Fleshmarket Alley - Ian Rankin   *m*   204

Clarkson, Odell (Outlaw)
The Law in Somos Santos - Ralph Cotton   *w*   471

Claudia (Twin; Parent)
Writing on the Wall - Lynne Sharon Schwartz   *c*   1223

Clavier, Sandra (Computer Expert; Businesswoman)
Saint Vidicon to the Rescue - Christopher Stasheff   *f*   626

Claxton, Beau (Cowboy; Drifter)
The Drifter - Lori Copeland   *i*   1018

Claye (Child)
The Prodigal Troll - Charles Coleman Finlay   *f*   570

Cleary, Lilly Bell Rose (Lawyer)
Wildcat Wine - Claire Matturro   *m*   163

Clem (Teenager; Handicapped)
Ghosts of Eden - T.M. Gray   *h*   662

Cleo (Health Care Professional; Lesbian)
Disability - Cris Mazza   *c*   1192

Cleopatra (Historical Figure; Ruler)
SPQR IX: The Princess and the Pirates - John Maddox Roberts   *t*   964

Clevis, Jimmy (Cowboy)
Rancho Alegre - John D. Nesbitt   *w*   505

Clifford, Noel (Nobleman)
My Lady Faire - Emily Hendrickson   *r*   328

Colbeck, Robert (Detective—Police)
The Excursion Train - Edward Marston   *t*   931

Colcernian, Diane (Military Personnel; Lawyer)
Treason - Don Brown   *i*   1008

Cole, Elvis (Detective—Private)
The Forgotten Man - Robert Crais   *m*   57

Cole, Geena (Detective—Private)
Who's Been Sleeping in My Bed? - Gemma Bruce   *r*   279

Cole, Gideon (Lawyer)
To Love a Thief - Julie Anne Long   *r*   373

Cole, Lola (Teenager)
Dreamspawn - Christa Faust   *h*   658

Cole, Virgil (Lawman)
Appaloosa - Robert B. Parker   *t*   944
Appaloosa - Robert B. Parker   *c*   1209

Colmes, Mack (Security Officer)
Flesh Gothic - Edward Lee   *h*   691

Colquitt, Michaela (Child)
Shadow Haven - Emily LaForge   *r*   365

Colter, Ben (Insurance Investigator)
Five in a Row - Jan Coffey   *r*   294

Colville, Kate (Detective—Homicide)
Killing a Unicorn - Marjorie Eccles   *m*   71

Conde, Mario (Detective—Homicide)
Havana Red - Leonardo Padura   *m*   184

Connable, Lucy (Spouse)
The Undertaker's Wife - Loren D. Estleman   *w*   479

Connable, Richard (Undertaker)
The Undertaker's Wife - Loren D. Estleman   *w*   479

Connable, Victoria (Child)
The Undertaker's Wife - Loren D. Estleman   *w*   479

Connelly, Mike (Lawyer)
Double Take - Joseph H. Hilley   *i*   1045

Conners, Libby (Pilot)
Dawn of a Thousand Nights - Tricia Goyer   *i*   1035

Connolly, Caroline Tabb (Real Estate Agent)
Underground - Craig Spector   *h*   728

Connor, Gail (Lawyer)
Suspicion of Rage - Barbara Parker   *c*   1208
Suspicion of Rage - Barbara Parker   *m*   189

Connor, Kate (Housewife)
Carpe Demon - Julie Kenner   *h*   677

Connor, Liz (Businesswoman; Political Figure)
Tangle of Lies - Patricia Potter   *r*   405

Fernandez, Elena (Spouse)
The Watcher in the Pine - Rebecca Pawel   *m*   192

Ferris, Llewellyn "Lew" (Police Officer; Fisherman)
Dead Jitterbug - Victoria Houston   *m*   132

Ferry, Catherine (Scientist)
Blood Memory - Greg Iles   *c*   1170

Fidelma (Religious; Scholar)
Badger's Moon - Peter Tremayne   *t*   985
Badger's Moon - Peter Tremayne   *m*   238

Field, Lindy (Lawyer)
Sins of the Fathers - James Scott Bell   *i*   1003

Fielding, Emma (Archaeologist; Detective—Amateur)
More Bitter than Death - Dana Cameron   *m*   39

Fielding, John (Historical Figure; Judge)
Rules of Engagement - Bruce Alexander   *m*   4
Rules of Engagement - Bruce Alexander   *t*   842

Finbow, Thomas (Animal Trainer)
The Mapmaker's Daughter - John Pilkington   *t*   955

Findabhair (Teenager; Cousin)
The Hunter's Moon - O.R. Melling   *f*   606

Fine, Urban (Nobleman)
A Factory of Cunning - Philippa Stockley   *c*   1232

Finn (Artist; Widow(er))
The Illuminator - Brenda Rickman
   Vantrease   *c*   1237
The Illuminator - Brenda Rickman Vantrease   *t*   989

Finn, Justin (Child; Clone)
Cast of Shadows - Kevin Guilfoile   *c*   1154

Fiora, Lee (Teenager; Student—High School)
Prep - Curtis Sittenfeld   *c*   1229

Fish, Jack (Spy)
Jack Fish - J. Milligan   *c*   1199

Fisher, John King (Rancher; Historical Figure)
Pendencia Creek - E. Lee Fisher   *w*   481

Fisher, Naomi (Young Woman; Clerk)
The Storekeeper's Daughter - Wanda E.
   Brunstetter   *r*   280
The Storekeeper's Daughter - Wanda E.
   Brunstetter   *i*   1009

Fisher, Phryne (Detective—Private)
Away with the Fairies - Kerry Greenwood   *t*   899
Away with the Fairies - Kerry Greenwood   *m*   108
Ruddy Gore - Kerry Greenwood   *m*   109

Fisher, Sarah Vivian (Spouse; Historical Figure)
Pendencia Creek - E. Lee Fisher   *w*   481

Fitz Hugh, Francine "Fancy" (Noblewoman; Ward)
Naughty or Nice - Melanie George   *r*   322

Fitzgerald, Maddie (Advertising)
Bait - Karen Robards   *r*   415

FitzHenry, Rhys (Warrior)
The Beauty Bride - Claire Delacroix   *r*   305

Fitzroy, Henry (Vampire)
Smoke and Mirrors - Tanya Huff   *h*   672

Fitzwalter, Alexa (Lawyer)
Guardian of Honor - Robin D. Owens   *f*   614

Flanagan, Brenna (Time Traveler; Witch)
Night's Kiss - Amanda Ashley   *r*   255

Fleet, Arlene (Murderer)
Gods in Alabama - Joshilyn Jackson   *c*   1172

Fleming, Pete (Police Officer)
Love Next Door - Anna Schmidt   *i*   1085

Fletcher, Miriam (Businesswoman)
The Hidden Family - Charles Stross   *f*   628

Fleur-du-Mal (Mythical Creature; Criminal)
The Meq - Steve Cash   *f*   551

Flic (Traveler)
Once upon a Summer Day - Dennis L.
   McKiernan   *f*   603

Flier, Suzanna (Musician)
The Kreutzer Sonata - Margriet De Moor   *c*   1133

Flint, Miles (Detective—Private)
Buried Deep - Kristine Kathryn Rusch   *s*   806

Floege, Emilie (Historical Figure; Artist)
The Painted Kiss - Elizabeth Hickey   *t*   909

Floyd (Detective—Private)
Century Rain - Alastair Reynolds   *s*   801

Fluck, Zelda (Spouse)
Trouble in Paradise - Pip Granger   *c*   1150
Trouble in Paradise - Pip Granger   *m*   106

Fludd, Edward (Scientist)
A Sundial in a Grave: 1610 - Mary Gentle   *t*   893

Flynn, Kelly (Accountant; Detective—Amateur)
Knit One, Kill Two - Maggie Sefton   *m*   219

Ford, Fargo (Outlaw)
Revenge of Eagles - William W. Johnstone   *w*   497

Ford, Marion "Doc" (Scientist; Single Parent)
Dead of Night - Randy Wayne White   *m*   243

Ford, Simon (Businessman; Inventor)
Stolen Memory - Virginia Kantra   *r*   351

Forder, Alice (Young Woman)
Natives and Exotics - Jane Alison   *t*   844
Natives and Exotics - Jane Alison   *c*   1103

Fordyce, Caroline (Writer; Detective—Amateur)
Wait Until Midnight - Amanda Quick   *r*   407

Forlo (Warrior)
Blades of the Tiger - Chris Pierson   *f*   616

Fortenberry, Annie (Innkeeper; Widow(er))
Full Bloom - Janet Evanovich   *r*   312

Fortunato, Michael (Child)
A Rumor of Gems - Ellen Steiber   *f*   627

Foster, Dylan (Professor)
When the Day of Evil Comes - Melanie
   Wells   *i*   1091

Foster, Laura (Teacher)
Like Death - Tim Waggoner   *h*   733

Foster, Laurence (Spouse; Parent)
No Place Like Home - Mary Higgins Clark   *c*   1125

Foster, Tony (Filmmaker)
Smoke and Mirrors - Tanya Huff   *h*   672

Foster, Willow (Lawyer)
The Dangerous Protector - Janet Chapman   *r*   291

Fox (Noblewoman)
A Factory of Cunning - Philippa Stockley   *t*   976
A Factory of Cunning - Philippa Stockley   *c*   1232

Fox, Dave (Police Officer)
November Mourns - Tom Piccirilli   *h*   709

Foxe, Colin (Vampire; Police Officer)
I Hunger for You - Susan Sizemore   *h*   727
I Hunger for You - Susan Sizemore   *h*   429

Frank, Anne (Historical Figure; Holocaust Victim)
The Boy Who Loved Anne Frank - Ellen
   Feldman   *c*   1142

Franklin, Dominic "Nic" (FBI Agent; Lawyer)
Dark Moon - Lori Handeland   *r*   325

Frazer, Katherine (Gentlewoman)
Miss Frazer's Adventure - Debbie Raleigh   *r*   409

Frederick II (Historical Figure; Ruler)
The Falcon of Palermo - Maria Bordihn   *t*   856

Freeman, Lanie Belle (Teenager)
The Homeplace - Gilbert Morris   *i*   1070

Freeman, Max (Detective—Private)
A Killing Night - Jonathon King   *m*   143

Fremont, Jessie Benton (Spouse; Historical Figure)
Dream West - David Nevin   *w*   506

Fremont, John Charles (Historical Figure; Explorer)
Dream West - David Nevin   *w*   506

Frevisse (Religious)
The Widow's Tale - Margaret Frazer   *m*   91

Freyl, Hugh (Lawyer; Friend)
Bleedout - Joan Brady   *c*   1115

Freytag-Loringhoven, Elsa von (Historical Figure)
Holy Skirts - Rene Steinke   *t*   975

Friant, Rene (Computer Expert)
Murder in Clichy - Cara Black   *m*   21

Friedman, Kinky (Detective—Private; Singer)
Ten Little New Yorkers - Kinky Friedman   *m*   92

Frost, Bridget (Editor)
A Ghost of a Chance - Peter Guttridge   *m*   112

Fry, Wendell (Drifter; Gunfighter)
Trapp's Mountain - Robert J. Randisi   *w*   517

Fulmer, Claudia (Parent)
Drive Like Hell - Dallas Hudgens   *c*   1168

Fulmer, Luke (Teenager)
Drive Like Hell - Dallas Hudgens   *c*   1168

Fulmer, Nick (Landscaper; Drug Dealer)
Drive Like Hell - Dallas Hudgens   *c*   1168

Fuyuki (Organized Crime Figure)
The Devil of Nanking - Mo Hayder   *c*   1159

Fyne, Juliet (Witch; Captive)
The Moon Witch - Linda Winstead Jones   *r*   347

G

Gabriel (Sailor)
Pieces of Hate - Tim Lebbon   *h*   689

Gabrielle (Scientist)
Building Harlequin's Moon - Larry Niven   *s*   795

Gagnon, Catherine (Abuse Victim; Parent)
Alone - Lisa Gardner   *c*   1148

Gagnon, Jimmy (Wealthy; Spouse)
Alone - Lisa Gardner   *c*   1148

Galatyn, Llyr (Ruler; Mythical Creature)
Master of the Moon - Angela Knight   *r*   360

Gallagher, Jax (Gambler; Genius)
Skintight - Susan Andersen   *r*   254

Gallagher, Wilhelmina "Willi" (Teacher;
   Detective—Amateur)
The Eye That Is Divine - Kat Goldring   *m*   102

Gallan, John (Police Officer)
The Crime Trade - Simon Kernick   *m*   141

Gambier, Alex (Child; Handicapped)
Phantom Nights - John Farris   *h*   656

Garcia, Juanita (Businesswoman)
Human Resource - Pierce Askegren   *s*   746

Gardner, Derik (Cook; Werewolf)
Derik's Bane - MaryJanice Davidson   *h*   654

Garner, Dallas (Student—College; Waiter/Waitress)
Lone Star Calder - Janet Dailey   *r*   300

Garner, Peyton (Agent)
Measure of a Man - Adrianne Byrd   *r*   283

Garrett, Luke (Saloon Keeper/Owner; Outlaw)
Her Bodyguard - Geralyn Dawson   *r*   304

Garrett, Mibby (Landscaper; Widow(er))
Always Green - Patti Ann Hill   *i*   1044

Garrett, Owen (Military Personnel)
The Dark Crusade - Walter H. Hunt   *s*   777

L

M

Mannet, Eddie (Cowboy)
The Wrangler - Frank Roderus   *w*   519

Manning, Ty (Innkeeper)
Look Closely - Laura Caldwell   *r*   284

Manningtree, Titus (Gentleman)
The Exploits and Adventures of Miss Alethea Darcy - Elizabeth Aston   *t*   848

Manoso, Carlos "Ranger" (Bounty Hunter)
Eleven on Top - Janet Evanovich   *m*   80

Mantilini, Paul (Organized Crime Figure)
The Devil's Wind - Richard Rayner   *c*   1218
The Devil's Wind - Richard Rayner   *t*   961

March, John (Religious; Military Personnel)
March - Geraldine Brooks   *c*   1117
March - Geraldine Brooks   *t*   860

March, Marmee (Spouse)
March - Geraldine Brooks   *c*   1117
March - Geraldine Brooks   *t*   860

Marguerite of Alencon (Noblewoman)
The King's Mistress - Terri Brisbin   *r*   272

Marion, David (Convict)
Bleedout - Joan Brady   *c*   1115

Mark (Divorced Person)
Lost in the Forest - Sue Miller   *c*   1198

Mark, Lennox (Publisher)
My Name Is Legion - A.N. Wilson   *c*   1243

Markby, Alan (Police Officer; Fiance(e))
That Way Murder Lies - Ann Granger   *m*   105

Markham, William (Sea Captain; Spirit)
Spirited Away - Pamela Labud   *r*   364

Markos, Nicholas (Businessman)
Code Name: Fiancee - Susan Vaughan   *r*   443

Marlowe, Christopher (Historical Figure; Writer)
Tamburlaine Must Die - Louise Welsh   *t*   992

Marlowe, Milton (Magician)
Guardian of the Freedom - Irene Radford   *f*   617

Marques, Alberto (Writer)
Havana Red - Leonardo Padura   *m*   184

Marsh, Jeremy (Writer)
True Believer - Nicholas Sparks   *c*   1230

Marsh, Pepper (Computer Expert; Unemployed)
Hard Day's Knight - Katie MacAlister   *r*   379

Marshall, Lucius (Nobleman)
Simply Unforgettable - Mary Balogh   *r*   261

Martin (Television Personality; Convict)
A Long Way Down - Nick Hornby   *c*   1166

Martin, Fitzhugh (Businessman)
Acts of Faith - Philip Caputo   *c*   1122

Martin, Jessie (Student)
Galveston Rose - Mary Powell   *w*   514

Martin, Thomas (Religious)
City of the Dead - Brian Keene   *h*   675

Martinez, Elisa (Refugee; Maintenance Worker)
Endless Chain - Emilie Richards   *r*   412

Martynov, Mikhail (Scientist)
Sunstorm - Stephen Baxter   *s*   748

Marx, Groucho (Historical Figure; Actor)
Groucho Marx, King of the Jungle - Ron Goulart   *t*   897

Mary (Parent)
Milk - Darcey Steinke   *c*   1231

Masefield, Genevieve (Gentlewoman; Detective—Private)
Murder on the Salsette - Conrad Allen   *t*   845
Murder on the Salsette - Conrad Allen   *m*   5

Maslow, Meyer (Holocaust Victim; Businessman)
A Changed Man - Francine Prose   *c*   1214

Mason, Matthew "Mutt" (Mentally Ill Person)
Wrapped in Rain - Charles Martin   *i*   1063

Massing, Welstiel (Warrior)
Sister of the Dead - Barb Hendee   *h*   667

Masters, Lily (Thief)
To Love a Thief - Julie Anne Long   *r*   373

Masters, Torrie (Spaceship Captain; Businesswoman)
Unmasked - C.J. Barry   *r*   264

Masterson, Grace (Artist)
Empire Rising - Thomas Kelly   *c*   1177
Empire Rising - Thomas Kelly   *t*   920

Matekoni, J.L.B. (Spouse)
In the Company of Cheerful Ladies - Alexander McCall Smith   *c*   1193

Mathers, Bevand (Musician)
The Demonologist - Michael Laimo   *h*   683

Mathers, Kristin (Young Woman)
The Demonologist - Michael Laimo   *h*   683

Mathers, Violet (Teenager)
Oh My Stars - Lorna Landvik   *t*   924

Mathewar (Wizard)
The Divided Crown - Isabel Glass   *f*   573

Matthews, Daniel (Teenager)
New World Order - Ben Jeapes   *s*   778

Matthews, Dayne (Actor)
Fame - Karen Kingsbury   *i*   1054

Matthias (Secretary)
The Hidden Family - Charles Stross   *f*   628

Maureen (Single Parent)
A Long Way Down - Nick Hornby   *c*   1166

Mavra (Vampire)
Dead Beat - Jim Butcher   *h*   647

May, John (Detective—Police)
The Water Room - Christopher Fowler   *m*   89

Mayer, Willard (Spy; Professor)
Hitler's Peace - Philip Kerr   *m*   142
Hitler's Peace - Philip Kerr   *c*   1178
Hitler's Peace - Philip Kerr   *t*   922

Mayovskyj, Kolya (Widow(er); Engineer)
A Short History of Tractors in Ukrainian - Marina Lewycka   *c*   1188

Mayovskyj, Vera (Young Woman)
A Short History of Tractors in Ukrainian - Marina Lewycka   *c*   1188

McAllister, Antonio (Police Officer)
Terminal 9 - Patricia H. Rushford   *i*   1083

McAllister, Seth (Businessman)
Protected Hearts - Bonnie K. Winn   *i*   1097

McBride, Grace (Computer Expert)
Dead Run - P.J. Tracy   *m*   237

McBride, Mari (Store Owner)
Her Bodyguard - Geralyn Dawson   *r*   304

McCabe, Cash (Bully)
The Relentless Gun - Pete Peterson   *w*   512

McCabe, Hunter (Architect)
Never Tell - Karen Young   *r*   450

McCabe, Sam (FBI Agent)
Bait - Karen Robards   *r*   415

McCaffrey, Selena (Martial Arts Expert; Criminal)
The Assassin - Rachel Butler   *r*   282

McCain, Truman (Police Officer)
Truly, Madly, Dangerously - Linda Winstead Jones   *r*   348

McCain, Wynter (Twin)
Moon of the Sleeping Bear - K. Celeste Bryan   *w*   466

McCall, Treena (Dancer; Widow(er))
Skintight - Susan Andersen   *r*   254

McCarthy, Lou (Spouse; Businesswoman)
Winners - Eric B. Martin   *c*   1190

McCarthy, Shane (Chimneysweep)
Winners - Eric B. Martin   *c*   1190

McClellan, Doris (Psychic; Grandparent)
True Believer - Nicholas Sparks   *c*   1230

McClintoch, Lara (Antiques Dealer; Detective—Amateur)
The Moai Murders - Lyn Hamilton   *m*   118

McCormack, Calvin (Political Figure; Spouse)
Flesh Wounds - John Lawton   *m*   149

McCoy, Jane (FBI Agent)
In the Company of Liars - David Ellis   *m*   75

McCoy, Lukas (Contractor)
Random Acts of Fashion - Nikki Rivers   *r*   414

McDonald, Cal (Detective—Private)
Savage Membrane - Steve Niles   *h*   706

McGee, Connel (Military Personnel)
Camp Ford - Johnny D. Boggs   *w*   458

McGorran, Siobhan (Scientist)
Sunstorm - Stephen Baxter   *s*   748

McGuire, Sean (Sports Figure; Guardian)
Table for Five - Susan Wiggs   *r*   445

McIntyre, Chris (Veteran)
Wounded Healer - Donna Fleisher   *i*   1028

McKenna, Abbey (Farmer)
Gunsmoke: The Last Dog Soldier - Joseph A. West   *w*   533

McKenna, Cassie (Widow(er); FBI Agent)
Bloody Point - Linda J. White   *i*   1092

McKenzie, Eli (Spy; Detective)
The McKenzie Artifact - Alison Kent   *r*   356

McKenzie, Rushmore (Detective—Private)
Tin City - David Housewright   *m*   131

McKeon, Hart (Fugitive; Convict)
Blood Atonement - J.D. Harkleroad   *w*   493

McKie, Jamie (Heir)
Whence Came a Prince - Liz Curtis Higgs   *i*   1042

McLean, Ewan (Nobleman)
Lord of Sin - Madeline Hunter   *r*   338

McMillan, Carlisle (Carpenter)
High Plains Tango - Robert James Waller   *w*   529

McNair, Eric (Vampire)
Wicked Nights - Nina Bangs   *r*   263

McNair, Mike (Scientist)
The God Particle - Richard Cox   *s*   757

McNally, Skye (Gambler; Addict)
Double Down - Tess Hudson   *r*   334

McNelly, Leander (Lawman; Historical Figure)
Pendencia Creek - E. Lee Fisher   *w*   481

McPhail, Walker (Knight)
Hard Day's Knight - Katie MacAlister   *r*   379

McQueen, Steve "Danny" (Musician)
Goodnight Steve McQueen - Louise Wener   *c*   1241

Meade, Lois (Businesswoman; Detective—Amateur)
Weeping on Wednesday - Ann Purser   *m*   203

Meadowlark (Spouse; Indian)
Dancing with the Golden Bear - Win Blevins   *w*   457

Medici, Marie de (Historical Figure; Royalty)
A Sundial in a Grave: 1610 - Mary Gentle   *t*   893

Meehan, Margaret (Immigrant)
The Keeners - Maura D. Shaw   *t*   971

Character Name Index

Muse, Loren (Detective—Homicide)
The Innocent - Harlan Coben   *c*   1127

Mykel (Military Personnel)
Alector's Choice - L.E. Modesitt Jr.   *f*   607

Myrren (Witch)
Myrren's Gift - Fiona McIntosh   *f*   602

N

Nakata, Satoru (Friend; Aged Person)
Kafka on the Shore - Haruki Murakami   *c*   1203

Nameless Detective (Detective—Private)
Nightcrawlers - Bill Pronzini   *m*   202

Nash, Charlotte (Spy; Gentlewoman)
My Surrender - Connie Brockway   *r*   275

Natalie (Student)
Someone Comes to Town, Someone Leaves Town - Cory Doctorow   *f*   563

Natasha (Teenager; Girlfriend)
Upstate - Kalisha Buckhanon   *c*   1118

Navarre, Jackson "Tres" (Detective—Private; Professor)
Mission Road - Rick Riordan   *m*   208

Naysmith, William (Writer)
The Portrait - Iain Pears   *t*   948

Nell, Mary (Young Woman)
One Sunday Morning - Amy Ephron   *t*   883
One Sunday Morning - Amy Ephron   *c*   1140

Nelle (Aged Person; Mentally Ill Person)
The Mermaid Chair - Sue Monk Kidd   *c*   1179

Netta (Captive)
Tahn - L.A. Kelly   *i*   1053

Neville, Margaret (Housewife)
The Wounded Hawk - Sara Douglass   *f*   565

Neville, Thomas (Religious)
The Wounded Hawk - Sara Douglass   *f*   565

Niamor (Spy)
The Aware - Glenda Larke   *f*   592

Nicci (Healer)
Chainfire - Terry Goodkind   *f*   574

Nicholas, Lee (Actor)
Smoke and Mirrors - Tanya Huff   *h*   672

Nicholas of Dunkeathe (Nobleman)
Lord of Dunkeathe - Margaret Moore   *r*   391

Nichols, Alex (Police Officer)
Runaway Mistress - Robyn Carr   *r*   286

Nichols, Tallulah "Lu" (Journalist)
A New Lu - Laura Castoro   *r*   290

Nina Bronca (Indian)
Wild Girl - Jim Fergus   *t*   887

Nixon, Richard (Historical Figure; Military Personnel)
The Ambassador's Son - Homer Hickam   *t*   908

Nofret-te-en (Ruler)
Sanctuary - Mercedes Lackey   *f*   591

Nolan, Alex (Spouse)
No Place Like Home - Mary Higgins Clark   *c*   1125

Nolan, Donna (Radio Personality)
Wicked Nights - Nina Bangs   *r*   263

Nolan, Vincent (Volunteer)
A Changed Man - Francine Prose   *c*   1214

Norbanus, Titus (Military Personnel)
The Seven Hills - John Maddox Roberts   *t*   963
The Seven Hills - John Maddox Roberts   *s*   804

Nordhagen, Roger (Doctor)
Finishing Touches - Thomas Tessier   *h*   731

Nori (Young Woman)
Wolf in the Night - Tara Harper   *s*   775

North, Cleo (Consultant; Military Personnel)
The First Mistake - Merline Lovelace   *r*   376
The Last Bullet - Merline Lovelace   *r*   377
The Middle Sin - Merline Lovelace   *r*   378

North, Marcus (Nobleman; Bastard Son)
To Pleasure a Prince - Sabrina Jeffries   *r*   343

Novak, Alexandra (Writer)
Lord Byron's Novel - John Crowley   *t*   871

Novak, Renata (Government Official)
The Prometheus Project - Steve White   *s*   832

Nubey, Jeb (Religious)
Whisper Town - Patricia Hickman   *i*   1041

Nudge (Teenager; Genetically Altered Being)
Maximum Ride: The Angel Experiment - James Patterson   *s*   798

Nyvysk, Alexander (Religious)
Flesh Gothic - Edward Lee   *h*   691

O

Oak-Lord (Deity)
Heartwood - Barbara Campbell   *f*   550

O'Bannon, Xanthier (Sea Captain; Nobleman)
Across a Wild Sea - Sasha Lord   *r*   374

O'Brian, Callie (Businesswoman; Restaurateur)
Detours - Bette Nordberg   *i*   1074

O'Brien, Emerald (Psychic; Store Owner)
Murder under a Mystic Moon - Yasmine Galenorn   *h*   659

O'Brien, Tommy (Worker; Thief)
Terminal - Brian Keene   *h*   676

O'Conner, Grace (Businesswoman)
Second-Chance Hero - Justine Davis   *r*   303

O'Conner, Marilyn "Marly" (Teenager)
Second-Chance Hero - Justine Davis   *r*   303

O'Connor, Carson (Detective—Police)
Dean Koontz's Frankenstein. Book 1: Prodigal Son - Dean R. Koontz   *h*   681

O'Connor, Conn (Journalist)
Bloodlines - Jan Burke   *m*   37

O'Connor, Drew (Farmer)
A Bride Most Begrudging - Deeanne Gist   *i*   1034

Od (Wizard)
Od Magic - Patricia A. McKillip   *f*   604

Odysseus (Nobleman; Traveler)
Odysseus on the Rhine - Edward S. Louis   *f*   596

O'Gamhna, Beatrice (Gang Member)
Metropolis - Elizabeth Gaffney   *c*   1147
Metropolis - Elizabeth Gaffney   *t*   891

O'Hara, Grace (Teenager)
Cryptid Hunters - Roland Smith   *s*   814

O'Hara, Marty (Teenager)
Cryptid Hunters - Roland Smith   *s*   814

Old, Rose (Foundling)
Misfortune - Wesley Stace   *t*   974

Old Knight (Knight)
Tilting at Windmills - Julian Branston   *t*   859

Olga (Noblewoman)
The Hidden Family - Charles Stross   *f*   628

Oliver, Gideon (Anthropologist; Detective—Amateur)
Where There's a Will - Aaron Elkins   *m*   74

Olmos, Christina (Computer Expert)
Cusp - Robert A. Metzger   *s*   791

Olmos, Xavier (Computer Expert)
Cusp - Robert A. Metzger   *s*   791

Olsen, Timothy (Scientist)
Jason X: The Experiment - Pat Cadigan   *h*   649

Olson, Lanny (Police Officer)
Velocity - Dean R. Koontz   *h*   682
Velocity - Dean R. Koontz   *c*   1182

O'Mahoney, Peter (Teenager)
Suffer the Children - David Bishop   *h*   643

O'Malley, Rourke (Banker)
Really Hot - Jennifer LaBrecque   *r*   363

O'Mara, Ronan (Historian)
Ireland - Frank Delaney   *t*   875

O'Neill, Rafe (Businessman; Vampire)
Vampire Beach - Alexa Hayes   *h*   666

Onkar (Health Care Professional)
Afterburn - S.L. Viehl   *s*   826

Onslow, Judith (Nurse; Detective—Amateur)
The Black Smith - Constance Little   *m*   154

Opari (Mythical Creature)
The Meq - Steve Cash   *f*   551

Orr, Jane (Prostitute; Reincarnated Person)
Darkwitch Rising - Sara Douglass   *f*   564

Orrick of Silloth (Nobleman)
The King's Mistress - Terri Brisbin   *r*   272

Osborne, Paul "Doc" (Dentist; Fisherman)
Dead Jitterbug - Victoria Houston   *m*   132

O'Shea, Mattie (Worker)
The Hunter's Moon - O.R. Melling   *f*   606

O'Shea, Torie (Genealogist; Detective—Amateur)
Thicker than Water - Rett MacPherson   *m*   157

Ostvan (Artisan)
The Carpet Makers - Andreas Eschbach   *s*   769

Owen, Faith (Single Parent)
Jamie - Lori Foster   *r*   318

Owen, Gareth (Government Official)
The Point in the Market - Michael Pearce   *m*   193
The Point in the Market - Michael Pearce   *t*   947

Owens, Marty (Store Owner)
Her Man Upstairs - Dixie Browning   *r*   277

Owens, Simon (Archaeologist)
The Midas Trap - Sharon McClellan   *r*   386

P

Pada (Military Personnel)
Talyn - Holly Lisle   *f*   595

Pagone, Allison (Writer)
In the Company of Liars - David Ellis   *m*   75

Pamir (Spaceman)
The Well of Stars - Robert Reed   *s*   799

Paola (Spouse; Psychologist)
The Mysterious Flame of Queen Loana - Umberto Eco   *c*   1139

Pardoe, Dan (Police Officer)
Postscript to Poison - Dorothy Bowers   *m*   27
Shadows Before - Dorothy Bowers   *m*   28

Parker (Sailor)
Pieces of Hate - Tim Lebbon   *h*   689

Q

Character Name Index

S

Scott, Jimmy (Widow(er))
Veterans Way - Robin Lee Hatcher   *i*   1038

Scott, Kate (Professor)
The Effects of Light - Miranda Beverly-
Whittemore   *c*   1114

Scott, Stella (Store Owner)
Hot Spot - Susan Johnson   *r*   345

Scott-Olson, Sharyn (Police Officer)
Buried Deep - Kristine Kathryn Rusch   *s*   806

Scudder, Matt (Detective—Private)
All the Flowers Are Dying - Lawrence Block   *m*   22

Scythe, Jackson (Detective—Homicide)
Sprayed Stiff - Laura Bradley   *m*   30

Sealy, Olivia (Amnesiac; Wealthy)
Bloodlines - Dinah McCall   *r*   384

Sebastian (Nobleman)
A Lady of Talent - Evelyn Richardson   *r*   413

Seebeck, August (Traveler; Worker)
Godplayers - Damien Broderick   *f*   545

Selavy, Rose (Prostitute; Spirit)
Kiss the Goat - Brian Stableford   *h*   729

Selgrin, Lucy (Relative)
The Sad Truth about Happiness - Anne
Giardini   *c*   1149

Selgrin, Maggie (Health Care Professional)
The Sad Truth about Happiness - Anne
Giardini   *c*   1149

Seltzer, Nathan (Store Owner)
Boogaloo on Second Avenue - Mark
Kurlansky   *c*   1185

Sema (Animal)
Unspoken - Angela Elwell Hunt   *i*   1047

Semenkaru, Danilo (Professor; Immortal)
The Blood of Kings - John Michael
Curlovich   *h*   653

Semerket (Detective—Police)
Year of the Hyenas - Brad Geagley   *t*   892
Year of the Hyenas - Brad Geagley   *m*   97

Senneth (Religious)
Mystic and Rider - Sharon Shinn   *f*   623

Sev, Brano (Amnesiac; Spy)
36 Yalta Boulevard - Olen Steinhauer   *m*   227

Seward, John L. (Doctor)
The Book of Renfield - Tim Lucas   *h*   694

Sha'ik (Religious; Rebel)
Deadhouse Gates - Steven Erikson   *f*   567

Shakespeare, William (Historical Figure; Writer)
Murder in Stratford - Audrey Peterson   *t*   953
Murder in Stratford - Audrey Peterson   *m*   199

Shamas (Spouse; Immigrant)
Maps for Lost Lovers - Nadeem Aslam   *c*   1108

Shannon, Elizabeth (Young Woman; Captive)
Comanche Crossing - Harold G. Ross   *w*   521

Shannon, James (Farmer; Sailor)
Comanche Crossing - Harold G. Ross   *w*   521

Shannon, Mark (Sports Figure)
Double Down - Tess Hudson   *r*   334

Shannon, Rick (Radio Personality; Detective—
Private)
Highway 61 Resurfaced - Bill Fitzhugh   *m*   86

Shapiro, Desiree (Detective—Private; Widow(er))
Murder Can Mess Up Your Mascara - Selma
Eichler   *m*   72

Shapiro, Paul (Young Man)
Fear Me - Stephen Laws   *h*   685

Shardlake, Matthew (Lawyer; Handicapped)
Dark Fire - C.J. Sansom   *m*   214

Sharpe, Gil (Artist)
The Fyre Mirror - Karen Harper   *t*   905

Shaughnessy, M.K. (FBI Agent)
What She Can't See - Hunter Morgan   *r*   392

Shaw, Mally (Nurse)
Phantom Nights - John Farris   *h*   656

Shaw, Samantha (Businesswoman; Detective—
Amateur)
Batteries Required - Jennifer Apodaca   *m*   8

Shay (Teenager; Rebel)
Uglies - Scott Westerfeld   *s*   831

Shedara (Mythical Creature)
Blades of the Tiger - Chris Pierson   *f*   616

Sheffers, Margaret "May" (Gentlewoman)
The Marriage List - Dorothy McFalls   *r*   387

Shefford, Zoe (Psychic)
Intimidation - Wanda L. Dyson   *i*   1026

Shelley, Wollstonecraft "Wollie" (Store Owner;
Detective—Amateur)
Dating Is Murder - Harley Jane Kozak   *m*   146

Shelton, Rebecca (Spouse)
Monster - Frank Peretti   *h*   708

Shelton, Reed (Police Officer)
Monster - Frank Peretti   *h*   708
Monster - Frank Peretti   *i*   1078

Shelton, Vivien (Lawyer; Animal Lover)
First Dance - Karen Kendall   *r*   353

Shemov, Pavel (Warrior)
The Rite - Richard Lee Byers   *f*   549

Shepher, Shulamit (Scholar)
The Genizah at the House of Shepher - Tamar
Yellin   *t*   996

Shepherd, James (Friend; Teenager)
The Diezmo - Rick Bass   *c*   1112

Shepherd, Lori (Volunteer; Detective—Amateur)
Aunt Dimity and the Next of Kin - Nancy
Atherton   *m*   9
Aunt Dimity and the Next of Kin - Nancy
Atherton   *h*   638

Sherbourne, Edmund (Religious)
Sweet Violet - Catherine Palmer   *i*   1076

Sheridan, Charles (Scientist; Nobleman)
Death at Blenheim Palace - Robin Paige   *m*   186

Sheridan, Kathryn Ardleigh (Writer; Noblewoman)
Death at Blenheim Palace - Robin Paige   *m*   186

Sherwood, Ray (Musician)
Swing - Rupert Holmes   *m*   130
Swing - Rupert Holmes   *c*   1164
Swing - Rupert Holmes   *t*   912

Shi Chongming (Professor)
The Devil of Nanking - Mo Hayder   *t*   907
The Devil of Nanking - Mo Hayder   *c*   1159

Shipton, Cassandra (Businesswoman; Fiance(e))
The Divine Circle of Ladies Making Mischief - Dolores
Stewart Riccio   *r*   410

Shoshannah (Captive)
A Crown in the Stars - Kacy Barnett-
Gramckow   *i*   1001

Shostakovich, Dmitri (Composer; Historical Figure)
Europe Central - William T. Vollmann   *c*   1238

Sibbechai (Vampire)
Witch Finder - C.L. Werner   *f*   631

Signy (Royalty)
A Mankind Witch - Dave Freer   *f*   572

Silar (Religious)
Demonsouled - Jonathan Moeller   *f*   609

Silva, Leilani (Researcher)
Black Sands - Colleen Coble   *i*   1015

Silver, Harry (Spaceman)
Rogue Berserker - Fred Saberhagen   *s*   808

Silver Feather (Indian)
Silver Feather - Cassie Edwards   *r*   311

Silverhair, Pasgen (Mythical Creature)
Ill Met by Moonlight - Mercedes Lackey   *f*   590

Simpkins, Brenda Marlene (Care Giver)
The Only Road There Is - Rebecca Bailey   *w*   455

Simpkins, Dennis Ishman (Relative)
The Only Road There Is - Rebecca Bailey   *w*   455

Simpkins, Mauda Belle (Aged Person)
The Only Road There Is - Rebecca Bailey   *w*   455

Sims, Christabel (Noblewoman; Widow(er))
One Night with a Prince - Sabrina Jeffries   *r*   342

Sinclair, Eric (Vampire; Ruler)
Undead and Unappreciated - MaryJanice
Davidson   *r*   301

Singer, Alma (Teenager)
The History of Love - Nicole Krauss   *c*   1184

Singer, Charlotte (Parent; Linguist)
The History of Love - Nicole Krauss   *c*   1184

Sissy (Addict)
Sex with the Serpent Girl - Matthew
Carnahan   *c*   1123

Skirmig (Diplomat)
Talyn - Holly Lisle   *f*   595

Sloane, Sydney (Detective—Private; Lesbian)
Son of a Gun - Randye Lordon   *m*   155

Slyekin (Animal)
One for Sorrow, Two for Joy - Clive
Woodall   *f*   633

Smith, Jake (Detective—Private; Single Parent)
Her Fifth Husband? - Dixie Browning   *r*   276

Smith, Jedediah (Mountain Man; Explorer)
Dancing with the Golden Bear - Win
Blevins   *w*   457

Smith, John Stephen (Plantation Owner)
No Holier Spot of Ground - John Warren
Smith   *w*   525

Smith, Kelly (Journalist)
The God Particle - Richard Cox   *s*   757

Smith, Ricky (Gambler)
Mr. Lucky - James Swain   *c*   1233

Smith, Robert (Cousin; Plantation Owner)
No Holier Spot of Ground - John Warren
Smith   *w*   525

Smyth, John (Editor)
Mountaintop Drive - James R. Coggins   *i*   1016

Snapdragon, Luther (Maintenance Worker)
The Spoon in the Bathroom Wall - Tony
Johnston   *f*   586

Snapdragon, Martha (Child)
The Spoon in the Bathroom Wall - Tony
Johnston   *f*   586

Snorri (Chieftain)
Saga: A Novel of Medieval Iceland - Jeff
Janoda   *t*   918

Snow, Emma (Governess)
A Summer's Day - Lisa Noeli   *r*   399

Snow, Mia (Warrior; Detective—Police)
Awaken Me Darkly - Gena Showalter   *r*   426

Snow Flower (Young Woman)
Snow Flower and the Secret Fan - Lisa See   *t*   970

Snowstealer, Raryn (Warrior)
The Rite - Richard Lee Byers   *f*   549

Solomon, Sasha (Advertising; Detective—Amateur)
The Belen Hitch - Pari Noskin Taichert   *w*   526

T

Z

Zachary, Zoe (Government Official)
Dexta - C.J. Ryan *s* 807

Zael (Teenager)
Ravenor Returned - Dan Abnett *s* 739

Zakolyev, Dmitri (Military Personnel)
The Journeys of Socrates - Dan Millman *t* 935

Zalos, Rehanne (Student)
When the Beast Ravens - E. Rose Sabin *f* 620

Zapata de Leon, Cesar (Revolutionary)
Rebel Gun - Lyle Brandt *w* 462

Zeinab (Spouse)
The Point in the Market - Michael Pearce *t* 947

Zeno (Philosopher)
The Seven Hills - John Maddox Roberts *s* 804

Zero, Nina (Photographer; Criminal)
Digging James Dean - Robert Eversz *m* 81

Zezen, Zianno (Mythical Creature)
The Meq - Steve Cash *f* 551

Zhao-ji (Orphan)
Paradox - John Meaney *s* 788

Ziani, Antonio (Adventurer; Businessman)
The Lion of St. Mark - Thomas Quinn *t* 959

Zical (Military Personnel)
The Dare - Susan Kearney *s* 779

Zileri, Paolo (Military Personnel)
The Way to Glory - David Drake *s* 765

Zillis, Steve (Saloon Keeper/Owner)
Velocity - Dean R. Koontz *h* 682

Zipporah (Historical Figure; Biblical Figure)
Zipporah, Wife of Moses - Marek Halter *t* 904

Znora, Burn mu (Health Care Professional)
Afterburn - S.L. Viehl *s* 826

Zou Tun (Religious; Nobleman)
Hungry Tigress - Jade Lee *r* 368

Zuckerman, Adam (Widow(er); Single Parent)
The Butterfly Garden - Annette Blair *r* 267

Character Description Index

This index alphabetically lists descriptions of the major characters in featured titles. The descriptions may be occupations (astronaut, lawyer, etc.) or may describe persona (amnesiac, runaway, teenager, etc.). For each description, character names are listed alphabetically. Also provided are book titles, author names, genre codes and entry numbers. The genre codes are as follows: *c* Popular Fiction, *f* Fantasy, *h* Horror, *i* Inspirational, *m* Mystery, *r* Romance, *s* Science Fiction, *t* Historical, and *w* Western.

ABUSE VICTIM

Deveraux, Gally
High Plains Tango - Robert James Waller   *w*   529

Gagnon, Catherine
Alone - Lisa Gardner   *c*   1148

Swensen, Charity
A Land of Sheltered Promise - Jane Kirkpatrick   *w*   501

ACCIDENT VICTIM

Boudreaux, Bernie
The Professor's Daughter - Emily Raboteau   *c*   1215

Caine, Gillian
Random Acts of Fashion - Nikki Rivers   *r*   414

John
Lost in the Forest - Sue Miller   *c*   1198

Rael
Everything Changes - Jonathan Tropper   *c*   1235

ACCOUNTANT

Decker, Simon
Intimate Knowledge - Amanda Stevens   *r*   434

Flynn, Kelly
Knit One, Kill Two - Maggie Sefton   *m*   219

Le Noyer, Claire
Kissing Adrien - Siri L. Mitchell   *i*   1068

Spinelli, Sydney
First Date - Karen Kendall   *r*   354

ACTIVIST

Kincade, Sam
Endless Chain - Emilie Richards   *r*   412

Quinette
Acts of Faith - Philip Caputo   *c*   1122

Tegge, Del Jr.
By Summer's End - Pamela Morsi   *r*   393

Ulysses, Joe
The Divine Circle of Ladies Making Mischief - Dolores Stewart Riccio   *r*   410

ACTOR

Blaize
Tamburlaine Must Die - Louise Welsh   *t*   992

Booth, John Wilkes
The Curse of Cain - J. Mark Powell   *t*   956

Harrington, Jack
Worlds Collide - Alison Strobel   *i*   1088

Marx, Groucho
Groucho Marx, King of the Jungle - Ron Goulart   *t*   897

Matthews, Dayne
Fame - Karen Kingsbury   *i*   1054

Nicholas, Lee
Smoke and Mirrors - Tanya Huff   *h*   672

Revill, Nicholas
An Honorable Murder - Philip Gooden   *t*   896
An Honorable Murder - Philip Gooden   *m*   104

Waterston, Michael
Owl's Well That Ends Well - Donna Andrews   *m*   7

ACTRESS

Anderson, Catherine
Director's Cut - Alton Gansky   *i*   1031

Douglas, Kiki Sonntag
First Kiss - Kylie Adams   *r*   251

Hart, Katy
Fame - Karen Kingsbury   *i*   1054

Loring, Lisel
Nothing More to Lose - Kathryn Shay   *r*   423

Miller, Zee
Glimpses of Paradise - James Scott Bell   *i*   1002

Troy, Haila
The Frightened Stiff - Kelley Roos   *m*   211

ADDICT

Burns, Roberto
Badwater - Clinton McKinzie   *m*   171

Lawson, Alex
Hidden River - Adrian McKinty   *m*   170

McNally, Skye
Double Down - Tess Hudson   *r*   334

Sissy
Sex with the Serpent Girl - Matthew Carnahan   *c*   1123

ADMINISTRATOR

Vedreaux, Miryam
When the Beast Ravens - E. Rose Sabin   *f*   620

ADOPTEE

Brannock, Earl
Windward West - Matt Braun   *w*   465

ADVENTURER

Braithwaite, Douglas
Acts of Faith - Philip Caputo   *c*   1122

Casanova, Giovanni Giacomo
What Casanova Told Me - Susan Swan   *t*   978

Kovacs, Takeshi
Woken Furies - Richard Morgan   *s*   792

Leigh, Ariel
Take My Breath Away - Tina Donahue   *r*   307

Moreland, Theo
An Unexpected Pleasure - Candace Camp   *r*   285

Standish, Harrison
Mission: Irresistible - Lori Wilde   *r*   446

Ziani, Antonio
The Lion of St. Mark - Thomas Quinn   *t*   959

ADVERTISING

Cooper, Cassie
Mission: Irresistible - Lori Wilde   *r*   446

Dansky, Michael
Wildwood Road - Christopher Golden   *h*   661

Fitzgerald, Maddie
Bait - Karen Robards   *r*   415

Jones, Marlee
Detour Ahead - Cindi Myers   *r*   394

Mahoney, Chris
Fashion Victim - Sam Baker   *r*   257

Polito, Teddy
Wildwood Road - Christopher Golden   *h*   661

Solomon, Sasha
The Belen Hitch - Pari Noskin Taichert   *w*   526

AGED PERSON

Arrowgrass, Eolacha Kingfisher
The Iron Tree - Cecilia Dart-Thornton   *f*   560

Beacham, Elizabeth
Aunt Dimity and the Next of Kin - Nancy
   Atherton   *h*   638

DuFresne, Eliza
Four and Twenty Blackbirds - Cherie Priest   *h*   711

Gursky, Leo
The History of Love - Nicole Krauss   *c*   1184

Herndon, Lydia
The Belen Hitch - Pari Noskin Taichert   *w*   526

Jane, Thomas
Old Man's War - John Scalzi   *s*   811

Morgan, Virginia
Aprons on a Clothesline - Traci DePree   *i*   1023

Moses
Ghosts of Eden - T.M. Gray   *h*   662

Nakata, Satoru
Kafka on the Shore - Haruki Murakami   *c*   1203

Nelle
The Mermaid Chair - Sue Monk Kidd   *c*   1179

Parrish, Rose
Galveston Rose - Mary Powell   *w*   514

Perry, John
Old Man's War - John Scalzi   *s*   811

Simpkins, Mauda Belle
The Only Road There Is - Rebecca Bailey   *w*   455

Stuart, Henry
The Poet of Tolstoy Park - Sonny Brewer   *c*   1116

Tansy
Godplayers - Damien Broderick   *f*   545

Trumbull, Victoria
The Paperwhite Narcissus - Cynthia Riggs   *m*   207

Wilson, Harry
Old Man's War - John Scalzi   *s*   811

AGENT

de Quincy, Justin
Prince of Darkness - Sharon Kay Penman   *t*   949
Prince of Darkness - Sharon Kay Penman   *m*   196

Garner, Peyton
Measure of a Man - Adrianne Byrd   *r*   283

ALCOHOLIC

Taylor, Jack
The Magdalen Martyrs - Ken Bruen   *m*   34

ALIEN

Banichi
Destroyer - C.J. Cherryh   *s*   756

Corvax
Natural History - Justina Robson   *s*   805

Dingo
Formidable Enemy - Terry Bramlett   *s*   753

Draycos
Dragon and Slave - Timothy Zahn   *s*   839

Eesyan, Porthik
Mission to Minerva - James P. Hogan   *s*   776

G'Kaan
Slaves Unchained - Susan Wright   *s*   837

Jago
Destroyer - C.J. Cherryh   *s*   756

Jarrikk
Lost in Translation - Edward Willett   *s*   833

Kahn
The Challenge - Susan Kearney   *r*   352

Kyrin en Arr
Awaken Me Darkly - Gena Showalter   *r*   426

Liana
Afterburn - S.L. Viehl   *s*   826

Saluu-hir-lek
The Light-Years Beneath My Feet - Alan Dean
   Foster   *s*   771

Sarpedon
Crimson Tears - Ben Counter   *f*   558

Tchar
Into the Looking Glass - John Ringo   *s*   802

AMNESIAC

Birdsong, Tess
Shadows of Myth - Rachel Lee   *f*   594

Eldi, Rosa
The Rose of the World - Jude Fisher   *f*   571

Mackay, Juliana
Only for a Knight - Sue-Ellen Welfonder   *r*   444

Sealy, Olivia
Bloodlines - Dinah McCall   *r*   384

Sev, Brano
36 Yalta Boulevard - Olen Steinhauer   *m*   227

Stewart, Erica
Never Tell - Karen Young   *r*   450

ANGEL

Goodnight, Augusta
Too Late for Angels - Mignon F. Ballard   *m*   10

Turner, Andrew
Heaven Sent - Montre Bible   *i*   1004

ANIMAL

Bete
The Rose of the World - Jude Fisher   *f*   571

Chica
Jemez Spring - Rudolfo Anaya   *w*   452

Dante
Sight Hound - Pam Houston   *c*   1167

Dulcie
Cat Cross Their Graves - Shirley Rousseau
   Murphy   *m*   175

George
The Light-Years Beneath My Feet - Alan Dean
   Foster   *s*   771

Grey Rishte
Wolf in the Night - Tara Harper   *s*   775

Ji-Stu
Rabbit and the Wolves - Deborah L. Duvall   *w*   478

Joe Grey
Cat Cross Their Graves - Shirley Rousseau
   Murphy   *m*   175

King
The Winning Hand - C.K. Crigger   *w*   472

Kirrick
One for Sorrow, Two for Joy - Clive
   Woodall   *f*   633

Koko
The Cat Who Went Bananas - Lilian Jackson
   Braun   *m*   31

Midnight Louie
Cat in a Hot Pink Pursuit - Carole Nelson
   Douglas   *m*   68

Moon Dancer
Horse of Seven Moons - Karen Taschek   *w*   527

Mrs. Murphy
Cat's Eyewitness - Rita Mae Brown   *m*   32

Phil
Dog - Michelle Herman   *c*   1162

Redbird
Rabbit and the Wolves - Deborah L. Duvall   *w*   478

Sema
Unspoken - Angela Elwell Hunt   *i*   1047

Slyekin
One for Sorrow, Two for Joy - Clive
   Woodall   *f*   633

Stanley
Sight Hound - Pam Houston   *c*   1167

Tee Tucker
Cat's Eyewitness - Rita Mae Brown   *m*   32

Traska
One for Sorrow, Two for Joy - Clive
   Woodall   *f*   633

Wa-Ya
Rabbit and the Wolves - Deborah L. Duvall   *w*   478

Yum Yum
The Cat Who Went Bananas - Lilian Jackson
   Braun   *m*   31

ANIMAL LOVER

Chilton, Sarah
Horse of Seven Moons - Karen Taschek   *w*   527

Shelton, Vivien
First Dance - Karen Kendall   *r*   353

ANIMAL TRAINER

Arnold, Jessie
Murder at Five Finger Light - Sue Henry   *m*   127

Finbow, Thomas
The Mapmaker's Daughter - John Pilkington   *t*   955

ANTHROPOLOGIST

Brennan, Temperance
Cross Bones - Kathy Reichs   *m*   206

Costard, Aisha
Buried Deep - Kristine Kathryn Rusch   *s*   806

Oliver, Gideon
Where There's a Will - Aaron Elkins   *m*   74

ANTIQUARIAN

Yambo
The Mysterious Flame of Queen Loana - Umberto
   Eco   *c*   1139

ANTIQUES DEALER

Anderson, Julia
The Pleasure Slave - Gena Showalter   *r*   427

Keane, Sebastian
A Rumor of Gems - Ellen Steiber   *f*   627

McClintoch, Lara
The Moai Murders - Lyn Hamilton   *m*   118

BASTARD SON

Bowden, Raymond
Rancho Alegre - John D. Nesbitt   w   505

Byrne, Gavin
One Night with a Prince - Sabrina Jeffries   r   342

de Quincy, Justin
Prince of Darkness - Sharon Kay Penman   t   949
Prince of Darkness - Sharon Kay Penman   m   196

North, Marcus
To Pleasure a Prince - Sabrina Jeffries   r   343

Rochester, Trevelyan
Much Ado about Magic - Patricia Rice   r   411

BEACHCOMBER

Jackson, J.W.
Second Sight - Philip R. Craig   m   55
Vineyard Prey - Philip R. Craig   m   56

BIBLICAL FIGURE

Abigail of Carmel
Abigail's Story - Ann Burton   r   281

David
Abigail's Story - Ann Burton   r   281

Moses
Zipporah, Wife of Moses - Marek Halter   t   904

Zipporah
Zipporah, Wife of Moses - Marek Halter   t   904

BIKER

MacAllister, Wade
Heartbreak Hotel - Jill Marie Landis   r   366

BODYGUARD

Feor
The Hidden Queen - Rachel Lee   f   593

Jarom
The Crimson Sword - Eldon Thompson   f   629

Torchay
The Compass Rose - Gail Dayton   f   561

BOUNTY HUNTER

Keller, Martin
Ride the Red Sun Down - Thom Nicholson   w   507

Law, J.T.
Showdown in Austin - Tom Calhoun   w   467

Manoso, Carlos "Ranger"
Eleven on Top - Janet Evanovich   m   80

Plum, Stephanie
Eleven on Top - Janet Evanovich   m   80

BOYFRIEND

Aguilar, Silvio
Savage Garden - Denise Hamilton   c   1157

Dawson, Roger
Return to Abo - Sharon Niederman   w   508

Dwayne
The Untelling - Tayari Jones   c   1175

John
Milk - Darcey Steinke   c   1231

Lister, Reuben
The Real Mother - Judith Michael   c   1196

Mac
The Baker's Apprentice - Judith Ryan
   Hendricks   c   1161

BRIDE

Hardy, Tasmin
The Penrose Treasure - Janet Tanner   r   439

Renshaw, Meg
Without a Clue - Trish Jensen   r   344

BULLY

Ballard, Lafe
The Trampled Field - Jeanne Williams   w   536

McCabe, Cash
The Relentless Gun - Pete Peterson   w   512

BUSINESSMAN

Alan
Someone Comes to Town, Someone Leaves Town -
   Cory Doctorow   f   563

Avery, Ben
The Cold Trail - Phillip Gessert   w   487

Bishop, John
The Spirit Box - Stephen Gallagher   h   660

Braithwaite, Douglas
Acts of Faith - Philip Caputo   c   1122

Brannock, Virgil
Windward West - Matt Braun   w   465

Broussard, J.J.
Galveston Rose - Mary Powell   w   514

Byrne, Gavin
One Night with a Prince - Sabrina Jeffries   r   342

Cheng, Winston
Rogue Berserker - Fred Saberhagen   s   808

Chung, Lin
Away with the Fairies - Kerry Greenwood   m   108
Ruddy Gore - Kerry Greenwood   m   109

Conover, Nick
Company Man - Joseph Finder   c   1145

Coughlin, Alex
Exes and Ohs - Beth Kendrick   r   355

Crist, Victor
Imprint - Paul L. Bates   s   747

Dalton, Rob
Least Likely Wedding - Patricia McLinn   r   388

Fallon, Tom
Sudden Rain - Maritta Wolff   c   1245

Fergusson, Dylan
Mostly a Lady - Lisa Manuel   r   382

Ford, Simon
Stolen Memory - Virginia Kantra   r   351

Goulet, Lucien
The Transformation - Catherine Chidgey   t   867

Gozan, Shiloh ben
The Turquoise Ring - Grace Tiffany   t   983

Hoffmeir, Caleb
The Storekeeper's Daughter - Wanda E.
   Brunstetter   r   280
The Storekeeper's Daughter - Wanda E.
   Brunstetter   i   1009

John
Lost in the Forest - Sue Miller   c   1198

Keeley, Steve
The God Particle - Richard Cox   s   757

Kitterage, Jason
The Pleasure Garden - Regan Allen   r   253

Kittre
Wolf in the Night - Tara Harper   s   775

Laidlaw, John
Hosack's Folly - Gillen D'Arcy Wood   t   993

Lanning, Thomas
The Lady and the Cit - Blair Bancroft   r   262

Lawton, Jason
Spin - Robert Charles Wilson   s   835

Levin, Dale
Loving Promises - Gail Gaymer Martin   i   1064

Lim, Johnny
The Harmony Silk Factory - Tash Aw   t   849
The Harmony Silk Factory - Tash Aw   c   1109

Lister, Reuben
The Real Mother - Judith Michael   c   1196

Lubin
Behemoth: Seppuku - Peter Watts   s   827

Markos, Nicholas
Code Name: Fiancee - Susan Vaughan   r   443

Martin, Fitzhugh
Acts of Faith - Philip Caputo   c   1122

Maslow, Meyer
A Changed Man - Francine Prose   c   1214

McAllister, Seth
Protected Hearts - Bonnie K. Winn   i   1097

Mendez, Rafael
The Transformation - Catherine Chidgey   t   867

Moarkan
The Carpet Makers - Andreas Eschbach   s   769

Morrison, Erik
Fall Girl - Pierce Askegren   s   745
Human Resource - Pierce Askegren   s   746

O'Neill, Rafe
Vampire Beach - Alexa Hayes   h   666

Prager, Moe
The James Deans - Reed Farrel Coleman   m   49

Ramsey, Darren
City of the Dead - Brian Keene   h   675

Randolph, Dan
Powersat - Ben Bova   s   752

Ritchie, Julian
Love of My Life - Meredith Bond   r   268

Roarke
Origin in Death - J.D. Robb   r   416

Ryker, Clay
Expiration Date - Eric Wilson   i   1095

Soranzo, Giovanni
The Lion of St. Mark - Thomas Quinn   t   959

Stanley, Daniel
The Tea House of Mulberry Street - Sharon
   Owens   c   1206

Sullivan, Blake
The Best Gift - Irene Hannon   i   1036

Vikorn
Bangkok Tattoo - John Burdett   c   1120

Walker, Marcus
The Light-Years Beneath My Feet - Alan Dean
   Foster   s   771

Westbrook, Ethan
Pickup Lines - Holly Jacobs   r   340

Wilson, Paul
No Hiding Place - Janet Tanner   r   438

Yamagata, Saito
Mercury - Ben Bova   s   751

Schiller, Esau
The Center of Winter - Marya Hornbacher   *c*   1165

Schiller, Katie
The Center of Winter - Marya Hornbacher   *c*   1165

Snapdragon, Martha
The Spoon in the Bathroom Wall - Tony
   Johnston   *f*   586

Swensen, Charity
A Land of Sheltered Promise - Jane
   Kirkpatrick   *w*   501

Talcott, Margaret
The Lost Mother - Mary McGarry Morris   *c*   1202
The Lost Mother - Mary McGarry Morris   *t*   936

Talcott, Thomas
The Lost Mother - Mary McGarry Morris   *t*   936
The Lost Mother - Mary McGarry Morris   *c*   1202

Unnamed Character
Enchantments - Linda Ferri   *c*   1144

Vrabec, Kazi
The Abandoned - Douglas Clegg   *h*   650

CHIMNEYSWEEP

McCarthy, Shane
Winners - Eric B. Martin   *c*   1190

CIVIL SERVANT

Mitchell, Meredith
That Way Murder Lies - Ann Granger   *m*   105

CLERK

Fisher, Naomi
The Storekeeper's Daughter - Wanda E.
   Brunstetter   *r*   280
The Storekeeper's Daughter - Wanda E.
   Brunstetter   *i*   1009

CLONE

Finn, Justin
Cast of Shadows - Kevin Guilfoile   *c*   1154

Kathy
Never Let Me Go - Kazuo Ishiguro   *c*   1171

Ruth
Never Let Me Go - Kazuo Ishiguro   *c*   1171

Tommy
Never Let Me Go - Kazuo Ishiguro   *c*   1171

COLLECTOR

Kessler, Ana
The Icon - Neil Olson   *m*   182

Rees, Danny
Hot Spot - Susan Johnson   *r*   345

COMPANION

Bernardo
Zorro - Isabel Allende   *t*   846
Zorro - Isabel Allende   *c*   1104
Zorro - Isabel Allende   *w*   451

Hermes
SPQR IX: The Princess and the Pirates - John
   Maddox Roberts   *t*   964

Logan, Sarah
On Winding Hill Road - Diane Tyrrel   *r*   442

Merrit, Lilias
My Lord Beast - Mary Lennox   *r*   371

COMPOSER

Charpentier, Marc-Antoine
Emilie's Voice - Susanne Dunlap   *c*   1137

Lully, Jean-Baptiste
Emilie's Voice - Susanne Dunlap   *c*   1137

Prentice, Gail
Swing - Rupert Holmes   *c*   1164
Swing - Rupert Holmes   *m*   130

Shostakovich, Dmitri
Europe Central - William T. Vollmann   *c*   1238

COMPUTER EXPERT

Belinsky, Annie
Dead Run - P.J. Tracy   *m*   237

Clavier, Sandra
Saint Vidicon to the Rescue - Christopher
   Stasheff   *f*   626

Doyle, Emily
Five in a Row - Jan Coffey   *r*   294

Friant, Rene
Murder in Clichy - Cara Black   *m*   21

Marsh, Pepper
Hard Day's Knight - Katie MacAlister   *r*   379

McBride, Grace
Dead Run - P.J. Tracy   *m*   237

Montana, Steve
The Quantum Connection - Travis S. Taylor   *s*   818

Olmos, Christina
Cusp - Robert A. Metzger   *s*   791

Olmos, Xavier
Cusp - Robert A. Metzger   *s*   791

Quinlan, Adam
Just Peachy - Jill Winters   *r*   447

Quintera, Isabella
Jigsaw - Kathleen Nance   *r*   395

Ricci, Tony
Saint Vidicon to the Rescue - Christopher
   Stasheff   *f*   626

Scheer, Wendy
Human Resource - Pierce Askegren   *s*   746

Whiteside, Erik
Resurrection Road - Kathryn R. Wall   *m*   241

COMPUTER GAME PLAYER

Waterford, Larry
The Quantum Connection - Travis S. Taylor   *s*   818

CONSULTANT

Archer, Annabelle
Better Off Wed - Laura Durham   *m*   70

Augustus
The Myriad - R.M. Meluch   *s*   789

Broussard, J.J.
Galveston Rose - Mary Powell   *w*   514

Kendricks, Andrea "Andy"
The Good Girl's Guide to Murder - Susan
   McBride   *m*   164

Kincaid, Carnegie
Death Takes a Honeymoon - Deborah
   Donnelly   *m*   66

Leigh, Ariel
Take My Breath Away - Tina Donahue   *r*   307

North, Cleo
The First Mistake - Merline Lovelace   *r*   376

The Last Bullet - Merline Lovelace   *r*   377
The Middle Sin - Merline Lovelace   *r*   378

Stevens, Hope
Cut and Run - Ridley Pearson   *m*   194

Strano, Mya
A Pinch of Cool - Mary Leo   *r*   372

Waterhouse, Salome
Evil Intentions - Denise Osborne   *m*   183

CONTRACTOR

McCoy, Lukas
Random Acts of Fashion - Nikki Rivers   *r*   414

Stevens, Cole
Her Man Upstairs - Dixie Browning   *r*   277

CONVICT

Blackman, Joel
The Broker - John Grisham   *c*   1153

Brown, Lorenzo
Drama City - George P. Pelecanos   *c*   1211
Drama City - George P. Pelecanos   *m*   195

Faiser, Henry
Now You See Her - Cecelia Tishy   *c*   1234

Jenkins, Shad
November Mourns - Tom Piccirilli   *h*   709

Marion, David
Bleedout - Joan Brady   *c*   1115

Martin
A Long Way Down - Nick Hornby   *c*   1166

McKeon, Hart
Blood Atonement - J.D. Harkleroad   *w*   493

Trapp, John Henry
Trapp's Mountain - Robert J. Randisi   *w*   517

COOK

Brinkman, Craig
Detour Ahead - Cindi Myers   *r*   394

Gardner, Derik
Derik's Bane - MaryJanice Davidson   *h*   654

Heaney, Bridget
The Spice Box - Lou Jane Temple   *m*   231
The Spice Box - Lou Jane Temple   *t*   980

Randazzo, Phil
The Year of Past Things - M.A. Harper   *h*   665

COUNSELOR

Coombs, Natalie
Saving Grace - Denise Hunter   *i*   1049

Hunter, Amanda
Love Next Door - Anna Schmidt   *i*   1085

COUSIN

Findabhair
The Hunter's Moon - O.R. Melling   *f*   606

Smith, Robert
No Holier Spot of Ground - John Warren
   Smith   *w*   525

COWBOY

Calloway, Hewey
Six Bits a Day - Elmer Kelton   *w*   499

Calloway, Walter
Six Bits a Day - Elmer Kelton   *w*   499

DIPLOMAT

DIRECTOR

DIVORCED PERSON

DOCTOR

Chandler, Vicki
Resurrection Dreams - Richard Laymon   *h*   686

Dupree, Tyler
Spin - Robert Charles Wilson   *s*   835

Hoffmann, Heinrich
98 Reasons for Being - Clare Dudman   *t*   879

Hosack, David
Hosack's Folly - Gillen D'Arcy Wood   *c*   1246
Hosack's Folly - Gillen D'Arcy Wood   *t*   993

Kerr, Larson
When the Lion Roars - DiAnn Mills   *i*   1067

Mangioni, Gianni
Alibi - Joseph Kanon   *t*   919

Moore, Davis
Cast of Shadows - Kevin Guilfoile   *c*   1154

Morelli, Mark
Dark Angel - Karen Harper   *r*   326

Nordhagen, Roger
Finishing Touches - Thomas Tessier   *h*   731

Perowne, Henry
Saturday - Ian McEwan   *c*   1194

Rofocale, Arthur
In Darkness Waiting - John Shirley   *h*   725

Ruiz, Cicero
Sympathy between Humans - Jodi Compton   *c*   1129

Seward, John L.
The Book of Renfield - Tim Lucas   *h*   694

Sutherland, Tom
Finishing Touches - Thomas Tessier   *h*   731

Templeton, William
A New Lu - Laura Castoro   *r*   290

Watson, John
The Italian Secretary - Caleb Carr   *t*   862
The Italian Secretary - Caleb Carr   *m*   41
Mrs. Hudson and the Spirits' Curse - Martin
   Davies   *t*   874

Wise, Lorna
Valley of Bones - Michael Gruber   *m*   110

DRIFTER

Claxton, Beau
The Drifter - Lori Copeland   *i*   1018

Fry, Wendell
Trapp's Mountain - Robert J. Randisi   *w*   517

Lassiter
Ambush for Lassiter - Loren Zane Grey   *w*   490

Pooder, Zebulan A.
The Death of Desert Belle - Phil Dunlap   *w*   477

Price, Matthew
Rebel Gun - Lyle Brandt   *w*   462

Prine, Jeremy
The Treasure of Jericho Mountain - Cameron
   Judd   *w*   498

Reacher, Jack
One Shot - Lee Child   *m*   45

DRIVER

Miner, Kit
Kiss the Goat - Brian Stableford   *h*   729

Turner, Diana
Silver Feather - Cassie Edwards   *r*   311

DRUG DEALER

Fulmer, Nick
Drive Like Hell - Dallas Hudgens   *c*   1168

EDITOR

Archer, Harry
Sex & Sensibility - Rosemarie Santini   *r*   420

Frost, Bridget
A Ghost of a Chance - Peter Guttridge   *m*   112

Hinton, Emily
Emily Ever After - Anne Dayton   *i*   1021

Jensen, Tim
Boogeyman - Jeff Marriotte   *h*   697

Lord, Emma
The Alpine Quilt - Mary Daheim   *m*   60

Milano, Roy
The Shooting Script - Laurence Klavan   *m*   145

Smyth, John
Mountaintop Drive - James R. Coggins   *i*   1016

EMPATH

Bircher, Kathryn
Lost in Translation - Edward Willett   *s*   833

Jarrikk
Lost in Translation - Edward Willett   *s*   833

EMPLOYER

Andrews, Rachael
Bloody Hills - Charles G. West   *w*   530

Tarpley, C.C.
Six Bits a Day - Elmer Kelton   *w*   499

ENGINEER

Holman, Jim
Sudden Rain - Maritta Wolff   *c*   1245

Hubbard, Theodorus
That Anvil of Our Souls - David Poyer   *t*   957

Madison, Mark
Fiesta Moon - Linda Windsor   *i*   1096

Mayovskyj, Kolya
A Short History of Tractors in Ukrainian - Marina
   Lewycka   *c*   1188

Sachs, Perry
Submerged - Alton Gansky   *i*   1032

ENTERTAINER

Bones, Frank
Bones - Seth Greenland   *c*   1152

Eelie
Sex with the Serpent Girl - Matthew
   Carnahan   *c*   1123

Magenta
Desolation - Tim Lebbon   *h*   688

Murphy, Tom
Fairy BrewHaHa at the Lucky Nickel Saloon - Ken
   Rand   *f*   618

Sagara, Lune
Godplayers - Damien Broderick   *f*   545

ENVIRONMENTALIST

LeDeux, Rene
The Red-Hot Cajun - Sandra Hill   *r*   330

EXECUTIONER

Cotterill, Simon
The Hangman's Hymn - P.C. Doherty   *t*   877

EXPATRIATE

Eremon
The White Mare - Jules Watson   *t*   991
The White Mare - Jules Watson   *f*   630

EXPLORER

Anturasi, Jorim
A Secret Atlas - Michael A. Stackpole   *f*   625

Anturasi, Keles
A Secret Atlas - Michael A. Stackpole   *f*   625

Fremont, John Charles
Dream West - David Nevin   *w*   506

Smith, Jedediah
Dancing with the Golden Bear - Win
   Blevins   *w*   457

FARMER

Bannon, Jim
The Forbidden Hills - Al Lacy   *i*   1056

Beede, Josiah
Die Like a Hero - Clyde Linsley   *m*   152

Dancer, Jack
The Relentless Gun - Pete Peterson   *w*   512

Granger, Jacob
The Sugar Camp Quilt - Jennifer Chiaverini   *t*   866

McKenna, Abbey
Gunsmoke: The Last Dog Soldier - Joseph A.
   West   *w*   533

O'Connor, Drew
A Bride Most Begrudging - Deeanne Gist   *i*   1034

Shannon, James
Comanche Crossing - Harold G. Ross   *w*   521

Tobler, Paul
The World Still Melting - Robley Wilson   *c*   1244

Ware, Christy
The Trampled Field - Jeanne Williams   *w*   536

Wilmarth, Ruth
Mad Cow Nightmare - Nancy Means
   Wright   *m*   249

FBI AGENT

Bevere, Donnie
Intimidation - Wanda L. Dyson   *i*   1026

Bhagat, Max
Breaking Point - Suzanne Brockmann   *r*   274

Blackwell, Cece
Dangerous Curves - Pamela Britton   *r*   273

Cortez, Jeremiah
Before Sunrise - Diana Palmer   *r*   402

Demarkian, Gregor
The Headmaster's Wife - Jane Haddam   *m*   113

Franklin, Dominic "Nic"
Dark Moon - Lori Handeland   *r*   325

McCabe, Sam
Bait - Karen Robards   *r*   415

McCoy, Jane
In the Company of Liars - David Ellis   *m*   75

McKenna, Cassie
Bloody Point - Linda J. White   *i*   1092

Moore, Brady
Comes a Horseman - Robert Liparulo   *i*   1060

Mueller, Sharon
Dead Run - P.J. Tracy   *m*   237

Rivers, Dutch
Better Read than Dead - Victoria Laurie   *m*   147

Shaughnessy, M.K.
What She Can't See - Hunter Morgan   *r*   392

Thomas, Adam
What She Can't See - Hunter Morgan   *r*   392

Wagner, Alicia
Comes a Horseman - Robert Liparulo   *i*   1060

FIANCE(E)

Cahill, Francesca
Deadly Illusions - Brenda Joyce   *r*   349

Gibbs, Lavinia
Twilight - Katherine Mosby   *t*   937

Lavery, Edith
Snobs - Julian Fellowes   *c*   1143

Markby, Alan
That Way Murder Lies - Ann Granger   *m*   105

Petya
The Turkish Gambit - Boris Akunin   *c*   1101

Shipton, Cassandra
The Divine Circle of Ladies Making Mischief - Dolores Stewart Riccio   *r*   410

Ulysses, Joe
The Divine Circle of Ladies Making Mischief - Dolores Stewart Riccio   *r*   410

FILMMAKER

Baldini, Eric
A Pinch of Cool - Mary Leo   *r*   372

Bell-Rivers, Hugh
The Mysteries - Lisa Tuttle   *h*   732

Foster, Tony
Smoke and Mirrors - Tanya Huff   *h*   672

FINANCIER

Sullivan, Jacob
Mindscan - Robert J. Sawyer   *s*   809

FIRE FIGHTER

Adams, Flex
Measure of a Man - Adrianne Byrd   *r*   283

Carver, Trey "Lincoln"
Measure of a Man - Adrianne Byrd   *r*   283

Gum, Jason
The Smoke Room - Earl Emerson   *m*   76

Woodward, Ian
Nothing More to Lose - Kathryn Shay   *r*   423

FISHERMAN

Dowd, Noel
The Season of Open Water - Dawn Clifton Tripp   *t*   986

Ferris, Llewellyn "Lew"
Dead Jitterbug - Victoria Houston   *m*   132

Osborne, Paul "Doc"
Dead Jitterbug - Victoria Houston   *m*   132

FOREMAN

Moran, Craig
Ambush for Lassiter - Loren Zane Grey   *w*   490

FOSTER PARENT

Britton, Tamara
Plenty Good Room - Cherie Paris Edwards   *i*   1027

FOUNDLING

Old, Rose
Misfortune - Wesley Stace   *t*   974

Tuala
The Dark Mirror - Juliet Marillier   *f*   598

FRIEND

Aaron
The Best-Kept Secret - Kimberla Lawson Roby   *c*   1220

Aguila
Comanche Crossing - Harold G. Ross   *w*   521

Behan, John
Trouble in Tombstone - Richard S. Wheeler   *w*   535

Benteen, Susanna
High Plains Tango - Robert James Waller   *w*   529

Brewer, Lanier
The Same Sweet Girls - Cassandra King   *c*   1180

Cardoza, Wendy
Mambo Peligroso - Patricia Chao   *c*   1124

Caro
Ya-Yas in Bloom - Rebecca Wells   *c*   1240

Dunne, Rosie
Rosie Dunne - Cecilia Ahern   *c*   1100

Freyl, Hugh
Bleedout - Joan Brady   *c*   1115

Huck
My Jim - Nancy Rawles   *c*   1217

Iverson, Gil
Hardwater - Steve Sherwood   *w*   523

Jensen, Will
Out of Range - C.J. Box   *w*   460

Nakata, Satoru
Kafka on the Shore - Haruki Murakami   *c*   1203

Queenie
Small Island - Andrea Levy   *c*   1187

Rael
Everything Changes - Jonathan Tropper   *c*   1235

Shepherd, James
The Diezmo - Rick Bass   *c*   1112

Stewart, Alex
Rosie Dunne - Cecilia Ahern   *c*   1100

Thomas
The Mermaid Chair - Sue Monk Kidd   *c*   1179

Trask, Nathan
Last Resort - Hannah Alexander   *i*   999

Walker, Vivi Abbott
Ya-Yas in Bloom - Rebecca Wells   *c*   1240

Whitman, Teensy
Ya-Yas in Bloom - Rebecca Wells   *c*   1240

FRONTIERSMAN

Brannock, Clint
Windward West - Matt Braun   *w*   465

Lewis, Andrew
Sons of Texas - Elmer Kelton   *w*   500
Sons of Texas - Elmer Kelton   *t*   921

Lewis, Michael
Sons of Texas - Elmer Kelton   *t*   921
Sons of Texas - Elmer Kelton   *w*   500

Lewis, Mordecai
Sons of Texas - Elmer Kelton   *w*   500

FUGITIVE

Casey, Jenny
Hammered - Elizabeth Bear   *s*   749

Cowl
Cowl - Neal Asher   *s*   743

de Noche, Tylar
Shadowfall - James Clemens   *f*   554

Falconer, Quellcrist
Woken Furies - Richard Morgan   *s*   792

Grant, Angie
Shadowed Secrets - Lois Richer   *i*   1080

Hawthorne, Helen
Just Murdered - Elaine Viets   *m*   239

McKeon, Hart
Blood Atonement - J.D. Harkleroad   *w*   493

Phoenix, Shaun
Stargazer - Colby Hodge   *r*   331

Popescu, Miranda
A Princess of Roumania - Paul Park   *f*   615

Ritter, Warren
Eight of Swords - David Skibbins   *m*   223

Tenragen, Tarja
Harshini - Jennifer Fallon   *f*   568

GAMBLER

Gallagher, Jax
Skintight - Susan Andersen   *r*   254

Hill, Ellie
The Marriage Trap - Elizabeth Thornton   *r*   441

McNally, Skye
Double Down - Tess Hudson   *r*   334

Smith, Ricky
Mr. Lucky - James Swain   *c*   1233

GAME WARDEN

Jensen, Will
Out of Range - C.J. Box   *w*   460

Pickett, Joe
Out of Range - C.J. Box   *w*   460
Out of Range - C.J. Box   *m*   29

GANG MEMBER

Ball, Virgil
Canaan's Tongue - John Wray   *t*   995

Dolan, Johnny
Metropolis - Elizabeth Gaffney   *c*   1147

Harris, Frank
Metropolis - Elizabeth Gaffney   *c*   1147
Metropolis - Elizabeth Gaffney   *t*   891

Morelle, Thaddeus
Canaan's Tongue - John Wray   *t*   995

O'Gamhna, Beatrice
Metropolis - Elizabeth Gaffney   *t*   891
Metropolis - Elizabeth Gaffney   *c*   1147

Vesta, Vinny
Mafia Summer - E. Duke Vincent   *t*   990

GARDENER

Arai, Mas
Gasa-Gasa Girl - Naomi Hirahara   *m*   129

Grandparent (continued)

London, Diana
Master of the Moon - Angela Knight   r   360

Lukacs, Andreas
Cagebird - Karin Lowachee   s   784

Mallory, Dev
Bad Money - Ed Gorman   w   489

M'Tal
Dragonsblood - Todd McCaffrey   s   786

Novak, Renata
The Prometheus Project - Steve White   s   832

Owen, Gareth
The Point in the Market - Michael Pearce   t   947
The Point in the Market - Michael Pearce   m   193

Rhinehart, Vladislav
Dexta - C.J. Ryan   s   807

Thornton, Jane
Powersat - Ben Bova   s   752

Trojanowski, Nikolai
Migration - Julie E. Czerneda   s   759

VanDeen, Gloria
Dexta - C.J. Ryan   s   807

Wade, Vanessa
Code Name: Fiancee - Susan Vaughan   r   443

Zachary, Zoe
Dexta - C.J. Ryan   s   807

GRANDPARENT

Branch, Geneva
Who Does She Think She Is? - Benilde
  Little   c   1189

George
Natives and Exotics - Jane Alison   c   1103

McClellan, Doris
True Believer - Nicholas Sparks   c   1230

Violet
Natives and Exotics - Jane Alison   c   1103

Watson, Sadie
My Jim - Nancy Rawles   c   1217

GUARD

Joplin, Meager
Ambush for Lassiter - Loren Zane Grey   w   490

Wild, Iain
London Revenant - Conrad Williams   h   736

GUARDIAN

Elliot, Sara
The Real Mother - Judith Michael   c   1196

Jansen, Colby
Dark Secret - Christine Feehan   r   313

Kendall, Lucien
Naughty or Nice - Melanie George   r   322

McGuire, Sean
Table for Five - Susan Wiggs   r   445

Moreland, Hayden
Unveiled - Kristina Cook   r   296

GUIDE

Carson, Kit
Dream West - David Nevin   w   506

Jellic, Kurt
Stranded with a Stranger - Frances Housden   r   332

GUNFIGHTER

Avery, Harliss
The Cold Trail - Phillip Gessert   w   487

Dancer, John
The Relentless Gun - Pete Peterson   w   512

Ellis, CC
Guns of Wolf Valley - Ralph Cotton   w   469

Fry, Wendell
Trapp's Mountain - Robert J. Randisi   w   517

MacCallister, Falcon
Revenge of Eagles - William W. Johnstone   w   497

HAIRDRESSER

Burlingame, Tracie
Expired - Evie Rhodes   h   714

Sawyer, Reyn Marten
Sprayed Stiff - Laura Bradley   m   30

HANDICAPPED

Alannah
Across a Wild Sea - Sasha Lord   r   374

Clem
Ghosts of Eden - T.M. Gray   h   662

Gambier, Alex
Phantom Nights - John Farris   h   656

Holbrook, Gabriel
Stranger in Town - Brenda Novak   r   401

Kerry, Ethan
Death Rides a Red Horse - Cotton Smith   w   524

Rhyme, Lincoln
The Twelfth Card - Jeffery Deaver   m   64

Ruiz, Cicero
Sympathy between Humans - Jodi Compton   c   1129

Shardlake, Matthew
Dark Fire - C.J. Sansom   m   214

Summers, Holly
Unspeakable - Graham Masterton   h   699

Woodward, Ian
Nothing More to Lose - Kathryn Shay   r   423

HANDYMAN

Andrews, Nick
A Sheltering Love - Terri Reed   i   1079

Donovan, Luke
Josie Day Is Coming Home - Lisa Plumley   r   404

HEALER

Kirra
Mystic and Rider - Sharon Shinn   f   623

Lazar, Cally
Cruel and Unusual Intuition - Claire Daniels   m   62

Makepeace, Zinnia
Trouble in Paradise - Pip Granger   m   106
Trouble in Paradise - Pip Granger   c   1150

Nicci
Chainfire - Terry Goodkind   f   574

Teresita
The Hummingbird's Daughter - Luis Alberto
  Urrea   t   988
The Hummingbird's Daughter - Luis Alberto
  Urrea   c   1236

HEALTH CARE PROFESSIONAL

Cleo
Disability - Cris Mazza   c   1192

Onkar
Afterburn - S.L. Viehl   s   826

Selgrin, Maggie
The Sad Truth about Happiness - Anne
  Giardini   c   1149

Teri
Disability - Cris Mazza   c   1192

Znora, Burn mu
Afterburn - S.L. Viehl   s   826

HEIR

Broughton, Charles
Snobs - Julian Fellowes   c   1143

Donovan, Luke
Josie Day Is Coming Home - Lisa Plumley   r   404

Glennshannon, Hadley
Riders to Moon Rock - Andrew J. Fenady   w   480

Kennesaw, Sam
Sealed with a Kiss - Mae Nunn   i   1075

McKie, Jamie
Whence Came a Prince - Liz Curtis Higgs   i   1042

Penrose, Adam
The Penrose Treasure - Janet Tanner   r   439

Uhtred
The Last Kingdom - Bernard Cornwell   t   870
The Last Kingdom - Bernard Cornwell   c   1130

HEIR—LOST

Bowden, Raymond
Rancho Alegre - John D. Nesbitt   w   505

HEIRESS

Elliott, Tara
Sealed with a Kiss - Mae Nunn   i   1075

Kendricks, Andrea "Andy"
The Good Girl's Guide to Murder - Susan
  McBride   m   164

Portia
The Turquoise Ring - Grace Tiffany   t   983

Pruett, Caroline
The Winning Hand - C.K. Crigger   w   472

Reed, Carley
A Table by the Window - Lawana Blackwell   i   1006

Rose, Abby
A Wedding to Die For - Leann Sweeney   m   230

Somerset, Sophie
Lord Will and Her Grace - Sophia Nash   r   396

Trevor, Aurelia
The Lady and the Cit - Blair Bancroft   r   262

Winters, Elizabeth
Marriage Minded - Julia Parks   r   403

HERBALIST

Appleton, Susanna
Face Down Below the Banqueting House - Kathy
  Lynn Emerson   m   77
Face Down Below the Banqueting House - Kathy
  Lynn Emerson   t   882

Bayles, China
Dead Man's Bones - Susan Wittig Albert   m   3

HERO

de la Vega, Diego
Zorro - Isabel Allende   *t*   846
Zorro - Isabel Allende   *c*   1104
Zorro - Isabel Allende   *w*   451

HEROINE

Applebaum, Sophie
The Wonder Spot - Melissa Bank   *c*   1111

Teresita
The Hummingbird's Daughter - Luis Alberto
   Urrea   *c*   1236
The Hummingbird's Daughter - Luis Alberto
   Urrea   *t*   988

Ware, Christy
The Trampled Field - Jeanne Williams   *w*   536

HIPPIE

Tomlinson, Sighurdhr
Dead of Night - Randy Wayne White   *m*   243

HISTORIAN

Duiker
Deadhouse Gates - Steven Erikson   *f*   567

O'Mara, Ronan
Ireland - Frank Delaney   *t*   875

HISTORICAL FIGURE

Adams, Asked For
What Casanova Told Me - Susan Swan   *t*   978

Aetius, Flavius
The Sword of Attila - Michael Curtis Ford   *t*   889

Akhmatova, Anna
Europe Central - William T. Vollmann   *c*   1238

al-Idrisi, Muhammed
A Sultan in Palermo - Tariq Ali   *t*   843

Alfred the Great
The Last Kingdom - Bernard Cornwell   *t*   870
The Last Kingdom - Bernard Cornwell   *c*   1130

Anderson, Tom
Jass - David Fulmer   *m*   93

Andre, John
Shadow Patriots - Lucia St. Clair Robson   *t*   965

Arnold, Benedict
Shadow Patriots - Lucia St. Clair Robson   *t*   965

Attila
The Scourge of God - William Dietrich   *c*   1135

Attila the Hun
The Scourge of God - William Dietrich   *t*   876
The Sword of Attila - Michael Curtis Ford   *t*   889

Austen, Jane
Jane and His Lordship's Legacy - Stephanie
   Barron   *t*   852
Jane and His Lordship's Legacy - Stephanie
   Barron   *m*   14

Austin, Stephen F.
Sons of Texas - Elmer Kelton   *t*   921

Berard
The Falcon of Palermo - Maria Bordihn   *t*   856

Bierce, Ambrose
Ambrose Bierce and the Ace of Shoots - Oakley
   Hall   *t*   903
Ambrose Bierce and the Ace of Shoots - Oakley
   Hall   *c*   1155

Ambrose Bierce and the Ace of Shoots - Oakley
   Hall   *m*   115

Bonny, Anne
Kingston by Starlight - Christopher John
   Farley   *t*   885

Booth, John Wilkes
The Curse of Cain - J. Mark Powell   *t*   956

Brutus, Marcus Junius
Emperor: The Field of Swords - Conn
   Iggulden   *t*   914

Byron, George Gordon
Lord Byron's Novel - John Crowley   *t*   871

Caesar, Julius
Emperor: The Field of Swords - Conn
   Iggulden   *t*   914

Carson, Kit
Dream West - David Nevin   *w*   506

Casanova, Giovanni Giacomo
What Casanova Told Me - Susan Swan   *t*   978

Catherine de Medici
The Dark Queen - Susan Carroll   *t*   863

Cecil, William
The Fyre Mirror - Karen Harper   *t*   905

Cervantes, Miguel de
Tilting at Windmills - Julian Branston   *t*   859

Charles II
Darkwitch Rising - Sara Douglass   *f*   564
Darkwitch Rising - Sara Douglass   *t*   878

Charpentier, Marc-Antoine
Emilie's Voice - Susanne Dunlap   *c*   1137

Churchill, Winston
Hitler's Peace - Philip Kerr   *c*   1178

Cicero, Marcus Tullius
A Gladiator Dies Only Once - Steven Saylor   *t*   967

Cleopatra
SPQR IX: The Princess and the Pirates - John
   Maddox Roberts   *t*   964

Custer, George Armstrong
An Obituary for Major Reno - Richard S.
   Wheeler   *w*   534

Doyle, Arthur Conan
What Rough Beast - H.R. Knight   *h*   680

Duchamp, Marcel
Holy Skirts - Rene Steinke   *t*   975

Earp, Wyatt
Trouble in Tombstone - Richard S. Wheeler   *w*   535

Edward IV
The Exiled - Posie Graeme-Evans   *t*   898

Eleanor of Aquitaine
Prince of Darkness - Sharon Kay Penman   *t*   949

Elizabeth I
Face Down Below the Banqueting House - Kathy
   Lynn Emerson   *t*   882
The Fyre Mirror - Karen Harper   *t*   905
The Fyre Mirror - Karen Harper   *m*   119
Ill Met by Moonlight - Mercedes Lackey   *t*   923
Ill Met by Moonlight - Mercedes Lackey   *f*   590

Emerson, Lidian Jackson
Mr. Emerson's Wife - Amy Belding Brown   *t*   861

Emerson, Ralph Waldo
March - Geraldine Brooks   *t*   860
Mr. Emerson's Wife - Amy Belding Brown   *t*   861

Fielding, John
Rules of Engagement - Bruce Alexander   *t*   842
Rules of Engagement - Bruce Alexander   *m*   4

Fisher, John King
Pendencia Creek - E. Lee Fisher   *w*   481

Fisher, Sarah Vivian
Pendencia Creek - E. Lee Fisher   *w*   481

Floege, Emilie
The Painted Kiss - Elizabeth Hickey   *t*   909

Frank, Anne
The Boy Who Loved Anne Frank - Ellen
   Feldman   *c*   1142

Frederick II
The Falcon of Palermo - Maria Bordihn   *t*   856

Fremont, Jessie Benton
Dream West - David Nevin   *w*   506

Fremont, John Charles
Dream West - David Nevin   *w*   506

Freytag-Loringhoven, Elsa von
Holy Skirts - Rene Steinke   *t*   975

Gerstein, Kurt
Europe Central - William T. Vollmann   *c*   1238

Gordon, Charles George
The Triumph of the Sun - Wilbur A. Smith   *t*   973

Grant, Ulysses S.
Never Call Retreat - Newt Gingrich   *t*   894

Hathaway, Anne
Murder in Stratford - Audrey Peterson   *m*   199
Murder in Stratford - Audrey Peterson   *t*   953

Hitler, Adolf
Cavalcade - Walter Satterthwait   *t*   966

Ho Chi Minh
Nam-A-Rama - Phillip Jennings   *c*   1174

Hoffmann, Heinrich
98 Reasons for Being - Clare Dudman   *t*   879

Holliday, John Henry "Doc"
Trouble in Tombstone - Richard S. Wheeler   *w*   535

Hosack, David
Hosack's Folly - Gillen D'Arcy Wood   *c*   1246
Hosack's Folly - Gillen D'Arcy Wood   *t*   993

Houdini, Harry
What Rough Beast - H.R. Knight   *h*   680

Houston, Sam
The Rivers of War - Eric Flint   *s*   770

Innocent III
The Falcon of Palermo - Maria Bordihn   *t*   856

Jackson, Andrew
The Rivers of War - Eric Flint   *s*   770
The Rivers of War - Eric Flint   *t*   888

Jethro
Zipporah, Wife of Moses - Marek Halter   *t*   904

John
Prince of Darkness - Sharon Kay Penman   *t*   949

Jonson, Ben
An Honorable Murder - Philip Gooden   *t*   896

Kennedy, John Fitzgerald
The Ambassador's Son - Homer Hickam   *t*   908

Klimt, Gustav
The Painted Kiss - Elizabeth Hickey   *t*   909

Lee, Robert E.
Never Call Retreat - Newt Gingrich   *t*   894

Lincoln, Abraham
The Emancipator's Wife - Barbara Hambly   *c*   1156
Never Call Retreat - Newt Gingrich   *t*   894

Lincoln, Mary Todd
The Emancipator's Wife - Barbara Hambly   *c*   1156

Louis IX
The Crown Rose - Fiona Avery   *f*   539

Luti, Margherita
The Ruby Ring - Diane Haeger   *t*   902

Lynch, William
Sailors in the Holy Land - Andrew C.A.
　Jampoler　*t*　917

Madison, James
The Rivers of War - Eric Flint　*t*　888

Mahdi, Mohammed Ahmed
The Triumph of the Sun - Wilbur A. Smith　*t*　973

Marlowe, Christopher
Tamburlaine Must Die - Louise Welsh　*t*　992

Marx, Groucho
Groucho Marx, King of the Jungle - Ron
　Goulart　*t*　897

McNelly, Leander
Pendencia Creek - E. Lee Fisher　*w*　481

Medici, Marie de
A Sundial in a Grave: 1610 - Mary Gentle　*t*　893

Monroe, James
The Rivers of War - Eric Flint　*t*　888

Morton, Jelly Roll
Jass - David Fulmer　*m*　93

Moses
Zipporah, Wife of Moses - Marek Halter　*t*　904

Nixon, Richard
The Ambassador's Son - Homer Hickam　*t*　908

Pompey the Great
Emperor: The Field of Swords - Conn
　Iggulden　*t*　914

Potter, Beatrix
The Tale of Holly How - Susan Wittig Albert　*t*　841

Rackam, Calico Jack
Kingston by Starlight - Christopher John
　Farley　*t*　885

Ramses III
Year of the Hyenas - Brad Geagley　*t*　892

Raphael
The Ruby Ring - Diane Haeger　*t*　902

Reno, Marcus
An Obituary for Major Reno - Richard S.
　Wheeler　*w*　534

Roosevelt, Franklin Delano
Hitler's Peace - Philip Kerr　*c*　1178
Hitler's Peace - Philip Kerr　*t*　922

Roosevelt, Theodore
Dakota - Matt Braun　*w*　463

Ross, John
The Rivers of War - Eric Flint　*s*　770

Rujari
A Sultan in Palermo - Tariq Ali　*t*　843

Shakespeare, William
Murder in Stratford - Audrey Peterson　*m*　199
Murder in Stratford - Audrey Peterson　*t*　953

Shostakovich, Dmitri
Europe Central - William T. Vollmann　*c*　1238

Thoreau, Henry David
Mr. Emerson's Wife - Amy Belding Brown　*t*　861

White, Walter
The Moon in Our Hands - Thomas Dyja　*t*　880

Wirz, Henri
Devil's Domain - Tim Champlin　*w*　468

Wycliffe, John
The Illuminator - Brenda Rickman Vantrease　*t*　989
The Illuminator - Brenda Rickman
　Vantrease　*c*　1237

Zipporah
Zipporah, Wife of Moses - Marek Halter　*t*　904

HOLOCAUST VICTIM

Frank, Anne
The Boy Who Loved Anne Frank - Ellen
　Feldman　*c*　1142

Maslow, Meyer
A Changed Man - Francine Prose　*c*　1214

HOMOSEXUAL

Adams, Flex
Measure of a Man - Adrianne Byrd　*r*　283

Dunn, Jamie
The Blood of Kings - John Michael
　Curlovich　*h*　653

Ingram, Somers
The Linnet Bird - Linda Holeman　*t*　911

Murphy, Adam
Light Before Day - Christopher Rice　*c*　1219

Walter
Milk - Darcey Steinke　*c*　1231

HORSE TRAINER

DeMoss, Redford
My Favorite Mistake - Stephanie Bond　*r*　269

Kiran
The Light of the Oracle - Victoria Hanley　*f*　576

Lewis, Mordecai
Sons of Texas - Elmer Kelton　*w*　500

HOTEL OWNER

Brody, Tyler
Murder in the Hamptons - Amy Garvey　*r*　321

Potter, Tracy
Heartbreak Hotel - Jill Marie Landis　*r*　366

Tomba, Fabrizio
First Kiss - Kylie Adams　*r*　251

HOUSEKEEPER

Hudson, Emma
Mrs. Hudson and the Spirits' Curse - Martin
　Davies　*t*　874

Iorga
The Book of Renfield - Tim Lucas　*h*　694

HOUSEWIFE

Connor, Kate
Carpe Demon - Julie Kenner　*h*　677

Dupont, Laura
Carpe Demon - Julie Kenner　*h*　677

Fallon, Killian
Sudden Rain - Maritta Wolff　*c*　1245

Henshaw, Susan
Death in Duplicate - Valerie Wolzien　*m*　248

Neville, Margaret
The Wounded Hawk - Sara Douglass　*f*　565

Thompson, Kate
The Mommy Fund - Madeleine Jacob　*c*　1173

Tiptree, Jacobia
Tool & Die - Sarah Graves　*m*　107

HUNTER

Darak
Heartwood - Barbara Campbell　*f*　550

IMMIGRANT

Briody, Michael
Empire Rising - Thomas Kelly　*c*　1177
Empire Rising - Thomas Kelly　*t*　920

Grillo, Wilfredo
Hour of the Cat - Peter Quinn　*t*　958

Harris, Frank
Metropolis - Elizabeth Gaffney　*t*　891
Metropolis - Elizabeth Gaffney　*c*　1147

Heaney, Bridget
The Spice Box - Lou Jane Temple　*t*　980
The Spice Box - Lou Jane Temple　*m*　231

Kaukab
Maps for Lost Lovers - Nadeem Aslam　*c*　1108

Meehan, Margaret
The Keeners - Maura D. Shaw　*t*　971

Murphy, Molly
In Like Flynn - Rhys Bowen　*t*　857
In Like Flynn - Rhys Bowen　*m*　26

Riordan, Tom
The Keeners - Maura D. Shaw　*t*　971

Salcido, Procopio
Music of the Mill - Luis J. Rodriguez　*c*　1221

Shamas
Maps for Lost Lovers - Nadeem Aslam　*c*　1108

van Pels, Peter
The Boy Who Loved Anne Frank - Ellen
　Feldman　*c*　1142
The Boy Who Loved Anne Frank - Ellen
　Feldman　*t*　886

IMMORTAL

de Towaji, Bruno
To Crush the Moon - Wil McCarthy　*s*　787

Semenkaru, Danilo
The Blood of Kings - John Michael
　Curlovich　*h*　653

Tall John
47 - Walter Mosley　*s*　793

IMPOSTER

Bridges, Wes
Full Bloom - Janet Evanovich　*r*　312

Kent, Eliza
Mostly a Lady - Lisa Manuel　*r*　382

Kent, Sophie
The Beauty of Bond Street - Jacqueline
　Navin　*r*　397

Penny, Jenny
Lady in Waiting - Kathryn Caskie　*r*　287

Turner, Diana
Silver Feather - Cassie Edwards　*r*　311

IMPOVERISHED

Mac Gordon, Riona
Lord of Dunkeathe - Margaret Moore　*r*　391

INDIAN

Bin-daa-dee-nin
Horse of Seven Moons - Karen Taschek　*w*　527

Bird, Xavier
Three-Day Road - Joseph Boyden　*t*　858

Boans, Annie
Mending Skins - Eric Gansworth　*w*　485

Boans, Dougie
Mending Skins - Eric Gansworth   w   485

Clah, Ella
White Thunder - Aimee Thurlo   m   234

Crow, Mary
Legacy of Masks - Sallie Bissell   m   20

Drinkwater, Roger
The Lake, the River and the Other Lake - Steve
   Amick   c   1106

Gray Wolf
Moon in the Water - Stan Gordon   w   488
Rebel Gun - Lyle Brandt   w   462

Iron Hawk
Gunsmoke: The Last Dog Soldier - Joseph A.
   West   w   533

Keytano
Revenge of Eagles - William W. Johnstone   w   497

Lassiter, Quannah
The Eye That Is Divine - Kat Goldring   m   102

Leather Hand
People of the Moon - Kathleen O'Neal Gear   w   486

Lone Wolf, Jacob
Warrior's Heart - Jackie Kramer   r   361

Lozen
Moon in the Water - Stan Gordon   w   488

Meadowlark
Dancing with the Golden Bear - Win
   Blevins   w   457

Mountain Witch
People of the Moon - Kathleen O'Neal Gear   w   486

Mounter, Shirley
Mending Skins - Eric Gansworth   w   485

Nina Bronca
Wild Girl - Jim Fergus   t   887

Silver Feather
Silver Feather - Cassie Edwards   r   311

Whiskeyjack, Elijah
Three-Day Road - Joseph Boyden   t   858

Young Ripple
People of the Moon - Kathleen O'Neal Gear   w   486

INNKEEPER

Clark, Alexandra "Lexy"
Sexy Lexy - Kate Moore   r   390

Fortenberry, Annie
Full Bloom - Janet Evanovich   r   312

Manning, Ty
Look Closely - Laura Caldwell   r   284

Yoder, Magdalena
Assault and Pepper - Tamar Myers   m   177

INSURANCE INVESTIGATOR

Colter, Ben
Five in a Row - Jan Coffey   r   294

INTERIOR DECORATOR

Bryce, Emily Murdock
The Green Plaid Pants - Margaret Scherf   m   217

Bryce, Henry
The Green Plaid Pants - Margaret Scherf   m   217

Gilbert, Erin
False Premises - Leslie Caine   m   38

Gray, Pamela
Goddess of Light - P.C. Cast   r   289

Harding, Maggie
Murder in the Hamptons - Amy Garvey   r   321

Lasiter, Sasha
Her Fifth Husband? - Dixie Browning   r   276

Sullivan, Steve
False Premises - Leslie Caine   m   38

INVALID

Drelincorte, Aubrey
My Lord Beast - Mary Lennox   r   371

INVENTOR

Ford, Simon
Stolen Memory - Virginia Kantra   r   351

INVESTIGATOR

Bridges, Wes
Full Bloom - Janet Evanovich   r   312

Mallory, Dev
Bad Money - Ed Gorman   w   489

White, Walter
The Moon in Our Hands - Thomas Dyja   t   880

JOCKEY

Callie
The Great Inland Sea - David Francis   t   890

Day
The Great Inland Sea - David Francis   t   890

JOURNALIST

Ackroyd, Laura
Dead Reckoning - Patricia Hall   m   116

Anderson, Annie
Fashion Victim - Sam Baker   r   257
Fashion Victim - Sam Baker   c   1110

Antonelli, Tony
The Hot Kid - Elmore Leonard   c   1186

Bierce, Ambrose
Ambrose Bierce and the Ace of Shoots - Oakley
   Hall   c   1155
Ambrose Bierce and the Ace of Shoots - Oakley
   Hall   t   903

Blackbird, Nora
Cross Your Heart and Hope to Die - Nancy
   Martin   m   159

Bowes, Lynne
Jason X: The Experiment - Pat Cadigan   h   649

Brunetti, Monica
The Road to Home - Vanessa Del Fabbro   i   1022

Chilton, Maggie
Return to Abo - Sharon Niederman   w   508

Corrigan, Jack
Bloodlines - Jan Burke   m   37

Denby, Frank
Groucho Marx, King of the Jungle - Ron
   Goulart   t   897

Diamond, Eve
Savage Garden - Denise Hamilton   m   117
Savage Garden - Denise Hamilton   c   1157

Dulaney, McLeod
Unholy Death in Princeton - Ann Waldron   m   240

Grant, Phoebe
Dreaming in Black and White - Laura Jensen
   Walker   i   1089

Hasbro, Enola
Fall Girl - Pierce Askegren   s   745

Ireton, Richard
Qi - David Aikman   i   998

Kelly, Irene
Bloodlines - Jan Burke   m   37

Kennedy, Andrew
Once upon a Bride - Jean Stone   r   435
Twice upon a Wedding - Jean Stone   r   436

Lanyard, Carl
Cellars - John Shirley   h   723

Lenoir, Christine
A High and Hidden Place - Michele Claire
   Lucas   t   929

Leonard, Isabelle
See Isabelle Run - Elizabeth Bloom   m   23

Madrid, Nick
A Ghost of a Chance - Peter Guttridge   m   112

Malek, Steve
Three Strikes You're Dead - Robert
   Goldsborough   m   103

Montgomery, Kate
Close to You - Christina Dodd   r   306

Mulcahey, Megan
An Unexpected Pleasure - Candace Camp   r   285

Murphy, Adam
Light Before Day - Christopher Rice   c   1219

Nichols, Tallulah "Lu"
A New Lu - Laura Castoro   r   290

O'Connor, Conn
Bloodlines - Jan Burke   m   37

Post, Nikki
Journey to Forever - Carol Steward   i   1087

Qwilleran, James "Qwill"
The Cat Who Went Bananas - Lilian Jackson
   Braun   m   31

Rain, Tucker
Wrapped in Rain - Charles Martin   i   1063

Raymond, Scott
Like Death - Tim Waggoner   h   733

Richler, Joseph
An Obituary for Major Reno - Richard S.
   Wheeler   w   534

St. James, Sydney
Death Watch - Jack Cavanaugh   i   1013

Smith, Kelly
The God Particle - Richard Cox   s   757

Trumbull, Victoria
The Paperwhite Narcissus - Cynthia Riggs   m   207

Vonner, Hunz
Death Watch - Jack Cavanaugh   i   1013

Yablonsky, Bubbles
Bubbles Betrothed - Sarah Strohmeyer   m   228

JUDGE

Fielding, John
Rules of Engagement - Bruce Alexander   t   842
Rules of Engagement - Bruce Alexander   m   4

Yarbrough, Joe Riddley
Who Killed the Queen of Clubs? - Patricia
   Sprinkle   m   226

Yarbrough, MacLaren
Who Killed the Queen of Clubs? - Patricia
   Sprinkle   m   226

KIDNAPPER

Denzer, Lucette
Moon of the Sleeping Bear - K. Celeste Bryan   w   466

Ryn of Anwyn
The Moon Witch - Linda Winstead Jones   r   347

KNIGHT

Bryan, Guy de
The Sinner's Tale - Will Davenport   t   873

Budoc
The Last Companion - Patrick McCormack   t   933

de Noche, Tylar
Shadowfall - James Clemens   f   554

Ehrling, Liam
Return of the Exile - Mary H. Herbert   f   581

Geraint
For Camelot's Honor - Sarah Zettel   f   637

McPhail, Walker
Hard Day's Knight - Katie MacAlister   r   379

Old Knight
Tilting at Windmills - Julian Branston   t   859

St. Simeon, Conon
My Lady's Favor - Joanne Rock   r   419

LABOR ORGANIZER

Salcido, Johnny
Music of the Mill - Luis J. Rodriguez   c   1221

LAIRD

MacKenzie, Robbie
Only for a Knight - Sue-Ellen Welfonder   r   444

Reaganach, Hector
Lord of the Isles - Amanda Scott   r   421

LANDLORD

Bligh, Queenie
Small Island - Andrea Levy   t   927

Peter
Desolation - Tim Lebbon   h   688

Queenie
Small Island - Andrea Levy   c   1187

Turner, Jack
No Strings Attached - Millie Criswell   r   298

LANDOWNER

Courtenay, Robert
The Wounded Hawk - Sara Douglass   f   565

Leo
The Madness of Love - Katharine Davies   c   1132

Speke, Edward
The Keeners - Maura D. Shaw   t   971

LANDSCAPER

Fulmer, Nick
Drive Like Hell - Dallas Hudgens   c   1168

Garrett, Mibby
Always Green - Patti Ann Hill   i   1044

LAWMAN

Behan, John
Trouble in Tombstone - Richard S. Wheeler   w   535

Brown, Jefferson
Marshal of Medicine Lodge - Stan Lynde   w   502

Burrack, Sam
Killing Plain - Ralph Cotton   w   470

Carter, Hooney
The Law in Somos Santos - Ralph Cotton   w   471

Cole, Virgil
Appaloosa - Robert B. Parker   c   1209
Appaloosa - Robert B. Parker   t   944

Dawson, Cray
The Law in Somos Santos - Ralph Cotton   w   471

Dillon, Matt
Gunsmoke: The Last Dog Soldier - Joseph A. West   w   533

Earp, Wyatt
Trouble in Tombstone - Richard S. Wheeler   w   535

Fanshaw, Merlin
Marshal of Medicine Lodge - Stan Lynde   w   502

Hitch, Everett
Appaloosa - Robert B. Parker   c   1209
Appaloosa - Robert B. Parker   t   944

Iverson, Gil
Hardwater - Steve Sherwood   w   523

Jones, Hadley
Killing Plain - Ralph Cotton   w   470

Kelly, Piedmont
The Death of Desert Belle - Phil Dunlap   w   477

McNelly, Leander
Pendencia Creek - E. Lee Fisher   w   481

Ramey, Jed
Devil's Kin - Charles G. West   w   531

Ridgeway, Chance
Marshal of Medicine Lodge - Stan Lynde   w   502

Satterfield, Ben
The Death of Desert Belle - Phil Dunlap   w   477

Spratte, Johnny
Devil's Kin - Charles G. West   w   531

Thulin, Marv
Blood Atonement - J.D. Harkleroad   w   493

Webster, Carlos
The Hot Kid - Elmore Leonard   t   926
The Hot Kid - Elmore Leonard   c   1186

LAWYER

Allegretti, Vicki
Devil's Corner - Lisa Scottoline   m   218

Anglin, J.B.
First Dance - Karen Kendall   r   353

Ballentyne, Kendra
Sit, Stay, Slay - Linda O. Johnston   m   137

Beede, Josiah
Die Like a Hero - Clyde Linsley   m   152

Brewer, Zack
Treason - Don Brown   i   1008

Cleary, Lilly Bell Rose
Wildcat Wine - Claire Matturro   m   163

Colcernian, Diane
Treason - Don Brown   i   1008

Cole, Gideon
To Love a Thief - Julie Anne Long   r   373

Connelly, Mike
Double Take - Joseph H. Hilley   i   1045

Connor, Gail
Suspicion of Rage - Barbara Parker   m   189
Suspicion of Rage - Barbara Parker   c   1208

Connor, Stuart
Carpe Demon - Julie Kenner   h   677

Cooper, Alexandra
Entombed - Linda Fairstein   m   83

Corbin, Ben
Dead Man's Rule - Rick Acker   i   997

Cortez, Quinn
Killing Her Softly - Beverly Barton   r   265

Coyne, Brady
Second Sight - Philip R. Craig   m   55

Crow, Mary
Legacy of Masks - Sallie Bissell   m   20

Crowder, Lauren
Missing Persons - Stephen White   m   244

Cunningham, Gil
The Nicholas Feast - Pat McIntosh   m   168
The Nicholas Feast - Pat McIntosh   t   934

D'Angelo, Erin
The Sign of the Book - John Dunning   m   69

Docherty, Merlyn
The Graveyard Position - Robert Barnard   m   11

Dresden, Beau
Where the River Runs - Patti Callahan Henry   r   329

Farrell, Johnny
Empire Rising - Thomas Kelly   c   1177
Empire Rising - Thomas Kelly   t   920

Field, Lindy
Sins of the Fathers - James Scott Bell   i   1003

Fitzwalter, Alexa
Guardian of Honor - Robin D. Owens   f   614

Foster, Willow
The Dangerous Protector - Janet Chapman   r   291

Franklin, Dominic "Nic"
Dark Moon - Lori Handeland   r   325

Freyl, Hugh
Bleedout - Joan Brady   c   1115

Goldstein, Miles
Detour - James Siegel   c   1227

Hairston, Samuel
You Made Me Love You - Shirley Hailstock   r   324

Hardy, Dismas
The Motive - John Lescroart   m   151

Hirsch, David
The Mourning Sexton - Michael Baron   m   12

Jones, Guy
Eye of the Beholder - Kathy Herman   i   1040

Landry, Jarrod
Shadow Haven - Emily LaForge   r   365

Law, Eric
Goodnight, Sweetheart - Suzanne Simmons   r   428

Mendoza, Inez
With Red Hands - Stephen Woodworth   h   738

Monroe, Parker
Forests of the Night - James W. Hall   m   114

Piretti, Katerina
The Open Channel - Jill Morrow   h   705

Quintana, Anthony
Suspicion of Rage - Barbara Parker   m   189
Suspicion of Rage - Barbara Parker   c   1208

Shardlake, Matthew
Dark Fire - C.J. Sansom   m   214

Shelton, Vivien
First Dance - Karen Kendall   r   353

MINE OWNER

MODEL

MOUNTAIN MAN

MURDERER

Blevins, Billy Ray
Bloody Hills - Charles G. West   *w*   530

Fleet, Arlene
Gods in Alabama - Joshilyn Jackson   *c*   1172

Gee, Victorio
Death Rides a Red Horse - Cotton Smith   *w*   524

Hulett, Al
Ride the Red Sun Down - Thom Nicholson   *w*   507

Joplin, Meager
Ambush for Lassiter - Loren Zane Grey   *w*   490

Malin, Flynt
Riders of Deathwater Valley - James C. Work   *w*   537

Moran, Craig
Ambush for Lassiter - Loren Zane Grey   *w*   490

Rain, John
Killing Rain - Barry Eisler   *m*   73

Raven
Jemez Spring - Rudolfo Anaya   *w*   452

Riker, Harvey
The World Still Melting - Robley Wilson   *c*   1244

Rix, Nathaniel
Hangman's Song - Charles G. West   *w*   532

Scatieri, Ray
Citizen Vince - Jess Walter   *c*   1239

MUSEUM CURATOR

Harper, Benni
Delectable Mountains - Earlene Fowler   *m*   90

Keller, Phoebe
Before Sunrise - Diana Palmer   *r*   402

Montgomery, Camille
Wicked - Shannon Drake   *r*   309

Moon, Penelope
Intimate Knowledge - Amanda Stevens   *r*   434

Spear, Matthew
The Icon - Neil Olson   *m*   182

MUSICIAN

Blades, Roland
Horn of Plenty - Thomas F. Monteleone   *h*   703

Du Pre, Gabriel
Stewball - Peter Bowen   *m*   25

Flier, Suzanna
The Kreutzer Sonata - Margriet De Moor   *c*   1133

Gingras
Pay the Piper - Jane Yolen   *f*   635

Golden, Jess
Dead Reckoning - Natasha Rhodes   *h*   715

Harman
Everran's Bane - Sylvia Kelso   *f*   588

Hedstrom, Kjel
Oh My Stars - Lorna Landvik   *t*   924

Jamie
Dead Reckoning - Natasha Rhodes   *h*   715

Lester, Everett
Dark Star - Creston Mapes   *i*   1061

Mathers, Bevand
The Demonologist - Michael Laimo   *h*   683

McQueen, Steve "Danny"
Goodnight Steve McQueen - Louise Wener   *c*   1241

Morton, Jelly Roll
Jass - David Fulmer   *m*   93

Moss, Laurus
Leeway Cottage - Beth Gutcheon   *t*   901

Richards, Damali
The Bitten - L.A. Banks   *h*   639
The Forbidden - L.A. Banks   *h*   640

Ross, Satchel
Horn of Plenty - Thomas F. Monteleone   *h*   703

Scooter
The Magic Keys - Albert Murray   *t*   938

Sherwood, Ray
Swing - Rupert Holmes   *c*   1164
Swing - Rupert Holmes   *t*   912
Swing - Rupert Holmes   *m*   130

Sykes, Austin
Oh My Stars - Lorna Landvik   *t*   924

Thurston, George
Horn of Plenty - Thomas F. Monteleone   *h*   703

MYTHICAL CREATURE

Avatre
Sanctuary - Mercedes Lackey   *f*   591

Cel
A Stroke of Midnight - Laurell K. Hamilton   *f*   575

Cross, Nathan
Carved in Stone - Vickie Taylor   *r*   440

de Wintershinn, Gossamyr
Gossamyr - Michele Hauf   *f*   578

Eldi, Rosa
The Rose of the World - Jude Fisher   *f*   571

Fleur-du-Mal
The Meq - Steve Cash   *f*   551

Galatyn, Llyr
Master of the Moon - Angela Knight   *r*   360

Kestrel
Tumbling After - Paul Witcover   *f*   632

Lara
Lara - Bertrice Small   *r*   431

Leesil
Sister of the Dead - Barb Hendee   *h*   667

Lessel
Sister of the Dead - Barb Hendee   *f*   580

Mistral
A Stroke of Midnight - Laurell K. Hamilton   *f*   575

Opari
The Meq - Steve Cash   *f*   551

Red Lady
Gossamyr - Michele Hauf   *f*   578

Rhoslyn
Ill Met by Moonlight - Mercedes Lackey   *f*   590

Shedara
Blades of the Tiger - Chris Pierson   *f*   616

Silverhair, Pasgen
Ill Met by Moonlight - Mercedes Lackey   *f*   590

Stardust, Sparkle
Wicked Nights - Nina Bangs   *r*   263

Undercraft
The Widow and the King - John Dickinson   *f*   562

Windy
The Prodigal Troll - Charles Coleman Finlay   *f*   570

Zezen, Zianno
The Meq - Steve Cash   *f*   551

NARRATOR

Balboa, Inigo
Captain Alatriste - Arturo Perez-Reverte   *c*   1212

Georgia
The Red Hat Club Rides Again - Haywood Smith   *r*   432

Jasira
Towelhead - Alicia Erian   *c*   1141

Kathy
Never Let Me Go - Kazuo Ishiguro   *c*   1171

Leland, Dakota
By Summer's End - Pamela Morsi   *r*   393

Unnamed Character
American Purgatorio - John Haskell   *c*   1158
The Earth and Sky of Jacques Dorme - Andrei Makine   *t*   930
Enchantments - Linda Ferri   *c*   1144
The Ice Queen - Alice Hoffman   *c*   1163
The Kreutzer Sonata - Margriet De Moor   *c*   1133
The Society of Others - William Nicholson   *c*   1204

NEIGHBOR

Houghton, Daniel III
A Lick and a Promise - Jo Leigh   *r*   370

Riker, Harvey
The World Still Melting - Robley Wilson   *c*   1244

Stuart, Leslie "Stu"
The Yada Yada Prayer Group Gets Real - Neta Jackson   *i*   1050

Vuoso
Towelhead - Alicia Erian   *c*   1141

NOBLEMAN

Adoula, Jackson
We Few - David Weber   *s*   829

Ambrose
The Widow and the King - John Dickinson   *f*   562

Arvad, Caelith
Mystic Quest - Tracy Hickman   *f*   582

Austrey, Deveron
Ironcrown Moon - Julian May   *f*   599

Bastien
Guardian of Honor - Robin D. Owens   *f*   614

Boscastle, Grayson
The Seduction of an English Scoundrel - Jillian Hunter   *r*   336

Boscastle, Heath
The Wedding Night of an English Rogue - Jillian Hunter   *r*   337

Breckland, Dominic
The Love Affair of an English Lord - Jillian Hunter   *r*   335

Bridei
The Dark Mirror - Juliet Marillier   *f*   598

Broughton, Charles
Snobs - Julian Fellowes   *c*   1143

Campbell, Callum
Lady in Waiting - Kathryn Caskie   *r*   287

Carsington, Rupert
Mr. Impossible - Loretta Chase   *r*   292

Clifford, Noel
My Lady Faire - Emily Hendrickson   *r*   328

Cravenlock, Mazael
Demonsouled - Jonathan Moeller   *f*   609
Demonsouled - Jonathan Moeller   *h*   702

Deathstalker, Lewis
Deathstalker Coda - Simon R. Green   *s*   774

Deathstalker, Owen
Deathstalker Coda - Simon R. Green   *s*   774

Silar
Demonsouled - Jonathan Moeller   *f*   609

Sparks
Pieces of Hate - Tim Lebbon   *h*   689

Summers, Ethan
Central Park - Debra White Smith   *i*   1086

Swenson, David
Heavens to Betsy - Beth Pattillo   *i*   1077

Thia
Storms of Destiny - A.C. Crispin   *f*   559

Thomas
The Mermaid Chair - Sue Monk Kidd   *c*   1179

Vicosz, Bill
Steel Ghosts - Michael Paine   *h*   707

Vidicon
Saint Vidicon to the Rescue - Christopher Stasheff   *f*   626

Walter
Milk - Darcey Steinke   *c*   1231

Wycliffe, John
The Illuminator - Brenda Rickman Vantrease   *c*   1237
The Illuminator - Brenda Rickman Vantrease   *t*   989

Zou Tun
Hungry Tigress - Jade Lee   *r*   368

RESEARCHER

Adams, Luce
What Casanova Told Me - Susan Swan   *t*   978

Keane, Owen
The Confessions of Owen Keane - Terence Faherty   *m*   82

Silva, Leilani
Black Sands - Colleen Coble   *i*   1015

Strandman, Perry
In Darkness Waiting - John Shirley   *h*   725

RESISTANCE FIGHTER

Everett, Langdon
Sons of Liberty - Marie Jakober   *t*   916

Winslow, Gabrielle
The Gypsy Moon - Gilbert Morris   *i*   1069

RESTAURATEUR

Carmichael, Stephen
The Open Channel - Jill Morrow   *h*   705

O'Brian, Callie
Detours - Bette Nordberg   *i*   1074

REVOLUTIONARY

Halloran, Barry
1972 - Morgan Llywelyn   *t*   928

Zapata de Leon, Cesar
Rebel Gun - Lyle Brandt   *w*   462

ROBOT

Goldhawk
Metallic Love - Tanith Lee   *s*   782

Verlis
Metallic Love - Tanith Lee   *s*   782

RODEO RIDER

Daniels, Ali
A Thousand Tomorrows - Karen Kingsbury   *i*   1055

Gunner, Cody
A Thousand Tomorrows - Karen Kingsbury   *i*   1055

ROOMMATE

Rebecca
The Sad Truth about Happiness - Anne Giardini   *c*   1149

ROYALTY

Beynor
Ironcrown Moon - Julian May   *f*   599

Borel
Once upon a Summer Day - Dennis L. McKiernan   *f*   603

Catherine de Medici
The Dark Queen - Susan Carroll   *t*   863

Eleanor of Aquitaine
Prince of Darkness - Sharon Kay Penman   *t*   949

Eremon
The White Mare - Jules Watson   *t*   991
The White Mare - Jules Watson   *f*   630

Hal
The Unhandsome Prince - John Moore   *f*   610

John
Prince of Darkness - Sharon Kay Penman   *t*   949

Kazanov, Viktor
Seducing the Prince - Patricia Grasso   *r*   323

Kevleren, Maddyn
Empire's Daughter - Simon Brown   *f*   546

Lilly
Stargazer - Colby Hodge   *r*   331

Medici, Marie de
A Sundial in a Grave: 1610 - Mary Gentle   *t*   893

Michiko
Heretic Betrayers - Scott McGough   *f*   600

Raodon
Elantris - Brandon Sanderson   *f*   621

Rennsellaer
A Brother's Price - Wen Spencer   *s*   815

Rhiann
The White Mare - Jules Watson   *f*   630
The White Mare - Jules Watson   *t*   991

Sarene
Elantris - Brandon Sanderson   *f*   621

Signy
A Mankind Witch - Dave Freer   *f*   572

Tayyichiut
Lords of Grass and Thunder - Curt Benjamin   *f*   543

RULER

Alfred the Great
The Last Kingdom - Bernard Cornwell   *t*   870
The Last Kingdom - Bernard Cornwell   *c*   1130

Attila
The Scourge of God - William Dietrich   *c*   1135

Beryx
Everran's Bane - Sylvia Kelso   *f*   588

Bran Mak Morn
Bran Mak Morn: The Last King - Robert E. Howard   *f*   584

Brutus
Darkwitch Rising - Sara Douglass   *t*   878

Celimus
Blood and Memory - Fiona McIntosh   *f*   601
Myrren's Gift - Fiona McIntosh   *f*   602

Charles II
Darkwitch Rising - Sara Douglass   *f*   564
Darkwitch Rising - Sara Douglass   *t*   878

Cleopatra
SPQR IX: The Princess and the Pirates - John Maddox Roberts   *t*   964

Conrig
Ironcrown Moon - Julian May   *f*   599

Duanbai
My Life as Emperor - Tong Su   *t*   977

Durandal, Finn
Deathstalker Coda - Simon R. Green   *s*   774

Edward IV
The Exiled - Posie Graeme-Evans   *t*   898

Elizabeth I
Face Down Below the Banqueting House - Kathy Lynn Emerson   *t*   882
The Fyre Mirror - Karen Harper   *t*   905
The Fyre Mirror - Karen Harper   *m*   119
Ill Met by Moonlight - Mercedes Lackey   *t*   923
Ill Met by Moonlight - Mercedes Lackey   *f*   590

Frederick II
The Falcon of Palermo - Maria Bordihn   *t*   856

Galatyn, Llyr
Master of the Moon - Angela Knight   *r*   360

Grus
The Scepter's Return - Dan Chernenko   *f*   553

Jerret
The Divided Crown - Isabel Glass   *f*   573

Lanus
The Scepter's Return - Dan Chernenko   *f*   553

Louis IX
The Crown Rose - Fiona Avery   *f*   539

Mergen-Khan
Lords of Grass and Thunder - Curt Benjamin   *f*   543

Nofret-te-en
Sanctuary - Mercedes Lackey   *f*   591

Ramses III
Year of the Hyenas - Brad Geagley   *t*   892

Rujari
A Sultan in Palermo - Tariq Ali   *t*   843

Saetan
Dreams Made Flesh - Anne Bishop   *f*   544

Sinclair, Eric
Undead and Unappreciated - MaryJanice Davidson   *r*   301

Spithaera
The Crimson Sword - Eldon Thompson   *f*   629

Taylor, Betsy
Undead and Unappreciated - MaryJanice Davidson   *r*   301

Valentyna
Blood and Memory - Fiona McIntosh   *f*   601

Wenceslas, Basic
Scattered Suns - Kevin J. Anderson   *s*   740

RUNAWAY

Avery, Ben Jr.
The Cold Trail - Phillip Gessert   *w*   487

Beacon, Vanessa
Every Waking Moment - Brenda Novak   *r*   400

Character Description Index

Varyl, Kallista
The Compass Rose - Gail Dayton *f* 561

SPACEMAN

Aari
First Warning - Anne McCaffrey *s* 785

Cameron, Bren
Destroyer - C.J. Cherryh *s* 756

Morgan, Jack
Dragon and Slave - Timothy Zahn *s* 839

Mursk, Conrad
To Crush the Moon - Wil McCarthy *s* 787

Pamir
The Well of Stars - Robert Reed *s* 799

Silver, Harry
Rogue Berserker - Fred Saberhagen *s* 808

Stinson, Trent
Anywhere but Here - Jerry Oltion *s* 797

Viktor
The Sunborn - Gregory Benford *s* 750

SPACESHIP CAPTAIN

Axelrod, Shanna
The Sunborn - Gregory Benford *s* 750

Bo-Sheng
Cagebird - Karin Lowachee *s* 784

Deter, Qaade
Unmasked - C.J. Barry *r* 264

Elliot, Trilby
Finders Keepers - Linnea Sinclair *s* 813

Farragut, John
The Myriad - R.M. Meluch *s* 789

Li Wing, Xiomara
To Crush the Moon - Wil McCarthy *s* 787

Masters, Torrie
Unmasked - C.J. Barry *r* 264

Mir
The Well of Stars - Robert Reed *s* 799

yos'Phelium, Cantra
Crystal Soldier - Sharon Lee *s* 781

SPACEWOMAN

Ames, Tabitha
The Quantum Connection - Travis S. Taylor *s* 818

Julia
The Sunborn - Gregory Benford *s* 750

Khoriilya
First Warning - Anne McCaffrey *s* 785

Stinson, Donna
Anywhere but Here - Jerry Oltion *s* 797

Washen
The Well of Stars - Robert Reed *s* 799

SPINSTER

Allard, Frances
Simply Unforgettable - Mary Balogh *r* 261

Lapp, Sara
The Butterfly Garden - Annette Blair *r* 267

Rosemoor, Jane
Unveiled - Kristina Cook *r* 296

SPIRIT

Bingham, Rachel
After the Midnight Hour - Linda Randall
   Wisdom *r* 448

MacLeod, Hamish
A Cold Treachery - Charles Todd *m* 235
A Cold Treachery - Charles Todd *t* 984

Markham, William
Spirited Away - Pamela Labud *r* 364

Selavy, Rose
Kiss the Goat - Brian Stableford *h* 729

Westwood, Dimity
Aunt Dimity and the Next of Kin - Nancy
   Atherton *h* 638
Aunt Dimity and the Next of Kin - Nancy
   Atherton *m* 9

SPORTS FIGURE

Burdette, Cassie
Fairway to Heaven - Roberta Isleib *m* 133

Holbrook, Gabriel
Stranger in Town - Brenda Novak *r* 401

Magee, Kell
Her Passionate Plan B - Dixie Browning *r* 278

McGuire, Sean
Table for Five - Susan Wiggs *r* 445

Sanders, Blain
Dangerous Curves - Pamela Britton *r* 273

Shannon, Mark
Double Down - Tess Hudson *r* 334

SPOUSE

Andrews, Rachael
Bloody Hills - Charles G. West *w* 530

Asterius, Arcadia
The Cybelene Conspiracy - Albert Noyer *m* 181

Barton, Liza "Celia"
No Place Like Home - Mary Higgins Clark *c* 1125

Baxter, Jodi
The Yada Yada Prayer Group Gets Real - Neta
   Jackson *i* 1050

Black, Curtis
The Best-Kept Secret - Kimberla Lawson
   Roby *c* 1220

Black, Ellie
The Other Woman - Jane Green *c* 1151

Blakely, Mary June
Sweetgrass - Mary Alice Monroe *r* 389

Blakely, Preston
Sweetgrass - Mary Alice Monroe *r* 389

Bon
No Man's Land - Thu Huong Duong *c* 1138

Breibard, Paul
Detour - James Siegel *c* 1227

Claiborne, Catherine
That Anvil of Our Souls - David Poyer *t* 957

Connable, Lucy
The Undertaker's Wife - Loren D. Estleman *w* 479

Cooper, Dan
The Other Woman - Jane Green *c* 1151

Crowder, Lauren
Missing Persons - Stephen White *m* 244

Dallas, Eve
Origin in Death - J.D. Robb *r* 416

Darcy, Elizabeth Bennet
Suspense and Sensibility - Carrie Bebris *m* 18
Suspense and Sensibility - Carrie Bebris *h* 641

Darcy, Fitzwilliam
Suspense and Sensibility - Carrie Bebris *h* 641
Suspense and Sensibility - Carrie Bebris *m* 18

Darling, Max
Murder Walks the Plank - Carolyn Hart *m* 123

Dickerson, Patty
The Good Wife - Stewart O'Nan *c* 1205

Dupont, Julia
The Same Sweet Girls - Cassandra King *c* 1180

Emerson, Lidian Jackson
Mr. Emerson's Wife - Amy Belding Brown *t* 861

Emerson, Radcliffe
The Serpent on the Crown - Elizabeth
   Peters *m* 198
The Serpent on the Crown - Elizabeth Peters *t* 952

Eva
Lost in the Forest - Sue Miller *c* 1198

Fallon, Tom
Sudden Rain - Maritta Wolff *c* 1245

Fernandez, Elena
The Watcher in the Pine - Rebecca Pawel *m* 192

Fisher, Sarah Vivian
Pendencia Creek - E. Lee Fisher *w* 481

Fluck, Zelda
Trouble in Paradise - Pip Granger *c* 1150
Trouble in Paradise - Pip Granger *m* 106

Foster, Laurence
No Place Like Home - Mary Higgins Clark *c* 1125

Fremont, Jessie Benton
Dream West - David Nevin *w* 506

Gagnon, Jimmy
Alone - Lisa Gardner *c* 1148

Gibbons, Sara
Showdown in Austin - Tom Calhoun *w* 467

Hathaway, Anne
Murder in Stratford - Audrey Peterson *t* 953
Murder in Stratford - Audrey Peterson *m* 199

Hayden, Maggie
Hot Flashes and Cold Cream - Diann Hunt *i* 1048

Hill, Judy
Unlucky for Some - Jill McGown *m* 167

Hoan
No Man's Land - Thu Huong Duong *c* 1138

Hunter, Matt
The Innocent - Harlan Coben *c* 1127
The Innocent - Harlan Coben *m* 48

Ingram, Somers
The Linnet Bird - Linda Holeman *t* 911

Jim
My Jim - Nancy Rawles *c* 1217

Jones, Ellen
Eye of the Beholder - Kathy Herman *i* 1040

Jordan, Jan
Always Jan - Roxanne Henke *i* 1039

Joseph, Hortense
Small Island - Andrea Levy *t* 927
Small Island - Andrea Levy *c* 1187

Kaukab
Maps for Lost Lovers - Nadeem Aslam *c* 1108

Lim, Snow
The Harmony Silk Factory - Tash Aw *c* 1109
The Harmony Silk Factory - Tash Aw *t* 849

Lloyd
Unlucky for Some - Jill McGown *m* 167

MacKenzie, David
Expectations - Melanie M. Jeschke   *i*   1051

MacKenzie, Kate
Expectations - Melanie M. Jeschke   *i*   1051

Mallory, Cora
Bad Money - Ed Gorman   *w*   489

March, Marmee
March - Geraldine Brooks   *t*   860
March - Geraldine Brooks   *c*   1117

Matekoni, J.L.B.
In the Company of Cheerful Ladies - Alexander McCall Smith   *c*   1193

McCarthy, Lou
Winners - Eric B. Martin   *c*   1190

McCormack, Calvin
Flesh Wounds - John Lawton   *m*   149

Meadowlark
Dancing with the Golden Bear - Win Blevins   *w*   457

Mein
No Man's Land - Thu Huong Duong   *c*   1138

Mosely, Callie
Guns of Wolf Valley - Ralph Cotton   *w*   469

Nolan, Alex
No Place Like Home - Mary Higgins Clark   *c*   1125

Paola
The Mysterious Flame of Queen Loana - Umberto Eco   *c*   1139

Pendragon, Gwen
Riders of Deathwater Valley - James C. Work   *w*   537

Pickett, Marybeth
Out of Range - C.J. Box   *w*   460

Pitt, Charlotte
Long Spoon Lane - Anne Perry   *t*   951
Long Spoon Lane - Anne Perry   *m*   197

Powerscourt, Lucy
Death of a Chancellor - David Dickinson   *m*   65

Randazzo, Phil
The Year of Past Things - M.A. Harper   *h*   665

Saint-Martin, Paul de
Lethal Beauty - Charles O'Brien   *t*   942

Shamas
Maps for Lost Lovers - Nadeem Aslam   *c*   1108

Shelton, Rebecca
Monster - Frank Peretti   *h*   708

Stanley, Penny
The Tea House of Mulberry Street - Sharon Owens   *c*   1206

Terra, Julia
The Cigar Roller - Pablo Medina   *c*   1195

Thornton, Rebecca
For the Love of the Land - Bonnie Leon   *i*   1058
The Heart of Thornton Creek - Bonnie Leon   *i*   1059

Tobler, Arlene
The World Still Melting - Robley Wilson   *c*   1244

Unnamed Character
American Purgatorio - John Haskell   *c*   1158

van Vlooten, Marius
The Kreutzer Sonata - Margriet De Moor   *c*   1133

Ware, Melissa Jardine
The Trampled Field - Jeanne Williams   *w*   536

Wickham, Michelle
The Year of Past Things - M.A. Harper   *h*   665

Yarbrough, Joe Riddley
Who Killed the Queen of Clubs? - Patricia Sprinkle   *m*   226

Zeinab
The Point in the Market - Michael Pearce   *t*   947

SPY

Allon, Gabriel
Prince of Fire - Daniel Silva   *m*   222

Amara
Academ's Fury - Jim Butcher   *f*   548

Anwar, Nikolai
Final Justice - Jasmine Cresswell   *r*   297

Atkins, Wendy
Thieves of Mercy - James L. Nelson   *t*   940

Beecham, Melody
Final Justice - Jasmine Cresswell   *r*   297

Begay, Joe
Vineyard Prey - Philip R. Craig   *m*   56

Blaze
The Aware - Glenda Larke   *f*   592

Carmichael, Caroline
Blown - Francine Mathews   *m*   162

Darby, Kate
Shadow Patriots - Lucia St. Clair Robson   *t*   965

Devaney
The Prometheus Project - Steve White   *s*   832

Dietrich, Jed
The Unknown Soldier - Gerald Seymour   *c*   1224

Fish, Jack
Jack Fish - J. Milligan   *c*   1199

George
With Red Hands - Stephen Woodworth   *h*   738

Harris, Julie
A Season of Shadows - Paul McCusker   *i*   1066

Holmes, Mycroft
The Italian Secretary - Caleb Carr   *m*   41

Jones, Abel
Rebels of Babylon - Owen Parry   *m*   191
Rebels of Babylon - Owen Parry   *t*   945

Kirkwood, Georgina
Guardian of the Freedom - Irene Radford   *f*   617

Lauria
Freedom's Apprentice - Naomi Kritzer   *f*   589

Mayer, Willard
Hitler's Peace - Philip Kerr   *c*   1178
Hitler's Peace - Philip Kerr   *t*   922
Hitler's Peace - Philip Kerr   *m*   142

McKenzie, Eli
The McKenzie Artifact - Alison Kent   *r*   356

Mundy, Adele
The Way to Glory - David Drake   *s*   765

Nash, Charlotte
My Surrender - Connie Brockway   *r*   275

Niamor
The Aware - Glenda Larke   *f*   592

Rain, John
Killing Rain - Barry Eisler   *m*   73

Ravenor, Gideon
Ravenor Returned - Dan Abnett   *s*   739

Ross, Dand
My Surrender - Connie Brockway   *r*   275

Sagara, Lune
Godplayers - Damien Broderick   *f*   545

Schellenberger, Walter
Hitler's Peace - Philip Kerr   *t*   922

Sev, Brano
36 Yalta Boulevard - Olen Steinhauer   *m*   227

Soraya
Rise of a Hero - Hilari Bell   *f*   542

Tanner, Jack
The Curse of Cain - J. Mark Powell   *t*   956

Tarleton, Basil
The Curse of Cain - J. Mark Powell   *t*   956

Tavi
Academ's Fury - Jim Butcher   *f*   548

Thonius, Carl
Ravenor Returned - Dan Abnett   *s*   739

Travante, Megan
Against the Tide - John Ringo   *f*   619

Wroughton, Eddie
The Unknown Soldier - Gerald Seymour   *c*   1224

STOCK BROKER

Holman, Preston
Every Waking Moment - Brenda Novak   *r*   400

STORE OWNER

Ace
Resurrection Dreams - Richard Laymon   *h*   686

Browning, Theodosia
Chamomile Mourning - Laura Childs   *m*   46

Caine, Gillian
Random Acts of Fashion - Nikki Rivers   *r*   414

Darling, Annie Laurance
Murder Walks the Plank - Carolyn Hart   *m*   123

Devonshire, Betsy
Embroidered Truths - Monica Ferris   *m*   85

Hart, Alexandra
Vampire Beach - Alexa Hayes   *h*   666

Holly, Jean
The Golden Box - Frances Crane   *m*   58

Janeway, Cliff
The Sign of the Book - John Dunning   *m*   69

Knight, Abby
Slay It with Flowers - Kate Collins   *m*   51

Lee, Peggy
Pretty Poison - Joyce Lavene   *m*   148

Malloy, Claire
The Goodbye Body - Joan Hess   *m*   128

McBride, Mari
Her Bodyguard - Geralyn Dawson   *r*   304

Moore, Rebecca
Dangerous Curves - Judith Skillings   *m*   224

O'Brien, Emerald
Murder under a Mystic Moon - Yasmine Galenorn   *h*   659

Owens, Marty
Her Man Upstairs - Dixie Browning   *r*   277

Savoy, Janet
Grave Intent - Deborah LeBlanc   *h*   690

Scott, Stella
Hot Spot - Susan Johnson   *r*   345

Seltzer, Nathan
Boogaloo on Second Avenue - Mark Kurlansky   *c*   1185

Shelley, Wollstonecraft "Wollie"
Dating Is Murder - Harley Jane Kozak   *m*   146

Williams, A.J.
The Best Gift - Irene Hannon   *i*   1036

TELEPATH

TELEVISION PERSONALITY

TERRORIST

THIEF

TIME TRAVELER

TOUR GUIDE

TOURIST

TRAVEL AGENT

TRAVELER

Diomedes
Odysseus on the Rhine - Edward S. Louis *f* 596

Flic
Once upon a Summer Day - Dennis L. McKiernan *f* 603

Icarium
Deadhouse Gates - Steven Erikson *f* 567

Jarred
The Iron Tree - Cecilia Dart-Thornton *f* 560

Josiah
According to Crow - E. Sedia *f* 622

Odysseus
Odysseus on the Rhine - Edward S. Louis *f* 596

Philoctetes
Odysseus on the Rhine - Edward S. Louis *f* 596

Seebeck, August
Godplayers - Damien Broderick *f* 545

TRUCK DRIVER

Gudmundsen, Goldie
Hardwater - Steve Sherwood *w* 523

TUTOR

Mulcahey, Megan
An Unexpected Pleasure - Candace Camp *r* 285

TWIN

Burton, Ethan
No Direction Home - Marisa Silver *c* 1228

Burton, Will
No Direction Home - Marisa Silver *c* 1228

Claudia
Writing on the Wall - Lynne Sharon Schwartz *c* 1223

Denzer, Sage
Moon of the Sleeping Bear - K. Celeste Bryan *w* 466

McCain, Wynter
Moon of the Sleeping Bear - K. Celeste Bryan *w* 466

Renata
Writing on the Wall - Lynne Sharon Schwartz *c* 1223

Valentina
The Madness of Love - Katharine Davies *c* 1132

UNDERTAKER

Connable, Richard
The Undertaker's Wife - Loren D. Estleman *w* 479

Savoy, Michael
Grave Intent - Deborah LeBlanc *h* 690

UNEMPLOYED

Joseph, Elliott
Unspeakable - Graham Masterton *h* 699

Marsh, Pepper
Hard Day's Knight - Katie MacAlister *r* 379

St. John, Sydney Marie
Goodnight, Sweetheart - Suzanne Simmons *r* 428

VACATIONER

Graves, Eleanor
Down Time - Lynn Abbey *f* 538

Merrigan, Emma
Down Time - Lynn Abbey *f* 538

VAMPIRE

De La Cruz, Rafael
Dark Secret - Christine Feehan *r* 313

DeLongpre, Roshan
Night's Kiss - Amanda Ashley *r* 255

Earl
Gil's All Fright Diner - A. Lee Martinez *h* 698

Fitzroy, Henry
Smoke and Mirrors - Tanya Huff *h* 672

Foxe, Colin
I Hunger for You - Susan Sizemore *h* 727
I Hunger for You - Susan Sizemore *r* 429

Gideon
Fear Me - Stephen Laws *h* 685

Kirby-Jones, Simon
Baked to Death - Dean James *m* 134

Kopernik, Jadzia Vilma
Fiend - Jemiah Jefferson *h* 673

Laurent
I Hunger for You - Susan Sizemore *h* 727

Lee, Magnus
Vampire Hunter D - Hideyuki Kikuchi *h* 679

Magiere
Sister of the Dead - Barb Hendee *h* 667
Sister of the Dead - Barb Hendee *f* 580

Mavra
Dead Beat - Jim Butcher *h* 647

McNair, Eric
Wicked Nights - Nina Bangs *r* 263

O'Neill, Rafe
Vampire Beach - Alexa Hayes *h* 666

Ricari, Orfeo
Fiend - Jemiah Jefferson *h* 673

Rivera, Carlos
The Bitten - L.A. Banks *h* 639
The Forbidden - L.A. Banks *h* 640

Rufford, Ian
The Companion - Susan Squires *r* 433

Sibbechai
Witch Finder - C.L. Werner *f* 631

Sinclair, Eric
Undead and Unappreciated - MaryJanice Davidson *r* 301

Taylor, Betsy
Undead and Unappreciated - MaryJanice Davidson *r* 301

VAMPIRE HUNTER

Richards, Damali
The Bitten - L.A. Banks *h* 639
The Forbidden - L.A. Banks *h* 640

Thulman, Mathias
Witch Finder - C.L. Werner *f* 631

Vampire Hunter D
Vampire Hunter D - Hideyuki Kikuchi *h* 679

VETERAN

Alatriste y Tenorio, Diego
Captain Alatriste - Arturo Perez-Reverte *c* 1212
Captain Alatriste - Arturo Perez-Reverte *t* 950

Begay, Joe
Vineyard Prey - Philip R. Craig *m* 56

Bon
No Man's Land - Thu Huong Duong *c* 1138

Chandler, John
The Wrangler - Frank Roderus *w* 519

Drinkwater, Roger
The Lake, the River and the Other Lake - Steve Amick *c* 1106

Grayson, Erin
Wounded Healer - Donna Fleisher *i* 1028

Joseph, Gilbert
Small Island - Andrea Levy *t* 927
Small Island - Andrea Levy *c* 1187

Kapostash, Howard
The Ha-Ha - Dave King *c* 1181

Lacey, Gabriel
The Sudbury School Murders - Ashley Gardner *m* 95

Lawrence, Doyle
Glimpses of Paradise - James Scott Bell *i* 1002

McIntyre, Chris
Wounded Healer - Donna Fleisher *i* 1028

Penrose, Adam
The Penrose Treasure - Janet Tanner *r* 439

Pike, Joe
The Forgotten Man - Robert Crais *m* 57

Rutledge, Ian
A Cold Treachery - Charles Todd *m* 235
A Cold Treachery - Charles Todd *t* 984

VETERINARIAN

Calvert, Sam
The Long Way Home - Sarah Storme *r* 437

Popper, Jessica
Lead a Horse to Water - Cynthia Baxter *m* 15

Wolfe, Travis
Cryptid Hunters - Roland Smith *s* 814

VILLAIN

Raven
Jemez Spring - Rudolfo Anaya *w* 452

VOLUNTEER

Dresden, Meridy McFadden
Where the River Runs - Patti Callahan Henry *r* 329

Nolan, Vincent
A Changed Man - Francine Prose *c* 1214

Shepherd, Lori
Aunt Dimity and the Next of Kin - Nancy Atherton *m* 9
Aunt Dimity and the Next of Kin - Nancy Atherton *h* 638

WAITER/WAITRESS

Garner, Dallas
Lone Star Calder - Janet Dailey *r* 300

Riddle, Jordan
The Sound of My Voice - Jo Kadlecek *i* 1052

Spivey, Roberta Jones
Sex and the Serial Killer - Jennifer Skully *r* 430

WANDERER

Cair, Jarl
A Mankind Witch - Dave Freer *f* 572

WARD

Fitz Hugh, Francine "Fancy"
Naughty or Nice - Melanie George   *r*   322

Jimmy
War at Home - Kris Nelscott   *m*   180

Moreland, Madeline
Unveiled - Kristina Cook   *r*   296

WARLOCK

Gerachtyent, Kayne
Heir of Stone - S.L. Farrell   *f*   569

Kirion
The Duke's Ballad - Andre Norton   *f*   611

WARLORD

Lucivar
Dreams Made Flesh - Anne Bishop   *f*   544

Vortepor of Dyfed
The Last Companion - Patrick McCormack   *t*   933

WARRIOR

Allion
The Crimson Sword - Eldon Thompson   *f*   629

Attila the Hun
The Scourge of God - William Dietrich   *t*   876
The Sword of Attila - Michael Curtis Ford   *t*   889

Autshumao
Islands - Dan Sleigh   *t*   972

Blackcloak, Archer
Shadows of Myth - Rachel Lee   *f*   594

Cameron, Sigimor
Highland Conqueror - Hannah Howell   *r*   333

Daol
Blood of Wolves - Loren L. Coleman   *f*   556

Darthassian, Lanther
Return of the Exile - Mary H. Herbert   *f*   581

Doroga
Academ's Fury - Jim Butcher   *f*   548

Else
The Tyranny of the Night - Glen Cook   *f*   557

Feor
The Hidden Queen - Rachel Lee   *f*   593

FitzHenry, Rhys
The Beauty Bride - Claire Delacroix   *r*   305

Forlo
Blades of the Tiger - Chris Pierson   *f*   616

Graybrook, Dorn
The Rite - Richard Lee Byers   *f*   549

Grimnir
Blood of Wolves - Loren L. Coleman   *f*   556

Hakkonsen, Erik
A Mankind Witch - Dave Freer   *f*   572

Hidetsugu, Yamagushi
Heretic Betrayers - Scott McGough   *f*   600

Iron Hawk
Gunsmoke: The Last Dog Soldier - Joseph A. West   *w*   533

Jezzil
Storms of Destiny - A.C. Crispin   *f*   559

Kern
Blood of Wolves - Loren L. Coleman   *f*   556

Kiron
Sanctuary - Mercedes Lackey   *f*   591

Massing, Welstiel
Sister of the Dead - Barb Hendee   *h*   667

Philoctetes
Odysseus on the Rhine - Edward S. Louis   *f*   596

Qutula
Lords of Grass and Thunder - Curt Benjamin   *f*   543

Ragnar
The Last Kingdom - Bernard Cornwell   *t*   870
The Last Kingdom - Bernard Cornwell   *c*   1130

Ravenson, Raven
Mists of Everness - John Wright   *f*   634

Shemov, Pavel
The Rite - Richard Lee Byers   *f*   549

Snow, Mia
Awaken Me Darkly - Gena Showalter   *r*   426

Snowstealer, Raryn
The Rite - Richard Lee Byers   *f*   549

Tamar
Freedom's Apprentice - Naomi Kritzer   *f*   589

Tristan ar Malik
The Pleasure Slave - Gena Showalter   *r*   427

Umezawa, Toshi
Heretic Betrayers - Scott McGough   *f*   600

Villon, Jean Cesar Ulrich III
Gossamyr - Michele Hauf   *f*   578

WEALTHY

Christian, Howard
Mammoth - John Varley   *s*   825

Custis, Josh
Underground - Craig Spector   *h*   728

Defalle, Gatien
On Winding Hill Road - Diane Tyrrel   *r*   442

Gagnon, Jimmy
Alone - Lisa Gardner   *c*   1148

Gold, Wally
Diana Lively Is Falling Down - Sheila Curran   *r*   299

Grantforth, Jagan
Finders Keepers - Linnea Sinclair   *s*   813

Hardesty, Adam
Wait Until Midnight - Amanda Quick   *r*   407

Hart, Calder
Deadly Illusions - Brenda Joyce   *r*   349

Kimball, Alex
First Date - Karen Kendall   *r*   354

Lawton, Diane
Spin - Robert Charles Wilson   *s*   835

Lawton, Jason
Spin - Robert Charles Wilson   *s*   835

Parrish, Rose
Galveston Rose - Mary Powell   *w*   514

Roarke
Origin in Death - J.D. Robb   *r*   416

Rossi, Matt
Without a Clue - Trish Jensen   *r*   344

Sealy, Olivia
Bloodlines - Dinah McCall   *r*   384

Teeny
The Red Hat Club Rides Again - Haywood Smith   *r*   432

Whitefield, Riley
Falling for Gracie - Susan Mallery   *r*   381

Woodlock, Olivia
Crimson Moon - Rebecca York   *r*   449

WEREWOLF

Duke
Gil's All Fright Diner - A. Lee Martinez   *h*   698

Gardner, Derik
Derik's Bane - MaryJanice Davidson   *h*   654

Hanover, Elise
Dark Moon - Lori Handeland   *r*   325

Kavanaugh, Sim
To Tame a Wolf - Susan Krinard   *r*   362

London, Diana
Master of the Moon - Angela Knight   *r*   360

Morgan, Sam
Crimson Moon - Rebecca York   *r*   449

Ryn of Anwyn
The Moon Witch - Linda Winstead Jones   *r*   347

WIDOW(ER)

Brandt, Sarah
Murder on Lenox Hill - Victoria Thompson   *m*   233
Murder on Lenox Hill - Victoria Thompson   *t*   982

Burk, Charity
The Drifter - Lori Copeland   *i*   1018

Culver, Victoria
Warrior's Heart - Jackie Kramer   *r*   361

Davis, Mary
A Garden in Paris - Stephanie Grace Whitson   *i*   1093

Deveaux, Gabriella
Shadow Haven - Emily LaForge   *r*   365

Deveraux, Gally
High Plains Tango - Robert James Waller   *w*   529

Duvere, Emma
Protected Hearts - Bonnie K. Winn   *i*   1097

Fairfax, Claudia
My Lady Faire - Emily Hendrickson   *r*   328

Finn
The Illuminator - Brenda Rickman Vantrease   *c*   1237
The Illuminator - Brenda Rickman Vantrease   *t*   989

Fortenberry, Annie
Full Bloom - Janet Evanovich   *r*   312

Garrett, Mibby
Always Green - Patti Ann Hill   *i*   1044

Gold, Wally
Diana Lively Is Falling Down - Sheila Curran   *r*   299

Harris, Julie
A Season of Shadows - Paul McCusker   *i*   1066

Jamison, Marissa
The Perfect Family - Carla Cassidy   *r*   288

Kennedy, Kate
Who Killed Swami Schwartz? - Nora Charles   *m*   43

Kent, Eliza
Mostly a Lady - Lisa Manuel   *r*   382

Madison, Kate
Mother of Prevention - Lori Copeland   *i*   1019

Mancroft, Violet
By the Grand Canal - William Riviere   *t*   962

Mayovskyj, Kolya
A Short History of Tractors in Ukrainian - Marina Lewycka   *c*   1188

McCall, Treena
Skintight - Susan Andersen   *r*   254

McKenna, Cassie
Bloody Point - Linda J. White   *i*   1092

YOUNG MAN

YOUNG WOMAN

Author Index

This index is an alphabetical listing of the authors of books featured in entries and those listed within entries under the rubrics "Other books by the same author" and "Other books you might like." For each author, the titles of books described or listed in this edition and their entry numbers appear. Bold numbers indicate a featured main entry; light-face numbers refer to books recommended for further reading.

A

Abbey, Lynn
Behind Time 538
Cinnabar Shadows 624
Daughter of the Bright Moon 581
Down Time **538**
Jerlayne 538, 593
Out of Time 538
Sanctuary 538
Taking Time 538
Unicorn and Dragon 564

Abbott, Megan
Die a Little **1**

Abe, Shana
The Truelove Bride 421

Abella, Alex
Final Acts 24
The Killing of the Saints 1208

Abnett, Dan
The Guns of Tanith 739
Ravenor 739
Ravenor Returned 558, **739**
Riders of the Dead 619
Sabbat Martyr 739
Straight Silver 739
Traitor General 739
Xenos 616

Abraham, Ken
The Prodigal Project Series 1037

Abrahams, Peter
Crying Wolf 1098
Down the Rabbit Hole 1098
Lights Out 1098
Oblivion **1098**
Revolution No. 9 1098
Their Wildest Dreams 1098

Acker, Rick
Dead Man's Rule **997**, 1045

Ackroyd, Peter
The Clerkenwell Tales 877, 898
The Trial of Elizabeth Cree 951

Acres, Mark
Dark Divide 631
Dragon War 591
Dragonspawn 588

Adair, Cherry
Dare Me **250**

On Thin Ice 332

Adams, Alice
After the War 1206
Almost Perfect 1110, 1155
Medicine Men 1247
A Southern Exposure 1190, 1245

Adams, Kylie
First Kiss **251**
Fly Me to the Moon 251, 254, 334

Adams, Richard
Watership Down 633

Adamson, Lydia
The Dr. Deirdre Nightingale Series 15

Adamson, M.J.
The Burning Tree 152

Adcock, Thomas
The Neal Hockaday Series 22

Adichie, Chimamanda Ngozi
Purple Hibiscus 1228

Adicks, Richard
A Court of Owls 956

Adkins, Patrick
Lord of the Crooked Paths 596

Adlard, Mark
Volteface 747

Agee, James
A Death in the Family 1198

Agnello Hornby, Simonetta
The Almond Picker **1099**, 1109, 1237

Ahern, Cecelia
P.S. I Love You 1100
Rosie Dunne **1100**

Aickman, Robert
Cold Hand in Mine 652

Aiken, Ginny
The Bellamy's Blossoms Series 1043

Aiken, Joan
Black Hearts in Battersea 617
Eliza's Daughter 848
Jane Fairfax 848

Aikin, Jim
The Wall at the Edge of the World 831

Aikman, David
Qi **998**
When the Almond Tree Blossoms 998

Airth, Rennie
River of Darkness 235

Akenson, Donald H.
At Face Value 974

Aksyonov, Vasily
The Winter's Hero 1203

Akunin, Boris
Murder on the Leviathan 2, 840, 1101, 1155
The Turkish Gambit **2**, **840**, **1101**
The Winter Queen 2, 840, 1101, 1216

Alarcon, Daniel
War by Candlelight **1102**, 1105

Albert, Bill
Death at Blenheim Palace **186**

Albert, Susan Wittig
Bloodroot 3, 841
Chile Death 177
The China Bayles Series 33, 46, 51, 85, 90, 107, 185, 219, 224
Dead Man's Bones **3**, 659
Death at Blenheim Palace **186**
A Dilly of a Death 3, 841
Indigo Dying 3, 841
Mistletoe Man 3, 841
Rueful Death 102
The Tale of Hill Top Farm 841
The Tale of Holly How **841**
An Unthymely Death and Other Gardening Mysteries 3

Alcorn, Randy
Lord Foulgrin's Letters 1046
Safely Home 998

Alcott, Louisa May
Little Women 860, 1117

Aldington, Richard
The Romance of Casanova 978

Aldiss, Brian W.
Dracula Unbound 679, 743
Enemies of the System 749
Greybeard 811
Non-Stop 799
Seasons in Flight 758

Aikman, David
Qi **998**
When the Almond Tree Blossoms 998

Aldridge, Ray
The Orpheus Machine 833

Alers, Rochelle
Beyond Business 276
Island Magic 339
Just Before Dawn 324
No Compromise 324

Alexander, Bruce
The Color of Death 4, 842
Death of a Colonial 4, 842
An Experiment in Treason 4, 842
The Price of Murder 4, 842
Rules of Engagement **4**, **842**
The Sir John Fielding Series 101, 852, 895
Smuggler's Moon 4, 842

Alexander, Carly
The Eggnog Chronicles 290, 298, 350

Alexander, Carrie
The Chocolate Seduction 370, 372
Honk If You Love Real Men **252**

Alexander, David
Fane 577

Alexander, Hannah
The Crystal Cavern 999
Hideaway 999
Last Resort **999**
Necessary Measures 999
Safe Haven 999
Urgent Care 999

Alexander, Marc
The Mist Lizard 814

Alexander, Trisha
Falling for an Older Man 298

Alexie, Sherman
Reservation Blues 1164
Ten Little Indians 513

Ali, Monica
Brick Lane 1108, 1141

Ali, Tariq
The Book of Saladin 843
Fear of Mirrors 843
Redemption 843
Shadows of the Pomegranate Tree 843
The Stone Woman 843
A Sultan in Palermo **843**

Author Index

Author Index

Face Down Beneath the Eleanor Cross 77
Face Down under the Wych Elm 77, 882
Face Down upon a Herbal 882
Murders and Other Confusions 77
The Susanna, Lady Appleton Series 119, 905

Emery, Clayton
Sword Play 559

Emshwiller, Carol
I Live with You **768**
Joy in Our Cause 768
The Start of the End of It All 768
Verging on the Pertinent 768

Enger, Leif
Peace Like a River 1202

Engh, M.J.
Rainbow Man 815

Enoch, Suzanne
London's Perfect Scoundrel 406
A Matter of Scandal 270
Meet Me at Midnight 335

Ephron, Amy
Biodegradable Soap 883, 1140
Bruised Fruit 883, 1140
A Cup of Tea 883, 1140
One Sunday Morning **883**, **1140**
White Rose 867, 883, 1140

Erdrich, Louise
The Beet Queen 924
Four Souls 518, 525, 1176
The Last Report on the Miracle at Little No Horse 988
The Master Butchers Singing Club 514, 891, 986, 1103
Tales of Burning Love 1161

Erian, Alicia
The Brutal Language of Love 1141
Towelhead 1111, **1141**, 1188, 1221

Erickson, Lynn
The Eleventh Hour 405
The Ripple Effect 405

Erickson, Steve
Amnesiascope 566
Arc d'X 566
Days between Stations 566
Our Ecstatic Days 563, **566**
The Sea Came in at Midnight 566
Tours of the Black Clock 566

Erikson, Steven
Blood Follows 567
Deadhouse Gates **567**
Gardens of the Moon 567, 629
The Healthy Dead 567

Eschbach, Andreas
The Carpet Makers **769**

Esquivel, Laura
Like Water for Chocolate 1236

Estes, Rose
Troll Taken 570

Estleman, Loren D.
The Amos Walker Series 202
Any Man's Death 78
Black Powder, White Smoke 468, 471, 479
Bloody Season 944
Kill Zone 78
Little Black Dress **78**, 479
The Peter Macklin Series 73
Poison Blonde 479
Port Hazard 479
Retro 479

Roses Are Dead 78
Something Borrowed, Something Black 78
The Undertaker's Wife **479**

Etchells, Olive
No Corners for the Devil 79, 174

Etchison, Dennis
Shadow Man 661

Etherington, Wendy
My Place or Yours? 277

Evanick, Marcia
Christmas on Conrad Street 291

Evanovich, Janet
Eleven on Top **80**
Full Blast 312
Full Bloom **312**
Full House 312
Full Speed 312
Full Tilt 312
Hard Eight 80
Hot Six 899
Metro Girl 163
Seven Up 80
The Stephanie Plum Series 23, 30, 63, 146, 159, 164, 228, 239
Ten Big Ones 80
Three to Get Deadly 1127
To the Nines 80
Visions of Sugarplums 80

Evans, Linda
Sleipnir 572

Evans, Mary Anna
Artifacts 39, 241

Even, Aaron Roy
Bloodroot 880, 924

Everett, Percival
Big Picture 1242
Damned If I Do 1102
My Existing Condition 1198
Walk Me to the Distance 1181

Eversz, Robert
Burning Garbo 81
Digging James Dean **81**
Killing Paparazzi 81
Shooting Elvis 81

Ewing, Jean R.
Valor's Reward 422

F

Faber, Michel
The Crimson and the White 981

Faherty, Terence
Come Back Dead 1
The Confessions of Owen Keane **82**
Die Dreaming 82
Live to Regret 82
The Lost Keats 82
The Ordained 82
Orion Rising 82

Fairbanks, Nancy
The Carolyn Blue Series 87, 124

Fairstein, Linda
The Alexandra Cooper Series 161, 206
The Bone Vault 83
Cold Hit 83
The Deadhouse 83
Entombed **83**
The Kills 83

Likely to Die 83

Falconer, Colin
The Sultan's Harem 843, 906
When We Were Gods 914, 964

Fallon, Jennifer
Eye of the Labyrinth 568
Harshini **568**
The Lion of Senet 568
Lord of the Shadows 568
Medalon 568, 598
Treason Keep 568

Farhi, Moris
Children of the Rainbow 884
Journey through the Wilderness 884
The Last of Days 884
Young Turk **884**

Farland, David
The Lair of Bones 595
Wizardborn 567, 598

Farley, Christopher John
Kingston by Starlight **885**
My Favorite War 885

Farmer, Jerrilyn
Dim Sum Dead 84
The Flaming Luau of Death 74, **84**
Immaculate Reception 84
Killer Wedding 66, 70, 84, 239
The Madeline Bean Series 38, 47, 183
Mumbo Gumbo 84, 187
Perfect Sax 84

Farr, Diane
Falling for Chloe 387

Farrell, J.G.
The Troubles 853

Farrell, James T.
Studs Lonigan 1177

Farrell, S.L.
Heir of Stone **569**
Holder of Lightnings 569
Mage of Clouds 569

Farren, Mick
The Time of Feasting 727

Farrer, Matthew
Legacy 739

Farris, John
All Heads Turn When the Hunt Goes By 690
Dragonfly 656
The Fury and the Power 656
The Fury and the Terror 656
Phantom Nights 656
Solar Eclipse 656
Soon She Will Be Gone 656

Fasman, Jon
The Geographer's Library 1183

Faulkner, Colleen
What She Can't See **392**

Faulkner, William
Light in August 1215

Faulks, Sebastian
Birdsong 858, 962
Charlotte Gray 847

Faust, Christa
Burned/One Night at Mercy **657**, 658, 737
Control Freak 657, 658
Dreamspawn 657, **658**
Hoodtown 657, 658

Fawcett, Quinn
The Mycroft Holmes Series 232, 862, 872, 874

Fawkes, Richard
Face of the Enemy 807
Nature of the Beast 802

Feather, Jane
Velvet 275
The Widow's Kiss 214

Feehan, Christine
Dark Fire 313
Dark Guardian 313
Dark Melody 263, 313, 433, 440
Dark Secret 255, **313**
Dark Symphony 313, 429
Hot Blooded 664
Lover Beware 314
Mind Game 274, 282, 314
Oceans of Fire **314**, 325
The Only One 440
The Scarletti Curse 313
Shadow Game 274, 314, 395
The Twilight before Christmas 314
Wild Rain 314, 347

Feintuch, David
The King 602
Prisoner's Hope 765
The Still 574

Feist, Raymond E.
A Darkness at Sethanon 607
Exile's Return 611
King of Foxes 601
Krondor: Tear of the Gods 567
Krondor, the Betrayal 568
Rage of a Demon King 602, 629

Feldhahn, Shaunti
The Veritas Conflict 1033, 1046

Feldman, Ellen
The Boy Who Loved Anne Frank **886**, **1142**
Conjugal Rites 886
God Bless the Child 886, 1142
Looking for Love 886, 1142
Lucy 886, 1142, 1156
Rearview Mirror 1142
Too Close for Comfort 886, 1142

Fell, Doris Elaine
Always in September 1068

Fellowes, Julian
Snobs **1143**, 1232

Fenady, Andrew J.
Claws of the Eagle 480
Double Eagles 480
Riders to Moon Rock **480**
The Runaways 480
There Came a Stranger 480

Ferber, Edna
Cimarron 926

Fergus, Jim
One Thousand White Women 887
Wild Girl 854, **887**

Ferguson, Jo Ann
Her Only Hero 285
A Model Marriage 413
Valentine Kittens **315**
A Valentine Waltz 315
Wedding Day Kittens **316**

Ferrarella, Marie
An Uncommon Hero 286

Ferri, Linda
Enchantments **1144**

Spanking Watson 92
Steppin' on a Rainbow 92
Ten Little New Yorkers 92

Friesner, Esther
Child of the Eagle 615
Druid's Blood 597
Elf Defense 606
Gnome Man's Land 618
Majyk by Accident 610
The Sherwood Game 626, 779
Sphynxes Wild 632

Frommer, Sara Hoskinson
The Joan Spencer Series 172
Witness in Bishop Hill 157

Frost, Gregory
*Attack of the Jazz Giants and Other
   Stories* **772**
Fitcher's Brides 772
Lyrec 772
A Pure Cold Light 772
Remscela 772
Tain 569, 584, 772

Frost, Mark
The List of 7 680

Fuentes, Carlos
The Old Gringo 903

Fuentes, Leonardo Padura
Havana Red **184**

Fuhrman, Holly
Pickup Lines **340**

Fuller, Dean
A Death in Paris 21

Fuller, Jack
The Best of Jackson Payne 912

Fuller, Roger
Sign of the Pagan 876

Fulmer, David
Chasing the Devil's Tail 93
Jass **93**

Fulton, Eileen
The Nina McFall Series 187

Funderburk, Robert
The Dylan St. John Series 1083

Furey, Maggie
Echo of Eternity 555, 568, 582
The Spirit of Stone 622

Furst, Alan
Blood of Victory 222, 922
Dark Voyage 1178, 1216
Kingdom of Shadows 139, 1107

Furutani, Dale
The Ken Tanaka Series 129

Fusilli, Jim
The Terry Orr Series 49

G

Gabaldon, Diana
Lord John and the Private Matter 4,
   101, 976

Gabhart, Ann H.
A Chance Hero 1029
A Forbidden Yearning 1029
A Heart Divided 1029
The Look of Eagles 1029
The Scent of Lilacs **1029**, 1052

Gabriel, Kristin
Dangerously Irresistible 394

Gaffney, Elizabeth
Metropolis **891**, 1103, **1147**, 1187,
   1246

Gaffney, Patricia
Flight Lessons 329, 389
Saving Graces 380

Gaines, Ernest J.
*The Autobiography of Miss Jane
   Pittman* 1217
A Lesson Before Dying 938

Galef, David
Flesh 1121, 1222

Galenorn, Yasmine
Embracing the Moon 659
The Emerald O'Brien Series 62, 102,
   147, 221
Ghost of a Chance 46, 638, 659
Legend of the Jade Dragon 659
Murder under a Mystic Moon **659**

Gallagher, Stephen
The Boat House 660
Nightmare, with Angel 660
Rain 660
Red Red Robin 660
The Spirit Box **660**
Valley of Lights 706
White Bizango 660

Gallison, Kate
The Mother Lavinia Gray Series 225

Galloway, Janice
Clara 1133, 1137

Gamble, Terry
The Water Dancers 513

Gansky, Alton
Before Another Dies **1030**, 1031,
   1032
Beneath the Ice 1030, 1031, 1032
Director's Cut **1031**
The Incumbent 1030, 1031, 1032
The J.D. Stanton Series 1060
Out of Time 1030, 1032
The Ridgeline Series 1013, 1017
Submerged 1030, 1031, **1032**, 1078
A Treasure Deep 1030, 1031, 1032
Vanished 1073

Gansworth, Eric
Indian Summers 485
Mending Skins 451, 453, **485**
Nickel Eclipse: Iroquois Moon 485
Smoke Dancing 451, 453, 485

Garbera, Katherine
Let It Ride 334

Garcia, Cristina
Monkey Hunting 1195

Garcia, Eric
Matchstick Men 1123, 1150, 1218

Garcia, Ricardo L.
*Brother Bill's Bait Bites Back and
   Other Tales from the Raton* 491,
   511, 522

Garcia-Aguilera, Carolina
Havana Heat 184, 189
The Lupe Solano Series 35
A Miracle in Paradise 110

Garcia Marquez, Gabriel
Chronicle of a Death Foretold 94
One Hundred Years of Solitude 988,
   1203, 1236

Garcia-Roza, Luiz Alfredo
December Heat 94
The Silence of the Rain 94
Southwesterly Wind 94

A Window in Copacabana **94**

Gardam, Jane
Crusoe's Daughter 886
The Flight of the Maidens 927

Gardner, Ashley
The Glass House 95
The Hanover Square Affair 95
A Regimental Murder 95
The Sudbury School Murders **95**

Gardner, Craig Shaw
A Disagreement with Death 587

Gardner, James Alan
Expendable 773
Gravity Wells **773**
Hunted 773
Radiant 773
Trapped 773
Vigilant 773

Gardner, Lisa
Alone **1148**
The Killing Hour 1148
The Next Accident 1148
The Survivors Club 1148
The Third Victim 1148

Garfield, Brian
The Paladin 142, 149

Garland, Mark
Sword of the Prophets 553

Garlock, Dorothy
Mother Road 936

Garner, Alan
The Moon of Gomrath 606
The Weirdstone of Brisingamen 579,
   632

Garnett, Gale Zoe
Visible Amazement 1111

Garnett, Juliana
The Laird 444

Garrett, George
Entered from the Sun 992

Garrett, Randall
Lord Darcy 575

Garrique, Sheila
All the Children Were Sent Away 850

Garrison, Peter
The Magic Dead 609
The Sorcerer's Gun 621

Gartner, Chloe
Drums of Khartoum 973

Garton, Ray
Crucifax 683
*The Nightmares on Elm Street: Parts 4
   and 5* 643, 658

Garvey, Amy
Murder in the Hamptons **321**
Wicked Women Whodunit **302**

Garwood, Haley Elizabeth
Swords Across the Thames 870, 900

Garwood, Julie
Murder List 415
Saving Grace 421

Gash, Jonathan
Jade Woman 200

Gaskell, Elizabeth
*Mrs. Gaskell's Tales of Mystery and
   Horror* 720

Gaskell, Jane
Strange Evil 636

Gaspar de Alba, Alicia
Desert Blood **96**

Gates, Patrick
Grimm Memorials 661

Gauger, Rick
Charon's Ark 750

Gautreaux, Tim
The Clearing 986

Gay, William
*I Hate to See That Evening Sun Go
   Down* 1116
The Long Home 1244

Geagley, Brad
Year of the Hyenas **97**, **892**

Gear, Kathleen O'Neal
People of the Masks 486
People of the Mist 486
People of the Moon **486**
People of the Owl 486
People of the Raven 486
People of the Silence 486

Gear, W. Michael
Coyote Summer 457
The Morning River 457
People of the Moon **486**
Starstrike 829

Gearino, G.D.
Blue Hole 114

Gedge, Paula
House of Illusions 943

Gedney, Mona
Lady Diana's Daring Deed 295
Waltz with a Rogue **260**

Gelb, Jeff
Shock Rock 703
Shock Rock II 703

Gellis, Roberta
Ill Met by Moonlight **590**, **923**

Gemmell, David
The Dark Prince 595
The Jerusalem Man 554
The Knights of Dark Renown 582
The Last Sword of Power 553
The Midnight Falcon 624, 625
Ravenheart 543
Stormrider 557, 571
The White Wolf 594, 601

Gent, Peter
North Dallas Forty 1172

Gentle, Mary
The Architect of Desire 893
Carthage Ascendant 893
Golden Witchbreed 893
A Hawk in Silver 893
Rats and Gargoyles 621, 893
A Sundial in a Grave: 1610 **893**

Gentry, Christine
Carnosaur Crimes **98**
Mesozoic Murder 98

George, Anne
The Southern Sisters Series 226

George, Catherine
The Right Choice 273

George, Elizabeth
Deception on His Mind 99
In Pursuit of the Proper Sinner 99
In the Presence of the Enemy 99, 899
A Place of Hiding 99
A Traitor to Memory 99
With No One as a Witness **99**

Murder at San Simeon 897, 903

Hall, Russ
Bent Red Moon **492**
Blue-Eyed Indian 492
No Murder Before Its Time 492

Halter, Marek
The Book of Abraham 904
The Children of Abraham 904
Sarah 904
The Wind of the Khazars 904
Zipporah, Wife of Moses **904**

Hambly, Barbara
The Benjamin January Series 93, 152
Bride of the Rat God 597, 617
Days of the Dead 1156
Dead Water 1156
Die upon a Kiss 945, 1156
The Dog Wizard 613
Dragonsbane 591
Dragonstar 1156
The Emancipator's Wife **1156**
Icefalcon's Quest 602
The James Asher Series 121
The Magicians of Night 601
The Rainbow Abyss 548
Wet Grave 1156
The Witches of Wenshar 589

Hamill, Pete
Forever 920, 1147, 1177, 1187, 1246
Snow in August 891

Hamilton, Denise
The Eve Diamond Series 220
The Jasmine Trade 117, 1157
Last Lullaby 117, 1157
Savage Garden **117**, **1157**
Sugar Skull 117, 1157

Hamilton, Edmond
City at World's End 835
The Star Kings 774

Hamilton, Laurell K.
The Anita Blake Series 121, 134
Bite 255, **664**
Burnt Offerings 575
Cerulean Sins 575
Cravings 664
Death of a Darklord 667, 702
Guilty Pleasures 639, 666, 724, 727
Incubus Dreams 301, 575, 640
The Laughing Corpse 647
Narcissus in Chains 575
Seduced by Moonlight 575, 614
A Stroke of Midnight **575**

Hamilton, Lyn
The African Quest 118
The Celtic Riddle 118
The Etruscan Chimera 118
The Magyar Venus 118
The Moai Murders **118**
The Thai Amulet 118

Hamilton, Peter
Fallen Dragon 789
Pandora's Star 740, 801

Hamilton, Steve
The Alex McKnight Series 131
Winter of the Wolf Moon 13

Hammett, Dashiell
The Thin Man 211, 217

Hammond, Gerald
The Keith Calder Series 17

Hamner, Earl
The Twilight Zone Scripts of Earl Hamner 712, 713, 718, 719

Hancock, Karen
Arena 1072

Hand, Elizabeth
Bibliomancy 721
Mortal Love 732

Handeland, Lori
Blue Moon 325, 449
Dark Moon **325**
Dreams of an Eagle 325
Full Moon Dreams 325
Hunter's Moon 325
The Husband Quest 325

Handler, David
The Berger & Mitry Series 88, 145
The Man Who Would Be F. Scott Fitzgerald 61

Haney, Lauren
A Curse of Silence 892
The Lieutenant Bak Series 97

Hanley, Victoria
The Healer's Keep 576
The Light of the Oracle **576**
The Seer and the Sword 576

Hanlon, Emily
Petersburg 935

Hannah, Kristin
Between Sisters 393
On Mystic Lake 366
Summer Island 380, 393

Hanner, Mary K.
Rapid Growth 660

Hannon, Irene
The Best Gift **1036**, 1075
Crossroads 1036
It Had to Be You 1036
Never Say Goodbye 1036
One Special Christmas 1036
The Way Home 1036

Hansen, Valerie
Blessings of the Heart 1036
The Perfect Couple 1064
The Troublesome Angel 1079

Harbaugh, Karen
Cupid's Kiss 289

Hardwick, Gary
Cold Medina 42, 180

Hardy, Kristin
Scoring 370
Slippery When Wet 269

Harfenist, Jean
A Brief History of the Flood 1144

Harkleroad, J.D.
Blood Atonement **493**
Horsethief Trail 493

Harkness, Lucy
The Happy Pigs 140

Harlan, Thomas
The Gate of Fire 565
The Shadow of Ararat 539, 615

Harness, Charles L.
Lunar Justice 809
An Ornament to His Profession 760

Harper, Karen
The Baby Farm 326
Dark Angel **326**
Dark Harvest 326
Dark Road Home 326
The Elizabeth I Series 77, 882, 896, 955
The Empty Cradle 326
The Fyre Mirror 119, **905**

The Poyson Garden 214
The Queene's Christmas 119, 905
The Queene's Cure 119, 905
The Thorne Maze 119, 905
The Tidal Poole 119, 905
The Twylight Tower 119, 905
Wings of the Morning 326

Harper, M.A.
The Worst Day of My Life, So Far 665
The Year of Past Things **665**, 705

Harper, Tara
Cat Scratch Fever 775
Cataract 775
Grayheart 775
Silver Moon, Black Steel 775
Wolf in the Night **775**
Wolf's Bane 775

Harper, Tom
Knights of the Cross 906
The Mosaic of Shadows 120, **906**

Harries, Ann
Manly Pursuits 972

Harrigan, Stephen
The Gates of the Alamo 506, 854

Harrington, Jonathan
The Danny O'Flaherty Series 17

Harrington, Kathleen
Cherish the Dream 311

Harris, Charlaine
The Aurora Teagarden Series 226
Bite **664**
Club Dead 121
Dead as a Doornail **121**, 647, 677
Dead to the World 121
Dead Until Dark 121, 301, 666
The Lily Bard Series 50, 241
Living Dead in Dallas 121
The Sookie Stackhouse Series 134

Harris, E. Lynn
Any Way the Wind Blows 1220

Harris, Fred
Coyote Revenge 864
Following the Harvest 523

Harris, Joanne
Five Quarters of the Orange 980

Harris, Lee
The Christine Bennett Series 248
Murder in Alphabet City **122**
Murder in Hell's Kitchen 122

Harris, Narelle M.
Witch Honour **577**

Harris, Robert
Enigma 149, 881

Harris, Thomas
Red Dragon 682, 738

Harrison, Harry
One King's Way 572
The Stainless Steel Rat 784
The Stars and Stripes Forever 822

Harrison, Jamie
The Jules Clement Series 25, 111

Harrison, Janis
The Bretta Solomon Series 3, 51, 148

Harrison, Jim
Legends of the Fall 1212
Wolf 1162, 1167, 1169

Harrison, Kathryn
The Binding Chair 970
Exposure 1114

Harrison, Kim
Dead Witch Walking 677

Harrison, Ray
The Sergeant Bragg/Constable Morton Series 65, 197

Harstad, Donald
The Carl Houseman Series 24, 111
A Long December 75

Hart, Carolyn
April Fool Dead 123
The Death on Demand Series 241
Engaged to Die 123
The Henrie O Series 43, 60, 172, 240
Letter from Home 58
Murder Walks the Plank **123**, 845
Sugar Plum Dead 123
White Elephant Dead 123

Hart, Ellen
Death on a Silver Platter 124
Dial M for Meat Loaf 124
The Jane Lawless Series 155
Murder in the Air 124
No Reservations Required **124**
The Oldest Sin 124
Slice and Dice 124

Hart, Jillian
Heart and Soul 1087
Malcolm's Honor 391

Hart, Neesa
End of State 1037
Her Passionate Pirate 1037
Impeachable Offense 1037
Necessary Evils **1037**
Want Ad Wedding 1037
You Made Me Love You 1037

Hart, William
Never Fade Away 1138

Hartman, Elizabeth
The Truth about Fire 113

Harvey, Caroline
The Brass Dolphin 937

Harvey, John
The Charlie Resnick Series 141, 204
Flesh and Blood 79

Harvey, William Fryer
Midnight Tales 642

Harwin, Patricia
Arson and Old Lace 125
The Far Wychwood Series 203
Slaying Is Such Sweet Sorrow **125**

Harwood, John
The Ghost Writer 729

Haskell, John
American Purgatorio **1158**
I Am Not Jackson Pollock 1158

Hastings, Macdonald
Cork on the Water 132

Hatcher, Robin Lee
Beyond the Shadows 1028, 1038
Catching Katie 1038
Legacy Lane 1038
Patterns of Love 1029
Promise Me Spring 267
Promised to Me 1038
The Shepherd's Voice 1041, 1070
Veterans Way **1038**
The Victory Club 1038
Whispers from Yesterday 1085

Hauck, Stephanie Bond
My Favorite Mistake **269**

Author Index

Pastime 944
Potshot 190
The Spenser Series 57, 208
Valediction 944
Widow's Walk 190

Parker, T. Jefferson
California Girl 37, 153, 220
Silent Joe 48, 195

Parkhurst, Carolyn
The Dogs of Babel 1167

Parkinson, T.L.
The Man Upstairs 688

Parks, Julia
The Devil and Miss Webster 403
Fortune's Fools 403
A Gift for a Rogue 403
His Saving Grace 399, 403
Marriage Minded **403**
To Marry an Heiress 403

Parks, Suzan-Lori
Getting Mother's Body 1175

Parks, Tim
Goodness 1192

Parr, Delia
The Trinity Series 1094

Parrish, Frank
The Dan Mallett Series 17

Parry, Owen
The Bold Sons of Erin 191, 916, 945
Call Each River Jordan 191, 945
Faded Coat of Blue 191, 945
Honor's Kingdom 191, 945
Rebels of Babylon **191**, 945
Shadows of Glory 191, 231, 945

Parry, Richard
That Fateful Lightning 894

Parshall, Craig
The Chambers of Justice Series 997, 1003, 1008, 1045

Parsons, Alexander
In the Shadow of the Sun **946**
Leaving Disneyland 946

Parsons, Julie
Eager to Please 1211

Patchett, Ann
Bel Canto 1137

Paton Walsh, Jill
Fireweed 850
The Imogen Quy Series 201

Patten, Lewis B.
Back Trail 511
Blood on the Grass 511
Guns of Vengeance 461, 511
Ride the Red Trail 511
Sundown **511**
The Woman at Ox-Yoke 511

Patterson, James
2nd Chance 899
3rd Degree 75
The Alex Cross Series 213
Kiss the Girls 1227
The Lake House 1184
Mary, Mary 1157
Maximum Ride: The Angel Experiment **798**

Patterson, Richard North
Conviction 151

Pattillo, Beth
Heavens to Betsy **1077**
Princess Charming 1077

Pattison, Eliot
The Shan Tao Yun Series 36

Patton, Fiona
The Golden Sword 585

Pawel, Rebecca
Death of a Nationalist 192
The Inspector Tejada Series 246
Law of Return 192
The Watcher in the Pine **192**

Paxson, Diana L.
Ancestors of Avalon 630
The Lord of Horses 889
The Sea Star 573

Peale, Cynthia
The Caroline Ames Series 212
Murder at Bertram's Bower 233
The White Crow 26, 982

Pearce, Michael
A Cold Touch of Ice 193, 947
A Dead Man in Trieste 947
Death of an Effendi 193
Dmitri and the Milk-Drinkers 2
The Face in the Cemetery 193, 947
The Fig Tree Murder 947
The Last Cut 193
The Mamur Zapt Series 198, 952
The Point in the Market **193**, **947**
The Snake Catcher's Daughter 193, 947

Pearl, Matthew
The Dante Club 861

Pears, Iain
Death and Restoration 948
The Dream of Scipio 948
The Immaculate Deception 948
An Instance of the Fingerpost 948
The Jonathan Argyll Series 245
The Last Judgement 948
The Portrait **948**
The Titian Committee 150

Pearson, Ridley
Beyond Recognition 76
The Body of David Hayes 48
Chain of Evidence 194
Cut and Run 75, **194**
Hard Fall 194
Hidden Charges 194
The Lou Boldt Series 64, 213
Parallel Lines 194
Probable Cause 194

Pearson, T.R.
Blue Ridge 1210
Call and Response 1210
Cry Me a River 1210
Glad News of the Natural World **1210**
Gospel Hour 1163
Polar 1210
True Cross 1210

Peart, Jane
Autumn Encore 1038
The Brides of Montclair Series 1069
Courageous Bride 1012, 1035
The Senator's Bride 1020

Peck, Robert Newton
Hallapoosa 867

Pelecanos, George P.
The Big Blowdown 195, 1216
Drama City **195**, **1211**, 1227
Hard Revolution 1211
Hell to Pay 1211
King Suckerman 195, 247
The Nick Stefanos Series 59
Right as Rain 53, 1211
Shame the Devil 195, 1211, 1233

Soul Circus 1211
The Sweet Forever 195

Pelevin, Viktor
Homo Zapiens 1143

Pella, Judith
The Daughters of Fortune Series 1012, 1035, 1066

Pence, Joanne
The Angelina Amalfi Series 63, 124

Pendergrass, Tess
Colorado Twilight 491

Pendleton, Ford
Gunmaster 498, 504, 512

Penman, Sharon Kay
Cruel as the Grave 196, 949
Dragon's Lair 196, 949
Here Be Dragons 900
Prince of Darkness **196**, **949**
The Queen's Man 196, 949
Time and Chance 949
When Christ and His Saints Slept 949

Perabo, Susan
The Broken Places 937

Perdue, Lewis
Daughter of God 19

Peretti, Frank
Monster **708**, 1072, **1078**, 1095
The Oath 708, 1078
Piercing the Darkness 708, 1078
Prophet 1078
This Present Darkness 708
Tilly 1078
The Visitation 708, 1078

Perez-Reverte, Arturo
Captain Alatriste **950**, **1212**
The Club Dumas 950, 1212
The Fencing Master 2, 846, 859, 950, 1212
The Flanders Panel 1212
The Nautical Chart 950, 1212
The Queen of the South 950, 1212
The Seville Communion 110, 246, 950

Perkins, Diane
The Improper Wife 270

Perkins, Wilder
The Bartholomew Hoare Series 14, 18
Hoare and the Matter of Treason 852

Perrin, Kayla
An All Night Man **339**
If You Want Me 339
In an Instant 339

Perry, Anne
Bedford Square 197
A Christmas Visitor 951
Half Moon Street 197
Long Spoon Lane **197**, **951**
No Graves as Yet 915, 951, 984
Seven Dials 197, 951
Shoulder the Sky 951
Slaves of Obsession 191
Southampton Row 197, 951
The Thomas and Charlotte Pitt Series 65, 186
The Whitechapel Conspiracy 197, 951

Perry, Marta
Hero in Her Heart 1047
Hunter's Bride 1087
A Mother's Wish 1044, 1064
Promise Forever 1036
Unlikely Hero 1075

Perry, Steve
The Tularemia Gambit 785

Perry, Thomas
The Butcher's Boy 78
The Jane Whitefield Series 162

Peters, Elizabeth
The Amelia Peabody Series 144, 186, 947
Children of the Storm 198, 952
The Crocodile on the Sandbank 292
The Golden One 198, 952
Guardian of the Horizon 193, 198, 952
He Shall Thunder in the Sky 198, 952
Lord of the Silent 198, 952
The Serpent on the Crown **198**, **952**

Peters, Ellis
The Brother Cadfael Series 196, 934

Peters, Ralph
Rebels of Babylon **191**

Peterson, Ann Voss
Accessory to Marriage 434

Peterson, Audrey
Dartmoor Burial 199, 953
Death Too Soon 199, 953
Elegy in a Country Graveyard 953
Lament for Christabel 199
Murder in Stratford **199**, **953**
The Nocturne Murder 953
Shroud for a Scholar 199
An Unmourned Death 199, 953

Peterson, Pete
Cowboy Years 512
Reckoning at Raindance 512
The Relentless Gun 512, **512**

Peterson, Tracie
The Bells of Lowell Series 1076, 1094
The Desert Roses Series 1002, 1020
The Heirs of Montana Series 1018
A Slender Thread 1054, 1071, 1088

Petit, Caroline
The Fat Man's Daughter 126, **200**, **954**

Philbrick, Rodman
Coffins 689

Phillips, Arthur
The Egyptologist 1183

Phillips, Max
The Artist Wife 909

Phillips, Michael
The Heathersleigh Hall Series 1020
King's Crossroads 1040
The Rift in Time Series 1032
The Russians Series 1058, 1059
The Secret of the Rose Series 1069

Phillips, Susan Elizabeth
Ain't She Sweet 430
Heaven, Texas 278
Honey Moon 299

Piccirilli, Tom
A Choir of Ill Children 709
Dark Father 709
Hexes 709
A Lower Deep 709
Night Class 709
November Mourns **709**

Pickard, Nancy
The 27-Ingredient Chile Con Carne Murders 177
The Blue Corn Murders 980

Author Index

Author Index

Author Index

Title Index

This index alphabetically lists all titles featured in entries and those listed within entries under "Other books by the same author" and "Other books you might like." Each title is followed by the author's name and the number of the entry where the book is described or listed. Bold numbers indicate featured main entries; light-face numbers refer to books recommended for further reading.

Title Index

Title Index

Title Index

Title Index

Title Index

Title Index

Title Index

G

Title Index

Title Index

Title Index

Q

R

R Is for Ricochet
Grafton, Sue   1153

Rabbit and the Bears
Duvall, Deborah L.   478

Rabbit and the Wolves
Duvall, Deborah L.   **478**

Rabbit Goes Duck Hunting
Duvall, Deborah L.   478

Rabid Growth
Moore, James A.   **704**

Race to the Altar
Hagan, Patricia   273

The Rachel Alexander and Dash Series
Benjamin, Carole Lea   72

The Rachel O'Connor Series
Freeman, Mary   148

The Rachel Porter Series
Speart, Jessica   13

Racing against the Clock
Wilde, Lori   446

The Rackets
Kelly, Thomas   920, 1177

Radiant
Gardner, James Alan   773

Radio Activity
Fitzhugh, Bill   86

The Rag and Bone Shop
Cormier, Robert   840

The Rage
Byers, Richard Lee   549

Rage
Smith, Wilbur A.   972

Rage of a Demon King
Feist, Raymond E.   602, 629

Rage of Eagles
Johnstone, William W.   497

A Rage to Live
O'Hara, John   1232

Ragtime
Doctorow, E.L.   869, 1143, 1147

Ragtime in Simla
Cleverly, Barbara   868

Rahab's Story
Burton, Ann   281

The Raiders
Wallace, Willard M.   940

Raiders of the Western & Atlantic
Champlin, Tim   458, 468, 521

The Railroad Detective
Marston, Edward   931, 932

Rain
Gallagher, Stephen   660

Rain Fall
Eisler, Barry   73

Rain Storm
Eisler, Barry   73

Rain Valley
Paine, Lauran   510

The Rainbow Abyss
Hambly, Barbara   548

Rainbow Man
Engh, M.J.   815

Rainbow Mars
Niven, Larry   795

Rainbow Rider
Overholser, Wayne D.   509

The Rainmaker
Grisham, John   12

Raise the Red Lantern
Su, Tong   977

Raiser of Gales
Kikuchi, Hideyuki   679

Raising Holy Hell
Olds, Bruce   860, 995

Raisins and Almonds
Greenwood, Kerry   108, 109

A Rake's Vow
Laurens, Stephanie   261, 322

The Ramage Hawk
Pilkington, John   955

Rancho Alegre
Nesbitt, John D.   **505**

Rancho Vermejo
Warlick, Gary   468, 471

Random Acts of Fashion
Rivers, Nikki   344, **414**

The Ranger and the Green Derby
Clason, Dick   493

Ranger's Trail
Kelton, Elmer   499, 500

Rape
Oates, Joyce Carol   1105

Rapid Growth
Hanner, Mary K.   660

The Raptor Zone
Moffat, Gwen   174

A Rare and Curious Gift
Holdstock, Pauline   902, **910**

A Rare Sensation
DeNosky, Kathie   278

Raspberry Crush
Winters, Jill   447

Rats and Gargoyles
Gentle, Mary   621, 893

The Rats, the Bats, and the Ugly
Freer, Dave   830

Rattle His Bones
Dunn, Carola   841

Rattlesnake Mesa
Dawson, Peter   475

Ravelstein
Bellow, Saul   937

Raven
Baker, Laura   402

Ravenheart
Gemmell, David   543

Ravenor
Abnett, Dan   739

Ravenor Returned
Abnett, Dan   558, **739**

The Ravenous
Gray, T.M.   662

RavenShadow
Blevins, Win   457

Ravished
Henley, Virginia   439

Rawhide
Flynn, T.T.   482

The Rayford Goodman Series
Cutler, Stan   92

Real Men Sell Bras
McDavid, Cathy   414

The Real Mother
Michael, Judith   **1196**

Really Hot
LaBrecque, Jennifer   363

Realm of Shadows
Drake, Shannon   309

Reap a Wicked Harvest
Pilkington, John   955

Rearview Mirror
Feldman, Ellen   1142

Reason and Riots
Bly, Stephen   1007

Reason and Romance
Smith, Debra White   1086

Reasons to Live
Hempel, Amy   1160

Rebecca
Du Maurier, Daphne   442

Rebel Dawn
Crispin, A.C.   559

Rebel Gun
Brandt, Lyle   **462**

Rebel Ranger
MacDonald, William Colt   503, 504

The Rebel Worlds
Anderson, Poul   781

Rebels of Babylon
Parry, Owen   **191**, **945**

Reckoning at Raindance
Peterson, Pete   512

Reckoning Infinity
Stith, John E.   776

Reconsidering Riley
Plumley, Lisa   312, 404

Red
Ketchum, Jack   678

Red Beans and Vice
Temple, Lou Jane   231, 980

Red Dragon
Harris, Thomas   682, 738

The Red Eagle
Hogan, Ray   494

Red Grass River
Blake, James Carlos   867

The Red Hat Club
Smith, Haywood   432

The Red Hat Club Rides Again
Smith, Haywood   **432**

The Red-Hot Cajun
Hill, Sandra   **330**

Red Lily
Roberts, Nora   417

Red Limit Freeway
DeChancie, John   834

Red Mesa
Thurlo, Aimee   234

The Red Queen
Drabble, Margaret   1189

The Red Raider
MacDonald, William Colt   503, **504**

Red Red Robin
Gallagher, Stephen   660

The Red River
Bean, Frederic   457

Red River
Nagle, P.G.   487, 500

The Red River of the North Series
Snelling, Lauraine   1018

Red River Stage
Grove, Fred   491

Red Sky at Morning
Bradford, Richard   946

Red Slippers
McKiernan, Dennis L.   603

The Red Tent
Diamant, Anita   281, 904

Red Thunder
Varley, John   825

The Red Unicorn
Lee, Tanith   782

Red Wind Crossing
Nesbitt, John D.   505, 530, 532

Redemption
Ali, Tariq   843

Redemption Ark
Reynolds, Alastair   801

The Redemption of Althalus
Eddings, David   547

Redemption Street
Coleman, Reed Farrel   49

The Reed Bennett Series
Wood, Ted   24

The Reeve's Tale
Frazer, Margaret   91

The Refuge
Cresswell, Jasmine   297

Regeneration
Barker, Pat   858

The Regeneration Trilogy
Barker, Pat   962

The Regiment
Dalmas, John   765

A Regimental Murder
Gardner, Ashley   95

Title Index

Title Index

Title Index

Title Index

Title Index

Title Index